Søren Kierkegaard's Journals and Papers

SØREN KIERKEGAARD'S JOURNALS AND PAPERS

Volume 3, L-R

EDITED AND TRANSLATED BY

Howard V. Hong and Edna H. Hong

ASSISTED BY GREGOR MALANTSCHUK

INDIANA UNIVERSITY PRESS

BLOOMINGTON AND LONDON

This book has been brought to publication with the assistance of a grant from Carlsberg Fondet.

Published in Canada by Fitzhenry & Whiteside Limited, Don Mills, Ontario
Manufactured in the United States of America

Library of Congress Cataloging in Publication Data

Kierkegaard, Søren Aabye, 1813–1855.
Søren Kierkegaard's journals and papers.

Translation of portions of the 20 volume Danish work published 1909–48 under title: Papirer.
Includes bibliographies.
1. Philosophy—Collected works. I. Hong, Howard Vincent, 1912– ed. II. Hong, Edna (Hatlestad) 1913– ed. III. Malantschuk, Gregor.
B4372.E5H66   198'.9   67–13025
ISBN 0-253-18240-9 (vol. 1)
ISBN 0-253-18241-7 (vol. 2)
ISBN 0-253-18242-5 (vol. 3)   1 2 3 4 5 79 78 77 76 75

Contents

v

Chronology

1813

May 5   Søren Aabye Kierkegaard born at Nytorv 2 (now 27), Copenhagen, son of Michael Pedersen Kierkegaard and Anne Sørensdatter Lund Kierkegaard.

June 3   Baptized in Vor Frue Kirke congregation (meeting in Helliggeist Kirke) in Copenhagen.

1821

Enrolled in Borgerdydskolen in Copenhagen.

1828

Apr. 20   Confirmed in Vor Frue Kirke congregation (meeting in Trinitatis Kirke) by Pastor J. P. Mynster (later Bishop of Sjælland).

1830

Oct. 30   Registered as student at University of Copenhagen.

Nov. 1   Drafted into Royal Guard, Company 7.

Nov. 4   Discharged as unfit for service.

1831

Apr. 25   Finishes first part of second examination (Latin, Greek, Hebrew, and history, *magna cum laude;* mathematics, *summa cum laude*).

Oct. 27   Completes second part of second examination (philosophy, physics, and mathematics, *summa cum laude*).

1834

Apr. 15   Entry I A 1 of journals and papers.

July 31   Mother dies.

1835

Summer in north Sjælland.

1837

Between May 8 and May 12. On a visit to the Rørdams in Frederiksberg meets Regine Olsen for the first time (see II A 67, 68).

Autumn.   Begins teaching Latin for a term in Borgerdydskolen.

Sept. 1   Moves from home to Løvstræde 7.

1838

"The Battle between the Old and the New Soap-Cellars," (a philosophical comedy drafted but not completed or published; see *Pap.* II B 1–21).

May 19   About 10:30 A.M., S.K.'s entry concerning "an indescribable joy" (see II A 228).

Aug. 8/9   Father dies, 2:00 A.M.

Aug. 14   Father buried in family plot in Assistents Cemetery.

Sept. 7   Publication of *From the Papers of One Still Living, published against his will by S. Kierkegaard.* (About H. C. Andersen as a novelist, with special reference to his latest work, *Only a Fiddler.*)

1840

Feb. 1   Census list gives address as Kultorvet 132 (now 11).

Apr. or Oct.   Moves to Nørregade 230A (now 38).

June 2   Presents his request for examination to theological faculty.

July 3   Completes examination for degree (*magna cum laude*).

July 19–Aug. 6   Journey to ancestral home in Jutland.

Sept. 8   Proposes to Regine Olsen,

Sept. 10   Becomes engaged to Regine.

Oct. 8   First number of *Corsaren* (*The Corsair*) published by M. Goldschmidt.

Nov. 17   Enters the Pastoral Seminary.

1841

Jan. 12   Preaches sermon in Holmens Kirke (see III C 1).

July 16   Dissertation for the *Magister* degree, *The Concept of Irony, with Constant Reference to Socrates,* accepted.

Aug. 11   Returns Regine Olsen's engagement ring.

Sept. 16   Dissertation printed.

Sept. 28   10 A.M.–2:00 P.M., 4:00 P.M.–7:30 P.M. Defends his dissertation. (Around mid-century Magister degrees came to be regarded and named officially as doctoral degrees such as they are now.)

Oct. 11   Engagement with Regine Olsen broken.

Oct. 25   Leaves Copenhagen for Berlin, where he attends Schelling's lectures.

1842

March 6   Returns to Copenhagen.

Nov. 11   S.K.'s brother Peter Christian Kierkegaard ordained. *Johannes Climacus, or De omnibus dubitandum est* begun but not completed or published.

1843

Feb. 20   *Either/Or,* edited by Victor Eremita, published.

May 8   Leaves for short visit to Berlin.

May 16   *Two Upbuilding* [*Edifying*] *Discourses,* by S. Kierkegaard, published.

July   Learns of Regine's engagement to Johan Frederik Schlegel.

Oct. 16   *Repetition,* by Constantin Constantius; *Fear and Trembling,* by Johannes de Silentio; and *Three Upbuilding* [*Edifying*] *Discourses,* by S. Kierkegaard, published.

Dec. 6   *Four Upbuilding* [*Edifying*] *Discourses,* by S. Kierkegaard, published.

1844

Feb. 24   Preaches terminal sermon in Trinitatis Kirke.

March 5   *Two Upbuilding* [*Edifying*] *Discourses,* by S. Kierkegaard, published.

June 8   *Three Upbuilding* [*Edifying*] *Discourses,* by S. Kierkegaard, published.

June 13   *Philosophical Fragments,* by Johannes Climacus, published.

June 17   *The Concept of Anxiety* [*Dread*], by Vigilius Haufniensis; and *Prefaces,* by Nicolaus Notabene, published.

Aug. 31   *Four Upbuilding [Edifying] Discourses,* by S. Kierkegaard, published.

Oct. 16   Moves from Nørregade 230A (now 38) to house at Nytorv 2, Copenhagen.

1845

Apr. 29   *Three Discourses on Imagined Occasions,* by S. Kierkegaard, published.

Apr. 30   *Stages on Life's Way,* edited by Hilarius Bogbinder, published.

May 13–24   Journey to Berlin.

May 29   *Eighteen Upbuilding [Edifying] Discourses* (from 1842–43), by S. Kierkegaard, published.

Dec. 27   Article "The Activity of a Travelling Esthetician . . .," containing references to P. L. Møller and *The Corsair,* by Frater Taciturnus, published in *Fædrelandet [The Fatherland].*

1846

Jan. 2   First Attack on S.K. in *The Corsair.*

Jan. 10   S.K.'s reply by Frater Taciturnus in *Fædrelandet.*

Feb. 7   Considers qualifying himself for ordination (VII^1 A 4).

Feb. 27   *Concluding Unscientific Postscript,* by Johannes Climacus, published.

Mar. 9   "Report" (*The Corsair*) begun in first NB Journal (VII^1 A 98).

Mar. 30   *Two Ages: the Age of Revolution and the Present Age. A Literary Review [The Present Age is part of this work],* by S. Kierkegaard, published.

May 2–16   Visit to Berlin.

June 12   Acquires Magister A. P. Adler's books: *Studier og Exempler, Forsøg til en kort systematisk Fremstilling af Christendommen i dens Logik,* and *Theologiske Studier.*

Oct. 2   Goldschmidt resigns as editor of *The Corsair.*

Oct. 7   Goldschmidt travels to Germany and Italy.

1847

Jan. 24   S.K. writes: "God be praised that I was subjected to the attack of the rabble. I have now had time to arrive at the conviction that it was a melancholy thought to want to live in a vicarage, doing penance in an out-of-the-way place, forgotten. I now have made up my mind quite otherwise" (VII^1 A 229).

Date of preface to *The Book on Adler* [*On Authority and Revelation*], not published; ms. in *Papirer* (VII² B 235–70; VIII² B 1–27).

Drafts of lectures on communication (VIII² B 79–89), not published or delivered.

Mar. 13 *Upbuilding Discourses in Various Spirits*, by S. Kierkegaard, published.

Sept. 29 *Works of Love*, by S. Kierkegaard, published.

Nov. 3 Regine Olsen marries Johan Frederik Schlegel.

Dec. 24 Sells house on Nytorv.

1848

Jan. 28 Leases apartment at Rosenborggade and Tornebuskgade 156A (now 7) for April occupancy.

Apr. 19 S.K. notes: "My whole nature is changed. My concealment and reserve are broken—I am free to speak" (VIII¹ A 640).

Apr. 24 "No, no, my reserve still cannot be broken, at least not now" (VIII¹ A 645).

Apr. 26 *Christian Discourses*, by S. Kierkegaard, published.

July 24–27 *The Crisis* [*and a Crisis*] *in the Life of an Actress*, by Inter et Inter, published.

Aug. Notes that his health is poor and is convinced that he will die (IX A 216).

Reflections on direct and indirect communication (IX A 218, 221–24).

Sept. 1 Preaches in Vor Frue Kirke (IX A 266–69, 272).

Nov. *The Point of View for My Work as an Author* "as good as finished" (IX A 293); published posthumously in 1859 by S.K.'s brother, Peter Christian Kierkegaard.

"Armed Neutrality," by S. Kierkegaard, written toward the end of 1848 and the beginning of 1849 (X⁵ B 105–10) but not published.

1849

May 14 Second edition of *Either/Or;* and *The Lily of the Field and the Bird of the Air*, by S. Kierkegaard, published.

May 19 *Two Minor Ethical-Religious Essays*, by H. H., published.

June 25–26 Councillor Olsen (Regine's father) dies.

July 30 *The Sickness unto Death*, by Anti-Climacus, published.

Nov. 13   *Three Discourses at the Communion on Fridays,* by S. Kierkegaard, published.

1850

April 18   Moves to Nørregade 43 (now 35), Copenhagen.
Sept. 27   *Practice [Training] in Christianity,* by Anti-Climacus, published.
Dec. 20   *An Upbuilding [Edifying] Discourse,* by S. Kierkegaard, published.

1851

Veiviser (directory) listing for 1851; Østerbro 108A (torn down).
Jan. 31   "An Open Letter ... Dr. Rudelbach," by S. Kierkegaard, published.
Aug. 7   *On My Work as an Author;* and *Two Discourses at the Communion on Fridays,* by S. Kierkegaard, published.
Sept. 10   *For Self-Examination,* by S. Kierkegaard, published.

1851–52

Judge for Yourselves!, by S. Kierkegaard, written. Published posthumously, 1876.
Veiviser listing for 1852–55: Klædeboderne 5–6 (now Skindergade 38).

1854

Jan. 30   Bishop Mynster dies.
Apr. 15   H. Martensen named Bishop.
Dec. 18   S.K. begins polemic against Bishop Martensen in *Fædrelandet.*

1855

Jan.–May   Polemic continues.
May 24   *This Must Be Said; So Let It Now Be Said,* by S. Kierkegaard, advertised as published.
First number of *The Moment.*
June 16   *Christ's Judgment on Official Christianity,* by S. Kierkegaard, published.
Sept. 3   *The Unchangeableness of God. A Discourse,* by S. Kierkegaard, published.

Sept. 25 Ninth and last number of *The Moment* published; number 10 published posthumously. S.K. writes his last journal entry (XI² A 439).

Oct. 2 Enters Frederiks Hospital.

Nov. 11 Dies.

Nov. 18 Is buried in Assistents Cemetery, Copenhagen.

Translators' Preface

We are indebted to the University of Copenhagen not only for the working arena of the Kierkegaard Library but also for invaluable and pleasant associations with scholars at the Library. We think especially of Dr. Alessandro Cortese, University of Milan, Dr. Georg Balan, Bucharest Conservatory, and the library director, Professor Niels Thulstrup. A Fulbright grant, a grant from the St. Olaf College Humanities Research Fund, and the cooperation of the U.S. Educational Commission, Copenhagen, were of great importance in making possible this valuable period of work in Denmark during part of 1968.

Dr. Gregor Malantschuk has again contributed portions of the notes and has been a constant critic on particular troublesome issues. Acknowledgment is gratefully made to Carlsberg Fondet for this collaboration and also to Rask-Ørsted Fondet for its assistance.

Dr. Oliver Olson has continued to assist by providing translations of the German, Hebrew, and Greek quotations; Gertrude Hilleboe has again translated the Latin portions. Grethe Kjær has given helpful counsel and assistance in various ways. Gail Sundem Noller aided in the preparation of the manuscript, and J. M. Matthew and Susan Fernandez of Indiana University Press carefully guided the manuscript through the long process of preparation.

St. Olaf College
Northfield, Minnesota

H.V.H.
E.H.H.

A history of Kierkegaard's journals and papers and a full account of the principles of this selection from them are given in the translators' preface to Volume 1. Briefly, the entries in the first four volumes of this edition, including the present one, are arranged topically, and chronologically within each topic. Volumes 5 and 6 will contain the autobiographical selections. There will be a complete index. Those who wish to follow the serial order of the entries in the present volume, insofar as that can be done on the basis of the *Papirer*, will find appended a table which collates the entries of this volume with the *Papirer* (see pp. 781 ff.).

Within the entries, a series of five periods indicates omissions or breaks in the Danish text as it stands. A series of three periods is used in the few instances of the translators' omissions.

Brackets are used in the text to enclose certain crucial Danish terms just translated or to enclose material supplied by the translators.

Footnote numbers in the text refer to the editors' footnotes, which appear in serial order at the end of the volume. Kierkegaard's notes and marginal comments appear at the bottom of the particular page, at the end of the entry, or in a few special cases as a bracketed insertion within an entry.

Diacritical markings, which Kierkegaard rarely used in writing Greek words, have been added.

Kierkegaard's consciously developed punctuation (VIII[1] A 33–38) has been retained to a large extent. This is evident in the use of the colon and the dash and a minimal use of question marks. Pedagogical-stylistic characteristics (change of pace, variation of sentence length, and the architecture of sentences and paragraphs) have also been carried over in the main. They are intended as an invitation to reflection and rereading—ideally, aloud.

Søren Kierkegaard's Journals and Papers

LANGUAGE

« **2304**

The difference I have sought to find in the ancient languages (of quantity[1]) and the modern (of accentuation[2]) with respect to the romantic, Steffens (in an entirely different connection, in *Caricaturen des Heiligsten,*[3] I, p. 350) expresses as follows: *"Die europäischen Sprachen sind nur Ton; die Buchstaben, die Sylben, die Worte haben nur Bedeutung für das Ohr, der Klang schliesst sich an das innerste, lebendigste, beweglichste Dasein an, und diejenige Sprache vor allen, die den Ausdruck betont, wo die Töne sich, steigend und fallend, hervorgehoben oder zurückgedrängt, an die innere Bedeutung an jede Gemüthsbewegung eng und leicht anschmiegen, kann recht* [p. 351] *eigentliche eine* christliche* *Sprache, genannt werden, und deutet auf den Sieg der Liebe über das Gesetz."*[4]

* what I would call: romantic.

I A 250   September 28, 1836

« **2305**

There could be some very interesting investigations of the various uses of metaphor[5] in various languages and at various levels of development. In living language we use images more casually; there is a certain fragrance which is shed over the style but which generally does not actually displace the essential expression, a sheer gleam which pleasantly affects the mood during the reading. The Latins and the Greeks, however, halt the movement of the tale and develop the figure so completely that in a sense one has to hunt for the essential expression, as in Virgil, for example: "Like a wanderer who suddenly plunges" etc. It should also be noted that the nature philosophers who see in all nature a metaphor of human life (for example Steffens, *Karikaturen des Heiligsten,*[6] II, Introduction) constitute a special mode.

I A 251   *n.d.*, 1836

« **2306**

The musical quality lies in the rhyme and rhythm.

The great importance of the refrain, especially in antiquity (*Knabens Wunderhorn*[7]), for example, Bürger's *Lenore.*[8]

3

On a smaller scale the theory of a written language is the same as the theory of a universal language for scholars.

I A 261   *n.d.*, 1836

« 2307

O God, grant that the strength I feel at this moment may not be like that of a powerful army, countless as the dust and well-equipped, but which was only like an impotent dream in the night; grant that the reassurance I feel may not be comparable to the army's performance, which was like a hungry man's dream in which he believed he could satiate himself with imaginary food and then he woke up all the weaker.

I have taken these expressions from Schubert's *Symbolik des Traums*,[9] second edition, p. 27, which cites them as images that frequently emerge in various forms in symbolic language and precisely thereby point to an underlying archetype.

II A 62   *n.d.*, 1837

« 2308

To write in Latin about romantic subjects in an appropriate mood is just as unreasonable as asking someone to use squares to describe a circle—the humorous hyperboles of life's paradoxes exceed every schematization, burst every straitjacket; it is like putting new wine in old leather flasks; and if Latin eventually dominates by a forced marriage to the bound young lover, then the toothless old crone who cannot articulate her speech must put up with it if he seeks his satisfaction in other ways.

II A 111   July 8, 1837

« 2309

A remarkable transition occurs when one begins to study the grammar of the indicative and the subjunctive, because here for the first time one becomes conscious that everything depends upon how something is thought, consequently how thinking in its absoluteness supersedes an apparent reality [*Realitet*].

II A 155   September 4, 1837

« 2310

The indicative thinks something as actuality [*Virkeligt*] (the identity of thinking and actuality). The subjunctive thinks something as thinkable.

II A 156   *n.d.*, 1837

« **2311**

Was not the reason that the Latins used an indicative in such sentences as: should, ought, could, it would be too tedious—that the modern languages involve far more (or more correctly, first developed) reflection, whereby every expression again becomes pregnant.*
It occurred to me on another occasion that this is also the reason why it must be much easier to catechize in Greek (it was the Greeks, after all, who raised up the greatest of all catechists, Socrates), because in the modern languages the single expression, be it ever so simplified, still contains a reflection which must be sorted out.

II A 157 September 5, 1837

« **2312**

In margin of 2311 (II A 157):
* Hegel also talks about the *Ernsthaftigkeit*[10] of Latin . . . . . perhaps this is the reason.

II A 158 *n.d.*, 1837

« **2313**

The grammar of the indicative and subjunctive contains basically the most esthetic concepts and gives rise to almost the highest esthetic enjoyment (it borders on the musical, which is the highest), and of the subjunctive the hackneyed proposition *cogito ergo sum* holds true: it is the subjunctive's life principle (therefore one could really present the whole of modern philosophy in a theory about the indicative and the subjunctive; it is indeed purely subjunctive).

II A 159 *n.d.*, 1837

« **2314**

It should be possible to write a whole novel in which the present subjunctive is the invisible soul, is what lighting is for painting.

II A 160 September 13, 1837

« **2315**

This is why it may legitimately be said that the subjunctive, which occurs as a glimmer of the individuality of the person in question, is a dramatic retort in which the narrator steps aside as it were and makes the remark as true of the individuality (that is, poetically true), not as factually so and not even as if it may be that, but it is presented under the illumination of subjectivity.

II A 161 September 13, 1837

« **2316**

The Greeks' dual number—what relation to parallelism—what relation to the tonic of Greek Music. (See Bindesbøll.[11])

II A 665   *n.d.,* 1837

« **2317**

Ussing[12] is an exclamation point at the end of a sentence, which, it should be noted, is supposed to give the mark its meaning. In this respect the writing style of our age is in remarkable contrast to that of the Middle Ages and antiquity. They produced words which merited exclamation points but did not get them except in the heart's amen; as a substitute our age produces nothing but exclamation points.

II A 722   April 14, 1838

« **2318**

A person really feels how much he lacks when he cannot speak a language the way he speaks his native tongue[13]—all the intermediate shades.

III A 156   *n.d.,* 1841

« **2319**

In the old days, as is well-known, they wrote one word after the other without a break, one sentence after another without any separation. One shudders to think of reading such writing! Now we have gone to the opposite extreme. We write nothing but punctuation marks, no words, no meaning, but simply exclamation and question marks.

III A 222   *n.d.,* 1840–42(?)

« **2320**

In immediacy, then, everything is true; but cannot consciousness remain in this immediacy? If this immediacy and that of animals were identical, then the problem of consciousness would be annulled, but that would also mean that man is an animal or that man is *inarticulate.* Therefore it is language which annuls immediacy;[14] if man could not talk he would remain in the immediate.

This could be expressed, he [Johannes Climacus] thought, by saying that the immediate is reality [*Realiteten*], language is ideality, since by speaking I produce the contradiction. When I seek to express sense perception in this way, the contradiction is present, for what I say is something different from what I want to say. I cannot express reality [*Realiteten*] in language, because I use ideality to characterize it, which is a contradiction, an untruth.

The possibility of doubt, then, is implicit in the duality of consciousness.[15]

IV B 14:6   n.d., 1842–43

« 2321

. . . . . but this much is certain, it will not do to assume that man himself invented language or, as Professor Madvig has expressed* so superbly in a prospectus, that men reached an agreement on what language they would speak.[16]

In margin: * with profound irony.

V B 53:12   n.d., 1844

« 2322

I do believe that Young is wrong and Talleyrand after him when they say that language is for the purpose of concealing thoughts;[17] I believe also that a later writer is wrong when he says that the purpose of language is not for concealing thoughts but for concealing the fact that one has no thoughts . . . . .

V B 115:2   n.d., 1844

« 2323

The actual difference between men is merely the way in which they talk nonsense. It is universally human to do so.

VIII[1] A 110   n.d., 1847

« 2324

It is all well enough that "language" distinguishes man from the animal; no doubt simply because all instruction takes place directly through language, man is also easily led astray. Speech is in fact an abstraction and always presents the abstract rather than the concrete.[18]

Approaching something scientifically, esthetically, etc., how easily a person is led into the conceit that he really knows something for which he has the word. It is the concrete intuition which is so easily lost here.

And now the ethical approach! How easily a person is led to think of man (an abstraction) instead of himself, this tremendous concretion. Herein lies the truth in Pythagorean instruction, to begin with silence. This was a way of gaining consciousness of the concrete.

X^2 A 235   n.d., 1849

« 2325

ψ 10:14[19]

The Vulgate translated this: *tibi* (namely, *Deo*) *derelictus pauper.*

Scriver[20] (pt. 1, p. 35) explains this as follows: that the world chose all the distinguished, powerful, etc.—thus there was nobody left for God but the poor and the forsaken.[*]

Our translation translates it differently: the poor entrusts himself to you.

x[4] A 197   *n.d.*, 1851

« 2326

[*] *In margin of 2325* (x[4] A 197):

As a commentary these words could be added: God has chosen the poor and the spurned[21]—chosen them—no, this was no choice, there was no one else for him to choose, for the world had chosen all the powerful and the prestigious.

x[4] A 198   *n.d.*

« 2327 *Scriver*

somewhere[22] (pt. 1, p. 40) translates Job 13:15 thus: Even if he (God) slays me, I nevertheless hope in him.

A beautiful translation, but not correct.

In pt. 1, p. 42, Scriver says that the soul, the human soul, is God's rest, or that God rests in it—that this glorious gift to man is just as extraordinary as it would be for a subject if a powerful prince were to rest his head on his breast.

x[4] A 199   *n.d.*, 1851

« 2328 *That the Word of God Is Written in Poor Language*

Calvin puts his finger on the right spot. "It is with diligence or deliberation that the greatest secrets of the kingdom of God are given to us in very contemptible clothing. Read Demosthenes, Cicero, Plato —they will capture and transport you— . . . . . Holy Scripture will bore into your heart . . . . . *Ut promptum sit perspicere, divinum quiddam spirare sacras scripturas.*"[23]

Institutiones, I, ch. 8, quoted according to Henry, *Calvins Leben,*[24] pt. 1, p. 295.

I think there is also another side to this—that it is divine eminence, so to speak, which writes in poor language. His majesty writes in a poor hand on a scrap of paper, etc.—the more subordinate one is, the more he must cling to direct eminence or dignity—the other is just the opposite.

x⁴ A 313   n.d., 1851

« 2329 *The History of Expressions—Demoralization*

Among the various characteristics of a demoralized age is its tendency to use expressions of pathos with a kind of pandering refinement just when it becomes aware that they no longer mean anything.

Take, for example, the way we use the word "shepherd" [*Hyrde*] for a bishop nowadays. I have noticed that this has come into use only very recently, and it certainly will become a practice now that Martensen[25] has become bishop, because the public regards him as utterly harmless to its sovereignty (and quite correctly, for he is indeed the obedient servant of the public), and for this very reason he is panderingly called "shepherd."

So it is also with the expression "father" or "sire" for a king. At first there is a period when this expression is used with great pathos. Then comes a period in which the expression is abominated and therefore is not used. When the people have won out and have become sovereign *de facto,* although keeping a king *de nomine,* the expression suddenly pops up again and even becomes very popular. But why? Because now it means nothing—well, actually it means, by a mystification, that I "the people" am sovereign and amuse myself by playing blindman's buff with you, play the game of calling you "sire."

XI¹ A 80   n.d., 1854

« 2330 *Christianity*

There are foods which get their names simply from the way they are prepared—for example, marinated beef [*Suursteeg*].

Suppose, now, that someone took a notion to prepare it with sweet ingredients rather than sour—would I not be right in saying that it is not marinated beef? Now suppose he turned the affair in the following way: knowing that his sweetened steak was meant to taste good, if it turned out bad and he then offered it as his marinated or sour beef—would this not be an evasion in order to divert attention?

So it is with Christianity. The rascals have abolished Christianity and in its place cooked up something which appeals to the taste of the natural man and which they call Christianity. If one says: This is not Christianity, then I dare say they will turn the thing around and drag in numbers and ask you whether this which they are proclaiming as Christianity does not entirely please them—and this is supposed to prove that it is Christianity.

XI¹ A 205   n.d., 1854

« 2331 *A Gauge To Measure Existential Specific Gravity*

What confuses everything is the thoughtlessness and knavishness of our pretending that everything is changed because we have picked up some expressions and phrases, but existentially [*existentielt*] everything remains the same.[26]

We have instruments for physical measurement. If one took a barrel of water, colored it, and then tried to sell it for cognac, it would be tested and pronounced a fraud.

Thus it would be desirable to have a similar instrument for testing existence. If we did, we would be surprised to see that we in Christendom have not moved at all but existentially are pagan or Jewish.

XI¹ A 361   n.d., 1854

« 2332 *Christianity—Christendom*

In talking with a pupil a teacher sometimes expresses himself in lower terms and means something higher, and in such a way that the pupil understands it. He says, for example: Tomorrow will be a fun day, and means thereby that it will be a rigorous day with much to do, which in a certain higher sense can also be fun. Suppose that the pupil takes the liberty of pretending he did not understand and loafs all day long and when the teacher remonstrates with him answers: Didn't you say that tomorrow should be a fun day?

A teacher usually speaks in higher terms about being diligent in trying, about really making an effort; he calls it a joy and a pleasure, which in a higher sense it is. But I wonder if he would put up with the boy's taking the liberty of exploiting these higher terms *joy* and *pleasure* by taking a vacation?

Thus also with Christianity. In his majestic language God has proclaimed a great joy to us men—a great joy. Yes, God cannot speak in another way about the high goal he sets in Christianity. And what is Christendom? Christendom is a tricky boy who pretends he does not understand what God meant but thinks that since it is a great joy the task must be to enjoy life thoroughly.

Christendom is sheer high treason against Christianity, an impertinent insolence, and this is public worship in this country.

XI[1] A 520   n.d., 1854

« 2333 *"Speaking in Tongues"*

Consistent as Christianity naturally is (so consistent that I am still far from having grasped how consistent it is—so that it does not occur to me to speak of it as almost everyone nowadays speaks, patronisingly like a supercilious critic), it also admits to having its own language, speaking in tongues; this is the Christian language,[27] altogether different, not as one language is different from another, different from all human language, the qualitative difference of a difference of concept.

The more I pursue the matter, the more I see that the confusion is not only in Denmark, not only in Protestantism, and not only in Christendom, but the confusion is in the nature of man, and thereby in the slang which we human beings speak.

The Christian language uses the same words we men use, and in that respect desires no change. But its use of them is qualitatively different from our use of them; it uses the words inversely, for Christianity makes manifest one sphere more or a higher sphere than the one in which we men naturally live, and in this sphere ordinary human language is reflected inversely. For example, Christianity says that to lose the earthly is a gain,[28] that to possess it is a loss. We also use the words *loss* and *gain*. But we do not in any way include the sphere of the spirit, and therefore by *"loss"* and *"gain"* we understand the opposite of what Christianity understands. And so we let Christianity talk away—and afterwards preach it in our own language and call it Christianity.

As in music we speak of transposing a part to a key different from that in which it was originally written, so the Christian language is wholly and entirely qualitatively different from our language at every point, even though we use the same words. Christendom's great feat was to transpose Christian language back into the old wretched gabble —and in this way we all have become Christians.

And now we are waiting for new apostles, for now presumably mankind has finished and thoroughly learned the lesson assigned by the apostles—what insolence!

XI[2] A 37   n.d., 1854

« 2334 *Flesh and Blood—Language*

There is much talk nowadays about flesh and blood being man's enemy, but I am more and more inclined to look upon language, the ability to speak, as a still more dangerous or as an at least equally dangerous enemy of every man.

There was, after all, something very true in that ancient view that character training begins with silence (Pythagoras).[29]

Perhaps still more tempting to a man, in any case just as tempting as the impulses of flesh and blood, is the ability to use the highest expressions, to inflate them and thus to make it appear as if one himself were such a person or as if one's life really were related to them.

If, for example, I compare Luther with Pythagoras from this point of view, the comparison is not to the advantage of Luther with his insistence that the important thing is that the doctrine be proclaimed unadulterated—that is, objectively.

No, the misuse of language (alas, if one is going to be absolutely scrupulous about it, perhaps the most famous historical figures are not exempted—yet always with the exception of Socrates)—the misuse of language in a way that makes a person seem [to be] more than he actually is, in a way that is not altogether scrupulous as to whether or not one is using too high an expression—this sin, the misuse of language, is undoubtedly as prevalent as the sins of flesh and blood, possibly even more widespread, embracing all men.

The police thoroughly frisk suspicious persons. If the mobs of speakers, teachers, professors etc. were to be thoroughly frisked in the same way, it would no doubt become a complicated criminal affair. To give them a thorough frisking—yes, to strip them of the clothing, the changes of clothing, and the disguises of language, to frisk them by ordering them to be silent, saying: Shut up, and let us see what your life expresses, for once let this be the speaker who says who you are.[*]

The poisoning of wells in a country or a city is used as an example of an odious crime—but the sin of using language dishonestly is just as dangerous—alas, the only difference is that one person is not supposed to say much to another about it.

This, you see, is why the race has sunk and is sinking more and more into dishonesty—and even world-famous historical figures who are given prominence as servants of truth are found on close inspection to be careless of how they used language.

This explains the entire nonsense of Christendom. If the New

Testament had been taken literally, this confusion would not have been possible.

For what is Christendom? It is this indulgence continued from generation to generation, whereby first of all a little bit is knocked off of what it means to call oneself a Christian, and then the next generation knocks off a little more of the already reduced price, and the next generation again knocks off a little of what had been knocked off of the already discounted price, etc.—all through the misuse of language, by continuing to use the highest and most decisive expressions while continually investing them with less and less meaning, continually committing themselves less and less to what the words say.

XI^2 A 128   *n.d., 1854*

« **2335**

[*] *In margin of 2334* (XI^2 A 128):

A big uproar is made about moving road signs—but the person who treats language dishonestly actually falsifies the road signs.

XI^2 A 129   *n.d.*

« **2336** *Language*

is an ideality which every man has gratis. What an ideality—that God can use language to express his thoughts and thus man by means of language has fellowship with God.

But in the relationship of spirit nothing is ever a direct gift in the way a material gift can be; no, in the sphere of spirit the gift is always also a judge—and by means of language or by means of what this ideality becomes in his mouth a man judges himself.

And in the sphere of spirit irony is always present. How ironical that it is precisely by means of language that a man can degrade himself below the inarticulate—for a twaddler is actually a lower classification than an inarticulate being.

XI^2 A 147   *n.d., 1854*

« **2337** *If Only Man Could Not Talk!*

Animal life is so simple, so easy to understand, because the animal has the advantage over man of not being able to talk. The only talking in animal existence [*Tilværelse*] is its life, its actions.

When, for example, I see a deer in heat, I see what it means, that the deer is in the grip of a powerful drive, and there is nothing further to say about it. If it could talk, we would perhaps hear some rubbish about its being motivated by a sense of duty, that out of duty to society and the race it wants to propagate the species, plus the fact that it is performing the greatest service etc.

When I see a spider spinning its fine web, truly a work of art, I see —for the spider has the advantage over man of not being able to talk —I see what it means, the spider is seeking a living. If the spider could talk, I would probably hear—while it sits hungrily watching the web to see if a fly would come—a long discussion about its enthusiasm for art which lay behind the production of this fine web, which actually is a work of art.

And so it is everywhere in the animal world.

Take the power of speech from man—and you will see that human existence will no longer be so difficult to explain.

The thing that confuses everything is this advantage man has over the animal, his ability to talk. It permits a person's life to express the lowest while his mouth prattles about the highest and *to give assurances* that this is what determines him.

Language, the gift of speech, engulfs the human race in such a cloud of drivel and twaddle that it becomes its ruination. God alone knows how many there are in every generation who have not been ruined by talking, who have not been transformed to prattlers or hypocrites. Only the most outstanding personalities of the human race are able to bear this advantage, the power of speech.

So dubious is this advantage which man has over the animal, an advantage which often, ironically, means that he is what the deer is not: a babbler or a hypocrite.

XI^2 A 222   *n.d.,* 1854

LEAP

« **2338**

Descartes' philosophy has a birthmark. Having eliminated every-thing in order to find himself as a thinking being in such a way that this very thinking is myself, he then finds that with the same necessity he thinks God. Then in the meantime his system also calls for the rescue of the finite world in some way or other. The development toward this end is as follows. God cannot deceive; he has implanted all ideas within me, and therefore they are true. Incidentally, it is noteworthy that Descartes, who himself in one of the meditations[30] explains the possi-bility of error by recalling that freedom in man is superior to thought, nevertheless has construed thought, not freedom, as the absolute. Obviously this is the position of the elder Fichte—not *cogito ergo sum*, but I act *ergo sum*, for this *cogito* is something derived or it is identical with "I act"; either the consciousness of freedom is in the action, and then it should not read *cogito ergo sum*, or it is the subsequent consciousness.

IV C 11 *n.d.*, 1842–43.

« **2339**

In margin of 2338 (IV C 11):

N.B.

This transition is manifestly a *pathos-filled*[31] transition, not dialecti-cal, for dialectically nothing can be derived. To me this is important.

A pathos-filled transition can be achieved by every one if he wills it, because the transition to the infinite, which consists in pathos, takes only courage.

There is a similar transition in Plato's positing God's uniting of the idea with matter. (See Tennemann, *Geschichte der Philosophie*,[32] I, p. 78 n.)

This is also comparable to what is expressed in the phrase *systema assistentiæ*.[33]

What Leibniz later developed in his *harmonia præstablita*.[34]

The Platonic doctrine of ideas. See Tennemann, II, pp. 370–71.

Strangely enough, he denied it with respect to the origin of language. See Tennemann, II, p. 343.

IV C 12   n.d.

« 2340

Addition to 2339 (IV C 12):
The pathos-filled transition also in Spinoza.

> See *Cogitata metaphysica*,[35] part I, ch. III, end (on freedom and predestination).

IV C 13   n.d., 1842–43

« 2341

Basic principles[36] can be demonstrated only indirectly (negatively). This idea is frequently found and developed in Trendlenburg's *Logische Untersuchungen.*[37] It is significant to me for the leap,[38] and to show that the ultimate can be reached only as limit.[39]

In margin: See Trendlenburg, *Elementa,*[40] pp. 15 n. and 16 and many passages in *Logische Untersuchungen.*

The possibility of concluding negatively far outweighs that of affirmation in modes of concluding. See Trendlenburg's *Erlaüterungen*[41] on Aristotelian logic, p. 58.

By analogy and induction the conclusion can be reached only by a LEAP.[42]

All other conclusions are essentially tautological.

Trendlenburg does not seem to be at all aware of the leap.[43]

V A 74   n.d., 1844

« 2342

Lessing[44] uses the word *leap;* whether it is an expression or a thought is a matter of indifference—I understand it as a thought.

Sämtl. W., VI.
V B 1:3   n.d., 1844

« 2343

Here again we see an example of how far immanence reaches, and that with exclusive validity one succeeds only in confusing everything.*

* Note. On this point compare with *Fear and Trembling,*[45] where the necessity of "the leap" is emphasized numerous times with respect both to the dialectical and to pathos, which is the substance of the leap.[46]

V B 49:14   n.d., 1844

« 2344

Rötscher[47] has quite rightly interpreted him [Hamlet] as being morbidly reflective, and it is incredible that Goethe[48] has taken such great pains to adhere to Hamlet. Rötscher's development is excellent, and it also has something else of interest for one who wants[*] to check the systematicians a bit more closely, for R. is, as is known, a Hegelian, but in the psychical development of characters he is different and is constrained to use and does continually use existential categories such as the leap, for example, although he does not emphasize it as much as Vigilius Haufniensis[49] does, and to me it is inconceivable that one can use them without noting the consequences for the system.

[*] *In margin:* to see how the systematicians are constrained to use existential categories such as the leap, for example.

V B 150:21   *n.d.,* 1844

« 2345

*How does a new quality
emerge from an unbroken
quantitative determinant?*[50]

        I am a poor man who does not have many ideas; if
        I get one, I must take care that I hold onto it.
   A leap.[51]
The Platonic moment.
        unsre Zuthat.[52] (See a passage in the *Phänomenologie*[53]).
        hinter den Rücken
Every quality consequently emerges with a leap.
   Is this leap then entirely homogeneous.
        The leap by which water turns to ice, the leap by
        which I understand an author, and the leap which is
        the transition from good to evil. More sudden, Les-
        sing's Faust,[54] the evil spirit, who is as hasty as the
        transition from good to evil.
   A qualitative difference between leaps.
   The paradox.
   Christ's entry into the world.
(1) Effect[55] upon Hegel's whole contribution[56]—to have thought
    through a skepticism—method—impossible.
(2) Transition from esthetics to ethics
(3) from ethics to religion

The paradox presumably can be conquered and digested, as it were, for retrogressive thinking.

Is there not something comparable with regard to world history?

Can we forget that we have come into Christianity by a paradox?

That which did not originate in any man's heart,[57] even though he can grasp it afterwards but never forget that it did not originate in his heart.

Dialectical and pathos-filled transitions.

What follows from this for logic.

V C 1   *n.d.*, 1844

« 2346

Addition to 2345 (V C 1):
Hegel's Transition in Relation to Kant

The younger Fichte[58] and others express it this way: that philosophy arises in *Erkennen als selbst-Erkennen*[59]—Schelling[60] (in Berlin): "Hegel disapproved of the bad intellectual intuition" (which is nevertheless a composite viewing of contrasts, but spontaneously, by a leap) and invented the logical idea—consequently the method.

V C 2   *n.d.*, 1844

« 2347

Addition to 2345 (V C 1):

Who has forgotten the beautiful Easter morning when Prof. Heiberg[61] arose to understand Hegelian philosophy, as he himself has so elevatingly explained it[62]—was this not a leap? Or did someone dream it?

V C 3   *n.d.*, 1844

« 2348

Addition to 2345 (V C 1):
In the older skepticism.

The doctrine of motion. (Transition) (Not on the spot[63] and not beyond the spot) Here is the leap. Therefore man's walking is a falling.

The doctrine of what it means to learn[64] (Sextus Empiricus. See Tennemann,[65] V, p. 297).

The transition from probability to truth.

The different kinds of change and transition (κίνησις, μεταβολή[66]).

> See Aristotle. Tennemann, III, p. 126
>
> V C 6   *n.d.*, 1844

« **2349**

Addition to 2345 (V C 1):
> The thought of God[67] emerges with a leap.

> The results (*resultare,* to leap backwards) in the proofs for the existence of God occur with a leap.

> The way Hegel[68] cuts off the bad infinity is a leap.

> The leap of sin-consciousness.[69]

>> The leap of inference in induction and analogy.

> The leap of the Atonement.

> The transition from eudæmonism to the concept of duty is a leap, or, assisted by a more and more developed understanding of what is most prudent, is one finally supposed to go directly over to virtue? No, there is a pain of decision which the sensuous (the eudæmonistic), the finite (the eudæmonistic) cannot endure. Man is not led to do his duty by merely reflecting that it is the most prudent thing to do; in the moment of decision reason lets go, and he *either* turns back to eudæmonism or he chooses the good by a *leap*.

> Lessing[70] uses the word *leap*.

> Jacobi[71] on Lessing (the well-known discourse.)

>> Jacobi [has] something similar in connection with Claudius Wandsb. B. See S. W.,[72] III, p. 331.

> V C 7   *n.d.*, 1844

« **2350**

Addition to 2345 (V C 1):
Basically all acknowledge the leap and use it in psychological and ethical formulations but explain it away in logic. Thus I note that Rötscher, *Cyclus dramatischer Charaktere* (Berlin: 1844), p. 105, uses the category: *qualitativer Sprung*—although he is a Hegelian.

> V C 8   *n.d.*, 1844

« **2351**

Addition to 2345 (V C 1):
> On the question: *How does a new quality emerge from an unbroken quantitative determinant?*

See H. Steffens, *Was Ich Erlebte,*[73] X, p. 118 *et passim.*

One cannot see whether it is a reflection on nature, a bold expression of wonder, or whether the objection against a *generatio æqvivoca* or spontaneous transition is drawn from ethics, from which it should be drawn.

The dialectical point is completely lacking.

V C 9   *n.d.,* 1844

« 2352

Trendlenburg resorts all too frequently to examples from mathematics and the natural sciences. Regrettably one finds almost no examples of the ethical in logic, which arouses in my thought a suspicion about logic and serves to support my theory of the leap, which is essentially at home in the realm of freedom, even though it ought to be metaphorically suggested in logic and should not be explained away, as Hegel[74] does.

V C 12   *n.d.,* 1844

« 2353 *Conclusion—Enthymeme—Decision*

A Trilogy

This will be an investigation of importance for my theory of the leap and of the difference between a dialectical transition and a transition of pathos.

In the final analysis, what I call a transition of pathos Aristotle[75] called an enthymeme. Perhaps. How remarkable, since I am now reading about enthymeme for the first time in Aristotle's *Rhetoric.*

VI A 33   *n.d.,* 1845

« 2354

I will now take the floor where he [*Lessing*] speaks of the leap. Contemporaneity or noncontemporaneity makes no essential difference; a historical point of departure (and this it is also for the contemporary, the historical, that the God [*Guden*] exists [*er til*]—that is, exists by having come into the sphere of actuality [*bleven til*]), for an eternal decision is and remains a leap.[76]

VI B 35:30   *n.d.,* 1845

« 2355

Note. . . . Perhaps it is also cunning on Lessing's part to employ the word *ernstlich,* for in connection with leaping, especially when the metaphor is developed for the imagination, earnestness is droll enough, because it has no relation, or a comic relation, to the leap, since a leap is dialectically decisive. That is to say, being about to make the leap is a nothing in relation to the leap, and to have been most earnestly very close to the leap, that is, to have executed this nothing with utmost earnestness, is a jest.

In margin: if one does not have sufficient earnestness to do as Munchausen[77] did.[78]

VI B 98:26   *n.d.,* 1845

« **2356**

The ironic subtlety lies in turning the attack into a self-revelation through a negative approach. The attacker rushes to the attack and makes a great commotion; in the eyes of foolish men it looks as if he were the strongest, and yet he achieves nothing else—and irony slyly sees to that—he achieves nothing else than the revealing of his own nature, his own wretchedness or insignificance. Thus, for example, one uses irony against an ill-tempered woman, and her ill-temper becomes more and more obvious. Thus, when a man says something extraordinary about himself—for example, that he has had a revelation —it is ironically correct to believe him (the negative approach—not to contradict him directly, which only foolish men do) in order in this way to help him find out for himself that he has had no revelation. If a man actually has ataraxia and self-control, he will be capable of using a negative consistency to make apparent any phenomenon however dia-lectically complicated. Therefore if A. seems pleased as Punch over the profundity that the law got carried away in condemning Christ and thereby did away with itself, the whole thing is nothing more nor less than an example of the flopping over of the concept, executed with a little ironic coloring. It is well known that Hegel is anything but ironi-cal; for him the flopping over of the concept is always a serious matter. That irony thrives on a similar dialectic is an impoverished discovery in 1846. Hegel believes that the concept, by means of immanental necessity, overthrows itself, itself flops over;[79] irony, however, is aware of the transition inasmuch as it is aware of its drollness or its ingenuity. The qualitative dialectic is in essential harmony only with the category of the leap, a category in which A. also dabbles.[80]

VII[2] B 261:22   *n.d.,* 1846–47

« **2357**

We ought not despise the leap. There is something extraordinary in it. Therefore among almost all peoples there is a legend about a leap whereby the innocent are saved, whereas the evil are plunged into the abyss—a leap which only the innocent can perform.

VIII[1] A 681   *n.d.*, 1848

« **2358**

In the sermon on the Gospel for Easter Monday, in the final passage, Luther[81] makes the distinction: You have the right to argue the Bible, but you do not have the right to argue the Holy Scriptures. This is the old view that something may be true in philosophy which is not true in theology.[82] The Bible and Holy Scriptures are the same book, to be sure, but the way in which it is regarded makes the difference.

Here as everywhere we must pay attention to the qualitative leap, that there is no direct transition (for example, as from reading and studying in the Bible as an ordinary human book—to taking it as God's word, as Holy Scripture[83]), but everywhere a μετάβασις εἰς ἄλλο γένος,[84] a leap, whereby I burst the whole progression of reason and define a qualitative newness, but a newness ἄλλο γένος.

X[1] A 361   *n.d.*, 1849

« **2359** *Playing at Christianity*

The medium in which one is a Christian has decisive significance for the Christian life.

To be a Christian in the medium of imagination (hidden inwardness—the artistic pomp and ceremony on Sunday and the like) is playing at Christianity.

To be a Christian in the world, as Christianity calls it, this evil, sinful world—that is what is meant by being a Christian according to the New Testament.

The consequence of this, prophesies the New Testament, will be suffering. But on the other hand, according to the New Testament, God is willing to enter in, to help, admittedly according to the enormous yardstick he always uses, which makes it so strenuous for us human beings.

But God will not be taken for a fool and the last thing he wants is that making a fool of him should be called Christianity. God, who is himself actuality [*Virkelighed*], wants this actual world to be the setting for being a Christian.

An illustration: when the swimming instructor himself leaps into the deep water and then says to the beginner that he will help him, that there is nothing to be afraid of—the teacher expects one thing—that the beginner will leap out into the deep water. If the beginner gets the notion of walking out in the shallows and playing at swimming—that makes a fool of the swimming instructor, who is ready and waiting out in the deep water.[85]

XI[2] A 103 *n.d.,* 1854

LEIBNIZ

« **2360**

At the very beginning of the *Theodicy*,[86] Leibniz says there are two things especially which cause problems for man—the relationship between the free and the necessary and the continuity of substance and its separate parts. The first problem has engaged all men; the latter, the philosophers.

IV A 11   n.d., 1842–43

« **2361**

What Leibniz[87] says about lazy reason is excellent: *"la raison paresseuse."* See Erdmann's edition, p. 470, second column.[*] Chrysippus has also used it. See Tennemann, *Geschichte der Philosophie*,[88] IV, p. 300.

[*] *In margin:* and p. 518, para. 55, *le sophisme paresseux* (λόγος ἀργός) *sophisma pigrum.*[89]

IV A 12   n.d., 1842–43

« **2362**

Leibniz[90] tells about a Baron André Taifel who had a satyr and the following inscription on his coat of arms: *mas perdido y menos arrepentido, plus perdu et moins repentant,*[91] and that later a Count Villamedina, who was in love with the queen, used the same motto to indicate a hopeless passion which one nevertheless will not give up.

See Erdmann's edition of Leibniz, p. 652, column 2.

IV A 26   n.d., 1842–43

« **2363**

"What I predict will either happen or it will not happen; for Apollo granted me the gift of prophecy."

Tiresias[92]

(These words are found somewhere in Leibniz, in his *Theodicy*,[93] quoted from Bayle, I believe.)

IV A 29   n.d., 1842–43

« **2364**

Part One,[94] about evil, God's goodness, etc.:
To illuminate God's relation to evil he uses the metaphor of a river and the familiar natural law *l'inertie naturelle des corps*; see para. 30.[95]
Leibniz believes that the ground of evil is not to be sought in matter but in the ideal nature of creation (see para. 20, para. 31; the different expressions must be compared; in the latter passage he says: *les raisons ideales qui la bornent*[96]) what he understands by that . . . . .

IV C 30   *n.d.*, 1842–43

« **2365**

The idea of many possible worlds[97] is the one whereby he [Leibniz] really attributes consciousness to God, for if there are many possible worlds, a choice is presupposed, and a choice presupposes consciousness (para. 7[98]). He thereby also explains God's foreknowledge of the fortuitous; it is a factor in a whole possible world. —*scientia simplicis intelligentiae, scientia visionis, scientia media.*[99]—
By the principle of sufficient reason he shows that there is no *indifferentia æquiliberii.*[100]
He goes back to Aristotle. (See para. 34.) I have picked this out myself in his *Ethics*, where the essential portions are noted.

IV C 31   *n.d.*, 1842–43

« **2366**

The difference between necessity and *la raison du mellieur* and that a completely indifferent freedom is nonsense are the two cardinal ideas in Leibniz's *Theodicy.*[101]

IV C 36   *n.d.*

« **2367**

Leibniz[102] makes the very important observation (para. 212) that there are great difficulties involved in the inference of quality from quantity,[103] just as from equals to similars.[104] One Mr. Sturm is supposed to have written a book (*Euclides Catholicus*) in which he advances the thesis: *si similia similibus addas tota sunt similia.*[105] Leibniz thinks one ought to say: *si similia similibus addas similiter, tota sunt similia.*[106] —It is the distinction between nature and size, quality and quantity. A part of the shortest path between two points is also the shortest path between the points of this part, *mais la partie du mellieur tout n'est pas nécessairement le mellieur, qu'on pouvait faire de cette partie*[107] (para. 213).

IV C 37   *n.d.*, 1842–43

« **2368**

The English prelate mentioned by Leibniz (para. 270[108]) can be none other than *King*. He gives hell a comic touch; the passage deserves rereading. Fecht's work[109] on the state of the damned also seems to have something similar. This and the following paragraph are well worth reading.

IV C 38   *n.d.*, 1842–43

LESSING

« **2369**

A Spanish Song.   (Lessing, vol. XVII, p. 281[110])

Gestern liebt ich,
Heute leid' ich,
Morgen sterb' ich,
Dennoch denk' ich,
Heut' und morgen,
Gern an gestern. [111]

III A 200   *n.d.,* 1842

« **2370**

This [an historical point of departure for an eternal conscious-ness] is and remains the main problem with respect to the relationship between Christianity and philosophy. Lessing is the only one who has dealt with it. But Lessing knew considerably more what the issue is about than the common herd [*Creti and Pleti*[112]] of modern philoso-phers.[113]

V B 1:2   *n.d.,* 1844

« **2371**

(1) *Lessing, as a subjective thinker, is aware of the dialectic of communica-tion.*[114]

VI B 35:7   *n.d.,* 1845

« **2372**

It probably cannot be called anything but a squabble, for there has been no crucial battle since Lessing if the usual requirements for a scholarly battle hold—namely, that the points of difference between religion and speculation be clearly defined and not that a half-baked philosophical idea bows [asks a lady for a dance] to the first religious expression as the best and is then clapped together with all kinds of scholarly improprieties.[115]

VI B 136   *n.d.,* 1845

27

« **2373**

Lessing's whole book "On the Fable" must be read again. Like everything he writes, it is masterly. It is found in *Sämtl. W.,*[116] vol. XVIII. On pages 204, 205, especially, and others, there is something about Aristotle's teaching about actuality and possibility, and Lessing's teaching concerning it. It agrees so perfectly with what I have developed through several pseudonyms; therefore I have preferred "the experiment" to the historical-actual.

x^1 A 363   *n.d.,* 1849

« **2374**

What De la Mott says of Aesop's fables is excellent: His rendition is extremely precise; he never wastes any time on descriptions; he comes straight to the point, and every word hastens to the end; he knows no alternative between the necessary and the useless.

Quoted by Lessing in "On the Fable," *Stl. W.,*[117] vol. XVIII, p. 242.

x^1 A 371   *n.d.,* 1849

« **2375**

It is also certain that Christ never established the distinguishing mark "Orthodox" or "Heterodox"—but "by their deeds you will know them."

I read this someplace in the Wolfenbüttel Fragments, *Von dem Zwecke Jesu und seiner Jünger,*[118] para. 6, end.

x^1 A 379   *n.d.,* 1849

« **2376**

The commentary on Peter's denial in the Wolfenbüttel Fragments (*Vom Zwecke Jesu und seiner Jünger,*[119] para. 54, p. 235) is rather witty: The twelve stools on which they had clamored to sit were now suddenly set aside, and no one clamored any more to be on his right or on his left.

Generally speaking, this paragraph and the one following by a scoffer are not without boldness and ingenuity.

x^1 A 449   *n.d.,* 1849

« **2377** *About Lessing and the Fragments*

Even though Lessing can be forgiven everything in the Fragments,[120] only in a different sense can he be forgiven for making the attack anonymously (alas, and in this respect, too, he set the tone for the modern age); here he obviously was not sufficiently developed dialectically to know what he was doing.

The matter is quite simple—it is impossible to fight anonymously against what claims to be [the authority] and itself declares authority to be the source of its power—i.e., if that is permitted, then everything is lost for the authority before the battle begins, then even the biggest fool can dispose of the authority.

Authority's manner of fighting is as follows: Let me get a look at you, you who are speaking this way; step right up before me face to face, and then repeat that I am a deceiver etc. In other words, authority is related to pathos.

But could not the pathos-filled, perhaps, also be a truth just as well as the so-called objective. I wonder if Lessing himself did not believe that, in case he were attacked anonymously, the attacker would be disarmed by being placed face to face with Lessing, in other words, that the attacker would be silenced.

Whether Christianity is truth, that is, whether Christ is the one he says he is, can actually be decided only in the situation of contemporaneity, which really draws forth the pathos.

Therefore, if a person wants even an approximate idea of it, he must first use all the imagination he has to get even an impression of the tension of contemporaneity.

But instead not even one scholar, no, scarcely one branch of knowledge, sits down and ponders what there really is to understand in terms of pathos. Furthermore, we are now removed 1800 years from the tension of contemporaneity—and we are almost totally apathetic. But on top of it we become anonymous; this is a distance of possibly 18,000 years; it is the greatest possible distance of qualitative misunderstanding. This must be the issue itself. What issue? The issue, in fact, is [to be] for or against what has presented itself as an authority and consequently wants to influence pathos. If this is taken away, the issue *in casu* is also taken away. What would one think of a district judge who read an order from his chief not as an order but as a literary production, evaluating it and examining it critically, under the impression that this was his task, and then even submitted his "well-written" critique to the chief. I wonder if he would not be put in a mental institution.

If there is a question about an authority, then the issue is one of authority—ergo, it can be contested neither objectively nor anonymously. I must be contemporary with it, and in my own private person go to Christ and say: You are a deceiver.

x¹ A 465   n.d.,   1849

« **2378**

In margin of 2377 (x¹ A 465):

At most Christianity may be defended anonymously, for the defender takes a lower position, after all, and perhaps does it deliberately in order not to be confused with an apostle, an exceptional Christian, and the like. But it cannot be attacked anonymously, for the attacker takes a position directly opposite to the authority, which is essentially personality. The attacker conducts himself thus: he says, "I will attack this authority," but by being anonymous he has decided the matter in advance and expressed that this authority is an authority. Consequently, the whole thing is confusion.

x¹ A 466   n.d.

« **2379** *The Hidden Attack upon Christianity*

What has harmed the cause of Christianity so much is that for a long time, because of the prevailing respect Christianity now enjoys, attacks have been made upon it with subtlety and cunning.

As example of this I refer to Lessing, who cannot be found guiltless in this matter.

A recently published book by Professor Schwarz, *Lessing als Theologe*, [121] emphasizes again, especially with reference to *Nathan the Wise*, that Lessing abhorred all fanaticism. On the other hand he was, of course, no enemy of Christianity.

Here is the example. One sets up the concept fanaticism—harangues against it, and people think that is great. But Christianity—it is given its due.

Wait a moment. If fanaticism were to be defined, we would see that what actually constitutes fanaticism is exclusiveness, that there is one specific condition for blessedness, one and one only, exclusively, that without this condition there is no salvation. Furthermore, we learn that fanaticism is characterized by its zeal in wanting to save others and its condemnation of others.

But if this is so, then Christ is really the greatest fanatic of all. Why, then, not make an attack like this: Christianity is fanaticism; Christ is a fanatic.

Christianity has been harmed incalculably by being given a deep bow and meaningless respect. Meanwhile it has been deprived of all its characteristic marks, which have been stamped as errors and corruption. This, again, has prompted the defenders of Christianity to step out of character and to alter Christianity. If the attack had been made directly upon Christianity, the issue would have become recognizable and it would have forced the defenders into character. As it was, the ones who attacked it bowed most respectfully before it, and the ones who defended it actually attacked it. Lessing attacks fanaticism—but Christianity, God forbid, no, he has respect for that. The defenders of Christianity make additional claims that what Lessing says is true, Christianity is not fanaticism. And when you look more closely, you see that the result is that Christianity is no longer Christianity, that gradually something entirely different from New Testament Christianity has been placed under the name of Christianity. With regard to Lessing the defenders should have turned the matter something like this: No, thank you, Christianity is fanaticism. Tertullian would have done it. But nowadays it seems far too lofty and audacious; when the attacker is so polite as to express respect for Christianity, then to reject his respect and pressure him into the attack would never occur to anyone in the Christendom of our age, where the majority have a pecuniary interest in Christianity and thank God that it is not attacked.

XI^2 A 39   *n.d.,* 1854

LOVE

« 2380

All true love is grounded in this, that one loves another in a third[122]—all the way from the lowest stage, for example, where they love one another in a third, to the Christian teaching that the brothers should love one another in Christ.

II A 24   n.d., 1837

« 2381

In margin of 2380 (II A 24):

If there were no higher individuality in whom the single individual rests and through whom spiritual reciprocity is realized, the same would happen with individuality in this love as happened at one time with Catholics and Protestants who disputed and persuaded one another: namely, the one would become the other, just as the Catholic became Protestant and the Protestant Catholic.—

II A 25   n.d.

« 2382

The most interesting time is the period of falling in love, when, after the first magical sweeping sensation, one fetches something home from every encounter,[123] every glance (however fleetingly the soul hides, so to speak, behind the eyelid), just like a bird busily fetching one stick after the other to her nest and yet always feeling overwhelmed by the great wealth.

II A 273   October 11, 1838

« 2383

Fear and trembling (see Philippians 2:12) is not the *primus motor* in the Christian life, for it is love; but it is what the oscillating *balance wheel* is to the clock—it is the oscillating *balance wheel* of the Christian life.

II A 370   February 16, 1839

« 2384

It is often claimed that Christianity makes no assumptions at all about man. It does clearly presuppose something: *self-love.* Surely

32

Christ clearly presupposes it when he says that love to one's neighbor ought to be just as great as the love to ourselves.[124]

II A 462   June 29, 1839

« **2385**

Kornmann: *Mons Veneris*[125]

II A 704   *n.d.*, 1838

« **2386**

Woman's love is Yes and Amen; man's love is talk-talk. Woman's consciousness is far more universal or at least far less subjectivized and therefore more a community-consciousness (an Amen). —Of course I do not refer to the love of a young immature girl.

II A 498   *n.d.*, 1839

« **2387**

It certainly is an indescribably wonderful presentation of the power of love to ennoble a person, or of a person's rebirth through Eros, which is found in the *Symposium.*[126]

III A 61   *n.d.*, 1840

« **2388**

. . . . . and we sometimes hear, frequently enough, those wild cries of grief: If this or that desire is not fulfilled, then what is life, what is the very bliss of heaven, how could it compensate me for the loss of the only thing I desired in the world—but we must not *love the world* in this way.[127]

III A 89   *n.d.*, 1841

« **2389**

Narcissus[128] was so cruel that he was inattentive to the nymph's (Echo's) love. She grieved to death, and only her voice remained. Presumably it has continued to echo in his ears. No matter what variations there may be of the Narcissus legend, they all agree that in the end he saw himself in a river, became enamored with himself, and thus in a horrible manner became a sacrifice to unhappy love.

III A 120   *n.d.*, 1841

« **2390** *What it means to love God*

. . . . . and you who feel so far removed from your God, what else is your seeking God in repentance but loving God.

III A 137   *n.d.*, 1841

« 2391

Her many sins were forgiven her because she *loved much.* [129]

III A 138   *n.d.,* 1841

« 2392

They say love makes one blind; [130] it does more than that—it makes one deaf and it makes one lame; the person suffering from it is like the Mimosa plant, which closes up and no skeleton key can open it; the more one uses force, the more tightly it shuts.

III A 157   *n.d.,* 1841

« 2393 *Contribution to a Theory of Kissing* [131]

a prize essay
dedicated to
all doting lovers
by
the author.

There are many things between heaven and earth, they say, which no philosopher has explored. Among those things is also this realm. This might be because philosophers do not think about such things. More likely there are other reasons.

The most ambiguous kiss is the one given in the Christmas game of forfeit—it can be all or nothing—

the masculine kiss
a stolen kiss
the conjugal domestic kiss with which married people wipe each other's mouth.

III B 106   *n.d.,* 1841–42

« 2394

Kissing [132] can be classified according to duration. Musical tones are also classified in this way. Here we see the different meanings of time. In the tonal world time is also asserted, but abstractly; it enters into no relationship to the idea, and the historical does not manifest itself. With respect to the kiss, the first one, for example, the fact that it is the first one, has enormous significance, and the last one, the fact that it is the last one. This has no place in the tonal world; it would be ridiculous.

III B 114   *n.d.,* 1841–42

« 2395

. . . . . Perhaps you express yourself more as a child, perhaps you say: God, to be sure, is all-powerful, it's an easy matter for him, and for me it is so very important that I get my wish; my future, my joy, and everything depend on it. It is charming of you not to lose your childlikeness even though sufferings threaten; you captivate us. And yet is it not true that you could not wish to captivate God in the same way, for if you got what you wanted, you would obtain it as a child does, and you could not love God with your whole heart, could not love him with all your passion—but only this love is becoming to a man, only this love makes him happy.

III A 237   *n.d.*, 1842

« 2396

This is how love changes to hate. The sculptor Phidias had two disciples—Alkamenes from Athens and Agorakritos from Paros. Both of them made a statue of Aphrodite. When Alkamenes won the prize, Agorakritos sold his work on the condition that it not remain in Athens and changed it to a *Nemesis* which was erected in Rhamnus.[133]

IV A 195   *n.d.*, 1842

« 2397

III[134]

God's Love Hides a Multitude of Sins

Is this reason to sin. Christianity is a religion for *all*, for it pardons a woman who was taken in *adultery* and condemns the man who looks at a woman to lust after her.

When the Pharisees surrounded that woman,[135] they *discovered* the multitude of sins, but Christ wrote in the sand—and hid it.

In Christ everything is revealed—and *everything is hidden.* Christ's love which indulgently hides the multitude of sins and Christ's love of God, a love which is pleasing to God and under which he hides a multitude of sins.

He who hides a transgression[136] seeks love. Proverbs 17:9.

IV B 144   *n.d.*, 1843

« 2398

Addition to 2397 (IV B 144):
Love conquers all—more accurately characterized: *striving love.*

(1) It strives with itself.[137]

Therefore a clear and definite conception of his own weakness is required of him who is to be possessed [by love]—and then to rejoice in happiness—I wonder if it is so easy.

(2) It strives with time.[138]

Therefore a concrete conception of time is required of him—and then to rejoice in happiness—O! I wonder if it is so easy.

(3) It strives with vicissitude.

Therefore he must have undergone a religious change—and then really to rejoice in his happiness—I wonder if it is so easy.

IV B 146   *n.d.*, 1843

« **2399**

Addition to 2397 (IV B 144):

Love Casts Out Fear

Perhaps you would like to do much for another person whom you think you love, but you want to be recognized for it, admired if not by others at least by the particular person; but you are honest enough to confess to yourself that even with the greatest effort you are able to do only a little. This little you do not want to do, because it is so humbling—consequently you do not love the other person as yourself.

Perhaps love requires that you shall yield. If a father said to his son: We must be separated—would it be a proof of his love for his father if he said: Should I forsake you?—it is indeed the father's wish.

Self-love is egotism unless it is also love for God—thereby love for all.

IV B 147   *n.d.*, 1843

« **2400**

Addition to 2397 (IV B 144):

Above All Have a Heartfelt Love for Each Other

Christianity has been accused of assuming too little in man, of making a clod of him—yet it assumes that man loves himself; for it says that we must love our neighbor as we love ourselves.[139] This is not merely a hard truth but a profound connecting point.

> See index to Augustine,[140] first part, under the article *amor probus—improbus*.

For love can express itself in many external deeds, but all these deeds can also be lacking in love. We can gain friends by unrighteous mammon, but everything disappears; this is not the love being discussed here; it must be an abiding love since it is to have power to hide a multitude of sins.

> And only that one is unhappy who is either too vain to be able to love what he may admire or whose inclination governs him so that he loves what he despises.

The qualification of *heartfelt* inwardness. For whatever does not proceed from faith is sin; the same holds for love. Romans 14:23. ψ15:4.

> The love which, if it has bound itself to its own detriment, nevertheless does not change it [the promise]; but if it has bound itself to the detriment of another person, changes it.

Along margin:

Preliminary:

When an apostle talks about love, it is something different from the frequently disappointing, frequently confusing talk we generally hear—and yet he adds: a *heartfelt* . . . . .[141]

IV B 148   n.d., 1843

« 2401 *You Loved Us First*

Father in heaven, let us never forget that you are love, neither when joy claims to make everything comprehensible without you, nor when sorrow's dark speech . . . . . nor . . . . .

that nothing may take this assurance away from us, neither the present nor the future, nor we ourselves with our foolish desires, but let us hold on to this assurance and you in it. But then grant also that we might remain in you, convinced that he who remains in love remains in you and you in him.

And when anxieties seek to terrify us, then hasten, God, to give us a testimony

> that this assurance might also form our hearts, that our hearts might remain in love and thereby remain in you, convinced that he who remains in love remains in you and you in him.

> might be victorious over the lust of the world, over the restlessness of the mind, the need of the moment, over

the anxiety of the future, over the terrors of the past, this full assurance.[142]

IV B 150   n.d., 1843

« 2402

The Incarnation is so very difficult to understand because it is so very difficult for the absolutely Exalted One to make himself comprehensible to the one of low position in the equality of love (not in the condescension of love)—in this lies the erotic profundity, which through an earthly misunderstanding has been conceived as if it had occurred unto offense and degradation.

—If a prince loved a poor peasant girl, the task of finding equality would be very difficult.[143] He would not only conceal his royal rank (not allow it to peep through) but, if she then desired him to reveal himself as king and to elevate her to his side, he would say that it is unbecoming, and his deep erotic love would be manifested precisely by his concern not to wound her and also not to satisfy her earthly vanity (which in a certain sense would be a wrong against her, even though she begged for it) but in truth to love her and become completely equal with her.

IV A 183   n.d., 1844

« 2403 *Love Is the Fulfilling of the Law*

(a) the law is the skeleton, the bony structure, the dehydrated husk. Love is the fullness.

(b) love is not malingering in fulfilling the law—partiality—softness—no, it truly fulfills the law and more.[144]

VII[1] A 225   n.d., 1847

« 2404

In margin of 2403 (VII[1] A 225):
The law articulates with difficulty (μογις λαλων) (the demoniac who was dumb[145]), but love speaks the word plainly.

VII[1] A 226   n.d.

« 2405

Erotic love dedicates the two to union, but death dedicates them to separation.

VIII[1] A 51   n.d., 1847

« 2406

Even more dismal than to misunderstand the truth is to be misunderstood by the beloved.

VIII[1] A 86   n.d., 1847

« **2407**

We should learn from God what love is. He is indeed the one who first loved[146] us—and thus is our first teacher, who by loving us taught us love so that we could love him. And when at last the couch of death is prepared[147] for you and you lie down never to get up again, when it grows still around you, when those close to you gradually withdraw, and the stillness grows because only those closest to you remain, and then those closest to you quietly leave and the stillness grows because only the most intimate ones remain, and when the last one has gone —then there still remains one by the deathbed, he who was the first— God.

VIII[1] A 89   *n.d.,* 1847

« **2408**

It was on the occasion of a banquet (the *Symposium*[148]) that the conversation was about love; it was also on the occasion of a banquet that Mary Magdalene came to Christ.[149]

VIII[1] A 149   *n.d.,* 1847

« **2409** *From a Preface to* **Works of Love**

That great Eastern emperor intended to perform so many and so great exploits that he had to take along a large number of writers in order to make complete and accurate reports. This would all have been fine and would have worked if the emperor's numerous and great exploits had amounted to something and if in any case he had taken along an adequate number of writers. But Christian love! It is so unlike that mighty Eastern emperor; it does not have the slightest notion of being able to do big things and therefore has no idea at all of having a staff of writers along. Christian love is so very unlike that mighty Eastern emperor, because it has the good fortune and grace to per- form deeds which all the mighty ones of the world put together have not performed—so numerous and so glorious are they. Christian love is so very much unlike that mighty Eastern emperor—it remains de- voutly oblivious of its works and therefore feels no need at all of a writer to record—the very things that love forgets. After all, even the poorest act of love has the essential quality of being beyond words, of being indescribable.[150]

VIII[1] A 173   *n.d.,* 1847

« **2410**

I must once again deal with erotic love and friendship. It is obvi- ous that in Christendom we have completely forgotten what love is

We pander to erotic love and friendship, laud and praise it as love, consequently as a virtue. Nonsense! Erotic love and friendship are earthly happiness, a temporal good just like money, abilities, talents, etc., only better. They are to be desired for happiness but should not be made delusively important. Love is self-denial, rooted in the relationship to God.[151] Finally we abolish this. Scribe has now abolished erotic love, and now we impudently (like Emilie Carlèn[152]) want to explain God's love as too visionary. Well, we must make allowance for a female who in all kindness wants to abolish God and make us happy by getting a little virgin married.

Imagine a novel like this. The apostle Paul was really in love with a captain's wife. But Paul was a visionary; he did not want to marry her even though she was a widow. Now avenging fate overtakes Paul, for he was a visionary. One day he saw her pouring tea and, lo, she was pregnant—then Paul was distressed (that it was not by him that the widow had become pregnant), and he despaired.

Nothing is more ridiculous than an author's arbitrary use of Nemesis, presenting an individual as acting rightly and then bringing Nemesis upon him—because the author unfortunately has not understood that he acted rightly, because the author does not know which way is up.

VIII[1] A 196   n.d., 1847

« 2411

He who is to speak of self-denial's love does not need to take great pains to appear to be a self-lover, for if he is the true lover, the world must regard him as a self-lover.[153]

VIII[1] A 295   n.d., 1847

« 2412

To be married, to have children, to be a public official and have subordinates—in short, to have a lot of people sharing in one's life and giving it point is, of course, a heightening of self-esteem. People complain about being lonesome and therefore get married etc.—but is this love; I should say it is self-love.[154] Most of what people of this kind say about believing in God and feeling God close to them is simply delusion, an intensified self-esteem and sense of vitality which they confuse with religiousness. They believe themselves to be, as they say, the object of the fatherly care of providence. Ultimately it is nothing more nor less than a sense of coziness in life, that they would be missed, which in a certain sense they feel every moment of their lives.

VIII[1] A 393   *n.d.*, 1847

« **2413**

Blosius,[155] p. 613.
Amor Jesu me afficit; Ejus odor me reficit;
In hunc mens mea deficit; Solus amanti sufficit.

VIII[1] A 437   *n.d.*, 1847

« **2414** *Text for a Wedding Ceremony*

Ephesians 5:20[156]: He who loves his wife loves himself.
This is self-love in a good sense.

VIII[1] A 521   *n.d.*, 1848

« **2415**

"The moment" can never at some moment get the notion into its head that someone could be put to death because he is one who loves. The moment understands, and quite rightly in its own way, that one who loves must be loved. But the moment lacks self-understanding, does not understand that what it calls love is self-love ("the moment's" love is self-love) and that it has always been "the moment" which has put to death the one who loves.[157]

VIII[1] A 610   *n.d.*, 1848

« **2416** *Something about Loving*

What human being, ideally, can be loved the most? The one who makes me unhappy,[158] but in such a way that I am fervently convinced that it is according to his best conviction, that in truth he honestly intends to do the best. All the elements of love must be set in motion by him who is to be loved the most, and this occurs only according to the formulation here developed. I love such a person because I feel the love in him, but the fact that he made me unhappy through something he intended to be the best for me awakens my sympathy—and I love him even more. In sorrow over my own unhappiness, when I consider how it must be for him who loves now that he has made the beloved unhappy, in sorrow over this I love him even more.

This is the most perfect formula for loving. I have never seen it presented. It has the remarkable paradox that I love the most—because he made me unhappy.

In this formulation there is more reflected sympathy than is usually thought of.

This is the scale.

(1) To love someone *because* he makes me happy—is egotism.

(2) To love without further qualifications, which is higher than (1) in the sense that a general is higher than a major general. Simplicity is more than the gradations. The identity of simplicity and the superlative. (To love *because* is like "major" added to "general"; it diminishes.)

(3) To love—and in addition to love even more—because he made me unhappy. When a "because" in relation to loving is like a plus (as in no. 1), it subtracts from and is a minus. But if in relation to loving a "because" seems to be a minus (that he made me unhappy is indeed like a subtraction), it is a plus, the only, the absolutely fervently moving plus in relationship to loving.

VIII[1] (A 680   *n.d.,* 1848

« 2417 *Theme for a Wedding Meditation*
What You Love is Yours, and It Remains Yours.

If someone were to complain about loving a person who deceived him or her—if you really love him or her, then he (or she) is *yours.* Anyone who cannot understand this does not really love, is trapped in the unholy confusion that erotic love is love, instead of recognizing that it is self-love.[159]

IX A 30   *n.d.,* 1848

« 2418

Unhappy love[160] is the highest form of erotic love. The lover still says: I would ten times rather be unhappy with him and ten times as unhappy again than to be happy with someone else.

So also with the religious person. It just has to be that one becomes unhappy, humanly speaking—it lies in the misrelationship between God and man; but still, still—what blessedness!

IX A 88   *n.d.,* 1848

« 2419

Just as "faith" is a dialectical qualification, so also is true Christian love. Therefore Christianity teaches specifically that one ought to love his enemy,[161] that the pagan, too, loves his friend. One can love his enemy only for God's sake or because one loves God.[162] The mark of one's loving God is quite rightly, therefore, the dialectical, for one spontaneously hates his enemy. When a person loves his friend, it is by no means clear that he loves God; but when a person loves his enemy, it is clear that he fears and loves God, and only in this way can God be loved.

IX A 306   *n.d.*, 1848

« 2420

What men love is the human pity that helps only humanly (for example, by giving money, with sympathy, in short, only in connection with earthly or purely human misfortunes, pains, sufferings.) It is true that men love one who pities in this way. But if as a Christian or if he were a Christian and he were then also to add a few words about Christ, that there is salvation only in him, then persecution would start. In view of his philanthropy, which is approved, there would be a tendency to let him off on easier terms, reckon his Christianity to his credit—as an oddity.

IX A 327   *n.d.*, 1848

« 2421

The martyrdom in being a Christian is seen here also. Tax-gatherers and sinners are in fact human beings who actually are unable to reciprocate[163]; to love them is therefore true love—and yet Christ *is reproached* for this, and he must suffer because he is truly loving.

To love those who can reciprocate—the distinguished and the respected ones who confer prestige by association—this the world calls love. The relativities can be of many kinds, but in one way or another there must be a little profit involved with love, otherwise the world does not regard it as love and makes it even less profitable by punishing it as if it were an offense.

X^1 A 444   *n.d.*, 1849

« 2422

Luther[164] makes an utterly masterful distinction in his sermon on the Gospel about the lilies and the birds.

Faith is indeed without care and concern [*Bekymring*]. Why, then, do the Scriptures elsewhere commend being concerned?

Luther replies: In Christianity everything revolves around faith—and love. In relation to faith, care and concern are sinful. In relation to love, however, care and concern are altogether in place.

Masterful! But the sad thing about us human beings is simply that we usually have care and concern in the wrong place (i.e., in relation to faith, then care and concern are doubt, disbelief, etc.) and so rarely in the right place! O, how rare is genuine love-concern, and how common is [worrying] concern.

x^1 A 487   *n.d.*, 1849

« 2423

Here again Luther[165] is completely right. No one can see faith, it is unseen; therefore no one can decide whether or not a man has faith. But faith shall be known by love. Nowadays we have wanted to make love into an unseen something, but against this Luther, together with Scripture, would protest, for love is Christianly the works of love. To say that love is a feeling and the like is really an unchristian conception. This is the esthetic definition of love and therefore fits the erotic and everything of that nature. But from a Christian point of view love is the works of love. Christ's love was not intense feeling, a full heart, etc.; it was rather the work of love, which is his life.

x^1 A 489   *n.d.*, 1849

« 2424

Sometimes I could almost become anxious and fearful when I consider that it is commanded in the Law[166] that one shall love God, something which at those moments seems to me to be an all too frightful foolhardiness. At such moments I wonder how a person can do that, and it seems that the maximum is rather to hold fast to the blessed thought that God loves him. What extravagant audacity for a human being in relation to God to dare say of a single act in his life, let alone of any portion of his life or of his entire life: This I have done for God's sake. Even when I sacrifice most for a good cause, I still depend on God's helping me to see it through, and therefore I still have not done it for God's sake but at best have acted in reliance upon God, with him in reserve.

x^1 A 514   *n.d.*, 1849

« 2425

Much that is said praising a mother's love for her child[167] is, of course, rooted in a misunderstanding, since maternal love as such is simply self-love raised to a higher power, and thus the animals also have it. That this kind of love in its initial state is self-love is apparent also in other analogous relationships where the foolishness of this kind of praise is obvious to everyone—for example, an author's love toward his work.

In the scriptures it is never maternal love as such which is compared with God's love for a human being; the comparison is only with the strength of maternal love. One could also use other figures—for example, the passion of the miser and the like. But such a figure would be inappropriate. Maternal love, on the contrary, is a beautiful figure.

x^1 A 635 *n.d.*, 1849

« **2426**

We eulogize it as true love—the more sacrifices a person makes the more he loves the object of his love. But this, too, is still a form of self-love[168], for the sacrifices remind a person of himself.

x^1 A 638 *n.d.*, 1849

« **2427**

Even in relation to loving a human being, it holds true that everything, even the most hopeless, works for good for you, if you genuinely love him. Why, then, should it not be true in relation to God. It is actually God who makes it what it is in the first case. God who sees your love and who is love permits even this, your love for a human being, to work for your good.

x^1 A 675 *n.d.*, 1849

« **2428** *The Way It Really Should Be Said*

As for erotic love and friendship, it ought to be said that Christianity does not really extol them. You should not be in too much of a hurry but only hold out with God a little, or, better, as long as you can—but if you discern that God overstrains you, then accept these humans means as an aid. It is the same with earning a living, occupation, and all such things.

But the relationship must not be turned around[169] as it is done in Christendom; we must not be permitted to make out that erotic love and friendship are the truest love; and we must not be permitted to make out that earning a living and everything connected with it are the true earnestness of life.

In short, the Christian contention is that God quite simply must have first priority[170] for a man's life at every point in existence [*Tilvæ-relsen*], in every relationship of his life. And this must be in earnest—not Sunday platitudes. But on the other hand God is no cruel creditor and mortgage holder, nor should a human being presume to want to be more than a human being, a demon or God-man.

But men, or a man, should not live in such a way that they tumble out into life from a frivolous upbringing and never in a deeper sense really give a thought to God and to his priority-demand, but instead regard erotic love, friendship, making a living, and the like, as the earnestness of life. No, stretched to the utmost by the most rigorous religious upbringing, after persevering in a demanding God-relationship with youthful confidence and trust, a man should have learned that this is the earnestness of life. But then, presumably, he has also been humbled in such a way that he may accept this human aid and alleviation, accept it as something beautiful which God blesses; but he does not become enamored with it, does not forget what is truly the earnestness of life.

x^2 A 63　*n.d.*, 1849

« 2429

Justice avenges itself—love is avenged.

x^2 A 107　*n.d.*, 1849

« 2430

"What you have not done to the least of these, my brothers, you *have* not done to me either."[171] It could perhaps also read: You *would* not *have* done to me either. Christ is suffering humanity, even though, more sharply defined, he is suffering humanity precisely because of his fear of God.

Here is the criterion. Men say: If we had been contemporary with Christ, then etc. Christ answers, as he will answer on the day of judgment: Have you not been contemporary with the sick, the poor, the despised, the suffering, and the like, and done nothing for them, which would have been considerably easier than doing works of love toward me when I lived, I, who exposed to danger anyone who dared to listen to me or acknowledge me.—

x^2 A 247　*n.d.*, 1849

« 2431

This is also one of the expressions in which Christ's consciousness of his divinity is boldly evident: And whoever gives to one of these least ones even a cup of cold water for my sake[172] shall receive it again tenfold.

x^2 A 262　*n.d.*, 1849

« 2432 *Offense*

Simply take the statement that Christ as a child "was submissive to his parents"—consequently, as Luther[173] properly phrases it, shared their work, gathered chips, etc. The immediate and inherent offense is in the fact that his divinity does not find a distinctive external expression.

The world will always be offended in this way on a lesser scale even by the extraordinary, humanly speaking, if such a person does not find external expression[174] but fits in completely with people in general. If he is the extraordinary, is called that, then he is supposed to have the mark of distinction and live among the distinguished—but he must not live with us; that would be eccentricity, affectation.

This is how difficult it is to love one's neighbor. O, if God had not commanded it[175]—one would rather put up with falling among robbers than express love to one's neighbor in this world—but prating about it, well, that is profitable.

x³ A 19   n.d., 1850

« 2433

Nullae sunt inimicitiæ nisi amoris acerbæ. Propertius[176]

x³ A 489   n.d., 1850

« 2434

"He who sees his brother in need, yet shuts his heart"[177]—yes, at the same time he shuts God out.

Love to God and love to neighbor[178] are like two doors that open simultaneously, so that it is impossible to open one without opening the other, and impossible to shut one without also shutting the other.

x³ A 739   n.d., 1851

« 2435 *Distance*

St. John[179] declares that it is our duty to lay down our lives for the brethren—that really means for every human being, since, to be sure, we are all Christians—and just think how we are living!

x³ A 741   n.d., 1851

« 2436 *God Terrifies—but out of Love*

Think of a lover—but a deeply earnest man. Do you believe that when he is talking with the girl he will praise himself, entice, persuade—no, on the contrary, he will speak against himself. Does this mean he does not want the girl? Certainly he does, but he is earnest.

So it is with God. Though he himself does not terrify, he allows a man to be afraid of walking the way he nevertheless *wills* that a man shall walk, even though he will forgive him for not having ventured upon it. In his infinite love God is that earnest.

x⁴ A 309   n.d., 1851

« 2437 *"Also"*[180]

Christianity believes that it is the greatest possible high treason to want to love God *also,* to enjoy life, be attached to the world, and *also* love God—even a mere man is not satisfied with *also* being loved, with being loved *also.* Dreadful presumption for a miserable nothing like man to want to venture *also* to love God!

This could be said in another way—I do acknowledge that I ought to love God wholeheartedly, but because of human frailty I cannot entirely let go of the world, something I believe God will make allowance for. Such a position, which undeniably is more forgivable than that unashamed brashness of mediation, Christianity nevertheless cannot become involved with. It must say: My little friend, how can you be so childish; yet perhaps you may come to something better.

"But," I hear someone say, "is not the God I am supposed to love the same God who has created this whole wonderful world? How, then, could he possibly object to my loving it, rejoicing in it, in his gifts? Do not the sparrow and the lily and all of nature rejoice?" To which Christianity must reply: Rubbish! In the first place, do you really know whether the lily and the sparrow rejoice? Secondly, if you are able to rejoice in the same way as the sparrow and the lily, go ahead, please. But you cannot. The sparrow, the lily, and the life of all nature are simple essence [*Væsen*]. The sparrow is not a double essence, is not a synthesis. There is no either/or for the sparrow, and consequently no arrogant "also" is possible for it either. Only man is a double essence. Furthermore, it is a question whether God can be said to have created the whole world you speak of; the whole world of culture is a human creation.

"But then is man the most wretched of all creatures, destined from God's hand to be unhappy or to be obliged to make himself unhappy?" To this I must answer: This is not what we are talking about; the discussion is only about: what is Christianity's understanding? Furthermore, Christianity certainly understands that hating the world and oneself this way in order to love God, that precisely this is blessedness, something entirely different from enjoying the world *au niveau* with the sparrow and the lily.

Paganism, however, knew that there is a fork in the road (Hercules), and Christianity teaches that the way is narrow, that only a few find it, but Christendom has invented the idea that God and the world are one and the same.

x^4 A 482   *n.d.,* 1852

« **2438** *To Love Christ*

What does it mean to love? It is to want to be like [*ligne*] the beloved, or it is to move out of one's own [interests] into the beloved's [interests].

Suppose someone, with the greatest sacrifice, has done me the greatest service, and I now say that I love him—well, observe how I express it and see whether or not I do love Christ who suffered and died for me. Now then, happy that he gained for me the forgiveness of my sins and eternal salvation, I will properly enjoy life but also thank him and again thank him. Hold on there—is that what it means to love Christ? No, it is the very opposite, the most frightful egotism. Or do I not know the way Christ wants me to express my gratitude—that is, by imitation [*Efterfølgelse*]. If I love him, then I must express that love in his language and not rattle away in my own language and try to make him believe that this is supposed to signify how much I love him.

x⁴ A 589   *n.d.*, 1852

« **2439** *Love—Cruelty*

Is it not cruel to say to a man who asks only that he might first bury his father: Let the dead bury their dead[181]—and yet it is love which says that.

But, of course, for us Christianity has become something entirely different from what it was, for nowadays Christianity is supposed to be that very love which lovingly buries and remembers the dead. In Christendom at present Christianity makes no cleavage—no, no, it joins. If I love the beloved very much, it is no longer as it was once in Christianity—relinquish her; no, now Christianity says love her, for Christianity means precisely to love her and to comply with her desire.

It certainly is clear that Christianity has essentially disappeared from the world. Christianity has become an irrelevant motto over the whole. Nowadays Christianity does not have even the self-awareness possessed by a friend or a girl in love, who desire that loving them shall be expressed by giving up the rest.

Christianity has disappeared; "the race"[182] has been put in the place of the individual; in official preaching Christianity has become mythology, poesy.

x⁴ A 642   *n.d.*, 1852

« **2440** *Psychological*

A child who obediently does his father's will which is directly opposite to his own wish—well, the child is a long way from doubting his father's love, but yet there is not much trumpeting and ingratiating talk about how doting father is. —On the other hand, the child who knows full well that he is really the one who gets his way and that the father's will is not fulfilled—yes, yes, then there is trumpeting and shouting and ingratiating talk about what a doting father he has.

It is the same with us human beings in relation to God. Imagine a man who knows very well that it is God's will, and also Christianity according to God's concept of it, to live in poverty and abasement— *aber,* he cannot reconcile himself to that, but on the contrary he desires to have abundance, to be a brilliant success in the world, and on his own takes the liberty of making this into Christianity—just look and listen, he will trumpet about God's love, about how God is love,[183] how blessed it is that God is love—all calculated, as it were, to dupe God, like the clever child who ingratiatingly wants to dupe its father so that he may not notice that he is being fooled. Such a man is then zealous —zealous to win thousands and thousands for Christianity—yes, it may very well be necessary, because he himself exempted himself from doing God's will. But you will always hear him talking about God's love, that God is love, how blessed it is that God is love.

x⁴ A 655   *n.d.,* 1852

« 2441 *Egotism*

The more one thinks about it, the more he will see that the examples of love usually mentioned are examples of self-love.

Aristotle has already shown this very well in his *Nicomachean Ethics,* book 9, chapter 7.

To be specific, he who has produced something loves it more than the production loves him. Why is this? Because there is more "being," more egotism, in the first relationship than in the second, because author-love is the highest egotism.

Therefore the father loves the child more than the child loves the father; therefore the mother loves the child even more than does the father, for she is more egotistically interested in its existence (moreover, as Aristotle naïvely says, she also knows more surely that the child is really hers); therefore the benefactor loves the one benefited more than the latter loves him, because there is an egotistical satisfaction in having done a good turn.

This whole chapter by Aristotle is valuable.

In margin: see also the *Ethics,* book 8, chapter 14, in the beginning or a little farther on.

x⁵ A 34   *n.d.,* 1852

« **2442** *To Love Christ*

Think of it something like this. By his holy suffering and death, by his Atonement, Christ has made full satisfaction for your sin, won God's love for you, assured your eternal salvation—this you believe—and now nothing at all is said of anything additional. On the contrary, you are living in sheer joy and happiness and ineffable enjoyment of all the benefits of this life which fall to your lot in every way and to your posterity thereafter—how you must love this your Savior and his infinite love, how intoxicating your love and your gratitude must be!

And yet, yet—suppose now that you had a hunch that Christ did not really want it that way, that he would like to be thanked in an entirely different way—could you still love him then? And if you and your gratitude were honest, would you not think he wronged you by concealing it from you? Take the relationship between man and man. If there were someone who had done you the greatest favor, and your gratitude and love truly approached the magnitude of the benefaction, is it not true that you would expect something more of him, that he honestly tell you the way in which he would prefer to be thanked? It would grieve you if he concealed it from you. For to deceive—of course, one ought never deceive—but to deceive the person who niggardly and pettily watches out for himself and never does a thing without proper payment—that is human. But to deceive love because it is love, to exploit its being love—how terrible! Well, to be sure, it was somewhat unkind of love to let it happen, something it might do only to those it did not love, those who by their ingratitude grieved love.

But if "imitation" [*Efterfølgelsen*], willingness to suffer, is the thanks—so that in a way Christ becomes the person who makes you unhappy—answer me this: Do you then believe you could become happier by having to acknowledge within yourself that in order to become happy you deceived him, the loving one, who not even in the remotest way did the least thing to protect himself against being deceived?

Thus there is no coercion here, none at all, not the slightest—unless you are coerced by the very fact that it is so totally left entirely to you yourself. O, my friend, every better man understands full well that this is indeed thy most coercive of all, understands the Apostle's words, "The love of Christ constrains me"[184]—yes, it constrains as no law and as no punishment and no power can constrain.

Consequently, precisely in order to love Christ, you must demand of him that he let you understand the way in which he would prefer to be thanked, so that you, even though you do not manage to thank him in the right way, at least do not in ignorance of it take on new guilt, your ingratitude to him, namely, that your jubilating thanks was not loving him but loving yourself.

Alas, we human beings have no conception of divine sublimity! If we can just live on the fat of the land and God does not crack down on us—then we completely forget that his very calmness, just this, can signify his disfavor. We drag God down to the pettiness of someone who stingily watches out for himself and promptly makes a fuss if he does not get what he wants—but the very fact that he lets us get drunk on a life of ease and frothy gratitude can be an expression of his contempt and disfavor, whereas the lives of his beloved ones express that they must suffer, that they are willing to suffer, because they have understood this to be God's will which he has proclaimed clearly enough to us and which we know, but which we harden ourselves against, and clubbing together with others we fortify ourselves in this state—for in solitariness you will become aware.

$$\text{X}^5 \text{ A } 50 \quad n.d., \text{ 1852}$$

« 2443 *To Love God*[185]

No one has loved God in a Christian way who has not had sufficiently both a painful and a nauseating impression that men are bestial. God's love in the Christian sense is not of the same order as human love for one another; the relationship is one of contrast.

This must be carefully understood. In every generation a not inconsiderable number of men who conceitedly and arrogantly want to despise men and love God announce themselves, if I may put it this way—no, thanks, it is not to be understood in that way.

No, the matter has a different structure. The beginning is simply this: with deep sympathy, disinterestedly, and in true love to have loved men.

Alas, if it were not the case—which it all too surely is—if men were not so asinine that just this kind of love is repaid with bestial treatment —if this were not so, then I might be tempted to assume that it would happen the following way. God in heaven would take note of such a man, simply on the basis of his love for men; he would, as it is said of the rich young man in the gospel, look upon him and love him.[186] Then God would say to himself: I could wish that this man would love me; for he pleases me. There is nothing else to do than to let his relationship to men become embittered through their rewarding him with bestial treatment, since I cannot be loved in direct unison with love to men.

This is how the painful, nauseating impression of man's bestiality is to be understood. This does not mean that he ceases to love them. No, but the relationship of contrast is to make the God-relationship negatively recognizable.

From a Christian point of view, to love God and to be happy and fortunate in this world are not possible. No, the God of Christianity is in contrast to this world; therefore one who loves God Christianly cannot be happy and fortunate in this world.

XI[1] A 279   n.d., 1854

« 2444 *To Be Loved by God—To Love God*

What Alcibiades[187] said about Socrates, that from being the lover he became the beloved, also expresses God's relation to a human being—it ends with God becoming the beloved.

XI[1] A 356   n.d., 1854

« 2445 *Infinite Love!*

You take a person captive—and then you deceive him.

Yes, but you do it out of love; consequently you do not deceive him after all, O infinite love.

No, no, no, you do not get me to believe anything else about you; you—there it is again—you do not deceive me, for you are infinite love!

You want to deceive me, that is true. You want to test whether or not you can get me to believe that you are anything but love, which, however, if it happened, would grieve you, O infinite love, more than me—consequently you do not deceive me, O infinite love!

XI[1] A 405   n.d., 1854

« 2446 *God in Heaven*

No lover knows how to conceal the identity of the beloved, their mutual understanding, and their meetings and being together as does God in heaven!

To all appearances things are like this: this person is the most wretched, unfortunate, and miserable of all; everything combines to harass and plague him, to mock and ridicule him, and he even cries out, God has forsaken me—and this phenomenon conceals the fact that he is the very one who is the beloved. This is the way God covers up the understanding with the beloved.

No human being was ever as dignified, as majestic, as concerned about his love and concerned for the understanding of every outsider; therefore no human being could ever think of concealing who the beloved is, to hide this beneath the beloved's becoming the most unfortunate of all.

And yet only this God is the God of love! The pagans' love gods went around among men, and even though it was not immediately known who the beloved was, the discovery was soon made—because their favor was sufficiently discernible, and to that extent the gods were drawn out of hiding and recognized.

But the God of love, who is spirit, hides his love better. The beloved becomes the unfortunate and unhappy one. The majesty of his personality, which must seek the most unconditional concealment, also requires this.

Just as the concealment is the most reliable, so also is the love: not for this life, no, but for eternity.

XI[1] A 406   *n.d.*, 1854

« 2447 *The Majesty of God*

It has occurred to me (and I shall use it as an illustration) that the best criterion for an individual's personality would be the way in which he proposes to the beloved, if this could possibly be known. Simply because to be loved engrosses the lover so exceedingly, he is likely to lose himself at such a moment; only a very superior and pronounced personality, who is always himself, will maintain himself entirely in his own conception of himself.

So much for introduction. Now let us see how God proposes, so to speak, to a human being—God, who Christianly may in no way be considered a-pathetic, for he is such pure passion and pathos that he has only one pathos: to love, to be love, and out of love wanting to be loved.

Let us now see how he proposes to a human being, what Christianity tells us about this. He proposes by saying to a person: I love you, I who am love; be my beloved—the consequence of this will be, and I tell you this at the outset, the consequence will be that you become an unhappy, piteous, wretched man, a byword among men, hated, exiled, persecuted by men, and finally deceived by me.

Truly such a proposal is either the speech of a mad man (and eminent in that category, transcending in originality all hitherto known fixed ideas and mad pranks), or it is majesty.

If a human being dare speak about such things, I should say that it makes a person dizzy to think of such majesty, which, infinitely moved in love, is itself even at the very moment that it affirms itself majestically in this degree. But on the other hand, if this majesty is love itself, how he must suffer in love because there is this sad misrelationship between God and man, so that for the beloved (the human being) it must be so painful to love and to be the beloved!

XI[1] A 411   *n.d.*, 1854

« 2448 *The Intensive—the Extensive—Christianity*

God is love, and God wants to be loved—this is the Christianity of the New Testament.

Now everyone knows that to be loved is dialectical only in the direction of intensity. It would be nonsense, yes, an insult, if instead of loving unconditionally a person offered a half dozen, as if one could love to a certain degree, as if in love a four shilling down payment were possible.

Yet this is the turn we have given to Christianity in Christendom.

What I declaim against in particular is the dishonesty of claiming that this is the Christianity of the New Testament, let alone an advance.

XI[1] A 414   *n.d.*, 1854

« 2449 *The Examination by Existence*[188]

The main question in the examination existence [*Tilværelsen*] gives to men is this: Do you have love?

We shall now proceed to find out, says Christianity, and to that end gets everything ready.

Is a man able to hold out in loving the one who makes him unhappy, continue to believe that this one, precisely this one, is love, and also that he is doing this out of love—yes, then there is love in you.

In Christianity God's relationship to us human beings is just like this. Humanly speaking he makes a person unhappy—this he knows very well, and the New Testament says this clearly enough. But nevertheless believe, believe that I, this very one, am love, and that precisely out of love I make you, humanly speaking, unhappy—if you do, there is love in you.

The love with which a human being loves the one who makes him happy—this love cannot be called having love in onself, because such love is continuously induced from without and can therefore also be self-love.

But when the object becomes the one who makes you unhappy, the love in you is denied all supply from outside, and consequently we shall get to see whether there is love in you or not, something which will be recognized by your continuing to believe that the object is love and is treating you this way simply out of love for you.

That this is a frightful examination for a poor human being is granted. However, that Christendom, out of consideration of this, has falsified all Christianity and has made something else out of it cannot be approved.

What can be said with truth is that God in infinite love is more concerned than is the poor human being he is examining in love—O infinite love. But this does not mean the syrupy nonsense that God therefore alters the condition.

Yes, he is infinitely concerned on this occasion, far more than the one examined. But one could be tempted to say that Christendom long ago relieved God of this kind of concern, because the kinds of louts and boors who are now called Christians really do not get along far enough for the question of an examination to arise. This, again, in another sense deprives him of the infinite love which has offered the condition indiscriminately to every human being.

Throughout my childhood I heard that there is great joy, pure joy, in heaven. I believed it, too, and thought of God as being blissful in pure joy. Alas, the more I think about it the more I conceive of God as sorrowful, he who more than all others knows what sorrow is.

XI[1] A 459   n.d., 1854

« 2450 *God Is Love*

It is this, transformed into a motto and dressed up in babytalk,[189] which has completely confused Christianity and made garbage of Christendom.

The law of loving is quite simple and familiar: to love is to be transformed into likeness to the beloved.

Aber, aber,—this law holds only on the ascending and not on the descending scale. Example. If someone is superior in understanding and wisdom, the law for his love in relation to a person far inferior in understanding and wisdom is certainly not that he be transformed into likeness with the latter.[*] To love in this way is to be ridiculous, and if he is actually superior it will not happen. No, the law is to want to do everything to draw the beloved up to himself, and if then the beloved wills it, then the law for his lover is to be transformed into the likeness of the beloved.

This law is applicable and is to be enforced in all possible situations.

In Christendom only one exception has been made, God in heaven; in the babytalk interpretation, God is supposed to be pure love —which is pure nonsense. Here it is clamorously affirmed to be egotism and deception if the superior one is not transformed into likeness to the one of less understanding; in one case this is supposed to be valid, that is, here the law of love does not apply, for God is indeed pure love —which is sheer nonsense!

In this way for the good of children and "childlike souls" Christendom has transformed God into such a fabulous monstrosity that everything known by the ancients about monstrously compounded creatures, everything the most dissolute Arabian fantasy has hit upon, is but a bagatelle compared to this conglomeration: to be omnipotent, omniscient, all-wise, and so on—all this united with being love, but love, it should be noted, in the sense of being nonsense, so that even the silliest woman, for example, in loving her child as a mother, is indeed less nonsensical, is less remote from pure love.

No, that God is love means, of course, that he will do everything to help you to love him, that is, to be transformed into likeness to him. As I have frequently said, he knows very well how infinitely agonizing this transformation is for a human being; he is willing to suffer with you—yes, out of love he suffers more than you, suffers all the deep sorrow of misunderstanding—but he is not changed.

But just as an older person, wishing to win a child's love, begins by becoming an object of affection to the child according to the child's understanding, and to that end gives the child cookies etc., so Christianity, too, provides an inducement.

The inducement is the proclamation of the forgiveness of sins. Every human being who is not integrated enough as a person to sorrow over his sins, to note that the tragedy really lies at this point, every human being who does not have that much of the eternal in him—of every such person it holds true that he cannot come to love God, God cannot become involved with him, God cannot, if I may put it this way, hunt him down.

Consequently the forgiveness of sins is preached and, if I dare say so, with a magnificence which is without parallel.

Now Christianity really begins. From this the transition is to be made to loving God or to be remade into likeness with God. And thus begins what I characterize in this way: God must make you unhappy, humanly speaking, if he is to love you and you are to love him.[190]

Like the child who eats the cookies and ignores the giver, Christendom has done the supposedly deft trick of taking the divine magnificence away and then using it as a piquant ingredient in living this life pleasantly according to its own lights. This is the swindle, the most foolish thing possible, of course, since the most foolish thing of all is to try to fool God.

XI² A 8   n.d., 1854

« 2451

[*] *In margin of 2450* (XI² A 8):

Note. Of course it must be remembered that any conceivable superiority in the relation between man and man is still only a very imperfect analogy to the relation between being God and being human. And since we nobly and piously suppose the equality of all men, we are quite right in straightway equalizing the reciprocity so that the law for both parties is to be changed into likeness to the beloved.[191]

XI² A 9   n.d.

« 2452 *God Is Love*

When I have said that there is a doubleness in this, that he loves a person and wants to be loved, it should be remembered with regard to the latter that this is again a qualification of his love for the person, because God knows that the highest blessedness for a human being is to come to love God properly.

In the relationship of erotic love between two human beings this naturally cannot be the case because of the egotism in wanting to be loved, for it does not follow that for the other party it is the greatest happiness and benefaction to come to love this person.

XI² A 105   n.d., 1854

« 2453

God wants to be loved. This is why he wants Christians. To love God is to be a Christian.

God, of course, knows best how agonizing this is, humanly speaking, for a man. He says it as clearly as possible. To love God is possible only by clashing with all human existence (hating father and mother, hating oneself, suffering because one is a Christian etc.)

"Man's" rascally interests these days center on securing millions of Christians, the more the better, all, if possible, for in this way the whole difficulty in being a Christian vanishes; being a Christian and being a human being are synonymous, and we stand where paganism left off.

"Christendom" is that cowardly, hypocritical, rascally attempt to make a fool of God in a nice way, as if this kind of Christians by battalions were good enough for God (who wants to be loved—and what this means he himself knows well enough). This is a swindle, and it is hypocritically concealed by those velveteen liars under the pretence that their zeal for this kind of extension is Christian zeal for the extension of the doctrine.

Christendom has mocked and still mocks God just as much as if someone were to bring a nut-lover tons and millions of tons of hollow nuts instead of one nut with a kernel in it, and thereby give the appearance of zeal for fulfilling his desire.

If there were no eternity we should have to say that nothing as untrue as these words has ever been said: God is not mocked.

XI² A 390   *n.d.*, 1854–55

« **2454** *Dying to the World*¹⁹²

July 2

Even an adult is not wholly at ease when the dentist takes out his instruments—and it is his tooth which is to be pulled. And even the most courageous man gets a strange feeling around his heart when the surgeon takes out his instruments—and it is his arm or leg which is to be amputated.

Yet in every man there is something that is more deeply rooted than a molar, that is most deeply rooted, something to which he clings more tightly than to an arm or a leg of his body—this is a man's zest for life.

Therefore all experience shouts: Above all, see to it that you don't lose your zest for life; whatever you lose in life, if you keep only this, there is always the possibility of regaining everything.

God is of another mind. Above all, he says, I must take away a man's zest for life if there is to be any possibility of becoming a Christian, of dying to the world, of hating onself, and of loving me.

It is terrifying when God takes out the instruments for the operation for which no human being has the strength: to take away a man's zest for life, to slay him—in order that he can live as one who has died to life.

Yet it cannot be otherwise, for in no other way can a human being love God. He must be in a state of agony so that if he were a pagan he would at no time hesitate to commit suicide. In this state he must —live. Only in this state can he love God. I am not saying that everyone in this state therefore loves God, by no means. I only say that this state is the condition for being able to love God.

* *

And this religion has become a national religion, on which 1000 oath-bound Falstaffs or veterinarians and their families are living, etc.

XI^2 A 421   July 2, 1855

« 2455 *To Love God or to Love the Ugly*

July 10, 1855

In everything essentially Christian, if it is to be kept the Christianity of the New Testament, there is a serious *nota bene* which has the effect, if this *nota bene* is to stand, that almost all flee from it.[193] Christendom's genius, working on the theory that Christianity is perfectible, has been and is the elimination of all these *nota bene's*. In this way Christianity has become nonsense, and now it goes in one ear and out the other; now we get millions of Christians and the preacher industry is flourishing.

To love the ugly[194]—yes, quite right! For if I am flesh and blood, a sensuous being, an animal-creature (all of which I actually am), then "spirit" is the most frightful of all to me, as frightful as death, and to love spirit is the most frightful of all. This is also the way Christianity understands it; it teaches that to love God is: to die, to die to the world, the most agonizing of all agonies—blessed is he who is not offended.

This is why in those times when people were still fairly earnest about Christianity a human skull was used as an object of prolonged meditation. We surely cannot say that spirit resembles a skull, for spirit resembles no physical object. But a human skull was nevertheless the most suggestive symbol.

* *

In "Christendom" it is different! The human skull—O, heaven help us, there is nothing people avoid more than anything that reminds them of death, even more so than they did in paganism. No, the death's head, that curious room decoration, is seen no more. On one cabinet there is now a naked Venus and on the other the crucified Savior—and a young woman and a speculative clergyman, both, of course, Christians, argue the question of which form is more beautiful.

Lectures are delivered in Christendom, in the name of Christianity, on the subject that to love God is to fill one's life, one's time, one's thoughts with the pursuit of the earthly, to thank God when one succeeds and pray to him for success. In other words, loving God is loving the beautiful. Therefore there also flourishes in Christendom —something it is very proud of and calls Christianity's newest development and most beautiful flower—Christian family life. Splendid! New Testament Christianity had a decided preference for the single state —and yet family life has become its culmination.

The whole thing, of course, is a lie, and to prevent as far as possible anyone from getting the idea that it is a lie, an appropriate device has been hit upon—having the minister take his oath upon the New Testament.

XI^2 A 426   July 10, 1855

LUTHER

« 2456

An old saying that the Antichrist would be born of a nun and a priest (originated and used at the time in connection with Luther's marriage) . . . . .

I A 283   n.d., 1836

« 2457

In v. Dobeneck (<i>des deutschen Mittelalters Volksglauben und Heroensagen,</i> II; Berlin: 1815) I, p. 149 fn., I find a remarkable quotation from Luther's <i>Table Talk</i> about a person who sold his soul to the devil: <i>Endlich b e t r o g ihn der Teufel r e d l i c h</i>[195] (what distressing irony for those concerned).

II A 145   August 26, 1837

« 2458

The same thing happened to Catholicism that happened to the entire globe. Another Copernicus (Luther) came along who discovered that Rome is not the center about which everything revolves but merely a peripheral point.

II A 289   November 2, 1838

« 2459

When in our day some dogmaticians make such a strong appeal to the Augsburg Confession as contrasted to the Formula of Concord,[196] they forget that the difference between them is more like that between the minute hand of a clock and the hour hand, which can never be as exact, and that generally many things which were questions in the Formula of Concord were not questions at all in the Augsburg Confession.

II A 434   May 20, 1839

« 2460

* When one reads Luther he definitely gets the impression of a wise and assured spirit who speaks with a decisiveness which is <i>"gewaltig"</i> (<i>er predigte gewaltig</i>—ἐξουσία—Matthew 7).[197] And yet it seems to me

this assurance has something alarming about it, in fact an uncertainty. It is well known that a mental state frequently seeks a hiding place in its opposite. We bolster ourselves with strong words, and the words tend to become even stronger simply because we ourselves are vacillating. This is not some kind of deception; it is a pious attempt. We do not even want to put the uncertainty or anxiety into words, we do not even want (or dare) to name it properly, and we force out the very opposite in hopes that it will help. Thus Luther makes dominant use of that which the New Testament uses very moderately—the sin against the Holy Spirit. In order to force himself and the believer forward, he uses these words directly and dramatically about everything. If this is the case, then ultimately there is not one single human being who has not merely once but many times sinned against the Holy Spirit. And since the N.T. maintains that this sin cannot be forgiven, what then? —I know very well that most people would cross themselves if I were to compare Luther's assurance with Socrates', for example. But would not this be an expression of the fact that most people have a greater sensitivity and inclination to the alarming? Luther, as you know, was very shaken by a stroke of lightning which killed the friend at his side, but his words always sound as if the lightning were continually striking behind him.[198]

VI A 108   *n.d.*, 1845

« **2461**

⟩ What Luther[199] says is excellent, the one thing needful and the sole explanation—that this whole doctrine (of the Atonement and in the main all Christianity) must be traced back to the struggle of the anguished conscience. Remove the anguished conscience, and you may as well lock the churches and convert them into dance halls.[200] The anguished conscience understands Christianity. In the same way an animal understands when you lay a stone and a piece of bread before it and the animal is hungry: the animal understands that one is for eating and the other is not. The anguished conscience understands Christianity. If we first have to prove the necessity of being hungry before we eat—well, then eating becomes finicky.

But you say, "I still cannot grasp the Atonement." Here I must ask in which understanding—in the understanding of the anguished conscience or in the understanding of indifferent and objective speculation. How could anyone sitting placidly and objectively in his study and speculating ever be able to understand the necessity of an atonement,

since an atonement is necessary only in the understanding of anguished conscience. If a man had the power to live without needing to
eat, how could he understand the necessity of eating—something the
hungry man easily understands. It is the same in the life of the spirit.
A man can acquire the indifference which renders the Atonement
superfluous—yes, the natural man is actually in this situation, but how
could someone in this situation be able to understand the Atonement?
It is therefore very consistent for Luther[201] to teach that man must be
taught by a revelation concerning how deeply he lies in sin, that the
anguished conscience is not a natural consequence like being hungry.

VII[1] A 192   *n.d.*, 1846

« **2462**

Luther[202] says somewhere that if one wishes to be a Christian, he
must also wear the court ceremonial dress (the cross).

Found quoted in my concordance[203] in the article *Kreuz*, para. 7.

VII[1] A 209   *n.d.*, 1846

« **2463**

Wonderful! The category "for you" (subjectivity, inwardness)
with which *Either/Or*[204] concludes (only the truth which builds up
[*opbygger*] is truth for you) is Luther's own. I have never really read
anything by Luther. But now I open up his sermons[205]—and right there
in the Gospel for the First Sunday in Advent he says "for you," on this
everything depends (see second page, first column, and first page,
fourth column).

VIII[1] A 465   *n.d.*, 1847

« **2464**

What a relief for the person who hears and reads the contemporary pastors and almost has to say to himself, "I understand from you
what I am to do—simply take it easy, because I have already become
too perfect"—what a relief to read Luther. There is a man who can
really stay by a person and preach him farther out instead of backwards.

VIII[1] A 541   *n.d.*, 1848

« **2465**

Saturday
Today I have read Luther's sermon according to plan;[206] it was the
Gospel about the ten lepers.[207] O, Luther is still the master of us all.

VIII[1] A 642   April 22, 1848

« **2466**

"Your sins are forgiven"—this is what the Christians call to each other, with this call Christianity proceeds through the world, by these words it is known, just as a people, a nation is always known by the language it speaks. One person shouts these words to another just as a night watchman in chain-series shouts a watchword to the next one, etc.

> See Luther's sermon[208] on the Gospel for the 19th Sunday after Trinity, the end.

> VIII[1] A 664   *n.d.,* 1848

« **2467**

I have frequently pointed out the confusion in modern philosophy with regard to faith. But even in Luther's interpretation there is a basic confusion in his understanding of faith. If faith is the immediate, a vitality, a kind of persevering genius with respect to this life so that one does not lose hope and confidence (in which one person is by nature equipped differently from another) or if it is a qualification of reflection, then the whole ethical idea of being willing to surrender desire has been compromised, with the result that faith is just as much the willingness to relinquish as to remain fast or to desire. This never becomes clear for Luther. Consequently he never does interpret or illuminate that around which everything revolves, that without which Christianity is neither more nor less than a doctrine pertaining to some few people who happen to have a genius for believing. That which is of utmost importance: you shall believe, and thus that every man can believe, whether or not he has the genius—away with it! But this is not faith at all; it is something which the world also esteems—this confident clinging to life. No, you shall believe.

Strangely enough, the examples in the New Testament (the gospels) which are of immediate faith—for example, the centurion, the hemorrhaging woman—here Luther[209] is inexhaustible in his praise of such faith. But this is not really faith; this is a spontaneous devotedness to Christ (hardly ever as the very Son of God) as the man who may be able to help, and this immediacy has a remarkable power to persevere. But is this faith? It is not clearly evident that Christ means anything more to them than a man who is able to help. If their immediacy is faith, then, to be sure, every young girl sincerely in love also has faith.

But every Sunday the preacher declares that when it comes to earthly desires one must add: If God wills it, if it is possible—that is, make it dialectical—that is, be willing to accept the opposite—that is, see to it that one makes the movement of resignation [*Resignationens*]. Luther usually talks about all this, too, but not when he explains gospels like these—that is, Luther is no dialectician; sometimes he has one thought, then again another. If this were to be applied to those gospels, it would have to be pointed out that it is dubious whether that centurion and that woman had faith, whether it was not rather an immediacy which, although laudable and touching, nevertheless rushed forth too impetuously.

But then a new difficulty arises, for Christ[210] himself praises the centurion's and the woman's faith.

But this difficulty is only apparent; for he could see into their hearts and therefore see that their faith was *after* resignation. And Christ himself expresses the dialectical definition of faith. He says: If it is possible.[211] And from Christ we are to learn.

But Luther is somewhat confused—that is, somewhat dialectically confused. It is upon this point among others that I must concentrate all my strength as I have been doing—the dialectical definition of faith.

IX A 11   *n.d.*, 1848

« **2468**

Luther[212] makes the excellent observation (the Epistle for New Year's Day) that just as the heir does not work to get possession, for he has it, just so with the works of the believer—they are training exercises; for in faith, to be sure, he owns everything, just as the heir owns the inheritance.

IX A 22   *n.d.*, 1848

« **2469**

They are words worthy of Luther (but he actually became too much involved with secular things, which is why the fruit of the Reformation became politics and political development), the words he spoke to one of the princes who wanted to help him: It is rather you who need my help; it depends on who is able to pray the best.

Task for thinkers: How far is present-day Christendom from finding meaning in this.

IX A 96   *n.d.*, 1848

« **2470**

Luther's sermon[213] on the Epistle for the Third Sunday after Easter is a true expression of his concept of conformity and heterogeneity between what is Christian and what is secular. But even here we already see how the natural outcome of the Reformation had to be a political development. The whole inward orientation in what I usually call "hidden inwardness" was not made dialectically secure enough, and thus it is quite natural to become preoccupied by secularity again and to make the former, which is presupposed, a cancelled element.

IX A 145 *n.d.*, 1848

« 2471

This [nonreducibility of Christianity] does not contradict Christ's statement[214] about one shepherd and one flock, for essentially this simply says that it shall be made possible for all to become true Christians.

See Luther's sermon[215] on the Gospel for the Second Sunday after Easter (I am the good shepherd), the conclusion: You must not understand it to mean that the whole world and all people are going to become believers. It means rather: we must always have the holy cross; the majority will always persecute the flock who believe, etc.

IX A 274 *n.d.*, 1848

« 2472

Luther[216] makes the fine observation (in his sermon on Nicodemus) that the bronze serpent looked exactly like other snakes, yet with the difference not only of not being poisonous but of being liberating. In the same way Christ looks like all other men, belongs to the fallen race, and yet he is not merely without sin, but is the Savior.

IX A 377 November 26, 1848

« 2473

When Luther,[217] speaking of the Gospel about the lost sheep,[218] says that it is the same with a mother who has many children ("When one child is sick, at the time it looks very much as if she loved only the sick child")—this is really misinterpreting the Gospel. For a mother certainly is attached to the other children nevertheless, and she merely seems to love only the sick child. But in God's relationship to the sinner, whom he loves, it is not like this; he does not, after all, love the 99 righteous ones just as much.

IX A 389 *n.d.*, 1848

« 2474

In Luther's sermon[219] on the Gospel for the Twelfth Sunday after Trinity (*Ephata*) there are some excellent observations about faith on behalf of others, but also the usual dialectical unclarity when he says that only when we are able to add "It surely will happen" does it then happen. The fact is that every prayer must be made dialectical, but Luther vacillates between the immediate definition of faith and the dialectical.

IX A 433   *n.d.*, 1848

« 2475

Luther's commentary[220] on this text is wonderful. The very moment when the faith of the synagogue leader is tempted most severely —that is, when the message comes that his daughter is dead and that consequently it is pointless to bother Christ—at that very moment the woman suffering from a hemorrhage is healed, as if to strengthen his faith.

X[1] A 10   *n.d.*, 1849

« 2476

The observation which Luther[221] makes (the Gospel for the Twenty-Seventh Sunday after Trinity) is entirely right—that the parable of the wise and foolish virgins[222] does not distinguish between Christians and pagans but between Christians and Christians, i.e., Christians who are that only in name.

X[1] A 21   *n.d.*, 1849

« 2477

It is just as Luther[223] says somewhere in the sermon on the Epistle for the First Sunday in Advent: Either a man indulges the flesh too much so that he sophistically manages to place far too much under the heading of life's necessities, or he mortifies himself, but then there is the lurking error of thinking that this is something meritorious. In the first case the man very likely is aware of it himself but makes God out to be all too loving, somewhat like an all too lenient father. At the same time, if he honestly confesses before God that he just does not dare venture out further and puts it up to God whether or not he will withdraw this sanction from him, although he will rejoice in it as long as he has it with God's permission—then the situation is not as dangerous. The other error of meritoriousness is always more dangerous. If one is weak, it is easier [than for the strong] to be weak before God. But if one is such a robust devil of a fellow that he can manage things himself, he only too easily becomes self-important.

X[1] A 25   *n.d.*, 1849

« **2478**

Luther[224] says (in the sermon on the Epistle for the Second Sunday in Advent) that Paul calls Scriptures the Word of the Cross. This is not entirely true, but the name is good.

x^1 A 32   *n.d.*, 1849

« **2479**

What Luther[225] says (in the sermon on the Epistle for the Fourth Sunday in Advent) is excellent: To pray God for something and then not believe that he will give it means to make a fool of God.

Also at the end of the same sermon: God is to be everything to us, and we are to be everything to the neighbor.

x^1 A 47   *n.d.*, 1849

« **2480**

The conclusion of Luther's sermon[226] for Quinquagesima Sunday on I Corinthians 13, where he makes out that faith is superior to love, is sophistry. On the whole Luther always interprets love only as love toward one's neighbor, just as if it were not also a duty to love God. Essentially Luther had substituted faith for love toward God and then called love—love toward one's neighbor.

x^1 A 85   *n.d.*, 1849

« **2481**

Since the Middle Ages had gone farther and farther astray in accentuating the aspect of Christ as the prototype—Luther came along and accentuated the other side, that he is a gift and this gift is to be received in faith.[227]

In other respects, the more I look at Luther the more I am convinced that he was muddle-headed. A reform which amounts to casting off burdens and making life easy is appreciated—and one can easily get friends to cooperate. True reforming always makes life difficult, lays on burdens, and therefore the true reformer is always slain, as if it were enmity toward mankind.

Just that line of Luther's—Hear me, O Pope, etc.—to me is almost disgustingly secular-minded. Is this the sanctified earnestness of a reformer who, concerned for his own responsibility, knows that all true reforming consists in inward deepening. Such words are so very reminiscent of a journalist's slogan and the like. That unfortunate politicizing, that business of dislodging the Pope, is and still remains Luther's confusion.

But now in our time it is clear that what must come to the fore is the aspect of Christ as prototype. The main point is to have learned from the Middle Ages to avoid the errors of this approach. But it is this side which must come to the fore, because the Lutheran emphasis on faith has now simply become a fig leaf for the most unchristian shirking.

x^1 A 154   *n.d.*, 1849

« 2482

Luther's sermon[228] on the Epistle for the Third Sunday in Trinity may be cited as an example of his incorrectness. In his first point about humility he says that both God and the world resist the proud but love the humble. In his next point he shows how the pious man must suffer, why he needs consolation. (Cast all your cares upon God.) Here Luther has in the first place obviously forgotten to define accurately the Christian collision. It simply is not true that the world loves the humble person. The world ridicules the humble person. And essential Christianity continually means: to do the good and for that very reason to suffer.

x^1 A 172   *n.d.*, 1849

« 2483

Luther[229] rightly says (in the sermon on the Epistle for the Eighth Sunday after Trinity) that if the forgiveness of sins was intended to make good works superfluous, the doctrine should not be called the doctrine of the forgiveness of sins but the doctrine of the permission of sins.

x^1 A 197   *n.d.*, 1849

« 2484

The tragedy of Christendom is clearly that we have removed the dialectical element from Luther's doctrine of faith, so that it has become a cloak for sheer paganism and epicureanism. We completely forget that Luther urged faith in contrast to a fantastically exaggerated asceticism.

x^1 A 213   *n.d.*, 1849

« 2485

Luther's sermon[230] on the Gospel for Epiphany is worth reading again and again, especially the first part.

x^1 A 297   *n.d.*, 1849

« **2486**

Deuteronomy 33:9—"who said of his father and mother, 'I regard them not'; he disowned his brothers, and ignored his children." Here, indeed, the subject is a religiousness which corresponds to Christianity: to hate father and mother for Christ's sake.

I became aware of this passage in Luther's sermon[231] on the Gospel about the marriage at Cana.

x^1 A 303 *n.d.*, 1849

« **2487**

"Faith made us masters; love made us servants," says Luther[232] in the sermon on the Gospel for the Third Sunday after Epiphany.

In the same Gospel[233] (about the leper) we read that Christ says to the leper: Go, show yourself to the priests *as a witness to them.* In the last phrase there is a double meaning which Luther also hints at. "Witness to them," i.e., that they may bear witness to it, but also, that it may become a witness to them that they themselves ought to believe in Christ.

x^1 A 304 *n.d.*, 1849

« **2488**

In Luther's sermon[234] on the Gospel about Christ boarding the boat, there are excellent things, among them his reference to the delusion of that piety which is so busy about "peace of mind" and seeks in this a proof of piety.

Bishop Mynster's entire leadership is neither more nor less than worldly prudence, and to that extent he has done much harm.

x^1 A 314 *n.d.*, 1849

« **2489**

Precisely when the religious is most true it is true in such a way that reason almost has to smile at it—and stop believing. How refreshing and invigorating what Luther[235] says about praying boldly, rightly imploring and pestering God—he likes this, it pleases him very much. Here reason might say: Yes, this is all right, but still it is dangerous to pray in this way if my primary desire is to get something; since my praying pleases God, he could decline to give me what I pray for simply in order that I could become more and more pleasing to him, in so far as my imploring becomes more and more fervent.

To this must be answered: Rubbish! This is one of Luther's immortal services and the surest testimony of how tried and tested he was

—the fact he invented the category of rubbish as the only reply one ought to give to doubt,[236] unless one prefers to say with Hamann: Bah! Yet I prefer Luther's expression, which expresses quite differently the momentum of a striving which in fear and trembling will listen to no rubbish. Hamann's expression is more humorous but also more careless and to that extent less earnest. Perhaps one thinks it is a jest if one says "Rubbish" to doubt—O, truly, he who has had to defend himself with this answer, he knows what earnestness is. To become involved in doubt is a jest, to listen to it a little is also jest—but to say nothing but "Rubbish" shows that the matter is earnest and that one takes it seriously.

x^1 A 324   n.d., 1849

« **2490**

"But these things are written for our consolation, that we might know: where *one* devil tempts us, there are *many* angels to minister to us."

Luther[237] in the sermon on the gospel account of the temptations of Christ.

x^1 A 326   n.d., 1849

« **2491**

In his sermon on the Gospel for the Second Sunday after Easter ("I am the good shepherd"), Luther[238] very movingly develops the way the true Christian becomes unrecognizable, as it were, through all the persecution and mistreatment etc. he suffers—but Christ still knows him and recognizes him as his own.

What Luther[239] says in the same sermon about hirelings deserves to be reprinted. It is so very appropriate—and this was said by someone now dead.

x^1 A 370   n.d., 1849

« **2492**

The conclusion of Luther's sermon[240] on the Gospel "I am the good shepherd" deserves to be printed just in order, if possible, to put an end once and for all to all the nonsense that there are supposedly pure Christians, and consequently Christianity quits striving.

x^1 A 376   n.d., 1849

« **2493**

It might sometime be appropriate to memorize one of Luther's sermons and deliver it without giving any hint of it—and then see how furious the clergy would become—and then say: This is a sermon by

Luther, word for word. As a precaution one could let two persons in on the sworn secret who could testify that this was one's original intention—so that the whole thing would not turn out to be a case of plagiarism.

X^1 A 403   n.d., 1849

« 2494

Luther[241] is entirely right in saying (in the sermon on the Gospel) that these are strong words about God—for God so loved the world—because "the world is an abomination to God"; but this is just to show that no one is excluded except one who excludes himself.

X^1 A 419   n.d., 1849

« 2495

"Faith is not everybody's business"—but this is a peculiar use of language by Luther[242] in his translation of II Thessalonians 3:2. Faith is thereby superficially defined as a kind of genius, a disposition, a talent. I also recall that Schelling[243] in his lectures said something to the effect that faith is a talent—and cited Luther.

X^1 A 420   n.d., 1849

« 2496

The Gospel about the great banquet[244] (second Sunday after Trinity) begins with the statement by one of the guests: Blessed is he who shall eat bread in the kingdom of God. But Christ takes the occasion for a parable, showing that he might not make it to the table in the kingdom of God. Humanly speaking, this is somewhat harsh. In his sermon Luther[245] himself takes note of this discourtesy.

The same Gospel presents marriage as an excuse for not seeking God's kingdom.

In his sermon on this Gospel Luther[246] introduces a really remarkable proof of the immortality of the soul, which he himself, however, does not rightly emphasize. He declares that Christ himself is the food, is the banquet, is the meal. If, then, we eat of this meal, even though we die, we are unable to remain in death, for—our food lives. Usually we conclude that we live because we eat; here the conclusion is that we may live because the food lives. There is something remarkable about this syllogism.

X^1 A 439   n.d., 1849

« 2497

In Luther's sermon[247] on the Pharisee and the publican, a beautiful passage from Psalm 50:23 is quoted:

He who brings thanksgiving as his sacrifice honors me; to him who orders his way aright I will show the salvation of God.

Therefore "thanksgiving" is essentially the God-pleasing "sacrifice."

x¹ A 474   *n.d.,* 1849

« **2498**

Luther[248] uses a very good category in his sermon on the Epistle for Christmas Day (Hebrews)—that "Christ is the radiance of his glory and the express image of his nature."

"These words are better understood with the heart than they are expressed with pen or tongue." And then comes this:

"Intrinsically they are more intelligible than all explanations and the more one explains them the more obscure they become." That is, they *are not supposed to be comprehended.*

x¹ A 526   *n.d.,* 1849

« **2499**

Luther[249] makes a good distinction in the sermon on the second Sunday after Epiphany (Epistle) between reproving or punishing and cursing. The one who curses desires that evil may come; the one who punishes desires that evil will disappear.

x¹ A 545   *n.d.,* 1849

« **2500**

Luther's words[250] at the very beginning of his sermon on the Epistle for the First Sunday in Lent are true.

Experience also teaches that the gospel never remains pure and unadulterated anywhere in the world longer than within living memory; but as long as those who first brought it into being lived, it endured and increased—when they were dead and gone the light went out. Then came the sects and false teachers.

The latter remark is less important. The former is entirely true, except that Luther himself seems not to have been entirely clear about the implicit categories of thought. The relation of contemporaneity[251] to Christ is the true relationship, is the truth of situation. Next comes the derived: contemporaneity with true Christianity in an even stricter sense. Second-hand Christianity is nonsense, because it is Christianity without the tension of actuality.

x¹ A 595   *n.d.,* 1849

« **2501**

In the sermon on the Epistle for the Sixth Sunday after Easter, Luther[252] expresses very beautifully that the Christian must maintain the practice every day either of God's speaking with him (by reading God's Word) or of speaking with God (by praying).

x[1] A 630   *n.d.*, 1849

« **2502**

Even Luther does not put it together properly.

In the sermon[253] on the Epistle for the Second Sunday after Trinity, he preaches on the text: Do not wonder that the world hates you. The next Sunday he preaches about humility[254] (God resists the proud), that without humility one is loved neither by God nor by men. But he forgets that the Christian ratio is: do good and suffer for it—consequently, be humble and you will be or will continue to be hated by men. Then in another portion[255] of the same sermon, "Cast all your cares upon God," Luther says something about that the Christian must suffer.

But it is completely undialectical to speak this way. In animatedly exhorting to humility, one leaves out the difficulty and establishes an unchristian relationship; another Sunday one provides consolation.

I have spoken of this at the end of part I of *Works of Love.*[256] But I cannot emphasize it enough. It is no easy matter. Over the years I have unceasingly trained myself in it, and yet I frequently catch myself veering away unchristianly.

The life of the spirit is extremely strenuous. To prove that I am right about this, that I am ridiculed, that I am in the minority—what extreme strenuousness. And suppose, then, that the majority were to come over to one's side—then to remember that this, indeed, would be proof, or in any case an indication, that one was wrong. And to have to endure this in a world where one lives in company with these thousands and thousands who understand no more about spirit than they understand Chinese!

x[1] A 651   *n.d.*, 1849

« **2503** *A Point of View in Luther's Direction*

Luther is entirely right in what he says in the preface to his sermons[257] about the distinction between Christ as pattern [*Exempel*] and as gift. I am quite conscious of the fact that I have moved in the direction of Christ as pattern.

But something must be kept in mind in this regard. Luther was confronted by the exaggerated misuse of Christ as pattern; therefore he accentuates the opposite.[258] But Luther has long since been victorious in Protestantism and Christ has been completely forgotten as the pattern, and the whole thing actually has become pretence in hidden inwardness.

In addition, I have also thought that Christ as example must be used in a way different from what Luther or the Middle Ages had in mind. Christ as pattern ought to jack up the price so enormously that the prototype [*Forbilledet*] itself teaches men to resort to grace. The error of the Middle Ages was in imagining that men could possibly manage to be like Christ. From this came sanctification by works and the like. Then came Luther and quite rightly emphasized Christ as gift and made the same distinction[259] between Christ as gift and as pattern as between faith and works. But I wonder if Luther ever dreamed of the pretence involved in the hidden inwardness which this has engendered. I also wonder if Luther ever dreamed when he got married that this would eventually go so far that a pastor would almost think that if he only married he then would have done all that God required of him.

I see very clearly how I could be attacked from Luther's own position, but, truly, I have also understood Luther well—and therefore I have also taken care not to tumble around in a fog, as if everything were still as it was in Luther's day.

x^2 A 30   *n.d.,* 1849

« 2504

At the close of Luther's sermon[260] on the Gospel for the day after Easter, there is a remark about the incomprehensibility of faith and that it is not to be a matter of speculation.

x^2 A 123   *n.d.,* 1849

« 2505

Luther[261] makes a superb observation on the great draft of fish: the apostles got it not because of their toil and labor—no, on the contrary they got it only after they had labored and toiled in vain.

x^2 A 162   *n.d.,* 1849

« 2506

Luther[262] makes a fine distinction when he says: The gospel does not read, "*Your hand* shall not kill" but "*You* shall not kill"—and thereby shows that the thought, the cast of mind, is decisive.

x^2 A 173   *n.d.,* 1849

« **2507**

Luther's teaching is not only a return to original Christianity but a modification of the essentially Christian. He onesidedly draws Paul[263] forward and uses the gospels less.[264]

He himself best disproves his conception of the Bible, he who throws out the epistle of James. Why? Because it does not belong to the canon? No, this he does not deny. But on dogmatic grounds. Therefore he himself has a point of departure superior to the Bible, which probably was his idea, too, since he posited Scripture just before the conflict with the Pope, in order to have a firm basis, conceding a willingness to be convinced if they could convince him by the Scriptures. And this was all right, for what he wanted eliminated was the balderdash of tradition, which they no doubt would not find in the Bible.

x^2 A 244   *n.d.*, 1849

« **2508**

Odd that Luther[265] declares so often in his sermons that we should pay the clergy and the schoolteachers. He refers to it even in his sermon on the Gospel for the 26th Sunday after Trinity (Matthew 25) about the day of judgment, when Christ will divide the sheep from the goats.

x^2 A 245   *n.d.*, 1849

« **2509** *Luther is really not clear,*

not about the doctrine of free will, either, and thus in his sermon[266] on the Epistle for the First Sunday after Epiphany (Romans 12) he definitely gets into asceticism.

Nor is Luther entirely clear concerning another aspect of free will. It is common knowledge that the cunning orthodox abolish it solely out of fear of tempting God. But Luther rants against free will at times and then preaches how everyone ought to obey the authorities etc.[267] But as for Luther himself! Was it not of his own free will that he exposed himself to certain danger by opposing the Pope? It certainly was not the Pope who attacked Luther; it was Luther who attacked the Pope.

Or I wonder how Luther would judge the theory which Peter [Christian Kierkegaard] has formulated in order to give a gloss to whimpering: one ought to witness for the good but not against the evil. And then according to this theory I am judged. Consequently, when evil is shrewd enough to ignore all one's witness to the good, perhaps even so audacious as to make capital of it, extolling it, then one would not dare to witness against the evil without tempting God. In that case almost every one of the martyrs of the Church is to be judged guilty of having tempted God. Instead, formulating such theories, which hide one's lack of courage and faith and confidence, is enough to tempt God. Is it not also tempting God if a person sneaks away, stays at home, when he expects an encounter; is this not tempting his patience, just as much as it is tempting God to plunge rashly ahead? Was Napoleon angrier when a general ventured on his own responsibility than when a general cautiously failed to appear—or incautiously and indefensibly. Ultimately pusillanimity's greatest virtue is to sleep[268]—in order not to sin or to tempt God.

But back to Luther. Luther acted rightly, but his preaching is not always clear or in agreement with his life—a rare occurrence—his life is better than his preaching!

The fact of the matter is that we must acknowledge that in the last resort there is no theory. As the king was the law and the end of the law, so our Lord is ultimately all theory. Consult with him, you single individual—this is the theory.

x^2 A 263   *n.d.*, 1849

« 2510 *Proportions*

Luther[269] rightly says (in the sermon about Stephen) that there should be no preaching in the churches. It is an accommodation with a kind of idolatry. It is a concession to our weakness. —Alas, we are so far behind that not many even go to church—and nevertheless this is Christendom!

x^2 A 334   *n.d.*, 1850

« 2511

In the beginning of the sermon on the Epistle for the Third Sunday after Easter, Luther[270] rightly shows that it is Jewish to cling to this life, the wish that one may prosper in everything and that he may live long in the land; it is Christian to regard oneself as a pilgrim here in this world, even though Luther finds it necessary in view of the extremes of the Middle Ages to warn against running to the monastery and the like.

The consequence of the Jewish view is intensified nationalism—and now (yes, as in every respect Christianity is turned around)—now it has become the true orthodoxy to be as nationalistic as any politician.

This is a counterpart to what I have pointed out some other place: Christianity praises the unmarried state—nowadays married life is earnestness, the unmarried state fanaticism. Christianity was proclaimed by men who demanded no wages—in Christendom today when a man has a son who cannot do anything else they say: Let him become a theologian, it is the surest way to make a living, real breadlearning.

x^2 A 364   n.d., 1850

« **2512**

Luther was no dialectician. In his sermon[271] on the Epistle for the Sixth Sunday after Easter, he develops (something he develops elsewhere also) the theme that in relation to faith the concern should not be with persons but only with the word: Even if it were an apostle and he taught anything different from Holy Scripture, one ought not follow him.

Well and good—but Luther should still have been a little more careful. Indeed, Christianity has obviously come into the world conversely so that the person is higher than the doctrine. How am I going to find out if something is God's word or doctrine? Luther answers: By testing the doctrine—then all is lost and Christianity is a human invention. It happens the other way around, that I submit to a person's authority; but consequently the person is higher than the doctrine.

Luther ought to have been mindful of this, although he may be right in other respects in what he says about man's presumption over against the word of God.

x^2 A 448   n.d., 1850

« **2513** *The Fraudulent Use of Luther*

The fraud is this: what Luther did in opposition to and in some defiance of a mistaken, deluded inflation of asceticism[272]—this has been made into the truth in and for itself; and now although everything has become secularized (so that the contrast has disappeared completely), Luther is appealed to nevertheless.

Precisely in contrast to the exaggeration and deluded meritoriousness of the ascetic, Luther devoutly marked out a simple secularity in the good sense of the word. But here the contrast is the very point. Now Christianity has been completely homogenized with unadulterated secularism—and still we continue to appeal to Luther.

x^2 A 558   n.d., 1850

« **2514** *Luther*

When I look at Luther, I often come to think that there is something dubious about him—a reformer who wants to throw off the yoke is questionable. This is precisely why he was promptly taken in vain *politically;* for he himself as well as his whole position share a common boundary with politics—not attacking "the crowd" but a high-ranking individual.

This is why the battle was so easy for Luther. What is difficult is simply having to suffer because one has to make things more difficult for others. When one is fighting to throw off burdens, he is, of course, promptly understood by a whole mass of people who are interested in having burdens thrown off. Consequently the proper Christian mark of double danger is missing here.

In a certain sense Luther took the matter too lightly. He ought to have made it obvious that the freedom he was fighting for (and in this battle he was right) leads to making life, the life of the spirit, infinitely more strenuous than it was before.

If he had rigorously kept to that, then surely no one would have cared to line up with him, and he would have experienced the double danger; for no one joins forces with someone—in order to have his life made more strenuous.

But he swung off too hastily. Jubilantly, politically jubilating, the contemporary age embraced his cause, joined the party—Luther wants to topple the Pope—bravo! Well, all I can say is that this is pure political bargaining.

The only important thing to me in this is to get it dialectically clarified. As for the rest, I have the deepest respect for Luther—but was he a Socrates? No, no, far from that. When I talk purely and simply about man I say: Of all men old Socrates is the greatest—Socrates, the hero and martyr of intellectuality. Only you understood what it is to be a reformer, understood what it meant for you yourself to be that, and were that.

X^2 A 559   *n.d.,* 1850

« **2515**

There is something very striking in Luther's observation[273] in his sermon on the Gospel for the day of Mary's Annunciation: Men doubt that God will provide adequately for their physical needs and then believe that he will surely bestow eternal salvation upon them.

Alas, the truth is that we let eternal salvation stand at a distance; we make use of physical necessity right away.

The relationship is quite different, however. Just because eternal salvation is so great a good, we feel such a great need for it—for that very reason the need helps us. Sometimes it is more difficult for a person to associate earthly need with thought of God in the right way —God is very easily too spiritual for him.

x³ A 58   n.d., 1850

« **2516** *Luther as* **point de vue**

I could be tempted to take Luther's book of sermons and extract a great many sentences and ideas, all of which are marked in my copy, and publish them in order to show how far the preaching nowadays is from Christianity, so that it shall not be said that I am the one who hits upon exaggerations.

x³ A 127   n.d., 1850

« **2517** *Judaism—Christianity*

Even Luther was not sure about the difference between Jewish religiousness and Christian religiousness.

Judaic religion relates to this life, has promise for this life—the Christian religion is essentially promise for the next life, since essential Christianity is suffering truth.

In one and the same sermon[274] (the sermon on the Gospel for the first day of Pentecost)—yes, with only a few periods between—Luther represents the Christian "as a man of God, a man for whose sake God spares country and people," and he also says that "the world must regard the Christian as the bird of ill omen which brings corruption and damnation upon country and people." Luther speaks this way in other places where he speaks about storms coming as soon as there is a true Christian and true Christian confession—"If Christ is along in the ship, there is stormy weather at once"—thus the Christian simply cannot be acceptable to the world "which lived in peace and quiet until that man came and disturbed everything," as it is stated also in one of Luther's sermons.[275]

x³ A 138   n.d., 1850

« **2518** *Luther*

The place where we really have to begin again is with Luther.

It went a little too fast with this lumping together of secularity and religiousness.

Luther was perhaps right as far as he himself was concerned; he certainly possessed the inward truth to dare to venture doing the opposite and yet be completely free in it, to be married and yet be as if not married, to be in the world and yet be as a stranger, although taking part in everything, etc.

Ah, but it was a dangerous matter to extend this teaching beyond himself, for this made the matter all too easy for all secular minded- ness, which is satisfied with merely giving verbal assurances and thus remains purely and simply secularism.

How many are there really in any generation of whom it can be truthfully said that even though they own all earthly goods, they own them in such a way that they still do not possess them, that they are willing to surrender them at any time, that they do not cling to them at all, would willingly let them go?

O, dangerous spirituality. It is far more simple to say: I am afraid of myself, afraid that the whole thing might be a complete fraud in me, so I would rather give them up.

Incidentally, Luther himself was severely tried in external strug- gles, did not entirely conform to the secular mentality, and was tested by the enormous scandal his marriage aroused.

Ah, but now all testing has vanished!

Luther's true successor will come to resemble the exact opposite of Luther, because Luther came after the preposterous overstatement of asceticism; whereas he will come after the horrible fraud to which Luther's view gave birth.

X^3 A 153   *n.d.*, 1850

« 2519 *The Pharisee—and the Tax-Collector*

In his sermon on this Luther[276] properly points out that the Phari- see's guilt was that since he felt superior to the tax-collector he did not give a thought to helping him toward salvation but was satisfied with his feeling of superiority; thus he used the tax-collector, if I dare put it this way, to illustrate his virtue and piety by contrast.

———

It is also noteworthy that the Gospel puts a purely Christian prayer in the tax-collector's mouth and thus actually introduces the essentially Christian before Christianity. Therefore Luther is of the opinion (in the same sermon) that we must assume that the publican had heard the Christian proclamation. Thus the parable does not show the difference within Judaism but shows the difference between Judaism and Christianity.

x³ A 170   n.d., 1850

« 2520 *O, Luther, too*

does not think consistently but talks enthusiastically about one thing in one place and forgets that somewhere else he says something else —thus it is difficult to act on such instructions.

In the Gospel about the woman who was hemorrhaging he says right at the end[277] that even the greatest of all will happen if a man believes it will happen. This, he says, is apparent from the two miracles in the Gospel.

But in other places Luther declares that to expect miracles is to tempt God.

x³ A 211   n.d., 1850

« 2521 *Luther*

When Luther said: Voluntary poverty, the single state, to spend the larger part of the day in prayer and supplication, fasting, etc.—all these are not the crucial factors—it is faith (in this connection it must be remembered that faith could also be combined with the monastic life and originally was part and parcel of it, and the degeneration was not so much the monastic life as the meritoriousness it was presumed to have), this was certainly true of Luther. In addition, to keep the record straight, he was also the man who had shown that he knew and at every moment how to do the former.

Ah, but Luther was not a dialectician; he did not see the enormous danger involved in making something else supreme, something which relates to and presupposes a first and for which there is no test whatsoever. He did not understand that he had provided the corrective and that he ought to turn off the tap with extreme caution lest people automatically make him into a paradigm.

This is exactly what happened. It was not long before the secular mentality understood: Aha! There is just the man for us,[278] that Luther! Aided and abetted by his theory, we get permission to hang on to a thoroughgoing secularity, to arrange our lives so secularly that it is a pleasure, and then we add: "To give everything to the poor, to live in the monastery is not the best thing—that is what Luther said"—not even one of our most cunning schemers would have had the courage to contrive that. And it is true—it takes great courage, great faith and fearlessness, devoutly to venture such things—on the other hand, it requires only a very ordinary scoundrel to take it in vain.

Poor Luther! To think that every fellow appeals to you, how all those job-holders, "gentlemen, fathers, and champion rifle-shots,"[279] members of the Friendship Club, et al., and also the clergy, appeal to you.

For my part, among all the people I know I have not found a single one whom I dared believe capable of voluntarily giving up everything to live in a monk's cell, no more than I dare assert it of myself. It is really hard when one is 37 years old, a theological candidate for many years, already for some time a recognized author—then to discover that he is not capable of doing what he knew at sixteen, due to his upbringing, people had far surpassed.

X³ A 217   n.d., 1850

« 2522

In margin of 2521 (x³ A 217):

No wonder Luther very quickly got such great support! The secular mentality understood immediately that here was a break. That this was true of Luther was beside the point to them; they understood at once how with a little lying this could be used to great profit. They invented the assurance, they assured that in their deep inwardness they were willing to give everything to the poor, etc., but since it was not the highest, they did not do it, kept every penny and grinned in their beards at our Lord, the New Testament, Luther—especially at Luther, that chosen instrument of God who had helped men so splendidly to make a fool of God.

Curiously enough, after the gospel had been given its rightful place and all this about voluntary poverty etc. had been removed, Luther himself had to undergo the experience of scarcely being able to get a little money for the pastors and schoolteachers. People probably answered: To give your goods to the poor or the Church is not the highest good—this is what Luther says—therefore we do not do it. If it were the highest, we would surely do it. Thus in his sermon[280] on the Gospel for the 26th Sunday after Trinity (other places as well), Luther complains that it was much better before, even though the gospel had been brought out into the light of day.

On the whole Luther struck too hard. He should have done everything to remove self-righteousness from such works and then otherwise have left them standing, should have regarded his marriage as an act of awakening. But he went too far; the result was that getting married and not giving to the poor came to be regarded as a great step forward in religious life.

Also in *Tischreden* (ed. Benjamin Lindner; Salfeld: 1745) (in a piece with the title *"von einem Fürsten, der in seinem letzten Ende Geld auf Wucher ausliehe,"*[281] part II, p. 229) Luther says: *"also ist es jetzt* (namely, since the gospel was disclosed) *leider dahin kommen, dass man sagt: oh, gute Werck, meine frommigkeit macht mich nicht selig, darum wil ich geitzen, wuchern, und thun, was mir gefällt und wohl thut etc."*[282]—

X³ A 218   *n.d.*

« 2523

In his sermon on the Gospel for the 26th Sunday after Trinity, Luther[283] wants to point out as a matter of course that in Matthew 25:31, etc. pagan acts of compassion are out of the question, because it says the acts are directed to Christians "and a pagan would scarcely show compassion toward a Christian". This is a somewhat precipitous and mistaken conclusion. In a relationship still more bitter than that between pagan and Christian, the relationship between Jew and Samaritan, the Samaritan certainly showed compassion to the Jew.

X³ A 221   *n.d.,* 1850

« 2524 *Luther's Metamorphoses*

Luther's contemporaries, especially his intimates, received the strong impression that he was a hero of the faith, at first excessively melancholy and then dreadfully tested in the most frightful spiritual trials [*Anfægtelser*], a devout, God-fearing man, and as such essentially a stranger in the world.

Soon afterward the impression of Luther changed; he actually came to be construed as a political hero, and the key phrase by which he was remembered came to be: Hear, O Pope, etc.

Once again the impression changed, now that the Pope was humbled, and Luther was construed as a happy man of the world and good company; the key phrase by which he was remembered by both the clergy and the lay people became: *Wer nicht liebt Weiber, Wein, Gesang,*[284] etc. To use the vernacular, one can say today that the significance of the Reformation is construed as follows: Luther set girls and wine and card-playing in their rightful place in the Christian Church, as an essential ingredient, yes, as the true consummation in contrast to the defectiveness of poverty, prayer, and fasting. To that extent the best way to celebrate his memory is as follows. Chorus of clergy and lay people: A toast to Martin Luther! Hurrah! hurrah! That was a good toast! Hurrah! Once again, hurrah! hurrah! To preserve his memory his portrait could also be put on cards as the jack-of-clubs. It is not enough to erect monuments to him. No, make him into the jack-of-clubs, and there will be hardly a clergyman who will not have occasion again and again to be reminded of Martin Luther and the Reformation.

X^3 A 234   *n.d.*, 1850

« 2525

In the sermon on the Epistle for the Fourth Sunday after Epiphany, Luther[285] interprets Christianity as if in a certain sense it were the wrath of God.

He explains that love to God means to love one's neighbor—for two reasons. The first is that God does not need our love. The second is that God has made folly of the world and wants to be loved under the cross and amidst lamentation. I Corinthians 1:21 ("For since, in the wisdom of God, the world did not know God through wisdom etc."). Therefore, says Luther, he has sacrificed himself amidst lamentation and in death on the cross and has given his faithful followers the same to suffer, so that all those who have not willed to love God previously, when he gave them food and drink, honor and prestige, now are to love him in hunger and distress, in trouble and ignominy.

The category is as follows: the God-relationship is not directly recognizable (Judaism) but inversely. The mark of offense is also here —to love God, not only when things go wrong (for this is not sufficient to constitute the possibility of offense, categorically understood, for opposition and everything belonging to it can very well come from something other than God)—but when the opposition arises from the God-relationship itself, originates from one's relating himself to God. As it says in the Gospel:[286] when persecution arises on account of the Word.

X^3 A 302   *n.d.*, 1850

« 2526 *Jest in Earnest*

In one of Luther's table-talks[287] he tells how he acts when the devil tempts [*anfægter*] him during the night. He says to him: My good Satan, you must really let me have peace now, for you know it is God's will that man shall work by day and sleep by night.

X^3 A 335   *n.d.*, 1850

« 2527 *Luther—and the Course of Protestantism*

Luther[288] laments (in the sermon on the Epistle for the Fourth Sunday in Lent) that there are many more who want to hear the law proclaimed rather than the gospel.

In our day it is exactly the opposite. They want to hear nothing at all except gospel, gospel.

But then, to be sure, our age has made extraordinary progress in Christianity. Alas, no, there is quite another explanation. When there is any authentic interest in the religious, the most immediate thing a person so inspired wants to do in order to realize it is to make himself worthy, etc. No doubt this can very easily degenerate and become a dangerous error, but nevertheless it always indicates that there is desire and concern for the religious.

Then came Luther. In contrast to this adolescent behavior, Luther stressed faith. It was obviously too high for men; they could better understand and would rather hear that they should fast, make pilgrimages, etc., but wanting to hear this and to act accordingly always indicates that there is desire and concern for the religious.

After Luther came Protestantism. It found that Luther was glorious; it did not even have enough desire and concern to choose to begin to strive, to fast, to give alms, etc. It had something quite different to attend to—and men wanted only to hear the gospel, the gospel.

O, Luther, Luther, did you not know that Draconian law simply has the result that no one is executed—and the same is the case on a higher level. However true it was of Luther—and however Christianly true it still is—it must be tested with the greatest rigor; otherwise the secular mentality takes it in vain and it continues to be not merely pure and simple secularity but even brags that this is the highest spirituality.

x^3 A 336   *n.d.,* 1850

« 2528 *Direct Attack*

If the established order wants to have a direct attack, well, here it is—

In order not to say too much and in order not to leap too quickly to the highest things, the established order has taken Luther in vain. The guilt of the established order is that it has nullified Luther's positive contribution. Luther rescued "discipleship, the imitation of Christ" from a fantastic misunderstanding—but the present age has completely secularized Luther, as if this were what Luther meant.[289]

x^3 A 510   *n.d.,* 1850

« 2529 *An Inconsistency in Luther*

In his sermon on the Gospel for the First Sunday in Advent, right at the beginning, Luther[290] states that every legitimate gospel proclaims first faith and then works, and every gospel in which this is the case is legitimate gospel.

But what about appealing to Scripture as the only norm? Here Luther has himself made a norm by which he determines what is a legitimate gospel.

x³ A 516   n.d., 1850

« 2530 *Experiment*
Mynster—Luther

In order to understand what I mean when I say that the established order must make a little admission,[291] let us make this experiment.

Some Sunday let Mynster, instead of preaching himself, take one of Luther's sermons, particularly one of the characteristic ones, and read it aloud—and the whole thing will sound like a satire on Mynster, unless he hurries and makes a little admission [*Indrømmelse*] concerning himself.

Perhaps Luther's preaching, too, is excessive—so we have become Lutherans to a degree!

Yes, one can easily eulogize Luther—but read Luther aloud!

x³ A 533   n.d., 1850

« 2531 *Even Luther*

does not properly relate the existential ideas; therefore he has only one thought at each point and this one thought alone at each point; he is also rhetorical.

When he wants to exhort children to obey their parents, servants to be faithful in the lowly task, the poor to fear God, etc., he declares that we also see (particularly if the persons concerned fear God) that God makes a famous doctor out of a poor wretch, a powerful man, a rich man out of a poor hired man, etc. This is Jewish piety. The mark of piety is that everything goes well in life. The fruit of godliness is that everything goes well.

When he speaks in other passages of being a true Christian, we learn something altogether different—the true Christian must suffer in every way in this world, poverty and persecution, etc.

How, then, shall I order my life according to these instructions? Where Luther exhorts to piety, he must certainly mean Christian piety.

But now if he were to say at this point what he says about the fate of the true Christian in the world—well, there goes the encouragement to amount to something in this world.

Where, after all, is the preacher who has only one thought about being a Christian and about the Christian's fate in this world?

On this point, as with so many existential points, Luther contradicts himself when one puts his thoughts together.

x^3 A 605   *n.d.*, 1850

« 2532 *A Dialectical Qualification by Luther*

In the sermon on the Epistle for the 11th Sunday after Trinity, Luther[292] quite rightly, as usual, characterizes faith. He says it is diametrically opposed to feeling (the qualification of immediacy). For example, you feel your sin—and now you are to believe that it is entirely forgiven and consequently be sheer joy, although you feel the very opposite.

Suppose someone raises an objection to Luther: But if this is the way it is, how can you incessantly talk about having to experience faith when we experience the very opposite.

So Luther must quite rightly make the distinction that there is still an experience of faith.

This is precisely how it is. But care must be exercised constantly so that experience A and experience B are not confused, so that the qualification of faith as the absurd always comes between.

But the careless treatment of Christianity permits these two kinds of experience to run together and then is oblivious to the fact that the entire sphere of faith vanishes and with it Christianity.

x^4 A 7   *n.d.*, 1851

« 2533 *The Brightness of the Law—The Brightness of the Gospel*

When Moses[293] descended the mountain with the law, no one could bear to look at his face—because of the brightness [*Klarhed*]. When Christ[294] was transfigured [*forklaredes*] upon the mountain, the disciples could not only endure this brightness but even found it infinitely salutary.

The brightness of the law is fatal, that of the gospel infinitely salutary.

This observation is found somewhere in Luther's sermon[295] on the Epistle for the 12th Sunday after Trinity.

x^4 A 12   *n.d.*, 1851

« 2534 *Luther's Marriage*[296]

Its significance, of course, is that it is one of those exceptional actions which are awakening, one of those exceptional actions in which the absolute, which has to bear all these relativities and relativities which actuality [*Virkeligheden*] is, weary of bearing them, exhales for a moment and establishes a new quality.

Underneath all the relativizing of actuality is the absolute. And those exceptional actions, which are recognizable by the break of the absolute with something ethical, are like the sigh of the absolute.

But what do men do! They erect a learned science upon such an exceptional action. For example, right at present Luther's marriage is attracting attention. It is being researched and researched. If someone discovers that Luther, for example, happened to be unshaven on his wedding day, they will believe that this belongs to a true evangelical Lutheran marriage.

X^4 A 25   *n.d.,* 1851

« 2535 *Armor*

In the beginning of his sermon on the Epistle for the 21st Sunday after Trinity (Ephesians 6) Luther[297] says: There are two kinds of armor: the one makes us *unconquerable;* the other makes us conquerors.

X^4 A 54   *n.d.,* 1851

« 2536 *Luther*

declares: If I am going to be deceived, I would rather be deceived by God than by men, for if God deceives me, he no doubt can defend it.

See Petersen, *Die Idee der Kirche,* [298] III, p. 420 fn.

X^4 A 237   *n.d.,* 1851

« 2537 *Luther—Catherine von Bora*[299]

Luther really could not have been what we call "in love." I can imagine him saying to Catherine: My dear girl, the purpose of my marriage—as I told you—is to defy Satan, the Pope, and the whole world. This being the case, you can understand that I could just as well marry your kitchen maid—for the important thing is to make my marriage generally known. I could just as well marry a doorpost, if it were possible for the doorpost to be regarded as my wife in a real marriage; for I am not particularly eager for the bridal bed, but only for a way of defying Satan, the Pope, and the whole world.

One could say the very opposite: My dear girl, the fact that I do not marry you must not grieve you. In my sight you are and continue to be the one and only beloved, but to defy Satan, the public, the newspapers, and the whole nineteenth century, I cannot marry.

x^4 A 324   *n.d., 1851*

« 2538 *Luther*

I have read somewhere in Henry's *Calvins Leben,*[300] III, a note on Luther, that when he was about to die and wanted to make a will and others thought there should be witnesses, Luther said, "It is not necessary, for I am well-known both on earth and in heaven and hell, so my signature is enough." (*In margin:* see Henry, *Calvins Leben,* III, p. 582, note.) Here Luther is so naïvely humorous that it is almost showing off.

x^4 A 325   *n.d., 1851*

« 2539 *Indulgence—Popularity*

Christianity has never really been more popular than when the Pope stated plainly: If you want to be saved, it will cost 4 marks and 8 shillings and a tip to the priest; if you want to be completely saved, then 5 marks; but that you will be saved is absolutely guaranteed, and you will get a receipt. Basically this is and continues to be popular.

To think of Luther as popular is a total misunderstanding. No, no. By what means did Luther become so popular? Well, look more closely and you will see the connection. It was found that the Pope had become too expensive—and then Luther was taken in vain and through the turn which he gave to the matter men thought to get salvation a little cheaper, absolutely free. It is never popular to enter earnestly into the way Luther took. No, the object of popular rage was that the Pope was too expensive, especially when word got around that there was the possibility of getting the same thing completely gratis without any expense whatsoever.*

The Pope was, after all, a man who understood the popular mind, as surely as Peer Degn[301] understands it, as surely as all classes and ranks are basically one. Luther's way in its essential truth, with its more precise understanding, is infinitely too high, much much too intended for "spirit," ever to become really popular.

x^4 A 371   *n.d., 1851*

« 2540

[*] *In margin of 2539* (x^4 A 371):

Among the contemporaries there was certainly many an innkeeper who had his suspicions about Luther's way, whether it could actually be that one "really" is saved at so low a price, that is, free. Because the conception of having to pay in "spirit," in spiritual struggle—that is never popular. Suppose that the Pope's fee had been 10,000 dollars! That would be expensive! Yet, free in the sense which Luther means it is infinitely more expensive, because it is spirit and spiritual trial [*Anfægtelse*]. However, for one who has no conception of spirit, the accounting is 10,000 dollars or gratis, purely and simply gratis. No doubt Luther abolished the payment of money—but he was earnest about the spiritual cost, and that is incomparably more expensive.

x^4 A 372   *n.d.*

« 2541 *Luther's Swing Away from the Monastery*

Away, shouts Luther, away with all these fancied pious acts of fasting etc. Everyone remain in his calling [*Kald*]; this is the true worship of God.

But wait a minute, dear Luther. So everyone remains in his occupation [*Stilling*]. But is every secular occupation compatible with Christianity—for example, being a stage actor? There are some great conflicts here. In the next place, how is he to live in his secular occupation, is social morality as such enough for a Christian. If not, is he to express the Christian ethic in his secular occupation: if he does, then *ein, zwei, drei,* he is reduced to poverty and persecution.

Seen from the angle of contrast to monastic error, Luther's swing away from the monastery looks very simple, but on closer inspection what huge conflicts there are here, because true Christianity is characterized by not fitting into this world.

But then Luther was no dialectician; he always saw only one side of the matter.

x^4 A 394   *n.d.,* 1851

« 2542 *Luther*

Everyone will admit that there is an enormous difference if someone at the peak of all scholarly achievement suddenly stops and says: No, it does not depend on science and scholarship—and if a bricklayer's apprentice leaps up and says the same thing.

But why, then, do we not want to understand that there is this kind of difference when someone (Luther, for example), after having fasted and disciplined his flesh for twenty years and consequently conscious of being able to do this and able at any time to do this if necessary, says: No, it does not depend on this—and when we say the same thing, we who have not even tried. Are there no grounds for being suspicious about oneself if one has not tried at all?

x^4 451   *n.d.*, 1852

« 2543 *That the Principle of Works is Simpler than the Principle of Faith*

To mention "works" suggests Catholicism. In order not to be misunderstood, I point out something which is perhaps not necessary and in any case ought not be necessary—namely, that everything Catholicism has thought up about the meritoriousness of works of course has to be rejected completely.

But then I declare that the principle of works is *simpler* than the principle of faith. And why?

Because the principle of works begins with the beginning, and begins with what is common to us men; the principle of faith begins so far ahead that there are not many in any generation who come so far—therefore this principle must become completely meaningless if one wants to begin at once with it.

The principle of works begins with the beginning and with what is generally true—namely, that we ought to be treated as beginners—yes, it is even to our advantage.

A scoundrel is treated this way—quite simply: May I see your works. If he comes and protests that in his hidden inwardness he is willing to sacrifice everything, in hidden inwardness he longs to sit and sing hymns and fast in the stillness of a monastery, while outwardly he reaps profit and cuts quite a figure in society, then we say to him—this is the simplicity of it—no, my good Morten Fredriksen,[302] excuse us, but we say as Hummer[303] says to Klister when he assures him that he has the money: Do you have it here, and when Klister answers: I don't have it here, Hummer says: I see! (very drawn out), I see! So we also say: May we see your works. Alas, but for us men this is sorely needed!

O, dear Luther! Are they not two completely different things: a scholar who, after having devoted the twenty most vigorous years of his life (the years in which one really studies) to the most strenuous study and in his 48th year, standing at the peak of his scholarship, still has not found the satisfaction he sought and suddenly, as it were, comes to the breaking point, to the opposite extreme, and closes his books and says: No, it is not scholarship that matters—is this not something completely different from the innkeeper who happened to walk by just then and heard the scholar say it (for he roomed there, the windows were open, and the scholar said it very loudly and passion-ately), an innkeeper who could not even write his own name and could scarcely read it when someone else wrote it—is it not something en-tirely different if he goes his way, takes that remark as a result, and says: It is not scholarship that matters.

The discipline which Luther underwent (in fact, it was carried to an immoderate degree) is precisely what guarantees that what he says about his inwardness can be the truth. But it is infinitely high, and thus not simple, for it is infinitely high to dare be so sure of one's inward-ness that keeping the things of the world does not signify that one wants to keep them—no, but that one wants to do something still higher than to give them away. Yet where there are such guarantees —well, this is another matter—such a man knows what it is to renounce this world, he has attempted it, he is convinced within himself and in God that he can do it; yet, this is something else.

But is it not something entirely different when someone begins immediately (not where Luther began, because many years earlier Luther quite simply began at the beginning, with works), there where Luther, so to speak, ended in order to begin the new beginning, this new beginning which, if it is to be true in any way, must always presup-pose that the simple beginning has gone before.

And just as I, if I were an innkeeper who could neither read nor write, just as I then—because I would be aware of not having the presuppositions that scholar had, presuppositions which gave him the right to say "It is not scholarship that matters"—would not dare to take it as a result and repeat it, just so would I far less (for the matter is far more important) take the Lutheran principle as a result, since I am convinced that I am completely inexperienced in that which may be called the presupposition which can make the Lutheran principle truth in me.

When the gospel asks us to renounce this world (nowhere in the gospel does it say anything about this being meritorious; this is a fraudulent invention, but it is also a treacherous invention that out of zeal to impress upon us that meritoriousness is a wicked human inven-tion it comes to be forgotten that to renounce this world is quite literally demanded in the gospel), the simple thing is to do it. If one does not do it, the next simple thing to do is to confess that it is because one is too weak to do it, still clings too much to this world. But it is stupendously high to retain it, to acquire it, and then dare maintain that one is like the person who does not possess it, that the man who fasts, the ascetic, is a lower position.

Considering that we are what we seem as a rule to be, is it not likewise simpler for us to be incessantly halted and checked on the way to eternity by the question of works instead of getting permission to wander along as if every one of us were such a hero who dared to believe himself to be on this infinitely high plane of hidden inwardness, etc. And is not this the real reason we are a little afraid of the principle of works, for it will prevent us (ah, but the real danger is in getting permission to do so)—will prevent us from unperturbedly imagining all sorts of things about our inwardness while we unperturbedly go on living for secular goals.

———

It is not my intention—assuming I were able to do it—to prompt anyone to attempt literally to renounce everything—no, I merely wish to contribute to our coming into relationship to the truth by means of confessions; I hold to No. 2, this simple thing to do: that when one does not do it, he confesses that it is because he does not have the strength to do it, is too weak, clings too much to the world.

Luther purchased his situation of appreciation at an infinitely costly price, for fear and trembling and spiritual trials such as his are indeed frightfully costly—a situation of appreciation, inasmuch as secularism received him with open arms as the most welcome of persons (even if this was a mistake). No doubt one who has the task of reminding people of the Christian demands can purchase at a far cheaper price, for he does not need to be tested by spiritual trials in this way, but then, again, he comes into a situation where he is not appreciated, is not welcome, since this is regarded as rigorousness (although it is a misunderstanding), although it is merely what every man who does not and will not fancy himself to be a hero must wish for himself.

XI² A 301   *n.d.*, 1853–54

« 2544 *Luther*

Just as one can become accustomed to doing something, for example, accustomed to taking a walk every day along the same path, but gets tired of it and says to himself, "This time you are going to go another way," puts on his hat and coat, and before he knows it is off again on the same path—so it is also in things of the spirit. There is something one has thought about, at first only on occasions, and later has considered it properly and then laid it aside, but he cannot get rid of it and says to himself, "You simply must quit coming back to that point incessantly"—but it will not work.

So it has been with me regarding a certain thought about Luther.

Has not a great confusion actually come about through Luther, however innocent in a certain sense that honest man was in the matter?

Let us see how things went with Luther! After about 20 years of fear and trembling and spiritual trial [*Anfægtelse*] so terrible that—note this well!—there is hardly one individual in a generation who experiences anything like it, his human nature reacted, to put it this way, and this fear and trembling was transfigured into the most blissful and happy confidence and joy—wonderful!

But now what happens? In Protestantism this principle is made into the universal. In this way and only in this way (for this is true Christianity) is Christianity to be presented, this extremely powerful resource and reassurance which Luther, in fear and trembling and spiritual trials, fighting unto death, discovered in the extremity of his anxiety [*Angst*]—this is to be proclaimed as the one and only means for all, and yet there is not one individual in each generation who is put to the test in this way—yet if we take this presupposition away, this frightful antecedent, this fear and trembling and spiritual trial, it all too easily becomes a lie, a frightful lie. If this fear and trembling and spiritual trial are present, it is truly wonderful to have the confidence to be able to rejoice in this life. But suppose, now, that there is no fear and trembling and spiritual trial (and there is not one in each generation who experiences this the way Luther did)—is it then so wonderful to want to enjoy this life, and can it not very easily become a dreadful deceit if everyone who likes to enjoy this life gets permission (and we cannot control it) to counterfeit this inwardness [*Inderlighed*] of Luther's?

Is it cogent to make a principle for all out of what to such a degree is based on a particular situation (which fear and trembling and spiritual trials are, particularly to the degree in which Luther experienced them)?

In Luther it was the truth, but was it justifiable to universalize it? I wonder—and let us be honest—if we do not come a little closer to actuality by assuming that the original situation (foreground or background, as you wish) is: sloth, sensuousness, a deficiency of fear and trembling—but this indeed infinitely changes the matter; then it is precisely awakening which the proclamation generally ought to call for. Further—I wonder if we really do not come a little closer to actuality by assuming that as a rule the original situation (and this, to be sure, determines ordinarily how the preaching ought to attack the matter) is not only sloth, sensuousness, etc.; but that this—yes, it is the same with all of us, Luther perhaps an exception—is mixed with a certain tendency toward hypocrisy. But then is it not terribly dangerous to universalize what was true for Luther, to give such a foothold to that swindler inside of us, that what he needs is to be reassured—aha!! Is this not terribly dangerous—and it happens easily when what was true for Luther becomes the universal principle, almost tempting us men to pretend that what we need is reassurance, because was not this what Luther needed—after some twenty years of spiritual trials such as not one in each generation experiences? Was society really benefitted by having a man who was so honest—yes, he was honesty itself—so honest that it did not occur to him that anyone could want to steal; was society —or only just the thieves—benefitted by his writing laws which naturally bore the mark of his assumption that thievery does not take place—in the same way as Luther's approach presupposes that men are suffering under fear and trembling and spiritual trials, therefore console, console them, reassure them, reassure them so that no such poor Christian man sits in mortal anxiety and doubts his salvation—O, I know what this means—therefore reassure them. O, dear Luther, where are these Christian men you speak of? And if such an individual is found ever so seldom, can and ought this be made the universal principle which we swindlers have made it by taking advantage of Luther?

XI² A 303   n.d., 1853–54

« 2545

Addition to 2544 (XI² A 303):

At the end or in a note to the heading "Luther" should be added: It is not my intention here to reintroduce the monastery, even if I were able to do so. My proposal is merely that we become conscious of the truth which may be in monasticism and that we see to it that we move into a relationship to the truth by making some admissions about ourselves.

XI² A 304   n.d., 1853–54

« 2546 *Luther*

Luther has actually done incalculable harm by not becoming a martyr.

For one thing it is odd for a person designated to be God's man to the degree he was to end up in ordinary comfortable association with adoring admirers and followers. It can so very easily get to be pointless. Normally the life of such a person is so dangerous while he is living that pointlessness cannot set in, and when he is snatched away in a violent death pointlessness is again avoided. It was different with Luther. Although it is true that for some years he was salt, his later life was not devoid of pointlessness. The *Table Talks* are an example: a man of God sitting in placid comfort, ringed by admiring adorers who believe that if he simply breaks wind it is a revelation or the result of inspiration.

But if he had this harmful influence even in his own generation, how much more in succeeding generations, when everything became thinner and thinner, worse and still worse, mimicking [*Efterabelse*]. By halting halfway, Luther debased the mint-standard for being a reformer and thereby gave birth in later generations to that mob, that rabble of nice cordial people who also want to be reformers a little. Furthermore, he gave birth to the confusion of being a reformer with the help of politics.

The result has been the deepest confusion of the highest concepts and the most dangerous demoralisation, which is naturally the case when something as fine, noble, and delicate as the concept "reformer" decays.

For the sake of God in heaven Luther should have seen to one thing (which he did not do): that it was emphatically driven home that to be a reformer in this manner (halfway) is something inferior. This he did not do, with enormous confusion resulting. Not only will it be more difficult to get an integral reformer in the future—no, it is made almost impossible. Secularity has exploited Lutheranism to turn the relationship completely around so that being a reformer in this fashion, coming out on top, is regarded as being superior. You see, there went the whole thing, there the nerve of Christianity broke!

If the Christian view is not firmly maintained, that the martyr is the highest, the true, and that coming out unscathed is something inferior, which with indulgence can be conceded—then Satan is not only rampant but he has conquered. Just as all the nerves converge in the fingertips, so the entire nervous system of Christianity converges in the reality [*Realitet*] of martyrdom. If this is reversed, you have what we are now stuck in—fundamentally we live in such a nice world that reforming therefore means coming out unscathed, for the world (which is not immersed in evil, as Christianity teaches—and thus the martyr) wills the good and therefore the reformer wins—yes, therefore Satan wins!

By his later life Luther accredited mediocrity. It should be noted that in a certain sense it takes a hero to accredit mediocrity—and in Protestantism we are blessed with this beyond all measure.

XI^1 A 61   n.d., 1854

« 2547 *How Satirical!*

In contrast to Catholicism, Luther emphasizes the gospel—and even during his own life he is obliged to observe (quite rightly!) that this high spirituality is taken in such a way that he is not even able to get a little for the pastors to live on. Alas, Luther, in a way you have deserved this satire. Just imagine, dear Luther, what knavish tricks this high spirituality must lead to now, hundreds of years later.

That Luther complains about the turn of events can be seen in many of his sermons. At the moment I recall, for example, the one on the Gospel for the 26th Sunday after Trinity.[304]

XI^1 A 77   n.d., 1854

« 2548 *O, Luther*

Luther, you do have an enormous responsibility, for when I look more closely I see ever more clearly that you toppled the Pope—and set "the public" upon the throne.

You altered the New Testament concept of "the martyr" and taught men to win by numbers.

XI^1 A 108   n.d., 1854

« 2549 *Luther*

Was it not really a misunderstanding on Luther's part to think that Satan was in ferocious pursuit of him. It seems to me that Satan must rather have been well pleased with Luther for bringing about a confusion which is not very easy to achieve, because it requires a noble and upright man to put it in motion, and, as is known, noble and upright men are rare.

XI^1 A 127   n.d., 1854

« 2550 *Being a Christian in the New Testament Restlessness—the Martyr—Luther*

In the New Testament the apostles express what it is to be a Christian; to be Christian is, as spirit, the utmost restlessness of spirit, the impatience of eternity, nothing but fear and trembling, intensified by being in this evil world which crucified love, intensified by trepidation over the accounting when the Lord and Master will come again and judge whether they have been faithful.

If this is so, then having to become a martyr—something Christ predicts for the Christian—is so far from being an intensification that it is rather a mitigation. One could say that only external sufferings like this and finally a martyr's death are able to mitigate and soothe the soul-agony which is the strain of being a Christian according to the New Testament. Therefore martyrdom is not cruel but, on the contrary, is what physical suffering so often is in relation to mental torment. On the other hand it would have been cruel if Christ had said to the disciples: After I am gone you will have no more to do, so get married, get yourself a nice little job and scrape some money together, be a good, decent fellow who goes to church once a week and to the Lord's Supper three times a year.

Thus in the New Testament the two belong together: restlessness in the Christian requires martyrdom as a kind of mitigation—and martyrdom is the requirement.

But soon the restlessness is diminished in "Christendom," this dead mass devoid of spirit.

Then in the Middle Ages asceticism came into favor (people thought there no longer was occasion or opportunity for martyrdom). As I have frequently pointed out [i.e., x⁵ A 146, A 159; XI¹ A 7], this was not the mistake but rather that instead of confessing that Christianity had retrogressed and been diluted, a compromise was made with Christendom's vapid mass of millions of Christians to the point that the ascetic came to be honored as the *extraordinary* Christian.

Thus it became more and more evident that if a person wanted to live quietly and enjoy life, Christianity would bring troubles.

— —and this ultimately finds expression in Luther (who otherwise certainly was right in his opposition to Catholic abuses).

Luther discovers that Christianity exists to soothe and reassure.

I have frequently pointed out [i.e., x³ A 153, 217, 336] that Luther altered Christianity. As I note now, Schopenhauer[305] maintains that by altering virginity Luther altered Christianity. I have shared this view inasmuch as I thought that Luther should have scrupulously made it clear that his marriage was an exception, a corrective. But my main point has been that Luther altered Christianity by altering martyrdom.

Thus Luther turns Christianity upside down. Christianity exists to soothe and reassure, Christ came to the world to soothe and reassure, it is added, anguished consciences.

This is completely opposite to the New Testament. Christ comes to the world to save a sinful world, a world immersed in evil. But a sinful world really does not suffer from an anguished conscience. Here it is a question of arousing restlessness.

But the tragedy about Luther is that a condition in Christendom at a particular time and place is transformed into the normative. Luther suffered exceedingly from an anguished conscience and needed a cure. Well and good, but must Christianity therefore be converted *in toto* to this, to soothing and reassuring anguished consciences.

The more I see of Luther the more clear it is to me that he also is a part of this confusion of mistaking the patient for the physician. He is an exceedingly important patient for Christendom, but he is not the physician; he has the patient's passion for expressing and describing his suffering and what he feels he needs to relieve it, but he does not have the physician's comprehensive view. And to reform Christianity requires first and foremost a comprehensive view of the whole of Christianity.

XI[1] A 193   n.d., 1854

« 2551 *Augustine's View of Election by Grace*

The idea that a man's eternal salvation is to be decided by a striving in time, in this life, is so superhumanly heavy that it will kill a man even more surely than massive sunstroke. The weight of it is so great that it is impossible even to begin, for the moment in which one is going to begin is already a wasted moment—alas, and one single moment is enough for the decision of salvation, consequently to his damnation.

I now interpret Augustine as having hit upon election by grace simply in order to avoid this difficulty; for in this case eternal salvation is not decided in relation to a striving.

Luther understood the problem thus: No man can endure the anxiety [*Angst*] that his striving will decide his eternal salvation or eternal damnation. No, no, says Luther, this can only lead to despair or to blasphemy. And therefore (note this!), therefore it is not so (Luther apparently alters New Testament Christianity because otherwise mankind must despair). You are saved by grace; be reassured, you are saved by grace—and then you strive as well as you can.

This is Luther's variation of the matter. I will not speak here of the swindle concocted by a later Protestantism. No, I will stand by this Lutheran principle. My objection is this: Luther ought to have let it be known that he reduced Christianity. Furthermore, he ought to have made it be known that his argument: "otherwise we must despair"—

is actually arguing from the human side. But, strictly speaking, this argument is without foundation when the question is what the New Testament understands by Christianity; strictly speaking, the fact that Luther could argue thus shows that for him Christianity was not yet unconditionally sovereign, but that this sovereignty, too, has to yield under the assumption that "otherwise a man must despair." But I always come back to this—that Luther should have made the true connection known. In my opinion, subjects who cannot honestly pay the taxes are not rebellious subjects if they openly say to the monarch: We cannot pay the taxes. But on the other hand they do not have the right to falsify the amount of the taxes, quietly decrease them, and then honestly pay them.

O, what Christendom has needed for at least 1500 years is the human, bold forthrightness[*] to make an honest admission about itself but not to change a jot or tittle of Christianity—O, if this had just been done, how completely different the picture would be!

XI[1] A 297   n.d., 1854

« 2552

[*] *Addition in margin of 2551* (XI[1] A 297):
And instead of this human, bold forthrightness, we got this tragic, pusillanimous, as well as crafty, underhanded Bible interpreting which plagues and torments the Scriptures to find passages from which a tortured person can get what he wants.

XI[1] A 298   n.d.

« 2553 *Luther*

has, after all, occasioned a great confusion. What actually happened because of Luther? The same thing happened that so often happens. There is something that the secular mind, politics, and the lower elements want accomplished, but for one thing these contenders do not have very much courage but are only cravenly shrewd; and for another, they fear all the more opposition if it is originated or initiated by them. Thus they lie in wait just in case a religious person on religious grounds apparently wants the same thing, and then they exploit him.

XI[1] A 442   n.d., 1854

« 2554 *Law and Gospel*

The way in which even Luther speaks of the law and gospel is still not the teaching of Christ.

[*In margin:* Luther's sermon[306] on the Gospel for the Third Sunday in Advent can be used as an example.]

Luther separates the two: the law and the gospel. First the law and then the gospel, which is sheer leniency, etc. This way Christianity becomes an optimism anticipating that we are to have an easy life in this world.

This means that Christianity becomes Judaism. The law corresponds, for example, to what being tempted and tried by God was in the Old Testament, but then comes the gospel, just as in the Old Testament the time of testing came to an end and everything became joy and jubilation.

But, as I have frequently said [i.e., IX A 24; X³ A 139, 157; X⁴ A 572], every human existence in which the tension of life is resolved within this life is Judaism. Christianity is: this life, sheer suffering—eternity.

It does not help that we men get angry ten times over and say: No human being can endure that. This does not help. God is not impressed. The error in Luther's preaching is that it bears the mark of this consideration for us poor human beings, which shows that he does not hold Christianity at the level which is found in the New Testament, specifically in the gospel: the unconditioned. No, God is not impressed; he changes nothing. Yet believe that it is out of love that he wills what he wills. He himself suffers infinitely in this, but he does not change. Yes, he suffers in love more than you do, but he does not change. He sets everything in motion to bring a human being to what most surely is the greatest agony possible for a man—to hate himself (for to hate himself and the world and so on are the condition for loving God). He sets everything in motion, entices, moves, persuades, sometimes almost as if he were begging, as if he were the one in need. At other times he terrifyingly lets go of you momentarily so that a moment's relapse into sin may teach you both new strenuousness and not to take his love in vain, or he alternately approaches you and withdraws from you—in all this he suffers infinitely more than you do, even when it is you who distress him by new sin—but he does not change, O, infinite love!

But it is easy to see that Luther's preaching of Christianity changes Christianity's life-view and world view. He has one-sidedly appropriated "the apostle" and goes so far—as he frequently does with this yardstick (turned the wrong way)—that he criticizes the gospels.[307] If he does not find the apostle's teaching in the gospel he concludes *ergo* this is no gospel. Luther does not seem to see that the apostle has already relaxed in relation to the gospels. And this wrong tack Luther made has been continued in Protestantism, which has made Luther absolute. When we found the apostle to be more rigorous (which he is) than Luther, we concluded: Here the apostle is wrong, this is not pure gospel. In this way we have systematically, step by step, cheated —that is, attempted to cheat God out of the gospel by turning the whole relationship around.

XI^1 A 572   *n.d.*, 1854

« 2555 *The Unconditioned; Luther*

The turn which Luther gave—namely, that Christianity must first and foremost *quiet* and *reassure*—is really the language of revolution, even though in the language of the greatest possible submission.

The Christian demand presses to the utter extremity, and then the purely human reacts: We cannot; this is sheer death-agony—Christianity must first and foremost quiet and reassure.

But this kind of talking cunningly attributes a quality of deference to the unconditioned. And as soon as the unconditioned acquires a deference or as soon as it is assumed that something is able to set itself in relationship with the unconditioned, that the unconditioned defers to it, the unconditioned is no longer the unconditioned.

Fundamentally, Luther's view makes the decisive factor in Christianity whether or not men are able to be comfortably disposed by it, but then Christianity is not the unconditioned and God is only a relative majesty.

The law for revolution is declared in Luther's view.

XI^2 A 194   *n.d.*, 1854

« 2556 *Luther—the Reformation*

Luther is the very opposite of "the apostle."

"The apostle" expresses Christianity in God's interest, comes with authority from God and in his interest.

Luther expresses Christianity in man's interest, is essentially the human reaction to Christianity in God's interest. Thus Luther's formula: I cannot do otherwise,[308] which is not at all the apostle's formula.

What confusion just at this point when Luther has been made an apostle!

On the whole, what Christendom has always lacked is a diagnostician of the disease and a dialectician.

XI^2 A 266   *n.d.*, 1855

MAJESTY

« **2557** *Solidarity*

The basis of all solidarity lies in needing one another. This is why a man cannot in this sense have solidarity with God—for God needs nothing and nobody; to hold to God means to be up for examination continually, and in love God [is] most severe with the one who comes closest to him. O, how many there are who have deceived themselves about this and have thought that God needed them.

God's majesty seems to be forgotten; therefore, instead of the customary expositions on God's qualities, I could be tempted to concentrate on God's majesty, in order that there might be proper appreciation of—love.

X^4 A 443   *n.d.,* 1851

« **2558**

Addition in margin of 2557 (X^4 A 443):

Paganism has no concept of God's majesty, which is the case with Judaism, too, although to a lesser degree. This explains how paganism (for example, Cicero in *de natura deorum,* III, end[309]) claimed to disprove the existence of a God [*at en Gud er til*] on the grounds that evil men prosper in the world just as Diogenes[310] did in saying of a robber, Harpalus, who was regarded as lucky: Your existence [*Tilværelse*] disproves the existence of gods. This is the shallow concept of human gods, who are believed to strike immediately, presumably because they are unsure of themselves. But Christianity! This infinite majesty, that the God of love simply lets those whom he loves fare badly in the world and lets the evil ones have good fortune for the time being: infinite majesty. Take a weak human analogy. The merely human is to be hard on one's enemies and opponents but tender with one's associates. On a somewhat higher level you will find one who is very gentle with his enemies and opponents but severe with those who would be his friends! Perhaps this is culpable pride, but in the relationship between God and man it cannot be otherwise if God in truth shall be God, God with majesty. And yet in this prodigious majesty he is love.

X^4 A 444   *n.d.*

« **2559** *God's Majesty—Grace in the First Place*

The fact that the more a person holds to God, the closer he comes to him, and the more he wills as God wills, the more strenuous everything becomes for him, the greater his suffering in this world—that this is so, that this is certain, that this is Christianity, that this is spirit have their basis in God's majesty, and it cannot be otherwise. That God nevertheless is—or, more accurately, precisely then—is infinite, infinite love, is just as certain—O, those blessed glorious ones who could endure being involved with God in this way. That their salvation, for all that, is "grace" is just as certain, for the expression of majesty is again this: No one can be saved except by grace. But those glorious ones do not have grace in the first place: their lives express the strenuousness of spirit in the strict sense; and while they themselves admit before God that they are saved by grace, we all should bow deeply before them.

Then comes the second relationship.[311] A man realizes how frightful it is to come close to God (which, however, is God's requirement) but admits his weakness, admits that he does not dare, at least not yet—and then shifts "grace" into first place, and thus grace gets permission to be lenient with regard to the most extreme exertions.

And in his infinite love God can and will be open to this kind of thing—but then he does desire honesty and truth and wants us to admit this. I must humbly and straightforwardly admit that the fault lies in me, that I am afraid to be spirit in the strict sense and therefore shirk a bit. What is wrong about preaching is the nonsense about "I am so very willing." Rubbish. No. I am the one who is not very willing—and in "grace" God will forgive me. Infinite love that he is—he is still willing to have something to do with a man on these conditions also.

My God, my God—I do not cry "My God, my God, why have you forsaken me"—no, it was only the highest one, the unique one, your beloved one, he who stood closest to you and next to him the ones especially chosen—no, I cry: My God, my God, that you stay by me this way, are willing to stay by me, are willing to have anything to do with me, even though I am so weak and do not dare venture out very far.

But present-day preaching is wrong, essentially wrong; all true preaching is essentially self-accusation. To say, "I am very willing" is to insult God: either I must venture way out—or I must confess that I am a poor child, so weak.

$$\text{x}^4 \text{ A } 446 \quad n.d., \ 1851$$

« 2560 *The Majesty of God*

What a wretched conception of the majesty of God, that his right-eousness should be directly recognizable by his immediately smiting and punishing those who do not will as he wills.

No, no, it is the very opposite, just as all recognizability with regard to God is inverted. His disfavor, his punishment, in this world is to ignore the ungodly—O, you who have a conception of God, understand his punishment!—they are as if nonexistent for him—and this is why they prosper so well in this sinful world.

Only to those whom God loves and who love God, only to them does he send sufferings; in love he does not have it in his heart that they should fool their lives away and not become aware that God is spirit, that for him this world is immersed in evil. Therefore he calls to them through sufferings that they might become heterogeneous with this world; he calls to them, he wants to be present for them and them to be present for him—while in the disfavor of his infinite majesty he ignores and by ignoring punishes the ungodly.

In the human situation there is only a very, very weak analogy. A person of genuine majesty is rigorous only toward those he loves, points out their errors, makes them aware, almost plagues them. His enemies, especially the more stupid ones, he ignores—and their punishment is to become more and more confirmed in their error.

x^4 A 612   *n.d.,* 1852

« 2561 *God's Majesty*

In a certain sense it would certainly be an injustice to our age to say that it has no conception of respect for God in the sense of approaching God too closely and minimizing him. No, it is rather the opposite. God has been made so majestic and has been so fantastically infinitized that he really has been smuggled out of everything to some point infinitely distant from actuality. But except for this there is still no conception of true respect for him. It is quite right that a certain type of anthropomorphism weakens the expression of respect for God, but it is also clear that he can be elevated in this way beyond the anthropomorphic so that in another sense the true expression of respect vanishes.

x^5 A 47   *n.d.,* 1852

« 2562 *The Enormous Illusion—God's Majesty*

It all looks so settled—all these people, these thousands and thousands and millions—and that I shall be saved just as they are, that I am a Christian just like them—but consider God's majesty and how for him millions and millions of people are a zero when it is question of the extent to which they have fulfilled his will or not. Consider that he let a whole world be flooded and saved only three!

But it is only all too obvious that in "Christendom" the conception of respect for God's majesty has dwindled, yes, is almost obliterated. And only when in unconditional fear and trembling this conception of respect comes to life again, only then can a person come into the position where he alone, alone, unconditionally alone, can ask about his salvation and in infinite anxiety on his own behalf infinitely forget all the conflicts of sympathy, such as not wanting to be saved if his father, mother, and beloved are not also saved.

Christianity has come into the world as the unconditioned, and this unconditioned fear and trembling on his own behalf also corresponds to the unconditioned.

But in "Christendom" we are all dulled by the thought that we shall all be saved—just like that!

x^5 A 86   *n.d.*, 1853

« 2563 *Hypocrisy*

People usually are much inclined to ridicule someone who religiously pioneers a new way, because they understand that such a person does not get a chance to enjoy life, to accumulate money, and so on and on.

What we want in fact is the most convenient religion possible, a kind of accompaniment to all our finite striving.

This slackness and absence of spirit is hypocritically prettied up (especially by hypocritical clergymen) into the solemnity of holding fast to the faith of our fathers.

But take a closer look and you will see, however, that it is as I have said. If someone were to lose sight of all the finite by holding fast to the faith of our fathers, we should regard it as ridiculous. You see, what we want is that religion should be about nothing at all or a divine strengthening of the pursuit of the finite.

The very reason we talk so much about the majesty of God is that we think of him as being so extremely elevated that he willingly tolerates our making a fool of him.

Incidentally, there is considerable truth in this, but in quite another sense. It is much easier to fool God than my neighbor. Why? Because my neighbor is insignificant enough to keep a sharp eye on me. But, but, but that God is easiest to fool means: God punishes by ignoring—what genuine majesty!

But here is the sting. In times past God has punished frightfully
—and this meant that he still found something which pleased him so
that he did not give men up entirely. Now the most horrible punishment of all has come upon us, the truly majestic punishment upon
"Christendom," whose guilt is high treason [*Majestæts-Forbrydelse*,
crime against His Majesty] itself—God ignores us entirely. And therefore—what dreadful punishment!—secular life goes on splendidly and
mankind makes great strides in physical discoveries etc.—but God ignores us.

XI[1] A 37   *n.d.*, 1854

« 2564 *Majesty—"It is Only a Manner of Speaking"*

The majority undoubtedly relate to the New Testament and all its
strong expressions and reckon something like this: Since God is so
infinitely exalted, what he says must not be taken so scrupulously; it
is not strictly literal, it is a certain manner of speaking.

But this is completely turned around. Indeed, the more insignificant the speaker, the more relevant the phrase "It is, after all, only a
manner of speaking" may be to his strong words, but the more significant, the less relevant. For example, if a grocery clerk gives someone
his word and his promise in the strongest terms—well, it is probably
only a manner of speaking; but when a king does it, one is less inclined
to take it that way. The rule is: The more insignificant the speaker, the
more likely what he says is a manner of speaking; the more significant,
the less likely it is a manner of speaking.

The relation is such that God is the one of whom it must be said
unconditionally that what he says is not a "manner of speaking" but
must simply be taken strictly literally. Majesty is simply to speak literally truthfully. To exaggerate (what he says, after all, "is only a manner
of speaking") is not suitable to Majesties, least of all to the absolute
Majesty.

This also shows itself thus—one can insult insignificant persons by
taking them at their word, for they talk in idiomatic phrases and therefore take it for granted that one has a right to blabber a bit; one insults
Majesties by not taking them at their word, for it betrays a small-
mindedness which does not have a cheerful openness in the presence
of the Majesty.

But this is certainly the crime we commit by the millions against
God—namely, that we are sufficiently craven and paltry not to dare to
take him at his word. No one, no one, no one talks with God, takes him
simply at his word. Among the few who still, as they see it, concern

themselves about relating to God, there is probably no one who does not first of all consult his neighbor or this one and that one about how he should talk to God—and then he talks to God—and this is called talking with God.

XI¹ A 65   *n.d.*, 1854

« 2565 *Time—Eternity*

To satisfy eternity—with this task man was sent out into the world, and later the order was unconditionally enjoined by Christianity.

But then for a long time from generation to generation the infamous falsification was perpetuated—that the task is to satisfy the times.

The gifted ones, who should maintain the standard, became cowardly and infamously falsified the standard, found it more comfortable to flatter their contemporaries.

Finally, it was declared or at least practiced with great bravado by such villains as Goethe, Hegel, and among us, Mynster, that to satisfy the times is the greatest earnestness.

The times finally comes to mean the dregs, the rabble among contemporaries, because there are more of them, they are numerically strongest.

This is what must be changed, and Governance, as it is wont to do, dialectically applies the very opposite in its extreme form. Alas, but it is dreadful to be commanded to make the true law binding upon such a demoralised generation.

To no human Majesty could it occur in the remotest way to act in this way. When he detects an attack upon his sovereignty, he plunges in as quickly as possible.

But this sublime Majesty, God is merely amused at losing the game, so to speak—so sure he is of his sovereignty. He lets century after century go by; the race grows more and more conceited—and then, just to show his majesty, he uses a nothing to halt the whole thing, to cashier these millions.

XI¹ A 435   *n.d.*, 1854

« 2566 *The Crowd—the Single Individual*

Never has the category of the race been so overwhelming, never have the crowd, the numerical, the abstractions been so overwhelming as now in our time. And never has the single individual [*den Enkelte*] been so strongly accentuated as by me, for Socrates did have disciples. The two correspond to each other and are related to the majesty of the divine.

After all, God is not a Majesty who reduces the conditions when faced with mounting rebellion; no, he jacks up the conditions. Take an illustration. If someone stood ready with a big, heavy club to fight ten men and those ten were reinforced by ten more, it would be majestical to lay the thick club down and pick up a slender stick to fight the twenty. True majesty is that remote from buckling under.

Precisely because the mutiny is so aggravated and is so powerful, for that very reason—how majestic!—the nearest thing to nothing is used.

Alas, but in a certain sense it is terrible for the poor human being who is to be used in this way, who is constantly kept on the very verge of being nothing in every sense of the word, in order that the Majesty can be seen properly—the Majesty which in proportion to the growth of the rebellion becomes, if I dare put it this way, playful—and thus demonstrates the sure superiority of its infinite power. In a certain sense it is terrible for the poor human being—yet this is love, O you of infinite love.

XI^1 A 486   n.d., 1854

« 2567 *God's Majesty*

Elsewhere [XI^1 A 227] I have pointed out how God's majesty is secured against the numerical—which otherwise would be the ruin of majesty—by being related inversely to the numerical—the greater the number the less one enters into relationship with God.*

His majesty can be seen from another side, namely, that unlike other Majesties he needs no police or guard to punish offenses against him, no, he is better secured, because the pattern is as follows: to sin against God is to punish oneself—this is how sure God is that punishment falls upon his enemies. Perhaps someone may think this makes all punishment natural punishment, thereby abolishing *positive* punishments, and therefore that this is frivolous talk. Take care. With regard to crimes which do not punish themselves, it is human to imagine that the sinner can get away with them if justice does not catch up with him in time, because a man's life has a time-limit and by dying he can avoid punishment. But God has eternity. And so it still holds that to sin is to punish oneself; one does not get by when there is an eternity lying ahead of him. Consequently, to sin against God is to punish oneself, and in this way God's majesty is assured. But not only this—he must also repent of the punishment he suffers (his sin) if he wants to come to an understanding with God—what tremendously majestic distance!

To say thanks for gracious punishment is the limit of human conceivability—but that the sinner is to repent of the punishment, suffer the punishment, and then beg forgiveness for it—how majestic!

XI^1 A 589   n.d., 1854

« **2568**

[*] *In margin of 2567* (XI^1 A 589):

The greater the number, the farther from God—the single individual is the one closest to him. Here he is again secured against this closest one—the closer he comes to the single one, the greater the single one feels his distance.

XI^1 A 590   n.d.

« **2569** *The Son of Man Shall Come as a Thief in the Night*[312]

———

In Prof. Jacobi's little article[313] on the Irvingites, I see that their explanation of this [text] is that Christ will come so unobserved that no one will notice it, no one will notice that he has been here.

This is not without discernment—after all, a thief does not make a big racket when he comes. And on the other hand there is something majestic about the stringency which lets judgment fall upon men in such a way that they merely go on living and never detect that the whole thing is decided.

As I have pointed out elsewhere [i.e., XI^1 A 439], one cannot warn against this sufficiently. Men are so inclined to fabricate for themselves a somewhat plebian and almost chummy idea of divine majesty that God (like one boon companion to another) is supposed to make a big racket in order to get his due and therefore comes making a great noise. No, precisely because the divine is so infinitely elevated, the most vigilant attentiveness is required lest God hand us over to ourselves. We always forget that we men are the ones who need God, not God who needs us; we forget that God in his majesty does not care at all for our earthly and temporal busyness. This accounts for the universality in Christendom of the false—yes, almost brutish and irrational—consolation that if God does not intervene with punishment, then one is in excellent standing with him. We forget that the divine Majesty has a punishment which he himself, of course, regards as the most dreadful: to ignore, majestically to ignore, to hand men over to themselves.

This on the occasion of that interpretation by the Irvingites, which I otherwise leave open.

XI² A 43   *n.d.*, 1854

« 2570 *God's Majesty*

This I have said frequently [x⁵ A 86; XI¹ A 37], that all the confusion in Christendom centers in our having lost a conception of God's majesty, what majesty of spirit is. Consequently the guilt of Christendom is the guilt of high treason; we have actually degraded the God of Christianity to the level of having a human cause, or in the human sense a cause in which he can still reach only the superlative of human majesty[314] and whatever worship he may demand or wish to have becomes something else, something most convenient to human nature: being busy about finite matters, in the finite sense fighting for his kingdom but still as a kingdom of the world—instead of the worship related to the unconditioned, undeniably the most strenuous kind of worship for flesh and blood.

God is pure subjectivity,[315] sheer unmitigated subjectivity, and intrinsically has no trace at all of the objective, since everything with such objectivity still comes thereby within the realm of relativities.

This had been completely forgotten; this is why in Christendom it is commonly thought that small matters do not concern God (something like the old pagan notion), but, on the other hand, that there is something so important that in and by itself it must concern God, attract his attention, interest him, if you please, whether he wants to or not.

Both conceptions are equally unchristian. But it is particularly the latter view I shall consider inasmuch as it is high treason; the other will be elucidated and illuminated in the process.

The pagan considered small things to be too insignificant to concern God; a single human being does not concern God, but a nation, for example, the enterprise of a nation, does; consequently there is something which because of its own significance must concern God—whereas in the Christian view God is infinite majesty in such a way that nothing in and for itself can concern him but only insofar as it pleases his majesty. Consequently the smallest trifle can concern him just as much as what we humans call the most significant of all, because it is his pleasure and not the object which determines his concern—he is infinite subjectivity.

That the lower concept of God's majesty is, from a Christian point of view, high treason is readily seen by looking at human majesty. Take the mightiest emperor who ever lived. It certainly is true, we must admit, that a good many things in and for themselves could not concern him. No, whether they concern him depends upon whether it is agreeable to his majesty. Since even the mightiest emperor is nevertheless not pure subjectivity but has an objectivity in his world, he is obligated under the law, and a situation, event, or the like can be so significant and crucial that it must concern his majesty willy-nilly. Here, you see, is the limit to his majesty, and the high treason consists in applying this limitation to God.

Yet there are men in Christendom who hold this view completely. The single individual utterly despairs of existing for God—but let's join together, make a crowd, a whole nation, an enormous enterprise—well, this in and for itself or by itself concerns God no more than the most forsaken, poor, stupid person—if it does concern God, it is only because it so pleases him. One might say, "You men could just as well save yourself the trouble insofar as these great enterprises are calculated to interest God—God is interested in what pleases him, for he is pure subjectivity and sheer subjectivity has no interest at all in anything except what pleases him."

If not only a European war broke out but a war with Asia and then Africa, America, and Australia were forced to take part—in and for itself, by itself, this would not concern God at all—but that a poor human being sighs to him, this would concern him, for his majesty is so disposed and this would move him subjectively.

But now suppose that all of Europe's emperors and kings issued an edict commanding thousands of ordained hired servants (I mean the clergy) *officially* to invoke the support of heaven, and suppose a gigantic united church service with 100,000 musicians, 50,000 organ pumpers, and 1,000,000 ordained hired servants was arranged for the purpose of officially invoking the support of heaven. This does not concern the heavenly majesty at all—but a poor man walking along Kjøbmagergade, sighing out of the depths of his heart to God—this concerns him infinitely, ineffably, for his majesty is so disposed, and this would move him subjectively.

And why would the other not concern him, the inordinate official noise which could be heard for miles and obviously, then, must be able to pierce heaven—why would this not concern him at all, why? My friend, whatever other conception you have of God, you surely do not doubt that he is what could be called a "connoisseur," a sensitive connoisseur, he who is sheer subjectivity, and being subjectivity is directly related to being a connoisseur. This is why women (who are superior to men in subjectivity) are generally regarded as sensitive connoisseurs, connoisseurs who know immediately how to distinguish between the official and the personal, know that the official is really an insult, a pompous way of making a fool of someone. Therefore what an infinite distance from God—an emperor who by means of an edict concocted by a prime minister orders 10,000 ordained hired-servants to bawl officially to God—what an infinite distance in comparison with a poor man who sighs to God out of the depths of his heart.

But this true Christian conception of God is not to the world's taste; insolent as it is, in addition to all other pleasures it wants the additional one of having worldliness stand in direct proportion to God; it turns a deaf ear to what Christianity wants, that worldliness be inversely related, that there is only one access to interesting the heavenly majesty—being a poor single individual human being. But only God knows how long the earthly emperor can stand this deathly silence, he who is perhaps accustomed to believing that the official bawling of 10,000 ordained hired-servants signifies something else, which of course they encourage in the emperor, for it is after all their living.

This is how Christianity has been proclaimed in Christendom—and this all goes together with the degrading of God's majesty. Money, power, and the like, these are what count in the world. Art and scholarship and all such higher things must put up with bowing and scraping before money. If a wealthy man wants to make a contribution, he is bowed to and feted as an art connoisseur and patron of poets, although he understands neither art nor poetry at all. One might think that the omnipotence of money would run aground at one point on Christianity, which, proclaimed in poverty, celebrated poverty as blessed and taught that a rich man would have difficulty entering the kingdom of God. Yes, so it was originally, but then the ordained hired-servants and the sworn in timeservers, the money changers of Christianity, got hold of things, and then Christianity was improved practically and it triumphantly spread over kingdoms and countries—and the majesty of God was degraded.

XI² A 54   *n.d.*, 1854

« 2571 *God's Majesty—God's Cause*

As I have said,[316] the guilt of Christendom is high treason; we have degraded God to being a superlative of human majesty; this has been done by the way we have served Christianity.

How has Christianity been served in Christendom? I wonder if it has not been simply as politics? Served through the prudential use of human expedients—therefore God has a cause in a human sense, therefore God is degraded, is merely some human Majesty.

But where in this kind of serving is there the least trace of resemblance to Christ's admonition[317] in the Sermon on the Mount? Is there any thought here that it is supposed to be *blessed* to be persecuted, blessed? No, suffering is precisely what we avoid in every way, and this is praised as *Christian* wisdom. We avoid suffering in every way and thereby forsake the cause of Christianity, or we change it in order to avoid suffering. Is this the commentary on: It is *blessed* to suffer? —It does not read that you must put up with suffering; no, it reads[318]: Rejoice, and be glad—it is blessed. —Where is there the slightest reminder of Christ's admonition[319]: If someone takes your coat, give him your cloak also—or is Christendom's commentary on this passage rather this: When you have taken someone's coat away from him, take his cloak along with it, too. —Where is there the slightest reminder of Christ's admonition[320] to be as indifferent to tomorrow as the lillies and the birds—or is Christendom's commentary on this: Studying theology is the surest way to a snug berth.

No, we have served Christianity just as if God were some human Majesty who aspires to extend himself and become the mightiest, that is, just as if Christianity were politics.

But the God of Christianity, the God of the New Testament, is infinite majesty and has not the thinnest thread of a cause in the human sense. That is why he demands to be served in another way: namely, by disdaining the use of human means, by scorning human cleverness, and by not wanting to accept human assistance. To the secular mind this of course is inconceivable; this is a sublimity of which it has no intimation, the infinite sublimity which in a human sense does not have a cause.

But simply because God is infinite majesty in this way and in the human sense has no cause, he has no use at all for the crowd of politicians in velvet and silk, who have charitably wanted to serve Christianity and to serve God by serving themselves. No, God has no use for politicians, only worshippers can serve him. Worshippers—yes, and to worship means simply to disdain human cleverness because it is blessed to suffer for God.

When Christianity is served in this way, it becomes qualitatively different from what it has become in Christendom, where it has become a flat, trivial, ordinary cause just like the rest of politics.

From the way Christianity was first served, it was understood that Christianity is something so infinitely sublime that all existence, the angels, the devil, and so on are interested in this event. On the other hand, a cause served by human means, and in which one does not venture out farther than the politicians, naturally degenerates into bagatelles *ad modum* a European war etc.: some nonsense we human beings cook up among ourselves.

Only when a cause is served in contempt for human means and human cleverness does the superhuman appear. But this service again expresses that the cause one serves is in the human sense not a cause.

No, humanly speaking, God has no cause whatsoever—spare yourself the effort, for God is not in hot water at all, in dire need of your intelligent efforts on behalf of him and his kingdom. He is not aspiring to expand his power, because it cannot be expanded. No, God wants to be worshipped. And to worship means simply that you adore him in such a way that you look only to him, disdaining human means. To worship him means simply that your desire is not, through human means, to avoid suffering; but rather that you look only to him and find it blessed to suffer.

But this sublimity, which is the Christianity of the New Testament, is not convenient for us human beings, and that is why we have dragged God down into the filth, have built beautiful churches for him, countries and kingdoms of Christians, which means to drag him down into the filth, for he is infinitely more elevated, so sublime that only the disdaining of human means corresponds to his sublimity, the disdaining of human means, which means the same as being willing to be sacrificed. Christendom, however, not only does not disdain human means; it imputes the same mind to God, that he thinks that they are what must be used. Christendom, itself spineless, has made God into an ordinary spineless human Majesty.

Humanly speaking, God has no cause at all. Eternal, unchanged, he sits and surveys all existence [*Tilværelsen*] and looks to see if there is anyone who wants to worship him. To worship him means to relate oneself unconditionally to him. But all who want to relate themselves unconditionally must *eo ipso* collide with this world, collide, for this world is precisely the world of the conditioned. Thus worship becomes *eo ipso* suffering—and to find it blessed is to serve God.

However, he who is unwilling to worship, unwilling to suffer, unwilling to serve God, hits upon the notion that God has a cause in the human sense; consequently it is a question of getting it to fit into the world of relativities, for which cleverness and human means are used—and this is called serving God.[*] This is how we have degraded God and, in addition, made Christ into a visionary, for he disdained the use of human means, the use of human cleverness, to avoid suffering (suffering is inseparable from the unconditioned and from unconditionally serving God—human cleverness therefore avoids suffering by changing the unconditioned to the conditioned), and he was visionary enough to prescribe the same for his disciples.

XI^2 A 55   *n.d.*, 1854

« **2572**

[*] *In margin of 2571* (XI^2 A 55):
The axiom is this: in relation to the unconditioned or by unconditionally serving the unconditioned, suffering is unavoidable in this world, which is the world of the conditioned. This must be held to firmly. Cleverness wants very much to give the impression that the cause is the same, only that cleverness knows how to avoid suffering. But this is a lie. The cause is not the same, is not the unconditioned, for no cleverness can invent a way by which suffering can be avoided if one actually relates himself unconditionally to the unconditioned.

XI^2 A 56   *n.d.*

« **2573 God's Majesty**

A stronger expression than this for the sublimity of God, the degree to which, humanly speaking, he has no cause, cannot be conceived: He makes the beloved unhappy, those who want to take their stand with him—precisely those, and they become unhappy to the same degree that they more honestly and more inwardly devote themselves to him. Infinite majesty! But here again we have the sign of the sphere of paradox, the marks of inversion.

In a certain sense this is too superhuman for a man to endure. At the same time it must be remembered that God is love, infinite love, and suffers with, yes, suffers more than the beloved, but does not change. No, he is not like an earthly Majesty who has the power, so to speak, of suspending protocol, his majesty, for the sake of the beloved —has the power, which means that precisely this is his weakness, for he has the power because his superiority and majesty, and consequently the protocol, are a kind of prank and not a qualification of essence, for an earthly majesty is only an accessory, a change of clothes, for a poor wretch like the rest of us.

But such majesty! —merely to point it out is to become anxious and fearful!

O, when I consider how from earliest childhood I have been isolated in special torments appointed for the extraordinary, when I consider how I had to suffer later, how bitter my life had to be, when I consider how in a certain sense I was gripped hard (for it is still love which takes this hard grip) — — and that only then did I really become aware of Christianity and God's majesty—when I consider this and then think of the rubbish about millions and millions and centuries and centuries of millions of Christians! Yes, men really know how to corrupt everything!

So sublime, then, is God's majesty.

And when all is said and done, this is what first and foremost has to be drilled into Christendom: What is to be understood by God's majesty, what it means. It is sufficiently obvious that the perpetual talk that God is love, this official nonsense, has so dragged God down into the nonsense that, properly stated in the mildest way, the concept of God abroad in Christendom is obscene.

One does not know whether to laugh or to cry when, skimming through paganism, one sees what incongruous, strange, and baroque ideas of God men are able to concoct— —but Christendom almost takes the negative prize for invention. There is always some salt in the pagan gods, but it is hard to imagine anything more fat, flat, and insipid than to make (for as the man is, so is his God, "he makes God in his image") God into hearty nonsense, a fuddy-duddy any preacher can twaddle about. This concept of God makes a man so insipid that I know no better way of expressing it than to say: It is so insipid it is obscene. To change God into such an embarrassing vapidity is worse than to change him into a bull, as the pagans did. To change God into such an embarrassing insipidity that a man becomes insipid on his behalf is, of course, far worse than all mocking of religion.

XI² A 118   *n.d.*, 1854

« 2574 *Divine Aristocracy*

How moving, how indescribably moving: precisely the most exalted is always the object of the boldest address, without any beating around the bush, without any problems—indeed, almost as if language had exhausted every possible gradation of titles, so that when we come to God the relationship turns about and to him we unreservedly say "*Du.*"[321]

On the other hand, how ironical that it is man himself who creates all the problems and makes his access to God so difficult, because, because—yes, because man is petty and small-minded.

God's aristocracy is curiously reversed. Regular aristocracy protects itself in all sorts of ways against direct advances. God, on the contrary, says: Come, dear man, come without any formalities at all—but look, man himself produces the formalities, and God is removed from man by the infinite distance of aristocracy.

It is the same with God's aristocracy as it is with taking hold of nettles. The main thing is to take hold quickly. But when all is said and done, man does not find it very smart to take hold too quickly: discretion is the better part of valor etc.—and he burns himself. Similarly, the God of love says: "Approach me directly"—yes, this is how God speaks, he who is infinite love. But man thinks: discretion is the better part of valor; the smartest thing for a person to do is to see if he can get one of God's valets to become interested in him and, if possible, get an audience with His Majesty. Thus the result is that God becomes the most aristocratic of all in a direct sense.

XI² A 144   *n.d.*, 1854

« 2575 *The Greatest Danger to Christianity*

is, I contend, not heresies, heterodoxies, not atheists, not profane secularism—no, but the kind of orthodoxy which is cordial drivel, mediocrity served up sweet.

The very being of Christianity is opposed to nothing, nothing, more than to this mediocrity, in which it does not so much die as dwindle away.

This particular kind of orthodoxy is high treason against Christianity, because despite its cordiality and inoffensiveness and good intentions it still does not have the imprint of fundamental respect for majesty.

There is nothing which so insidiously displaces the majestic as this very cordiality. Perpetually cordial, so small, so petty, tampering and meddling and tampering some more—the result is really that majesty is defrauded a little bit. A little bit—right here is the danger, for majesty is more disposed to a violent attack than to becoming a little bit degraded—amid cordiality.

This kind of orthodoxy is related to the cordial drivel of family life and essentially has its abode in the cordiality of family life. This, again, is the most dangerous of all for Christianity. Christianity is not as opposed to debauchery and frightful passions and the like as much as it is to this flat mediocrity, this nauseating atmosphere, this together-ness, where admittedly great crimes, wild excesses, and powerful aber-rations cannot easily occur—but where majesty has even greater difficulty in finding what it requires: the majestic expression of submis-sion. Nothing is further from obeying either/or than this flat, cordial family drivel.

XI^2 A 152 *n.d.*, 1854

« 2576 *God's Majesty*

Just as the effect of the Draconian law was that no one was pun-ished, so also we can elevate God into a kind of majesty whereby in a rascally way we are completely rid of him.

This is the kind of majesty into which Christendom has got God removed.

Therefore it is necessary to stress that God is pure subjectivity in the sense that if he is so inclined the most insignificant triviality can draw his attention. Of course it is quite another matter that he, as I have frequently discussed [XI^1 A 37; XI^2 A 43], majestically punishes men by ignoring them and all their striving, but this certainly is not because he is so removed in his majesty that he cannot detect it, as it were. Yet he is not, of course, subjectivity in the sense that something would have the power to influence him. No, the greatest and the least are equally incapable of this. But, as mentioned, the least triviality can draw his attention if it so pleases him. If it so pleases him. It all centers on this. For he indeed sees all, knows all, the greatest and the least or the most insignificant triviality. Therefore no one should deceive him-self. Even if a person heaps crime upon crime and it goes unpunished, yes, his life is sheer good luck and conquest, he should not be de-ceived, for God sees it, God is very near but he overlooks him; he is punished with the most frightful punishment of all—he is ignored by God. If the religious person thinks that one triviality or another could be so trivial as to go unnoticed by God, let him not be deceived, for God sees all, and if it so pleases him he can take note of it.

The formulation of the catechism that God is in heaven and does what he pleases is quite right, if this is understood as I have presented it here: God is pure subjectivity. For him everything is nothing if it so pleases him and nothing is everything if it so pleases him. But this middle term—if it so pleases him—is the infinite distance which God has, he who nevertheless in another sense is infinitely the closest. Everywhere and at every moment he is closest of all, yet infinitely secured against impertinence, for, whether or not he lets his nearness be noticed or whether or not he subjectively wills to be near depends solely on whether it so pleases him.

XI^2 A 166   *n.d.*, 1854

« **2577**

. . . . . The most frightful high treason against God is to make him and his Word ridiculous, not by ridicule—no, but by imputing in the twaddle of mediocrity that he also is a twaddler.[322]

XI^3 B 260   *n.d.*, 1855

MARRIAGE

« **2578**

It is a remarkable contrast: paganism levied a tax upon bachelor-hood[323]; Christianity recommended celibacy.

II A 244   August 11, 1838

« **2579**

Our age is losing more and more the teleological[324] factor which belongs to a view of life—and among the educated classes* there are no doubt a great many who regard a marriage without children as the best—in this connection one thinks contrariwise of the Jews, who almost completely surrendered their own existence and sought it only in another.

II A 374   February 25, 1839

« **2580**

In margin of 2579 (II A 374):
* In this area there is frequently a completely egotistic eudæmonism which will not tolerate the resignation [*Resignation*][325] which consists in having one's life purpose centered in another person. Marriage seems to require a comparable resignation, except that, for one thing, the fruit comes more quickly and almost simultaneously with the seeding, and also that with such a frame of mind the mutual resignation is not based upon a third as it ought to be but rather calculatingly seeks a *gain*. It is otherwise, for example, in Augustine; see p. 27 [i.e., II A 469–470].

II A 375   *n.d.*

« **2581**

Whereas the clergy by celibacy demonstrated ultimate indifference toward women, the other side attained its ideal in chivalry—and yet there was a parity, which we note also in this, that the knight could be buried as a clergyman if he requested it.

See Busching.[326]

II A 429   May 17, 1839

« **2582**

Marriage is a physical unity, not a unity in spirit and truth; therefore it says in Genesis of man and woman that "they are to be one flesh." Therefore the possibility of a second marriage, etc. See p. 7 [i.e., II A 375, 376].

II A 469   July 7, 1839

« **2583**

Addition to 2582 (II A 469):

And precisely because the Church sought to make marriage into something more, it disapproved of a second marriage. Athenagoras says: ὁ δεύτερος γάμος εὐπρεπές ἐστι μοιχεία—[327] precisely because with this view of marriage the Church sought to make the Greek esthetic element as well as the teleological element of Judaism* a matter of indifference, and because it allowed the real existence [*reale existents*] of man and woman to become a brother–sister relationship (specifically, in Christ), it made the marriage relationship an organic process, and as a result it either had to construe repeated marriage as completely ἀδιάφορον[328] or it had to assume that repetition of the marriage introduced a reflection upon it which made it inadmissible. It is true that there was the brother–sister relationship in the Jewish system also, but yet it was more of an external relationship and in contrast to other nations, but for the Christians in this relationship the similarity to angels which Christ speaks about had already begun, at least as an inner qualification, even though it was not in perfect harmony with external existence.

II A 470   July 7, 1839

« **2584**

In margin of 2583 (II A 470):

* As when Augustine,[329] in his ardor for the perfection which commences at the end of the world, says that without marriage: *multo citius civitas dei compleretur et acceleraretur terminus seculi.*[330]

See p. 7 m [i.e., II A 375].

II A 471   *n.d.*

« **2585**

On the way to Aarhuus, I saw a very comical sight. Two cows yoked together trotted past us; the one gadded about and flourished her tail very smartly; the other appeared to be more prosaic and more despondent over having to share in these same motions. —Are not most marriages so proportioned?

III A 82   n.d., 1840

« 2586

The universalized interpretation of the particular thesis[331]—Marry or do not marry, you will repent both—is, so to speak, the epitome of all the wisdom of life; and the personal relationship a teacher should always have to his pupil is best designated by: May it be to your good [*Velbekomme*].[332] We cannot, however, say to a person what would otherwise be considered the very best: The best thing for you is to go and hang yourself, for we have to say: Hang yourself or do not hang yourself—you will repent both.—

III A 117   n.d., 1841

« 2587

It takes courage to get married, and we ought not extol virginity —for Diana[333] herself did not remain a virgin because she felt the superiority of that state but because she feared the pains of giving birth. Indeed, Euripides[334] declares somewhere that he would rather go into battle three times than give birth once.

III A 144   n.d., 1841

« 2588

But marriage is impossible without confidence. [335]

III B 39   n.d., 1841

« 2589

If God gave Adam sociality by giving him Eve, this by no means entails extensive marital sociability, for Eve did not bring along a swarm of women friends.[336]

III B 41:25   n.d., 1841

« 2590 *Aristotle's* Politics

In Book I, Chapter 8,[337] there are some observations on marriage which adequately show that the Greek mentality [*Græciteten*] was unable to comprehend marriage.

Book I has general observations on the origin of the state, domestic life, its significance in politics since the state is an association of families. How the different forms of government are mirrored in the relationships of domestic life (master–servant–man–woman–parents–

children). Book II contains historical surveys, partly of ideal plans for a state, partly [of] historical states.

Book III begins with a development of what a citizen is, what constitutes a state, to what extent a state remains the same when the form of government is changed.

IV C 28   *n.d.*, 1842–43

« **2591**

Today there was this advertisement in the paper:[338] "Because of other plans, will sell 16 yards of heavy black silk cloth." God knows what the first intention was. A good response for a girl who was deceived in the final days before the wedding could be to have her advertise 16 yards of heavy black silk etc. which had been intended for a bridal dress.[339]

IV A 78   *n.d.*, 1843

« **2592**

When asked why he did not wish to be a father, Thales is supposed to have answered: Out of love for children. When his mother pressured him to get married, he said: By Zeus, it is not the time for that yet. After he came of age and she again kept on with this, he said: Now it is no longer the time for that.

See Diogenes Laertius, I, para. 26.
Kleobulos gave the maxim: Daughters should be married when they are maidens in age and women in understanding.

See Diogenes L., I, para. 91.[340]

IV A 237   *n.d.*, 1843

« **2593**

The second marriage is only a mediocre reprinting, a mediocre second edition.

V A 64   *n.d.*, 1844

« **2594**

My relationship to marriage is like Diana's to those giving birth: herself unmarried, she assisted.[341]

VI A 36   *n.d.*, 1845

« **2595**

There is a picture which portrays Rousseau and a young girl. The caption reads: "Rousseau's first love." Alongside hangs another picture with the caption, "Rousseau's last love." What an epigram! Suppose there had been only one picture with the title, "Rousseau's one and only love."

VIII[1] A 52   *n.d.*, 1847

« **2596**

Erotic love and marriage are really only a deeper confirmation of self-love by becoming two in self-loving.[342] For this very reason married people become so satisfied, so vegetatively prosperous—because true love does not fit into earthly existence [*Tilvær*] the way self-love does. Therefore the solitary lacks self-love; married people express this by saying: He is selfish, loves himself—because married people presume that marriage is love.

VIII[1] A 190   *n.d.*, 1847

« **2597**

If I were to base a wedding ceremony on some portion or other of ancient pastorals[343]—yet, please note, with permission to include the name of God and of Christ five or six times along with the cake—the marriage ceremony would be such that the bride and groom as well as the others would be deeply moved by the rare discourse. —And if I were to be scrupulous about the scriptural teaching concerning marriage and use it as the basis for a wedding, the bride and groom and others would become so embarrassed and embittered that they would like to massacre me. —See, one sticks his finger into the earth in order to smell what country he is in: when one discovers this, he smells that he is in Christendom.

VIII[1] A 198   *n.d.*, 1847

« **2598**

Oddly enough, I find an especially good observation in my old journal for 1839 (E. E.) [i.e., II A 469], which on the whole does not have much which is really felicitous or thorough: Marriage is not really love, and therefore it is said that the two become *one flesh*—but not one spirit, since two spirits cannot possibly become one spirit. This observation would have lent itself very well for use in *Works of Love.*

VIII[1] A 231   *n.d.*, 1847

« **2599**

Just as it was, no doubt, entirely right for Luther to marry, expressly to proclaim and establish temporality and earthly life as pleasing to God in contrast to fantastic abstraction, so in these times it might be beneficial for a person to refrain from marrying, expressly in order to declare that spirituality still has so much reality [*Realitet*] that it can be enough, more than enough, for a life. Nowadays men have become so secularized that they must learn in time to play cards and also get married and other such things—in order to have something to fill up time. O, this jealous secularity, which wants all men to be uniform, becomes angry when someone will not marry. There is something epigrammatic in not marrying, not socializing, not playing cards, not getting involved with others. In order to make his way in these times, one must be married—otherwise people become suspicious that it might be an attempt to make their own lives strenuous.

VIII[1] A 369   *n.d.*, 1847

« **2600**

Christendom is in dire need of an unmarried person to take up Christianity again—not as if there were something objectionable in marriage, but it certainly has come to be highly overrated. Getting married has finally become the highest and truest earnestness. But this is not Christian. You are permitted to marry; Christianity blesses it; but never forget the place for the more decisively religious persons. Otherwise, to be consistent, one would have to object to Paul on the grounds that he was not married.

On the whole it would be good to scrap completely that exception common in sermons: It applied at those times, in those situations, etc.

IX A 237   *n.d.*, 1848

« **2601**

Established Christendom, insofar as it has any fear of God, is essentially Judaism. Upon closer inspection, it is apparent that conventional Christians have recovered once more this whole business of having a good life here on earth—which is God's benediction upon a person—amassing of money, having success with whatever one undertakes, etc.

Peter[344] has always been very determined to get an heir; he has finally become so Judaic that he believes that the blessing of God does not rest upon an unmarried person.[*]

On the whole it would be good once again to touch on marriage from this angle. Ordinarily there is but very little religiousness in

Christendom with regard to marriage, but what is there is essentially Judaic, this business of having it good here on earth, this earthly life as directly commensurable with the blessing of God—and misfortune and the like as being God's punishment.

This kind of Christianity assumes that Christ has finished the whole matter once and for all—one believes on him—and then arranges his own life along the lines of Jewish piety.

IX A 245   n.d., 1848

« **2602**

[*] *In margin of 2601* (IX A 245):

In established Christendom this extreme, ridiculous from a Christian view, is soon reached—that marriage as such is holiness, in quite the same sense as the single state was regarded in the Middle Ages. Here the Jewish element is apparent.

IX A 246   n.d.

« **2603**

The question, however, is whether monastic orders have not become necessary again in order to get pastors or men who live only to preach. It was really an error arising from the Reformation and its whole political direction, that because Luther got married (in contrast to celibacy), it has almost become a perfection to get married. If remaining single is only properly understood, then religion always needs the unmarried, especially in our time.

IX A 434   n.d., 1848

« **2604**

What stupidity! In a little article about the propensity of men to heed warnings, which I find in paging through Jens Møller's journal[345] (VI, pp. 118, passim), I note that he says[346] that the drawing of lots has been sanctioned in a Protestant congregation, the United Brethren.

Aber. Among other reasons, the United Brethren do this simply to cool off flesh and blood. Therefore marriage is decided by lot. From an erotic point of view, it is impossible to imagine a more cruel and revolting method, a method better calculated to destroy erotic ardor. However, I think that in a certain sense the United Brethren have touched Christianity. Christianity demotes the erotic to the level of indifference and makes marriage a duty; therefore what girl you get is a matter of complete indifference. It is your duty to be married.

X¹ A 310   n.d., 1849

« **2605**

The Middle Ages went astray and believed that it was a sacrilege for a priest to marry. Then came Luther—and married. Now things have gone so far that it is regarded as a fault if a clergyman does not marry. One cannot very well be a pastor if he is not married. The congregation will have no confidence in someone as a spiritual adviser etc. if he is not married. —And this obviously is said in the same sense that one says of a physician: "families" prefer having a married man as their physician, that is, they are afraid that an unmarried man will be lecherous.

In the Middle Ages, therefore, celibacy corresponded to holiness (this was the idea, quite apart from the question whether there was a lecher among them); nowadays an unmarried man is suspected of being a lecher with whom wife and daughters are not safe.

Truly the world has advanced in spirituality. In the Middle Ages there was the greatest confidence in the unmarried man; his unmarried state was thought to be a guarantee—this is the syllogism of the Spirit. Nowadays we have most confidence in the married man; we regard the fact that he is married as a guarantee that he will not seduce one's wife and daughters—this is the syllogism of the flesh.

x^1 A 440   *n.d.*, 1849

« **2606**

I Timothy 5:11 seems to disagree with 14. In the first portion it reads that the young widows, when out of wantonness they become disobedient toward Christ, *desire* to marry; in the other portion, I (Paul) am of the opinion that they *should* marry. If they themselves wish it, everything seems to be in order.

I do not entirely understand this passage, unless I simply take it as the most evident argument against the erotic, so that to want to marry (falling in love, the erotic) is reproved and the Christian view is posed in contrast: they should marry—but not, please note, as a uniting of *desiring* and *should,* but in such a way that this *should* is the strongest contrast to that *desiring.*

x^1 A 445   *n.d.*, 1849

« **2607**

The error in the Middle Ages (which has commonly repeated itself) is that someone who acts in a special way wants to make his way the norm for others. Not to marry is obviously to act in a special way.

With regard to the person concerned, this may be entirely pleasing to God. But it is something else to establish this as the norm, yes, even if only to initiate others into it for the sake of the cause. The special one is the exception and ought to be conscious of himself as such, and rather than advising others to do the same, the exception should instead advise others to do the universal. The special one is genuine only when he has primitivity in the God-relationship. Only the primitive God-relationship can be defended over against the universal. Everything which does not have this primitivity is *eo ipso* unjustified when it wants to be an exception.

To continue with the example, not to marry—it is easy to show how this ought to be done. The individual remains absolutely silent about his resolution. He goes on living unmarried—quite right—but if he remains silent, no third person can check up on this.

This *non-faktum* can be interpreted in 17 ways. For a long time no one notices it at all, for there certainly is no standard age for getting married. They think he is going around like the others looking for a girl. Time passes—and he remains unmarried. This *non-faktum* can be interpreted in 17 ways.

The error of the Middle Ages was to make it known, and then, even crazier, to make it out to be a perfection or merit.

Even I have experienced this collision.[347] In her suffering and distress—and, alas, she suffered far too much—my betrothed finally asked me: Tell me just one thing—that you will never get married. Here was the collision. She was so agitated that she was very close to moving toward religion in a decisive sense. I could, and with good conscience, have said: No. And then what? Then I, who was conscious of having very particular determinants, would have intervened disturbingly in her life. Therefore I replied with a jest.[348] If she was going to do anything like that, i.e., if it was to be her own truth and therefore permissible, it must dawn upon her with radical primitivity.

The truth soon became apparent; she married—for which I have thanked and praised God. On the other hand, if this had truly been her truth, everything might have turned out differently. She would not have said a word to me about such things but would have determined primitively in her own God-relationship not to marry, and perhaps she would have been right. But as she possibly meant it, she probably did not have a clear God-relationship but only a God-relationship at second hand. But if one does not have the God-relationship first hand, one is unjustified in being an exception. With all her heart she desired the relationship with me. For her it almost amounted to our being united whether we married or remained unmarried. As far as I was concerned, this perhaps was entirely in order, because in me this was something primitive, but in her it would have been derived; she had not come into a God-relationship but found rest in a kind of platonic love relationship to me. But such a relationship is not religious and consequently is inadmissible. Only the primitive God-relationship is the justified exception.

x^1 A 485   *n.d.*, 1849

« **2608**

The error of the Middle Ages was to regard poverty, the unmarried state, etc. as something which in and for itself could please God. This has never been Christianity's understanding. Christianity has recommended poverty, the unmarried state, etc. so that by being occupied with finite things as little as possible, men could all the better serve the truth. It is clear enough that a person who can live on roots, be unmarried, etc. has more time and can less calculatingly serve the truth.

But we have found it most convenient to set the whole matter aside by pretending that the error of the Middle Ages is the teaching of Christianity.

x^2 A 181   *n.d.*, 1849

« **2609**

It is dubious to argue as Ambrose[349] argues some place in order to prove that a Christian has the right to serve the state (something which occupied them very much at that time)—appealing to Scriptures that he who has a public office must be faithful in the office—for it is one thing to have it and another thing to seek it. It is the same as proving that Christianity recommends marriage on the basis that Scripture says: What God has joined together no man shall separate —for it is one thing to stipulate the sanctity of the contracted pact; it is another to recommend contracting the pact. Take another example. A rashly signed bond—since I put my signature to it, I ought to honor it. Now, if ethics enjoins this, does this mean that it recommends reckless signing of bonds?

This is purely illustrative; I by no means believe that Christianity has anything against marriage—but Christianity is always very much against such dishonest arguments.

x^2 A 566   *n.d.*, 1850

« **2610**

One reason, among others, that marriage is unbearable for those who want to be separated is certainly this—the possibility of divorce. If divorce were impossible, things would perhaps go better.

The dove-keeper knows that if he were to take the two most quarrelsome doves (but a male and a female) and shut them up together, they would eventually mate.

How reliable is everything God does! With two males it probably would not work; they would kill each other; but male and female *shall* adapt to one another, and if it is only made impossible for them to be separated, they settle down.

X^3 A 113   *n.d.,* 1850

« **2611** *The Marriage in Cana*[350]

Christendom has been so terribly preoccupied with this marriage, but I do not know what it has proved by it.

In the first place, the circumstance that Christ was present at the wedding proves nothing at all about marriage. It was his task as a teacher to be present everywhere, always looking for the opportunity to instruct. For indeed he was not a professor who with a manuscript lectures from a podium at certain hours. Consequently nothing is proved by this. Otherwise, from the fact that Christ was more often present at banquets and with Pharisees it could also be proved that Christ was an advocate of banquets and the Pharisees.

But he changed the water into wine to enliven the party. True, yet we observe that it was his mother who had to prompt him to do it and who first of all had to take a reprimand—therefore he was not particularly disposed to do it.

If we are to get any judgment of Christianity upon marriage out of this story, then we must say: Marriage is related to Christianity in the same way Mary is to this miracle—actually Christianity does not care to get involved in it; is quite indifferent whether one marries or not. But the woman asks for it—and so Christianity gives in and for a moment takes the woman's conception of marriage.

X^3 A 316   *n.d.,* 1850

« **2612**

The preachers rant against celibacy—and at the same time the secular mentality adopts it, journalists and the like—in short, those who really are to pull in the harness are quite naturally unmarried. But the preachers, to be sure, do not think there is anything to be done to put Christianity through—it won the victory long ago.

x³ A 419   *n.d.*, 1850

« 2613 *Marriage of the Clergy*

If it were not for this deplorable, stagnant tradition that a pastor must be married, that it cannot be otherwise, for then he is not a proper pastor—it might very well happen that some theological candidate would begin as a pastor without being demoralized by this running after a position.

x³ A 468   *n.d.*, 1850

« 2614 *Marriage*

If marriage really were a duty—as the moralists are now prating—what arbitrariness, then, to forbid women to propose to men just as well as men propose to women.

Indeed, not to fulfill an obligation means guilt. A girl dies unmarried—but she says in her defense: No one proposed to me.

Is this a defense—if marriage actually is a duty?

What nonsense: duty as the major premise; as the minor premise, however, custom and usage do not permit the woman herself to propose. How in the world can custom and usage exempt me from fulfilling a duty? If it is duty, then custom and usage must be changed.

Ah, there still survives in us from remote times an anxiety about the strenuous life which has an eye on the unmarried state. Nowadays, for the sake of security, we go so far that we even make marriage a duty. In our distraction we then forget that if this is so, the esthetic or traditional notion that women may not propose to men is invalid.

x³ A 553   *n.d.*, 1850

« 2615 *Marriage*

In the symbolical books (one of them) there is a passage somewhere[351] which states that because of the prevailing sensuality and lechery marriage has now been made so universal.

This certainly is an entirely different way of looking at it than we are accustomed to.

xi¹ A 52   *n.d.*, 1854

« 2616 *Protestantism*

Protestantism is dubious even in its symbolical books.[352]

We now live in such a way that all this business of fasting, celibacy, etc. is ridiculous extremism, madness, unreasonable worship of God.

But marriage is the true and reasonable worship of God.

Fine. Yet even in the symbolical books there is the casual remark which escaped Luther or one of the reformers, which says that because the world has now become so old and lechery so out of hand, it is no longer possible to live chastely outside of marriage and therefore marriage must be given a place. But, good Lord, this is an altogether different way of speaking; consequently marriage is a concession they felt obliged to make to lechery.

And it is on these symbolical books the pastor takes his oath—and not a single one has called out: I cannot take an oath on a book like this which contains two such outright contradictions as: marriage is divine, a step forward in reasonable Christian worship—and marriage is a concession on the basis of the rising tide of lechery.

On the whole, there has been an ambiguity in Protestantism from the very beginning: has human nature in its degeneration been obliged to seek alleviation since it can no longer bear the divine—or is marriage a forward step in true religiousness?

XI¹ A 129   n.d., 1854

« 2617 Marriage

The way marriage is regarded is decisive for every religious view of life, for every religion, and by marriage I mean the moral [sædelige] expression for the propagation of the species.

Besides the sexual drive and everything pertaining to it which may determine a person to marry, there is another view which I shall emphasize here. In Plato[353] and Aristotle[354] as well as in the older Church fathers (in Böhringer[355] on occasion and marked in my copy) the view is expressed that to leave posterity is a consolation for not being immortal, that propagation of the race is a substitute for the immortality of the individual, and therefore the person who clings to life, if he does not assume his immortality, still strives to extend his life by leaving a family.

This has never been expressed as strongly as in Judaism, where everything revolves around: Propagate and be fruitful—everything revolves around the line of descent and genealogy—and this is divinely sanctioned. Therefore, according to Judaism, there is no immortality either.

Then comes Christianity and introduces virginity—that is, religion of the spirit.

There will always be a swinging between the individual, immortal, and the individual without immortality but consoling himself with his posterity. Between or within these two lie the identifying differences among all religions.

XI[1] A 150   n.d., 1854

« 2618 *A Christian Nation*

Associated with this rubbish is all the indecent—from a Christian point of view—promotion of child-begetting as the most worthwhile thing we can think of, in contrast to—the single state.

Christianly, marriage is merely better than burning. No more. Therefore stand back, Mother, stand back my good Mrs.!

But they convince themselves that they are begetting Christians— and this explains the importance of all this nonsense about children.

On the other hand the one for whom Christianity has concern (as it is always concerned for the abandoned, the rejected), the unmarried girl who is not lucky enough to marry–she is overlooked and mini- mized. No, no, my good Mrs.—look at her and please stard aside with your flock of children. We are not Jews, nor has Christianity offered a prize to the one who can have the most children, nor does Chris- tianity believe the story we tell children about the stork bringing chil- dren. Christianity knows full well where children come from and that we are merely clothing our lust in pompous platitudes (about marrying only for the sake of having children)—but, to repeat, it is better to marry than to burn.[356]

XI[1] A 169   n.d., 1854

« 2619 *Marriage*

That Christ meant that the Christian obviously would not marry is discernible even more clearly in the following indirect way than in all that is said directly.

When Christ points out the degree in which he wants to be loved by the Christian, he puts the collision in this way: He who loves father, mother, sister, brother and so on more than me is not worthy of me. Generally he does not say: One who loves his child more than me—he does not think of the Christian as married, for otherwise he might have aimed in quite another way at precisely this collision.*

It is clear that the most disturbing difficulties later in Christianity are related to marriage and concern for children. It is really with the help of "the infant" that Christianity has been seesawed and the unconditioned has been rocked: a genuine piece of human rascality—by introducing "the infant," we have intended to get God to relax.

In margin: *Note. Insofar as mention (for example, Matthew 19:29) is made of forsaking "wife and children for Christ's sake," it must always be remembered that there is a great difference between married men with wife and children who want to be Christians and Christians who want to marry and have children.

XI¹ A 253   n.d., 1854

« 2620 *Christianity—the Single State*

According to Christianity the world is a world of sin, the consequence of a fall.

Christianity is salvation, but it is also a *cessation;* it wants to stop all the perpetuation which is oriented toward the prolongation of this world.

Therefore Christianity is partial to the single state. It is the characteristic expression for the Christian's breaking with the world, and therefore the New Testament constantly uses words which imply a stopping, words such as: to be salt, to be sacrificed, etc.

Yet it was not long before marriage was going strong among Christians—and here begins the confusion of producing in the rear what is being fought up front. In marriage the Christian immediately takes on a relationship to the world different from that of being a stranger, an alien, salt, a sacrifice, of having an arresting effect.

If anyone says that he marries to beget children and to make true Christians for God by bringing them up from the start in Christianity, I would answer—rubbish! The fact of the matter is that you feel the desire to beget children. But as far as this method of making true Christians is concerned, there is nothing Christianity is more opposed to than to be anticipated in this way and thereby to be turned into rubbish, for generally speaking it is almost impossible for a man brought up from childhood in Christianity to become a Christian.

XI¹ A 295   n.d., 1854

« 2621 *Celibacy*

At the time the Pope ordered that the clergy should remain unmarried, the Christian view had already been long lost and a confusing accommodation or accord with the world had set in. It is not a matter of the priest having to be unmarried; no, the Christian is to be unmarried. The distinction between clergy and laiety is unchristian, *aber—aber* —not upside down, so that the clergy must also be married.

For Christianity this world is a sinful world; a child is conceived in iniquity and born in sin. Christianity wants to stop, atone for the past, but it does not then actually want to start all over again right away. When someone pays another's debts, he makes one stipulation —no more debts again—so it is with being unmarried in relation to being Christian.

But in Christendom married people are consecrated, and the consecration sanctifies this relationship. Charming! In the same way bandits in the South sanctify their murders by kneeling in advance at the altar.

By consecration married people sanctify their resolution. Splendid! At the foot of the altar where the savior of the world hangs upon his cross, he who by his death atoned for the sins of the race, original sin, and taught: imitate me, imitate me [*følg mig efter*], which is what it means to be a Christian—there the lovers kneel and resolve, resolve to perpetuate original sin. If it is true that consecration sanctifies sexual relations, then it must be true of the child which is born that it is not conceived in iniquity and born in sin.

"But Christ himself attended a wedding." Incomparable! Consequently he, who was so rigorous about what it means to be a disciple that he did not permit a disciple to bury his father[357] lest he get too involved with the world, he supposedly thought that being a disciple was consistent with marrying and begetting children, which means settling down as deeply as possible in this life—all this then is proved by his attendance at a wedding? By the same token we supposedly can demonstrate true Christianity by putting on banquets because Christ attended a banquet, or even that being a Christian is to be a deceiver, because Christ was surrounded by tax collectors and sinners.

"But the apostle nevertheless permits marriage." Yes, he permits it. Consequently you see that he is infinitely far from the view of marriage which flourishes now in Protestantism, especially in Denmark. He permits it, and if you are honest, you cannot deny that there is a certain reluctance in the apostle when he does it. He would rather not give in; he says: It is better to marry than to suffer being burned, that is, if worst comes to worst, all right, better marriage than to burn.[358]

But we are happy in this religion which consists of begetting children. Therefore we do not come in shame to the baptismal font with the children, so that baptism might possibly make good the parents' wrongdoing. No, with conceited self-satisfaction we produce children and feel that even if we are not lucky enough to produce twins, God is pleased with us for having one child—and this is New Testament Christianity!

Generally speaking, the conception of the propagation of the race is decisive for every religion. Either the world is essentially a splendid world and it is very pleasing to God that its being is perpetuated or —and this is New Testament Christianity—God is very opposed to the existence [*Tilværen*] and being of this world. Christianity has been introduced to call a halt, and therefore propagation also is immediately blockaded.

The only reliable concepts of what Christianity is are (principally) the proclamation of Christ and of the apostles and also contemporary Judaism's and paganism's judgment of it. With one voice they say: Christianity is hatred of men. And so it is in the New Testament. Christ expresses by his life: to love God is to hate men. Hate men?—how can this be for him who was sheer love of mankind! Yes, certainly—he understood from the outset and maintained to the last that he was sacrificed to men, and therefore he was sheer love toward all that suffers, is abandoned, is rejected, and the like—but not in the sense of helping them with money, power, and other earthly means. But this kind of love for mankind—and this is what we men call humanitarianism, helping men to enjoy this life—this kind of love was alien to him. He knew only too well that Christianity makes men unhappy in this life, because to love God means to be willing to suffer.

In this way we can understand Christ's concern in talking with his apostles about their not being offended by him; likewise we can understand that what he prophesied to them had to take place—namely, that they would be mistreated, expelled, persecuted, killed—in order truly to express that to love God is to hate men, or to love them in such a way as human egotism simply does not want to be loved. It is easy to understand that this love had to be rewarded as it was rewarded.

But that enormous lie which Christendom puts under the title: to love men—this turns Christianity completely around. The truth about our way of living is really this: we love ourselves—and hate God. This is what nowadays is called Christianity. Naturally we take care not to say it. We even expect ultimately to be able to make God believe that this is Christianity.

XI[1] A 313   *n.d.*, 1854

« **2622 *Propagation of the Species***
** *Christianity Wants to Close the Way***

Christianity might speak in this way to a person who wants to get married: In what capacity do you want to propagate the species—is it *qua* animal creature or *qua* man of spirit? In the first capacity the matter is all too simple.

But if it is in the second capacity, stop a moment. Do you not think that to be a father requires that you have reached the maturity of really having a view of life which you dare vouch for and dare commend to your child when, with the right it has in being a child and in owing you its life, it asks you about the meaning of life? Or supposing that what nature takes care of, breast milk, etc. happened to be the woman's special task to attend to—would it not be loathesome to want to be a mother, to satisfy one's desires, but not to have in readiness what the child needs? But from the father a child has the right to demand a view of life, that the father really has a view of life.

However, if a person is to attain this maturity, a long time will pass before he marries; the years will pass, the very years in which desire is strongest. If he finally reaches maturity and his view of life is Christianity, it might very well never occur to him to want to bring a child into existence [*Tilværelsen*]. To bring a child into existence! The child is born in sin after being conceived in transgression, and this existence is a vale of woe—is this what you are going to tell the child, is it this which gives you confidence toward the child who owes his existence to you?

O my God, the more I think about it the more I think Protestantism has fundamentally confused Christianity.

By nature man centers existence around the propagation of the species; this constitutes all his egotism *qua* animal creature or here it culminates. Christianity would decentralize this relationship—and what a battle it has been! How frightfully true, just in this connection, Christ's words[359] to the apostles: I am sending you as a sheep among ravening wolves—yes, ravening wolves are what men become, all right, as soon as someone touches this point in earnest and in earnest wants to wrench from them what for them is the whole content of life.

And then along comes Protestantism and applies Christianity—precisely in relation to marriage—and marriage becomes particularly well-pleasing to God. What loathsomeness in this falsified Christianity which lies to men partly because it is more pleasant to play up to men and partly because "the parson" in the capacity of stud master and breeder is egocentrically interested in increasing the flock and in promoting having as many children as possible.

The error in Catholicism is not that the priest is unmarried—no, the error is that a qualitative distinction has been introduced between laity and clergy which is directly opposed to the New Testament and is a concession of weakness in the direction of numbers. No, the error is not that the priest is unmarried—a Christian ought to be unmarried.

"But if this is going to be stressed, you won't get any Christians"—what difference does it make!

"If, on the other hand, you make marriage into Christianity, you will get millions of Christians"—again, what difference does it make!

$$XI^2 \text{ A } 150 \quad n.d., \text{ 1854}$$

« 2623 *One More Reason for Marrying!*

Christianity says: Refrain from marrying; this is pleasing to God and is a natural consequence if you are really a Christian.

To this the human species replies: But if we all do that, the species will die out.

Of course the species regards the extinction of the species as the greatest misfortune.

The result is that men not only do not refrain from marrying—no, they get one more reason for marrying: to prevent this frightful development (which is so imminent!), this frightful development (which almost everyone is engaged in preventing!), this frightful development, that the race might die out.

This is one more reason for marrying!

$$XI^2 \text{ A } 153 \quad n.d., \text{ 1854}$$

« 2624 *The Single State*

To create is reserved for God, and this, if one dares speak of such things, is the highest autopathetic satisfaction.

The giving of life is a weak analogy to this and is conceded to man—human egotism culminates at this point.

As the nerve ends lie under the nails, so human egotism is concentrated in the sexual relationship, the propagation of the species, the giving of life.

According to Christian teaching, God wants only one thing of us human beings—he wants to be loved. But in order that a human being may love God he must give up all egotism, first and foremost the intensified egotism: propagation of the species, the giving of life.

That sexuality is the center of human egotism God knows too well, of course, and therefore this became the locus of attention. A person does not have to look very hard to be convinced that here human egotism is total.

So God demanded the renunciation of this egotism—then God pointed to immortality. As I have often discussed in these journals [i.e., XI¹ A 150], propagation of the species was a substitute for immortality (which both Plato and Aristotle[360] explicitly state) both in paganism and in Judaism.

Sexuality is the culmination of human egotism. Therefore, in a purely human sense, not only the woman but the man also feels life to be lost, a failure, unless he is married. Only the married are genuine citizens in this world, the single person is an alien (which is precisely what Christianity wants the Christian to be—and what God wants the Christian to be, in order to love him). Therefore the Jews (who knew all about the propagation of the species) regarded sterility as a disgrace for a woman. Therefore no mishap touches a person so painfully as one which affects propagation of the species; everything else (being blind, crippled, deaf, etc.) does not violate him, does not touch the tender point of his egotism. Self-esteem *qua* animal creature is connected with propagating the species, the giving of life. This is why people who through natural or unnatural excesses have lost the power of procreation are so extraordinarily concerned with getting it back again in order to regain self-esteem, etc.

Consequently God wants the single state because he wants to be loved.

But man says: "I cannot give you this sacrifice—but let me get married and with your cooperation I will beget ten others to love you." Wonderful! But look a little more closely—these ten, if this begetter of children and vendor of human beings finally delivers ten, do these ten become single human beings who renounce the potentiated egotism? No, these ten behave in the very same way and each one perhaps furnishes ten more, always within the same formula that instead of one God gets ten—whereas in truth God gets none at all but is continually led around by the nose.

In Protestantism all the wrappings have been taken off of this matter. Protestantism teaches "short and sweet" that marriage is well-pleasing to God—and I foresee that learned theology will discover some day that the God of the Christians is called neither Jehovah nor Adonai, is not even neuter gender, but is a female called Minnie the Matchmaker!

What has Christianity come to in the course of the centuries! In the old version of *Don Juan*,[361] Elvira's servant says to Don Juan concerning Elvira: In an out-of-the-way corner I met my deceased master's daughter dressed in a man's shabby suit—what a terrible sight! So it is with Christianity! The only sovereign, the divine Majesty—must now make music at weddings and christening parties.

The single state, says Christianity. No, replies man, but I would like to make arrangements for a wedding ceremony. Charming! It is *ad modum:* Refrain from murder! —No, and I would like to have you consecrate the dagger.

The single state, says Christianity. No, says Protestantism. Marriage is precisely what is well-pleasing to God. He leaps for joy the more humans he can get to be married.

Have we not reached the point where Christianity has become the very opposite of what it is in the New Testament? It has been "attained," for a lot of work has been put in on it—what are Christendom's 1800 years other than the history of the continued striving by the numerical to get Christianity re-edited; the history of how Christianity, served less and less, has steadily made more and more concessions to the numerical, has bargained until everything has been reversed. This is the history of 1800 years—in which the student is carefully taught not to make a mistake about what true Christianity is.

In the Christianity of the New Testament God wants to be loved and therefore wants man to give up the egotism which the giving of life is.

The fall is the satisfaction of this egotism—and the history of temporality really begins at this point, a constant repetition of the same guilt, continually working against or hindering what God is aiming at, the halting of this false step—by means of the single state. Every time the single state, motivated by love to God, makes its appearance, this is a move in the direction of complying with God's intention.

But I almost shudder when I think how far I went in this direction and how amazingly I was halted and turned back to the single state, and how I, certainly with self-understanding but understanding myself as an exception, knew how to conceal from my contemporaries what I knew until at long last I see how here again providence has been with me and wants some definite outcome.

O, infinite majesty, even if you were not love, even if you were cold in infinite majesty, I could still not keep from loving you, I need something majestic to love. What others have said about not finding love in this world and therefore feeling the need to love you because you are love (which I agree with completely), this I also want to say about majesty. There was and is in my soul a need for majesty, a majesty which I can never weary or tire of worshipping. In the world I found nothing of majesty, no more of majesty than of beard on a young girl's cheek, or even less, for I found it ridiculous.

XI^2 A 154   *n.d.*, 1854

« 2625 *The wedding in Cana*

Christendom's *repeated* and *repeated* reference to this and to Christ's being present at a wedding and providing the wine proves indirectly that men have a suspicion that Christianity is opposed to marriage, and therefore this story becomes as important to them as their reasoning based on it is ridiculous.

XI^2 A 160   *n.d.*, 1854

« 2626 *Christianity as Doctrine*

If it actually was God's intention that Christianity be only a doctrine, a few propositions, then the New Testament is a ridiculous book —to set everything in motion in this way, to have Christ suffer in this way—in order to introduce a few doctrinal propositions. Mankind might well say: For heaven's sake, if that is all you want, if that can concern you so much, we are glad to take on whatever you want; we can do it just as easily as if you wanted us to wear three-cornered hats instead of round ones.

Truly, if it were God's idea that Christianity be merely a doctrine, the whole apparatus of the New Testament and Christ's life betrays that God as a student of human nature is, to put it bluntly, a complete bungler.

No, God, who knows the swindler, "man," has his sights on something else: the transformation of character.

Therefore God aims first and foremost at the cardinal point—the single state.

Heterogeneity is what God wants, heterogeneity with this world. A dying away instead of the lust of life, the single state instead of weddings and birthings.

There was a time when the Christian adorned his house only with —a skull. Now it is Venus one sees in every house; now it is (Christian?) culture to bring a refined allusion to sex into everything; the education of women is refined coquetry.

Yes, either a Venus as the symbol, or the Jewish view that child begetting is the blessing of this life—one or the other is the whole point in Christendom's life or life in Christendom.

The wonderful result of making Christianity into doctrine is that the earnestness of life in Christendom is—the relationship to the opposite sex—and this is supposed to be Christianity, the Christianity of the New Testament.

XI² A 172   n.d., 1854

« 2627 *Marriage*

That propagation of the species is related to human egotism or, more accurately, is human egotism is seen in countless ways—here only a couple of items— —

Most men do not have enough self-esteem to live as single individuals; their egotism craves to toe an auxiliary line for the potentiation of their self-esteem—that there are those who owe their lives to them. Now they think that their lives do have significance. Then, too, as mentioned before [XI² A 154], this is a substitute for immortality.

Most men lack self-esteem adequate to hold their own over against other men; their self-esteem requires that they have a few people who must unconditionally obey them, a few people whom they have entirely in their power, who feel that they are their masters. Their children fill this need. God have mercy on the cruelty and egotism hidden in family life, since it is all too true, unfortunately, that parents more often need upbringing than the children.

XI² A 176   n.d., 1854

« 2628 *Christianity—Christendom*

The New Testament presents the matter in such a way that if a person reads the gospels with only the slightest primitivity or openness, he will get the impression that even if there were no other hindrance to marriage on the part of Christianity, the Christian does not have time to marry. A Christian is committed to God to such a degree that there can be no thought of time for delay because of marriage.

In Christendom the situation is such that if a theological student has come so far that he is really ready to collect himself in concentration upon what Christianity is, it turns out that he has no time for that —because he is engaged and must get married as soon as possible, and therefore he has no time to collect himself in concentration upon what Christianity is—because he has to get married. And it is on Christianity's expense account that he marries, for he and his family are going to live off it!!!!

So he gets married, becomes a pastor and—do not forget this, which can be done so easily, for of course it means nothing—takes an oath on the New Testament, an oath which he understands to mean that he serves as do all the others; then he takes a few books with him to the country, begets a few children—and now you can be sure to find out what Christianity is from him and his wife.

And this is the way Christianity is spread "all around the world," as the late Mynster has said.

O, would that we had hypocrites, brazen liars, insolent cads to deal with! But this spinelessness, this twaddle, this triviality, and yet a certain inoffensive willingness which, please note, is just as unfortunate as if a needle without an eye wanted to substitute willingness for the lack of an eye, but in this connection it must be observed that the needle can innocently lack an eye, but this trivial, inoffensive willingness is lack of character, originating in never having willed to any purpose—and this is supposed to be Christianity.

Everywhere, those swarms of inoffensive nonentities who are bold and brazen in a crowd but otherwise willing enough. If your idea is to get men dressed up in a new outfit—such a reformation can easily be managed—they are willing enough. But watch out—such a reformation is an illusion because it is still the old nonsense or the old nonsense in a new outfit.

XI^2 A 231   *n.d.*, 1854

« 2629 *The Single State*

The exalted view which regards sexuality as not really constituting man's superiority, man's ideality as lying deeper, and sexuality as his degradation and that consequently the task, if the ideality is to be achieved, is precisely to forsake sexuality, to play the piece backwards as one must do to counteract witchcraft—all this has been lost in Christendom, especially in Protestantism, in such a way as if it had never been.

In the course of centuries the movement, especially in Protestantism, has been full sail ahead into the lower levels, downward where marriage constitutes the meaning of life, relationship with the opposite sex the earnestness of life, etc.; therefore the tendency in Protestantism is to regard a single person as ridiculous, something like a single shoe, that is, something which falls short of its definition, something which essentially is not if there are not two of them.

* *

Luther declared that it was impossible to live chastely outside of marriage—the early Church declared that it was impossible to live chastely within marriage, which therefore was "tolerated fornication."

* *

In the meantime we are all Christians and Christianity flourishes "all around the world."

* *

Is it Luther's idea that because men have become as lecherous and sensuous as they now are it is impossible to live chastely outside of marriage? That may be. But then the Reformation becomes something odd, especially when there is the continual trumpeting about the great Christian advance which is said to have taken place. It becomes all the more a concession to lechery or sensuousness.

XI² A 238   *n.d.*, 1854

« 2630 *"The Child"*

In Christendom's confusion this point is like the white spot in a corn or the black spot in a target—in one way or another it is all epitomized here.

Where in all the world did Christendom get "the child"—for it is easy enough to see that Christ unconditionally holds the view that to be a Christian naturally means the single state.

But then the child was brought in.

Now it begins. First of all—so it goes—it would be cruel, untenable, for the parents to believe themselves saved and not to know that their child is saved also.

Therefore something had to be concocted to pacify the parents (despite the fact that the New Testament does not dissolve such collisions by conceding, since Christianity tightens the collision to the point of hating father and mother and wife and children).

Then they hit upon infant baptism—that when the child receives water on its head everything is decided, the child is a Christian, eternally saved.

Then the child should be brought up in Christianity. For that purpose Christianity must be made into the opposite of what it is in the New Testament, since it is entirely impossible for a child to grasp *punctum saliens* of Christianity: original sin—and since the parents would be in a peculiar light if the child were able to grasp it.

Consequently Christianity was made over into an optimism, "enjoy life,"[362] Judaism with an admixture of falsified Christian ingredients.

And so, from a Christian point of view, demoralization continues in the family with the help of the child.

It began by giving in to the parents and taking up the game that the child is a Christian. Soon the parents discovered that since it was certain and true that the child becomes eternally saved simply by baptism, to be a Christian like a child is fundamentally the most enjoyable way to be a Christian.

And then it was made into the sentimental dogma of faith: the child is the true Christian.

Christendom got a child to lie to and then utilized the lie to lie also to itself, and thereby Christianity became just the opposite of what it is in the New Testament.

One sees how necessary it is to affirm the single state. As soon as we get the child of Christian parents, all Christianity is turned upside down—and then out from professors and preachers, men and women —as from a horn of plenty—flows profound nonsense, sentimental, speculative nonsense.

This basic confusion of Christianity and this incalculable load of theological questions and problems and battles and accusations of heresy, all this rests upon these two fulcrums! (if they may be called that): that Christ was present at a wedding (therefore, the Christian must marry, marriage is the meaning of life, true Christianity is impossible outside of marriage) and Christ made a casual remark to some women when the apostles wanted to keep them back: Let the little children come unto me (ergo, the significance of Christ's coming into the world was to establish marriages in order to get little children).

Christ came into the world to set it afire; therefore celibacy was required of Christians in order to maintain the fire. Christendom has become a breeding ground where, as for a Jew or a pagan, having children has become—true Christianity.

XI^2 A 241   December 13, 1854

« **2631** *Inversion*

A young state might place a premium on the fruitfulness of marriage; in an overpopulated state a premium might be placed on bachelorhood; and, as I read in the last part of the younger Fichte's *Ethics*, [363] celibacy is recommended eventually for purely communistic reasons.

So also with Christianity. It is one thing when Christianity is to be introduced into a pagan country; it is another matter when it is in "Christendom," where all are Christians, or, more correctly, where the tragedy is that far too many are Christians, that it has become nonsense —then the method must be completely reversed—instead of doggedly acting as if nothing were wrong and going on producing, if possible, still more Christians for Christianity in this nonsensical way.

XI^2 A 372   *n.d.*, 1854–55

MARTYR

« 2632 *Reply*

Just as in a large shipment of herring the outermost layer gets crushed and ruined, just as the outermost fruit gets bruised and damaged by the crate, so in every generation there are a few persons who stand farthest out and suffer from the crate, who alone protect those who are in the middle.

VI A 110   *n.d.*, 1845

« 2633

It has been said that nowadays it is impossible even to be persecuted,[364] but this is not true. The reason is that the leaders today do not know how to incite people. If they suffer an injustice, they complain, they criticize men, but it is simply to make themselves concentric with them; we censure those we have not given up. But speak of the idea in the court language and with its elegance—then persecution is sure to come. If you are ridiculed, then do not scold—say: I have the honor of being ridiculed—that is: You are thoroughly repudiated, and it is therefore an honor to be persecuted by you. You will have the honor of being scourged, the honor of being executed. All the outpouring of passion is inconsequential compared to the elegant court language of the idea.

VII¹ A 175   *n.d.*, 1846

« 2634

It is well-known that the clergy introduced burning at the stake in order to avoid "the shedding of blood" (thus when Giordano Bruno was given over to the secular court, advice was given to proceed as mildly as possible and in any case to avoid the shedding of blood, that is, he was to be burned[365]); so now the world has also taught the clergy this specious sanctity—no longer is there persecution to the point of shedding blood; shedding blood is avoided, but there is all the more torturing.

VIII¹ A 240   *n.d.*, 1847

« **2635**

Paul is the only apostle who speaks of a thorn in the flesh.[366] But the others also suffered martyrdom at the hands of their contemporaries. —O, this rubbish and preacher-prattle about having been contemporary with Christ. Uffda!

VIII[1] A 396   *n.d.,* 1847

« **2636**

What the age needs is not a genius—it surely has had geniuses enough—but a martyr,[367] one who in order to teach men to obey would himself become obedient unto death, one whom men put to death; but, see, just because of that they would lose, for simply by killing him, by being victorious in this way, they would become afraid for themselves. This is the awakening which the age needs.

VIII[1] A 418   *n.d.,* 1847

« **2637**

The category of "those glorious ones whom the world repudiated because it was not worthy of them"[368] has gone out of use; such men scarcely appear in the last three centuries. It is essentially stupid to go on eulogizing them, for the world is so changed that it prefers prudence and consequently cannot admire or praise anyone as great unless he triumphs[369] in a secular way in this world and during his own lifetime. Self-sacrifice becomes comical, a kind of insanity.

How ironical that a person whose life expresses that he is great in this latter sense speaks with tears in his eyes and moves others—to tears —with his masterly discourse on those glorious ones; and at the same time there lives a poet who also in the understanding of our time is great, and he gets the audience to laugh at those glorious ones.

IX A 46   *n.d.,* 1848

« **2638**

At the moment it seems as if much, much more is accomplished when an honored and respected man declares some truth or other— people then flock around him by the hundreds. But the despised martyr preaches with emphasis in a quite different way, for all the contempt has an intensifying effect when the injustice men did to him is recalled.

IX A 98   *n.d.,* 1848

« **2639**

The influence of no man's life is as great as a martyr's, for he does not begin to be effective until they have put him to death. This way the generation is left with him or is captive within itself.

IX A 102   *n.d.*, 1848

« **2640**

From now on there will appear no prophets, judges, etc. who go ahead and lead the generation onward, but there will continue to be martyrs who by hurling themselves against the human invention called progress force the generation back. Only in this way will there be progress—in intensity. The lesson has been given us once and for all; there is nothing further to add to that. But it is a matter of inward deepening.

With the help of this human going-further, everything merely becomes thinner and thinner—with the help of God's governance everything becomes more and more inward.

IX A 126   *n.d.*, 1848

« **2641**

That Christ suffered for our sins is essentially to be understood as the Atonement, and this is mainly what ought to be discussed.

However, an historical accretion may be pointed out here. The impiety of men, wherein men have taught each other a scaling down of the good, yes, have set evil (selfishness) in place of the good, has precisely the result that the one who is to express the good again must suffer; in order to indicate the standard, he must suffer and consequently suffers for the offenses of others.[*] If men had been good, they would have related themselves forthrightly to him and he would not need to suffer. But now he suffers, and why? —because the others are sinners.

On a smaller scale it may be pointed out how the error can be so small at a given time that it can be removed without a martyrdom. But if this is not the case, if a martyrdom is necessary in order to get truth rightfully reinstated, then this martyr indeed suffers for the sins of others.

[*] *In margin:* Some observations on this may be found in H. Steffens, *Anthropologie.* [370]

No doubt this was mentioned earlier in journal NB², in the latter part [i.e., VIII¹ A 337].

IX A 141   *n.d.*, 1848

« **2642**

What Christendom needs at every moment is someone who expresses Christianity uncalculatingly or with absolute *recklessness*. He is then to be regarded as a measuring instrument—that is, how he is judged in Christendom will be a test of how much true Christianity there is in Christendom at a given time. If his fate is to be slain, then Christendom is even worse than Judaism at the time of Christ, for then the collision was infinitely greater, since Christianity was the absolutely new; whereas in Christendom men at least have knowledge of it. If his fate is to be mocked and ridiculed, to be regarded as mad, while a whole contemporary generation of clergy (who, note well, do not dare to speak uncalculatingly or recklessly) is honored and they are also regarded as true Christians—then Christendom is an illusion. In short, his fate is the judgment. The judgment is not what he says but what is said of him.

This is the thoroughly modern type of judge.

IX A 165   *n.d.*, 1848

« **2643** *Behold, This Is Christianity*

Christianity says: You are to love men, be kindly disposed toward them, surround them with the most sacrificial love. Strive after this, strive to resemble your prototype [*Forbillede*]. If so, to the extent that you succeed in resembling your prototype, it will go with you as it went with him. To the same degree that you resemble him, to the same degree you will suffer abuse. When you become momentarily weary along the way, when you are groaning because of the mistreatment you have already suffered and, troubled, ask: What shall I do? Then Christianity answers: You certainly do not imagine yourself to be already perfect; all right, then, keep on striving, love men more—and, of course, the mistreatment will then become even greater. Before you, then, if you live 70 years, lies a day-by-day increase of mistreatment, that is, if you advance in being a Christian, and if not, woe unto you.

This is the second constraint Christianity uses: If you do not love men in the way Christianity requires, you are eternally condemned and go to hell.

Actually, this is what Christ kept from the apostles and disciples; he let them continue in the purely human idea: maybe—maybe not, continue in the purely human thought that in a while things would be all right again, etc. The necessity of its happening this way, that uninterruptedly to the very last it could only be a matter of suffering abuse, the necessity of it, the unavoidability of it—this he kept from them.

That it is necessary and unavoidable is demonstrated in part by the prototype (whose life otherwise comes to express something accidental), in part by Christianity's express teaching that to love God is to hate the world. If this really is the relation between God and the world, then every intermediary hope is treason against God, a regression.

The tension of Christianity, or the tension in which Christianity brings a Christian, can consistently only lead to and give rise to the impatience of martyrdom, which then craves to drain the cup of death, the sooner the better.

This impatience, however, is by no means approved by Christianity. If you wish to call Christianity cruel, which, merely humanly understood, it is, then it is systematic in its cruelty. It requires martyrdom, but not its impatience, no, its protraction.[371] With the same protractedness of a fortune-blessed person regarding a long life ahead of him, the martyr step by step must suffer daily torment, and even then, humanly speaking, the everlastingly unmitigated prospect of its continuation or increase for the rest of his life.

I promise to give a reward of ten dollars to anyone who can explain to me what it means that this teaching came to be and continues to be introduced under the name "gentle grounds of comfort."

IX A 325   n.d., 1848

« 2644

The person who is put to death because he wants to seduce the people is surely not a martyr, but only the person who is put to death because he wants to guide or save them when he also could have seduced them—otherwise what he intends is perhaps a conceited fancy without a home anywhere, an impotent thought, and the like.

IX A 385   n.d., 1848

« 2645

If Christ were to come to the world today, he would probably not be put to death but would be ridiculed. This is the martyrdom of an age of reason. In an age of passion and feeling martyrs were put to death.

IX A 435   n.d., 1848

« **2646**

In a certain sense the world is so cunning that it half understands that a martyr would be the most dangerous man of all. This is why so much is said about there being no martyrs any more these days. What the world fears is precisely the strenuousness of a person's staking his life on the truth, that it will come too close; therefore all prudence which consists of "to a certain degree" goes up in smoke.

But a spontaneous enthusiast can no longer become a martyr, that is, even if he did, the world would protest it, would deny it. Therefore the art now is to be a reflective martyr, a person who from the beginning moves in all consciousness toward this, employing all capacities (which otherwise are used to gain earthly advantage) to engage in everything in such a way so that men cannot get rid of him—and then becomes a martyr. This is a protracted and difficult process, to do all this and to hold on year after year, simply to achieve one's downfall, but to fall, of course, in such a way that truth is decisively victorious.

This is the ultimate means for extricating men out of the self-satisfied fascination with prudence and shrewdness.

Such a martyr I would call "truth's secret agent."[372]

This is the ultimate power a man has over others. He can say: Yes, yes, you must eventually take my life or treat me in such a way that you yourselves will regret it.

IX A 495   *n.d.*, 1848

« **2647**

"Upbringing"[373] is the one thing needful*: once again there must be upbringing in Christianity. But "the race" cannot "be brought up" in Christianity; this is just as impossible as adding disparate quantities. "To bring up" is not commensurate with "the race," and "to bring up the race" is not commensurate with Christianity. "To bring up the human race" veritably means to transform "the human race" into "the single individuals" in order to begin "upbringing," because "single individuals" are brought up, or "single individuals" are "brought up in Christianity."

———

* Note. Parenthetically, no one can know this better than I do, I who have always reckoned my principal advantage among my contemporaries to be that I have been well brought up in Christianity from childhood. Again, no one can know this better than I, whose entire activity as an author, at least from one point of view, can be regarded as a reflection of the author's having been brought up rigorously in Christianity and then educated once again.

[*In margin:* So that at least from one point of view I, the author, am myself the one who has been educated. Therefore I, the author, if I think of being in relation to the age, am far from calling myself the educator—no, I myself am the one who has been educated or brought up. This is one of the reasons I have been so scrupulous about avoiding admiration, adherents, cheers, and other hoopla, for, good heavens, there is no point in shouting hurrah because someone is brought up and one certainly does not become an adherent of—a disciple. On the other hand this is one of the reasons I have been willing to submit to all the very opposite; like a volunteer I have even risked becoming, alas, the poor "master of irony"!—becoming a sacrifice to laughter—all of which is connected with being brought up, and one who is to be brought up and is willing can benefit greatly from it. By God's help and with wise teachers one learns wisdom *directly* in the first lesson. The person who, in order to go through such a course ventures into the second lesson and does not become a distracted but an attentive, diligent, hard-working, obedient pupil, learns profound wisdom from God through having had the courage to expose himself to fools as his teachers.]

But if there is to be "upbringing" in Christianity—and the stage is not the hidden enclosure of family life or the fenced-in school yard or the peaceful security of the Church, where the educator has the upper hand, but the stage is historical actuality, where the educator is weakest, weakest of all—what is the educator called here? He is not called "priest" or "parish clerk" or even "professor," although he may possibly have these names, too, but essentially he is called "the martyr." On the stage of historical actuality the martyr brings up or educates in Christianity, and since it is in "Christendom," where all are Christians, he consequently educates Christians in Christianity. Through his own obedience he teaches obedience. He is not a teacher who teaches by beating the pupils; the main characteristic of his teaching is to teach by letting himself be beaten. The learners do not, I dare say, get his agreement and consent, but they do get the permission of his patience and thus have leave to do with him as they will. Finally they put him to death—and now the real instruction begins, now they learn obedience from him, or from their having put him to death.

IX B 63:11 *n.d.*, 1848

« 2648

"The martyr" ("the missionary") will by all means have within himself what is appropriate to the age, "the age of reflection"—an infinite reflection as a servant in respect to becoming a martyr, so that, knowing the times from the bottom up, he succeeds in falling at the right spot and assures that his death wounds in the right spot.[374] This superior reflection and this infinitely reflected work of reflection in *becoming* a martyr will constitute his distinction from all earlier martyrs, from the martyr of immediacy who simply required the faith and courage to risk his life but perhaps did not need it over a long period, in any case did not need the extremely complicated labor of reflection involved in dialectically determining the place where he shall fall. Whole volumes could be written about this alone.[375]

IX B 63:12 *n.d.*, 1848

« 2649

"The martyr," this "martyr of the future" ("the missionary"[376]), who uses the category "the single individual" educationally, will by all means have within himself what is appropriate to the age ("the age of reflection")—a superior reflection[377] and, in addition to the faith and the courage to risk, will need the work or the preliminary work of infinite reflection in *becoming* or in order to become a martyr. In this he will be different from any previous martyr (of immediacy), who simply required the faith and courage to risk his life. Differing from all previous martyrs, the martyr of the future will possess a superior reflection as a servant to determine freely (of course unconditionally obedient to God) what kind of mistreatment and persecution he is to suffer, whether he shall fall or not, and if he is to fall, the place where he shall fall, so that he succeeds, dialectically, in falling at the right spot so that his death wounds in the right spot, wounds the survivors. It will not be "the others," as it was previously, who assault the martyr, who simply has to suffer—no, "the martyr" will be the one who determines the suffering.[378] Just as in a parade the provost marshal gives the orders and marches at the head of the procession, just as the forestry expert goes ahead when trees are to be cut and points: "Cut there, and there, so and so much"—so this martyr of the future will himself be the one who goes ahead of his persecutors and—knowing the specific sickness of the particular age, knowing how it is to be healed, together with the kind of suffering to which he will have to expose himself—arranges everything himself with the cunning of a superior reflection. He will be just like that hero who himself gave the firing orders to the soldiers at his own execution. Actually, the persecutors only obey his orders, but the real truth of the matter is hid from their eyes. Sick as they are, they do what they do according to their sickness. —Whole volumes could be written about this alone.

The first form of rulers in the world was "the tyrants"; the last will be "the martyrs." In the development of the world this is the movement [*in margin*: toward a growing secular mentality, for secularism is greatest, must have achieved a frightful upper hand, when only the martyrs are able to be rulers. When one person is the tyrant, the mass is not completely secularized, but when "the mass" wants to be tyrant, then the secular mentality is completely universal, and then only the martyr can be the ruler]. No doubt there is an infinite difference between a tyrant and a martyr; yet they have one thing in common: the power to constrain. The tyrant, with a craving for power, constrains by force; the martyr, unconditionally obedient to God, personally unconditionally obedient to God, constrains by his own sufferings. Then the tyrant dies, and his rule is over; the martyr dies, and his rule begins. The tyrant was the egotistic individual who inhumanly ruled over the masses, made the others into a mass and ruled over the mass. The martyr is the suffering single individual who in his love of mankind educates others in Christianity, converting the mass into single individuals—and there is joy in heaven for every single individual he thus rescues from the mass, from what the apostle himself calls the "animal-category." —Whole volumes could be written about this alone, even by me, a kind of poet and philosopher,[379] to say nothing of the one who is coming, the philosopher-poet or the poet-philosopher, who, in addition, will see close at hand the object of my presentiments at a distance, will see accomplished what I have only dimly imagined will be carried out sometime in a distant future.

There are really only two sides to choose between—either/or. Well, of course, there are many parties in the practical world [*In margin*: Not really but only *figuratively* is there any question of "choosing," since what is chosen makes no difference—one is just as wrong as the other. In the practical world there are many parties]—there are the liberals and the conservatives, etc.—and all the strangest combinations, such as the rational liberals and the rational conservatives. Once there were four parties in England, a large country; this was supposedly also the case in smaller Odense. But in the profoundest sense there really are only two parties to choose between—and here lies the category "the single individual": *either* in obedience to God, fearing and loving him, to take the side of God against men so that one loves men in God— *or* to take the side of men against God, so that by mutilation one humanizes God and does not "sense what is God's and what is man's" (Matthew 16:23). There is a struggle going on between man and God, a struggle unto life and death—was not the God-man put to death! — About these things alone: about what constitutes earnestness, about "the single individual," about what constitutes the demonic, whether the demonic is the evil or the good, about silence as a factor contributing to evil and silence as a factor contributing to good, about "deceiving into the truth,"[380] about indirect communication, to what extent this is treason against what it is to be human, an impertinence toward God, about what one learns concerning the demonic by considering the God-man—about these things alone whole volumes could be written, even by me, a kind of philosopher, to say nothing of him who is coming, "the philosopher" who will have seen "the missionary to Christendom" and at first hand will know about all this which I have only gradually learned to understand ever so little.

IX B 63:13   n.d., 1848

« **2650**

The world's basic tragedy is the confounded pontificating and that one discovery supersedes another and places men in the position of pontificating even more impersonally on a progressively greater scale. There are no human beings anymore, no thinkers, no lovers, etc.—but the daily press has enveloped the human race in a kind of atmosphere of thoughts, feelings, moods, even decisions and intentions, which are nobody's and belong to nobody and to everybody.

It is agonizing to see the hardness or callousness with which a man is able to worm his way in where he supposes truth to be, in order to learn to recite it, in order that his hand organ can include this piece, too, but it never occurs to him to do something.

Truly there is only one thing to do with respect to serving the truth: to suffer for it. This is the only possible awakening. Such an appalling, all-engulfing web of reflection as now envelops the generation cannot be exploded by reflection;[381] greater powers are needed.

And martyrs are the only ones who are needed. But of course no such adventurers as a Robert Blum,[382] who has nothing at all of the martyr in him. For not only was he active in the service of untruth, but apart from this, looked at quite formally, he did not have the slightest idea of wanting to be anything like that—he is apprehended and shot. This is what in our times is called a martyr. We no doubt think that it takes great sagacity and extraordinary perseverance to become a cabinet officer, but, truly, in our time, a time of reflection, the preparation of one who in truth is to be a martyr is a gigantic labor of reflection, although his absolute pathos always transcends his eminent reflection, for otherwise he will not become a martyr; but if he has not employed the most eminent reflection, he is actually no good as a martyr.

x^1 A 16   *n.d.*, 1849

« 2651

Why cannot Christ be called a martyr? Because he was not a witness to truth but was "the truth," and his death was not martyrdom but the Atonement.[383]

x^1 A 119   *n.d.*, 1849

« 2652

A true martyrdom, *omnibus numeris absolutum*,[384] is really possible only in opposition to "the many," "the crowd," that is, the martyr must fall at the hands of "the many." The person who becomes a martyr by attacking an individual (king, emperor, pope, etc.) is not bereft of the idea of support; he has the idea of "the many" as support.

Socrates is the only one, is "the martyr" in the eminent sense, the greatest man; whereas Christ is "the truth," and it would be blasphemous to call him a "martyr."

x^1 A 220   *n.d.*, 1849

« 2653 *The Relationship Between Two Small Essays— by H.H.*[385]

To let oneself be slain for the truth is the expression for possessing absolute truth; corresponding to this is a qualitative difference [*in margin:* or as it is called in the second essay, a specific qualitative difference] from other human beings—there we have the apostle.

Therefore *no human being has a right* to this—there we have the genius.

Authority is precisely what is required, but the genius has no authority.

x^1 A 333   *n.d.*, 1849

« **2654**

Thus one sees that to be a Christian is a martyrdom, is to be sacrificed. Other men soon discover that the religious man is bound in a different way than they are: he dare not become angry, quarrel, take revenge, or repay like with like, because he is *before God*, who can immediately do to him what he does to another. Others take advantage of this. Humanly speaking, by being *before God* the religious man is abandoned to suffering every injury, injustice, degradation, and deception at the hands of the others, who say "Goodbye" to God and do not give him a thought. Yes, humanly speaking, to be put in prison (provided one still has the right to defend himself and use his human common sense or powers) is not nearly as tormenting and agonizing as to be a religious man in this world, a religious man who by being before God is defenseless while the others harass and torment him, and while in addition he still continually suffers anguish (because he is before God[386]) over whether he actually is being good enough to the others, whether he is repaying all the evil they do to him with all the good he can think of—for if not, God might wash his hands of him.

X[1] A 382   *n.d.*, 1849

« **2655**

One who is to be a teacher of the existential must himself always bear the mark of having exposed himself to what in the ordinary sense is the greatest danger.

When Christianity battled with the spontaneous passions, when the lust of the flesh and everything connected with it was the greatest danger for men because to them it was the highest, then the teacher had to show that he was the teacher by being unmarried and in other ways.

In a rationalistic age the laughter of ridicule is the danger feared most. In our time a man can more easily endure everything else, but to be made a laughing stock—not to mention having gone through the experience of being laughed to scorn every day—men shrink from this danger more than from the most tortured death, and only in a kind of mad or demonic rapport with the horror do they say of one who encounters such danger: It is nothing—which is simply part of the torture.

This, then, is the danger. And therefore the teacher in our time must be marked by his having been tried and tested in this danger.

Others, it is true, prove that they are teachers by pointing to important offices, high rank, medals and ribbons, etc. By the step of exposing myself to ridicule I proved at least that I had a conception of what it means to be a teacher.

x^1 A 623   *n.d.*, 1849

« **2656**

As a rule "the clergy" seldom talk about "the martyrs." But if they were to speak and be consistent with their usual twaddle, they might occasionally cite as warning examples those who "by reading that dangerous book, the New Testament, ended by making themselves unhappy"—that is, they became martyrs. Humanly speaking, it may indeed be said that no one makes himself as unhappy as a martyr for the truth.

x^2 A 190   *n.d.*, 1849

« **2657**

During the time of the persecution of Christians there was also the cruel practice of smearing the martyrs with pitch and the like, igniting them as torches, and using them to illuminate the festivities. Basically the same thing is always repeated in Christendom—the unbloody martyrs in particular have had to burn slowly—and their suffering has thus been the light in the Church.

x^2 A 289   *n.d.*, 1849

« **2658** *Mood (Poetic)*

O, once upon a happier time when "the name of Jesus" was full of pathos, when it as yet had not been misused by false piety and thoughtlessness, was not yet smudged by constant use to the point of being nothing at all—then it was blessed to confess that one belonged wholly to this name. But nowadays, now it would indeed almost be sincere and heartfelt pathos to suppress it, to plan one's life as scrupulously as possible according to the Christian rules, suffer if possible what a Christian suffers, and yet never name the name of Christ, keeping it as the heart's secret. Thus here again it is almost as if everything were reversed, so that the true Christian might feel obliged to suppress this disgustingly misused name, this name most precious to him, in order that he may then live intimately with Him.

O, once upon a happier time when the enemy did not claim to be Christian—but nowadays they would, in a frenzy, put the true Christian to death—they, the Christians, and because—he is not a Christian. What comfort for those martyrs that even in the moment of death they had the blessed consolation and satisfaction of having their guilt announced to them—that they were put to death for being Christians—what more blessed words could they wish to hear; but what frenzy, what frenzied fear and trembling, when the verdict upon the Christian martyr sounds like the one and only charge that could give him anxiety: You are being put to death because you are not Christian!

x^2 A 323   *n.d.*, 1849–50

« 2659 *Martyrdom*

In the present age even the martyrs will be different. To die from spiritual overexertion, from soul-suffering, etc.—could not happen in the past, when it was a matter of life or death from the beginning. But then there was not the enormous bulk of reflection to lift, either—the purely intellectual problems, the complication of speculation, along with the counterfeit version of Christianity and the millions of titular Christians.

The fewer thoughts, the less reflection, the closer the issue lies to life and death. It is the same everywhere. To give only one example from another area: therefore the quick recourse to the physical in education of former times.

Consequently a bloodless martyrdom. Yet it is perhaps even more tormenting, for the more reflection there is around, the more slowly-tormenting vileness there is, and at the same time the bloodless martyrdom has nothing like the catastrophe of life and death to give supporting powers or to denote one's position and keep him on the spot.

x^3 A 303   *n.d.*, 1850

« 2660 *"But We Cannot All Be Martyrs, Can We?"*[387]

Answer: is it then better that we all, every single one of us, say: I cannot do it. If it is wrong that everyone should be a martyr—then it certainly is also wrong that nobody is willing to be one.

x^3 A 498   *n.d.*, 1850

« 2661 *The New Thing*

Martyrs in the future must become long-distance martyrs.

The battle must be against prudence and cleverness. How frighteningly cunning and sly the world is today. If there is among men someone whom they must admit is in the service of the good, such a sight is far from inspiring them to want to support him or be like him. No, with great prudence they quite calmly say: he must fall—and then they just wait for the moment to plunge in and make speeches.

Consider the short-run martyrs. The catastrophe comes to a climax as quickly as possible. The martyr is concerned simply and solely for his idea; now he falls as a sacrifice—and see, the speechifiers rush in and exploit the martyrs, and it becomes a big question as to how much good the martyr has really done.

No, the martyrs must become long-distance martyrs, particularly now when the world is so thoroughly prudential and so thoroughly demoralized. The martyr's task will be to embarrass the secular mentality and worldly common sense, in the same way as constant surveillance by the police can be embarrassing.

The martyr will have to occupy a position a couple notches above that of the best man in the establishment—inasmuch as he himself possesses the power to become top rank. But this he does not do; he remains in completely ordinary categories, he is as nothing, and thus he gradually provides room for the ideal, brings it to mind. This embarrasses the secular mentality, for it wants to get rid of the ideal. Thus it regards as a kind of traitor the person who, instead of becoming top rank himself and relinquishing the ideal, decides to be as nothing, merely to show how high the ideal is. It is, humanly speaking, treason for someone who can be number one—and if he undertakes to be number one, he would place a crown on relativities and on this "to a certain degree" as the highest, something which would please flesh and blood—to decide to be number zero merely to provide a place for the ideal, by which he embarrasses the relativities, which would not have anything against him if he became number one in earnest (for then the relativities would become something earnest) but have very much against his decision—they still must concede that he is superior to them—to be number zero.

This is police work, extremely strenuous. I am convinced that no one will be able to carry it through unless he is supported in a special way by very definite daily suffering and a very definite break with life; for otherwise flesh and blood and the environment will still cajole him into becoming top rank, something he has in his power every moment.

This is protracted martyrdom, and, to repeat, the martyr must by definite daily suffering be so much in the power of providence that this is what presses him every moment and keeps him awake; otherwise it cannot be done. He must be in the power of providence like the clipped bird, the decoy, which the birdcatcher has completely in his power in order to catch the others. He must be in the hand of providence in this way, and then his work is comparable to that of a secret agent[388] or a police detective.

x^3 A 511   *n.d.*, 1850

« 2662 *How Christianity Is Slackened*

First there is Christ. This is the existential impetus of the eternal itself, who comes—in order to suffer and die.

Then come the apostles, who are unconditionally willing to die—longing for martyrdom.

Then come the martyrs. But the dialectic has already begun—whether it is unconditionally required of the Christian to suffer martyrdom, whether it is not just as truly Christian to want to live—the extensive as well as the intensive.[*]

Then Christianity is slackened by a full quality—now there are only apologists.

Then Christianity essentially comes to a standstill.

Then science and scholarship and the theory of the Church begin.

x^4 A 108   *n.d.*, 1851

« 2663

[*] *In margin of 2662* (x^4 A 108):

As early as the time of Cyprian, to be a Christian in a stricter sense became representative (which Cyprian did not sanction): the blood witnesses issued receipts which freed others from risking their lives and permitted them to make sacrifices and in this way to avoid persecution.[389]

x^4 A 109   *n.d.*

« 2664 *The Human Race*

It goes with the race as with the individual; the older it becomes the more apparent becomes the corruption residing in it—youth conceals much and mitigates much.

The manner in which the exceptional, the truer, is persecuted in these times is therefore far more infamous than formerly.

In the age when they put the exceptional to death because they did not understand him[390]—what an excusable guilt compared to the situation we find most often nowadays.

Today it is most often simple, unadulterated, conscious envy. They know very well that this one and that one is the exceptional; they understand that renown awaits him—and this is what they envy. They are beside themselves with envy because no immortal name is waiting for them—thus they give themselves the joy of mistreating him——

——O, you fools, this is precisely the way he becomes immortal; every mistreatment adds a year to his renown. If you envy him his immortality, then honor and glorify him, spoil him with a good life, and he will not become immortal.

XI¹ A 114   n.d., 1854

« 2665 *Martyrdom*

New Testament Christianity rests in the thought that the martyrdom has worth in and for itself, unconditional worth, as the prototype [*Forbilledet*] also makes manifest.

Christianity wants to move existence at the most profound level. But for such a movement, as Archimedes[391] has properly said, a point outside is needed.

But the one and only point outside is martyrdom, and, please note, martyrdom with the idea that martyrdom has worth in and for itself, unconditionally. A martyrdom and 1000 martyrs but without the idea of the worth of martyrdom in and for itself—they suffer martyrdom, to be sure, but try to avoid it or wish that it were not necessary —all such martyrdoms are only points of movement or fulcrums inside the world, not the fulcrum outside the world. To a degree they are carried through in homogeneity with the world and make use of human shrewdness and help, etc., and then only when it cannot be avoided, then martyrdom. On the other hand, martyrdom which is a point outside the world is carried through in such a way that the martyr, as it says in the Epistle to the Hebrews,[392] will not let himself be helped, refuses help to avoid martyrdom—this martyrdom indeed has worth in and for itself.

Martyrdom carried through, please note, in accord with the conception mentioned here is *cardo rerum* in Christianity.

The history of Christendom is therefore the progressive alteration of the conception of Christianity with respect to martyrdom.

First of all the conception of martyrdom is changed, but martyrs still fall, yes, by the thousands. But changing the conception already approaches homogeneity with the world.

Then the martyrdoms decrease—the Church does not want to be too rigorous in the demands upon Christians—martyrdom vanishes.

So it goes, step by step—we do not want our Christianity to be too rigorous and exacting, so we make more and more concessions.

Finally the whole outlook shifts so that not being a martyr becomes the very mark of wisdom. Then we put on that most beautiful cloak called pedagogical consideration for the weak, a humanitarianism, and also the wisdom which (unlike the fanatics and the crackpots) does not will more than is possible at the particular moment.

Good night, Ole! There went Christianity, completely lost in homogeneity with the world! Not to will more than is possible at the particular moment is simply the formula for politics and secular-mindedness. But such a view is so remote from moving the world or being a fulcrum outside the world that it belongs, hide and hair, entirely to this world.

But Christianity is and continues to be—clergymen begetting children, bishops like Engeltoft[393] having triplets, and everything is just fine. And yet such a change has taken place that language is inadequate and no visual image could signify it adequately.

XI[1] A 462   *n.d.*, 1854

« **2666** *Martyrdom's*

high thoughts, all such higher things, all the higher things related to a polemical and pessimistic view of life have, as a whole, disappeared from the race, and to compare the race to the great understanding of what it is to be human is like comparing chaff to grains of wheat. Everything culminates in this wretched itch for being happy in this world. There are two classes of people: those lucky enough to make their fortune and those who fail.

This recurs to me because I have been reminded these days of Lessing and the *Fragments.*

He puts the matter in this way: in various parts of the gospel there is a hint that Christ really wanted the earthly, to be king, etc., but he failed.

No, no, but precisely in order that the repulsion may be all the stronger, precisely to point out all the more passionately that this was what he did not want, he makes a move as if he did—in order to repel it, so that true spirituality may be seen, which is related specifically to voluntary repulsion.

The truth remains that in pronouncing judgment a person manifests what is within him. And because there is none of the more ideal passion in men of our time, and certainly not in Lessing, the matter takes such a miserable shape for them. In our time there is no one at all who could conceivably believe a person could want to seek, to gain, fame, for example, with a pessimistic intention, that is, in order to brush the filth off and the more deeply to wound polemically. No, no one believes in such a thing—and then they want to understand Christ or meddle with interpreting him.

"Spirit" has gone out of the race entirely. Ideal passions which have—and precisely this is the ideality—a potentiation in them, a looming quality, so that such a person in ideal passion is continually related inversely to the world, appear no more. And therefore Christianity, too, is dragged down into the most wretched, diddling mediocrity. Truly it can be said that Christ would really never acknowledge being the founder of this kind of Christianity. But with a new swindle men turn the matter around, consistently, and recast Christ in likeness to what we call Christianity. So in our time the greatest we have is one who craved the world, made a mess of it, and now the only chance he has for a little profit is to reinterpret his life and aspire to the kind of fame and esteem associated with suffering. And the prototype for this turns out to be—Jesus Christ!

XI[1] A 511   n.d., 1854

« **2667 *A Church Father in the Fourth Century***

(no doubt Basil[394] or one of the Gregorys, in any case the passage is marked in my copy of Böhringer) says: A martyrdom is impossible[395] —for the enemies are also called Christians.

Absolutely right. There it is. The tragedy lies in the untrue kind of propagation. Even at that time one must have been able to see with half an eye: We are no longer salt, we are a mass.

There was not the openness or Christian courage to turn the situation around and see that there still was the possibility of manifesting martyrdom at the hands of Christendom.

So it went, further and further, and, with the nonsensical extensity which Christendom has, became more and more wretched, more and more meaningless with every century.

But no one wants to see where the tragedy lies. No thanks, says shrewd secularity, which now has gotten a liking and taste for Christianity, since it has become the very opposite of what it is in the New Testament—no, thanks, we are not that crazy, this is magnificent, almost heavenly.

And the few who have the integrity to see the lay of the land are disspirited and dubious about daring to risk such a decisive step as turning against Christendom, against what Christianly is infinitely more dangerous to Christianity than all of paganism. But the Christian order is still to turn in the direction of the danger.

XI^2 A 68   *n.d.,* 1854

« 2668 *"After All, We Cannot All Be Martyrs"*[396]

To which God probably would answer: "Leave that to me." [*In margin*: For the objection is actually an impertinent shrewdness.]

But man fools himself by means of the numerical. In this life it is quite rightly the most prudent thing always, if possible, to be just like the others. But eternity disperses the crowd and requires what in a certain sense, quite true, it is impossible for all to become.

XI^2 A 262   *n.d.,* 1854

MARY

« **2669**

In margin: Note. The necessary protraction is also a cross which the chosen one has to bear with faith and humility. When the angel had announced to Mary that she would bear a child by the Spirit—well, the whole thing certainly was a miracle—why should the child take nine months like other children? Why could it not happen at once, for, after all, she had grasped and agreed that the birth was a miracle. In other words, let us not make Mary a composite of two natures: a temporal and temporally-minded woman who thinks it fitting that it lasts nine months, and the believing Mary who humbly understands that this birth was a miracle. No, she understood that it was a miracle; but why should it then in a certain way be in accord with the order of nature? Yes, here is the cross. Neurotic impatience becomes dazed by the extraordinary and simply cannot recover in faith and humility. Only humility is capable of bearing, as did Mary, the fact that the miraculous must take its time. I wonder if Mary, after receiving the announcement, did not remain the same quiet, humble woman; I wonder if she became preoccupied with asking what time it was, when the month was over —out of fear that it [the miracle] might be revoked.[397]

VII[2] B 235, p. 63 fn. *n.d.,* 1846–47

« **2670**

Imagine Joseph, Jesus' stepfather. Imagine him in the situation of contemporaneity. I wonder if one would not laugh at the silly fool who believed Mary; I wonder if one would not regard Mary as being all the more astute because she put one over on him—that is, I wonder if everybody would not talk more or less blasphemously.

VIII[1] A 338 *n.d.,* 1847

« **2671** *The Virgin Mary*

. . . . . Even if it varies in degree, this is the fate of all whose lives are singled out to have historical significance—they are not happy—but they adoringly praise God for what has been granted to them or for what it pleased God to let happen through them. Mary says: All generations will call me blessed.[398] Mary thought of herself as sacrificed; happy she was not; and the prophecy also said that a sword would pierce her heart.[399]

[*In margin:* The true religious existence is to be as if demolished for this life—but still to consider oneself blessed. Mediation is an invention of the secular mind.]

Here again, by the way, is a sample of what the sermon accomplishes. Nowadays the preacher orates about the humble faith disclosed in Mary's words. Take the situation of contemporaneity—indeed, I wager it became a big scandal that a despised virgin behaved this way and announced that all generations would call her blessed. The talk among her contemporaries was: "You could even have a little sympathy for the poor girl if only she were not so crackbrained conceited."

O, this sermonizing, this sermonizing, it has absolutely deranged Christianity. In the realm of possibility we flirt with the holy and thereby become all the more capable of persecuting it in actuality.

X³ A 57   *n.d.*, 1850

« 2672 *The Annunciation*

Theme: that the angel made the right choice—for Mary made the right choice.

To be sure she was the chosen one, and thus it was settled that it was she. But yet there is also a moment of freedom, of acceptance, wherein it is demonstrated that someone is the right one. If the angel had not found her such as he did find her to be, she would not have been the right one.

She said:[400] Behold, I am the handmaid of the Lord; let it be to me as you will.

We are so accustomed to hearing this that we easily overlook its significance and even imagine that we would answer just this way under the same circumstances.

Let us ponder on what she could—ah, far more naturally—have answered. It is good for us to ponder quite differently from the way gentle piety—not without gracefulness—has embellished this scene with its own sentiments and, for example, dwelt on the thought that when the angel had spoken to Mary, it was as if the whole creation cried to Mary: O do say "Yes"! Hurry and say "Yes"! etc.

She could, then—yes, as Sarah did[401]—she could have smiled, and she had just as good reason to. And if she could not have smiled, she could have felt herself dishonored by this salutation and dismissed it.

Or she could have said: This is too exalted for me; I cannot do it; spare me, I am not up to it. The angel is clearly of the same opinion, too—that it is beyond her power. Therefore the power of the Holy Spirit must overshadow her. Well, fine, but it is precisely this, in faith to become nothing, a mere instrument—it is precisely this which goes beyond a human being's power, beyond even the utmost, utmost exertion of a person's ultimate strength.

x^4 A 454   *n.d.*, 1852

« 2673 *"For Behold, Henceforth All Generations Will Call Me Blessed"*—Luke 1:48

Quite right, generations henceforth—but not her own generation, which has seen in her the most wretched of all women.

But we skip over this and assume that Mary was the extraordinary in pleasure and happiness. We skip over this and thereby miss the point, Mary's faith or the greatness of her faith, that she humbly and gladly found the situation to be sheer blessedness. And we deceive ourselves, as if it were modesty and humility on our part not to aspire to something akin to the extraordinariness which has befallen Mary; and we cheat the prototypes by not even slightly remembering with gratitude their sufferings.

Just about the most important thing to us, to the average man, is what kind of a time we are going to have during our life here on earth. We must already be "spirit" before we are able [without temptation] to have anything to do with the assignment of praise from later generations.

But the more I think about this the more clearly I see how mendaciously we avoid the holy. This I will not and cannot do. I shall live here on earth at most only 70 years—but in eternity I shall live with those glorious ones—and how will they regard me, how will they look upon me, if I try to cheat them and lie my way out of the true relationship to them.

x^4 A 520   *n.d.*, 1852

« 2674 *The Virgin Mary*

Yes, honor to her! O my God, when the message comes to her: You will live your life scorned by other maidens, treated as a frivolous, conceited wench or a poor, half-crazy wretch or a loose woman, and so on—after that you will be exposed to all possible suffering, and finally, because it seems as if God, too, has deceived you, a sword will pierce your heart[402]—this is the glad tidings.— —Yes, honor to her—to be able to say promptly, without a moment's consideration: Behold, I am the handmaid of the Lord, and then to be able to sing the song of praise: Henceforth all generations will call me blessed.[403] O my God, this is quite different from being able to speak perfectly all the living and dead languages (as our educated girls do); this is speaking in tongues.

XI[1] A 40   n.d., 1854

MEDIOCRITY

« **2675**

The world always wills the good only to a certain degree.[404] Men never want it said of them that they are hard-hearted; on the contrary, they prefer being called compassionate. But they are compassionate only to a certain degree; they are not truly so. If someone is absolutely compassionate, that is, truly so, they persecute him and say: It is vanity. In this way the world wins two advantages: *first,* it is exempted from all the sacrificing which is involved in being truly compassionate, and *then* it is honored and esteemed for being compassionate.

This is how the world operates, and it is really the secret of its evil. It is too clever—perhaps also too good—to want to abolish goodness and greatness; it wants to pay a moderate price for the honor and reputation of being great and good. This is why it is so important for the world to persecute the true good—otherwise this whole traffic is made impossible.

IX A 149 *n.d.,* 1848

« **2676**

..... But is it not just as unreasonable of me to demand that mediocrity should change as it is of mediocrity to demand that I should change?

Yes, but only when regarded esthetically and intellectually, only then is the one just as unreasonable for me as the other is for mediocrity.

From a Christian point of view the matter is quite different. For Christianity is supported by faith in what a human being can become, that he can be changed from what he is, infinitely changed—and therefore I am right in my demand and mediocrity is wrong in its demand.

XI¹ A 250 *n.d.,* 1854

« **2677** *Hypocrisy—Nonsense*

It probably was dangerous and precarious enough at the time when the accusation which might be made against the teachers was that they were hypocrites. Oh, but it is far more tragic if they must be declared to be peddlers of nonsense. Hypocrites are not as far from what Christianity is, from spirit, as one is who in all cozy mediocrity[405] steadily habituates himself in nonsense and believes that this is Christianity.

What I have said elsewhere [XI[1] A 167] is true—namely, that being changed into a genial muddlehead must be regarded as the most dangerous kind of demon possession. Among other things the danger lies in the fact that one does not realize it as easily as if, for example, the transformation consisted of becoming a werewolf.

But the evil in the world is exactly proportioned to the good. When Christianity came into the world as spirit and at the time when it was spirit, Satan had to exert himself and he shaped hypocrites or ambitious, grandiose errors. Now, since Christianity has not existed as spirit for a long time, Satan amuses himself with the kind of sorcery which produces genial nonsense—he knows very well that he has never been as victorious as now.

XI[1] A 549   n.d., 1854

« 2678 *Offense*

Mediocrity will perhaps console itself with the thought that if Christianity is not elevated too high (which it obviously is not), there is at least the advantage of not causing offense.

No, thanks. If exaltation can be guilty of occasioning offense by elevating Christianity too high, mediocrity is always guilty.

Mediocrity remembers only what Christ[406] says to Peter: You are an offense to me (words which, incidentally, it never dares appropriate, for Peter, after all, was as different from mediocrity as possible).

How often, in lesser circumstances and on a smaller scale, has not someone who in truth willed the truth had occasion to say to that cursed, miserable, hearty, swindling mediocrity which wanted to hold him back: You are an offense to me.

You see, O mediocrity, that you are perhaps least of all exempt from the guilt which you thought yourself absolutely safeguarded against—the guilt of giving offense. Could not this observation be of some help, could it not rouse you up and rout you out of your restful rut.

XI[2] A 1   October, 1854

« 2679 *Humility—Insignificance*

Because Christianity continually lays a claim upon humility and relates everything to humility and the tasks of humility, mediocre insignificance therefore immediately thinks: This is something for me—and does not consider that Christian humility, as with everything Christian, involves a dialectic, so that its humility presupposes a pride which carries its head higher than proud human humility but which then humbles itself.

Examples: "Do not seek the high places but associate with the lowly."[407] Splendid, says mediocrity, this is something for me. I don't crave to be king; I am satisfied with being a cabinet member or a well-to-do citizen, a true Christian who does not seek the high places. Humbug! Look more closely at what Christianity understands by the lowly and you will see that in another sense men declare that such seeking done in all earnestness is the most frightful pride, arrogance, coveting of something higher than being both king and emperor. — "Do not sit down at the head of the table."[408] Splendid, says mediocrity. I don't pine for such things. I am satisfied with a place in about the middle or even a bit toward the lower end—I am a true Christian who does not sit at the head of the table. Wrong again. If a person really gets serious about the humility which abases unconditionally, you will see that it will be condemned as the most frightful arrogance, much worse than wanting to sit at the head of the table. Just as dumb Gottlieb[409] in the fairy story always makes a mistake, so will mediocrity falsify Christianity for all eternity.

But is must always be remembered that Christianity is in no way whatsoever associated with differences between man and man, the differences of capacities and endowments. No, no, it offers itself unconditionally to every human being. But it demands of him the passion to venture everything. "That's all you have to do," says God; "I will do the rest." Therefore the apostle James[410] says: If anyone of you lacks wisdom, let him pray for it. Therefore Christ used very simple men as apostles in order not to prompt the confusion that Christianity is related essentially to genius and talent.

But "man," who is a professional swindler or has an innate instinct for swindling, has naturally pretended that he did not understand about Christianity's equality for all men, because he does not like the part about the will's changing or the changing of the will.

The equality of Christianity for all men has been altered to: insignificance. No, thanks. Certainly Christianity is equally for all so that genius and talent are mere caprices here, but it is nevertheless so far from being mediocrity (and the equality of insignificance for all) that what Christianity demands (and which every human being is capable of, if he wills—therein is the equality) is so great and perfect, so rare, that among a dozen talented people there may not be a single Christian, although they all still have the possibility of being able to be true Christians.

XI² A 91   *n.d., 1854*

« 2680 *Christendom's Dishonesty*

How shall I explain the dishonesty of all these millions, on what basis shall I explain it! As hypocrisy—and in that sense evil? No, no, I interpret it as mediocrity, as a lack of human frankness and openness.

Consider an illustration, a powerful prince, as princes were in the days when it meant something to be kings or emperors, and you will notice what men regard as the most sensible way to deal with him: Say nothing but good of him but, in addition, never have anything to do with him. This is the life-wisdom of mediocrity.

And this is the pattern for fabricating the whole proclamation of official Christianity: Speak well of God, sounding the trumpets and bassoons sweetly, the more the better, but sensibly avoid getting involved with him.

There is nothing mediocrity fears as much as the genuinely lofty, the infinite—but it is not crazy enough to say this outright. No, no, mediocrity is sensible and prudent: it speaks of it in the most glowing terms—but as for becoming involved, no thanks. Bluntly to state: I am afraid of this loftiness—would be regarded by mediocrity as being very imprudent, for that would mean becoming involved with it. No, pure, unadulterated eulogy—and then sensibly and prudently avoid becoming involved with it.

XI² A 138   *n.d., 1854*

« 2681 *Mediocrity*

What makes it so enormously difficult to get Christianity hauled through the mire in our time is that it is stalled in mediocrity, passionlessness, and absence of spirit, something far more dangerous than heresies and schisms, where there nevertheless is passion.

This mediocrity dresses itself up in various ways. Now as modesty, humility, which supposes that we all will be saved, just as we are all Christians. No, the devil with it, this is not modesty, humility—no, it is sloth, indifference, which does not want to be inconvenienced by the matter and therefore for the sake of indolence assumes that we are all Christians, and thereupon this indolence demands to be regarded as humility, modesty.

And mediocrity dresses up as cordiality or heartiness. It is so very cordial that it judges everybody else leniently. No, the devil with it, it is not cordiality, it is self-love, which quite correctly understands that the surest way to spare yourself is to spare others, especially in these times which will hardly tolerate that anyone assumes he is saved apart from others.

XI^2 A 323   n.d., 1854

« 2682 *Cunning Humility*

Lutheran religiosity, especially in the next generation after Luther and following, is undeniably the kind we human beings like best of all, the kind that whines and whimpers to us and to God—and then everything is all right. "What is man, a miserable wretch, unable to accomplish anything, etc." O, but I get another impression reading the New Testament;[411] I get the impression that according to God's idea man is a giant—but he is to be stretched, not spared.

Otherwise, does not Luther's position easily become a cunning swindle. Permit me to use an analogy. Take the leaseholders, hired men, and renters in relation to the owner of a large estate. Is there a single one of them, no matter how prosperous, who does not whine. It is regarded as the shrewdest thing to do. And when the owner meets Martin Hansen one day and says, "Well, how are things going?" Martin Hansen replies, "Oh, rather poorly" (which is a lie, for he has thousands). But M. H.'s father told him on his deathbed: Never give the appearance of having anything—and least of all to the owner of the estate.

XI^2 A 326   n.d., 1854

« 2683 *The Well-intentioned!*

Imagine a kind of medicine which in a full dose has a laxative effect and in a half dose has a constipating effect.

Suppose someone is suffering from constipation. But—for some reason or other, because there is not enough for a dose or because it is feared that such a large amount might be too much—in order to do something he is given, with the best intentions, a half dose: "After all, it is something." "Aha, it certainly is something, for the full dose has a laxative effect and the half dose a constipating effect, and he suffers from constipation."

So it is with Christianity. It is the same with this as with everything qualified by an Either/Or—the half has the very opposite effect of the whole.

And we go on practising this well-intentioned act from generation to generation, produce Christians by the millions, are proud of it—and have no inkling that we are doing just exactly the opposite of what we intend to do.

However, this never becomes popular. It takes a physician to understand that a medicine can be such that a half dose can have an effect which is the opposite to that of a full dose. Common sense, levelheadedness, mediocrity never catches on but until the end of time undeviatingly continues to say of the half-dosage: "After all, it is something; even if it doesn't work very well, it is still something." But that it should have an opposite effect—no, mediocrity does not grasp that.

But all the benefits and advantages of this earthly life are to be found in "mediocrity"; therefore if you want them, you must see to it that you maintain good relations with mediocrity. Therefore reassure mediocrity—and how ironical even this, that mediocrity really needs reassurance!—reassure mediocrity, make the well-intentioned move, "After all, it is something." As a matter of fact, you are in one sense doing something, and not a little—you are doing the worst thing you can do.

XI² A 385   n.d., 1854–55

« 2684 *Mediocrity*

Individually, mediocre people certainly are not pushy toward each other, are guilty of no insolence; indeed, they mutually respect each other's mediocrity.[412]

But these mediocrities all together, this whole mass of mediocrity, or mediocrity *en masse,* is insolence toward God, because it wants to set itself up [*opkaste sig*] as the highest and to vomit up [*opkaste*] the ideal. Just as we are mutually insured for fire, so also mediocrity wants to make mediocre individuals completely sure that mediocrity is the truth.

XI² A 278   n.d., 1855

« 2685 *According To the Christian View, the Mediocre, Mediocrity, Up-to-a-Point-Ness, the Merely Human, What We Men Call Cordiality—It Is Just This Which Christianly Is the Offense— the Intrusion of Satan*

August 13, 1855

It is of utmost importance to hold fast to this; if you cannot. you will never get a perspective on Christianity, never detect the swindle which the whole of Christendom is.

The essential Christian truth of what stands above in the heading you learn from Christ himself in his relation to Peter, something I cannot sufficiently drill and stress—in order, Christianly, to strike a blow right at the most dangerous kind of nonchristianity: cordial mediocrity, hearty rubbish, etc. Just as almost every child has an innate gift (very displeasing to the earnest parent) for buttering up his father— acting in a certain way and "I will, I will, I will be good," but never doing what his father wants—so Christian orthodoxy has excelled in buttering up God, sparing itself, and then calling it cordiality toward others etc.

Now to Christ and Peter (Matthew 16:23). Christ says that he now must go to Jerusalem and suffer and be put to death. Consider first Peter the apostle. He is an apostle and therefore measures a good two feet taller than what we call the mediocre, even though according to Christ's judgment (again a criterion of what Christ understands by being a Christian, a crushing criterion for all the rascality of Christendom) Peter needs to be converted, for Christ says to him after he had already been an apostle for some time: "When you are converted." When Christ deliberately seems to expose himself voluntarily to death (which according to the universally human conception is not even permissible), Peter—motivated by personal love for his master from whom he is very reluctant to be separated—takes the occasion to rebuke him. And Christ[413] says (listen, you battalions of mediocrity, you who are ants compared to Peter and yet are duped by the preachers to thinking that you are Christians and that by this kind of Christianity you get to heaven): Get behind me, Satan! You are an offense to me, for you do not perceive the things of God, but of men.

According to Christ's judgment, Christianity and being a Christian are so high that to want to dissuade his teacher and friend from voluntarily exposing himself to death is: the offense, the intrusion of Satan.

Nothing more is needed to see that the kind of leveling Christendom does is neither more nor less than the offense, the work of Satan, and all of mediocrity's teachers of Christianity are: the offense, instruments of Satan.

Therefore flee from this offense, flee from those thousands of jobholding teachers of Christianity, flee from Satan's instruments in the most dangerous form, the form of cordiality.

No, the mark of truly relating oneself to Christianity has not been concealed by Christ—it is: to hate oneself. Hatred of oneself is the only passion which can bear the divine, but in the process you are crushed in the most appalling way.

There is, therefore, only one true relationship to Christianity: loving God to hate oneself. If you shrink away from this most appalling of appalling agonies, this lifelong soul-breaking—well, be truthful enough to admit, then, that you do not truly relate yourself to Christianity.

Christendom has not made this admission, although it is easy enough to show that in 1800 years of Christendom there has not been a single proclamation of Christianity without the mark of inverted Christianity: in love of oneself to love God, for which reason all Christendom is offense, the intrusion of Satan, invented by perceiving only the things of men.

XI² A 427   August 13, 1855

« 2686 *Criminal Mediocrity*

In one sense, particularly from a Christian point of view, all mediocrity is a crime.

Unfortunately, at the same time it is quite in order and very natural that the majority—mediocrely equipped by nature and not educated to anything higher—advance only to mediocrity. Who could think of wanting to pass judgment—that is, if this mediocrity is not inveigled by journalists and agitators, as is the case in our day, into wanting to play the judge of what truth is etc.

Consequently, as mentioned, this mediocrity cannot be called criminal.

No, this kind is quite different. There are always individuals (more or fewer, according to the higher or lower criterion) who by nature and by all other conditions are so placed (situated) that they are able to work for something higher. But, shrewd as they are, they soon perceive that greater and greater strenuousness results only in making them conflict (collide) more and more frequently with all the mediocrity, whose self-seeking is not served by the introduction of something higher; on the other hand they see that by indolence and minor performances they very easily manage to become admired, loved, esteemed, and rewarded in every way by all the mediocrity, which is the great power in society.

Then these low villains commit against the higher life the treason of proclaiming mediocrity, in order to become themselves the top men in mediocrity's class, instead of being on the receiving end of all mediocrity's racket, opposition, and hatred by truly serving something higher.

O, it is so villainous! And also so utterly corrupting for the whole; simply because such a traitor to the higher life had the capacity to serve the higher life, has elements of it (although it certainly is evident that he lacks what is essential, the will), for this very reason his treachery against the higher life once more reinforces mediocrity, which makes out that he belongs to their company.

The category "criminal mediocrity" has differences of degree, and the culmination point is what is called a Prince of the Church. From the Christian point of view such a fellow is a highly qualified criminal. It is not customary to regard him this way, and, naturally, the majority find it almost deranged to talk this way. This is especially the case with us in our limited context; we do not even have the analogy from civil life which is well-known on the continent: that the very distinguished, decorated Lord Baron who lives in a splendid palace, surrounded by gallooned servants, turns out to be, when the police come, a runaway galley slave, and thus for a moment it looks as if the detective were a madman, something the gracious Lord Baron, if he is brash and nervy, perhaps will try to make him out to be. And so it is, *Christianly,* with these princes of the Church, the vanguard of criminal mediocrity, who, falsifying, give religion a wrong turn; instead of themselves becoming suffering imitators of Christ in the New Testament sense, they sell cheap what it means to be a Christian, and then all this mediocrity fancies itself to be Christian. They utilize the battalions of mediocrity to elevate themselves as the extraordinary, who are directly admired, praised, and rewarded, whereas the extraordinary (which, however, is solely the ordinary or regular) from the Christian point of view is known in the opposite way, by suffering. A velveted His Grace, starred, elevated to princely rank, exuding refinement and sanctity, turns out —when the police come—to be, in the Christian sense, a galley slave or something much, much worse and more revolting. What wonder, then, that the majority regard the detective as a deranged man, whereas his detective's eye is manifested particularly by his ability to see that such a person is a most consummate criminal precisely because he, disguised in a fabric of lies and hypocrisy, is regarded by the majority as being holiness personified.

Consequently this is the pinnacle of criminal mediocrity. But with differences of degree it is present wherever a man, shrewdly or in fear of men, prefers (perhaps even covering up his crime against God, the idea, the higher life, by calling it love of humanity) prefers, in order to have profit (men's money or their friendship, their regard) to scale down the larger truth, instead of coming to suffer at the hands of men by being loyal to the larger truth, to the higher life.

Just as there is eternal enmity between fire and water, between mouse and cat, so is there eternal enmity between the idea, the higher life, and mediocrity. But it must be said to the excuse of the battallions of mediocrity that they do not know what they are doing. It is different with the traitors, with criminal mediocrity.

The categorical degree of this crime is apparent in the fact that it actually cannot be punished in this world. For he wins men (the number depends on the degree of the crime) to himself precisely by betraying the highest, the idea. The battalions of mediocrity cannot understand it in any other way than that he is the great one; they have no intimation that the truly great look the very opposite. But eternity is all the better informed about this fellow's true situation.

XI^3 B 177   *n.d., 1855*

« **2687 Brief Observations**

September 23, 1855

Being a Christian out of Fear of Men

In the New Testament the formula for being a Christian is: fear God more than men. In this lie all the specific Christian collisions. As soon as one can be a Christian out of fear of men, yes, when out of fear of men one does not even dare stop calling himself a Christian, then *eo ipso* there is no Christianity.

From this we see what nonsense it is to believe that true Christianity is found in "the Church" with its large numbers. The spirit of Christianity is opposed to nothing more than to this, this human mediocrity, this animal-man's faith in human numbers. No, whatever true Christianity there is to be found in the course of the centuries may be found in the sects and the like, except that being a sect or outside the Church is no proof of being true Christianity. But what is to be found may be found in the sects and the like. The only thing resembling the Christianity of the New Testament is a sect, which, indeed, is what Christianity is called in the New Testament.

Be Especially Afraid of Going Astray
by Calling Evasion Humility.

Every human being is a born hypocrite. And in each generation there is perhaps not a single one who in the course of his whole life gets everything hypocritical knocked out of him by providence.

That hypocritical creature, man, has no greater propensity than to dodge strenuousness by assuming the appearance of humility and modesty. When man sees what agonies are involved in being an apostle, he says: I am too humble to aspire to be an apostle. The hypocrite! When he reads Christ's description of how difficult it is to enter the kingdom of heaven, he says: I am humbly satisfied just to approach the threshold of heaven. The hypocrite! The idea behind such humility and modesty, whereby we make things easy and actually fool ourselves, is to butter up God, who supposedly is pleased with such humility and modesty. But it does not please him at all. Neither does it please a teacher to hear a pupil who does not feel like putting in time and effort say: I am too humble and modest to wish for a high mark; I am humbly and modestly satisfied with just barely passing. "You scoundrel," says the teacher, "you dare call that humility and modesty!" If you loaf and dawdle instead of putting in time and effort and consequently do no better than you have, it certainly would be insolent to expect a high mark—but I demand that you do work which deserves a high mark.

XI^2 A 435   September 23, 1855

MELANCHOLY

« **2688**

Just as a woman who is unhappy at home spends a lot of time looking out the window, so the soul of a melancholy person keeps on the lookout for diversions. Another form of melancholy is the kind which keeps its eyes shut in order to have darkness all around.

VIII^1 A 239   *n.d.*, 1847

« **2689**

Christianity certainly is not melancholy—on the contrary, it is the glad news for those who are melancholy. It certainly is not glad news for the thoughtless and light-minded; it wants first of all to make them earnest.

VIII^1 A 341   *n.d.*, 1847

« **2690**

What people regard as selfishness and lack of participation may sometimes be melancholy. When a person is gay and happy, he is also more open, but when he feels deeply and inwardly unhappy, he shuts himself in, but it does not follow that this is selfishness. Sometimes it can almost be thoughtfulness of others, in order not to let them feel how unhappy he is.

IX A 366   *n.d.*, 1848

« **2691**

In Book 3, Chapter 23, where the Lord himself teaches one how he shall find peace. Thomas à Kempis[414] says:

"Be desirous, my son, to do the will of another rather than thine own." This struck me. But the question is, where does one find clergymen such as these nowadays. If I were to submit myself to any clergyman, I am sure he would secularize my whole endeavor by promptly getting me into the establishment, into the moment, into an office, into a title, etc.

In other respects there is something very appealing to this. A melancholy person is generally inclined to declare himself incapable in such things—for then it is as if his responsibility were lessened, but it must not be forgotten that one's responsibility becomes all the greater if one has thus declared himself incompetent.

One can discern similarities in other areas. A melancholy person has a strong tendency to become the henpecked partner in the marriage relationship; he wants it; he finds gratification in it. Here again one sees how close irony and melancholy are to one another, for an essential ironist would also always be henpecked in his marriage.

x^1 A 400   *n.d.*, 1849

« 2692 *Question: Whether It Would Be Psychologically Correct, Whether It Is Even Psychologically Conceivable*

A basically melancholy individual who otherwise had never been tormented or tempted by the thought of suicide.

He takes a walk one day in a beautiful wooded area. It has just been raining; everything smells fresh and fragrant; it occurs to him that he never or only rarely had felt so indescribably, so ineffably good.

As he walks along the thought comes to him *en passant:* what if you took your life—and he does it.

Here there is no premeditation about such a step, no sequence of events, nor any violent agitation. The thought comes to him something like this: see, there is a delightful little flower; he commits the deed in about the same state of mind as that in which one bends down and picks a little flower; therefore death in this case would be a kind of well-being carried to a higher power.

Is such a thing conceivable?

Melancholy's point of contact with insanity is, as in so many other respects, that one himself becomes an object. What is peculiar and unusual is the almost idyllic objectivity, idyllically to mistake oneself for a little flower etc. This would be an extreme example of being loosely attached to life.

x^1 A 642   *n.d.*, 1849

« 2693 *Hypochondria*

The saying goes: When garbage comes to be honored, no one knows what will happen. The hypochondriac experiences the truth of this. When the hypochondriac throws himself into trifles—whether the light has been put out properly at night, the fire in the stove, the door properly shut, whether one's underwear is properly buttoned over the stomach, and all that—it is unbelievable how insolent such garbage can be when it notices that it has arrived at the honor of having attention paid to it; no despot tyrannizes worse than such trifles.

XI[1] A 569   *n.d.*, 1854

METHODISTS

« 2694 *The Pastoral Appointment*

All by itself it would be entirely different from and provide a satire upon the current way of calling clergymen—namely, Wesley's (See *Joh. Wesleys Leben*[415] etc., translated from English, published by Krumacher, Hamburg, 1841, II, p. 203) required threefold test: (1) their theological competence (2) their ability to speak (3) *Their reasons for believing themselves called by God to preach.* The last is never asked these days. The whole thing has become as secular and profane as possible, a matter of making a living, a job for which one qualifies by taking three examinations.

With respect to the third test, successfully bringing others to conversion qualified as proof of the call [*Kaldelsen*].[416]

If the applicant passed, he was accepted first for a shorter trial period and later for a four-year probation.

x^3 A 517   *n.d.*, 1850

« 2695

Wesley[417] puts it very well when he recommends the Methodist hymns above others: It is not these miserable doggerels but the singing which is more likely to make a Christian of a critic than a critic of a Christian.

x^3 A 518   *n.d.*, 1850

« 2696

Walsh, a Methodist, formerly a Catholic, extraordinarily gifted, but whose weak body could not bear his spirit and spiritual exertions, said of himself: The sword is too sharp for the scabbard.[418]

x^3 A 520   *n.d.*, 1850

« 2697 *Very Good!*

Wesley had been unmarried for a long time and had even written a book about the unmarried state. As an older man he wanted to get married. He himself felt the incongruity of his situation. "For the sake of appearance he called in or counselled with several religious friends so that they might encourage him to follow his inclination." (See *Wesleys Leben*,[419] translated from English, published by Krummacher, Hamburg, 1841, II, p. 295.) You see, this is why we have friends. This is what I have always said.

X³ A 523   *n.d.*, 1850

MIDDLE AGES

« 2698

The duality which I have pointed out [i.e., I A 145] in the role of the fools in the Middle Ages can also be seen in this—that they had one language for science and scholarship and one for poetry (Latin-Romance languages).

I A 213   August 2, 1836

« 2699

The duality I have noted [i.e., I A 145, 213] in the Middle Ages in other respects can also be seen in the way nature and art are involved in the formation of a great poet. The Middle Ages therefore had the two poles developed separately—the nature-poets and the art-poets—and they *seldom* or *never* overlap. For the most part it seems characteristic of the Middle Ages that the two forces which ought to be united, to merge with each other, are kept apart, are represented as two directions—(for example, the scholastic—the life of chivalry, etc.)

I A 226   August 21, 1836

« 2700

The mythology[420] produced by the Middle Ages was, if I may say so, humanistic—that is, mythology in the proper sense is the creation of God in human form; this mythology creates man in his image (more epic); it was life which was supposed to clarify itself.

I A 269   November 3, 1836

« 2701

The children's crusade[421] should be regarded as a very sarcastic comment by world history on the whole chivalric movement.

I A 281   *n.d.*, 1836

« 2702

The duality of the Middle Ages is apparent also in the fact that the congregation ate the bread and the priest drank the chalice.

I A 284   November 20, 1836

« **2703**

Prompted by a remark by von Raumer[422] in the fifth volume of his historical *Taschenbuch,* p. 137, where he seems to present a view similar to one I developed some time ago, I decided, since his remark is prefaced by a quotation: *"Ueber das wahrscheinliche Alter und die Bedeutung des Gedicht vom wartburger Kriege,* [423] by Koberstein,[424] p. 57," to examine this, and the book now lies before me. Since V. Raumer himself does not go into it further, I must stick to Koberstein, which poses the problem that I do not have the slightest knowledge of the poem he mentions. He disassociates [p. 53] *"das Räthselspiel zwischen Wolfram v. Eschenbach und Klinsor"*[425] from the Wartburger rivalry [p. 56]. *"Und so ist denn, wie gesagt, aus der Neigung, die auf Wolframs Verherrlichung gerichtet war, und aus dieser Vorliebe für das Allegorische und Räthselhafte auch unser Räthselspiel entsprungen, in welchem dem tüchtigen in dem Glauben an die Untrüglichkeit und Allgemeingültigkeit des Christenthums erstarkten Wolfram die neckende, hämische Magie in dem Klinsor entgegentritt, die aus dem Naturglauben hervorgegangen und nach dem heidnischen Orient, als ihrem Vaterland zurückweisend, den Christen an sich selbst irre zu machen,* [p. 57] *die Unzulänglichkeit der chr. Offenbarung zu erweisen versucht, und da ihr dies nicht gelingen will, den Teufel selbst zu Hülfe ruft, als das Element des ewigen Verneinens, Aufhebens und Zerstörens"* [426] etc. He thinks [p. 57] "that already here we see the first appearance of the idea which in the centuries following, especially since the Reformation, developed and centered about a specific individual as its focal point, and finally was grasped in its full profundity by Goethe in his *Faust,* yet in such a way that while both poets have understood the deep cleft in man, the older one, in accordance with the Middle Age's view of the world, has represented the cleft in two individuals, whereas Goethe has let it develop in *one* individual."

On closer inspection I do not find the content I expected, and the whole comment seems to dissolve into a trifle. To be specific, viewing life as a struggle and consequently viewing the life which is essentially moved by the religious as a struggle between the devil and God is, if I may say so, a conceptual mode in no way specifically different from that of the modern period, and merely by abstracting from a Goethian poetic development (whether this is actually the case with Faust, about that later) which sees these two worlds more as being in and with each other and views these two forces in a higher concentricity, not in a phenomenological eccentricity, it would be easy to give examples here

of a newer as well as an older development than the Middle Ages. —
If we ask in the next place how the difference between the older and
the Goethian view is to be understood, we do not get much more
enlightenment, for the specific difference between them—something
our author has not seen—is that Goethe has written a second part of
F., but I cannot see that he has let this struggle take place within the
individual himself; in fact, he is comparable to Klingsor, who also had
his better beginning, and F. is first F. when in his development his
conflict with the world conjures up the devil (when I say that he is then
F. for the first time and thereby suggest, as it were, a previous existence, this is due to the frailty of language, which continually must
allow a mistaken identity of F. as individual and as idea; the Biblical
expression "he was in the beginning" applies to the latter), only that
now F. is developed more lyrically (everything is therefore shoved
aside), whereas the older poet has conceived him more epically, but
this difference of conception can, of course, also be repeated within the
characteristically modified sphere of every age.

My main point is that it is not a question at all of the poets'
conceptions, although these also ought to be considered* as representatives, but of how time lies before us in a world-historical sense, and
here I believe that, although multiple tendencies intersected in time,
they did know each other and did not see how, if I may put it this way,
since I speak only of the world's side, how the one ironized over the
other. Nevertheless, the modern period, more *umsichtig* and without
such an inspiring illusion, becomes conscious of that which the earlier
age externalized as nisses, trolls, and the devil as the cold irony of the
world, which perhaps in the next moment is itself both a part of and
a stage toward something else.[†] Therefore the Middle Ages, rooted
in its entire nature, could very well conceive of life as a struggle and
thus also between the childlike, pious Wolfram and the cunning Klingsor. But it never found rest,[‡] for if Christianity conquered, a life-view
conquered which proclaims itself simply as a struggle, and therefore
the striving must begin anew, even though within another sphere,
which does not concern us here.[§]

I C 113   December 3, 1836

In margin: * and the question arises whether or not these, just as
they themselves made the world and its movements take form for
them, must not repeat the same two-sidedness for the observer who
in his development has outlived the Middle Ages.

† *In margin:* in this way, that along with the one effort its opposite also arises in consciousness.

‡ *In margin:* see in this connection Schlegel's observations on the three kinds of tragedy.

§ *In margin:* therefore Faust, conceived world-historically, has in *one sense* his counterpart in the one saving Church.

« 2704

The Danish word for *ingenuity [Sindrighed*—literally, mind-riches] characterizes poetry of the Middle Ages superbly; ingenuity—the marvelous leaps—illogical—thus one could say that bee hives are ingenious —not rational—the same with all of nature's spontaneous works, to which also belong the poetry and folk songs of the Middle Ages.

> There stands a tree on my father's farm
> It bears such wonderful branches.
> And all the girls got men this year
> And I must walk here alone[427]

See Thiele, *Danske Folkesagn,*[428] pt. II, coll. 3, p. 152:

> Laddie, laddie, peppercorn
> The kitten blows on a silver horn.

II A 631   n.d., 1837

« 2705

Within the medieval Church people felt so indissolubly bound to its past that they were almost fettered by it (chains).[429]

II A 268   October 5, 1838

« 2706

It is very significant that an Amen from the mouth of one who did not understand the prayer to which he answered Amen was called ἀμὴν ὀρφανόν יְתוֹמָה. [430] by the rabbis. Was not the congregation's Amen throughout the whole Middle Ages like this, was not the congregation itself truly ὀρφανός.

II A 380   March 11, 1839

« 2707

The cleft I have on so many occasions [i.e., I A 145, 213, 226] pointed to in the Middle Ages was so radical that one could say that simultaneously with the dogmatic distribution of the Lord's Supper *sub una specie* there entered *into all life a corresponding living   s u b   u n a s p e c i e* (the monastic life—chivalry—clergy—laity—scholars and fools —bread for the laity, wine for the clergy) instead of the individual's synthesis of these elements, which is reserved for a later age.

II A 468   July 5, 1839

« 2708

The theater was divine service not only in Greece but also in Persia, *ni fallor.*[431] People took it for granted that one who produced plays at his own expense was rewarded in heaven. Therefore it was about the same as building churches and cloisters in the Middle Ages.

VI A 37   *n.d.,* 1845

« 2709

The mistake[432] in the Middle Ages was to regard the forsaking of external goods as something meritorious. The next step, to renounce them entirely *in abstracto,* was regarded as Christian. Both are unchristian. It is something quite different if, by confessing Christ and being occupied only with this, one actually does give up everything, does not have time to look after his property, does not require a wife in marriage etc., and runs the risk of having the government or the people confiscate his property.

VIII^1 A 592   *n.d.,* 1848

« 2710

The fault[433] with much of what the Middle Ages practiced in order to express the heterogeneity of Christian life to worldliness was that one became important to himself by doing it, yes, even important before God. Christianity believes that the Christian should be so spiritual that he could do such things as easily as if they were nothing. If he can do them this way, Christianity looks upon it favorably. If he cannot, then he had better make an honest confession [*Tilstaaelse*] and admission [*Indrømmelse*] and abstain from dabbling—and then also Christianity is gratified.

x^2 A 464   *n.d.,* 1850

« 2711 *The Middle Ages—the Modern Age*

The error[434] and also the vanity of the Middle Ages was running to the monastery, scourging oneself—and then being admired for it.

No, stay where you are—but witness for truth and against untruth, do not become engrossed in all sorts of earthly and finite aims, but work for the truth and the kingdom of God, and you will see, you will see how, humanly speaking, you will very soon become unhappy in the world, scourged in one way or another—and yet, note well that it nevertheless is simply and solely unconditionally by grace that one is saved, quite the same as it is grace that saves the person who is converted just before death.

But when one busily occupies his time with all sorts of finite efforts and then on ultimate matters gives assurances of his inwardness etc. —well, then he immediately conforms to the secular mentality and does not collide with it.

Humanly speaking, Christianity must make a person unhappy if he is earnest about Christianity. It immediately directs his whole mind and effort toward the eternal; he thereby becomes heterogeneous with the whole secular mentality and must collide.

And then, without further ado, appointments to be preachers of this doctrine are made by the dozens, this doctrine which, humanly speaking, is like a plague to the natural man. Of course, the natural man probably does not exist any more. We are all Christians.

x^3 A 175   *n.d.*, 1850

« 2712 *Middle Ages—Mynster*

The Middle Ages thought Christianity meant renunciation, dying to the world, asceticism.

Mynster thinks Christianity is almost the same as culture and education (the modern view, generally).

Taken without qualification, this conception "culture" is highly dubious and, if it means pleasure, refinement, merely human culture, is perhaps directly counter to Christianity.

If Christianity is supposed to be culture, it must be the culture of character, or education and culture aimed at becoming persons of character.

This, in part, is the way I understand it. Here there will also be a place for self-denial, renunciation, dying to the world, only not in the extravagant sense of those who flagellated themselves into the monastery. The person who is to remain standing in the world to witness to the truth will bring appropriate asceticism into his life.

The Middle Ages has been accused of a-cosmism—but in no case is cosmism Christianity. And yet the kind of culture and education supposedly identifiable with Christianity is almost the kind of culture which quite ingeniously is characterized by the phrase—to possess the world.

x^3 A 588   *n.d.*, 1850

MIRACLES

« 2713

Clausen[435] and a great number of scholars before him stop with an exclusively *moral consideration* of the concept *miracle*[436] (the beneficial results for men, and therefore they have difficulties with miracles in which someone suffers loss, for example, the Gaderenes). But if one does not want to enter into the far more profound inquiry whereby miracles are viewed as part of the new order of things, which in the New Testament is called the Kingdom of Heaven, then it seems to me that the *purely esthetic side* of miracles could make just as strong a case as the moral. This appears, for example, in the wedding at Cana, in Christ's walking on the water, and in many other places, and it seems to me that this observation at least points to a far more ideal infinity than the notion that raising Lazarus from the dead was a miracle because it was beneficial to Lazarus. This *finite* view deprives miracles, as it deprives everything higher, of their true infinity, their true divine freedom.

January 14, 1839

He who cannot understand the *royalty,* so to speak, implicit in miracles as seen from this side must either be a philistine or a Judas (John 12:4).

II C 5   *n.d.,* 1839

« 2714

The widow[437] who put three pennies in the temple treasury box performed a miracle just like the miracle[438] of the five loaves and three fish; she gave more than the rich—consequently the three pennies were transformed into abundance.

VI A 69   *n.d.,* 1845

« 2715

The meaning of the miracle[439] of the five loaves and two fish is not that a person should expect something similar, nor is it that preacher-prattle about how frequently even a little has proved to be sufficient

196

—this is nothing more than an attempt to explain the miraculous by the nonmiraculous, by substituting something which is not a miracle. The meaning is that the troubled person should let himself be *quieted*, should be edified or built up by the thought of the power of the Almighty, be built up and quieted by the release which miracle provides. The miracle has esthetic significance. It is like a drama, except that it must be *believed*, but it should have a cleansing and quieting effect on the troubled person's passions, so that he does not remain completely prosaic and petty of heart.

VIII^1 A 26   *n.d.*, 1847

« 2716 *The Daughter of Jairus*[440]

Shall we say: Such a thing is a miracle, and it does not happen any more? Or shall we say: Once in a while medical science is able to do wonderful things; once in a while there is an unusual case like this. In other words, shall we say that the resurrection of Jairus's daughter is a miracle and appeal to what is not a miracle in order to explain it?

No, let us rather speak in this way. Whose joy is really more beautiful and well-pleasing to God, the joy of one whose desire is fulfilled (Jairus in this case) by the miracle *or* the joy of one who quietly suffers the pain of having his request denied but, gently moved and touched, rejoices with him whose lot has been extraordinary joy? Whose joy is really more blessed, the joy of him who learns from the report that his desire is fulfilled *or* the joy of him who by the report is reminded once again of his pain but yet, although saddened, is devoutly built up by the presentation of a more perfect existence [*Tilvær-else*] where the miracle is at home? Who listens more worthily to the poet's song, he who possesses what the poet celebrates or he to whom that is denied but who in truth is not denied—the inspiration of the poet's song?

VIII^1 A 39   *n.d.*, 1847

« 2717

In the feeding of the five thousand (John 6:1–15) there is presented a remarkable example of the union of wealth and economy.[441] After sufficient food for the five thousand had been procured by a miracle (what abundance compares with this!), one would expect the left-overs to be wasted. But God is never like that—everything was carefully gathered together, according to the gospel. The human way is to be unable to work miracles and at the same time to waste the leftovers. The divine way is miraculously to create the abundance and then to gather up the crumbs.

VIII¹ A 65   n.d., 1847

« 2718 *The miracle of the five loaves and the three small fish is an example of the unity of divine abundance and economy.*[442]

I wonder if a man who could perform miracles would think of having the crumbs collected. Alas, only at a lavish banquet is there the practice of smashing the glasses in order to indicate affluence. But Christ performs a miracle and can perform a miracle at any moment —and he has the crumbs collected; he does not disdain the crumbs. It is no surprise that a poor person says: The scraps, too, are bread—but that the richest one gathers up the scraps as if he were the poorest of all—this is divine.

VIII¹ A 340   n.d., 1847

« 2719

There has been enough talk that if we had been the ones who were healed by a miracle etc. or, on the other hand, that this does not happen among us now and we must be satisfied with less. But suppose that things were now as they were then 1800 years ago, that to be healed in this way also meant being put out of the synagogue (see John 9, the man blind from birth). Ah, it is not as easy as the garrulous, rambling, slapdash preacher makes it out to be. We cannot use Christ to worldly advantage. Would there not be many who would rather remain blind than to have their eyes opened to the conditions!

VIII¹ A 428   n.d., 1847

« 2720

After all, both are equally meaningless: *either* (this is what Lessing[443] himself does, that is, by publishing the Wolfenbüttel Fragments[444]) to employ all one's acumen to show the *unreasonableness* of a miracle and then on that basis (that it is unreasonable) conclude that it is ergo no miracle—but would it be a miracle if it were reasonable? —*or* (this is the wisdom of speculation) to employ all one's profundity and acumen to understand the miracle, to make it understandable, and then conclude that it ergo is a miracle because it is understandable— but then it is indeed no miracle.

No, let miracle be what it is: an object of faith.

The whole calamity is that Christianity has comfortably become a thought project for clever heads and cogitators who have absolutely nothing essential to do with Christianity—rather than being a consolation of the suffering which no human wisdom can alleviate, a consolation of the anguish and pain of the consciousness of sin, and in any case it is only for those who suffer.

What should we think of the fate of a medicine if, by some curious error, instead of being used by a sick person for whom it was intended, it was made the object of a test by a chemist, who then discovered that it was not a remedy—and was mistaken simply in saying: I am not sick.

It is the radical fall of man that we permit ourselves to regard and treat Christianity in this way and that faith long ago really became extinct, the faith which would defend itself in a life-and-death struggle. But what is all this current lifeless Christendom? And how remarkable that the mission enterprise of the whole recent period amounts to nothing. Why? Because Christianity itself really does not exist [*er til*] anymore. This observation on the mission enterprise I have found in the Wolfenbüttel Fragments, and I agree.

In margin: It is just as inconceivable for the mission enterprise to secure adherents as for an oldster to have procreative powers.

x^1 A 373   *n.d.*, 1849

« 2721 *Miracle*

That Christ makes something big out of something small, as at the feeding of the 5000,[445] is usually referred to as a miracle.

But Christ also works a miracle inversely—makes something big (everything that wants to be something) into something little, makes it infinitely nothing in humility.

We may think that this miracle is much easier, but it is not so. Every qualitative change, every infinite change in quality, is genuinely a miracle. A human being can perhaps point out another's weakness, but to show it to be infinitely nothing, that only the divine can do, and man cannot even by himself humble himself in this way.

x^3 A 532   *n.d.*, 1850

« 2722 *An Observation by Abelard*

In Neander's biography of Bernard[446] (2 ed., pp. 246 and 247) Abelard's view of miracles is presented, including his interpretation of the later absence of miracles as a proof of the decline of faith and the secularization of Christianity. "And," he adds, "right now miracles are needed more than when the teaching came into the world, now when a dead faith prevails."

Here Neander cannot refrain from pointing out that apparently Abelard is merely looking for arguments against his opponents, since the need for miracles when the teaching came into the world was an entirely different matter and since, in addition, a dead faith most readily clings to miracles.

Alas, no, Abelard is right. It is absolutely true that more miracles, if possible, are needed when it is a matter of tearing people out of the illusion that they are believers, for the battle conditions and the task are far more difficult than when Christianity had to deal with pagans. As for the point that a dead faith greatly prefers to cling to miracles, this holds only in relation to miracles at a historical distance. Dead faith cannot get involved contemporaneously with miracles.

x^3 A 594   *n.d.*, 1850

« 2723 *Miracle*

Conceited sensibleness considers itself qualified to protest the miracle when it does not appear to have a finite teleology, is not beneficial, for example.

Christ's commanding the sea[447] to be calm and quiet is not judged to have any such finite teleology—ergo.

O human sensibleness! No, the miracle is to be regarded from another side. It is a part, especially by way of contrast, of making Christ the object of faith, the sign of contradiction, wherein lies the possibility of offense. The miracle comes again in the passion story. Here the tension arises precisely from his being impotent this way—he who commanded even the waves and the wind, almost as if merely for the enjoyment of his divine power.

x^5 A 130   *n.d.*, 1853

« 2724 *Miracles Are No Longer Needed Now*

It was not long before there came to be discussing and explaining in Christendom concerning the absence of miracles: miracles are not needed any more; that was only when Christianity was first introduced.

This again is part of the naturally cunning hypocritical rascality which is inseparable from being human and which therefore fools the Church Fathers as well as others if they do not watch out.

First of all it is meaningless to say that they were needed in the early period of Christianity but not later, just as if Christianity were an historical phenomenon in the sense that it had to be developed, take on a history in the course of time, instead of its being the examination of every generation, so that every generation begins from scratch, every generation is tested to find whether there are some among its millions who want to be Jesus Christ's disciples.

As soon as a person gets clear on this he readily sees how confusing this talk is about an alteration in the course of time.

No, Christianity is a definite and, in the New Testament, accurately stated intensification in existing[448] [*i at existere*]. Thus miracles are needed in every generation just as much as in the first.

But now comes the rascality. We human beings prefer to be free from strenuous effort and this, again, we hypocritically prefer to conceal.

No one wants to be an apostle, because we have a conception of the anguish involved in being one, that it really means to be sacrificed to others, and we have no inclination for this. But we hypocritically express it thus: I am too humble to want to be an apostle.

To be contemporaneous with a miracle is extremely strenuous—therefore we prefer to avoid it. But with natural cunning we know how to hide it hypocritically, and we say that we are too humble to crave a miracle now, and it is not needed any more, either—of course not, for we have peace and quiet for the enjoyment of life, or peace and quiet for open and obvious fasting and all that, but, please note, open and obvious so that one can sit in state, fasting in all security, and be admired—which is very different from the strenuousness of being an apostle.

But in Christendom everything that involves strenuousness with respect to being a Christian is continually, continually, everlastingly continually being abolished—but, please note, hypocritically, under the pretence of humility.

Therefore Christendom is like a child's top, if I may use a queer but suggestive figure. The operator makes the top spin with a whipping string, but after some years the top hits upon a score of polite excuses (the ones Christendom also uses)—for one thing, that it has now developed so much that the whipping-string is now no longer needed (this corresponds to the rascality which abolishes Christianity under the heading of perfectibility)—and so the top takes it easy, which it prefers to do. Then, too, it is too humble to aspire to perform the remarkable trick which is reserved for only the very extraordinary tops, the trick of spinning around on the point—that is, it does not like the whipping-string, but, with familiar human honesty, it expresses this by saying that it is too humble to aspire to such a thing.

XI[1] A 186   *n.d.,* 1854

« **2725** *Miracle*

In the New Testament miracle is presented as inseparable from being Christian (Mark 16:17), and this is also the view of Christianity, so instead of the rubbish about miracles not being needed any more, the thesis can be stated bluntly that when there are no longer any miracles Christianity no longer exists at all.

But miracles have their own context. Miracles are not for getting money or for profit or for avoiding dangers and suffering. On the contrary, in this respect, God continually leaves "the apostle" or "the disciple" utterly in the lurch, brings him into all sorts of anguish, requires that he voluntarily expose himself to them—and then he has the gift of miracle. Yes, understood in a purely human way, having the gift of miracle involves the condition of one more misery: to be starving—and then to have the gift of miracle. Furthermore, the gift of miracle is calculated to arouse men's opposition to him.

See, this is why miracles are needed no more. No, we prefer to be the teachers of Christianity on the condition that it is a good, fat, secure job with easy advancement for an educated man with a family.

My proposal has always been that we should be honest enough to put an end to this hypocritical way in which we—humbly—shirk Christianity. I do not go further; at least until now I have not gone further. But the hypocrisy is perhaps so deep and malignant that men cannot be persuaded to agree to the honesty which I have desired both on my account and on theirs.

XI[1] A 187   *n.d.,* 1854

« **2726**

. . . . ."Now that Christendom is so widespread miracles are no longer needed." Rubbish and hypocrisy! Miracles are needed now more than ever, but we are cunning enough to want to be exempted from being able to work miracles; we are partial to what is regular, external, and literal. We are cunning enough to understand how strenuous life might become if we were to include miracles, and then we are hypocritical enough to make it look as if we were too modest to aspire to anything like that.

XI[2] A 339   *n.d.,* 1854

MISSION

« 2727 *The Extension of Christianity*

The spread of other religions is related to politics, just as they are also more or less connected with a nationalism.

In the mission work particularly characteristic of Christianity we see that it relates to the whole human race.

A single individual, gripped by Christianity, becomes a missionary, and that is why Christianity has spread so remarkably, something scarcely to be found in any other religion, no more than it occurs to the single individual in any other religion to want, *mir nichts und Dir nichts,* [449] to spread his religion.

Actually, the only attempt to connect the spread of Christianity and politics is the papacy, but the Roman idea still lies beyond nationalism and is related to the whole human race.

x^3 A 676   *n.d.,* 1850

« 2728 *Commissioning the Disciples*

When the disciples are sent to fetch the ass and the colt, Christ says: Go to the village opposite you.

This is like a motto for the commissioning of the disciples and for the universalism of Christianity, because with these words one can circumnavigate the globe. This is a specification of place just like the time specification *printed in this year.* [450]

x^4 A 103   *n.d.,* 1851

« 2729 *Curious Self-Contradiction*

Just when the Church really settled down and got it effectually made into dogma that outside the Church there is no salvation—strangely enough, just then there was a settling down. How cruel, then —the more strictly it is taken that there is no salvation outside the Church—not to become a missionary. [451] But this was not done, but instead the doctrine that outside the Church there is no salvation was learnedly developed.

In repose and possessing the doctrine that outside the Church there is no salvation, and especially the more eruditely it was lectured about, the Church became analogous to the Jewish people or even to

203

pagans, with God a kind of national God, and even though the Church was composed of various nations, it was still like a nation for the one born within the Church and baptized as a child.

X⁵ A 102   *n.d.*, 1853

« 2730 *The Established Order of Christendom*

Where is the scripture text that substantiates the rightness, the authorization, of any such galimatias as the *established* order of Christendom? According to the New Testament, Christianity is a continuing mission, every Christian a missionary: Go out and proclaim my teaching—and nowadays we are all Christians in such a way that it never even remotely occurs to any one of us to become missionaries, except for a few unfortunate characters who grab at it as the last way out (either the foreign legion or missions)—horrible satire!

X⁵ A 122   *n.d.*, 1853

« 2731 *Suffering For the Doctrine*

If someone were to say: But if I lived some place where everybody is a true Christian (an impossibility), then the answer must be: If this were the case (although it cannot be)—then you are *eo ipso* a missionary. But we have completely forgotten that to be a Christian means essentially to be a missionary.

Christianity in repose is *eo ipso* not Christianity. As soon as anything of that sort appears, it means: become a missionary.

Christianity in repose, stagnant Christianity, creates an obstruction, and this formidable obstruction is the sickness of Christendom.

XI¹ A 345   *n.d.*, 1854

« 2732 *Christianity—Diffusion*

Christianity is inversely related to diffusion.

Christianity implies a contrast between God and man.⁴⁵² When Christianity has become a human affair, which is "Christendom's" goal, then it *eo ipso* is no longer God's affair.

God wants individuals [*Individer*]. But the individual either good-naturedly and sympathetically or cunningly and slyly always wants to have the crowd along. But God wants individuals.

XI¹ A 489   *n.d.*, 1854

« 2733 *Christendom is a Sickness*

This sickness has come about by obstructing the mission.

Christianity is always restless; Christendom is like constipation after a surfeit of food.

XI² A 397   *n.d.*, 1855

MOHAMMEDANISM

« 2734

No prophet, no historian could find a more descriptive expression for Mohammedanism than the one Mohammed himself has given in the suspension of his sacred tomb between two magnets,[*] that is, between the divine which did not become human (incarnation) and the human which did not become divine (brothers and coheirs in Christ").[453] Here there is neither individualized polytheism nor concretized monotheism (Jehovah), but abstract monotheism—"God is one"[454]—in which it is specifically the number which must be *affirmed*, not like the Jewish God who to a certain degree was unpredicated, yet still more concretized: "I am who I am."[†] It is not incarnation (the Messiah), not merely prophet (Moses), for there were many prophets among the Jews without any difference in power even though with a difference in degree; but Mohammed demanded a specific superiority (approximating an incarnation, but, of course, like everything else in Mohammedanism, stopping at the halfway point).

II A 86   June 3, 1837

« 2735

[*] *In margin of 2734* (II A 86):
An attempted ascension, but no one ascends to heaven except him who descended from heaven.

II A 87   *n.d.*

« 2736

[†] *In margin of 2734* (II A 86):
It is therefore very interesting to see the Mohammedans in a curiously ironical manner bearing the coat of arms which so appropriately characterizes their relationship to Christianity—the moon, which borrows its light from the sun. (From a scrap of paper dated Jan. 5, 1837, which I found in my desk drawer.)

II A 88   *n.d.*

« **2737**

[†] *In margin of 2734* (II A 86):

In the words, I am who I am, the personal eternal consciousness has already taken precedence and therefore does not develop a fatalism as does the cold "unity."

Furthermore, these words, "I am who I am," are an excellent answer to out-of-place questions.

II A 89   *n.d.*

« **2738**

It seems to me that Napoleon resembles Mohammed more than any of the great generals of the past. Napoleon felt himself to be or at least played the part of a missionary, one who brought with him and proclaimed and fought for certain ideas (the gospel of freedom which is now heard clearly and distinctly in his native country). Many of his proclamations in Italy show this. Then Napoleon's expedition went in a direction opposite to Mohammed's expansion but through the same countries—Mohammed from the east toward the west, Napoleon from the west toward the east.

II A 262   September 17, 1838

MOMENT, THE MOMENTARY

« **2739**

Solon's statement[455] that no one may safely consider himself happy as long as he is alive contains a profound grief over life, for it actually says that no one is happy before the moment he has been happy, and then he is in a way unhappy, for he knows his happiness as something that is gone.

IV A 3   *n.d.*, 1842–43

« **2740**

. . . . . for the moment is really time's atom, but not until eternity is posited, and this is why one may properly say that eternity is always ἐν ἀτόμῳ.[456]

V B 55:6   *n.d.*, 1844

« **2741**

To chase after the applause of the moment[457] is like chasing one's own shadow. It eludes the one who chases after it. I am reminded of a picture in a devotional book of a child running after its own shadow and the shadow runs right along with it.

VII¹ A 38   *n.d.*, 1846

« **2742**

Everyone who is to exist [*existere*] with a perspective other than that of the moment[458] must above all take care to stay clear of a close relationship to the moment. As long as such a person lives together with supernumeraries and choristers who generally, it is well to note, are forgotten as soon as they die, the prospect looks rather disappointing. But at a distance the person of distinction stands alone, and the chorus has vanished. But if he has become involved with the chorus, he stands in a fatal position. He is like a dancer doing by himself a dance which is supposed to be danced by two; his words, his utterances have reference to the chorus, but at death the chorus has departed.

The best showing at a distance is made when everything is arranged so it becomes apparent that the contemporary age has been made to look like a fool.

VII¹ A 170   n.d., 1846

« **2743**

The idea that everything depends upon a minute—that everything depends on one minute or a half hour—otherwise everything is lost—is really nothing but demonic superstition and the most intensified passion of superstition. Such a thing can torture the extraordinariness out of a man, but it is not faith. Is not God present in every moment, or is God perhaps like Isaac,[459] and when like Esau one has been fooled by the younger brother and has not received the blessing—does Isaac have no more blessings? But even Isaac had one more for Esau as well. And God, who is sheer blessing, should he then have none, and should he not have new blessings, and new blessings at every moment?

IX A 35   n.d., 1848

« **2744**

"The moment" occurs when the person is there, the right person.[460]

XI² A 405   n.d., 1855

MONASTICISM

« **2745**

Precisely because life's disparate factors were not unified either in the single individual or in the whole race, life had to end with the heroes' entering the monastery, and although they highly disapproved of anyone's making that decision in his youth (see the story of the beautiful Melusina:[461] Geoffrey murders his brother Freymund), they considered it quite natural for themselves to do so after knocking around for a lifetime. For example, Geoffrey.

I A 267   November 1, 1836

« **2746**

With the Jesuits the monastic orders are at an end, for here in a completely secular operation they achieved a parody of themselves.

II A 292   November 3, 1838

« **2747**

[Excerpts from] *Encyklopaedie der theologischen Wissenschaften* by Rosenkranz.[462] Halle, 1831.

. . . . . The Roman C[hurch] is correctly pictured as the one with a predominantly negative orientation, the Church which finitized the elements of the idea but precisely thereby also imprinted these all the more deeply upon the people. Pp. 187–216 . . . . .

R. is quite right in observing that the Quakers, Methodists, Herrnhutters, etc. can be regarded as Protestantism's monasticism, since by abstraction from wider ranges of secular life they hope to present the Christian life in its purity . . . . .

Very appropriately R. says that the Greek worship [*Cultus*] is comparable to the Jewish, the Catholic to the Greek religion (classical), because in the first two the awe-inspiring predominates, but in the latter two religion has gone over into art and is seized with the idea of the beautiful . . . . .

II C 61   November 9, 1838

« **2748**

The flower *nymphæa alba* is a beautiful image of an *Einsidlei.* [463] Seeing them floating in great numbers alongside each other, each one with its equally vast setting (namely, the leaves), one is carried back to antiquity's beautiful idea of an equal distribution of the land, and the white color is reminiscent of the robes of the religious order, the leaves of the cloister with its peaceful gardens—the water of innocence—and just as cloister life seems without attachment in the world, without family and race, so also the flower, but far down in the bottom of the pond it is deeply rooted.

II A 483   July 20, 1839

« **2749**

Meanwhile I willingly concede the dubiousness of the monastic movement, for it went too far in externalizing what ought to be inward;[464] but then, instead of comprehending the dubiousness and rejoicing in the truth, to get mediation established in the place of honor makes a poor solution.[465]

VI B 58:8   *n.d.,* 1845

« **2750**

There is no doubt that our age and Protestantism especially may need the monastery again or that it should exist. "The monastery" is an essential dialectical element in Christianity; therefore we need to have it out there like a buoy at sea in order to see where we are, even though I myself would not enter it. But if there really is true Christianity in every generation, there must also be individuals who have this need. What would Luther think if he were to look around now? —That there are not very many in our time overwhelmed by the religious, that we have all become so strong—or so weak, in religiousness! That the few analogies to such men are nowadays sent to the lunatic asylum.[466] What would Luther think upon seeing that the office which alone decisively (*si placet*) represents essential Christianity, that of the pastors, has been so secularized in the service of the state (to say nothing of their inner being) that they are almost more occupied with counting sheep and pigs, and *à la* Augustus with counting men, and with tending to the awakening of those apparently dead than with wrenching Christendom out of its apparent death or, worse yet, out of its apparent life. For the appearance of death is not so dangerous, simply because it still seems to have the danger of death, but the appearance of life is the most dangerous of all—is apparently without danger.

VIII[1] A 403   n.d., 1847

« 2751

The Reformation abolished the monastery.[467] Fine! At present I will not elaborate on the Reformation as giving rise to the whole politics of secularism. But take Christendom—if there is to be any mention of Christianity, where is it to be found, except in the quiet ones among the people? The quiet ones[468] among us are the only tiny fragments of Christians we have. But in a decisive sense the quiet ones are actually not Christians; their lives are not exposed to double danger.[469] The quiet ones actually are a more secular edition of the monastery;[470] they are people who tend to their businesses, beget children, etc. And then in the quietness of their minds they also occupy themselves with Christianity—in short, they are the religious of hidden inwardness.[471] But they completely avoid the other danger—suffering for the sake of truth; they shun being led out into the actual Christian situation.

There is much that is beautiful in their lives, but their quietness is still not Christianity, not in the deepest sense. It resembles the view which makes Christianity into a gentle doctrine of truth.

IX A 362   n.d., 1848

« 2752 *Highbrow Sensuality*

Under this heading it is possible to treat the whole modern conception of the clergy. There has been so much wailing about debauchery in the monastery. The modern debauchery is just as depraved and far more dangerous, because it is not as abominable in the eyes of men as was unchastity. It is, indeed, not specifically sensuality but is simply out-and-out secular-mindedness for a shopkeeper, a businessman, and the like to want to amass money, for a lawyer, a doctor, and the like, in short, a secular office holder, to covet worldly esteem—no, the sensuality, the debauchery comes first when one wants to be spiritual to boot, when one wants to gorge on worldliness and sandwich holiness in between. All this tear-jerking, all this ecstatic declaiming and describing of how truth has suffered in the world is—if one is himself secular-minded—sensuality.

How true the Old Testament expression[472] which calls such ones —whores.

IX A 403   n.d., 1848

« **2753**

What shabby deceit in preaching![473] They say Christ did not go out into the desert or enter a monastery; he remained in the world: ergo—by saying this they think they have justified the unlimited worldliness in which the clergy live. No—but hold on! Undoubtedly Christ did not go out into the desert, did not enter a monastery; for him that would have been pure mitigation. He remained in the world—but not, however, to become decorated, a cabinet member, an honorary member of this and that, but to suffer. This was the advantage he had from remaining in the world, and this very advantage he would have avoided by entering a monastery.

Naturally the congregation listens to all this with sheer joy—the whole thing is secular-mindedness, and the only miracle is God's longsuffering, that such a rascal of a preacher does not suddenly get a stroke in the pulpit. Actually, he should have it there, just before he takes off his clerical gown to go over to the club.

IX A 404   *n.d.*, 1848

« **2754**

Today, the first day of Pentecost,[474] Mynster preached against monasteries and hermits—good Lord, to take the trouble to play on that string now in the nineteenth century in order to be rewarded with applause. He did not polemicize against a single one of the forms of evil prevailing today—heavens, no, that could have serious consequences for him—no, he polemicized against the monastery.

X³ A 56   *n.d.*, 1850

« **2755** *The Fraud*

If Cato Uticensis[475] had not taken his own life because it would have been greater not to, this would be significant. But that every grocery clerk who does not do away with himself is automatically greater than Cato is nonsense.

It is the same with Christianity in our day in relation to the ascetic and the candidate for the monastery.

X³ A 216   *n.d.*, 1850

« **2756** *Human Nonsense*

Today I spoke with an eminent ecclesiastic. He explained enthusiastically that what is really needed is mendicant monks and the like. But why is His Eminence himself not a mendicant monk? On that point it is not feasible to say: I *cannot,* for it depends solely upon the will. Consequently His Eminence prefers to occupy one of the high offices. But next Sunday he will preach movingly that what is really needed is mendicant monks.

And, in addition, suppose such a mendicant monk arose or emerged from among us—what would His Eminence do then? He would immediately use the occasion to exclaim: This is what I have said all along—and then he would almost come to think of himself as being the man, rather than of the ever greater guilt the longer and louder he had said that this was needed but without acting accordingly.

And in addition, if the mendicant monk were to live only one year, His Eminence would be among those crying that it is an exaggeration, an exaggeration—because now the matter would begin to be serious.

See, this eminent ecclesiastic comfortably holds a good appointment, watches carefully for better vacancies in order to make application. Amazing human nonsense! Just go in for nonsense—*there* is advancement and preferment. In this world there is no advancement for the truth; there is only demotion.

> X³ A 337   *n.d.*, 1850

« 2757

In answer to the charge that if we are all supposed to be monks the matter would become far too earnest, Chrysostom says: "In truth, it is not earnestness but a lack of earnestness which has destroyed everything."

> Neander, *Chrysostom,*[476] I., p. 22.
> X³ A 752   *n.d.*, 1851

« 2758 *Immured Monks*

I read in Neander's *Chrysostomus*[477] (II, p. 230) that there were even monks who went so far in their zeal that they had themselves walled in with just a little hole left through which they received food. The exiled Chrysostom met such a *monachus monachorum*[478] (μόναχος ἐγκεκλεισμένος, immured monk) in Nicæa and convinced him that it would be more God-pleasing to do something beneficial, and he became a missionary.

> X⁴ A 4   *n.d.*, 1851

« 2759 *Ruysbroek*

characterizes the corruption of the monks and says: "Was all this (the wholly secular way of life) the rule of Benedict or of Augustine? Many glosses and commentaries would be required to establish this."

I say the same: the way we are living—is this Christianity? There will have to be a great many glosses and commentaries, entire sciences, to get this out of the New Testament.

The passage by Ruysbroek is quoted from Ullmann, *Reformatoren vor der Reformation*[479] (1842), II, pp. 58–59.

x⁴ A 374   *n.d.*, 1851

« 2760 *"The Monastery"*

The error of the medieval monastic movement[480] was this. Asceticism, renunciation, and the like, were still an expression of an infinite passion and of Christianity's heterogeneity with the world. Therefore it all should have been done very simply; it should have explained to the monastic candidate that this alone was the requirement.

But instead something else occurred. The monastic candidate nevertheless made himself homogeneous with the world, for he allowed himself and his [conduct] to be regarded as the extraordinary, which was directly honored with the admiration of his contemporaries. This meant that the monastic candidate shared in the general scaling down of the Christian requirement. He did not make asceticism the requirement but made it a criterion of the way others lived and thus reaped admiration for doing the extraordinary. But such extraordinariness was made homogeneous with everything else secular.

In a similar manner the monastic candidate avoided persecution, suffering for the doctrine, etc. It is easy to see that asceticism and the like, existentially presented simply as the requirement required of everyone, would simply have made men furious. But when the ascetic is willing to accept the admiration of others and to let the others be exempted because of their admiration of him, then one can get involved even with asceticism.

The sign that Christianity had been reduced is the very emergence of the rank of extraordinary Christian. That helped! Instead of there being, Christianly, only one requirement for all of us, there was a progression: the Christian who was directly honored by admiration came to be the extraordinary, and flat secularism became the universally Christian.

Christianity received its first blow when the emperor became a Christian. The second, and far more dangerous blow, came when the category of the directly recognizable extraordinary Christian emerged. The error lay, as stated, not in entering the monastery but in the title of extraordinary Christian, which was directly honored with the admiration of the contemporaries.

$$X^4 \text{ A } 531 \quad n.d., \ 1852$$

« 2761 *The Monastery*

The usual interpretation is that it is cowardice which makes a person flee from the world into the monastery.

Well, perhaps it is the case sometimes that a person has doubts about being able to endure the bestial grinning and sniggering, the persecution and mistreatment, which are the necessary consequence of expressing "spirit" among animal creatures.

Yet it can also be looked at from another side: he flees because he does not have the heart to disturb the others, who he knows cannot be brought all the way out, and to whom he therefore will only be an affliction. Or, if you are honest, you who still prefer to delight in this life, enjoying it, bearing children who are also to enjoy it—would you really not prefer to get rid of a person who speaks of only one thing: to die, to die to the world? And would it not be a kind of consideration on his part to hide away, since the result of his remaining among you might be that you become far more guilty than you perhaps ever had thought possible, because the result would be that in order to protect yourself against such a person, you might have to persecute him bestially and thereby sink down to and into bestiality. When that idyllic enjoyment of life does not come in touch with "spirit," it becomes something even more beautiful, but, alas, in relation to spirit it becomes either spirit itself or bestiality.

$$XI^1 \text{ A } 85 \quad n.d., \ 1854$$

« 2762 *The Retreat*

It is a special sort of a retreat we should make.

Back to the monastery—the question must be brought back to the monastery from which Luther broke out (this is probably the truth). Yet this is not to say that the Pope is to be victorious or that the papal police should take over.

The monastery's error was not asceticism, celibacy, etc.[481] No, the error was that Christianity was reduced by allowing this to be regarded as pertaining to extraordinary Christians—and then all the purely secular nonsense as ordinary Christianity.

No, asceticism and everything belonging to it is merely a beginning, a condition for being able to be a witness to the truth.

Therefore the swing Luther made was in the wrong direction. There ought to be an increase, not a reduction.

This is why I have always wondered if there really isn't something wrong with the notion that God was with Lutheranism, for wherever God is along the advance to be made is marked by an increase in the demand and by greater difficulties. The mark of the human, on the other hand, is always that things are supposed to be made easier and that this relaxation is regarded as the forward step.

Consequently the error in the Middle Ages was not the monastery and asceticism but that basically the secular mentality had conquered in the monk's parading as the extraordinary Christian.

No, first the ascetic—this is the gymnastics—and then the witness to the truth—this very simply is what it means to be a Christian—and goodnight to all you millions and trillions and quadrillions.

Therefore Luther should either have made the turn in this way or should have made it clear that by his turn a further reduction was being made because of the increasing wretchedness of the human race.

XI[1] A 134   *n.d.*, 1854

« 2763 *Denmark*

Back to the monastery, from which Luther broke away, is the first cause for Christianity to take up.

Essentially providence uses only one power: time; it grants time and on a scale incomprehensible to a poor human being it grants errors time to develop completely in all their consequences.

In order to make apparent what nonsense, what dishonesty, and what corruption Protestantism is—if it is supposed to be religion, to be Christianity, rather than a necessary corrective at a given time—in order to make this properly apparent a country was needed which was not aided even by having Catholicism at its side, which was the case in Germany and other countries.

No, Protestantism had to go on its own, left completely to itself, in a country with even a language all its own.

This was needed in order to make it all apparent—a worldly-wise, pleasure-hungry, artistically-gifted Epicurean, a master in creating and maintaining appearances—such a man was required as a church-leader. Then, if he is granted a long life, the total depth of nonsense and confusion will be made manifest.

This has happened under Bishop Mynster—but of course the

country, the people, do not see it; they are completely satisfied with his kind of Christianity and with the Christian condition of the country.

Christianly this is just about as bad as it can be—yes, to use the predicate "Christian" for the condition of Denmark, even with the addition that the conditions are very poor, is really saying too much. If applied to Denmark the predicate Christian is ridiculous. Take an illustration. If a man comes along leading the most miserable nag of a horse, it is not ridiculous for him to declare it to be a horse. If, however, he comes along with a cow and says it is a horse, that is ridiculous. It does not help for him to concede that it is a poor horse. No, it is a cow.

Religiously Denmark is so low that it is not only inferior to what has been seen of Christianity hitherto but is inferior to Judaism—yes, the only analogy is found in the lowest forms of paganism—to such a degree has self-denial, the point in Christianity, been forgotten and to such a degree have earthly well-being and comfortable mediocrity been idolized.

Religion in this country consists essentially of getting married and then being active in earning a living, acquiring for oneself and his own, and yet—this is characteristic of Denmark—not without sympathy for those in need, especially the needy with families, for the business of family and livelihood is the earnestness of life. And if one is so fortunate as to acquire wealth, it is assumed in Denmark that he is particularly beloved of God.

And then, incidentally, one goes to church occasionally, once or twice a year to communion, pays the pastor his due—and that is Christianity.

$$\text{XI}^1 \text{ A } 198 \quad n.d., \ 1854$$

« 2764 *The Monastery*

dropped out. In place of monasticism's unreasonable worship there appeared the true Christian worship, for we, we Protestants, we do not flee like cowards from life, and neither did Christ—no, we remain, as did Christ, in the world—lost in unmitigated profane secularism, worse than paganism.

What great and true Christian progress! The truth is that the secular mentality won out so completely that it no longer would tolerate the presence of the monastery, which was still a reminder of the heterogeneity of Christianity.

We remain—just as Christ did—in the world! What a superb big lie for hypocritical, lying orators! If great achievements are the theme for speakers generally, this duplicity and falsification is for hypocritical orators.

XI¹ A 263   n.d.,   1854

« 2765 *To Enter a Monastery Is Cowardly— No, Remain in the World!*[482]

What the world wanted and wants is to have Christianity abolished. But in its shrewdness the world has instinctively understood that Christianity is most effectively abolished when the appearance of having it is still maintained.

Therefore "to enter a monastery is cowardly; no, remain in the world" became the watchword. For the world shrewdly understood that the kind of people who are able to express Christianity's heterogeneity on the street, in the midst of the actuality of life, are no longer to be found; the race has long been too corrupt for that. Consequently, let us just prevent them from entering the monastery; then we will surely have the upper hand and can force them to express our own world in the name of Christianity.

And it succeeded. It has been achieved, particularly in Protestantism, particularly in Denmark. The end result achieved is that every predicate which Christianity uses to indicate what it is to be a Christian, heterogeneity with the world, is like a satire upon a Christendom which has become completely homogeneous with the world.

XI¹ A 443   n.d.,   1854

MONEY

« **2766**

The public would rather have a Jewish peddler[483] of buggy whip ribbons as an author, because him they can really treat shabbily. The most gracious public is amused and gratified that they can dignifiedly purchase the gifts of the mind and spirit for a few dollars and then kick the Jew. Of course no one but an author can offer such terms, to stand in his shop grovelling and bargaining to this extent—just so he earns money.

VII[1] A 67   *n.d.*, 1846

« **2767**

That there are publishers, that there are men whose virtually entire existence expresses that books are a commodity and an author a merchant, is an altogether immoral situation. Inasmuch as the monetary factor enters into an intellectual undertaking (which being an author is) in that he is paid, gets honoraria etc., the one who essentially carries out the intellectual undertaking should himself take over the financial side, not because of a possibly greater financial reward, far from it, but in order that there can be a little modesty. If the financial arrangement is formulated as a way of making a living by a total outsider, this so easily leads to impudence and effrontery. There are plenty examples of publisher-effrontery; the effrontery consists of unreservedly going to the extreme in regarding intellectual productions as commodities. Then again the money factor gives the public power over the publisher, and the financial relation gives the publisher power over the author, and therefore the author (who in money matters ought to be as bashful and modest as a girl with respect to selling her virtue) perhaps at times sits and blushes and feels violated but has no power to prevail.

Let us assume that it became customary for a clergyman to have a business manager who would collect his money, tithes, offerings, etc., which is quite all right inasmuch as the business manager is in the clergyman's service. But let us suppose that this became an independent way of making a living and that such a business manager would pay the clergyman his wages and now himself made the plans and had only a financial interest in the pastor's standing with the congregation. What then? Well, this would result in the practice that the pastor, every Saturday night upon finishing his sermon, would go over to the business manager and let him see it. And the business manager would say: "If your Reverence talks this way, no one will come to church, and, damn it all, there goes the offering plate money, and in that case I can't guarantee much for this year, which, after all, is to your own interest. No, you must butter up the congregation a little; let me tell you how. If I am not quite up to writing a sermon, I do understand very well the times we live in and what the congregation wants."

I imagine the pastor would flush with embarrassment and say: "Have I been appointed teacher in order to flatter the congregation and for you to earn money?" But the business manager answers: "I have no time for hysterics, high-mindedness, and all that. Everyone is a thief in his own job, and my job is to see to it that Your Reverence satisfies the times."

So it goes between the clergyman and the business manager. The nauseousness of the moneyman's sniffing at the sermon and judging it commercially is revolting enough. And yet is not the business manager supported in the same way as a publisher, whose financial outlook finds acceptance by all the mercenaries of the daily press.

But without modesty there is no true intellectual–spiritual relationship; but how is the author's possible modesty to be of any good to the reader when it has to go through this medium of effrontery: money, money, money, the demands of the time, money, money.

VII^1 A 77   *n.d.*, 1846

« **2768**

Money is the numerator; mercy[484] the denominator. But the denominator is still the more important.

VIII^1 A 209   *n.d.*, 1847

« **2769**

δίκαιος actually means: equal, and according to what Rosenvinge[485] has told me, somewhere in Xenophon's *Cyropædia*[486] it is found used in this way about a carriage.

In the Gospel about the unfaithful steward the expression "unrighteous mammon" is understood to mean unequal mammon—that is, mammon, which has the quality of confirming the distinctions between man and man and in an altogether indifferent way (that is, unrighteous). For this is the very nature of "money."

x^1 A 55   *n.d.*, 1849

« 2770 *Aphorism*

See p. 158 in this journal [i.e., x^1 A 666].

It is one thing to be a prophet (*profiteri*) of a faith, a science, a capability, and something else to make a profit (*Profit*) on it.

x^2 A 5   *n.d.*, 1849

« 2771 *Finite Aims*

Yes, when you live together with men in the herd, if you have financial means, how completely natural it is for you to enjoy life by means of it, and if you have no financial means, how completely natural for you to see about getting something to live on, devoting most of your time to acquiring an ample income and enjoying life as much as possible.

But be alone with God and then see if it is so natural, see if he does not confiscate your financial assets and either require you to give them up or take your life into his service to such an extent that you become an outright laborer. And if you have no financial assets, will he not ask if you cannot restrict your necessities, use less, in order to get all the more time to work in his service. Is it not like swindling God when you too quickly and too energetically arrange your life so as to serve finite goals and thereby your own convenience, your own enjoyment of life.

This, you see, was the meaning of "poverty," as found also in paganism.

But by erecting a caricature of the Middle Ages it is so very easy to get the whole matter shoved to one side.

x^4 A 263   *n.d.*, 1851

« 2772 *Indignation*

In dead seriousness I require that everyone who wants to be involved with me shall double his pledge to the church budget.

Nothing weakens the impression made by moral pathos more than bringing money[487] into the matter. If someone wanted to express indignation by refusing to pay his church contribution, the whole thing can be explained as his desire to save the money. No, double the church contribution—but stop going to church.

The punishment[488] I should like the clergy to have is a tenfold increase in salary for each one—but not a person in church. But this, of course, like everything of mine, according to Bishop Mynster, is "much too high." I am afraid that neither the world nor the clergy would understand this punishment. At the same time it is the truest punishment and entirely within the idea.

Let us make a thought experiment—if someone could prove conclusively (not in the sense in which I speak of the nonexistence of Christianity)—no, if he could prove that Christ had never existed at all, nor the apostles, that the whole thing is a fabrication, and then if nothing was done by the state and the congregations, no hint of abolishing all these clerical jobs—I wonder how many clergymen would resign. If the matter were not so serious, it would be exceedingly ridiculous for the preachers and their families to go on calmly living off Christianity.

Yes, in the long run, perhaps the greatest support Christianity has in our time is not the cleverness of the government etc., but the fear of an enormous financial upheaval.[489] It is also entirely certain that the bankruptcy of ten Rothschilds would not result in such a great upheaval as would occur if Christianity went out of business.

XI² A 22   n.d., 1854

« 2773 *Sigh*

Would to God that there were not one single person with a pecuniary interest[490] in our being Christians—that is, in our calling ourselves Christians. If that day ever comes, Christianity will once more become a possibility!

What a dreadful responsibility—to appoint by the thousands men who have a pecuniary interest in our calling ourselves Christians; what a dreadful responsibility, and doubly, doubly confusing that it is done, as they say, in the interest of Christianity.

Suppose the state got the idea of appointing, by the thousands, men who have a pecuniary interest in our calling ourselves poets. Would this not mean that from then on there would be no more poets? O, if poetry did not completely forsake us men, would it not shout: Away with them, away with them, for Satan's sake or in God's name; get rid of these thousands so that there is not one single man with a pecuniary interest in our being, that is, in our calling ourselves, poets —and on that day a poet will once again be possible.

XI² A 363   n.d., 1854

« 2774 Where Does the State Get the Money with Which It Pays Teachers of Christianity?

Somewhere else [i.e., xɪ² A 263] I have pointed out what dreadful confusion has arisen because someone got the disastrous idea of introducing the pecuniary element into Christianity, which has produced an enormous illusion, to the ruination of Christianity, and created an ambiguity that has fostered hypocrites or troubled consciences. O, if Christianity ever shakes off this ambiguity, it will be like awakening from a hard, heavy sleep of troubled dreams!

I have always thought of the role of the state as being similar to that of, for example, a millionaire who got the idea of paying thousands of teachers of Christianity out of his own pocket and to whom one then must say: For God's sake, stop! Do not risk this blasphemy! Don't you know it is high treason against Christianity! Don't you know it is not Christianity you are serving but Satan, for one can give all his money to the poor in order to serve Christianity in poverty, but one cannot serve Christianity with contributions of money—this confuses Christianity with precisely that which it is not, an ordinary human enterprise. And yet by paying thousands of teachers of Christianity a private individual could not occasion as great a confusion as the state does when it pays them. The private individual, after all, has no authority, he has only money, but the fact that the state pays teachers has created the additional confusion of abolishing the authority of Christianity and substituting the authority of the state, thus creating the idea —infinite confusion!—that one cannot be a proper teacher of Christianity unless he is a public official, that is, unless he is authorized by the state.

Thus I have assumed the state, which pays the teachers of Christianity, to be like a private millionaire. But now I will raise the question: Where does the state get the money with which it pays the teachers of Christianity? Now we see from a new angle how infinitely confusing and corrupting this whole thing is, since the state itself acquires the money by falsifying Christianity in one way or another; the falsifying of what Christianity is brings in the money, and this money again buys the falsification of what Christianity is.

Actually it may be said that the state has turned the suffering and death of Christ into money. The fact that Christ by his suffering and death has saved men and won an eternal salvation (which, however, in the New Testament is always proclaimed in such a way that it is just as much, just exactly as much, a commitment as it is a gift to men, which is why instead of becoming a gift it becomes most demoralizing to all who do not receive it rightly by relating to it in commitment) this has been made simply and solely a gift. Had attention been called to the other side, to the commitment, it would never have occurred to any reasonable man to behave as the state has behaved [*changed from:* to force this upon men directly].

The suffering and death of Christ has been made pure gift; by letting all obligations and commitment be removed, all *Notabenes* have been disposed of, and thus Christianity has become utterly and outrightly an outright gift, a present. The state then took over or availed itself of this infinite gift, this colossal good, and interposed itself as the middle term between Christ and the individual, which confuses Christianity at the deepest level.

This is how that state has taken over Christianity; it has said something like this: We are going to see to it that men share in this great, priceless good (salvation by Christ); not only are we responsible for your getting a Tivoli, but an eternal salvation, too, is obtainable only from us. According to the size of the country, it will cost so and so many thousands—and now an estimate is made of how many thousands of dollars the teachers need—this is how the money is procured.

But if it is assumed that the value of Christ's suffering and death is measurable (commensurable) in money, then it is really simply and solely Christ's prerogative to say: It costs so and so much. On the other hand, it is a dreadful outrage for a third party to force himself in between Christ and the individual and say: It costs so and so much.

But this is what the state has done, it has perpetrated what according to the New Testament must be called a robber-assault or a swindle, and on a grand scale, on so grand a scale that the robbers, the swindlers, do not, as is customary, end up in prison, but the person who will not voluntarily let himself be assaulted and swindled ends up in prison. And it is the state that does it, the state from which one usually seeks help against robbers and swindlers! And the state thinks it is doing this in the interest of Christianity—yes, of course, if it can be in Christianity's interest to be thoroughly confused.

Thus, again, how infinitely confusing and corrupting it is for the state to want to help Christianity financially! No good will come of it until the relationship becomes natural again. Let Christianity take care of itself; it can do so very nicely; by the living God, it is not in bad straits. You have a fixed idea, most Honorable State, if you think it needs your help, or is it one of your tricks that in the name of serving Christianity you have wanted to utilize Christianity, perhaps in order to dominate men all the better, as if the state controlled or had the slightest influence on the decision: an eternal salvation. No, let Christianity shift for itself. And if there are some who want to use Christianity to swindle people, blackmail them, then let us just turn to the state, the police, to get protection against swindlers.

XI³ B 115   *n.d.,* 1855

MONTAIGNE

« 2775

Montaigne[491] put it well: "I have not studied in order to write a book, but I have studied what I have written in the book." IV, p. 270 (book 2, chapter 18).

VIII[1] A 289   n.d., 1847

« 2776

A good observation by Montaigne,[492] bk. 2, ch. 12 (III, p. 263): *Wir* (we Christians) *sollten uns schämen, dass noch nie ein Anhänger einer menschlichen Sekte erfunden ward, so sonderbar und schwer auch ihre Behauptungen waren, der nicht gewissermassen sein Betragen und Leben darnach einrichtete! Und eine so göttliche und himmlische Lehre* (Christianity) *zeichnet die Christen durch nichts anders aus als durch die Sprache.*[493]—See Spinoza *Tractatus theol. pol.*, Intro., p. 85: *jam dadum enim res eo pervenit, ut neminem fere, quisnam sit, num scilicet Christianus, Turca, Judæus vel Ethnicus noscere possis nisi ex corporis externo habitu et cultu, vel quod hanc aut illam ecclesiam frequentet, vel denique quod huic aut illi opinioni addictus est, et in verba alicujus magistri jurare solet. Caeterum vita eadem omnibus est.*[494]

VIII[1] A 315   n.d., 1847

« 2777

It is a good proverb:

> *Wer spinnt zu fein*
> *Haspelt sich ein,*[495]

which is actually an Italian proverb:

> *Chi troppo assotiglia, si scavezza.*[496]

VIII[1] A 318   n.d., 1847

« 2778

In Montaigne,[497] bk. II, chapter 16 (about honor, renown) these splendid words by a sailor are to be found:

My God, you can save me if you will; if you want to, you can also let me sink: but I constantly hold my rudder straight.

That was a good motto.

X[3] A 371   n.d., 1850

« **2779**

Nothing fastens a thing deeper in our memory than the wish—to forget it.

> Montaigne. Somewhere in book 2, chapter 12, in German translation I am reading; it is page 395.
>
> x^3 A 412   *n.d.*, 1850

« **2780**

Montaigne[498] says somewhere (in vol. V): It is not enough for those who are supposed to govern to have a sound understanding of human nature, not enough to be able to do what we are able to do. If they do not stand high above us, they stand far below us.

> x^3 A 459   *n.d.*, 1850

« **2781**

Montaigne:[499] Everyone is careful in going to confession—one should rather be careful in acting. Boldness in making mistakes is put right again to a degree and is held in check by boldness in confessing one's mistakes.

> x^3 A 480   *n.d.*, 1850

« **2782** *Montaigne*

It is superbly stated (book 1, chapter 28, on solitude[500]): As far as the smooth words behind which ambition and covetousness (perhaps he ought to have added addiction to sensual pleasures) hide are concerned, "we are not in this world for our own sakes but for the sake of the universal best" (and that we therefore must not withdraw into solitude); therefore we want to appeal to your conscience, you who are about to lead off the dance (you who are now playing an official role) and have you lay your hand on your heart and say: I wonder if it is not just the opposite, I wonder if position and office and the hubbub of the world are not sought in order to profit from the universal; the wretched means used to push oneself ahead clearly show that the aims do not amount to much.

This is excellent; also this—that by using inferior means one proves pointblank mediocre aims, which is extraordinarily t ue.

> x^3 A 503   *n.d.*, 1850

« **2783** *Aristotle's proverbial saying:*

O, my friends, a friend is not to be found any more.

> (Montaigne,[501] book 1, chapter 27.)
>
> x^3 A 508   *n.d.*, 1850

« **2784**

Montaigne[502] declares somewhere that as far as he knows man is the only creature whose worth is determined by what he has on (titles, external circumstances, etc). It would never occur to anyone to determine a horse's worth by its saddle or a dog by its collar.

x³ A 513   *n.d.,* 1850

MOZART

« **2785**

Elvira[503] (in *Don Juan*) is really not a character; she lacks the required definite and more explicit contours; she is a transparent, diaphanous figure, through which we see the finger of God, providence, which in a way mitigates the impression of the all too vindictive nemesis in the Commander, because it continually opens for D. J. the possibility of escaping it. Elvira is all too ethereal for a character; she is like the fairy maidens who have no back.

I A 240   September 13, 1836

« **2786**

How is the Page in *Figaro* related to D. Juan?

I A 270   November 10, 1836

« **2787**

The old man I met in the theater who had been going to see *Don Juan* for thirty years (tradition).

I A 278   *n.d.*, 1836

« **2788**

If Mozart lived now and were to compose music for *Don Juan* and consequently were in the position of having to use dance music, would it be proper to use galop music, or would the surging, hopeless music be in direct contrast to Don Juan's character; on the other hand, the charming, graceful, unfolding minuet harmonizes splendidly with D. J.'s enjoyment, just as its propriety is splendidly satirized by D. J.'s laxity. The only time D. J. could dance a galop would be with the Commander in the last act, if his vitality would be adequate to whirl him and instil in him the requisite zest for life.

I A 291   *n.d.*, 1836

« **2789**

In certain respects I can say of Don Juan what Elvira says to him: "You murderer of my happiness"[504]—

for to tell the truth it is this piece which affected me so diabolically that I can never forget it; it was this piece which drove me, like Elvira, out of the cloister's quiet night.

II A 491   *n.d.,* 1839

« **2790**

Those two familiar violin strains, which Mozart uses with his boundless genius to dialecticize his Don Juan out of morality's substantial, inexplicable, mute depths, show him vanishing or, more correctly, let him vanish far off in the horizon, in a twinkling let him run away like a shadow far beyond the farthest streak of horizon, as if there were an infinity between these two powers, as if the whole world lay between these two worlds— those two violin strains, this very moment, here in the middle of the street——have I lost my mind?——Is it my ears, which for love of Mozart's music have ceased to hear?——Is this the reward of the god, to give unfortunate me, who sits like the lame and the blind at the entrance to the temple of music and begs from those who enter, to give me ears which themselves present what they hear? Only those two violin strains—for now I hear nothing more. Just as in that immortal overture they spring forth from the deep choral tones, so here they leap at me from the din and hubbub of the street with the complete surprise of a revelation. It must be close by, for now I hear his light dance again. Those passing by probably think I have lost my mind; I imagine that my face looks like a question mark, asking: Don't you hear anything? Answer: I beg your pardon? —There is of course a confounded racket. ——Now I see them: So it is to you, you two unfortunate artists, I owe this surprise! —One was probably 17 years old, wearing a green Kalmuk coat with large bone buttons; the coat itself was too large for him. He held the violin tightly under his chin, his cap was pulled down over his eyes, his hand was concealed in a fingerless glove, and his fingers were red and blue with cold. The other one was older and wore a chenille coat. Both were blind. A little girl, who presumably guided them, stood in front of them and thrust her hands under her scarf. We gathered one by one, a few admirers of these melodies—a postman with his mailbag, a little boy, a couple of dock workers. The elegant carriages rolled noisily by; the carts and wagons drowned out the melodies, which occasionally emerged fragmentarily from the engulfing noise.

For me it was a tryst.[505]

III B 179:34   *n.d.,* 1841–42

« **2791**

[*Underlined in copy of* Either/Or:]

Immortal Mozart! You to whom I owe everything, to whom I owe *the loss of my mind.* [506]

Added:

This is no mere phrase; it is an expression for the imagination's wild melancholy, which in the next moment reveals itself as tranquil melancholy and thus alternates.

IV A 224   *n.d.,* 1843

MYSTERY

« 2792

. . . . . how the doctrine of God's justice and of man's sin concentrically merges in the mystery of the Atonement.[507]

VIII² B 133:5   n.d., 1847

« 2793

There has been much discussion about the passage in Scripture:[508] All is revealed in the mystery; and a certain speculation has affirmed that it was not profane speculation but in the mystery.[509]

In relation to Christianity, I would emphasize another side of the concept *mystery:* the ethical-religious. Christianity entered as a mystery; the greatest possible human guarantee was required for admittance—how profane Christianity has been made now by the slipshod way in which everyone is made a Christian as a matter of course and everyone is assumed to be one!

Christianity understood very well that serving the truth depends particularly upon the transformation of the individual so that he becomes shaped to be an instrument of the truth. But in our objective, activist age no one gives a thought to such things. Therefore this woeful preaching of Christianity—objectively quite correct—by men who really have no intimation of Christianity. Nothing, nothing has to such a degree confused, yes, abolished Christianity as the unchristian way in which it is preached.

Certainly Christianity has never been a mystery, has in fact abhorred mystery, in the sense of being only for a few superlative people who have been initiated. No, God has chosen the poor and the despised[510]—but the initiation was not lacking. It is not an intellectual initiation but an ethical initiation, personality's enormous respect for being admitted into the Christian community, a respect expressed not in assurances and frills but existentially in action.

Do not I, a poor insignificant human being in my scrap of existence, experience something comparable? Transform me into a few doctrines and let every dabbler teach them, although his life is a satire on what he says: would not this be meaningless? How am I different? I wonder if it is not in this, that in striving I nevertheless have transformed my individuality in order existentially to serve my thought. That is, I have had an initiation. Therefore the little I have has been a power, and to pontificate about it would merely add a little nonsense to all the other nonsense.

Therefore I never forget that in Christianity a shoemaker, a tailor, a manual laborer is just as much a possibility as the greatest scholar and the keenest intellectual. Yes, in general the Church must always expect its salvation from a layman, simply because he is closer to the ethical initiation.

x^2 A 341   *n.d.*, 1850

MYSTIC, MYSTICISM

« 2794

May not Matthew 11:12 properly be interpreted as referring to the mystics (here I am giving this verse a wider meaning, whereby it can apply outside the sphere of theology also), who think that they have a direct relationship to God and consequently will not acknowledge that all men have only an indirect relationship (the Church—in the political domain, the state.).

I A 168   June 6, 1836

« 2795

Mysticism does not have the patience to wait for God's revelation.

III A 8   July 11, 1840

« 2796

As with certain bird cries, we hear[511] a mystic only in the stillness of the night; for this reason a mystic generally does not have as much significance for his noisy contemporaries as for the listening kindred spirit in the stillness of history after the passage of time.

III A 70   n.d., 1840

« 2797

The system *begins* with "nothing"; the mystic always ends with "nothing."[512] The latter is the divine nothing, just as Socrates' ignorance was devout fear of God, the ignorance with which he did not begin but ended, or which he continually reached.

X^2 A 340   n.d., 1850

MYTH, MYTHOLOGY

« 2798

What is involved in the concept *myth* and *mythology*—does not every age have its mythology—Novalis etc.—how is it different from poetry (the subjunctive—the novel, poetic prose)—a hypothetical proposition in the indicative.[513]

I A 241   September 13, 1836

« 2799

Mythology is the compacting (suppressed being) of eternity (the eternal idea) in the categories of time and space—in time, for example, Chiliasm or the doctrine of a kingdom of heaven which begins in time*; in space, for example, an idea construed as being a finite personality. Just as the poetic is the subjunctive but does not claim to be more (poetic actuality), mythology, on the other hand, is a hypothetical statement in the indicative[514] (see p. 1 of this book [i.e., I A 241]) and lies in the very middle of the conflict between them, because the ideal, losing its gravity, is compacted in earthly form.—

* Therefore it is in a certain sense basically comical to think of Pastor Stiefel (contemporary with Luther), who predicted the end of the world at a certain hour and gathered his congregation in the church, but nothing happened; however, it could easily have become the end of him, because the people became so embittered that they nearly killed him.

I A 300   *n.d.,* 1836

« 2800

Scandinavian mythology killed itself, just as Solon ordered his laws to be burned 100 years after his death.—

II A 587   February, 1837

« 2801

The legend found among various peoples concerning their most distinguished men, their heroes, bring to mind those words in Genesis[515] (You shall bruise its head when it wounds your heel), because these heroes are vulnerable only in the heel—(Krishna, Hercules, Baldur).

II A 99   June 26, 1837

« **2802**

. . . . . just as when certain geniuses abrogate the whole meaning of mythology in their zeal to bring every myth before their "eagle eye," to make it a capriccioso for their "mouth organ." This is the way concepts and myths are frequently prostituted in the world.[516]

V B 53:35   *n.d.,* 1844

« **2803**

Faith is quite correctly "the point outside the world" which therefore also moves the whole world.

It is easy to perceive that what bursts forth through a negation of all points in the world is the point outside the world.

The syllogism that there is no righteousness in the world but only unrighteousness and from that to prove that there is righteousness—this must indeed be outside the world. Here, then, is the point outside. This is the syllogism of faith.

Consider the absurd. The negating of all concepts forces one outside the world, to the absurd—and here is faith.

Alas, but faith has not been found in the world for a long, long time—and therefore neither does it move the world. Faith has let itself be fooled and has become a point within the world, and therefore at best it moves as does any other point within the world, occasioning transactions of modest probability and initiating a few minor incidents —but it does not move as the point outside.

Christianity did move in this way when it entered the world, but the world, which certainly does not want such a point out there which would hold the world in continuous fear and trembling, fooled itself or Christianity and brought Christianity inside. From being a point outside the world Christianity—they imagine—became the established.

Everything came to a halt. Lately they have been busy proving that early Christianity is myth[517]—well, why not, since we are not aware that the later version is more like a myth or a fable. It all depends upon the point of departure. But to me it seems illuminating that Christianity in its present form is the most fabulous thing imaginable.

If a one-time king now lives on Knabro Street as a bartender, one is easily tempted, especially if he finds him to be a slap-happy, self-satisfied, contented bartender, to regard his original kingship as a myth. And this may be right, for the person's identity in this case is certain. But we should be careful about applying this directly to Christianity. To be sure, there is something called Christianity. The fact that millions happen to call something Christianity which does not resemble Christianity any more than the bartender resembles a king certainly does not make it Christianity.

Now the matter takes a turn. In its original form Christianity is in its proper medium— its form is the reduplication of its content. There is nothing mythical here. Now reduplication has been taken away—and therefore Christendom is simply myth.[518]

There are two kinds of incognito:[519] in the form of a servant Christ was God; in the form of the God-man Christendom [Christenheden] is paganism [Hedenskab]. In the former incognito there is no contradiction; in the latter hodgepodge there is a self-contradiction and from this arises the mythical—unless one wishes bluntly to call it a lie. Sweep in front of your own door first, get rid of the lie, and then this matter of myth will be settled—that is, the minute it is seen that Christendom is a lie, a deception, the very same minute it will be seen that original Christianity was anything but myth.

Here again the tactic runs counter to custom. There should be no counterarguments demonstrating that Christianity is not myth; it is not to be defended etc. No, there should be attack; Christendom should be proved to be a fable, and then we will be rid of this question of myth.

x^2 A 529 _n.d.,_ 1850

« 2804 _Fraud_

Even with the best of intentions a child cannot grasp Christianity except as mythology;[520] the eater alters the meat.

This is why we are so preoccupied in Christendom with child-faith, the childlike, for in this way we get a sentimental mythology for Christianity—but what about "imitation" [Efterfølgelsen]!

Basically Christendom has made an attempt to let "the child" decide what Christianity is—and then we exploit the child's transformation of Christianity into mythology—which was done innocently by the child—and we use it in order to shirk from whatever does not please us, and we wallow in sentimentality.

x^4 A 519 _n.d.,_ 1852

« 2805 _A Christian Nota Bene_

Anyone whose life [Leven], whose existence [Existeren], is not characterized by the existence-form defined in the New Testament thereby expresses—regardless of what his mouth babbles, declaims, assures—that for him Christianity is mythology, poetry.[521]

The existential is the characteristic that distinguishes between poetry and mythology—and Christianity. Indeed, the reason Christ proclaimed Christianity is discipleship or imitation [*Efterfølgelse*] was to prevent a merely imaginary relationship to the essentially Christian.

Only in relation to poetry and mythology can the individual reasonably have the freedom to plan his life accordingly or not. But here again it is implicit that what the individual applies this freedom to is for him merely mythology, poetry.

But if Christianity is merely mythology, poetry, then the individual is no doubt exempted from the strenuousness of a judgment and an accounting, but he has also exempted himself from Christianity's promises of eternal salvation.

The only thing the individual will be unable to exempt himself from is the punishment eternity will be obliged to set on this; for no matter how much the individual exempts himself, Christianity nevertheless takes the freedom of giving him to understand, if possible, that Christianity is not poetry or mythology.

XI^1 A 217   *n.d.,* 1854

NATURAL SCIENCES

« **2806**

There are probably few branches of knowledge which bestow on man the serene and happy frame of mind as do the natural sciences. He goes out into nature and everything is familiar to him; it is as if he had talked previously with the plants and animals. He not only sees what use man can make of them (this is something quite subordinate), but he sees their significance in the whole universe. He stands like Adam[522] of old—all the animals come to him, and he gives them names.

I A 31   November 22, 1834

« **2807** *The Highest Potentiation of Immediacy or of the Dialectic of Feeling—in Relation to Natural Science*

If I were to imagine a girl very much in love and some man who wanted to use all his reason and knowledge to ridicule her passion, there could scarcely be any question of the enamored girl's having to choose between keeping her treasure and being ridiculed for it. Not at all. But if an extremely cold and calculating fellow calmly told the young girl: I shall explain to you what love is, and if the girl confessed that everything he said was absolutely correct, I wonder if she would choose his miserable common sense instead of her treasure. I wonder if the young girl would not say to him, "What you say is quite right; I, too, can understand it very well, and yet there is one thing which I do not understand. I do not understand how you can speak so calmly and coldly about this, something which affects me so deeply. Obviously we must not be talking about the same thing, since the effects are so very different." All honor to the young lady for this appropriate retort —on her lips so moving, and on the lips of a wise man so ironical— impugning reason and the relationship of reason to enthusiasm and rapture. It is easy to see that one loses out by choosing reason when this so-called reason (enlightenment, speculation, etc.) puts something presumptuous in place of faith and immediacy. But even when reason seemingly would provide the same thing, only in a different form, it is still a great loss. Here it is a question of choice. One can choose not to let himself be chilled by reason, can choose to hold on to rapture and enthusiasm, in faith and in confidence.

There might seem to be a difficulty here insofar as science and the zeal to understand have inspired devotees and followers, and inasmuch as understanding and enthusiasm in this sense do not seem to be opposed to one another. At the same time it should be noted that an observer, a natural scientist, etc., for example, who is really enthusiastic about grasping and understanding, does not himself discern that he continually posits what he seeks to abrogate. He is enthusiastic about understanding everything else, but the fact that he himself is enthusiastic he does not come to understand, i.e., he does not conceptualize his own enthusiasm at the same time that he is enthusiastic about conceptualizing everything else.[523]

One or the other must be the case: *either* the conceptualizer has grown cold, but then all his conceptualizing is a loss in comparison with his enthusiasm, even if he conceives it correctly, *or* he must be enthusiastic in his striving to conceptualize, but then he presupposes the enthusiasm itself as an ultimate inexplicable which sustains him.

In our time it is the natural sciences which are especially dangerous. Physiology will ultimately extend itself to the point of embracing ethics.[524] There are already sufficient clues of a new endeavor—to treat ethics as physics, whereby all of ethics becomes illusory and ethics in the race is treated statistically by averages or is calculated as one calculates vibrations in laws of nature.

A physiologist takes it upon himself to explain all mankind. The question here is, first and foremost, *principiis obsta:* What do I have to do with this. Why should I need to know about afferent and efferent nerve-impulses, about the circulation of blood, about the human being's microscopic condition in the womb. *The ethical has tasks enough for me.* Do I need to know the digestive process in order to eat? Do I need to know the processes of the nervous system—in order to believe in God and to love men? And if someone now says: Well, true enough, for this one does not need such knowledge, then I shall ask again: I wonder if I am not weakening my whole ethical passion by becoming a natural scientist? And I wonder if, with all this diverse knowledge of analogies, of abnormalities, of this and that, I do not lose more and more the impress of the ethical: the *you shall,* it is *you* yourself, you do not have to do with a single other person; even if heaven and earth collapse, YOU SHALL. I wonder if it is not a way of providing myself with a lot of sly evasions and excuses. I wonder if my gaze is not turned away from the most important thing by letting myself begin with physiology, instead of assuming the whole of physiology and saying: Begin.

Think of a brilliant physiologist (those mere butcher-apprentices who think they can explain everything with a knife and with a microscope are an abomination to me)—what does he do? First and foremost he grants that every transition is a leap, that he cannot explain how a consciousness comes into existence [*bliver til*] or how a consciousness of the environment becomes self-consciousness or God-consciousness; he concedes that no matter how much he explains the nervous system, he cannot explain the essentially constitutive, the idea. A brilliant physiologist admits that there is no analogy between animals and men; in short, he admits the qualitative dialectic. Consequently he admits categorically that he really cannot explain anything. But what does he do then? He skeletonizes, he dissects, he pierces with knives as far in as he can, in order to show—that he cannot! If someone knew that even though he picked every leaf from the flower, separated the fibers of the stem, and observed every part microscopically, and still could not explain what is constitutive in plants—why does he do it then? Or is he not keeping the student in a completely wrong kind of self-contradiction? Instead of saying summarily, "I cannot understand this," he encumbers the student with a mass of detail and very fascinating, engaging knowledge, which nevertheless always ends with the fact that he cannot, after all, explain the ultimate. But it is precisely this kind of preoccupation with much knowledge which results in one's losing the impress of the purely ethical. Instead of hungrily beginning to eat, instead of enthusiastically beginning with the ethical, lightly armed and unencumbered with any knowledge about the nervous system, ganglia, and blood-circulation etc., one becomes preoccupied with knowledge about digestion and the quasi-knowledge that in spite of all *this* one is still unable to explain the ultimate.

Let us consider the problem of freedom and necessity. Let the physiologist begin to explain fully how the circulation of the blood influences so and so in a specific way and how pressure upon the nerves has such and such effects, etc., etc.—ultimately he is still unable to explain that freedom is an illusion. When he had completed his four volumes full of statistics and oddities, he is forced to declare: But ultimately we must stop in wonder. Why then all this knowledge? Actually, isn't this playing a hoax on man? Isn't this tricking him little by little out of enthusiasm and maintaining him in the delusion that

some day, with the aid of bigger and better microscopes, he will succeed in discovering that freedom was an illusion and that it is all a
mechanism of nature?

All knowledge has something captivating about it, but on the
other hand, it also alters the entire state of the knower's mind. The
objectivity, the disinterestedness with which a physiologist counts the
pulse-beats and studies the nervous system has no relationship to
ethical enthusiasm.[*] And when the physiologist has written the extraordinary, the most extraordinary four volumes full of the most
amazing observations, he nevertheless personally admits—if he is truly
honest and brilliant—that he has not explained the ultimate, the ultimate which is the beginning and the end of ethics. And when the
reader has read through the four-volume set and has admired the
physiologist, his mood has really altered little by little. One does not
therefore say that the ethical is obscurantist, fearful of light, etc.—no,
but that the ethical is an enemy of a knowledge which, after occupying
a man's whole life, finally ends with his not being able to explain the
most important thing of all.

Imagine the most infamous criminal who has ever lived and suppose that physiology at the time had on its nose the most wonderful
pair of spectacles there ever was so it could now explain the criminal,
that the whole thing was a natural necessity, that his brain was too
small, etc. —how horrible this exemption from subsequent indictment
in comparison with Christianity's judgment upon him, that he will go
to hell if he does not repent.[525]

VII[1] A 182   n.d., 1846

« 2808

[*] In margin of 2807 (VII[1] A 182):
Scientific admiration of the subtlety of nature in human physiology is completely heterogeneous, yes, is heresy, with respect to the
ethical, which has nothing to do with admiration but only with YOU
SHALL.

VII[1] A 183   n.d.,

« 2809

Most of what flourishes nowadays under the name of science and
scholarship (especially the natural sciences) is not science at all but
curiosity. —Ultimately all corruption will come from the natural sciences. —
Many admirers (Un sot trouve toujours un autre sot qui l'admire[526]) believe

that carrying out investigations microscopically is synonymous with scientific earnestness. Foolish superstitious belief in the microscope—no, with the aid of microscopic observation curiosity simply becomes more comical. That a man simply and profoundly says: "I cannot see with the naked eye how consciousness comes into existence" is entirely in order. But for a man to peer through a microscope and look and look and look—and still not see it—this is comical, and that this is supposed to be earnestness is especially ridiculous. To regard the invention of the microscope as a bit of fun, a minor diversion, may be all right, but to regard it as earnestness is exceedingly obtuse. The art of printing books is already an almost satirical invention, and, good Lord, has it really proved that there are very many who actually have anything to communicate? Consequently, this tremendous invention has aided the broadcast of all that rubbish which otherwise would have perished at birth. —If God were to walk around with a cane in his hand, it would fall particularly upon all those earnest observers employing the microscope. With his cane God would pound all the hypocrisy out of them and out of the natural scientists. The hypocrisy is namely this —that natural science is supposed to lead to God. Yes, it certainly does lead to God—in this *imposing* way, but this is exactly the impertinence. It is not hard to convince oneself that the natural scientist is hypocritical in this way. Tell him that any man has all he needs in his conscience and in Luther's *Small Catechism,* and the natural scientist will look down his nose. In an imposing way he wants to make God into a coy beauty, a devil of a fellow, whom not everyone can understand—stop, the divine and simple truth is that no one, absolutely no one, can understand him, that the wisest of men must humbly take his stand on THE SAME as does the simple man. —Herein lies the profundity in Socratic ignorance—truly to *forsake* with TOTAL PASSION all curious knowledge, in order in all simplicity to be ignorant before God, to forsake this show (which, after all, is something between man and man) of making observations by way of the microscope. —On the other hand, Goethe, who was no religious mind, cowardly held fast to that differentiating knowledge.

But all such scientificalness becomes especially dangerous and corruptive when it wants to enter into the realm of the spirit. Let them treat plants, animals, and stars in that way, but to treat the human spirit in this way is blasphemy, which only weakens the passion of the ethical and of the religious. The act of eating is itself far more reasonable than microscopic observation of digestion. And to pray to God is not, like eating, something inferior to observations but is absolutely the highest of all.

Thus we learn from the physiologist[527] how the unconscious comes first and then the conscious, but how then is the relation finally reversed and the conscious exercises a partially shaping influence upon the unconscious? Now the physiologist becomes esthetic and sentimental and talks about the noble expression of a cultivated personality, character, attitude,[528] etc.—good Lord, what is all this? A little triviality and at most a little paganism (the inner is the outer; the outer is the inner). Paul[529] does not speak of becoming beautiful through praying and preaching etc. Simply let the external man decay; the inner man grows in magnificence.

Materialistic physiology is comic (to believe that by putting to death one finds the spirit which gives life); the modern, more mental-spiritual physiology is sophistic. It admits itself that it cannot explain the miracle,[530] and yet it wants to continue; it becomes more and more voluminous, and all these volumes treat of this and of that, numerous and very remarkable things—and still it is unable to explain the miracle.

Then sophistic physiology declares it to be a miracle that consciousness comes into existence, a miracle that the idea becomes mind, that mind becomes spirit (in short, the qualitative transitions). If this is supposed to be taken downright seriously, then this entire science is at an end, this science which accordingly exists only as a jest. Its essential task is the miracle, but this it cannot explain. What good is it then to explain everything else? And now to get a chance to be sophistical or, more correctly, in order to exist as a voluminous science, physiology carries on in this fashion. It declares that the transition (from unconsciousness to consciousness etc.) is indeed a miracle, but it takes place very *almählig*,[531] i.e., little by little. Dialectically it is very easy to detect the sophistry. The question is not whether or not, when it occurs, it occurs as a miracle. Here is the sophism; the entire science is a parenthesis. It is not a greater or lesser miracle because a long or a short time has passed before it occurred. It was obviously consistent with this science for a physician, writing on the history of trepanning, to divide the history into two parts, the first treating of that time when there was no knowledge of the subject. The whole of physiology treats what is qualitatively irrelevant. But to call this a science is a sophism. This *"Almählige"* can have different meanings in different contexts. It can signify the plant world, the animal world. It can signify the world's 6,000 years, statistics on procreation, and God knows what else.* But as a whole, qualitatively, it signifies nothing, absolutely nothing, if the fact remains clear that the miracle nevertheless cannot be explained. The whole thing is an approximation process: almost, almost and as good as; it is almost, as it were, almost etc. —And this is what is treated in many volumes, this is what the microscope is used for.

Thus we learn from sophistical physiology that "The key to the knowledge of conscious mental life lies in the unconscious" (Carus).[532] But if one cannot explain the transition from unconsciousness to consciousness, what does this say about the key? On the contrary, the transition is a leap (to which wonder corresponds), which no key can unlock. —Then we learn that *"das Gesetz des Geheimnisses"*[533] is supposed to be of special help—in explaining. But this law can do nothing more than to emphasize the miracle as such—what then does it explain? In dogmatics it is understood that a miracle is explained as a miracle and that it cannot be understood, but an exact science cannot function this way. Therefore it wants to conjure up an appearance, as if it nevertheless could almost, as good as, as it were, for the most part, just about —explain the miracle.

Thus physiology spreads out over the plant world and animal world and exhibits analogies,[534] analogies which still are not supposed to be analogies, inasmuch as human life from the beginning, from the first trace, is qualitatively different from the plant kingdom and the animal kingdom. What then are all these analogies supposed to amount to, especially all the prodigious details of analogies through the use of microscopic observations?

O dreadful sophistry which expands microscopically and telescopically in volume after volume and yet, qualitatively understood, yields nothing but does deceive men out of the simple, profound, passionate wonder and admiration which gives impetus to the ethical.

The only certainty is the ethical-religious. It declares: Believe—you shall believe. And if anyone were to ask me if by its help I have always danced on roses, I would answer: No, but nevertheless, nevertheless it is an indescribably blessed certainty that all is good and God is love; either I must be to blame that things go wrong—and then God is still love, or it will turn out well and evil will prove to have had its significance—but then, too, God is love. —Just for a joke let us say to hysterical sentimentality: Does not the whole question go back to the fact that you have not had a bowel movement? But let us also know how to jest about microscopic, meaningless seriousness.

When all is said and done, what do the physiologist and the physician really know in the medium of actuality, in the medium of becoming? Through observation (consequently in the medium of imagination, where everything is at rest) it is easy enough to explain that mind and body[535] are not opposites but one self-developing idea and that the relation is therefore an *In-einander.* But in the situation of actuality, where then is the beginning to be made? Shall the sufferer first take some drops or shall he first believe? O you often repeated masterly satire on the physician when he still does not know which is which. But the ethicist says: Believe, you shall believe. Only the ethicist dares to speak with enthusiasm; the physician believes neither in his medications—nor in faith. The ethicist says with enthusiasm: In a certain sense all medical science is a jest. The fun of saving a man's life for a few years is merely fun—earnestness is to die blessed.

VII[1] A 186   *n.d.,* 1846

[*] *In margin:* Therefore there are many internal contradictions. See Carus, *Psyche,*[536] see pp. 156 and 159 marked in my copy.

« 2810

To me there is something repulsive when a natural scientist, after having pointed to some ingenious design in nature, sententiously declares that this reminds us of the verse that God has counted every hair of our heads. O, the fool and his science, he has never known what faith is![537] Faith believes it without all his science, and it would only become disgusted with itself in reading all his volumes if these, please note, were supposed to lead to faith, strengthen faith, etc.

VII[1] A 188   *n.d.,* 1846

« 2811

Of all scholarship, the natural sciences are the most banal. It has always amused me to reflect on how year after year that which once aroused amazement becomes commonplace, for this is always the fate of discoveries within the sphere of the bad infinity.[538] What a sensation the stethoscope made![539] It will soon come to the point that every barber does it, and when he has finished shaving you he will ask: Would you also like to be stethoscoped? Someone will invent an instrument to listen to the heart beat. It will create a great sensation until after 50 years every barber will be able to do it. Then after one has had a haircut and been stethoscoped (by this time it will be quite common) the barber will ask: Would you also like to have me listen to your heartbeat?

VII[1] A 189   n.d., 1846

« 2812

It is simple and beautiful and moving that the lover gazes, enamored, at his beloved, but it is fashionable and superior to peer at her through a monocle. The natural scientist uses the microscope[540] the way a fop uses a monocle—only the microscope is turned toward God.

VII[1] A 190   n.d., 1846

« 2813

If there were anything by way of the natural sciences which would help define spirit, I should be the first to get hold of a microscope, and I think my perseverance would equal anyone's. But when by qualitative dialectic I easily perceive that, qualitatively understood, in 100,000 years the world will not have advanced one single step, I shall do the very opposite, preserve my soul and not waste one single second of my life on curiosity. When at some time I lie at death's door, I shall console myself by saying: Probably I have not understood the slightest about this kind of thing, not one bit more than my Anders[541] or a chambermaid; I have perhaps only wondered and adoringly praised God more often. I certainly do understand that it is God who has given man the kind of acuteness with which he makes discoveries by means of instruments and such, but it is also God who has given man the reason by which in the qualitative dialectic he might perceive the self-contradiction inherent in this quantitative, approximating almost—thus man ought devoutly and humbly to renounce curiosity, renounce the kind of equanimity which is required for microscopic research and rather pray to God and relate himself to him only through the ethical.

VII[1] A 191   n.d., 1846

« 2814

If the natural sciences had been as developed in Socrates' time as they are now, all the Sophists would have become natural scientists. One would have hung a microscope outside his shop to attract customers; another would have had a sign reading: Look through our giant microscope and see how a man thinks;* another: See how the grass grows. Excellent motifs for an Aristophanes, especially if he has Socrates present and has him peer into a microscope.

In margin: *And Socrates, after reading the notice, would have said: From this advertisement one sees how a man behaves who does not think.

                                        VII¹ A 194   *n.d.*, 1846

« **2815**

All natural science, like all modern scholarship, is sophistical. Do an experiment using Socrates' simple question: "Does natural science know something or does it not?" It can answer neither Yes nor No, for the whole secret of it is that it is almost and as good as and not very far from and almost, just as if it knew something.

                                        VII¹ A 195   *n.d.*, 1846

« **2816**

Natural science is sophistical in the same way nature is sophistical (all its greatness and beauty captivates one as if this were the explanation rather than that the explanation of this greatness and beauty is the invisible which cannot be seen but can only be believed). Its explanation lies solely in stipulating the qualitative invisibility of the miracle, but instead (rather than falling down and perishing like the sphinx before the word) it creates the illusion that this whole enormous apparatus of knowledge is the explanation. As Proteus changed shapes in order to prevent anyone from seizing him, so natural science captivates, interests, elevates, charms, teaches, enriches, seduces, persuades—at one time with knowledge of the stars, now of the rare little bird, now of a special aptitude, now of a mysterious profundity, etc. By all these charms it prevents man from dialectically thinking it through. But there are so few dialecticians in each generation, and there will be fewer—then natural science will harness all mankind.

                                        VII¹ A 196   *n.d.*, 1846

« **2817**

From the natural sciences a tragic distinction will spread between the simple folk who believe simply and the learned and half-learned —who have looked through a microscope. No longer as in the old days shall one confidently dare to speak about the one and undivided highest and address all, all, all men, regardless of whether they are black or green, have big heads or little ones—we must first see if they have brains enough—to believe in God. If Christ had known about the microscope, he would have examined the apostles first.

                                        VII¹ A 197   *n.d.*, 184ᵉ

« **2818**

I am happy to acknowledge that Carus's book (*Psyche*)[542] is excellent, and if he will give the qualitative its due, then I will gratefully take a few of his good psychological observations. At all decisive points he makes unqualified room—for the miracle, for the creative power of God, for the absolute expression of worship, and says: This no one can grasp, no science, neither now nor ever. Then he commmunicates the interesting things he knows. But there must never be any proximity between these two categories; above all they must never be brought into dangerous sophistical proximity to each other. If that happens, I will not read or buy a single one of his psychological observations; it is too costly.

VII[1] A 198 *n.d.*, 1846

« **2819**

On the whole the extravagance of the natural sciences could make excellent comedy.

It is market day for the Sophists; each one comes on such a day and puts up his booth; a curious crowd flocks to the place.

We hear three trumpet blasts; then a herald walks in front of a kind of triumphal carriage carrying the great scientist. The herald shouts: It is now proved to us as a necessary fact that in 1,000 years there will be a Spanish astronomer who will prophecy as a necessary fact that in 1,000 years a new star will appear. That it exists can be theoretically demonstrated, but it is so far away that it will be a long time yet. This remarkable presentation, ladies and gentlemen, is also noteworthy because His Majesty, the King of France, has been convinced of it and declares it the most remarkable thing he has heard—also the Pope. The play could end with a revolt by some of the craftsmen who rip down the booths and smash everything to pieces.

The situation is this—someone had invented a giant microscope which was supposed to surpass all wonders hitherto known, whether one considered the microscope itself or looked through it. But a tremendously huge apparatus was necessary for this and six month's labor, and the labor cost huge sums. There is still three months of work left. But that very day a report comes that someone in China (by a series of remarkable discoveries communication had been amazingly accelerated) had discovered a microscope of even higher magnifying power which could be constructed very easily. Thus the giant microscope had lost all its worth (before it was even ready!); the promoter is ruined and the workers are without bread.

The insane speed by which one discovery displaces another.

VII[1] A 199   n.d., 1846

« 2820

It does no good to get involved with the natural sciences. We stand there defenseless and utterly without control. The researcher immediately begins to distract us with his particular projects—now to Australia, then to the moon, then into an underground crevice, then the devil knows where—looking for an intestinal worm. Now we use the telescope—now the microscope. Who in the devil can stand that![543]

Joking aside, let us talk earnestly. The confusion lies in the fact that it never becomes dialectically clear which is which, how philosophy is to use natural science. Is the whole thing an ingenious metaphor (then one might as well be ignorant of it), is it an example, an analogy, or is it of such importance that *philosophical* theory should be revised in relation to it?

For a thinker there is no more horrible anguish than to have to live in the tension that while one is heaping up details it continually seems as if the thought, the conclusion is just about to appear. If the natural scientist does not feel this anguish, he must not be a thinker. This is the most dreadful tantalization of the intellectual! A thinker is literally in hell as long as he has not found certainty of spirit: *hic Rhodus, hic salta,*[544] the sphere of faith, where you must believe even if the world burst into pieces and the elements melted. Here there is no waiting for the latest shipping reports or news by mail. This certainty of spirit, the most humble of all, the most mortifying for the conceited mind (for it is so superior to peer through a microscope), is the only certainty.

The main objection, the whole objection to the natural sciences can be expressed formally, simply, and unconditionally in this way:[545] It is incredible that a human being who has infinitely reflected about himself as spirit could then think of choosing the natural sciences (with empirical material) as the task for his striving. An empirical natural scientist must *either* be a man of talent and instinct (it is characteristic of talent and instinct not to be profoundly and fundamentally dialectical but only to pry into things, to be ingenious, but not to understand oneself*), *or* he must be a man who from early youth half-unconsciously becomes a natural scientist, and now by force of habit has come to be at home in this way of living—the most dreadful way of living there is: to fascinate and astonish the whole world by his discoveries and his ingeniousness and then not to understand himself. Of course such a natural scientist has consciousness, consciousness within the range of his talents, perhaps an amazing acuteness, the gift of synthesizing, an almost superhuman ability to associate ideas, etc. But at its very best, the situation will be this: such a pre-eminently talented man, unparalleled in his intellectual endowment, explains the whole of nature—but does not understand himself. He does not become transparent to himself in the decisiveness of the spirit, in the ethical appropriation of his talents, and so on. But it is easy to see that this is simply skepticism (for skepticism means that an unknown, an X, explains everything. When everything is explained by an X which is not explained, then, viewed as a whole, nothing at all is explained). If this is not skepticism, then it is superstition.

In margin:

*And to be able to live on happily this way without feeling any misgivings because the deceptive variety of observations and discoveries continually conceals the total unclarity.

VII^1 A 200   *n.d.*, 1846

« 2821

What the "race" tends toward is apparently the establishment of natural science in the place of religion.

X^2 A 362   *n.d.*, 1850

« 2822 *Das christliche Bewusstseyn*[546]

This is Schleiermacher's phrase, and Neander, praising it, explains that the Reformation was an act of this Christian consciousness (See Petersen, *die Idee der Kirche,* [547] III, p. 346 n).

That may be all right, but there is something very dubious about it.

To be specific, Christianity ideally relates to the single individual.

When, however, what it is to be a Christian is expertly minimized, when all kinds of illusions are tolerated in order to keep up the appearance that all are Christians, whole countries and states, a Christian diffusion is marketed—this is a collective consciousness—but that this is supposed to be Christianity—no thanks.

In the same way, no doubt, the world also wants to market a new culture-consciousness, a Christian diffusion, therefore a Christian consciousness, —and it probably will make natural science its religion.

You see, this Christian consciousness means so much that ultimately the falling away from Christianity will become the Christian consciousness, and there will be a Christian consciousness over the whole world at the same time, at the very same time, that Christianity does not exist at all.

X⁴ A 232   n.d., 1851

« 2823 The Objections of the Natural Sciences to Christianity and Scholarship (Theology)

Christianity teaches that there is a conflict between God and man.

And natural science is the most conceited of all, and, please note, in the direction of mutiny against God (note: that there are indeed some humble and devout natural scientists is another matter; my concern is particularly with that whole class of society which appeals to natural science), probably boasting of their experiments to which nature responds, probably boasting of their computations and predictions and the like, thus *either* wanting to make God completely superfluous and to substitute natural laws which—since the natural scientists have made such incomparable progress—must most humbly obey science, consequently man, so that man really becomes God, *or* they force God, so painfully embarrassed, into his own laws, so that, if I dare say so, the devil himself must be God.

The conflict between God and "man" will therefore culminate in the withdrawal of "man" behind natural science. And it is perhaps the trend of the future that Christianity now wants to shake off illusions, with the result that there will be hosts of people whose religion will become natural science.

At present natural science shows that a whole range of ideas about natural phenomena found in Holy Scripture are not scientifically defensible: ergo, Holy Scripture is not God's Word, is not a revelation.

Here theological scholarship gets into trouble, for the natural sciences are perhaps right in what they say—and theological scholarship is also eager to be a science, but then it loses the game here, too. If the whole thing were not so serious, it would be extremely comical to consider theology's painful situation, which it certainly deserves, for this is its nemesis for wanting to be a science.

Otherwise the matter is not difficult at all. To be specific, the medium, the only medium, through which God communicates with "man," the only thing he will talk about with man is: the ethical. But to speak ethically about the ethical (and if one does not speak ethically about it, it does not become the ethical; and on the other hand God must be assumed to be unconditionally the master in speaking ethically about the ethical) means unconditionally to render everything else infinitely unimportant. Stick to the point, stick to the point; the watchword is stick to the point—that is, stick to the ethical. If those who are to be addressed call an apple a pear, forget it—this is really not the time to waste time in explaining, waiting; the ethicist also calls an apple a pear—for he is nevertheless able to say what infinitely concerns him—the ethical. But the person who is not an ethicist perhaps cannot make himself do this; he has to put in a few words, at least in passing, about this mistake in regard to apples and pears, for he is vain about his knowledge—that is, he is not an ethicist, is not capable of speaking ethically about the ethical.

As soon as anything other than the ethical is even faintly accentuated in discussing the ethical, the discussion is no longer an ethical discussion of the ethical and there is the risk that this other factor will draw attention to itself and away from the ethical, thus if the men to whom the ethical is to be addressed assume that the earth stands still and the sun goes around it—this is of no importance whatsoever if the discussion is to be ethical—so infinitely important is the ethical—this sort of thing must not be allowed to interfere in the slightest way. No, only the ethical is to be accentuated—and as far as the ethical is concerned the natural sciences have really made no discoveries at all.

Or imagine a revelation now in our time! The natural sciences certainly do not dare maintain that everything has been discovered already, that it will not be discovered after a thousand years that in many respects we have lived and discoursed in illusion. Imagine a revelation. It will concern itself essentially with the ethical—for, as already stated, this is the medium of communication for the divine. And in order really to speak ethically about the ethical, in order not to interfere in the remotest way by drawing attention away from the ethical, it will speak about natural phenomena in exactly the same way we do, for there is no time to waste on such matters, and the teacher (God) is not like a conceited human teacher who wants to show what he knows. On the contrary, the teacher (God) is earnestness itself and therefore wants to do everything to prevent the disciple from being distracted; therefore the teacher in no way whatsoever draws attention to anything other than the ethical and in everything else speaks just as do the men whom he addresses. Otherwise philology, veterinary medicine, and the like would have the same right as natural science to demand that a revelation occupy itself with what can be of interest to all these sciences.

But there is a deep cunning involved in the objections of the natural sciences. In regard to that which remains completely unchanged—even if one on the largest possible scale concedes that the natural sciences have a case against the revelation—namely, the Christian ethic, its requirements to die to the world, etc., natural science has yet to make any rectifying discoveries. But this *the Christian ethic* is what is not wanted; the desire is to enjoy life in pagan fashion and for that purpose to be rid of Christianity—yet half afraid of Christianity as men still are, they hypocritically want to do this—on scientific grounds.

The joker is and remains scientific theology. It is actually in real trouble and with the help of the natural sciences it will get into trouble more and more. For scientific theology is without faith, without open confidence before God, without a good conscience in the presence of Holy Scripture. Therefore it is unable devoutly to get air as Luther would promptly do with the help of the following decree: "Our Lord does not give a damn for the natural sciences; if it pleases God to let himself be born and to suffer in order to speak to men about the one thing necessary, then there are not even a fugitive time and occasion and mood to communicate a hint about natural science, or to divulge that he is already informed about the art of printing and the steam engine. Yes, it is so far from being the case that, on the contrary, where God wants to communicate to men something of this kind by means of a revelation, he—in order to tempt men—intersperses a bit of balderdash, calculated to scandalize all contemporary scientific researchers and the whole honorable scientific public and all societies for the propagation of scientific knowledge, the whole lot, one for all and all for one."

The conflict with the objections of the natural ciences and the struggle related to this are generally analogous to the conflict with the system. The objections themselves do not have much significance, but a strong opinion and secular training will embarrass the theologians so that they do not dare to do anything else than give the appearance of also being a bit scientific; in this respect they are afraid of being left holding the bag as was the case vis-à-vis the system in its day. A sense of humor and personal courage are what is needed—a sense of humor to show how ridiculous the objection is, since no matter how scientifically justified natural science is, it misses the point in "religion," and lacks the personal courage to dare to fear God more than men.

X[5] A 73   *n.d.,* 1853

« **2824** *The Natural Sciences*

The enormous upswing of the natural sciences in our day proves that the race has despaired of being spirit; it is a distraction.

Analogies in the lives of individuals are easily noted.

XI[1] A 94 *n.d.,* 1854

NATURE

« **2825**

The moon is the earth's conscience.

II A 633   *n.d.,* 1837

« **2826**

A forest is seen to its best advantage at a distance, for then it is an interesting secret; close at hand it is a solved riddle. Water, on the other hand, is a profound truth which becomes more interesting the more one plumbs its depths, and the smallest drop of water has the same effect on the attentive mind, so that there is no need of quantity as with trees.

II A 475   July 14, 1839

« **2827**

Sometimes when the whole sky is overcast, one sees a little strip, a little patch, which seems to dream of a bliss of its own and to radiate a glory from within itself.

II A 494   *n.d.,* 1839

« **2828**

Trees carry on the most pleasant, the most refreshing conversation, and although all the leaves talk away at the same time (in spite of all the rules of etiquette), it is not at all disturbing; instead it lulls the external senses and awakens the inner ones.

II A 505   *n.d.,* 1839

« **2829**

Standing right outside the gate to this little place[548] in the late twilight amid the aroma which hay always exudes—the sheep drifting home and forming the foreground—dark clouds broken by a few intense streaks of light, characteristic of clouds indicating a storm—in the background looms the heath— —if only I could recall adequately the impression of that evening.

III A 76   *n.d.,* 1840

256

« **2830**

The heath must be particularly adapted to developing vigorous spirits; here everything lies naked and unveiled before God, and here is no place for a lot of distractions, those many odd nooks and corners where the consciousness can hide, and from which earnestness often has a hard time recovering vagrant thoughts. Here consciousness must come to definite and precise conclusions about itself. Here on the heath one must truly say, "Whither shall I flee from thy presence?"[549]

III A 78   n.d., 1840

« **2831**

When the moon is reflected on the ocean this way, it seems as if it were playing upon strings.

III A 152   n.d., 1841

« **2832**

No wonder the ocean is called the mother of all—when it cradles a ship between its motherly breasts the way it does.

III A 153   n.d., 1841

« **2833** *In Praise of Autumn*[550]

poetic . . . . .

When autumn comes with its brisk, invigorating coolness, when the remnant of summer heat in the atmosphere is like a possibility, a motherly solicitude lest the indulger be chilled, when one always has, so to speak, a light coat at hand, and the autumn winds increase—when autumn comes and the transitoriness of life elicits longing, when the forest does not stand secure as if it would stand thus to all eternity but changes color even as one is looking at it, for change inflames desire. If a woman remains secure and quiet, she does not arouse desire, but when she changes colors, the change signifies: hurry, hurry! It is the same with autumn. In the summer the clouds never float as hurriedly as in the autumn. And in the autumn the echo never thinks of pausing to relax in the warm air of the woods—no, it rushes by without pausing.

VI A 89   n.d., 1845

« **2834**

Addition to 2833 (VI A 89):

Everything which is present prompts criticism, but memory disarms and allows one to use ideality not to reject but to embellish the past.

VI A 90   n.d., 1845

« **2835**

In margin of 2833 (VI A 89):

Everything during autumn indeed reminds us of decline—and yet it strikes me as being the most beautiful of seasons. When I begin to decline, would that someone might think as well of me as I do of autumn!

VI A 91   n.d.

« **2836**

Walk along the beach and let the movement of the ocean accompany the indefiniteness of your thoughts—but do not stand still, do not discover the uniformity; if you hear it for just a half-second, it is already difficult to tear yourself away from its spell. Sit in a boat and let the lapping of the water commingle with a single thought in your mind so that sometimes you hear the lapping and sometimes not—but do not let your eyes become enamored of the motion of the waves; if you surrender for only a half-second to its uniformity, nature's persuasion is almost like a vow for eternity.

VI A 126   n.d., 1845

« **2837**

It is a singularly pitiful sight to see a poor old nag straining before a wagon, with a nosebag on and not even able to eat. Or when a poor old horse has got the nosebag askew and cannot reach its food, and nobody thinks of helping it!

VI A 138   n.d., 1845

« **2838** *From an Occasional Discourse*[551]

. . . . . The forest does not want to become involved with the solitary. Therefore it returns his word without change, without sympathy; its echo is like a "no," and even though it re-echoes many times it is still only a repeated "no." If the forest wanted to speak with him, it would answer; if the forest were sympathetic with him, it would retain his word, preserve it unchanged.—

VII[1] A 46   n.d., 1846

« **2839**

Making a visit in the country is pleasant if a person is of such an age that the host and hostess's only desire is that he make his own plans and they merely see to it that he comes to no harm.

                                                          VII^1 A 88   n.d., 1846

« **2840**

See journal JJ, pp. 216–17 [i.e., VI A 89–91]
Eulogy on Autumn

(in the French Style)*

> * N.B. I think this mode
> of mystification should
> be effective.

Autumn is: the time of longings, the time of colors,
            the time of clouds, the time of sounds
            (sound is transmitted far more animatedly
            and swiftly than in the oppressive summer
            heat), the time of recollections.

                                                          VII^1 B 205   n.d., 1846

« **2841**

Addition to 2840 (VII^1 B 205):
Long live autumn! There is only one glass of the champagne worth drinking, only one piece of the roast worth eating, at only one time is a girl worth loving, and there is really only one girl worth this one time—and only autumn is *the season of the year.*

                                                          VII^1 B 206   n.d., 1846

« **2842**

Eulogy on Autumn
by 5 persons
ending with a *tutti*
to be used as a reply
by a humorous individual.

No. 2
Autumn Is the Time of **Clouds**.
According to familiar Norse mythology, clouds are formed by the giant [Ymer]'s brain.[552] And truly there is no better symbol for clouds than thoughts and no better symbol for thought than clouds—clouds are brain-weaving, and what else are thoughts. That is why we become weary of everything else but not of the clouds—in the autumn, which again is the time for reflecting. Long ago I wearily abandoned man-

kind, although I had or simply because I had made a thorough study of the subject. I began as a youth by loving older men—and grew weary of that. Then I loved somewhat older youth like myself and grew weary of that. Then came the young girls—and then matrons, undeniably the best, but it is sheer vanity, even when they are past their time as matrons. Wearily I turned away from humanity and humorously turned to those creatures which, unlike the human kind, do not have the pretensions of being the marvel of creation, but yet, perhaps for that very reason, are very entertaining because they do not pretend so much. I mean cows. And no doubt I made as many interesting acquaintances in the meadows as anywhere—I will never forget the dun colored cow—the happy hours, and so forth—but yet I grew weary of that.

But of the clouds—during autumn, never. They are scarcely recognizable, so changed are they, and he who never saw clouds during autumn has never seen them. In the winter it is too cold to see clouds —in the summer they are too indolent and sleepy—but during autumn —dreaming (to be developed). —In the summer they stand still and are bored—in the autumn they hurry like vagabond dreams. In the summer it is as if they do not care to hang up there—in the autumn it is obvious that they wantonly enjoy floating. In the summer one cloud scarcely bothers to get out of the way of another. In the autumn they play with each other in jolly games, dodge each other, meet, separate, long for each other again, blend colors (as friends blend blood) with each other, become one, although the individuality of each cloud shines through.

Stand still, you who call yourself a thinker, and watch the clouds —during autumn. If you have ever thought about it before, think about it again. Consider what you might wish to be—a human being? Such a thought could hardly occur to a human being. An angel? Tiresome! A tree? Takes too long and is too quiet. A cow? Too stolid a life. No —a cloud—in the autumn. Would I were that, and the rest of the year I would stay hidden somewhere—or in nothingness, which could also be expressed in this way: I do not want to be, but every autumn I would like to live the one month.* In itself a cloud is a rather impressive thing (I would not want to be a little bitty mackerel cloud); I would like to be a large, shapely cloud. In spite of its size, a cloud is lightness itself, bouyant, and insofar as it does not have a musical sense (but it does) it does have a sense of color—it knows how to bathe in colors.

To you, then, Autumn! With this glass I greet you, *recollecting* you, your profound and yet so fleeting thoughts, you, my best thoughts, whom we may completely appropriate without plagiarizing. When autumn comes, I leap into a carriage, pull the fur robe up over my head, put on a cap—showing only the eyes with which I grasp at you. When the driver drives as fast as the horses can go (Ah, what is that compared to the clouds!), then it seems as if I had almost become a cloud.

Along margin: Or I would live hidden as a thought until autumn; then I would become a cloud.

VII^1 B 207   *n.d.*, 1846

« **2843**

No. 3
Autumn Is the Time of **Sounds**.
If you imagined a trumpeter who has fallen asleep with the trumpet at his mouth, could you then say you heard anything? —How boring to be an echo in the summertime. The suffocating air in the woods drives echo itself away. But autumn! Only then does echo hear the beloved's voice—everything is in love with echo, is merely waiting to give answer. For autumn means elation. When you shout, answers come from myriads of places.

VII^1 B 208   *n.d.*, 1846

« **2844**

No. 4
Autumn Is the Time of **Colors**.
What is color? That is, what is the meaning of color? Color is motion and disturbance made visible, just as sound is motion made audible. Everything characterized by immobility, repose, would therefore not have color. A mathematician would not color a triangle; summer is repose, serenity, is therefore colorless—the unremittingly blue heaven is certainly not color. For what is color? Color is contrast, but contrast is disturbance, movement; even if two contrasts stand ever so still directly opposite each other, the fact that they contrast is disturbance. Thus summer is repose. But then comes autumn, and with autumn come passions, and with passions disturbance, and with disturbance color, and with passion's disturbance the shifting and changing of colors. To change color is indeed the expression of disturbance, the

disturbance of passions. And autumn changes colors. In contrast to summer, we may say that the distinguishing feature of autumn is that it changes colors. If you say that autumn is a longer season and therefore this changing lasts some time, I reply: the contrasts during autumn are so intensely in motion every moment that it is like a constant shifting. It is impossible to see all the contrasts at once, and the change appears as one sees the same contrasts together with a new contrast and so on further.

The "dusky-hued autumn" is therefore not merely melancholy—it is heroic—for it is nature's doom, its battle for life. It bows under the annihilation—this is the sadness—but then again it is as if the delight of summer is momentarily remembered and echoed, but far more intensely, for the time is short.

Look—at your feet the straw withers; if you will look very carefully, you will see that every straw has its own color. Meanwhile the beech tree holds itself erect. It will not bow; it will not yield; it wistfully shakes its head, but then it proudly shakes off the withered leaves again; it would rather have a few leaves which are not withered than all those withered ones. How curious it is that in the summer time no one really sees that a green leaf is really green, no one sees the poetry in the green of the summer, in all the green—it is almost as if one eats green. But in the autumn! When the birch tree stands bare, with only one single green but freshly green leaf on its naked branch, then you see the color *green,* you see it by contrast.

VII¹ B 209   n.d., 1846

« 2845

No. 5
Autumn Is the Time of **Recollections**.

> N.B.—this discourse should be delivered in the purest and noblest spirit, in order to create a contrast to the despair in the others.

It is a familiar fact that the person who is an expert in the art of cooking knows how to make a delicacy out of even the most unpalatable ingredients. So it is with memory; what it has prepared and serves is delicious.

> N.B.—the tone must be raised a little or this does not come to have pathos.

VII¹ B 210   n.d., 1846

« **2846**

Adler's [553] dizziness is apparent also in his careless, loose thinking and believing that greatness will prevail even if wrong and injustice also occur, and the best proof of this dizziness is his constant appeal to analogies from nature, for nature simply is not the ethical; nature allows rain to fall on good and evil alike, but the ethical makes the qualitative distinction. . . .

VII² B 256:20   *n.d.,* 1846-47

« **2847**

for nature takes the child from the mother's womb and lays it at her breast.

VIII¹ A 263   *n.d.,* 1847

« **2848**

What remarkable things are told about the stork—that when the water is so low that it cannot drink, it throws in stones until the water is deep enough. I read this in several authors from antiquity, then in Montaigne,[554] and now finally in Steffen's *Religions-philosophie.*[555]

VIII¹ A 411   *n.d.,* 1847

« **2849**

There is something much more compassionate in gray weather than in sunny weather. It is like a development of the theme that even insignificant things, yes, discarded things, can amount to something. And gray weather appears more beautiful the more one looks at it.

VIII¹ A 427   *n.d.,* 1847

« **2850**

When the butterfly departs from the cocoon—and gets wings— everything it loses, all its wrappings, is nothing; it loses nothing.

VIII¹ A 474   *n.d.,* 1847

« **2851**

. . . . . and when I go out under the arch of heaven, behold the myriad stars—I do not feel at all alien in this enormous world—for, truly, it is my Father's. Nor do I feel abandoned on the crossroad of life and in the misery of life, for I am always under my Father's eye.

IX A 19   *n.d.,* 1848

« **2852**

In a book *Nanna oder*[556]—it is on the mental life of plants—by one Fechner (which I am reading in the Athenæum)—there are several good things. For example, this splendid observation of analogy: the pupa lives on the leaf—the butterfly on the flower, and, as the author sentimentally remarks,[557] it perhaps pains the leaf to be eaten, but it is sweet for the flower, and consequently the pain is remunerative.

X^1 A 34   *n.d.*, 1849

« **2853** *God*

Not even a sparrow falls to earth without his will[558]—yes, in a quiet hour when, dressed in silk and velvet, you play Christianity with us and present this in your resonant voice and magnificent oratory, and the rest of us enjoy it—then this can be very simple. But take an actual situation in nature: in a storm, when a hurricane rages and uproots trees, and the birds in death-agony plunge to the ground. Or suppose that the wind blows away the pollen of millions of flowers, or that the earth opens up and swallows entire cities—then say that not even a sparrow falls to earth without the will of your heavenly father, yes, that even the hairs on your head are numbered.

Really, we need to live more with nature if for no other reason than to get more of an impression of God's majesty. Huddled together in the great cultural centers we have as much as possible abolished all overwhelming impressions—a lamentable demoralization.

X^4 A 483   *n.d.*, 1852

NEW TESTAMENT

« 2854

Inspiration may be considered *either* as restricted exclusively to the activity of the apostles as they were writing the New Testament *or* also as extended over their whole lifetime. We find no basis in the New Testament for the former view; on the contrary, what is referred to, the communication of the Holy Spirit, is something which must be regarded as being stretched out over their whole lifetime. (Something which on the whole is characteristic of the New Testament—this continuing across.) If we are to consider inspiration in the strictest sense of the word, it must be as something extended over their whole lifetime. But if we cannot assume that those whom Christ himself had chosen and instructed were able to interpret Christianity properly, then they were indeed assured by this inspiration, but then the following generation would misunderstand it, and so on, unless we also again assume the next generation's infallibility through inspiration and thereby declare that Christianity is something which absolutely cannot be reconciled with human life, for by inspiration they would have moved beyond the universally human position. —The doctrine of the infallibility of the Pope was not adequate, since the pure doctrine became for him merely something like a relic, but when it was declared it was misunderstood. Nor was it enough to extend it to the teachers, for their actual work as teachers would avail nothing, and it became necessary to presuppose infallibility for every single human being, and then, to be sure, teachers were no longer necessary.

I A 26　October 10, 1834

« 2855

What do these words[559] mean: If they do not believe Moses and the prophets, neither will they believe if someone arose from the dead.

I A 298　December 3, 1836

« 2856

The element of knowledge which future eternal happiness must necessarily contain is implied after a fashion in Ephesians 1:21: "Above every name that is named, not only ἐν τῷ αἰῶνι τουτῷ, but also ἐν τῷ μέλλοντι"[560] where, indeed, it is also implied that one will become acquainted with names which have greater meaning than even the greatest of all historical names.

II A 149   August 28, 1837

« 2857

The majority of people pass by Christianity as the voice from heaven (John 12:29); they hear it but do not understand it and take it to be thunder—or they hear the voice but do not see who it is who speaks (Acts 9:7).

II A 368   February 12, 1839

« 2858

In Christianity everything has dropped to a lower level because a higher factor has entered in. In the Old Testament προφετεία was the highest, but in the New Testament ἐν γλώσσῃ λαλεῖν[561] is, so that προφετεία possesses consciousness in itself, not as in the Old Testament.

II A 379   March 9, 1839

« 2859

The merciful Samaritan could be characterized by comparing him with two English lords who, when they saw a poor wretch coming down the highway on a runaway horse in full gallop, about to be thrown off at any moment and shouting for help, calmly looked on. One lord said to the other: "I'll wager 100 pounds he falls off," and the other answered, "I'll take you up on that." Thereupon they spurred their racers, hurried ahead to open the gates along the way and pay the tollgate keepers so that nothing should stop the unfortunate rider.[562] The Levite and the priest not only went by—but made a bet instead of helping.

VI A 111   n.d., 1845

« 2860

It is incomprehensible that a hymn writer like Kingo[563] could ever think of writing hymns which are historical corruptions of the gospels, in which the versifying appears as annoyingly ludicrous contrasted to the brief, simple gospel narrative.

VII¹ A 83   n.d., 1846

« 2861

In the Gospel about the Pharisee and the tax collector[564] it says that the Pharisee "stood by himself," but in the next gospel lesson (about the deaf mute) it says that Christ took him aside.

VIII[1] A 248   *n.d.*, 1847

« 2862

. . . . . But now suppose that the victim, whom the merciful Samaritan took care of, died in his hands,[565] and then suppose that consequently the Samaritan had to report it to the police, and suppose the police had said: Of course we must keep you under arrest for the time being. What then? His contemporaries would have laughed at him for being stupid enough to let himself in for all that nonsense and would think either that he must be quite an "idiot" and ignorant of the ways of the law or, if he did know in advance what could happen, he must indeed be "crazy."

Behold, these are the wages of mercy.

VIII[1] A 311   *n.d.*, 1847

« 2863

John 14:27: I give not as the world gives; let not your hearts be troubled and do not let them be afraid. Consequently there is reason to be troubled and to be afraid when the world gives. It is here as with the words in Hebrews:[566] to shrink back to one's own destruction.

IX A 355   *n.d.*, 1848

« 2864

When Laurentius Valla was in Rome and read this Gospel (Matthew 5:7, Blessed are the merciful, for they shall obtain mercy), he is supposed to have said: Assuredly either this is not true, or we are not Christians.

See Arndt,[567] II, chapter 5, para. 2.

IX A 384   *n.d.*, 1848

« 2865 *A Christian Prescription*

It is a very simple matter. Pick up the New Testament; read it. Can you deny, do you dare deny, that what you read there about forsaking everything, about giving up the world, being mocked and spit upon as your Lord and master was—can you deny, do you dare deny, that this is very easy to understand, indescribably easy, that you do not need a

dictionary or commentary or a single other person in order to understand it? But you say, "Before I do this, however, before I risk such a
decisive step, I must first consult with others." Insolent, disobedient
one, you are cheeky! You know very well that it is nothing but blasphemy, for you, you cheat, you are looking for a way out, an excuse,
since you know very well that every human being will recommend
whatever indulges you and advise you to follow what best pleases flesh
and blood, and will say: For God's sake, spare yourself.

But the situation is this—what tragic confusion! —men think that
God is far away, that it is 1800 years since Christ died. What would a
father think if his son, instead of immediately obeying a command
which was easy enough to understand, first of all consulted with—
another boy—as to whether he should do his father's will or not. Would
the father not say: The very fact that you have the nerve to talk to a
single one of your comrades about whether or not you should do what
I have commanded, that alone is guilt enough to deserve every punishment.

And even if it were so (which you yourself have not admitted is so
and in truth is not at all the case)—if it were so that the order, the
command, is too difficult to understand, it is still disobedience to want
to consult with someone other than God himself. Thus the father
would also say to the child: What is the meaning of consulting with the
other boys—you certainly can come to me.

x¹ A 221   n.d., 1849

« 2866

What it means actually to be Christian is seen here (John 12:10):
the Jews wanted to kill Lazarus—because Christ had raised him from
the dead. So dangerous it is to be raised from the dead—by Christ!

x¹ A 287   n.d., 1849

« 2867

Zacharias Werner[568] mentions in a sermon that the old Church
Fathers represented the three resurrections from the dead symboli-
cally as degrees of damnation from which men are aroused by Christ:
the daughter of Jairus—she is only sleeping; the son of the widow of
Nain—he has already been carried out; Lazarus—he already stinks.

x¹ A 288   n.d., 1849

« 2868

The words so often misused: "Blessed are the eyes and ears which saw and heard what you saw and heard"—these words—O, how right they are—these words are spoken "to the disciples privately." I have always maintained this, but I had forgotten that it is in the New Testament—see Luke 10:23.

Usually there is more than enough stress upon what is said to the disciples in private—for example, what is said in the Sermon on the Mount about renouncing the world, about suffering persecution etc. No pastor forgets to point out that this is said to the disciples in private. But in the second passage this is forgotten; here supposedly everyone is summarily blessed by having been or by being contemporary with Christ, by seeing—yes, what only the believer can see and what naturally can never be combined with the frightfulness of seeing as in contemporaneity.

x^1 A 482 *n.d.*, 1849

« **2869**

Just as one who plays the lottery dreams only of numbers and concocts the most remarkable combinations because his imagination is preoccupied day and night with that alone, so also there is a way of exegeting the Bible which is, in the good sense, as if possessed and therefore is able to find types and so on everywhere. This is not at all erroneous. The error in the first instance is to fill one's imagination with such rubbish as numbers and possible winnings.

x^1 A 655 *n.d.*, 1849

« **2870** *The Confusion in "Christendom"*

Here is a new insight or the same insight from a new angle.

The teachers in Christendom commit themselves to conform to the New Testament in their teaching. Splendid. Later a prolix controversy arose over the question whether and to what extent the symbolical books are binding, a controversy which has extended over a long period of time and about which whole libraries have been written.

But good Lord, Christianity is no "doctrine." Why, then, that oath? If an oath had to be given, it ought to have read that they pledged themselves to act according to the New Testament, to live in conformity with the New Testament.

Or does it perhaps mean that "the teacher" is simply to teach according to the New Testament, but he is then to bind his listeners to act according to it.[*] Fine, then we get the rare situation in which the teacher of a doctrine convinces the listeners, inspires them to do what does not inspire him, convinces them of what does not convince him.

Or should we perhaps say: To be sure, it follows as a matter of course, if care is taken that the doctrine is taught in its purity it goes without saying that one will act according to what one learns. Well, thanks for that! If that were true, then Christianity would actually be fundamentally and totally in error, for Christianity understands that it by no means necessarily follows automatically that one does what he learns. Christianity maintains that there is actually an infinite distance between the two. But the world's tactic is continually to lead attention away from doing, from acting, over to the subject of doctrine.

x^3 A 32   *n.d.*, 1850

« 2871

[*] *In margin of 2870* (x^3 A 32):

Incidentally, it becomes more and more clear that the "voluntary" is really what characterizes the essentially Christian and is also that which creates difficulties—but we have completely done away with it.

x^3 A 33   *n.d.*

« 2872 *The Heart of the Matter*

The matter is quite simple. The New Testament is very easy to understand.[569] But we human beings are really a bunch of scheming swindlers; we pretend to be unable to understand it because we understand very well that the minute we understand we are obliged to act accordingly at once. But in order to make it up to the New Testament a little, lest it become angry with us and find us altogether wrong, we flatter it, tell it that it is so tremendously profound, so wonderfully beautiful,so unfathomably sublime, and all that, somewhat as a little child pretends it cannot understand what has been commanded and then is cunning enough to flatter Papa.

Therefore we humans pretend to be unable to understand the N.T.; we do not want to understand it.

Here Christian scholarship has its place. Christian scholarship is the human race's prodigious invention to defend itself against the N.T., to ensure that one can continue to be a Christian without letting the N.T. come too close.

Christian scholarship was invented to interpret, clarify, more sharply illuminate, etc., the N.T. Well, thanks! Yes, we human beings are a bunch of scheming swindlers—and our Lord the simple soul—but, you may be sure, the simple soul who cannot be fooled.

Take any words in the N.T.; forget everything except pledging yourself to act accordingly. Heavens, you will say, if I do that my whole life will be ruined in this world for all time.

What is to be done? Priceless scholarship, what would we do without you? Dreadful it is to fall into the hands of the living God—but it is dreadful even to be alone with the N.T. I do not make myself out to be better than I am; I admit (and yet it may well be possible that I am one of the more intrepid souls around here) that as yet I do not dare unconditionally to be alone with the N.T.[570] Alone with it, that is, to be with it in such a way that it is as if I were all alone in the whole world, and as if God sat beside me and said: Will you please pay attention to what it says and act accordingly. Alone with it, that is, as if I were all alone in the whole world and as if Christ stood beside me lest there be anything irregular with respect to doing what it tells us to do, so that one is obliged to do what the example [*Exempel*] of Christ points to.

Ah, how many have there been in Christianity's 1800 years who have had the courage to dare to be alone with the N.T. What dreadful consequences it could drive me to—this stubborn and domineering book—if I were to be alone with it this way!

How different it is when I take a concordance to help me, a dictionary, a few commentaries, three translations[571]—all to help me thoroughly understand this profound and wonderfully beautiful and unfathomably sublime book—"for," I frankly declare, "if I only understand the N.T., as far as this business of doing accordingly is concerned, I will surely do that." Truly, how fortunate, O rare consolation —that the N.T. is so difficult to understand. It is man's cause I speak of when I say: Let us stick together, by all that is holy let us promise and hold each other [to the promise] to spare nothing, spare no pains, no late midnight hours, to make the N.T. more and more difficult to understand. If the scholarly sciences we have so far invented are not sufficient, let us invent more of them in order to explain and interpret Holy Scripture.

I open the N.T. and read: "If you want to be perfect, then sell all your goods and give to the poor and come and follow me." Good God, all the capitalists, the officeholders, and the pensioners, the whole race no less, would be almost beggars: we would be sunk if it were not for scientific scholarship! Scientific scholarship! Those words have a magnificent sound; honor be to everyone who dedicated his abilities to the service of scientific scholarship. Praise be to everyone who works to consolidate the reputation of scientific scholarship among men—scientific scholarship, which helps to restrain the N.T., this, as scientific scholarship says, this "inspired" book—that is, this confounded book which would *ein, zwei, drei,* run us all down if it got loose, that is, if scientific scholarship did not restrain it.

In vain does the N.T. raise its voice higher than the blood of Abel, which cries out to heaven; in vain does it command with authority; in vain does it admonish and implore—we do not hear it, that is, we hear its voice only through scientific scholarship. Just as a foreigner face to face with royal majesty protests his rights in a foreign language and passionately dares to say the bold words—but see, the interpreter who is to translate it to the king does not dare translate it and substitutes something else—just so does the N.T. sound through scientific scholarship. Just as the cries of one tortured in the bull of Phalaris sounded like music in the tyrant's ears, so the divine authority of the N.T. sounds like tinkling bells or like nothing at all through scientific scholarship—yes, for we humans are crafty. Just as we lock up the insane so that they do not disturb the world, just as the tyrant removes the outspoken person so that his voice will not be heard, so also we have locked up the N.T. with the help of scientific scholarship. In vain does it shout, cry out, wave its arms and gesticulate—it does not help, for we perceive it only through scientific scholarship. In order to secure ourselves completely we declare that scientific scholarship exists specifically to help us understand the N.T., in order that we may better hear its voice. Ah, no insane man, no prisoner of the state was ever so confined; as far as they are concerned, no one denies that they are locked up. But with regard to the N.T. the precautions are even greater: we lock it up but say we are doing the opposite, that we are busily engaged in helping it to gain power and control. But then, of course, no insane person, no prisoner of the state, would ever be as dangerous to us as the N.T. if it were set at liberty.

It is true that we Protestants go to great efforts so that every person, if possible, can have the N.T. Ah, but what care we take to impress upon everyone that the N.T. can be understood only through scientific scholarship! To want to open the N.T., to understand what one reads there as an out-and-out order, to promptly act accordingly —what a mistake! No, the N.T. is a doctrine, and scientific scholarship is required to understand it!

This, then, is the situation. The little bit I have wanted to do is easily stated: I have wanted to make people a little aware and to make the admission that I find the N.T. very easy to understand, but so far I have found tremendously great difficulties in my own self when it comes to acting literally according to what is not difficult to understand.

I perhaps could have taken another direction and invented a new scientific scholarship; but I am much more satisfied to have done what I have done—made an admission about myself.

x^3 A 34 *n.d.*, 1850

« 2873 *The Parable of the Lost Sheep*[572]

This parable no doubt expresses most strongly that man has nothing to do toward his own salvation: the shepherd takes the sheep, lays it upon his shoulder, carries it, etc.—the sheep merely has to lie perfectly still.

Ah, but that is only one factor. If the sheep does not die right then, he will have to strive again himself. And is it not extremely difficult to lie perfectly still so that no new guilt arises or that anxiety for the old guilt does not get the upper hand again, etc.

Christianity is mildness in severity. Since severity is the dialectical factor in this way, men have completely done away with it and have made out that Christianity is mildness.

The tremendous danger in everything that has a dialectical factor which is to be resolved, transformed into its opposite (severity into mildness), is that the whole thing is made far too easy through a transformation of the dialectical into something about which one at the very most makes assurances, that deep within etc. etc.

The greatest deception and slyness in the realm of the spirit will be connected with malpractices regarding such a dialectical factor, so that simply because it ought to be resolved, the matter is then made all too easy, whereby the other clause (mildness here) becomes untruth.

x^3 A 165 *n.d.*, 1850

« 2874 *The Only Way the New Testament Is To Be Read—Captivatingly*

As I have so often said, the basic confusion in Christianity is that it has been made into doctrine. With respect to a doctrine, a person must first and foremost totally master the whole thing. It is just the opposite with the N.T. It pertains solely to the ethical, and therefore it wants you to begin quite simply by taking a single ethical point—but then see to it that you do it.

When a person becomes self-important in wanting to understand the whole thing first etc. and pretends that this is love of truth instead of a cunning which wants to be free from implementation, the following steps may be taken (and if he himself is the guilty one, he can also take steps against himself): take one or another of the passages in the N.T. which contain a demand for self-denial and renunciation, words which are always as simple as possible to understand but so difficult to carry out—and say to him: Why don't you act, then, on these words which are, after all, so easy to understand—and then you will see the cunning.

Ethically the question is never one of understanding, comprehending; it is a matter of doing what one understands, and the thing which a man actually ought to do is always easy to understand.

But this is precisely what human cunning always sets aside—in order to go into the matter profoundly, adding that a person really ought not to act on something he does not understand. Yes, of course, and that is why God has also arranged things in such a way that whatever is to be acted upon is very easy to understand, that the most stupid person of all can understand it right away. What is easier to understand than: Give your fortune to the poor—but there are other difficulties. What is easier to understand than all the demands pointing to self-denial and renunciation?

But we do not want such things to be mentioned. On the contrary, we have turned things around, as if the profundity were that according to which we should act. If that were the case, God would then really be a second-rate partner of a legislator who—probably in order to experience the joy of not having his law complied with—made his laws so deep and profound that men had to devote a lifetime to interpreting them—and thus would be legally innocent because they did not have time to comply with them, not even to begin—for even at the last minute it would not have become clear to them what was required.

"But is it not of absolute importance, then, first of all to understand?" No, ethically the important thing is that you do it, that which is so infinitely easy to understand that you understand it immediately, but which flesh and blood want to keep you from doing.

X³ A 169   *n.d.*, 1850

« 2875 *The Prodigal Son—the Only Begotten Son*

In the Gospel story the prodigal has an older brother, but he will not do a single thing to save the prodigal.

But Christianity itself is, indeed, κατεξόχην the gospel. And in this gospel the prodigal son (the human race) has an older brother (the only begotten Son), and he does everything, loses his life, in order to save the prodigal, in accord with the Father from the beginning.

X³ A 214   *n.d.*, 1850

« 2876 *Clerical Use of the Bible*

How often I have heard the clergy explain that the requirements found in the Sermon on the Mount were exclusively for the apostles and not meant for us (yet it may be recalled that it reads[573] "He turned to the disciples" and that he did in fact have seventy disciples, and we also see how absolute the requirement is in the instances of persons who came to him wanting to be disciples; but between "apostle" and disciple there is the distinction that the apostle has divine authority, whereas the requirement of giving up everything is uniform). On the other hand, the clergy make unqualified use of the words, "Blessed are the eyes which see what you see," as if they were said unqualifiedly to all, and yet it reads expressly that he addressed the disciples in particular: "Blessed are the eyes" etc.

X³ A 233   *n.d.*, 1850

« 2877 *A New Proof for the Divinity of the Bible*

Up until now we have done as follows: we have declared that Holy Scripture is divine revelation, inspired, etc.—ergo, there must then be perfect harmony between all the reports down to the least detail; it must be the most perfect Greek, etc.

Let us now look at the matter from another side. God surely knows what it is "to believe," what it means to require faith, that it means the rejection of direct communication, the positing of an ambiguity.

Now we are getting to the point! Precisely because God wants Holy Scripture to be the object of faith and an offense to any other point of view, for this reason there are carefully contrived discrepancies (which, after all, in eternity will readily be dissolved into harmonies); therefore it is written in bad Greek, etc.

Take another aspect. As the ruler of the world, God also wants to be the object of a faith, he wants you and me to believe that he is the loving Father, etc. A theory which would correspond to that harmony-theory must require that the world also be equally as devoid of ambiguity, so that it is humanly possible to sense *directly* that God is love. But the world is far from being like that. And why not? Because God wants to be believed in faith.

[*] It is the same with Holy Scripture. But "faith" went out of style; the tension of passion which is faith seemed to men to be an exaggeration—and so if men were going to get involved at all in accepting a revealed word of God it had to be on the condition that they could *directly* sense that it is God's word, there would have to be perfect harmony throughout, etc.

They did not spare scholarly efforts—yes, but even the most scholarly efforts are still always indolence compared to the kind of strenuousness which goes with faith.[†]

X³ A 328   n.d., 1850

« 2878

[*] *In margin of 2877* (x³ A 328):

The Middle Ages taught that the visible symbols in the sacraments were to "tempt" faith, that is, by means of the possibility of offense to form the opposition out of which faith can emerge so that the individual *chooses* faith, but there is no direct connection —Clement of Alexandria[574] taught that Holy Scripture used allegories—in order that heretics might not understand it—that is, in order that it could be only for faith.

X³ A 329   n.d.

« 2879

[†] *In margin of 2877* (x³ A 328):

And in scientific scholarly absentmindedness they made God into a rather stupid God who—because they themselves had forgotten what it is to believe or never knew—has also forgotten or perhaps never knew how to arrange that which is to be the object of "faith."

X³ A 330   n.d.

« 2880 *The Gospel about the Paralytic*[575]

Spiritually understood, this applies to the person who thinks that he has to do the managing himself, must himself do the reckoning etc. —alas, after many years he perhaps drags around in torment because of all these calculations, drags around like a paralytic, until faith comes and he hears the words: Stand up and walk.

Take up your bed and walk—this is the expression for how strong he has become, that what previously carried him he now carries, to that extent he now finds he does not need such support.

x^3 A 537   *n.d.*, 1850

« 2881 *The Old Tactic—My Tactic*

The method now is to leave out the existentially strenuous passages in the New Testament. We hush them up—and then we arrange things on easier and cheaper terms. We probably think that since we do not mention these passages God does not know that they are in the New Testament.

I think that it is better to take them along, to acknowledge [*tilstaae*] that these qualifications are found in the New Testament—and then make confession of our own weakness.

x^3 A 541   *n.d.*, 1850

« 2882 *God's Sublimity*

He gives men a holy book which contains his will but contains no middle terms in relation to the ideal—and then he leaves it up to each one how he is going to understand it. He is not to be heard from, keeps perfectly quiet, testing the single individual, for it actually seems to be left completely up to us how we are to understand Scripture. But it goes without saying—judgment is coming.

x^3 A 549   *n.d.*, 1850

« 2883 *The Strongest Expression for God's Most Stringent Rigorousness*

This is found in the Gospel about the hardhearted fellow servant,[576] which ends by saying that if we do not forgive each other's sins, God will be just as severe with us as we are with others—alas, alas, what a blow, for we know very well how severe we can be with others.

The point is that God plays along and thus acts toward us as we act toward others.

x^3 A 582   *n.d.*, 1850

« 2884 *How the New Testament Is Read*

We are, after all, very accustomed to the fact that there is a New Testament—and we have a mutual understanding that we are not to act according to what it says.

For example, when I write a book in which the requirements are set fifty per cent lower than they are in the New Testament, I know of men who say to their wives: "You must not read that book"; they are afraid that reading it would overstrain them. The same men never think of hesitating to let their wives read the N.T.—they of course are confident that it is very unlikely for anyone to think of acting according to what it says.

x^3 A 590   *n.d.*, 1850

« 2885 *The New Testament*

is, however, like a satire on us.

The New Testament contains consolation and again consolation for those who must suffer for Christ's sake—from the outset it presupposes that the Christian suffers for the doctrine, and now it gives consolation—and these texts are supposed to be used in preaching to us, who are not willing to suffer at all.

x^3 A 722   *n.d.*, 1851

« 2886 *Our Way of Reading the New Testament*

Think of one of the older Church Fathers—and let him be an eyewitness to the way we read the New Testament! We leave out everything existential [*det Existentielle*], literally act as if it were not there at all—this we literally do; the early Christians took what they read there absolutely literally.

I am so much closer to the early Christians than to the average Christians of today that I acknowledge that it is in the N.T. and make an admission.

I cannot really work up momentum to do any more, because I, too, am crippled by the illusion that we are all Christians. But nevertheless I am like a shout of alarm, the cry of conscience, warning us where we are.

In order to do more, one must have authority; in order to find out what it means to be a Christian, one must begin at the beginning.

x^4 A 122   *n.d.*, 1851

« 2887 *John the Baptist*

Somewhere[577] in the gospel it states that John said of Christ: I myself did not recognize him—but when he saw the Spirit in the form of a dove hovering over him, he recognized him. And yet, when Christ comes to him to be baptized, John says:[578] I need to be baptized by you, and you come to me. However, this can be reconciled, for John could very well have recognized Christ as someone or the one who stood far above him without therefore having recognized him as God's only begotten Son.

X^4 A 157 *n.d.*, 1851

« 2888 *The Divine—The Human*

Perhaps you say, "But, after all, it is God himself who has created this world with all its delight and joy; therefore it is a self-contradiction on his part that Christianity comes and changes it all to sin and lays down the requirement of dying to the world."

In a certain sense I have no answer to this; such things are no concern of mine. If it simply remains firm that this is the teaching of Christianity, then I have nothing to do with this sort of objection.

But, incidentally, is it not a self-contradiction on your part that you accept Holy Scripture to be the word of God, accept Christianity as divine teaching—and then when you bump up against something which you cannot square with your ideas and feelings—then you say that it is a self-contradiction on the part of God, rather than that it is self-contradiction on your part, inasmuch as you must either dismiss entirely this divine doctrine or take it just as it is.

X^4 A 260 *n.d.*, 1851

« 2889 *Contrast*

God's word was spoken (simply communicated orally) by a single man and later was written down—nowadays any fool gets his rubbish printed in 10,000 and 10,000 copies.

According to the mentality of our day one would think that God at least might have postponed being born until after the invention of printing, that before that it was not the fullness of time, and that he then would have gotten himself one, two, three high-speed presses.

What a satire on the human race that God's word was put into the world as it was! What a satire on the human race that everything grows worse and worse as communication and that by means of ever new inventions dissemination grows greater and greater!

X^4 A 315 *n.d.*, 1851

« 2890 *The New Testament*

Luther[579] expressly says somewhere that what had confused the Church was the continual accent upon the teachers in the Church and upon their writings.

He believed, as he also says, that when the New Testament was brought out of hiding, translated into the native language, and consequently made available to everyone, scholarly reading of the Bible no longer should take place.

Yes, there it is. But just as the Pope secured himself by forbidding the reading of the New Testament, so Protestantism secured itself with the aid of—scholarly exegesis. It all centers around preventing us from or protecting us against getting the impact of God's word.

x⁴ A 428   n.d., 1851

« 2891 *The Gospel of the Good Shepherd*[580]

Theme: the difference between the hireling and the shepherd first becomes clearly evident—when the wolves come.

This is aimed at "Christendom." In calm weather, when everything is secure, when there are no dangers for Christianity, yes, in fact all the advantages are bound up with it—then it is easy to confuse the shepherd and the hireling, then it suits the hireling perfectly to be the shepherd. But when the wolves come—. Thus it is really the hirelings who have invented the kind of security which "Christendom" is. They know very well that when the wolves come it will become evident that they are not shepherds. This being the case, they are interested in keeping the wolves from coming. This can give them a superficial likeness to shepherds.* Because—when the wolves come, when they can no longer be kept away, then it will become obvious that the hirelings are hirelings.

*Yet it is easy to see the difference: the hireling fears the coming of the wolves not for sake of the sheep but for his own sake, that he will lose the gain and that, in addition, it will become evident that he is a hireling.

———

Incidentally, it is worth noting that the Gospel of the good shepherd is accompanied by the Epistle of Peter[581] which treats of the imitation [*Efterfølgelse*] of Christ, although those who selected this Epistle were probably influenced by the closing words: You were like sheep without a shepherd.

x⁴ A 526   n.d., 1852

« 2892

In margin of 2891 (x⁴ A 526):

Introduction

"The hireling" and "the shepherd" are not different from one another as, for example, red and black are different, so that one can see the difference immediately with half an eye. It must be remembered that the secret and the art of the hireling consists precisely in doing everything to resemble the shepherd as deceptively as possible. The hireling does not put the label "hireling" on his hat—heavens, no, on no account must anyone find out that I am anything but the shepherd.

x^4 A 527   n.d.

« 2893 Christianity in the New Testament— Christendom

In the New Testament becoming a Christian is presented (as in Matthew 10) as the most terrible collision with every most intimate relationship: to hate father and mother,[582] to slay one's child, etc.—in "Christendom" Christianity is applied inversely precisely to knit these natural intimate relationships more intimately together—Christianity means specifically to love father and mother.

In the Gospel about the great banquet[583] one man excuses himself, saying: I have married a wife, and another says: I have bought a yoke of oxen, etc.—consequently the invitation comes in such a way that to accept it would disturb one's getting married and running his business, etc. In "Christendom" Christianity is applied as a consecration formula, and one goes to church on Sunday to get God's help in making a living.

x^4 A 607   n.d., 1852

« 2894 The Compassionate Samaritan

"How do you read?" Christ[584] asks the lawyer, and then leads him to see that by reading the Law he himself ought to understand it essentially as Christ now interprets it to him.

And then we read again the parable of the Samaritan—but let us imagine that this parable had been transcribed at the time of Christ and after reading it someone came to Christ again, just like the lawyer —then Christ must again say: How do you read? and in this way he always adds a new interpretation and always in such a way that the "How do you read?" which preceded this new commentary now again at the end turns to the reader: How do you read? And so it must continue—until action follows; for anyone who does not act accordingly will most likely hit on some escape or other which necessitates a new reproachful "How do you read?" and a new commentary. Action is the true understanding of the law.

The parable of the compassionate Samaritan[585] could be understood metaphorically: (1) It is I who am the priest and the Levite; (2)

It is I to whom it is said: Go and do; (3) It is I who have fallen among robbers (the power of sin over me, also the fact that I have not acted according to this Gospel) and Christ is the Samaritan.

x[5] A 15   *n.d.*, 1852

« 2895 *Christianity*

Whoever you are, take the New Testament, put aside all commentaries and human doctrinal concepts and symbolic books, pick up the New Testament and read it—and then say whether what is taught here is actually anything for a child, do you dare preach it to a child? You will no doubt answer: No. Then I ask: What is it, then, that we are doing in Christendom? Actually, we cook up something ourselves which we call Christianity—that is, we distill all the mildness out of the New Testament and leave the rigorousness behind. This mildness we call Christianity and offer it to children. What wonder, then, that this mildness (which is almost mythology and poetry) pleases children! And when the concoction pleases the children, we turn the thing around and say that just because it pleases the children it is proved to be true Christianity, and we talk about child-faith as the highest.

Or think of a young girl on the day she is to be confirmed and strengthened in her sense of being a Christian—think of her, so hopeful and happy, in childlike loveliness overflowing in expectation—and it is indeed New Testament Christianity in which she is to be confirmed. Now, then, do you have the courage to tell her what it is she is doing, that by a sacred oath she is committing herself for life to the doctrine that commands one to renounce this world, to hate oneself, and presupposes sheer suffering for the doctrine? Do you have the courage to do this? No, you do not. So what do you do? You alter Christianity, distill sweetness out of it and offer it to the girl—and it suits her completely. Then finally we turn the thing around and in later years say we are not the true Christians we were at confirmation—alas, and that was not Christianity at all.

x[5] A 48   *n.d.*, 1852

« 2896 *The Christianity of the New Testament— The Proclamation of Official Christianity*

It is not just a matter of speaking in tongues[586] on that Pentecost day; no, the whole language of the New Testament, although using the same words and the same language we use, is a speaking in tongues.

To be persecuted from city to city, flogged, and so on, and then to say that this is sheer joy, to thank God for the grace to be whipped etc.—that is speaking in tongues.

The official preaching, or the official nonsense for which thousands are salaried and earn a wage just as well as the Capitoline geese, consists in omitting any mention of this, as if it were nothing—or, it amounts to the same thing, in parodying what was said. Christianity is sheer joy—I got a good festival offering last year; Christianity is sheer joy—I was knighted by the king; Christianity is sheer joy—I shall now go home and eat Christmas rice pudding and ham and roast goose and drink punch and so on and so on.

It seems to me that we could at least point out in church how infinitely far we are from resembling Christianity.

x^5 A 66 *n.d., 1853*

« **2897** *How "Christendom" Reads the New Testament, Especially the Gospels*

This is how the New Testament is divided: every word Christ spoke pointing toward the strenuousness and suffering related to being a Christian, of this we say: This does not apply to us; this was spoken expressly to the disciples. We make capital, however, of every word of consolation, of promise. Whether the New Testament records that Christ spoke to the apostles or expressly to the apostles or not makes no difference to "Christendom." No, if in the very same passage in the New Testament where it says that Christ spoke to the apostles there is found one word pointing toward strenuousness and also a word of promise, the actual situation in "Christendom" is that the first word is almost never heard—after all, it was spoken to the apostles— and the other is heard incessantly, even though it, too, was spoken particularly to the apostles.

If the matter were not so serious, one might be tempted to say it is ridiculous to see such Christians as generally are found in "Christendom" consoling themselves with such promises and words of consolation. For even if it were not cheating to appropriate those words to themselves, the words nevertheless still do not fit them. O, in the world of the spirit there is an eternal consistency: words like those strong words of consolation really fit only a corresponding strenuousness.

"Christendom" falsely appropriates the words of consolation and encouragement—and in the long run still never uses them. For in the world of the spirit everything hangs together: if I truly were to use such a prodigiously exalted consolation, the first effect the consolation would have would be to make my life more strenuous. The first thing the consolation does is to give me strenuousness.

But "Christendom" lives in imagination and dreams. It is obvious that one can cheat his way to money and power etc., and it is actual money and power that he gets; but one cannot cheat his way to the consolation of the eternal.

Yet *mundus vult decipi*—not only is Christendom deceived, no, it *wants* to be deceived; it becomes furious and hates, persecutes, slays the person who does not want to deceive it. Therefore "Christendom" would surely become furious if someone showed that this kind of Christianity is a chimera. No, Christendom wants to have the delusion of being a Christian—therefore the place where it will really make a difference whether one has been a Christian or not is—eternity, where delusions are of no help.

But Christianity has become so inverted that men actually believe that Christianity is part and parcel of the proper enjoyment of this life; we need this reassurance of eternity in order to enjoy this life properly, and this Christendom gives us.

How extremely preposterous!

X^5 A 78   *n.d.*, 1853

« 2898 *The unconditioned—an immediate relationship to God—the New Testament neither is nor can be absolutely directly or literally normative for us ordinary men—grace—Luther.*

For a person to be able unconditionally to express the unconditioned, he must have an immediate relationship to God, and God must *in concreto* say to him what he *in concreto* is to do, so that he is exempted from all responsibility for what his task is, what he is to do, and is entirely blameless if God commands him, for example, to fast for ten days, which is fatal, etc. etc.

It is different with us ordinary men who do not have an immediate or direct relationship to God but must try to find out on our own what *in concreto* we are to do.

From this we also see that the New Testament cannot absolutely directly and literally be normative for us, for what does the New Testament express? First of all, the life of Christ, but he, indeed, is the God-man. Furthermore, everyone who lived contemporary with Christ and saw in him the God-man had *eo ipso* an immediate relationship to

God, and Paul was called by a revelation and therefore had an immediate relationship to God.

Alas, what I have suffered in this regard, because I dejectedly intended to make the New Testament literally normative for my life, I, who did not have an immediate relationship to God. But, O, God is not one who places the same requirement upon a person who knows directly from God what he is to do and the one who on his own responsibility must himself discover what the task is. If God commands me directly, *in concreto,* to run this or that risk, do this or that (*in concreto*) with my death as the result—well, I have no responsibility. But, if I have no immediate or direct relationship to God, then it is my own responsibility—do I have the right to do it? If I have an immediate or direct relationship to God and God *in concreto* tells me what I am to do and also tells me in advance how I shall suffer because of it—well, then I know clearly by the suffering that I am on the right path. But, if I have no immediate relationship to God, can I on my own responsibility presume to recognize my God-relationship by suffering; a God-relationship can also be recognized by prosperity, etc.!

We see from this that the New Testament is not literally regulative for us ordinary human beings, that is, the lives portrayed in the New Testament are a whole quality different from what it is to be an ordinary man.

Here the doctrine of "grace" emerges. If I do not have an immediate and direct relationship to God, so that he *in concreto* tells me what I *in concreto* am to do, then, in order to find rest and peace of soul, I must *eo ipso* have *grace in the first place.* Grace in the first place! What frightful afflictions and struggles these words bring to my mind. And yet I would not wish to be rid of a single one of these sufferings; God be praised and thanked that in one sense I came to be aware of grace in such a severe way; it is all too easy to take it in vain. But it is entirely true: grace in the first place. Grace for the future, not only for the past. Yet what does it mean—grace in the first place, grace for the future? This is what it means: since I am only an ordinary human being and do not have an immediate relationship to God but must try on my own responsibility to find (*in concreto*) my task, what I am to do, I must use my understanding as well as I can, and I have responsibility in this respect, and on the other hand, even though I use it as well as I am able, alas, it is still foolishness—therefore I need grace in the first place —if not, I must literally go mad or despair.

Next to the New Testament, Luther is the truest figure. What does

Luther express? Luther expresses a halt, an act of awareness. In him mankind or Christendom comes to be aware that between the God-man and us other men, yes, between the apostle and us other men, there is a qualitative difference, and that therefore "grace" must be introduced. The first Christians, the old Church fathers, did not understand it this way; they naively went all out for imitation [*Efterfølgelse*]. Honor and praise to them! But at the basis of all their striving there nevertheless was an ignoring of the fact that between the God-man and an ordinary human being there lies a qualitative difference, that an ordinary man cannot or dare not (even though he ever so honestly would) decline his life according to that paradigm.

With Luther, therefore, there is a kind of thinning out of Christianity, compared with the earliest Christians; in another sense there is an advance with respect to the naïveté that an ordinary man, however honestly he would try, can have the God-man literally as the prototype.

Luther reduced Christianity. What I blame him for is that he did not make this manifestly apparent, that the most we have is a casual note in the *Augsburg Confession*,[587] in the articles on abuses: no. 2, *de conjugio Sacerdotum*, 14: *Et cum senescente mundo paulatim natura humana fiat imbecillior.*

In Luther there is a reduction. Yet hatred toward oneself still remains, but in another form. Fundamental to the earliest Christians' striving lay the naïve idea that they really were able to come up to the prototype, and that to hate oneself was to fast and flagellate oneself or become a martyr. In Luther's position, to hate oneself has another locus, refers specifically to slaying the understanding, to how a man needs grace, something which can be equally as difficult for flesh and blood, for flesh and blood can also be willing to fast and flagellate oneself and let oneself be burned, if it only remains fixed that likeness to the God-man, to the apostle, can be attained.

X[5] A 96   *n.d.,* 1853

« **2899** *Nonsense*

Böhringer, in the biography of Bernard of Clairvaux (*Die Kirche und ihre Zeugen,* II, part I, p. 550) discusses Hildegard and relates that the Pope fully accepted the claim that she had actually had divine revelation.

Charming, what charming absent-mindedness. The Pope does not realize at all that this puts her a whole quality higher than he is. No, the Pope sits there quite impassively and acknowledges divine revelations in the same way as one customarily acknowledges that a person has great talents.

x⁵ A 135   *n.d.*, 1853

« 2900 *The Laborers in the Vineyard*[588]

The wages were the same for all of them. The wages are eternal salvation—the category of quality. Those who want the wages to be different want to finitize and secularize the eternal. In worldly affairs a scaled wage is quite proper; in the sphere of the purely qualitative, the eternal, the wages are uniform. In any case, if there is to be a difference, it must be made by the giver himself; it cannot be demanded by the laborer.

x⁵ A 140   *n.d.*, 1853

« 2901 *Christ Said This Particularly to the Apostles*

This is what we usually say about everything Christ said which we do not find convenient.

If what he said suits us, then nothing is said about Christ's having spoken particularly to the disciples—as for example: Blessed are the eyes that see what you see.[589]

At the very end of Luther's sermon[590] on the Gospel for the Nineteenth Sunday after Trinity, I also note that he clearly appropriates to himself and to every Christian Christ's words to the apostles: Receive the Holy Spirit. If you forgive the sins of any, etc.

But in the same manner we might also claim the gift of miracle.

XI¹ A 26   *n.d.*, 1854

« 2902 *A Crime Story*

Christianity not only does not exist, no, it is nonexistent in such a way that what we admonish against at every single solitary point as being detestable, impious—that, precisely that, is New Testament Christianity. Aha, it is ingenious and reassuring, all right, but it is also very criminal. Given the ever so many thousands who are participating thoughtlessly in it and the many, many who are doing it *bona fide*, there must have been and must be some real rascals among them, since otherwise the situation could not have arisen or advanced in this way.

The matter is very simple. What the New Testament understands by Christianity is shockingly opposed to flesh and blood, the natural man, is mortally against him, yes, there is nothing which opposes him in this way; and there is nothing the natural man shrinks from more than he shrinks from that which the New Testament calls Christianity.

This we must leave to God, since in his view to love God is to hate the world; Christianity expresses this also in the New Testament with complete accuracy, with a divine accuracy.

But we do not want to act in this way, do not want to be honest in this way, do not want to admit (which is my proposal) what Christianity is and that in this sense we are not Christian. Man, even the most stupid, is a very clever creation where flesh and blood are concerned; where they are concerned he has an extraordinarily keen instinct. And his instinct has taught him: it does not pay to do things this way; you will find that the *summa summarum* will happen, you will become a Christian if you are just that honest about Christianity.

Consequently we need to be better protected. This is achieved by inventing something which is convenient for us and then with every imaginable art loading it with scripture passages—and this we call Christianity. But for perfect security we turn New Testament Christianity around in such a way that we admonish against it as the most detestable and impious of all.

This is the case at every single, solitary point in official Christianity. This can be demonstrated at every point, but consider here only one which is related to one [on Spirit] treated from another angle in the previous journal entry [i.e., XI^1 A 72]. To venture on the scale which the New Testament understands by venturing, if there is to be praying in earnest for the Holy Spirit—this is not convenient for us human beings. "Then we could certainly admit this." No, that is really not enough—it gets us nowhere, does not secure us sufficiently against becoming Christian. Ergo, we turn the relationship around: to spare ourselves and enjoy life is true Christianity. To venture according to the criterion is— — —to tempt God. See—now we are safe, perfectly safe. Should I be so presumptuous as to tempt God? God forbid!

O, of all crime stories, this is the most frightful!

XI^1 A 73   *n.d.*, 1854

« **2903** *A Difficulty with the New Testament, That in One Sense It Seems Unusable in Actual Life*

The dimensions in the New Testament are all on a large scale. From this it follows that the dimensions of error, corruption, etc. are also on a large scale, are structured ideally.

That, unfortunately, is why the greatest and most widespread error and misunderstanding, the most triumphant in every age, is barely warned against in the New Testament; it is as if the New Testament were so ideal that it neither could nor would give any thought to the idea that men could sink so deep, become so lamentable.

The New Testament[591] denounces wrong doctrine, hypocrisy, works-righteousness, etc.—but there is really not a passage in the New Testament against the orthodoxy which is nonsense, mediocrity, tripe, and balderdash, a playing at Christianity and living in platitudes. It is almost as if the New Testament regarded thinking about such things as beneath its dignity.

But, alas, such is the true Christianity and orthodoxy of millions and millions and of the official preachers. And they exploit the fact that the New Testament does not speak of such things to make themselves out to be the true Church.

The New Testament contains the divine truth. Just as it is high above all errors, extravagances, etc., so mediocrity, chatter, pettiness, and nonsense are low in their onesidedness. But since nonsense nevertheless has the tendency not to be onesided, it capitalizes on this in making a claim to be the truly divine, which rises above all onesidedness.

This is the way history marches on—millions and millions of Christians. Yet the New Testament is a wonderful book; it is always right, even if the opposite seems to be the case. When one considers "Christendom," these millions of Christians, and then reads in the New Testament: The way is narrow and those who find it are few; you will be hated by all; whoever kills you will think he is offering service to God —it certainly seems that the New Testament is wrong and has been proven untrue. Relax, my friend, for the New Testament is all too right. In the course of time there will have lived a single individual among these millions, a number of single individuals—the way is narrow and they come to be hated by all and killing them is regarded as serving God—yes, these single individuals are the Christians—see the New Testament.

XI[1] A 107   n.d., 1854

« 2904 *Our Distance from New Testament Christianity*

In the New Testament the relationship is: God—man; an individual man relates himself quite simply and directly, without any distancing middle term, to every single solitary man of these countless millions —thus he could, if God so willed and he himself as well, become an apostle, a disciple.

Nowadays the relationship is as follows: between Christ and the individual an enormous abstraction is introduced—the state, or the race. This state (which only figuratively can be called Christian—for otherwise it would have to be formed by individuals who relate themselves first of all to Christ) takes it upon itself to hire—according to the size of the state—1,000 or 10,000 clergymen who objectively proclaim the teachings of Christ.

Objectively!—again an enormous distance from the individual's relating himself to Christ.

Then "the pastor" preaches objectively. And since he has plenty to do preaching, how in the world could he ever find the time to do anything he says.

The congregation exempts itself by declaring that the kind of religiousness which can be required only of the pastor cannot be required of it.

But then Christianity is nothing but mythology, poetry—it is not the atheist who says this—no, on closer inspection it is the orthodox Church itself which expresses it.

XI¹ A 110   n.d., 1854

« 2905 Law—Gospel

In the New Testament the relationship of the gospel to the law is that of the radical cure. All those commands and orders of the law avail nothing; nothing comes of them; a person is never saved by them. No, come in all earnestness to a breaking point, a breakthrough; break with all that within you with which the law with all its commands is quarreling; break with it entirely—all of your past has been forgiven (grace) and God will help you (grace). Become a new man, perfect as the truth (the gospel is the truth).

But in the New Testament, especially in the gospels, there is no trace of what we have made of it—that grace is a discharge from the law.

But here as always we exploit the words. We take the word "grace" and what pleases us we call grace, the Christian doctrine of grace. We do not consider that Christianity is God's invention and in relation to his infinite majesty and our great guilt we ought to rejoice over what he, out of his genuine love to us, calls grace.

XI¹ A 138   n.d., 1854

« 2906 The New Testament

What makes it so difficult for us human beings to get the right impression of the New Testament is that the redoubling [*Fordoblelse*] which belongs to divine majesty is so entirely foreign to us that we have no criterion for the "I-ness" [*Egoitet*] which is always just as great in affirmations as it is in denials, just as great in divine prodigality as it is in divine economy, just as great in giving as it is in holding back.

When One says: Come unto me, all of you;[592] and further: I have come into the world not to judge it but to save it[593]—at once we get confused and immediately conceive of millions and millions saved, the whole world, etc. We fail to see that while the Savior of the world holds to what he has said, at the same time the divine is that tremendous I-ness, so that, *summa summarum*, only very few will be saved, and yet, even if not a single one were saved, he would still not change what he said: Come unto me, all of you; I have not come into the world to judge it but to save it.

Therefore in "Christendom" Christianity has become almost what we call barbershop talk. We have taken separate sentences (without their counter sentences), especially those sentences which appeal to us —and thereby the endless nonsense of "Christendom" has come into existence. Surely it was an injustice to Columbus that America was not named for him; it is another kind of injustice to Jesus Christ that Christendom is named for him.

As already said, the New Testament is the divinely majestic, and therefore there are always the sentence and the counter sentence, with the implication of the requirement of faith and the prevention of outright impertinence and chumminess.

XI[1] A 154 *n.d.*, 1854

« 2907 *Perhaps All of Christianity Could Be Thought of This Way*

With divine intention the New Testament is so constituted that with the same God-pleasing honesty all sorts of men (every man) can interpret it each according to his own wisdom. That is just the way God wants it to be, for he is spirit and wants to be worshipped as spirit; therefore he wants the person, the Christian, to be an individual and thus to endure the enormous strain of not being able to get information from other men but having to involve himself with God primitively, taking before God the responsibility for his interpreting the New Testament the way he does. God does not want those specimen-men [*Exemplar-Mennesker*] who fritter their lives away as specimens and mimickers [*Efterabere*], sneaking off from the strenuousness which, however, is not beyond human power, for every human being is intended and outfitted [*lagt an*] to become an individual—that is, primitively relating himself to God, not sharing in the nonsense of generations and of millions, not using it for cover or for excusing himself, but alone, conscious of his responsibility, relating to God, without all the clothes-changing and disguising, responsible to God for how he understands what it is to be a Christian.

But as soon as an individual relates himself primitively to God according to the New Testament and interprets it according to his own wisdom, he will have a collision if he does not let go of it. This is why, as it says in the New Testament, the Christian must suffer for the doctrine.

Glancing through the history of Christendom, we see that those single individuals who primitively related themselves to God according to the New Testament thereby suffered for their Christianity—they were, *summa summarum,* the Christians.

For every single one of these there are perhaps thousands or, as the case might be, millions and trillions of specimen-men. As a matter of fact, there are also specimen-martyrs—that is, martyrs who risk life and limb on someone else's word and gown[594] and consequently without the primitive strenuousness which, after all, is the decisive thing.

O, it is so easy to run in the herd as a specimen, as a number among the millions, as a parrot and mimic who lets another person apprehend some truth in the most horrible agony—and then play act it, take him as a result and a guarantee that they can busy themselves with filling their lives with every possible earthly goal.

Is this not the enormous forgery: to jumble and confuse the strenuousness of primitivity in order to get rid of it—the primitivity which every human being can have, for he is primitively intended and outfitted for it, intended and outfitted to understand that he stands alone, alone, alone with God—to jumble and confuse this with differentiating factors of genius, talent, etc.?

Is it incorrect to regard almost the whole history of Christendom (with the exception of the early period) as an enormous swindle on the part of "man," inasmuch as, knowing the enormous strenuousness (and also loftiness) of that which God required and commanded—to become a disciple—and in order to get out of it, man craftily confused disciple and apostle with genius and talent, and then—then was humbly satisfied with not aspiring to anything as high as being a disciple or an apostle.

Christ chose men from the people, from the common class, to be apostles and disciples, in order to express that every human being is able to be one. But we see that "man" is clever; he quickly turned the whole thing around and said: Well, fine, but it is confoundedly strenuous to be an apostle or disciple, so I, as far as I am concerned, would rather be exempted from that great distinction. But in addition to being clever, man is also cowardly and hypocritical; therefore he did not say it aloud, no, he adulterated what it is to be an apostle and a disciple to being a genius, etc.—and so we are happily rid of Christianity in a nice way. And when things really got rolling, this whole business of millions and millions of Christians began in earnest.

What isn't being done (by way of erecting great, impressive buildings to the memory of those apostles, countless crowds parading on their festival days), what isn't being done to hide that which, after all, embarrasses us—namely, that every one of us could also be a disciple, an apostle—but it is so confoundedly strenuous.

As far as I know there is a creature which lives in the water and has no other means of defense than to muddy the water and slip away. Presumably there are also land creatures which defend themselves by raising clouds of dust. In the same way "Christendom" takes the prize for water-muddying and dust-raising in order thereby to get away from the New Testament. Except that human beings are hypocrites, which animals are not, and therefore they have given this great enterprise the appearance of being zeal for Christianity.

And is it not zeal for Christianity, after all, to make millions and millions of Christians—and then, in that great swarm, to be able to sneak away from the New Testament's criterion and requirement for being Christian?

Is it not zeal, true zeal for Christianity, to erect Herculean buildings in memory of an apostle, a disciple—and thereby bury in forgetfulness the idea that one could himself be an apostle, a disciple, and that what hinders a person is actually not humility but something else which can be forgiven if one is honest enough to admit the true situation but which cannot be forgiven when one hypocritically hides it.

XI^1 A 155 *n.d.,* 1854

« **2908** *Christianity*

With a keenness reserved only for the divine majesty, Christianity in the New Testament (consequently, Christianity) is designed to wound the natural man so bitterly that nothing, nothing is able to enflame him the way it does. Therefore the completely correct, true, the only reliable judgment on Christianity, the judgment of contemporary paganism—namely, that Christianity is hatred of mankind, *odium generis humani*[595]—for according to Christianity there is a life-and-death struggle and battle between what it is to be God and what it is to be man, and to love God is to hate oneself and this world and everything the natural man loves, loves with the passion of his whole soul. Nothing, therefore, is more certain than what the New Testament predicts, that the true Christian will come to be hated, despised, put to death, and with a passion expended on no one else who is put to death.

But since the time of the martyrs God has not once had a single one among the extra-ordinary officials (the ordinary or ordained tradesmen, the preachers and professors, naturally cannot be counted as officials except insofar as they are officials in the counter-party, against God in the name of being for God), not a single solitary one, who in the crucial moment did not become humanely soft-hearted or blinked his eyes and became a little afraid, in short, who did not in one way or another chisel off a little of what Christianity actually is, thereby helping more and more to become Christians.

Finally "man" has so browbeaten the proclamation of Christianity that today Christianity is the very opposite of what it is in the New Testament.

Take some present-day examples. No honest man with the New Testament in his hand (and a pastor, after all, by oath is bound to it) can conduct a marriage ceremony as it is done nowadays. No! Remember, the New Testament is intended to wound the natural man deeply with divine penetration. The pagan ranked it as the greatest happiness to fall in love, to be happily in love; humanly speaking, the most happy of all sights is a pair of happy lovers. But Christianly! Christianly, it is a wake—if there must be a celebration, it must be as if at a funeral. How tragic, declares Christianity, that once again there are two who want to be united this way in order to belong more firmly to this sinful world and to propagate this sinful race further by their progeny.

Consequently, from a Christian point of view the kind of celebration which is used now—and where the clergyman is along—is a lie, the scurviest sort of lie. No honest man can get it out of the New Testament—and the clergyman in fact is bound by oath to the New Testament.

With the New Testament instructing him, the clergyman must conduct himself as follows. He must first of all call the lovers into his presence, admonishing them that the solitary life is more pleasing to

God, is a truer life for the Christian, whose life, after all, is to be a crucifixion. Then he can read aloud to them Paul's words[596] that nevertheless it is better, consequently more pleasing to God, to marry than to burn.

This then becomes the wedding text—and from a Christian point of view a quiet sorrow ought to be the keynote for this sorrowful occasion.

Conversely, no honest man with the New Testament in his hand —and the clergyman is in fact bound by oath to the New Testament— is able to take part in the kind of graveside ceremony we have nowadays. No, from a Christian point of view there ought to be delight and cheerfulness, here we should be dressed in white—and that is the way it was in the early Church, whereas now we use white at weddings. Here the sounds of joy should be raised, joyfullly, joyfully, joyfully, as nowadays at the celebration of a birth (but that is the way the day of death was regarded in the early Church) or as at a wedding ceremony (but in the early Church that was looked upon almost as a person's day of death; by the death the soul is united with the beloved).

Thus at every possible point present-day Christianity is a villainous lie inasmuch as it passes itself off as New Testament Christianity.

XI[1] A 157   *n.d.*, 1854

« 2909 *The Unconditional Condition for Becoming Christian*

This is, in unconditionally obedient silence and submission to the New Testament, to get to know what Christianity is—whether it seems sweet or bitter to us men, terrifying or joyous, desirable or frightening, etc.

This is simply the way one relates himself to Christianity.

But in the course of time the unconditional respect for God dwindled. The relationship was turned around and became modified in this syllogism: This would surely be frightful, a nightmare, for us men— therefore this cannot be Christianity, i.e., mankind decides what Christianity is, i.e., Christianity is abolished.

XI[1] A 316   *n.d.*, 1854

« 2910 *The Wrong Turn in Christendom*

Yes, if it were only yesterday that true Christianity was proclaimed and today that the wrong turn was made, how very easy it would be to show where the mistake lies.

But it has gone on now for a long, long time. And for many, many people the error has been changed, *bona fide,* into this solemn slogan: Hold fast to the faith of the fathers, which again the ecclesiastical rogues know how to make use of. How slyly even Bishop Mynster knew how to use it.

And yet, from a Christian point of view, all that about the faith of our fathers is a fallacy, a fallacy in any age. Christianly, the faith of our fathers can never be spoken of as something conclusive. Christianly, there is only the question of the New Testament, with which every generation has to begin. The confusion which has produced "Christendom" and taken Christianity back to Judaism is that in the course of time, instead of beginning with the New Testament, each separate generation began with "the faith of our fathers," with clinging to the faith of the fathers. Always this swindle of the historical and the category of the race instead of what is essentially Christian—ideality and the single individual.

XI[1] A 392   n.d.,   1854

« 2911 *God's Word*

This word of God, very simply, contains God's will for us and his commands—and this we evade in such a way that we pretend as if everything were in order. We have God's word, we are a Christian nation, and so on—and the only things which occupy us are the artistic, the scientific-scholarly.

All this is fundamentally matchless insolence.

And yet it is so. While the pastors dispute about who can write most beautifully, while journals and periodicals with deep seriousness criticize the artistic aspects of the language, the construction, etc., we completely forget that we are to act according to this, that God has not really given his word as material for a literary exercise to see who is able to present it most elegantly. This is so completely forgotten that to say it in earnest would be regarded as ridiculous. In earnest, that means some place other than in a church or in a sermon, for in being said there it does not become earnest but naturally comes under the heading of art, a matter of whether or not it has been expressed elegantly.

XI[1] A 395   n.d.,   1854

« 2912 *God's Word*

"After all, we have God's word." Yes, of course, namely, in such a way that between every single individual and the word of God is

inserted 1800 years of opinions about how God's word is to be understood—to have it in this manner is just about like "having the reward"
—"elsewhere."

"And, after all, we have oath-bound teachers who individually
have taken an oath upon the New Testament." Yes, of course, but
between the oath of each and every one of these teachers and the New
Testament is inserted 1800 years of opinions about how the New Testament is to be understood; further, there is inserted the idea: I take my
oath just as do the other clergymen of the time—in a way which makes
it preferable to do away with the oath.

XI¹ A 452   n.d., 1854

« **2913**

Matthew 12:34: How can you speak good when you are evil?

In a certain sense one might say that precisely this is a kind of evil,
this dissimulation which prevents what Christ adds—the mouth speaks
out of the abundance of the heart. The passage must therefore not be
interpreted to mean that Christ asserted that they did not do it; neither
should it be interpreted negatively, that they did not speak good, that
precisely this dissimulation was the heart's abundance from which
their mouths spoke evil (good words).

XI¹ A 571   n.d., 1854

« **2914** *"Christendom" a Conspiracy*

"Christendom" is a conspiracy against New Testament Christianity.

The problem is to see this, for it is not readily seen, even though
once it is said it is extremely easy to see. But it is not easily seen, for
no one dreams of a conspiracy along such lines. But it is a conspiracy
nevertheless and, as pointed out elsewhere [i.e., XI² A 39], is in a certain
sense an expression of respect for Christianity in that we do not conspire to rebel openly but conspire cunningly to falsify the concept of
being a Christian and make the world Christian (the world with which,
according to the New Testament, one should be engaged in battle and
by which one should be persecuted).

"Christendom" is a conspiracy against New Testament Christianity. I know very well that Christendom would like to make us
believe that they are wonderful Christians, that the atheists and the
sectarians etc. are the conspirators. No, no, it is an old dodge—for
example, when a thief is being chased, he hits on the idea of himself

shouting: Stop, thief!—in order to divert attention from himself. Thus "Christendom" is feverishly defending orthodoxy against sects and atheists etc., but one is not fooled by that; Christendom itself is the conspiracy against New Testament Christianity and is far more dangerous than all the atheists and sects.

Christendom is a conspiracy against New Testament Christianity. What was Catiline's conspiracy, what was any well-known historic conspiracy, what were all of them together compared to this conspiracy.

But now the next point—what is to be used against this enormous conspiracy, where can sufficient recruits be found to take up arms against these masses? Well, this point is enough to throw especially the public and persons of a good, decent sort into a rage—the next point is that it is the single individual, a single individual, who is to be used.

Frightful! And yet it is the only legitimate thing, the only logical thing, to do. For if a combination of two is used, the conspiracy is not radically broken up; if a combination of two is used, then that which is used against the conspiracy contains the seeds of a new conspiracy against New Testament Christianity; for where there are two there are also ten, and then a hundred, etc.—and when it gets to be a million, we have the conspiracy. The numerical is actually the conspiracy, for the numerical craftily suffocates the point in Christianity. Under the guise of zeal for Christianity the numerical smothers Christianity; just as a mother under the guise of solicitude might lie on her child and smother it, just so does the numerical lie on Christianity and smother it to death.

The numerical is the conspiracy. Just as in civil life, when crowds of people collect in the street, the police pitch in immediately, regardless of whether or not a crime has been committed, for the massing together of men is a crime—so also, and with a completely different kind of right, the higher police immediately and directly attack wherever millions of Christians show up—the greater the number, the more certain that it is a lie, the more certain that there is a falsification here.

This can be regarded as a counter-proposition to what has delighted the clergy for a long time now—the spread of Christianity.

XI^2 A 174   *n.d.*, 1854

« 2915 *Christianity*

What makes it so extremely difficult even to become merely aware of what Christianity means is that by nature we have a viewpoint flatly contrary to that of the New Testament, a completely different kind of eyes, so to speak.

The New Testament's viewpoint is simply and solely—the eternal. That is the subject matter with which it is concerned—and it declares (which is the truth) that if an eternal damnation is involved, then whatever you suffer during these few years of temporal life is nothing, yes, sheer grace if you get off with suffering as much as possible these few years and then become eternally blessed. That is, the New Testament is immersed in the eternal to such an extent that it treats this life as a mere bagatelle.

It is just the opposite with us men. We are so preoccupied with this life, with having it good in this life, with avoiding suffering in this life, that we really prefer to defer the matter of eternity, or wish to take the easiest way to get a kind of certainty that endorses our preoccupation with enjoying this life.

Thus eternal life is the single important matter for Christianity—for us [it is] something close to our present life.

This viewpoint also sheds light on my thesis that Christianity does not exist at all.

When Christianity truly exists, it means that the eternal is of such importance to a man that this life is a bagatelle to him, this life with all possible sufferings is still only a bagatelle compared to escaping eternal damnation.

Ergo, when the temporal has become the most important, yes, when the eternal is even exploited by the temporal, is obliged to do a job connected with enhancing the desire to enjoy this life—then Christianity is so falsified that it simply does not exist.

Christianity in the New Testament puts it this way: Before God human existence is so culpable that there can be no question of altogether escaping punishment. Consequently choose, choose to suffer in this life—become a Christian in the New Testament understanding of what it means, and hope then for an eternal salvation, the offer of which is still sheer grace.

In Christendom everything has become so twisted that the Christian uses the blessedness of eternity as a refinement within the enjoyment of this life.

XI^2 A 181   *n.d.,* 1854

« **2916**

"The way is narrow, and there are few who find it"[597]—thus in the New Testament.

In Christendom we all walk along one and the same way, which is supposed to be the right way.

$$XI^2 \text{ A } 316 \quad n.d., \text{ 1854}$$

« 2917 *Is This the Education or the Demoralization of Teachers of Christianity?*

From a Christian point of view, everything, everything depends upon the individual's reading the New Testament as primitively as possible.

Every effort is made to prevent just that—in the name of educating teachers in Christianity.

He is educated—that is, he is initiated into all the countless fads which human mediocrity has devised in order to escape the Christian requirement (this is more or less the history of Christendom), he is initiated into them, and he is, if possible, made callous by the idea that there are millions and millions who have carried on this way.

And this is called educating! I should think that it is—from a Christian point of view—demoralizing.

An example. Read the New Testament primitively and you will get the impression very plainly that Christianity does not want you to marry. But that is not what men want. Thus the history of Christianity is everything men have devised over the centuries to enable them to make marriage compatible with the New Testament, and men are initiated in this (yes, somewhat like being initiated by going to the dance hall), in this they are initiated, in this educated (how elevating!) to become teachers of Christianity.

It is the same at every point. By nature man is against the Christianity of the New Testament. So people are educated, that is, people are initiated into all the swindles men have devised in order to outsmart the New Testament. And this education is altogether necessary.

Thereupon the educated teachers go out and educate the congregation.

It is really dreadful, for the confusion is continually raised to a higher power. Would it not be something to despair over if the situation were such that we not only had dance halls as now but young girls supposedly were to be educated in the dance halls, and therefore it was recommended that more dance halls be established.

*   *

In order to be a teacher in Christianity it is necessary that the New Testament be read primitively—and then character-education.

XI² A 364   *n.d.*, 1854–55

« **2918**

"Cyprianus"[598] and such works are prohibited on the grounds that they encourage the superstitious belief that spirits can be conjured forth, for we are afraid of spirits—but the New Testament is propagated on the grandest possible scale—the idea is to get it into everybody's hands, if possible. Yet what book is more capable of evoking the spirits than this—if you only have the capacity to read it.

Yet there is perhaps an unconscious but very refined cunning, an instinctive cunning, involved here—which reckons that distribution of this book to everyone, if possible, is the best protection against it, the best guarantee that it becomes worthless. Right! Hurry up, then, get on with it—if possible, pave the streets with New Testaments, sell them for fuel, cheaper than peat, tile your houses with them, sell them ever cheaper than sand so they can be used as ballast in ships—then you are absolutely protected, then you will be able to assemble at a great festival and a speaker will step forward and praise us and our age for our labor and zeal in extending Christianity.

XI² A 386   *n.d.*, 1854–55

« **2919** *Official Christianity (the Christianity*
of Christendom) New Testament Christianity

(1) The official ("Christendom's") Christianity is quite simply a *fraud,* is a way of defrauding God.

New Testament Christianity is a gift to man but equally as much a commitment for man, and the commitment is so heavy that to be a Christian is, humanly speaking, the greatest misery and wretchedness.

Christendom's Christianity takes Christianity only as gift. That is why it is so busy with the sacraments (superstitiously) and pretends ignorance of any commitment in relation to the sacrament.

This defrauds God, just as it is fraud when someone is designated as an heir but with a definite commitment, and he accepts the inheritance—but shrugs off the commitment, and at most, instead of fulfilling the commitment, returns compliments in insipid thanks for the inheritance.

(2) Official (Christendom's) Christianity is social Christianity, the New Testament's Christianity is anti-social.

This is easy to see, because the formula for New Testament Christianity is in hatred of oneself to love God: but to hate self is really a part of killing and hating the urge, the itch, for sociality, which is something most precious to the natural man. To hate oneself in association with others is not hating oneself—for association expresses loving oneself.

Consequently it is a *swindle* on official Christianity's part to use what the New Testament Christianity says about loving God and the neighbor to convert Christianity into the pagan or Jewish principle of society, by which Christianity becomes just the opposite of what it was in the New Testament.

XI² A 387   *n.d.*, 1854–55

« **2920**

That "Christendom's" Christianity not only dilutes, waters down Christianity, but falsifies its principle, makes it, Christianly understood, the most dangerous poison, so that Christianity of this kind not only does not save but kills.

A

According to the New Testament Christianity is *restlessness*.

Implicit in the New Testament is the view that man, conceived in transgression, born in sin, is a shrewd animal-creature, infatuated with this physical world as if in a kind of bewitchment and enchantment, *loving tranquillity.*

Then Christianity introduces eternity as the most intense restlessness—in order to rescue man from this bewitchment, from this tranquillity.

In Christendom's Christianity Christianity is introduced as a tranquilizer.

As a result, the condition of Christendom is a secularism one whole quality lower than it ever was in paganism; for in Christendom even eternity is used to tranquilize and to lend zest to the enjoyment of life.

B

According to the New Testament God hunts men because he wants to be loved by them.

That is why Christianity is restlessness. In a similar way the fisherman, too, makes a noise in order to scare the fish out of the deep water and the holes.

Christianity, then, is restlessness for the purpose of capturing.

And Christianity is restlessness because God wants to be loved in a contrasting relationship (conflict with "the others").

In "Christendom" Christianity is used to tranquilize, Christianity is used in support of the very principle Christianity is against.

And in Christendom there are Christian peoples, kingdoms, countries, a Christian world. This means that the contrasting relationship (to the others) by being Christian and loving God disappears, and we have paganism.

C

According to the New Testament a person's eternal salvation is determined here in this life. (The decision of eternity is also related inversely to time, the shorter the time the better.)

In Christendom we play the game that this life is merely a first one, all eternity is a striving: we waste this life, and wasting this life is supposed to be Christianity.

XI^2 A 395   *n.d.*, 1855

« 2921 *This Is the Movement in the Deterioration in Christendom*

May 19, 1855

To become [*changed from:* to be] what the N. T. understands by Christian is something the natural man shrinks from more than from being killed—and he has a right to shrink, for to become a Christian, spirit, is to go on living after the natural man in a person has been slain, or to live while slaying the natural man, and consequently the natural man has reason to shrink more from becoming Christian than from death, for death, after all, is only a moment.

To impress the animal creature, the natural man, in such a way that it actually becomes earnest about becoming Christian—for this divine authority is required.

As early as "the apostle" the scaling down process begins, and it seems as if the natural man gets off a little easier in becoming a Christian.

Then the human throng gradually flocks in—all in proportion to the change that takes place in the definition of what it is to be a

Christian, and the definition of "Christian" is continually changed more and more by the influx.

Nowadays whole countries and kingdoms are called Christian.

There are a few who still preserve a true idea of what it is to be Christian—that it means to die to the world—but despair of expressing it in public, for they understand that the natural man becomes enraged when dying to the world is supposed to be earnestness and in this enraged condition wants such a person put to death.

Therefore these few flee the world in order to express what is indeed somewhat truer at a distance from men and from their persecution.

Then the world hits on the idea that to flee is cowardly, that one should remain among men—for the world knows very well that men are not born these days who have the courage, the stamina, to be able to hold out expressing what Christianity is in an environment of millions of natural men disguised as Christians.

XI² A 403   May 19, 1855

NUMBERS, CROWD, MASS, PUBLIC

« 2922

What is really behind the tendency, apparent in people who in one respect or another have deteriorated, to rush pellmell into the world just then instead of shunning it. J. Jürgensen,[599] for example, says that when he is drunk he feels an almost irresistible impulse to be with people, to go just where the crowd is.

See Goethe's *Faust*,[600] p. 197.

I A 165   *n.d.*, 1836

« 2923

A man of considerable understanding will always be regarded by the mass as imprudent. The objection they will raise against him, whereby their understanding presumably surpasses his, will, in fact, be no more or no less than one of the points he himself has thoroughly considered.

VII¹ A 100   *n.d.*, 1846

« 2924

More and more the tendency will be toward writing for the crowd, which understands nothing, and by those who know how to write—for the crowd.[601]

VIII¹ A 132   *n.d.*, 1847

« 2925

Yet I wonder if the voice of the people really was also the voice of God[602] when the Jews cried out: Crucify!

VIII¹ A 199   *n.d.*, 1847

« 2926

. . . . . The crowd spit on him (Christ). You shudder, you would perhaps prefer that such a thing be left unmentioned because it is so horrible, because the fact that it happened shakes one out of his customary soft way of thinking. —But now imagine yourself contemporary with that event. Are you quite sure you would have had tl ᐧ courage to side openly with Christ, to stand by a man mocked by every glance, betrayed by all—on whom the crowd spits. But you were present! Perhaps you were moved to compassion by the sight of the mistreatment of this man, but you stood in the crowd. Far be it from you to participate in those diabolical doings. But look, those standing near you noticed that you did not shout along. Enraged in their wild passion, a couple of them standing nearby grabbed hold of you—your life was at stake, more surely than if you had been attacked by wild animals —and at the moment you had neither the courage nor the resolution to risk your life, at least not for such a man, despised and rejected by all—and you went along with the crowd,* you, too, shouted insults at him, and you, too, spat upon him.[603]

O, we warn young people against going to dens of iniquity, even out of curiosity, because no one knows what might happen. Even more terrible is the danger of being along in the crowd if you are not so unconditionally resolved within yourself concerning what you want that you are willing to sacrifice your life. Ah, but those who are so resolved seldom run with the crowd. In truth, there is no place, not even one most disgustingly dedicated to lust and vice, where a human being is more easily corrupted—than in the crowd.

VIII[1] A 296   n.d., 1847

« **2927**

In margin of 2926 (VIII[1] A 296):

* Consequently you gave in; you participated in the mockery—to save your life, it is true. O monstrous contradiction—the very one whom you mocked died to save your life.[604]

VIII[1] A 297   n.d.

« **2928** *The Impenitence of the Public*

The procedure is quite simple. By means of some anonymous somebody or someone who really is not anything (the ethical—responsibility) but in private life a poet of sorts, a charming little fellow or chap (for example, an author of an amateur comedy for students, that is, for the whole public), the public manages to get said the slander and evil it wants said and then assumes the guilt or the paternity of what its amiable little protege has produced. But to get justice over against the public is an impossibility, just as impossible as catching a fart. The public is nonsense. This is law and order![605]

VIII[1] A 456   n.d., 1847

« 2929

There never has been and there cannot be a Christian reformation which turns against authority as if all would then be well; that would be much too secular a movement. No, the essentially Christian reformation means to turn against the mass, for the essentially Christian reformation means that each person must be reformed,[606] and only then is the most ungodly of all unchristian categories overthrown: the crowd, the public.

VIII^1 A 461   n.d., 1847

« 2930

Of all horrible contrasts this is the most horrible—that the crowd shouted: Let Barrabas live![607] So far was Christ from getting justice in the world! Analogies are not lacking. Usually we call more attention to the analogy "Crucify him"—sometime I will emphasize the analogy "Let Barrabas live!"

VIII^1 A 471   n.d., 1847

« 2931

. . . . . And so *He* was mocked, spit upon, crucified—so deeply degraded. And yet there is still one little aspect which perhaps indicates the degradation most powerfully and horribly. Possibly you do not recognize it, have never heard it talked about, or have heard it so often—that you nevertheless do not recognize it. You see, there was a notorious bandit under guard—the people demanded that he be freed. Is it not true that the contrasts illuminate each other: Christ and Barrabas—yes, and the contrasts: Crucify—Let him live![608]

VIII^1 A 477   n.d., 1847

« 2932

. . . There is a view of life which holds that where the crowd is, there also is the truth, that it must have the crowd on its side. There is another view of life which holds that wherever the crowd is there is untruth.[609] Thus (to carry the matter to its ultimate conclusion for a moment) even though all the individuals quietly, each by himself, possessed the truth, if they got together in a crowd (in such a way that "the crowd" came to have any deciding, balloting, noisy, audible significance), untruth would nevertheless be present at once.[610]

For the crowd (not this one or that, living or dead, but understood ideally) is untruth [changed from *evil*], since the crowd either produces impenitence and irresponsibility or at least weakens the individual's sense of responsibility by making it a fractional category. Notice that no single soldier dared lay hands upon Caius Marius[a] but only three or four women with the consciousness or notion of being a "crowd", with a kind of hope that possibly no one could say definitely who started it[b]—they had the courage to do it.[c] Consider the highest, think of Christ and the entire human race, all the human beings who have been born and ever will be born, but in the situation of singleness— each one as a single individual, all alone with Christ in lonely sur- roundings—and then as a single individual to walk up to him and spit upon him—no human being has ever been born or ever will be born who would have the courage or the audacity to do that.[d] But then they became a crowd, then it went on apace, then they had the courage to do it—dreadful untruth!

For the crowd is untruth. Therefore no one basically has more contempt for what it means to be a human being than those [changed from *one*] who are in the forefront of a crowd. Suppose a single ordi- nary, perhaps impoverished, person comes to such a one—no, he is much too insignificant[e]—no, there have to be at least 100. And if there are 1,000, he prostrates himself before the crowd, bowing and scrap- ing, the cowardly, impious monster [changed from *wretch*]![f] No, when you are visited by a single individual human being—perhaps, as we cruelly say, a poor, miserable human being—you ought to invite him into the best room, and if you have more than one tone of voice, use the most friendly and loving one.[g] If, however, there is a meeting of 1,000 or more,[h] then,[i] you ought proudly[j] to turn up your coat collar as high as possible, and if you are so unfortunate as to be applauded, you ought to gather all possible sarcasm and satire in your demeanor (or, if you prefer, pray the Lord's Prayer in complete silence) and not say, as did that quasi-wise man: Did I say something stupid, but, more accurately, I must have said something stupid. This is the truth.

For the crowd is untruth. Christ was crucified because he would not have anything to do with the crowd (even though he addressed himself to all),[k] because he did not want to form a party, did not allow balloting, but he wanted to be what he was, the truth, which is related to the single individual. —Therefore everyone who will in truth serve the truth is *eo ipso* a martyr, and if it were possible for one still in the womb to resolve in truth to serve the truth, he would be *eo ipso* a martyr still in the womb. To win a crowd is no art; for that only untruth is needed, nonsense, and a little knowledge of human passions. But no witness to the truth dares get involved with the crowd. His work is to be involved with all men, if possible, but always individually, speaking with each and every person on the sidewalk and on the streets—in order to split apart.[1] But he avoids the crowd, especially when it is treated as authoritative in matters of the truth and its applause, hissing, and balloting are regarded as judges—he avoids the crowd more than a decent young girl avoids the dance halls in the harbor. Those who speak to the crowd, coveting its approval, those who deferentially bow and scrape before it (although they either must understand what they are talking about and therefore ought not bow and scrape or they do not understand it and therefore should not speak)—such people he regards as being worse than prostitutes, as instruments of untruth.

Therefore I teach that the crowd is untruth [changed from *evil*]. And I could weep, even want to die, when I am mindful[m] that the daily press and anonymity make things crazier with the help of "the public." That an anonymous person by means of the press day in and day out can say what he wants to say, what he perhaps would not have the courage to say at all as an individual, and can get 10,000 X 10,000 to repeat it—and no one has responsibility; that not even the relatively impenitent crowd is omnipotent as in ancient days, but the absolutely impenitent one—and no one [has responsibility]!

My God! What sort of tomfoolery is it, after all, for the states to maintain police who capture a few thieves and robbers if the public life [changed from *the state*] itself and the communication of truth are basically untruth. We do not say that the truth can overtake[n] the lie and error. Impossible! The truth is not so fast on its feet. In the first place it cannot influence by means of fantasy (which is untruth). Its communicator is only an individual, and furthermore its communicated content is related to the single individual—for this view of life (the single individual) is precisely the truth.[o]

With regard to every single individual human being who lives in this country with me, unconditionally every single individual human being, if I could manage it,[p] I for my part[q] am willing to humble myself before him as deeply as possible, both orally and in writing, as a suppliant imploring him to think of his God-relationship.[r] Whether it is an assembly of 10,000[s] or it is a public of 100,000,[t] I pray God (and hope he will do it) to give me, the weakest of all, the pithiness to express all my abhorrence; for the mass, the crowd, is untruth.

[a] This was the truth.
[b] Or who it was.
[c] What untruth!*

* The untruth is first of all that it is the crowd which does what either only an individual can do or in every case each individual does. For a crowd is an abstraction with no hands; whereas every individual ordinarily has two hands, and when he, a single individual, puts his two hands on C. M., they are that single individual's two hands and not his neighbor's, even less the hands of the crowd, which has no hands. Second, the untruth is that the crowd had "courage" to do this; whereas the most cowardly person was never so cowardly as the "crowd" always is. For every individual who escapes into the crowd also cowardly escapes from being the single individual who either has the courage to lay hands on C. M., or at least the courage to confess that he does not have the courage; he contributes his share of cowardice to "the cowardice" which is the crowd.

ᵈ This is the truth.

ᵉ He proudly turns him away.

ᶠ What untruth!   .

ᵍ This is the truth.

ʰ Where truth is to be a matter of balloting.

ⁱ One ought to say "Hello" and ignore them.

ʲ God-fearingly

ᵏ Because he in no way wanted the help of the crowd, because in this respect he unconditionally thrust them away.

ˡ Or talk to the crowd, not in order to cultivate the crowd but in order to split it up, so that one individual and another may go home from the assembly and become the single individual.

ᵐ The wretchedness of our age, comparable only to the worst of the ancient period.

ⁿ With the aid of the press.

ᵒ The truth can neither be communicated or received without the help of God**, without God as accomplice, the middle term, since he is the truth. Therefore it can be communicated and received only by "the single individual," who for the sake of the cause could be every last human who lives. The category is simply the category of the truth in contrast to the abstract and fantastical, the impersonal, the mass, the public, which excludes God as the middle term and thereby the truth, for God is the truth and its middle term.***

** Before God's eyes, so to speak.

*** For the personal God cannot be the middle term in an impersonal relationship.

ᵖ In God's name.

q Serving my cause.

r To honor every individual human being is to fear God; whereas every gathering consciously or unconsciously has a tendency to want to be God, to want to be feared more than God.

s Claiming to be authoritative with regard to the truth.

t Claiming to be authoritative with regard to the truth.[611]

VIII[1] A 656   n.d., 1847–48

« 2933

Here, again, is the tragedy of history: once again the principle of the crowd (and now, with the prevalent culture and aided by the press this concept will have an utterly more frightful power than in ancient times) has been established. "The crowd" is the authority.[612] "The crowd" is god; "the crowd" is truth; "the crowd" is power and honor. As a result it is now merely a matter of gambling with this "crowd," just as one gambles with money; thus "the crowd" is everything, and the only thing that matters is getting control of it, getting it on his side. All things bow before this power.[*]

Consequently men cannot become aware of my teaching about "the single individual,"[613] and yet, things being as they are, no wonder they cannot become aware.

From now on every witness of the truth will direct his attack against the crowd,[614] every true martyr will fall before the crowd. From now on this very willingness to stand alone in God's name in order to witness that there is a God, this very thing for which he will be reproached—that he does not want anyone's help—is his task.

But they do not want to understand me; they do not have the courage and the fear of God for that. My task is fearfully strenuous—thanks be to God who helps me.

The majority are still standing on that old front, opposing the king, the emperor, and the nobility instead of the crowd. Everything the crowd does, the most horrible cruelty, is good; it is the will of God. No eastern despot has ever been as obsequiously served and flattered by cringing courtlings as "the crowd" by journalists, by all the men of the moment.

And so they are unable to understand my teaching about the single individual. Well, the fact is, they do not dare.

VIII[1] A 538   n.d., 1848

« **2934**

* *In margin of 2933* (VIII[1] A 538): And if a person will have nothing to do with the crowd, in unalloyed striving for the truth covets it alone and not the favor of the crowd, money, etc., such an effort is considered to be something like playing cards for nothing. The truth is believed to be nothing, the idea is nothing, but the crowd—that is something.

VIII[1] A 539   *n.d.*

« **2935**

According to its definition, "the crowd" is always misled—for if it is genuinely led, there is no crowd; where there is genuine leading, eternally understood, there is no crowd.

VIII[1] A 571   *n.d.*, 1848

« **2936**

What I wrote about "the crowd" was understood at the time by the liberals, by the opposition, by *Fædrelandet*[615]—now they presumably understand it no more. That means they never have had any essentially ethical outlook. They want to have the crowd on their side—otherwise they are angry with it. But it is not understood that the crowd itself is the evil.

VIII[1] A 611   *n.d.*, 1848

« **2937**

In the old days it was like this. There was a single individual who had arrived at an understanding of some truth.[616] Precisely because he carried that enormous responsibility so solitarily and perhaps also in ever greater suffering, he discovered the truth ever more inwardly, for that is the very tension in which it is discovered.

Now, however, one includes the crowd immediately, takes a shortcut, and instead of suffering and winning wants to win immediately. But to win by means of the crowd is simply a lie, is to betray the truth.

VIII[1] A 620   *n.d.*, 1848

« **2938**

I long for the more perfect. Open before God in the faith that my sins are forgiven, I also hope to be matured for something higher. But if I go on living, and even if I have but one hour to live—I will use it to the best of my ability for that for which I have up to now used it— to work against the stronghold of evil—the crowd, the unholy blather between man and man, the unholy contempt for being an individual human being.

IX A 63   n.d., 1848

« 2939

The wisdom of always doing as "the others" do is very convenient. It brings all the earthly advantages, and esteem to boot—because one is wise. Each one flatters the other by admiring it as wisdom.

IX A 143   n.d., 1848

« 2940

The treatment of the whole question of the popularity of Christianity, whether or not it is popular, betrays a basic misunderstanding.

Christianity is not unpopular in the sense that art and science and scholarship are, that is, with respect to the differences between man and man. It is unpopular with respect to what all men have in common. Thus it is and always will be very unpopular to see a person who is truly in love, who dares and suffers everything for love, satisfied and happy only in his love; it is extremely unpopular, for most men would regard it as madness. Likewise Christian self-renunciation, magnanimity, etc. are highly unpopular; the majority interpret it as madness.

With respect to accidental unpopularity (based on the differences between man and man), it must be said that the others do not understand it, and with that—period. With respect to the essentially unpopular (to live passionately in something, in and for itself absolutely passionately) one must say: The others regard it as madness.

IX A 146   n.d., 1848

« 2941

One must see it for himself (otherwise he would not believe it), how even nice, good-natured people become like different creatures as soon as they form a "crowd."[617] One must see for himself the lack of character even in otherwise upright persons who say: It is a disgrace, it is shocking to do or to say anything like that—and then contribute their own little share to envelop city and countryside in a snowstorm of blather and town gossip. The hardheartedness with which otherwise kind people act in the capacity of the public, because they regard their participation or nonparticipation as a small matter—a small matter which becomes enormous through the contribution of the many. One must see how no attack is as dreaded as that of laughter, how even the man who courageously would risk his life for a stranger would well nigh betray his father and mother if the risk is laughter, because that attack isolates the one attacked more than any other and at no point supports its victim by being done with pathos, but silliness and curiosity and sensuality grin, and cowardice which itself trembles before such an attack, continually shouts that it amounts to nothing, and the cowardice which contemptibly buys its way out of an attack with bribing or kowtowing to those involved says: It is nothing, and the participants say: It is nothing.

IX A 277   *n.d.*, 1848

« **2942**

Pantheism is an acoustical illusion which confuses *vox populi* and *vox dei*,[618] as when the shout went up: Crucify! Crucify! —*vox populi.*

IX A 294   *n.d.*, 1848

« **2943**

If a person is going to do battle in the world, from the standpoint of immediacy he recognizes only one danger—whether or not he has the strength to fight. The insidious danger—that he might be admired and exploited in support of the very point he wants to fight—this danger immediacy does not know. In immediacy, therefore, there is an urge to polemicize; one does not know his own strength, has an idea that his opponent perhaps has greater strength: here is the whole round of conflicts. How much more exhausting to fight when one has superiority and has to contend only with the numerical, the practical and external opposition of spiritlessness.[619]

IX A 452   *n.d.*, 1848

« **2944**

In every generation there perhaps are not twenty people who, when the showdown comes and they must make a judgment in life instead of hortatory and poetizing assertions, do not regard earnestness as an extravagance. A preacher of penitence who is truly earnest naturally exposes himself to danger, even reaps misfortune for his efforts—precisely that is earnestness; but look, all his contemporaries are unanimous about its being an extravagance. On the other hand, if among his contemporaries there is one of those half-depraved flirtatious characters who learn a little bit from the preacher of penitence and then play the preacher of penitence, he naturally creates an enormous stir and everybody says: This is earnestness, true earnestness. Naturally they all say it, for what else is there to say when he creates an enormous stir. It is the same with a satirist. But with the help of a preacher of penitence like this and a satirist like this, the world naturally does not advance but merely sinks deeper. And if one will examine it, one will see here as everywhere that what men are attentive to is finitude. That is why they say he is a clever and earnest satirist or preacher of penitence—because he makes something out of it—indeed, he does create a stir.

O, it is so deeply rooted in every man's nature—the view that the truth is directly recognizable by way of the majority, by way of the acknowledgement it wins, *etc.* I have experienced this myself and can still often catch myself being carried away momentarily by this immediacy.

IX A 490 *n.d.*, 1848

« **2945**

There are crimes which are of no concern to the police, such as slander, backbiting, gossip, etc.; when it gets out of hand, then the clergy are to take hold. Well, well, thanks to the clergy! Mob-vulgarity began by attacking the police and, if possible, incapacitating them altogether; but the pastors—indeed, thanks to the clergy!

The pastors in particular and, insofar as there was a misuse of the press, the other journalists bear the responsibility for the fact that mob-vulgarity spread so fast and so furiously.

X¹ A 231 *n.d.*, 1849

« **2946**

It is also a self-contradiction in striving with "the crowd" that if one strains with all his might to express that it is nothing—then "the crowd" says: It is nothing; one can see that he does not mind at all—and so the whole thing becomes crazier than ever. On the other hand, if it is detected that one suffers, sympathy is immediately at one's service. Alas, but even Christ had to endure being pitied.

X¹ A 268 *n.d.*, 1849

« **2947**

After all, it is very convenient to be "one with the age," especially in the sense of the public, for then we act in the first person but judge ourselves in the third person as if we were not ourselves. We give ourselves every leeway to obstruct the extraordinary; if it succeeds, it is concluded that this person and that person are not the extraordinary. But the entire role and behavior of the age, how it dealt with him —this the age itself talks about objectively.

There is a curious kind of self-contempt in wanting to go along with the world this way; it is the public which actually despises itself most profoundly; to be irresponsible, somewhat like the wind or a horse and a dog, is the most pitiful of privileges.

x^1 A 458   *n.d.,* 1849

« 2948 *Speech by a Poetic Personality*

It so happens that I own a very rare book. Perhaps I am the only one here in the city who has a copy of this book—the New Testament of our Lord Jesus Christ. It so happens that as a child I learned to read in the local school, something I must strongly emphasize, since, unfortunately, I am also a Ph.D., Th.D., and member of various learned societies. It so happens that in later years I have limited my reading almost to this one rare book. Out of this continued reading the following thought came to me.

If I were to convene an assembly of 100,000 people, if I could speak loudly enough to be heard by such an assemblage, and if I then were to say: I cannot live on air, and not only that, I regard it as my duty to safeguard my future—there surely would be no resounding applause, but people would almost think me mad to bring up what every sensible person knows to be sensible. However, if I lock my door and in a private room take out this very rare book, it is as if a voice said to me: "You insolent scoundrel! When I, God in heaven, command something in my Word, you are to obey immediately. Who has asked you to live on air? What an impudent, arrogant exaggeration in order to make my word ridiculous. Go to the penitentiary and find out how much a man needs in order to live—more than that you do not need." —If this is the way it is, where is the passage in the New Testament which constitutes a point of departure for plush jobs?

On the whole, I think I have discovered that Christianity can be communicated relevantly only in a private room, and the larger the group the less the essentially Christian comes forth, and it becomes almost ridiculous.

x^2 A 121   *n.d.,* 1849

« 2949

It is quite certain that the more costly something is made, the more people value it. If it cost money to go to church, there would be many in church, etc. Common sense might suppose it was serving Christianity by executing or introducing this idea. But there is another difficulty: the divine will not be supported in this way. The infinite superiority of the divine is veritably in its wanting to be squandered without being supported by illusion—yet, of course, infinitely aware that it is the divine, and sadly aware of how little attention is paid to it for that very reason. But it would never be possible that the divine would want to be aided by an illusion.

x^2 A 294   *n.d.*, 1849

« 2950 *The Dialectics of my Polemics*

Others, at the head of the crowd, attack the single individual; I, qua single individual, attack the crowd and have never felt it justifiable or worth the trouble to attack an individual. But to attack an individual in the name of the crowd, of the public, is cowardly secular-mindedness. Generally speaking, no campaign has ever been as cowardly as that of the daily press. When in a long bygone age the government was the power, it took courage to attack it; but now it is public knowledge that the crowd wields the power, and yet people go on playing the game that it is courageous to attack the government, or, even better, a single official in the government.

What a lie! Every time the press is attacked, when one says Grüne, Ploug,[620] etc., they get angry and explain that they are a principle, demand to be designated by abstract names. However, as soon as they make the attack, they continually take only one single public official and aim at him the enormously disproportionate weapon of the daily press. What profound cowardice if it were called duelling when one party as a single individual equipped with a pistol meets the other sitting behind a battery, or behind a regiment.

It is easy to see that my polemics are in the service of the truth; for it is *eo ipso* suffering. This is why it is not understood—that is, most people actually do not understand it; a few do not wish to understand it.

x^2 A 369   *n.d.*, 1850

« 2951

The idol, the tyrant, of our age is "the many," "the crowd," statistics. Just as the religious man at an earlier time might regard with sorrow and with the idea that "he is lost" everyone who sided with the "ungodly emperor," the "ungodly pope," the "ungodly bureaucracy," and cringed for the fellow, or as pious parents regarded their children's going to work at the castle, so one ought to sorrow deeply over everyone who resorts to voting. No matter how much competence he may otherwise have, even though he were a genius, this would only make it all the worse, because formally he abets an evil—voting by ballot.

This idolatry which worships voting by ballot is, spiritually understood, almost like that execrable service of lingam,[621] for voting by ballot is the productive power in relation to the deification of statistics.

Alas, but how long will it be before the individual appears who will stand against this!

X^2 A 383   *n.d.*, 1850

« 2952 *The Difference between "the Crowd," the "Public"—and Community*

In the "public" and the like the single individual is nothing; there is no individual; the numerical is the constituting form and the law for the coming into existence [*Tilblivelse*] of a *generatio aequivoca;* detached from the "public" the single individual is nothing, and in the public he is, more basically understood, really nothing at all.[622]

In community [*Menighed*] the single individual [*den Enkelte*] *is;* the single individual is dialectically decisive as the presupposition for forming *community,* and in *community* the single individual is qualitatively something essential and can at any moment become higher than "community," specifically, as soon as "the others" fall away from the idea. The cohesiveness of community comes from each one's being a single individual, and then the idea; the connectedness of a public or rather its disconnectedness consists of the numerical character of everything. Every single individual in community guarantees the community; the public is a chimera. In community the single individual is a microcosm who qualitatively reproduces the cosmos; here, in a good sense, it holds true that *unum noris, omnes.* In a public there is no single individual and the whole is nothing; here it is impossible to say *unum noris, omnes,* for here there is no *one.* "Community" is certainly more than a sum, but yet it is truly a sum of ones; the public is nonsense— a sum of negative ones, of ones who are not ones, who become ones through the sum instead of the sum becoming a sum of the ones.

X^2 A 390   *n.d.*, 1850

« 2953

How rare would be the person who is literally able to speak to a gathering[623] in the same way one speaks to an individual because he has tempered his mind and thoughts not to surrender to the illusion of numbers and the dizziness of animal qualifications.[624] And in how many different ways it can be observed that as soon as men are in a crowd they feel themselves unconstrained as animals. When two men are talking together, it would never occur to one of them to say: Bravo, or hiss. But in a crowd it is done almost involuntarily.

Now in what capacity does the individual do this—for, confound it, the crowd *qua talis* does not, after all, have a mouth. He does not do it as an individual, for the person who is really conscious of himself as the single individual does not do it; and yet it is an individual who does it, or a few individuals, but in such a way that each individual among them does it. In what kind of state is such an individual? In a state of confusion of sorts, somewhat like a school when the teacher cannot properly look after things and see the individuals, and the boys take advantage of the fact to have a lark because there is no one, or in an animal state, or in a devil-may-care state, so one confuses himself with an abstraction.

Experience will also show that it is the most mediocre, the most foolish, the most immature, the least conscious persons who go in for being an organ in this sense—and an organ in this sense can only be compared with what breaking wind is for an organism.

This is why the newspaper always scrupulously reports every instance where there is hissing or hurrahing—great significance is ascribed to it.

Thus the lunatic authority is ventriloquism; the decisive voice in public life is not that of the mouth—but the stomach, or still more accurately, the rump.

$$x^2 \text{ A } 485 \quad n.d., 1850$$

« 2954 *The Fate of the Extraordinary*

There is a little trick in the doing; it depends on how the intermediate authority takes it. For the majority the extraordinary (when he is not propped up by illusion—and in that case he is not actually the extraordinary) is a piece of foolishness. But the majority do not really credit themselves with the right to have an opinion. The majority look inquisitively to the intermediate authority. If this [opinion] is lacking, the majority conclude: Ergo, the man is really crazy. If the intermediate authority is envious of the extraordinary and is in collusion with the mass confusion, then the end is even more certain. Then the most dissimilar people unite in overthrowing the extraordinary. The prestigious people pretend to recognize and appreciate the extraordinary, but they hoist him so high, so extraordinarily high, that it all actually becomes a kind of madness. However, they do not call it that; for the most part they officially maintain profound silence—but then they let the majority pronounce judgment.[625] And while everyone who ought to supply the middle authority is silent, the majority are permitted to judge quite unabashedly, and they pronounce it madness, eccentricity, pride, etc.

x^3 A 20   *n.d.*, 1850

« **2955** *The Public*

The sum and substance of the public life is actually, from first to last, lack of conscience.

There exists a hungry monster—whether it is still bloodthirsty I do not decide; however, recent times have indicated how easily blood-thirstiness can arouse—a hungry monster: the public. It hungers with a desperate passion "to get something to chatter about." The journalists are animal-keepers who provide something for the public to talk about. In ancient days people were cast to the wild animals—now the public devours someone tastefully prepared by the journalists as the tastiest dish of all for the public—twaddle.

A public personality is *eo ipso* the victim; the "journalist" knows how to determine precisely how long he can be served up, how many times a week the public will relish him as twaddle. If the public personality is an egotist who endures all this because it is, after all, inescapable, if he wants to obtain other earthly benefits, then he suffers less, is not a martyr, is free of sadness, is better understood. But the public devours him just the same, prepared as twaddle; the benefit "the public" actually has of celebrities is that it gets something to chatter about, a meal of twaddle. No one knows how it happens; those who know nothing about the public life sometimes are of the opinion that the public personality ought to defend himself, explain himself, etc.— that it is pride on his part not to do it—O you ignoramuses, you poor ignoramuses, not so; the public demands anything but, it demands only twaddle, "something to chatter about." There is only one sensible avenue of escape and that is to live one's personal life as secluded as possible and only show oneself in the character of a public person in appropriately solemn situations—but Christianity actually does not permit a person to live in this manner.

It is said that social differences make a happy and harmonious love-relationship impossible between man and woman. Maybe, maybe not! But this difference [is not problematical]; to be a private man in a civil position, in a subordinate post, in short, the kind of person who does not belong in the interest-sphere of the public and of journalists, and to be a public person—these two can never understand each other; there is a qualitative difference between them every moment of their lives, so much the more when the public person actually is a servant of truth who, not because of his own personal inclination or for the sake of his own earthly aims, endures being the public's fodder so it can get something to chatter about.

Something to chatter about![626] God created man in his own image; he also gave him the gift of the word and wanted man to talk, each man with his neighbor, the lover with the beloved, friend with friend, also several men with each other—and about what? O you Almighty One, you set heaven and earth in motion to create a world over which eternity eternally marvels, over its wisdom and grandeur—and over your love; but man found it to be nothing worth talking about. O, you infinite sublimity, for whose sublimity the heavenly hosts are still struggling to find an expression, you brought yourself to stoop to man, as the adult to the child when in order to make the child happy he promises to play with him, you acted out what by your participation became more than play, that wonderful interplay which is called history—and those serving spirits who stand closest to you, help you in arranging the whole thing and look into it most deeply, they have not yet fathomed it, even less have grown weary of marvelling over it: but man found it was not anything worth talking about. Man—that is, the public. It demands only something to chatter about, and this is understood to mean finding something about each other to chatter about, something about our meaningless lives, particularly the trivialities in our lives. Anything else nauseates the public, which knows only one lust—the desire for self-pollution by talking, a lust in which it indulges with the help of the "journalist."

X³ A 21   n.d., 1850

« 2956 *Christianity's Collision*

When Christianity is once again placed in all its truth into actuality, a remarkable thing will happen, the clergymen and the parishes will unite to defend themselves against Christianity. People do not want to give up Christianity entirely; they have gotten it into their heads that it can be very expedient to be a Christian at such a fairly cheap and moderate price—and never in all eternity will the parish go in for

Christianity in all its truth. "All right," they say, "let's spend what it costs to keep pastors the way we usually do," pastors who for a low price and fair treatment endeavor to insure themselves the approval of a most worthy cultured public by waiting upon them and serving them Christianity.[627]

x^3 A 262   *n.d.,* 1850

« 2957 *The System*[628] *—Hidden Inwardness*

"The system" has just about disappeared. When two students converse and mention the system, they almost involuntarily begin to smile.

I hope that "hidden inwardness"[629] will, with the help of God, go the same way. When two preachers talk together and mention hidden inwardness they involuntarily begin to smile.

"The public," too, is headed the same way. What joy when once the concept drops out, along with the concepts "the majority," "the ballot," etc.

x^3 A 451   *n.d.,* 1850

« 2958 *That Christianity Simply Does Not Exist*

This thesis, which Anti-Climacus[630] posits, has aroused some rage, as if it were a frightful exaggeration.

The fact is that no doubt most people let themselves be taken in by the illusion of numbers.

Let us make the following experiment. All of us who could be said to be really interested in Christianity—let us, every single one of us— yes, just as in the Christmas game one is sentenced to go out and look at the stars—go into a room alone. Each one shuts the door behind him, is now alone, summons to his mind the thought that God is present, states his own full name and says: Do you dare here before God, do you dare maintain that you in the most rigorous sense are a true Christian? I vouch that there is not a single one—everyone says: No, God forbid—I appeal to grace and continue striving. —Then we all come out again. Perhaps someone shows that it tormented him to make the confession; another shows nothing; but it makes no differ- ence—in brief, every single one of us made the confession and there- fore we can very well play together, or perhaps for that very reason we can play together best, since children who are alike play together best.

Of those, then, who really are interested in Christianity there was no one who dared say that he was a Christian in the most rigorous sense. But the whole crowd who have no interest at all in Christianity, their lives can certainly not be taken as any proof that Christianity exists [*er til*].

But if there are no Christians in the most rigorous sense, then there is no Christianity either.

Hardly anyone is provoked as soon as the numerical mass is broken up, simplified. But each one should himself simplify the numerical mass and not let himself be awed by an illusion.

This is the thesis—as soon as one single true Christian in the most rigorous sense exists, Christianity exists; and on the other hand, if there were 7 billion, 5 million, 696,734 or 35 Christians of the up-to-a-certain-point kind—Christianity for that reason does not exist.*

The numerical does not constitute quality; on the contrary, it is the indifferent quality. It holds true—*unum noris omnes.* We are not enraged when someone says: I am just as good a Christian as all the others. But we are enraged when someone says: In the strictest sense I am not a Christian, *and* the others probably are not either—and yet basically the two statements are one and the same.

But the fact is—the numerical exercises a sensate power over us men. "Number," which never changes, that is, never produces a new quality, changes us. Every single individual confesses that in the most rigorous sense he is not a Christian and that to this extent Christianity does not exist, but then we still want the sum of such individuals (who do not prove that Christianity exists or prove that Christianity does not exist) to be proof that Christianity exists.

The numerical exercises a sensuous power and changes the man. Take a very simple example, a store clerk, who is accustomed to having 300 dollars in cash sales go through his hands every day. Every evening he quite mechanically counts the money and never makes a mistake. But suppose one evening there is 10,000—then he is changed, the blood mounts to his head, his heart almost pounds, his hands tremble, he has to count it over many times, and still there is only a larger number of the so familiar 5 dollar bills. And so it is with respect to the number of men. The same men and women, known individually to know the extent to which they are informed or not about this or that matter—the same men and women (yes, for they are the same men and women) sitting in an auditorium, and I am standing at a lectern—they change me and appear changed to me; I am awed; I think: Wow!

The numerical changes men, intoxicates them, obsesses them, as if by being many they were something altogether different from what each single individual is. They are intoxicated and interpret everything differently. If someone in such a noble public happens to pass gas loudly (something everyone knows very well is usually frowned upon), people are startled, begin to wonder if it is not the voice of a spirit—so intoxicated are we when we are a public.

On the other hand, the numerical intoxicates the speaker, and he evaluates altogether differently than he usually would.

And since so many love this confused, intoxicated state, they love to be in a gathering and to talk at a gathering.

x^3 A 656   n.d., 1850

« 2959

In margin of 2958 (x^3 A 656):

*Seen from the other side, very likely we are fortunate that there is not, in the strictest sense, one true Christian, for one true Christian would explode existence [*Tilværelsen*] and presumably have the effect that all the rest of us desert completely.

This is why it is the pseudonym[631] who says that Christianity does not exist; I (through the Preface) merely say of myself that I dare not call myself a Christian in the strictest sense.

x^3 A 657   n.d.

« 2960 *The Old Orthodox*

are now completely without qualities. They are blind to what the year 1848 has made sufficiently clear—that the crowd, the mass, are evil. They still live in the obsolete notion that one battles against the established order with the help of the people.

x^4 A 93   n.d., 1851

« 2961 *"The Apostle"*

True enough, many attached themselves to the apostle. But the apostle did not *first* confer with them, ascertain how many there were, make arrangements, etc.—no, he went into action, period; and then the majority sided with him, taking advantage of the fact that the apostle had acted.

When Rudelbach[632] (in the article in *Fædrelandet*) says that the apostle is surrounded by a cloud of witnesses, R. makes a mistake, since he sees the cloud—and not the apostle.

x^4 A 100   n.d., 1851

« **2962**

. . . . . appealing *politically* to being a mass, a crowd, or even a flock, a herd, or even a lump, the leftovers of men, forgetting that, religiously, one person is enough.

x^4 A 105   *n.d.*, 1851

« **2963** *Character*

Anyone who believes that to be in the majority is truth has the problem, if he factually is in the minority, of being able to continue speaking and acting as if he were in the majority; at this very point it becomes evident whether his views on being a majority are a matter of character or of shabby opportunism.

Inversely, anyone whose view is to be in the minority, if he factually is in the majority at some moment, must unalterably express that he is the minority; otherwise it would be obvious that he does not have character but really prefers to be in the majority.

The temptation in the first case (to be cowed and concede that he is in the minority) is essentially the same, that is, just as great, as the second temptation: to become untrue, deluded by numbers, and admit that he is in the majority.

Perhaps there are more who could withstand the first temptation better than the second, just as assuredly as there are very few who have the character to be in the minority.

x^4 A 107   *n.d.*, 1851

« **2964** *The Public*

Here are some of the abuses perpetrated by and with this concept.

(1) Authors speak with deepest respect about the public, request its lenient consideration etc. But the public is an abstraction which does not exist at all. Then each individual reads and flatters himself with the thought that all this is being said to him. It is demoralizing. If authors wrote for the single individual, it would not occur to him to flatter himself.

(2) The industrialists in literature,[633] the party men, etc., write for the public, in the name of the public etc. in order to give the impression that they are many, a palpable power.

(3) The majority of people are not so afraid of holding a wrong opinion, but they are afraid of holding an opinion alone. They are protected on this point through the practice of writing for the public; in this way they know that they do not stand alone in their opinions.

This also is demoralizing, everyone should learn to stand alone with his opinion, even though it be the case that the opinion is shared by many.

X^4 A 225   *n.d.,* 1851

« 2965 *The Single Individual–the Public*

The thesis "the public, the crowd, is untruth"[634] can consistently and truly be fought through to the finish only by one person; it would categorically not be a fighting through to the finish if there were even two who join together to fight that thesis through to the finish, for two is a number, is an orientation toward the crowd, the public; whereas one is not a number but a qualitative determinant. —And the thesis that "the public, the crowd, is untruth" is a thesis of Christianity; in every generation where this thesis is not fought through to the finish, in every such generation Christianity does not actually exist.

But from the one side, the surrounding world into which the thesis is to be introduced naturally finds it foolish, ridiculously foolish, that one person wants to do it—"Yes, if there were even a few,"—perhaps "several" or perhaps *(risum teneatis!)* "the public." That is, the surrounding world moves in the direction of the dialectic that the public is truth; therefore the thesis "the public is untruth" can be regarded as true (capital!) only if it has the public on its side.

From the other side, a few individuals will no doubt become aware of the whole communication, this struggle oriented to the thesis that the public is untruth. Then they will join up—yes, here we have it again —with that one person—in order (wonderful!) to help him! Either they are unable to understand that this sets the cause back or they do not want to understand it but find it easier to join up with the one person after he has carried the cause so far along that—by an ingenious, officious shift!—there can be profit in winning the public over to it.

O, to endure this solitary battle year after year, to have the power to make it easy to win all simply by compromising—this is asceticism. It is a solitary battle in which one also fights to stand alone. This the surrounding world finds absolutely ridiculous, the surrounding world which is all too familiar with the way one should behave: that one should begin by pretending to be many—for then one becomes many, just as all the sheep run to drink water when one of them runs to drink.

But how sad it is when someone intensely engaged in this solitary battle goes on hoping and hoping for just one honest man who also takes hold, solitarily. But no! They all want profit—they are utterly indifferent to truth and Christianity.

And when they find out that they can no longer protect themselves against this solitary warrior by finding it ridiculous, they begin to shout that it is arrogance, frightful arrogance—and we are all Christians!

X^4 A 405   n.d., 1851

« 2966 The Frightfulness of Having the Universally Human Be the Standard by Which We Are Judged

Everyone, everyone is so prone to set his mind at ease in a relativity. Anyone who is a little better than his family and relatives or the others in the provincial town where he lives or among his peers, etc., promptly sets his mind at ease and feels superior.

Consider then the judgment coming in eternity, where there will be millions and millions just of blood-witnesses in the strictest sense of the word.

We live comparatively with a few or a hundred or a few thousand or a hundred thousand—or—to carry this on—a few million (the mind is already dizzy)—and we will be judged according to the most terrifying standard of the tried and tested blood-witnesses, and there will be millions of just them alone.

O, it is so natural for a man, this wretched idea that God will not be so severe, after all, for if he were he would be in the awkward situation of having to condemn us all. My friend, even if the point which you believe that God could not go beyond without excessive severity has been left far behind, even then he still has millions who have discharged the task.

What is the bourgeois mentality? Comparing oneself with a specific number. But Christianity abolishes the bourgeois mentality: the standard is all, all men. Even in Copenhagen there is a big stir if someone is willing to suffer a little for Christianity—and on judgment day there will be billions who have suffered far, far more.

X^4 A 535   n.d., 1852

« 2967

To keep together—in order to be sacrificed.
To keep together—in order to avoid being sacrificed.
To keep together—in order to win the things of this earth.

The Unchristian Anticlimax

Christ is born, comes to the world—in order to suffer and die, in order to be sacrificed.

Thereupon he sends out the twelve apostles. He has prepared them, told them their fate in advance. "You will be hated by all for my name's sake; indeed, the day is coming when whoever kills you will think he is doing God a service"—and then they are *sent out—in order* to be sacrificed. —The apostles go out; let us keep together, they say to each other, let us keep together in order to strengthen each other in accomplishing our task—to be sacrificed.

But soon thousands are won for Christianity. Nevertheless they are still so unevenly matched that there is still a probability or at least a possibility that being a Christian comes to mean: to be sacrificed, although the early situation is already altered in such a way that they do not in the strictest sense keep together—in order to be sacrificed, for the numerical factor is already beginning to make it improbable that they will all be sacrificed.

Now there come to be more and more thousands—the farther we get away from the essentially Christian: keeping together in order to be sacrificed; by keeping together when there are thousands of them, they are more likely to avoid being sacrificed.

Finally—and at most it took only two centuries—the watchword is: Let us keep together—in order to avoid being sacrificed.

Here already is the qualitative change. Nowadays we go farther— nowadays, imagine the joy: Christianity has conquered; it has become a state religion—let us keep together in order to obtain the things of this world.

This means that today the momentum of Christ's life and the lives of the apostles and martyrs has been spent; we have happily and comfortably arrived at nonsense and meaninglessness. Happy the man who is to lead men onward! For who is ever as loved, esteemed, appreciated, and rewarded as the inestimable, noble man who regards it as his task to lead men deeper and deeper into meaninglessness, and no wonder, for if the fish is happy in water and the bird in air, man feels even happier—in meaninglessness, where he feels at home.

From this moment on, of course, all of Christianity becomes gib- berish—and as a matter of course it now for the first time really takes on mammoth proportions, with millions, millions, and billions of Christians. From now on, of course, the thing to be concerned about is to get a steady stream of greater and greater numbers, because in the same degree it will become more difficult, finally impossible, to bring transparency into this meaninglessness—and the real reason they keep together these days (they have kept together in order to secure the things of this earth and have secured them) is: Let us now keep together to make it impossible for the truth to illuminate this situation. Let us become millions and more millions of Christians, thousands and more thousands of preachers and professors, and there will be all the more confusion, all the more impenetrable darkness.

x⁵ A 123   *n.d.*, 1853

« 2968 *"Beware of Men"; the Monastery; To Suffer Persecution*

Man is *by nature* an animal-creation.[635] All human effort is therefore in the direction of running together in a herd—"Let us join together," etc. It goes on, of course, under all sorts of high-sounding names, that it is out of love, sympathy, and enthusiasm, in order to do something really great, etc.—this is the usual villainous human hypocrisy. The truth is that in the herd one is free from the criterion of the individual and of the ideal.

From a Christian point of view the law is this: Either go out into solitude, away from men, so that you may be able to acquire the criterion of the ideal undisturbed by the nonsense and the haggling of numbers (for here to count is to haggle); or if you remain among men, then you must suffer persecution—in order to preserve heterogeneity, which again insures individuality and the criterion of the ideal. But Christianity is impossible in direct continuity with the herd.

Here again we see how false it is that what we are now living in (direct continuity and conformity with "the others") is supposed to be higher than the monastery.

XI¹ A 16   *n.d.*, 1854

« 2969 *The Congregation*

Here, again, the cheating which pervades everything in our times.

We have a bad conscience; each one of us knows very well: I am no Christian—but is it not true that a sum of such Christians gives a Christian congregation.

Then the argument runs like this—all, each one, will say: Well, in the strictest sense I do not dare call myself a Christian, but nevertheless there certainly is a Christian congregation.

Always this statistical cheating to avoid the obvious truth—that each single individual is not a Christian.

And then for protection the congregation, of course, is cosmeti-
cized as "the objective," "the utmost earnestness," etc.

XI[1] A 64   *n.d.*, 1854

« 2970 *As Upside Down as Possible*

Everything, and also everything having to do with Christianity,
pushes in the direction of extensiveness, of bigness, towards mass.
People think they definitely will be saved if they are the mass, that one
is saved *en masse*.

O, my friend, from the Christian point of view everything that is
mass is *eo ipso* lost, for "mass," from the Christian point of view, is the
category of perdition. Salvation means to be saved out of the mass, and
only if all have become single individuals and there is no mass left, only
then can there be talk about all being saved.

But the emphasis upon the mass, this superstition of being safe
and sure when one is *en masse*, hangs together with the animal-defini-
tion of what it means to be a human being, corresponds exactly to the
animal's notion of being safe when it is in the flock, that danger consists in being separated from the flock. Here again it is apparent that
"the mass" is, Christianly, the category of perdition, because it corresponds to the "animal-man," whereas Christianity considers that salvation is to become spirit.

Yet the natural man, the animal-man, shrinks from becoming one,
even more, if possible, than he shrinks from death, particularly if there
is hope of—how ironical!—dying *en masse*. But Christianity stands immovable, more immovable than the north star, on this point that the
first condition of salvation is to become a single individual.

That being the case, one could be justified Christianly in categorically throwing out or discarding almost the entire eighteen hundred
years of Christendom as labor tending toward illusion rather than
Christianity.

The mass would consider this to be terrible arrogance; but that
helps neither me nor the mass, for Christianity does not change. The
sovereignty of God rests with eternally immovable firmness on this
point: Everything that is mass is *eo ipso* perdition. And he holds this
immovably fixed simply because all human power resides in mass.
Mass can destroy every human sovereignty—but not God's sovereignty.
The mass can, as it has continually done, persecute, mistreat, and kill
the instruments whom God uses to express this sovereignty of his—but
his sovereignty continues eternally unchanged, resting on the point

that everything which is mass is *eo ipso* perdition. Although no human power has succeeded in shutting out cholera, the eternal succeeds, and with infinite ease, in shutting out everything which is mass; only the eternal itself is *eo ipso* the blockade against everything called mass.

The natural law of the eternal, which is just as unchanging as the natural law of temporality, is this: If you want to have happiness in this world, have profit, pleasant days, temporal reward, you must work in the direction of mass, for admittedly that is where the good things are; thus what the animals believe is true—the good is to be in the flock. And since the proclaimers of Christianity want to have earthly advantage, there has been an influence, false, toward mass.

But if someone thinks that eventually there will be such a mass of millions, billions, and trillions that the eternal will ultimately get weary and tired of obstructing them and that the mass will force its way through—my friend, this is a mistake. As far as the eternal is concerned, number is the infinitely indifferent, or more accurately, number simply does not exist at all for the eternal. It is related inversely to the eternal —the greater the number, the easier—if I dare say so—it is to discard it. It is very hard for the eternal to discard a single individual. By being a single individual (alas, outside the mass, as it is called) he is the object of the eternal's concern, which wants infinitely to save him and is infinitely reluctant to thrust him back. On the other hand, as soon as there are 100,000 trillion billions, the eternal blows it away more easily than a storm blows pollen.

Christianity holds firm on this point. It does not help that you pretend humility as your reason for being in the mass, that you are too humble to want to be a single individual. O my friend, divine sovereignty knows human rascality only too well, that it is a matter of becoming mass, even under the name of humility, because in "mass" lies man's power. But the God of love is also an infinitely shrewd sovereign. He is well-informed about the arrogant mutiny, also about the rascally mutiny, which with the art of humility and modesty gets power through trickery, and this he knows perhaps even before the man knows it, the man who out of humility wants to remain in the mass. God knows it, understands his remote thoughts, and does not alter the law of the eternal.

When the populace rises *en masse* against the sovereign, a bodyguard is of no help; he is in the power of the mass. God is more secure; one can never get hold of him that way—as soon as the mass appears,

God becomes invisible. This almighty mass can, *si placet,* batter its nose against the front door, but it gets no farther, for God is present only for the single individual—that is his sovereignty. With him it is not the same as with the human sovereign to whom the adjutant comes and says: Your Majesty is obliged to appear on the balcony; there must be 20,000 people on the street. No, when there are 20,000 *en masse,* God does not appear—when it is the single individual—yes, then the divine majesty, divine also in this, is elevated above all forms in such a way that not even an angel is needed to announce that single individual. No, his majesty becomes—infinite love!—immediately visible, because for the single individual he is present.

You servants of lies—you who go about in long clothes—happy over having arranged (or that it has been arranged) the profitable lie about a Christian nation, a Christian state, a Christian country—you only incite the crowd against me because I say this, because I say of the poorest, most wretched, most miserable, most pitiable, most stupid, most sinful human being who has ever lived—if he wills to be a single individual, if he is willing to be helped to understand what human cruelty is prepared to help him understand (in the Christian state, the Christian country, the Christian nation)—that he does not belong to the flock, that he is a single individual, if he wills to be a single individual, and that the divine majesty then will immediately become visible in his infinite love. You are inciting the crowd upon me, you liars, because the profit you want can be had only with the help of the crowd, by means of preaching that where the crowd is God is present, that God is pleased by the masses.

XI[1] A 227   *n.d.,* 1854

« 2971 *My Judgment of Men*

It is just as it stands in my little book about my activity as an author: when one can get men as individuals, there is much about them that is lovable; but as soon as they become the public, the crowd etc., all the detestable features appear.

"The journalist" is really the corrupter; he (worse than any brothel keeper living off men's debauchery) lives off promotion of the evil principle in man: the numerical.[*]

As far as the clergy are concerned (I am speaking of Denmark), I believe that in a certain human sense they are just as fine as any other social class. But what makes them so harmful is that Christianity is something so infinitely high that it will not do at all for such ordinary nice people to undertake the task of representing Christianity. Either they must step more into the character of the New Testament Christianity (and most of them will then find it convenient to give up being a pastor) or (as I propose) by means of an admission make room for the Christianity of the New Testament.

I cannot stop being fond of the common man, even though journalistic scurrility has done everything to confuse him in his relationship to me and spoils for me what I loved so unspeakably, what to me was the most salutary respite from my intellectual endeavors—living together with the common man.

XI^1 A 234   *n.d.*, 1854

« 2972

[*] *In margin of 2971* (XI^1 A 234):

It is true what I once said—it is some place in the journal [i.e., X^2 A 314] —that if I were a father and had a daughter who was seduced, I would by no means abandon her; but a son who became a journalist I would regard as lost.

XI^1 A 235   *n.d.*

« 2973 *"The Others"*

To be like the others expresses mankind's degeneration, its degradation to copies, numbers—this is well known. But since this form of existence is the coziest and most convenient, it is hypocritically prettied up to be true moral earnestness.

That everyone knows this to be fiction, however, is seen very simply in the boundless, ever vigilant envy poured out upon any person who differs from the others. If it were actually regarded as an excellence to be like the others, it would be impossible to envy a person for not being like the others; after all, only the excellent, a good, is envied. And if we were convinced that not being like the others intellectually and spiritually is no more a good than being physically hunchbacked, we would not envy anyone for being that.

But, as said, we ourselves know full well how wretched it is to be "like the others." In a certain sense one would like very much to shake off the chains of slavery himself—but since he has neither the strength nor the courage to do it, it must also be certain that being like the others is a truly earnest, glorious, and noble thing, etc.

XI^1 A 287   *n.d.*, 1854

« 2974 *To Be Salt*[636]—*To Be the Crowd— the Judgment of the Eternal*

According to the New Testament to be Christian means to be salt. As we now live, especially in Protestantism, and especially in Denmark, to be Christian means to be the crowd, or to be the crowd means to be Christian—as different from the New Testament as possible.

It surely cannot be the meaning of the New Testament that only the apostles were to be salt once and for all and that no more salt would be needed, even though the world were to continue many thousands of years. No, in every generation in which Christianity is proclaimed, Christianity addresses the question to each single individual: Will you be a Christian, that is, are you willing to be salt, that is, are you willing to be sacrificed—instead of belonging to the crowd which inhumanly wants profit from the sacrifice of others. Are you yourself willing to be salt, to be Christian?

But the abolition of being Christian in the sense of being salt and the equating of being Christian with being the crowd (which brought about the utterly unchristian phrases like Christian nations, states, lands, and similar masses) are connected with our abolition of the judgment and accounting of eternity.

The way we are living in Protestantism presupposes that grace atones, but also that we then live a bourgeois life not subject to punishment. Consequently it is still as if salvation were linked to a stipulation, to a condition directed toward the existential. We perhaps assume that flagrant sinners are lost in spite of their so-called faith and in spite of grace. The moment we assume this we cannot stop with social morality, because if there is a condition, a stipulation directed toward the existential, social morality is no more adequate than flagrant sins. In that case we cannot stop short of what the New Testament provides as the condition: imitation and asceticism pointing toward martyrdom. Either grace atones unconditionally and saves us all, also flagrant sinners, even those who are not Christians at all—or we cannot stop short of what the New Testament defines as the condition: renunciation, imitation [*Efterfølgelsen*].

But it is easy to see that when regarding the mass as Christian came in, the judgment and accounting of eternity essentially went out. It is taken for granted that we are all saved; it is taken for granted that we are Christians from birth on—and in place of the terrible tension of having to use this life for an eternal decision, it is taken for granted that all has been decided and at most it is a matter of behaving somewhat decently as a kind of "Thank you," which incidentally is the smartest thing to do from a purely earthly and secular point of view.

To repeat, as soon as there is to be a condition, a stipulation, crucial to one's eternal salvation, directed toward the existential, social morality has nothing to do with the matter. We must either extend grace to the point of absurdity or we must come to stand by the stipulation, the condition given by the New Testament: imitation.

Here again is the distinction: to be salt and to be the mass. This is a qualitative distinction: confessing a religion from which one expects to profit both temporally and eternally and confessing a religion for which one suffers.

But then we arrive at the difficulty that truly to be a Christian means such heterogeneity with men that in all eternity they can never come to an understanding. To have lived this human life in such a way that we have let others be sacrificed for us and to have lived this human life in such a way that we have been sacrificed for others—between these two lies an eternal qualitative difference. To hear sheer worldlings talk about entering into the Christians' eternal happiness is enough to make one both laugh and cry. They have no idea that if they do make it, they will be in the company of persons whose lives are and were qualitatively different from theirs.

XI[1] A 325   n.d., 1854

« 2975   The Master—the Disciple—the Muddlehead

The disciple who became a fisher of men cast out his net and in one haul caught 3,000 souls—the Master during his whole lifetime caught only 12.

Is the disciple greater than the master, then? Yes, if everything from a Christian point of view were not reversed. The disciple catches thousands by watering down what Christianity is.

And when some day a disciple lives one hundred and twenty-seventh hand from that first disciple's twenty-seventh hand discipleship—a muddlehead—he will catch the whole world for Christianity.

That is the way things are moving ahead with Christianity.

XI[1] A 346   n.d., 1854

« 2976   Fear of Men—Fear of God

The collision toward which Christianity continually aims is to fear God more than men, consequently to fear men less than God. It does not consist in fasting or in celibacy and so on. No, if you fast out of fear of men, it is precisely not Christianity, and if men seek to browbeat you to give up fasting, then Christianity can mean fasting.

God is the one and only sovereign. In order to express this he chooses a very simple man as his envoy—that is the highest distinction. And then he requires that he, his ambassador and apostle, express that the great power whom he has the honor to represent is the one and only, which is the truth. This he is to express unconditionally over against kings, emperors, the public, and the Pope and whatever all of the authorities are called who browbeat men into the fear of men. And in order to do a thorough job of it, in order to express unconditionally the degree to which he is the one and only sovereign, God joins in beating up his own ambassador—yet out of love, yes, out of love, O you infinite love!

Only once has Christian love been proclaimed unconditionally in the fear of God—by the God-man.

Proclaimed entirely in the fear of men, Christianity is no longer Christianity.

Herein is the falsification in all Christendom. As soon as Christianity is proclaimed unconditionally in the fear of God, all fall away. When Christianity is proclaimed in the fear of men, all become Christians—this means, of course, making a fool of God, and an accounting will come.

The falsification is accomplished easily. Instead of proclaiming Christianity in the fear of God, the millions of falsifiers operate in this way: they change what I am speaking about, for example, into a thesis. The thesis reads as follows: True Christianity can be proclaimed only in the fear of God, or true Christianity cannot be proclaimed in the fear of men. Splendid! Then there is a talk, a lecture, a sermon—and if the speaker is living in a time when kings, emperors, popes, and the like are the powerful ones who browbeat men into the fear of men, he is careful to bow and scrape before them in order to declaim with a deep bow that true Christianity cannot be proclaimed in the fear of men. If the public, the many, the crowd are the powers that be who browbeat men into the fear of men, the speaker bows and scrapes before them and declaims that true Christianity cannot be proclaimed in the fear of men.[*]

This is the kind of Christianity which flourishes in Christendom: Christianity proclaimed in the fear of men—but Christianity is precisely the fear of God in contrast to the fear of men.

XI[1] A 372   *n.d.,* 1854

« 2977

[*] *In margin of 2976* (xi¹ a 372):

And this again can be lectured about and declaimed about by a sophist[637] who bows deeply before kings and emperors or before the public and the crowd according to the times—and so there is again the swindle, the acknowledgement of how cunningly we have deceptively proclaimed Christianity, and, alas, this acknowledgement is an even more refined deception.

xi¹ a 373   n.d.

« 2978 *To Want To Be Exactly Like the Others*

might seem to be a kind of loyalty to the others and naturally is hailed and acclaimed as such in the world—but of course it is the very opposite; for just as every man, from a spiritual point of view, is usually a rogue and the generation is a generation of rogues, so also human language is first and foremost a thieves' slang which hypocritically always twists everything the wrong way.

No, wanting to be exactly like the others is a cowardly and comfortable dishonesty toward the others.

That is why the race is punished by having these millions who, in the long run, mutually understand that the whole thing is not to be trusted, because the one is always just exactly like the others. This explains their anxiety and perplexity and suspiciousness when life pinches a bit.

Every primitivity, on the other hand, is honesty toward the others. Anyone who has carried a primitivity through has reliable knowledge about existence, is a person of experience, has something he dares vouch for. If a blushing youth (O Socrates![638]) turns to such a person, he will neither put him off with a lot of talk nor offer him this false reliance: just like the others.

At the moment there is in all Christendom no reliance superior to this: just like the others. No one, of course, says it, everybody talks loftily as if he had the highest reliability—but when the catastrophes come, then it is evident that the whole thing is: just like the others.

xi¹ a 387   n.d., 1854

« 2979 *The Great Catch of Fish*

"You shall catch men." During 1800 years, kingdoms, countries, nations, etc. have been caught, a continent became Christian and has been Christian through these many centuries—an enormous catch, enormous catch, a marvellous fulfillment of our Lord's prophecy!

Suppose a fisherman got an order to catch some pike and trout and then caught a million small carp—an enormous catch, an enormous catch! Or if he got an order to catch whales and then caught a million sardines—an enormous catch, an enormous catch!

The method increasingly used in the course of centuries is this: we have lowered the standard for being a Christian and thus have caught all the more. Instead of whales, we caught sardines—but countless millions of them. Instead of sardines, we caught sticklebacks—but countless millions of them—instead of whales. How wonderfully our Lord's prophecies have been fulfilled: I wonder, when I come again, will I find faith on earth!

XI^1 A 454   *n.d.*, 1854

« **2980** *The Trustworthiness of Numbers*

is, of course, deceptive, untrustworthy. And yet this is what is offered in the world, counted upon, so that you are fooled and go along with numbers.

There are millions of Mohammedans—but if you look a bit more closely you will see that they are Mohammedans of this sort: Yes, I am just like the others—and Mohammedans in the sense that if they were born into Christendom they would be Christians. There are millions of Christians—how trustworthy! Yes, they are so trustworthy that if the same ones were born in those countries they would be Mohammedans.

If there is a certain truth in the saying that man has received speech in order to conceal his thoughts or, as I put it, in order to conceal the absence of thoughts,[639] if there is a certain truth in this, namely, that he has not received it for this purpose but he uses it for this purpose—something like this can truthfully be said about the numerical: The numerical is used in order to conceal how empty all existence [*Tilværelsen*] is;* the numerical transfers mankind to an exalted state just as opium does, and he is so tranquillized by the tremendous trustworthiness of millions. And yet in truth millions are just as untrustworthy, wholly as untrustworthy, as *one*. But *one* does not have a drugging effect, which millions have, and thus, it is clear to see, one is wholly trustworthy. That is, "millions" transfer man into a drugged state; he sinks under the force of numbers; he expires *qua* spirit; he is thrown into the deal—but that is not the way it is expressed; no, he feels perfect trust and confidence—to such an extent is he deceived.

This, again, is related to the synthesis which man is. He is an animal creature and the possibility of spirit. *But the animal creature needs no higher certainty than numbers.* [†] To feel the need for a kind of certainty other than numbers is related to spirit. Therefore governance has so structured man that this urge toward spirit (for truth's sake) promptly gets its tensing contrast, for the numerical naturally picks up such a thing and ungraciously calls it arrogance.

XI[1] A 512   *n.d.,* 1854

« **2981**

In margin of 2980 (XI[1] A 512):

* Note. And just as we promptly get suspicious that there is a dearth of content when a man begins to run at the mouth and spill out a lot of rubbish, so also we ought to become most suspicious precisely when there get to be millions and millions, suspicious that this enormous number simply points to something wrong.

XI[1] A 513   *n.d.*

« **2982**

[†] *In margin of 2980* (XI[1] A 512):

In relation to everything finite and temporal, in relation to eating, drinking, etc., in relation to all kinds of secular activity and commerce in this world, no trustworthiness superior to that of number is needed, since in a certain sense number is the power in this world, where ideas may seem to be just as frail as number actually is in the world of ideas. In relation to the temporal, sensible, and finite there is (in the very nature of things) no eternal trustworthiness; consequently the trustworthiness of number is entirely trustworthy, yes, the only possible trustworthiness, and is a genuine trustworthiness, except that one is cheated by it—of the eternal, the infinite, the ideal.

XI[1] A 514   *n.d.*

« **2983** *The Numerical*

is like an envelope. One receives a large package, thinks it is something important, but look, it is a package of envelopes. So it is with all these thousands and thousands, who then again confuse having overt power with relating oneself to the idea.

XI[1] A 582   *n.d.,* 1854

« **2984** *Weakness—Strength*

According to the conception of our age I am the weakest of all, not only not a great party, not a small party—indeed, not even as much as two.

And yet among those of this age I am the only one who is strength —for the numerical, in the sphere of the idea, is weakness, yes, the greater the weaker.

XI² A 17   n.d., 1854

« 2985 *The Public*

is the most idea-less of all. In fact, it is the very opposite of the idea. For the public is numbers.

That is why the Jews are especially suited to be publicists, as our times indicate and which Poul Møller[640] was well aware of without explaining it, however. The Jew generally lacks imagination and sensibility, but abstract understanding he does have—and number is his element.

For the publicist the battle of opinions in public life is neither more nor less than the business of a stock exchange. Just as with the quotations on stocks and bonds, he is concerned only with the opinion having the highest percentage. He believes that numbers are ideas— which is the very extremity of idea-emptiness.

XI² A 26   n.d., 1854

« 2986 *Living by Comparison*

The law of existence for the numerical or for mass men is that they live by comparisons.[641] We see from this that the numerical is the sophistical, a self-extending factor which, inspected more closely, dissolves into nothing.

To have it just as good as the others—this is called being happy. Whether or not the lives of contemporaries are utterly shabby or are actually worthwhile does not concern the numerical one bit—no, he only wants to be just like the others.

The right thing is to behave just like the others. Whether something is all wrong makes no difference to the numerical man—it only has to be what the others are doing to be right. —To have the same religion as the others is to have the true religion, etc. etc.—always this "just like the others."

"Just like the others." This phrase expresses the two characteristic marks of being man in general: (1) sociality, the animal-creature which is linked to the herd: just like the others, (2) envy, which, however, animals do not have.

This envy is very characteristic. To be specific, animals are not envious because each animal is only a copy or specimen [*Exemplar*].

Man, on the other hand, is the only animal species in which every specimen is ($\kappa \alpha \tau \grave{\alpha} \ \delta \acute{v} \nu \alpha \mu \iota \nu$) more than the race, is an individuality, intended [*lagt an*] to be spirit. Number or the numerical man, of course, does not become spirit but still retains this feature which distinguishes him from other animal creatures—envy.[642] If man were merely a copy or specimen he would not have envy. But even the man who degrades himself the most to achieve the grand objective toward which the race, with the special assistance of the daily press, is striving —to become a specimen, even he will still be so different from the others that he will distinguish himself from the animal by—envy.

I maintain that it is the daily press in particular which works toward degrading men into copies or specimens, and nothing is more certain. Just as in a paper factory rags are worked together into a mass, so the daily press tends to grind all the differences of individuality away from men, all the spirit (for spirit is differentiation *per se* and, of course, from others) in order to make them happy *qua numerus* by means of this life which is the life of the numerical or mass men: in everything, just like the others. Here the animal creature finds peace and tranquillity, and here envy is quieted.

If the daily press reaches its grand objective, it is conceivable that the mass-men might suddenly feel a need for a few who are not just like the others—in order that envy might still have a little to live on.

In a certain sense I could wish this punishment upon the human race—that the daily press would achieve its objective and make everybody a specimen—what a frightful punishment: one million men each of whom is exactly like the others. It could be presented in a moral story and called: Envy Gets Its Due. The punishment would, of course, turn out to be the most excruciating boredom.

XI^2 A 88 *n.d.*, 1854

« 2987 *Christian Courage*

is one person holding out alone, as a single individual, against the opposition of the numerical (and this corresponds to the fact that the truth was in one person, in Christ, in opposition to the whole race), is conceptual heterogeneity, character heterogeneity with the numerical; Christian courage increases in proportion to the number, and the longer the opposition is endured the more inward the courage becomes.

This moral courage in the area of concepts, of truth and spirit, is qualitatively different from all other courage. To go courageously and alone as a plucky soldier against even 1,000 men or against cannons, into certain danger, etc.—all that has nothing at all in it of the collision of concepts.

Christian courage begins first of all where concepts are involved in the battle.

Therefore paganism did not really know this kind of courage. After all, the purely human principle that the numerical constitutes the concept is implicit in paganism. (Socrates was an exception, the only one who understood that the task was: the individual against number.)

Christianity introduced the concept "spirit" and now the collision is postulated: the single individual against number, that the truth can be in one single person, unconditionally one single person over against and in contrast to all, unconditionally all.

This collision is the most intensive collision possible. This explains why existence itself is interested wherever this collision is found, for a concept has such capaciousness that it can accommodate millions, yes, all, for the sake of a cause. Therefore the person who battles in the realm of concepts, wants to transform concepts, battles, after all, with the possibility of millions.

And the fact that all these countless men, in many respects good and kind, are all of them living a lie makes this collision so terribly strenuous. Alas, how human to want rather to give in and be himself the one who is living a lie. But precisely right here is the Christian battle, the Christian courage, both with regard to the impulses of fear and of compassion.

If I dared to speak like a pagan, I would say that existence is like a monstrous giant who lies perfectly still and has a good time watching men, just as we men enjoy watching birds or domestic animals—so he lies perfectly still and amuses himself watching human beings play their games, watching Ludvig and Mary noticing each other, falling in love, getting married, becoming parents of a numerous flock, all very nice and pleasant—existence keeps perfectly calm. Yes, even if someone were so precocious that he wanted to play the game of being regarded by the others as the person who really was concerned with concepts (as Bishop Mynster, for example, played Christianity), existence would keep perfectly calm, for, actually, it is not affected, and it is still only a game.

But the minute someone touches concepts in earnest—existence gets to its feet. And in order to defend itself, also in order to examine this man, there is a collision. The collision of a single individual with the numerical.

And of all those who have actually become involved with existence and actually been touched by concepts, there is no one, even the bravest, who has not shrunk back from the *tête à tête* with existence itself, and from the collision with the numerical in the battle of concepts.

XI² A 89   n.d., 1854

« 2988 *Arithmetic Problem*

"100,000 millions, each of whom is just like the others," = one.

Only when some one comes along who is different from these millions or this one, only then are there two.

In the world of number unity counts; in the world of the spirit there is no counting at all, or there differentiation counts, and consequently there is no counting.

But this must be practiced, just as a horse learns to be steady under fire. This must be drilled. This practice is especially important for the young officers of Christianity. One must learn not to be afraid of the numerical, learn that it is nothing, just as a child learns not to be afraid of ghosts: See, my child, it is nothing to be afraid of; it is nothing, there is nobody, or it is nothing, only the night fog. In this way one must learn not to be afraid of the numerical and learn this inverted group-arithmetic with which one can reckon the whole group to be neither more nor less than one, a trick such as Schlemihl's tall thin man does when he takes the entire tent and puts it in his pocket.

In "spirit" everything is turned around. In the material world, things are added together and make a large number; in the world of spirit adding results in a mystifying disappearance of number. For number is a hocus pocus hoax—the hoax that there are more than one. Hoaxing under the disguise of the many is rarely thought about.

XI² A 90   n.d., 1854

« 2989 *The Numerical*

Let me talk figuratively. Suppose there were—let us not be stingy with the number—100,000 Latin words declined like *mensa.* Suppose these words got the idea of getting an enormously long sheet of paper manufactured and getting themselves listed on it, one after the other —all in order to impress a grammarian. Would he be at all impressed? No, not the slightest. *Mensa,* he would say, is the declension. The others and the sum total of them are such a matter of indifference that it is a waste of time for me to get acquainted with the whole list—the next declension does not begin until *dominus,* but *dominus* does not have *mensa* as its model. These 100,000 words, he would say, may have their importance as vocabulary in a dictionary—but grammatically, no, none at all. —Or (to change the figure a little) if *mensa* got the notion of placing itself at the head of all these 100,000 words—in order to impress a grammarian, would he be impressed? Not the slightest. My good *mensa*, he would say, what concerns me is the declension, and you are mistaken about yourself and your significance when you think that you become more significant at the head of 100,000 words which are declined as you are. You are really mad, my good *mensa*, if you think one can put himself at the head of nothing, for the 100,000 are grammatically equal to 0. Therefore you are not at the head of something. It is just something which you make yourself and the 100,000 believe, or they you.[*]

This is the nature of the numerical. But the metaphor does not express—and to that extent is not suitable—that in the world of glossology it is accidental which of the 100,000 words becomes the paradigm. In the world of spirit the model for the declension is not accidental; but the vocabulary, the words which are declined according to this declension, the mimicking, have no significance at all.

Yes, this is how it is. And yet how sad, alas, that I must be the one to say such things, I who, sick at heart, so deeply loved the multitude of men. Alas, it is they themselves who have constrained me, under the influence of providence, to this indeclinability. But surely, if law and order are to be maintained, the matter depends upon an eye for quality, an eye for the model, for the declension and the utter insignificance of the number of words, the perhaps enormous number which belong to this declension.

XI^2 A 92   *n.d.*, 1854

« 2990

[*] *In margin of 2989* (XI^2 A 92):

To think that one stands at the *head* of what is nothing is the very same sort of madness as crazy Meier's[643] when he walked around with pockets full of stones thinking they were coins and boasting of his money, proud of *owning* what was nothing

XI^2 A 93   *n.d.*

« 2991 *The Numerical*

Just as a human being cannot maintain uninterrupted labor but needs diversion, so the numerical is diversion, mitigation.

The inversion consists in making diversion—into earnestness.

$$\text{X}^2 \text{ A } 109 \quad n.d., 1854$$

« 2992 *The Battle of the Human Race against God*

According to the New Testament there is conflict between God and man—and the way in which people are Christians in Christendom cannot have altered the situation; in fact, people have made it even worse, because "Christendom" is or "in Christendom" there is a far more serious battle against God than man's battle against God in paganism ever was.

The disproportion in this battle is not that man is only a little power compared with infinite divine power. No, the misrelationship is much greater and quite different and to that extent there is something very comical about this battle. Man's way of strengthening himself, his tactic, gravitates toward becoming a crowd, a mass, more and more, and still more, and so on. But before God mass is a subtraction; the greater the mass the less significance before God.

The tactic of the human race is therefore just as curious as if a runner were to get ready for the race by cutting off one leg, and then, not quite sure that he was strong enough yet, cutting off the other leg.

So disproportionate is this battle, so secure is God in his majesty.

Objectively the battle has absolutely no reality for God. Judaism and paganism downgraded the concept of the majesty of God because they thought this battle was objectively an object and that God had a kind of cause in a human sense.

No, what gives God an interest in this battle is subjectivity, for the highest is subjectivity—God is pure subjectivity[644] and in love it pleases God to be concerned about man. In this way the cause has God's interest, yes, to the highest degree—after all, what could possibly arouse God's infinite interest in anything except his own subjectivity, or the qualification of his own subjectivity.

Paganism and Judaism either trivialized God as having a cause in direct relationship[645] to man, or they elevated God into an abstract majesty so that all human affairs had absolutely no interest for him. Christianity elevates God in infinite majesty above everything objective, above having a cause in every sense, but then again he is interested, with infinite pathos—because he himself in love has so willed it.

$$\text{XI}^2 \text{ A } 116 \quad n.d., 1854$$

« 2993 *The Deepest Fall of the Human Race*

is nevertheless reserved for later times.

"Man" has made a discovery and rejoices in this discovery: the way to make life easy is to make it meaningless.

In character, this means becoming personally, existentially, a spineless fellow, or rather a shrewd animal creature who lives for finite ends—and then becomes important and interesting to himself and to others by way of *interesting* knowledge about the highest, being able to characterize it, present it, praise it, orate it, systematize it, etc.

With this as its background, martyrdom for being a Christian, when it appears again, will be martyrdom by laughter. In a sense there was still something superior in those bloody persecutions, for there was still a kind of vitality, and there was passion. But the miserable power and cowardice of contemptibleness are the power and cowardice of the smirk.

This also accounts for the modern tactic used against all character, the tactic of getting the man declared mad. The fact of the matter is that to have meaning face to face with character is to be forced oneself into having to have character. Therefore meaninglessness and cowardice, the refuse of the race—which is what the later generations are—invented the method of interpreting all such qualities as madness, because in the face of madness or insanity there is no need to act with character born of conviction.

The deep fall of the race is that there are no individualities any more, but in a certain wretched sense everyone has become two. When a book has become old and shabby, the binding separates and the pages fall out. Similarly in our time men are disintegrated; their understanding, their imaginations do not bind them in character—no, thanks. No, existentially they are spineless fellows who flirt learnedly, rhetorically, poetically, systematically, and so on with the highest.

To such entities, elevated discourse about involvement with God as being in a certain sense sheer anguish, the most intense anguish, elevated discourse or, rather, the fact that someone wants to become involved with God, must appear to such entities as the most ridiculous madness.

And this mass of otherwise very nice, decent, even fine people, the great majority, is led by the clergy to think that they are Christians—which naturally is to the interest of the preacher because of his appointment. If they were to be told that they are not Christians, they would become furious and with the best of good will would not be able to grasp it as anything but an insult and would thereupon become insulted and insulting. But the mass of men are not really like this. They do not get insulted when they are told that they are not poets. No, but the clergy have gotten them to imagine that they are Christians, that is, they so shockingly reduce what being a Christian is supposed to mean that in a certain meaningless sense it is true that they all are Christians. This, you see, is why they become insulted. And thus the mass of good, decent people is used to set upon the Christian. Thus they become the guilty ones and yet in a sense are not guilty, insofar as they are acting according to their best conviction, but the tragedy is that their best conviction is one of the lies palmed off and impressed on them by the preachers.

XI² A 127   n.d., 1854

« 2994 *Popularity*

Anything that is to become popular must tend toward extensiveness and multiplicity; the intensive never becomes popular. The intensive is only for men of character, and they are even more rare than geniuses and men of talent, except that the most simple man can be a man of character.

Thus if I were to make an attack on the present conditions among us in Christendom today and say: The Christianity we teach is a different brand of Christianity than New Testament Christianity, such an attack could become popular. Why? Because there is a dose of nonsense mixed into it, as if we were talking about several kinds of Christianity. This can get to be popular, people are able to comprehend this sort of thing: there are several kinds of Christianity, just as there are grade A butter and good butter and plain butter and margarine, which is almost as good as butter. The law of popularity is that a certain dose of nonsense must be mixed in.

A tightening up in the direction of either/or, on the other hand, never gets to be popular.

Multiplicity, extensiveness, expansiveness, and from another angle, the numerical—this is what becomes popular. For example, if I were the leader of an adequate number of adherents (proportionate to the population)—popular approval could be gained for my position as being right[646] and I could prove to be right. But for me to be right as a single person can never become popular. For me to procure an adequate number of mere ciphers as adherents to show that I am many would already be an accommodation on my part.

XI² A 146   *n.d.*, 1854

« 2995 *Christianity Bars the Way for Propagating the Race*

A metaphor. When the fire chief arrives at the scene of the fire, the first thing he does is to say to the police: Put up a blockade; close off the side streets—we can't have hordes of people around.

In the same way Christianity scrutinizes existence and promptly sees that evil is bound up with the numerical, the predominance of animal qualification[647] over spirit qualification—consequently, block off. That is, it follows as a matter of course that no Christian gets married. The tragedy is that there are dreadfully too many men, and all of them are engaged in supplying new millions of human beings.

A Christian is salt[648]—that is, it follows as a matter of course that no Christian gets married. The mass, which is to be salted, the mass —yes, worse luck, it is a horrible body, and all are busily engaged in producing the mass. Salt is needed there, salt: A Christian of course is unmarried.

Yes, here it is. These good, decent people who have hit on the idea of getting married and then, by bringing up children from childhood in Christianity, populating the earth with such uncommonly good, decent Christians, so thoroughly Christian—these good decent men are a bunch of drivelers or swindlers. In fact, Christendom supplies a glorious population of Christians by means of these good, decent people who have so kindly wished to instruct God in heaven how one goes about getting Christians, that it goes best when they are born and brought up in Christianity from childhood. Excellent! Christianity is simply this—the qualitative break of the divine with the human in the breakthrough which constitutes becoming a Christian, becoming salt —and then they want to bring up Christians from childhood—that is, they want to avoid the break with this existence, the break with this world.

No, thank you, good people! This is an invention of veterinarians —not of Christianity! It does not help one bit to protest that it is all meant sincerely, honestly, piously and at a cost for the sake of Christianity—no, no! Remember the metaphor of the fire chief! Whenever a fire breaks out, a horde of people, a horde of nice, sincere people storm up to help put it out—some with a pail, others with a glass of water, others with a squirt gun—in short, nice, sincere, decent people. But what does the fire chief say? He says: Get those people out of here, and if they don't leave on request, then drive them away.

Thus the situation at a fire is so serious that well-intentioned nonsense is not particularly welcome—no, well-intentioned nonsense is treated like a kind of crime. It is not taken to court—no, the police dispose of the whole thing by flogging the well-intentioned nonsense home—where it really belongs. But Christianity is taken to be such a meaningless affair that it does not even have the earnestness of a fire; Christianity is taken to be so meaningless that hearty nonsense and well-meaning silliness are given a warm welcome, are consulted.

Truly, truly, the thing that has wrecked humanity in Christendom for a long time is the lack of an authority capable and daring enough to transform hearty nonsense and well-meaning silliness into—guilt, disorderly conduct, and the like.

XI^2 A 151   n.d., 1854

« 2996 *Christendom*

Actually, there are two factors which have worked together to produce this nonsense, Christendom: on the one hand the over-the-years increasing number of those who want to be Christians—Christians, all right—but of course they do not want to be Christians in the New Testament sense of the word. (A zeal to become Christians like that of the Jew among us who was so zealous for the introduction of the Norwegian constitution, which expels the Jews—"I surely didn't know that.") —And this number so impressed by its quantity that more and more ground was yielded and the concept of a Christian became more and more falsified. On the other hand there has been the egotism of the egotistical clergy, who correctly saw that profit and numbers go together.

XI^2 A 155   n.d., 1854

« 2997 *The Religious—the Christianity of the Millions*

The life of the religious person is the most intensive agony—the shriek of the woman in labor or the scream from the operating room in the hospital is not as fearful—so excruciating is the agony of actually becoming involved with God. It cannot be otherwise, although it still remains unchanged that God is love—and yet, to take the supreme example, the life of the prototype shows on the most dreadful scale what it means to become involved with God, to be true to him.

So it is with the religious man. Examples are few and far between.

Meanwhile more and more millions uninterruptedly play the religious game that being involved with God is sheer bliss, sweet, sweet, and lovely—and thousands of preachers live well by declaiming it.

And both of these are Christianity! But the classification is anything but unreasonable; for since these millions only imagine that they are involved with God, consequently are fooled, it seems reasonable that they find it sweet, sheer sweetness, also that the clergy, who are in the same situation, live well.

XI² A 156   *n.d.,* 1854

« 2998 *Spontaneous Enthusiasm in Preaching Christianity; Reflection; Man's Instinctive Cunning*

Spontaneous enthusiasm in preaching Christianity is related to winning everybody,[649] if possible.

People extol this zeal as praiseworthy, extol it as love to win everybody in this way. Fine, but watch out lest man's instinctive cunning be knavishly implicit in this eulogizing. For men understand, perhaps instinctively, that if one can only get the numerical decked out in ideality, one can very well acquire power with it—and become a Christian at a better price. The numerical is fatally dangerous to ideality. Maybe the preacher becomes fascinated at the sight of all the Christians he is winning—this is dangerous to ideality. Or he is overwhelmed by the impression made by the statistical and thinks: How is it all going to end, this crowd, and only remotely related to Christianity; I must slack off a bit—in order to win all the more. And so ideality is lost.

O Socrates,[650] you saw things so correctly. In reflection the task becomes one of standing in the midst of men and then expressing: The crux of the matter is that I personally become a Christian. Here statistics are unable to enter in to play tricks; and here also it is properly expressed that God is not a busy Majesty who insists on having adherents, but that God is the unconditioned.

XI² A 159   *n.d.,* 1854

« 2999 *The Numerical*

The numerical (which as numbers increase more and more has become the law of human existence [*Tilværelsens*][651]) also has the demoralizing effect that the sight of these thousands and thousands prompts men to live merely comparatively, all human existence dissolves in the nonsense of comparison, the mud of numbers, which then is even prettied up to look like something under the name of history and politics, where the whole point (the mark of spiritlessness) is always that what counts is a large number of participants, that numbers confer significance, almost as if the idea were like a teller in a bank, who ponders numbers.

Alas, in ancient days there still lived men who thought primitively about being human, what it means on the whole to be a human being, what meaning it has within itself and within the whole of existence. Lost as everyone now is from the earliest years in the man-made nonsense of numbers, no one thinks of such things.

That is why there lives scarcely a man who has even an intimation of the dimensions of Christianity, that Christianity was established by God and has the dimensions or proportions of all existence, the proportions of the whole cosmos, that Christianity is an event which literally interests heaven and earth, as Christ portrayed it (for example, what he says in Luke 21 about his return). But here again the nonsense about "Christendom," these millions times millions of Christians, has jabbered Christianity down to a sorry state so that being a Christian is regarded as nothing, something we all are—thus beginning this mutual nonsense in which the whole point is always how great a number has been set in motion—always numbers.

But how ironical, the law is this—everything which needs numbers in order to become significant is *eo ipso* insignificant, and the greater the number it needs, the less significant it is. Everything which can be arranged, executed, completed only with the help of great numbers, the sum of which startles men in amazement, as if this were something important—precisely this is unimportant. The truly important is inversely related, needs a progressively smaller and smaller number to implement its completion, and for the most important of all, that which sets heaven and earth in motion, only one man is needed, and a need for more becomes a subtraction. European wars and revolutions and art exhibitions and gigantic newspapers and the like certainly cannot be operated by one person. This is why people believe that such things are the important rather than that their very unimportance makes large numbers necessary, that their lack of importance forces them to acquire importance from numbers. But what is most important of all, what interests angels and demons, that a person is actually involved with God—for this one single human being is enough.

Shudder, then, when you consider how we live—and that the truth is that every human being can be that one single person.

XI² A 167   n.d., 1854

« 3000 *Giant Enterprises*

Ah, what a change! Once it was true that when one thought of a giant enterprise he thought of one person, one man—a giant.

Nowadays we boast of giant enterprises and these giant enterprises actually are pigmy enterprises—a few million pigmies united together. The whole point is simply number.

XI² A 168   n.d., 1854

« 3001 *That Christianity Simply Does Not Exist*

The following considerations will also shed light on this my only thesis.[652]

Precisely because Christianity is the unconditionally significant it follows, according to the law of significance, that one person is sufficient.

Now, however, Christianity has been shifted over into the sphere of the insignificant, where the law is: Numbers confer significance. For Christianity to amount to something these days there have to be countries, nations, millions of people who call themselves Christians.

No doubt people would *bona fide* break into a horselaugh if it were stated that from a Christian point of view one man is sufficient. From the point of view of Christianity, the idea of Christian kingdoms and states, a Christian world, is just as laughable (provided Christianity used the category of the laughable).

What men perpetually seek in the numerical is what Adam sought among the trees—a hiding place. A person may secretly shrink from the truth that he is not a Christian, that Christianity simply does not exist —so he hides in "Christian states, nations, kingdoms," fleeing from the truth that Christianity simply does not exist.

XI² A 169   n.d., 1854

« 3002 *The World Is What You Make It*
(the Numerical)

Elsewhere [i.e., XI¹ A 301-302] I have shown how this expression should actually be understood, but I would like to add that it can have another interpretation or be construed another way. The world is what you make it, that is: no matter who you are, you will always find a number of your own kind. You will never stand alone; there will always be the group solidarity, always the world. Therefore the kind of a world you will have depends upon you yourself.

Part of the concept of the world (a mixture which providence watches over[*] just as a bath attendant sees to it that the water is properly mixed) is just this, that at all times all possible gradations and nuances are represented, numerically represented; this belongs to the world as the medium of examination. Wherever you look, everwhere there are all possible gradations of fallacies, wrong turns, etc., in all possible nuances and always numerically represented. It is infinitely easy to go wrong in the world and yet in such a way that one is covered by being like the others. Only willing the good is never numerically represented. This is consistent with the examination, for to will the good in truth involves the strenuousness of being one. On the other hand, it is precisely fallacies, wrong turns, and corruption which involve being numerically represented, simply in order to lure with numbers.

XI^2 A 184   n.d., 1854

« 3003

[*] *In margin of 3002* (XI^2 A 184):
When I say that providence takes care of it, it must of course not be overlooked that it is still man's own fault that at every moment all possible gradations of error, corruption, etc. are numerically represented.

XI^2 A 185   n.d.

« 3004 *God—"Man"*

"Just like the others"—this is "man's" sovereign idea; it is the animal qualification.[653]

Everything that is not just like the others is either madness or arrogance. Whether it is in fear and trembling before God, in quaking before eternity's accounting and hell's punishment, whether it is in the most dreadful self-torment, whether it is in the most high-minded self-sacrifice—as soon as it is not just like the others, it is either madness or arrogance. This is the rule in contemporaneity.

God, however, does not stand merely just as firmly but even more firmly on his principle: Not like the others. No, "God's kingdom first of all."[654] With the aid of this, God has protected himself in a marvelous way. To be specific, "God's kingdom first of all" can be understood *in concreto* by every concerned individual in his own concrete way, and the concretion of existence is so great that it adequately encompasses countless numbers. Consequently, each in his own way. On the other hand, there is no doubt that no one who has actually been in earnest about seeking the kingdom of God first of all can remain "just like the others"—it is forever impossible. In a certain sense it is like a lottery or the drawing of lots, except that the number of lots is far greater: everyone can draw his own or everyone is allotted his own in respect to how he is to interpret *in concreto* before God "God's kingdom first of all," but it can never happen that two people draw no. 99—that is, that two people get the same number.

Consequently "not just like the others"—and Christianity does not sentimentally understand this to mean shades of difference in coloring —no, Christianity interprets this to mean that one must suffer at the hands of others, must suffer because one is not like the others.

XI^2 A 211   *n.d.*, 1854

« 3005 *The Numerical*

In everything human lurks the transformation of concepts by numbers.

This is the law for mutiny:[655] numbers change a capital crime so that it is punished more leniently.

This law has many gradations until the number (in revolution) changes injustice to justice, crime into heroic acts, which are rewarded with all earthly benefits.

So it is also with "Christendom."[*] Numbers have changed the definition of what it is to be a Christian, from signifying that the true Christian life means to suffer and to be sacrificed to signifying the most intense and most refined enjoyment of this life, including the possession of all the goods of this life, plus having all this lionized and idolized as piety.

Therefore everything human is basically nonsense or sophistry. It looks as if it were something—it can look this way for a long time, but fundamental to it all is this: numbers transform the concept.

Only true Christianity makes the concept steadfast, the concept stands so firm that one becomes—a martyr for it.

XI^2 A 214   *n.d.*, 1854

« 3006

In margin of 3005 (XI^2 A 214):

Christendom is therefore mutiny[656] against Christianity, but a very special kind of detective's eye is required to see that it is mutiny, because the mutiny does not consist in no one's wanting to call himself Christian—no, the mutiny is precisely this "Let's all of us call ourselves Christians"—and thus by numbers alter the conception of Christian.

XI² A 215   n.d.

« 3007 Beware of Men[657]

In the purely human world the rule is: Seek help among men. Christianity says: Beware of men.

Christianity was indeed a fire which was lighted by Christ and which should be maintained, but in the physical world water puts out fire and in the spiritual world the many, the mass of men, put out fire —beware of men!

XI² A 220   n.d., 1854

« 3008 A Hypothesis

Let us suppose that Socrates had received an appointment to be an apostle—suppose that one of the apostles came to him and said: "Today within one hour we have caught 3,000 souls." I wonder if Socrates would not have doubted seriously that 3,000 could be caught in one hour by an ideality such as that of being a Christian.

XI² A 230   n.d., 1854

« 3009 The Numerical—the Proclamation of Christianity

For the true proclamation of Christianity it is necessary to shut your eyes to statistics—whether there are millions or ten millions, it must only mean one person.

But nevertheless Christianity must not be changed for the sake of one man—and from a Christian point of view, millions are qualitatively equal to only one person.

If, therefore, a Franz Cutler, or whoever it is in collegium politicum,[658] in a consideration of abstinence as a punishment for women, declares that he cannot stay away from them—Christianity should not be altered for this reason and its position on the single state reversed. No, for the sake of one Franz Cutler Christianity does not change. But from a Christian point of view ten million Franz Cutlers are the same as one.

Any proclamation of Christianity which concedes in the slightest to the numerical forgets what a Majesty the Christian has the honor of serving, also forgets the hatred this Majesty has for the numerical.

Therefore, my good Luther, you were not completely sober but somewhat drunk, or your brain somewhat befuddled by the numerical, by millions of Franz Cutlers, that time when you altered Christianity and declared that it was impossible to live chastely outside of marriage. Such things do not concern Christianity at all; it is too lofty and serene to be impressed by one or a million Franz Cutlers. In any case, dear Luther, you ought to have made it clear that this was not a matter of Christian progress but of scaling down.

XI² A 243   n.d., 1854

« 3010 Which Is It? Do "Numbers" Reassure or Disturb?

Nowadays we live rather tranquilized in the thought that since there are so many millions of us who call ourselves Christians (no matter how far we are from being that), simply because there are so many millions of us, God (like every other potentate) has to make a deal, knock off the price of Christianity more or less—in short, take us as genuine.

I find precisely these many millions to be so far from reassuring that these very millions are what disturb and in anxiety alarm. Since there are Christians galore, billions and trillions of Christians and there must be millions of blood-witnesses alone, truly God will not get into a fix by scrapping whole generations. No, if I were the only person in the world or if we at most were two, then it seems conceivable to me that God, if I dare say so, in view of the fact that he had no more than these two human beings who are far from fulfilling his requirement, would knock off a little from his requirement.

We human beings want to reassure ourselves with the help of numbers (and quite rightly numbers are impressive to all relative sovereigns). But look, for God the number is so great that, inversely, for us men number itself becomes the disturbing factor.

XI² A 324   n.d., 1854

OBEDIENCE

« 3011 *Yes and No*
or
The Two Brothers[659]

Which of the two sons was the prodigal, the one who said "No"
—and did the will of the father, or the one who said "Yes"—but did not
do the father's will, and perhaps even flattered himself for having been
willing enough to say "Yes."

VIII¹ A 29   n.d., 1847

« 3012

Moriz Carriere (*Die philosophische Weltanschauung der Reformationszeit;* Stuttgart, Tübingen: 1847, p. 181) cites a portion of *Theologia
Germanica;*[660] *"Und in dem Paradies ist Alles erlaubt was darinnen ist ohne ein
Baum und seine Frucht, das heisst von Allem ist nichts verboten und Gott zuwider,
denn Eines allein, eigner Wille."* That is, the forbidden tree could just as
well have had another name than the tree of knowledge. It makes no
difference which it is. This only remains fixed—there belongs in paradise a tree which is the forbidden tree.

VIII¹ A 69   n.d., 1847

« 3013

It cannot be denied (this, too, is connected with Christianity as
being radically polemical[661]) that Christianity teaches that the world is
going backward. For the clergy to bustle about reassuring people that
Christendom is progressing in the same sense as the world progresses
and that it almost happens automatically is just another way of flattering the world. No, from a Christian point of view, communion with
God rests in the possibility of being able to separate oneself from God.
The more human understanding and self-assertiveness and the like
become developed (and in this sense the world goes forward), the less
obedience there is to Christianity. At this time it has already gone so
far that Christianity is proclaimed in Christendom in such a way that
obedience is taken away and reasoning is put in its place. This is why

357

Christianity teaches with utter consistency that Christianity is so far from progressing that it may end with "apostasy"!

[*In margin:* Christ[662] himself says: I wonder if I shall find faith upon earth.]

But as always men prefer to make Christianity and the world homogeneous. That the world progresses cannot be denied, but it is in a way which does not truly please God; he must feel about it as does a father about a child who has become sophisticated about life—that is, he has lost the best.

When Christianity and the world come to amount to the same thing and all the tension is taken away, men will let it go—I really believe a Christianity like that is nothing but plain secular-mindedness.

IX A 273   *n.d.,* 1848

« **3014**

What is the meaning of the history of Christianity? Its meaning is the epitome of the excuses and evasions and compromises which are the contribution of humanity which does not wish to break openly with Christianity but still wants to maintain the appearance of being Christian, the epitome of all these excuses, evasions, and compromises by which a person becomes a Christian without quite literally breaking with the world. The history of Christianity is retrogression, an affinity between the world and Christianity.

It is quite simple. Take the New Testament[663]—lock your door, talk with God, pray—and then do what it says simply and plainly in the New Testament, actualize it by expressing it existentially—this is Christianity.

But the history of Christianity—"But first of all we have to find out what other enlightened Christians have thought, earnest, experienced Christians; we ought to make use of the experience of history." —How shameful it is to hear a man show off this way; he wants the experience of history to help him act as an individual man. And next. All these millions of so-called earnest, experienced Christians—has any one of them or have all of them together understood the matter any better than the God-man, have they known better what true Christianity is than Jesus Christ. Imagine that someone wanted to get to know the teachings of a philosopher and to that end went to his housekeeper instead of to the philosopher himself, to the housekeeper, who, to be sure, would have much information about the habits of this philosopher etc. but would know nothing about his teaching, to say nothing of knowing it better than the philosopher himself. And so it is with all this scholarly theology—instead of sticking to the New Testament, simply—that is, *doing* what it says.

x^1 A 396   *n.d.*, 1849

« 3015

This is how Christianity wants to rule. It requires nothing in particular—just when the man almost in impatient passion is most keen on wanting to do this particular something Christianity says: It is not needed; it is not required.

That is, Christianity wants unconditioned obedience[664] as a disposition.

The idea of pleasing God by doing this or that was a childish misunderstanding which did not properly conceive of God as the infinite sovereign whose sublimity does not permit such a relationship, as if one could do him a service instead of being required to ask permission to dare risk oneself in danger, ask permission to have the honor of serving the truth, etc.

x^2 A 582   *n.d.*, 1850

« 3016 *Obedience—the Power To Command*

As long as a man is personally obedient to something higher, so long he can also command.

But as soon as it becomes doubtful whether or not he must obey any longer—he is no longer able to command, and then he begins to give reasons.

To give reasons is an indirect indication that the obedience of faith is lacking.

Thus we see that the fact that the whole preaching and proclamation of Christianity is transposed into reasons is an indirect proof that faith has disappeared.

x^3 A 383   *n.d.*, 1850

« 3017

People go right on clamoring for mildness and leniency with respect to the proclamation of Christianity. The better ones among the clergy are almost ashamed at how low the bid has to be in order to get men to accept Christianity in a small way. They shudder at the thought that it might be necessary to shave off even more. But is it not inexplicable that one can be in such a position and then completely forget what plain experience generally teaches—namely, that the more one compromises the worse things get, and that the only thing that helps is rigorousness.

But to use rigorousness requires faith, and to have faith presupposes obedience to something higher—and this the preachers do not have—thus all the confusion.[665]

x³ A 384   n.d., 1850

« 3018 The Tragedy of Christendom Is That It Has Made Christianity into Nothing but a Doctrine

In an older age, when Christianity was understood to be an existing, a discipleship or imitation [Efterfølgelse], the preparation for becoming a teacher was also essentially of a disciplinary nature: learning to be obedient, practicing renunciation and self-denial, the ascetic life, etc.

When Christianity became nothing but doctrine, the test for becoming a teacher became a scholarly examination—existence was never asked about at all.

Then there gradually appeared those vast sciences and with the sciences new doubts etc.—for the life of imitation, which would have given men something altogether different to think about than doubt —was cancelled out.

What are all these sciences? They are the human race's attempt to defend itself against Christianity—but under the guise of really searching out what is acceptable and well-pleasing to God. Well, thanks! No, each person must confess: The New Testament is basically easy enough to understand—but difficult for us human beings, for flesh and blood, as we are, to do. "Give all that you have to the poor"—is that difficult to understand? Essentially not. But I prefer to be free, and yet I do not have the courage to say a blunt "No." So I hit upon a science. I say: I am perfectly willing to do it as soon as it is certain that it is in the New Testament; but there must be variants, and the ways of interpreting it are not absolutely sure. Here, you see, the whole apparatus of textual criticism is helpful, etc. etc.

Wherever there is anyone who in any measure manages to make existence strenuous, people will promptly concoct a science in order to defend themselves against him and convert him into pure doctrine. If he is someone who stands so high that they do not dare admit openly that the science is intended as a defense against him, they will introduce it as a means toward properly understanding him.

x³ A 496   n.d., 1850

« 3019 *Also in This Way Have They Contrived To Abolish the Proclamation of Genuine Christianity*

The pastor declares that there is indeed a God in heaven, a father who literally does concern himself about even the most minute aspects of a man's life. Well, if a man believes that, then I know that he needs neither more help nor help of some other kind.

As for the question: What is Christianity?—it is God's will that each man relate himself before God to Holy Scripture in this matter, and in particular God does not want all this chattering and prattling between man and man.

Such an individual who relates himself to God in this way becomes an authentic individual; what he introduces into life will be the fruit of long silence, and as he himself becomes a person of character in this manner his actions will acquire the power to excite and arouse, a propulsive power unto catastrophe in the surrounding world.

But men found it too rigorous to live this way (not to jabber about it on Sunday). Crafty as human nature always is, instead of holding to God—something every person can and ought to do—they made out that it is well-pleasing to God, it is humility, modesty, and cordiality to prattle together among themselves about what Christianity is, thereby setting aside the sovereignty of Christianity.

Only in character do I actually have the right to talk about what Christianity is; to confer (cordially!) with others about it in easy jargon is an assault upon Christianity, a lack of respect.

The true relation, obedience, what God wants—namely, that an individual shall look to him—this is labelled as detestable pride, arrogance—moreover, the false and indolent jargon is God-pleasing cordiality and humility.

x^3 A 497   *n.d.,* 1850

« 3020 *Fear and Trembling Abraham*[666]

. . . . . And he split the firewood; and he bound Isaac; and he lit the fire; and he drew the knife—and thrust it into Isaac!

The very same moment Jehovah stands visible beside Abraham and says: What have you done, you poor old man! That was not required of you at all; you were my friend, and I merely wanted to test your faith! And I also shouted to you in the last moment, I shouted: Abraham, Abraham, stop!

Then, in a voice faint with the solemn low tones of adoration, faint also with the broken feebleness of a deranged mind, Abraham answered: "O, Lord, I did not hear it; yet now that you speak of it, it seems to me that I did hear such a voice. O, when it is you, my God, who commands, when it is you who commands a father to murder his own son, one is somewhat overstrained at such a moment—therefore I did not hear the voice. If I had heard it, how would I have dared believe that it was yours? When you command me to sacrifice my child —and at the critical moment a voice is heard which says "Stop," I am obliged to think it is the tempter's voice which wants to keep me from carrying out your will. One of two alternatives: either I had to assume that the voice which told me to sacrifice Isaac was the tempter's voice, and then I would not have set out——. But since I was convinced that it was your voice, I had to conclude that the other voice was the voice of the tempter."

Then Abraham set off for home. And the Lord gave him a new Isaac. But Abraham did not look at him with joy; when he saw him, he shook his head and said: This is not Isaac.

But to Sara he said, "It was a strange business! It is certain, eternally certain, that God asked me to sacrifice Isaac; God himself cannot deny that—and yet when I carried it out, it was a mistake on my part, it was not God's will!"

But not so with the father of faith, Abraham! Obedience consists precisely in obeying promptly in the unconditional, the crucial moment. When one has come so far as to say A, he is, humanly speaking, very prone to say B and to act. Even more difficult than setting out for Moriah to offer Isaac is the capacity, when one has already drawn the knife, in unconditional obedience to be willing to understand: It is not required. With respect to decisions such as to sacrifice one's own child and to spare him, to maintain even in the final moment the same obedient, if I dare say so, agile willingness, like that of a servant who is already practically at the goal and then has to run back again and consequently had run in vain—O, this is greatness; "No one was as great as Abraham; who can comprehend him?"

x^4 A 338   *n.d.*, 1851

« 3021 *The Dialectic of Quality*

The more important a work, it is said, the more it is made an object of investigative exegesis. This is done according to a fixed scale:

the more important, the still more important, the most important of all—this is God's Word: ergo.

Rubbish—here in fact quality takes a turn: as soon as it is God's Word, all you have to do is to obey. If you want permission to do research, then never say that Holy Scripture is God's Word—if you do you trap yourself.

X^4 A 403   *n.d.,* 1851

« 3022 *Obedience*

It is obedience which has disappeared from the world, and this explains the absence of character.

As a rule the relationship should be thus: Man understands what God requires of him—and obedience or obligation knocks: Will you do this at once—and obedience does it, dares not do otherwise, and this is character.

But not so in our time. We understand very well what God requires of a man, are well-informed about the demands of ideality—but it comes to nothing. We do not strike fire—no, we regard ourselves as masters over our understanding—should we do it or not, is it prudent or not, and if so, how much, etc. Instead of becoming a person of character we are split in two: a kind of a poet—and a worldly sophisticate.

X^5 A 12   *n.d.,* 1852

« 3023 *The Christian Thesis*

is not: *intelligere ut credam,* nor is it *credere, ut intelligam.*[667]

No, it is: Act according to the command and orders of Christ; do the will of the Father—and you will become a believing person.

Christianity in no way lies in the sphere of intellectuality.

XI^1 A 339   *n.d.,* 1854

« 3024 *Promises without Commitments*

are candy and sweets, and candy and sweets are what Christianity has been made into in "Christendom."

But promises cannot be separated from the commitments. Man has wanted to do the same with Christianity as a person might do with medicine which, for the sake of taste, has been combined with raspberry syrup—he gets the bright idea of taking the raspberry syrup alone and calling it the medicine; in the same way man has wanted to take the promises without the commitments, accept the promises and say goodbye to the commitments.

But this cannot be done. Christianity's promises are related to commitments quite differently than raspberry syrup to medicine. If one separates the promises from the commitments, he gets the promises only as confection—that is, as illusion—that is, in such a way that he in this very way defrauds himself of the promises. But to get raspberry syrup as a confection does not mean to be defrauded, inasmuch as raspberry syrup, after all, is a sweet (although he certainly would be defrauded if he needed the medicine and took only the raspberry syrup), but to receive the promise of eternity as sugar and sweets is to be defrauded of them.

Accepting raspberry syrup as a confection is not being defrauded, but taking the promises of eternity as sugar and sweets means *eo ipso* to be defrauded.

XI¹ A 523   n.d., 1854

OFFENSE

« **3025**

The various occasions on which Christ[668] himself says: Blessed is the one who is not offended in me. These passages could be gathered together to show how Christ himself at various points sets the possibility of offense alongside. For example, as soon as he speaks of his glory,[669] he promptly adds as an antidote that he must suffer, and then again adds again: Blessed is he who is not offended. Likewise in the answer[670] to John's disciples.

VIII[1] A 381   n.d., 1847

« **3026**

The human dialectic cannot advance further than to the admission that it cannot think this [revelation], but also to the admission that this does not imply anything more than that it cannot think this. But the human dialectic, if it wants to understand itself, consequently, be humble, never forgets that God's thoughts are not man's thoughts, that all this about genius and education and reflection makes no difference but that divine authority is the decisive factor, that the apostle is the one whom God calls as such, be he fisherman or shoemaker (for nowadays it is perhaps all too easy to understand that Peter became an apostle, but at the time it was far easier to understand that he was a fisherman!)

The divine authority is the category, and here, also, quite appropriately, is the characteristic mark of it: *the possibility of offense.* Undoubtedly a genius can be an offense, *esthetically,* for a moment or 50 years or a 100, but he can never be an offense *ethically;* the offensive factor is that a man has divine authority.

But with regard to the qualification of being called by a revelation, just as with everything Christian, in the course of time indolence and habit and want of spirit or absence of spirit and thoughtlessness were allowed to dampen the coiled spring. At one moment a hysterical female had a revelation, then a sedentary handworker, now a professor, who became so *profound* that he could almost be said to have a revelation, then a peering genius who peered so deeply that he almost

365

just about had revelations. This gradually came to be the common understanding of being called by a revelation, and in this sense Paul also had a revelation, except that he also had an uncommonly good head on his shoulders.

No, the divine authority is the category. Here there is very little or nothing at all for instructors and assistant professors and paragraph eaters to do. The assistance of these gentlemen is needed here no more than a maiden needs a barber to shave her beard and no more than a bald man needs a hairdresser to style his hair. The matter is very simple: will you or will you not obey, will you submit in faith to his divine authority, or will you take offense—or will you perhaps not take sides—be careful, that, too, is offense.

But as mentioned, the coiled spring has been dampened or relaxed in the parenthetical. Exegesis was the first parenthesis. Exegesis got busy: how was the revelation to be comprehended, was there an inner fact, perhaps a kind of *Dichtung und Wahrheit,* and so on and on. Strange that Paul, whom this concerns most, does not seem to have spent one single second on *wanting to comprehend* in this sense—but the rest of us, well, we are not Paul and so we have to do something—for to obey him is not doing anything. Now, obviously, from generation to generation at every university, in every semester one course on how this and that, from generation to generation every other year a new book about how this and that—yes, it is an excellent diversionary means; in this way the prospect of obeying Paul is put more and more at a distance.

Philosophy, and along with it dogmatics, which mimics philosophy, was the second parenthesis. As befits a noble, high-born, human science, it said: "By no means am I going to get involved pettily in or let myself be disturbed by the question of who the author of the book is, whether he is only a fisherman and an insignificant man. No, away with all pettiness! The principal thing is the content, that is all I ask about. Just as the esthete does not ask who wrote a play but only what it is like, so, too, I am indifferent to who the author is"—also indifferent to the fact that he is "the apostle." Indeed, it is easy to speculate this way. For "the apostle," a man with divine authority—just there is the hitch. It is easy to be done with Paul in this manner—after all, one never gets around to begin with him, or to begin with his having divine authority. Scripture is handled so scientifically that it could just as well be by anonymous persons.

From the moment the parenthetical got underway there was, of course, plenty for instructors and assistant professors and paragraph eaters and peerers to do. As things went more and more in this direction, the category of being called by a revelation gradually receded more and more; it became a triviality, something indifferent, which eventually almost everybody could fool around with; and then it went so completely out of fashion that finally it became a rarity to see anyone in this "equipage."

And then Magister Adler proclaimed that he had had a revelation.[671]

VIII² B 15   n.d., 1847

« 3027

When he has done that he opens his arms to every one who seeks rest. But the discourse which omits this deterrent abolishes Christianity.

In margin: When Christianity entered the world it was not necessary to call attention to the offense, but nowadays we miss out on Christianity because we miss out on the possibility of offense—this is why Christianity can no longer satisfy men—alas, in fact it can no longer offend them.

Here use something which is enclosed in the previous notebook [i.e., VIII² B 38].[672]

VIII² B 40   n.d., 1847

« 3028

The possibility of offense[673] in relation to Christ has perhaps become greater in Christendom (with the help of the diffused Christian tradition in which one lives without being Christian) than ever before. Everything depends on how developed a person's idea of God is. The Jews' idea of God was not nearly as developed and as pure and spiritual as it has become through Christianity. But the tension of offense—that a man was God—is also greater.

The whole problem arises from being brought up in Christianity. It cannot be otherwise, but no one pays any attention to the problem.

Offense is never mentioned these days—alas, and even to the disciples, the believing disciples, Christ[674] said: You will be offended in me.

VIII¹ A 585   n.d., 1848

« 3029

All this about the possibility of offense,[675] in short, this which makes Christianity as divinely rigorous as it is, depends again upon another aspect of the doctrine of sin; it becomes an expression of respect for the battle of the anguished conscience, what it means, for this alone can bring a man through all these terrors (the possibility of offense) to the Savior.

IX A 244   *n.d.,* 1848

« **3030**

[*Inside the front cover of NB⁷:*]
Why Has Christianity Come into the World?
  The opposite of an apology.

IX A 253   *n.d.,* 1848

« **3031**

All this talk about Christianity which instead of introducing the middle term of offense at every point directly fits Christianity in with the natural man, obligingly and complimentarily, under the rubric of satisfying the deepest in him—is treason. Granted that the natural man has some sort of idea about God, the characteristic of the natural man is always willfulness as far as his feelings are concerned. Once in a while when he really is in the mood for it, he wants to luxuriate emotionally a little in his thought about God. But now Christianity! Merely to make the relationship to God, this feeling, an object of discipline and schooling—is this not enough to scandalize the profound depths of the natural man? Would it not also be an offense to the natural man to learn that his feelings in erotic love should be disciplined in a definite school.

But this is precisely what Christianity teaches. Instead of submitting the God-relationship to man's *libitum* in luxuriating hours of mood or in "quiet times,"[676] Christianity teaches that a man must first of all find out from God or by revelation how deeply he has sunk, what patience means, along with the fact that if a man wants to be a Christian he must arrange his life accordingly, not think about God in the same way a person goes to the Deer Park once a year or when he has the inclination, but that a person has to take the power away from nature, constrain it.

This is why Christians experience what the natural man does not perceive, simply because he always talks and thinks about God imaginatively at a distance. The Christian comes to experience what it means not to feel at all in the mood and then to be obliged for that very reason to think about God. Here we have it: it is the natural man's invention to fantasize a little thinking about God when he feels like it; Christianity is to think of God in spite of everything, to pray to him to help you think of him precisely when you feel cold and far away from God.

Here, then, are the roots of the possibility of offense, depicted as clearly as possible, and this is indeed the fundamental structure.

IX A 322   *n.d.*, 1848

« **3032**

The Gospel about the Pharisee and the publican. Luther's sermon.[677] Luther rightly says that God's judgment, that the publican went home justified in preference to the other, not only goes against reason but is *offensive*—that is, must be offensive to human understanding, the secular mind.

Luther admires the publican for putting side by side in his prayer such *contradicting* words as: me a *sinner—merciful.*

But he is wrong in thinking that the publican must have heard the gospel; such prayers are often found in the Psalms.

He is very illuminating concerning sin, that first of all evil entices, as if it were nothing, and then, when one has let himself be enticed, it terrifies. This is why I said somewhere else that the second repentance is the true repentance.

IX A 427   *n.d.*, 1848

« **3033**

In a certain sense it is enough to lose one's mind over, and here is where the possibility of offense really lies.

How often have I not caught myself thinking and saying to myself: Even if, humanly speaking, you know yourself to be well-meaning toward men, you must make an effort to be more loving; then things will go well and you will get along better with men. And what then— then Christianity steps up and says: You fool, what humbug is this, wasn't Christ love—and what happened to Him? Humanly speaking, there is something frightfully cruel in this thought. And yet this is Christianity. To be specific, Christianity declares: You must by no means refrain from doing what you had in mind—but you must know that it will lead you directly to the opposite goal.

X¹ A 565   *n.d.*, 1849

« **3034**

The concept "offense" or, as it is called, scandal, is the truth, is most often regarded as untruth. Thus if untruth has become entrenched in "an established order" and cozily settles down, and then the truth stirs, the latter is denounced as a scandal. When in the course of time literary infamy got the prescriptive right to exist, when such a thing was accepted instead of being a scandal every day it existed on such a disproportionate scale, absolutely no one dared say a word because all were afraid of arousing scandal. Well, thanks for that. And then when I said something, many people thought and said: It's a scandal, a scandal he should have avoided. Take a higher example. How many thousands considered it a scandal when Luther began to tamper with the Pope.

It is the same in other situations. When a person has cozily settled down in the established order and has all possible profit from it, when the truth as such has become a kind of luxury and jumbling every possible point of view has become supreme wisdom, then to raise up the truth is a scandal.

And if it is a professor against a professor—well, that's great—then it is a frightful scandal. But that the whole false peace and unity was the real scandal must not even be mentioned.

X^2 A 117   *n.d.*, 1849

« 3035 *The Possibility of Offense— the Single Individual*

What is commonly called Christendom (these thousands and millions) has made Christianity into utter nonsense.

But, in addition, established Christendom's orthodoxy has actually transformed Christianity to paganism.

Christ is the paradox;[678] everything Christian is marked accordingly, or as the synthesis it is such that it is marked by the dialectical possibility of offense. Orthodoxy (especially emotional and vigorous Grundtvigianism, for there is still power in Grundtvig[679]) has now taken this away and set in its place everywhere: the wonderful-glorious, the glorious, the incomparably glorious and deep etc.—in short, *direct* categories.

Thus Christ acquires direct recognizability, but direct recognizability means Christ is not "the sign"; with direct recognizability Christianity is paganism.

Then casually to work in something about the sign and the offense, although extremely rarely, is of no help, for the possibility of offense is the dialectically decisive factor, is the "boundary" between paganism, Judaism–Christianity.

It is clear that this fundamental confusion [*Grundforvirring*] is connected with upbringing in Christianity from childhood. Everything thereby acquires direct momentum; the repulsion of opposition is not there.

We also perceive that, because of the possibility of offense, Christianity in any case has only single individuals to deal with dialectically, for the possibility of offense separates and isolates each one as the channel to becoming a Christian.

x^2 A 389 *n.d.*, 1850

« 3036 *To Give Offense—To Take Offense*

Christ cries woe to them who give offense, to them by whom offense comes—and yet the possibility of offense is inseparable from every qualification of the essentially Christian, and Christ frequently repeats: "Blessed is he who is not offended in me."

The difference is this—the divine truth is "the truth," but in such a way that the world takes offense at it. It cannot be otherwise. But it cannot therefore be said that it gives offense.

To give offense is something else, for example, deliberately intending to wrench faith away from the believer. When the possibility of offense is shown in order to strengthen in the faith, this is the truly Christian proclamation of Christianity.

x^3 A 333 *n.d.*, 1850

« 3037 *The Dialectic of Offense*[680]

When a given age has gotten Christ changed over into esthetic categories and venerates him esthetically—when someone then, in the interest of the essentially Christian, must affirm debasement, the cry goes up that he is actually debasing and insulting Christ.

So it is everywhere. When Dr. A. Arnauld wrote against frequent going to communion (which the Jesuits irresponsibly defended) [*in margin:* Reuchlin, *Geschichte Port-Royal,*[681] I, p. 521 etc.], the cry went up that it was desecration, it was leading people away from religion—very fine, indeed, but it was rather an attempt to prevent them from taking it in vain.

It would be the same if someone today were to show that the trouble lies in the abundance of preaching that goes on, that it would be much better if there were not so much of it.

x^3 A 622 *n.d.*, 1850

« 3038 *John the Baptist*[682]

He sits in prison and sends the disciples to Christ to ask: Are you he who is to come?

Perhaps it could be understood in this way.

He has attacked Herod and therefore now is imprisoned! But Christ has paid no attention at all to the whole affair.

Perhaps it did not even have the approval of Christ, who did not want him to be regarded as either prophet or judge but only as one preparing the way for Christ.

Now he sits in prison, is perhaps impatient because Christ does not do anything for him.

Thus the words "Blessed is he who is not offended"[683] may be understood as applied to John's impatience.

x³ A 674   n.d., 1850

« 3039 *True Christianity—the Possibility of Offense*[684]

As I have constantly pointed out, the mark of Christianity is that at every point it shows the possibility of offense.

Originally it happened like this: Judaism is optimism—and now Christianity, which is pessimism, comes along and presents itself as the fulfillment of the prophecies and expectations of the Jews; thus God is supposed to be the same, although the change is the greatest possible. Here as plain as possible is the possibility of offense.

In Christendom the same is achieved by upbringing in Christianity. The Christianity in which a child is brought up and which the child assimilates is—Judaism is optimism—and now the question is whether as an adult he wants to become a Christian, which involves changing from optimism to pessimism, and the possibility of offense is just as intensive as in Judaism, because the child has been taught that it was Christianity, and the child has grown up in and with the idea that this optimism is Christianity; whereas the relationship is thus: precisely in order to be properly tightened and tensed for pessimism, optimism is necessary for the foreground, for the dialectic in contradistinction to which it is defined.

But one also sees what nonsense and what a swindle, from a Christian point of view, this sentimental rubbish in Christendom is— namely, that the adult longs to be the kind of a Christian he was as a child, that he admits (you driveller, or you scoundrel!) that as an adult he is not the Christian he was as a child.

XI¹ A 360   n.d., 1854

« 3040 *To Recommend Christianity in Such a Way That in a Sense One Cautions against It.*[685]

This is the formula for my proclamation, which has been offensive enough.

However, take another case. Will anyone deny that Epictetus was a Stoic, or that he knew how to recommend Stoicism, or that he did it magnificently? Yet he also continually cautions against it, against becoming involved in it if one is not whole-hearted.

But let a job-holding silk-clad pastor be hired to proclaim Stoicism and you will see that he will simply recommend it—exactly as a shopkeeper does. A shopkeeper will of course say: To caution against products is certainly foolish—in fact, I run the risk of getting no customers, or of losing the good business I previously had, or of driving customers away instead of keeping them in the store.

How revolting such a pastor, and this is called Christian earnestness!

XI^2 A 16   *n.d.,* 1854

OPTIMISM–PESSIMISM

« 3041 *Optimism——Pessimism*

If, as Christianity teaches, the world is a sinful world and is immersed in evil, then, from a Christian point of view, the good citizen is the person who does not propagate this sinful race.

Pessimistically, this has the same consistency as the optimistic deification of this world as a nice world which declares the one who begets many children, the more the better, to be the good citizen.

Optimism mulcts confirmed bachelorhood; pessimism mulcts marriage.

XI^1 A 204 *n.d.*, 1854

« 3042 *Christ and His Apostles*

I dare say there is a difference between the apostles' teaching and Christ's teaching, or between the apostles' Christianity and Christ's Christianity, but nothing can be farther from the truth than the conjecture in the *Wolfenbüttel Fragments*[686] that Christ had nothing but worldly motives, and thus when his tragic life and death had taught the apostles that everything was lost, they made a new version and presented him now as one whose primary thought was to want to suffer. Thus Christ would actually be the optimist and the apostles the "reluctantly voluntary" inventors of pessimism.

But nothing can be farther from the truth; and the pessimism one reluctantly concocts is itself a poor kind of pessimism.

No, Christ understood pessimism much better. And the difference between Christ and the apostle is that Christ unconditionally expresses unconditional pessimism which will have nothing to do with the wretched, miserable, sinful world except to be put to death, sacrificed. The apostle on the other hand plants the very first seeds of a new optimism: that is why a congregation is established. Of course, it would never occur to me that the apostle should be held responsible for what has grown out of this possibility over the centuries, particularly in Protestantism, particularly in Denmark, where Christianity (*sit venia verbo*) does not have the slightest trace of a long lost resemblance to

374

Christ's Christianity but, to the contrary, is just like the drinking song which Jeppe on the mountain sings: Merrily, merrily, round and around.[687]

Incidentally, with regard to Christ's almost seeming to give the appearance in the earlier part of his life that he intended to establish an earthly kingdom, it must always be remembered—something I have frequently emphasized—that this belongs precisely to achieving a properly thorough pessimism. But what do men know about pessimism, these wretched vermin we call men these days, who are so keen on getting a bit of happiness in this world that they naturally could never have an intimation of what pessimism is, that it seeks first of all to win everything simply to throw it away. This is the passion of martyrdom; imagine it intensified as it is in the God-man, and you have a faint notion of this pessimism. The kind of pessimism invented by men who have aspired to success but failed is not pessimism; it is a kind of optimism, an attempt to make the most of the given situation. And with this kind of pessimism they fancy themselves able to measure the passion of martyrdom in the God-man!

No, to have had the earthly in one's power is always a part of true pessimism.

XI[1] A 482   n.d., 1854

« 3043 Christianity—Judaism—Christendom

Even in the Old Testament (which has no intimation of what the New Testament requires: mortification, etc.) the nature of the matter is still such that Sirach[688] says: If you will serve the Lord, then prepare your soul for temptation—consequently wanting to serve the Lord is not simple optimism; bad weather does accompany it, although but slightly compared to when Christ comes on board—which, incidentally, is the origin of the saying common to sailors (a satire on modern Christendom and the clergy, in whose company one certainly can be completely safe): There's always a storm when there's a preacher on board. But the saying itself is sound and characterizes Christianity as it is: restlessness.

Compared with Judaism, then, Christianity is complete pessimism, a severity of which Judaism has no knowledge.

Do I hear someone say: How in the world has it come to be called grace, the gospel, and in contrast to law? I am able to answer this very adequately but must explain something I have never seen set forth. It is called grace because Christ introduces and promises the blessing which is called immortality. Please note this. Judaism did not know immortality. Immortality is proclaimed in Christ—note this well if you desire to become a Christian—and then the law's requirement of the utmost is intensified, but nevertheless this cannot be said to be related to such a blessing as immortality.

This is how it stands in Christianity. How, then, is it possible that Christendom has made Christianity out to be optimism—it is a riddle, or, well, it is easily explained, it is a swindle. Incidentally, this swindle proves indirectly that Christianity is truth and power; it is corrupted the way it is precisely so that no one dares to throw it out or to put a new religion in its place. No, Christianity flourishes all over the country—but, it must be admitted, it is exactly the opposite of Christianity. I doubt that there is anything analogous, that any other religion is corrupted in this way.

XI^1 A 585   n.d., 1854

« 3044 *Christianity Converted into Optimism*

Provided that converting Christianity into optimism is neither utter thoughtlessness nor simple knavery, the thinking behind it must go something like this.

For God the world is immersed in evil—in fact, Christianity teaches this—indeed, we also admit that such was the case with paganism and Judaism. But if we Christians will behave ourselves, be good, decent people, it could still be a wonderful world[689] and we would rejoice in this life—after all, Christ has made satisfaction for original sin.

"Man" is constantly occupied with getting this world made into a wonderful world and getting away from God's criminal view that it is immersed in evil, is for him a criminal existence.

I shall not at present dwell on whether current Christendom can be said to have managed in any way whatsoever to behave itself and be good, decent people, or whether the ethical situation in Christendom is not the same as it was in paganism, Judaism, Mohammedanism. But if this is not the case, then it is necessarily still unchanged that the Christian—if there happen to be any in this wonderful Christendom!!! —becomes a sacrifice, falls a sacrifice, in order to advance the cause of Christianity.

But I shall not dwell on this. No, the reason God does not change his view of this whole existence is that for him time has no meaning, to him the ancient past is perpetual present, likewise that ancient past event—the fall.

This whole human existence which dates from the fall and which we men are so conceited about is a devilish piece of work—this whole existence is against him, is simply the consequence of a stumble which, in view of the vast consequences, we would be most happy to forget, something God does not do.

This whole human existence is against God, is a falling away from him, a stumble away from him, and now he simultaneously wants to have mercy on it (for he is, in fact, love), but he also wants to pick a quarrel with it.

To this end Christianity—which for that reason promptly bars the way for propagation. The fact that Christianity bars the way for propagation means: Stop; I have endured this world-historical process long enough. Of course I will take pity on you, but I will not have any more consequences of the stumble.

Thus even if one became a Christian and died celibate, he would still be a criminal, for his existence by propagation was a crime.

The world can never become a wonderful world for God in this way, for either there is a given generation—but in that case it exists by propagation, or also——well, that disposes of the question whether this is a wonderful world or not.

Consider this illustration. Suppose there were a family whose ancestor had offended the king of the country—now if this were carried on from generation to generation by the respective successors to the throne, if the family is never forgiven, there would be many objections to this. In the first place, kings are only human beings and consequently time here has significance. In the next place, the second generation, the seventh, etc. actually does not have the same persons any more than the corresponding king is the same; perhaps the present-day members of that family actually are fine people, anything but enemies of the king.

Compare this with God's relation to the race. In the first place, for God time has no power to change; for God the incident with the ancestor essentially happened "today." And yet he will forget it—but, of course, on the condition that one will not *interere culpa*. In the illustration the crime was not that the later generations of that family derived from the ancestral father by propagation. But when the crime consists of that, then it is really too much to demand forgiveness with permission to *interere culpa*.

And yet this is the new version of Christianity which flourishes expecially in Protestantism. Christianity has, as it were, said to God:

Just let us be the boss here and you will see that you will be delighted with us, you will see what wonderful children we will bring up, true Christians, for this must be accepted in good time (Christianity properly holds that since to become Christian is a break, one does not accept it so early that it is nonsense to talk about breaking with the world, as if one would say that the infant in baptism breaks with the world, consequently the break is avoided—that is, becoming a Christian is avoided—that is, it becomes a fantasy, a little bit of sentimentality and a little bit of a childish joking).

No, Christianity stands firm on the single state—it has not needed empirical proofs; but Christendom's grand performance of obtaining Christian children, real Christians from childhood on, the result of this grand performance has adequately justified its aims, with the help of a deft turn, beginning anew upon the old view that it's a wonderful world, and it would be a shocking sin to stop the stream of legions of good, decent people by blocking off propagation.

No, Christianity stands firm on the single state—and I will not do as Luther did (I watched out for that!); if it seems that Paul does not agree with Christ, I will not say: Christ must be set aside; Paul is the man. No, should it happen that Paul does not agree with Christ, I will say: Well, then Paul must excuse me.

God's kingdom is not of this world; the Christian must be a stranger and an alien in this world, this world which to God is immersed in evil, the consequence of a guilt which for God, however, was perpetrated today . . . . .

This world, the selfishness of this whole existence is concentrated in, culminates in: propagation of the race, a selfishness which (as I have shown elsewhere [i.e., XI^2 A 154], since after all it cannot create (which is God's royal prerogative), nevertheless at least wants to give life. This selfishness God does not want; he wants it stopped—therefore Christianity blocks the way at once; God's kingdom is not of this world; the Christian is a stranger and an alien.

XI^2 A 163   *n.d.*, 1854

ORTHODOX, ORTHODOXY

« **3045**

The same thing is done with the concept "orthodoxy" as with the concept "consistency." Many think that being consistent means always doing the same thing and presumably would have us go around with umbrellas in sunny weather because we use them in rainy weather.

I A 45   January 28, 1835

« **3046**

. . . . . from the letter-case I have frequently had presentiments of losing.*

I A 193   n.d., 1836

*If orthodoxy continues to define itself restrictedly, it will begin to look like the grocer's stack of cone-shaped sacks, the smaller one inside the other.

I A 195   n.d., 1836

« **3047**

For a long time now rigid letter-of-the-law orthodoxy has reverted to being a counterpart to Don Quixote,[690] whose various ridiculous hair-splitting sophistries will provide excellent analogies.

V B 1   n.d., 1844

« **3048**

Giordano Bruno[691] put it very well in saying that narrow-minded orthodoxy worships and adores the tail of the donkey on which Christ made his entry [into Jerusalem].

VIII[1] A 118   n.d., 1847

« **3049**

Henrich Steffens[692] is a good example of a well-meaning orthodoxy which does not hesitate to assert that if there is in Christianity only the slightest thing which is to be subjected to the corrective of thinking in the sense that thinking is supposed to decide anything, then everything is lost—and which nevertheless itself *am Ende* remains in

379

confusion. He shows (in *Religions-Philosophie*, I, p. 440 *et passim*) that miracles are an obstacle to thought. If thinking is now going to have the right to decide something because it cannot grasp it, then Christianity is lost. What does Steffens do then? He provides a theory which, *thinking*, finds the inclusion of miracles to be entirely in order. Alas, alas. Is this not the primacy of thought if it decides that I may very well believe miracles. Dialectically, is there the slightest difference between the power which decides that I shall reject something and that which decides that I may accept it? How can this power decide that I may believe it without latently having the opposite decision at its disposal. The whole thing is a delusion, just exactly like Heiberg's thinking that "public" is a confused concept when it is against him—but a sensible one when it is for him—instead of the public in itself being nonsense. And this is how intelligence and thinking are Christianly dethroned, regardless of whether it will say yes or no.

Christianity is related neither to thinking nor to doubt,[693] but to will and to *obedience;* you shall believe. Wanting to take thinking along is disobedience, no matter whether it says yes or no.

VIII¹ A 331   n.d., 1847

« 3050

Now when everything in our day is supposed to be so dashing, sensible with a jaunty swing, so extraordinarily shrewd with a humorous touch—I read among other things the following words by someone who nevertheless regards himself as being orthodox: "He would never think of undertaking or beginning the utterly useless work of wanting to convert the world." Splendid! Clearly "the world" means the world or worldliness existing in Christendom. And now Christianity, which began with wanting to change the world at the time when there was not one single Christian—at that time Christianity did not say: What foolishness to begin such an enormous and useless task which can never be completed. But present day Christianity among the Orthodox is a gorged self-satisfaction which avoids every inconvenience involving risk and swims in all this about profundity and profundity and the wonderful-glorious and depth and depth.[694]

VIII¹ A 529   n.d., 1848

« 3051

But men are cowardly, the orthodox as well. Humanly speaking, Christianity is indeed foolishness. Therefore one does not dare be alone in it, alone in it with God and Christ. Therefore this clinging to history, to these countless thousands and thousands who have been just as foolish. But this is pandering and is unchristian.

VIII[1] A 566   n.d., 1848

« 3052

Almost with every word they say and about everything they undertake the orthodox usually are in a hurry to add: with God's help. On the whole they do not mean much by it, which is why they cackle so loudly. —In my private thoughts I deeply and sincerely believe that God helps me, but I do not dare say it, lest God become angry with me for showing off and cease helping me.

IX A 136   n.d., 1848

« 3053

The extent to which Christianity is lost is best seen in the tolerance on the part of the strict orthodox. Their watchword is: If we may only keep our faith to ourselves,[695] then let the rest of the world take care of itself. Merciful God, and this is supposed to be Christianity. This is the power which once broke into the world and by being willing to suffer forced Christianity upon the world, forced it more powerfully than any tyrant.

The orthodox do not suspect that this tolerance of others is the influence of the purely secular, that it stems from their not actually having the understanding or respect or courage for martyrdom or a proper faith in eternity but really prefer to have it good in this world.

And what makes the situation even more dreadful now is that this "tolerance" is willing to let the enormous forgery prevail—that the whole world calls itself Christian—when the orthodox nevertheless believe that the world is pagan.

How low Christianity has sunk, what an impotent poor thing it has become! It is reason which has triumphed, reason which has bullied enthusiasm and the like down to the level of the ludicrous. This is why people do not dare be enthusiastic, do not dare assert that martyrdom is an incomparable glory; they are more afraid of being laughed at than of being slain—and so they compromise; they wrap themselves up in their donkey skins, merely ask permission to dare be Christians themselves, call this tolerance, and boast about being the true Christians.

X[2] A 133   n.d., 1849

« **3054**

O, the world is so shrewd, and everything is supposed to be so lofty and elevated, and the orthodox are not so much better.

Everything is supposed to be so lofty and objective that something is equally true whether the person acts accordingly or not—but let us become a little stupid and understand that it is a lie in your throat, a fabrication of evil.

Everything is supposed to be so lofty: I am working for the truth —but that I admittedly also have every possible earthly advantage from it—who could be so prosaic as to think me so low that I would work for that reason. But let us be a little stupid and prosaic and at least look at this a bit suspiciously.

But in the state the police see to it that "poisons" are not issued without great precaution—in spiritual matters everyone handles poisons in the most reckless and careless manner.

Truly what the world needs is a really stupid Socrates, who was so very stupid that he dared not risk putting everything on such a high level.

What the noblest character who daily lived in fear and trembling perhaps dared risk in an emergency—this is something else again when it is the going thing in a world of shrewd and dubious persons. When a well-known honest man finds something on the street and says: I'll advertise it—well, this is all right. But when one of the dubious persons finds something and says: I'll make an announcement about it—the police think it would be better for him to hand it over immediately.

Alas, and who is so good that he must not deal with himself as a dubious person—and he who does not do so—well, he is the most dubious of all.

X^2 A 553   *n.d.*, 1850

« **3055**

It is easy enough for the orthodox here at home to charge me with exaggerating, with being all too rigorous,[696] etc. (which, incidentally, is not true, since according to the gospel I still have not reached more than 50%) and then advantageously forget that if such were the case, they are, in fact, themselves accomplices. I did not, after all, begin this way; it is a steady ascent. Now if the orthodox had done their duty and immediately or opportunely been supportive, I would hardly have become so rigorous (which, incidentally, might possibly have been a mistake, but excusable, because the greater truth was hidden from me). But their silence and petty opposition was, among other things, a factor in my having to set the price higher.

x^2 A 554   *n.d.*, 1850

« 3056 *Sterile Orthodoxy*

Melanchthon says in his *Sermons* (III, p. 118): *Es ist nicht nöthig zu disputiren, ob die Zerknirschung aus Liebe zur Gerechtigkeit oder aus Furcht vor der Strafe entspringe, weil diess gemischt ist. . . . . . Ich erinnere mich, dass gerade jene Leute welche darüber disputirten* (there was conflict over this in 1538), *hier eine ganze Nacht hindurch tranken und sangen; "Da trunken sie die liebe lange Nacht, biss dass der helle Tag anbrach: Sie sungen, sprungen und waren voll.* "[697]

See Galle, *Melanchthon als Theolog*[698] (Halle: 1840), p. 243.

x^4 A 413   *n.d.*, 1851

« 3057 *The Old Orthodox*

What keeps me from getting involved with them is, of course, not what they *say* about the apostolic but the fact that all the time they are saying it they are sitting and squawking in government jobs, with families and everything else—and then they squawk about apostolics.

One of two alternatives: either one should stop his tongue about the apostolic or step out in character.

x^4 A 662   *n.d.*, 1852

PAGANISM

« **3058**

Paganism never comes closer to the truth than Pilate:[699] What is truth—and thereupon they crucify it.

II A 676   October 16, 1837

« **3059**

Paganism is the sensuous, the full development of the sensuous life—its punishment, therefore, as we see in Prometheus, is that the liver is pecked [by a vulture] and continually grows [again], the continually awakening and yet never satisfied desire—Christianity is the *cerebral*, therefore Golgotha is called *the place of the skulls.*

II A 789   n.d., 1838

« **3060**

It is quite remarkable that the tendon which God touched in wrestling with Jacob is generally called *"tendo Achillis"* by physicians, and thus it bears the name of paganism's most powerful and valiant hero; paganism never came in such close contact with the divine that its physical strength suffered under it, and yet it must be said that Jacob was far more powerful.

II A 545   August 28, 1839

« **3061**

It is shameful how we have used even the essentially Christian for refinement in worldly things. We crave worldly things—as much as any pagan—but we also cover it up with Christian disdain for all worldliness. Thanks, that means harvesting twice.

X¹ A 600   n.d., 1849

« **3062** *Paganism*

At the very end of book II of *De natura deorum* Cicero articulates the essence of paganism: There is a providence which is concerned about the whole and also about individual men—but, note well, superior men. He says the gods are concerned about weighty matters, not insignificant matters.

What frightful hopelessness, or what frightful high treason against God! How in all the world would I dare to believe that God is concerned about me if he is concerned only about the eminent; how frightful for a man ever to believe that God is concerned about him, consequently that he is important to God.

No, Christianity turns the matter around. The more wretched, the more abandoned, the more insignificant, the more unhappy you are— be assured, the more God is concerned about you.

Paganism is comradeship with God; God is merely the superlative of what it is to be man.

x^4 A 442   *n.d.*, 1851

« **3063** *Paganism*

said (see *De natura deorum*,[700] end of book III, also Horace:[701] *æquam mentem mihi ipsi præstabo*[702]): We should thank God for good fortune; wisdom is to one's own credit.

Christianity teaches that the Pharisee sinned most deeply by thanking God that he was righteous. Yet it automatically follows (something Luther[703] points up in the sermon on the Pharisee and the publican) that one is not to ascribe sins falsely to himself but simply avoid confusing the merely human criterion with God's criterion.

x^4 A 448   *n.d.*, 1851

PARABLES (S. K.)

<< **3064** *A Fable of Sorts*
or
A Simple Story[*]

In a town in the provinces there once was an organization of tightrope dancers. Most of them were ordinary dancers, able to spring just about   [*sic*] high above the rope. But there was one of them who could rise   [*sic*] in height with his leap. He was regarded by all as the top-ranking dancer, the object of admiration, who was always hailed with jubilation, who always reaped a storm of applause. But there was yet another dancer in that organization in that town; he could rise   [*sic*] above the rope. Now he was not only not the top dancer—no, he was not even a dancer, but only a substitute and was used in that capacity as infrequently as possible, since the director scarcely dared use him. As soon as he came forward and made his leap, the audience, from orchestra to gallery, hooted and yelled and whistled at him, threw fruit and whatever else they had at hand at him, all with the idea that his performance was a kind of madness or possession and that he really ought to be confined to an institution for mental illness. Even in its most magnanimous mood the crowd could not get it through its head that this dancer's performance was extraordinary. That something which was so extremely different from the ordinary, something which was so extremely different from the performance of the dancer everybody regarded and admired as the number one dancer, that this should be extraordinary—no, this the crowd could not grasp; something like this, the crowd concluded, must be madness, and there was no one who sought to enlighten the crowd as to its error. The so-called number one dancer (whom we will here call A to distinguish him from the other dancer, whom we will call B) had, in fact, been very close to doing it, but he did not care to do it —for good reasons.

Dancer A said to himself: "I see very well that B performs the extraordinary, but I would be crazy to point that out to others. At times even I feel that it is a kind of betrayal on my part, but everything is at

386

stake, not just a triviality. If men take notice of him and that his accomplishment is the extraordinary, then I am as good as nothing, instead of my being everything as I now am (praise be to the folly of the crowd and the invention that the crowd is the judge)—and he a half-mad, crazy something or other. True enough, my having achieved more distinction than the other dancers I owe to him or to my having learned from him. But no one knows that and it must be kept quiet. And it is easily done if I just keep silent, for he is too proud to say a word or even to hint at it. A dead man would be more likely to tell tales out of school or make faces than he would be likely to say a word or betray in the slightest way with a look. Then, too, even if he were to say something, the crowd would not understand him. Oddly enough, he himself made me aware of this—in order to show me how safe and secure I can be in the deception. Incidentally, I need only ask him what the smartest thing is for me to do, and he would tell me this himself (which is most harmful to him), and no one knows this as he does. No doubt he despises me secretly, but his innermost being seems to be outside of this world; it is similar to being scorned by a man in China. And, finally, he is great and proud enough not to bother at all about recognition or, more correctly, great and proud enough to find satisfaction precisely in this mad situation. And I profit from it. And who knows, perhaps he is inwardly too lofty even to despise me; in any case it is clear that he always treats me in a very friendly way."

Dancer B, however, said to himself: "It is obvious that I could hold myself back and rise only a half-length above the rope, just a shade higher than A—then I would be the object of admiration. It would also be a deserved punishment for the traitor who is now number one by suppressing the truth. But to dance is my art, and to be able to dance is my genius, the gift of a higher power, a gift which must honestly and honorably be expressed for what it is, to do otherwise is treason against Providence." —"In view of the fact that I live in a market town," he said to himself, "it could be called, humanly speaking, a duty toward myself to hold back somewhat; indeed, I could hold back so much that I would become the admired number one dancer and little by little accustom men to understand the extraordinary. But, no, this is contemptible shrewdness whereby one does not God-fearingly love his genius but cravenly and wretchedly loves himself." So in maintaining his extraordinariness he remained true to himself—so he lived and so he died—alas, even a dancer can become a martyr.

Moral

The direct comparatives—greater, greatest, this greater, greatest —make a big hit in this world, are the objects of admiration, etc., for this greater, greatest are but gradation distinctions, quantitative qualifications within the quality and standard common to the majority of men—and, like everything human, the admiration of men generally and essentially is self-love. The extraordinary is a different quality. Naturally, the extraordinary has it in his power to hide, in a craven, worldly way, what extraordinary capacities he has, the power to hold himself back so much that he becomes the greatest of all in relation to the greatest; he has the power of shrewdly recognizing that the contemporaries constitute the court which judges the extraordinary; he has the power to misrepresent himself by abandoning that which, serving an ethical function, corresponds to the extraordinary: the recklessness and ruthlessness of elevation and self-denial. If he does not do this, if he loves God and the truth, if in gratitude he honors God by being wholly and fully what he is, then he is *eo ipso* a martyr. This will always be the fate of the extraordinary in a market town—and, after all, what is this world but a market town where the crowd, which understands nothing and has no standards, at least not for the extraordinary, is the court, and where the individuals who occupy the positions "greater," "greatest," in conspiracy with the ignorant crowd betray in their own self-interest the extraordinary. Yet in fairness no more can be required of the greater, the greatest, for when one himself is the "greater" or "greatest," he in truth acknowledges the extraordinary; he has extraordinary resignation and in another sphere would be the extraordinary. In the world of ideality, in the fantasy of youth there is no collision. There the question is: Are you the extraordinary—since you are ever so scrupulously striving to be that, there is in all eternity no doubt that you will also be regarded as the extraordinary. It is different in this world where a youth who is the extraordinary would fall into a tragic mistake: he would exert himself more and more, sacrifice himself more and more in the belief that he would thereby achieve recognition, ignorant that he is working against himself, is only hastening his destruction all the more, because in this world the extraordinary has only one way to success and recognition: to hold himself back. In this world the collision is not as if the world hated the extraordinary —no, but the world's envy is invariably directed against everyone who contemporaneously is and wants to be the extraordinary, therefore against the extraordinary, against the contemporary extraordinary. Yet the world's envy is in a way in the service of the truth by helping to expose someone who without justification wants to be the extraordinary. In this world the collision is between the extraordinary and the egotism of the ignorant crowd and the egotism, in the form of envy, of the somewhat more knowledgeable. And this conspiracy—the ignorance of the crowd and the envy of the knowledgeable—is the martyrdom of the extraordinary. The ignorant crowd generally becomes the obviously guilty party who mocks, persecutes, slays the extraordinary, but the envy of the knowledgeable who in secret treachery insidiously side with the ignorance of the crowd is a far more terrible guilt. For the crowd the prayer must in truth be said: Forgive them for they know not what they do. But how shall there be a prayer for the knowledgeable who, to be sure, do not do it but know very well what the crowd is doing and do not prevent it.

*In margin: Alluded to in another journal [i.e., IX A 12].

x^5 A 159   n.d., 1849

« **3065** *The Wild Goose*
A Metaphor

Anyone who knows even a little bit about bird-life knows that there is a kind of understanding between wild geese and tame geese, regardless of how different they are. When the flight of the wild geese is heard in the air and there are tame geese down on the ground, the tame geese are instantly aware of it and to a certain degree they understand what it means; this is why they also start up, beat their wings, cry out and fly along the ground a piece in awkward, confused disorder—and then it is over.

There was once a wild goose. In the autumn, about the time for migration, it became aware of some tame geese. It became enamored of them, thought it a shame to fly away from them, and hoped to win them over so that they would decide to go along with him on the flight.

To that end it became involved with them in every possible way, tried to entice them to rise a little higher and then again a little higher in their flight, that they might, if possible, accompany it in the flight, saved from the wretched, mediocre life of waddling around on the earth as respectable, tame geese.

In the beginning the tame geese thought it very entertaining and liked the wild goose. But soon they became tired of it, drove it away with sharp words, censured it as a visionary fool devoid of experience and wisdom. Alas, unfortunately the wild goose had become so involved with the tame geese that they had gradually gained power over it, their opinion meant something to it—and *summa summarum* the wild goose finally became a tame goose.

In a certain sense there was something splendid about what the wild goose wanted, but it was, nevertheless, a mistake, for—this is the law—a tame goose never becomes a wild goose, but a wild goose can certainly become a tame goose.

If what the wild goose did is to be commended in any way, it must above all unconditionally watch out for one thing—that it hold on to itself; as soon as it notices that the tame geese have any kind of power over it—then away, away in migratory flight.

The law for genius is this: A tame goose never becomes a wild goose, but on the other hand a wild goose can certainly become a tame goose—therefore watch out!

Christianity is not like this. It is true that the true Christian who is under the Spirit is as different from the ordinary man as the wild goose is from the tame goose. But Christianity does indeed specifically teach what a person can become in life.[*] Consequently there is hope here that a tame goose can become a wild goose. Therefore remain with them, these tame geese, stay with them, occupied with only one thing—wanting to win them for the transformation—but for God in heaven's sake watch out for one thing—as soon as you see that the tame geese begin to have power over you, away, away in migratory flight, so that it does not all end with your becoming like a tame goose, blissfully sunk in wretched mediocrity.

XI^1 A 195   *n.d.*, 1854

« 3066

[*] *In margin of 3065* (XI^1 A 195):
Being a Christian is not an original state in the sense of genius, but it is what one comes to be—here, therefore, there is not the arrogance of exclusiveness but the equality of humility.

XI^1 A 196   *n.d.*

« 3067 *The Tame Goose*

A Meditation for Awakening

Imagine that geese could talk—and that they had planned things in such a way that they, too, had their divine worship services.

Every Sunday they gathered together and a goose preached.

The gist of the sermon was as follows: What a high destiny geese have, to what a high goal the creator—and every time this word was mentioned the geese curtsied and the ganders bowed their heads—had appointed geese. With the help of their wings they could fly away to distant regions, blessed regions, where they really had their homes, for here they were but aliens.

It was the same every Sunday. Thereafter the assemblage dispersed and each one waddled home to his family. And so to church again the next Sunday, and then home again—and that was the end of it. They flourished and grew fat, became plump and delicate—were eaten on St. Martin's Eve—and that was the end of it.

That was the end of it. Although the Sunday discourse was so very lofty, on Monday the geese would tell each other what had happened to one goose who had wanted to make serious use of the wings given by the creator and intended for the high goal set before it—what happened to it, what horrors it had to endure. The geese had a shrewd mutual understanding about this. But of course they did not talk about it on Sunday; that, after all, was not appropriate, for then, so they said, it would be obvious that our Sunday worship actually makes a fool of God and of ourselves.

There were a few individual geese among them who looked poorly and grew thin. The other geese said among themselves: There you see what happens when you take seriously this business of wanting to fly. Because they secretly harbor the idea of wanting to fly, they get thin, do not prosper, do not have God's grace as we have it and therefore become plump, fat, and delicate, for by the grace of God one becomes plump, fat, and delicate.

Next Sunday they went again to the worship service, and the old gander preached about the high goal to which the creator (here the geese curtsied and the ganders bowed their heads) had appointed geese and for which their wings were intended.

So also with Christendom's worship services. Man, too, has wings, he has imagination, intended to help him actually rise aloft. But we play, allow our imagination to amuse itself in a quiet hour of Sunday daydreaming, and otherwise stay right where we are—and on Monday regard it as a proof of God's grace to get plump, fat, delicate, get layered with fat—that is, accumulate money, get to be somebody in the world, beget many children, be successful, etc. And those who actually become involved with God and who therefore are obliged to suffer, appear concerned, and have torments, troubles, and grief (it cannot be otherwise, nor is it, according to the New Testament)—of these we say: There is proof that they do not have the grace of God.

* *

And if someone reads this, he will say: This is delightful—and that's the end of it. He will waddle home to his family, will remain or will strive with all his might to become plump, delicate, fat—but on Sunday the pastor will preach and he will listen—just exactly like the geese.

XI² A 210   *n.d.,* 1854

« **3068**

"Looking at the Stars"

Before the end of 1854.

It is not astonomy I intend to discuss; that is enough by itself. It is about Christianity, about being a Christian; I allude to the penalty in the Christmas game of looking at the stars.

1.

"Who forfeits?" "H. H." "What shall his penalty be?" "He must go into a dark room and look at the stars."

So he goes in. Now let him forget everything and fervently think of one thing only—that he is not alone in the room, that God is present and asks him, "Are you a Christian? Answer me—but the decisive factor will not be what you say but how you say it, whether you answer honestly. If you do not answer honestly, I will strike you dead here on the floor—and you will never again play the Christmas game or look at the stars—and you know that I, the Almighty, can do it." He answers, "You dreadful one, I never imagined this question to be so crucial. I go to church every time Senior Pastor Petersen preaches—that is, every sixth Sunday; it is more than some of my friends do. Now and then I read some religious writing. I really believed that I had faith and was a Christian, so much more since I have had to put up with my friends' sarcasm and teasing about my going to church. But if it is going to be taken so seriously, then I confess in all honesty that I actually am not a Christian." Thereupon we open the door and he goes back and joins the company.

2.

"Next! Who forfeits?" "Miss T." "What shall her penalty be?"
"She shall go into a dark room and look at the stars."

Let her now forget everything and think fervently of one thing
only, that God is present and says to her: "I know that you are hiding
deep in your soul a secret desire. You have never talked to anyone
about it—you do not dare. Yet this desire is actually the content of your
whole life, you live on and for this desire. All right, then, this desire
will be fulfilled and entirely as you wish if you answer this question in
all honesty: Are you a Christian? Do not be afraid; what you answer
is not decisive—no, the main thing is whether you answer in all honesty." She answers, "You, God of love, do not be too hard on me. I
am only a poor girl. I grew up in my parents' home, have turned out
just like the other girls, and have not thought about this question in
this way. I am getting worried—it seems to me that there must not be
very many capable of earnestness enough to take this matter so seriously. You place such an enormous weight upon my answer by saying
that the fulfillment of my desire depends upon it. Yet the very fact that
I believe it to be an enormous weight is no doubt proof that I really
am not a Christian, for otherwise the question about myself would be
even more important intrinsically than my wish." And if it were not
dark in there, I believe one would see that God's eyes rested on this
girl with exceeding delight, for there was more wisdom in her unso-
phistication than in the great knowledge of many a scholar.

3.

"Next! Who forfeits?" "Pastor F." "What shall be his penalty?"
"He shall go into a dark room and look at the stars."

Let him now forget everything, especially all the pressure about
its being important for the state, diplomacy, and politics that there be
Christianity in the country, that it is needed to buttress the throne, etc.
Let him think fervently of one thing only, that God is present and asks
him: "Are you a Christian? You have taken a sacred vow as a teacher;
you have in a holy act accepted the assistance of the Holy Spirit—
therefore, if you are not a Christian, you have a great responsibility.
Yet this is not decisive, no, but your honesty is. Answer honestly! If
you do not, then I will let the great responsibility which hangs by a hair
over your head fall upon you with the crushing impact of more than

a hundredweight." He answers, "Thank you, God, for posing the matter that way for me, for then I dare confess honestly that I really am not a Christian. It has gone with me as with many another. A man becomes a pastor at an early age. Then he marries—becomes involved with a family. Then comes doubt. But now it is too late, a man has to —as we say—keep up a bold front; he is forced farther and farther into untruth, becomes less and less a Christian, while all the time he obstinately boasts that of course he is a Christian, since he is a teacher of Christianity. Therefore thank you, God, for setting me straight." Thereupon we open the door, and he goes back and joins the company.

* *

There were twenty-five persons at the party. Each one went into the dark room, which became a witness to the confession: "I really am not a Christian." Now all twenty-five are gathered in the reception room. Is this a company of Christians? Yes, of course—we are all Christians, we are a Christian nation, etc.[704]

XI[3] B 43   *n.d.,* 1854

« 3069 *The Climate of My Contemporaneity with Bishop Mynster*[705]

In Three Pictures [*changed to* "Two"][706]

In a deeper sense I have no desire to initiate others into what I have suffered in this relationship. But inasmuch as these sufferings are related to Christianity's cause, they may well have meaning for others. But I shall present it in such a manner that it may quite generally be read with interest.

First Picture[706]

Imagine a very large ship, even larger than the great ships we have today. Let it have room for one thousand passengers and, of course, everything planned as conveniently, comfortably, and luxuriously as possible.

It is evening. In the lounge there is gaiety, everything is beautifully illuminated, everything glitters; the orchestra is playing; in short, all is merriment, frivolity, enjoyment—and the racket and noise from the happy, hilarious fun rings out into the night.

Up on the deck stands the captain, and with him the second in command. The latter takes his binoculars from his eyes and hands them to the captain. He answers: I do not need them; I see it all right —that little white speck on the horizon. It will be a frightful night.

Thereupon, with the noble, resolute calmness of the experienced seaman, he issues his orders: The crew will remain on duty tonight; I myself will take command.

He goes into his cabin. He has not taken an especially large library along, but he has a Bible. He opens it and, strangely enough, he opens it up to the passage: This night your soul is required of you. Curious!

After his prayers he dresses for night duty, and now he is the full-fledged able-bodied seaman.

But the frivolity goes on in the lounge. There is song and music and conversation and noise, the clatter of plates and dishes, the champagne bottles pop, toasts are drunk to the captain, etc. etc.—"It will be a frightful night"—and perhaps in this night your soul will be required of you.

Is this not frightful? And yet I know something still more frightful.

Everything is the same, only the captain is someone else. The lounge is full of gaiety, and the gayest of all is the captain.

The white speck on the horizon is there; it will be a frightful night. But no one sees the white speck or suspects what it means. But no (this would not be the most dreadful)—no, there is one person who sees it and knows what it means—but he is a passanger. He has, after all, no command on the ship; he cannot do anything. But in order to do the one single thing he can do, he asks the captain to come up on deck, only for a moment. It takes a while, but finally he comes—but does not wish to hear anything and, passing it off as a joke, hurries down to the noisy, hilarious company in the lounge, where the toasts are being drunk to the captain with the usual enthusiasm, for which he thanks affably.

In his anxiety the poor passenger decides to dare once again to inconvenience the captain, but this time he is even impolite to him. But the white speck is still there on the horizon: "It will be a frightful night."

Is this not even more frightful? It was frightful to have the thousand carefree, noisy passengers, frightful to have the captain be the only one who understands—but, ah, it is still more significant that the captain knows it. Consequently it is more frightful to have the only person who sees and knows what is imminent—be a passenger.

*　*

That there is a white speck on the horizon which signifies (from a Christian point of view) that frightful weather threatens—this I knew, but, alas, I was only a passenger.

Second Picture[706]

Imagine a young woman, no splendid lady, she—no, let us imagine her as a capable housewife.

"We certainly do need a general housecleaning," she says, "but," she continues, "I say with Magister Kierkegaard 'either/or,' one of two alternatives; either we must nicely get old Auntie away for a few days, or we must let the general housecleaning go, for to do the housecleaning when she is at home is out of the question."

But this is the situation with the old aunt. She is the young woman's mother's sister; as a matter of fact she is a beautiful and lovable old woman and the household dotes on her, especially the young wife, who wants in every imaginable way to honor and almost worship this old woman—

—"but if there is to be a general housecleaning we must find a nice way to get old Auntie away while we do it."

Imagine that time goes by and it is not possible to get old Auntie away.

Time goes by, the young woman becomes depressed. The husband explains to her in vain that the whole thing is not so perilous. "Aha," she answers, "you don't understand at all; you have no idea of what I am suffering. Only a woman understands how frightfully I am suffering, what an agony it is to have to look perpetually at all this dirt everywhere and not be able to get at a thorough cleaning." "But my dear girl, you can certainly go ahead and do it, for Auntie is home, and I can go away for a few days." "That's a fine proposal! What do I care about you; you can stay home and help with the scrubbing. No, Auntie is the either/or; if Auntie is here I understand my task to be seeing to it that not a breath of air blows on her—and to do a scrupulous cleaning in that frame of mind—no, my friend, impossible!"

*   *

That from the Christian point of view the opposition is [*corrected from:* That from a Christian point of view we are] in dire need of a scrupulous housecleaning and scrubbing is certain. But as long as the old Bishop lives: no, either/or! What we desperately need, from a Christian point of view, is to get everything exposed—and the fact that the late Bishop's strength lay in his ability to conceal, an art in which he was really a master, is precisely why he has to be followed by a master in the art of exposing.

Third Picture [changed to "Second"][706]

The Climate of My Contemporaneity with Bishop Mynster

Imagine a young officer; let us imagine him a competent young officer.

There is a battle. Our young officer commands half a battery.

He perceives (and we can suppose that he is correct): God in heaven: Aim my three cannon right now this second at that spot—and the victory is ours.

But precisely on that spot (or if not on that spot then situated in such a way that it is impossible to aim the cannon toward that spot) on that spot his own general, the venerable Fieldmarshal Friedland, is standing with his staff.

Think what this young officer must suffer! "I am young," he says to himself. "My future would be made for me if I could get to use my cannon . . . . . O, my God, this is the time to act." A second goes by. "Never mind myself," the young officer says to himself, "but the battle could be decided if only I could use my cannon: O, my God, it's terrible that it is my own general who is in such a position that I am unable to use my cannon."

* *

That the only way, Christianly, to pressure the opposition was to apply ideals—this I saw; but then not to be able to do it because the old Bishop (my general!) did not want the reflex from the application of ideals! Or if I did it nevertheless (for, after all, I was not his subordinate in the way an officer is to his general), that it perhaps would be interpreted by him as a traitorous act, faithlessness, because he did not want that reflex! This I understand, he had his good reasons not to want it. For although I did everything and was willing to do everything to draw attention away from this reflex, he nevertheless understood that even if only a very few saw it, the reflex must needs show that, Christianly, the old Bishop's own Christian proclamation was not just what it should be. But the situation is as heartbreaking as possible, just about what one would imagine in the following incident. It is dark, and there is danger. Someone comes hurrying, willingness and devotedness personified, and, quite properly, with a lantern. And now it becomes clear that the people he wants to help do not want a lantern, for if there is a light they cannot avoid being seen—and that they do not want.

XI^3 B 109   *n.d.*, 1855

PARADOX

« **3070**

Paradox[707] is the real *pathos*[708] of the intellectual life, and just as only great souls are exposed to passions, so only great thinkers are exposed to what I call paradoxes, which are nothing other than rudimentary majestic thoughts.

II A 755   n.d., 1838

« **3071**

. . . . . But there is a view of the world according to which the paradox is higher than every system.

II A 439   May 22, 1839

« **3072**

Philosophy's idea is mediation[709]–Christianity's, the paradox.

III A 108   n.d., 1841

« **3073**

Leibniz's *Theodicee übersetzt mit Anmerkungen v. Gottscheden.* 1763.[710] *Hanover und Leipzig.*

The introduction deals with the harmony between reason and faith.

On p. 52 he uses the expression "to see" for that which is known *a priori* on the basis of genuine causes, "to believe" for that which is concluded only from the effect.

What I usually express by saying that Christianity consists of paradox, philosophy in mediation,[711] Leibniz expresses by distinguishing between what is above reason and what is against reason.[712] Faith is above reason. By reason he understands, as he says many places, a linking together of truths (*enchainement*[713]), a conclusion from causes. Faith therefore cannot be *proved, demonstrated, comprehended,* for the link which makes a linking together possible is missing, and what else does this say than that it is a paradox. This, precisely, is the irregularity in the paradox, continuity is lacking, or at any rate it has continuity only in reverse, that is, at the beginning it does not manifest itself as conti-

399

nuity. In my opinion nothing else should be said of the paradox and the unreasonableness of Christianity than that it is the first form, in world history as well as in consciousness.

The whole conflict between Leibniz and Bayle is very much to the point, and one is astonished if he compares it with controversy in our time, for we have actually gone backward, and I believe that Hegel has not really understood what it was all about.

In margin: Bayle's argument is found in his *Dictionary*[714] under the articles on Manicheans, Rorarius, and Xenophanes.

IV C 29   n.d., 1842–43

« 3074 *The Absolute Paradox*[715]

Insofar as philosophy is mediation,[716] it holds true that it is not complete before it has seen the ultimate paradox before its own eyes.

This paradox is the God-man[717] and is to be developed solely out of the idea, and yet with constant reference to Christ's appearance, in order to see whether it is sufficiently paradoxical, whether Christ's human existence [*Existents*] does not bear the mark of his not being the *individual* human being in the profoundest sense, to what extent his earthly existence does not fall within the metaphysical and the esthetic.

IV C 84   n.d., 1842–43

« 3075

Christ's appearance is and still remains a paradox. To his contemporaries[718] the paradox lay in the fact that this particular individual human being, who looked like other human beings, talked like them and followed the customs, was the son of God.[719] For all subsequent ages the paradox is different, for since he is not seen with the physical eye it is easier to represent him as the son of God, but the shocking thing now is that he spoke within the thought world of a particular age. And yet not to have done so would have been a great injustice to his contemporaries, for then his own age would have been the only one to have had a paradox as the occasion of offense.[720] —It is my opinion, at least, that his contemporaries had the most difficult paradox, for the sentimental longing to have been contemporary with Christ, which many people express, has no great significance; to be witness to such a paradox is an extremely earnest matter.

IV A 47   n.d., 1843

« **3076**

That the Son of God became man is certainly the highest meta-physical and religious paradox,[721] but it is nevertheless not the deepest ethical paradox.[722] Christ's appearance contains a polemic against existence. He became a human being like all others, but he stood in a polemical relationship to the concrete–ethical elements of actuality. He went about and taught the people; he owned nothing; he did not even have a place to lay his head. Truly it is uplifting to see the faith and trust in providence which makes a man carefree as the birds of the air and the flowers of the field, but to what extent is this an ethical expression for a human life? Shall a man not work in order to live; is it not superior; do I dare ignore providing for tomorrow in this way? Here the most difficult problems come together. Christ's life had a negative-polemical relation to church and state. It would be the highest ethical paradox if God's son entered into the whole of actuality, became part of it, submitted to all its triviality, for even if I have the courage and trust and faith to die of starvation, it is worthy of admiration, and in each generation there probably are not ten who have it, but all the same we teach and proclaim that it would be even greater to submit to the actualities of life.

God help the poor head which entertains this kind of doubt, the unhappy man who has sufficient passion to think, the silent letter incapable of doing anything for other men except to keep still about what he suffers and possibly to smile so that no one may detect it.

IV A 62 *n.d.*, 1843

« **3077**

The absolute paradox would be that the Son of God became man, came into the world,[723] went around in such a way that no one detected it, in the strictest sense became an individual human being who had a trade, got married, etc. (on this point the various observations would show how Christ's life is patterned according to a higher criterion than the ethical). In that case God would have been the greatest ironist, not God and Father of mankind. (If my most worthy contemporary theologians and philosophers had four cents worth of ideas in their heads they would have discovered this a long time ago, perhaps made a big song and dance about it.) The divine paradox is that he became noticed, if in no other way than by being crucified, that he performed miracles and the like, which means that he still was recognizable by his divine authority, even though it demanded faith to solve its paradox

—foolish human understanding prefers that he had advanced, influenced his age, inspired it, etc.: good Lord, probably something big would have happened in the world through influencing his age.

IV A 103   n.d., 1843

« 3078

If by repenting one can remain in a love relationship to God, then it is essentially still man himself who does it all, even if repentance is defined at its outermost boundary as a suffering. Repentance is no paradox, but when it lets go, the paradox begins; therefore he who trusts in the atonement is greater than the most profound penitent. Repentance[724] always entraps itself, for if it is to be the highest, the ultimate in a man, the saving factor, then it enters into a dialectic once more—whether it now is deep enough, etc.

IV A 116   n.d., 1843

« 3079

All *Problemata* should end as follows: This is the paradox of faith,[725] a paradox which no reasoning is able to master—and yet it is so, or we must obliterate the story of Abraham.

IV B 75   n.d., 1843

« 3080

Gradually a little more is coming to be said about the paradox; soon there will be all sorts of loose talk about it, thereby making the paradox an ἔνδοξον. How comical those men are whose talking permanently excuses them from thinking and who are only eager to get a new word to fool around with.

V A 79   n.d., 1844

« 3081

Let us agree about this difficulty, whether it would not be necessary for the understanding that the god [*Guden*] would reveal himself only in order to become discernible through difference, for you recall from the foregoing that if the teacher is to be something other than an occasion (under which assumption man would remain the highest), the learner must be untruth, and of this he could not be conscious by himself. It is the same with his knowledge of the god. First he must know the difference, but this he cannot know by himself. The difference which he himself provides is identical with likeness, because he cannot get outside himself. If, then, he comes to know the difference,

he comes to know it absolutely and comes to know the absolute difference, and this is the first paradox. Now follows the second, that in spite
of this absolute difference, the god must be identical with man, and not
with humanity but with this individual human being. But the moment
he comes to know that the God is absolutely different from him, he also
comes to know that he himself is absolutely different from the god.
Therefore we said that when the paradoxical passion of self-knowledge
is awakened, it would have a disturbing reflexive effect upon the man,
so that he who believed he knew himself would become doubtful as to
whether he was a human being or a more artfully constructed animal
than Typhon. But if the human being is absolutely different from the
god, this difference cannot be rooted in what the god himself has given
to him but must be rooted in himself. Therefore we said that the
untruth is also self-deserved. The difference, then, becomes sin.
But if he is now to become like the god, is this not the absolute paradox?

In the foregoing we have poetized the god as teacher and savior.
Thus he did indeed become an individual human being. But his purpose was certainly not to mock men by revealing himself and then
dying in such a way that no human being ever came to know his
revelation. Every clue of the understanding was in itself no clue, and
therefore it would have been no clue at all if he had gone triumphantly
through the world and dominated all kingdoms and countries. Therefore in our poem a collision was included: he was not entirely like other
human beings; in little things he was different. This we could easily
have developed further if we had extended the poem. He did not labor,
in this way he did not concern himself with human affairs. And there
was yet another difference: he suffered.[726]

In margin: For the next chapter.[727]

V B 5:10   n.d., 1844

« 3082

If the learner does not collide in *the moment* in the collision of
understanding, as we have shown, then the paradox thrusts him away,
and he takes *offense* or is scandalized.[728]

V B 11:4   n.d., 1844

« 3083

..... because all Christianity is rooted in the paradox,[729] one
must accept it (i.e. become a believer) or reject it (precisely because

it is paradoxical), but above all one is not to think it out speculatively, for then the result is definitely not Christianity.[730]

VI B 35:36   n.d., 1845

« **3084**

Christianity does not want to be understood[731]—but the rude speculator does not want to understand this. He cries incessantly: "From the standpoint of the eternal, there is no paradox."[732]

Christianity entered into the world not to be understood but to be existed in.[733] This cannot be expressed more strongly than by the fact that Christianity itself proclaims itself to be a paradox. If the horror in the beginning of Christianity was that one could so easily take offense, the horror now—the longer the world exists—is that Christianity, aided by culture, abundant knowledge, and objectifying, can so easily become sheer nonsense. The longer the world continues the more difficult it becomes to become a Christian.

VI B 43   n.d., 1845

« **3085**

The forgiveness of sin is indeed a paradox[734] insofar as the eternal truth is related to an existing person;[735] it is a paradox insofar as the eternal truth is related to the person botched up in time and by time and who nevertheless is an existing person (because under the qualification of sin existence is registered and accentuated a second time), but forgiveness of sin is really a paradox only when it is linked to the appearance of the god [Guden], to the fact that the god has existed [existeret]. For the paradox always arises by the joining of existing and the eternal truth, but the more often this occurs the more paradox.*

* Note. Reminiscent of *Fragments*,[736] in which I said that I do not believe that God exists [er til, eternally is], but know it; whereas I *believe* that God has existed [har været til] (the historical). At that time I simply put the two formulations together in order to make contrast clear and did not emphasize that even from the Greek point of view the eternal truth, by being for an existing person, becomes an object of faith and a paradox. But it by no means follows that this faith is the Christian faith as I have now presented it.

VI B 45   n.d., 1845

« **3086**

And the difficulty involved in the miracle of creation as something happening to an existing person is thrust aside as much as possible by being baptized as a child. The thinking probably goes something like this: An infant of eight days is scarcely an existing being [*Tilværende*] and if by being baptized it becomes a Christian (at an age when usually it is hardly looked upon as a human being), all difficulties are over. But this reasoning is not the paradox; it is much, much easier to show that it is nonsense. It attempts to thrust becoming a Christian so far back esthetically that to be born and to become a Christian amount almost to the same thing. And the dark discourse about grown men becoming children again is cozily exchanged for a little very charming flattery and baby talk about an eight-day infant's superabundant meritoriousness in being an infant of eight days, not a bit older.[737]

VI B 98:82   *n.d.*, 1845

« 3087

... Therefore Christianity must be foolishness to the Greeks,[738] because God's revelation of himself in suffering was precisely the paradox;* suffering is abnormality, weakness, and yet it is the negative form of the highest—the direct form is beauty, power, glory, etc., but for the highest to have its adequate form in the direct form shows thereby that the highest is not the extraordinarily highest. ...

In margin: * Note. This relationship is as a rule the prototype for being a chosen one in the religious sense, because in the Greek view the chosen one was a Pamphilius of fortune. Furthermore it is self-evident that there is and remains an infinite qualitative difference between Christ and every chosen one. Christ is himself the sphere of the paradox, and the chosen one is a derivative who bears the mark of belonging to this sphere.

VII² B 235, pp. 66–67   *n.d.*, 1846–47

« 3088

As a genius Paul does not compare with Plato or a Shakespeare; as an author of beautiful metaphors he is a rather inconspicuous person. But he is the apostle, and as apostle he has no affinity whatsoever with Plato or Shakespeare. The genius is the primitive, the original, the primeval point of departure[*] *within immanence;* an apostle is the point of departure *within transcendence*—that is, by virtue of a revelation, or by virtue of the paradox. The paradoxes of a genius are symptomatic, anticipatory, and they vanish; an apostle's paradox is qualitative. A genius is great because of the fertility of his ideas, an apostle is what he is by his divine authority. I do not listen to Paul because he is brilliant or incomparably brilliant, but I submit to him because he has divine authority. Paul should not appeal to his brilliance, for then he would be a fool *a la* Adler, but he should appeal to his divine authority; he should not commend his learning by using beautiful imagery, but he should say: Whether the imagery is beautiful or not, you shall obey, for I speak with authority; I cannot and dare not counsel you to obey, but I make you eternally responsible by speaking with the divine authority to which I am called. Authority, then, is the qualitatively decisive factor, authority is inconceivable within immanence.[739]

VII[2] B 256:9   *n.d.,* 1846–47

[*] *In margin:* The genius's point of departure is within his own personal identity; the point of departure of revelation is paradoxically beyond the personality.

VII[2] B 256:10   *n.d.*

« 3089

Kant's theory of radical evil [740] has only one fault: he does not definitely establish that the inexplicable is a category, that the paradox is a category. Everything turns on this. It is customary to say something like this: To say that we cannot understand this and that does not satisfy scholarship and science, which insist upon comprehending.[741] Here is the error. We must say the very opposite, that if *human* scholarship and science refuse to acknowledge that there is something they cannot understand, or, more accurately, something that they clearly understand that they cannot understand, then everything is confused. It is specifically the task of human knowing to understand that there is something it cannot understand and to understand what that is. Human knowing usually has been occupied with understanding and understanding, but if it will also take the trouble to understand itself, it must straightway posit the paradox. The paradox is not a concession but a category, an ontological qualification which expresses the relation between an existing cognitive spirit and the eternal truth.

VIII[1] A 11   *n.d.,* 1847

« 3090

N.B. The real paradox must not be overlooked—namely, that Christ came to the world in order to suffer. (See *Concluding Unscientific Postscript,* p. 460 etc.).[742]

VIII[1] A 273   *n.d.,* 1847

« **3091**

It is impossible that what I have to say regarding the paradox should become popular. To assume the ability to comprehend is flattering to human vanity. The other is the blessedness of humility. Yet, for example, how many girls are there in each generation who are truly capable of loving. Ninety-nine out of a hundred prefer to love "for reasons." The subtle way in which "reasons" subtract from instead of grounding or heightening [love] is not detected—in fact, the more reasons she has for her love the less is her love.

But here again it is apparent how reticence comes of itself. Such a girl truly in love without any reasons—if she were to speak of it with the other girls—would be regarded as inferior.

And therefore the marvelous love of providence, which has provided every animal with one or another means of defense, has also made every deeper nature reticent. Through reticence he saves his life, and saved he possesses his blessedness in reticence.

X^1 A 680   *n.d.*, 1849

« **3092** *Chaos—and Category*

It makes a vast difference if one first of all makes a move as if wanting to comprehend, speculatively grasp and comprehend—and then finally comes up with the idea that there is something incomprehensible in faith,[743] or if he from the very beginning categorically grasps that faith cannot be comprehended and is not supposed to be.

All speculative comprehension in the sphere of Christianity (if it does not totally emancipate itself and is obviously pagan) always ends with: there still remains, it must be admitted, something incomprehensible. But what confusion, why all this yielding to speculative curiosity, instead of dutifully and Christianly indicating immediately that a paradox cannot possibly be comprehended and is not supposed to be, since then it is not a paradox—and then concentrate on that. Cracking a peach stone is difficult; let us assume it is impossible: what would one think of a group of people, each one of whom put it in his mouth and tried to crack it: "Well, now, wait a minute—it's coming—" and finally said, "To a certain degree, however, I cannot crack it." Well, my friend, if you cannot crack it to a certain degree, that obviously means that you cannot crack it. What is one to think of that? Would it not be better to refrain from trying and begin by saying: I cannot—and perhaps then at most show why it is an impossibility for human teeth. But people go for drivel. It is their lack of character.

x^2 A 484   *n.d.*, 1850

« **3093**

[*In margin:* Julius Müller[744]–Johannes Climacus]

Julius Müller has invented the theory that original sin (*peccatum originale*) is traceable to a timeless fall before the lives of all men in time.

This is a basic dislocation of Christianity. Johannes Climacus[745] comes immediately with his problem: that an eternal blessedness or unblessedness is decided in time by a relation to something historical.

J. Müller believes that he has extricated himself from the first difficulty of getting sin and guilt into the world and in every man.

But now the next: the decision of salvation, since it is an eternal decision, becomes just as incommensurable for a decision in a moment of time as the former one. So it presumably became necessary for J. M. to place this decision outside of time also, in a timeless decision in every individual before the lives of all men in time.

The consequence comes to be that man has timelessly lived through his whole life in a kind of ideality before he lives it in time.

Such things can be pondered, to be sure—but then what is Christianity?

The whole thing is simply an indirect proof of the rightness of my view: posit the paradox. The dubiousness of speculation is revealed by Müller's theory. The paradox is that an eternal decision is decided in time. I say: it cannot be comprehended; it must be believed—that is, it is a paradox. Now comes speculation, saying: Of course I can comprehend it. I do it like this—I imagine a timeless decision prior to time—understand? Yes, my dear friend, but the problem was an eternal decision—in time, not an eternal decision in a timeless manner outside of all time.

Kant[746] with his radical evil was essentially more honest, for he never pretends that his theory is supposed to be a speculative comprehension of the Christian problem.

But the trouble with all the speculation of the period is that it cannot formulate and stick to the problem—but comprehend it—yes, that it can do all right. It is just as ridiculous as to take up sketching and have a man sit a long time for the picture—finally the sketch is ready—and the drawing turns out to be, say, a tree, an excellent likeness of a tree which stands outside the man's window—but supposedly it was a man who was to be sketched, not the tree; why then have the man sit for him such a long time! The problem is set up, and now the speculation begins; a long time elapses during which the problem, so to speak, must endure sitting for speculation; finally it is ready—here it is—and it is merely another problem. The difficulty or objection has become the problem. How can it be comprehended that an eternal decision is decided in time? The speculative answer: it can be decided in such a way that it is in a timeless mode—that is, not in time. Speculation's secret is really in the fact that it takes such a long time before the answer comes; if it were to come right away (in an almost timeless mode, instead of taking an inhumanly long time), the nonsense would appear for what it is. But if it were to come right away, how could it then be a speculative answer! But then it would indeed be a popular answer. The speculative way is to take many years, to write a folio and quote many scholarly treatises—then the answer is speculative and is the solution. It is speculative, at least it is very well contrived, and displays knowledge of men and of the world.

x^2 A 501 $n.d.$, 1850

« **3094**

In margin of 3093 (x^2 A 501):
The difference between the popular and the speculative lies in how long a time is taken. If a man is asked: Do you know this and that, or do you not—and he immediately answers "Yes" or "No," then it is a popular answer, and he is a college student. If it takes ten years for the answer to come, if it comes in the form of a system and in such a way that it is not quite clear whether he knows it or not, then it is a speculative answer, and he is a philosophy professor, or at least he ought to be.

x^2 A 502 $n.d.$

« **3095** *"Christian" Simplicity*

is not, I am sure, *literally* simplicity, or outright simplicity, a paradox (that an individual human being is God is nothing less than downright simple), but the simplicity is that the paradox is for the sake of influencing movement away from speculating and reasoning etc. and in the direction of existing [*at existere*],[747] of existentially expressing the essentially Christian. The simplicity is simply to exist. That is why Christianity is everywhere characterized by the paradox, lest the mistake be made of thinking that one has to speculate.

To exist, to act according to the command—that is the simplicity; to speculate, to reason—that is the opposite of the simplicity. Therefore what is expressed here by means of the paradox is not something to speculate about; act according to it—that is, be simple. There is nothing to speculate about here—believe it—and then do not go away and speculate about faith, for then you will forsake simplicity again. No, believe—act according to it—and then you will continue in simplicity.

Even Socratic simplicity was no literal simplicity: ignorance in this sense is very complex. But the simplicity was to get all this speculating (the sophistry) out of the way in order to act, to exist, which is simplicity.

But speculation is the incessantly recurring sophistry in relation to existing.

x^3 A 424   *n.d.*, 1850

« 3096 *Paradoxical*

The greatest possible striving—for nothing. This is as paradoxical as possible. But this is indeed the way it is if it is "grace" alone, only "grace"—and consequently the greatest possible striving is for nothing, signifies nothing.

It was different when men believed that salvation was earned: then there was no paradox, for there is nothing paradoxical in the greatest possible striving—and the highest good to be achieved thereby.

x^4 A 641   *n.d.*, 1852

« 3097 *The Paradox*

That Christianity is paradoxical can be seen from this fact alone —it answers the question: What is life's destiny? What is life's task? with: To die, to die to the world.[748] God created this world of living beings, placed man in it, planted this enormous lust for life in him— and the meaning of life, the task of life—is to die, to die to the world!

What a paradox! And again how paradoxical and how consistent! To die and to die to the world are the very signs of being related to an eternal life. Therefore the fact that eternal life is stirring within a person is not indicated directly by an intensified lust for life, but negatively, paradoxically, by being dead to the world, by being a dead and departed one!

Such is Christianity! O, but here is a point to which I continually return—suppose it is granted me to die to the world in this way—yet how far I still have to go!—but suppose it is granted me to be obliged to proclaim this to others—this seems to me to be too hard! How am I going to get them to accept it, and on the other hand, how dreadful if eternal salvation is bound up with this condition, how dreadful if there is a person you love as much as you love yourself and there is no discernible way to get him to accept it.

Alas, we who are brought up in Christianity from childhood, we all live in the soft, superficial, humanly benevolent idea that we are all going to be saved—the N. T. lives and breathes in the opposite: a little flock which will be eternally saved, and then the remainder. O, my God! I can become deathly anxious thinking about whether I will be saved—ah, but I can become almost as anxious, yes, just as anxious, thinking whether another person may not be eternally saved, another person whom one loves as much as one loves himself, a person for whom one would do everything.

Alas, we are brought up from childhood in Christianity; we have no inkling of the great Christian collisions—this hating father and mother, etc., for is it not hating father and mother to live in a faith according to which one believes himself to be saved, and then not get the others to enter into it, and consequently according to the same faith must believe that they are eternally lost—is it not the same as hating them to choose not to abandon his faith and choose to follow the loved ones! But collisions of this sort are not suspected in "Christendom," where, to be sure, we are all Christians and will all be saved!

X^5 A 142   n.d., 1853

« 3098 Judaism—Christianity

In Judaism God is in a certain sense not as hard as in Christianity; he is not qualified as spirit—therefore it comes to be only a "testing" —that is, the testing lasts a few years, and then one is granted what he desired—yes, even more than he desired.

In Christianity God is spirit—and therefore so extremely hard—out of love, for he craves spirit from man.

Incidentally, there is a paradox here similar to what Pascal[749] says about God's becoming more obscure in a revelation than he was before, the revealed God as more incomprehensible than the unrevealed God; in the same way here, the God of love is harder than the God of the law.

But the difference between Judaism and Christianity is rooted in the different relationship to eternity. In Judaism temporality is actually without eternity; in Christianity everything is aimed at eternity—therefore a lifetime of suffering, therefore no help in this life, no victory in this life.

But the person who has been brought up in Christianity from childhood finds it impossible to believe that God can be as hard as he is in Christianity, he, "the God of love" one knows so well from childhood on; and therefore it is almost impossible for the person brought up from childhood in Christianity to become more than a Jew.

In the Old Testament God is never so hard with those he loves as he is with the apostles, for example, whose life is sheer suffering and then martyrdom. [In the Old Testament] it lasts only a few years, or he quietly helps them some other way. But Christianity really bears down on having to hunger, thirst, suffer every possible evil, then persecution, finally to be put to death as a criminal——and through it all God is the God of love. In the Old Testament[750] when Daniel refuses out of piety to eat the king's rich food, God sees to it that he thrives just as well on what he gets to eat. When in the Old Testament the prophet is in need, God always finds a way out——but for the apostle there is only the prophecy: He who gives him a cup of water for my sake shall receive a prophet's reward. Thus there is no mention of unexpected help which will provide for his extreme needs. No, God abandons him completely, until he perishes from hunger and thirst——it can become that severe. And yet it is the God of love, yes, what is more, it is out of love. For everything, everything here is reflected in eternity. The more anguished temporality, the more blessed eternity.

Alas, I shudder when I think such thoughts! I notice all too well how mixed up I am because of having been brought up in Christianity from childhood. What a distance from our life to that of an apostle's. God is love. Remember that this was proclaimed by him who suffered more than anyone else in the world, was proclaimed by the Savior of the world! God is love—this was then proclaimed by apostles whose lives were suffering from beginning to end, as the lives of the pious under the law never were—and yet early and late the apostles talked about having a gospel to proclaim, a gospel, not the law.

Deny if you can that Christianity is a paradox.

XI[1] A 299   *n.d.*, 1854

« 3099 *Spirit—Appearance (Phenomenon)*
The Nearness of God—The Remoteness of God

God is spirit. As spirit God relates *paradoxically* to appearance (phenomenon), but paradoxically he can also come so close to actuality that he stands right in the middle of it, right on the street in Jerusalem.

It is impossible for God to be identified directly.[751] His majesty is so great that the most audacious imagination in its most audacious inventiveness could not invent a phrase adequate to describe him as directly identifiable, for his majesty is a quality higher, therefore only paradoxical; indeed, were he to be directly identifiable, he would actually become ludicrous. —If I were a German professor, I would no doubt break in here to point out that I was the first person to point out how God could become ludicrous, also that paganism actually is ludicrous insofar as it is ludicrous to say of God as directly recognizable: Either what I see is not God or if it is God it is ludicrous. —There is, after all, no analogy between humanity and this majesty, whose elevation is simply that nothing directly recognizable can express it and it can only be identified paradoxically. To suggest a poor analogy —at certain times in the history of mankind, especially when everything was confused, rulers have arisen who have ruled, if I dare say so, in their shirt sleeves. This constitutes a far more elevated majesty than an emperor's direct recognizability; here there is something paradoxical—that the ruler is identified by his going about in shirt-sleeves—which also leads to the thought that were such a ruler later to establish himself as emperor with direct recognizability, he would be laughable (the comic element in direct recognizability) if he believed he had become more, for he had become less.

Consequently God can relate to appearance only in a paradoxical way, but God can also come so close that he can stand right in the middle of actuality, right in front of our noses.

The law for God's nearness and remoteness is as follows: The more the phenomenon, the appearance, expresses that here God cannot possibly be present, the closer he is; inversely, the more the phenomenon, the appearance, expresses that God is very near, the farther away he is.

The more the phenomenon, the appearance, expresses that here God cannot possibly be present, the closer he is. This is the case with Christ. The very moment the appearance expressed that this man could not possibly be the God-man—no, when the appearance expressed that, men even refused to recognize him as a man (See, what a man![752]), then God was the closest to actuality he had ever been.

The law for God's remoteness (and the history of this is the history of Christendom) is as follows: Everything that strengthens the appearance distances God. At the time when there were no churches and the few Christians gathered together in catacombs as refugees and persecutees, God was closer to actuality. Then came churches, so many churches, such great, splendid churches—to the same degree God was distanced. For God's nearness is inversely related to phenomenon, and this ascending scale (churches, many churches, splendid churches) is an increase in the sphere of appearance. When Christianity was not doctrine, when it was one or two affirmations expressed in one's life, God was closer to actuality than when Christianity became doctrine. And with every increase and embellishment of doctrine etc., to the same degree God was distanced. For doctrine and its dissemination is an increase in appearance, and God relates himself inversely. —When there were no clergy but the Christians were all brothers, God was closer to actuality than when there came to be clergymen, many clergymen, a powerful ecclesiastical order. For clergymen are an increase in appearance, and God relates inversely to phenomenon.

And this is how it happened that Christendom has step by step become just about the farthest distance possible from God, all under the claim that Christianity is perfectible, that it progresses. Christendom's history is one of alienation from God through the strengthening of appearance, or (as in certain situations we speak of removing someone tactfully and politely) Christendom's history is one of progressively removing God tactfully and politely by building churches and monumental buildings, by a monstrous doctrinal system with an incalculable host of preachers.

Thus Christendom is just about the greatest distance possible from God.

Now if I say this to anyone, I know that there is not one of those who appear to be concerned about such matters (for those who are unconcerned about such things would, of course, give me the brush-off) who will not say: Then something must be done—there are definitely too few pastors in proportion to the population; let's get a thousand more (excellent—in order to get farther away from God!), a good many more churches (excellent, in order to get farther away from God!), and get a permanent committee of pastors and professors to make the doctrine more strictly accurate—excellent—in order to get farther away from God.

No, no, no, if you are really in earnest about getting God closer, then consign the whole lying gang of preachers and professors to death and the devil, these fellows who *en masse* provide an excellent commentary on the Bible passage:[753] Seek first God's kingdom, venture right into the middle of actuality, risk—and instantly God is there on the spot. O, believe it, be confident in quite another way than one is confident that a doctor summoned at night will get up, be confident in quite another way that the instant one actually ventures for the sake of God, he is immediately there on the spot, he who is infinite love.

So willing is he, infinite love, so willing to become involved with a man that he has written love letters to us in his word, has proposed to us and said: Come, Come. And now he sits and watches to see if there is one single person who will venture.

Absolutely every single human being is able to venture, and God is willing to become involved with absolutely every single human being who ventures. But it stands to reason that he, infinite love, is also majesty—and he is a connoisseur; with his dreadful sharp-sightedness he is able to see whether a person wants to exploit him or is venturing. Thus when a milksop dressed in velvet wants to lead God by the nose with fat, flabby, solemn phrases about loving God, then surely God sees with frightful clarity that such a man has his own private interpretation of the verse about seeking God's kingdom first.

But where is there one who will actually venture—whereas there are preachers and professors by the hundred thousands who want to make a profit, at most are willing to venture a tiny little bit if they can count on a proportionate increase in profit. But that is not venturing in the Christian way. But where is there one person who will actually venture, who, trusting in God and in the power of God, will dare relate inversely to appearance—something Christendom does not seem to accept but seems to assume that God relates directly to appearance—where appearance is greatest, God is nearest. Therefore spiritual Christendom builds great, spacious churches for God, presumably so that he can really have enough room. But from a Christian point of view it is true that even the smallest space is too large for God—to such an extent does he relate paradoxically, inversely, to space and place.[*] One single, poor, abandoned, simple man who, trusting in God, will venture absolutely—there God is present and makes him, humanly speaking, more unhappy. This God must do in order to be able to be there—to such an extent does God relate negatively to phenomenon——and then we build huge edifices for him, and hundreds, yes, thousands of pastors and bishops, deans and professors, are summoned together in an enormous Church council, convinced that when such a colossal body is assembled and sits at unbelievable cost to the state—that God is present, that he is closest there, that his cause is advanced there—and God relates inversely to phenomenon.

XI² A 51   n.d., 1854

« 3100

In margin of 3099 (XI² A 51):

The least possible of all places or phenomena—one solitary, destitute, abandoned human being—this is the place for God; to such an extent does God relate negatively to appearance; and if God is to be present in this man, he must make him more unhappy, humanly speaking—to such an extent does God relate negatively to appearances; he has to have as little appearance as possible, and in addition he must negate this little bit.

XI² A 52   n.d.

« 3101 *Christianity—Rebirth*

Christianity holds that the central issue is a qualitative transformation, a total character transformation in time (just as qualitative as the change from not being to being which is birth). Anything which is merely a development of what man is originally is not essentially Christian existence.

Christendom, which is constantly interested in getting rid of the paradox[754] (to be born as adults is the paradox) and thereby exclude strenuous efforts. With that in mind the stage for becoming a Christian has been transferred to the period of infancy. This in itself is ridiculous if the idea is to dodge the paradox, for if a child has lived only five minutes the mere fact it has been born makes a second birth or being born a second time just as paradoxical as the rebirth of a man forty years old.

But what Christendom has intended and achieved is to exclude strenuous efforts. Rebirth is shifted so far back in time that just as we may say of birth: We don't know how it happened, so also with rebirth: We do not know how it happened. Thus we are happily rid of all Christianity's qualitative strenuous efforts.

This implies that we are also rid of all Christianity's promises, and yet Christianity does indeed teach that rebirth is eternal life, is immortality.

By displacing the paradox Christendom has quite simply managed to restore the old paganism—trimmed with Christian expressions and phrases.

Confirmation does not help much, for it also takes place in childhood, and it is incredibly ridiculous to hear pastors address little boys on confirmation day as—little Christians. I propose that we introduce the custom at confirmation of having the boys wear false beards and mustaches—to make them look like men.

XI² A 81   n.d., 1854

« 3102 *A Reversal of Concepts is the Sign of the New Quality*

Wherever a new quality appears, concepts are reversed.

Take, for instance, the quality of the divine. Men in fact do a lot of thinking about the divine. But all such human thought does not go beyond the idea that the divine is the superlative of the most superlative superlative of the human. This is easy to see. Quantity—this is why the quality of the divine is not to be found here.

Christianity introduces the quality of the divine, which is immediately signified by a reversal of all concepts; thus the divine and the relationship to it become exactly the opposite of what they are in the sphere of the direct. Being involved with God and being his favorite, instead of meaning sheer happiness, as imagined by the pagan and, indeed, by direct thought, means, in the Christian view, sheer suffering; instead of the enjoyment of life, as in the direct view, it means to die, to die to the world; instead of God's beloved's becoming powerful as in the direct view, the Christian view holds that he becomes abased etc. etc.—this I have pointed out in numerous ways. But here we see that everything essentially Christian is paradoxical and that it is precisely the paradox which is the form for the quality of the divine.

Christendom's great service to Christianity (which, after all, according to the professors, is perfectible) is to prate and palaver it back into the sphere of the direct, to slacken the paradox in the hiatic, most superlative superlative of the direct, yet with the *assurance* that the qualitative change has taken place.

XI² A 212   n.d., 1854

PASCAL

« 3103

Pascal says: The reason it is so difficult to believe is that it is so difficult to obey.

VII¹ A 151   n.d., 1846

« 3104

That the horses once ran away with him made, it is well known, an extraordinarily deep impression and had a decisive result in Pascal's life.[755]

VII² B 257:9   n.d., 1846–47

« 3105 *The Abasement of Christ*

Pascal says somewhere (in his *Pensees*, XIV, Jesus Christ)[756] "that it is ridiculous to be scandalized by the abasement of Christ, just as if this abasement were of the same kind manifested by his loftiness." One might rather say that it actually would be comical or ridiculous if Christ had come in earthly loftiness and splendor, because the loftiness he was supposed to express was the very opposite of that. Existential transparency requires being what one teaches. It would be comical if someone about to compete in a race were to come wearing a suit and a heavy coat and carrying an umbrella, just like someone going for a ride in a carriage and wishing to wrap himself up well. In the very same way earthly loftiness would have continually embarrassed and parodied Christ's true loftiness.

The mode which ideally corresponds best to being the ideal in the sense of truth is simply to be nothing at all.

X³ A 542   n.d., 1850

« 3106 *Established Christendom*

Pascal[757] says somewhere that it is dangerous to know God and not know one's own wretchedness.

But is not this danger actually deserved, this danger brought about in established Christendom by the frivolous and indiscriminate way all are permitted to become Christians, are given an idea of God, especially of his love—but are not made inwardly contemplative at all unto the recognition of their own wretchedness.

By being taken in vain Christianity has spoiled and demoralized men.

x^3 A 543 *n.d.*, 1850

« 3107

Pascal says (in his *Pensees*,[758] XXIX, Moral Thoughts, 24): Very few men speak humbly about humility, few modestly about modesty, few doubtfully about doubt—there is nothing but lies, duplicity, contradiction in us.

This expresses what I advance in a still higher relation—reduplication. With Pascal it is still almost esthetic; I press it farther in the direction of existence.

Incidentally, it is comical to think of the words "few speak doubtfully about doubt" in reference to the recent past—when doubt was *taught.* Martensen[759] was just as dogmatically rigid when he lectured on *de omnibus dubitandum* as when he lectured on a dogma.

x^3 A 544 *n.d.*, 1850

« 3108 *Pascal*

He categorizes it very well. He says (in *Pensees,* XXXI, Miscellaneous Thoughts, 5)[760] that from the literal agreement of many in one the tremendous conclusion of an ideal agreement is drawn. But this does not absolutely convince that one can wager on his assertion.

This distinction: to convince absolutely and to wager on something.

x^3 A 546 *n.d.*, 1850

« 3109 *Pascal*

In the Athenæum[761] there is a fine little essay by Neander: *Uber die geschichtliche Bedeutung der pensees Pascals* (Berlin: 1847).[762]

I see by the essay that not until just recently has Pascal's *Pensees* been published in its complete and original form by Prosper Faugère, 1844, that the older editions had omitted and altered portions, that similarly Anton Arnauld (Port Royal), who published them, took the liberty of making changes, thinking it was better to make minor changes than continually to have to write apologies: *il est bien plus à propos de prévenir les chicaneries par quelque petit changement, qui ne fait qu'a doucir une expression, que de se reduire à la necessité de faire des apologies.*[763]

Neander correctly points out that Pascal divides the theoretical and the practical in man and established the practical as the highest.

Cousin regards Pascal as an enemy of all philosophy, since, despairing of finding truth through reason, he throws himself into the arms of authoritative faith and combines "boundless scepticism with convulsive piety." Neander shows quite correctly that this is a complete misunderstanding, that Pascal merely insists upon the practical and "finds it ridiculous for reason to demand from the heart proofs for its first principles, just as it would be for the heart to demand that the reason should feel all the propositions it proves in order to embrace them."

Pascal declares (this is something which appears first in Faugère's edition): "One ought to have these three qualities: Pyrrhonist, geometrician, and a Christian submitting in faith. And these three stand in harmony with each other and temper each other, inasmuch as one doubts when one should, affirms when one should, and submits when one should. The last act of reason is to acknowledge that there are many things which exceed its powers; if reason does not reach this point, it is merely weak."

Pascal declares that knowledge of the divine stands in an inverse relation to knowledge of the human. One must first know the human, then love; the divine one must first love and then know. By this Pascal means that knowledge of the divine is essentially a transformation of the person; one must become a different person in order to know the divine. This is what is completely forgotten in our time when there is so much nonsense about knowing and knowing, but ethical transformation (the slower kind of knowing) is regarded as superfluous, not to mention religious transformation. We want to know and to know in order to satisfy the proud and vain and inquisitive or curious mind— but the divine will never be known this way. Men would be anxious and fearful if they ever really got to know how dangerous it is to know, how obligating it is—although it is true that only in the reverse order can the divine be known. God does not conduct clearance sales, does not entrust the religious to every frivolous or curious observer, but only to a person in proportion to his being existentially transformed.

X³ A 609   *n.d.*, 1850

« 3110 *Pascal*

writes in a letter to Mademoiselle Roannes (on the occasion of the miraculous healing of little Perrier in Port Royal):

Only rarely and for a few does God appear out of nature's secrecy which hides him. Until the Incarnation he kept himself hidden under it. Then he hid himself even more by enveloping himself in humanness. For he was more knowable as long as he was invisible. Now he has hid himself still more deeply in the Sacrament. Everything is a veil which hides God; but the Christians should know him in everything, and we have so much more to thank him for because he has revealed himself to us in sufferings while he hides himself for others. (See Reuchlin, *Geschichte Port Royal,* I, pp. 680–81.)[764]

Here is the dialectic which Johannes Climacus[765] maintained: A revelation, the fact that it is a revelation, is recognized by its opposite, that it is a mystery. God reveals himself—this is known by his hiding himself. Thus there is nothing of the direct.

x^3 A 626   *n.d.,* 1850

« 3111

The French phrase *seul à seul* is a good expression for solitude or for being absolutely alone.

I found it in Reuchlin, *Pascals Leben*[766] (Stuttgart: 1840, p. 30), in Jacqueline's (Pascal's youngest sister) letter to her father about permission to enter the cloister, in which she asks permission to withdraw (*retraite*) for fourteen days or three weeks into a religious house (Port Royal) to contemplate the step all alone (*seul à seul*).

x^3 A 630   *n.d.,* 1850

« 3112

Ein Wahn, der mich beglückt,
Ist eine Wahrheit werth, die mich zu Boden drückt.[767]

Quoted in Reuchlin, *Pascals Leben,*[768] book II at the end (of the *Provincial Letters*), p. 72.

x^3 A 631   *n.d.,* 1850

« 3113 *The Jesuits*

What Reuchlin says about the Jesuits in *Pascals Leben,*[769] book II, is very significant. They were not like the Pharisees, who enjoined heavy burdens and laid them on others but did not put a finger to them themselves. No, the Jesuits themselves lived rather austerely—but they preached a lax morality for others.

This is extremely significant. The Jesuits wanted only one thing: to have power, influence, domination over men. The surest way to achieve that end is to live more austerely oneself—otherwise all esteem is lost—and to demoralize men by making life easy for them.

What Reuchlin says (p. 98) about the change which the Jesuits made in the discipline is also significant—namely, that Eskobar calls the father-confessor "the confessor's advocate," *Defensor*—previously he was the judge.

x^3 A 632   *n.d.*, 1850

« **3114**

(See Reuchlin, *Pascals Leben*, pp. 135 and 136.)[770]

In the Tenth Letter (of the *Provincial Letters*) Pascal declaims against the attitude that the dispensation from the command to love God is supposed to be the advantage Christ brought to us men, so that before Christ's becoming man and his death we were pledged to love God in deed, but not any more now.

In den zerstreuten Gedanken Pascals heisst es: Die Liebe ist kein bildliches Gebot. Sagen, Christus, welcher gekommen, die Forbilder wegzunehmen und die Wahrheit an ihre Stelle zu setzen, sey nur gekommen, um das Bild der Liebe aufzustellen und die wirkliche Liebe, die Verpflichtung dazu wegzunehmen, welche zuvor galt, das zu sagen, ist abscheulich.

Der Messias soll nach den Fleischlichen Juden ein grosser, weltlicher Fürst seyn; nach den fleischlichen Christen ist er gekommen, uns von der Verpflichtung zur Liebe Gottes zu befreien und uns die Sacramente geben, welche Alles ohne uns wirken. Dieses ist so wenig die christliche Religion, als jenes die jüdische.[771]

Yet it must always be borne in mind that everything depends on to whom one is speaking. To the troubled and melancholy, to them who sink under the enormous task of loving God absolutely, yes, almost tempted by the thought that it might even be presumptuous arrogance to want to venture such a thing, to them one should talk about grace, that it is God who loves me.

On the other hand, Pascal declaims against the Jesuits' callous irresponsibility which would even make a profession of demoralizing men in this manner by means of Christianity's mildness—this, you see, is another matter.

x^3 A 633   *n.d.*, 1850

« **3115** *Pascal*

[*In margin:* See Reuchlin, *Pascals Leben*, p. 137][772]

Pascal is right in pointing out (Letter XI of the *Provincial Letters*) that the fact that people declaim so much against his opposition to the corrupting of morals is proof that they are indifferent to the truth and secularly cling to this life. If someone warns against poisoned meat or a city where there is a plague, people do not take it with ill will or interpret it as lack of love.

In the same letter he says to the Jesuits that in the ten earlier letters he has been all but facetious, he has shown them the wound that could be inflicted but has not yet inflicted it.

x^3 A 634 *n.d.*, 1850

« 3116 *Pascal*

. . . . . In short, if we say that man is too insignificant to associate with God—we must be very great to be able to decide such things.

Some place in *Pensees,* quoted in Reuchlin,
Pascals Leben, p. 238.[773]
x^3 A 639 *n.d.*, 1850

« 3117 *Pascal*

To know God only speculatively is not to know him at all.
Reuchlin, *Pascals Leben,* p. 243.[774]
x^3 A 640 *n.d.*, 1850

« 3118 *Christianity*

Once upon a time all the other branches of knowledge drew their prestige from Christianity, from theology: a natural scientist, a physician, etc.—for him to be a doctor of theology as well was a recommendation. Alas, men have turned this almost completely around. The fact that Pascal was a famous mathematician is almost a benefit to Christianity, because of that people feel that they can listen to and reflect on what he says. Alas, what a change.

x^3 A 641 *n.d.*, 1850

« 3119 *Mynster*

If I had to find a beautiful expression for the Mynsterian approach and one which would please him, I would quote a passage from Pascal's *Pensees,* where he speaks of how one should approach those who repudiate religion or are ill-disposed toward it:

One should begin with proofs, showing that religion does not quarrel with reason; next, show that it is venerable and try to inspire respect for it; then make it pleasant and appealing (ingratiate it) and awaken the desire in them for it to be true, something one shall then drive home with irrefutable proofs; but it mainly depends on making it pleasant and appealing in their eyes.

Quoted from Reuchlin's
Pascals Leben, p. 223.[775]
x³ A 642   *n.d.*, 1850

« 3120 *Jacqueline Pascal*

She said it superbly (in her reflections on the mystery of Christ's death) where she speaks of good works:

Nothing is so dangerous as that which pleases both God and man, for such acts have something which pleases men and something else which pleases God. For example, St. Theresa's greatness—her humility pleased God, her superior enlightenment (*Erleuchtung*) pleased men.

See Reuchlin, *Pascals Leben,*[776] p. 258, Appendix I.[*]

Incidentally, I interpret her words somewhat differently than she herself. The danger in something which is pleasing both to God and man or the danger in practising such works is that there is a lulling-to-sleep element in them; when, on the contrary, what I do pleases God but not men, or vice versa, I am kept more awake, in the first case am kept in the right heterogeneity.

Incidentally, too, there might be a question about its proving to be true that God and man actually are in such agreement.

x³ A 644   *n.d.*, 1850

« 3121

[*] *In margin of 3120* (x³ A 644):
She also says:
Fear death when there is no danger, but not in danger, for we ought to be men.

See ibid., 259.
x³ A 645   *n.d.*

« 3122 *Virgin Mary*

Reuchlin (either in his *Geschichte Port Royal* or in *Pascals Leben*) observes somewhere[777] that it was a proof of the moral laxity which the Jesuits introduced that they understood Mary as a symbol of the world's pain, immersed themselves in this world's pain, which went through her heart.

x³ A 646   *n.d.*, 1850

« 3123 *"To Leave the World"*

In *Pascals Leben und der Geist seiner Schriften*[778] by Reuchlin (available in the *Athenæum*),[779] in one of the supplements, there is this remark by a pious man: "From a Christian point of view it is not required to have a special call to leave the world, but only a special call to remain in the world: the former is no more necessary than a special call to run away from a fire."

This is truly the way it is. But the situation is that we men prefer to remain in this world, and therefore the exact opposite of the essentially Christian has quite appropriately been made into true earnestness—that is, mendaciously and hypocritically. From a Christian point of view, leaving the world is prior; a special call is required to remain in the world, for the person who is to remain in the world and express the essentially Christian will become a martyr. This is mendaciously and hypocritically turned around in this way: remaining in the world —that is, in the sense of conforming to the world—is the highest; leaving the world is inferior.

O depth of hypocrisy! As I have often observed, the secular mind will never rest until it has managed to make the opposite of the truth into dogma. Therefore any time a person wishes to find true Christianity he merely has to take what is customarily presented in Christendom, especially in Protestantism, give it a couple turns, and he has essential Christianity.

The secret lies in the fact that anything essentially Christian is characterized by a dialectical middle term, and the mendacity lies in leaving this out and thus getting no. 1 as no. 3—that is, getting that which is lower (no. 1, the worldly) than the dialectical middle term as that which is higher (no. 3) than the dialectical middle term.

X^5 A 75 *n.d.*, 1853

« 3124 *Christianity*

The trustworthy judgment of the nature of Christianity is and will be the paganism and Judaism contemporary with Christianity's entering into the world. That Christianity is hatred of mankind is easily seen from Christianity's demanding that a man shall hate himself. On the whole the unconditioned relationship to the unconditioned is fatal to whatever we naturally think of when we think of humanness.

In "Christendom" we never really get to know what Christianity is, for Christendom is a society of men who neither have the faith truly to become Christians or the courage to break with it, and to that end have made their own Christianity.

Pascal's remark[780] about Christendom is very striking—namely, that it is a society of men who by means of some sacraments exempt themselves from the duty to love God.

Christendom is precisely the very thing Christ wanted to throw out entirely, the very thing he came into the world to annihilate.

XI² A 327   *n.d.*, 1854

PASSION, PATHOS

« **3125**

Sentimentality is to true and genuine feeling [*Følelse*] as the sparrow to the swallow. The sparrow lets the swallow build its nest and get everything ready and thereupon lays its young in it. (I don't know for sure if this is exactly the case with sparrows and swallows, but I know this much—that there are twenty kinds of birds which do this sort of thing.)

I A 117   January, 1836

« **3126**

Zeno distinguished among the passions [*Lidenskaberne*] on the basis that apparent virtues and apparent evils could be regarded in two ways with respect to time present or to time future:

ἡδονή–λύπη.

The rational operations of the mind are:
βούλησις (willing the good)
χαρά (joy in possessing the good)
εὐλαβεία (prudent precaution against evil).[781]

IV C 57   *n.d.*, 1842–43

« **3127**

Let no one misinterpret all my talk about pathos [*Pathos*] and passion [*Lidenskab*] to mean that I intend to sanction every uncircumcised immediacy, every unshaven passion.

V A 44   *n.d.*, 1844

« **3128**

It is rather odd how men whom I generally regard as good-natured and who generally are not unfriendly toward me, when they get into a passion are then able to lie to the high heaven and scarcely be aware of it themselves. Passion [*Lidenskaben*] does have a strange power, and therefore how foolish all this modern thing about systems and systems, as if there were help in them; no, passion must be purified. Occasionally these days I come across expressions of this.

VII[1] A 102   *n.d.*, 1846

427

« **3129**

What our age needs is *pathos* [*Pathos*] (just as scurvy needs green vegetables); but, truly, the work of boring an artesian well cannot be more artful than all my dialectical reckoning of the comic, the pathos-filled, and the passionate in order to get, if possible, a beneficial pathos-filled breeze blowing. The tragedy of our age is reason and reflection. No spontaneous enthusiast will be able to help us any more, for the reflection of the age is consuming him. That is why there has to be a man who is able to short-suit reflectively all reflections, a man of reason who with prudence and ruthlessness and with an incognito[782] of mockery and wit conceals an enthusiasm of top quality. In order to champion marriage in our day we must be able to enchant the licentious lust of the age with a seducer's diary,[783] and so on throughout.

VIII[1] A 92   n.d., 1847

« **3130** *An Observation about Something in*
"Fear and Trembling"[784]

Johannes de Silentio is right in saying that in order to show the various psychological stages a passionate concentration is needed.

So it is with the decision whether or not I shall assume that this or that is, humanly speaking, impossible for me. I am not thinking here even of the highest collisions, where the expected is altogether opposed to the order of nature (for example, that Sara gets a child although far beyond the natural age to bear children). That is why Johannes de Silentio constantly repeats that he cannot understand Abraham, since in addition the collision here is so high that the ethical is spiritual trial [*Anfægtelsen*].

No, in lesser situations, there are many people, surely by far the majority, who are able to live without any real consciousness penetrating their lives. For them it is certainly possible that they never come in passionate concentration to the decision whether they should cling expectantly to this possibility or give it up; they live on this way in unclarity.

It is otherwise with the individualities whose nature is consciousness. They can very well give up this or that, even if it is their dearest wish, but they must have clarity on whether they should expect or not.

It is forever impossible to make this comprehensible to immediately spontaneous or half-reflective natures. Therefore they never come to distinguish between resignation [*Resignation*] and faith.

This is precisely what Johannes de Silentio has again and again enjoined. Everything, he says, depends upon passionate concentration.

Thus when someone comes and wants to correct him by taking the matter back into ordinary intellectual unclarity (which undeniably is common among men)—then, yes, then he of course succeeds in being understood by many.

So it goes always when that which an authentic thinker has pushed to its logical conclusion is corrected with the help of that "which he rejected before he ever began."

x^2 A 594 *n.d.*, 1850

« 3131 *The Inverse Relation between the Greatness of a Passion and the Insignificance of the Object*

It is often pointed out (today, too, by Pastor Visby[785] in his sermon on the hardhearted fellow servant, whom he used as an occasion to preach about enmity) that it takes just a little trifle to arouse the greatest passion [*Lidenskab*]. In my opinion this can be explained by the fact that there is an unsound or half-demented relationship between passion and the object; once passion has arisen, it is inflamed by the senselessness that the whole thing revolves around a mere trifle.

If, as an example (such as Visby's) of how a trifle sets the strongest passions in motion, reference is made to the fact that partisan or schismatic disputes, religious disputes, and civil wars always are the most violent—and this despite the fact that the contenders are so close to each other that it must indeed be a trifle which most often disunites them—it must be pointed out that here the matter is altogether different, because at the root of this disunity lies all the passion which also had expected or desired unity. At the root of controversy or enmity between strangers lies indifference—at the root of the other controversy lies friendship, a spirit of solidarity.

x^3 A 583 *n.d.*, 1850

« 3132

In margin of 3131 (x^3 A 583):

For this reason one cannot dispute with a stranger over a trifle, for indifference does not permit it. On the other hand, when friends or neighbors get into a dispute about a trifle (which can happen precisely because they are friends and neighbors) then it is no trifle, for the fact that it is between them, that the relationship may now be broken, is no trifle.

x³ A 584   n.d.

« 3133 *For Contemporary Orthodoxy in Protestantism Christianity Is Mythology, Poetry*

For a moment let us concede that Christianity exists [*er til*] objectively, although this is not quite true, because even its objective existence is far from being exactly Christianity.

We assume, then, that objectively it exists. What does not exist, however, is the kind of passion [*Lidenskab*] which is the formal condition of being able to receive the content of Christianity, unconditioned passion, the passion of the unconditioned.

This kind of passion quite literally does not appear in the world any more. Yes, it is so long since it has been that even the novel writers and poets in our time do not dare (for fear of being regarded as mad men, liars, or laughing-stock) to portray a passion of such loftiness.

But if the formal condition of being able to receive the content of Christianity [does not exist], then the objective existence [*Væren-til*], so to speak, is an existence which nevertheless in another sense is not an existence, that is, Christianity is mythology, poetry, which is what it is for so-called orthodoxy.

*   *

And how difficult it will be to get Christianity back again I can see merely from the experience of my fragment of striving. It is not difficult to discover that I have an advantage in relation to the current mess, and this means that the few who do have the capacity to see this, instead of helping me to forge ahead, want to snatch something of mine, adapt it, and thus come to be in opposition to me. Further, in private conversation there are very many who with great interest are willing to listen to me develop the theme that Christianity does not exist—and if someone thinks this can be an ingredient in his next sermon he is very ready to use it. But it never occurs to him, not in the remotest way, that he is supposed to make some sacrifice.

Just as in a confused, flabby age an officer in desperation may say: Nothing of any good will come until we get capital punishment again, so too a religious officer in our time might say: Nothing of any good will come before we in all earnestness get hell-punishment again. Alas, but I tremble when I think of the agonies in which the man who is supposed to reintroduce it must be hardened and martyred. War does not batter men any more, or epidemics; against all such things they are spiritlessly armed by their spiritlessness.

XI[1] A 126   *n.d.*, 1854

PASTORS, CLERGY

« 3134

..... for what hope is there, indeed, for the Christian teachers of our day, or what prospects are there for the proclamation of the gospel in the world we have made for ourselves, where the servants of the Word with their Christian tenets soon become like watchmen with their edifying verses ("For the sake of Jesus' wounds, forgive us our sins, O gracious God,"[786] which is a remarkable contrast to all the buying and selling on the streets and sidewalks), to which no one pays any attention and whose song is of interest only because it tells the time—as unheeded as watchmen, except for the statistical information on who has had their banns read for the first, second, or third time in order to give them one more year of grace in which to vegetate.

> January 9, precisely at 9 o'clock in the evening, provided the watchman here on the square is crying out the right time.

II A 325   January 9, 1839

« 3135

One may very well be the court preacher in the ostentatious sense; it is not even dangerous, although it is never Christian. But then he must admit that it is for the sake of his weakness, because he does not feel the strength and the courage to serve truth in the true way. If one is brash and wants such ostentatiousness to be earnestness, a fantasy existence *a la* witness-of-the-truth, then a protest is due.

The same holds true of the bread-and-butter attitude, the odiousness lies in the brashness with which a person wants to dress up as earnestness the human weakness which requires a steady occupation.

I truly do not wish (and in my fear and trembling I always think like this) to disturb a single person, to upset him so that he cannot see his way. But brashness is the downfall of all Christianity.

IX A 201   *n.d.,* 1848

« 3136

Since the European catastrophe, has any stronger attack on Christianity been made than before? By no means. But formerly all the

432

clergymen kept silent, for then their livelihood was secure—then it was only Christianity which was betrayed—never mind that! Nowadays Christianity is not being attacked (the rebellion in our time really does not do that) but the living is—and this brings the clergy to its knees. *Quod erat demonstrandum.*

IX A 406 *n.d.,* 1848

« **3137**

Pastors are no longer spiritual counselors—physicians have become that; instead of becoming another man by means of conversion one becomes that nowadays by water cures and the like—but we are all Christians!

x^2 A 238 *n.d.,* 1849

« **3138 *The "Preacher" and the Schoolteacher***

A Kind of Idyll

Changed from: An Essay in Dialogue

———

A summer house in the country, luncheon table all prepared. The schoolteacher and Peer Hansen

———

Schoolteacher: Tell me now, P. H. What in the world are you doing in our neighborhood?
P. H.: No, first things first. A glass of schnaps to open the meal and the heart. (Drinks a schnaps.) Well, to be brief, I am out here on behalf of the Temperance Society.
Schoolteacher: Then at least I understand why you had to have a glass of schnaps "first," for if you had told me that first I certainly could not even have offered you a schnaps.
P. H.: Please don't misunderstand me. I have by no means joined the Temperance Society, anything but. I will drink a second glass in honor of the Temperance Society and I always do that; I always drink a second glass in honor of the Temperance Society. (They clink their glasses, both drink and say: Long live the Temperance Society!) Now to the business at hand. You see, it is well known that from the beginning I have had extraordinary speaking ability, really have the gift of gab. The Temperance Society became aware of my talents and in the interest of the Society decided not to let them go to waste. To put it briefly, I have been called and installed

as "Pastor" to the Temperance Society. That this is as far as
possible from going in as a member but just the opposite is clear
from the fact that I have been engaged to go out from the Temperance Society. The Temperance Society Board has been and is of
the opinion: What does it matter if the pastor, as I am usually
called, drinks a schnaps or two or four or, in one word, drinks;
what does it matter if by using his gifts he is able to win scores of
members for the Society, members of which do not drink.

Schoolteacher: The Society is right about that. Even the strictest
teetotaler must find that every such glass of schnaps for the pastor
is well utilized, presupposing that you do get members for the
Society and that your experience is not like that of the man who
said, "It pays off," when he fed pork to his pig, but he reckoned
wrong, because he fed it three sides of pork and got back only two.

P. H.:   So you agree. I, of course, am completely convinced it is right,
and if I had not already done it I would drink another schnaps in
honor of the Temperance Society. To go on with my story, I have
made an agreement with the Society, whose activity involves diet,
that I have my diet: 4 schnaps every day, 2 glasses of punch, and
an extra dram for every one who signs up as a member. It all goes
on the expense account, and just as I believe that the society is
satisfied with me, so I am also satisfied with it. I really don't want
to make any alteration or to leave. Like Peer Degn,[787] I grieve to
think of leaving a congregation which I love and esteem and which
loves and esteems me in return.

Schoolteacher: You, who are like Degn and more to boot, have
become a "pastor" and somebody in this world, maybe you can
tell me one thing. I have often imaged myself in a pastor's robe,
but now I can find out from you what it is to be a pastor. It must
be wonderful to stand and preach the very opposite of what one
does himself—after all, you certainly cannot feel what you are
saying.

P.H.: Why should I not be able to feel what I am saying. I can assure
you—and every one of my many, many listeners is able to testify
—that I sometimes am so moved that I can scarcely talk for emotion. In the first place, I think of the 4 drams, the two glasses of
punch, an extra dram, and also the fact that I have really done well
in the world and have a good living—isn't that moving! Next I
think of my useful and beneficial activity. While I stand there
talking I look at the people I am talking to and can read their eyes:

there sits one who as sure as my name is P. H. will go right out
of this meeting and sign up as a member, and I get so emotional
over this that I start to cry, and this has such a powerful effect that
I can see on his neighbor's face that he is going to do the same
—if that isn't moving then I don't know what is. If I were a saint,
would it be nearly as moving for me to produce such an effect? Am
I right?

Schoolteacher: Perhaps, but isn't it untrue to call yourself a pastor?

P.H.: Not at all.* If a person can proclaim the teaching that we should
not aspire after earthly honor, esteem, wealth—if a person can
proclaim this in such a way that he convinces men to live their lives
accordingly, does it make any difference if he himself does just the
opposite? Or isn't the best proof of his extraordinary talent for
speaking, of his being truly a great orator, the fact that although
he does just the opposite he has such an enormous influence?

Schoolteacher: But doesn't it ever happen that exception is taken to
your not being a member and you are reproached for it?

P. H.:   Yes, of course, but I dismiss it. I explain it as an indulgence
in personalities, an insulting indulgence in personalities; it is my
job to preach, and one should stick to the subject. That slays them.

It ends with P. H.'s saying to the schoolteacher:
Listen, and I will give a speech as I usually give it.

This discourse is delivered in good form with a certain appearance
of pathos, yet with a little fantasy, yet as it could be given by someone
not utterly lacking in talent. He speaks of the highmindedness of
arriving at a resolution at all, especially this one, pictures what goes
on in the soul of one who resolves to become a member of the Temperance Society.

This makes so deep an impression on the schoolteacher that he
resolves to become a member, and P. H. gives himself an extra dram.

End.

x⁵ A 163   *n.d.*, 1849

« 3139

Addition to 3138 (x⁵ A 163):

*What is a pastor? A pastor is one who is paid by the state to
proclaim the doctrine of poverty. A pastor is one who is respected and
honored and esteemed in society for proclaiming that we should not
seek after worldly honor, esteem, and wealth. The state thinks this way

—and curiously enough, when I said earlier that the Temperance Society thinks this way, you thought them right—if the pastor can get the congregation to act according to his teaching, what difference does it make if the pastor is an exception? There was a time when it was required that the pastor should do it and the congregation was exempted. The state reckons more accurately—the pastor is exempted if he simply takes care of the congregation.

x^5 A 164   *n.d.*, 1849

« 3140

Always the same. For some years the clergymen have been busy "patterning the pastoral robe so that it would almost look like a professor's academic gown"; this would be scholarly. Now they are withdrawing and wanting to get into parliament—to be a pastor does not amount to anything. And this is embellished by the high-sounding name of working for the whole—that is, staying in Copenhagen and enjoying oneself, whetting the appetite, voting, and all that. —And this is earnestness! If someone all on his own gave up his official income and worked night and day for an idea—it would be [regarded as] fanaticism.

x^2 A 357   *n.d.*, 1850

« 3141

What an infinite difference: sheltered by the illusion that it is one's office and job, within the illusion of a Sunday worship service for the sort of people who come to listen to it—to declaim a few Christian truths—and oneself, attractive in the eyes of the world, existentially living one's daily life in purely secular categories, on the go as a politician, a voting and dancing member of everything—what an infinite difference between this and being expected to place the Christian ideas into the middle of actuality, breaking through the illusions, accenting personal existence in the power of these ideas! Then the conflict will, it must, manifest itself, must manifest how far "actuality" is from essential Christianity. As long as the clergy are satisfied with having insured themselves a living and as long as they are legally or theatrically permitted one day a week, as well as at funerals, to talk a jargon of their own which makes no demands whatsoever as soon as the shop is closed—well, then it is tolerated, of course. This is precisely what the world finds attractive. No one, perhaps no one is as attractive as a clergyman who is a politician. For the world understands very well that a pastor ought to be a witness for the religious in the midst of "actuality," but now it triumphs. Most of his time and thoughts are directed to elections etc.—thus he expresses that being a pastor is only a means of making a living. And then the sanctimoniousness of such a minister's explaining his participation in politics as zeal and religiousness. O, you blind preacher, if you want to be more than "a pastor," then be a Christian witness in the midst of actuality, but not a politician.

The essentially Christian first of all requires that what is said in church be expressed in "actuality," that it penetrate lives; it is this which distinguishes the essentially Christian from theatricality and the like. This is why the pastor should go out among them, look after them, make them aware. But does the pastor go there—he avoids it. As soon as the pastor has taken off his gown on Sunday he as much as says: For heaven's sake, let us not talk about that. I am just like all of you, a member of the club, voting member in all secular societies, a pleasant social companion, shrewd about my advantages, just like the rest of you. How unseemly, how uncultured it would be of me to recall or even existentially bring to mind the essentially Christian outside of the church; it would be as if an actor were to keep on acting a comedy out in company and in everyday life.

x^2 A 418   *n.d.*, 1850

« 3142 *A Satirical Collision*

Sometimes the world, in an egotistical attack of "spirituality," shouts that if the teachers of religion were as they were in the time of the apostles, renouncing earthly advantage, doing it for nothing, etc., the congregation would imitate them—and then when someone stands among them and does it even at a financial sacrifice, the world shouts, "He is crazy." —This is how far secular mentality has come to dominate. The world cannot identify in "actuality" the very thing it asks for and quite rightly finds it insanity for someone to do something without having any profit——*aber* this was exactly what it asked for.

This, you see, is the genuine Christian collision for the person who dedicates himself in this way.

x^2 A 550   *n.d.*, 1850

« 3143

Clergymen are an intolerable lot to talk with. They are quite ridiculously spoiled by declaiming the highest. And then a perpetual equivocation about the quiet virtues which are effected in secret.

x^3 A 40   *n.d.*, 1850

« 3144 *A Pastor—a Policeman*

A policeman does not have the right to be a private man. If he goes by a place where a disturbance is going on or a crime is being committed—and it perhaps would be most convenient for him to slip away without identifying himself as a policeman—if a bystander recognizes him, he has the right to say to the policeman: Will you please do your duty.

Similarly a pastor does not have the right to be a private man and limit himself to orating one hour once a week and otherwise be private. If he is contemporary with corruption, he is obliged to witness.

x^3 A 62   *n.d.,* 1850

« 3145 *An Actor—a Pastor*

An actor[788] portrays the man of nobility, the hero, the witness of the truth, and the like; he expresses all these noble, elevated, heroic feelings and thoughts. Would anyone deny that it would be jolting if the actor did this in person. But why is a pastor supposed to have the right to do this? The actor may also be a believer just like the rest of us and the pastor; to be sure, in Christendom we are all Christians, and yet our conformity is to the secular mentality. Why then is a pastor supposed to have the right to declaim in person all these wonderful virtues and continually create the confusion that he himself is the one who carries them out?

A very logical mind could be tempted to make the following proposal: Completely abolish the pulpit and the clerical vestments, ordination, and the like. Arrange a little stage[789] in the church, with the usual kind of curtain. There is no objection to using the organ if desired. A prelude is played. The curtain goes up, and "the pastor" comes out, or if a combined performance is wanted, several "pastors" come out in historical costumes. One of them would play the role of Luther. The stage director (incidentally, he could just as well be borrowed from the theater, since the Secretary for Ecclesiastical Affairs is also the Theater Secretary) has seen to the authenticity of the costume —he would declaim one of Luther's sermons. There would be some tears, of course, just as there are tears in the theater when a tragedy is presented; but for the most part crying in church is believed to be different from crying in the theater, which may well be true sometimes but as a rule is not true.

x^3 A 93   *n.d.,* 1850

« 3146 *Ordination*

We make much of ordination in Christendom. A new teacher is going to be ordained, and events proceed awesomely, solemnly during the "still, solemn hour."

Now he is ordained. Thereupon he arranges his life quite secularly, just like the other secular professionals or ordained men.

This kind of religiosity is actually a counterpart to that mentioned earlier in this journal [i.e., x³ A 73]—a thief declares: On Sunday, God willing, I intend to burglarize on Amagertorv.

Incidentally, the zealous clergy keep a tight rein on ordination, that is, on every occasion when it is not embarrassing but can be put to ecclesiastical use to con others. If a layman wants to preach, God forbid, then the clergy fuss about ordination, the gifts of grace communicated to them by ordination.

Meanwhile there is an erudite theological debate about the nature and significance of ordination from a speculative point of view—and we await from our profound thinker, genius, and ecclesiastical saloon-keeper, Senior Court Chaplain John Doe, a book which will cast a new light on this mystery.

Fortunate Christendom! Anyone who loves stuff and nonsense is invited to settle down in Christendom. In Christendom every cause means 17 different things, and the basis of all these meanings is that it means nothing. The silliness of the whole thing is that it is upside down and around every which way *ad libitum* simply according to whim and occasion. This going-to-pot of all concepts is established Christendom.

X³ A 120 *n.d.,* 1850

« 3147 *To Ignore the Rabble*

It may well be the smartest thing to ignore the rabble, existentially (consequently every day, every single day of one's life—and on a rare and occasional Sunday formally discourse on loving one's neighbor) expressing that only a very small fraction of society exists. But a Christian clergyman has no right to do this.

God in heaven, how does a clergyman dare say: It is beneath my *dignity* to become involved with the rabble. Wretch, do you know what you are saying, that it is blasphemy, that you mock Christ, who introduced a new concept of dignity, Christian dignity, which consists in doing just this—existing for the rabble, suffering its misunderstanding, perhaps its persecution, but all to help it forward.

x^3 A 132   *n.d.*, 1850

« 3148 *All Christianity Has Become a Way of Speaking*

How many clergymen are there who dare personally confess that they pray, they themselves personally pray, personally relate their lives to God, pray to God in that connection. No, just like the others, the pastor adapts his life according to prudence and probability, and in a deeper sense it never occurs to him that God would intervene directly in his life—but on Sunday he preaches that the Christian (*in abstracto*) prays, that the pray-er (*in abstracto*) takes everything to God.

The whole thing has become a way of speaking which everyone finds quite appropriate for "the pastor" to use on Sunday (just as the doctors and lawyers also have a special language) but which they would not permit the pastor or layman to use personally on Monday—that would be ridiculous.

The sensibleness of the age has presumably come a long, long way from this childishness—nowadays it is a mode of speaking which is used in the sermon, similar to the undertaker's demeanor.

x^3 A 176   *n.d.*, 1850

« 3149 *Ecclesiastical-secular Nonsense*

This crops up in various forms again and again because of the perfect conformity of the clerical and the secular.

There is a clergyman. He is a very mediocre clergyman, as everyone knows. But he is also supposed to be a remarkable farmer or horse and cattle breeder. The government (I leave undecided whether it is the ecclesiastical or the secular arm of the government, for the only thing lacking would be that the ecclesiastical branch, that the Bishop, who himself perhaps was an outstanding veterinarian, was the one who had recommended him and drawn the government's attention to him) became aware of his merits—and he becomes a Knight of Denmark.

Instead of arranging his removal from ecclesiastical office and finding a place for him where he belongs, he remains in the ecclesiastical office—and is decorated to boot.

The fact that he is decorated should signify that he is a more than ordinary pastor, but here it means a minus; it is in another capacity that he is a knight.

What priceless nonsense! In any case it seems to me he should be forbidden to wear the decoration on his pastoral gown. It is bad enough for a pastor to wear a decoration that signifies he is an unusually competent pastor; but to wear a decoration that reminds the congregation that he is something quite different from a pastor is utterly mad.[*]

This comes from a total lack of respect for what it means to be a clergyman, which again is a result of the perfect conformity between the clerical and the secular.

Suppose a pastor had the luck of becoming the champion bird-hunter—then everybody would find it inappropriate for him to wear the symbol of his rank on his pastoral gown. And yet, after all, that is not as ridiculous as for a pastor constantly to wear a decoration which reminds the congregation that he is an outstanding veterinarian or something like that. Actually, it is not in the capacity of veterinarian that he wears the pastoral gown—and yet it is in the capacity of veterinarian that he wears the cross of the Knight upon his pastoral gown.

The government has an eye for merits—on the other hand, it has no eye for what it ought to mean to be a clergyman.

X^3 A 242 _n.d._, 1850

« 3150

[*] _In margin of 3149_ (X^3 A 242):

Recently I read that a lieutenant and Knight of Denmark became a clergyman (presumably he had been in the war as a volunteer and had distinguished himself). Just as he is now permitted to wear the Knight's cross on his clerical gown, he could very well be permitted to wear epaulets on his clerical gown, too.

X^3 A 243 _n.d._

« 3151 _Where Are We?_

Here: if a man is not married, it is inappropriate, yes, it is shocking for him to want to be a pastor. Yes, come to think of it, we have gone even farther, we have come so far that we prove by the New Testament that this is the way it should be.

Here: experience teaches that it is quite proper for a father to let his son study theology, "for it is the most secure way to make a living."

X^3 A 244 _n.d._, 1850

« 3152 *The Impossibility of Christianity Here Today*

1.

Even if there were no other hindrances—and God knows there are plenty—this alone would be sufficient: there exist [*existerer*] 1,000 men with a very strong interest that people do not get to know what Christianity is.

If they do get to know what it is, the [pastoral] livings will not necessarily go down the drain—that is not my point—but an interpretation will be necessary, and if a person is very hot-tempered and impetuous, he does not take the time to hear that it is merely a matter of an interpretation and thinks that it implies the elimination of his livelihood—and then there's the devil to pay.

It is not unlikely that this will happen, that these 1,000 men will not even take the time to hear that it is merely a matter of interpretation. The same burning zeal and glowing enthusiasm with which in former times a believing clergy held fast to "the faith" and on this point would not listen to a word—the same zeal and enthusiasm still exists—praised be the clergy—but it has taken another direction—not toward the "faith" but toward a livelihood and the security of that livelihood.

The same clergy who with inconceivable—yes, inconceivable for someone who has no concept of the clergy—with inconceivable tranquillity have calmly seen and heard that Christianity has lost one position after the other in the nineteenth century, the same clergy who with the same inconceivable tranquillity have calmly seen that society (Christendom, where we are all Christians) is frightfully more corrupt morally than it was at any time in antiquity, while the clergy calmly go on living off our all being Christians! These same clergy are simultaneously armed and battle-ready when their livelihood is touched. Not one word, they say; we hold fast with all the passion of orthodoxy—to our livelihood; naturally, if everything remains as it is, we are willing to preach about the glory of giving away everything in order to belong wholly to Christ, that one should seek the kingdom of God first, etc.; and of course we appeal with good conscience to the life we have lived up until now, but we are too earnest to stand for witticisms and pranks, that on Monday anyone gets serious about taking away our livelihood.

Behold these 1,000 men—and if the superior officers are also included, whose passion and zeal of faith are even greater, in proportion to their larger incomes, and if inclusion is also made of those who stand *a la suite*[790] but, in the aspiring passion of possibility, are still interested in a livelihood, then there are no doubt a good 1,100, a holy number, reminiscent of the 1,100 martyrs—behold, these 1,100 are ready to risk unto martyrdom for the sake of their bread and butter—actually, they will make Christianity impossible.

2.

And if this is not the case, if someone wants to situate Christianity in the context of actuality, then the daily press, which battles for the sovereignty of the public over both God and Christ, would set everything in motion to make Christianity impossible.

x³ A 260   n.d., 1850

« 3153 *The Necessity for a Clergy (but More Vigorously Christian) as a Middle Term in Christendom*

The more I think about it, the more I return to the thought that a clergy in an older form (of the Middle Ages) is essential as a middle term in Christendom. By far the majority of men feel no need for Christianity in the strictest sense; on the contrary, it would make them unhappy and confused. Looking at it ideally we of course have to say that all of them should feel the need, and this is my blessed consolation, that no one, no one is excluded. But actually this is not so. Christianity's consolation really begins on the other side of all universally human troubles and concerns; its consolation is really the forgiveness of sins and alas, for that matter, is so far from being an alleviation, that it requires that one suffer for the doctrine. The majority cannot get involved in this; it would disturb life for them. Essentially they need a relationship to Christianity. Then life is a joy, a pious joy, to them. And we should all remember that in the end, that is, in eternity, we essentially will all be equally blessed.

Catholicism's error was that the clergy egotistically, domineeringly, made itself into an intermediate authority in order to rule. Instead of the exact opposite, which is and ought to be the case—to take care that the passage to the more rigorous Christianity stands open for everyone who desires it.

Thus Catholicism's error was the clergy, that is, a severe, more monastic clergy egotistically wanted to be an intermediate authority.

Then Luther rose up in order to shake off this intolerable yoke in the name of the ordinary Christian and to secure for everyone the immediate relationship to God. Splendid! Honor to him!

However, Luther was no dialectician. He failed to see that he was the extraordinary, that when all was said and done he was perhaps the only one who could bear this immediate relationship to God. Yet he made himself the norm. Protestantism's watchword became: We are all priests—which had to result either in tragic excesses or a sinking into sheer secularism.

Look at the situation in Protestantism. Yes, of course, it is a given, it is fixed, that the ministers we have now are priests. Well, so we are all priests—these ministers are not to be distinguished from other landlords or merchants, or from other secular career men; in short, they are exactly like everybody else—ergo, we are all priests.

The high spirituality which Luther entered into—ah, there is nothing in the world easier to counterfeit (and no one can convince me to the contrary, that when the gospel tells us to give everything to the poor, the simple thing is simply to do it; high spirituality does just the opposite, saying, I do not do it, but in my inwardness I am like the one who has done it, and at all times I am willing to do it).

Luther was perfectly right in smashing the egotism of the clergy domineeringly wanting to be the intermediate authority; but, O, he had very poor knowledge of mankind if he could think that it was possible for all of us to become priests, that the only way of doing it in this world was—and this is what happened—for priests to become landlords—and all of us priests.

There should be a clergy as the middle term. The clergy should be rigorously Christian, should express the most strenuous demands of Christianity, at least approximately, for otherwise the whole thing is destroyed and everything becomes secularism through and through, which is the actual case. Draconian laws amount to nothing, and the magnificent sublimity that we are all priests—leads to the tragic nonsense we see before us.

This clergy must be recruited from such persons who have been brought to break completely with the world, either by great sins or very severe misfortunes, and the like. But now, instead of broodingly and misanthropically making others unhappy by demanding the same of them, they should—loving what it is to be human—treat the weaker ones, or those who are unable to go out so far, leniently, as far as truth allows. Surely it is not imperiousness to be bound by the more severe terms oneself—and of course readily allowing everyone who desires it to enter into the more strenuous Christian life.

x³ A 267   n.d., 1850

« 3154 Can a Theological Candidate Demand To Be Ordained without Wanting To Have a Clerical Appointment?

As the situation is at present, I do not see that a theological candidate could be denied ordination if he demanded it, even if he did not want an appointment.

It was the state Church which linked ordination to an appointment and to a livelihood, but today the state Church is essentially dissolved.

x³ A 325   n.d., 1850

« 3155 The State-Church

How fortunate for poetry that the state has not decided that poetry is a necessity, that a poet must be appointed for every thousand men —for then poetry would have been destroyed. We would have gotten civil service poets, and men would have been spoiled by such continual poet-nonsense and would never feel inclined to hear a genuine poet.

It is the same with Christianity. The state paternally appoints 1,000 civil service officials—and Christianity perishes in nonsense.

x³ A 436   n.d., 1850

« 3156 Pastors

If anybody wants to say that the majority of the clergy, after all, barely make a living and that there is really nothing from a Christian point of view to make a fuss about, not even by the strictest standards, the answer must be: Provided these gentlemen could have gotten a better living some other way, or provided that this is not the maximum they would be able to achieve with their abilities and qualifications, to be specific, provided that they do not *pro virili* aspire to get a bigger and better living as soon as possible. From a Christian point of view their "bare living" would essentially only have any meaning if they were men who could have gotten a bigger and better living some other way but chose the more meager living in order to serve Christianity.

Incidentally, one could also ask where it says in the New Testament that a minister absolutely must get married, must absolutely have so much that he can support a wife and children, must be absolutely guaranteed the excuse and the escape when he dares venture nothing that he does it out of concern for his wife and children—that is why in proclaiming Christianity he must adapt himself to the others, that is why he has to refrain from witnessing for the truth and against the untruth, etc.—perhaps that is even the reason he has a wife and child. Just as in the literary world certain set phrases are used: This is merely a rough outline; I have not had the time to develop it further, etc. etc. —thereby protecting oneself against the critics: so also we have 1,000 married clergymen, all of whom, each one individually, would show what men they are—if only they did not have a wife and children. And to keep everything in good order, we are most scrupulous about seeing to it that as far as possible every pastor gets married. We do not want to have unmarried pastors, declare the congregations and the church authorities; we do not want to be unmarried, say the pastors—this way we are all guaranteed cozy security, for the pastors cannot get around to doing anything because of wife and children, and the candidate can hardly get to be a pastor without having a wife and children.

To castrate a man is called emasculating him; from the spiritual point of view, from the side of spirit, the question is whether we do not intend to emasculate him, inasmuch as it takes a most extraordinary man to have a wife and child and actually to serve the idea.

X^3 A 502   *n.d.*, 1850

« **3157**

Pastors have finally ceased to be what they actually ought to be to the point that, in relation to what it really means to be a pastor, the factors by which they make a big hit and become honored, respected, and esteemed etc. are completely irrelevant—namely, that they are good mixers, people who can take part in anything, administer, deliver occasional addresses, in short, be a sort of more elegant edition of an undertaker. —Or in another manner, that for which they actually come to be regarded—for example, being somewhat scholarly, etc.—is irrelevant to what it is to be a pastor.

Christianity has actually been abolished,[791] and therefore we really have not known what to do with a pastor; being a pastor has practically become a charade, and no one can definitely say what it is; it is an indefinable something, but someone who as such is present at all kinds of solemn occasions, a nice man, *neutrius generis* (neither ecclesiastical nor secular) or *generis utriusque*, an ecclesiastical-secular hermaphrodite.

X^3 A 514   *n.d.*, 1850

« 3158 *A Modern Analogy to Something in the Time of the Reformation*

I have heard that the number of theological students has dwindled strikingly—presumably because of apprehension that the old idea of studying theology as the surest way to bread is going out.

It was just the same in the time of the Reformation. Luther's concept of the pastor was not as appealing as the Catholic concept. I see that he explains this (in *Theobald Thamer* by August Neander; Berlin: 1842, p. 5): "*In den vorigen Zeiten, da nicht eine theologia sondern matheologia* (μαθαιολογία) *vorgetragen wurde . . . . . welche Schaaren von Priester streiften damals durch die Welt; jetzt aber . . . . . fliehen wir dieses Studium, so dass man kaum unter Tausenden in der ganzen Schaar der Studenten, der mit diesem Studium sich beschäftigen will . . . . .*"[792]

x^3 A 606   *n.d.*, 1850

« 3159 *"Training in Christianity"*[793]

I have heard that some pastors object: "This can't be preached to congregations." "Well, it is also for pastors."

But the confusion of our age is so profound that it seems plain as day to everyone that the pastors presumably must be Christians. It is accepted as an axiom. Nobody demurs if someone insists that a large share of the congregation are not Christian. But the pastors—should not absolutely every single pastor be a Christian, he who is a teacher in Christianity, has his bread and butter as a teacher—and should he not know what Christianity is? Well, that would certainly be precarious —especially for them who commission him as such as a matter of course.

x^3 A 610   *n.d.*, 1850

« 3160 *The Turn in the Proclamation of Christianity Corresponding to the Situation of the Clergy*

As long as the clergy were exalted and sacrosanct in the eyes of men, Christianity continued to be preached in its rigorousness. For even if the clergy did not take it so rigorously themselves, no one dared criticize them and they could very well impose burdens and dare to be severe.

But little by little, as this nimbus vanished, the clergy got into the situation of being themselves controlled. Thus there was nothing to do but compromise Christianity. They compromised so much that they finally achieved perfect conformity with flat, secular aspirations—which was then proclaimed to be Christianity. This is approximately Protestantism today.

The good aspect of this is that one can no longer be rigorous with others when he is not rigorous with himself. Today only someone who is rigorous with himself can dare to be rigorous or to proclaim a more rigorous Christianity—even so things may go badly for him.

Incidentally, the same thing that happened on a large scale to the clergy happens also in lesser situations. A power arises which in the public mind acquires the prescriptive right to be a rigorous power, rigorous with others—and there arises the idea of being rigorous in opposition to it. This is how the opposition arose in various nations. No demands at all were made on the opposition—that it should be disinterested, etc:—no, attention was directed to the idea that the opposition should be severe with the government. And then the manner in which the opposition reimbursed itself was new, was not a matter of getting offices etc., and thus people fancied that the opposition was truth. This is now water over the dam—and it is always to the good.

x^3 A 698   n.d., 1850

« 3161 *Chrysostom*

declaims against the habit of regarding clergymen merely as orators and the view common in the great cities dominated by Greek culture that religious address is practically the same as the Sophists' deluxe oration. "The majority behave during sermons like spectators at a race, and we see how the crowd divides into parties, with one party declaring itself for this pastor and the other party for that one, and how they listen to the address in different moods, depending on how they feel about the pastor."

Neander, *Chrysostomus*, I, p. 62.[794]

Further: "What should we say about the internal squabbling and badgering of the believers, which is just as prevalent as attacks from without and which make even more difficulty for the teacher. In his conceitedness the one will arrogantly and vainly dig into things the knowledge of which would accomplish nothing and of which knowledge is impossible. Others demand of him an accounting of God's judgment and compel him to measure the immense abyss. There are few who are really earnest about faith and life, but many who speculate about things which we cannot possibly grasp, yes, which call down God's wrath on us for wanting to speculate on them."

Neander, *Chrysostomus*, I, p. 63,
x³ A 751   *n.d.*, 1851

« 3162 *Origen*

warns against clergymen receiving earthly wages and becoming, as he says, Pharaoh's priests instead of God's.

Pharaoh, the earthly king, wants his priests to have earthly goods, to be concerned about the earthly, not for souls. But what commands does Christ give to his own? He who does not give up everything he possesses cannot be my disciple. I shudder in uttering these words. I accuse myself first of all. I must declare my own condemnation first of all. How do we have the audacity to preach such truths to people, yes, even merely to read them, we who not only do not give up everything we possess but struggle to gain more? But if our consciences condemn us, should we therefore hide what is written? No, I will not make myself guilty of a double crime, I will confess, confess before the entire people what the gospel says and what I still have not fulfilled.

See Böhringer, *Die Kirche und ihre Zeugen*,[795]
Origen, I, pt. 1, p. 109.
x⁴ A 121   *n.d.*, 1851

« 3163 *Erasmus of Rotterdam*

says somewhere in Ἐγκώμιον μωρίας, "The princes hand piety over to the common man; the comman man hands it over to the clergy; the secular clergy (*seculares*) shove it over to the ecclesiastical orders; these shove it over to the monks; the more lenient of these shove it over to the more rigorous; the more rigorous shove it over to the mendicant friars; and these shove it over to the Carthusian monks, among whom alone is piety to be found and in such a way that it is not easily found."

See Adolf Müller, *Erasmus Leben*[796]
(Hamburg: 1828), p. 235.
x⁴ A 332   *n.d.*, 1851

« 3164 *The Pastor—the Congregations*

If it were really so that eternal salvation could be bought at the bargain price the clergy usually offer, anyone who did not accept it would be crazy. But the fact is that deep within him every man in Christendom has a far more earnest idea of Christianity and understands this much, that it is no great help to them that the clergy want to have a clearance sale. Men are afraid of Christianity, afraid that it will get a finger on them and they will not be able to get rid of it.

x⁴ A 368   n.d., 1851

« 3165 *"Reasons"*

One must give reasons[797] in order to get people to accept Christianity, says the pastor; it is an accommodation but a necessary one.

At this time I will not discuss the fact that this is rubbish, that if one gets people to accept Christianity by giving them reasons, then it is not Christianity they accept. I will say something else: Look more closely, and you will see that "the pastor" has still more reasons than those he gives, has reasons why he gives reasons, reasons about which he keeps silent. To be specific, he has the reason that he wants to have a good standing with the people, who would perhaps get angry if he represented Christianity more truthfully. He has the reason that it is his bread and butter, and he must take care to speak in such a way that the congregation is not niggardly with the offering. In short, he has the reason that he himself is stuck in the same worldliness as the congregation.

x⁴ A 393   n.d., 1851

« 3166 *Characterlessness*

How often one hears—yes, this is something everyone is willing to talk about—that pastors ought to be more in the character of the essentially Christian.

Do you believe that is what people really want? In truth, no, no! What they want is precisely that the pastor be without character; precisely such characterlessness is popular and beloved—partly because by his help one wins indulgence from the existential [implications], partly because one has the advantage of feeling himself to be better than the pastor or at least to have the right to judge him.

But woe to him if he dared to be earnest about this and to walk in character.

O abyss of deceit and hypocrisy!

To be a person of character, then, must at best mean that it is obviously advantageous in gaining a reputation; one step farther and you are a disgrace in the world (and this very step is the critical one which decides that this is an authentic character; the other is an invention of hypocrisy).

x⁴ A 502   n.d., 1852

« **3167** *For a clergyman to esteem being a*
consummate man of the world, participating
in all secular activities as much as anyone,
can be the most refined self-indulgence.

1. For example, there is a lobster banquet at Cabinet Secretary
H.'s house. The Bishop is also there—and the verdict on him is: There
is an exceptional man; he can do everything; at a lobster banquet he
can heap invective as well as anybody. —And did you hear him on
Sunday? The way he described those exalted virtues was marvelous.

The Portuguese minister is also a *tout à fait* man at a lobster
banquet—but he has no refinement. The clergyman has the advantage
—of also being able to describe so marvelously. It is like having lobster
with a very special *sauce piquante—no wonder it tastes so marvelous.*

2. Julie and Fanny are the Cabinet Secretary's daughters. They
discuss the banquet (they were not present, for ladies are not likely to
be at such affairs) and Julie says: You can be sure it is very difficult and
burdensome for the Bishop to take part in such banquets; he would
much rather live in poverty—did you hear him on Sunday? He cried
when he was describing etc. etc. And so Julie and Fanny worshipped
him—and this is the woman's verdict.

This, too, is refinement; the Portuguese minister is not worshipped because he eats lobster with genuine voluptuousness. And
women's worship—yes, and *in specie* their divine worship, is again a *sauce
piquant,* served with the lobster only to this incomparable ecclesiastic.

3. We thank none of the other guests at this lobster banquet—we
thank only the Bishop for making the sacrifice of taking part in such
an affair, doing it so completely that no gourmet could relish his
lobster more, he, the man of God who on Sundays—and consequently
would rather live in poverty but adapts himself to us, which is why we
thank him (for condescending to us and the lobster), thank him for not
suddenly becoming earnest (as he inwardly is—did you hear him on
Sunday!) and disturbing our lobster banquet etc., something he easily
(did you hear him on Sunday?) can do without.

Such a clergyman acquires everywhere a refined superiority to
himself. If the foreign minister is a Knight of the Elephant—well, that
is the earnestness of his life. But if this clergyman also becomes a
Knight of the Elephant, you can be sure that for him it is a childish
game—didn't you hear him on Sunday! Therefore he is different from
the other Knights of the Elephant in that he is infinitely elevated above
"such childishness," yet in such a way that he is also (as a precaution)
a Knight of the Elephant.

This can be the most dreadful refinement. Then a conscious hedonist might say: All the pleasure and glory of the world will not satisfy me if I am not also a clergyman; it is an intensification which I would know how to savor. Then a Greek hedonist might say: I understand that Christianity has made possible a refinement I did not suspect; for what was all my enjoyment of life compared to what it would have been if I were a Christian ecclesiastic!

It can be a refinement. It is also possible that in the beginning he embraced it innocently—alas, and then was unable to resist it. It can also be a completely foolhardy venture in the direction of inwardness —alas, and which then completely forgot to subordinate itself occasionally to control.

x^4 A 510   *n.d.*, 1852

« 3168 *Ananias—Sapphira:*[798] *the Clergy*

The sin of which those two were guilty can easily become the sin of the clergy. The indefensible thing is not that they gain earthly advantages but that they give them the appearance of piety, the appearance of being zeal for Christianity. So it was also with Ananias and Sapphira—they could very well have kept all their wealth, no one demanded it of them—what they should not have done was to have given a part under the pretence that in love and fear of God they were giving the whole. As far as I am concerned, the clergyman is welcome to take a tenth instead of a twentieth or thirtieth—but he may not pretend that it is Christianity he actually wants if it is the tenth that he wants.

x^4 A 622   *n.d.*, 1852

« 3169 *Proclamation*

Pastor: You must die to the world—that will be ten dollars.

Novice: Well, if I must die to the world, renounce all the things of this world, I certainly understand that I will have to put out more than ten dollars for the sake of the cause, but there is just one question: Who gets the ten dollars?

Pastor: Of course I get it; it is my wages; after all, I and my family have to make a living out of proclaiming that one must die to the world. It is a very cheap price, and very soon much more will have to be charged. If you are fair, you yourself will understand that it takes a lot out of a man to proclaim that one must die to the world if the proclamation is made with earnestness and zeal. Therefore it is very necessary for me and my family to spend the summer in the country in order to recuperate etc.

x^4 A 627 *n.d.,* 1852

« 3170 *Christianity—No Christians*

Qua career man and job holder the "pastor" (the legion) proclaims Christianity objectively—naturally (yes, it actually is natural; the opposite would, indeed, be Christian!), it does not occur to him to act accordingly. He says: My job is to proclaim Christianity—*ad modum* that customs clerk[799] who scribbled a few words no one could even read and, when he was censured for it by his co-workers, answered that it was not his business to read; his business was only to write; it was the co-workers' business to read——so that consequently the summation that "no one could read what he wrote, not even he himself" is incorrect, for that was the last thing he thought should be demanded of him —and in the same way the pastor would certainly also protest the summation that no one does what the sermon says, not even the pastor himself, for he will say: I am the last one of whom this could be demanded; I am hired simply to preach.

And so it is with "the pastor's" proclamation. The congregation on the other hand excuses itself from doing what the sermon says by declaring: We have so many other things to take care of; such a stringent Christianity can be required only of "the pastor," the man of God.

And thus we arrive at the result: Christianity—but no Christians.

But now Socrates[800] says that it is impossible that there can be flute playing if there is no flute player; the reverse is also true, if there is no flute player, there is no flute playing. But nowadays there are no Christians—ergo, Christianity does not exist, or the kind of Christianity we have is a sham, a deception.

Yet beware of rashly assuming that only the clergy are egotistically interested in this deception (a shift the congregation would gladly make). No, on closer inspection we see that the congregation is no different; for if one actually loves the things of the world, it is no advantage to him to have pastors who, by personally expressing Christianity, are earnest about proclaiming Christianity.

x^5 A 10 *n.d.,* 1852

« 3171 *Naïveté (Vinet)*

In his *Pastoral-Theologie*[801] Vinet says quite naïvely: "Priest" is the only ecclesiastical name which does not appear at all in the New Testament.

Incredible to be able to say this naïvely! In my opinion this is a splendid satire.

XI¹ A 53   n.d., 1854

« 3172 *Beware of Those Who Go Around in Long Garments*[802]

As soon as the proclaimer is someone who goes around in long garments, in one way or another Christianity is on the way to becoming official Christianity.

But there is nothing Christianity is more opposed to than everything which even tastes of "official Christianity." Christianity is not opposed even to the most desperate heresy as much as it is to official Christianity.

For Christianity is heterogeneity with this world—the very instant it starts, even in the remotest way, to become official Christianity, that same instant Christianity starts to become homogeneity with this world.

Official Christianity is diametrically antithetical to true Christianity; it turns every relation around, even the most minor ones. The temporal, the human, the finite always come *first of all*—and then a little bit of Christian oratory; but Christianity is: *first of all* Christianity, and then we get to see what can happen with the temporal, the finite, the human.

Christianly, it goes like this: Go out and proclaim Christianity—and there will be a living all right. Officially, it goes like this: First of all a living is assured for a man and his family, with the possibility of advancement—then, then comes the matter of preaching Christianity. So it is in everything, everything. Christianly it reads (to take this example): Go out just as you are; officially: No, one must first have a clerical gown tailored, the vestments, the costume. Christianly, the most important is always put first (precisely this is Christianity); officially, the most unimportant is always put first—that is, all official Christianity is *eo ipso* not Christianity, for the most unimportant in first place is *eo ipso* not what Christianity is: the most important in first place.

XI¹ A 68   n.d., 1854

« 3173 *Life—Death*

To live, of course, is enjoyable; to die is a nightmare.

O, but when the requirement is to live as one who has died to the world, then to live in this life is the most terrible, terrible torment; but then, again, to die is a blessing, yes, an unspeakable blessing, since it means coming into one's proper element.

And if a Protestant preacher were to read this, he would very likely find it beautiful, wonderful—and use it as a sublime passage in his next sermon.

The odiousness, the odiousness of these Protestant preachers who at most read what has cost others death throes and then use it as beautiful passages in their sermons.

XI[1] A 86   n.d.,   1854

« 3174 *Sheer Trickery*

A theological candidate becomes a minister—why? Indeed, he is going to be married and has to have something to live on.

So he acquires a congregation. He has scarcely gotten it before he begins to use it as a pretext, that he must proclaim Christianity as consolation for the sake of the congregation.

The whole thing is very simple: he entered the priesthood mendaciously—thus he guards against ever coming to understand what Christianity is; indeed, he runs the risk of having this understanding running him out of his job and career.

XI[1] A 88   n.d.,   1854

« 3175 *The Clergyman*

The fact that the "clergyman" goes around in female attire is not, after all, devoid of deeper significance.[*]

For the "clergyman's" characteristic fault ordinarily tends to be the same as woman's: cunning, subtlety, and lies. Yes, just as one may say that a woman's element is lies (although when said of woman it has a more innocent significance), that wherever there is a woman there definitely is a little lie as well, so may it also be said of the official clergy.

Also characteristic of the clergyman are swooning and fainting and the coquettishness which wants not and yet wants so very much. This is especially true of the top-ranking prelates. Not long ago I read of someone who had become an archbishop somewhere in Germany. In his installation address he said, of course, that he had prayed to God that this cup (becoming archbishop) might be taken from him, but, alas, in vain. That is just exactly like a woman who can be dying to get into the bridal bed and yet she swoons and will not, something that would be misinterpreted if the bridegroom took it seriously. But it must be remembered that the woman is innocent, it is a part of her nature, and therefore it is meant† to treat her with irony. It is different with the prelate. But his analogy to feminine nature is found in the synthesis present in the sexual relationship: sin—and yet desire. The prelate is well aware that from a Christian point of view this matter of a secularly high-ranking clergy is sin—but he does desire it. This is then expressed by his official swooning. By swooning he satisfies after a fashion the Christian indignation over his high secular status, just as the woman's chastity and modesty are satisfied by her opposition. But as stated, with the woman it is something different from this ecclesiastical coquettishness.

XI[1] A 228   n.d., 1854

« 3176

[*]*In margin of 3175* (XI[1] A 228):

When I speak this way about the "clergyman" it is, of course, with the reservation that, after all, there can always be just as many honest men in this profession as in any other. The point is that they enter it *bona fide* and live in it *bona fide,* but the dubiousness is that such a profession should not be entered into in this sense of *bona fide.*

If the long robes did not promptly bring to mind the Pharisee, the official clergy, and all the ambiguity attached to them (and it is this very ambiguity which makes him analagous to the feminine nature), one could be tempted to find in him some symbolism of his belonging to a neuter sex, something of a hermaphrodite.

XI[1] A 229   n.d.

« 3177

In margin of 3175 (XI[1] A 228):

† In my opinion this meanness is so shocking and disgusting that if it would help a punishment should be placed on it. After all, the woman is by nature less free in the sex-relationship than man (that is why she is also called κατεξόχην: the sex, woman is the sex). But because the man is more free in this respect, it is so loathsome (ever so much worse and revolting than striking her or using physical force) to be ironical about her lesser freedom in the sex-relationship. This meanness in the upper classes corresponds to what appears in the lower classes as beating her with brute force, but, as always, something worse, as all sins become the higher we go up the social scale. The more refined classes take advantage of not having the crudeness of the

lower classes, but oh, their more refined sins are all the more malignant.

XI[1] A 230   n.d.

« 3178 *The Oath-bound Pastor*

If it can be shown that from a Christian point of view the state has no right to pay teachers of Christianity a salary, then the pastor, who is bound by oath[803] on the New Testament, is obliged to say: No, it does not help him at all that the state is willing. The oath makes the pastor accountable before God, directly to the New Testament.

XI[1] A 344   n.d., 1854

« 3179 *The Pastoral Oath*[804]

Seek first the kingdom of God[805]—this is Christianity. And the pastor is bound to this by oath on the New Testament.

Now we all know how things go in practical life, that it does not in the remotest way have the remotest resemblance to this: Seek *first* the kingdom of God. It takes the student four years to graduate, then he becomes a graduate. Now he has to wait four or five years before he gets appropriate seniority. Then he seeks. And finally he gets an appointment and a job—this is seeking the kingdom of God *first*.

Is not such an oath perjury, and would it not be far better to do away with it completely? Or is an oath which in no shape or manner means a thing more reliable than no oath?

Humanly speaking, in a certain sense we cannot call the pastor's oath a perjury. It is the same with this oath as with other oaths. When it is commonly accepted and mutually understood that an oath in a given situation means nothing, we do not regard it as perjury to take the oath even though one does not keep it. Such an oath is regarded as a formality. But can Christianity be served by such a thing? Is it not far better to let the oath drop out completely?

XI[1] A 389   n.d., 1854

« 3180 *The Clergyman*

When the candidate has become a public official, perhaps then his subsequent efforts will be a striving in the direction of: First the Kingdom of God.[806] A striving, this is the turn we would like to give the matter, for it is so difficult to control a striving.

Let us see now! "First the Kingdom of God." But does not the clergyman's whole activity rather follow this law: Money first of all, and then—. Whatever he involves himself with, it is: May I first ask for my money—and then.

Furthermore, if it is a matter of the clergyman's life being a striving toward New Testament Christianity, then advancement in the ecclesiastical establishment should proceed inversely. One would begin with 1,200 dollars and after being fifteen years, for example, in service, would get only 800, and soon the biggest and richest appointments would go to the beginners.

XI[1] A 390   n.d.,   1854

« 3181 *The Clergy*

If a comic poet were to come up with what clergymen in all seriousness regard as their task we would all burst out laughing.

Of all magnitudes you, O God, are the most troublesome, an enormous weight—as soon as you are present, along comes the storm, distress at sea, suffering—you know that very well yourself, you infinite love. That is why in love you suffer so much with the religious person, without thereby being changed yourself.

The task the clergy have assigned themselves is to apply God in such a way that he makes life easy; having anything to do with him makes life easy, gives pleasure, etc.

But no one laughs. Yet we would all laugh if someone announced that he would undertake to perform amputations, pull teeth, so it not only would not hurt but would be pure pleasure—yes, he merely lamented that he was not equally adroit at putting the leg back on again, for if he could he would know for sure that every man of means would indulge in the pleasure, the luxury, every day (as one now takes a bath, etc.) of having a leg amputated or a tooth extracted.

XI[1] A 417   n.d.,   1854

« 3182 *God's Word Must Be Proclaimed To the People The Medium (the Clergy)*

"The people" is always the health which is able to engender some good; what has amounted to something in the world and what derives from something which has amounted to something is generally already corrupted, for everything human is frail and the generations are quickly corrupted.

This, among many other reasons, is why God's word must be proclaimed before the people.

But to proclaim it there must, after all, be some men. These, then, are the medium through which God's word sounds to the people. This medium is the clergy.

Now it is easy to see that if this medium were entirely selfless, it would be perfect, for then God's word would almost spontaneously and directly sound to the people, since the medium would be free of all disturbing elements.

But the tragedy has always been and still is in the medium.

Catholicism correctly saw that it was good for the medium to belong as little as possible to this world. Therefore celibacy, poverty, asceticism, etc. That is absolutely right and is intended to remove selfishness from the medium. But what happens—Satan slips into the clergy and in spiritual arrogance it occurs to them to want to be something other than the medium, to be the intermediary authority between God and man and thus be repaid for what they temporarily renounced.

Protestantism sees this error. In order to preclude such spiritual arrogance it hits upon the idea that the clergy must be just like every-body else. Thus we get a completely secularized clergy: public officials, bigwigs, men with wives and families, just as trapped in all the tempo-ral nonsense as anyone else. And this is supposed to be the medium through which God's word should sound! Well, if this medium is intended to transmit sound, a mattress is also appropriate! No, such a clergy, such a medium, obstructs God's word or renders God's word sounding through it into something entirely different.

XI[1] A 532   n.d., 1854

« 3183 *A Protestant Clergyman*

That such a fellow should be a teacher of Christianity is just as ridiculous as to see a chest of drawers dance. The chest of drawers— well, as a chest of drawers it is a very respectable piece of furniture, I really am not depreciating the merits of a chest of drawers, but it does lack those very qualities which are necessary for dancing. It is the same with the Protestant clergyman in respect to being a teacher of Chris-tianity—he lacks all the very qualities and possesses all the opposites, is a husband, father, public official, status figure, a knight, wears flow-ing robes. —The chest of drawers considered as a chest of drawers is very respectable and creditable, but a chest of drawers is not cut out for dancing, and the clergyman is not suitable for being a teacher of Christianity.

XI[1] A 548   n.d., 1854

« 3184 *A Presumed Prescriptive Right*

It is quite amusing to see the shamelessness with which the official clergy, confronted with something arising out of the sects, knows how to call attention to the fact that it actually is a question of money. And this is universally accepted by the congregations—for the official clergy now has the prescriptive right to make a profit for itself.

But if profit with respect to religion is reprehensible, then the official clergy are much worse than the sect-makers, inasmuch as the official clergy have profit assured in a different way, and in addition also have the profit of honor and esteem.

XI[1] A 584   *n.d.*, 1854

« 3185 *"The Priest"*

As in so much of what Peer Degn[807] said, there is something typical in these lines also: "If you want fine sand, it will cost so much; if you want coarse sand, it will cost so much."

Basically, this explains the existence of the entire clerical official-dom.

In vain does God have it proclaimed that he is love, that everyone, unconditionally everyone, is able to address him directly, that God is very glad to have him do it.

In vain. This is too high for man; he cannot get it into his head; dares not believe it. Then "the priest" comes to his aid and sets things right, satisfies man's deep need to be fooled—Peer Degn was very accomplished in this. "The priest" introduces intermediate authorities and gradations, a whole caste of officials—and everywhere there is money to be paid. This, you see, man can get into his head. Now his soul finds peace and satisfaction, his mind is at rest, now for the first time he is perfectly sure that he has a God—and his certainty is proportional to how much he pays the clergyman. The average man never comprehends that Heaven's Majesty—if I may put it this way—sits and waits up in heaven for someone to address himself to him, almost mournful that no one wants to understand his love. "No," says Martin Frandsen, "that is a figment of the imagination, it can never be like that. It is difficult enough just to get to talk with the Chancellor, and he is only a human being—and then it is supposed to be so easy to get to talk to God! No, no, this is a figment of the imagination." But if the clergyman explains that it costs $100 and $10 to the priest, then Martin Frandsen says, "Well, now, this makes sense. Sure, it's a lot of money, but when a man has paid out $100 he can be sure that he is involved with God."

This is precisely what God wants to do away with, and this is precisely what man introduces, and in this respect it is the "priest" who satisfies man's deep need.

God in heaven may assuredly say with truth of the world of humans: *Mundus vult decipi.*[808]

XI² A 148   *n.d.*, 1854

« 3186 *That from the Christian Point of View the Life of "the Pastor" Is an Irregularity*

May 16

I suggest this not merely because his whole life cannot be said to resemble the imitation [*Efterfølgelse*] of Christ.

No, I allude especially to the fact that he is a government official. What nonsense, then, to proclaim a kingdom not of this world which wants to be of this world at any price.

And the fact that he is a governmental official is so fundamentally confusing, interferes so profoundly.

The common man, the people, always consider anything that is governmental (stamped by the state) as being better; it is better to be a royal hat maker than to be a pure and simple hat maker, etc., etc.: at every point social life is stamped by the state.

And now comes "the pastor." The fact that he is authorized by the crown gives him status in the eyes of the people; they believe that to be the maximum—the higher the rank, the more status, the more badges—how utterly nonsensical this kind of Christian proclamation is. The pastor stands and walks and lives and enjoys status by virtue of the very thing Christianity is diametrically opposed to.

XI² A 400   May 16, 1855

« 3187 *What We Call the Pastor Is the Unhappiest of All Persons*

May 17, 1855

It is often said that to be a pastor [*Præst*], especially a rural pastor, must be a most pleasant life.

From the other side there is frequently heard the cry that the clergy are the most ungodly of all hypocrites, etc.—and to that extent perhaps the most unhappy.

It is my opinion that to be what we understand by pastor is to be the unhappiest of persons.

For what is a pastor? A pastor is a man just as goodnatured and kindly as the rest of us—but no more, and the way it is nowadays, because he is pledged by oath to something as high as the New Testament, he brings his life into the most tormenting self-contradiction, bears his whole lifelong a conscience oppressed not by the past but by a constant present, from which death cannot free him, which he in death takes with him to the accounting in the next life.

Frightful punishment for the superficiality with which the human race has taken Christianity. Frightful! Because man in his void of spirit has deluded himself into thinking that being a Christian is something everybody is—therefore it is necessary to have these great numbers of clergy, and this is why the state creates these unhappy creatures by the thousand, these unhappy creatures who in the days of their youth get a wrong perspective of Christianity and as adults do not have the strength to tear themselves out of the error into which they have come —and now do the greatest harm in the name of Christianity, since more and more men are becoming increasingly doubtful of the pastor, that what he says is not his conviction but is something official, with the result that the pastor is more and more habituated to putting on a bold front. Thus society is demoralized at the deepest level with the aid of —the proclamation of Christianity.

XI² A 401   May 17, 1855

« 3188 *Brief Observations*

1

The atheist—and I

The atheist wants to get rid of "the priest," for in his shortsightedness and prejudice he believes that then we will also be rid of Christianity.

I want to get rid of "the priest"—in order that Christianity can emerge again; as long as there is "the priest" Christianity is an impossibility.

In his blind hatred of Christianity the atheist is sufficiently courteous to assume that from a Christian point of view the priest is justified. I see that the "priest" and the atheist are allies, except that the priest is the more dangerous enemy.

2

"The priest" as the boundary line

Thus do these millions of Christians in Christendom live: "The priest" or "the minister" is regarded as furnishing the superlative of what it is to be a Christian; a man is a Christian, then, within this boundary; it would perhaps even be regarded as presumptuous to want to be a better Christian than the clergyman.

No, anyone who imagines that being a Christian within the boundary line set by "the minister," that being a Christian by running along with the herd or in the operation set by "the minister" deceives only himself. Instead of playing at jumping hurdles inside the rail fence by jumping over a straw, a Christian from the earliest period of Christianity would immediately understand that, inasmuch as there has to be a criterion for the hurdle, the very first task is to jump over the very low rail fence "the clergyman" provides, and he would understand this to be the very first, the weakest and easiest beginning.

3

Where God builds a church, the devil builds a chapel

If this were true, the world we live in would almost be quite nice.

But it is not true; no, the devil builds churches and chapels where truth has suffered.

It is just one of the devil's tricks to get the rumor going that churches are God's buildings, which is just as sure as that clergymen are God's servants.

4

"Christendom's" striving toward the ideal

We laugh to see a man busily searching for his glasses—which are sitting on his nose.

But in its way Christendom's striving is more laughable.

The truth about the essentially Christian ideal is that it has existed; Christ has indeed lived, and the prototype has been portrayed. And this ideal relates to the single individual; only as a single individual can there be any question of striving toward it; and if the single individual is going to strive toward it he must, of course, turn in the direction of the ideal that has existed, turn back toward it—if he is actually to strive toward it.

Christendom has turned things around in such a way that the ideal for being a Christian and toward which one strives is a far-off goal in the infinite future—consequently, in its striving toward the ideal, Christendom turns its back on the true ideal, who has indeed lived, consequently, under the name of striving toward the ideal, strives away from the ideal. And in order that this striving toward that remote far-off-in-the-future ideal may amount to anything, all unite in order to strive with united effort, for then it will surely succeed—yes, it will surely succeed with everybody working together; whereas the truth is that only the single individual, every individual—but only as a single individual—can strive. "New courage!" Christendom shouts enthusiastically. "Let us strive together; it will surely succeed; just don't lose courage but strengthen our hearts with the thought that Christianity is perfectible, and that it advances. Therefore onward, onward toward that goal ahead of us, far off in the future!" —and from a Christian point of view the ideal has existed for 1800 years.

5

"Does Christianity not exist?"[809]

"It is, after all, pure nonsense to maintain that Christianity does not exist at all; the very fact that there are 1,000 teachers in Christianity is sufficient to disprove this nonsense: if there are 1,000 teachers of Christianity, Christianity must certainly exist."

Perhaps the same argument can be used to prove that the busybody has a lot of business, for, after all, he employs five secretaries, and if a person employs five secretaries he must certainly have a lot of business.

No, the existence of 1,000 teachers of Christianity proves that there are 1,000 job openings for teachers of Christianity, something I have never denied, no more than I doubt for a single moment that if there were 10,000 job openings, there would be 10,000 teachers of Christianity, which I doubt no more than I doubt that Christianity does not exist at all, and that the busybody has no business.

XI^3 B 197   *n.d.,* 1855

PAUL

« **3189**

Romans 4. Some have wondered why Paul, in accentuating Abraham[810] as an example of faith, did not rather take the moment in his life when he was about to sacrifice Isaac, but in my opinion it is entirely consistent with the whole spirit of Paul and the syllogistic implications of the passage to take the example of Sara's barrenness, for there absolutely everything was handed over to God, and in Paul's eyes all life outside of Christianity, Jewish as well as pagan, was just as barren.

II C 8   April 3, 1839

« **3190**

The Christian life has aphorisms with their own characteristic quality which falls outside the range of all esthetic qualifications—for example, Paul in Romans 1:1: ἀφωρισμένος εἰς εὐαγγέλιον.[811]

II A 396   April 23, 1839

« **3191 *Our Communion with Christ***

A Homily

on Romans:[812] "Neither angels, devils, ... "
Angels (Galatians 1:8)
Devils (Ephesians[813])
Things present
Things to come
Height
Depth
. . . . . Paul has named everything, but there is one thing he has not named—but he was, after all, an apostle of the Lord. We will name it: that not *we* ourselves. There is still one enemy.

III C 23   *n.d.*, 1840–41

« **3192 *Something about Devotional Eloquence***

The whole mistaken way in which we read the Bible—imagine Paul's apostolic energy loaded and weighted with 1800 years of erudi-

465

tion and scholarship. What a comical misunderstanding! How lacking in a primitive impression of Paul. Either what he has written is inspired or it is not; thus exegetical scholarship and collating are not the way by which we come closer to inspired writing.

A Paul, whose life rhythm has the quickest tempo, whose every moment is valuable, writes some lines to a congregation to give them momentum toward existing [*at existere*] in the faith—these lines, no longer urgent messages and beckoning announcements, are now perishing in the scholarship of 1800 years.

VI A 163   *n.d.*, 1845

« 3193

Was Paul a public official? No. Did he have a bread-and-butter job? No. Did he earn much money? No. Was he married and did he have children? No. Well, then Paul certainly was not an earnest man![814]

VIII[1] A 206   *n.d.*, 1847

« 3194

Whatever does not proceed from faith is sin, says Paul.[815] Thus in a certain sense the sin against the Holy Spirit becomes acting deliberately against one's conviction.

It is quite striking that if everything which does not proceed from faith is sin, then one would think that everything which proceeds from faith (subjective conviction) is not sin. This being the case, then in one sense sin would be Socratic ignorance[816]—that is, if a person can have so erroneous a conviction that his action objectively becomes sin. But otherwise Paul (just the opposite of Socrates) lays stress on consciousness. Sin is not ignorance but is doing what does not proceed from faith.

Here the point of conflict between Paul and Socrates would be that Socrates says it is impossible for a person really to have understood, grasped, perceived the good and then do the evil—for the proof that one has actually comprehended the good is precisely this, that understanding exercises such power over a person that he does it; otherwise the fact that a person does not do the good demonstrates that he has not understood it. This is pure intellectuality, from which Socrates does not emerge; he does not make room for the will, or room within which the will can stir and move.

X[1] A 392   *n.d.*, 1849

« 3195 *An Experiment in Crazy Comedy*

The apostle Paul examined in theology by a theological professor.

He is, of course, rejected; although it is not absolutely true, there is still some truth in the passage in the *Wolfenb. Fragments* (*Von dem Zwecke Jesu und seiner Jünger,*[817] para. 24, end): *Nun aber bekennt man* (in baptism) *eine Dreieinigkeit in Gott, eine Menschwerdung der anderen Person in Gott, und ein Haufen mehr andere Catechismus-Artikel dabey, worauf die ersten Christen und vielleicht die Apostel selbst zum Theil nicht würden haben zu antworten wissen.*[818] The untruth lies in the use of baptism, but otherwise it is true, particularly in relation to theology—yes, there are many questions in the catechism an apostle would not know how to answer.

X^1 A 401   *n.d.,* 1849

« 3196

How much easier and milder Christianity is when it is not a contending teaching but the relationship to Christians is already evident in the pastoral letters, where Paul simply portrays a Christian teacher's relationship to fellow Christians. Basically the task and the tone are therefore gently hortative.

But for one thing it must be noted that with respect to the few Christians at that time everything was in order, for they were true Christians or at least fairly so. Furthermore, the Christian Church itself was still such a small plant that it was a sect in the world, which does help in keeping alert.

But from the moment Christianity conquered *in the worldly sense* and all became Christians in the ridiculous manner which nowadays is jealously guarded by secular-ecclesiastic authorities—so that everyone is baptized as a child—from that moment on the prime polemical target must be the illusion that we are all Christians, and this polemical sighting must be sharper and sharper with each century that "established Christendom" stands, for with every century the illusion grows.

X^1 A 451   *n.d.,* 1849

« 3197

In I Corinthians 9:18 Paul says: My reward is that in my preaching I may present the gospel *free of charge;* consequently his wage is simply that he takes no payment. This is talk befitting an apostle.

X^2 A 41   *n.d.,* 1849

« **3198**

It is easy enough to defend the use of prudence in achieving something by appealing to Paul, who, after all, also used prudence. Well, let's take that. A life which has qualitatively and totally secured its own heterogeneity as madness (something, in fact, achieved by acting in total opposition to prudence), such a life can use prudence without any danger. But it is dangerous for a person not so distinguished to act prudentially, for then prudence makes capital of him *in toto.* Such a person has not secured for himself any heterogeneity (which, relative to Paul, is achieved only by acting decisively against reason at some time). Religious people do not think of this. Religious persons undistinguished in this way religiously defend acting prudentially by appealing to Paul, without noticing or wanting to notice that the "total madness" of Paul's life, that is, its dissimilarity with prudence, adequately safeguarded him, while their crumb of religiosity drowns in the total prudence of the world and the secular mentality.

x^2 A 441   *n.d.,* 1850

« 3199 *An Apostle—and a Pastor Today*

Paul's introduction to becoming an apostle was "not to confer with flesh and blood" (Galatians[819]). Nowadays a candidate uses a dozen years in which he scurries from Herod to Pilate[820] continually on errands in the category of conferring with flesh and blood—this is his introduction.

x^3 A 467   *n.d.,* 1850

« 3200 *The Dying Paul*

Legend tells us that when Paul was beheaded, his head still cried out the name of Christ three times.

This signified that his preaching essentially began with his death. It is traditional to say that in death the beloved's picture is found in the lover's heart—but Paul's concern was to proclaim the word.

I read this historical observation in Scriver.[821]

x^4 A 17   *n.d.,* 1851

« 3201 *The Extensive and the Intensive in the Proclamation of Christianity*

It is clear that a complete change, a world-change, has taken place in Christianity since the time when they diverted attention away from inward deepening leading to the development of character and directed it to external change, removal of the pressure of life, etc. The subsequent advance in the direction of this change has had the effect that Christianity hardly exists at all any more.[822]

Paul[823] writes, "Were you a slave when called? Never mind. But if you can gain your freedom, avail yourself of the opportunity." This is divine loftiness, genuinely Christian. But what justified the apostle in this infinite indifference to everything external? Very simple—his life was even more wretched than the slaves in that he lived a life of poverty and also of persecution[824] according to Christ's example. One is then justified in speaking this way; his speaking therefore becomes genuine loftiness and far different from the shameful talking of one who enjoys all the goods of life and then speaks this way to one who suffers.

This was Christianity; this is the way Christianity must really be served in order to be Christianity.

Then they knocked down what it means to be a Christian, and the rich and the powerful, who wanted to enjoy life—they too became Christians. And then—perhaps out of shame—a little was done for slaves and the poor etc.

This is the corrupting of Christianity.

People flounder around in all this; the rich and powerful Christians at times quote Paul on poverty! What insolence! Yes, if one himself lives in voluntary poverty as Paul did he can talk loftily about poverty.

Consequently one of two things: the Christian must either live in the same condition as the poor and wretched and subsequent elevation of spirit or, if being a Christian is going to be merged with the enjoyment of life, then much, much more must be done for the poor and the suffering.

If Christianity would have held continually to the intensive, if no one had been allowed to call himself a Christian unless his life expressed equality with the wretched (without making this the mark of the "extraordinary Christian" as in the Middle Ages), well, then Christianity would have continued to be the salt of the world instead of being frightfully diluted in these millions and millions of Christians and rendered unrecognizable through politicizing evaporation.

$$X^4 \text{ A } 541 \quad n.d., 1852$$

PERFECTIBILITY

« 3202

... But a man who begins with a revelation and the Savior's dictation can hope for perfectibility only in an *inessential* way; he must rather fear that in the sequence of time this First will lose the vividness and intensity it had before; but if such a person dares hope *essentially* for perfectibility, this, then, is blasphemy. Admittedly Adler declares that he does not himself regard those words in the preface and the sermons this way, but (if he really believes what the preface says) how does he dare get so involved in such accommodation as to say: "even if my sermons and studies may be regarded merely as a child's first lisping, babbling, imperfect voice" and to get involved in such a way that "he really believes that the Word witnesses that an event has taken place." Consequently when his solemn pronouncement about Jesus having commanded him to write down the words does not get him a hearing, he wants to take up with the person who does what in Adler's eyes (if he really believes what the preface says) must be the most dreadful presumption—to regard it as an infant's babbling. Or have the authorities probably given the affair the turn, have the authorities so missed the point that they have gone ahead and regarded the whole performance to be Adler's and now esthetically ask him to admit that it was an imperfect something. By no means, they have quite properly argued *e concessis*. Where Adler got this about "an infant's babbling voice" is incomprehensible. In the preface to the sermons it is not Adler's voice which is heard at all; it is, in fact, Jesus who dictates to Adler's pen. Adler's reply, then, has meaning only when it is presupposed that the whole preface is fiction and mental derangement; thus Adler's first attempt, his invention of a revelation, must be regarded as an infant's babbling voice. What may we hope for Adler's continued efforts in the future; dare we hope for better work the next time he composes a revelation. But in any case the preface to the sermons must be withdrawn and retracted as solemnly as possible.

Adler's *hope of his perfectibility essentially implies the retraction of the preface and of the sermons since it defines both parts as his own production*. ...[825]

VII² B 235, pp. 113–14   *n.d.,* 1846–47

« 3203

But now what if the authorities had asked him if he would admit that he had been in a rapturous and confused state of mind when he wrote the preface and the sermons. And if one has begun in a rapturous state, it can be altogether proper to hope for a certain perfectibility,* to hope, was Adler himself said, "that by adapting and calmly developing the ideas over a period of time I will be able to allow the Christian content to unfold in a more appropriate form and more in accordance with the specific words of Holy Scripture." Well, if one has begun in a rapturous and confused condition—but in that case one has not, after all, begun with the plainest and clearest of all, a revelation, with Jesus himself dictating what one is to write down. Even in strictly human endeavors it holds true for all competent men that the first is the best—the decision made in enthusiasm is the best, first love is the best, likewise the dialectically first estimate in a case. Only for confused men is it true that they first of all come staggering through the door like a drunk man—and at times it may very well happen that some good may come out of it all when they gradually sober up. But in that case the first is not something which should be allowed to stand but, on the contrary, should be retracted.

In margin: *Note. The whole matter of Adler's perfectibility is just another one of those unhappy residues of the colleges. If only Adler had been a layman, for it is one of his various misfortunes that his fervor has no relationship to his poor theological capacities. Christianity is a revelation—1700 years later they really begin to develop the theory that it must be perfectible—after all, the many hundred years do amount to something; but to experience a revelation in his own life and then to go through this exegetical course concerning what one has himself experienced—that is really comical.[826]

VII² B 257:12, p. 288 *n.d.,* 1846–47

« 3204

But in comparison with a modern theological confusion and *in specie* the Hegelian confusion of concepts, the Adlerian confusion has a purely comic value. It is now about 1800 years since Christianity came into the world—as a revelation, and about as long since Paul declared himself called by a revelation to spread Christianity. But then 1600 or 1700 years later there arose an exegetical and dogmatic wisdom which understood all this differently. It knew how to explain a revelation as an inner fact, as incantation, ethusiasm, possession—as the spontaneous and immediate. The next discovery was the theory of perfectibility, that a revealed teaching is perfectible. Well, now, there is always a little excuse in the great distance and the significant change in the world since that time. It is no longer possible to get hold of Paul and confront him with the interpretation of his own words by such an exegesis and dogmatics, and on the other hand the exegetes and dogmaticians do not themselves maintain that they have had a revelation. It is different with Magister A.! In his own life to have gone through a world-historical cycle—to receive a revelation to begin with, then for two years to explain exegetically what a revelation is (something no one could understand better than he), and then two years later to have a full-blown theory of the perfectibility of the teaching* revealed to him (for that which Christ has dictated to him was still imperfect)—such an originality certainly has never been heard of before!

*(i.e., dictated to him, according to his own declaration, by Christ or written down by him at Christ's command).[827]

IX B 5: 2 y   *n.d.*, 1848

« 3205 *"In the Fullness of Time"*[828]

What does this mean? It means that when the human race had reached the point that from then on "spirit" could be made the criterion: then Christianity came.

There the matter must rest. But in order to get rid of Christianity, the idea was invented of making Christianity into doctrine in the historical sense and of regarding the history[829] (like the history of Platonic philosophy) of this doctrine as important—yes, it has even been thought that this doctrine is perfectible! Splendid! Let us just get going with this perfectibility and we will easily abolish Christianity completely. And this is really what man wants—but it is done hypocritically under the name of the perfectibility of Christianity. If it is the death of Christianity they want, this is always done best (which has happened) under the name of protecting it, defending it, perfecting it. Incidentally, this constitutes an indirect proof of the tremendous power of Christianity—that this dangerous attack is always made under the guise of defending, protecting, perfecting it. In this way the whole situation is altered, and it looks as if it were the true Christians who betrayed, attacked, and corrupted it.

X[4] A 522   *n.d.*, 1852

« 3206 *Upside Down*

Take a solid, scholarly presentation of the history[830] of Christianity—I agree with all of it, I am even learning something, for the author is more learned than I am, but there is one thing I do not agree with: he explains everything in such a way that he regards regression as an advance.[831]

Take a circle—someone more sharp-eyed than I shows me that here is a bend, consequently an approximation of a polygon, and the approximation increases, for there are steadily more and more bends. I agree wholeheartedly with him, but I disagree on one point—that for a circle to become a polygon is an advance. It is the same with Christianity's presumed perfectibility and its becoming perfect.

X^5 A 100   *n.d.*, 1853

« 3207 *Epigram*

I

Christianity Is Perfectible—It Goes Forward!—
Now the Consummation Has Been Reached!

What Christianity presents as the ideal, that Christians are a priesthood of believers—whether or not it was achieved in apostolic days—has now been achieved, particularly in Protestantism, particularly in Denmark.

If what is now called a priest is what a priest truly is—well, then we are are all priests.[832]

II

We Are All Priests!

When paganism disintegrated, it was inconceivable that one priest could see another without bursting into laughter. Now the situation is such that it is inconceivable that a clergyman can see a layman or a layman a clergyman without bursting into laughter—but we are indeed all priests!

X^5 A 111   *n.d.*, 1853

« 3208 Christianity Is Perfectible

See, there the whole thing went to pieces, there triumphed rascality, which became more and more unrestrained.

We have abolished Christianity, but note well the rascality of doing it (not in mutiny against Christianity) with the help of—its perfectibility.[833]

XI^1 A 246   *n.d.*, 1854

« 3209 *Christendom*

Instead of all this shameless rubbish which—after first reducing Christianity to a simple historical phenomenon (O, the high treason of it!) then hit upon the idea that Christianity is perfectible—ah, yes, just as if, when a drop of attar of roses falls into the ocean, the ocean would insist that the addition was a perfecting process—that progress is being made (impudent affrontery)—not at all, but just as the ocean in relation to that drop, so the world in relation to Christianity is only able to devour it, corrupt it.

Instead of all this shameless rubbish, the truth is this: Christendom is the fall from Christianity.

What is deceptive is that a fall or falling away is thought of as involving a solemn, genuine renouncing of Christianity. O, dear friend, the world is not that honorable and good, not at all; the lie is its element, and therefore the fall is in the form of a lie, the fall is the lie of apparently being that [which is denied].

I have pointed out above [i.e., xi^1 A 551] that every demoralization is related to something which was sound and healthy—therefore, since Christianity is the truth, demoralization goes in the direction of a lie. After asceticism comes—not simple sensuality, but unnatural lusts—and after Christianity is introduced as truth comes—not simple paganism—no, then comes the lie of being Christian, paganism refined by dishonestly having appropriated one side of essential Christianity in an epicurean way to the advantage of this life, and this falsification is prettied up to be Christianity.

Christendom is the fall from Christianity—and a fall so deep that it would have been far better to have fallen by directly and honorably renouncing Christianity. And the very fact that the fall is so deep is deceptive, just as the most dangerous crimes deceptively look like virtues—the first thing that must be done is to make it apparent that they are crimes.

Christendom is the fall from Christianity. The few better Christians included are so far from being beneficial that they rather do harm since they have not had the energy and character to make the true state of affairs apparent and to risk their lives. They are therefore useless—they are merely taken up in the counting, just like ten policemen wearing their badges at a riot of 10,000 people—it does not help; strictly speaking, they merely add to the number, and thus if the number of rioters were to be scrupulously given, it would have to be said that there were 10,010. But there is a difference in that the policeman, after all, is unable to resist, but every Christian is able to extricate himself from Christendom's falsities, demonstrating to the uttermost, and if he does not, then it is quite in order to count him along in corruption's mob.

XI^1 A 552   n.d., 1854

« 3210 *The Supposed Epochs in Christendom*

Since New Testament Christianity has been made into simple history and since the notion has been developed that Christianity is perfectible, the notion that there have been different epochs followed as a matter of course. New Testament Christianity was the epoch of the Son, and now we stand before—the epoch of the Spirit!

No, no, no! Christianity in the New Testament is Christianity. And Christianity is life's final examination. The test is that God desires to be loved. But the *summa summarum* of it all is that Christendom is to be considered to have flunked the examination *in corpore*.

In retaliation Christendom has been inexhaustible in inventing nonsense and tricks.

An epoch of the Spirit! Any kind of meaningful talk about this should begin with the apostles. But to have it begin later, during the progress of Christendom—well, there we have it, the progress of Christendom—from a Christian point of view there is absolutely no meaning in talking about any progress from generation to generation. Every generation begins at the beginning; the final examination is the same. And when the generation is buried, eternity looks to see how many there were in it who took the divinely ordered final examination. And then the next generation can begin.

But man's trick is always to manage to introduce the numerical in order to hide himself in numbers. The individual hides by taking refuge in the crowd of contemporaries, the contemporary generation. And to hide still better each generation hides in the linear series of generations. Always the coward, when a man is thus hidden, when he feels himself safely concealed, he becomes brash, forward, and impudent enough to talk about the progress of Christianity, about a new epoch—the epoch of the Spirit. This certainly does look as if it resembled Spirit: this most cowardly flocking together in shoals of herring or herds of animals, impersonality from first to last. If this period, our age, is supposed to be the age of Spirit, then it must get its name (*ad modum lucus a non lucendo*) from being entirely devoid of spirit; thus the age of spirit comes to be the one distinguished by being totally devoid of spirit. Among all the millions who constitute the public, there is not a single one who has the courage to become involved with God all by himself alone; few have even an idea of anything like this—and this bunch is supposed to be the age of Spirit.

XI² A 38   *n.d.,* 1854

« 3211 *Children and Women—the Man—Christian Earnestness*

Christianity is earnestness. Obviously therefore the criterion is applied to the man; the Christian requirement is related to the man, to God's very conception of what this means; the man is the human.

But everyone who has the slightest practical experience in life, in the commercial world, knows that whenever anyone wants to sneak out of something the tactic is to bring in women and children.

Here is a new explanation of the old theme, how Christianity, by an inversion which men like to call perfectibility, has become the very opposite of what it was originally.

Christianity, so it goes, certainly is for human beings; a child certainly is also a human being—ergo the child is the criterion of what Christianity is.

This is now a lie of such proportions that it is downright unprincipled to bring up a child in Christianity, for the child cannot possibly appropriate to himself what Christianity really is (how can the child have any conception of original sin when it is brought up to regard father and mother as benefactors, to thank them for the great blessing of having come into existence, etc.?). Consequently we must *either* make Christianity into something other than what it is in order to enable the child to appropriate it (but have we the right to fool the child in the name of teaching?) or the child itself alters Christianity because it cannot do otherwise (but have we the right to give the child occasion to become entrenched in these fancies, and have we the right to do it in the name of teaching and instructing?).

No, the whole business about the child in relation to Christianity is a swindle. Just as in the commercial world, for example, when the authorities come looking for the man, he manages to sneak away and bring in the wife and children, who are supposed to touch and soften the authorities, so Christendom's more recent history is this swindle of the man sneaking away from Christianity, getting it made into something for children and women. And when it is done and religion has become all-day suckers, the man comes home, the sneak, and licks the sucker, too, and talks about religion, Christianity, as being especially for children and women.

What insolence, and what a loathesome lie—that religion is something for women and chilren, presumably because its task is too easy for the strong, for the man! Well, thanks a lot, especially for the sort of men around nowadays!

No, religion, Christianity, is an ideality, a task, under which the greatest ideality of what it is to be man must almost collapse. That is what Christianity was originally. It came out of the Orient. What was the relationship there? There the man was the human; women and children were almost a kind of domesticated animal. But just as the whole world-historical process is a masterstroke of botching God's whole design, it was reserved for romantic Protestant Christendom to make children and women "the human" and the man zero. I foresee the attainment of perfectibility in the form of polyandry, the counterpart of the earlier polygamy. This alteration where children and women have become "the human" has also altered Christianity to the exact opposite of the original; it has become sheer gift—it was sheer task.

$$XI^2 \text{ A } 187 \quad n.d., 1854$$

« **3212** *The method must be changed;*
            for the truth is not that Christianly there is progress
            (the method used up to now fits this assumption),
            but the truth is that Christianly there is retrogres-
            sion—consequently the method must be changed.

Some place in a recent author (Böhringer,[834] I think) I have read some remark like the following. The discussion is about one of the critical points in the history of the Christian Church, and the writer says: There was only one of two things for the Church to do here: either it must straightforwardly declare itself not to be the Christian Church (but this, indeed, would be suicide), or it must keep its wits about it and insist that it is the true Christian Church.

So it would be suicide—yes, in truth a suicide, yet a God-pleasing act that there still is sufficient truth to do away with itself this way in order to make room for truth instead of suffocating truth by blanketing it with its bestial propagation which insolently pretends to be Christianity.

But the Church had neither the courage nor the truth for this, for this heroic suicide—it preferred to slay Christianity with its lie.

But the very thing which the writer casually dismisses as preposterous, something the Church could not dream of doing, that is the very thing that ought to be done.

The method must be changed. Instead of the general lie that Christianity is perfectible (which completely denies Christianity and makes an outright fool of God), instead of the insolence which thinks it is going farther, instead of the slyness and cunning which, no less insolent, stops at nothing in order to hide the truth about the retrogression of Christianity—instead of all that, in the future an admission must be made, each generation must make its own admission, in order thus to relate to Christianity.

XI² A 325   n.d., 1854

« 3213   *That Christianity has not entered the world—which "Christendom" expresses in its slang in this way: Christianity is perfectible; it progresses.*

Think of the beginning: "the apostle"—and it is high time and of great importance, especially in Protestantism, that a word be said about the apostle in order, if possible, to counteract the confusion that Luther has occasioned in his justifiable zeal against malpractice—and yet not justified—by turning the matter in such a way that it becomes the disciple who decides what Christianity is, not the master, not Christ but Paul, something that in the foolish jargon of Christendom has not been called a reduction of Christianity—there would be some meaning in that—but, meaninglessly, has been called a forward step.

The apostle obviously is moved by human concern. In his joy and enthusiasm over Christianity he wants to make Christians of as many as possible, the more the better, and therefore perhaps is a little flexible about what it means to be Christian. In the next place, struggling with such high seas as Christianity did at the beginning, with the opposition of the whole world, the apostle in human concern perhaps feels that there is a need for the Christian cause to be strengthened by more people becoming Christians—and therefore, as he inflexibly fights against the world, he is a little flexible about what it means to be a Christian.

Thus in a very short time—triumph, triumph, triumph! —Perhaps 30 to 40,000 Christians.

With dialectical accuracy it may be said that now Christianity is actually lost. One apostle cannot control 30 to 40,000. Here is the first germ of Christians-in-name, the ruin of all Christianity.

The result is inevitable. The human aggregate of "Christians" gets to be a kind of a power directly opposite to the apostle. He who does not fear the whole world, does not retreat a hair's breadth before the opposition of all paganism and Judaism, has created here a force which becomes dangerous to himself and to Christianity; indeed, he himself has agreed that these thousands are Christians.

Now it comes. It soon becomes obvious that these 30 to 40,000 Christians have not exactly intended to comply with Christianity's unconditioned demands; it is not so easy to become a Christian as it is to accept the name of Christian, even if there is still mortal danger bound up with the name, but there are also the enthusiasm of risks and perils and an apostle's power to grip men in a mood—and yet they have been allowed to call themselves Christians.

Here it is. The apostle perhaps does not even have the courage of the idea to drop them; in a way they are his own work—and already the human aggregate exercises its power; God's will and his Word, the prototype's, no longer unconditionally decide what Christianity is, not for the apostle himself, rather for the apostle in relation to the human aggregate of "Christians," but the human aggregate exercises an influence.

Some examples. "The prototype" (which for him is always the one) teaches and expresses the single state. If millions X trillions, like [Gert] Bundtmager in *The Political Tinker*, [835] "are unable to endure it" and do not want to be Christians, he does not alter a jot; for him millions X trillions do not exist at all, something The Society of the Lost, the public, the very honorable cultured public, naturally never gets into its statistic-filled head. "The apostle," however, who does not retreat before all paganism and Judaism, has directly in front of him a force, produced by him, which becomes dangerous to him: 30 to 40,000 "Christians"—who are unable, at least some of them, to commit themselves unconditionally. And yet they are, after all, Christians! Here it is. They have been allowed to call themselves Christians, there has been joy over the mounting number, and now comes the bill for the joy, now the number exercises its power. The apostle cannot make up his mind to drop them. Thus we already have here the sophistry of turning the matter in such a way that if someone who has gotten permission to assume the name of Christian later proves not to will entirely as Christianity wills, he still has permission to call himself Christian, and the dubious character of the thing comes to light; you see that there are many among the Christians who are not willing to accept this or that and who still are Christians, ergo, it can not be Christianity. It is still true: if he will not accept it, then he is not Christian.

But the human aggregate of "Christians" exercises its power over the apostle; he gives in: After all, "it is better to marry than to burn."[836] It is better, for to burn is something unpleasant; so it is better to marry, in a pinch it is better to marry. It is like the craving to eat strawberries during a cholera epidemic, to which the physician may say, "It is not good to eat strawberries." "Yes, but we would like to. Please, may we not eat strawberries." "Well, in a pinch eat them, but eat them without cream; it would be best not to eat strawberries, but in a pinch it is better to eat them without cream than with." This is not Christ's proclamation of Christianity. His unconditioned proclamation (as in Matthew 5:28: "Everyone who looks at a women lustfully has already committed adultery with her in his heart") does not really concede in the remotest way a consultative voice to the immediacy of human nature, does not really change a jot for its sake; on the contrary it is precisely this which he, in a rescue (so that man may become spirit), wants to slay; he does not tolerate a syllable of reasoning such as this: I cannot restrain my lust; ergo, to satisfy it in this human, most inoffensive manner gets to be Christianity. No, this reasoning, containing the seeds of the destruction of Christianity, this reasoning to him is scandalous, the impulse of Satan, just as Peter's friendly advice[837] to spare himself and the others was to him scandalous, the impulse of Satan. The apostle's proclamation, however, made a concession to the human aggregate. The consequences will appear in the course of centuries, when, in consideration of the millions of Christians who find it most agreeable to marry, it will be discovered that true Christianity, the only thing pleasing to God, is to get married. The more often the better. When that time comes, Christianity will have won a total victory: Christians will be produced by the millions, the consumption of clergymen will be enormous, we will have Christian kingdoms, countries, Christian houses of prostitution—in short, all will be Christian, a Christian world, and velvet-clad pork peddlers or, as I was about to say, cross-bearers, to steer Christ's Church as oath-sworn teachers in Christendom.

Another example. "Use a little wine for the sake of your stomach," Paul writes to Timothy (I Timothy 5:23). Strictly speaking, this is not Christ's proclamation of Christianity, comes out of another view of life, does not have the passion of the master's proclamation, is not: "Hate yourself; if your right hand tempts you, cut it off," etc. No one, unless he deliberately wants to, can misunderstand me, as if I did not show the apostle the honor due him, something no one does more willingly or promptly than I. No, but the observation is true. I am like a person who, with scarcely a piece of dry bread in his house, for once sits down to dinner in a prosperous middle-class hotel, and the hostess, who once had dined at Court, says to him, "Isn't this just like the food at the royal table?" And he answers: "The food is excellent, and for one who himself scarcely has a piece of dry bread in the house, it is, of course, a royal banquet, but it is not the same as the food served at the royal court." And so it is with my observation (which is so extremely necessary, particularly in Protestantism, because all Christendom's knavish tricks are connected with a continued effort, under the name of progress, of getting rid of the master and taking one's stand with the disciple, and then taking advantage of the fact that the apostle, who personally did not compromise, gave in a little, and while perfecting Christianity, threw Christianity away completely, turning it upside down, getting it to be just the opposite of what it is in the Christian proclamation)—my observation that the apostle's proclamation in the quoted examples does not have the passion of the unconditioned, as the master's did.

But examples, incidentally, are not necessary, for nothing is easier to see than that when one hastily gets perhaps 30 to 40,000 "Christians," the human aggregate is already overwhelming, that if one does not immediately resolve to dump just about the whole aggregate again, the result will be that these thousands become a force which restamps Christianity, because the apostle, the teacher, who has plenty of courage over against paganism and Judaism, does not have courage to dump them. What Christianity is the Christians must certainly know; but nowadays it is not maintained rigorously enough to prevent Christians-in-name-only from slipping in; thus eventually (thanks to the perseverance of the enterprising oath-bound ones) in the course of centuries the Christians-in-name-only, the battalions of them, the prodigious human aggregate, will decide what Christianity is, and what they call Christianity will be declared to be true Christianity—otherwise the preacher-band (*ad modum* the gypsy-band) will not be able to live by the thousands with families.

What helped Christianity at first was the enormous opposition from without, having to fight in a life and death struggle with a whole world. Yet this also contributed at the outset to giving Christianity a wrong stance by diverting attention from the fact that Christianity intrinsically is a religion of suffering, and it came to seem almost as if the world's opposition were the sole cause of the sufferings, and in this way Christianity almost adopted the tactics of a political power, which in the course of centuries recurs and becomes the dominant policy.

*   *

Only when a person immoveably maintains that earnestness is that *he* become Christian, that this is his task for his whole life, that all his activity on behalf of others' becoming Christian is only part of his own becoming Christian—only then can a person be related to the unconditioned. As soon as he thinks: Now I am a Christian and my task is to make Christians of others—Christianity is lost. He insists it is unavoidable, he gets busy, and with human gladness he will rejoice over the thought of having won—think of it!—thousands for Christianity. Here it is again! To catch men for Christianity is not like catching birds or fish—if you have caught them, the matter is finished. But beware of these thousands! If you have allowed them to call themselves Christians, perhaps rejoicing over the thought of their great number, you will see that it becomes the ruination of Christianity. Probably you yourself do not have the courage to dismiss them when the implications of their being Christians become clear. Then they will take the power away from both you and Christianity and will restamp Christianity.

XI^3 B 175   *n.d.*, 1855

PERSON, PERSONALITY

« 3214

Actually it is the conscience which constitutes a personality; personality is an individual determinateness confirmed by being known by God in the possibility of conscience. The conscience may sleep, but the possibility of it is constitutive.[838] Otherwise the determinateness would be a transitory feature. Not even the consciousness of the determinateness, self-consciousness, is constitutive, inasmuch as it is only the relationship in which the determinateness relates itself to itself; whereas God's shared knowledge [*Guds Samviden*] is the stabilization, the confirmation.

VII[1] A 10   n.d., 1846

« 3215

Finally all purely human qualifications are abolished.[839] Yesterday Pastor Visby,[840] in reading the lists of births and deaths within Our Savior's Parish, stated that the number of dead was so and so large, but that the number was not entirely reliable since it referred only to the ones "buried." How inhuman to identify dying with being buried! No wonder that poor people are so concerned about being buried! Suppose that among those listening to the sermon there was a poor man who (according to what Visby stated, that the dead did not include those buried by the welfare department) could not expect to be buried, that is (O inhumanity), to die. And what a parody that Visby in his sermon, in which he garrulously went to extremes to individualize his New Year's greetings (something like the cards one buys: Greetings to Father, Mother, Brother-in-law, Son, Daughter, to a Twenty-Four-Year-Old, a Fifty-Year-Old, etc.) spoke also of those who probably would not celebrate the next New Year's Day, that is, would die during the coming year, but did not draw the distinction between those who would die and those who would be buried during the year just beginning.

X[1] A 2   January 2, 1849

« **3216**

Curious—the use of the word *personal* to signify an impertinent utterance. So far removed are we from the personal (and yet it is the secret of all existence) that the personal, speaking personally to a person, is "being personal"—that is, an insult.[841]

X^1 A 18   *n.d.*, 1849

« **3217**

[*In margin:* Martensen]

It is mighty fine nonsense that Martensen prattles somewhere in his *Dogmatics*.[842] saying that even if the apostles' writings were anonymous, we would still recognize their divine character, their qualitative difference from all other writings.

Here we have heresy, without Martensen's being aware of it. The divine, therefore, is supposed to be directly recognizable,[843] after all.

No, the divine has everywhere a paradoxical recognizability.

An apostle's tactic is not this—to propound a teaching—and thus the rest of us recognize that the teaching is divine. No, an apostle goes among the people with his teaching and says: This teaching is from God. That puts a stop to all intellectual deliberations and it now depends on whether the apostle carries through the consequences of this step.

But nowadays, for God knows how many years, the world has been completely weaned from achieving "actuality" at all or perceiving an actual personality. Everywhere sheer illusion, which takes all attention away from personality. Sometimes it is the public, sometimes the press, sometimes science and scholarship, sometimes speculation, etc. It is always, as it is called, "the cause"—in any case there is no person, and in every case this way of doing battle was perhaps chosen because there is no cause.

In relation to everything divine, there is always the paradox,[844] and that is why there always needs to be this personality who by affirming that it is divine, by imperatively forcing himself in among actual men, forces them into a decision.

I know no man of whom it is in the strictest sense true that his life has achieved actuality. There is a deceptive appearance, but on closer inspection hundreds of illusions are discernible, with the result that he does not exist altogether personally, that actuality cannot get hold of him altogether personally. No one says: *I.* One person talks in the name of the century, one in the name of the public, one in the name of science, one by virtue of his office, and everywhere their lives are guaranteed by the "tradition" that "others," "the others," are doing the same thing.

The majority in our time will, I dare say, quite *bona fide* be of the opinion that an apostle—if the art of printing had been invented at that time—could just as well have worked through the press, published his *"Ideas and Maxims"* etc., and himself lived as a regular man of letters, as hidden as possible, and above all he would not have perpetrated such an extravagance as I have by talking with people on the streets and avenues. Alas, and my bit of extravagance is, of course, but an infinitely weak and imperfect remote intimation of the apostolic extravagance.

x^1 A 628   *n.d.*, 1849

« **3218** *Luther*

Here the consequences of not being dialectical are apparent. In a sermon Luther[845] inveighs most vigorously against the faith which looks to the person[846] instead of to the Word; true faith looks to the Word, no matter who the person is.

Well and good in the relation between man and man, but in other respects Christianity is abolished by this theory. Then we get a doctrine or teaching in the ordinary sense in which the teaching is more than the teacher instead of Christianity's being a paradox and that the important point is the person. Why, I wonder, does Paul[847] so zealously insist that he is apostle οὐκ ἀπ' ἀνθρώπων οὐδὲ δι' ἀνθρώπων except to show the heterogeneity which, again, is the authority. In another connection Paul[848] quite consistently abandons this distinction of his when it is a matter of setting forth the person of Christ, as when he declaims against the practice of some who call themselves followers of Peter, others of Apollo, others of Paul, etc., instead of all being followers of Christ.

On the whole this is again the paradoxical heterogeneity of Christianity from all teachings or theories in the scientific-scholarly sense—it posits authority. A philosophy with authority is nonsense. For a philosopher extends no further than his teachings. If I can show that his teachings are self-contradictory, faulty, etc., he has no significance. The paradox is that personality is above doctrine or teaching. Therefore it is nonsense for a philosopher to require faith.

x^2 A 312   *n.d.*, 1849

« 3219 *To Have a Cause—the Objective: Hypocrisy*

It has occurred to me that here again there is something hypocritical in all the talk about having a cause, being an earnest man who has a cause, etc.

Indeed! The fact is that no one in our day dares to be a person. The one is so afraid of "the others"[849] that he does not dare to be an *I*—that is, no one dares to be an *I*.[850] Fear of men is dominant; indeed, as antiquity has already declared (Aristotle[851] somewhere in *Politics* or *Ethics*): Tyranny and democracy hate each other just as the one potter hates another—that is, it is the same form of government, only in tyranny one is the tyrant, in democracy, the masses.

But back to the matter of having a cause. From fear of the others, one dares not be an *I* and therefore strives to become an impersonal something, a cause, the cause, a principle, and the like.

This again has led to anonymity. In a setting as limited as the Danish, anonymity is almost necessary if envy and the tyranny of the masses are not to be set in motion all too powerfully.

Everything tends toward the abolishing of personality, but naturally it takes place in the hypocritical fiction that this is, of course, a great step forward, that this is quite another kind of earnestness than when we are *I*'s and personality.

How hypocritical! No, it is cowardice, and moreover it is whimpering and whining in order always to manage to be many—and one never dares to be alone, never dares to be an *I*. But if it is a "cause," then there are many right away—and there is protection first of all against the danger we fear most in our wretched, wretched, demoralized age —to be alone, to be a solitary *I*.

XI¹ A 51   *n.d.*, 1854

« 3220 *Officialdom*

Nothing, nothing, nothing, no error, no crime, is God so unconditionally against as everything that is official. Why? Because the official is the impersonal,[852] and therefore the deepest insult to offer a personality.

Take a feeble analogy: a woman will put up with a defect in her beloved, his weaknesses, however ineptly he expresses his feelings—if only it is personal and primitive. But one thing arouses her profound indignation, one thing she feels as the deepest insult, one thing she never forgives—even though it be executed with ever so much virtuosity and expertness—the hint that she is loved officially, that it is the official thing to do. Perhaps a virtuoso is able to fool her so that she never finds out, but—well, after all it was only an illustration, for no virtuoso or expert ever fools God—if she discovers it, she never forgives it.

XI^1 A 97 *n.d.*, 1854

« 3221 *The System*

Personality is aristocratic—the system is a plebian invention; by means of the system (that omnibus) everyone comes along.

That is why they always say (in the human thieves' slang which always talks a lot of nonsense): He was only a personality; he did not have any system—that is, they make the inferior the superior.

XI^1 A 341 *n.d.*, 1854

« 3222 *The Going Rate or the Market Price of Men*

When the National Pension Fund[853] (*ad usus publicos*) gets going, it would be entirely proper to list once every month the going rate or the market price of men: the government offers so much; the National Fund, so much.

XI^1 A 354 *n.d.*, 1854

« 3223

The proclamation of official Christianity is every proclamation which is by virtue of and in the character of anything else than the personal, the purely personal, the personal conviction of the one who proclaims

When the one who proclaims is in the service of the state, a royal office-holder, we have official proclamation, an ambiguity about whether he is teaching the doctrine, whether everything he has to say is in the capacity and power of being a public official or whether it is his personal conviction, for which he offers his personal existence as security.

And since Christianity is precisely the personal and entered into the world for this very reason—to introduce "personality, being a person," to put an end to all abstractions, ambiguities, hoaxes, impersonalities, in which, according to Christianity, evil has its very home, it is readily apparent that the official proclamation of Christianity does away with Christianity.

Every man shrinks from becoming personality, from standing face to face with the others as a personality; he shrinks from it because he knows that doing so makes it possible for the others to take aim at him. We shrink from being revealed; therefore we live, if not in utter darkness, then in twilight, hoaxes, the impersonal. But Christianity, which knows the truth, knows that it means: revelation. That is why Christianity points so decisively at being a personality. And that is again why an impersonal proclamation is the abolition of Christianity. It is its abolition and, of course, the most dangerous; it takes place in the name of proclaiming and spreading Christianity, just as Christianity's retrogression became most dangerous when men discovered that Christianity was perfectible, and the retrogression, the retreat, was covered up by: Christianity is progressing, Christianity is perfectible—in one sense such an expertly concealed retreat that neither Xenophon's nor Moreau's retreat[854] can stand comparison.

XI[1] A 393   n.d., 1854

« 3224 *Ventriloquism*

It occurs to me that mankind would be mighty happy if it managed to find a way for everyone to be a virtuoso in ventriloquism—how satisfied we would be with anonymity!

As a matter of fact, the inventions which really please mankind are either tinged with the rebellion of the race against God (the tower of Babel, railroads, mass-mindedness) or, if they are related to the individual, they are inventions which satisfy his boyishness.

Yes, school boys find great sport in being able to say something without the teacher's being able to discover who said it.

Boyishness is related to the impersonal, and it is impersonality which pleases man—that is, personally being impersonal, being a person but without any danger or responsibility,[855] being an ill-tempered, malicious person perhaps, venting all one's spite—but anonymously or by ventriloquism.

And a man's salvation lies precisely in his becoming a person. Yes, this rule could be formulated: One who becomes a personality, one who succeeds in coming that far, or who comes that far, is ordinarily saved. Why? Because he is so illuminated that he cannot hide from himself—yes, illuminated as if he were transparent.[856] The municipality is already of the opinion that gas-illumination at night helps to prevent a lot of crime because light frightens crime away. Consider, then, the piercing illumination of being personality, light everywhere.

By nature man loves dusk, the impersonal; when there gets to be too much light the situation easily becomes far too serious for him, especially if the light does not fluctuate but is steady—not so many hours of light and then dusk and darkness, but uninterrupted light, intensely bright.

In margin: "Personality" is derived from sound (*personare*); in another sense personality could be called transparency.

XI² A 107   n.d., 1854

« 3225 *Human Training*

Every man is endowed with individuality or distinctiveness by providence. The meaning of life, then, should be to fulfill this distinctiveness, strengthened and matured in the collisions which it must generate in the world around it.

But human training is demoralizing, designed to teach a person the trick of not batting an eyelid, of not saying a word, of not doing the least thing without having the guarantee that many others before him have behaved in the same way. The point is to avoid all dangers, all collisions, all the strain bound up with being distinctive.

Just as in the world of opinions newspapers demoralize men by breaking them of the practice of having a view of their own and of being developed by carrying through their view in opposition to the views of others, breaking them of this, and on the other hand, habituating them to have for every view the guarantee that a significant number of people have the same view (wide circulation of the newspaper provides this)—the so-called human training demoralizes in the same way.

Such a trained man of good taste is actually a detriment; whereas every distinctive character (which every one is originally) who is fulfilled in life is a veritable enrichment, a plus which enters into the world, such a trained man is a deleterious mimicking.

Such a molded man, this deleterious mimicking, thinks, of course, that he, too, is immortal—guaranteed by the fact that he is conducting himself exactly as many others before him conducted themselves.

A man's whole salvation lies in becoming personality—but no one is farther removed from personality than this trained man. It is true that he is usually exempted from everything that can happen to individuality, from having to stand alone, from the tension of primitivity, perhaps from running crosswise in life in some significant way, becoming ridiculous, perhaps, a laughing stock, perhaps coming to be persecuted, perhaps put to death; but he is fundamentally demoralized, a nonhuman, a monstrosity; in a way he has ceased to be God's creation and has become a creature which—loathsome thought!—has the human race for its creator. Only God, creating, can give individuality; if man is going to imitate God's feat, it consists of taking away individuality. Such a trained man is changed into a human creation, who also bears his maker's (man's)—not his image, no, but his stamp—that he is just like the others, the basest being of all—yes, the most insignificant animal is worth more than such a being, which is in no way chargeable to God but through guilt is man's own work.[*]

XI² A 177   *n.d.*, 1854

« 3226

[*] *In margin of 3225* (XI² A 177):

The utter baseness of being just like the others makes its appearance only in the human world and was not there originally but came later, a demoralization—the creator did not equip any living being so meagerly.

XI² A 178   *n.d.*

« 3227 *Meaning—Meaninglessness*

Exactly to the same degree that one is a significant personality, to the same degree nothing is insignificant or without meaning for him. This is because for him everything has the impress of his person. To err in an insignificant trifle means nothing to an insignificant personality—but for a significant personality it means at once that he is able to err in something significant also. A bartender, for example, does not get excited about making a small mistake in arithmetic whereas the eminent astronomer immediately gets the impression that he is also capable of making a mistake in the most important matters of all, and he is very sensitive about such a mistake, for in everything he feels the impress of his own person.

Properly understood, this is very relevant to God's idea that for God nothing is insignificant or without meaning.

XI² A 217   *n.d.*, 1854

« 3228 *The Personal—the Official*[857]

May 17, 1855

Christianity is rooted in the view of existence which says that all salvation is related to becoming personality.

The New Testament insists that the person who is to be a teacher in Christianity should be prevented in every way from being permitted to slip into objectivity, from withholding, hiding his personality. No, everything is done to the end that his proclamation may become a pure and personal transparency, that his life may be his teaching.

It is otherwise with state Christianity. The state is so good as to provide 1,000 teachers in Christianity and to arrange things for them in such a way that all sorts of escapes are possible for them: remaining personally uninvolved, what they say is a function of their office, and so on—

XI² A 402   May 17, 1855

« **3229** *The Church—the Public*

August 30, 1855

The fundamental corruption of our day consists in our having abolished personality.[858]

No one in our day dares to be a person; cravenly fearful of men, everyone shrinks from being an *I* in the presence of, perhaps in contrast to, others.

So it is that politicians make the best of it with the public. The politician is no *I*—heaven forbid! No, he speaks in the name of the public.

"The Church" is used in exactly the same way. All that is wanted is a shielding abstraction whereby one avoids being an *I*, which in our day is the most dangerous of all.

This abstraction (the Church) is decked out to be a person; one speaks of the life of the Church, and so on—one is intellectually brilliant and at the same time also manages to remain apart personally.

XI² A 431   August 30, 1855

PETER

« **3230**

If Christ had been only a man, then it is clear that Peter would not have denied him. Peter was too deep and honest for that. But whereas the pastors usually prate inconsistently, saying that it was doubly inexcusable of Peter because Christ was God, one must rather say: No, this is precisely what explains Peter. Had he regarded Christ only as a man, then he could have tolerated the thought that he should be treated in this way, and Peter would not have forgotten himself but would have remained loyal to him. But the madness, as it were, that Christ is God, that he has the power to call legions of angels at any desired moment —this is what completely overwhelms Peter. Just as out of fright one can lose his tongue, so all of Peter's ideas freeze, and in this partial paralysis he denies him.

VIII[1] A 370   *n.d.*, 1847

« **3231**

A witness was needed, a witness before whose thought the crucified and risen one could hover day and night. Peter became that witness. The memory of that most shocking sight might not have been able to arouse his zeal adequately. But Peter had one more memory —the denial, which reminded him of the same thing. What he had seen and experienced could not possibly ever be forgotten. It was quite impossible that Peter's testimony to it could ever be silenced. But that look of love which overtook Peter on the path of perdition reminded him day and night of what he had to make up for. —But let us not forget what is the object of this story: Christ loved the man he saw, the man who had changed in such a way that he denied Christ.

VIII[2] B 36:11   *n.d.*, 1847

« **3232**

Peter's state of mind must have been dreadful during the days when Christ was dead—and Peter had denied him—and then they were separated from each other in this way.

This occurred to me while reading Luther's sermon[859] on the Epistle for the Third Sunday in Trinity.

It would be of value to present Peter in this light.

X^1 A 173   *n.d.,* 1849

« **3233**

Insofar as it is permissible to think about such things and in such a purely human manner, one might say that a man in Christ's place, when Peter denied him, would have one more reason to be angry—that is, no human being can intentionally will to die. Peter's betrayal is wholly irrelevant to Christ's chief aim for his life—to die; in that respect the disciple's betrayal cannot be a hindrance. This is consistent with the fact that Peter does not have—and no man could—common cause with Christ.

On the other hand, if a man has a disciple or friend upon whom he has depended and that person then betrays him, the action ordinarily must be assumed to be detrimental to the former's cause, because no man, after all, can simply and solely have the cause: to be slain.[860]

X^1 A 237   *n.d.,* 1849

« **3234**

What Peter must have endured the three days Christ was dead! To be separated from Christ that way after denying him. Horrible.

And yet Peter was not repudiated, he resorted to grace and became the apostle he was.

Compared with Jehovah's relation to Moses, who did not enter the Promised Land simply because he doubted, that is gentleness and leniency beyond measure.

O, infinite gentleness, of which I am almost afraid lest it captivate me so that I take it in vain.

My greatest disquietude about Christianity, almost, is its gentleness and mildness; I become so anxious about the possibility of taking it in vain.

X^3 A 149   *n.d.,* 1850

« **3235** *Simon Peter*

"Could you not watch with me one hour?"[861] Here, for one moment, Christ is the suffering human being who for his own sake craves the sympathetic participation of another human being. But in the same moment he is again the teacher: "Watch and pray that you do not fall into temptation"—therefore not for my sake but for your own.

x⁴ A 163   *n.d.*, 1851

« 3236 *Peter Went Out and Wept Bitterly*[862]

That was fine of Peter! Here, also, the measure is a distance from what is common among men! If there lives a man whom you have treated unjustifiably, victimized, etc.—if he then is noble enough not to reproach you for it, not to reprove you for it, and you then exploit the situation, pretend that nothing is wrong, and everything is fine—this is the universal.

xI¹ A 31   *n.d.*, 1854

« 3237 *The Apostle Peter*

They speak disparagingly of his denial and then magnify his later life.

But there is one thing not sufficiently noted—that for him one glance was enough. There is scarcely one in a million for whom, under the circumstances, one glance would be enough. The way men are nowadays each one would probably have smugly counted himself very lucky to have left the Master high and dry *so cleverly,* and if the Master had cast a glance at them, each would have thought self-complacently: I'm smart enough to pretend I didn't notice anything.

xI¹ A 274   *n.d.*, 1854

« 3238

Get behind me, Satan! —You are not on the
side of God but of men.[863]

———

Thus Christianity is so very lofty that even the best-intentioned humane act (and Peter certainly meant well) is not a mistake, an error of judgment—no, it is "of Satan."

What, then, is "Christendom"—what else but a human good intention not nearly as honest as Peter's.

Consequently Christendom is Satan's invention.

xI¹ A 375   *n.d.*, 1854

PETRARCH

« 3239

In Petrarch's poem "The Triumph of Love"[864] there are many small incidents of which much could be made in an erotic sense, but it would be too bad to charge Petrarch with being a past master of eroticism. For him it is something historical, something external, which he notices, not the beating heart of the idea, and while observing it he does not have the concupiscence of the idea or the voluptuous exhilarated shiver of the moment of conception.

IV A 95   *n.d.*, 1843

« 3240

If he himself wanted to return to Eden, the angel with the flaming sword stood there; the same angel did not stand before his memory.

It was hard for Petrarch that Laura belonged to another, but he dared, however, think of her. He had no reproach other than the fact that the more he dreamed the more bitter the pain, but no higher power forbade him that.[865]

V B 116:3   *n.d.*, 1844

« 3241

Petrarch says it beautifully: Anger is a brief rage, and if one does not constrain it—a long rage, which ends in disaster.

X^2 A 412   *n.d.*, 1850

« 3242

> *Les desirs innocens, et les chastes attraits,*
> *Passant dans l'Elysée, et ne meurent jamais.* [866]

I have read the passage quoted but not the source; it is quoted in Fernow, *Petrarcas Leben.* [867]

X^3 A 683   *n.d.*, 1850

PHILOSOPHY

« 3243

The stone which was laid before Christ's grave could well be called *the philosophers' stone*,[868] it seems to me, inasmuch as its removal has given not only the Pharisees but now for 1800 years the philosophers a good deal to do.

I A 35   November 24, 1834

« 3244

The critical period is related to the present as a hydraulic gold mine is to the bank which mints the gold nuggets and puts them in circulation.

I A 87   October 7, 1835

« 3245

Philosophy and Christianity can never be united, *[869] for if I am going to hold fast to what is most essential in Christianity—namely, redemption, and if it is really going to amount to anything, it of course must be extended to the whole man. Or should I regard his moral powers as defective and his cognition, on the other hand, as sound? In this way I can indeed conceive of a philosophy after Christianity or after a man has become Christian, but then it would be a Christian philosophy. Then the relationship would not be one of philosophy to Christianity but of Christianity to Christian knowledge or, if one insists, Christian philosophy, unless one holds that philosophy, previous to or within Christianity, must conclude that one is not able to solve life's riddle; for if philosophy as a self-accounting for the relationship between God and the world denied itself, if it came to the conclusion that it could not explain this relationship, then philosophy at its highest perfection would involve its own total destruction, namely as evidence that it could not fulfill its own definition. Yes, seen from this standpoint, philosophy would not even serve as a transition to Christianity, for it would necessarily have to stop with this negative result, and the whole idea of redemptive need would of necessity have to enter a man from

496

another side altogether, that is, first of all it would have to be felt and then be known. And if philosophy became aware of the great throng of men who maintain a lively conviction of their need for redemption, actual redemption, it would be able to kneel before it—(although it would probably be difficult, since before such a test Christianity requires a personal-living-within-it, but in the same way, too, a consciousness of redemption, and if he adheres to it in the moment of reflection, he would surrender his philosophy and attach himself to the latter and then he would lack the substratum for his reflection and at most could look back on it as something in the past, the true reality of which he at this moment would have to deny,[†] that is, as philosopher) —and attempt to understand the conviction of these men, but it would still not acknowledge the necessity of redemption. Generally speaking, the yawning abyss is *here* where Christianity posits man's cognition as defective on account of sin, which is rectified in Christianity; the philosopher *qua* man tries to expound the relationship of God and the world; the result can readily be acknowledged as limited, inasmuch as man is a limited being, but also as the greatest possible result for man *qua* man. To be sure the philosopher can arrive at the idea of man's sin, but it does not follow that he knows that man needs redemption, least of all a redemption which, corresponding to the sinfulness of ordinary creatures, must be left to God, but a relative redemption (that is, it redeems itself). Yes, he would call out to man to forget the past, because for his powerful activity there is no time for that.

* Compare the scholastic thesis: "Something can be true in philosophy which is false in theology."[870]

† The philosopher must either embrace optimism—or despair.

I A 94   October 17, 1835

« **3246**

—The results of such a union[871] (of Christianity and philosophy) are seen in rationalism, of which conception confusion of language is one variety, and just as we have observed that many words spread through the different languages, the rationalists, even though they tear each other to pieces, likewise have these words in common: philosophical, reasonable Christianity (Christianity and everything about Christ's appearance are an accommodation).

I A 98   *n.d.*, 1835

« 3247

I have attempted to show why Christianity and philosophy cannot be united.[872] In order to show the correctness of this separation I have taken into account how Christianity—or more correctly, the Christian life—must appear from the standpoint of reason. To provide additional confirmation I shall now sketch how man as man outside of Christianity must appear to the Christian. In this connection it will be enough to bring to mind how the Christians regarded the pagans, considered their gods as the work of the devil and their virtues as glittering vices, how one of their coryphi declared man to be a block of wood, a stone, before Christ, how they in no manner linked preaching of their gospel to man as such, how they always began with "Repent" and how they even declared that their gospel was foolishness to the pagans and an offense to the Jews. And should anyone possibly think that by taking the extremes I may have placed them in too sharp contrast to each other, and that one ought to pay attention to the countless pertinent and present nuances, I shall take note of them a little just in case there really are any. Why is it there are really a good number of people who claim to find Christian impulses in their consciousness but on the other hand neither are nor pretend to be Christians? No doubt it is because *Christianity is a radical cure* from which men shrink, and these people do this without the need for the external representations which led many of the early Christians to postpone the decisive step to the last moment —they no doubt lack the strength to make the despairing *leap*. Add to this the queer suffocating atmosphere which meets us in Christianity and which exposes everyone to an extremely dangerous climatic fever (spiritual trials—see above [i.e., I A 95]), before he becomes acclimatized. If we turn first of all to life here on earth, they meet us with the explanation that everything is sinful, man as well as nature. They talk about the broad way as compared to the narrow way. If we turn to the other world, we find—so the Christians teach—the problem solved (Act V). And even if Christians do not have such a grandiose imagination as that of the northmen who pictured Loki bound to a rock with poison dripping down on him but still placed his wife at his side—the Christians on the other hand knew how to deprive the unfortunate one of every relief—not even a drop of water to quench his burning tongue. Almost everywhere that the Christian occupies himself with what is to come, there is punishment, devastation, ruin, eternal torment and suffering before his eyes. In this respect the Christian's imagination is exuberant and wayward, but when it comes to describing the bliss of the faithful and chosen ones, it is proportionately meager. External bliss is described as an ecstatic staring with lusterless staring eyes, enormous fixed pupils, or a moist, swimming gaze which hinders any clear vision. There is no mention of a vigorous spiritual life. Beholding God face to face, full comprehension in contrast to our seeing in a mirror darkly here on earth—this has not concerned them very much. It seems to me to be like the way love is treated in a certain kind of romantic novel. After a long and tedious struggle with dragons and wild animals, the lover finally succeeds in falling into his girl's arms, and then the curtain falls on a marriage just as prosaic as all the others, instead of there now being an increased awakening of love, an intimate, mutual reflecting of each other. I have always found it far more salutary to think of seeing gathered together in one place all the great and gifted men of the whole world, all those who have put a hand to the wheel of man's development. I have always been inspired by the thought of a university (in the most profound sense) of the human race, a sort of scholarly republic where—in eternal struggle between opposites—we would grow in knowledge every moment, where the often hidden and little known causes and effects of the past are unveiled in their full light. The Christians, however, have been afraid of admitting these great men into their fellowship in order that it should not become too mixed, in order that one single solitary chord could always be struck and the Christians can thus sit like a Chinese council and rejoice that they have erected that high, insurmountable wall against—the barbarians. And why all this? Not to criticize the Christians but to show the accepted *de facto* contrast in the Christian life, to caution everybody who is still not tightly laced in this kind of a spiritual corset from imprudently entering into such a thing, to protect him against such narrow-chested, asthmatic representations. To be sure it is hard to live in a land where the sun never shines above the horizon; but neither is it especially gratifying to live in a place where the sun stands so perpendicularly over the top of our heads that it does not allow either us or anything around us to cast a shadow.

I A 99 *n.d.*, 1835

« **3248**

About the significance of participles in philosophical language—the opposite is a parenthesis—a system in *one* sentence. —Even if a single person were to be found who could write one, it would be almost impossible to find one who could read it

I A 127   *n.d.*, 1836

« 3249

There are metaphysicians of a certain kind who, when they are not able to proceed any farther, take themselves by the scruff of the neck, like Münchausen,[873] and thus acquire something *a priori*.

I A 153   April, 1836

« 3250

Philosophical knowledge is first complete (with nothing left over) in the system—idea and form—therefore no absolute principle? No— there is only the form.

I A 253   October 6, 1836

« 3251

Philosophy sheds its skin every step it takes, and the more foolish followers creep into it.

II A 11   *n.d.*, 1837

« 3252

Philosophy is life's dry-nurse, who can take care of us—but not suckle us.

II A 59   *n.d.*, 1837

« 3253

If one does not maintain strictly the relation between philosophy (the purely human view of the world, the *human* standpoint) and Christianity[874] but begins straightway, without special penetrating investigations of this relationship, to speculate about dogma, one can easily achieve apparently rich and satisfying results. But things can also turn out as with marl at one time, when, without having investigated it and the soil, people used it on any sort of land—and got excellent yields for a few years but afterwards found that the soil was exhausted.

II A 77   *n.d.*, 1837

« 3254

For many men, including philosophers, arriving at a result is like the plot in novels: to see her and to love her are one and the same.

N.B. One finds this, of course, only in cheap novelists, who do not know what love is and therefore leap over it.

II A 586   February, 1837

« **3255**

Beware of false prophets who come to you in wolves' clothing but inwardly are sheep[875]—that is, the phrasemongers.

II A 176   October 10, 1837

« **3256**

In margin of 3255 (II A 176):
That is to say, the systematic wolves.

II A 177   *n.d.*

« **3257**

There is a kind of reflection in which the object is lost completely, and then one behaves like the raven when it lost its object (the cheese) because of its eloquence. In this respect it is a picture of idealism, which when everything was lost had only itself left.

II A 198   November 24, 1837

« **3258**

These recitation assistants of modern philosophy seem to be like scorekeepers, yet not like scorekeepers in a rifle match who do nevertheless participate somewhat in a kind of danger, although in a very superficial way, but rather like scorekeepers in billiards, who repeat their *quatre à pointe* in their sleep etc.

II A 701   February 8, 1838

« **3259** *Concerning the Relationship between Christianity and Philosophy*

Motto: When a man meets a man on a road, and one man has a rake and one man has a spade, can one man do the other man any harm?—

II A 239   August 1, 1838

« **3260**

Excerpt from:
Der historische Christus und die Philosophie Kritik der Grundidee des Werks: das Leben Jesu von Dr. D. F. Strauss. v. Julius Schaller Dr. d. Philos. u. Privatdocent an der Universitæt Halle. Leipzig 1838. . . . [*]

[*] *In margin:* Begun July 23—finished August 21, 1838

II C 54   July 23–August 21, 1838

« **3261**

Addition to 3260 (II C 54):

Since I have come to this point I cannot withhold the observation that the reason many works of recent philosophy, after the admiration which their brilliance must elicit from everyone has subsided, leave such a meager genuinely satisfying yield, is that they concentrate entirely on questions which never arise in the Christian consciousness, that they revolve around problems which ought to assume the actuality of a relation between God and men; whereas the Christian consciousness, without inquiring about this *conditio sine qua non*, seeks to grasp the concretions which this relation has supplied. Thus when Schaller develops the concept of redemption, he merely develops the possibility of God's relation to men, the occurrence of which surely can be granted to him with good reason within the assumption of the presence of a personal God; but the God of wrath is still not reconciled thereby, and the satisfaction and peace found in such a reply is merely illusory, because this question does not have real [*real*] significance for the Christian consciousness, but it does have great importance for philosophical "preliminary studies."

II C 55 K.   August 13, 1838

« **3262**

Continuation of 3259 (II C 54):

The personal immanence of God in man is primarily the all-penetrating and all-*"übergreifende"* human personality. This alone is the basis and presupposition of every man's knowledge of God. If God actually were only substance or only abstract subject, no creature would possess even a mere intimation of God; therefore there is some point in characterizing every religion as a revelation of God, but only that religion may be called absolute revelation in which God as person, therefore as he is in and for himself, has become revealed and has entered into human consciousness according to his full infinite essence. In this way every contrast between God and the world is actually annihilated.

II C 56   *n.d.*, 1838

« **3263**

Addition to 3262 (II C 56):

But if every contrast between God and man is abrogated in this way, it shows that the contrast was a purely logical contrast and that the contrast within the sphere of religious-moral views (sin, etc.) is not touched, for the simple reason that it has not been reached.

II C 57   n.d., 1838

« **3264**

I dare say the unphilosophical mind can manage to comprehend the defectiveness of a foregoing position; but then this presents itself as something hard and impenetrable to him. Thus we also see that many men first have to give vent to a mass of polemics before they are able to arrive at their real subject—the philosophical mind mitigates the foregoing views, propitiatingly diminishes them to elements.[876]

II A 299   November 22, 1838

« **3265**

The dialectical aspect of the modern development is certainly predominant but ought not therefore enervate the substantial. It ought to be like Vaulunder's sword, so limber that he could turn it around his body and so sharp that it would split boulders like clay.

II A 706   n.d., 1838

« **3266**

Telegraph message from an effervescent to a clairvoyant about the relation between Christianity and philosophy.

Motto: When a man meets a man on a road and one man has a rake and one man has a spade, can one man do the other man any harm?

II A 786   n.d., 1838

« **3267**

Addition to 3266: (II A 786):

Preface

The problem is to find the clairvoyant who is able to solve for me all the problems to which I, who only see in a mirror darkly,[877] am exposed. Whether there actually is such a person now or when he will put in his appearance, I am too much of an effervescent to tell.

II A 787   n.d., 1838

« **3268**

Addition to 3266 (II A 786):
Motto: and they cast lots for his seamless woven tunic.[878]

II A 788   n.d., 1838

« **3269**

Addition to 3266 (II A 786):

Motto *"Maledictus qui porcum alit et filium suum docet sapientiam græcam,"*[879] a Jewish saying 60 years before Christ.

Christianity does not want to negotiate with philosophy, even if philosophy is willing to share the booty with it; Christianity does not want to have the King of Sodom say: I have made Abraham rich.[880]

II A 790   *n.d.*, 1838

« **3270**

It seems as if philosophers in their accounts of modern philosophy since Descartes have adopted a form sometimes found in the fairy story,[881] which, through a repetition of everything that went before every time a new part is added, finally develops into an interminable series: stick won't beat dog, dog won't bite cow, cow won't go home, etc.

II A 353   February 5, 1839

« **3271**

The latest work by Günther (*die juste-milieu der Philosophie*)[882] has such a felicitous title that I have become so infatuated and preoccupied with it that I pause at the title and almost do not get the book read.

II A 356   February 7, 1839

« **3272**

To remind philosophers and dogmaticians in our day about the significance for speculation of the words: Repent, you—is about the same as shouting "Hep" after a Jew.[883]

II A 426   May 15, 1839

« **3273**

The trouble with philosophers in respect to Christianity is that they use continental maps when they ought to use special large-scale maps, *for every dogma is nothing but a more concrete extension of* the universal human consciousness.

II A 440   May 22, 1839

« **3274**

The situation of philosophy in relation to Christianity is like that of one who is being interrogated; face to face with his interrogator he makes up a story which coincides in all essential elements and yet is completely different.[884]

II A 493   n.d., 1839

« **3275**

It is now apparent that the formal systems in their categorical rigor resemble the Slavic language, which by a perpetual prelude of a half-dozen consonants makes the language so difficult to speak that the idea is often suppressed and at best is audible in a tolerated *sheva*[885] —and on the other side the mystic suffers a perpetual hiatus.

II A 511   July 22, 1839

« **3276**

If one looks at philosophy's latest endeavors (in Fichte,[886] et al.) with reference to Christianity,[887] one cannot deny an earnest endeavor to recognize the uniqueness in Christianity; it even takes time to *pray* a little along its toilsome way; it momentarily pauses in its haste; it even has the patience and the place for a monologue by Christianity, although it does wish that it would be as brief as possible. Nevertheless, in all this the endeavors of philosophy obviously tend toward a recognition of Christianity's harmony with the universally human consciousness and, according to this view, the concentric doubleness of Christianity and philosophy, with their merely historical differences abrogated in the concept. But the true Christian view, that universally human existence does not explain Christianity and that Christianity is not simply another factor in the world, but that Christianity explains the world and that the pre-Christian development cannot therefore be regarded as concentric with Christianity because neither Christianity nor Christ had any such center but were simply the infinite, discontinuous, straight line, the continuously repeated ex-centric seeking—this is not understood. In his *Aphorismen über die Zukunft der Theologie* (in his *Zeitschrift*, III, pp. 200 ff.),[888] Fichte[889] very competently points out, however, that monotheism can never be explained by polytheism; but however correct this statement is, one must with just as much rigor press the point that Christian monotheism never in all eternity can be explained by pagan* monotheism, yes, even more rigorously in order that the concept of revelation shall not be volatized and wrested from us by such tricks. It contains not only something which men have not themselves given, but something which has never occurred to the mind of any man even as a wish, an ideal, or anything else.

II A 517   July 28, 1839

« 3277

In margin of 3276 (II A 517):

* But Fichte does not do this (see p. 252,[890] where he presents Judaism), and yet in a way he does it when he says (same page) that Christianity *ist nicht nur der Besluss und Vollender des jüdischen Kultus, sondern ebenso der Schlüssel und Deuter des heidnischen Polytheismus.*[891] This seems to place paganism on an equal level with Judaism in relation to Christianity.

II A 518   *n.d.*

« 3278

In margin of 3276 (II A 517):

(On p. 252[892] Fichte also expresses himself in opposition to the current method of regarding the one as proceeding from the other in a dialectical process. And this vindicates the significance of what Sibbern calls the collateral.[893])

II A 519   *n.d.*

« 3279

Philosophers treat dogmas, the sacred affirmations of Scripture, in short, the whole sacred consciousness, the way Appius Pulcher[894] treated the sacred hens. One consults them, and if they predict something bad, then like the general one says: If the sacred hens won't eat, then let them drink—and thereupon casts them overboard.

II A 529   August 7, 1839

« 3280

Hip, hip, hurray, ecstasy—to sneeze—the solemnity of our systematic advancement forbids it, just as it is forbidden under arms—nevertheless I allow myself to, and to cough, too; in short, I allow myself all *secernationes et quidem sensu metaphysico*[895]

II A 814   *n.d.*, 1839

« 3281

If it were the case that philosophers are presuppositionless,[896] an account would still have to be made of language and its entire importance and relation to speculation, for here speculation does indeed have a medium which it has not provided itself, and what the eternal secret of consciousness is for speculation as a union of a qualification of nature and a qualification of freedom, so also language is [for speculation] partly an original given and partly something freely developing.

And just as the individual, no matter how freely he develops, can never reach the point of becoming absolutely independent, since true freedom consists, on the contrary, in appropriating the given and consequently in becoming absolutely dependent through freedom, so it is also with language, although we do find at times the ill-conceived tendency of not wanting to accept language as the freely appropriated given but rather to produce it for oneself, whether it appears in the highest regions where it usually ends in silence or in the personal isolation of jargonish nonsense. Perhaps the story of the Babylonian confusion of tongues[897] may be explained in this way, that it was an attempt to construct an arbitrarily formed common language, which, since it lacked fully integrative commonalty, necessarily broke up into the most disparate differences, for here it is a matter of the *totum est parte sua prius*, which was not understood.

III A 11   July 18, 1840

« **3282**

Si philosophi hujus ævi jure contenderint, disputationes ipsorum et magna eorundem de ph. merita ignorare immo non in succum et sanguinem convertere non impunite licere, equidem non negaverim mihi persuasum esse, melius veritati consultum iri, si illorum vestigia non secuti non vitam ex systemate disponere et interpretari, sed systema tandem ex experientia evadere atque prodire conamur ab utrimque enim pugnandum est—[898]

III A 24   n.d., 1840

« **3283**

If there is anything to be praised in the marvellous progress of modern philosophy,[899] it certainly is the power of genius with which it seizes and vigorously *holds on to* the phenomenon. Although it is fitting for the phenomenon (which as such is always *foeminini generis*) by reason of its feminine nature to surrender* to the stronger sex, yet among the knights of the modern age there is frequently a lack of deferential propriety, profound enthusiasm, in place of which one sometimes hears too much the jingle of spurs etc.—and at times it shrivels before the fellows.

In margin: *And with justification one nevertheless—in contrast to what has often been said, that the observer ought to surrender himself —ought to remember that it is rather up to the phenomenon; and we will say that history, so to speak, rejoices in this embrace.

However sterile history is, its embrace is fertile, like that of the old witch in the fairy tale by Musæus,[900] and just as those three armor bearers of Roland's with a certain aversion decided to share the bed with the old crone, yet they did not regret it afterwards.

In the arms of philosophy history rejuvenates itself unto divine youthfulness.[901]

III B 12   n.d., 1840–41

« 3284

Aristotle's view* that philosophy begins with wonder, not as in our day with doubt, is a positive point of departure for philosophy.[902] Indeed, the world will no doubt learn that it does not do to begin with the negative,[903] and the reason for success up to the present is that philosophers have never quite surrendered to the negative and thus have never earnestly done what they have said. They merely flirt with doubt.

In margin: *διὰ γὰρ τὸ
θαυμάζειν οἱ ἄνθρωποι
καὶ νῦν καὶ τὸ πρῶτον
ἤρξαντο φιλοσοφεῖν.[904]
Also Plato in *Theætetus.* μάλα γὰρ φιλόσοφον
τοῦτο τὸ πάθος, τὸ θαυμάζειν.
οὐ γὰρ ἄλλη ἀρχὴ
φιλοσοφίας ἢ αὐτή.[905]
See Hermann, *Geschichte und System der Platonische Philosophie,* I, p. 275, note 5.[906]

III A 107   n.d., 1841

« 3285

The doctrine of revelation as presented by Marheincke in his *Dogmatik*[907] serves to illuminate the philosophic volatilization of Christian doctrinal concepts—the logical proposition that the finite is the infinite, together with the explanation Werder[908] gives, that the stress is on the last word. All this must be gone through meticulously in order, if possible, to bring clarity into the confusion. —The doctrine of the image of God according to Marheincke's lecture[909] is also such a volatilization.

III C 32   n.d., 1841–42

« 3286 *The Skeptic*

Just as the seducer should give a reflected picture of the abortive endeavor which wishes to carry out its purpose in relation to "woman," so also the skeptic in relation to man as an attempt to wrench everything away from him.

III A 244   n.d., 1842

« **3287**

a stocky little man with a head bigger than an ox's. Jovial from his youth, he had only received a bare pass in his theological examination. His oratory would have appalled the capital city—now he had become a pastor out on the Jutland heath.[910] Yet this satisfied him—the heath was a playground—as to a swamp bittern—he had given a talk on the occasion of a crop failure, maintains that every peasant can understand it; he writes that he has given it word for word in pure Jutland dialect. —"Every man is by nature a philosopher," every peasant lad learns, and also the words, "What does it profit a man etc. and not damage his own soul"—he who has understood this has essentially understood all philosophy.

At a pastoral conference in one of the provinces.

III B 183   n.d., 1842

« **3288**

All of the numerous discussion group leaders, assistant professors, and survey people who nowadays in Germany take it upon themselves to introduce people to philosophy and to characterize philosophy's present position are just as distasteful to me with their devoid-of-all-pathos newspaper information about the situation of philosophy as dull, sleepy billiard game scorekeepers with their monotonous cry: *dixe à ons.* And strangely enough, philosophy advances steadily, and despite the fact that in the whole crowd of philosophers there is not one single player but simply scorekeepers. I wait in vain for a man to appear who would have the power to say: *à point.* In vain —we are already far along in *quarant,* and the game will soon be over and all the enigmas explained. If only the German philosophers could explain the enigma that the game goes on although there is no one who plays. —What wonder then, when this is the situation with the Germans, that I set my hopes on Danish philosophy.[911] My barber, too, an older but well-read man, who has followed the movements of modern Danish philosophy with energy and interest, maintains that Denmark has never had such philosophers as it has now; the beginning of Danish philosophy should now be at hand. The other day he was so good as to utilize the ten minutes he uses for my shave to give me a

short survey of modern Danish philosophy. He assumes that it begins
with *Riegels, Horrebov,* and *Boie.* He knew Riegels intimately; he was his
friend and Du-brother, a little square-built man, always cheerful and
contented. He remembers distinctly what a sensation his debut
aroused. He advanced many remarkable truths. What they were my
barber has forgotten—it was many years ago; yet he remembers as
vividly as if it were yesterday what a sensation he made. Horrebov and
Boie always came to his barber shop, where he then had the opportunity to become familiar with their philosophy. These three men must
be regarded as the coryphi in modern Danish philosophy. Riisbright
should also be mentioned although his work as a teacher at the University of Copenhagen was quieter and less noticed. On the whole, however, he stood outside the great movements in modern Danish
philosophy. But what my barber could not recall without deep emotion
was that through untimely death Denmark should lose the most gifted
philosopher it had. The man is now forgotten. Many people perhaps
do not know he ever lived. His name is Niels Rasmussen, and he was
a contemporary of the three great philosophers. He had conceived the
eminent idea that all European philosophy might unite around the
Danish, and this again around his philosophy. To that end he worked
energetically on a subscription plan; but the work took all his strength
to the extent that he died of over-exhaustion. If, said my barber, if his
subscription plan had been finished, if the work it heralded had been
finished, if it had been read, if it had been translated, if it had been
understood by the European philosophers, then without any doubt the
hopeful Niels Rasmussen would have brought Denmark to the heights
it does not occupy even in this moment. But—he died, Denmark's
philosophical hope. —The barber and I offered him a tear, whereupon
he continued to shave my beard as well as to communicate a survey of
modern Danish philosophy. What Riegels in a jovial moment had
confided to him, what Horrebov, Boie, and he had whispered about in
the barber shop—this he spread all around the country. —He paused
a moment in his barbering to wipe off some lather; he used the moment to show me on a map which hung on the wall how modern Danish
philosophy in its grand movements spread across Sjælland, yes,
pushed way up into Norway as far as Trondhjem. Everyone justifiably
dared to expect something extraordinary from this great stir, but then
came the unhappy years of the war, which shattered everything. But
now once again he had gained the courage to hope. The present epoch
in Danish philosophy showed clearly that it stood in an essential rela-

tion to the previous epoch in modern Danish philosophy; it had contact with it and forsook its conclusion only to find one higher. The first epoch worked toward a sound understanding of man and achieved it as well; philosophy today abandons more and more this relative superficiality in order to reach something higher. It has perhaps discovered that there is something more and something different, something it provisionally calls the anterior Innermost or that which is behind the Innermost Being.[912] As soon as it has discovered what this is or, as my barber more correctly put it, as soon as it has gotten back there behind, it will gain the European reputation which Niels Rasmussen had intended it to have. My barber is of the opinion that one may safely dare hope so, confident in the extraordinary powers of Danish philosophy.

III B 192 *n.d., 1842*

« **3289**

Apollonius[913] of Tyana's development of the motto "Know thyself" is sheer sophomoric pretension. It was regarded as difficult and as the ultimate, and yet he was not satisfied with it but says that Pythagoras not only knew himself but also knew who he had been, which he then would also like to apply to himself.[914] In a curiously comic way the profundity of the first sentence is thereby dissipated. So it goes in our time with many philosophers; they have to say something in addition, and they thereby make it all ridiculous, even though there are always a goodly number who take it to be profound wisdom.

In margin: See book VI, 11, p. 500.[915]

IV A 19 *n.d., 1842–43*

« **3290**

In margin of 3289 (IV A 19):
A similar sophomoric pretension by one of the disciples of Heraclitus.[916] Heraclitus had said: One cannot step into the same river twice. A disciple wanting to improve it said: One cannot even step into it once. Thereby the nerve is cut; as far as making any sense, the statement becomes the opposite, an Eleatic sentence, and denies motion.

IV A 20 *n.d.*

« **3291**

Then the philosophers are worse than the Pharisees,[917] who, as we read, impose heavy burdens but themselves do not lift them, for in this they are the same, but the philosophers demand the impossible. And if there is a young man who thinks that to philosophize is not to talk or to write but in all quietness to do honestly and scrupulously what the philosophers say one should do, they let him waste his time, many years of his life, and then themselves show that it is impossible,[918] and yet it has gripped him so profoundly that rescue is perhaps impossible.[919]

IV B 6   *n.d.*, 1842   43

« **3292**

To be sure, there is not a vigorous systematic development everywhere in Aristotle, but still there is hardly a work by him in which one does not discern the systematic thinker; whereas in our time there are plenty of systematizers in whom there is not a trace of systematic thinking. His *Ethics* falls into the following parts: books I–III on the good, virtue, and many other themes; books IV–V a development of the moral virtues, i.e., the virtues related to the irrational part of the soul: courage, moderation, magnanimity ($\epsilon\lambda\epsilon\upsilon\theta\epsilon\rho\iota\acute{o}\tau\eta s$). Book VI on the intellectual virtues: $\tau\acute{\epsilon}\chi\nu\eta$, $\dot{\epsilon}\pi\iota\sigma\tau\acute{\eta}\mu\eta$, $\sigma\omega\phi\rho\sigma\acute{\upsilon}\nu\eta$, $\nu\sigma\hat{\upsilon}s$, $\sigma\sigma\phi\acute{\iota}a$.[920] Here A. no longer uses his observation on the $\mu\epsilon\sigma\acute{o}\tau\eta s$[921] of virtue. Book VII on abstinence etc., pleasure. Book VIII on friendship; Book IX on friendship. Book X on pleasure.

IV C 25   *n.d.*, 1842–43

« **3293** *Scholasticism*

First period.
> From Scotus Erigena–Anselm.
> The contrast between object and consciousness not yet marked.

Second period.
> The contrast between nominalism and realism shifts over into realism by way of knowledge of Aristotle.

Third period.
> Realism. Trend again toward nominalism.

Fourth period.
> Nominalism
> William of Occam.[922]

IV C 61   *n.d.*, 1842–43

« **3294**

Ancient philosophy, the most ancient in Greece, was preëminently occupied with the question of the motion whereby the world came into existence [*blev til*], the constitutive relationship of the elements to each other. —The most recent philosophy is especially occupied with motion—that is, motion in logic.[923] It would not be without significance to collate the various theses from these two spheres. Modern philosophy has never accounted for motion. Similarly, in its otherwise profuse slates of categories there is no category which is called mediation,[924] which for the newest philosophy is nevertheless the most essential of all, in fact, the essential nerve in it, whereby it seeks to dissociate itself from every older philosophy.

IV A 54 *n.d.*, 1843

« 3295

Pythagoras said that the wisest man was the one who gave things their names and who discovered number.

See Tennemann, I, p. 101.[925]

IV A 55 *n.d.*, 1843

« 3296

There are many people in our day who possess the result of the whole of existence and do not know how to account for the least little thing.

IV A 163 *n.d.*, 1843

« 3297

In the realm of thought there is a haggling, an up-to-a-certain-point[926] kind of understanding, which just as surely leads to nonsense as good intentions lead to hell.

V A 9 *n.d.*, 1844

« 3298

Bacon says: *tempus siquidem simile est fluvio, qui levia atque inflata ad nos devehit, solida autem et pondus habentia submergit.*[927]

Jacobi, *S. W.*, II, p. 134 n.[928]

V A 31 *n.d.*, 1844

« 3299

Danish philosophy[929]—if there ever comes to be such a thing—will be different from German philosophy in that it definitely will not begin with nothing or without any presuppositions[930] whatsoever or explain everything by mediating,[931] because, on the contrary, it begins with the proposition that there are many things between heaven and earth which no philosophy has explained.[932]

By being incorporated in philosophy, this proposition will provide the necessary corrective and will also cast a humorous-edifying warmth over the whole.

V A 46   *n.d.,* 1844

« 3300

It is a very strange experience for me to read the third chapter of the third book of Aristotle's *De Anima.* [933] A year and a half ago I began a little essay *De omnibus dubitandum,* in which I made my first attempt at a little speculative development. The motivating concept I used was: error. Aristotle does the same.[934] At that time I had not read a bit of Aristotle but a good share of Plato.

The Greeks still remain my consolation. The confounded mendacity which entered into philosophy with Hegel, the endless insinuating and betraying, and the parading and spinning out of one or another single passage in Greek philosophy.

Praised be Trendelenburg[935]—one of the most sober philosophical philologists I know.

V A 98   *n.d.,* 1844

« 3301

... The question as we have presented it is simplified as much as possible, and in considering it we shall attempt again to simplify everything as much as possible; for even if something else received instead of the answer to this particular question were something absolutely glorious, it still would really be indulgence in an awful dissipation, and it would be a loss to get to know something else instead of getting an answer to the perhaps more insignificant question but, after all, please note, the one which was asked. No doubt this often happens in the most recent science and scholarship precisely because it has the pet idea of becoming concrete immediately. But this concretion often has a seductive effect and deprives thought of peace of mind, the scientific-scholarly contentment which is satisfied with thought itself. This is by no means to say that it is wrong of science and scholarship to assimilate concrete matter, but it does not begin simply with that. The mathematician is delighted with his algebra, which means nothing but the calculation itself. The sensate person may not be content with that, but would it therefore be proper for the mathematician promptly to give

up the letters and choose dollars, marks, and shillings merely in order
to arouse the sensuous man to participation through the stimulation
of his passion. This is the way it goes when one begins to make the idea
concrete immediately and does not first of all clarify in pure abstraction the idea he wants to make applicable in the concrete. The concrete
is multiplicity and as such exercises an enchanting power over men.
Suppose now it happened—and why should it not happen—that the
idea[*] which is to be demonstrated in the concrete remained unclear
and yet that the learner or the reader delighted in this diversion, forgot
the idea, was not enraged with the one who really had deceived[†] him
but even considered himself very indebted to him. The historical (concretely understood) inherently has various charms which the philosopher, however, if in general he wishes to be true to himself, ought to
reject. The historical to him means only the historical, not this historical, and one who merely wants to satisfy the demands of imagination
or curiosity turns to him in vain. If he then wants to demonstrate the
relation of the idea to the historical, the historical becomes purely
abstract and essentially is temporality.[‡] Whether temporality means
a single individual's life or the most wonderful world-historical
achievement is a matter of indifference to him. The philosopher therefore cannot fall into the misunderstanding, which is a result of sensuous astonishment[§] and of superstition, that the idea shows itself more
clearly in world history than in an individual man's life. It is the
philosopher's passion to reject all these distinctions and above all to
reject deceiving the reader by them, as if he had said something (*qua*
philosopher) because as historian he had instructed the learner. If this
is not the case, then everything is confused, and the learner is at a loss
as to whether he should thank such a man or not. If the method is
concrete from the very beginning, it either results in his instanta-
neously venturing out in the historical matter or, preoccupied with the
interpretations of others, he seeks to demonstrate the idea in them. In
the *first case*, for example, he speaks about China. Who would not be
happy to know something about China? He amazes us with his learning; one is overwhelmed by all the new things to be learned and thanks
him—if one is numbered among those who previously really did not
know anything in particular about the subject and to those who in their
rejoicing over it forget that this subject is not at all what they were
supposed to find out. Another reader, however, is by chance very
familiar with the Chinese and discovers that there is an error. This is
made known, and there is a controversy. One is curious, reads both

sides, finds out something new—and forgets even more what it is that he really wants to find out. —In the second case he speaks about Oriental philosophy, Greek, Jewish, etc. One acquires an indescribable amount of information, but unfortunately not what he seeks and what he as philosopher should achieve. He gets into a profound dilemma: he hardly dares confide his secret to anyone, for it would indeed seem as if he were ungracious toward a man who knows so much about everything. The philosopher wants to show how the god [*Guden*] enters guidingly into the historical. Consequently he settles upon one or another world-historical decision. He intensifies the dramatic interest; the interests of countries and kingdoms, the fates of millions are wrapped up in the conflict—and now the final judgment develops out of this: it is divine providence. Previously one was not so aware of that catastrophe; he thanks the philosopher for the enjoyment he has had, admires his art—and forgets that this is not at all what he wishes to find out, forgets that he who can see the god's guidance only in the world-historical decision (where it can be seen) but not in the most insignificant person's life—that he is no philosopher, that he does not have the philosopher's passion—he is merely superstitious. Soon everyone who knows anything or knows how to talk about the good becomes a philosopher; all unite in dragging men's minds down into multiplicity and, thus immersed, into forgetfulness of what is the philosopher's business and occupation, what Aristotle[936] expresses so beautifully, that philosophy is occupied with that which is related in only one way.[¹] Since the method has become so concrete no provisional reflection, of course, is necessary; one passes on at once to the main dish. At the conclusion of the system it will be seen that the method is correct. At the end, after every means of diversion has been employed to disturb the reader and bribe the judge. Even a logical problem cannot be handled without one side of the historical concretion immediately crowding in as the long-winded report on what others have thought about it, etc. —An instrument of distraction, nothing but an instrument of distraction.[937]

[*]*In margin:* which in the beginning one did not clarify for himself in the conciseness and unconcern of abstraction but which was supposed to become clear for the first time in the conclusion—that is, after having seen and understood the diverse things which are precisely the things which can distract the thought.

[†]*In margin:* had intruded upon him even more than by speaking to him about the highest and the holiest, which requires stillness of soul above all, in Dyrehaugsbakken amusement park.

[‡].*At bottom of page:* (as if a person wanted to show him how one instrument by its entry into the totality first produced the wholeness —and yet would not first perform the passage of that particular instrument for him but began immediately with the whole orchestra).

[§]*In margin:* delusions of phantasy, the indefinable frauds of indefinite feelings.

[‖]*In margin:* τὸ ἀεὶ κατὰ τὰ αὐτὰ ὡς αὐτῶς ἔχον[938]   (Plato)
V B 14, pp. 73–76   n.d., 1844

« 3302

This is the way a philosopher acted with whom I once had the honor of speaking. When I ventured to point out to him one or another minor difficulty which needed consideration before it would be possible to bring off dogmatic speculation, he replied: You may very well be right, but one should not think about it, because then he will never get around to speculating.[939]
V B 55:3   n.d., 1844

« 3303 *Popularity*

A person is not unpopular because he uses technical expressions, for that is something accidental, and they can be adapted, as they are for even the simplest of men.

He is and remains unpopular who thinks one thought all the way through. Although he used no technical expressions, Socrates[940] was unpopular because his ignorance, if it is to be maintained, is more strenuous for life than all Hegel's philosophy.
VI A 15   n.d., 1845

« 3304

Though the system were politely to assign me a guest room in the loft, in order that I might be included, I still prefer to be a thinker who is like a bird on a twig.[941]
VI A 66   n.d., 1845

« 3305

It is more difficult to describe a particular actor than it is to write a whole esthetic, more difficult to describe one single performance of his than to describe the particular actor. The more limited the subject matter is (all this about Chinese drama and the Middle Ages and Ancient Scandinavia, Spain, etc. etc.), the more difficult the task, because the task directly tests the descriptive powers. The more one dares use the method of general survey, the easier it is, for when the volume of material is so great, one still seems to be saying something with these completely abstract observations which everyone knows by rote. The more concrete the task is, the more difficult. God knows how long philosophers will continue to grow fat on the illusion they have gotten themselves and others to believe—namely, that surveys are the most difficult.

VI A 133   *n.d.*, 1845

« 3306   *The Dialectic of Beginning*[942] *Scene in the Underworld*[943]

Characters: Socrates
Hegel

Socrates sits in the cool [of the evening] by a fountain, listening.
Hegel sits at a desk reading Trendelenburg's *Logische Untersuchungen*,[944] II, p. 198, and walks over to Socrates to complain.
Socrates: Shall we begin by completely agreeing or disagreeing about something which we call a presupposition.[945]
[Sic] Hegel:
Socrates: With what presupposition do you begin?
Hegel: None at all.
Socrates: Now that is something; then you perhaps do not begin at all.
Hegel: I not begin—I who have written twenty-one volumes?[946]
Socrates: Ye gods, what a hecatomb you have offered!
Hegel: But I start with nothing.
Socrates: Is that not with something?
Hegel: No—the inverse process. It becomes apparent only at the conclusion of the whole process, when I have treated all the sciences, history, etc.
Socrates: How shall I be able to surmount this difficulty, for many remarkable things must certainly have happened which would captivate me. (Misuse of the oratorical element.) You know that I did not allow even Polos to talk more than five minutes at a time, and you want to talk XXI volumes.

VI A 145   *n.d.*, 1845

« 3307

Xenophon[947] tells of a young man who wanted to assume the government of a city. Socrates halted him by asking if he had the requisite preparation, if he knew how many ships the city had, etc. This preparation is of great importance if a mediation between Christianity and speculation is to amount to anything; to mediate between speculation and speculation is not so difficult but is rather meaningless.

VI B 54:33   *n.d.*, 1845

« 3308

Most systematizers in relation to their systems are like a man who builds an enormous castle and himself lives alongside it in a shed; they themselves do not live in the enormous systematic building.[948] But in the realm of mind and spirit this nonresidence is and remains a decisive objection. Spiritually understood, a man's thoughts must be the building in which he lives—otherwise the whole thing is deranged.

VII^1 A 82   *n.d.*, 1846

« 3309

In the main, the majority of people, also here in Copenhagen, regard philosophizing, reflecting on existence, scholarship, as a kind of mental derangement and a waste of time (as a North American[949] says quite naïvely of all North Americans; see *Theol. Maanedsskrift*[950] by Grundtvig and Rudelbach, XII, pp. 7 etc.)* The reason Sibbern, for example, is not regarded this way is primarily that he makes a living as professor of philosophy—that is, if it is one's livelihood, then one can philosophize just as others sweep chimneys, for example, but if one is a private person and then actually philosophizes for the sake of philosophizing (which Sibbern[951] certainly does, but people are not completely aware of it), it would be considered just as deranged as if a man of independent means were to sweep chimneys. That is, to sweep chimneys for the sake of sweeping chimneys is absurd: ergo, philosophizing for the sake of philosophizing is also absurd.

After all, the bread-and-butter outlook still plays the crucial role in the world; wherever this middle term falls away, people become confused. Nominal Christians who actually have no impression of the essentially Christian do not take exception at all to a minister's delivering orthodox doctrine, and why not? Because it is his bread and butter. They take no exception at all to the fact that that preacher makes strong demands upon their lives in his sermon—and why not? It is part and parcel of his trade, just as a military officer looks stern and a policeman strikes. —When, on the other hand, a private person is religious in the more rigorous sense of the word and expresses his religiousness, he is regarded as crazy—and why? Because the middle term of "livelihood" is missing.

When someone is regarded as living independently and does in fact, people have a great urge to say to him: "If I were in your place, I know exactly how I would run my life." And thereupon they come out with it and one sees that they have no impression at all of anything; meanwhile, in order to live they become grocers, chimney sweeps, artists, preachers, etc.

In margin: * It[952] also relates that the North American schools and high schools use summaries sometimes containing 20 branches of knowledge—in all brevity.

VII[1] A 152   *n.d.,* 1846

« **3310**

In the same book (p. 199) by Moritz Carriere[953] are quoted the following words by Sebastian Franck: *"Als ein Philosoph gefragt wurde, wann er angefangen ein Philosoph zu werden, antwortete er: da ich mir selbst anfing ein Freund zu werden. Wenn man einen Christen fragte, wann er ein Christ geworden, würde er antworten: da ich anfing mir selbst ein Feind zu werden."*[954]

VIII[1] A 70   *n.d.,* 1847

« **3311**

What pedantry there is in being a philosopher nowadays. One thinks of antiquity when a man was: philosopher and tyrant in Corinth.[955] This combination would be absolutely ridiculous to the present age.

VIII[1] A 152   *n.d.,* 1847

« **3312**

What Campanella says is very excellent: *Das Nichtseyn besteht aus den drei Principien der Onmacht, der Unwissenheit, und des Hasses.*[956]

Carriere, p. 567[957]
VIII[1] A 166   *n.d.,* 1847

« **3313**

In *Works of Love*[958] I said: The age of thinkers is passed. Soon one will have to say: The age of thought is passed.

VIII[1] A 627   *n.d.,* 1848

« **3314**

In the old days men loved wisdom (φιλοσοφία); nowadays we love the name of philosopher.[959]

IX A 148   *n.d., 1848*

« **3315** *Speculation—Faith*

Speculation can present the problems, can recognize that every individual problem is a problem for faith, is compounded and characterized in such a way that it is a problem for faith—and then can submit: Will you believe or not?

Furthermore, speculation can supervise and check faith—that is, what is believed in a given moment or is the content of faith—in order to see that there is no rattle-brained mixing with faith of categories which are not objects of faith but, for example, of speculation.

All this is a very protracted undertaking.

Speculation is sighted—and yet only to the extent that it says: Here it is; then it is blind; then comes faith, which believes; it is sighted in relation to objects of faith.

X^2 A 432   *n.d., 1850*

« **3316** *"The Professor"*

In the earlier ancient period the philosopher was a power, an ethical power, a [person of] character—then the empire protected itself by putting them on salary, by making them "professors." So has it gone also with Christianity.

The professor is a castrate, but he has not castrated himself for the sake of the heavenly Kingdom but just the reverse—in order to accommodate nicely into this characterless world.

X^4 A 450   *n.d., 1852*

« **3317** *Epigram*

IV

"Is this the road to London?" "Yes, if you turn around, for you are going away from London."[960]

I have read many theological works, some philological and philosophical works, particularly philosophical works related to Greek philosophy: I bow respectfully to the scholarship, the research, etc. which they manifest; I acknowledge with proper modesty that I am only an apprentice, but there is one thing with which I must disagree.

I have found the same way of thinking in every single one of these works without variation.

They say: In Socrates philosophy was *as yet merely* (pay attention to this *as yet merely*)—it was *as yet merely* a life.[961] In Plato, on the other hand (consequently it goes forward; we are ascending), it becomes (we are ascending) doctrine. Then it becomes scientific scholarship. And so it goes with philosophy, onward and upward, until in our time we stand at the pinnacle of scientific scholarship and look back on Socrates as inferior, for in him philosophy was, after all, as yet merely a life.

In Christ, in the apostles, in the first Christians Christianity was *as yet merely* (pay attention to *as yet merely*)—it was *as yet merely* a life. Then it advances, we are ascending; Christianity becomes doctrine, then scientific scholarship, we are ascending—and now we stand at the pinnacle of scientific scholarship and look back on the first Christians, for in them Christianity was as yet merely a life.

What is this, anyway? Is it an extremely profound cunning or an incomprehensible trap, involving, incidentally, all the mental faculties.

Is this the road to London? Certainly, but only if one turns around.

But how is this incomprehensible inversion to be explained?
Quite simply.

To be specific, if philosophy or religion is a man's life, his life (for philosophy and religion are his life) will miss all the earthly advantages and benefits, because philosophy and religion are heterogeneous with this earthly life.

We human beings have no inclination in this direction—which I find to be quite natural.

If we could only conveniently fix it some other way. Ah, yes! This way, for example: I exclude my personal life, make my personal life one thing and philosophy another. In this way my personal life is at my disposal, and now, like everyone else, completely unembarrassed by philosophy, like everyone else, a merchant, a shopkeeper, etc., I organize my personal life so as to acquire as much of earthly benefits and advantages as possible. Philosophy, on the other hand, is scientific scholarship.

In this manner we get (in place of that philosopher in whom philosophy was as yet merely a life, in place of those first Christians in whom Christianity was as yet only a life), we get an instructor, a professor of philosophy, a clergyman, etc., someone who, from the point of view of scientific scholarship, the objective, superior position, looks back at Socrates and regards him as inferior, looks back at the first Christians and regards them as inferior, for in Socrates philosophy was as yet merely a life, and in the first Christians Christianity was as yet merely etc.

But is this not a bit too much—to want to have the earthly benefits and advantages—and then in addition want to stand above those glorious ones.

Is this the road to London? Certainly, but only if one turns around.

Turn around, make a beginning (I propose no more) by simply admitting that the present is not superior but inferior. On this road it is possible to come back to the truth, on the other road—or if one goes away from London on the road which leads to London—it is impossible.

X^5 A 113 *n.d.*, 1853

PIETISM

« **3318** *Pietism*

Yes, indeed, pietism[962] (properly understood, not simply in the sense of abstaining from dancing and such externals, no, in the sense of witnessing for the truth and suffering for it, together with the understanding that suffering in this world belongs to being a Christian, and that a shrewd and secular conformity with this world is unchristian)— yes, indeed, pietism is the one and only consequence of Christianity. And the mildest suggestion, it seems to me, is that we at least put up with its being said, without thereby judging anyone, but directing every individual, including me, to grace and indulgence.

x^3 A 437   *n.d.*, 1850

« **3319** *A Sly Twist That Will perhaps Be Given to My Cause.*

It will be made to seem as if I wanted to introduce pietism, petty and pusillanimous renunciation in things that do not matter.

No, thank you, I have never made the slightest gesture in this direction. What I want is to incite in the direction of becoming ethical characters, witnesses of the truth, of willing to suffer for truth and to renounce worldly shrewdness.

x^3 A 556   *n.d.*, 1850

« **3320** *How Christianity Is Going Backwards in Christendom*

When Spener made his appearance, the established was strictly orthodox, and Spener was charged with heterodoxy.

Now pietism is the only little stronghold orthodoxy has, the established is half-and-half.

The historical aspect of this observation I have read in Märklin, *Darstellung und Critik des modernen Pietismus*[963] (1839) and also in Hosbach, *Leben Speners,*[964] at the very end of part II.

x^3 A 682   *n.d.*, 1850

« **3321** *Francke*

He was charged with wanting to establish a new religion and the like. He answers: *"Ich verlange keine neue Religion sondern neue Herzen."*

In his *Abgenöthigte Fürstellung*, para. 41. See Guericke, *Franckes Leben*, p. 52, n.[965]

X^4 A 84   *n.d.*, 1851

« **3322** *Francke*

Francke observes correctly (in connection with dancing, to which, incidentally, he is opposed) that such matters are not primary subjects for discussion; the most important is the improvement of the heart. But the world prefers to talk about such things first, in order to label Christianity as extremism.

But Francke himself does not actually use the approach properly. He goes into the subject of whether dancing is permissible and gives reasons against it. No, it is actually a more sagacious approach to answer: I am so far behind in Christianity that I do not have time to get involved in the question of dancing, or to dance, either. This is an authentic religious approach. The trouble is we are so inclined to show that we are right and to come up with reasons, and thereby we abandon the essentially Christian position.

It is just the same with something a bit more weighty—science and scholarship. Anyone who gives reason to prove that there is no science and scholarship from a Christian point of view fools himself. No, take any Christian rule of life and say: Since, unfortunately, I must admit that I have not personally realized it, how can I have time for the question of science and scholarship. This is essentially the Socratic way.

The passage about dancing is found in Guericke's *Franckes Leben*, p. 178.[966] Among the reasons against dancing Francke gives there is one which is so lofty or high that one almost has to laugh—he says that dancing conflicts with "the imitation of Christ." No doubt a dancing partner really does not look like an "imitator of Christ," but here, as we say of the voice, Francke's argument breaks into a falsetto; it is too high.

X^4 A 94   *n.d.*, 1851

PLATO

« 3323

The great picture in *Phaedrus*,[967] in which the fourth kind of madness—the madness of love—is described, a description which is just as chaste as it is voluptuous, because voluptuousness is at all times conquered by the chasteness; the voluptuousness is the strong coloring.

It ends with a prayer.

The whole passage must be examined. Para. 244–57.

Hegel[968] touches on this picture.

Also Schleiermacher[969] in the preface to *Phaedrus*, but [he] thinks it ought not be insisted upon.

What is expressed here is love's moment of stimulation, which is so incomparably described.

III B 26   n.d., 1841

« 3324

The definition of being which Plato gives in *Parmenides*,[970] para. 151, the last words: Being is nothing other than participating in an essence in time present.

IV C 70   n.d., 1842–43

« 3325

The trilogy which is made so much of—art, religion, and philosophy[971]—Plato and especially Plotinus already had: music, love, philosophy.[972]

IV A 159   n.d., 1843

« 3326

This was the basic meaning of Gorgias's theory,[973] that the strongest is the just, and that it was a kind of self-defense on the part of the weak, who had taught them, to invent the chatter about virtue etc.

IV A 230   n.d., 1843

« 3327

The excellence of Plato's *Republic* is that he did not make the state higher than the individual, least of all in the manner of Hegelian jargon. In order to describe the individual, he describes the state; he describes a democrat by describing democracy; he constructs a state for the individual, *unum noris omnes*[974]—this is the proper human ideality; otherwise we get the confusion that many by being many produce something entirely different from what each one is individually.

VII[1] A 70 *n.d.*, 1846

« 3328 *Plato*

Is it not strange that Plato in his *Republic* wants to have "the poets" expelled from the state,[975] frequently attacks "the poets" in various ways, and yet actually was himself a poet, or a thinker who was predominantly poetic.

It is also strange that this is not an earlier stage and the crucial ethical stage a later one. Alas, no, it is the reverse. It is a reverse μετάβασις εἰς ἄλλο γένος.[976] It is reminiscent of Socrates, who was himself actually an ethicist and was right in wanting to be rid of the "poet." In the second generation (Plato) there is such regression that Plato is the poet who wants to be rid of the "poet"; he poetizes wanting to be rid of the poet—so far it has gone in reverse.

Some words of Aristippus (in Wieland's *Aristipp und seine Zeit*, IV, p. 34[977]), where he speaks of Plato's *Republic*, have impressed me: "You demand," he writes, "my opinion of this new *poetizing* by our avowed poet-enemies."

This aspect of Plato has been significant to me personally as well. I have always recognized that there is a poetic strain in me. But in me there is a struggling forward. I do not spontaneously imitate a Socrates and let the matter regress. No, in the boundless turbulence of the religious I am one position ahead. I point out the turn, the swing, which has to be made; but almost collapsing myself under the enormous intellectual task of clearing the terrain, I point out the simple ethical existence as the higher life.

X[2] A 608 *n.d.*, 1850

« 3329 *Inversion*

The Christian interpretation that here in the world everything is reversed, that the more I try my best to be virtuous the worse it goes for me etc.—all this is already to be found in the whole excellent presentation of the ethical in the first books of Plato's *Republic*.

[*In margin:* And if even a pagan conceived of the world in this way, one who did not have the highest, the true ideal—how dreadful must

Christianity's conception of it be, for the distance is in proportion to the elevation of the ideal, and the world therefore is completely good only for the wicked or for those who recognize no ideal.]

The Sophists teach that to do wrong is advantageous[978] and that everyone knows it, yet for safety's sake one maintains the appearance of willing the good—Socrates wants men to do the good and to avoid the appearance of it, does not want the reward to be a temptation.

Here, incidentally, is a little difficulty which is easily removed. When the Sophists teach that to do injustice is most advantageous and that everyone basically regards it this way—what then is the purpose of the show of being regarded as just. If this is supposed to be an advantage, the world must actually regard justice as the good, and the world cannot then be so evil that the relationship is one of inversion. The secret, however, lies right here. It is merely a show of being virtue, justice, etc., and in this weak form it pleases the world, primarily as an expression for cunning, which cunningly knows how to maintain the show. As soon as willing to be just really becomes something in earnest, the world cannot tolerate it, and things do not go well for the just man, but an interesting mystification, as if the world itself half believed, half disbelieved that it is profitable, precisely this hypocrisy is part of being very successful, as long as the world is willing to be a part of this mystification and honor this man as a just man.

x^2 A 609   *n.d.,* 1850

« 3330

In margin of 3329 (x^2 A 609):

What a superb eulogy on this world is placed in the mouth of the eulogist of injustice: "The just man will be whipped, stretched on the rack, put in chains; his eyes will be burned out, and after suffering every imaginable mistreatment he will be nailed to a cross, and now too late he will understand that in this world one ought to strive to *appear* just but not be mad enough *to be* just. On the other hand, what a glorious lot the unjust man has in this world if he is shrewd enough to gain public approval and is regarded as an upright man while under the mask of virtue he allows himself everything. The highest positions of honor in the state are his; he can marry whom he will and give in marriage to whom he will. Everyone counts it an honor to have associations and relationships with him, and since no means are too base for him to use in reaching his goal, he is successful in everything; in every situation he comes out on top—in short he becomes a rich and powerful man in the position to benefit his friends and to harm his enemies, yes, to win over even the gods with magnificent offerings and rich gifts, so that he will be dearer to them than the just man, who has nothing to give."[979]

x^2 A 610   n.d.

« 3331

Zeller, *Die Philosophie der Griechen*.[980] Tübingen: 1844. volume I, part 3, "The Sophists," p. 256. Plato attributes to the Sophists the general characteristic of debating for and against on any question (ἀ ντιλογικὴ τέχνη) and to instruct the listeners in this art (ἀμφισβη- τητικοὺς ποιεῖν[981]). And it is the same art of which Aristophanes accuses Socrates, that he gives instruction in both just and unjust discourse. This is the appearance of wisdom of which Plato accuses the Sophists, because its basis is that wisdom is not taught in objective knowledge but in subjective reflection, which can lean just as well toward one side as the other, or the capacity praised so highly by Hippias in Xenophon (*Memorabilia*, IV, 4, 6) of always being able to say something new about everything.

x^6 C 6:1   n.d., 1852

POLEMICAL, POLEMICS

« 3332

It is not accurate to say that meekness makes for our peace. We should rather say: If you are meek, you have peace, even though the whole world be at war and at war against you.

x¹ A 205   n.d., 1849

« 3333 *The Gospel of Peace*

This is what Christianity is called and calls itself—and yet it is that which disturbed existence [*Tilværelsen*] as never before.

Here again we see how far all direct categories can go in characterizing the essentially Christian, which is always inverse.

x³ A 428   n.d., 1850

« 3334 *Church—State*
Christianity—the World

For many, many generations men have continually kept on trimming and reducing Christianity, made it milder and milder, more and more domesticated, until finally it is not Christianity at all.

No wonder it is thought that Christianity must ultimately become identical with the world.

Never in all eternity can Christianity become identical with the world. Christianity will never become identical with the world[982] any more than the single individual's flesh and blood (natural drives, secular-mindedness) will ever as a matter of course ever become identical with the essentially Christian, so that the individual is perhaps born with self-renunciation instead of with flesh and blood (which on other grounds also would be nonsense, since self-renunciation presupposes something to fight against, specifically flesh and blood).

This everlasting nonsense about Christianity permeating the world more and more is a *quid pro quo,* a babbling of contradictions, for the truth of the matter is that the world is more and more wearing away and gnawing away the essentially Christian from Christianity.

x³ A 574   n.d., 1850

« 3335 *My Polemic*

Christianity cannot be developed on the conditions current official preaching employs in offering Christianity.

Yet I do not use this as a basis for denying that those who offer it on these conditions are Christians. No, not at all, for in quietness of mind before God it is possible that they make the admission for which alone I contend—namely, that in human weakness and sympathy there has been a scaling down, just as I myself do not try to pass as willing or able to realize [*realisere*] the most rigorous kind of proclamation of Christianity.

Consequently, what I contend for is that if the proclaimers of Christianity have made this confession in silence, then we ought to have it said and officially noted.

It must be said that we do scale down. If this admission is suppressed, then the whole matter is something quite different. And the tragedy is precisely that it is being suppressed.

x^3 A 580   *n.d.*, 1850

« 3336 *Christendom*

It can be stated *a priori* that in all Christendom today there is not one single official (clergyman, professor, teacher) who in one way or another does not avail himself of the counterfeit expansion of Christianity.

Efforts should be made to halt and work against this counterfeit expansion. It is nothing but a perfidious and hypocritical or scatterbrained and stupid adulteration. In the New Testament to be a Christian is a polemical concept,[982] identified by being the most strenuous life of suffering a man can possibly lead. Thus we humans could openly declare: We do not wish to get involved with this, we do not want to be Christians. But we neither dare nor are sufficiently honorable to do so. The same thing can be attained in another way. if we are all Christians, the polemic and the strenuousness resulting from it are abolished. If we are all Christians, being a Christian is no longer a battle but a game, all the identifications of being a Christian are not polemical but direct: the more Christians, the more worldly profit.

Thus efforts should be made to halt the false expansion. When I think about it, it seems to me that it cannot be done unless Christ himself comes again and once more gets twelve apostles to scrap Christendom altogether and in effigy the almost eighteen hundred years of Christendom.

But no one sees this. No, they go on as usual: there comes a new set of preachers and professors who marry and have children, from whom again there will come preachers and professors engaged in the further spreading of Christianity (that is, Christian nonsense): bright, smiling, happy, blissful prospect—from nonsense to nonsense!

And yet someday my vision may come true—Christianity will be reclaimed from the state, from the generation. Just as the still honest officials once approached the state imploringly, sometimes also im- periously, with authority, asking that it remove itself from Christianity, so officials will come who will say to the state: *manus de tabula;* don't risk it, don't give the patronizing four shillings this way, do you not know that it is high treason against Christianity's divine majesty; have you not considered the many souls whose welfare you have on your conscience because you lured them with a salary to become clergy- men.

The matter will take this serious turn as soon as men are able to understand it, for making a living and everything related to it will enter into the picture.

Incidentally, I could laugh when I think of the tragic-comic situa- tion of theology, which until now has been regarded as the most secure way, ceasing to be the way of life (for it is well-known that the way to life is something else). They probably will say of him: "He hasn't learned a thing" and mean that he has not made himself proficient in any trade or profession. Imagine a father with a twenty-four year old son who is a theological candidate—and hear the worried father say: "Ludwig is a good-for-nothing who hasn't learned a thing." "What do you mean—hasn't learned a thing—he has studied, hasn't he—he is a theological candidate." "But don't you know that that amounts to nothing since there isn't a theological living anymore!"

XI[1] A 156   n.d., 1854

« 3337 *The Enemies of Christianity*

In a way it is good that Christianity still has enemies, because for the longest time they have been the only ones from whom it has been possible to get any trustworthy information about what Christianity is.[*] The Christians, of course, reserve the right to make it conform to their taste.

Yet I dare say Christianity will soon—that is, if Christianity is represented by those now called Christians—become so meaningless that it will not even be able to make enemies. The reason Christianity still has enemies is probably mainly because of its past history, its historical significance.

XI[1] A 161   n.d., 1854

« 3338

[*]*In margin of 3337* (XI[1] A 161):

This is because the enemies hate the Christians and thus are able to depict what Christianity is; their hate helps them to see what Christianity in the New Testament is. Hatred toward being man on his own terms. But these days the Christian certainly does not hate himself, therefore he does not know either, does not want to know, what Christianity is.

XI[1] A 162   n.d.

« 3339

According to the New Testament the natural man is utterly opposed to being a Christian; in fact, according to the New Testament there is a life-and-death struggle between God and man.

That being the case, some transformation is already required—simply to become aware of the Christian requirement and to be able to present it.

If someone does this, then there promptly is not one but probably there are ten who get busy showing that it is an enormous exaggeration, that such a thing is not Christianity—which everyone can comprehend.

And the latter view prevails, because, after all, every one can comprehend that the former is wrong—what nonsense!

Since according to its own teaching Christianity relates conversely to being man, it follows as a matter of course that the syllogism "Everyone can comprehend it" must be reversed like this: That which everyone can comprehend is not Christianity.

The confusion has been fortified by the new confusion in the illusion that, after all, we are all Christians. For it does hold true of the universally human that everyone can comprehend that this is this and that, ergo.

For ages, now, the essentially Christian has not been served in character, and everyone who does not serve it in character completely accepts this: Everyone can comprehend it; ergo, a person without character finds it impossible to resist polemically.

Young man, you who may perhaps read this at some time, when you read it you will find it so obvious that it will almost seem redundant to make it so obvious. My young friend, if you are to carry it out you will constantly need, year after year, elementary drill and practice in it; otherwise you will be fooled and will end up fooling others, and even end in this "Every one can comprehend it." By means of the truth you lose out on all the benefits and advantages of this world; by going along with this "Every one can comprehend it," the benefits and advantages of this earth come to you.

Believe me! For me there is a singular coherence in all this; therefore I cannot be fooled; otherwise I, too, would be. Even the best trained decoy dove eventually ends up being fooled and flies away with the doves it is supposed to trap, but when it is fastened to the dovecot by a cord it is not fooled. And the little fish wriggling on the hook, painfully pierced by it so that a bigger fish can be caught—no matter how many of its kind come, even a whole shoal of fish—it is not fooled.

XI^2 A 347   *n.d.*, 1854

POSSIBILITY

« 3340

The more significant an individual is, the easier he will find actuality to be, the more difficult he will find possibility.[983] This is the expression of an ethical view. Viewed esthetically (that is, in relation to enjoyment), he will find possibility more intensive than actuality.

IV A 35   n.d., 1843

« 3341

Actually it is wicked—the sufferer's presumption when he has hoped and waited for a long time but receives no help and then abruptly stops and says: Now help is impossible. O, such a man does not know what he is saying; otherwise he would shrink from such high treason. What is a man's crumb of life before God—did not heaven move if Jupiter merely wrinkled his brow—should it be impossible then for God to help a man a little bit.

IX A 36   n.d., 1848

« 3342

Thale's words are like a motto on the whole modern method of proclaiming Christianity: Declare the probable but suppress the impossible.

Plutarch, *The Feast of the Seven Wise Men,* ch. 17.[984]

In margin: Christianity has been interpreted entirely on the basis of what is probable—and Christianity has been suppressed.

IX A 239   n.d., 1848

« 3343

It is a dangerous business to arrive in eternity with possibilities which one himself has prevented from becoming actualities. Possibility is a hint from God. A person must follow it. The possibility for the highest is in every man; he must follow it. If God does not want it, then let him hinder it; the person must not hinder it himself. Trusting in God, I have ventured, but I have failed—there is peace and rest and

535

God's confidence in that. I have not ventured—it is an utterly unhappy thought, a torment for all eternity.

IX A 352   *n.d.*, 1848

« **3344**

The miracle of the five loaves[985] is a beautiful commentary on the verse: Seek first his kingdom and his righteousness, and all these things shall be yours as well.[986] It was in order to hear Christ that the people had stayed so long—and the rest was added as well.

But perhaps someone says: A person can't wait for miracles. To that I would answer: No, certainly not. But would you then dare compare your reason and imagination with God, that is, because your imagination does not stretch far enough to think of possibilities, should God therefore not have possibilities? God has 100,000 possibilities at every moment without any of these possibilities being a miracle. But the arbitrariness is in your wanting to make a cutoff because you no longer see any possibility. This cannot be emphasized enough. Merely think of the relationship between a somewhat limited person and one brilliantly gifted. Perhaps there comes a moment when the somewhat limited man, who has confided in the brilliant one, says: No, it's all over now. There is no more help to be had. But in talking with the other the limited man would discover to his humiliation that he still has various possibilities. The ingratitude and the blameworthiness lies in this—that the man of limitations breaks off and says: There is no possibility, instead of saying: *I* see no possibility.

IX A 412   *n.d.*, 1848

« **3345**

Christ's own life manifests this difference between possibility and actuality:[987] one can understand in "possibility" what one cannot identify in "actuality." Did the prophets not prophesy that Christ would suffer—and then a person came along who suffered and said of himself that he was the Messiah—but what happened—they were unable to recognize him, the very one the prophecies fit; and yet they were able to understand the prophecies.

So is it always. If I invite a man to come to my house and then explain to him that I intend to take a magnanimous step of some sort, a step which will bring along with it loss and suffering for myself, he will completely understand me, he will think it wonderful, he will admire me, and he will go away excited and inspired—and if I then actually take the step and in no time at all actually come to suffer, he will be unable to recognize me.

Imagination[988] constantly wants to foreshorten and to slip in another picture, the picture of the noble sufferer admired by all. But in actuality things do not go that fast; actuality perhaps separates it by a distance of fifty years.

Very few succeed in receiving the impression of "actuality." The majority must be satisfied with being deceived by getting only the impression of the first (the magnanimous moment which precedes, when the actuality of suffering has not yet begun) or of the last, when the result is there and he has triumphed.

x^2 A 114   *n.d.,* 1849

« 3346 *The Relationship: Possibility—Actuality*

In margin: See p. 55n [i.e., x^2 A 205]

It cannot be expressed more precisely—the infinite difference which exists between understanding something in possibility and understanding the same in actuality.[989] Consider the apostles. They certainly are as honestly and uprightly willing as possible. Christ has told them in advance what is going to happen—predicted it so that they might not be offended. And yet when it becomes actual, they are offended just the same.

The fact is that when I understand something in possibility, I do not become essentially changed, I remain in the old ways and make use of my imagination; when it becomes actuality, then it is I who am changed, and now the question is whether I can preserve myself. When it is a matter of understanding in possibility, I have to strain my imagination to the limit; when it is a matter of understanding the same thing in actuality, I am spared all exertion in regard to my imagination; actuality is placed very close to me, all too close; it has, as it were, swallowed me, and the question now is whether I can rescue myself from it.

x^2 A 202   *n.d.,* 1849

« 3347

If I present in the sphere of possibility the way the extraordinary person must always suffer—everyone is moved. But in the situation of contemporaneity they would all say of an extraordinary: Well, as far as he is concerned, it is another matter; his pride is far too insufferable;

it is not our fault that he is as peculiar as he is, etc. This means that the extraordinary is permitted in possibility—is denied in actuality.

x^3 A 16   *n.d.*, 1850

« 3348 *Possibility—Actuality*

Mynster orates and says: And He did not withhold the great words, but He (Christ) said them: I am indeed a king—and then Mynster weeps, and I, Miss Jespersen, Student Møller, Chairman of the Board Nissen, Grocer Grønberg, etc. etc.—all of us weep and admire Mynster; many a one is not at all clear whether he is weeping at the thought of Christ or shedding tears of admiration for Mynster.

When He said these words, believe me, the Jews laughed and Pilate shrugged his shoulders—and the rest of us, what would we have done?

I think that I might be able to persuade a stone that this is so.

And yet not even this may be said—or you will see how actuality passes judgment. You will move not one; they will laugh you to scorn (alas, as the expert, the master of persuasion) and accuse you of conceit, pride, and impracticality.

And then ought you not be permitted the consoling thought of death!

x^3 A 290   *n.d.*, 1850

« 3349 *Possibility—Actuality*

I can never sufficiently stress how crucial to a true picture of the essentially Christian is the fact that what appears so extraordinarily inviting in possibility becomes just the opposite when made actual, or that the actualization, the realization, is not a superlative of the picture of possibility, but that here everything is reversed. A person is a great success if he is able to portray truth glowingly. One supposes that he will be an even greater success if he does the higher: act according to it. No, thanks, here comes the inversion: the more [you act accordingly], the more you will suffer.

x^3 A 482   *n.d.*, 1850

« 3350 *The Established Order of "Christendom"*
or
Possibility—Actuality

Permit me to use an illustration. Imagine a country by the sea.

In this land—let us imagine it this way—this doctrine was recited as an article of faith: man can swim, is lighter than water, does not drown. There were state-appointed teachers who recited the doctrine every Sunday, proved to men and persuaded men, reassured them, that they could be absolutely sure that it is certain that all of them are able to swim—for, naturally, this statement which seems so brief, when it became official doctrine, transmitted from generation to generation, grew into a whole science, with countless books written about it giving reasons and more reasons.

It was the official proclamation. Now there was another power in the state, the police, who with the most rigorous injunctions and punishment kept guard lest anyone should have the audacity to go into the water—in order to see if it were true that he was able to swim. Such an attempt was punished by imprisonment, and the clergy warned against it as being blasphemous.

This is the situation in "Christendom." We hold off Christianity as a possibility, prove it, persuade and convince ourselves that we are Christians, that we can be quite at ease—and then we denounce as presumptuous and cry "Woe!" to the person who would dare to make Christianity a reality (wants to go out into the water to see if it is true that he can swim, or wants to go out into the water out of joy over the fact that he can swim, as the clergy have proved with many reasons that he can do) and the authorities punish it.

Christianity is preached—and everything is used to strengthen us in the illusion that we are Christians and have faith— —but woe to him who dares to make the leap to see if he does have faith or wants to make the leap[990] on the basis of what the clergy say about his having faith.

You must believe that there is a providence, and "rest assured, you do believe it, you are a Christian"—but woe unto you if you dare venture to order your life according to it—if Christianity becomes in fact an actuality for you, such an attempt is blasphemy and is punished by jail.

And yet it surely is Christianity's intention that a person use this life to venture out in such a way that God can get hold of him, that one gets to see whether or not he actually has faith, and if not, to strive with God's help to get it.

What responsibility! In the last judgment, the question will surely be: Have you employed life[991] to test whether you have faith or not, in order then to gain it? And that is just what "Christendom" wants with all its strength to keep everyone from doing by (1) calming and tranquilizing in illusions, (2) by declaring venturing out to be presumption and blasphemy, and (3) by applying civil punishment.

Thus they storm and rage and rant against the freethinkers who want to make mythology out of Christianity—but when we hold off Christianity as a possibility in this way we ourselves make it into mythology, poetry, in short, into something to which we relate only through imagination. We are different from the atheists only in that we do not insidiously declare that Christianity is mythology, poetry—but conceal it.

X^5 A 143   *n.d.*, 1853

PRACTICALITY, SENSIBLENESS

« **3351**

In days of old when men were not so calculating and practical, one occasionally saw an inspired, enthusiastic act, true heroism. Nowadays calculating practicality stifles everything. If men do not succeed in breaking through and really learning profoundly to despise calculating practicality (the contemptible peddler who offers a person earthly advantage), to perceive that calculating practicality, that is, acting shrewdly, defiles a person much worse than stealing and murdering, simply because everything here is intended to suppress the conscience —if they do not succeed, then everything is lost.

VIII[1] A 188   n.d., 1847

« **3352**

Christ[992] says: Blessed is the one who is not offended in me. How enormously concerned—but at the same time how close at hand giving offense must lie to the essentially Christian [*Christelige*]. If what is called Christianity these days—this doctrine which particularly satisfies the cultured as the peak of culture—were Christianity, how in the world is there any place for this concern: Blessed is the one who is not offended in me. How in the world could any man be offended by modern Christianity! I know only one form (which is not sufficiently considered) that would be offensive to a simple man—that truth and Christianity should be inaccessible to him. But in this sense one could also be offended by art and science and by tightrope walking etc.

Has Mynster ever dared to say that this is Christianity: Do the good and then you will be punished for it. And why has he not done it? Because he himself wants to be honored and esteemed for doing the good, wants to convince himself that he deserves the esteem he enjoys since he is indeed doing the good. But that is paganism. In part it has yet another basis, because Mynster is taken up with a notion about practical [*praktiske*] life and actuality: that it does not help any to require so much.[993] Certainly it does not help any—except that it can help a person in such a way that precisely what Christianity speaks

541

about happens to him. But then Christ has been the most impracti-cal[994] of all.

For the most part there is great confusion in regard to what is practical.[995] In contrast to an empty formalism, a conceited scientific scholarliness etc., people talk about practicality and eulogize Chris-tianity for being practical. When one gets down to brass tacks he finds that practicing Christianity is not very useful and that it is highly impractical. Indeed, is there anything more impractical than offering one's life for the truth, anything more impractical than not looking to one's own advantage, anything more impractical than making one's life difficult and strenuous and being rewarded with insults, is there any-thing more impractical than being labelled—not with titles and honors —but with invective and ridicule? And yet I would certainly think that this is Christianity; and yet I would certainly think that old man Socra-tes was infinitely farther along than all the geographical Christendom of today. But, of course, Socrates, who is called practical in contrast to the theoretical philosophers, is just as impractical, almost just as impractical, as Christianity. How impractical not to take money for his teaching, how impractical not to defend himself in the way he himself knew would bring about his release, how impractical not to escape from the prison, how impractical to die for the truth! For a sailor to die at sea where he risked his life in the hope of profit, for the soldier to fall in battle where he risked his life in the hope of becoming a general—that is more like it, that is practical—but to die for the truth!

VIII[1] A 510   *n.d.*, 1848

« **3353**

Only then will history be cleansed and purified. When all these "practical realists" who perhaps have been bold and shameless enough in the situation of contemporaneity, availing themselves of the advantage, and also of the unconstraint granted them in regard to what history will say of them—when all these "practical realists" have fallen into decay and are no longer bold but dead and buried and forgotten as if they had never existed, then he remains, he whom history sowed, he who must humbly endure the tortures of contemporaneity.

IX A 133   *n.d.*, 1848

« **3354**

The various presentations (in the work "Come unto me all you who labor etc.")[996] of how the practical, sensible people, the statesmen etc., judge Christ in the situation of contemporaneity are merely the carrying out of finitude's judgment of the absolute.[997] Therefore there is constantly something prophetically insane in most of them, in that the most insane thing they can say of Christ is precisely what he wills. For example, when the shrewd and sensible say, "Unless he intends to be put to death."[998] But that is precisely what Christ had in mind. It is the same in many passages.

IX A 140 *n.d.*, 1848

« **3355**

A man cannot really be said to be truly able to serve the good until he disdains acting shrewdly,[999] even though it would bring him ever so much advantage—disdains it just as profoundly and in exactly the same way as an earnest married man would disdain staring at every female on the street.

IX A 409 *n.d.*, 1848

« **3356**

When a teaching or doctrine offers the learner advantages of one sort or another and for this reason it is proposed that he adhere to it —well, it is worth listening to. But when a teaching reverses the relationship, enters the world not to serve men but to be served by them, sacrificing everything for its sake—must not a practical man regard it as madness.[1000]

This is just about the situation of Christianity when considered by a practical man; for the business of eternal salvation does not mean much to a practical man, and for all relative $\tau \acute{\epsilon} \lambda \eta$[1001] Christianity actually reverses the relationship.

x^2 A 154 *n.d.*, 1849

« **3357** *Lines by a "Prudent Person"*

The first time is always the most expensive. The first time one buys spinach it is almost worth its weight in gold; later in the summer a person can get more than he wants for two shillings.

It is the same with Christianity. Thus a prudent person is not so dumb as to bet on Christianity the first time; no, but 1800 years later it will have properly fallen to the price where even prudence advises buying it. This is the case even in relation to a genius. Prudence holds back at first—the second and third time there may be mention of bidding, depending on how significant the genius is, for if he is a rather significant genius, then one must wait for the sixth or seventh time around.

This, you see, is prudence. It is precisely by means of this prudence that we prove the truth of Christianity these days—namely, that the sensible and prudent people are for it—which is precisely what proves that Christianity no longer exists.

X³ A 143   n.d., 1850

« 3358

Ea non media sed nulla via est, velut eventum exspectantium, quo fortunæ suæ consilia applicent.[1002] Livius 32, 21.

Splendidly spoken of those who "have to see results first"[1003] before they pass judgment.

X³ A 460   n.d., 1850

« 3359 Wanting To See the Results before Passing Judgment[1004]

This has its basis in the mistaken notion that the outstanding person is regarded as if he were merely up for an examination and that all the rest of us have to do is pass judgment on him—rather than that every living person by being alive is up for examination, so that *in casu* he himself is the one who is judged, together with his verdict that he would not pass judgment before he had seen the results.

X³ A 461   n.d., 1850

« 3360 Sensibleness[1005]—The Changed Form of the World

An enthusiastic person has an urge for decisiveness; perhaps he also believes that decisiveness will give him power; perhaps he also has illusions about his own abilities. But wherever there is enthusiasm, there is also a tendency toward making decisions, toward catastrophe.

"Sensibleness" [*Forstandighed*] has made another discovery. It has perceived once and for all that no man can go through with the idea to the end, that ultimately, if he does not abandon the idea and thereby save himself, a decision must come, a catastrophe, which will expose that he is a spineless fellow. In addition, sensibleness also makes an appeal to experience—numerous observations of what happened to an enthusiast when the chips were down. The difference between man and man, therefore, lies not so much in their capabilities, for no one can go through with the idea, as in their not getting involved in arriving at decisions. Therefore sensibleness maintains that wisdom is chiefly a matter of preventing decisions. Thus one can solemnly assert that if it is required, he will of course be the man—and at the same time take care, if possible, as far as he can manage, not to come to any decision.

The prevention of decision on the part of sensibleness has brought about an existential obstruction, so to speak, and a dreadful demoralization, which then ended with a dreadful catastrophe such as that of 1848.

x⁴ A 416   n.d., 1851

« 3361 Christianity—Mankind

While the human race these days has Christianity down on its level, underfoot, in such a way that one relates to it as a superior intellect relates to fantasies, it still has an evil conscience, a dark suspicion that Christianity still is really sovereign.

And therefore we do not want to let go of it, and at the same time we would make every effort to keep Christianity from becoming Christianity again. The world is smart enough to understand that it is best insured against this sovereign by having him down underfoot in this way; the world is smart enough to understand that to get rid of him entirely could lead to getting him back again in earnest. No, the world says, it is best the way it is now—now we have Christianity most advantageously, insofar as this can be done or, more correctly, insofar as this could be done.

XI¹ A 367   n.d., 1854

« 3362 The World's Conscience

In Plato's *Republic* (III),[1006] Phokylides is quoted as declaring that when a person has come so far that he has enough to live on he ought to practice virtue ($\delta\epsilon\hat{\iota}\ \zeta\eta\tau\epsilon\hat{\iota}\nu\ \beta\iota\acute{o}\tau\eta\nu,\ \grave{a}\rho\acute{\epsilon}\tau\eta\nu\ \delta'\ \ddot{o}\tau\alpha\nu\ \hat{\eta}\ \beta\acute{\iota}os\ \ddot{\eta}\delta\eta;$[1007] see the notes in Heise[1008]).

I am reminded here again of a statement I read in Schopenhauer[1009]—that an Englishman is supposed to have said that to have a conscience was such an expensive way of life that his circumstances did not permit it.

—And Englishmen, after all, are recognized as practical people; therefore an Englishman's judgment must certainly be regarded as conclusive concerning what practical people must understand by conscience.

And this again reminds me of a story Father[1010] told. In the old days when district judges and bailiffs were the gracious lord's sometime coachmen or servants, these subjects were still given a kind of examination, in which the chief administrative officer of the country questioned them—and the whole thing operated on "bribery." At such an examination the examiner said to the candidate: What do you understand by conscience? The candidate answered in a low voice: I have a fifty pound tub of butter in the carriage. "Fine," answered the examiner. "Quite correct, but still not adequate." "I have . . . . ." "Fine, fine, but still not completely adequate." "I have ten dollars in cash." "Excellent!"

So it is with the really practical man's conscience. And if one were to search thoroughly the consciences of the countless mass, one would probably begin to feel like a person rooting around in an ancient chest full of all kinds of trifles, as in that trunk in the play *Kjerligheden uden Strømper*[1011]—so that in a certain sense one is obliged to say that if the conscience is supposed to be the hiding place for such things and not for something else, it would almost be better not to have a conscience. Such men, of course, are far, far superior to those practical people, but, sad to say, they still in a deeper sense do not have a conscience; they are like the owner of an instrument intended for some very specific purpose, but he uses it for something else and actually does not know what it is for—thus only in an improper sense can he be said to own this instrument.

XI^2 A 7   *n.d.*, 1854

PRAYER, PRAYERS

« **3363**

When Adam lived in paradise, the word was: Pray. When he was driven out, the word was: Work. When Christ came into the world the word was: Pray and work (*ora et labora*).

II A 69   n.d., 1837

« **3364**

I have often wondered when I thanked God for something whether fear of losing it motivated the prayer or whether the prayer came out of the religious assurance which had conquered the world.

II A 201   December 8, 1837

« **3365** *On Perseverance in Prayer*[1012]

It is said that James, the leader of the congregation in Jerusalem, had tough skin like a camel's on his knees from continually praying, that he could keep on praying for several days.[1013] To our age this no doubt seems ridiculous, but we should remember, however, what eloquence of heart, what fullness, goes along with being able to pray so long without becoming weak, especially we who have enough trouble in making one heartfelt prayer.

II A 266   October 1, 1838

« **3366** *Prayer:*

Father in heaven, our thoughts turn to you, seek you again in this hour—not with the irresolute step of a traveler who has lost his way but with the sure flight of a bird to its familiar home. Let not our trust in you be a fleeting thought, a momentary fancy, the deceptive tranquilizing of the earth-bound heart. Let our longings for your kingdom, our hopes for your glory, not be unproductive birth pangs, not like rainless clouds, but let them in fullness of heart rise to you and, granted, be as the refreshing dew quenching our thirst and as your heavenly manna, satisfying us forever.

II A 285   October 30, 1838

« **3367**

May our words not be like flowers, which today stand in the meadow and tomorrow are thrown in the furnace, not like flowers, even if their splendor exceeds the glory of Solomon.

II A 308   December 24, 1838

« **3368**

In margin of 3367 (II A 308):
And if you grant us knowledge of the many glories of science, let us not forget in all this the one thing needful. And if you extinguish our mental powers or allow us to grow so old on this earth that our minds are dulled, there is one thing which never can be forgotten even if we forget all else—that we are saved by your son.

II A 309   *n.d.*

« **3369**

Father in heaven, awaken conscience within us, teach us to open our spiritual ears to your voice and to pay attention to what you say, so that your will may sound purely and clearly for us as it does in heaven, unadulterated by worldly shrewdness, undeadened by the voice of passions. Keep us vigilant in fear and trembling[1014] to work out our salvation. But also—when the law speaks loudest, when its earnestness terrifies us, when it thunders from Sinai—let there be a soft voice which whispers to us that we are your children, so that we may cry out with joy: Abba, Father.[1015]

II A 313   December 28, 1838

« **3370**

In margin of 3369 (II A 313):
Grant that in every hour like that there may be born anew in our hearts, (youthfully, hopefully,) the Abba,[1016] the father-name you wish to be called.

II A 314   *n.d.*

« **3371** *Christ Walks upon the Sea*

Prayer

Lord, calm the waves in this breast, subdue the storm! Be still, my soul, so that the divine can work in me! Be still, my soul, so that God may rest within you, that his peace may overshadow you! Father in heaven, we have experienced often enough that the world cannot give us peace. But let us feel that you can give peace; let us perceive the truth of the promise that the whole world cannot take your peace from us.

II A 318   January 1, 1839

« **3372**

Father in heaven! When the thought of you awakens in our soul, let it not awaken like a terrified bird that flutters about in confusion, but like a child from its sleep, with a heavenly smile.

II A 320   January 6, 1839

« **3373**

Father in heaven! Walk with us as you formerly walked with the Jews in antiquity. Let us not believe that we have outgrown your upbringing, but let us grow up to it and grow under it as the good seed grows in patience. Let us not forget what you have done for us, and when your help has been wondrously prepared, let us not seek it again like ungrateful creatures because we ate and became satisfied. Let us feel that without you we achieve nothing at all, but let us not feel it in craven impotence but in the strong confidence, in the glad assurance that you are powerful in the weak.

II A 327   January 16, 1839

« **3374**

Lord, make our hearts into your temple, in which you take up residence. Let every unclean thought, every terrestrial desire be found shattered, like the idol Dagon, each morning at the base of the Ark of the Covenant. Teach us to master our flesh and blood, and let it be blood sacrifice, so that we may say with the apostles: I die daily.

II A 334   January 20, 1839

« **3375**

God, give me the strength to think only of what I have to do and what you assign to me; bid me walk accordingly as in days of old you commanded the prophet Elisha: If you meet someone on the way, do not greet him, and if he greets you, do not greet him in return.

II A 336   January 22, 1839

« **3376**

Father in heaven, open the fountains of our eyes, let a torrent of tears like a flood obliterate all of the past life which did not find favor in your eyes; but also give us a sign as of old, when you set the rainbow as a gateway of grace in the heavens, that you will no more wipe us out with a flood; let sin never again get such power over us that you again have to tear us out of the *body* of sin.

II A 342   February 1, 1839

« 3377

Father in heaven! Teach us to walk in your sight and let not our thoughts and deeds be as strangers from afar paying a brief visit to your mansions, but as native-born, feeling that you live with us, for of what use would it be to us, however glorious such a visit might be, of what use would it be to us even though our faces shone like the face of Moses when he had talked with God, of what use would it be even though like Moses before the Jews we hid our faces in order not to detect how swiftly the splendor vanished—? Let us never forget that all Christianity is a *life course,* so that even if I stand at the farthest border of your kingdom, holy Father, far away by myself like the publican of old, if I only stand with my face *toward* you—not turned around like him who put his hand to the plow—with staff in hand ready to go, even if mountains and valleys and raging rivers lie before me, I still have the promise: The least in the kingdom of heaven is greater than what is born of women.

II A 377   March 2, 1839

« 3378

God in heaven, let me rightly feel my nothingness,[1017] not to despair over it, but all the more intensely to feel the greatness of your goodness.

(This wish is not, as the scoffer in me would say, an Epicureanism, as when a gourmand starves himself in order that the food may taste all the better.)

II A 423   May 14, 1839

« 3379

By talking so much about the unchangeableness of God[1018] we weaken the meaning of prayer, but I would like to ask: Do you really believe that the benediction which the pastor pronounces from the holy altar works just as powerfully on those who inquisitively* walk around admiring the works of man (the statues) in the church as it does on those who are gathered here in stillness to devote their attention to God?[1019] Or should the spiritual benediction be just as indifferent to who receives it as the fructifying rain which God lets fall on the righteous and the unrighteous? Or, to continue the figure of speech, is the rain really so indifferent, or does it not bring abundant fruit to the well-cultivated field but dries up without fruit on the barren field? Or are you who in unbelief deny the validity of prayer not guilty of superstition, for is it not superstitious to believe that God would act upon man in a purely external way.

In margin: * and this is something which often happens, particularly during communion.

II A 537   August 9, 1839

‹ 3380

Father in heaven! Turn your face from me no longer; let it shine upon me again so that I may walk in your way and no more go astray far from you, where your voice can no longer reach me. O, speak to me, let me hear your voice, even if it may terrifyingly run me down on my trackless way, where sick and defiled in spirit I live solitary and remote, far from fellowship with you and with other men. Lord Jesus Christ, you who came to the world to save the lost, you who left the ninety-nine sheep in order to search for the one gone astray, seek me out on my false path of delusions where I hide from you and from men; you, the good shepherd, let me hear your gentle voice, let me recognize it, let me follow it! Gracious Holy Spirit, manifest yourself also to me with inexpressible sighs, pray for me as Abraham prayed for corrupted Sodom, if there be but one pure thought, one good feeling in me, so that the time for testing the barren tree may still be extended —you gracious Holy Spirit, you who regenerate the extinct, who renew the outworn, renew me as well and create in me a clean heart. You who with motherly solicitude keep and preserve all wherever there is a spark of life, O bind me closer and closer to him, my Savior and Redeemer, so that healed, I may not, like those nine lepers, forget to return, as did the one leper,[1020] to him who has given me life, in whom alone salvation is to be found—yes, sanctify my thoughts and deeds that it may be seen and known that I am his bondservant now and for all eternity.

II A 538   August 16, 1839

« 3381

Father in heaven, from your hand we will accept everything.[1021] You stretch out your mighty hand and seize the wise in their foolishness; you stretch out your mighty hand, and worlds pass away. You open your gentle hand and satisfy everything that lives with blessing, and even if you seem at times to withdraw your hand from us, we nevertheless know that you are only closing it to hide the more abundant blessing in it, that you close it only to open it again and satisfy all that lives with blessing.

II A 554   September 4, 1839

« **3382**

Lord God, you know our cares better than we ourselves know them, you know how easily the apprehensive mind is predisposed to premature and self-induced worries. We beseech you to give us the insight to see through their prematureness and pride and to disdain them—these busy, self-induced cares, but we pray that we may humbly accept from your hand the cares that you yourself lay upon us and that you will give us the strength to bear them.

III A 32   *n.d.*, 1840

« **3383**

We turn our minds to you, O God, so that you may rule there, for it is you who uplifts and casts down. Even if we were honored in the world, highly trusted among men, if the destinies of many people were put in our hands and many perhaps enviously looked up to us, and still all our efforts, our achievements, our longing, our hope in the world, did not find favor in your eyes, O righteous God, what would all such glory amount to against this unblessedness. And if we were bowed down and troubled, misunderstood, abandoned, alone with our cares, and yet your eyes which see in secret rested with pleasure on our efforts, our achievements, our hope and longing for you, what would such amount to in the face of this blessedness. And if we were humbled and crushed by the thought of our own guilt, if our sins had alienated us from mankind, so that no word of consolation rested upon us, and yet our penitence had found its way to your throne, O merciful God, and had found favor in your eyes, O what would such sufferings amount to in the face of this blessedness.

III C 9   *n.d.*, 1840–41

« **3384**

Lord our God, teach us to pray aright so that our soul may open itself to you and not conceal a secret wish which it knows you do not want to fulfill or nourish a private secret fear that you might deny it something which could serve its peace and its salvation, so that it may seek and find its rest there, the only place it is to be had, in humble gratitude to you; for not until we understand how to thank you at all times, not until then have we conquered the world.

III C 19   n.d., 1840–41

« **3385 *7th Sunday a. T.*[1022]**

See journal from my journey[1023] [i.e., III A 66].

Lord our God! All creation looks to you and expects food and nourishment from you. You open your generous hand and satisfy all that lives with blessing.[1024] You hear the cry of the animal, you heed the lamentation of men. They lift their thoughts to you, those to whom you have given much, for they know that everything comes from you and that no superabundance satisfies when you do not bless it, those to whom you gave little, for they know that no gift from you is so poor that with your blessing it is less than superabundance.

III A 86   n.d., 1841

« **3386**

It still holds that in order to pray in truth to God out of an honest heart we cannot deceitfully hide anything in the secrecy of our being —not that we are trying to deceive God, but we do not have the courage to confide it to him.

III A 126   n.d., 1841

« **3387**

And when at times, O Lord, it is as if you paid no attention to my voice, paid no attention to my lamentation, my sigh, my thank-you— I will still continue praying to you until you hear my thanksgiving because you have listened to me!

III A 158   n.d., 1841

« **3388**

It is said that earthly love makes one eloquent—how much more should love of you, O God, make a man eloquent—you who yourself formed man's mouth for speech.

III A 162   n.d., 1841

« **3389**

As long as a person has a grudge against someone, he cannot become happy. Ilithyia[1025] was the goddess who came to assist women in labor. When she sat with folded hands the woman in labor could not give birth. In the same way if there is another person who folds his hands one cannot become happy; perhaps he is a man of prayer whom one has refused something.

III A 204   n.d., 1842

« **3390**

. . . . . For even if the prayer does not accomplish anything here on earth,[1026] it nevertheless works in heaven.

IV A 145   n. d., 1843

« **3391**

For No. 2[1027]

Lord, our God, you know all, the most secret thought, and when apprehensions would dismay us, when the grief of sin overwhelms us—then hurry, O Lord, and give the witness of love, that it may again be victorious in our soul and hide the multitude of our sins.

IV B 149   n.d., 1843

« **3392** *Be Vigilant in Prayer*

How difficult it is *actually* to be vigilant. One does not know whether he still is awake, actually is awake, is sleeping internally.

This lends itself to allegorical development in terms of physical awakening.

IV B 164   n.d., 1843–44

« **3393** *Be Sober in Prayer*

To pray (to collect oneself) is a task for the whole soul, no easy matter.[1028]

1) Conditions before prayer
2) During prayer and after it
3) About fulfillment

do not use many words
do not anxiously interrupt the prayer to see if it is happening.

IV B 165   n.d., 1843–44

« **3394** *Prayer*

Father in heaven! You loved us first. Help us never to forget that you are love,[1029] so that this full conviction might be victorious in our hearts over the world's allurement, the mind's unrest, the anxieties over the future, the horrors of the past, the needs of the moment. O, grant also that this conviction might form our minds so that our hearts become constant and true in love to them whom you bid us to love as ourselves.

IV B 171   *n.d.*, 1842–44(?)

« **3395**

Merciful God! We do know that all good gifts and all perfect gifts come from you[1030]—but you did not send us empty-handed into the world—let not our hands be closed, our hearts be hardened—but add your blessing so that our gift may be a gift from you above, good and perfect.

IV B 175   *n.d.*, 1842–44(?)

« **3396**

. . . . . Of course, when prayer is heard here on earth and mingles with busy human speech, it is idle talk, but it is working in heaven;[1031] and frequently prayer does sow in corruption, but nevertheless it harvests in incorruption.

IV A 171   *n.d.*, 1844

« **3397**

By striving properly in prayer, the miracle takes place that God in heaven and you are victorious, for you are victorious because God is victorious. [1032]

V B 221   *n.d.*, 1844

« **3398** *Prayer*

Father in heaven

We do indeed know that seeking always has its promise; why then do we not seek you, the one and only giver and guarantee of all promises.[1033] We know very well that the seeker need not always go far away, for the more holy the object he seeks the closer at hand it is, and if he seeks you, O God, you are closest of all. But we know also that seeking always has its terror; why then not seek you, you mighty one. Does not even he quake who trusts in the thought of his kinship to you when he ventures out in those decisions in which he seeks a trace of you in the powers of existence, does not even he whom you called friend because he walked in your sight seek with fear and trembling a friendly reunion with you, Lord of Heaven; does not even the one who prays, who loves you with his whole heart, venture with anxiety into prayer's engagement with you, you powerful one; does not even the dying one, for whom you yourself replace life, still not relinquish the temporal with a shudder when he seeks you, you terrifying one; does not even the wretch whom the world gave only suffering* proceed to God with dread—how then does the sinner dare seek you, you righteous one. But this is why he does not seek you in this way but seeks you in the confession of sins. For here is the place, how still.

(No one can see God without purity,[1034] and yet no one can get to see him without confessing his sin.)

* with sheer wretchedness behind him.

VI B 150   n.d., 1844–45

« 3399 *Prayer*[1035]

Father in heaven! What is all man's knowledge but a chipped fragment if he does not know you, what is all his achievement but half-finished work if you do not share the work, what are all his labors but sheer vanity if he does not seek you. We pray, then, that you will form the hearts of those who live without God in the world, so that they might seek you; the hearts of those who seek you that they might wait upon you; the hearts of those that wait upon you that they might find you; and the hearts of those that find you that they might give away everything in order to buy what they possess and that nothing might tear you from them or them from you until their final blessed end. And if, alas, though seeking, they did not find you as the years went by, if they did not find you when they were told in their youth to rejoice in the delights of the world and not to seek what will come in time, if they did not find you when they were cast down and were told to forget God and let the world heal them, and if they did not find you when they were told in their old age that they had lived in vain—Lord God, if he did not find you until the hour of death, if he had continually sought you, then he also found what we all seek: a final blessed end.

VI B 154   n.d., 1844–45

« 3400

And if the years went by and the way grew narrow and passed one point after the other where the path of desire turned aside—[teach him so] that he may wait

And if the years went by and the path of repentance grew narrow, and despair often beckoned to byroads—[teach him so] that he may wait for you.

Father in heaven![1036] What is man without you, what is all he knows but a chipped fragment if he does not know you, what are all his efforts but a half-finished work if you are not the master builder. So move those who live without God in the world that they might seek you, and discipline the minds of those who seek you that they might wait upon you. Well do we know that all seeking has its promise—why not, then, the seeking which seeks you; but we know, too, that all seeking has its pain, and also the seeking which seeks you. We know, too, that to seek does not mean that a man must go out into the wide world, for the more noble that which he seeks, the closer it lies to him, and if he seeks you—Lord, you are closest of all to him. But that is why he has not yet found you. Teach him to wait—if the years pass by, so that he may wait—if the season of joy passes, so that he may wait—and even if he loses everything which is not worth winning, if he still waits for you, he still has not lost.

VI B 160   n.d., 1844–45

« 3401

. . . . . Truly, O God, you will say to many a one who has done great deeds in your name: I do not know you—but I do not appeal to such things but to what I experienced in the quiet solitude when nothing distracted, when the best in me sought you—will you also say: It is not you; will you say that you do not know me? Do you not remember the time[1037] (to be completed)
was it not you who took it from me—and I sought you in tears.

> I seek and desire nothing in the world; I have renounced it to have fellowship with you. Were you to say to me now: I do not know you, then all is lost.

If I had the choice between being the greatest of men without you and being a hair which you count (and truly, before you, I am no more than that and do not wish for new disarrangement in order to be more than any other man), I would choose the latter. Even though I am only so very insignificant to you, to me this little is infinitely much, and to be nothing at all to you, although everything otherwise, is to me nothing, absolutely nothing.

VI B 161   n.d., 1844–45

« 3402 *On the Occasion of a Confession*[1038]

Father in heaven, we turn our minds and our thoughts to you, for it is you who raise up, and it is you who cast down. Even though we were honored in the world and trusted among men, what would all such glory be compared to the unblessedness if you, O righteous God, were not pleased with our own effort, our achievement, our longing, our hope in the world. If we were weighed down, demolished, unappreciated, abandoned, alone in the world, and yet your eye which sees in secret rested approvingly on our effort, our achievement, our longing, our hope in the world—what would these tribulations be compared to such blessedness! And if we were humiliated and crushed by the thought of our own guilt, if our sins had alienated us from men so that no word of consolation came to our ears, and yet our repentance found the way to your throne, O merciful God, and found grace in your sight —what would these sufferings be compared to such blessedness. Lord, we turn our minds and our thoughts to you, for it is you who raise up and it is you who cast down, to you Lord, Father, our Father, you who are in heaven.

VI B 164   *n.d.,* 1844–45

« 3403

The spontaneous, immediate person believes and imagines that when he prays the main thing, the thing he has to work at especially, is that *God hears* [*hører*] what it is **he** *is praying about.* And yet in truth's eternal sense it is just the opposite: the true prayer-relationship does not exist when God hears what is being prayed about but when the *pray-er* continues to pray until he is the *one who hears,*[1039] who hears what God wills. The immediate, spontaneous person uses a lot of words and therefore is actually demanding when he prays. The true pray-er is simply *obedient* [*hørig*].[1040]

VII[1] A 56   *n.d.,* 1846

« 3404

1.[1041]

Father in heaven, you speak to a man in many ways; you who alone possess wisdom and understanding, you nevertheless wish to make yourself understandable to him. You speak with him also in your silence,[1042] for he also speaks who is silent in order to examine the pupil; he also speaks who is silent in order to test the beloved; he also speaks who is silent in order that the hour of understanding, when it comes, might be all the more inward. Father in heaven, in the hour of silence when a man stands alone and abandoned and does not hear your voice, does it not seem to him that the separation will last forever. In the hour of silence when a man is prostrate in the desert where he does not hear your voice, does it not seem to him as if it had disappeared completely.

Father in heaven, is it not true that this is merely the moment of silence in the intimacy of conversation. Bless this silence, then, as you bless each and every one of your words to a man. Let him never forget that you also speak when you are silent. Grant him the confidence, if he prays to you, that you are silent out of love, just as you speak out of love, so that whether you are silent or whether you speak, you are still the same father, whether you instruct by word of mouth or educate with your silence, it is still the same fatherliness.

VII[1] A 131 n.d., 1846

« **3405**

2.

Father in heaven! Great is your infinite kingdom, you who support the heavens and steer cosmic forces in vast space; countless as the sand are they who depend upon you merely for life. And yet you hear the cry of all, also the cry of man, whom you fashioned in a special way; you hear the cry of all men, not in jumbled confusion, and not selectively as if you made distinctions. You do not hear only the voice of the one who has responsibility for many, in whose name he could pray to you, as if he stood nearer to you because he stands high. You do not hear only the voice of the one who prays for his loved ones, as if he could preëminently draw your attention, he who has the joyful preëminence of having loved ones. No, you hear the most wretched, the most forsaken, the most solitary of men—in the desert, in the swarm. And if oblivion had separated him from all the others, and if he had become undistinguishable in the crowd,[*] you recognize him, you still have not forgotten him, you remember his name, you know where he is hiding, where he hides in the desert or escapes in the crowd. And even if he sat with frightful thoughts in the deepest darkness of anxiety, forsaken by men, almost forsaken by human language, you still have not forgotten him; you understand his language, you know how to find a way to him at once, quick as the speed of sound, the speed of light. And if you delay, it is not your slowness but your wisdom. If you delay, it still is not slowness but because you alone know the swiftness of your help. If you delay, it still is not stinginess but fatherly thriftiness which lays aside the best for the child in the safest place and for the most opportune time. Lord God! A man cries to you in the day of need, thanks you in the day of joy. How beautiful to thank when a man readily understands that you give good and perfect gifts,[1043] when even the mortal heart is immediately disposed to understand, and even earthy common sense quickly agrees. Yet it is still more blessed to give thanks when life becomes a dark story, still more blessed to give thanks when the heart is oppressed, when the mind is darkened, when reason turns traitor in its ambiguity and memory deceitful in its forgetfulness, when self-love shrinks back in horror, when prudence resists—if not in defiance then still in despondency— then it is more blessed to thank God. For the one who gives thanks in this manner loves God; he dares to say to you, all-knowing God: Lord, you know all things, you know that I love you.

[*] Yes, not as one man more but only as a number in the census count.

VII¹ A 132   *n.d.*, 1846

« **3406**

3.

. . . . . Save me from becoming a fool who will not accept your discipline, or a defiant fool who will not accept your discipline, a fool who will not accept it as a blessing, a defiant fool who will accept it to damnation.[1044]

VII¹ A 133   *n.d.*, 1846

« **3407**

6.

Father in heaven! As a father sends his child out into the world, so have you put man here upon earth. He is separated from you as by a world; he does not see you with his eyes; he does not hear your voice with his mortal ears. He stands now in the world; and the way lies before him—so long in the dull moment of despondency, which does not wish to give itself time, so impracticable in the tormenting moment of impatience, which does not wish to give him time. At such a time you give to your child cheerful boldness in the wide world, cheerful boldness when there seem to be so many false tracks and the right road is so difficult to recognize, cheerful boldness when worry and anxiety seem to find a basis in the depraved raging of the elements, in the horror of events, in the disheartening human misery. Give him then the cheerful boldness to remember and believe that as a father sends his child out in the world so you have placed a man here upon earth. —Merciful God! As the prodigal son,[1045] when he sought the way back, found everything changed, even his brother's disposition—but not the father, whose love received him, the homecomer, with a banquet, whose fatherliness used the banquet to give him, the lost one, cheerful boldness. When a man comes back to you like that, then you give him cheerful boldness on the way of repentance, for his returning is not joyous in the same way as a beloved child's coming home, but is hard and heavy—if he is the lost one. Nor is he awaited in the same way by the loving father who gladly waits for the loved one—O, may he still have the cheerful boldness to believe that he is awaited by the merciful Father who is concerned and fearful of his damnation.

VII[1] A 136   n.d., 1846

« **3408**

7.
Father in heaven! Well do we know that you are everywhere present. If anyone at this moment calls upon you, perhaps from his sick bed, if someone in deep distress at sea cries out to you, or from the even greater distress of sin, we know well that you are close at hand to hear him. But you are indeed also here in your house, here where your congregation is gathered together, many perhaps fleeing from heavy thoughts or accompanied by heavy thoughts which follow them, but surely also many out of a quiet daily life of contentment, perhaps also someone enveloped in joyful thoughts because of fulfilled desires hidden in his grateful heart—yet all of them needing to seek you, O God, you the friend of the grateful in blessed intimacy, you, the consolation of the weak in strengthening association, you, the refuge of the anxious in secret solace, you, the secrete confidant of those who weep while you count the tears, you, the last person at the deathbed when you receive the dying one's soul. Let yourself be found, then, O God, in this hour; you who are the father of all, let yourself be found with the good gift of testimony for each one according to his need, so that the happy one might win the cheerful boldness to rejoice properly in you for your good gifts,[1046] that the sorrowing one might win the cheerful boldness properly to accept in you your perfect gifts. For us men, to be sure, there are differences among these things, the differences of joy and sorrow, but for you, O God, there are no differences among these things—everything that comes from you is a good and perfect gift.

VII[1] A 137   n.d., 1846

« **3409**

10.
Father in heaven! You are incomprehensible in your creation; you live afar off in a light which no one can penetrate, and even if you are recognized in your providence, our knowledge is still only weak and

obscures your clarity. But you are still more incomprehensible in your grace and mercy. For what is a man to you, O infinite one, that you are mindful of him—but still more, what is the son of the fallen race to you, you Holy One, that you nevertheless will visit him. Yes, what is a sinner that for his sake your Son would come to the world, not to condemn but to save, not to make known his place of residence so the lost could seek him, but to seek the lost one, without having a resting place as even the animal has, without having a stone on which to rest his head, hungering in the desert, thirsting on the cross. Merciful God and Father! What can a man do in return; without you he is unable even to thank you. Teach us, then, the properly humble discernment of understanding so that—like the broken sinner who sighs under his guilt, saying: It is impossible,[1047] it is impossible that God can have mercy on me in this way—in the very same way he who in faith appropriates this mercy to himself must say in his joy: It is impossible. If even death itself seemed to want to separate the lovers and they are once again given to each other, this, indeed, would be the first cry in the moment of their assured reunion: It is impossible. And the glad gospel of joy about your mercifulness, heavenly Father—yes, even if a man heard it from his earliest childhood, it would not therefore be less incomprehensible! Even if a man reflected on it every day, it would not therefore be less incomprehensible!* Would the incomprehensibility of your grace then be like that of a man which at one time existed but disappeared on closer acquaintance; would it be like the happiness of the lovers—once incomprehensible long ago, but no more! O lazy human discernment, O deceitful mortal wisdom, O dull, dead thoughts of slumbering faith, O wretched forgetfulness of a cold heart —no, Lord, preserve every believer in the properly humble discernment of understanding and deliver him from evil!

> * Should then the incomprehensibility of your grace
> be like a man's?

VII[1] A 142   *n.d., 1846*

« 3410 *Prayer*

Father in heaven! It sometimes happens that we say one thing about a man when he is present and, regrettably, something else when he is absent; we speak differently about him in his presence than in his absence. But you, our God, how could we possibly talk differently about you in your absence—you who are everywhere present;[1048] how could we possibly talk differently about you—you who always remain the same! Grant then, O God, that we may do our best to combat the absence of spirit which wants to delude us into thinking that you are absent, in order that, for the sake of collecting and building up the mind, disciplining and purifying the mind, we may keep in mind that you are always present.

VIII¹ A 55   *n.d.,* 1847

« 3411

How often have I reflected on what pests we men must be to God, inconveniencing him with all our little griefs and little joys, wanting him to rejoice with us when we thank him for the good. What is a man, after all, that you are mindful of him. There is a lot of preaching about our duty[1049] to pray to God, but would it not be more correct to point out to men the prodigious prerogative of being able to talk with God.

VIII¹ A 159   *n.d.,* 1847

« 3412

Father in heaven! Do not side with our sins against us, but side with us against our sins so that when the thought of you awakens in the soul, and every time it awakens, it might not remind us of our trespasses but of your forgiveness, not of how we went astray but of how you saved us!

VIII¹ A 247   *n.d.,* 1847

« 3413

Father in heaven! Have a little patience with us, for we often think in all sincerity that we are talking with you and yet talk so foolishly. Sometimes what happens to us is so good (in our way of thinking) that we do not have enough words to thank you—like a cunning child who thanks because it has gotten its way. Then again things go badly and we cry to you, if we do not wail and screech—alas, like a foolish child who is afraid of what benefits him. But no matter how childish we are, how far it is from the truth that we really are children if you really are supposed to be the father of these children—alas, as if an animal were to claim a human being as its father—no matter how childish we are, no matter how little our speech and our language resemble the language we should learn from you, this much we still understand—that it should not be this way, that we must see to learning something else. Have a little patience with us, then.

VIII¹ A 255   *n.d.,* 1847

« 3414

Christ wept blood when he prayed—nowadays the preachers give three reasons[1050] to prove that it is expedient to pray. —What if people were forbidden to pray; then they probably would no longer need three reasons. When parents have done everything to make their children happy and they still are not happy, the parents take everything away from them—it helps!

VIII[1] A 304   *n.d.*, 1847

« 3415

..... For we are not related to you, O God, as to a man from whom we buy—you must first of all give and only then can there be mention of our duty to buy from you—what you have given: faith, hope, love, longing, the opportune moment. You give all things and without payment, for nothing (only the pagan who did not know you believed that the gods did not give anything for nothing),* but when you have given, then you demand that we buy from you what you have given. Thus do you condescend to become involved with us men; you are not ashamed to be our God (Hebrews[1051]). —And yet it is, indeed, as when we give to a child and then, to delight the child, pretend as if he were giving to us—what we, in fact, gave the child, what really belongs to us. Yes, the relation to God is not even of this nature, for God is also the one who gives in order to make perfect. It must then be like that of a father or mother helping the child write the birthday letter which is then accepted on the birthday as a gift.

* Here is the whole mistake in paganism—namely, that man relates directly to God as to another person, a more powerful man, instead of man's first relating to God secondarily: after God has given everything for nothing.

VIII[1] A 342   *n.d.*, 1847

« 3416 *Prayer*

Even now today, O God, we would come to you .....

Text: Even now tonight I will require your soul of you.[1052]

VIII[1] A 364   *n.d.*, 1847

« 3417

..... O, God, there is so much in the outer world to draw us away from you.[1053] That is why we enter into your house, but even here there is at times a security which will deceive us, as if here all danger and terror were far away, here where the greatest danger of all is to be discussed—sin, and the greatest horror—Christ's suffering and death.

VIII¹ A 367   n.d., 1847

« 3418 *Prayer*

Lord Jesus Christ, there is so much that holds us back and attracts us; each has his own and yet all have much. But you are the eternally strongest one! Draw us,[1054] then, even more strongly to yourself. We call you our Redeemer, because you came to the world to unfasten all the bonds, the fetters of unworthy concerns which we ourselves have laid upon ourselves; you have come to break the heavy chains of sin. We call you our Savior, because you want to save us in this way and deliver us from all this. For this, indeed, was God's will, which you fulfilled and made possible, our sanctification. This is why you descended into the lower regions of the earth, and this is why you rose again into the heights in order to draw us to yourself from there.

VIII¹ A 372   n.d., 1847

« 3419

Father in heaven! Out there this one is strong[1055] and that one is weak; the strong one is perhaps arrogant in his strength; the weak one sighs and, alas, is envious; but in here we are all weak, here face to face with you, you mighty one, you who alone are strong.

VIII¹ A 380   n.d., 1847

« 3420 *Sermon Delivered in Frue Kirke One Friday*

Father in heaven! Just as the regular intercession of the congregation is that you will comfort all those who are sick and burdened, so too the intercession in this hour is that you will give rest to the souls of those who labor and are heavy laden. And yet, this is not an intercession—who would dare consider himself so sound that he would need to pray only for others? Alas, no, each one prays for himself, that you will give him rest of soul. You, O God, —as you see that he is laboring and troubled in the consciousness of sin, give him rest for his soul. Amen

Matthew 11:28.

. . . . . [*Text essentially the same as Christian Discourses, pp.* 269, *l.* 14–273, *l.* 15]. So heavy a burden no man has carried; however heavily his own guilt rests upon a man, it still is not that heavy, alas, even if it does not become lighter until he takes his burden to your mercy to find rest.

VIII² B 107   n.d., 1847–48.

« 3421

"Ask, and you will receive, that your joy may be full" (John[1056]). Here Christianity itself shows that prayer, however blessed it is in itself, still is not the supreme blessedness. Compared to earthly blessedness, prayer, praying, is a greater blessedness, but the blessedness of heaven is greater than praying.[1057]

VIII¹ A 532   n.d., 1848

« 3422 *Stephen*

When a man is about to die, there are a lot of last minute things to arrange before he gets permission to die; he has to make his will, etc.; then he turns over and dies. Stephen, too, had something to arrange; he had to pray for his enemies first[1058]—when that was arranged, he died. Actually he left nothing behind, for no one would accept his intercessory prayer, so he took that with him, also.

VIII¹ A 546   n.d., 1848

« 3423

From "The Sickness unto Death":

Prayer

In margin: N.B. Not to be used, perhaps, since a prayer here gives an almost too upbuilding tone.[1059]

Father in heaven! So often the congregation brings its intercession to you for all who are sick and sorrowing; and if any of us is lying at death's door in mortal sickness, the congregation sometimes makes a special intercessory prayer: Grant that each one of us may rightly become aware of which sickness is the sickness unto death, and of how we are all sick in this way! And you, our Lord Jesus Christ, you who came to the world to heal those who suffer from this sickness, which we all have but which you can heal only in those who are aware of being sick in this way: Help us in this sickness to turn to you to be healed! And you, God the Holy Spirit, you who come to our assistance if we honestly want to be healed: Be with us so that we never to our own ruination elude the physician's help but remain with him—saved from the sickness. For to be with him is to be saved from sickness, and only when we are with him are we saved from sickness!

VIII² B 143   n.d., 1848

« **3424**

Imagine a girl in love. Which do you think she appreciates more —that the beloved remembers her and thinks of her on a Sunday when he is loafing and has nothing to do—or that the beloved has the time to think of her when he is busiest of all and yet without neglecting anything: in the same way prayer to God in the day of need is most cherished and well-pleasing.

IX A 15   *n.d.*, 1848

« **3425**

To be able to say a total "Amen" to a prayer—O, how seldom, how extremely seldom this happens even with an otherwise diligent and constant pray-er! It is even more rare than the moment in erotic love when the lovers find each other to be perfectly ideal. To say "Amen" in such a way that not one single word more can be added, but the one single word which gratifies and satisfies is this very "Amen," consequently after having prayed in such a way that the soul's whole desire is gratified in the pouring out of prayer, after having said everything that lay on one's heart—that is, before God one has become transparent to himself in all his weakness but also in all his hope: O, if there comes a moment (and this perhaps one senses more often), a moment when it is as if the whole language is not sufficient to express what is tormenting one, nor sufficient to express how it is in one's heart—such a moment would be just the opposite of the moment when the whole language is superfluous, when it makes no difference if every single word in the language has been forgotten, since a person has no use for it, because there is nothing more to add than Amen.

IX A 24   *n.d.*, 1848

« **3426**

The Archimedean point[1060] outside the world is a prayer chamber where a true man of prayer prays in all honesty—and he will move the earth. Yes, if he is this true pray-er, it is unbelievable what he achieves when he shuts his door.

IX A 115   *n.d.*, 1848

« **3427**

The more a person prays, the more certain his final consolation is that God has commanded that we *shall* pray; for God is so infinite that many times a person would otherwise hardly dare to pray, however much he wanted to.

IX A 192   n.d., 1848

« 3428

But by praying a person also makes himself buoyant in relation to God; otherwise God would completely overwhelm him.

IX A 193   n.d., 1848

« 3429

Loving God! You have commanded us to forgive our enemies, our erring brothers, not seven times but 70 X 7 times:[1061] how would you ever then grow weary of forgiving an honest penitent.

IX A 328   n.d., 1848

« 3430

Perhaps some Sunday it might be vivifying and also a way of jolting the observational approach to choose a morning hymn which speaks only of the day at hand and then to take off from there; instead of commenting on all the lofty truths, to pray for the day at hand,[1062] instead of observations which range all over time and world history, to pray for the day at hand—and since family devotions[1063] presumably have fallen into disuse, to use Sunday in this way.

IX A 417   n.d., 1848

« 3431

Arndt, II, chapter 20, para. 5.[1064] When we pray we should forget everything else—on the other hand, when we do other, external things, we ought not be attached to them wholeheartedly but be distracted.

IX A 426   n.d., 1848

« 3432 *Something about What It Is To "Pray"*

The Church Fathers were right in observing that to pray is to breathe. Here we see the stupidity of talking about a *why,* [1065] for why do I breathe? Because otherwise I would die—and so it is with praying. Nor do I intend to change the world through my breathing—I simply intend to replenish my vitality and be *renewed*—it is the same with prayer in the relation to God.

IX A 462   n.d., 1848

« 3433

Hymn 22 in the Evangelical Hymnbook[1066] could be sung beforehand.

A Sermon
A sermon could be given on the theme*
that God is present[1067] **here** *at this moment.*

Prayer

You everywhere present One, when I was considering how I would speak and what I would say, you were present. When the single individual decided to go up into your house and went to it, you were present; but perhaps to him it was still not really being present—bless, then, our devotion that we all, each one individually, may in this hour apprehend your presence and that we are before you.

x¹ A 210   *n.d.,* 1849

« 3434

Addition to 3433 (x¹ A 210):
*We are not going to indulge in any observations; you are not going to learn anything you do not know (this I guarantee you); I am not going to entertain you—but we will consider together and, with God's help, you will get something to think about as we consider together . . . . .

x¹ A 211   *n.d.,* 1849

« 3435

They are beautiful, those words by St. Theresa which Fenelon[1068] often quotes:
"O, you blind ones, to abandon prayer just when it ought to begin." But that is how it goes. In good days, when everything is so easy to understand, or it is assumed that everything is so easy to understand, then they pray or think that they pray. When adversity comes and praying becomes a struggle, that is, becomes real prayer, then they abandon it.

x¹ A 291   *n.d.,* 1849

« 3436

To pray oneself out is something like crying oneself out, as we say.
And when you have prayed yourself out completely, then there is only one word left: Amen.

x¹ A 388   *n.d.,* 1849

« 3437

Theme for an edifying discourse:
The Art of Arriving at an Amen

It is not very easy. There always seems to be something to add.
A resolution, the resolution of faith.

x[1] A 389   n.d., 1849

« **3438**

In margin of 3437 (x[1] A 389):
How close the comic[1069] always is to the highest pathos; at this
point one could very well think of Peer Degn,[1070] who at one time
could recite the whole litany in Greek but now could only remember
that the last word was: Amen.

x[1] A 390   n.d.

« **3439** *Prayer*

From your hand we willingly receive all things.[1071] If honor and
glory are offered, we willingly receive them from your hand; if it is
ridicule and mockery, we willingly receive them from your hand. O,
that we might accept the one as we accept the other, with equal joy and
gratitude. There is no great difference—and there would be no difference for us if we concentrated on the main clue—that it comes from
you.

x[1] A 470   n.d., 1849

« **3440**

Father in heaven, when in the evening we get ready to go to sleep,
it is our consolation that you are the one who stays awake and watches
—and when we awake in the morning and stay awake throughout the
day—alas, how disconsolate if for all that you were not the one who
stays awake and watches. Therefore the distinction we make between
sleeping and being awake is only a jest—as if we needed you to stay
awake and watch only while we sleep and not when we ourselves
are awake.

x[1] A 633   n.d., 1849

« **3441**

What it means to pray in Jesus' name is perhaps illustrated most
simply in this way. A public official orders this and that *in the name of
the King*—what does it mean? In the first place it means: I myself am
nothing, I have no power,[1072] nothing to say on my own—but it is in
the name of the King. It is the same with praying in the name of Jesus:
I do not dare approach God except through an intermediary; if my
prayer is to be heard, it must be in the name of Jesus; it is this name

which gives it power. In the next place—when a public official commands in the name of the King, it follows as a matter of course that what he orders must be the King's will; he cannot command his own will in the name of the King. It is the same with praying in the name of Jesus. Praying in such a manner that it conforms to the will of Jesus, I cannot pray in the name of Jesus about my own will. The name of Jesus is not a casual endorsement but the decisive factor. The fact that the name of Jesus precedes is not praying in Jesus' name but is praying in such a way that I dare put the name of Jesus to my prayer, that is, picture him, his holy will, together with what I am praying about. Finally, when a public official commands in the name of the King, it means that the King takes the responsibility upon himself. So it is also with praying in Jesus' name: Jesus takes upon himself the responsibility and all the consequences; he steps forward for us, steps forward in place of the one who is praying.

x^2 A 77   *n.d.*, 1849

« 3442 *Prayer*

You who came into the world *to suffer*,[1073] you endured the hardest suffering of all: to be fully conscious of it in advance, you whose suffering was increased by the voluntariness of your suffering, by having it within your power at all times to prevent the suffering—you who suffered throughout your entire life until your ignominious death—we thank you for sanctifying suffering, for blessedly illuminating by your holy life and career something that to the natural man is utter darkness —what it is to suffer. We thank you for this, and [we pray] that no sufferer may ever forget the consolation which is able to strengthen and illuminate above all else, and that no sufferer may ever arrogantly forget the humbling distinction: that you suffered innocently for the guilty, the distinction which again is the supreme consolation—that your death was atoning death.

x^6 B 239   *n.d.*, 1849-51

« 3443 *Prayer*

Father in heaven! O, you who concern yourself with the sparrow and not in such a way that you cruelly require the sparrow to be like you, no, you who lovingly concern yourself with the sparrow in such a way that you put yourself in its place like a concerned father—you concern yourself with man[1074] as well. And if you require of him a striving to be like you, which you do not require of the sparrow, you nevertheless do not cruelly demand it. No, in fatherly concern you put yourself in his place, and you yourself are the one who gives him the energy to strive.

x^2 A 342   *n.d.*, 1850

« 3444 *Prayer*

Lord Jesus Christ! You endured suffering your whole life[1075] in order to save me also, and, alas, your time of suffering is still not over; but is it not true that you atoningly and redeemingly will endure this suffering, too, the patient suffering of having to do with me, I who so often go astray from the right path, or even if I stay on the right path so often stumble on the right path. Infinite patience, infinitely patient suffering! How many times have I not become impatient, wanted to reject, wanted to abandon everything, wanted to take the frightful, easy shortcut, the shortcut of despair—but you did not lose patience. Alas, what your chosen servant said does not fit me: that he completed your sufferings; no, all that fits me is that I increased your sufferings, added new sufferings to those you once suffered in order to save me also.

x^2 A 343   *n.d.*, 1850

« 3445 *Prayer*

We human beings carry the holy only in fragile jars, but you, O Holy Spirit, when you live in a man you live in what is infinitely inferior: you Spirit of Holiness, you live in our filth and impurity, you Spirit of Wisdom, you live in our foolishness, you Spirit of Truth, you live in our self-deception! O, stay here, and you who do not conveniently look for a desirable residence, which you would seek in vain, you, who creating and giving new birth, make your own dwelling place, O, stay here that it may at some time come to be that you are delighted with the house you yourself prepared for yourself in my filthy and foolish and cheating heart.

x^2 A 344   *n.d.*, 1850

« 3446

It is a beautiful, childlike remark Arndt[1076] makes somewhere (one of the twelve chapters by Weigel): "It is absolutely true, God knows very well what you need, and in a sense you do not need to say it to him in prayer, but God has so ordered it that he pretends he does not know if you do not yourself say it to him in prayer." Parents sometimes do the same with the child: they say he may have it with pleasure, but he must himself ask for it.

x^2 A 496   *n.d.*, 1850

« 3447 *An Example of Faith in Which Reflection Is To Be Sidetracked*

When the task is not to endure this or that, to work for and to will this and that, etc., where, praying to God for help, I consequently think specifically of this and that, which is the task.

No, let the task be to forget this and that. Inner experience will teach that there are many situations, especially those of spiritual trial [*Anfægtelse*] in which the greatest danger is to continue thinking about that which should be put aside, that it does not help at all to will with the greatest straining of the will to be rid of it, that one merely runs aground in it more deeply, that it is a question of getting away from it, a question of quiet humility which knows how to forget.

Consequently the task is: to forget. And the embattled individuality is a religious person who prays to God for help and assistance—consequently for help and assistance to forget. And now if the praying becomes prolix, verbose, it is just as anxious as before and is not capable of expressing the person's prayer—yes, the very opposite is the result—then I am reminded more and more of that against which I am supposed to defend myself by forgetting.

Here the important thing is a sigh of trust and confidence, which to God is simultaneously comprehensible—and then off to forgetting. (Incidentally, verbose, prolix praying may often conceal unbelief.) From such a situation a person may learn to muster most quickly the most intensive trust in God. Here there is no time to add a single word to the prayer, for then I am reminded of what I am supposed to forget. Here the prayer is the silent, trusting understanding with God.

This, therefore, is genuine education in praying, because talkativeness is dangerous. Even though a longer outpouring before God is characterized by inwardness, the question still is and continues to be whether or not the act of prayer easily becomes a postponement of acting.[1077]

There certainly is and ought to be a blessedness in prayer, but this blessedness can be dwelt upon too much.

Such collisions and conflicts can teach a person another aspect of prayer.

x^2 A 595   *n.d.*, 1850

« **3448**

Teach me, O God, so that I do not suffocate and torture myself in suffocating reflection, but that I may breathe healthfully in faith.

x^2 A 632   *n.d.,* 1850

« **3449** *The Religious*

Would that you might so fill my thoughts, Lord Jesus Christ, that people could look at me and tell that I am thinking of you. How would they see it? Would they see it in my eyes turned heavenward? That could also mean that I am looking at the stars or at visions and hallucinations. No, would that your image might prevail upon me in such a way that I proclaim your teaching, even though I am wretched, scorned, and ridiculed—then people would see (not by my glance but by my daily character) that I am thinking of you.

*   *

You, heavenly powers, you who undergird the good, you heavenly hosts, help me to raise my voice so that it can, if possible, be heard over the whole world. I have only one word to say, but if I am granted the power to say this one word or this one sentence in such a way that it might establish itself firmly and never be forgotten—my choice is made, I have it. I would say: Our Lord Jesus Christ was a nobody—remember that, Christendom!

x^3 A 11   *n.d.,* 1850

« **3450** *The Sigh of One Who Prays*

Loving Father, I am a total failure—and yet you are love. I even fail to cling to this, that you are love—and yet you are love. No matter how I turn, this is the one thing I cannot get away from or be free of —that you are love. This is why I believe that even when I fail to cling to this—that you are love—it is still out of love that you permit it to happen, O infinite love.

x^3 A 49   *n.d.,* 1850

« **3451** *The Sigh of One Who Is Struggling*

"O, my God, my God, this is beyond my strength; even in the most trivial matters, it seems to me as if you squeezed me with all your weight. It is constantly the same; I barely stir, and immediately it seems to be an enormous guilt, an atrocious sin which cannot help but have the most dreadful results, and I sink under the weight of you. No, I no longer have the strength to carry you." Reply: Allow me to tell you that you are making the same mistake as the man who believed he had gone blind when he had turned out the light. —Or is it you, then, who is supposed to carry God? I thought it was God who in infinite love wants to carry you—carry you just as lightly as he no doubt is heavy if you were to carry him.

X³ A 208   n.d., 1850

« 3452 *To God*

Even if it were true that I am grateful, humanly speaking, for every benefaction you show me insofar as I can comprehend[1078] how good you are to me—ah, this is actually not a relation between you, O God, and a man—that a man has to be able to *understand* that you are good. Help me to thank you as well when I do not *understand* that you are good but almost childishly want to understand that you now seem to love less. Nauseating thought—I could make myself eternally unhappy thinking this way!

———

Often it seems as if my relation to you resembled the relation to an examiner: I am obliged to use my reason, my strength, and then the question remains whether or not I gave the correct answer, and if I was wrong, you would merely say: You were wrong there, you made a mistake—it is your own fault. O, my God, is this a relation between God and man! No, God be praised, we do not stand so dignifiedly face to face with each other, you and I. O, no, even when I have made a mistake it was still your governance which permitted it to happen and promptly and lovingly lifted it up into your fatherly purpose for me, lovingly disposing of the millions of possibilities so that even the mistake would become truly useful to me.

———

You let me succeed in everything; then there came a time when you let me fail in everything. I understood it to mean that it was all over now and you literally did not want to have anything more to do with me. I believed, however, that I had one blessing left—to thank you unceasingly for the indescribable good you did for me, infinitely more than I had even expected or could hope to expect. —O, my stingy heart, which in spite of everything is so niggardly when it thinks of you. No, your intention was that I should go forward, that from the indescribable good you had done to me in such a way that I could understand it I should learn the blessedness to praise and thank you even when I am unable to understand nothing but the fact that everything goes wrong for me.

x^3 A 222   *n.d.,* 1850

« 3453 *The Way a Religious Man Speaks*

There was a time, O God, when you overwhelmed me with good gifts, and with every benefaction I was reminded of you; that time was blessed. Then everything changed; it seemed as if everything went wrong; and every time a new misfortune came along I was reminded of you, of the fact that you are love: that was even more blessed. For your love is not like human love, which proves that it is love by what it does for me. No, your love is above all proof: no matter what you do with me—it is infinite love. When am I most truly aware that you are infinite love? Certainly not when I am aided by the proof—O, no, when I perceive it without proof, when it is not a dogma which always requires proof but has become my axiom, which never needs proof. O, but when my soul grows weary, then may you not omit the proof.

x^3 A 223   *n.d.,* 1850

« 3454 *To God*

Deep down in my soul you placed the blessed assurance that you are love. Then, as a father deals with a child, you drummed the same thing into me again and showed me again and again that you are love. Then you took in the sails for a time. You wanted me to try my hand a little without proof—to see whether I could do the same without proof. Then everything became confused; I became anxious and afraid to the point that I felt it was all too advanced for me, and I was afraid that I had gone too far, had become too tactless, had stuck it out too long with you, and that what had happened to me was my punishment. Just take one worry away from me, I said—that it is not my responsibility. Ungrateful wretch that I am, as if it were my earlier goodness which was responsible for your showing your love to me up until now! Relieve me of one worry, I said, that it is all my many mistakes which were responsible for making you tired of me. Ungrateful wretch that I am, as if you had loved me previously because of my wisdom and merits! O foolish, conceited heart which even wants to counterfeit the past, is not content simply to have perceived the blessedness that God is love and that he shows it—but wants to have deserved it a little, even if only in comparison to his present unworthiness. O, no, no, God be praised that it has never been my worthiness which has made God love me. It is precisely this which gives me cheerful boldness, otherwise a man would die of anxiety this very moment, lest he prove to be unworthy in the next moment.

x^3 A 227   *n.d.,* 1850

« 3455 *To Pray in Christ's Name*

This is how it is pictured in Christendom. I have a God in heaven from whom I may expect every benefit (for he is infinite love)—alas, if only I were not a sinner. But now Christ by his suffering and death has made satisfaction and reconciled me with God—ergo, I now dare expect every benefit and pray God for it.

Here again we trim off too quickly. We forget that Christ is the prototype [*Forbilledet*].[1079] We alter the relationship as if God were a powerful prince and Christ the powerful, most intimate, courtier, whose influence is so great that when I pray in his name my prayer is heard. But this courtier does not pass himself off as the prototype—I merely use his influence.

If then I pray to God in Christ's name for one benefit or another or for exemption from one evil or another, there is implicit that *aber,* that in binding me to imitation [*Efterfølgelse*] Christ's name binds me to far greater suffering and privation by actually having to die to the world.

x^3 A 317   *n.d.,* 1850

« 3456 *Prayer—Faith*

While reading Scriver,[1080] I came across this excellent statement, which he attributes to another author without saying who:

Prayer is the daughter of faith, but the daughter must support the mother.

x^3 A 531   *n.d.,* 1850

« 3457 *A Pouring Out*

O, my God, how often have I not been happy, grateful, unspeakably happy in recognizing how strangely things have gone many times: that I started to do something—and not until later did I fully understand how right and full of meaning it was.

But at times the situation has been such that I had to say jubilantly: My God, it is your wisdom which rules—with the cooperation of my stupidity. I try to take everything into consideration the best I can—but then I do something imprudent and foolish—and I am ready to lose courage at the thought that now the whole thing is wasted—and then afterwards I understand that you changed this very foolishness into something very wise. Infinite love!

x^3 A 595   *n.d., 1850*

« **3458**

   "Bless the Lord, O my soul, and forget not all his benefits."
No, do not forget any—ah, but who has such a memory! Then let me at least not forget this benefit—that you bear with my forgetfulness.

x^3 A 700   *n.d., 1851*

« **3459**

Father in heaven, we pray we might remember that everything happening to us comes from you, and that nothing coming from you can harm us—no, no, it can only benefit us.

x^4 A 229   *n.d., 1851*

« **3460 Savonarola**

"The father of prayer is silence,[1081] its mother, solitude."
                    See Rudelbach, *Savonarola*, p. 428.[1082]

x^4 A 281   *n.d., 1851*

« **3461 Prayer——and Prayer**

What an infinite difference. One who prays—but in practice lives with the understanding that after a few days or a few years everything will turn out all right, and who therefore is essentially defined in finite categories, relates to God as to one who will help him finitely. And one who prays (and such a one the witness to truth must be!) and sees ahead of him an entire life of suffering until the very end, increasing as time goes on, and who prays to God to give him strength to endure—and therefore every time he prays to God he confirms and establishes all the more firmly the impossibility of the suffering being taken away.

x^4 A 562   *n.d., 1852*

« **3462 Prayer——Prayer**

"Every troubled, burdened, suffering human being can find consolation only by praying." —Very true, very true; nevertheless take particular note of this. We ordinary men pray God to end our suffering, to send us better times—and that is how we find consolation in prayer. The witness to truth prays God to give him strength to endure suffering; consequently he prays himself more and more deeply into suffering; the more inwardly and the more intimately he prays to God the more firmly he becomes immersed in suffering. —Do you have the courage to pray this way?

X⁴ A 565   n.d., 1852

« 3463 *Alas!*

I read in a devotional book (Arndt[1083]) that a person should think of God even in everything he normally undertakes. Alas, how often even in the devotional hour, when we ought to be thinking of God, we think of something else!

XI¹ A 11   n.d., 1854

« 3464 *O, God!*

O God, all you have from us men is trouble! Alas, when I consider all your kindnesses to me and want to collect my thoughts to thank you properly for them—alas, I often find myself so distracted that the most desperate thoughts crisscross my mind and it ends with my having to beseech you to help me to thank you—but a benefactor could ask to be at least spared the new inconvenience of even being asked to help someone thank him!

And when sin momentarily gets power over me in new sin—when my soul is inconsolable and I finally know of nothing else to do but say to you: You must help me, you must console me, [you must help me] think of something in which I can find consolation; then even my sin becomes transfigured and helps me farther along than I otherwise would have come. How shameless! It is you against whom I sinned, and then to ask you to console me for it!

And yet I know that does not displease you, infinite love, for in one sense it still indicates progress! If sin has complete power over a man, he dares not think of you at all. If he fights against it but not with all his strength, he dares at most only accuse himself before you and pray for forgiveness. But if he fights with all his might, honestly—then and only then it can dawn on him that you are on his side in such a way that it is you who must console him, so that before you, instead of merely accusing himself, he dares to complain, almost as if it were something which had happened to him.

XI¹ A 578   n.d., 1854

PREACHING, PROCLAMATION

« 3465

It is no doubt true that one learns by teaching others, but sometimes it can also be detrimental. Thus, when a young theological candidate makes too early a start in preaching to others, there is swift reprisal. It becomes a habit for him to depict the gloriousness of faith, for example, as glowingly and imaginatively as he is capable of doing. His actions, meanwhile, are unrelated to what he says, and up to now there has not been a chance for it because he has attempted so little. When it then becomes obvious that he just is not becoming an apostle right away etc., it is likely to end with his abandoning it completely.

V A 12 *n.d.*, 1844

« 3466

Today, when Spang[1084] stepped into the pulpit with all his aplomb and unctuousness etc., sawing the air with his gestures—a housemaid sat just under the pulpit. She had sung the hymn very serenely, but as soon as the sermon commenced she began to cry. Now it is usually quite difficult to reach the point of weeping over Spang, but particularly at the beginning of this sermon it was absolutely impossible; therefore I conclude that she came to church to cry. It was appalling —up in the pulpit all those pretentious airs and gesticulations, right under it a maidservant who does not hear a word he says or only occasionally plucks out a word, and regards God's house not as a house of prayer but as a house of mourning where she cries her heart out for all the vexations she has suffered since last she was here. It really ought to be stipulated that every servant is to have every Sunday free and is to go to church every Sunday morning. —I think serving maids are the most lovable lot to be found, both in Church and on Frederiksberg.

V A 17 *n.d.*, 1844

« 3467

From another manuscript but not used
(*Concluding Postscript*).

580

Everyone possesses the art of being able to speak his mother tongue; there are words in his mother tongue which express the highest things. Inasmuch, then, as every native-born person can speak the language, he can also say the word. On the other hand, if the sage uses the same word, it looks momentarily as if he had wasted his life by not having advanced beyond it. But the person who is very ingenious in listening when people are speaking also discovers what a fraud takes place when definite thoughts are not attached to the words, a fraud which does not disclose itself if we merely listen to the separate words but shows itself immediately if we hear the words together with others. The simplest of men is able to say: There is a God; and a child names the name of God, yet without perceiving that it is a task requiring a thinker's utmost effort to attach a definite thought to the word. I could easily write reams if I wanted to give examples of how people talk in such a way that their own words testify that they think nothing. I now take an example from devotional discourse.[1085] In the same sense as a general impression is associated with the idea of a forest, a theater, a fort, a prison, so the idea of quiet repose full of solemnity and devotion is immediately linked to the idea of the house of God. This is as it should be. For a score of years now I have heard and read sermons and have never found any other kind of talk than this: "The congregation here assembled now rests in a devotional peace of mind." But the person who is very much occupied with religion, who perhaps reads a sermon every day, goes to church every Sunday, may also have been distracted—yes, not only this, but according to the law that spiritual trial [Anfægtelse] increases proportionately to religious inwardness, he perhaps has been most disturbed of all when he counted on having peace of mind in this holy place, most disturbed because he himself was so fearful of becoming disturbed (for completely unthinking persons are usually free from spiritual trial.) Conversely, a man who enters a church now and then will be seized by a sensuous, esthetic impression in which the unfamiliar plays an essential role, and thus he will be solemn. He will therefore understand perfectly what the pastor says about solemnity. On the other hand, the person who is being tried, who at times does not succeed in getting properly in tune, will struggle and listen and listen, and if he listens and reads year in and year out but never hears anything except that one is solemn—he will feel abandoned, perhaps despairingly regard himself as trash. Who, then, is really being preached to? —Only God knows. Esthetically it holds that the less frequent, the more solemn. I love the Danish woods—but for that very reason I would never live in a wooded area. If I had to live there and be there every day, there would be days and times when it would not seem so beautiful to me, times when I would become despondent because at some time it did appear beautiful to me, and it would seem as if I had lost both it and myself. Therefore if the preachers want to be consistent, they ought to recommend going to church as infrequently as possible. If, on the other hand, I occupy myself *every day* with the religious (which the pastor does say now and then), something very grievous may happen to me, and yet I am supposed to struggle through. Here is where the pastor's task begins. He is not supposed to preach to arty dilettantes and let it come to the point that a man sitting there spiritually distraught, concerned because he has not managed to feel devotional during the time of devotions—that he then shall be excluded from the sermon. —Is it not true, then, that there is and is supposed to be solemnity in God's house? Yes, of course. And although every bungling preacher can say, "How solemn!"—is not the most experienced preacher supposed to venture to say anything else—and yet there should be an infinite difference between what they say, for the experienced preacher is supposed to know how to bring into his sermon and sermons what is needful for the one being spiritually tried. An experienced preacher preaches for those being spiritually tried; a preacher who relates himself to religion only on Saturday night will best satisfy the people who go to church only a few times a year. The ordinary preacherly, ecclesiastical solemnity is theatrical scenery and a theatrical operation, a parallel to the formality which prevails at funerals. — How does this solemnity come about unless the preacher who is preaching maintains a certain abstract idea about what is normal, that a person is solemn in just the proper way in God's house, yes, even in a special way according to the particular festival day (which is not often achieved, as is known by one who is in spiritual trial)—in short, what usually goes on in God's house is such that those assembled are almost not human beings but saints, that is, arty dilettantes who manage to feel solemn by going to church infrequently. On Saturday night the preacher thinks about this theme or that, does not himself exist [*existere*] in his thinking, for then he would be quite differently informed. If he is going to preach about spiritual trial, about human frailty, he scrapes together a few points (for in a curious way there is always something true in the peasants' superstition that the preacher has a book—not Cyprianus, however, but a handbook for preachers, just as in Germany there is even a handbook for lovers). But this he forgets completely when he speaks about solemnity in the house of God, where imperfect men, nevertheless, also come.

VI A 150   *n.d.*, 1845

« **3468**

The preacher says: It is good to be here in God's house. Would that we could remain here, but we must go out again into the confusion of life![1086] Lies and nonsense! The most difficult thing of all would be to remain day after day inside of God's house. The listener gets the impression that the trouble lies in the confusion of the world and not in the listener himself.

VI A 151   *n.d.*, 1845

« **3469**

Through a casual contact, by reading a book, or in some other acccidental way, it occurs to a pastor just as he is going to ponder a sermon Saturday evening that the hymn singing, the chanting of the liturgy, and other related matters have great significance, that so often the congregation handles them shabbily. So he preaches about that; he warns against neglecting that part of the service; he complains that for the most part people come to church only to hear the sermon; he appeals to his own experience, that people come to church late, etc. This is what he preaches about. What happens? Two weeks later someone gets the idea that what the age really needs is a new hymn book[1087] since the congregation cannot possibly find edification in the evangelical hymn book. Our pastor immediately goes along, and now it is clear to him that this is a long-felt and profoundly-felt need. Two weeks earlier it was he himself who observed that it was a bad habit for people to come so late, a bad habit which had a basis quite different from dissatisfaction with the official hymn book. This is altogether forgotten. Our preacher thinks only of the immediate moment; otherwise he would have to say: No, wait—let us first get people to come to church and sing hymns, and then we can always see if a profound need shows up, for the development of a long-felt, profound need involves a long view; but to say that a congregation which is indifferent to the divine service as a whole, except for the sermon, *höchstens,* feels a need for a new hymn book, feels a deep need for a new hymn book—this is preacher-prattle.

VI A 152   *n.d.*, 1845

« **3470**

A religious discourse should never be abstract truth, for all understand it and yet understand nothing. The task of the religious discourse is to deal with this thing and that, with this one and that one, Peter and Paul, potters and merchants and chamberlains—*aber* in order to lead it all (*in concreto*) to the absolute. Of course it does not name people by name and say Mads Sorensen from East Sundby, it is you I am talking about, but it recognizes the relativities and manifold concretions of existence so precisely that it nevertheless does talk specifically about this one and that one.[1088]

VI A 155   *n.d.*, 1845

« **3471** *For: Something about Devotional Eloquence*[1089]

A strange climax.

. . . . . I heard a pastor preaching about a miracle, who, in order to make the report of it credible, first developed that the disciples had seen it with the eyes of faith, but then, doubting the credibility of the argument himself, concentrated all his mimetic gifts, his eloquence, and perspiring efforts on the last point—that they had even seen it with their physical eyes. His Right Reverend Sir seemed to think that the certainty of the physical senses is higher than the certainty of faith (this is already confusing enough) even with respect to a miracle, which dialectically is directly counter to the senses. It was a good thing that he said Amen; it was the best thing he said, for he really seemed to be just as well informed about Christianity as Peer Degn,[1090] who once was able to say the whole Lord's Prayer in Greek but now could only remember that the last word was Amen. It all adds up to this definition for a sermon: It is a discourse given by a preacher and ending with the word *Amen*.

VI A 156   *n.d.*, 1845

« **3472**

It is especially difficult for *another* person to speak appropriately about concern for livelihood. Surely the place of honor as speaker always ought to be granted to the son of poverty if he speaks appropriately about poverty. But the mind of one who has experienced this kind of life is perhaps frequently embittered and unfree, so that by speaking he does not convey cheerful confidence but communicates troubled concern. When this is the case, the inexperienced one may also be permitted to speak if he has learned inwardly to speak appropriately.

May God grant that the right words may find their proper place; if this happens with one who is poor, then he is of course undeniably the more excellent speaker.[1091]

VII[1] B 177:4   *n.d.*, 1846

« **3473**

In margin: Note. The pastor who, when speaking about the one and only object (in the essential sense) of the sermon, the paradox,[1092] is unable to produce this effect [contemporary actuality] and hold his listeners in the tension of contemporaneity, is not essentially a pastor. Regarded essentially, all his knowledge and proficiency etc. amount to nothing, but the lack of a present tense[1093] is sufficient evidence that he is not himself a believer, for in faith the believer is wholly contemporary, as contemporary as any contemporary can be, with a paradox.[1094]

VII[2] B 235, p. 88   *n.d.*, 1846–47

« **3474**

A deep and vital religiousness is to religion-at-a-distance as being in battle is to a maneuver (where no danger is present on the training field); and just as an officer who has done a tour as observer of a foreign army is ordered on his return to plan a training maneuver representing the battle, so clergymen sometimes arrange some religious scenes instead of preaching—that is, they once again esthetically place religion at a distance; for as Aristotle[1095] has rightly said, all the esthetic is representation and thereby at a distance, not in the medium of actuality, but a sermon must be in the actual moment of the present. In a certain sense a preacher should be such a person that the listeners are obliged to say: Where can I get away from this man; his words run me down in every hiding place, and how can I get rid of him, for he constantly confronts me.

VII[2] B 235, p. 191   *n.d.*, 1846–47

« **3475**

Most men really never come into contact with the religious; they live out their lives in an imaginary notion of God's nice, cozy, pleasant goodness and love and the notion that if they ever did decide to enter his house their consolation and confidence would be extraordinary. O you fools—likewise you pastors, who know nothing at all about preaching effectively to men. A pastor should say: What do you really want in church; have you considered what you will discover here, what horrors will be spoken of here such as the world does not know, that it is not evil men who persecute and martyr the good but God himself who tests throughout the long years; do you have any intimation of the horrors of spiritual trials? Therefore stay at home instead; manage to sneak through the world, but watch out for God. —After all, what good is it that those slobbering preachers change God into sweets and moonlight and then call such sentimentality and rubbish Christianity.[1096] —But as far as that goes, the trouble stems from the clergy and from the whole miserable system of livings.[1097]

VIII[1] A 98   n.d., 1847

« 3476

The whole notion of a bread-winning clergy is a delusion. Why do people get disconcerted when a man who is not a clergyman but nevertheless has ability, insight, and leisure wishes to concern himself with proclaiming Christianity or with confessing Christ—and yet it does not bother them at all when a clergyman does it? For this reason—that for the clergy it is a paid occupation. That is basically what people think. Therefore it sounds rather foolish when a pastor brags about confessing Christ in a special way. For just as people find it quite in order that an attorney gets cases wherever he can, since that is his paid occupation, so they find it quite in order that a pastor as such preaches some Christianity, especially when he also watches his chances for a bigger and better position. If someone were to give up his position in order to proclaim Christianity *gratis*, people would be angry. What people want is worldliness, and therefore just as we have physicians, attorneys, et al., so we also want to have a few who are pastors, or whose paid occupation is to be pastors. But the impression of the spiritual we do not want.

VIII[1] A 310   n.d., 1847

« 3477 *N. B.*

The *summa summarum* of orthodoxy (which, incidentally, not only regards itself as orthodoxy but also becomes self-important by defending Christianity against speculation, against Feuerbach, against Anabaptists, and the like) is this: Christianity is the most elevated and the most profound[1098] and the one and only which can cast true luster over this life (this is important to plumbers); without it joys are indeed empty and sorrows drain one of energy; therefore anyone who is more than ordinarily profound takes his stand with Christianity. —Fine, and such being the case, it is no wonder that Christianity has successfully been introduced into distinguished and cultured circles, since it is itself so distinguished.

But where in the world in all this orthodox rigmarole is there room for the essentially Christian, the decisive issue, that the earnestness of eternity waits in the background, the judgment, that you must accept Christianity, that Christianity by no means presupposes a direct need and desire for Christianity in the natural man (be he profound or simple) and therefore believes that it must itself command every man to become Christian, for otherwise he never becomes one.

If there were an absolute monarch who had a shrewd minister who won all the subordinates over to the king's side by showing him to be the wisest and best and most profound and prudent and well-intentioned—what then? Was this victory of service to the king, and without knowing it himself was not this faithful minister perhaps a traitor? What does the absolute demand? Absolute submission—that is, submission which comes from a "Shall."[1099] As soon as there is deliberation about it, etc., absolute submission will never again be attained. Thinking it over cannot result in absolute submission, obedience, etc. any more than a round cannon designed for shooting round cannon balls can shoot a square cannon ball; the very first beginning of deliberation about it is defection, rebellion.

This is the mission in our time. It is not necessary to proclaim Christianity, it has been proclaimed enough, I am sure, but it is the "You shall" that is what the missionary in Christendom has to proclaim. But the bishops and preachers have not understood this, and, even if they had understood it, they would not have dared to do it. Of course, to go out into the world in the consciousness or at least with the hope and prospect that the "You shall" which one proclaims will make one influential, powerful: well, now, that is appealing to a man. But to go out in the world in the consciousness that for proclaiming this "You shall" they may put you to death, and even if they do not do that you will never get to rule over others, since the "You shall" applies to you yourself—this teaching has no appeal to men.

The whole modern age, especially politics, has lost the idea that there is a "shall." Because of orthodoxy Christianity has also lost its "shall." That is the tragedy. One does not need to be a prophet to see that it will cost a great deal to get the situation straightened out again; it will cost the authentic missionaries just as much as it once cost to introduce Christianity into a pagan land, for now it is a matter of introducing it into Christendom.

What is the specific character of "the sermon." First (1), that it is given by a *pastor.* He is a pastor by virtue of his ordination. Here is the possibility of offense. The paradox. This is so completely forgotten in our age that it might never have been known. Everything is talk-talk about genius and talent and studies and eloquence of speech and the fit of the pastoral gown, etc. Second (2), authority. A pastor *must* use authority; he *must* say to men: *You shall;* that he must do even if they kill him, that he must do even if everybody falls away from Christianity. But everyone will accept it if he were to say: I beseech the most honored, cultured public's lenient indulgence for these eternal truths.

VIII[1] A 434   *n.d.,* 1847

« **3478**

When a minister preaches about God and Christ and eternity etc. these days, the congregation listens in the usual way. But let him merely say "in these times, with the war"—presto, their ears prick up, that is something to preach about. Everybody sits up straight to get every word, the women take off their hats so they won't miss a thing —but it does not matter much what is said about God and Christ.

VIII[1] A 668   *n.d.,* 1848

« **3479**

It certainly is high time that Christianity be taken away from men in order to teach them to appreciate it a little. We picture the yield of 1800 years, what individuals have achieved over the long years, the chosen individuals who became more or less unforgettable, the entire yield of thoughts, moods, feelings, expressions, etc.: all this is at the disposal of preaching as something to comment upon—and all we do is get farther away from existing [*at existere*].

X[1] A 6   *n.d.,* 1849

« **3480**

When the compassionate Samaritan[1100] is preached about, the assumption is that someone who has a mistaken idea can nevertheless act rightly. But when Matthew 25[1101] is the text (deeds of compassion), the Gospel about the Samaritan is forgotten: here we learn that no one but believing Christians can perform deeds of compassion.

X[1] A 19   *n.d.,* 1849

« **3481**

Is it not, after all, a kind of inhuman cruelty or sadism (like that of the tyrant who contrived to have the shrieks of those being martyred transformed mechanically into music[1102]) to preach in an elegant church to an elegant, honored, cultured gathering about those noble ones who suffered for the truth[1103] etc.—and the general effect is that the auditors have passed a pleasant hour and the speaker is admired. Is it not brutish cruelty on the part of the auditors and blood money for the speaker—for he does in fact turn the martyrs into money.[1104]

It would be the right thing to do sometime to arrange such an address—everything would be in order, the pleasant hour would be almost over—and then suddenly let fly at them by showing what a lie the whole thing has been.

In fact, revival preachers must be cunning. "The cultured" shrewdly stay away when they hear that there is to be such a preacher, or if they come they come mentally armed with a thousand prudential rules and evasions. Therefore, if they are to get a showerbath, one must be able to trick them.

Or has the world (the actuality in which you and I live) now become so perfect that there is no occasion for you to suffer a little for truth? But see, the lie has been contrived that to be earnest about what is said is extremism.

A quiet, modest, retiring country pastor probably cannot preach differently; there is no setting for the larger decisions. Nevertheless he can see to humbling himself and his listeners under eminence and greatness so that it all becomes a little more than a pleasant hour.

But to preach this way in the great cities is treason against Christianity.

X^1 A 125   *n.d.,* 1849

« **3482**

In the *Evangelical Hymnbook,*[1105] no. 5, v. 6, *Te deum laudamus,* is the following:

> The prophets announced you,
> The apostles proclaimed you,
> And the martyr-flock glorified you
> In the hour of death, solemnly.

These words could be a theme for the various ways of proclaiming the Word.

x¹ A 144   n.d., 1849

« **3483**

The rhetorical "discourse"[1106] completely confuses the essentially Christian. We hear, we read a discourse which shows and finds fault with the fact that so many declare the highest but do not do it. We concentrate on it—alas, while we are looking at the speaker we see that he himself is just such a person, but the fallacy is raised to the second power. In the first is the fallacy: to declare the highest and not do it; in the second power is the fallacy: to preach about the fact that many declare the highest and do not do it. The fallacy can become more and more refined. The third power is not merely to preach about it but to weep while one is preaching—alas, and when we look at the speaker who even weeps while he preaches about the fact that so many declare the highest and do not do it—yes, that they even preach about the fact that so many declare the highest and yet do not do it, without doing it themselves—we see that he himself is such a speaker. The fallacy can mount higher and higher in refinement. However, it is not always refinement; most often it is stupidity.

x¹ A 182   n.d., 1849

« **3484**

In addition to having understood the truth, it is also required for the proclamation of truth that in proclaiming it one be completely independent of men. But even more rare than a person who has grasped the truth is the person who has such recklessness in proclaiming it. But without this the truth becomes warped, so that the true becomes untrue because the men to whom it is proclaimed are made the authority.

x¹ A 207   n.d., 1849

« **3485**

Surely that which is being preached these days is untenable as Christianity.[1107] The whole thing is a grand attempt to make fools of men. The pastor is not the one farthest out—he stands on land and commends and recommends Christianity, all those marvelous and inestimable grounds of consolation, the great good in being a Christian, but he betrays not wholly ambiguously that he adds in the quiet recesses of his mind: if anyone is so unfortunate as to be reduced to the possibility of being helped only by the consolation of Christianity —for I help myself along by having a living (whereas Christianity consoles the poor) and help myself along by having powerful friends, honor, and esteem (whereas Christianity consoles the despised etc.).

Courage and resoluteness and truth and the implications for personality must enter into the preaching.

[*In margin:* The clergy have merely an attorney's relation to Christianity; they are paid to defend the cause of Christianity, and if they do so it is regarded as very important—since they are not paid to attack Christianity.]

What discussion there is about miracles! Miracles are extolled— and then the addition: but miracles do not happen any more. This is really a way of making fools of people. Either we should abandon miracles completely or act accordingly. It is pointed out how miracles declare the omnipotence of God etc., and then we say: Would you be so narrow-minded that you cannot rejoice over God, because he does not perform miracles for you?

Just as the observation of nature (the lilies and the birds) ought to be a godly diversion, so a discourse on miracles ought to be a dithyrambic rejoicing over God. Upbuilding edification should be sought in this widening of the mind and spirit, this audacious exhalation of joy over God—and then never mind whether or not God does a miracle on my account. To speak quite humanly, I ought to be so infatuated with God the Almighty, who shows his omnipotence in performing miracles, that I completely forget myself over him.

X^1 A 540   *n.d.*, 1849

« **3486**

This is more or less the way preaching goes about it.[1108] Using the essentially Christian, it mildly entices—and then employs the terrifying element in Christianity to thrust back. Be humble, so it goes—be humble, for the proud man who wants to stand alone will come to stand alone as a punishment, because the manner of punishment is always the manner of the sin—but, but, but, Reverend Sir, Christ also stood alone, and therefore by imitating [*efterfølge*] him one is even more surely encompassed by the terrifying, which, however, is used as a deterrent which is supposed to frighten one toward the mildness. —Be conciliatory, so it goes, for the obstinate and the domineering will end up being mocked, scorned—but, but Christ ended up this way, too; he will be put to death—but Christ was in fact crucified.

So goes the whole confusion. And what betrays an even deeper confusion in Christendom is this—if I were to put this as poetic lines in the mouth of a witty character in a novel, it would be admired and relished by amateurs and professionals alike, because, after all, all are agreed that it is *perdü*. But if I were to say it and sign it, people would become furious, because it would appear almost as if the man were mad enough to want Christianity to be taken in earnest.

X^2 A 21   *n.d.*, 1849

« 3487

There is also this subtlety in preaching that in warning against "meritoriousness," the whole fantastic asceticism of the Middle Ages[1109] (flagellation and the like) is slyly confused with the exposing onself to danger, the strain and suffering which are connected with confessing Christ in any decisive way, and which are indeed demanded of the Christian in a decisive sense, that is, without all sorts of hallucinations about being a public official etc., so that it is *qua* public official and jobholder one proclaims Christianity and confesses Christ.

X^2 A 95   *n.d.*, 1849

« 3488

From the ethical point of view preaching, the preaching situation as it is understood nowadays, seems calculated to deceive the speakers and the hearers.

In a magnificent building where art and good taste have produced the esthetic effect[1110] of pomp and ceremony, when the organ's magnificent voice has filled the vaulted room and the last tones die away —a speaker steps forth who now sets everything in motion to create the desired effect at that moment; he himself is fired up by perceiving how effective he is; he is intensified, etc.

The deceased Spang[1111] once declared that he had had some of his most glorious moments in the pulpit. Yes, O yes, the intensification of mood and imagination is indeed something, esthetically. But I wonder if an actor does not speak in the same way about creating a hushed stillness in the theater so that one can hear a pin drop—and the next moment hear the applause; I wonder if an actor does not also say that he has had some of his most glorious moments on the stage, through the intensification which comes from electrifying and being electrified. And the pastor even more, he who is himself the *I* who speaks *qua* author.

And so they speak movingly about a pastor's feeling the need to preach; when he has not preached for a month or two he feels an emptiness, a great void, etc.—well, no wonder that he who is spoiled by such weekly esthetic intensifications during which in an inspired mood he exaltedly moves and is himself moved by depicting faith, hope, love, noble deeds, the blessedness of suffering, etc.—no wonder that he feels a void; when a person is addicted, it is not so easy to do without alcohol.

But where in all this is there a place for lowly ethical existing and acting.

It is just as impossible for Mynster, face to face with a merely tolerable dialectician, to show the difference between a preacher of his style and an actor, as it is to stand on his head. For the difference between a pastor and an actor is simply the existential, that the pastor is poor when he preaches about poverty, is derided when he preaches about suffering derision, etc.; whereas the actor simply has the task to deceive by doing away with the existential altogether—in the most profound sense the pastor has the task of preaching with his life. Yes, somewhat paradoxically he could say: Preaching is much like keeping one's mouth shut but expressing existentially, indeed, with his life, what is ordinarily expressed with words.[1112] The resounding organ, the splendid arm motions, etc. are really not needed: a mute can preach, and a cripple who has no arms. [In margin:] See p. 134 [i.e., x^2 A 151].

x^2 A 149   *n.d.*, 1849

« **3489**

See p. 133, middle [i.e., x^2 A 149].

In order to get rid of esthetic sensory illusions and stimulations, preaching should either be done only for a few at a time, somewhat as in a confessional, or it should be done for the "crowd" on the street[1113] —and not by a public official with a bread-and-butter job.

In order to justify preaching in crowded churches, appeal frequently has been made to Christ and the apostles, who did in fact cry out and witness and address themselves to the crowd. *Aber*: in the first place they did it on the street (and thus the esthetic sense-illusion cannot appear); next, when they did it in the synagogues they were neither in the service of the established order nor conforming to it. It would be somewhat analogous if someone who was not a public official and a bread-and-butter preacher would use one of our churches to preach against this whole decadent Christianity. Finally, both Christ and the apostles scrupulously expressed their teaching with their lives, were in the character of the teacher, not in the character of councilman, Knight of the Danish Order, second and first class.

Within an established order of public officials and bread-and-butter representatives, preaching in a magnificent church is, from a Christian point of view, actually nonsense; it becomes sheer sense-illusion, which is more than amply demonstrated by all the talk about the differences between preachers—the predicates used are always in the esthetic sphere.

X^2 A 151   *n.d.*, 1849

« 3490

Preaching the law is terrifying, for if it is done thoroughly and in truth it recoils worst upon oneself;[1114] the one who stands closest is always hit the hardest, and one must be most rigorous toward himself. Preaching grace is joyful.

X^2 A 218   *n.d.*, 1849

« 3491

A handsome court preacher,[1115] the cultured public's chosen one, steps forward in the magnificent castle church, faces a chosen group of distinguished and cultured people, and preaches movingly on the apostle's words: God chose the lowly and the despised. —And no one laughs.

X^2 A 227   *n.d.*, 1849

« 3492

Preaching particularly lacks the awakening *you* of authoritative application—that it is you who is being addressed.[1116] The awakening of the widow of Nain's son is always presented as a symbol of spiritual awakening—well, maybe, but Christ[1117] did not step up to the stretcher and deliver an address about the resurrection of the dead—no, he said: You, young man, I say to you, stand up. —Of course I do not mean that the pastor is able to perform miracles. The point, as Luther[1118] says in his sermon on this Gospel, is that you must hear Christ say it to you —but the usual discourse *about* it is of no benefit.

X^2 A 230   *n.d.*, 1849

« 3493

"The church," where the organ makes music, sometimes even with the assistance of trombones, is really not the place to proclaim

Christianity—no, when in actuality derision is making the music, then —from a Christian point of view—one is properly supported by the accompaniment—if one can preach at such a time.

x^2 A 288   *n.d.*, 1849

« 3494 *The Proclamation of Christianity*

Here is the problem that brings me to a standstill: for the proclamation of Christianity in its truth as it is in the New Testament, a divine language is required, and more than a human being is required to proclaim it. The contrariety of the spirit in relation to the universally human (that when the world goes against me I simply ought to rejoice, that this actually is fortunate, etc.)—well, even if by supreme effort I could even tolerably maintain this uncompromising position, it is still cruel to talk this way to other men.

This I understand. But what has happened? Yes, the authentic proclamation of Christianity has disappeared from the world. The Christianity which is proclaimed is anything but Christianity.

Consequently I have thought that there has to be a poetic presentation. In a poetic presentation Christianity is represented in its true superhuman elevation—and it must now be left to each and every person as to how far he can venture out.

But the matter becomes more difficult, for when he who has divine authority is along and gives the orders, his resolved command is just the thing that gives assistance in venturing out.

x^2 A 310   *n.d.*, 1849

« 3495

Since Visby[1119] lost the election[1120] it seems that Christianshavn folk do not want to listen to him at all. It is just too bad to have a church as empty as it was today.

The fools, of course, do not understand things in an essentially Christian way. When a person is a court preacher and has a great audience—everyone scurries over there. From a Christian point of view it is probable that they may perhaps get a little secular art—but not Christianity. If a man is persecuted it is probable, from a Christian point of view, that they may perhaps get a little Christianity.

He preached today (Christ in the temple at the age of 12) on the theme: "Search and you will find."[1121]

(1) What to search for
(2) How to search
(3) Where to search.

The sermon was cut a little short; otherwise it would have been excellent. He knew how to use the gospel for the day in an illuminating way. He did it quite nicely, but he could have done it better. Mary sought something which was not her own, something which was entrusted to her, and by God, something which she had had in the same way we should seek lost innocence, come like children into the kingdom of God. She sought it indefatigibly. She sought it in the temple.

x^2 A 363   *n.d.*, 1850

« 3496

Instead of preaching himself every Sunday, why does it never occur to a pastor to read a sermon aloud, one by Luther, for example! But there is a lot of nonsense about the living word,[1122] and then, too, he is afraid someone would take him for a parish clerk!

x^2 A 382   *n.d.*, 1850

« 3497

The present-day sermon is usually quite confusing. The "pastor" has at his disposal, in the form of platitudes, the thoughts and expressions of men whose lives were existentially expressive equivalents—but no one of us expresses it. Thus it becomes nothing but self-contradiction.

The pastor says, "It is so good to be in God's house—but a person's work does not allow him to remain there" etc. What work? How much does a man need to live? Yes, ask the ascetics. But we—we need ever so much more—and yet we talk like those ascetics, and the whole thing becomes a satire on ourselves.

The thing is—there must be admissions. We must admit that we are not so spiritually simple, that we are more developed both sensually and intellectually—and then, just the same, flee to grace.

x^2 A 581   *n.d.*, 1850

« 3498 *The Proclamation of Christianity*

One thing only I understand, that if Christianity is not at all maintained at its qualitative point (that its presupposition is a suffering and misery, together with repentance, such that this life is lost), then Christianity is actually an impossibility.

This is the way Christianity came into the world. But what then? Human affectation (long after the time of the martyrs) found that Christianity was supposed to be something extraordinary and thus it was supposed to make a game of Christianity—and this is Christendom.

Try to proclaim Christianity in Christendom. Be yourself wretched like one of those whom human pity for safety's sake keeps hidden from society so that we do not become anxious and afraid by knowing that such sufferings exist. Be such a one yourself and then dare to proclaim consolation for such suffering, consequently reminding society that such suffering does exist—and you will see what an uproar there will be. And then we are all Christians! But with the utmost circumspection we keep the lepers, the insane, the demoniacs, the publicans, and flagrant sinners far outside human society—and yet it was precisely to such people Christianity was proclaimed.

O, human pity or what amounts to the same thing, O human pity in Christendom, no different and just as cruel as any in paganism! Seneca tells of a man on whom a king took revenge by having his nose and ears cut off, by having him generally mauled, and then locked up in a cage where he was unable to stand upright—and what does Seneca[1123] say further? He relates that after leaving him in there amid his own excrement—people finally ceased to have pity on him because he was so loathsome. Wonderful pity!

But Christianity begins to console there where human society wishes to be ignorant that such sufferings exist. In Christendom there is no change at all. True Christianity would shock everybody, as it once did, because in proclaiming consolation for such horrible sufferings it embarrasses society by pulling out these horrible sufferings for a day, something we usually defend ourselves against so that we may remain ignorant of them—we Christians!

x^3 A 48   *n.d.*, 1850

« 3499 *Preaching*

There is an argument about what kind of address is the right one.

The situation now is that what we call the sermon (that is, a speech, a rhetorical oration)[1124] is a completely incongruous form of communication for Christianity.

Christianity can be communicated only by witnesses: that is, by those who existentially express what is said, actualize it.

But precisely when Mynster[1125] is most admired, in his most brilliant moments—precisely then he is, from a Christian point of view, most untrue. It is dreadful to imagine how this same crowd, which is silent with admiration, would rage against a poor mistreated apostle —who did what Mynster orates about.

x^3 A 59   *n.d.*, 1850

« 3500 *The Distance from the Prototypes in Christendom*

This is best seen indirectly in the preaching, which in a purely theatrical way does not make present and actual the difficulties involved in realization but lets the whole thing be one of those solemn uplifts in a quiet hour, the basis of which is the tacit unanimity that none of us has any intention of doing it,[1126] no more than it ever occurs to the pastor to begin trying to do it—otherwise he would have to speak differently.

x³ A 102   n.d., 1850

« 3501 *The Lenient, Untrue Proclamation of Christianity*

It is not merely untrue, but it therefore also bears a great responsibility.

To be specific, when Christianity is proclaimed so leniently, it does not have the degree of consolation which the person requires who is wretched in the strictest sense. The fact is that men do not wish to have anything to do with those who are wretched in the strictest sense but wish to remain ignorant of their existence—and it is right here that Christianity begins.

Take any contemporary sermon you choose and hand it to someone who is really suffering, to someone suffering depression bordering on insanity, to someone with an obsession, or someone suffering for the sake of the truth—it sounds like mockery of him; it does not dare to console him because it never dares to think of his suffering.

That there are sorrow and adversity and hardship etc.—yes, even the happiest of people must surely be aware of them. The sermon does consider them but, mind you, on such a low key that the total impression in no way whatsoever disturbs the impression of a cozy, pleasurable life. And happy, prospering people, if they have a shred of human intelligence at all, like to hear this. —And this is supposed to be Christianity!

Just the fact that Christianity drags these poor wretches into the picture, brings them, so to speak, into society's consciousness, offends the natural man; drags them into the picture—why?—to console them. Well, thanks, says the natural man; we prefer to know nothing about such sufferings; that is why we have places far removed and remote from society where we shove them away. And as soon as we detect how things are with a man, that he is wretched in this way, we volunteer—

presumably out of sympathy—to remove him far, far away from ourselves.

And this man is precisely one of those whom Christ is seeking. O, you fine preachers, you are admired and no doubt admire yourselves for your affinity with the classicity of a Goethe, he who knew how to put at a distance—but what do any of you actually understand of Christianity!

Originally I understood Christianity much better—ah, but what did it amount to, really, until the world itself taught me to be aware. My initial inner suffering, which registered the proper degree of anguish, helped me at first—and yet I was quite unaware of the most crucial strenuousness of the essentially Christian.

X^3 A 129   *n.d.*, 1850

« 3502 *The Various Degree-readings of Christianity*

Christianity may be regarded as a fluid which then can be measured.

The law is: the greater the rigorousness, the greater the consolation.

Rigorousness is the spirituous, but the spirituous is again consolation.

The usual sermon measures barely one degree if the New Testament is reckoned at fourteen.

The consequence is that the usual sermon is able to console only those who really need no consolation—whereas the N. T. is able to console the most wretched person of all, even if the most soaring fantasy imagined him more wretched than the most wretched of all who have ever been.

It would seem that consolation is something everyone would like to hear, the more consolation the better. No, no, this must be understood *cum grano salis.* The degree of consolation is continually reminiscent of the degree of wretchedness. But there is a kind of wretchedness[1127] of which the natural man wishes above all else to remain ignorant, that it exists—this kind of consolation he really does not want to hear. When wretchedness is portrayed, there is brought to mind the fact that it is something which has happened to many, something which can happen to any man—and so goes the enthusiastic discourse of consolation. Thanks all the same, says the natural man, but I would just as soon, as long as possible, remain ignorant that such wretchedness exists.

Venture to proclaim this kind of consolation and you will find that you are thrust out of good society, treated as an evil pest to be guarded against—but Christianity, that gentle doctrine, this the cultured society of zestful men of the world will surely want to keep.

Therefore it is obvious that a clergyman in our day must "be of the world" enough to proclaim Christianity—to suppress Christianity.

X³ A 130   n.d., 1850

« 3503 *Prudence—the Good*

Prudence hinders a man from willing the good in this way also.

We all know that it does not pay well to do good in this world, and thus to want to do it has all the appearance of stupidity. I have often pointed this out.

But here is a new form. If it is true that it does not pay to do good in this world (something of which we are all *nobly* aware), then why do we do it? It must then be because I *ought* to do it. But it is really extremely "embarrassing" to say that there is something one *ought* to do. We are adults, men, fathers, reasonable men—and should our relationship to our Lord then be something like that of a little snip of a child to his parents, a child who simply *shall* and that's all there is to it? That would certainly be ridiculous. The preacher may spout something about it on Sunday—but it is not actually to be realized [*realisere*].[1128]

If someone were to proclaim Christianity because he ought, it would surely be embarrassing and ridiculous to betray that he was so afraid of God that he did it simply and solely because he should do it. But if it is someone's bread and butter, perhaps a good, fat living—well, then it is earnestness to proclaim Christianity, there is nothing embarrassing or ridiculous about that.

O infinite depth, O horrible fecundity of deceit and cunning and fraud, conscious or unconscious, continued from generation to generation, practiced by thousands and thousands, maintained by practice —and then a poor lone man,[1129] a sickly person whose life hangs on a thread, who almost dies every day, at times every hour, an anxious and troubled conscience—and in the face of it all he is ordered, as it were, to take over the command. It is incredible, almost like the cruel stepmother in the fairy tale hitting upon some completely insurmountable task in order to torment the stepchild—except that here it is the God of love and it is out of love he grants me all this.

X³ A 141   n.d., 1850

« 3504 *The Good Books*

There a clergyman sits studying the works of these noble and devout souls; he learns them by heart—and orates.

If I had my way I would have good books like these burned and let the thieves plunder the bad ones. But this scurvy stealing: that such a scoundrel declaims what another came to know in terrible anguish, at the peril of his life, in anxiety and need—and does not resemble him in the remotest way.

x^3 A 154   *n.d.*, 1850

« 3505 *A Test of Christendom*

Order the preachers to keep quiet on Sunday. What is left? Well, then the essential thing is left: lives, the daily existence with which the pastor preaches.[1130] Seeing those, will you get the impression that it is Christianity they are proclaiming?

x^3 A 237   *n.d.*, 1850

« 3506 *The Proclamation of Christianity*

Essentially, Christianity cannot be proclaimed by talking—but by acting.[1131]

Nothing is more dangerous than to have all these high feelings and exalted resolutions go off in the direction of merely eloquent speaking. It then becomes an intoxication which is extremely dangerous, and the deception is that the whole thing becomes a glowing mood, and that, as they say, "He is so sincere!"—alas, yes, in the sense of the mood of the moment.

Preaching by means of acting is like a fast; the audience does not flock to it for intoxication; it is almost boring, and what is boring is that it promptly makes an issue of doing something about it, and one detects that the teacher is doing something about it.

x^3 A 246   *n.d.*, 1850

« 3507 *A Penitent Can Best Proclaim Truth*

This may be seen also in the fact that Peter's denial gave him momentum afterwards, because in repentance he had infinitely much to make up for. Paul's persecution of the congregation gave him momentum, for he had infinitely much to make good.

Incidentally, there are some observations on this thesis from another side, which last year were in the Bible case which lies on the desk and which now are in a packet by themselves in the wide middle drawer in the desk.

X³ A 271   *n.d.*, 1850

« 3508 *The Proclamation of Christianity as It Is Now Practiced*

is high treason against Christianity. Instead of (1) witnessing, (2) using authority,[1132] (3) then offering a life which is willing to take the consequences—in short, instead of keeping close to God and leaving the rest to him, we want—partly out of the stupid mediocrity which has never had a notion of the higher, partly out of fear of men, and finally for the sake of earthly profit—we want to stand in well with men and therefore incessantly change them into the authority which decides what truth is.

Obviously Christianity would have a hard time of it in our age. That a man should have a lord over him to the extent that every day of his life and every hour of his day is pledged to the service of God, that he should actually practice self-denial in this way, that his love of God should be so earnest that it actually means to hate the world—this, they would say, is revolting. Yes, quite correct. Christianity is also "the revolt," that is, as soon as Christianity is set forth in its truth people will revolt against it.

But where are they to be found these days, they who have even a mere notion of this. Just for that they need to be taken out of their relations to others in order to provide the possibility of coming close to God at all. But the majority are so tangled up in relations to "the others" from the cradle to the grave that it never occurs to them that absolute thoughts[1133] exist.

X³ A 288   *n.d.*, 1850

« 3509 *It Is Existence which Preaches,*

not the mouth. Take three clergymen from three different stations in life: a prelate, a well-to-do parish pastor, a mendicant friar who is actually an ascetic. All three preach about "the daily bread" for which we pray; perhaps they say the same thing—but the speaker, his character, his daily existence[1134] provide the interpretation here. It is the same everywhere. The prudent world shrewdly knows how to avail itself of this, too, just as Christianity knows how to emphasize that one must preach with his existence, lest the whole thing become shadowboxing.

X³ A 307   *n.d.*, 1850

« **3510**

There is a kind of preaching which corresponds to what a certain kind of lending-library novel is in the esthetic. Thisted[1135] has a good bit of it.

x^3 A 364   *n.d.*, 1850

« **3511** *Christianity Is Related to the One Who Proclaims It*

When Christ[1136] proclaims it, no man can bear being a Christian: they all betray him.

When an apostle proclaims it, then we men can begin to go along.

x^3 A 407   *n.d.*, 1850

« **3512** *A Memorandum for Preachers*

We ought to be reminded continually of what Quintilian[1137] says somewhere, that he has seen actors who let themselves be carried away so powerfully by their tragic roles that they were still crying when they got home. Quintilian[1138] goes on to say that he himself, one time when he had undertaken to arouse a certain passion in everyone, had put himself into it to such a degree that to his own utter surprise he had not only wept over it himself but had even become pale and felt just like one enduring pain.

One is reminded of what Hamlet says about the actor who is speaking of Hecuba.

Every true poet must have experienced the same thing.

The danger for the speaker is that he does not make the distinction, that he may be putting himself into it only poetically.[1139]

x^3 A 479   *n.d.*, 1850

« **3513** *The Proclamation of Christianity*

The truly Christian proclamation contains in its major premise that which is proclaimed and has within its minor premise,[1140] or as supporting premise, a dialectically qualified existing person (from which we see also how crucial personality is for the true proclamation of Christianity).

Let us consider such a well instructed person sent out by Governance to proclaim Christianity.

In the region assigned to him he finds that the main trouble is that "grace" is taken in vain. What does he do then? Does he stop proclaiming grace? No, by no means; that would be altering Christianity in another sense. Let us assume that he is rich: he gives everything to the poor—and then he proclaims "grace," that it is by grace that a man becomes saved, and he proclaims it more warmly, fervently, and enthusiastically than any clergyman. This proclamation is properly orchestrated: the major premise "grace," the minor premise, a person who has observed the most stringent requirements. But such a proclaimer, of course, is disturbing,[1141] for we want "grace" to mean that we have the right to keep our money. —Or he exposes himself to all kinds of persecution and mistreatment for the sake of truth, and then proclaims that a man is saved by sheer grace. This again is properly orchestrated: the major premise, grace, the minor premise, a person who complies with the most stringent requirements. But he is disturbing, for we want "grace" to mean that we get out of venturing.

x^3 A 484   n.d., 1850

« 3514 *The Pastor*

Someone who sits in state with all sorts of preferential treatment and composes a work of art which he delivers on Sunday and which we all admire. —But this, of course, is a poetic relationship. And that is just what it is. We have changed listening to the sermon into a matter of enjoyment.[1142]

To preach is: personally fighting against the troubles in life (and especially against those he speaks about) and then to find the occasion to and feel inclined to speak encouragement and to instruct others. But the main thing is the existence from which he goes forth to preach and to which he comes back from preaching.

x^3 A 515   n.d., 1850

« 3515 *A Proposal Aimed at the Improvement of Preaching*

They have been as miserly as possible in the matter of actually getting God's word to be heard. A little portion is read aloud—but the sermon drops it almost entirely.

My proposal, therefore, is:

(1) The whole New Testament (with the possible exception of the Book of Revelations) ought to be read aloud during every Church year.

(2) Sermons by the orthodox teachers of the Church from the different ages ought to be read aloud.

And it is not to be done in such a way that allows a possible choice (whereby one excludes what he does not like) but in such a way that when it is a Sunday for reading instead of preaching, that which is read is appropriate to the Gospel or the Epistle for the day and to the occasion, be it morning worship or vespers. Nor should the congregation know in advance on which day the pastor is not to preach but will read aloud.

There must be thorough control here. Every honest man has to confess that in a very short time even the most honest of men becomes enamored with his own method if he is not constrained to expose himself to a completely different light.

Let Martensen be obliged to read one of Luther's sermons aloud, not to mention one in which Luther talks about speculation—and no one will need to write against Martensen.[1143]

Of course, when the pastor has finished reading the sermon, he must not be permitted to tack on one word. He very likely would insist on doing just that, under the pretext that he had to make sure that the sermon he had read was properly understood. No, thank you, we are very well acquainted with theologians' concern for making sure of proper understanding. A sermon which Luther has delivered to a congregation is quite intelligible. And the pastor must not have permission to add one word to it.

x^3 A 534 *n.d.*, 1850

« 3516 *A Proposal toward a New Form of Preaching*

If we (making the admission[1144] that we do it out of human frailty, accommodating ourselves in the thought that what good does it do to raise the requirement so high that no one enters into Christianity at all—a view which is totally contrary to Christianity, since it is a way of serving Christianity by means of human whimpering and secular prudence) then keep the milder preaching of the gospel—yet in such a way, it is to be noted, that we continually recall the ideal[1145] (in order to stimulate the milder form, if nothing else)—then I also think that an annual Day of Penitence and Prayer ought to be introduced, at which time we would bring into consciousness the fact that we permit ourselves to make Christianity into something far more lenient than it really is.

The main point is always this—to regain an awareness of where we are, so that we do not make a fool of God by having Holy Scripture and then leaving out what we find to be too good and eventually thinking that it does not even exist.

x^3 A 547 *n.d.*, 1850

« **3517** *The Illusion Connected with Preaching*

The reason why sophists are so eager to preach in a chock-full church is that if they were to say what they have to say in an empty room they would become anxious and afraid for themselves, for they would notice that it pertains to themselves.

But the chock-full church creates two illusions: (1) the speaker, not thinking about himself, becomes important by the supreme earnestness of the fact that he is accomplishing something, is proclaiming the doctrine before these many thousands, is sowing the seed, etc.; (2) the illusion that when there are such myriads of Christians, then supposedly the old man himself, His Reverence, is a Christian.

X^3 A 692   *n.d.*, 1850

« **3518** *The Displacement of Christianity*

Christianity has been dragged down so low that it is supposed to have significance simply and solely as a consolation. Everyone arranges his life the best he can—and Christianity is taken along as consolation.

If Christianity were to be proclaimed in its truth, it would very likely appear to be keeping men from their tasks in life. And what would they most likely think if they were to hear that one must suffer for Christianity.

X^4 A 124   *n.d.*, 1851

« **3519** *The Proclamation of Christianity*

To the proclamation of Christianity belongs the word, speaking—and then an existing undergirding of the speaking, a witnessing.

If it is assumed that speaking is sufficient for the proclamation of Christianity, then we have transformed the church into a theater[1146] and can have an actor learn a sermon and splendidly, masterfully deliver it with facial expressions, gesticulations, modulation, tears, and everything a theater-going public might desire.

But, it is said, "The religous speaker, after all, declares that what he says is his faith, his conviction—the actor does not do that." Fine, but how am I to know that this is so, that it actually is the speaker's faith and conviction? Shall I be satisfied with the fact that he delivers it so beautifully, that he weeps and sobs—but after all the actor does that, too.

Thus the whole thing simply goes way back to what was primordial in Christendom: the speaker's life, his personal existence as the guarantee that what is proclaimed is the speaker's faith and conviction.

Thus both word and existence belong to the proclamation of Christianity. If one must be lacking, then preferably the former. If the latter is lacking, then the proclamation of Christianity is transformed into theatrical entertainment or enjoyment—however impressively His Reverence declaims, however impressively he depicts, however much he weeps does not help—Fru Heiberg also can do all that.

x^4 A 227   n.d., 1851

« 3520 *The New Thing, the Turning Point*

There are a great many churches around the country, and in every church there is an elevated place called a pulpit. A person ascends that pulpit in order to proclaim Christianity—that is what it is for.

Fine! That is, if the person who mounts it is so developed as a Christian that he dares call himself a Christian in the strict sense of the word.

But I have not come that far—whether others have I do not know —thus the pulpit actually becomes a place for bringing charges against oneself.

Is there anyone nowadays who is envious of daring to talk to people from a pulpit! At one time it was believed that by ascending the pulpit one came closer to God in such a way that he received the power to command others. This is not entirely so. By ascending the pulpit one does, no doubt, come closer to God—precisely for that reason one does not evade the self-accusation which the person in the congregation perhaps evades.

To preach from the pulpit means to bring charges against oneself, to preach from the pulpit ought to mean having the courage to let what he says recoil upon himself.

Then there is some truth in this kind of proclamation, but nevertheless, strictly speaking, real preaching or proclamation means preaching on the street[1147] or action.

x^4 A 287   n.d., 1851

« 3521 *Concerning Myself*

My relation is to inward deepening and not to dissemination. This voice with its subdued inwardness has convinced me; that which is true for one when said in this subdued tone becomes untruth for me as soon as I raise my voice to say the same thing. Why the roaring and shouting?

From the Christian point of view there should not be great churches but small chapels, and there should be preaching every day.

But an enormous auditorium, a mass of people, a scholar-orator, and then a roaring—it is appalling. It would be all right if it were a matter of market prices.

The loud voice of a missionary, not to mention an apostle's, where it is a matter of dissemination of the doctrine, is of course something quite different.

x⁴ A 317   *n.d.,* 1851

« 3522 *The First Day of Pentecost*

Paulli[1148] preached; he preached about joy in the Holy Spirit.

Then he showed how the apostolic Church was the great prototype: we must look back to "the first Church, when the apostles were the preachers." What is this? Nonsense. He is obviously trapped in an illusion himself and traps the congregation. It begins to look as if we really wished to have the apostles for preachers again. Foolishness! No, this is what should be said: Take a good look around you before you wish for that glorious time again when the apostles were preachers. You with your secularized lives are better served with plump career-preachers who are Knights of the Danish Order. Pray God that he will keep his hand over you lest you get apostles again, for then the fat would be in the fire.

Paulli continued: "The faithful lived in harmony together . . . . . and there were no poor among them; they shared everything in common." How touching or, more correctly, what touching rubbish! If it is so glorious that there are no poor—through everything being held in common—well, we have it in our power to bring it about. But I wonder if His Excellency is actually served thereby, or wishes it, or has any idea of what he is saying; or I wonder if the congregation does?

x⁴ A 330   *n.d.,* 1851

« 3523 *The Mild and Gentle Proclamation*[1149]

of Christianity has actually betrayed Christianity, and it no doubt became so mild and gentle out of fear of men.

Now it probably reckons that any opposition will run into many difficulties, for it must make Christianity rigorous—and men are not inclined to go for that.

But perhaps this craven, cowardly prudence miscalculates. For in times when superstition made men want to be Christian primarily out of precautionary considerations, made them afraid not to be Christian, it was natural for them to seek it at the cheapest price possible. But our age is much more free and easy, has some of the atheist's courage—and it may very well be that they will be willing to listen to a truthful presentation of Christianity in its authentic rigorousness. One of the good things about our age is that it takes a dim view of glossing over.

x^4 A 355   *n.d.*, 1851

« 3524 *The Proclamation of Christianity*

The law is this: If the proclamation is to be true, it must produce what it proclaims. For example, if the proclamation is that the Christian suffers in this world, then the proclaimer must also suffer. Otherwise, Christianity is transformed to mere teaching, an objective teaching, and this Christianity is not.

The order of precedence for proclamation is turned around: the more the proclaimer comes to suffer, the more perfect his proclamation; the more of a hit he makes, the more brilliant his career, the poorer his proclamation.

x^4 A 360   *n.d.*, 1851

« 3525 *Preaching*

It is easy to see that when the proclaimer of the essentially Christian is not in the character of the essentially Christian his proclamation evokes just the opposite effect.

Imagine two preachers, each delivering one and the same discourse, for example, about dying to the world, about renunciation. It is masterful, makes a deep impression, an almost overwhelming impression on the listeners. As they leave they are gripped by feelings, including gratitude to the speaker. How can we thank him, these honest, simple men wonder. One decides to send him 50 dollars as an expression of gratitude; another, a pair of silver candlesticks; a third, according to his humble best, a goose, etc. Imagine that one of the two preachers was, for example, an ascetic, living in character according to the essentially Christian—what then? Yes, here comes the earnestness —when the worthy gentlemen come with their presents, he cannot accept them, has no use for them. "If you want to thank me," he declares, "then do what I have proclaimed to you; for example, give this to the poor, and more yet." This is Christianity. It is quite true that the earnestness is greatest and truest at another point; the earnestness is not the discourse, but that which comes next. —The second preacher is a rhetorician, a cleric—he is pleased as punch over the presents; a few days later he goes around and thanks each one individually. Then, prompted by all these big gifts, he gives a great banquet with ten courses—this is playing at Christianity. This proclamation produces an actuality just the opposite of the essentially Christian actuality. The rhetorician does not die to himself, anything but; and the worthy gentlemen are led to believe that now they have done enough. Now they have scraped something together for His Reverence.

Or take two preachers. Each proclaims—it is one and the same discourse—how truth must suffer in this world. It is a masterful lecture and also produces an enormous effect; the listeners are carried away in audible admiration—but the one preacher is in character according to the essentially Christian; he says: What a blunder I have made—and then directs his attack at the listeners themselves, and receives boos and catcalls etc. This is Christianity; the earnestness is not the discourse, but what comes next. —The other preacher is a rhetorician, a cleric. He is delighted over the public's applause, bows and scrapes like those virtuosos who grant audience. More and more attention is directed to him because of his excellent discourse about how truth is derided in this world—he draws the attention of the government, becomes a Knight, ranking with the cabinet ministers, gets permission to have the velvet on the left arm, etc.—is this Christianity? No, this is playing at Christianity. The effect produced, or the actuality, is just the opposite.

This is playing at Christianity. And the fact that there are 600 trillions and billions and millions of such rhetoricians by no means proves that Christianity exists.

This play acting is permitted to go on from generation to generation; it looks as if Christianity existed on the largest possible scale of distribution—and it is a deception or mirage. What confidence can a young man be expected to get for daring to venture to shape his life according to Christianity when all he gets to see is such frightful untrustworthiness.

If there is any truth in this, that the relationship to God is the only blessing, that poverty and persecution are blessed in relationship to God—well, these millions of rhetoricians prove nothing with all their evidence; they merely prove that it can be very pleasant to have the benefits of money, honor, and esteem.[*]

X^4 A 495   *n.d.*, 1852

« **3526**

[*] *In margin of 3525* (x⁴ A 495):

In any case, as I have always said, the one who is not proclaiming Christianity in character at least must relate to the truth by confessing[1150] that this proclamation is not actually Christianity.

x⁴ A 496   *n.d.*

« **3527** *Preacher-prattle*

The whole proclamation as it is commonly represented by "the pastor" is and remains nonsense, although in saying that I do not mean that an end should be put to it, or that it cannot have its benefits, particularly because men as a rule do not have time to think about religion very much.

The confusion constantly centers in the fact that while the pastor is preaching the listener is substituting a lower level of thought and the pastor has no intention of snatching him out of it.

Take an example. The pastor preaches on the words: Christ did not rail and rant back when he was abused. He preaches about our doing just the same—not railing and ranting back. The listener listens devoutly and concludes something like this: If I do what the pastor is saying (not rail and rant back), then it surely will go well for me in this world.[1151] Here we have it. The whole thing turns on its going well for us in this world—and to that end we want to be involved with Christianity. What profound confusion! And that is the way 1,000 preachers preach and millions listen.

Take the words just read and ask yourself: Why was Christ crucified? Apparently because he did not rail and rant back. By railing and ranting back we always manage to get along well in this world. But no one is so sure of the most bitter persecution as one who manages to practice the elevation which does not rail and rant back; there is nothing the world hates so much. Take the example of Socrates;[1152] if he had brought himself to rail and rant back, he would not have been condemned.

Christ prays for his enemies. The pastor preaches on this. The listener concludes: If I do just the same, it will surely go well with me in this world. There we have it again! No, no, no, if you stood there accused and were sentenced to prison for life—if you then had the elevation to pray for your enemies, you would most certainly be put to death. Nothing creates as much bitterness as praying for one's enemies.

However, the fact that men essentially live all week long in totally different categories helps them not to perceive the nonsense in which they are immersed.

Christendom's basic confusion lies in the assumption by the official proclaimer and the official listener that Christianity is connected with the slogan: then it will go well with you in this world.

Well, I doubt very much that it goes well in this world for the true Christian.

For the clergy, however, things go very well in this world—but then that is not Christianity either.

x^4 A 597   *n.d., 1852*

« 3528 *The Good News Is Preached to the Poor*

When a king wishes to share a meal with poor folk, he has the good sense (and this is a royal trait) to eat the same food, drink the same poor wine or beer—if he does not care to do so, he stays away, for he perceives that it would be insulting to sit down at the table with them and not give an expression of equality.

So also with Christianity. There is no doctrine about God's adopting and loving the poor, the humble, the wretched, the unhappy—no, Christianity is the veritable act of God in Christ making himself equal with the humble and insignificant.

But we do it differently, we actually insult the poor with our proclamation of Christianity. Ourselves rich, powerful, happy to proclaim Christianity, to say nothing of having gotten it all by proclaiming Christianity—that is really insulting the poor.

x^4 A 671   *n.d., 1852*

« 3529 *Everything Depends upon How It Is Said*
The Falseness in the Preaching of Christianity

Take the rule of fasting. Have an Epicurean discuss it. He will point out that fasting is definitely needed in order to achieve more of a sense of pleasure, that it is praiseworthy on a dietetic basis and also for the sake of pleasure. A Stoic will say that one *ought* to fast in order to make a break with the sensate principle. Consider these two presentations—are they one and the same? And yet both of them recommend fasting, and the Epicurean is perhaps more persuasive than the Stoic. Yet these two presentations are infinitely (*toto coelo*) different.

So it is with the preaching of Christianity or the falseness therein (therefore where Mynster[1153] is involved). The expression of majesty in Christianity is set aside—it would not please men's tastes in our mutinous times; then a finite teleology is introduced and on that basis Christianity is recommended. And many go along—but it is a betrayal of Christianity.

Further. When Socrates[1154] was accused, he said that he knew he could very well have been released if he had been willing to weep and wail before the judges. What does this mean? It means that he was required to acknowledge the judges and his contemporaries as the criterion—but that he would not do, because he was on a divine mission. And now Christianity! It should indeed be served in a way commensurate with its character. But the falseness is rooted in actually making men the criterion in the proclamation of Christianity, appealing to their judgment, etc. When that is done, then men can be persuaded to go along with it in droves.

$$X^5 \ A \ 57 \quad n.d., \ 1852$$

« 3530 *The Christian Requirement*[1155]

The Christian requirement must be proclaimed in all its infinitude, not in such a way that I in self-torment bring myself into the thralldom of the law—no, it is grace; nor should it be proclaimed in such a way that I take it upon myself to pass judgment on anyone for not expressing the requirement in his life, for then I make Christianity into law, which takes its revenge by turning around and passing judgment on me.

Nevertheless the requirement must be *proclaimed* in all its infinitude; it must be heard.

As a result of neglecting it, of reducing the requirement, Christianity has become too mild for men, insipid, and order cannot be maintained.

And when there is an insurrection (as in 1848), what then? Then the enemies appropriate the New Testament and with the greatest ease show that the entire establishment is in no way Christianity. What then? Then the establishment is in a fix, for it has certainly passed itself off to be Christianity, true Christianity. What then? The end result— if the establishment is to prevail—would be that Christianity is lost. Instead, the establishment ought to be prepared for the attack by confessing and by having confessed that this actually is not Christianity, and thus Christianity does not stand and fall with the establishment.

But the establishment is *sophistical*. A distinction is made: in "quiet hours" and on Sundays there is talk about sublime things—but "this is not the way it is in practical life"[1156]—just like the sophist in Wieland's *Agathon* who, unlike Agathon, who believes that a person ought to order his life according to sublime ideals, believes that the sublime is something with which one diverts his soul, presumably in "quiet hours," but one is not to order his life according to it.[1157] The atheist, the scandalized, and the like bluntly declare that Christianity is poetry and mythology. What does the official preaching do? Good Lord, it harangues furiously in opposition, shouts loudly enough—in quiet hours—that Christianity is something else altogether. But then on Monday and outside of the quiet hours life goes on in completely different categories—as a result Christianity is still mythology and poetry, for the fact that it is not that to a person is not decided by shouting in quiet hours but by the actuality of a person's life or by at least admitting in the quiet hours that one's life expresses something entirely different. —What then is the difference between the atheist and the establishment? This—that the latter does all it can to suppress and hide with countless illusions the real truth of the matter. In that way it probably thinks it is more truthful than the atheist, and yet it is only because there is a deception, perhaps a pious deception, but still a deception—something of which the atheist is not guilty.

The official proclamation is Epicureanism.

It is the same old story from ancient times—the Epicurean and the Stoic can say exactly the same thing, except that the Epicurean ultimately defines virtue teleologically—that is, oriented to the enjoyment of life, *in order* to enjoy life, consequently does not arrive at the ultimate—and that the Epicurean will not break with desire but refines it.

So it is with the official proclamation of Christianity. It recommends the good—in order to enjoy life properly; it wants to refine desire (see Mynster).

x^5 A 62   *n.d.,* 1853

« 3531 *The True Elevation*

"Christ died once for the sins of all men and no sacrifice is needed any more"—so the "apostle" teaches and witnesses—and in order to get this proclaimed properly, the apostle's life is so strenuous that he himself becomes a sacrifice. O, noble, infinitely elevated, lovable, feminine modesty! This is how it should be understood: the apostle shrinks from calling attention to himself at God's side—no, there is no need of sacrifice any more—and yet his own life is also sacrificed. But by speaking as he does he diverts attention away from that; out of feminine modesty he conceals it! —The gospel is the glad message—and in order to proclaim it properly the apostle's life is so strenuous that no one suffers more than he (except the God-man). Infinite elevation, noble, lovable, feminine modesty! By speaking as he does the apostle draws all attention away from the nobility, conceals it—precisely that is the nobility. —"It is sheer grace"—and at the same time the proclaimer's life is more strenuous than that of any works-righteousness saint—yes, it is true, that is modesty.

The majority of men live otherwise; they use speech to hide their own inner squalor. Someone cries, "This cause is of infinite concern to me"—while his life expresses that it concerns him in a rather finite way. And so it is in everything.

X^5 A 117   *n.d.*, 1853

« 3532 *Preacher-jargon*

Christianity uses the same words and expressions, the same language we human beings use—but it understands each particular word the very opposite of what we human beings understand by it.[1158]

For example, Christianity says: Come to me, I will take away your burdens, make things easy for you, etc. By "burdens" Christianity understands wealth, might, power, earthly goods. Aha, this is a divine language—yet it uses the same word we use in human language—"burden."

We humans understand the matter differently. By "burdens" we understand poverty, want, social inferiority, etc. With our tongues hanging out we run after wealth, try to amount to something in order to avoid the ravages of time. Therefore we must find it quite ironic for someone to say to a millionaire: Come, my friends, and I shall relieve you of your burden, the burden under which you are groaning—give me your million and you will see how easy, etc. This is somewhat as in *Recensenten og Dyret*,[1159] where the juggler performs the amazingly deft feat—one, two, three—of drinking Klatterup's and Ledermann's wine.

Yet this is the way it is, so infinitely elevated is the divine language of Christianity—but, as stated, it is nevertheless the same language which we human beings use. Just as Socrates[1160] is said to have talked continually only about pack asses and leather tanners etc., but always with another meaning, so Christianity uses the same words and expressions we human beings use and yet says something entirely different from what we say.

Then with the help of 1,000, 10,000, 100,000 and millions of "preachers" the matter is prattled—with great solemnity—back into ordinary human jargon, and the result is called Christianity—this is "Christendom." By "burdens" the preacher understands poverty, want, social inferiority, etc., bows seventeen times before the millionaire—then reads something out of the New Testament and begins to orate—but Christianity understands "burdens" to mean the million dollars, the earthly goods, etc.

This is the way Christianity has gradually been introduced into the nations. Now there are Christian peoples, Christian states, Christian nations everywhere—but Christianity understands burdens as being a millionaire, possessing or seeking to possess worldly goods.

God in heaven, what abysmal nonsense!

XI[1] A 19   n.d., 1854

« 3533 *Sermonized Self-contradiction*

In order to win men for Christianity, the saying goes, attract them to it, make it inviting to them, and all that.

For example, when self-denial is presented, the pastor says: It is so blessed, O, so blessed—if you knew how blessed it is, you would aspire to this alone at all times, etc.

The congregation sits and listens, the majority of them, just as in the theater or as one listens to an orator.[1161]

But suppose there happened to be present a more earnest man, who said to himself: I am really going to begin, right now, today.

He does so[1162]—and what happens? He discovers the truth, that it is by no means blessed that way—but is extremely painful. What then? He is disgusted by the pastor's lie and completely loses his desire.

No, one must tell the truth, that it is extremely painful—it is precisely that which gives courage and endurance.

"Yes, but people will be scared away." Yes, people—those who only want all-day suckers—will be scared away, but they never enter into Christianity anyway.

XI[1] A 89   n.d., 1854

« 3534 *To Make Christianity Easy*

in order to get men to accept it (provided it is well-intentioned and not a swindle on the part of the clergy in order to make the whole business easy and profitable) still shows a deficiency in the understanding of human nature. The result has been that the ordinary person has a secret suspicion that all of Christianity is a lie—since it is so easy, since the highest can be had so cheaply.

This is how man is under the circumstances, and legitimately so.

Imagine that someone is willing to give on an enormous scale just as much money as anyone wants; all one needs to do is ask—the ordinary person will involuntarily suspect that he is giving away imitation money—for it cannot be on the level.

XI^1 A 172 *n.d.*, 1854

« 3535 *To Proclaim Christianity*

To proclaim Christianity really requires a person who combines personal character and dialectical power. (Socrates, for example, would be suitable.)

In the meantime it can limp along with a dialectician and go along tolerably well with a man of character.

But to entrust the proclaiming of Christianity to speech experts[1163] is *eo ipso* to do away with Christianity; and the fact that the proclaiming of Christianity at a given time is simply and solely represented by speech experts is sufficient proof that Christianity does not exist. A speech expert is just as suitable for proclaiming Christianity as a deaf-mute for being a musician. In order for it to become a theme for the speech experts, the characteristic aspects of essential Christianity (the dialectical, the sign of spirit) must be removed. But of course when that which makes Christianity Christianity is taken away, it goes fluently, swimmingly, enchantingly, convincingly—but it is not Christianity.

We do not object to the fact that many of the Church's great teachers were exceptional speakers—no, we do not object, but we remember that they also were ascetics or men of character or dialecticians. What I refer to is something quite different—the squad of speech experts who represent the proclaiming of Christianity these days.

XI^1 A 477 *n.d.*, 1854

« 3536 *Ideals for Preaching Christianity*

This is one ideal: The ideal for preaching is that all become Christians.

Another ideal is this (this is the reflection): The ideal for preaching is to gain one Christian.

XI[1] A 504   n.d., 1854

« 3537 *The Usual Preaching of Christianity*

If the matter were not so serious, it might be said that such preaching is about as ridiculous as one can imagine. The ludicrousness of it consists in bringing the expressions and concepts which belong in quite another sphere into relationship with the lives we live. Because essential Christianity, the solemnity of the Christian expressions, is just about as appropriate to us "as a tailor's child's being baptized Caesar, Alexander, Hannibal, Napoleon." If the preacher were a wag who talked in such solemn phrases just for the fun of it, it would have a humorous effect, just as when one uses a phrase that has a generally recognized official meaning and connection in a completely different and unofficial context, as if, for example, a man announced his wife's death and ended it thus: Burial will take place from St. Peter's Church, "notice of which is hereby announced." The latter is the language of the official announcement. But just as the solemnity of the official announcement is not appropriate in the minor events of everyday life, so the lofty Christian terminology does not fit the lives we live, although we nevertheless pass ourselves off as Christians. Every single one of the Bible's characterizations of being a Christian becomes ludicrous when applied to us—we who certainly are Christians! Try it, take any expression, take this one: To be a coworker with God, consequently to have a task in which one relates to God in such a way that he can be called his coworker—and now apply it to us Christians! The way we live our lives, our tasks ordinarily are detached from the idea of having God as a coworker; in fact, when we go to work, we might rather pray God (like children when they really want to play ask their parents either to go into another room or to let them go into another room, for the presence of the parents is too serious) to go into another room. We really sense this when we look at the morning hymns in the *Evangelical Hymnbook*[1164] and read again and again these expressions: "I hurry now to my task," "I hasten to my work,"—I hasten and I hurry, and I hurry and I hasten—but let us see if this task is of such quality that it is a case of being God's coworker.

It is very characteristic of Christianity in Christendom that it is a Sunday service. We dress up in nice clothes on Sunday, and in a more profound sense we disguise ourselves; we dress ourselves up in the whole Christian terminology, and the pastor is especially and remarkably well disguised—and in the quiet hour this Christianity will seem to fit the design rather well.

XI² A 27 *n.d.*, 1854

« 3538 *Service in Character—the Usual Preaching*

The former is the true service, but naturally also the dangerous one—therefore it is completely abolished. To be specific, it makes a beeline for the men one lives with, for the world one lives in, addresses itself directly to them, attacks them. The other kind of preaching turns into a talking-about. This is the difference: Sit in private conversation with a man and discuss how wretched the world and men are—he is very impressed with you, for of course he exempts himself and is eager to hear you talk *about.* But stand up and address your remarks directly to him, and you will see that it is quite another matter. —The swindle in Christendom these days is that here in Denmark, for example, the government has engaged 1,000 costumed, hired servants, each of whom in his own congregation talks *about,* perhaps about all the other congregations, but not about his own congregation—and so it is the country over. —Strictly speaking, this kind of preaching is actually a kind of slander: saying bad things about those who are not present. No wonder this kind of preaching of Christianity makes such a big hit. If this kind of a preacher gets militant about something, you can always be sure that it is something not right at hand. No wonder he is such a cozy man to listen to.

XI² A 71 *n.d.*, 1854

« 3539 *The Falsification of Christianity*

What has been falsified is the conception of what it is to be a Christian.

It is not so much the doctrine that has been falsified, but the proclaiming of Christianity, the role of teachers of Christianity. It is like water which in the reservoir is pure but is infected in passing through contaminated pipes—like taking someone to the water reservoir and telling him: "You see, the water is pure." "Yes, but it is contaminated by the medium through which it is brought to men." Whenever something can be shared only through a medium, the quality of the medium is almost as important as the quality of that which is communicated through the medium. This shows what a dubious thing is the talk about an objectively true proclamation of Christianity.

XI² A 249   n.d., 1854

« 3540 *To Sew without Knotting the Thread*[1165] *—or "It Is Quantity That Does It"*

As is well known, it was Till Eulenspiegel who summoned all the tailors in order to impart to them some very important erudition. They came. Thereupon he climbed a tree and said that they must not forget to tie a knot in the thread, for otherwise they would lose the first stitch.

I have no desire to summon the tailors and seamstresses, no! Nor do I entirely agree with Eulenspiegel[1166] that by not tying a knot one loses only the first stitch—he also loses the next, and so on and on, and the whole thing gets to be a mess.

I wish to discuss proclaiming Christianity without tying a knot in the thread.

Suppose that a speaker remarkably endowed in every respect preaches on the genuinely Christian theme of self-denial, renunciation of the world. Superbly, incomparably! He charms, enthralls, sweeps his audience off its feet in a matchless way. A rich man is in the audience; deeply, deeply stirred, really profoundly moved, he goes home and says to his wife: It was absolutely wonderful, and I want to show my gratitude by giving the speaker a present—a very expensive fruitbowl. Likewise another deeply moved rich man digs deep, deep, deep into his pocket and gives a gold snuffbox, and the speaker accepts them, gives courteous thanks.

Here, you see, a Christian knot was not tied in the thread. Christianity holds that "the sermon" comes on Monday, when the speaker sends the gifts back and says: After all, I teach self-denial—ergo, I cannot accept such things; otherwise the next time I speak about self-denial I run the risk of being inspired by the prospect of an elegant carriage.

This is how one sews without tying a knot in the thread, and this is how the whole mess comes about.

And this is how we are all Christians—not singly, but all together, a Christian nation.

"It is quantity that does it." Strangely enough, we all laugh when we hear the story of the bartender[1167] who sold beer a shilling below cost and when asked how that could pay answered: It is quantity that does it. He does perceive that it is a loss to sell for three shillings a bottle of beer that cost him four shillings, but it is his humble opinion that there is profit in selling at three shillings a bottle 100,000 bottles of beer which cost him four shillings per bottle. So also with being a Christian. Each individual is perhaps unwilling to admit that he is not exactly a Christian—but "quantity does it."

Do not do me wrong by misunderstanding me, wondering if in some way I envy that speaker his fruitbowl, golden snuffbox, embroidered armchair, the many lobster banquets where he sits at the head table (in gratitude for his sermon about self-denial), the elegant carriage, silk, velvet, gold and silver—no, no, that is not the way I take Christianity.

As far as I am concerned, if I could afford it, I would be happy to give a real lobster bust, serve ten kinds of wine etc.—but I have one everlasting concern. While entering the banquet hall with my guests and while shouting like Jeppe, "Strike up the music" (for I would also have dinner music), I would very softly say to myself: God in heaven, this is not Christianity! Or I would say to the guests: My friends, permit me to say one thing. In olden days it was the custom to say grace—with your permission, instead of saying grace I will merely say these words: My friends, this is not Christianity.

This is what I think can be done. I believe that God will make allowances for our frailty because we have been spoiled from childhood by being served Christian sweets and sweet Christian baby food with jam.

Therefore two things in particular must be required of such a speaker. (1) That he not look so terribly earnest, because to get silver fruitbowls etc. etc. etc. is not so terribly serious—or to talk three-quarters of an hour when one gets paid for it accordingly. (2) That he does not weep and still less sob. Actually, there is nothing to cry about. If he received no presents, was not banqueted, if instead he should live in poverty and wretchedness (and according to the New Testament, on which the speaker always bases his talk, God has reserved the right to be able to require that)—well, it would be inappropriate for a man to weep over such things, but I still think there would be some grounds for doing so. But in the other case there actually is no reason for it; whereas there is a very good reason for the audience to laugh.

Think of a father and his child. The child is eager to go out to Fredriksberg woods and play cops-and-robbers with his playmates. "Goodbye, my child, have fun, and here is some money to buy fruit

or whatever else you want." But if the child wanted going to Fredriksberg to mean working on his lessons, being earnest, not playing, the
father would probably say: Hand the dime back to me, you numbskull,
and stay home. You can go hungry and learn the index in Riises'
Geography by heart.

No, if in the Christian sense the end is to be tied, in order to keep
the whole thing from becoming nonsense, we must either have men
of character again who actually renounce the world, or we must at least
make admissions, and above all we must come out from behind the
mask: It is quantity that does it.

XI^2 A 281   *n.d.*, 1853–54

« 3541 *Playing at Christianity*

We all know how to play war, deceptively *to create an illusion* of
everything involved in war: the assigning of troops, taking the field
(everyone looks serious, but also full of courage and enthusiasm), the
orderlies dashing back and forth fearlessly, the officers' voices ringing
out. Signals, battle cries, musket volleys, the thunder of cannon . . . . .
everything, everything just as in war, only one thing lacking—the dangers.

Likewise with playing at Christianity—the creation of a deceptive
illusion of the Christian proclamation in such a way that everything is
simulated as accurately as possible—only one thing is omitted—the
dangers.

In the proclamation as we find it in the New Testament the whole
emphasis falls on the personal—this accounts for the dangers; when we
play at Christianity, the thing to do (but carefully, illusorily) is to draw
attention away from the personal—and in that way the dangers are
excluded.

The proclaimer, then, is—a public official! Aha, so perhaps it is not
his personal conviction he proclaims, but it is a function of his office!
—The proclamation is his means of making a living for his wife and
family, his career! Aha, so what he says is perhaps nothing more nor
less than a special jargon—like the lawyer's, physician's, etc. —And the
doctrine is proclaimed not on the street[1168] but in a church, an artistic
building where everything is set up to provide artistic tranquillity and
enjoyment and the kind of illusion the theater insists upon. Aha, so
perhaps we are actually in a theater when we are in church. —And the
address does not personally address those present, no, no, that would
be uncultured—it keeps a seemly distance from them, talks quite gener-

ally about, about, etc. Otherwise everything belonging to the proclamation of Christianity is simulated as well as possible—the upraised glance to call upon God, the hands lifted in prayer, the voice almost choked with tears, the loud voice defying the opposition of the whole world . . . . . Taratatata! Taratatata! And outside of the quiet hours it would be most inappropriate and uncultured to remind "the pastor" about what he said in the quiet hours; it would be just as foolish as if an actor[1169] were to draw his sword after the curtain had fallen and continue to be what he was in the play.

This is called playing at Christianity. By nature every man pursues the things of the world. Christianity wants to lift man to a higher life. To that end the state pays 1,000 clergymen, each one of whom—just exactly like the rest of secularity—is in pursuit of earthly things. This is how Christianity was introduced into the nations: it is not so much Christianity that has been introduced as a new way of making a living —being a pastor.

XI² A 289   n.d., 1853–54

PREDESTINATION

« **3542**

It seems to me that the doctrine of predestination, like an ant lion,[1170] pulls me down into a funnel; the first downfall conditions all the subsequent ones with a horrible consistency. Like the ant lion, it operates its funnel (surely an appropriate figure for such a logical train of thought) in the loose sand (pious religious feelings), and he who has once fallen is entwined by ultimate consequences as Laöcoon was entwined by snakes.

I A 10   September 11, 1834

« **3543**

The difficulty of embracing the theory of predestination will be obvious, I believe, by way of the following psychological experiment. Imagine that a man were told in advance that he would become one of the greatest scholars; if it were something he desired, he would promptly say: All right, I'll begin at once to study hard. Or—if he did not care for it, he would say: I will not look at a book. Both statements are equally wrong. In any case he would become what he was supposed to become, and he completely forgot that everything was predetermined, so that his statement also was predetermined, and he only got himself entangled in the worst contradictions.

I A 19   September 26, 1834

« **3544**

Addition to 3543 (I A 19):

If, on the other hand, I were to imagine that God's arrangement of everything is grounded in God's foreknowledge and consequently grants mankind actual freedom, then everything takes on a different aspect; if I then were to imagine that a person receives permission to look into the future and sees that he is destined to become a criminal, it could perhaps result in his making changes. There would be no objection to this with respect to God, for according to his foreknowledge he also must know that the man would change in this way.

I A 20   December 6, 1834

« **3545**

Incidental to the doctrine of predestination as that which, if it is maintained, brings a man into self-contradictions, the following could be cited: if one thinks that a person does everything out of egotism, he would promptly fall into contradiction; he would himself be aware that something is attributable to noble sacrifice, and according to his theory he would have to say it is egotism. (Fichte's doctrine of identity[1171] is also an example.)

I A 22   September 29, 1834

« **3546**

If predestination is explained solely as grounded in foreknowledge, one comes to assume that man deserves grace. Origen seems to imply this also, and defends this theory in his commentary on Romans:[1172] the basis of the predetermination lies in our own free will. Paul was destined for God's gospel! Why? Because he was *worthy* of it, by reason of his God-foreseen actions.

I A 43   *n.d.*, 1834

« **3547**

Here is the real solution of the problem of predestination. When it is said that they are chosen *"quos vocavit,"* they are chosen to salvation or are damned; for what else does the expression *quos vocavit* mean than those in whose consciousness Christianity emerged, and thus this view can be united with Schleiermacher's relative predestination; for those who have lived in this world but to whom no call came are obviously not predestined (since they are not called); nor is it enough to be able to say one is called,* but only the person in whose consciousness Christianity has emerged in relation to the rest of his life views. . . . . . .

* Unless one were to say that their not being called is predestination, but then one contradicts the first statement, which says that they are the called.

I A 295   December 1, 1836

« **3548**

Fundamentally, the doctrine of predestination and Montanism explain each other reciprocally, for both originate in a vital apprehension of the grand reconciliation of man with God provided by Christianity. In the glad assurance of that reconciliation the doctrine of predestination sees the inability of finite empiricism to shake it, which is then one-sidedly construed as a great immutability. Anxiously conscious of man's sinfulness, Montanism fears a relapse which would disturb everything, but because of this very fear it flees (not merely in the life of the individual but in thought itself) back again into that evangelical security; but this movement is construed one-sidedly when it is taught that a relapse makes it forever impossible to return. The mistake occurs when this doctrine momentarily roams into the practical domain and transfers qualifications from that area into its dogmatic concept, for if it were conceivable that *the whole human race* could sink back to the position of sin in which Christ found it, if God could once again enter into relationship with man as the punishing God, if the coming of Christ had no objective meaning for God and were not an immanent qualification of his being—well, then the Montanists would be right. But in the sphere of individuals this view has only relative significance; and the whole doctrine is simply an attempt to make fear and trembling, which has its truth in the life of the individual, into a scholarly-dogmatic qualification.

II A 399   April 26, 1839

« **3549**

Concerning God's cooperation with creatures, beginning with para. 377.[1173]

Velleitè is the expression for the suffering will, *volition* for the acting will. See para. 401.[1174]

Para. 406[1175] and following there is a dialogue which L. Valla has composed in order to penetrate Boethius. The difficulty is supposed to be to unite God's foreknowledge with freedom. He shows that knowledge neither adds to nor detracts from my action; consequently foreknowledge does not either.[1176] He explains all problems with respect to Apollo (the foreknower) but lets the matter run aground on Jupiter (on providence) and concludes with an admonition.

Thereupon L.[1177] develops the matter further with the aid of his theory about infinite possible worlds.

IV C 40   *n.d.,* 1842-43

« **3550 Christianity Turned Soft—the Doctrine of Predestination**

The emergence of the doctrine of predestination is also an unmistakable sign of how the existential momentum has been diminished.

By becoming soft Christianity has gotten the human mass to be Christian—and now the Christian sits and wonders how it is possible that a man can be saved. And then along comes the dogma of sedentary piety: predestination.

On the whole a distinction may be drawn between existential Christianity—and sedentary Christianity. The latter makes Christianity into doctrine, proceeds to get stubborn about doctrine, orthodoxy, and degenerates into fantasy.

X⁴ A 180   n.d., 1851

PRESENTIMENT

« **3551**

Cl. Brentano's little story, *Skjøn Ane*,[1178] is very interesting and is important with respect to presentiment. It has a strong folk character, and if it is not based on a legend, then Brentano has certainly proved himself a true master. That is, in addition to the lively, happy tone (*sana mens in sano corpore*), folklore is also permeated with a profound, earnest melancholy, a presentiment of the power of evil, a quiet resignation which allows every age to pay its tribute to this unyielding power;* that is why execution sites, ravens and crows, prisons, seductions, etc. play such a large role. Such a mood permeates this narrative: the simple devout verse which meanders through it in a wonderfully prophetic way; the executioner's fearful premonition when the sword moves by itself; the story of how beautiful Ane always puts on her apron in a characteristic way, etc. One ought to hear the story told by a tattered ragpicker in the cemetery of suicides on a foggy day of execution, amid the shriek of ravens and crows.†

(Incidentally, it resembles a poem in *Knaben Wunderh.*, II, p. 104,[1179] which, it is true, is quite commonplace, yet remarkable in that it is an ensign and that he brings a pardon, but too late.)

There is also something of presentiment in Steffens' *De 4 Nordmænd*[1180]—not scholarly research on it, but elements of it, only with him it becomes a little monotonous, almost as monotonous as his Norwegian mountains, for every one of his heroes begins almost every one of his more stirring and significant lines in the story by talking about the Norwegian mountains; similarly, their presentiment has something abstract about it beyond the vagueness[1181] which it indeed must have. There are not sufficient elements in their consciousness to permit even a suspicion of such things. All presentiment is murky and rises all at once in the consciousness or so gradually fills the soul with anxiety that it does not arise as a conclusion from given premises but always manifests itself in an undefined something; however, I now believe more than ever that an attempt should be made to point out the subjective predisposition and not as something unsound and

628

sickly, but as an aspect of a normal constitution.

In margin: *only stipulating burial in consecrated ground.

II A 32   n.d.,   1837

« 3552

In margin of 3551 (II A 32):

† or a family tragedy about the god who visited the father's sin upon the family unto 4 or 5 generations, told by a tattered stunted creature.

II A 33   n.d.

« 3553

Presentiment is not linked to the direction of the eye's orientation toward existence and its future but to the reflex of the eye's direction toward the past, so that the eye, by staring at what lies behind it (in another sense, ahead of it) develops a disposition to see what lies ahead of it (in another sense behind it).

$$C \overset{\frown}{\longleftarrow} A \dotsm B$$

For example, if A is the present, the time in which we are living, and B the future, then it is not by standing in A and turning my face toward B that I see B; for by turning thus I see nothing at all, but when C is the past, then it is by turning toward C that I see B, just as, in fact, in Achim V. Arnim's* novel[1182] the presentient eyes of Alrunen were situated *in the back of his head,* whereas his other two eyes, which were farsighted in the ordinary way—that is, regular eyes—were in his forehead just like the eyes of other men, or in that part of the head turned toward *the future.*

II A 558   September 10, 1839

« 3554

In margin of 3553 (II A 558):

See Isabella v. Aegypten, Keiser Carl des Fünften erste Jugendliebe.[1183]

II A 559   n.d.

« 3555

On the whole *De 4 Nordmænd*[1184] is remarkable with regard to presentiment—the oppressive presentiment which is here developed almost to monotony—is not presentiment usually found in connection with evil,[1185] original sin—

II A 588   n.d.,   1837

« **3556**

Presentiment's apparent polar altitude—
historic anticipations[1186]—

the prophetic statement[1187] is obscure because, just as in some
mirages, it can see distant regions (troops, for example) but sees them
upside down.

II A 589   *n.d.,* 1837

« **3557**

As far as I know, natural scientists[1188] agree that animals do not
have anxiety simply because by nature they are not qualified as spirit.
They fear the present, tremble, etc., but are not anxious. They have
no more anxiety than they can be said to have presentiment.[1189]

V B 53:9   *n.d.,* 1844

PRIMITIVITY

« **3558** *Aphorisms*

[*In margin:* see p. 187, top, this journal (i.e., x^2 A 5).]

1

One does not become an author nowadays through his primitivity, but—by reading.

One becomes a human being by aping the others.[1190] One does not know by himself that he is a human being but through an inference: he is like the others—therefore he is a human being. Only God knows whether any one of us is that!

And in our time, when people doubt and doubt about everything, no one hits upon this doubt—God knows whether any one of us is a human being.[1191]

2

Writing is done for "the many," who understand nothing, and by those who understand—how to write for "the many."

3

Philosophy has become fantastic, especially since we abandoned Kant's "honest way" and paid the well-known (honest) 100 dollars to become theocentric.

Note: The 100 dollars is the famous Kantian example of the distinction between what is thought and the actuality.[1192]

x^1 A 666   *n.d.,* 1849

« **3559**

Just as a rich man owning a valuable collection of art works or a splendid castle, etc., takes pleasure in having everyone come to see it and express his opinion about it, so God's joy in the world is that everyone should be a single individual who tells with primitivity what he wonders about most.

631

If there were a book in that rich man's house containing what the previous visitors had jotted down of their feelings and opinions, he would not want the next one to read the book before going in to see the collection.

Ah, but we men turn everything around. We get everything out of books.

This has finally consumed the nobility and the essential in being human.

X^3 A 52   *n.d.*, 1850

« **3560** *Primitivity*

Men are perfectible. They can be influenced to do one thing just as well as another, to fast as well as to live in worldly enjoyment—the most important thing is that they are just like the others, that they ape each other, do not stand alone.

But God wants neither one nor the other; what he wants is *primitivity.*[1193] Yet this is the effort we shrink from most of all, whereas we relish everything called aping.

From this it is apparent what little good it does to bring an objectively greater truth to bear—and then to allow aping. No godliness is achieved by this, for in the divine sense the truth is primitivity.

This is why God's word is ordered in such a way that every assertion is accompanied by its opposite. This demands primitivity.

But both teachers and followers feel best in aping and by aping —therefore they are *lovingly* unanimous about it and call it love.

XI^1 A 62   *n.d.*, 1854

« **3561** *One Must Take the World as It Is—*

this statement, or: The world is as one takes it, meaning please note, that one must take the world as it is, is the substance of these millions, the life and biography of the specimen-man [*Exemplar-Menneskets.*] They find everything given: concepts, ideas, thoughts, likewise custom and usage, in short, everything is given—the specimen-man brings nothing with him. So everything is given—and everybody hustles about his own business acquiring a fortune, getting to be somebody, getting married, etc. etc.

Life [*Tilværelsen*] actually pays no attention to the fact that these millions exist [*ere til*], is unaffected by them. All this existing [*Existeren*] is too trivial to affect life, which is planned [*lagt an*] for another kind of existing [*Existeren.*] In their relation to life these specimen-men are like little fish in a net set for bigger fish. The net is indeed a net (and in the same way life is also a net) set to catch fish—but the little fish have free passage. It does not help for specimen-men to become a great mass; they do not therefore weigh more: one specimen-man and one million have equally little effect on life, which pours out of that kind as from a horn of plenty.

But as soon as a man comes along bearing the quality of primitivity in himself, so that he does not say that one takes the world as it is (the sign of passing through freely like little fish) but says: Whatever the world may be, I relate to an original principle which I do not intend to change at the world's discretion—the moment this word is heard, a change takes place in the whole of life. Just as in the fairy tale when the castle which has been under a spell for a hundred years opens when the word is spoken and everyone comes alive, just so life becomes sheer awareness. Angels get busy, watch curiously to see what will come of it, for it is of concern to them. On the other hand, the somber, grumbling demons, proper limbs of the devil, who for a long time have been sitting inactive and chewing their fingernails, leap to their feet—for here is something to do, they say, and they have waited a long time for that, for specimen-men give neither them nor the angels anything to do.

This is what the apostle is talking about when he says that the Christian is not struggling with flesh and blood but with principalities and powers. This means that a Christian's existence radically affects life and thereby acquires the infinite ideality to set both heaven and earth in motion.

A Christian's existence affects life. He probably cannot be said to bring along with him a primitivity in the sense of genius,[1194] but he undertakes primitively Christianity's requirement for being Christian [*in margin:* And ethically, as pointed out elsewhere [i.e., XI[1] A 386], primitivity[1195] means to put everything into it, to risk everything, the kingdom of God *first and foremost*], in no way listens to the wretched business of taking the world as it is, but sticks to what Christianity wants the world to be—Christianity, which therefore is simply not a kingdom of this world because it will never respect the "One must take the world as it is."

XI[2] A 46   *n.d.,* 1854

PROFESSOR

« 3562

But the honorable speculative professor is absent-minded, is not existing [*er ikke existerende*], is not subjective, is not passionate—he is *sub specie æterni.* Yes, anyone who is as great as that is, of course, a lucky fellow.[1196]

VI B 40:31 n.d., 1845

« 3563

. . . . . No, assistant professors and instructors have nothing to do with the essentially Christian qualities. But there is no doubt so much to be done that Governance might see fit to send an attendant who in the most polite way of the world could remove these gentlemen, this crowd, from the holy. Perhaps I can illustrate this scene. I once witnessed a very magnificent funeral service. The coffin was to be buried in Garrison Cemetery with military honors. An immense following, an enormous mass of people had gathered [there]. The funeral procession began. So far the police officer in charge had managed by supreme effort, almost to the point of despair, to keep the huge mob from passing into the cemetery. He saw that it was touch and go; everything depended on getting the gate shut and confirming the yawning abyss, the *qualitative difference,* this *distinguendum est inter et inter.* The first part of the procession, the invited guests, had succeeded in getting in, and in solemn procession. But the long, long line of the uninvited mourners stood without—and it looked as if the police officer would be defeated. What did he do. Quickly he divided the policemen into two groups. Leading the one group himself, he once again threw himself against the noisy, excited mob; he ordered the other group to close in behind the uninvited mourners and get them, encouraged by nightsticks, to hurry into the cemetery. It worked. The gate was locked; quality was confirmed. Let us dwell on the situation. An earnest man, wearing mourning dress, too, who unrequested and uninvited has voluntarily decided to show a departed one the last honors—and then to be treated this way! When an uninvited mourner has the most beautiful prospect of receiving a formal note of gratitude the next day —and then today temporarily to be placed in this most ridiculous situation of a person in a mourning dress, an uninvited mourner, who is forced to jump and gallop to the beat of a police club! And so it is also when, generation after generation, it has become established that earnestness is all this profundity, this digging and delving about how Paul's conversion and revelations are to be interpreted; when an assistant professor, upheld by the centuries, with measured, earnest, long, solemn steps—(yes, like someone following a coffin; as Holberg[1197] says: He walks as measuredly and morally as someone following a coffin)—mounts the podium to lecture on this profundity—and then to have an attendant, using a club, transform him and all this earnestness into foolishness—in order to reinstate earnestness, quality!

VIII[1] A 441   n.d., 1847

« 3564

1. A dogmatic system, from a Christian point of view, is a luxury item; in calm weather, when one can count on at least the majority of men as being Christians, there can be time for such things—but when was that ever the case? And when it storms—then systematizing is evil, then all theology must be upbuilding or edifying. Systematizing contains an indirect falsification—as if everyone's genuinely being a Christian were entirely settled—since there is time to systematize.

2. A dogmatic system ought not be erected on the basis: *to comprehend faith,* but on the basis: *to comprehend that faith cannot be comprehended.* In a nutshell, from a Christian point of view, "the pastor" and "the professor" ought to say one and the same thing, only the professor should say it raised to the second power. If there are rebel spirits who are not willing to be satisfied with "the pastor," then they ought to come to something more rigorous by going to the professor. Christianly, everything is discipline; the ascending scale is to come to the more rigorous discipline. By running from "the pastor" we ought not slip into a speculative effeminacy but ought to come into an even more rigorous discipline.

X[1] A 561   n.d., 1849

« 3565 *The Difference between an Essential Thinker and a Professor*

The essential thinker always pushes the matter to the ultimate point—that is precisely his excellence—and only a few are able to follow him. Then along comes the professor; he takes "the paradox" away[1198] —a goodly number, almost the great mass, are able to understand him; and thus it is believed that now the truth has become more true.

Even if an eminent thinker hit upon the thought of "a system," he would never get it finished[1199]—so honest would he be. But just one little hint to the professor of what he intended—the professor promptly has the system finished.

It always seems that the professor is an altogether different sort of philosophic fellow—so it must appear when the task is reflected in the medium of the public—or when such a fellow and every second person are philosophers.

An essential thinker can conceive of the professor only as being comic. The professor is what Leporello is in relation to a Don Juan, only more so in that he falsely ascribes to himself an enormous esteem in the eyes of the half-learned.

X^1 A 573   *n.d.*, 1849

« **3566**

Take the paradox away from a thinker—and you have a professor. A professor has at his disposal a whole line of thinkers from Greece to modern times; it appears as if the professor stood above all of them. Well, many thanks—he is, of course, the infinitely inferior.

For example, a professor such as the sainted J. Møller.[1200] There was a real professor; he understood how to take away the paradoxes.

X^1 A 609   *n.d.*, 1849

« **3567**

The majority of men in any generation, even those who, as it is said, are occupied with thinking (professors and the like), live on and die in the illusion of a continuous process, that if they were granted a longer life the process would be a continued direct ascent of comprehending more and more. How many ever arrive at the maturity of discovering that a critical point comes where it reverses, where from now on the ascending comprehension is to comprehend more and more that there is something which cannot be comprehended.

This is Socratic ignorance, and this is what the speculation of our time needs as a corrective.

As Johannes Climacus[1201] rightly points out, the majority of men actually turn off there where the higher life should ascend for them, and they become practical people, "husband, father, and champion birdhunter;" as Anti-Climacus[1202] rightly points out, the majority of minds do not experience becoming spirit at all, and thus they do not experience this qualitative meeting with the divine. For them the divine is simply a rhetorical, nonsensical, hiatic superlative of the human —therefore their eudæmonia in the illusion of being more and more able to comprehend it, if they only had time and did not have to go to the office, the club, to talk with their wives, etc., if they only had time they would surely comprehend the divine perfectly.

Socratic ignorance, but, please note, modified in the spirit of Christianity—this is maturity, is intellectually what rebirth is ethically and religiously, is what it is to become a child again.

It is literally true that the law then becomes: increasing profundity is to comprehend more and more that one cannot comprehend. Here, then, comes all the childlikeness again, but raised to the second power. This sort of maturity has naïveté, simplicity, wonder, but has it essentially with humor, yet without being humor.

And that this life is blessed, as blessed as it is to worship, even more blessed than for a woman to be truly in love—well, those people with their eudæmonic illusions have no inkling of it. They never get an impression of quality but deceive themselves more and more.

X^1 A 679 *n.d.*, 1849

« **3568** *Lines for a Speech*

[*In margin:* "The Professor" in theology.]

O dreadful depth of confusion and misdirection, dreadfully entrenched through use and custom.

From generation to generation these hundreds and again hundreds of professors—in Christendom, consequently Christians, no doubt, to say nothing of their being professors in theology. They write books and then books about books, and books to give synopses of the books—periodicals arose merely to write about them, and book publishers flourish, and many, many thousands have jobs— — —and not a single one of these hired hands even remotely resembled in his life a truly Christian existence—yes, it did not occur to a single one of them to take the New Testament and read it directly and simply and before God ask himself the question: Does my life in any manner, even the remotest, resemble Christ's life, so that I dare call myself a follower or imitator—I, Professor of Theology, Knight of Denmark, honored and esteemed, with a fixed salary and free housing, an author of many learned books about Paul's three journeys.[1203]

There are passages in the N.T.[1204] whereby bishops, priests, deacons (no matter how little they approximately resemble the original sketch) can be justified, but find the passage in the N.T. which mentions professors of theology.[1205] Why does a person involuntarily laugh if to that passage which declares that God ordained some to be prophets, others to be apostles, others to be directors of the congregation, there is added: "some to be professors of theology?" Why could it not almost just as well say: God ordained some to be councilmen.

"The professor" is a more recent Christian invention—yes, a later Christian invention, for it began just about the time Christianity began to go backwards, and the culminating point for the professor has been reached in our day—when Christianity is completely abolished.

What does the "professor" express? The "professor" expresses that religion is a matter of learning; the professor is the greatest satire on the "apostle." Be professor of what? Of that which a few fishermen established in the world—what a splendid epigram! That Christianity would be capable of victory in the world—yes, the founder himself prophesied that, and the "fishermen" believed it. But the prize—that Christianity would triumph to such a degree that there would be professors in theology—this the founder has not prophesied, unless it might be where mention is made that the "falling away" will commence.

————

Eureka, I have it! The "professor" is really the analog to Don Quixote. Perhaps he will become an even more profound comic figure. Someone who has no idea or humanness in the direction of personally wanting to act and live in imitation of prototypes but who believes that it is a scholarly question. "The truth" is crucified as a thief, is scorned, spit upon before it cries out, dying: Follow me. But the "professor" (the un-man) does not understand a word of it; he conceives of it as a scholarly question.

In the pseudonymous works I have used only the expression "instructor" or "assistant professor," but "the professor" is a more authentic type, simply by the gravity of his life, His Eminence the Knight.

X^2 A 633   *n.d.*, 1850

« 3569

And they keep right on thinking that they can fight the boundless, bloated theological-scientific confusion of Christianity with a new book. No, no, little child, the matter is altogether simple. Get hold of one single genuine confessor—and get the theological professor to promise to meet in the confessional before God: and *ein, zwei, drei*, I will get every bit of theology confessed out of him, since the whole thing is part and parcel of the secular mentality and the secular-minded free and easy way of talking about Christianity. What is lacking is the conscience-relationship to Christianity. The "theological professor" must learn what the N.T. quite simply obliges him and every Christian to learn—so he learns to speak another language altogether, so he learns what indulgence he needs in order to continue being a professor, public official, a knight, etc. (instead of being a missionary and a martyr). That, you see, is what he ought to learn; then he reverses the relationship and makes his position the important thing.

But science and scholarship—yes, it is true, the confusion cannot be resolved by scientific and scholarly activity.

x^2 A 637 *n.d.*, 1850

« **3570** *Poetic*

Someone has the following Invitation advertisement printed in the newspaper

If there are five or six like-minded people who together with me and without any solemn ceremonies will pledge themselves simply to try to understand the New Testament and simply strive to express its demands in action, I propose to start religious meetings in which I will interpret the New Testament.

The meetings will be open and free to everyone but the clergy. A clergyman will pay each time an admission fee of ten dollars, which will be given to the poor. It is my opinion that those who have said goodbye to imitation [*Efterfølgelsen*] and have turned Christ into money ought to pay something extra if every once in a while they should wish to hear real preaching. If by any chance a theological professor should want to attend these meetings, the price for him will be twenty dollars each time. This does not seem unreasonable to me when one considers what it means to become a full professor of Christ's having been crucified or a guest professor in the stoning of Peter and Paul.

x^3 A 121 *n.d.*, 1850

« **3571** *"The Professor"*

Take mathematics. It is very possible that a famous mathematician, for example, was a martyr for his science—there is nothing in that to prevent me from becoming a professor in the subject he lectured about. For here the subject matter, the science, is the essential, the teacher's personal life the accidental.

But ethically-religiously, especially religiously, there is no subject matter in the sense that it is the essential thing and the person the accidental;[1206] here imitation [*Efterfølgelse*] is the essential factor. What nonsense, then, that—instead of imitating Christ or the apostles and suffering as they suffered—that one becomes a professor instead. Of what? Yes, of this—that Christ came to be crucified and the apostles were stoned.

The only thing lacking at Golgotha was a professor, who promptly would have appointed himself as professor—of theology? Well, we know that theology had not yet made its appearance at that time,[1207] and it would have been very obvious that if he were to become professor of anything it must be of this—that Christ was crucified. Consequently, professor of another person's being put to death.

It could be most curious to have such a professor go through the whole campaign. First of all he would become professor of Christ's being crucified. Then would come the apostles. Then Peter and Paul are brought to court and thereafter stoned—at once there is a new chapter, and on that very day the professor becomes a professor of Peter's and Paul's having been stoned. The council forbids the apostles to preach Christ. What do the apostles do? They do not let this interfere but continue preaching, for one must fear God more than men—and the professor lets nothing interfere either—he becomes professor of Peter's and Paul's not letting themselves be stopped from proclaiming the truth, even though they were stoned—for a professor ought to love the new chapter more than God and the truth.

"The professor" keeps following along—the professors' slogan is —to follow along [*følge med*], to follow along with the times, not, however, to follow [*følge efter*], to imitate [*efterfølge*] Christ. Supposing that there had been a contemporary theological professor (at that time, when theology had not yet made its appearance), one would be able to study the Acts of the Apostles and keep orientated by noting what he was currently professor of.

So it ended with the apostle's being crucified—and the professor became professor of the apostle's being crucified. After a while the professor departed this life in a quiet and peaceful death.

You see, the way to put an end to all this scholarly business when it gets all too important and pretentious is to seize "the professor" and isolate him until he makes admissions on this point—and then the whole established order may very well remain.

Moreover, "the theological professor" is a *point de vüe* in Christendom: to the same degree that "the professor" is regarded as supreme, to the same degree we are most disoriented in Christianity. In Christendom it is possible to see the level and estimate of Christianity by noting how "the professor" is regarded.

x^3 A 122   *n.d.*, 1850

« 3572 *Speculation*

They speculate themselves into Christianity—that is, they speculate Christianity out of the world.

x^3 A 392   *n.d.*, 1850

« 3573 *Crazy Comedy*

Scene on Judgment Day
Our Lord
A Theological Professor

Our Lord: "Have you sought the kingdom of God first and foremost?"

Professor: "No, I can't say that I have, but I know how to say 'to seek the kingdom of God first and foremost' in seven languages—(1) in Danish it goes like this, (2) in German like this, (3) in French like this, (4) in Greek like this, (5) in Hebrew like this, (6) in Latin like this, (7) in Arabic like this, (8) in Syrian like this, (9) in Phoenician like this —what am I saying, I actually know it in nine languages, two more than I said I did." Our Lord turns away while the Professor continues: "I have applied myself night and day to the best of my ability to searching and researching this matter." —Here he is interrupted by the trumpeting angel who with the words "You bungler!" gives him such a clout that he whizzes millions of miles away.

x^3 A 398   *n.d.*, 1850

« 3574 *The Existential*

Whenever someone existentially advances the cause one inch further—then a whole generation of assistant professors and lecturers appear who transpose this advance into doctrine—that is, the cause moves backwards.

x^4 A 236   *n.d.*, 1851

« 3575 *Those Who Become Merely Half-Witnesses-of-the-Truth*

I have often reflected that if anyone deserved a eulogy it would be one of those men who in a way became martyrs insofar as they failed to obtain the joys of life and yet did not reap the imperishable glory of the martyr's crown because in the crucial moment they became a bit frightened, perhaps recanted or accommodated a little, as, for example, Wessel, one of the forerunners of the Reformation. I find it nauseating to read a professor or someone similar who speaks condescendingly of such a person, or something I read in a book about the life of Calvin,[1208] where the author, quite like a master of ceremonies, censures poor Servetus and does not bear in mind that in the end Servetus did, however, go intrepidly to his death and even at the final moment remained true to what he professed. O, that disgusting gang of assistant professors who have never risked even a brass farthing and then censure such men.

I do not like to see a man venture more than he can carry through, but after all he is punished enough by having to live with this blow. But in any case such a man, unfortunate apprentice that he is, still has infinitely more value than millions of assistant professors and the whole herring shoal of men who make the sufferings of others into a paid career and a matter of interest, become professors of the subject, and then, to boot, censure them,[1209] as if they themselves were fellows of quite another sort—which, to be sure, they are—that is, trash.

X^4 A 389   n.d., 1851

« **3576**

Addition to "Christ as prototype." This note *perhaps* not to be used.

The passage which reads: "To the professor"* corresponds Christianity as objective teaching, doctrine

The passage, "The professor"! Nothing is mentioned about this character in the N. T., comes to read as follows:

The professor, the instructor, in relationship to taking over Christianity as mere scholarship, like mathematics, astronomy, geography etc.* Note. In better times there was indeed some Christian scholarliness up to a point; but the individual (the exception) who occupied himself with such scholarliness (perhaps because he himself felt the difficulty of relating Christianity to the scholarly and scientific, how close the bypaths lie, how necessary to prepare the greatest possible counterbalance)—had the Christian honesty etc. (expressive of the fact that for him it was decided that he himself would be a Christian and that for him the decisive thing was to be a Christian) to live himself as an ascetic, by his life to express far more strongly the contrast that

Christianity after all is something essentially different from a science like mathematics, etc., which is indifferent to the personal, and that Christianity is least of all brought to its highest when, homogeneous with the world, it is lectured upon by secularly successful assistant professors as an objective science—but the professor! Nothing is mentioned about that character in the N.T.—or when, more and more scholarly, the decision to become a Christian or the decision to become a Christian in a way not marked merely by "assurances" is put off, because one is continually expecting—a conclusion from science and scholarship.[1210]

X[6] B 17   n.d., 1851–52

« 3577 *"The Sacrifices"*

It is dreadful, one must surely say, dreadful that conditions are such that men must be slain in order to advance other men.

And yet this human slaughtering is not the most dreadful. No, even more abominable is the human slaughtering in which such a sacrifice is butchered and yields professors by the dozens or by the thousand—all in proportion to the significance of "the sacrifice."

X[4] A 503   n.d., 1852

« 3578 *Contemporaneity with Christ—the Poetic —Imitation*

If I had lived contemporaneously with Christ, would it ever have occurred to me to want to be a professor of it, to present it objectively —instead of sharing the suffering.

But now it is 1800 years later. All right. In order to have done with it, we must have the help of "the poet." What does the poet do? He has the kind of perspective-vision that sees very distant things as very near.

He succeeds in doing this, and now he wants to produce his masterpiece, the merit of which is precisely that the past is as if purely present. This is what he wants to "present"—and thus get to be admired by men, score a success, etc.

But the thing breaks down here. For if it really is so that the past has become purely present—how then can it occur to the poet to want to poetize[1211]—then you must become engaged, suffer, and act. Would it not be a shocking outrage if someone during a fire wanted (if this could be done) to occupy himself with "describing" the fire (instead of helping in the rescue work and fire fighting) and thus came to be admired for his art, made money, etc., alas, whereas the fire victims lost everything.

Christianity, in fact, will no longer tolerate the unabashed objectivity with which men want to play middleman, want to become professors of—that others were crucified—want to describe (in order to make money) how others have given everything to the poor.

O, inhaling and exhaling polluted air is no more dreadful than what I continually meet everywhere I look, this objectivity which sucks blood in the meanest way, or converts the sufferings of the glorious ones into money, honor, and prestige. And always ambiguity, ambiguity, ambiguity. The impression is always given that it is for the sake of science and scholarship, truth, and Christianity—that one first of all makes sure of his profit. Good God, can Christianity be served in this way? I wonder if one person who has never read a single learned work but has initiated an act of self-denial, I wonder if he has not contributed more to illuminate what Christianity is than 170,000 of the most utterly, utterly learned professors who first of all made sure of their earthly gain in order then to write of Christianity or ultimately to have profit from Christianity. Indeed, he has benefited it more. And if it were not for these 170,000 professors, what Christianity is would be recognizable, however faintly and imperfectly. But "the professors" completely conceal what Christianity is—under the guise of illuminating Christianity. They completely hide it by means of this most revolting concoction of learning, learned opinions, crisscrossed and strung together in and out.

$$X^4 \text{ A } 532 \quad n.d., \text{ 1852}$$

« 3579 *Distances*

Then one of God's chosen instruments sank in death. In agonies so intense they can scarcely be imagined, in passion far beyond all reason, something his own reason tortured him with in hours of spiritual trial, he resisted reason to the end, kept on passionately doing his utmost along the way where reason could discern, yes, could all too clearly see, that there was everything to lose. He persevered to the end, regarded by his contemporaries as deranged or as devil-possessed, hated, cursed, persecuted—then he finally sank in a martyr's death. Then something strange occurs; as if by magic all existence suddenly responds to this man of agonies—it turns out that he was right, this very man.

Let us now run through the distances.

The next generation stands as *in pausa*, in the *pausa* of admiration, for it is agitated under the pressure of this thing having happened on the other side of reason. Almost the same thing happens to this generation as happens to water when a stone is thrown into it. The water does not become still immediately but continues to be agitated for some time, although less and less.

The next generation still has admiration—yet at the same time a whisper is heard: Actually, when you really think about it, it was really not so inexplicable or incomprehensible; that glorious one can, after all, be explained. And it is not said deprecatingly, no, far from it; in fact, they intend to honor him.

What does it mean? It means men have moved so far away from the tension of passion that in tranquillity they begin to be loquacious.

Then this gets the upper hand, and finally the "professor" appears. By means of many arguments he is able to prove and substantiate and comprehend. That glorious one, his life included, is scientifically laid out in a paragraph. Candidates are examined in the number and kinds of arguments underlying an interpretation. And if they know the arguments, fine, then they are appointed or "called" to a nice little position with the possibility of promotion to lecture on the arguments to a congregation.

As soon as (at least this is how it was in old times), as soon as the prime minister entered the waiting room, the audience was over—and as soon as the "professor" arrives, it is clear that the life of that glorious one is used up, that now a new sacrifice is required. The "professor," of course, flatters himself and the respective candidates and the students and all their associates with the idea that the "professor" is the highest and richest flower of the whole development.

No, this is a misunderstanding. The professor is really the greatest human stupidity or inversion—that is, he is the arrogant human attempt to try to exhaust in reflection that which lies above reflection. The professor is deceived by being so far removed from contemporaneity with that glorious one, and by the fact that the agitation which contemporaries detected to the point of frenzy, the agitation in which the next generation trembled, has now diminished completely. When that happens, then comes the illusion: anyone who reasons straight can surely explain that glorious one and his life, and then the "professor" appears—and then it is all over for that time around.

An analogy may be drawn from the world of individuality. Take, for example, a person really in love; during the time he actually is in love it never occurs to him that he should be able to explain it—it rather seems to him, O lovable humility, incomprehensible that the girl is able to love him. Then let him win the girl. Then let the years go by and perhaps a time comes when he no longer trembles under the impact of his passion; no, it has completely subsided, and he has become exceptionally sensible—that is, utterly obtuse. Whether or not he is will be discernible in the extent to which he thinks he is able to explain his falling in love by giving this and that reason. It happens again and again in the world of individuality that a man or a woman who was once in love ten years later is professor or instructress in his or her love affair. Just as professors and assistant professors are always recognizable by their thinking themselves to be the most beautiful flower of the highest development, so also these professors and instructresses think that the stage in which they are at present is the highest.

x⁴ A 614   n.d., 1852

« **3580** *Theses*

According to New Testament teaching is not the life of the proclaimer (witnessing, witnesses) the real proclamation, and that with the mouth alone (professor's, speaker's) a dubious, not really Christian, "proclamation."

**

According to the New Testament, is not suffering in the world an inevitable consequence of truly expressing Christianity in this world, and therefore, according to the New Testament, is not the conclusion justified that if someone has not come to suffer in this world he must not have expressed Christianity truly in one way or other, not to mention that as a *teacher of Christianity* he has even made a brilliant career by being a teacher of Christianity?

**

According to the New Testament, is there not only one proof, only one thing that convinces—the fact that one's life expresses it?

**

Does not the New Testament hold that when the essentially Christian is placed into actuality it produces an effect which is described in the New Testament[1212] thus: "You will be hated by all for my name's sake" (persecution).

But in "Christendom" the essentially Christian is not placed into actuality; by means of speakers and professors (these are pretty much the official proclaimers) it is introduced only into possibility (rhetorically, dialectically, in the medium of imagination), while the speaker, professor, orients his life according to the secular rules of practical life, consequently does not place the essentially Christian into actuality.

X^6 B 227   *n.d.*, 1852

« **3581**

That the scholarly is the most dangerous of all for essential Christianity may become its disintegration.

———

The situation is like this. To you is proclaimed in the name of Jesus Christ the forgiveness of your sins, grace, eternal salvation—just believe it. If you then do not feel a deeper need to become involved with Christianity, then in God's name get out in the world, fill up your days and your time with one humanly beneficial enterprise or another, work, earn, marry, and so on.

If, however, you feel a deeper need to become involved with Christianity, well, then, get out in the character of the essentially Christian, in character in the strictest sense of the word—witness to the teaching like a missionary among the heathen or in "Christendom," suffer for the teaching, become a martyr.

In both cases the divine brevity of the Holy Scriptures' message, commands, promises, and assurances is not garbled; the ordinary Christian occupies his days and his time with other things and consequently does not have time to encumber Holy Scriptures with verbosity, and neither does the witness to the truth have the time for that.

But then a third alternative pushes forward: devoting oneself to the New Testament in a scholarly way. In former times, however, the propriety was observed that the person who so devoted himself to the New Testament was more scrupulously in the character of the essentially Christian, since he was an ascetic, etc.

But in our day the professor is just as much a man of the world as a professor of history, mathematics, Greek, etc.—in no way is he in the stricter sense of the word (than the ordinary Christian who certainly is not in the stricter sense in the character of the essentially Christian) in the character of the essentially Christian. But he does scholarly research on the New Testament.

And look, the divine brevity of the Holy Scriptures' message, commands, promises, and assurances, disintegrates into an infinite prolixity of pro's and contra's, an immeasurable host of doubtful questions arise and engender new doubts; as the "attorney" procures cases, so the "professor" develops the need for more and more professors in order to be able to make the survey, finally, perhaps, just to be able to make a survey of those whose business it is to make surveys. Truly, it is divine to be brief; this, yes, this is prolix! And yet this scholarship insists on ranking higher Christianly not only than the ordinary Christian (which, however, is false, since, Christianly, it is to his credit that when he will not in the stricter sense step forth in the character of the essentially Christian, at least he does not encumber it with prolixities) but even higher than the—unlearned—witnesses of the truth.

Such scholarship has the result that the ordinary Christian also gets wind of the pundits and now is no longer satisfied with what is his, yet without being able to become learned himself—therefore with him it becomes tripe. On the other hand, the result is that the person who feels the need to become involved with Christianity and consequently to step out in the character of the essentially Christian is led to want to immerse himself first of all in scholarship—that is, he never does come out in the character of the essentially Christian but perishes in the scholarly nonsense.

This is the putrefaction of essential Christianity. But a hypocritical appearance rests over the whole thing, as if it were nothing less than a deeply earnest interest in the essentially Christian. And care is taken to ensure the continuation of the putrefaction of the essentially Christian; therefore, if anyone were to try to get rid of it by ousting scholarship, the cry goes up: What impiety, for God's sake do not take away scholarship, this the truly Christian, the pride of our age.

XI^2 A 295   n.d., 1853–54

« 3582 *Culture*

It is not difficult to see that culture trivializes men, improves them as specimens but abolishes individualities. Here is but one example which occurs to me.

The distinguishing mark of man, according to Genesis,[1213] is to give animals names. While it is not generally customary now, the ordinary man, the rank and file man still has the power. When a simple man over a number of years notices a rarely seen bird, he promptly has a name for it, a characteristic name. Now take ten professors—how inadequate they are at giving names! What a satire it is to read the natural science journals (animals, plants, etc.) and see the names which originate with the common people and compare them with the wretched, silly names used when a professor on occasion is supposed to give a name. Usually they can think of nothing else than to designate the animal or plant with their own names.

XI[1] A 55   n.d., 1854

« 3583 Man-eaters

We do indeed live in civilized countries and consider ourselves far superior to cannibals—and yet it is easy to see that we are guilty of a more horrible and outrageous kind of man-eating than any cannibal's.

The "minister" (the Protestant clergyman) and the professor are man-eaters—yes, that is the word—they are man-eaters.

And they are more horrible and outrageous than the cannibals.

That they are man-eaters is readily seen in the fact that they live off others who have been slain, persecuted, and maltreated for the truth.

And this is more horrible than the man-eating of the cannibals, for evil is always more horrible in proportion to how long it lasts. The cannibals kill a man and eat him—then it is done. This is a briefer moment, and when it is done there is hope (until it happens again) that the cannibal might become different, improve. But the minister and the professor arrange once and for all (a cool and calm calculation) to live off the sufferings of that noble one. He marries on it, has children, and enjoys his nicely-fixed life—he lives off the agonies of that noble one. He counts on advancing in salary—to that extent has he arranged, with outrageous calmness, to live cannibalistically—no cannibal was ever so abominable. In vain does the voice of that noble one call out to us: Imitate me, imitate me [følge mig efter]. This call the pastor and professor suppress so that we do not hear it. And this is how he goes on living after having taken possession of his booty: the noble ones from whose sufferings he makes a living.

And not only that. The cannibal, of course, does not claim to be the best and truest friend of those he slays and eats. But the minister, the professor, also enjoys the honor and esteem of being the true friend and follower of the noble ones.

Truly, as it is written in the New Testament[1214] that publicans and sinners shall enter the kingdom of heaven before you (you Pharisees),

I also say that the cannibals shall enter the kingdom of God before the clergy and the professors.

XI¹ A 100   *n.d.*, 1854

« 3584 *The Official*

Nothing, nothing, nothing, not even the most hopeless atheist or a powerful persecutor of religion, nothing is as dangerous to Christianity as—an official clergyman and professor.

The New Testament (and this, after all, is Christianity) rests on the premise that there is a life-and-death struggle between God and men. An official clergyman and professor express that man has tricked God out of Christianity.

Anything that attacks Christianity in such a way that it lets it be what it is cannot be dangerous. Only that is dangerous which hypocritically falsifies Christianity.

XI¹ A 101   *n.d.*, 1854

« 3585 *To Live Off Christ's Having Been Crucified*

In the background the Savior of the world; his whole life was anguish; finally, in deepest anguish, he even cries from the cross:[1215] "My God, my God, why have you forsaken me."

In the foreground a theological professor. It is now twenty years since he became a professor and was married. His wife is still blooming, almost seductive. His house is attractively furnished—not luxuriously, for he cannot afford that, but tastefully, designed for gracious living in a select social circle. Thus he lives on, year after year. The children grow up; the next to the oldest is a girl, a lively creature of seventeen years, and the happy mother relives her youth in her awakening love————and all this is chargeable to the account of "My God, my God, why have you forsaken me." The professor is professor in what cost Christ a life of anguish and a death anguished to the point of despairing over God's help. The professor is professor of what the man of suffering taught: Imitate me.

And even if Christ never spoke a word about imitating him—it nevertheless seems to me that this idyllic life is dreadful, this idyllic life with the background: "My God, my God, why have you forsaken me."

It seems to me that to turn Jesus into money this way is worse than what Judas did. Partly because Judas, after all, came to be recognized as the traitor; he did not go and play the true, the really true disciple, which makes a great difference, and which the professor in fact does, since he will not take my suggestion and make an admission. Partly because there is always something mitigating about an event which occurs on the spur of the moment in contrast to something of long standing. And Judas—that settled the matter—he went (perhaps in passion) to the high priests, demanded the piddling thirty shillings, got them, betrayed him, hanged himself. But an idyllic life with a fixed annual income and a lovely wife, still enchanting at forty, and the blooming daughter of seventeen who has fallen in love—and it all is chargeable to the account of "My God, my God, why have you forsaken me."

XI^1 A 202   n.d., 1854

« 3586 *Suffering*

After all, suffering is not natural to man; consequently it naturally is painful.

But if one looks at the cause, at the cause which produces the suffering—then to suffer even has something persuasive about it.

If, on the other hand, one looks at those who cause the suffering —inasmuch as one suffers at the hands of men—the suffering becomes a bitter pain.

And yet the most embittering thought of all is of those cursed docents who consume other men, who live off others' having suffered, who beget children on that.

XI^1 A 203   n.d., 1854

« 3587 *The Human Race*

Real men are not being born these days; just as a certain kind of grain or a certain kind of fruit can be said to have the same name but be a completely different kind, so what is born these days is really not men. As far as spirit is concerned, the men born nowadays are as unusable as sewing needles without eyes.

Men are not being born, for they are without subjectivity. It is subjectivity which determines the relation to spirit, or it is the possibility of spirit. Subjectivity, the *I,* which ceaselessly reminds and arouses the *I,* the *I* which applies everything to itself, the *I* which on viewing the glorious or on hearing about it promptly applies it personally: How does it stand with you; are you striving in this way etc., the *I* that is the sleeplessness which defines the ethical.

But nowadays are born men without subjectivity, like knives without handles, arrows without tips. Millions are living solely occupied with the finite goals of this life. And those who ought to be the superior ones—well, they are the very ones I am thinking of when I say that men today are just as unusable for spirit as eyeless sewing needles are for sewing.

The superior ones are the assistant professors, that is, they are without subjectivity, truncated, obtuse objectivities, specimens. The very opposite of what is unconditionally intended to inflame subjectivity to the highest, if there is any, the very opposite of the divine suffering for the sins of the race and crying: Imitate me [*følge mig efter*] —they remain objective, inhumanly objective—yes, is it not as I say, they are not men!—they lecture about it. It is the same with respect to everything else magnificent which has had to suffer and which has demanded imitation: they remain objective about it and lecture about it.[1216] Yes, and still worse, such passivity is not achieved after a long battle with their better selves, with their consciences—no, their passivity is original, there is nothing better in them needing to be conquered; on the contrary, they think themselves glorious men who as such are able to lecture.

This is what it is to be devoid of spirit! For just as perpetrating a crime is not outright consciencelessness, but committing it *bona conscientia*, brutally thinking one is doing something glorious, is consciencelessness, so also it is indeed spiritlessness to be devoid of spirit in such a way that one thinks this is being spirit.

Alas, just as War Secretary General Neergaard[1217] continually reiterates: The noble Frederiksberg line of horses has died out, so also the human race has been dead for a long time now, and those being born now are no longer men.

XI[1] A 450   *n.d.*, 1854

« 3588 *Man*

The more I learn to know men, the more I doubt the accuracy of calling it an allegory to portray man as an animal (for example, Reynard the Fox)—when all is said and done, people are essentially nothing but animal creatures. Everything revolves around eating, drinking, propagating, having it good, etc. And the ones who ought to represent the life of the spirit, the teachers etc., are animal creatures in a still worse sense—they live off the sufferings of others, they make lollipops for themselves and produce offspring out of other people's agonies for the sake of the ideas and for the truth.

XI[1] A 467   *n.d.*, 1854

« 3589 *The Common Man*[1218]*—the Assistant Professors*

I love the common man—detest the professors.

The professors are the very ones who have demoralized the race. Everything would be better if the true relationship could prevail: the few who are truly in the service of the idea, or still higher, in the service of God—and then the people.

But the infamous situation prevails in which these scoundrels press in between these few and the people, this pack of robbers who in the guise of also serving the idea betray the true servants and confuse the people, all for the sake of paltry earthly advantage.

Were there no hell, it would have to be made in order to punish the professors, whose crime is such that it can scarcely be punished in this world.

XI[1] A 473   *n.d.,* 1854

« 3590 *The Two Ways*

One is to suffer; the other is to become a professor of another's having suffered.

The first is "the way"; the second is to go *roundabout* (that is why the preposition *about* is like a motto for all lecturing and professional prattling) and very likely ends with descending *downabout.*

XI[1] A 581   *n.d.,* 1854

« 3591 *"Christendom"*

is the most extreme insolence, the most shameless impudence toward God.

Are not all of us men, the whole human race, subject to one condition, equally obligated in obedience to the divine requirement? What boundless insolence, then, to divide and classify in such a way that one sits down and becomes a professor in what others have suffered in order to comply with God's requirement. Such a scoundrel-professor lectures, for example, on how a witness to the truth lived and worked. Here, says the professor, here we see the striking fact of how long he went about in frightful inner struggles before he resolved to venture; or here, so it goes, we cannot sanction his behavior, there was something weak about it, or something too hasty, or something violent, etc. And this professional nonsense is supposed to be spirituality. It does not occur to such an ass that instead of standing and babbling from a podium and criticizing, and with the same motivation also begetting children, he is himself committed to obedience to God's requirement.

XI² A 209   n.d., 1854

« 3592 *The Truly Religious Person*

Just as any cook knows, for example, that the strongest essence would be most revolting if taken alone or in large quantity, whereas a drop of it gives a lively flavor, so also the truly religious person these days is too powerful—he must first be put to death—and then stored by the assistant professors, who prepare the most rare and delicate concoctions by using him and his drop by drop.

This, however, is most loathsome. And for such a person to have to live blissfully in a better world together with—assistant professors —no, it is a revolting thought. Imagine dying by being eaten by cannibals and then having to live blissfully together, blissfully gathered together with those who ate you—shocking! Yet the other kind of cannibalism is still more abominable, especially because of its hypocrisy. [*In margin:* And if an assistant professor happens to read this, he will include it in his lectures.]

I steadfastly maintain that those who murder a witness to the truth cannot be as loathsome as assistant professors who turn his sufferings into profit.

XI² A 216   n.d., 1854

« 3593 *"The Assistant Professor"*

That Christianity does not exist at all[1219]—my persistent theme— that what is called Christianity is the exact opposite of what Christianity is—that is also seen in the fact that "the assistant professor" is now the representative of Christianity, is now Christianity's teacher and functionary. But "the assistant professor" is the exact counterpoint of what the New Testament means by being Christian.

Actually, "The assistant professor" is a nonhuman; I could almost be tempted to call him a nonanimal, inasmuch as in reason, intellectuality, etc. he stands far above the animal, who excusably lacks all such things and cannot be charged with sophistication—perhaps he can be properly called a nonthing. No suffering whatsoever prompts "the assistant professor" to think: Now I will suffer like that, and I am willing to suffer. No, just as a stone-deaf person is protected against hearing, the assistant professor is protected against the very thing Christ pointed to, the very thing he has required—imitation, discipleship [*Efterfølgelse*].

No suffering makes any impression on "the assistant professor." But he is on the go, extremely active studying the sufferings of others, getting all the details about them—for that is what he lives on, gets fat on, and along with his wife and children tastefully enjoys life by means of—the sufferings of others. He knows how to prepare them in such a way that the honorable public willingly pays an exorbitant price for his scholarship.

And not only does "the assistant professor" live this way, on the sufferings of the glorious ones—how repulsive!—but he also robs their lives of earnestness. If the people, the human throng, could get a direct impression of the suffering of a witness of the truth, much is thereby won. But this influence lawfully belonging to the deceased is what the assistant professor steals from him. The assistant professor thrusts himself between the glorious ones and the human throng and demoralizes the latter by pampering them, by serving up the sufferings of others as interesting information which is for sale quite as other delicacies are.

$$XI^2 \text{ A } 218 \quad n.d., 1854$$

« 3594 *Enlightened or Artificial Stupidity*

Just as we speak of artificial heat and light, artificial nature (in contrast to atmospheric warmth, daylight, natural flowers, natural beauty, etc.), so there is also an artificial stupidity.

No one, not even the most stupid man of all, is as stupid about Christianity as the "professor." His stupidity is artificially produced by much study.

In order to be preserved in this stupidity, constant and continued study of the writings of other professors* is required, for one thing, and for another, a strong opiate, the illusion that Christianity is perfectible.[1220] Anyone lucky enough to have his eyes opened to this wisdom is on the high road to becoming a professor.

In margin: * Note. I do not mean that the professor would be substantially benefited by reading other writings—he will still transform everything into his own stupidity.

$$XI^2 \text{ A } 233 \quad n.d., 1854$$

« 3595 *The Earnestness of Christianity*

The very moment someone has managed to spell out more clearly and to sharpen the characteristic marks of essential Christianity, it is utterly impossible to prevent the professors, swindlers, and twaddlers from immediately availing themselves of it—and lecturing on it.

It is impossible to prevent it, and so it has to be. If it were possible to define the essentially Christian in such a way that the professor's falsification of it would be impossible, then Christianity would be something other than it is.

No, falsification is continually possible. The earnestness lies elsewhere: eternity, and the professors cannot fool eternity. It cannot be denied that lecturing pays the best in time, but one cannot lecture himself into eternity.

XI² A 270   n.d., 1855

« 3596 *Shudder!*

One of Grimm's well-known fairy tales[1221] tells about someone who went out into the world to learn to shudder.

Perhaps he had to travel far away and perhaps still did not really learn to shudder. Let me tell you about something you do not need to go out in the world to find—no, stay where you are—and which nevertheless will make you shudder, if you are not so callous and devoid of spirit that mankind's most holy affairs do not concern you at all.

Think of all the erudite, learned nonsense, the mass of literature written by thousands and read by millions on the learned question about the extent to which the laity ought to be forbidden Christ's blood in the Lord's Supper—think about that. "Is it so appalling?" No, no, you interrupt me too soon, for surely this truck-load of pious, learned nonsense, surely it is always something to make one shudder, something one must shudder at on behalf of man, something which makes one shudder because of the judgment. But that is not what I meant. No, but think of the mass of scholarship and nonsense, the thousands and millions obviously occupied with writing, reading— think of it—and now let me tell you what you perhaps do not know, or if you do know it, let me make it very real and present to you.

In the early Church, when martyrs still shed blood, when to be a Christian was—if not personally becoming a martyr, at least like living next to a place that is on fire, so near that one can tell where the fire is, as they say, by feeling the wall—in the early Church the question whether the laity ought to be forbidden the blood in the Lord's Supper once came up. A bishop,[1222] who himself became a martyr, answered: If the Christian is asked to shed his blood for the Lord, how could he be forbidden the Lord's blood!

Shudder! When a person is a Christian like that, and when being a Christian is like that, then every question is infinitely easy to answer —then think of the professor-nonsense and those thousands writing and those millions reading! Do you believe the reason is that the question is difficult—in fact, it has become difficult, enormously difficult, because being a Christian has become dreadful nonsense.

XI² A 368   *n.d.*, 1854–55

« **3597** *Try it!*

(the evil of scholarship)

Imagine that it says in the New Testament that it is God's will that every human being is to have 100,000 dollars (we can surely imagine it!)—do you think there would be any question about a commentary? I wonder if everyone would not say: This is easy enough to understand; no commentary is needed; let us for God's sake stay away from commentaries—they might make the whole matter ambiguous. We prefer to have it as it stands—therefore, out, out with all commentaries.

But what stands in the New Testament (about the narrow way, about dying to the world,[1223] and so on) is no more difficult than this matter of 100,000 dollars. The difficulty lies somewhere else, in its not pleasing us—and therefore, therefore, therefore we must have commentaries and professors and commentaries. We are not "running the risk" of its becoming ambiguous—no, that is precisely what we want, and we hope that little by little, with the cooperation of commentaries, it will become ambiguous.

Is not, then, scholarship of evil? Is it not something we humans have invented because we do not want to understand what is only too easy to understand? Is it not an invention whereby we are strengthened in evil, in sneakery and hypocritical shirking?

We have invented scholarship in order to evade doing God's will. This much we certainly do understand—that face to face with God and his obviously understood will to say "This I will not do"—this no one dares to do. We do not dare do it that way, so we protect ourselves by making it seem as if it were very difficult to understand and that therefore we—he must indeed be flattered by this and regard it as praiseworthy in us—study and investigate etc., that is, we protect ourselves by hiding behind big books.

XI² A 376   *n.d.*, 1854–55

PROGRESS

« **3598**

Just as human progress is a constant falling,[1224] so all consistency is a constant inconsistency.

II A 763   n.d., 1838

« **3599**

It is the old story. A discovery is made—the human race is triumphant; everything, everything is enthusiastically set in motion to make the discovery more and more perfect. The human race jubilates and adores itself. After a long time there comes a halt—men pause: Is this discovery a good thing, after all, especially in its extraordinary perfection! And so once again the most eminent minds must set to speculating themselves almost crazy to discover safety valves, dampers, brakes, etc. to hold back, if possible, this incomparable and incomparably perfect discovery, the pride of the human race, lest it all end with running over and destroying the whole world. Just think of the invention of printing, perfected right down to the high-speed press which can make sure that no filth and scum goes unnoticed. Think of the trains. Think of the parliamentary constitutions, these matchless, perfected discoveries—the pride of the human race—which arouse longing for an oriental despotism as a more pleasant mode of life.

X^2 A 505   n.d., 1850

« **3600** *Historical Progress or Progress in Christendom*

What happens is *höchstens* something like this: there comes (with respect to the immediate past, which is less true—for with respect to original Christianity progress is impossible, and instead everything coming later is a continuous retrogression) a more truthful "what," but not a more truthful "how."

For example, a more truthful doctrine appears, or a particular dogma is more truthfully elucidated—and thereupon someone makes a hit, profits from it, etc. Then for a time we hear that sterile speculation has spoiled everything, and life, existence, must be emphasized—and this is accepted, and the one who discovered this makes a hit. Aha!

658

Lives and existences remain the same; the reduplications do not occur.

x⁴ A 414   *n.d.*, 1851

« 3601 *Progress through the Years*

There are people for whom life's progress or whose progress in life seems to mean that they become more and more stupid.

We know of their early youth, their childhood—no one suspected (this is the way we generally talk about the exceptional), no one suspected, who would ever have thought, that there resided in this child, who was just like the others, such a fund of stupidity as we now see developing ever more richly year by year.

XI¹ A 113   *n.d.*, 1854

« 3602 *The Human Race—Christianity*

Invariably when a man has turned 40 (husband, father, and champion rifle shot[1225]), he disavows his childhood fantasies as amusing—for now he has grown wise to the world, he has gained an understanding of reality, and he knows what earnestness is. Invariably a matron of 35 (mother, mistress of the house, and gossipmonger) disavows her childhood fantasies as amusing—for now she has grown wise to the world, has gained an understanding of reality, and knows what earnestness and true love are.

In like manner the race is now at the age where it is in the process of disavowing the high concepts of Christianity as a somewhat amusing something or other.

That the Sunday appearance of being a Christian is nevertheless maintained is, of course, quite consistent with ordinary human cowardice as well as with the ordinary human indolence which wants to stay in the comfortable old rut; finally, it is consistent with the presence of a social class which supports itself and family by maintaining the appearance that Christianity exists (I mean the clergy).

That Christianity does not fit in with the world, Christianity knew very well—O honored, enlightened Nineteenth Century—as you can see in the New Testament; it knew (see the New Testament) that it would be a matter of life and death—but it must enter into it.

Nowadays the situation is something like this: grandly patronizing, the world boasts of the conclusion, the ripe (to say nothing of rotten) fruit of sensibleness and experience—that Christianity does not fit into the world. The world boasts of this conclusion as if it had discovered this itself, as if Christianity (the eternal's idea) were *ein blutjunges Mädchen* who goodnaturedly fools around in life and now has to submit to having an experienced matron who knows the world patronizingly explain to her that she and her ways do not fit the world.

So the world grandly boasts of this prodigious conclusion (which, when regarded as the result of 1800 years of rigorous effort falls a little flat, something like a puff of gas instead of a birth, and, as far as novelty is concerned, faces the embarrassment that Christianity itself said it in the year 1) that Christianity does not fit in with the world—but grandly and patronizingly will perhaps allow it to remain like a piece of old furniture or old family servant. And when the clergy with professional, deferential dexterity bow and scrape before this patronizing world, the world will not be severe but will even protect this old junk.

XI[1] A 364   *n.d.,* 1854

« 3603 *God in Heaven*

Were I permitted to speak of such things, I would say that it is lucky for God that 1,000 years are as one day; otherwise it would be horrible to endure these centuries upon centuries, these hordes of millions, in which there is not an inch of progress or regression goes by leaps and bounds.

XI[1] A 466   *n.d.,* 1854

« 3604 *The Tragic Change in "Man"*

Once it was like this: He understood but little, but the little he understood moved him deeply.

Now he understands much, but it does not move him at all, or just superficially, or on the level of making faces.

Is this progress? Or is not this great understanding which makes no impression on man, does not move him, a kind of prostitution, like a smartly turned out woman, if you please, practised in all the devices of cunning and coquetry to please man—but lacking love?

XI[1] A 480   *n.d.,* 1854

PROOF

« 3605

The impecuniousness (for the awakening of conviction) of miracle in and for itself (then it is actually a contradiction, *sit venia verbo*), detached from its being a manifestation—for speculation merely something objective (*gegenständliche*)—a manifestation of eternal freedom under conditions it has given itself (time and space), is expressed in the words: "If they do not hear Moses and the prophets, neither will they be convinced if some one should rise from the dead." For they have simply pushed the question farther back. When, indeed, such a fact is told to them, they would either accept it as true, but it would be superstition, or they would be indifferent, or after having it completely proved they would accept it—but as a miracle?—unless they want to annul the concept at the very moment it is predicated of a concrete case.

Daub (in Bauer's *Zeitschrift*, I, 2, p. 103) observes quite rightly that doubt as well as unbelief would be very well served by getting involved in a proof of the truth of biblical miracles: "Bei dieser Forderung jedoch ist in der Geschichte *die Freiheit*—denn das gewisse und wahre Factum soll, damit das Wunder zu glauben stehe, ein durch dieses auf *nothwendige* Weise bedingtes sein, und in der Natur die *Nothwendigkeit* ignorirt, denn das Wunder, eine *freie* That soll als wäre es eine *Natur* Begebenheit gesehen—es soll erlebt werden; die bei der Himmelfahrt des Weltheilands Gegenwartigen *sahen nur,* dass er sich von der Erde entfernte, nicht aber die unbedingt Freiheit, sie, die Macht seiner Entfernung. Die Wahrheit, welche dieses Wunder ist, verwirklichte sich, und hat ihre Wirklichkeit in der *Macht,* nicht aber im vergänglichen und vergangnen Anblick dieser Bewegung. Der Zweifler also und der Unglaubige beweisen selbst so lange beide von jener Forderung eines auf dem Standpunkte der Geschichte oder der Natur, für die Wahrheit der Wunder zu fuhrenden [p. 104] Beweises nicht ablassen: dass in ihnen die bedingte Freiheit sich entweder unter das Gesetz der Causalität, wie in einer *pragmatisirenden* Geschichts-, oder, wie in einer

blos empirischen Natur-Kunde, unter die Sinnlichkeit die ihnen mit der
Thierheit gemein ist gestellt habe" ..... [1226]

II A 96   June 12, 1837

« **3606**

Note. It is true that I am not a poet and thus dare not claim to be
capable of an opinion, but would it not have an almost madly comical
effect to portray a man deluded into thinking that he could prove that
God exists—and then have an atheist accept it by virtue of the other's
proof. Both situations are equally fantastic, but just as no one has ever
proved it, so has there never been an atheist, even though there certainly have been many who have been unwilling to let what they knew
(that the God [*Guden*] exists) get control of their minds. It is the same
with immortality. —Suppose someone became immortal by means of
another's proving it*—would that not be infinitely ridiculous. Therefore there has never been a man who has not believed it, but there
certainly have been many who have been unwilling to let the truth
conquer in their souls, have been loathe to allow themselves *to be
convinced,* for what convinces me exists only by my becoming immersed
in it. —With respect to the existence of God, immortality, etc., in short,
with respect to all problems of immanence, recollection applies; it
exists altogether in every man, only he does not know it, but it again
follows that the conception may be very inadequate.

In margin: * (just as Nille became a stone and the deacon a
rooster[1227]) suppose there was someone who went around as a miracle
man, set up his booth, and proved the immortality of the individual for
a fee, just as indulgences were sold, and thus only the individual whose
immortality he proved became immortal.[1228]

V B 40:11   *n.d.,* 1844

« **3607**

(b) The Speculative View

3

The Proof of the Centuries

the fact that Christianity has endured for 18 centuries. (Mohammedism has endured for 12 centuries.)

Jean Paul is the one who has said that even if we eliminated all the
proofs for the truth of Christianity, there would still remain the fact
that Christianity has endured for 18 centuries.[1229]

VI B 25   *n.d.,* 1845

« 3608

Away with all this world history[1230] and reasons and proofs[1231] for the truth of Christianity: there is only one proof—that of faith.[1232] If I actually have a firm conviction (and this, to be sure, is a qualification of intense inwardness oriented to spirit), then to me my firm conviction is higher than reasons; it is actually the conviction which *sustains* the reasons, not the reasons which sustain the conviction. In this respect the esthete in *Either/Or* is right in his own way when he says in one of the Diapsalmata[1233] that reasons are curious things—when I do not have passion I proudly look down on reasons, and when I have passion reasons swell up immensely. What he speaks of and what he calls passion is the impassioned, the inward, which is precisely what a firm conviction is. "Reasons" can lay an egg no more than a rooster can, at most a wind egg, and no matter how much intercourse they have with each other they never beget or bear a conviction. A conviction arises elsewhere. That is what I meant someplace[1234] (in connection with a few problems written on a sheet of paper pasted on cardboard) by the problem of the difference between a pathos-filled and a dialectical transition.[1235]

It is impossible, then, for a person to hold back his conviction and push ahead with the reasons. No, the decisive factor is a person's conviction, or the fact that it is one's conviction, that it is my conviction, your conviction (personally). It is possible to talk half humorously about reasons: So, at long last you want to have a few reasons.[1236] I am happy to oblige. Do you want to have 3 or 5 or 7? How many do you want? But I can say nothing higher than this: *I* believe. This is the positive saturation point, just as when a lover says: She is the one I love, and he says nothing about loving her more than others love their beloveds, and nothing about reasons.

Consequently conviction must be at the top, and personality along with it; reasons are reduced to a lower rank—this, again, is just the opposite of all modern objectivity.

My development, or any man's development, proceeds in this way. Perhaps he does begin with a few reasons, but this is the lower stage. Then he chooses; under the weight of responsibility before God a conviction comes into existence in him through God. Now he is in the positive position. Now he cannot defend or prove his conviction with reasons; it is a self-contradiction, since reasons are lower. No, the matter becomes more fully personal or a matter of personality: his conviction can be defended only ethically, personally[1237]—that is, by the sacrifices which he is willing to make for it, the fearlessness with which he holds on to it.

There is only one proof for the truth of Christianity—the inward proof, *argumentum spiritus sancti.*

I John 5:9 intimates this: "If we receive the testimony of men" (this is all the historical proofs and considerations) "the testimony of God is greater"—that is, the inward testimony is greater. And then in verse 10: "He who believes in the son of God has the testimony in himself."

It is not reasons which justify the faith in God's son, but just the opposite—faith in God's son is the testimony. It is the movement of infinity within itself, and it cannot be otherwise. Reasons do not justify the conviction, but the conviction justifies the reasons. Everything previous is preparatory study, preliminary, something which disappears as soon as the conviction arrives and changes everything or turns the relationship around. Otherwise there would be no resting in a conviction, for then to have conviction would mean perpetually to repeat the reasons. The resting, the absolute resting in a conviction,[1238] in faith, is simply that faith itself is the testimony, faith is the justification.

x^1 A 481   *n.d.,* 1849

« 3609

And now Lic. Lind[1239] wants to lecture to the Craftsmen's Cultural Guild on proofs for the truth of Christianity!

No doubt well-meaning, but really, he does not know what he is doing.

This social class has already been pampered to feel itself an authority as soon as it is assembled in a meeting. The speaker is no "teacher" but someone who bows before the crowd, before this esteemed assemblage. And now "Proofs!" Fine, now everything is as it should be—"Let us now hear what Christianity can say in its defense" etc.—this is the impression, and this is the abolition[1240] of Christianity.

Pastors are what we need, pastors with courage and authority; the confessional is what ought to be used.

Alas, thus at every point well-meaning efforts—which add to the confusion.

x^2 A 430   *n.d.,* 1850

« 3610 *Faith—the Proof*

A person who is condemned to death as a criminal, a blasphemer; abandoned by all, he is scourged, scorned, spit upon, finally nailed to the cross—and he says: Believe on me. Yes, truly here is the place for faith, because all spontaneity and immediacy witnesses, crying to heaven, if you please, against this and says: Do not believe in him.

1,800 years later a speaker comes along who as a consequence of that man's life *proves* that he was the one he said he was. Well, if it can be proved, then he is no longer the object of faith.

If Christ had in any manner thought along these lines, he might have said to his disciples: Wait a while and you will surely come to see that I was right. But he did not do this, he did not appeal to results in the history[1241] of his life; he wanted to be the object of faith.[1242]

It is of no use to talk to anyone who, with this assistance, is unable to see the whole confusion in which Christendom is submerged.

x^2 A 446 *n.d.*, 1850

« 3611

In margin of 3610 (x^2 A 446):

Yet it must be remembered that simply because in "contemporaneity"[1243] the paradox is above human powers as the object of faith, the apostles are therefore also equipped with superhuman powers in order to be able to hold out in their faith. The rest of us have it somewhat easier, and then in addition have "grace" as the fruit of Christ's death. But it must never be forgotten that if it can be fully proved by results that Christ is the one he said he was, then he is not the object of faith.

x^2 A 447 *n.d.*

« 3612

This is the way Christianity entered the world: it presupposed want, distress, the suffering of the anguished conscience under the law, the hunger which cries out only for food—and then Christianity was the food.

And nowadays—now we think that we have to have appetizers[1244] to get people to enter into Christianity. What appetizers? The preaching of the law? No, no! Christianity must be served with appetizer seasonings: proofs, grounds, probability, and the like. And finally preaching has come to concentrate simply and solely on appetizers.

This means we betray Christianity, we actually deny that it is unconditionally the food, that the fault lies in men, that they should be properly starved out—then they would learn to need Christianity. But now it is Christianity which needs the appetizers in order to provide a little flavor—otherwise it presumably tastes like nothing. And what does it taste like with appetizers?

We have changed Christianity from a radical cure (which it is; therefore it presupposes in those concerned the resoluteness—*resolvere*, to open up—which is always required in a radical cure) into a minor precaution, like something used to prevent colds, toothaches, and the like. And strangely enough, although every inventor of drops, pills, etc., "which do neither good nor harm," trumpets his medicine as a miracle balm, Christianity is proclaimed in very muted tones: a host of grounds and reasons march right up in order to make it somewhat probable that there is something to Christianity. And this is called preaching, and therefore one is paid as a "servant of the Word." Truly, if worst comes to worst, I believe that Christianity would be better off served by a charlatan than by a legion of preachers of this sort.

x^2 A 461   *n.d.*, 1850

« 3613 *The Absoluteness of Christianity*

This alone is a proof of the divinity of Christianity, quite different from the proof of eighteen centuries.[1245]

A man comes to Christ and wants to be his disciple, asks only that Christ wait a few days while he buries his dead father, and then he will forsake everything and follow him. Christ[1246] replies: Let the dead bury their dead and follow me. God in heaven, to demand a breaking with everything on this scale is proof that a person has an absolute conception of his cause as the absolute cause. Truly no human being has ever talked like this. To be sure, the better one's cause, the more rigorous he is in choosing his disciples—but short of the absolute break, can anything more beautiful be imagined than this: simply to reserve a few days in order to bury a deceased father! Never has any man had a cause of such a nature that he could think of rejecting such a disciple; on the contrary, the very piety of the rejected disciple toward the dead father must recommend him. But only Christ had the absolute cause.

And what sublimity, which again can only be divine! Calmly resting in the idea of the absoluteness of his cause, to reject a disciple like that. Never has any man who has had a cause been so absolutely free from reliance upon another man for his cause; this, again, is the absoluteness of the divine.

Yet, of course, this has its distinctive compatibility with the cause Christ had. It was not the usual cause, which needs support to be victorious, if possible. No, his cause was specifically to see to it that he did not end up victorious; victory was easily his. It was certainly a reason for being severe; otherwise one might get disciples who would help him to be victorious. And Christ's cause was to make all the arrangements for his being put to death.

Remarkable cause! But here again is the expression for the absoluteness which is divine; in this sense no man has ever had a cause. Many a man has lost a cause, but never has any man had a cause embodying the stipulation that it should be lost, with all effort basically directed to that end. It is once again the superhuman which, completely heterogeneous with everything human, relates itself only to itself,[1247] does not come to the world to have its fate decided, but, eternally resolved within itself about what it wills, comes to the world —to be put to death.

X^3 A 193   *n.d.*, 1850

« 3614 *Augustine*

As a proof of the truth of Christianity Augustine[1248] also cites (in addition to the usual proofs of prophecy and historical consequences) the unity of Christians in contrast to the conflict and disunity among philosophers.

This argument does not mean very much, actually, since it is based on the difference between religion and philosophy, and to that extent every religion has this unity rather than the conflict which marks the philosophical.

X^4 A 162   *n.d.*, 1851

« 3615 *Anselm—the Modern*

Anselm's ontological proof[1249] has played a large role in modern times and is used especially by—free thought.

Curious! As Anselm himself relates, he won this proof (in *Proslogium*) by prayer and supplication. Incidentally, a peculiar method of praying! Anselm says: I want to prove the existence of God. To that end I pray God to strengthen and help me—but this is no doubt a much better proof for the existence [*Tilværelse*] of God—that it is so certain that one has to have God's help to prove it. If one could prove the existence of God without God's help it would be, so to speak, less certain that he exists.

The circle within which Anselm moves also becomes apparent in his reply to Gaunilo. G. has objected that "that beyond which nothing higher can be thought etc." is a mere thought. Anselm answers that it is not so, it is not merely a thought which can be thought and is thought and is rooted in the human mind—otherwise God would not exist. But, after all, this is the very thing to be proved!

See Böhringer,[1250] II, part 1, p. 350.

But what interests me about Anselm is that he also affirms the ascetic factor in relation to being a thinker. This is quoted somewhere earlier in Böhringer's life of Anselm.[1251]

And now think of modern philosophy, which gads about with this Anselmism, modern speculation, in which it is sadly only too true that God does not exist—and that it must be proved; and [think of] Anselm, who prays God for the proof.

x^4 A 210   *n.d.*, 1851

« **3616**

From a Christian point of view it is nonsense to offer as proof of the truth of Christianity the fact of its dissemination. It is not proved this way in the New Testament either; Christ and the apostles prove it conversely—that one is put to death for it. And this demonstration is also, from a Christian point of view, the only possible one, for inasmuch as Christianity is the polemical truth, the mark of its truth and the proof of it must correspond to this, consequently must be reversed, must be polemical.

But in "Christendom" the characteristic mark has become directness (dissemination), and this again indirectly declares that Christianity has been made into direct truth.

xi^2 A 338   *n.d.*, 1854

PROTESTANTISM

« 3617 *Catholicism—Protestantism*

Are not Catholicism[1252] and Protestantism actually related to one another as a building which cannot stand is related to buttresses which cannot stand alone, but the entire structure is able to stand, even very stable and secure, when the building and the buttresses together give it stability (this may seem a strange analogy, but this is the way it actually is in the physical world). In other words, is not Protestantism (or the Lutheran principle) really a corrective,[1253] and has not a great confusion been brought about by making this normative in Protestantism?

As long as Luther lived this could not readily be seen, for he constantly stood in the tension of combat, concentrated as a polemicist, stood in the smoke and steam of battle, for it is true of the battle of the spirit as well that as long as the struggle goes on there is something corresponding to smoke and steam which makes it impossible to find either the time or the quiet or the clarity to see whether what one has begun can be carried through. Luther battled, as the saying goes, constantly polemicizing against Catholicism: it cannot be done this way; then he is supposed to show how it should be done, but there is no time to pause for this, for now we have to go to the next point; we are in a battle; it cannot be done this way, and so on and so on— and nothing comes of it.

Then comes peace. Now it will become clear whether Protestantism can continue on its own. Whether or not it is possible perhaps cannot be seen accurately in a land where Catholicism exists alongside Protestantism, for although they do not fight but each takes care of its own affairs, there will nevertheless in many ways be a reciprocal relationship. To ascertain properly whether and to what extent Protestantism can stand alone, it is desirable to have a country in which there is no Catholicism. There it must be evident whether Protestantism— assuming that it degenerates—leads to a corruption which Catholicism —assuming that it degenerates—nevertheless does not lead to, and

669

whether this does not show that Protestantism is not qualified to stand alone.

Let us take a good look at this. It was after a heavy yoke had rested on men's shoulders for a long, long time, after men from generation to generation had been troubled about death and judgment and hell and with starving and flagellating themselves—and it was then that the bow broke. Out of the monastery cell broke the man Luther. Let us watch out now lest we separate things which really belong together, the background and the foreground, and get a landscape without background or something meaningless.

What Luther ventured was, given this presupposition, the truth; the opposite position had been brought to the point of false hypertension.

So Luther broke out of the monastery. But this was not an essentially good opportunity to see with reasonable level-headedness just how much truth lay in the opposite position when it is not overstrained. Luther did not know for sure, and it was rather a question of utilizing the advantage of having broken out and inflicting upon the opposite position as incurable a wound as possible.

Consider the situation when Luther broke out: there was falsification. Remove entirely this presupposition for Luther and Luther's position is completely meaningless. Imagine that what Luther in the utmost tension comprehended as the ultimate is taken as a kind of "conclusion" in such a way that people omit the tension completely—then Luther's position is utter nonsense. Imagine a country, far removed from all Catholicism, where the Lutheran "conclusion" has been introduced; there a generation lives who have never heard a single word about the side of the matter expressed by the monastery, asceticism, etc., the side which the middle ages exaggerated—but have been sentimentally reared and spoiled from childhood by Luther's "conclusion" about reassurance for the troubled conscience. But there is no one, note well, who even in the remotest way has this troubled conscience! What then is Luther's "conclusion"? Is there any meaning in reassurance for troubled consciences if the presupposition of the troubled conscience is not there? Does not Luther's conclusion thereby become meaningless, yes, what is worse, a refinement which makes the difference between degenerated Protestantism and the corruption of degenerated Catholicism.

This is just what I wanted to point out, also that this indicates that Protestantism is not qualified to stand alone.

When Catholicism degenerates, what form of corruption is likely to appear? Surface sanctity. When Protestantism degenerates, what form of corruption will appear? The answer is easy: spiritless secularism.

Place them side by side—surface sanctity versus spiritless secularism—but I maintain that here is one more refinement which cannot appear in Catholicism, and this is a result of Protestantism's being reckoned on the basis of a presupposition. This refinement is what I want to point out.

Let us make it very simple. Imagine a completely secularized Catholic prelate. Of course there is nothing extreme to the point of being punished by law or revenged by nature—no, he is all too worldly to be so stupid; no, the whole thing is reasonably and shrewdly calculated —and this is the worldliest of all—upon prudent enjoyment, and then again upon enjoying his shrewdness, and in this way his whole life is all possible enjoyment beyond that of the most secularized worldly-shrewd Epicurean. Now, how will a Catholic judge him? I assume (it is indeed proper) that he will say: It is not up to me to judge the high-ranking clergy; but otherwise the Catholic will easily see that this is worldliness. And why will he easily see this? Because Catholicism simultaneously expresses an entirely different aspect of Christianity in whose cause the high prelate must also acquiesce; side by side with him walks one who lives in poverty, and the Catholic has a pathos-filled conception of this which is sounder than the prelate's, which, alas, is only worldliness.

Now, on the other hand, imagine a Protestant country where there is no thought of Catholicism, where Luther's principle has been accepted long ago but without its presupposition, where ascetics and fasters and monks and those who proclaim Christ in poverty have been gotten rid of long ago, and not only that, but repudiated as ridiculous and foolish, so that if any such one were to appear, people would burst into laughter as they would at seeing an outlandish animal, repudiated as something inferior and imperfect—now imagine that in this Protestant country there lived a high Protestant cleric, an exact counterpart of the Catholic prelate: what then? Well, the Protestant cleric has a refinement—ah, a refinement the Catholic prelate hankers after in vain. Since among all his contemporaries there is not one last person with a pathos-filled conception of forsaking the world (a godliness which, incidentally, even though it was exaggerated in the Middle Ages, still has its truth), since all the religiosity of the country is built and rests

upon Luther's conclusion (without his presupposition) that religiousness is the frankness of rejoicing in life (which is wonderful, to be sure,
if one has Luther's fear and trembling and spiritual trials), because of
all this the Protestant cleric enjoys a refinement—by Jove, the Catholic
prelate perhaps says, golly!—the refinement that his contemporaries
understand his secular mentality and worldly enjoyment of life as—
religiousness! Look, one contemporary says to another (the situation
for the prelate was otherwise—there one person said to another, let us
not look at this or discuss it, for it is nothing but sheer secularity), look
at that Lutheran opennesss, see him at his turtle soup, there is someone who knows his way around; see how he can suck enjoyment out
of every situation in life, and how shrewd he is to his own advantage
—and admire this Lutheran frankness! He rides high in Lutheran frankness, high above the inferior and the imperfect, such as entering the
monastery, fasting, proclaiming Christ in poverty; he rides high above
all this in freedom of spirit and Lutheran frankness! The great thing
is not to forsake the world, to flee!—no, to be like the cleric is genuinely
Lutheran, for this is religiousness. The contemporaries not only tolerate it or make no effort to ignore it; no, they look upon it admiringly
—as religiousness.

Luther has established the highest spiritual principle—inwardness
alone.[1254] This can become so dangerous that we can sink to the very
lowest levels of paganism (yet the highest and the lowest are also alike)
where sensuous debauchery is honored as worship. Similarly, it can
come to the point in Protestantism where worldliness is honored and
venerated as godliness. And that, I maintain, cannot happen in Catholicism.

But why can it not happen in Catholicism? Because Catholicism
has the universal presupposition that we human beings are scoundrels.

And why can it happen in Protestantism? Because the principle of
Protestantism is related to a special presupposition: a human being
sitting in mental anxiety, in fear and trembling and great spiritual trial
—and of these there are not many in any generation.

* * *

It is not my aim here to reintroduce monasticism, even if I could;
I am merely attempting to help us along, by means of admissions, to
an understanding with truth.

XI² A 305   n.d., 1853–54

« 3618 *Protestantism*

If Protestantism is to be something other than a corrective[1255] (perhaps necessary at a given moment, therefore introduced only by an individual man under enormous responsibility and protected against any aping), is not Protestantism then actually a falling away from Christianity?

Indolent, villainous human nature wants to have peace and quiet, peace and quiet to enjoy life etc.; therefore it cries: I can't do it, I despair; if grace is not introduced in such a way that it basically abolishes Christianity, I despair.

This is a knavish trick, nothing but. It is just like females when they cunningly use fainting spells to get their way. And what does such a female need? She needs a man who calmly says, "Nonsense!"—then she does not swoon.

In the same way Protestantism is in dire need of a hard man who, when man begins the tricky business of saying that otherwise he must despair, can say: Fine, go ahead, but do despair, then![1256]

XI[1] A 87 *n.d.*, 1854

« 3619 *A Protestant Invention*

The clergyman gets into a dilemma by virtue of the fact that today there are no Christians at all who can be presented as prototypes [*Forbilleder*]; this can easily get to look suspicious.

Catholicism still always has a few who are Christians in character.

Then the Protestant pastors made this invention—that all around the country there are true Christians who very quietly are really true Christians—yes, at bottom, in hidden inwardness,[1257] we are all true Christians, all prototypes. Charming! If the New Testament shall decide what is to be understood by being a true Christian, then being a true Christian very quietly—cozily, enjoyably—would be just as impossible as firing a cannon very quietly.

XI[1] A 106 *n.d.*, 1854

« 3620 *To Become a Christian*

The Savior of the world, Jesus Christ, lives in poverty and abasement, then is persecuted and detested, finally is tortured in every way and is crucified.

Essentially, his teaching is his life. What he says, therefore, is essentially this: Imitate me [*følge mig efter*]; hate yourself; forsake all things; crucify the flesh; take up the cross; hate father and mother, etc.

Further: You will be hated by all for my name's sake, etc. Finally: There is an accounting in the world to come where I am the judge.

Alas, when one is born into Christendom, especially into Protestantism, especially in Denmark,[1258] when from childhood on one is in every way hypnotized into the illusion that he is a Christian, when from infancy one is poured full of this whole swindle which makes Christianity into optimism, when one lives in a so-called Christian state—that is, a society which in every possible way sees to it that a person is strengthened in the illusion that he is a Christian, even forces a person by means of civil punishment to be a Christian—well, then it is undeniably enormously difficult to become a Christian.

XI¹ A 199   n.d., 1854

« 3621 *All the Christianity of Men*

turns out to be rascality. People insert the religious as a possibility, and although their whole thought and effort are for earthly things and the enjoyment of this life—they insert the religious as a consolation in extreme emergencies, that is, as a guarantee for the proper enjoyment of this life. In this way Christianity becomes as horrible a contrast as possible to what it is in the New Testament. A telling example is the way the religious is taken along with erotic love into the wedding ceremony. This is the most revolting use of Christianity *contra naturam ejus.*[1259]

Otherwise life goes on and people take care not to get earnestly involved with God. With the help of dissipations and activity (which, incidentally, is dissipation from the Christian point of view), they keep themselves in turmoil of mind so that the divine can never get closer to them.

But if someone gets involved with God earnestly, they laugh at him as they do at someone foolish enough to let himself be tricked or at a maid who is fooled into thinking a prince is in love with her or that he intends anything other than to make a fool of her.

But for orators in the quiet hours it is a question of actually getting involved with God as intimately as possible—they describe and describe and it is all based on nauseating rapture and debauchery in the direction of refined pleasure.

As far as the ordinary man is concerned, what helps and saves him is his good nature and the fact that the clergy cannot completely demoralize him. As I have often remarked, here one sees nature's far-sighted care in equipping every child so richly because it knows in advance, alas, because it expects, that every child will most likely be brought up stupidly by the parents, and therefore a great original endowment must be squandered on the child in order for it to hold out. Something similar helps the common man in relation to the clergy, among whom—especially in Protestantism and especially in this country[1260]—there is rarely found a hypocrite but all the more droolers and diddling chatterboxes, who may very well be very good arithmetic teachers.

XI[1] A 213 *n.d.*, 1854

« 3622 *Lie after Lie*

The secular mentality has gotten the upper hand in Protestant Christianity to such a degree that if there is a suffering person who Christianly wants to console himself with the essentially Christian consolation that every day you live is one day less—God be praised—in this miserable existence, he does not, if possible, get permission to do it; the secular mentality will intimidate him so that he also makes this his dogma: Enjoy life etc.[1261] Yes, "the minister" (this scurvy liar who eats, drinks, and gets fat and begets children and advances in salary, all chargeable to the account: Christ's suffering and death) punishes the sufferer, points out to him that such thoughts are wicked, sinful. To be sure, the preacher has not bound himself by oath to the dogma "Enjoy life," but it is generally the case that one seldom takes an oath on something he is for but readily takes an oath on something he is against; it is a part of the lie-system. It would never do to let the preacher take an oath on: Enjoy life; but when he has taken an oath on the exact opposite, then one is, hypocritically, all the better assured that he can wholly sacrifice himself in order to proclaim: Enjoy life— sacrifice himself, but this of course must be taken with a grain of salt, for naturally he does not become a sacrifice but a soul in secularism's: Enjoy life. And this is Christianity.

XI[1] A 224 *n. d.*, 1854

« 3623 *Christianity—Christendom*

Imagine a funeral service staged as a ballet scene: this is how Christendom is related to Christianity (especially Protestantism).[1262]

Or take another illustration. In Ceylon[1263] there is said to be music in which the most sorrowful melodies are played with the beat of dance music. This is how Christendom is related to Christianity, especially Protestantism.

XI[1] A 247 *n.d.*, 1854

« 3624 *Christianity*

Christianity was a task given to the human race, a lesson assigned for an examination which had to be taken.

But finally, after a long, long preparation, in Protestantism, especially in Denmark, the race managed to turn the thing around thus: Let us act as if it were a game; let us play Christianity.

Just as a teacher assigns a lesson to a child and says: This is a hard lesson, and to learn it thoroughly will make tomorrow a strenuous day for you—so Christianity entered into the world, and in introducing Christianity, God said something like this to the human race: This is a hard lesson, and this temporal life will be a strenuous day for you. ——Now we act as if God said: This life is vacation time.

Thus to be a Christian, yes, even to be teachers in Christianity, became the coziest and most enjoyable of lives, an extraordinarily diverting and profitable game—and there was not even so much modesty left that it occurred to one single person that this kind of Christianity is not New Testament Christianity.

XI^1 A 437   *n.d.*, 1854

« 3625 *Protestantism*

is altogether indefensible. It is a revolution occasioned by proclaiming "the Apostle" (Paul) at the expense of the Master (Christ).

This may have significance as a corrective at a given time and in a given situation.

If in other respects Protestantism is to be maintained, it must be done in this way: We confess that Protestantism is a mitigation of Christianity which we men have allowed ourselves, appealing to God to put up with it.

And instead Protestantism is trumpeted as a forward step in Christianity! No, it is perhaps the most pronounced concession made to the numerical, this numerical principle which is the hereditary enemy of Christianity, which wants to be Christian but wants to be rid of ideality or have it downgraded, and which boasts of being so numerous.

XI^2 A 162   *n.d.*, 1854

« 3626 *The Guilt of Danish Protestantism*
The Corresponding Retribution

Certainly what Plato[1264] says of the highest being, that it can neither commit nor suffer injustice, is true of God, that how we men are can be a matter of indifference to God, how the Christians are a matter of indifference to the Christians' God—he does not suffer because of it.

Yet the apostle interprets it [how men àre] as if God suffered under it—he cautions the Christians against making God dishonored because of their immorality.[1265]

Looked at in this way, there have been times when it must be said that the Christian Church by its wild aberrations etc. has openly brought dishonor upon God.[1266]

But if it is to be stated wherein the guilt of Danish Protestantism lies, it cannot truthfully be said to be wild aberrations, conceited hypocrisy, etc.—no, its guilt, by dragging Christianity down into mediocrity and triviality and hearty nonsense, is that it has made God ridiculous.

Just as the punishment always fits the offense, the retribution will be proportioned to this guilt—Danish Protestantism must endure being seen for what it is: Christianly, something ridiculous. Precisely this is the only true and therefore the only God-pleasing cure. Anything else would be at fault in not fully and truly comprehending the sickness, the evil, and therefore the retribution would not fit properly.

XI² A 398   n.d., 1855

PROVIDENCE. GOVERNANCE

« 3627

Divine providence [*Forsyn*] moves, so to speak, according to a higher association of ideas; whereas the world moves according to its finite association of ideas. While finite individuals are thus realizing each his own idea, the deity does not meanwhile forget his great plans, and when no one is expecting it the miraculous enters history, and in so doing the deity through his association of ideas returns to his premise—somewhat the way a refrain in a ballad (especially in the balladry of the Middle Ages, in which the refrain often was not at all relevant to the content) comes again, and while it accumulates and within its accumulation lets the idea in the verse realize itself, it also develops itself independently.

II A 681   December 31, 1837

« 3628

†

A *providence* [*Forsyn*] is no easier to understand (to grasp) than redemption *[Forløsningen]*—both can only be believed. The idea of a providence implies that God concerns himself with the single individual and with his most individual aspect, which at most can be imaginatively (in the abstract) maintained as an everlasting concord in immanence between the infinite and the finite—but not in the process of becoming. Redemption is *continued* providence, that God will concern himself with the single individual and with his most individual aspect, although he has forfeited everything. Yet redemption is a transition εἰς ἄλλο γένος,[1267] inasmuch as it is also dialectical in a sign by which it is recognized, for providence is not recognized by a sign in the same way as Christ's death is the sign (the sign of the cross).

Providence and redemption are categories of despair—that is, I would have to despair if I dared not believe it, yes, if I were not commanded to believe. Thus they are not the occasion of despair—they keep despair away.

The historical aspect of redemption must stand fast and be certain in the same sense as any historical event, but not more so, for then the spheres are confused. The so-called historical, factual certainty would either have to be an autopsy[1268] of a contemporary or of a later person who had the statement from a trustworthy man; but if this then is overrated, the essence of faith is enervated. In respect to providence I have neither anything like this (something palpable to cling to) nor another man I can cling to; in addition I have against me a concerned view of existence with all that it knows of the wretchedness of existence —so I believe in a providence. The historical, factual presupposition of redemption must simply stand fast as any other historical fact, but then the passion of faith must determine the issue in quite the same sense as with providence.

For the crushed and contrite person, redemption's faith in the forgiveness of sins removes the middle term of anxiety, that his whole relationship to God will have to go through the middle term of punishment.

VII[1] A 130 *n.d.,* 1846

« **3629**

Voluminous and learned books have been written to justify God's management [*Styrelse*] of the world. As soon as a government has to be justified in print, it can run to a lot of words, but the relationship is still not quite the same between God and man, for God, to be sure, has the creator's right to require faith and obedience from the created, as well as that every creature may in his heart only think pleasing thoughts about him. On the other hand God is certainly not an elective king who could be set aside at the next assembly—if he does not adequately justify himself. The matter is quite simple. The punishment is devised by the loving God for the guilt of transgressions. But just as in a large household where there are many children the innocent sometimes share a little bit of it, too, so also in a great household where there are so many millions . . . . . no, not this way, for the reason this happens in a household where there are many children is that the father or the teacher is still only a man; but God is certainly well able to survey the whole scene, things do not get confused for him, he who counts the hairs on a man's head and sees to it that no sparrow falls to the earth prematurely. Therefore it is not so that under the management of God the innocent share some of the punishment, too—that is, are regarded as guilty, but the innocent may well share some of the suffering. But as soon as the innocent sufferer turns to God and asks if it is punishment, he promptly gets the answer: No, my dear child, it is no punishment; you certainly know that. Therefore instead of justifying God, an enterprise which is double-minded because it simultaneously wants to get to the same place by two roads, what is needed is to will only one thing and then everything is in order. He says to himself: The most abominable thing of all would be to let yourself insult God even in your most secret thoughts, to think that he did wrong. What does it matter to me if someone wants to write a big book to justify or accuse God—I believe. Where I seem to be able to understand his providence, I still prefer to believe, for faith is more blessed, and as long as a man lives in this world, understanding so easily becomes a matter of imagination and comradely obtrusiveness; and where I cannot understand—well, then it is blessed to believe.[1269]

VII[1] B 153:5   n.d., 1846

« 3630

..... But then the whole thing goes wrong and I fail to achieve anything. What foolishness. If I follow my orders and things go wrong as a consequence of that, then it is a part of governance [*Styrelsen*] and perhaps it will come to have meaning, although I do not understand it.

Suppose Stephen by his death achieved nothing else than to influence Paul—did he achieve nothing? And how often is it not the case that a brave man's downfall becomes itself an awakening. But the fact is that we want to play providence [*Forsyn*] ourselves.[1270] In that way history would certainly become only a farce.

VIII[1] A 329   n.d., 1847

« 3631 *Christendom*

One thousand pastors preach every Sunday: Not a sparrow falls to the earth without the heavenly Father's will; the hairs of your head are numbered,[1271] etc; and they say: It is salutary to believe this, and this you must believe.

What does this mean? It means: You must believe in a *providentia specialissima.*

And if on Monday a man lets it be known that he believes in a *providentia specialissima*—then he is thrown out of the community as a "fanatic."

And next Sunday one thousand men once again perform: You must believe etc.

X[4] A 602   n.d., 1852

« 3632 *Rascality Again*

Among people who possess something or have become something in the world there frequently or even usually is a tendency to be a little religious. They like to talk about believing in a providence [*Forsyn*], a governance [*Styrelse*]; on behalf of the providence and governance they are champions of the beautiful, uplifting conception that the world we live in is the best, and so on.

Charming! But if you analyze such piety a little more closely you perhaps will shudder instead at the kind of cruelty and egotism you find.

If a person does possess something or has become something in the world, he likes to have the enjoyment of this world refined by attributing it to God, and he becomes self-important by being the object of the concern, perhaps even the special concern, of providence. Aha!

Next, he is perhaps inclined to imagine that it is desirable that there be a providence and governance for the continuing possession of these earthly goods—the guarantee, perhaps. Aha!

Further, it flatters him to imagine that the something he has achieved in the world is, in fact, providence's reward because he has used life wisely and piously. Aha!

Finally, such faith perhaps helps (strange as it may seem) fortify him against the impression of the suffering and the unfortunate, the perpetual reminders of the wretchedness of this life. So he is always advising the sufferer to turn to providence—and this has a wonderful tranquilizing effect on him which enables him to enjoy life lavishly. If the sufferer becomes impatient, he goes perhaps a step further and explains that his sufferings are self-inflicted, a punishment—for there is a providence, a governance, which distributes rewards to the good (charming!) and punishment to the evil. Finally, in the existence of this providence he has a defense for not doing more for the sufferer than he is doing, because he fears to disturb the purposes of providence for every individual.

*   *

The idea of *providentia specialissima* belongs to Christianity. It is with the help of this idea that we devise subtleties.

In the New Testament the matter is presented differently. It is the Christian who is assumed to be the object of the *providentia specialissima*.

But in the New Testament a Christian is understood to be one who voluntarily has broken with everything called happiness in this world, has plunged into all sufferings, a sacrifice and sacrificed—and the promise of being the object of special care is given to him, that not a hair on his head will be hurt without God's will.

But here as everywhere we treat Christianity as arbitrarily as possible. We men select what seems able to suit our self-indulgence and throw away what does not please us—and thus we cook up a rascally religiosity which is supposed to be Christianity.

XI^1 A 267   *n.d.*, 1854

PUNISHMENT

« **3633**

In a way the eternity of hell-punishment[1272] is easy to prove, and in any case it can be shown again how difficult it is to get a historical point of departure for an eternal happiness in time, and also how thoughtlessly men behave. The first (the problem of *Fragments*) is supposed to be so easy to understand that everyone grasps it. The second (the eternality of hell-punishment—that is, an eternal unhappiness) no one will accept and the Church teaches it in vain, for it may be assumed quite safely that no one believes it. Well, well, well, what thinkers! It is absolutely the same problem. If anyone is able to think the one (eternal happiness decided in time), then he has *eo ipso* thought the second. If time is able to be an adequate medium for deciding eternal happiness, then it is also an adequate medium for deciding an eternal unhappiness. Here is the core of the problem, although the proofs which the orthodox have propounded are devoid of all elementary concepts.

The core is simply that the eternal eludes decision in time because it presupposes itself.

VI A 62   n.d., 1845

« **3634**

Montaigne[1273] expresses it well (III, p. 84): "Everyone who is expecting punishment suffers it; and everyone who has deserved it expects it."

VIII¹ A 278   n.d., 1847

« **3635**

Another way men excuse themselves either for shamelessly participating in some injustice committed against a man or for cravenly not daring to show sympathy for him, not daring to step forward, is to say: "It is God's punishment upon him." However solemn and sacred it appears, God's punishment is upon him—therefore you have permission to go ahead and commit injustice against him, therefore you are exempted from standing by him! Suppose it were God's punishment (although as a rule that kind of talk seems to appear on the occasions when the situation is just the opposite, when it merely expresses that men find it more comfortable to shunt guilt over onto the innocent one and say he is guilty rather than say: We others are the guilty ones)—is not my relationship, therefore, to such a person exactly the same as to every other man, is it for me to get mixed up in this situation? O, hypocrisy!

VIII[1] A 527   *n.d.*, 1848

« 3636

Here we see the difference between a pagan and a Chrisitan view. The fact that God defers punishment is explained by Christianity as his patience and compassion, his wanting to give the sinner time to repent and reform, and then even exempt him from the punishment, or in any case to let it come at a moment when it falls more gently because he is reconciled with God. Paganism represents God's patience in punishing as a kind of sadism which knows that later punishment pains the most. Thus, for example, Plutarch[1274] in a little essay about the slowness of divine punishment.

X[1] A 461   *n.d.*, 1849

« 3637

Forgiveness of sins and atonement do not mean simply that God waives every punishment but that the sufferer now suffers his punishment in an entirely different way because he knows that he is reconciled with God.

It is a crass misunderstanding to think that atonement should exempt one from punishment. No, the spiritual consolation in the forgiveness of sins is that the sinner gains the confident courage to dare to believe that God is gracious toward him, although he still suffers his punishment. But that is a genuine transubstantiation with regard to punishment.

X[1] A 462   *n.d.*, 1849

« 3638

The words which are found some place in the second part of *Either/Or*[1275] could be a good theme for a sermon.

It is not dreadful that I have to suffer punishment when I have acted badly; it would be dreadful if I could act badly—and there were no punishment.

X[2] A 115   *n.d.*, 1849

« **3639** *Collision*

A man may have sinned in many ways without therefore becoming liable to civil punishment, even if his guilt became notorious; but is God then not justified in requiring that a man expose himself to punishment of a kind different from that which could result if his guilt became evident.

I have thought about this immeasurably, and the collision is worked out after a fashion in some of the earlier attempts in the first journal, journal JJ, the one in octavo [i.e., VI A 31–32, 47, 55–59, 61; VII¹ A 6, 7, 21],[1276] under the title: *de occultis non judicat ecclesia.*[1277]

On the one hand it might seem analogous to tempting God if, when a person's guilt is not known, is not liable to civil punishment, he then wants to declare it. On the other hand it can be true religiousness. Suppose a man resolved for that reason to forfeit all his life's happiness, humanly speaking.

O that I lived at another time, when there was still a little bit of sympathy for these collisions of mine, which are truly Christian. But here I live in the middle of Christendom with thoughts like these, so alienated, so bereft of sympathy and understanding that I am practically treated as deranged if I seriously want to describe such collisions.

x^2 A 156 *n.d.,* 1849

« **3640** *The Measure of Distance*

Once it was like this: irresponsibly, obstinately, people tried to dodge the thought of an eternal punishment—nowadays even ludicrousness intervenes; the culture of the whole world gives one assurances that it is nonsense and that a person makes himself ludicrous by having such thoughts.

x^2 A 552 *n.d.,* 1850

« **3641**

The younger Fichte[1278] (in his *Ethics*, para. 249, in his evaluation of the Englishman Bentham, who defends the use of capital punishment for murderers and the leaders of an insurrection) observes in connection with the latter that it is a very fitting punishment and that it is a shortsighted softheartedness on the part of present lawmakers to abolish capital punishment for political criminals simply because the latter are impelled by a misguided conviction "quite as if only the subjective element, the opinion, were the crime and as if the enormous arrogance of wanting overtly to force others into his views by all violent means were not much more criminal.''

x^4 A 74   *n.d.*, 1851

« 3642 *Augustine*

declares that the words "Adam, where are you?" signify that God punitively reminds Adam that now he is no longer in God but outside of God.

Böhringer I, pt. 3, p. 498 top.[1279]

x^4 A 174   *n.d.*, 1851

« 3643 *The Distance Indicator*

The following can presumably be regarded as an essentially Christian observation, undiluted by human foolishness, nonsense, and knavery:

Man is born in sin, enters the world by a criminal act, his existence is a crime—procreation is the fall.

Since it is by means of a criminal act, a sin, it is not difficult to guess where one arrives at birth—he enters into a prison, this world is a prison.

And the punishment (as always, the punishment fits the sin)—yes, the punishment is: to exist [*at være til*]. Since to exist through procreation displeases God, the punishment is precisely this: Go ahead and have your fun; you will get tired of it eventually; you will get so sick and tired of this life that you will thank God for getting out of it sometime through death.

Thus, from a Christian point of view, death is not a punishment; on the contrary, it shows God's compassion for these miserable creatures in that it ends their existence [*Tilværelse*]. Another thing, as a painful catastrophe death can be regarded as a part of the punishment, the punishment the child suffers in punishment for the sin of his parents.

—Now measure the distance of this view from what we call Christianity: a purely pagan sensuality, where the propagation of the race is supposed to be life's earnestness, where the best thing one can do is to give a child life, etc.

xi^1 A 289   *n.d.*, 1854

« 3644 *The Divine Punishment: To Ignore*

That this is, according to God's conception (who is pure, infinite subjectivity),[1280] the most extreme, most frightful punishment, I have pointed out elsewhere [xi¹ A 381, 554]—also, the fact that one is not aware of it leads him into the nonsense that if something succeeds, then God has no objection, and this explains, for example, why Christendom (which is nothing else than the fall from Christianity) is [regarded as] well-pleasing to God—"for otherwise he would surely intervene and punish." But there is no sense of God's majesty and [in Christendom] (although Christian) the essentially Christian basic idea is completely foreign—namely, that God punishes only those he loves,[1281] only his beloveds become unhappy in this world, etc.

But I have discussed this sufficiently elsewhere.[1282] Here I wish to illustrate something marvelous, if I dare speak so, about God. One could say, for example: An omnipresent being—how is it possible for him to ignore anything, even the least little thing.

But here, you see, is where the truth that God is pure subjectivity bears down again. Even in relations between men it is readily seen that not much skill is needed to ignore someone who is not present. But when the task is to ignore someone who stands right in front of a person—well, only extraordinary human subjectivities can perform such a feat. And nothing is quite as deadly as having to endure, as having to put up with, being ignored, even though present, by a superior subjectivity.

It is the same with God. Although omnipresent, he is so self-contained that, ignoring, he can be related as if he were infinitely far away. But where the humanly superior subjectivity who punishes someone in his presence by ignoring him actually may be said to need the self-satisfaction of showing that he can ignore, God, again, is infinite subjectivity to the extent that he punitively ignores to the extent that the one so punished does not even notice it, which again in God's view is the worst punishment, even worse than if the sinner came to perceive it. For God considers (and he really cannot be blamed for it) that everything, everything centers on being happy to exist for him. The most terrible punishment, therefore, is that in which the sinner is not even aware that he is being punished.

O, but into what miserable wretchedness Christendom has dragged your majesticness, you who are the only majesty. It almost seems as if you were the one who needed us men, or as if you, as sovereign, needed us men—and thus it is forgotten to what extent you do not need us men, and also how infinite your love is if you become involved with men.

xi² A 96 *n.d.*, 1854

QUALITATIVE DIFFERENCE

« 3645

There is beauty and the power of the eternal in this single word of Luther[1283] on the Epistle lesson from Philippians 2: Christ humbled himself—not: he was humbled. O, infinite elevation, of which it holds true with categorical necessity: there was in heaven, on earth, in the abyss no one who could humble him—he humbled himself.

Here is Christ's infinitely qualitative difference from every man: he himself, without conditions, must give consent to every humiliation he suffers and approve that he will submit to this humiliation. This is infinite elevation over suffering, but also qualitatively infinite, more intensive suffering.

x^2 A 296 *n.d.,* 1849

« 3646 *Category*

With regard to everything human it holds true that the more one thinks about it, the better one understands it. With regard to the divine it holds true that the more one thinks about it, the less he understands it. There is a qualitative difference here, which makes it impossible for the relationship to be otherwise; the qualitative heterogeneity between God and man must manifest precisely this relationship.

Is one therefore supposed to give up thinking about the divine? Fool, no! If possible you are to use every moment for it, and with every moment properly used in this way you will learn to wonder more.

But if someone says to you that the relationship is otherwise, that the more you think about the divine the better you understand it, then you shall say: You lie in your throat.

Consider a purely human relationship. Consider a genuinely superior person. You will find that you seem at the outset to be very close to understanding him—and the more you are involved with him in earnest the more you will wonderingly admit that you do not understand.

Lies and untruth and deception always coyly pretend at the outset to be valuable; truth at the outset always seems very inexpensive, but something is sure to happen the more you become involved in it. Then the wondrous thing occurs—that which you bought originally at a lower price you now see is worth a higher price, and it continues to rise. In the relation between man and man, however, there is a limit; in the relation between man and God there is never any limit, least of all in eternity. No, when wonder has penetrated through the bottleneck of time, then in eternity it first becomes thoroughly limitless. Therefore the believer longs for eternity, so that he can get room in that boundlessness for his limitless wonder, with which he had difficulties in time just as one in close quarters cannot move about.

x^3 A 23   *n.d.*, 1850

« 3647 *What Is Human—What Is Christian*

"What is human and what is Christian are one and the same" has now become the slogan. It is the absolutely correct expression of the fact that Christianity has been abolished.[1284]

Voltaire is supposed to have said somewhere that he would not believe in the reality of hereditary nobility before it was historically verified that a child had been born with spurs. Likewise I say: Until further notice I intend to stay by the old idea that the essentially Christian and the human are contrasting qualities; I intend to stick to this until informed that a child has been born who is by nature or is innately characterized by self-denial. What Voltaire speaks of, being born with spurs, is not so impossible, at least involves no contradiction —but that self-denial is natural to man is utter nonsense.

Yet this kind of thing is written everywhere. Someone writes a book on the identity of the human and the Christian; another quotes it and modifies it a little, etc. The whole thing is utterly unhuman. No one on his own thinks of the simple experiment—to shut his door and in privacy talk with himself and ask himself: Is this really true, now?

x^4 A 258   *n.d.*, 1851

« 3648 *An Explanation Which Is Still Too Exalted for a Man*

How much easier it was in those times when some of the most difficult problems in Christianity were explained by means of the devil.

When a man genuinely wills to serve God and suffers misfortune because of it, when a man denies himself in order to please God and suffers misfortune for it, when it seems as if he would be far better off not involving himself with God—it was explained in former times by means of the devil. God was the giver of good gifts—the other came from the devil, who did it in defiance of God, so that God almost suffered together under it.

However, this explanation is inadequate, for if it comes from the devil then, to be sure, God is responsible for it.

The explanation lies elsewhere, in God's nature, in God's, if I dare say so, infinite distinction as spirit. The very fact that when one does his will and it appears (through the misfortune) as if he is displeased means: I am Spirit, infinite distance. On the other side it means: I require of you that you shall be spirit. This distance is qualitatively far, far removed from that of a father in relation to his son, for when the child simply does what the father wants, the father dances for joy. But God, who is love, is nevertheless spirit, and therefore there is an infinite distance, practically equivalent to a child's having to say of his father: He is crazy, for when I have nothing to do with him at all, don't do anything he wants me to do, I get along fine with him, and it seems as if he is very gracious and lenient, and not until I involve myself with him and really do what he wants me to do does he seem to get angry.

No man is able to comprehend this, and that is why the N.T. also teaches that God's spirit must help man to be able to comprehend that this is out of love, that "Spirit" is unable to love in another way.

Incidentally, this is relevant to something which is completely overlooked in our age. It is absolutely correct that in this world it seems that and is a fact that one can get along fine in the world just the same if he simply has nothing to do with God—this is nothing less than a Christian observation, and the ungodly and the hypocrite and the irresponsible as well can be deceived by it. But that is possible because God's punishment on man in this world is to ignore him[1285] —in the eyes of God a frightful punishment, of course, since God has an infinite conception of himself. On the other hand, one who adheres to God and whom God does not choose to ignore is unable to get along fine in this world. But the danger (in God's view, he who considers that this world is evil) is precisely in getting along fine in this world, coming through it triumphantly, and thereby being prevented from using this life well for entry, if possible, into eternity.

XI[1] A 2   n.d., 1854

« 3649 *A Mistake*

Since, according to God's Word, there must be a qualitative difference, yes, a difference of incongruity between God and man, it is certainly easy to see that one is able to find out what Christianity is only by unconditionally taking God's Word literally.

The alternative, which we humans like to avail ourselves of, is a mistake—namely, to apply what we ourselves are able to think up.

It is not convenient for us men to take Christianity literally; thus we have hit upon trying to improve it by patching it up. But for one thing patching simply does not make something better (when it is a matter of tearing up something whole in order to patch it), and for another it is unfortunate that we men are not cut out of the same cloth (indeed, there is a relation of incongruity between being God and being man), but then a patch is the worst of all mistakes.

XI^1 A 67   *n.d.*, 1854

« 3650 *An Arithmetic Problem*

Christianity predicates contrast between God and man, a contrast like that between life and death.

Now do a little calculating! If there are 1,000 Christians, is there not already a possibility that the contrast will disappear? The [possibility] grows with every 100,000, with every million—and ultimately when the whole world has become Christian, the contrast between God and man has disappeared—Christianity no longer exists.

Consequently one of two things: either the whole business of a million Christians is legitimate—in which case God has miscalculated, has established wrong ratios, or, or—the whole business of millions of Christians and a Christian world is a big swindle.

No, to be a Christian is to suffer in this world—and then eternity. On the other hand, God does not want to know about the swindle of the whole world's calling itself Christian in order to do away with suffering. Christianity is not a promise for this life (that is Judaism); it is a promise for eternity—but in this life a suffering.

XI^1 A 495   *n.d.*, 1854

REALITY, ACTUALITY

« **3651**

Where the poetic is concerned, a stronger and stronger effort is continually required in order to achieve actuality, just as in the experience of Pharoah when he dreamed a second time (after having been awake) and came closer to the actuality of his dream, as much closer as an ear of corn is a more concrete symbol of a fruitful year than a cow.

II A 551   August 31, 1839

« **3652**

What is contingency?
Its connection to the concept of actuality.
Aristotle's two requirements for voluntary action, that it must have spontaneity and knowledge.
The scholastics required still a third: contingency.
Leibniz[1286] has included this.

IV C 71   *n.d.*, 1842–43

« **3653**

[When the last part of the *Logic*[1287] is given the heading][1288] "*Actuality,*" which Hegel has done and the Hegelian school did again and again [the advantage is gained that it seems as if through logic the highest were already reached, or, if one prefers, the lowest.]

V B 49:1   *n.d.*, 1844

« **3654**

13. [Instead of recognizing that existing ethically is actuality,] actuality in the sense of existence [*Existents*], [the age has grown overwhelmingly contemplative . . . . .].[1289]

14. The only actuality which I do not change into a possibility by thinking it is my own, because my actuality *allem meinem Denken zuvorkomt,*[1290] so I do not get hold of my actuality by thinking and only by thinking, an actuality which is preserved essentially not by thinking it but by existing [*existere*].[1291]

VI B 54:13, 14   *n.d.*, 1845

692

« **3655**

From the religious point of view, to achieve "actuality" [*"Vir-kelighed"*] means: without being covered up by a doctrinal objectivity about the believer in general, what he does, without being covered up by an official and professional objectivity, promptly and directly to set one's God-relationship into actuality, not talking at all about how the believer takes everything to God but saying: In this matter I have deliberated with God and am acting out of confidence in God. One does not say: The believer believes this and that, but I believe this and that, and on the strength of this faith I act in this very concrete instance.

This is how actuality is achieved, this is how God can become present, this is how the spell is broken, this is how illusions are blasted, and God is able to communicate [*communicere*] with actuality.

x^2 A 197   *n.d.,* 1849

REASON, UNDERSTANDING

« **3656**

How little the understanding [*Forstanden*] can achieve in a speculative sense is best seen in this, that when it reaches the highest level it
must explain the highest by using a *self-contradictory* expression. Numerous expressions in the *Formula of Concord*[1292] serve as examples.

I A 243   September 19, 1836

« **3657**

If the understanding [*Forstanden*], feeling, and will are essential
qualifications in a man, belong essentially to human nature, then all
this chaff that the world-development[1293] now occupies a higher level
vanishes into thin air, for if there is a movement in world history,[1294]
then it belongs essentially to providence, and man's knowledge of it
is highly imperfect.

Therefore, however much the understanding advances,[1295] religion still can never be abolished, not only for those without authority,
who probably would continue, but also for those with authority.

The great individual is great simply because he has everything at
once.

Any other view overlooks the significance of the individuals in the
race and reflects only on the history of the race, from which it would
follow that *essentially* different men would be produced at different
times and the universal unity in being a human being would be abrogated.

Thus the great individual is not thereby different from the insignificant individual by possessing something essentially different or by
having it in another form (for this would also be an essential difference,
particularly according to modern form theory) but by having everything to a greater degree.

The collateral.[1296]

IV C 78   n.d., 1842–43

« **3658**

To what extent does the imagination play a role in logical thought, to what extent the will, to what extent is the conclusion a resolution.

IV C 89   *n.d.*, 1842–43

« **3659** *Understanding* [Forstand]—*Faith*

How far am I bound in responsibility to what my understanding says; I mean, to what extent does this responsibility apply: when my understanding tells me that I may not do this and this, then I must not do it.

This responsibility may hold in finite matters, but face to face with the Word of God it is impossible.

He who face to face with God's Word says: My understanding tells me I may not do this and this, consequently I will not get involved in this, denies and indeed denies God and God's Word and Christianity —obviously he may even have a brilliant career as a clergyman and teacher of Christianity—in "Christendom."

X^5 A 14   *n.d.*, 1852

REDOUBLING

« **3660**

In its elemental meaning (the expression itself) "dedication" is the concentrating of the individual within himself. When an individual begins an endeavor, conscious or in the consciousness that the endeavor, instead of leading to the achievement of finite purposes, will in fact prevent such fulfillment[1297]—he then becomes turned inwards in a self-redoubling [*Selvfordoblelse*]. This is the purely human; the religious depends upon to what extent the individual refers everything to God.

x^2 A 116   *n.d.,* 1849

« **3661**

Either qualitative redoubling [*Fordoblelse*], which in working also works against itself;[1298] *or* qualitative simplicity of character. *Tertium non datur.* [1299]

x^3 A 28   *n.d.,* 1850

« **3662** *God's Governance*

Even though God does not control everything from the outside by having the rest of the world in his power, he nevertheless wants to be governance in relation to every human being. For man is such a redoubling [*Fordoblelse*] in himself[1300] that to a degree he is his own fate insofar as he is untrue, insofar as he uses inadmissible means, etc., and despite all the protestations that it is not so, there is no one who is aware of it sooner than the person himself, and he then becomes insecure and finally trips himself. The same conditions in which a person now is he would have conquered earlier. The difference is that there was then more of truth in him, and he has now become unsure.

x^3 A 740   *n.d.,* 1851

« **3663** *Another Example of Redoubling*

Luke 21: 17–18.

"You will be hated by all for my name's sake"—consequently God will leave them in the lurch to that extent, expose them, and "yet not

696

a hair of your head will perish"—consequently they will, from another side, be the object of concern.

We human beings contrive something we call Christianity by knocking off on both sides, and thus we get the mediocrity of pure probability, where we feel most at home. But it seems to me we should nevertheless do one thing—we should admit that Christianity[1301] is not described this way in the New Testament.

XI¹ A 33   n.d., 1854

« 3664 *Double Meaning*

Everything essentially Christian has a double meaning [*Dobbelt-tydigt*], is a redoubling [*Fordoblelse*].[1302] And this is what is so strenuous, also what makes it difficult to have an understanding with others.

In the ordinary direct sense of being happy or suffering, how direct and easy it is to be understood.

But to say that suffering signifies blessedness has a double meaning. After all, one cannot straightforwardly complain about suffering if it signifies blessedness—and one is not understood if he talks about blessedness or about suffering, because the one is continually implicit in the other, and only the single meaning is directly understandable.

Incidentally, here we also see that essential Christianity is designed for a-sociality, designed to block off in the single individual's relation to God.

XI² A 65   n.d., 1854

REDUPLICATION

« 3665

No doubt there have been keener and more gifted authors than I, but I would certainly like to see the author who has reduplicated [*reduppliceret*][1303] his thinking more penetratingly than I have in the dialectic raised to the second power. It is one thing to be keenly penetrating in books, another to redouble [*fordoble*] the thought dialectically in existence. The first form of the dialectical is like a game played for nothing other than the game; reduplication is like a game in which the enjoyment is intensified by being played for high stakes. The dialectic in books is merely the dialectic of thinking, but reduplication[1304] of such thinking is action in life. But every thinker who does not reduplicate the dialectic of his thinking continuously constructs an illusion. His thinking never gains the decisive expression of action. He tries to correct misunderstandings etc. in a new book, but it is of no use, for he continues in an illusion of communication. Only the ethical thinker, by acting, can protect himself against illusions in communication.

VIII[1] A 91   *n.d.*, 1847

« 3666

A thinking person really cannot be blamed for wishing himself out of a world where literally there are not 10 in 100,000 who have thought about existence in such a way that they have been willing at all times to express in their existence what they have thought up to this time—and where, on the other hand there are certainly 99,995 who judge and condemn.

VIII[1] A 201   *n.d.*, 1847

« 3667

The curious thing about the way men talk with respect to God or about their relationship to God is that it never seems to occur to them that God also hears it.[1305] Someone says: At present I do not have the opportunity or the concentration to think about God—but after a while. Or even better, a young man says: "Now I am too young; I want to

698

enjoy life first—and then." I wonder if it would be possible to talk this way if they thought that God hears it.

But reduplication [*Reduplikationen*] is almost never seen. I really do not know one single religious author (except perhaps Augustine) who actually reduplicates his thought.

IX A 121   n.d., 1848

« 3668

Reduplication [*Reduplikationen*] is the essentially Christian; it is not different in the way one doctrine is different from another but is essentially different in that it is the doctrine which reduplicates, and thus the teacher[1306] is of importance. From the Christian point of view, the question is constantly raised not only of the Christian truth of what one says but also of the *how*[1307] of the one who says it.

Thus when someone in silk with decorations and stars declares that the truth must suffer persecution[1308] etc., then this combination, this juxtaposition produces only an esthetic relationship. His presentation is moving—while his character gives assurance that it is not like this any more, of course—that it was so in the old days. It is true the man-in-silk says (for he is orthodox—no one dares deny that): "Remember, you do not know at what moment you must suffer for the truth," and then the man-in-silk weeps (for he imagines that he is a martyr); but his listeners think something like this: Forget it! The man's character and his whole life assure us otherwise; it is no longer true that the truth is persecuted. Woe to him! —When out in the country in a quiet rural scene a Reverend Sir swears and thunders and crosses himself as he talks about how the world persecutes the Christian (His Reverence included), it is easy to see that this person is a rogue who flatters his vanity by imagining himself persecuted out here in rural peace and security, associating only with farmers and the like —no, old man, this, too, is comedy. If it is going to be earnest, then please take it to the metropolis and onto the big stage.

IX A 163   n.d., 1848

« 3669

If I could only have the experience of meeting a passionate thinker, that is, someone who honestly and honorably is constantly prepared to express in his life what he has understood![1309] But where are such thinkers? The majority all too soon find security for their lives in countless ways. They marry, have children, have a public office, have the prospect of a certain appointment, etc. Such a man perhaps reads and studies, understands that the only true situation for being in the truth, from a Christian point of view, is to become a martyr. That he understands, and that is what he lectures about. But even if it is merely a matter of giving up a little gratuity of ten dollars, he could not dream of it. Such a man does an enormous amount of harm—and why? Simply because he talks and lectures about the truth. Usually there is extreme controversy about the extent to which someone is speaking the truth. The next thing, the main point—whether a person does it [the truth] —is utterly forgotten in the zeal to fight the person who is presenting untruths.

IX A 344   n.d., 1848

« **3670**

An example of deficient reduplication in a situation.

A speaker at a public meeting says: I am not looking for applause (general applause!); I want only the truth etc. (applause from the left). I go straight ahead, looking neither to the right nor the left (applause from the right and the center) etc.

IX A 415   n.d., 1848

« **3671**

Men actually never get any farther than going around talking about the good, about what ought to be done, but that there is so much to hinder, and therefore etc. —and regard doing it as ridiculous exaggeration.

IX A 456   n.d., 1848

« **3672**

It is not inconceivable that Christ, in earlier conversations, simply to show the disciples that His kingdom was not of this world and simply to show them how easy it is to confuse the two, showed them that with one single stroke He could change everything into an earthly kingdom and himself into an earthly messiah. He then would have taken the occasion to warn them about the way they proclaimed his teaching, for the really decisive factor always resides in the *second time,* in the mode in which the truth is spoken, in the reduplication of existing [*at existere*] and acting. For example, one can proclaim a kingdom which is not of this world and not notice that the whole thing becomes secularized by the mode in which he proclaims it.

To repeat, Christ very likely showed his disciples in earlier conversations how close together the two are, that one little push is all that is necessary to secularize the whole affair. And that is perhaps what influenced Judas to betray him—to force him with a little push to give the undertaking another direction.

Another interpretation—Judas was a sceptic who doubted and could not wholly believe in the holiness of Christ but had a worldly-wise suspicion that there still might be some ambition lurking somewhere underneath it all. So he risked the experiment in order to expose the supposed ambition; in any event he did not think the catastrophe would turn out to be so frightful. Therefore his words:[1310] I have betrayed innocent blood. There is something about these words —as if he now for the first time had really been convinced that Christ was the pure one. Why? Because now, indeed, Christ had stood the test and remained true to himself.

On the whole, Judas must be construed as being far more than a mere scoundrel. When Christ said: I have chosen them myself, he said it of Judas, too. And the whole relationship must be made much more actual, far beyond appearances.

IX A 474   *n.d.*, 1848

« 3673

God's creative word creates omnipotently from nothing.

A speaker, an orator, produces an opposite effect: he talks about how the truth is scoffed at—and becomes honored and esteemed himself.

An existential thinker produces the effect he talks about. When he says the truth is persecuted—he hits so hard that he is hit in return and he can point to himself and say: You can see it on me.

X^2 A 541   *n.d.*, 1850

« 3674 *The Number Carried*

It is what I have repeated and repeated but can never repeat enough, and it was really this that alerted me to Christianity's collision with the world: the trouble, the hitch, the difficulty is not at all where it is thought to be. The difficulty is that if there is someone who wants to act according to what the pastor says, he is not permitted to do it, he is laughed to scorn (because he more or less expresses love to the neighbor), made fun of (because he is disinterested), persecuted etc.

O, shortsighted me, whom life itself had to grab hold of to open my eyes to this—otherwise I would have completely overlooked Christianity's collision further out. Christ was indeed the man who could fulfill his own teaching, he was, in fact, the existential expression of his own teaching—and he is the very one who collides, and so dreadfully. And after him all the martyrs etc.

But this, again, proves that Christianity has been abolished essentially. That can be seen in the proportions. We have the clergy, they proclaim the doctrine; the clergy's charge against the age is substantially this: There is no one who acts according to what we say. Consequently—for this is indirectly implied—all we demand is that you do what we say. Alas, here is where Christianity begins in earnest; it begins with the difficulties, sufferings, etc. bound up with following the doctrine, the fact that one is not permitted to do it but must suffer for it.

X^2 A 545   n.d., 1850

« 3675 *The Measure of Distance*

How far one is personally and existentially from the essentially Christian can be seen in this way: the same expressions, ideas, etc, used in the sermon (for example: that all life is an education, that we should take everything to God, etc.) and which are accepted there—if in actual life a person were to say such things about himself and his life (and the pastor does indeed say that we should live by what we have heard), people would find it either ridiculous and in bad taste or arrogant.

X^2 A 573   n.d., 1850

« 3676 *The Rigorousness of Reduplication*

If I am convinced about a matter and enthusiastically say so and then see how the great mass accept it, is it not asking too much of me that I, instead of promptly rejoicing over it, ought to take a look, become alarmed, yes, even become suspicious that I am on a wrong path, that there is a misunderstanding, because it has been so very easy to be understood and the truth is received with open arms?

Nevertheless, the truth is this rigorous.

X^3 A 124   n.d., 1850

« 3677

In margin of 3676 (X^3 A 124):

But it must be remembered that here, also, a kind of self-torturing can make its appearance; yet it can also be true of some that they actually do appropriate what they have heard. Luther[1311] declares that to Christian faith belong faith—works of love—and then persecution for the faith and love (the passage is marked in my copy of his sermons). He also says in another passage[1312] (which also is marked in my copy) that where there is no persecution there is something wrong with the preaching. However, it is my opinion that here again one has to be wary of self-torture, otherwise in bringing the teaching into the world it could become the task of incessantly taking care that it not enter in but that it be hurled back. Here we must commend ourselves to God and ask him to watch over us.

X^3 A 125   n.d.

« 3678 *About Myself*

Qvantum satis *of the Essentially Christian for the Purely Human*

Conscientiously and pertinently we perfect ourselves in our ability to present the right, the good, to depict the wrong paths. We think it is to be expected of a man: in any case it is good breeding.

But to want to start accomplishing it in daily life—that, indeed, would be silly, almost affected, approaching narrow-mindedness, scrupulousness, embarrassing to oneself and embarrassing to others. Besides, we think there is no point in beginning such things. If you embark upon it, Christianity becomes something dangerous which takes the whole hand when you give it a little finger—and then you have to quit anyway—so it was silly to begin. Consequently *principiis obsta.* The appropriate *qvantum satis* is that you know how to present and depict tastefully, beautifully, strikingly, that you are psychologist enough to point out human bypaths—but then no more.

X^3 A 220   n.d., 1850

« 3679 *Scandal*

Act just once in such a manner that your action expresses that you fear God alone and man not at all—you will immediately in some measure cause a scandal.

The only thing that manages to dodge scandal is that which out of fear of men and deference to men is completely conformed to the secular mentality.

X^3 A 225   n.d., 1850

« 3680 *Another Example of Craftiness*

If someone in serving the religious goes a little beyond the purely secular practice of treating it merely as a job and as a means to all kinds of earthly advantages, the cry promptly goes up: "Such things can only be required of an apostle; to attempt any such thing is to want to make oneself into an apostle." Aha, this way they win in two directions: not only do they find a brilliant excuse for refraining from such things— no, it is commendable, indeed, it is humility, but they also find a charge against the person who actually does such things—after all, it is presumptuous to make oneself into an apostle this way.

Yes, the world is crafty. But let us look a bit more closely. I do not know that it is in any way displeasing to God that in order to serve the truth a man is willing to make sacrifices, suffer for doing it, yes, even if it came to the point of being put to death. But I do know very well that God is not pleased when a man goes ahead and wants to make himself an apostle.

Here, you see, is the crux of the matter. The trademark of an apostle is not suffering but divine authority.[1313] All the witnesses of truth have also suffered, suffered unto death, without thinking of making themselves into apostles.

But the craftiness is promptly to pitch the matter so high that one is freed from doing it, wins honor and esteem for his humility in not doing it, and finds the occasion to indict the one who, without even remotely claiming authority, to say nothing of divine authority, makes sacrifices and then gets the added burden of being severely criticized because he makes sacrifices.

x^3 A 232   *n.d.*, 1850

« 3681 *"Grace"—Reduplication of the Essentially Christian*

A reduplication is always implicit in the essentially Christian. When "grace" is a matter of living a jolly, carefree life, then grace is taken in vain. Grace means that I must also die to the world, something the prototype [*Forbilledet*] expressed during his life, wheras his suffering and death was the acquisition of grace. I must also die to the world —and yet be saved by grace.

The human concept of grace is: Now you shall be completely free; that's why it is grace.

The essentially Christian is: Now you shall suffer and suffer—and then be saved by grace.

The mark of offense is readily seen. Just to have to listen to any talk about grace may be an offense to the natural man insofar as he wants to justify himself. But he says: All right, let it be grace then; I'll accept it humbly, but then I also want to be free. Alas, no, says Christianity. You will come to suffer and suffer—and then you nevertheless must humble yourself under the fact that it is by grace that you are saved.

Alas, only Christianity has God's idea of how infinitely sublime God is; we men make God rather trivial.

x³ A 278   n.d., 1850

« **3682**

Visby[1314] was right today in observing (in the sermon on the Gospel about the false prophets) that we sometime judge erroneously in believing a man's beautiful words and phrases while his life expresses the opposite, but that sometimes we also judge erroneously in concluding from what a man says that his life is corrupt, for sometimes a man's life is even better than what he says.

x³ A 299   n.d., 1850

« **3683 *Come Unto Me All of You*[1315]**

If the object is to say these words esthetically, then the art would be to say them in such a way that literally everybody, if possible, comes.

Christ said them in such a way that the effect was that everybody ran away from him.

Here again is the reduplication which is in everything essentially Christian.

Christ says: Come unto me all of you—but on the other hand he uses such means to repel that the effect is that everyone flees.

The merely human object would be to say: Come—and then use all the possible means to entice; Christianly, the object is to say: Come —and then use almost every means to repel.

O the unfathomable depth of pain and sadness in Christ—to say: Come to me, all of you—and know in advance what the effect would be.

Is any more proof for the divinity of Christ needed than his being able to bring himself to say these words: Come unto me, *all of you.* A man, Socrates, who understood that if he had invited all, just about everybody would have fled, a man, Socrates, therefore changes the invitation and talks about "the single individual." Prior knowledge of the effect changes the invitation for a man; but God changes nothing, he declares unchangingly: Come to me, *all of you.* Socrates also knew that all could benefit from his teaching, but he foresaw what the effect would be, and he changed the invitation. Christ knows eternally, divinely, that all need him; he knows in advance what the effect will be —but he does not alter the invitation. Divine!

x³ A 377   n.d., 1850

« **3684** *My Thesis*[1316]

My thesis is not that the substance of what is proclaimed in Christendom as Christianity is not Christianity. No, my thesis is that the *proclamation* is not Christianity. I am fighting about a *how,* a reduplication. It is self-evident that without reduplication Christianity is not Christianity.

x^3 A 431   *n.d.*, 1850

« **3685**

A passage in Anti-Climacus's *Practice
in Christianity, III*

He declares that Christianity cannot become the object of "observations."[1317]

To this it could be objected that in former days "Meditations" was a more common title.

This may be answered as follows: It all depends on the one who meditates—whether he is a witness of the truth, who suffers for Christianity, or someone who existentially expresses Christianity's heterogeneity with the world—well, why not?

But the danger comes when the author, the meditator, is an official, and the proclamation of Christianity becomes more and more secularized, an officially appointed job.

Anti-Climacus should therefore have been more thorough and said: Christianity cannot become the object of observations, particularly not the observations of officials whose entire existence is otherwise totally heterogeneous to the essentially Christian; whereas, to repeat, it is entirely another matter when one who meditates, the author, is someone whose life expresses that he understands superbly that Christianity actually cannot become the object for observations.

Observations on the part of one whose life expresses that he translates the observations into existence is one thing; observations on the part of one who lets his existence remain on the outside, yes, even has it in completely opposite categories, is something else again.

x^3 A 545   *n.d.*, 1850

« **3686** *Religiousness—Politics*

It is increasingly clear to me that the main issue is "how" something is introduced into the world, the reduplicating of the proposition in the operation-form related to the proposition.

Yes, in brief it can be said that the difference between politics and religion is that politics wants nothing to do with this reduplication: the politician is too busy, too worldly, too finite for that.

For reduplication is the slowest operation of all, is actually the operation of eternity.

What happened when Luther introduced the reformation idea? He, too, the great reformer, became impatient, did not reduplicate forcefully enough, accepted the aid of the princes—that is, he actually became a politician for whom winning is more important than "how" one wins. From a religious point of view, the only important thing is "how," simply because the religious person is absolutely assured that he or his cause will win—yes, that it actually has won—therefore he has to pay attention only to the "how," that is, to reduplicate.

Take a minor illustration. What is wrong with the Spandet-Grundt-vigian affair in parliament right now? This—that they do not reduplicate in relation to a religious cause—that is, they do not serve it religiously but politically, they call for the aid of Christianity's worst enemies so that they can force their way through by voting. But that is irreligious: on the other hand it was politically proper of Vespasian to say that one should not smell money—that tax money from a house of prostitution smells just as good as any other.

Here, again, is the impatience that understands that it takes long-range views to carry through if one is to reduplicate—that is, religiously serve a religious cause in our day. So one jumps at the advantages of a surface harmony with political radicalism and wants to win with its help.

Truly every such attempt paves the way more and more for the death of religion, for men become more and more contemptuous of religion. Momentarily it looks as if religion is helped, but it is simply the road to ruin, for afterward the politician, seeing that religion is demoralized, scorns it.

x^3 A 696   *n.d., 1850*

« 3687 *Reduplication*

In respect to finite and earthly goods (which precisely because of their inferiority do not relate to any reduplication), the manner in which I get them (provided it is not inadmissible[1318]) is more or less of no consequence; and it can easily become prudishness to be too strict.

But in respect to spiritual goods the manner in which they are obtained is itself the good, the expression for my concept of what constitutes a good thing. The manner may be of such a nature that I must say: No, on that condition I do not want to have it; it would be making a fool of myself.

X⁴ A 75 *n.d.*, 1851

« **3688** ***Private Conversation***

This, too, belongs to the demoralization—that in private conversations a person betrays that he knows very well how lunatic everything is; but officially—no, he is not such a lunatic as to say it officially.

Here it is again true that it is a grave self-denunciation to have understood something as right without acting on it, consequently that a person condemns himself with this kind of talking—if he does not also make the humbling admission.[1319] And that he is no doubt disinclined to do.

X⁴ A 128 *n.d.*, 1851

« **3689** ***Vinet***[1320]

As mentioned,[1321] he is not in character; he is really not even an author.

He lectures about individuality, about the *I,* the single individual, but he is infinitely far from the final reduplication, from saying: I, Vinet —that is, existentially tying the knot.[1322]

Yet this is certainly due in part to the enormous setting and the enormous means of communication. To use the French press for God knows how many millions—it would take a god to venture this final reduplication. Here again the fundamental defect in our time is apparent. In ancient days there was a division into smaller units, and so it was manageable: Socrates attended to Athens—and then it was I, Socrates.

What sort of presentation does Vinet make? It is rhetorical, to an extent actually socialistic. In his style one notes at once how far he is from the final existential reduplication—namely, that whatever happens he is himself a single individual. There is in his style nothing of that jabbing, gadflying, teasing which in lecturing about asociality is asocial—. No, Vinet writes like everyone else who wants to gain, *directly* gain, adherents to his point of view.

If I am not greatly mistaken, Vinet is so insecure in his theory that one could, if a crowd shouts its approval of it, get him to go along with them seriously and completely forget reduplication of what he has said about the single individual.

In observing Vinet I feel generally quite clear that what has helped me [go] somewhat farther out is that my setting has been so small.

X^4 A 190 *n.d., 1851*

« 3690 The Interesting—and Crime, a Reduplication[1323] in Being a Criminal

Adequate attention is not given to the fact that crime, like everything else, also has taken a step forward in reflection.

A reduplicated criminal of such a kind follows this pattern, for example. He is a young man, cultured, scientifically educated, musical, emotionally sensitive and impressionable,* writes poetry, moves in exclusive social circles, is interesting, women find a trace of melancholy in him, and if it is occasionally whispered about that there is something strange about him, women are of the opinion that it is something buried way back in his past and is the cause of his melancholy, but now he is upright, charming, "and so melancholy."

That is what he is like. But a fellow has to live, and live jauntily, live big. So he organizes a career—for example, he is secretly the leader of a little band of thieves, secretly devotes a certain time to managing and directing its operations, and claims 30–50% of the loot for himself. Under the circumstances it cannot be otherwise; just as a public official works his set hours every day, just as a merchant works in his own way —so, too, he manages his business, his way of making money, and money he must have, a lot of it.

Actually, there is no concept. With demonic callousness he has set a quota of so and so many crimes a year in order to live in style—no swerving from it; as for the rest, you can strive in every way to be charming and agreeable and enjoy life in the selected social circle.

The reduplication consists in the leading of a double life. Think of "a wasted talent," or "a young man gone astray," or "an out-and-out criminal," etc.—no such person leads a double life, no, during the time the talent is being wasted it is wasted in all its forms. The reduplication, however, is the demonic consciousness: the ability to be so and so much a criminal during the year according to definite quota control—and at the same time to be charming, cultured, etc.

A reduplicated criminal of this sort is, of course, most dangerous. But he will dupe women, the average run of men, even less skilled police detectives. Whoever does not catch him right in the act will always think: Well, maybe he was like that once, but now he is better

—"O, he is so genial, so sensitive, cultured, interesting, and melancholy."

In the meantime this takes place even if such criminals get involved in crimes of the kind the police are interested in, partly because there are few police detectives who understand such things, that their very deceptiveness makes such criminals the most skillful, and partly because there is scarcely the conception that these are real crimes.

But now to the reduplicated criminal who does not live by stealing and robbing—no, he lives on slander. For this he makes use of the press. Protects himself with extreme caution. Calculates: You need so and so much to live grandly. You can earn it by slander—and no swerving: it is your business, your living. Otherwise do everything to be charming, agreeable, try to win the select social group to which you belong.

Here there are no police to nab the criminal and no criminal courts to condemn him. Actually, it is a matter of public opinion formed by the thousands and thousands, among them all the nice but simple folk, above all the women etc., none of whom understand reduplication. They cannot conceive of such a person: "that he—no, he is interesting and charming and genial and sensitive and melancholy etc." And if eventually the situation may develop in such a way that if there is a quiet, keen observer who sees the criminal in him and treats him as such—then the observer will be looked upon as a maligner who wants to harm this charming man.†

How many understand the demonic—and this sort of reduplication is nothing but the demonic, and it is so far from being an excuse that it is in truth the dreadful element. But the demonic tempts, and even those who have misgivings about such a man are tempted to assume that he is, after all, a good man, that there is something good in him.

X^4 A 214   *n.d.*, 1851

« 3691

In margin of 3690 (X^4 A 214):
*Note. It is well known that as a rule there are few who are more benevolent and generous than prostitutes, and no one more easily moved to tears than a criminal—it is mood, which does not mean a thing.

X^4 A 215   *n.d.*

« 3692

In margin of 3690 (x⁴ A 214):

†And if it so happens that the conditions come to be such that a demoniac like this can achieve in a more honorable way the same earthly ends he wanted in the first place, then there is rejoicing as if it were a conversion. Highly doubtful! As soon as he can no longer get the money and influence he wants in an honorable way, he will revert, perhaps quite imperturbably, to his old ways. For this is the demonic, the imperturbability with which he maintains the fixed idea of so much a year to live on and so much influence which must be provided *a tout prix.*

x^4 A 216   *n.d.*

« 3693 *The Physical—the Spiritual*

Compare education as it was formerly and as it is now. Holberg[1324] declares somewhere that to be a physician nothing more is needed than to buy a black frock and write on the door: John Doe, General Practitioner. Similarly, it was also believed that to be a teacher and educator nothing more was needed than to buy a cane and start beating. —Peer Degn[1325] says that by the time Erasmus got it on the rump, speaking with respect, however, Peer had already been flogged three times in the presence of the school. This is no doubt commonly misinterpreted to mean that Peer is picturing himself as a bad boy who was frequently punished. No, no, Peer Degn has something quite different in mind. He is drawing upon the syllogism he himself as teacher now carries out: To educate is to flog, to be educated is to get floggings, ergo he has been excellently educated and can be proud of the fact; it is with self-esteem that he speaks of his education (the way a Magister talks about how many universities he has attended[1326]), and it is almost modest of him to speak of only three times, for seven times would be still more remarkable and a guarantee of a matchless education.

So it was with education formerly. Nowadays everything is admonition, directed only toward understanding, so that the child understands that one wishes him well, etc.—but it actually has no connection with existence.

Take a higher level. Religiously, attention has been directed entirely toward examining and understanding. No doubt this also can be strenuous, but strenuousness is, after all, essentially the transformation of existence, and that it is an enormous swindle to make it seem that if one were merely to understand the highest he would automatically do it. O, from understanding to doing there is an infinitely, infinitely greater distance than from not understanding to understanding; in the former situation there is a whole qualitative μετάβα-σις εἰς ἄλλο γένος.[1327] But we are very reluctant to move out existentially, and a whole lifetime may be spent in the work of understanding and understanding, and existence remains completely unchanged. We all laugh at the person who is supposed to come up for his matriculation examination and always says: Next time I'll take it. —But do we not all do the same—we work toward understanding and say: When we have simply understood it, we surely will do it; it will come, all right —and then we die. But if we were not hindered by death, we surely would get around to it—that is, as soon as we have properly understood it. O, the human cunning in the matter of understanding!

Fasting for a day, an action directed toward witnessing for the truth, all such things touch existence in a way quite different from studying for ten years and a hundred years. By working in the direction of understanding one takes the wrong turn, and there was more truth in the old method of promptly beginning in the sphere of action.

x⁴ A 289   n.d., 1851

« 3694   *Vinet's*[1328]   **Whole Theory**

that room must be provided so that one can reach the point of declaring his conviction is a sophism.

It all depends on what is understood by declaring's one's conviction. It ought to mean: to step forth existentially in character according to one's conviction, not to spout something about it in writing or talking.

Vinet actually pays no attention to this principle.

But this is utterly indefensible. It is far too easy to become informed about the apostolic way, to write about it, and then want to have praise for it.

No, no, you must either enter into it in character—or your task is to keep quiet.

Everything you communicate which is existentially higher than your own existence you dare communicate only in such a way that you use it to your humiliation, in such a way that no meritorious light falls on your saying it.

x⁴ A 295   n.d., 1851

« 3695

"You will be taken before kings and princes, but do not be anxious about what you are to say, for it will be given to you in the same hour."[1329]

This is then explained on the basis of the cooperation of the Holy Spirit, and quite rightly so.

But it also has a purely human interpretation. There is something artful and false in our speaking; we have our lives in completely different categories; we sit and torture ourselves to find expressions and are embarrassed in the presence of kings.

Imagine a man who has made up his mind, has understood: My life is sacrificed; there is nothing, nothing ahead of me but suffering —O, this makes him so earnest that he is unlikely to be at a loss for what he shall say, although it does not turn out to be eloquence or, least of all, oratorical technique (which does not concern him at all and right here is the secret). He is too earnest to trouble himself in the least about the world: if a person has integrity, he will not be at a loss for what he will say. The dilemma simply comes from loving ourselves and the world: the one who hates himself and the world soon makes up his mind what he will say.

X^4 A 336   *n.d.*, 1851

« 3696

It is customary to say that anyone who states that something is the will and command of God etc. and then does nothing about it makes a fool of God and mocks him who does not let himself be mocked, but I would maintain that he makes a fool of himself, for one makes a fool of oneself by saying: What I regard as supreme exercises no power over me—spineless me.

XI^2 A 332   *n.d.*, 1854

REFLECTION, THOUGHT

« **3697**

The novel has become reflective—

I A 128   n.d., 1836

« **3698**

Reflection can wind itself around a person in the most curious way. I can imagine someone's wanting to make a theatrical presentation of the fallaciousness of the age; but when he himself sits among the spectators he sees that no one, after all, takes it to heart except to detect the fallacy in his neighbor; he makes one more attempt and stages this very scene in the theater, and people laugh at it saying: Isn't it terrible how most people can see the faults of others and not their own, etc. etc.

In margin: Just as with King David,[1330] who did not understand the prophet's parable before he said: You are the man, O King!

II A 57   n.d., 1837

« **3699**

Fixed ideas are like a cramp, in the foot for example—the best remedy is to step on them.

II A 230   July 6, 1838

« **3700**

We should be able to speak of *drawing a thought,* just as we speak of drawing a breath.

II A 724   n.d., 1838

« **3701**

Real brooding [*Rugen*] over the idea ought to be concealed from all profane knowledge and interference on the part of strangers— likewise a bird will not hatch out [*udruge*] its eggs if they have been disturbed.[1331]

IV A 51   n.d., 1843

« **3702**

Self-reflection [*Selv-Reflexionen*] was a skepticism; it is overcome in pure thought. But pure thought is a still more extreme skepticism. Despite all the inwardness of self-reflection, it nevertheless could not forget its relation to actuality in the sense of actuality, its relation to the *an sich* which pursues it. Pure thought, however, is positive through having taken the whole matter imaginatively into a sphere where there is no relation to actuality at all. Pure thought does not even dream that it is skepticism—but this itself is the most extreme skepticism. If, without pressing the comparison, one were to compare skepticism with insanity,* a person who has a notion of being insane and whose life goes on amid this conflict is less mad, however, than one who triumphantly jubilates as the cleverest of all.[1332]

* *In margin:* And Danish readers will not forget that Poul Møller[1333] regarded Hegel as mad.

VI B 54:19   *n.d.*, 1845

« **3703**

[. . . the category of the apostle is specifically divine authority,] and it is precisely that which he should use. That is, in the idea of reflection he cannot become an apostle; the category of the apostle means specifically the use of divine authority.

In margin: In the idea of reflection an apostle is an impossibility; it [is] beyond it [reflection].

VIII² B 16:8   *n.d.*, 1847

« **3704** *N.B.*   *N.B.*

It has generally been thought that reflection is the natural enemy of Christianity and would destroy it. With God's help I hope to show that God-fearing reflection can tie knots again which a shallow, superficial reflection has toyed with so long. The divine authority of the Bible and everything related to it has been abolished; it looks as if one final unit of reflection is expected to finish the whole thing. But look, reflection is on the way to do a counterservice, to reset the trigger springs for the essentially Christian so that it may stand its ground—against reflection. Of course Christianity remains the same, altered in no way; not an iota is changed. But the battle becomes a different one; up until now it has been between reflection and the immediate, simple Christianity—now it becomes a battle between reflection and simplicity armed with reflection.[1334]

There is meaning in this, I believe. The task is not to comprehend Christianity but to comprehend that one cannot comprehend. This is the holy cause of faith, and reflection is therefore sanctified by being used in this way.

O, the more I think of what has been granted to me, the more I need an eternity in which to thank God.[1335]

IX A 248   *n.d.*, 1848

« **3705**

Accurate, clear, decisive, impassioned understanding is of great importance, for it facilitates action. But in this respect there is about as much difference among people as there is in the ways birds take flight. Some take off quietly and neatly from the branch on which they are perching and ascend heavenward in their flight, proudly, boldly. Others (the heavier and more indolent—crows, for example) make a big fuss when they are about to fly; they lift one foot and then promptly grab on again, and no flight takes place. Then they work their wings while they continue to cling fast with their feet; in this way they do not take wing but instead remain hanging on the branch like a lump—until finally they make enough headway to attain a kind of flight.

In so many ways men are just like this when it comes to achieving movement from understanding to action. On this point alone a sharp psychologist could have enough work for a lifetime if, after meticulous observation, he were to describe the abnormal motions which are made. For the lives of most men are and continue to be a simulated posture of a purely sensate existence. A few arrive at the proper understanding of what they should do—and then they pull back.

If one is going to act decisively in the ultimate sense of the word, he must have a boundless trust in God and venture to commit himself unconditionally to him alone. If such a person, endeavoring to love men according to the teachings of Christ, may be regarded as self-loving, he is then completely in God's power at every anxious moment, terrifyingly in a certain sense. He is perhaps worried about himself, whether or not he is loving. If he had the consolation that people regarded him as loving, it would be a relief. But people accuse him precisely because—it is a genuine God-relationship. And at any time he wishes God can agree with the people, and then the poor wretch is the most wretched of all. But surely God is not like that; yet, on the other hand, God is far out [beyond the ordinarily human] and in order to have a God-relationship one has to be completely in his power this way.

IX A 365   *n.d.*, 1848

« 3706

He who *could* not seduce men *cannot* save them either. This is the qualification of reflection.

IX A 383   *n.d.*, 1848

« 3707

If I am essentially reflective and am in the circumstance of having to act decisively, what then? Then my reflection will show me just as many possibilities *pro* as *contra*, exactly as many.[1336] And what does this mean? It means that I, the same as every other man, will please perceive that there is a providence, a guidance, a god; that the most my or any man's reflective powers achieve is to teach me to become aware of that; that here, if I dare speak this way, the toll fee must be paid. —And what do I run up against? The *absurd*. What then is the absurd? Quite simply, the absurd is this: that I, a rational being, must act in the situation where my understanding [*Forstand*], my reflection say to me: You can just as well do the one thing as the other, where my understanding and reflection say to me: You cannot act—that I nevertheless must act. But this situation will develop every time I must act decisively, for then I am in infinite passion, and this is precisely when the misrelation between acting and reflection appears. When I act something like this in the daily routine, I do not perceive the secret with regard to reflection and imagine that I am acting in the power of reflection, although nothing is more impossible, since it is reflection, in fact, which is the equilibrium of possibilities. —The absurd, or acting by virtue of the absurd, is then to act in faith, with confidence in God. Quite simply, I must act, but reflection has blocked the passage, so I take one of the possibilities and turn beseechingly to God and say: This is how I am doing it; bless it now; I cannot do otherwise, for I am brought to a halt by reflection.

Every man, whether he has much or little reflection, would experience this, for the nature of reflection is the same, regardless of its variation in degree in various individuals. But the reason it is seldom experienced is that an individual is seldom so inwardly oriented. When the difficulty begins he turns to another person for advice, and that then gives him a reflection, and so it goes. The process is quite simple.

A is in a mess: instead of persevering and acting by virtue of relation to God he goes to B. A is assumed to have 5 shares of reflection, B, on the other hand, 7. The reflection in A, if it were strictly held in confinement, would quite correctly have shown the balancing counter-weight to the 5 possibilities, or 5 counterpossibilities. Now he gets one possibility from B; since this possibility is not A's very own, he naturally has no counterpossibility (and B does not think it either, or is silent about it) and thus he acts with its help and thinks he is acting in the power of reflection. It is sheer fancy and hallucination.

Nothing is more impossible and more self-contradictory than to act (infinitely–decisively) by virtue of reflection. He who claims to have done it merely indicates that he either has no reflection (for the reflection which does not have a counterpossibility for every possibility is not reflection, which is indeed a doubleness) or that he does not know what it is to act.

x^1 A 66   *n.d.*, 1849

« 3708

Christ[1337] says to Paul: I will show you how much you must suffer for my sake.

So it always is in immediacy. But it is otherwise in reflection.[1338] In reflection a man is taken out of immediate relation to God, and that is why there must first of all be another movement of reflection[1339] which takes the man *so far out* that governance can get hold of him.

In our day men remain in the first reflection, in the reflection in which they are outside the immediate relationship to God; God and man therefore do not come into contact at all.

Besides, it goes without saying that when I mention Paul, his paradoxical distinction from every man must always be remembered —namely, that he is an apostle.[1340]

x^1 A 330   *n.d.*, 1849

« 3709

Psyche[1341] would not be satisfied with faith; it was, to be sure, possible that the invisible being who visited her was a monster—so she looked, and saw what she lost.

It is the same with the relationship of reflection in regard to God. You are perhaps able to see that what has been traversed is something extraordinary, and it was granted to you—if you will not be satisfied with it, satisfied with life past, if you want to have certainty for the future in order to be absolutely sure that the way you are going is not a wrong way—which is indeed a possibility (just as it was possible that the invisible being who visited Psyche was a monster who, precisely in order to conceal this, was willing to be seen only in the dark—that is, not seen but believed—): then everything is lost; in spite of everything you do not get assurance, only the assurance that now everything is lost.

x^2 A 614   *n.d., 1850*

« **3710** *The Conflict between "the Understanding"* ["Forstand"] *and "Faith" —Purely Psychological*

"The understanding" never comes into the domain of the absolute.

Take an example. I do indeed have a responsibility for my understanding. Fine—now take a man who wants to wean himself of some deeply ingrained habit. He says: You have gone around long enough saying tomorrow—begin now today, and he rushes fiercely to the attack. Then the understanding says: This is crazy: you must take it a little easy. We have examples of a man overstraining himself going at the rate you are. Relax a little and postpone it until tomorrow.

Here in the highest ethical sense it is true that a man has no responsibility for what happens to him if he fights against evil; he is supposed to act boldly, to cast responsibility upon God—that is, have faith and look at the danger of overstraining himself as a spiritual trial, a new cunning trick on the part of the evil habit.

Yet it is not to be denied that despite all this a person can also go astray in driving himself too hard in the battle against evil. I know this from personal experience; but then one relaxes, makes an admission to God and a promise to begin honestly again where one left off. Humility such as this (that one cannot do it all at once) can also play a part in saving a person from stoical conceit. I also know from my own experience (specifically because I am afraid of arbitrary whims) that I have to make a practice of defying with an advance notice this thing and that, this and that habit awaiting its turn. Suddenly to say "Today" can be very dangerous, can be illegitimate impatience.

It is the same with the understanding in relation to believing Christianity. It is in the interest of faith to make a final, absolute decision; it is in the interest of the understanding to keep "deliberation" alive. Just as the police would be embarrassed if there were no crimes, so the understanding would be embarrassed if deliberation were completed. "Faith" wants postulation of the absolute; the "understanding" wants prolongation of deliberation.[1342]

How difficult it is to have faith now in the nineteenth century when everything has become a chaos of reflections and deliberations.

This is really why it is always a great help to become perfectly clear that the object of faith is the absurd—it shortens things tremendously. Yes, one could say among other things that it is out of solicitude for men, to enable them to come to faith, that the object of faith is ordained by God to be the absurd, and that he let it be said in advance that it was and is and ever shall be the absurd.

x^2 A 624   *n.d.*, 1850

« **3711**

In some cases protracted reflection about willing or not willing in relation to a very decisive step is not simply to be explained as a lack of character. On the contrary, such continued reflection may be a necessary attrition which is the very condition for really acting decisively.

This, however, holds only with respect to religious decisions; esthetically and esthetically-ethically it is of particular importance to utilize the full vigorousness of the first moment. But religiously, loss of blood and attrition are necessary in order to become so devastated that action now becomes genuinely religious. It takes considerable strength of character, also, to keep oneself constantly at the same point of discrimination for the sake of the cause; to forget the whole thing or let it become less consequential is something else again. But to keep oneself at the point of decision with the same intensity day in and day out exhausts the physical man, the physical attachment to the world—and so it goes.

We often have examples of very great religious individualities [*Individualiteter*] who have gone on for several years holding themselves at the point of deciding whether or not to enter the cloister, and precisely that has helped them to do it; the step might otherwise have been the exaggeration of a momentary mood which they would repent of later; whereas now through attrition and the loss of blood they are in a condition which approximately corresponds to that of already being in the cloister, so empty and indifferent has every earthly and worldly thing become for them. If the bold resolution of a momentary mood had influenced them to enter the cloister, then the battle would begin right at that point. Now, however, they have kept their lives at the point of decision, have pledged themselves not to relinquish the thought about whether they should enter the monastery. This itself is an asceticism which may very well provide the transition. It is one thing to keep it in abeyance as a fanciful idea: Should you or shouldn't you enter the cloister; it is another thing to evoke the thought with the same intensity every single day, pledging yourself not to let your life meanwhile slip into any kind of distraction and to occupy yourself solely with the decision. To go through this is essentially to be in the cloister already.

x^2 A 636   *n.d.*, 1850

« **3712**

[*In margin: Fides humana and fides divina*]

The distinction which I thought should be made, the expression of reflection on the essentially Christian, that (just as the wise were first called σοροί and then φιλοσοφόι[1343]) instead of using the name or designation "Christian" we must admit that the task of truly being a Christian is so great nowadays and we so imperfect that we must be content with the designation Christ-lovers or something like that—this distinction is basic to the earlier one, in which a distinction was made between *fides humana* and *fides divina,* and it was nevertheless admitted that he who had only *fides humana* was also a Christian, although his faith actually was a proselyte-relation to being a Christian, convinced by all sorts of historical reasons, etc.

x^2 A 640   *n.d.*, 1850

« **3713** *Sickness—the Sickness of Reflection*[1344]

In book III of the *Republic*[1345] (in Heise's translation,[1346] I, p. 178 top *et passim*), Socrates takes issue with the misuse of the art of medicine, saying that rich people lie around and are sick a whole lifetime; he points out that medicine is properly used only for the poor, when a conclusion is reached and there is either recovery or death; he relates that Asclepius, in punishment for having healed a rich person lying at the point of death, was struck by lightning.

It is the same with religion. There is a misuse of religion, with the result that one goes on living in meditation, moods, etc. all his life. There is a proper use here, too—that it reaches a conclusion: either resolutely and mightily accepted—or rejected.

x^4 A 255   *n.d.*, 1851

« 3714 *Fear and Trembling*

..... Abraham sacrificed the ram and went home with Isaac, whom he spared.[1347]

But, Abraham said to himself, the whole experience has made me forever at variance with what it is to be human. If it had pleased you, O Lord, to let me be changed into the form of a horse, yet remaining human, I would be no more at variance with what it is to be man than I have become through what has just happened; having a dissimilar form is not as great a difference as not to have common concepts, and then to have them infinitely opposite at the most crucial points. —I cannot discuss this with Sara; she must regard this journey to Moria as the most horrible crime against her, against her beloved child, against you, O Lord. There will come a time when her wrath will subside and she will forgive me. And then I must thank her for this loving forgiveness. The same with Isaac; the time will come when he will feel strongly about what has happened—and he will hate me, until the moment arrives when he will forgive me, for which I must thank him. O Lord, my heart's sufferings when I brought myself to sacrifice Isaac has its compensation in this—the forgiveness of my crime, and I am humbly grateful for this loving forgiveness. And if I were to tell someone that this was your testing [*Prøvelse*] of me (something I would not do, lest I defile my relationship to you by initiating others into it) —O Lord, just to have such a relationship to you still sets me at variance with what it is to be man, more at variance than if I were changed into the shape of a horse.

But not so with Abraham, the father of faith. For to begin thinking such thoughts is to approach the boundaries of faith, even if one thought these reflections would help keep him inside the boundaries of faith: ah, reflections merely help one over the boundary. But Abraham, the father of faith, continues in faith, far from the boundary, from the boundary where faith vanishes in reflection.

x⁴ A 357   *n.d.*, 1851

« 3715 *Reflection*

The embarkation of the whole generation, the whole human race, upon reflection has changed everything.[1348]

In immediacy one was related to an unconditioned and unconditionally. No wonder, then, that a person risked life and death. —The secret of reflection is: there is no unconditioned; nothing is so untrue that there is not, after all, some truth in it, and nothing so true that there is not something untrue in it. Where then is there any room in this to risk one's life. Passion has vanished.

Christianity emphasized an unconditioned suffering—that of sin. Immediacy was laid hold of by it—and the result was passion in the movement of renunciation and self-denial. In reflection the suffering of sin is distinguished from all other suffering only by degree—and thus the individual [*Individet*] gets no impetus for venturing unconditionally.

The unconditioned, the eternal, etc. are really abolished—yet Christianity continues and we are all Christians—yes, what perhaps was not achieved even in early Christendom, that all are priests, has now been achieved—if what priests are now signifies what it means to be a priest, well, then of course we all are priests.

We all are Christians; Christianity continues. Amazing! Just an analogy from the ancient period. In ancient times it was essential to be educated in rhetoric, oratory, and eloquence. This education was related to the whole enterprise of public life in the republic; later this eloquence was put to executive use in the sphere of actuality. Then came the empire, and the sphere of actuality changed completely—the actions ceased, but the instruction and education of youth remained the same. In the schools of rhetoric they practiced orating on the same themes of freedom—*aber* in life there was no use for it. In the same way Christianity has been abolished in Christendom; but the priests are rhetoricians and the Sunday services are like exercises in schools of rhetoric. In appearance everything seems to be all right, but the sphere of actuality [*Virkeligheden*] has been abandoned by Christianity.

x^4 A 525 *n.d.*, 1852

« **3716** *The Law of Existence* [Tilværelses]

First of all comes life; then later or sooner (but afterwards) comes theory—not the reverse: first theory, then life. First art, the work of art, then the theory—and so it is in all things.*

Consequently, first life, then theory. Then, as a rule, there comes still a third: an attempt to create [*skabe*] life with the aid of theory, or the delusion of having the same life by means of the theory, which preceded, perhaps even of having potentiated life. This is the conclusion, the parody (as everything ends in parody), and then the process ends—and then there must be new life again.

Take Christianity, for example. It came in as life, sheer heroism which risked everything for the faith.

The change began essentially at the time Christianity came to be regarded as doctrine. This is the theory; it was *about* that which was lived. But there was still some vitality there, and therefore at times life-and-death disputes were carried on concerning "doctrine" and doctrinal formulations.

Nevertheless doctrine more and more became the adequate qualification of men's lives. Everything became objective. This is Christianity's theory.

Then followed a period in which the intention was to produce life by means of the theory; this is the period of the system, the parody.

Now this process has ended. Christianity must begin anew as life.

The catastrophe in 1848 is also very much along these lines.

x^4 A 528   *n.d.*, 1852

« 3717

[*]*In margin of 3716* (x^4 A 528):

This is why it is easiest to write a grammar of a dead language—because it has ended. The anatomist must have a dead body because, even if he in other respects could use a living body, it changes at every moment, is *in Flusse.* The guarantee that a theory can be produced is always that the object is in the sphere of being [*Væren*] or having been, not in becoming [*Vorden*]. It seems as if one has even more in theory than in life. In a certain sense that is the case. In the theory one has the whole thing in every detail and simultaneously; whereas life, poor life, is successive. But then again the theory does not have—life. That is the deception which ultimately makes the theory prey to the empty conceit that it is able to fashion life on a scale not known even by the life which preceded it.

x^4 A 529   *n.d.*

« 3718 *A Special Relationship to God in Immediacy and in Reflection*

In Holy Scripture we always find that God directly and immediately tells the person who has the special relationship to him what he has to do.

I do not understand this—that is, it is inconceivable; for thought this is impenetrable immediacy, but it still can be just as real.

In any case, this relationship is impossible in reflection. In reflection the relationship becomes dialectical. God must leave it up to the person who is to have the special relationship to him to decide for himself to venture into it.[*] God can indirectly and in many ways poke and prod a man to venture, but there cannot be an immediate, direct relationship in reflection. Consequently and ultimately the whole thing hinges on the person's venturing to become involved with God in a special way, always with the implicit possibility that he could have misinterpreted all the indirect influences. But on the other hand, all the indirect influences decide nothing—the venture must be made; and when it is made there is a complete qualitative change.

The person who has immediately a special relation to God has only the danger involved in carrying out what God has immediately and directly commanded. In reflection there is an additional qualitative danger, the possibility of having neglected to venture and the possibility of having ventured wrongly.

XI^2 A 273 *n.d.*, 1855

« **3719**

[*]*In margin of 3718* (XI^2 A 273):
In one sense it holds true of a special relationship to God in reflection that it can be known only afterwards; it is not something a man could appeal to directly and immediately, for at every moment there is a venturing, and thus at every moment there is the possibility of the danger of failing to venture or of venturing wrongly.

XI^2 A 274 *n.d.*

« **3720**

"Instead of the gifts of the spirit which were present in the Church in the beginning, we must use speculation and the like"—excellent surrogate, it is qualitatively different, and yet it is supposed to take its place, somewhat as if flying, for example, should take the place of swimming. Or do I come closer to the gifts of the spirit the more I speculate and develop in this direction? No, not any more than I come closer to swimming by becoming quite perfect in flying.

XI^2 A 340 *n.d.*, 1854

REFORM, REFORMATION, REFORMER

« 3721

Was not the Bohemians' and Moravians' opposition to accepting the Latin liturgy and the Spaniards' insistence upon keeping their old Mozarabic liturgy the first attempt at reformation?

I A 107   November 2, 1835

« 3722

Acknowledgment of the Reformation's negative aspect and the *possibility* of the return of the separated parties to the mother Church (without having to come back as prodigal sons) is expressed, although somewhat *schüchtern,* by their not having had the courage to do what the Catholics did to them—declare them to be heretics, [by their] not having had the courage to carry out to a conclusion the premises which they themselves have held historically and which they approved *as such.*

II A 76   June 2, 1837

« 3723

The post-Reformation period of conflict in the Protestant churches themselves is doubly interesting, for one thing because it proves that in the Reformation a world-historical element had gained momentum (one recognizes it from one angle also in the felt need for deliberating upon past experience in the world, which is another reason why these controversies provide a kind of compendious life-career of all dogmatics), for another because here all the dogmatic problems have been grasped in their most profound concretion, even though at times it approached paradox or caricature.

III A 2   July 4, 1840

« 3724

Note. If it happens, then the movement-man believes that the world has been helped. Even genuine reformers have been trapped by the illusion that changing uniforms (a change in externals) was a true reformation. This explains why reforming occurs so quickly and easily

726

–and, as Luther says, the world continues to be like the drunken peasant who, helped up on one side of the horse, falls off the other side. We believe that corruption comes from a king, an emperor, the Pope, a tyrant, or a national leader; if only he can be toppled, the world will be saved. A reformer now places himself at the head, points to the bearded man on the throne–he is the one. If that were true and not a fantastic illusion, the world would undeniably be an uncommonly wonderful world where one person is corrupt and all the rest of us are wonderful people. Let us recall a Socratic question raised in a similar Socratic situation: I wonder if with respect to horses there is only one who spoils them and everybody else knows how to ride. Any reformation which is not aware that fundamentally every single individual needs to be reformed is *eo ipso* an illusion. If one has a little ingenuity and chooses to use it in such a miserable way, one can easily win men over to his views, but he who believes that the world has become better because it has accepted his views in this way must be very stupid. Even the great reformer Luther cannot be entirely acquitted of a certain prejudice in this respect, because he did indeed know how to defend Christian freedom against the Pope with noble and elevated enthusiasm, but he was not sufficiently and dialectically alert to defend it and himself against stupid parrots and hangers-on. That is why, ironically enough, his reformation engendered the same evil he was fighting against–an exegetical spirit of bondage, a hyper-orthodox Lutheran coercion that was just as bad as the Pope's.[1349]

VII^2 B 235, pp. 48–49   *n.d.*, 1846–47

« 3725

This is the way such a revolutionary, who is an enemy of the established order (which one does not need to be in order to be a reformer and which a true reformer never is) seeks . . . . . [1350]

VII^2 B 249:4   *n.d.*, 1846–47

« 3726

Everyone who intends to influence men must be acquainted with two dangers: (1) men are lukewarm and indolent, difficult to set in motion; (2) once they are set in motion, there is nothing they are more inclined to do than to mimic.[1351] –The latter danger is absolutely just as great as the former, but the reforming gentlemen forget this, which is why we very rarely see a true reformer.

VIII^1 A 103   *n.d.*, 1847

« 3727

It is impossible to think of anything more foolish than the non-sense about a whole age being reformation-minded.[1352] Once again this is an expression of that nauseating flirtation[1353] with everything, that we want to be all things but always without danger and strain. Not only the danger but also the epigram and the renewal lie in this—that the reformer stands alone in the whole world—but this also expresses that God nevertheless achieves more than all individuals and general assemblies. And after all is said and done and the disorderly mob of reformers is taken individually and reduced merely to a little trifle, there has certainly never lived a more cowardly generation than this nauseating sweet-toothed generation which boasts of being the nine-teenth century.

VIII[1] A 429   *n.d.*, 1847

« 3728 *Anonymity*

Anonymity has also demoralized the time in this way, that by doing away with persons with character it has contributed to rendering the age characterless.

Anyone who in any way wants to play the reformer and in his displeasure with the established order wants to make a protest about it will speak the language of truth *extra ordinem,* that is, outside of the media which the state recognizes—he also ought to come forth and be recognized and bear the whole responsibility. He must not be afraid of danger, for the very danger shapes him, or in any case it is the examination which decides whether he is fit for such things or not.

But look, with the help of anonymity we have found a way of escape.

Let us assume that in one way or another an abuse or injustice occurs. This person and that person suffer under it. Agreed. But from the fact that one person suffers an injustice it still does not follow that he is the person really called to make the protest.

Now the rule should be that if I do not have the power earnestly and with integrity to stand up against the injustice, if I do not have the courage to witness in this way for the truth, then my task is to keep still and suffer. No impatience. The one who keeps still and suffers because he recognizes his unfitness to be a reformer, he, too, is a moral charac-ter. The true character does not emerge before the relations have been intensified during a long period of suffering and silence.

But with the help of anonymity a shortcut has been made. Every impatient coward who does not dare use his name—indeed, it might cost him his job or could occasion disgrace or some other loss—now becomes, anonymously, a witness to the truth.

Yes, no doubt it is very convenient. Then, to boot, anonymity was found to be something meritorious—it is "in order to stick to the issue." Well, well, I suppose it was "in order to stick to the issue" that an anonymity sometimes attacks a person by name. The anonymity was afraid to use his own name but was not afraid to attack the other by name. Today this kind of courage marks a brilliant advance for wretched cowardice.

Now the door was open. Every impatience and irritability came running with any triviality from the school of suffering—and became an anonymous reformer. Sometimes even school boys[1354] became—anonymously—reformers of public education or of the individual teachers, mentioning them by name. And although we have a police notice which prohibits innkeepers from serving liquor to boys, we have no order at all which forbids journalists—I almost said "to serve liquor to school boys"—we have no order forbidding boys to become co-workers on newspapers. Indeed, it cannot be prevented, since they can be anonymous.

Anyone who knows anything about human beings knows how much mediocrity and triviality and petty passions are tempted to play the reformer, to talk the bold language of truth.

And now this language is spoken from morning 'til evening—by all these cowards who in order to stick to the issue conceal their names. The following quite ordinary scene took place in a newspaper office. A man bluntly admitted that for various reasons he could not very well sign his name—so he remained anonymous. The editor and the author understood each other; and neither of the parties blushed. The article came out—one would think it was by one of the heroes of truth.

As a result, to want to be an authentic character who under his own name exposes himself to real danger would be ridiculous, stupid, since it is possible to do the same thing in a far more comfortable way and to deal only with the issue.

O, you wretches, yes, certainly one can do the same thing in a more comfortable way—one can demoralize all of society by speaking the gallant language of truth—if it is really the same as when a moral character is a benefit not only through the particulars of his protest but is infinitely beneficial by being a person of character.

A sight the world got to see in former times, a sight which has its positive side: a youthful agitator who bounces up and wants to be a reformer and then exposes himself to derision—this we no longer see. No, now things are more favorable for the agitators—they remain anonymous and are never compromised.

Meanwhile the anonymous ones thundered away—and they had to be listened to, for the public opinion here expressed, anonymously, was "simply to serve the cause of truth."

x^3 A 326   *n.d.*, 1850

« 3729 *The Way Things Are Going—and I*

Actually, I am getting to lie crosswise to the way things are going.[1355] The trouble is that a whole generation has wanted to dabble *en masse* at playing the reformer.[1356] With respect to the trend, the same thing will happen with me as is stated in one of the three small ethical-religious treatises (by F. F.) (which lies in the tin box)—first of all there must come a policeman who clears out all these false reformers.[1357]

The injustice in the relationship between the established order and me is that they want me to eulogize unreservedly the old establishment simply because it is old, just as if by its impotence in governing it were not also guilty of the whole generation's notion of playing reformer. No, the established must also be exposed, and if the established wishes to understand itself it must be thankful that it has happened, since it happened from a point of view which favors the position that there should be governing. Actually the established order ought to have made the admission[1358] on its own, before anyone on the outside reminded them of it, for it is the only way to get the reins of government again.

O, when a whole generation wants to trim off the government more and more—if only the Church leaders would gather together all their personal power and eloquence and say: We admit that we have erred, that we have not governed; we implore God's forgiveness and promise a change—truly it would make a great impression. It might then give the whole affair a turn.

x^3 A 608   *n.d.*, 1850

« 3730 *God's Thoughts Are*

not man's thoughts.

Once it was God's thought that a reformation was needed, and no one at that time wanted to be the reformer.

Now everyone wants to be the reformer—thus it is certain that a reformation is not God's thought.

x⁴ A 27   n.d., 1851

« 3731 *What We Are in for—*

It is not "doctrine" which ought to be revised, and it is not "the Church" which ought to be reformed, and so on—.

No, it is existences which should be revised. Our whole way of life is stuff and nonsense and lack of character; the point is that all of us ought to make a fearful admission[1359] to Christianity.

But we all shrink from this existential way—and thus there are all these escapes and inventions—that it is "doctrine" which ought to be revised, the Church and the state, etc.

x⁴ A 30   n.d., 1851

« 3732 *A Reformation—Without "a Reformer"*

The modern thing is—a reformation—without "a reformer."

Well, since everything has become impersonal, why not this, too?

But maybe it is not true that this reformation is without a reformer; after all, everyone has become a reformer[1360]—well, it amounts to the same thing. The concept "reformer" corresponds qualitatively to: one. If there are two, there is a qualitative loss. If there are ten, it is progressively a minus, and if everyone is a reformer, then no one is.

Consequently it is a reformation without a reformer. Yes, for the contemporary age a reformer is a nuisance, just about as much for those who are on his side as for those he is against. Thus he is abolished as old-fashioned. In his place is put a very different kind of complaint and, despite its apparent unsociability, sociable something —a voting machine—if something usable also for social entertainment is not preferred: a wheel of fortune.

And then the reformation begins. In sociable little clusters they sit —and ballot.

Nevertheless I still hope that a reformation will come once again. Just as Napoleon cleared the hall with his grenadiers, so there will come a poet who will clear the hall by means of ideals.[1361]

Incidentally, this matter of a poet who consumes the confused by introducing ideals is really Socratic.[1362]

x⁴ A 38   n.d., 1851

« 3733

. . . . . You have 1,000 pastors—if you had only one who had nevertheless a little to sacrifice for the sake of Christianity, you would be better served. You want to reform the Church—then get first of all one Christian, and let him reform the Church.

X^4 A 117   n.d., 1851

« 3734 *Our Age and the Age of the Reformation or the Age Before the Reformation*

It is said that these two ages resemble each other very much. Well, thanks for that! No, the evil in our age is the frivolous, profane conceit that we are fit to reform the Church; the evil in our age is simply wanting to take the concept of "reformation" in vain.

This is my thrust. I defend the established order to the extent that I understand it as my legitimate task to fight against the reformers in our age, all of whom are deceivers or confused people. Otherwise I am well aware of the deficiencies of the established.

My idea is: the true task in our age is not to reform but to get clear about our present situation, where we are.

X^4 A 345   n.d., 1851

« 3735 *Of the Reasons Which Make a Reformation a Requirement for these Times and thereby a Necessity*

A dialogue between a clergyman and an assistant professor: Mr. Babbler and Mr. Gabbler.

X^4 A 615   n.d., 1852

« 3736 *The Sign by Which a Given Situation Is Recognized To Be Ripe for Falling*

Suppose someone realizes something which is more true than what is contemporarily regarded to be true: it by no means follows that he must charge forth against the given situation.

No, if the given contemporary age does in fact *bona fide* regard what it calls the true to be that, he has to proceed more cautiously, for he first of all has to impart the needed knowledge to his contemporaries.

But when the contemporary situation is such that almost everyone knows *privately* that the whole thing is a mistake, is false, while no one will *officially* say so, when the tactic of the powers that be is: Let us just hold tight, pretend nothing has happened, give the silent treatment to every attack, for we know all too well ourselves that the whole thing is rotten, that we are playing false—well, then the prevailing situation is *eo ipso* condemned and it must fall. Just as someone is said to be marked by death, so also this situation is the symptom which invites unconditioned attack. Here there can be no question of whether something more true is encountering something which honestly thinks itself to be true. No, here the battle is against lies.

Basically, this is the situation in Christendom, especially in Protestantism, especially in Denmark.[1363]

XI[1] A 525   n.d., 1854

« 3737 *How I Understand the Future*

Certainly there must be reforming, and it will be a dreadful reformation—by comparison the Lutheran Reformation will almost be a jest —a dreadful reformation [*in margin:* a dreadful reformation which will have as its watchword: "I wonder if faith is to be found on earth." It will be identified by people "falling away" from Christianity by the millions, a dreadful reformation], for the point is that Christianity actually does not exist at all, and it will be horrible when a generation pampered by a childish Christianity, enthralled in the delusion of being Christian, once again gets the deathblow of what it is to become Christian, to be Christian.

Paganism was right in understanding Christianity to be hatred of mankind—so frightful it was to become Christian. But it is more horrible to have to learn it all over again when one has been pampered and made soft by the lollipop which is called Christianity, enthralled in the delusion of being Christian.

If this were to be brought to bear suddenly upon an individual, a generation, it would no doubt be beyond human limits, and it would also be beyond human limits if a person dared to speak this way, too rigorously, of the divine, for, good Lord, that poor pampered wretch cannot be blamed totally for what generations have been guilty of for a long time.

Therefore, as I understand it, since God is long-suffering, he sizes it all up, does not throw out the whole generation, nor does he set them a task which might be their ruin.

But it does not follow that everything is to go on as before. No, there must be a beginning:

We must thoroughly, completely, and truthfully draw up a balance sheet—and this is my task, this is how I see it.

In the New Testament salvation is bound up with being Christian —and in the New Testament interpretation of that, not a single one of us is Christian, not one. In the meantime—while we go on living carefree lives—God sits serenely up in heaven, with eternity's accounting in mind—and remember clearly that he is not impressed by the millions he has to dismiss, because we are not Christians by the millions, although we call ourselves that. What are we going to do about that? Furthermore, if the requirement were to be applied this moment, the requirement as it stands in the New Testament, there is not one of us, not a single one, who would not be crushed, annihilated, simply because we are all (and this is far more dangerous than to be a pagan or a Jew) pampered, softened, demoralized—and most dangerous of all, demoralized by means of Christianity—but God—remember this!—God is not impressed by millions.

Is it not forbearance, indescribable forbearance—O, that it may be true, but I dare to believe it is—that he allows us to count as Christians, but nevertheless at least requires one thing, that truth be brought into it, that a balance sheet must be made, that we should not try to find, if possible, an even greater artist than the late Bishop, an even greater artist in the art of concealing, veiling, covering with the aid of illusions, but that we should be honest enough to be willing to endure having the true situation uncovered.

XI^2 A 346   *n.d.*, 1854

« **3738** *Subtlety*

We commend it as fine and loving not to disturb (as the saying goes) others in their illusions, their religious illusions. This might also have its basis in our indolence and the fact that we are not really certain of something ourselves. For Christianity takes the very opposite view, regards it as its sacred duty to rip others out of their illusions (Socrates,[1364] too, feared most of all to be in error). But, of course, according to Christianity the Christian is himself a wise man.

XI^2 A 355   *n.d.*, 1854

RENUNCIATION, SELF-DENIAL

« **3739**

The ground and meaning of suffering: dying to immediacy and that a man achieves nothing at all himself, dying to immediacy and remaining in finiteness.[1365]

VI B 59:2   n.d., 1845

« **3740**

Self-denial [*Selvfornegtelse*]. To have everything within one's power and then to give up all power, and to give it up in such a way that one cannot himself do the least thing, yes, cannot even do anything for his adherents, and to maintain it so rigorously that one even constrains creation, nature, which wants to supply something—if this is not self-denial, then what is self-denial. Here is the place for one who denied himself, and just as a warrior may long to be gathered together with the heroes, where only wounds and battles and dangers and victories are talked about, so also the imitator [*Efterfølgeren*][1366] may long to be away from the confused opinions of the world to a place where all that is talked about is the suffering that is endured, misunderstanding, terror, mockery, and mortal danger—in short, the experiences of the one who takes up his cross and imitates Christ.[1367]

VII[1] B 181:2   n.d., 1846

« **3741**

Abraham of St. Clara[1368] tells about an old hermit to whom a rich man at his death willed his whole fortune, and when informed of the fact the hermit is supposed to have said: There must be a misunderstanding; how can he make me his heir when I died before he did.

VIII[1] A 211   n.d., 1847

« **3742**

The apostles[1369] say: "We who have given up everything to follow [*følge*] you—what reward shall we have?" An excellent vivifying sermon

735

could be preached on these words—for how many men are there in these times who have given up everything.

VIII¹ A 216   n.d., 1847

« **3743**

Love can be effectually praised only in self-denial, for God is love. What a person knows truly about love he must learn from God, that is, in self-denial he must become what every man can become (for self-denial is the claim upon the universally human), an instrument for God.[1370]

VIII² B 59:20   n.d., 1847

« **3744**

The pastors preach indulgence and teach that renouncing everything is required only of some individuals. No, it is required of all, but it is particularly required only of some individuals. But the one of whom it is not particularly required learns humility all the more.

The renouncing of all things has the spaciousness of freedom. God speaks something like this: It would give me great pleasure if you were to renounce everything for Christ's sake, but it is not absolutely demanded of you.

VIII¹ A 572   n.d., 1848

« **3745**

Thoroughly-reflected self-denial would avoid the appearance of willing the good. Consequently one is better than he seems. But then one must be pure. Suppose there were a man who, humanly speaking, was perhaps in one respect noble and disinterested, and when he reflected on it understood that the true thing to do was to avoid seeming to be that way. But now suppose that perhaps the same man was in other respects a greater sinner than many others—if he now in reflection hides or avoids the appearance of seeming to be as good and disinterested as he is but is not careful or cannot manage to reveal the other side, then here again there is untruth.

The self-denial of avoiding the appearance of being as good as one is is too perfect, is jacked up too high for a human being, is somewhat demonic—is not for sinners. A sinner must never delude himself into thinking that he can be so good that it would be dangerous for the world or men to find out how good he is. Christianity puts something else in place of this pagan idea of avoiding the appearance —namely, the confession of sins. If a person wants to be completely honest with respect to this, it can never be dangerous for the world to get to know all about how good he is.

Fine. But when knowing oneself as a sinner and confessing it again becomes a reflected expression for purity, then we are just as close to the same point. And so it was in the Middle Ages.

Thus it comes again—a man must use his reflection in fear and trembling.

IX A 224   n.d., 1848

« 3746

To talk grandiosely about truth and self-denial [*selvfornegtelse*] and then live in opposite categories[1371] is all wrong. But to intimate to others the nature of your self-denial, what you want and what you are sacrificing for it—that is human, and that is actually what all those I read about have done. Am I perhaps too preoccupied with the dialectical, with simply concealing the nature of my self-denial? On the other hand, if I myself describe my own self-denial, it seems to me I could just as well stop it, for it becomes nothing more than pretense. It is certainly true that when one adds reduplication, the additional dialectic, as I am doing, self-denial becomes as deeply inward as possible, and the God-relationship is absolutely, absolutely the only thing to which one can cling. In the other form[1372] of self-denial one has gradually assured himself of a little stronghold among men, witnesses—in case God should leave him in the lurch. Is that what it means to have faith; is that what it means to love God?

Here we see again that the hypothetical is infinitely more inward than all this positive certainty. Here in fact is an either/or. Either God is love: and then it is absolutely valid absolutely to stake absolutely everything on this alone, for bliss is just to have God alone; or God is not love: and then, yes, then the loss is so infinite that any other loss is of no consequence whatsoever, yes, then everything is so trivial that I must regard every moment I have lived in the illusion that he was love as infinite happiness, for which I must (what a strange way of speaking!) thank God from the bottom of my heart—as if he were love.

IX A 486   n.d., 1848

« 3747

It is easy enough to see that if a decision about the self-denial and renunciation of the worldly required in order to proclaim Christianity is to be made in the context of a forum called the great Christian public or the cultured Christian public, the matter is decided. The clergy themselves seem to understand this, which explains why they are so ready and willing on such occasions to take the matter to the great public. To vote by ballot on self-denial, whether and how much—well, it amounts to nothing.

The deception is rooted in this, that the clergy are supposed to take part in order to educate this great public and therefore to express self-denial existentially, so that merely by looking at the clergyman everyone sees at once what Christianity requires. But instead the clergy have joined up with the public, have utterly fallen out of character: teachers, God's servants—and nowadays they are really happy to be understood so well by their contemporaries.

x^2 A 509   n.d., 1850

« 3748

Is there not a necessary relation with respect to what results from what a man says and teaches so that he inevitably embraces the consequences, and thus if the consequences are not there, one is justified in concluding: Well, then he has not truly proclaimed this?

Take an example: proclaiming Christian self-denial. If someone truly proclaims it, does it not follow with necessity that it takes place in him, what he says takes place in him, so that the only authentic proof of the truth of the proclamation is that it brings forth what is proclaimed, perhaps not in such a way that anyone does what he says, but that what he says takes place in him—Christian self-denial takes place. If, however, someone makes a big hit preaching Christian self-denial —is that not direct proof that he is not proclaiming it in truth.

The sophists are so reluctant to stop here: they keep it ambiguous, saying: Sometimes truth must suffer in this world; sometimes it thrives.

But when Christian self-denial is proclaimed in such a way that the one who proclaims it makes a hit, then he is not actually proclaiming it; perhaps he declaims at a poetic distance[1373] from actuality, but he does not express it existentially, and therefore the consequences are omitted.

Here again we see how foolish it is to call Christianity a doctrine instead of calling it an existence-communication.

x^2 A 604   n.d., 1850

« 3749 *Christianity's Consolation—To Die to the World*

Christianity is said to be consolation and mildness. Fine. But Christianity nevertheless requires that a man shall die to the world.[1374]

Here we have it again. How many are there in any generation who would retain a suffering for which they sought consolation if they first of all endured all the sufferings which lie within the scope of dying to the world. For here lie just about all human concerns and troubles. There is only one gulf more, sorrow over one's sin, and how many have that, especially in the one and only sense of the word.

If one then says there is consolation in Christianity's intention to help a person to die to the world—but how many are there who really want it to the extent that they find it truly consoling to be helped into it.

No, Christianity actually exists [*existerer*] no more. The coiled spring—what spring?—the absolute itself—has long since been slackened, and the whole thing has become rubbish.

x^3 A 166   *n.d.*, 1850

« 3750 *Transforming Little into Much*

Learn to be satisfied with little—will you deny that this is much?

x^3 A 266   *n.d.*, 1850

« 3751 *Poverty*

It is one thing quite arbitrarily to make poverty into piety, as if poverty were something in and for itself. This, after all, is changing God into a kind of Grand Pasha who sits in idleness and to whom the pious say: Look at me now and you will see that I can live on bread and water.

It is another thing when poverty is related to the idea which a man serves with his life. Suppose, for example, that if the idea is to be served effectively there can be little time left over for earning a living; then it is surely one's duty to choose the curtailed time and the small income instead of acquiring more and then, of course, necessarily relinquishing the idea all the more. Or suppose that poverty is related to the idea itself. Take a theological student to whom a pastoral appointment is represented primarily as a way to earn one's bread and butter, but he hesitates lest he come in contact with all the worldliness in the forecourts of the temple, lest his life express his approval of this attitude. Here, you see, poverty is carried by the idea and carries the idea. The same holds true in many other ways.

X^3 A 306   *n.d.,* 1850

« 3752

Christ opens his arms and says: Come unto me. The pastor hurries and says: Simply dare to throw yourself into his arms—this is the life. Yes, of course, but watch out, for that embrace of his is first of all death. He calls himself life, he says come unto me—and if you give yourself over completely, you will also be dead, and to the world; for he is not life then and there, just like that; he is life through death.[1375]

X^3 A 351   *n.d.,* 1850

« 3753

Christ dies in order to save you—but on the condition that you die to the world. But then nothing is won, someone will say. How can that be? Is nothing won? Even if you died to the world ever so much, it would not follow that at the time of death you would enter into the eternal bliss which Christ has gained for you. But, you say, when someone has died to the world completely, he is then pure spirit and has essentially found the rest which Christianity offers, and then, to be sure, nothing is won by Christianity. Answer: Let us assume that to be true. It still remains that you will not succeed in dying to the world completely without Christ's help; yes, without his help you will not even manage to begin the task.

X^3 A 352   *n.d.,* 1850

« 3754

. . . . . And even if you did come to be eternally saved despite never having found occasion to concern yourself with the matter, it seems to me that some time, at least, it would become apparent to you that it was a sad and lamentable ingratitude that the good for which Christ suffered and died had not—yes, absolutely not—concerned you at all.

Thus you, you suffering one, must count yourself fortunate that God through heavy sufferings has prevented you from tossing your life away and has taught you to become attentive to the infinite good.

And this is what it means actually to die to the world—when an eternal blessedness shows itself unconditionally to be the one and only good and everything else to be nothing.

Alas, but we live in such a way that we find time to think of and be concerned with everything else, but we leave the question of eternal salvation completely open, or we apply "grace" in such a way that—as we say—we hope to be eternally saved by grace, which amounts to saying that we do not concern ourselves with the matter at all.

x^3 A 361   *n.d.*, 1850

« 3755 *The Voluntary*

That Christianity's pronouncements about suffering and self-denial are about the voluntary is implied in the very nature of the matter, for how in all the world could self-renunciation ever be unavoidable.

But self-denial has been completely abolished and the common human sufferings (sickness, poverty, etc.) have been substituted; thus Christianity has been reduced to a matter of teaching patience in these unavoidable things, which are then as far as possible avoided.

But what meaning is there then in Christ's words: "If any man would come after me, let him deny himself and take up his cross and follow me"—if by "cross" we are to understand some unavoidable suffering or other which happens to me. Suppose it is sickness—it is self-evident that as long as I am sick I am sick, and no admonition to take up my cross is really necessary if "cross" is supposed to mean this illness.

O, but the preachers have made the whole thing nonsense.

x^3 A 456   *n.d.*, 1850

« 3756

In margin of 3755 (x^3 A 456):

That the *essentially Christian* is the "voluntary" can be seen simply by the word which is used: self-denial. In regard to the unavoidable, the necessary, that which comes from the outside, etc., it is another power (providence, circumstances, other men, etc.) which denies something to me. But that which I deny myself (self-denial) is something voluntary, something I had power to get if I did not deny myself.

Here again we have an example of how Christianity has been abolished in Christendom—the fact that "cross"[1376] is understood to be suffering, instead of Christ's understanding of it as the suffering of self-denial.

x^3 A 457   *n.d.*

« **3757 *Human Cunning Again in Regard to
the Essentially Christian***

Actually to renounce all this life, to concentrate everything on the other side in such a way that one has nothing but trouble and work and suffering on this side—this is the most strenuous existence.

Well, if it gets too difficult, one can, with the help of grace, by praying for oneself, see about getting off a little easier.

But what have men devised? They have brashly invented the idea that concentrating everything on the other side in this manner is a very imperfect existence, is "living abstractly"—the perfect existence is the easier existence, or the easier existence is also the perfect existence.

This is brash mutiny against the essentially Christian—and it is here that the encounter must come.

The second lie is the great danger, and I do not believe any hunter can follow a trail more confidently than I am able instinctively to discover the whereabouts of this lie.

To be specific, this lie is the taking-in-vain of all Luther's efforts; it is Luther's spirituality transformed into brash secularism.

x^3 A 560   *n.d.,* 1850

« **3758 *You Will Be Hated by All for My Name's Sake***[1377]

No wonder! Is death so very welcome, after all, to men. And an apostle, an apostle's life, expresses quite literally dying, to die to—to what? To everything to which one can die. And it is precisely this, that to which one can die, which the natural man *naturally* and obviously loves as much as he loves his life.[1378]

x^4 A 261   *n.d.,* 1851

« **3759 *The Voluntary—To Die to the World***

It is thought that the voluntary is an exaggeration—but is not dying to the world Christianity's requirement for each and every one?[1379]

If there were nothing voluntary, the Christian would be tried only in the unavoidable tests of self-denial. But then it would be conceivable that one could live so favored by fortune that he would never find any occasion to die to the world, and he would then be able to say: It is not my fault. My life did not offer an opportunity.

No, if it is required of everyone to die to the world, it must not be circumstances or chance which decide to what extent someone dies to the world—thus we stand again before the voluntary.

x^4 A 266   *n.d.,* 1851

« 3760 *Double-Danger*

Here it is immediately evident. Calvin actually lived in poverty—yet he had many occasions to earn money and become a big man. Here then is an instance of self-renunciation to the first power.

If things were the way the preacher preaches today, Calvin would have been honored and esteemed for it. Well, hardly, it was just the opposite.

This is the double-danger. Because he wanted to live in poverty, he was exposed to slander on every side.

See *Henry Calvins Leben*, I, pp. 429 and 430.[1380] He himself says (p. 430 fn.): I would never have stopped if I had taken it upon myself to write a defense. Although this says a lot, something vast, it is only a hundredth part of the troubles I have every day.

x^4 A 316   *n.d.,* 1851

« 3761 *Human Perversity*

The secular mind is never quite satisfied until it has gotten a wrong made into a dogma, a duty.

The New Testament clearly has a preference for the unmarried state. This is unpalatable. Now, if we could only think of it this way—we could say: Christianity is much inclined in this direction, but it nevertheless does allow getting married as an indulgence. Or we could say that marriage can be regarded as adiaphorous—you may do as you like. But, no. The secular mind does not rest until it has made dogma out of—it is every person's unconditional duty to marry.

Christianity clearly has a preference for the voluntary, voluntarily to give up earthly things. Now one may say: I am not that strong, and I would rather hang on to earthly things and say with the fellow who declared: My dear brandy, if you do not forsake me, I shall never forsake you. One could say that and then keep the earthly but admit that it is a weakness. No, the secular mentality does not rest until it has gotten the opposite assertion made into a duty. They say: the voluntary, to sacrifice something of one's own free will is tempting God; no, sir, how could I be so wicked as to tempt God.

In the Middle Ages people did not know Greek. One could simply have acknowledged the fact and confessed that he did not care to expend the effort to learn it—but, no, the secular mentality did not rest until it had established the dogma that to know Greek was heresy. (See Adolf Müller, *Erasmus Rotterdams Leben;* Hamburg: 1828; p. 116).

x^4 A 326   *n.d.,* 1851

« **3762**

"Only if he can do it with joy, only then shall a man renounce the things of this world—otherwise it is not pleasing to God."

Splendid! —What fraudulent and hypocritical cunning to talk so much like Christianity and yet be so unlike it! For if this is to be taken straight, then it practically means that none of us will give up the things of this world, least of all in any decisive degree—for really and truly, it can in no way be done "with joy," that is in the sense that one regards it as renunciation's *quantum satis,* as something which can intensify pleasure.

Christianity speaks of dying to the world—this is something more earnest.

Think of undergoing a very painful operation. If it is agreed that one ought to undergo the operation only insofar as he can do it with pleasure, what then? Well, then the surgeon would say: This means that no one will ever submit to it, for it is silly, unthinkable nonsense to imagine that anyone would submit to it without groaning frightfully under the agonizing pain, to say nothing of being able to find pleasure in it. No, as far as undergoing this operation is concerned, it is a question of a person's having decided calmly and categorically to submit to the pain; if the surgeon, moved by the patient's pain, halted in the middle of the operation and asked if he would rather have him stop, it would be a question of the patient's quiet determination to stick it out—but it is rubbish and hypocrisy to speak of submitting to this operation only if it is enjoyable.

Christ[1381] says to the apostles: "You will weep and lament, but the world will rejoice." Here joy appears at another point—the world will rejoice, which is an intensification of the apostles' sufferings.

x⁴ A 504   *n.d.,* 1852

« **3763** *"Renunciation"—Demoralization*

The demoralization of our age (which quite simply has come about because "the understanding" has duped the whole generation, all of us) is this: renunciation, which is a Christian requirement, has been abolished—people go for the things of this earth. Not only that, no (this is the intensification) renunciation (which is shunned) is made a *aufgehobnes* factor and a refinement in the enjoyment and possession of the things of this earth. One takes, one covets the things of this earth —but is fastidiously above it all—although accepting it.

Renunciation's lofty idea of giving up the things of this earth as childishness is exploited in possessing the things of this earth. Someone wants to become a Knight of Dannebrog, a councilman, etc. etc. —achieves it—and then takes a lofty superior attitude toward it, as something childish—yet he is that.

"The understanding" inevitably nourishes the most revolting hypocrisy.

There must be some cutting, surgical cutting—the disjunction either/or must be asserted. If you want the things of this earth: surely I will not forbid you that. But then no more of the appearance of being far above such things. If you really are way above such things, you can express that by not taking them.

But this hypocrisy of "the understanding" is perhaps far more dangerous to Christianity than the raw brute passions it had to do battle with at first.

Incidentally, it is easy to see here what I mean when I say that I am "without authority." For I say: Go right ahead and get the things of this earth—but the hypocrisy must go. One with authority must say: Renounce the earthly.

x^4 A 517   *n.d.*, 1852

« 3764 *The Dangerous "Also"*[1382]

I can imagine a person well endowed in every respect. He has grasped the essence of Christianity and has understood that it can be proclaimed in truth only when it is served in self-denial and renunciation [*Forsagelse*]. Alas, but he cannot bring himself to such a life. I cannot, he says to himself, I cannot let go of the things of this world. And besides, I will not get anyone to accept Christianity. And finally, compared with what is generally called the proclamation of Christianity around here, my way is still a good deal more true.

So he accommodates and takes the things of this world *also*—but of course he does not declare the true situation publicly, for then he perhaps would lose the things of this world, and in any case, in such a situation they would probably lose their fascination for him. He pretends that his proclamation of Christianity is entirely as it should be, that it is true Christianity.

But in a mood of gratitude to God he says to himself: Since I also get the things of this world this way, I shall also work all the more zealously and tirelessly and will try to win more and more people for Christianity.

And he sticks to it. With a rare zeal and competence and endurance he proclaims Christianity throughout a generation and wins many, many for Christianity. And this moves him—it is honestly meant —he wants very much to show God his gratitude by working more and more zealously, by winning more and more.

Let us now draw up a balance sheet for him. Has the man benefitted Christianity? No, no, no. He has damaged it incalculably. He has made it doubly difficult for the true proclamation to pierce through when it does come; it must appear to be a ridiculous exaggeration. His false proclamation has given men a taste of Christianity without renunciation and as being just as true Christianity as the old—therefore one must be mad to want to get involved with the old Christianity. And the more zealously he has proclaimed his kind, and the more thousands he has won, the greater the danger. With regard to truth it is not the case that the falsification closest to it in a certain sense (closest in that it has the most truth in it) is an approximation of the truth, the closest to the truth. No, exactly the opposite; precisely that is the most dangerous and to that extent is the farthest from the truth, bars the way, and makes the truth unrecognizable. The utterly corrupt is closer to the truth. That is, it is easier to render the truth recognizable by way of a complete scoundrel and hypocrite than by way of a man who has used all his zeal and fervor to get as many as possible to follow his way and thought thereby to show his gratitude to God.

In a certain sense this is so extremely human, in another sense so dreadful. It is very human to want to scale down a little, but then also to be all the more zealous to extend it—and thereby to do the greatest damage. Such a proclaimer of Christianity goes to his grave with responsibility for himself, responsibility for these thousands he needed, if you please, in order to demonstrate his zeal and fervor, these thousands whom he won for Christianity, whom he imagined to be Christians and this way to be Christianity. Finally, with responsibility for the witness to the truth who at some time is supposed to introduce the true Christianity, whose life will now become doubly painful.

x^4 A 536   *n.d.,* 1852

« 3765

..... But someone will say: "What if someone actually expresses existentially that he has forsaken and does forsake this world, is it therefore absolutely certain that he will be saved? Maybe not? It could be arrogance or pride, to which God is very much opposed." True, it is not absolutely certain, nor will it ever be, for in the uncertainty is the striving. But in any case he has one advantage, one good, which is not possessed by one whose life expresses the very opposite of renunciation—he has not neglected to use the guidance which God in his Word has given to a man regarding what he is to do. Is it not peculiar that God tells us in his Word what he requires and then we exempt ourselves from it—and yet we are Christians just the same.

X^4 A 645   *n.d.*, 1852

« 3766

If requiring renunciation were, if I may put it this way, stinginess, pettiness, or punitive action on God's part, then I would have to revolt against it.

But that is not the case. Let me speak in a purely human way of how I understand it. God in heaven in all his fatherliness says to a man: "Little friend, if you call me Father (something I have in fact permitted), you may certainly say that you have a rich father and to that extent you may expect (reasonably so) that as a father I would never in all the world keep you on a scanty allowance—but, my little friend, consider the following: what is it that leads me not to act that way, for if I did, your lot would be one of inconceivable abundance. (1) If I did that for you, you could not become "spirit," but as a consequence you have come to have kinship with me. (2) The gospel is proclaimed to the poor, that is, the gospel is for the poor, but consequently (this you can understand and are honest enough to be willing to understand it) it must be proclaimed to one who is poor. It was not my intention with Christianity to go up and down creation giving money to the poor and health to the sick—no, poverty and sickness and suffering are part of this world, but the gospel is for the poor and can be proclaimed only by one who is poor. That, you see, is why—out of love for you—I require renunciation, and that is why, if I see that you cannot on your own initiative decide, and if I see a willingness in you (for otherwise I would not do this for you), I help you along with a little adversity to die to the world—but out of love.

X^4 A 649   *n.d.*, 1852

« 3767 *Renunciation*

We men are inclined to turn things in such a way that we say of renunciation: I cannot—and then all the more think that we need grace.

But that is altogether unchristian in the same way that the fiery vehemence with which a man wants to hold to God in order to enjoy the world, however much it might seem to outdo in fervency the quiet, humble obedience of renunciation, is not God-worship but idol-worship, and Christianity least of all.

x⁵ A 4   *n.d.*, 1852

« 3768 *Voluntary Suffering—Involuntary Suffering—Dying to the World*

That a man must be brought closer to the edge of suffering and misery to get the actual taste of Christianity is easy to see.

But when the suffering and misery which bring a man to the edge is involuntary, against his will (something to which he has not willingly exposed himself, something in which he is involved unintentionally), such a person—with respect to becoming and being Christian—seems to get off easier than the one whose suffering is voluntary. After all, the person whose suffering is involuntary merely expresses that he has become unhappy and that he is suffering and has found consolation in Christianity, but he does not disturb the others. And that, perhaps, is what sometimes hurts the most—namely, that the voluntary not only implicates the volunteer but actually sets the goal for others as well. It is as if he wanted to disturb or must utterly disturb others, those nice goodnatured people who, however, do not feel the need of great decisions—as if he must disturb their peace and happiness.

Note this. No one becomes a Christian if he is totally without voluntary suffering, for to become a Christian requires dying to the world, and dying to the world is an act of freedom (to die is inevitable, but to die to the world is free). It is not the kind of an equation where a certain extremity of wretchedness and misery = dying to the world. No, one may live his whole life in such misery without therefore dying to the world. Perhaps he also finds a certain consolation in Christianity, but still without dying to the world—which will become manifest if the earthly wretchedness is removed—whereupon he perhaps no longer feels the need of Christianity. That means that he has not died to the world; the natural man is still in him; for no suffering can compel a man to die to the world since it is free.

To want to have the consolation of Christianity and also enjoy life is the kind of Christianity the pastors live.

To have become unhappy and then find consolation in Christianity is perhaps an illusory relationship to Christianity.

To die to the world means voluntarily to give up the things of the earth. This is Christianity.

If the voluntary did not belong to becoming a Christian, then the kind of collisions the New Testament talks about—hating father and mother, etc. for the sake of Christ—would be impossible.

x⁵ A 19   *n.d.*, 1852

« 3769 *What It Means "To Die to the World"*

This is the requirement.[1383] On the other hand, it is something not even God can force a man to do, for even if God deprived a man of everything, saddled him with all sorts of sufferings and kept on doing so, it would not follow that a man thereby would die to the world, for to die to the world is an act of freedom.

And yet this is the requirement. We see from this how far our ordinary conception of Christianity is from essential Christianity, for we believe that if it begins with suffering, all we have to do is stick it out, hope, and then better times will come—O, what an infinite distance this is from dying to the world.

But God neither will nor can force a man to die to the world. He can help him along with sufferings, with adversity, etc.—but what God is waiting for is the act of freedom on man's part—to die to the world, freely relinquishing the world, not wanting to have it.

x⁵ A 25   *n.d.*, 1852

« 3770 *Rigorousness*

To die to the world is the requirement.[1384] But compel—no, says God, that I will absolutely not do, not at any price will I force a man to do that, and neither is it possible, since it is an act of freedom.

So we men merrily go on living. We play hooky—and since God does not seem to notice anything, does not use force against us (something he will not do), we eventually delude ourselves into thinking that we are on the right path, and we even thank God that everything goes so beautifully for us.

O, my God, and the requirement is to die to the world—and that will be the judgment.

We perhaps think that rigorousness would consist in God's taking a hard grip on us. No, no, the rigorousness is precisely God's pretending as if it were nothing at all—and that dying to the world is the requirement nevertheless and will be the judgment.

This is how Christianity understands the matter and therefore teaches quite consistently that the very fact that God takes a hard grip on a man is grace, something God does only for those he loves.

How is this to be understood? Very simply: Christianity assumes that before God the whole world is submerged in evil, is lost—ergo, mercy can manifest itself only in his being very hard and rigorous with an individual. This gives such individuals an advantage over the others, who go on living securely—in damnation.

There is nothing, nothing as consistent as Christianity. O, but how a man resists getting this consistency drummed into his head.

x⁵ A 29   n.d., 1852

« 3771 *To Hate Oneself*

This is how it should be understood: as soon as you discover you are selfishly or sensately attached to something, you must give it up in self-denial, and if you do not succeed right away you must be put under special police surveillance in the form of a striving toward giving it up.

But as you work more and more in that direction and feel greater assurance of eventual success, a new kind of self-love can suddenly awaken, which must be dislodged by hating one's self. To be specific, satisfaction over being able to do without can become a selfishness. Thus in a certain sense it can be hating oneself to be resigned to there being one or more particular things one cannot really manage to surrender. Indeed, it could be the greatest possible self-satisfaction ultimately to become pure spirit: thus it can be hating oneself to resign oneself humbly and yet happily to there being some particular things one is unable to conquer, some specific things one cannot manage to do without—yes, it can be hating oneself to let a few such things stand as a memento of one's impotence.

Yet this matter must be left up to each person's honesty, for it could so easily become a mask. And it is most dangerous (as Arndt[1385] somewhere in the first book of his *True Christianity*, observation no. 12 toward the end, illuminates with many illustrations and examples) that one does not *break* with everything in self-denial. Here also is the difference between Epicureanism and Stoicism: to want to refine, as they say, pleasure, desire—and to break with it absolutely.

x⁵ A 53   n.d., 1852

« 3772 *To Hate Oneself—the Proclamation of Christianity—the Official Proclamation*

According to the New Testament, there is only one kind of Christian: "the disciple" ["*Discipelen*"].

The requirements[1386] for being a disciple of Christ can be found in the New Testament (forsaking everything, hating oneself, one's own life, etc.).

What happens in the world to the person who takes this seriously (forsaking everything, hating himself)—that is, to the disciple—can also be found in the New Testament, which makes no attempt to conceal that he will be hated[1387] by everybody, cursed, detested, etc.—thus a person must really hate himself (how consistent Christianity is, after all!) to be willing to expose himself to such things.

————

To hate oneself. Christianity specifically teaches that a person can love God only if he hates himself—and Christianity requires that he love God.

————

To hate oneself. This must not be understood, however, as a demand of the law, for it is God one must love—consequently it is the expression for love.

Still less is hating oneself a way of achieving perfection or even meritoriousness. No, no, the requirement is always infinite, and infinitely changeable; thus if someone brashly claims to God's face that he has fulfilled the requirement, it can only lead to the folly of wanting to exhaust the infinite requirement through finite striving.

No, the purpose of the requirement to hate oneself is to teach one rightly to depend upon grace. Thus at the proper time and place the person who honestly strives to hate himself will also be reminded of the words: Be content with my grace[1388]—that is, love yourself, yet not as if it were hereby decided once and for all.

————

The New Testament teaches that Christianity is hating oneself.

The official preaching of Christianity has gained these millions of Christians by teaching that to love God is to love oneself, that in order really to enjoy this life one must have the cooperation of God, that the expectation of an eternal salvation is the primary factor in adding flavor to the joys and blessings of this life (Mynster).

Thus the average man can never be brought to espouse Christianity if Christianity means to hate oneself, or even if it is simply required that one recognize and acknowledge that this is the requirement.

———

Has a man the right to attack another man because his life does not meet the requirement of being a Christian?

No, never. Why not? Because he thereby changes (alters) Christianity and makes it into law. Furthermore, if he makes it into "law" for another man, God does the same—for him[1389]—and, after all, we are all in the situation of not fulfilling the requirement.

How, then, can the attack be made?[1390] Quite simply. When "the proclamation" either reduces the demand or keeps silent about it, the attack is made at the proper point—then the attack is not made upon the individual's life but upon his teaching. It is precisely here that the dubious character of the proclamation is most frequently to be found: it keeps silent about the requirement—and no wonder, since, officially, Christianity is to love oneself, to enjoy life, etc.

Consequently the requirement is suppressed. Whereas the requirement is expressly to hate oneself, which, however, must be understood to mean that it can never be done successfully by any man, and that I can have recourse to grace, since it is a matter solely between God and myself—whereas this is the way it is, it is indeed conceivable that I would recognize and acknowledge the requirement and humble myself under it, but that my striving to hate myself would really never amount to anything, so that I still would not lose out on life's joys and blessings. Well, no one but God has the right to judge this. But men are far from satisfied with this. Worldly craving and striving still do not satisfy a person if one does not dare give it the appearance of being earnestness and wisdom; worldly craving and striving would not satisfy a person at all if one were solemnly to admit what the requirement actually is, that one knows it but yet cannot bring himself to strive to meet it. This, you see, is why the requirement must be altered or suppressed—and here is where the attack can be made.

———

To hate oneself. In order to be able to proclaim Christianity one must already hate himself, because really to want to present the requirement—and consequently thereby to expose oneself in his deficiency (when the requirement is reduced, one becomes obviously more of a somebody)—means that one already hates himself.

It is eternally certain that the person who actually takes seriously the New Testament requirement for being a Christian will experience what is predicted in the New Testament.

But I wonder if the person who simply limited himself but at least did present, proclaim unconditionally, the requirement without either personally expressing it rigorously or binding others to it will slip out of it scot-free. It is very doubtful.

But suppose that as far as striving to hate myself is concerned I dare relax my effort, trusting in grace: has one then also the right—trusting in grace—to reduce the requirement, Christianity's requirement, to the point that one actually keeps silent about it—and this is still supposed to be Christianity.

X⁵ A 58   *n.d.*, 1852

« 3773 *"He Who Does Not Hate Father and Mother and His Own Life etc. Is Not Worthy of Me."*[1391]

"Alas, this I do not do, but simply because I am not worthy of you I come to you; you are my Savior and Redeemer; if I were worthy of you I would seem to need you less."

Quite right. One may legitimately pray in this way, and this prayer would also be heard. But in the very same moment there is heard: But from now on you must begin to hate father and mother and your own life etc. That is, through grace there is unceasingly forgiveness for the past but no exemption from the future, no exemption from striving, and so that this may be done in earnest, my life must be ordered in such a way that I can begin to strive. To secure one's life in all possible earthly respects and then protest that one will strive in the future is to make a fool of God and is just as foolish as if a person about to run a race were to put on one coat after another and try to make us think that now he is really going to run. No, it is just the reverse, the coats are removed—otherwise a person's protestations are untruth.

X⁵ A 68   *n.d.*, 1853

« 3774 *The Infinite Change in the God-concept Corresponding to Dying to the World*

The spontaneously devout life is lived somewhat as follows. A man —this is the natural man—wishes and desires in human innocence to rejoice in this life, to enjoy its benefits, the good things of the earth —O God is love, infinite love, and he has all the good gifts in his hand. This giver of good gifts is very close to man, so infinitely, blessedly close that in him we live, move, and have our being, and he is the Almighty who at all times has millions of possibilities—and the man has an understanding with this God that he has nothing against rejoicing in this life and enjoying its benefits.

The man goes on living in this fashion. Essentially his life and work are spent in gaining these innocent (humanly speaking) earthly benefits—and then he prays to God—fervently, ardently, eloquently—and there is no change in his understanding that on God's part there is nothing, nothing at all, against wanting to enjoy this life and desiring the things of the earth, nothing at all, no, God will even give them himself—therefore he prays and prays for these things.

Perhaps years pass by, and he does not get what he wants; perhaps he dies without getting it—but through it all he steadfastly continues to believe that on God's part there is nothing against a man's wishing to enjoy this life and craving for such enjoyment. The fact that he fails he can then explain in other ways, as part of God's prodigious plans, but his God-picture is and remains unchanged.

Then Christianity comes along. All at once it says: No, stop. To be sure God is love—but he is spirit, and he has a completely different idea about good gifts than you do. If you wish to be in harmony with him and as a consequence be able to pray to him, he requires that you find it more blessed to do without than to get, more blessed to suffer than to enjoy, etc. He is far from leaving you without any help in this respect. No, if you yourself will only venture out, he promises you a spirit[1392] who will actually make it more blessed for you to suffer than to enjoy.

Here is the fatal stroke which corresponds to dying to the world. For no matter how utterly hopeless the outlook, as long as a man relates spontaneously to God he maintains the hope that they will surely come—the earthly things he wants—for God, after all, has millions of possibilities and is love. But when it is God himself who will not, when he has a completely different idea—that is death. If you hanker after the things of this earth, then God is precisely the one you must avoid—how dreadful, therefore, that he is so near to you, and that at all times he has millions of possibilities—of bringing to nought all your efforts to achieve your aspirations.

You see, dying to the world means that if you do not will as God wills when you first suffer the death, he has millions of possibilities for constraining you—if he wants to—until you surrender and believe that it is just as he promises, that his spirit will make suffering more blissful for you than enjoying.

That the spirit will make suffering more blissful than enjoying, of course, must not be interpreted to mean—and Governance will certainly prevent you from doing that—that the instant you freely deny yourself you feel bliss, and a bliss akin to that which the man of immediacy desires. No, in that case the self-denial becomes a *shrewd* transaction.

No, first, first of all, you will feel suffering—and then, yes, even if it is not said, you can go on believing and relating yourself to it, assured that it will come, the moment will come when the Spirit will make it more blessed to do without than to get—not the moment when you get what you want—no, no, then it would still be the same old thing —no, the moment when it actually becomes more blessed to do without than to get.

This is New Testament Christianity. Whoever you are, answer me —do you believe that a man automatically embraces this way, and do you believe that there is nothing wrong with the fact that people are Christians by the millions.

x^5 A 79   *n.d.*, 1853

« 3775 *Picture—Contrast*

Once upon a time, in the first days of Christianity,[1393] to dare call oneself a Christian was something which was bought with the renunciation of everything and then was maintained at such a price that a strict discipline watched over morals and in extreme cases there was the punishment (and it is well to note that it was regarded as a severe punishment) of being expelled from the Christian community—that is, of losing the name of Christian, for at that time the Christians had no political power.

Nowadays the situation is such that it is impossible to free oneself from being called a Christian. An atheist can declare Christianity to be a lie as loudly and clearly as possible, and it does not help a bit—he must, declares the state, be regarded as a Christian just the same; here no doting mamma can be of any help—he is officially a Christian. We will not get anywhere if we let people get out of being Christians this way; the thing could spread, and what do we do then for all the various public officials and the like who have a financial interest in our calling ourselves, all of us, Christians.

XI^1 A 79   *n.d.*, 1854

« 3776 *Luke 14, the End*

The end of this chapter has always made a curious impression on me, as if Christ strongly advised a person against becoming his disciple, recommended that he use his native intelligence.

But that is not the meaning. The meaning is this: if you will not renounce everything, you cannot be my disciple—for the world's opposition to you will become so great that you will do best to come to terms now with him "who comes against you with 20,000." The world will knock over your tower or laugh at you for beginning.

Thus it is not a matter of Christ's rejecting a person; no, Christ merely prophecies what the result will be if a person renounces everything and still wants to be Christ's disciple.[1394]

XI[1] A 116   *n.d.*, 1854

« 3777 *Christianity in the New Testament Is Renunciation;*

we, to the contrary, have got Christianity reversed in such a way, as I have often pointed out, that it is the enjoyment of life, so that the blessedness of eternity, once and for all assured for all of us, must really give us the desire to want to enjoy and be gladdened by this life.

And not only that, but many times this point of view has made Christians, in thoughtlessness or in actual corruption, more callous toward the suffering, the poor, the forsaken—in short, all who are unable to share in enjoying life— than even pagans and Jews are. We have put them aside and comforted ourselves on their behalf with the thought that it will last only a few years—and then the poor, the suffering, and the like will become just as blessed as everybody else.

XI[1] A 143   *n.d.*, 1854

« 3778 *A Breach* [et Brud]—*A Bride* [en Brud]

With his demonic wisdom, the Seducer[1395] says: A bride [*en Brud*] and a breach [*et Brud*] correspond to one another as male and female.

With a quite different meaning, Christianity says (when one reflects on its calling the believer a bride and Christ the bridegroom): A breach [*et Brud*] and a bride [*en Brud*]—that is, in order to become a bride you must make a breach between the world and everything and yourself. Consequently, not a [*en*] bride and a [*et*] breach but a [*et*] breach and a [*en*] bride.

XI[1] A 283   *n.d.*, 1854

« 3779 *To Hate One's Self*

is Christianity's requirement; to hate oneself is the only passion which can carry the divine through.

Human nature, even the best-intentioned person, is always in one way or another honest enough, if you please, to love itself.

Consequently human nature cannot carry Christianity; it always reverses the relationship, evades the demand, avoids what Christianity really is: to carry Christianity through the world—and cunningly turns it around to mean that Christianity is supposed to carry us through the world.

This means that Christianity, instead of being in the divine egoity, is adroitly shifted into human egotism. Even the most honest of mankind do this, not to mention base, knavish, demoralized mankind.

XI[1] A 376   *n.d.*, 1854

« 3780 · *Service with Character—Respect for Christianity*

This is essentially Christian, this teaching: to abandon the world, to renounce the world.

When a person proclaims it in such a way that he actually renounces the world, then that is Christianity.

Imagine such a person—he actually gives up his salary, profit: my, how wonderful! "That will certainly be appreciated." Now if eventually this act is appreciated, then he himself will have to take care and manage to avoid such appreciation, lest he reap a benefit, a salary which he did not renounce. Meanwhile it no doubt will not be necessary for him to do anything on his part, because actually to give up salary and profit is far from being esteemed by one's contemporaries; it is precisely how a man brings down upon himself every possible trouble in this life. When Christianity as renunciation of the world is proclaimed in such a manner that the proclaimer actually renounces the world—and it is not Christianity otherwise—then Christianity becomes a disturbing force which must be guarded against, if in no other way, then at least by disparaging it and calling it unchristian extremism etc.: ". . . . . and by such ridiculous extremism such a proclaimer of course deserves it when even with the deepest good will men can respect neither him nor Christianity."

If, however, the essentially Christian (renunciation of the world) is proclaimed in such a way that it pays off splendidly for the proclaimer, *das ist was Anders!* Now Christianity gains prestige, people open their eyes, respect Christianity more and more, are more and more attracted to it and accept it, want to embrace it, etc.

Now imagine that a proclaimer has huge success with this kind of proclamation: imagine the advancement Christianity thereby gains for itself, what respect and prestige! Even the most miserly of all businessmen says: "That man instils respect for Christianity! It's clear to me —and the more I think of it the clearer it is—that neither wheat nor butter, meat, fish, salt, brandy—in short, no commodity, nor speculating in government bonds, pays so splendidly or yields as much as Christianity. You have to hand it to him—that man knows how to create respect for Christianity. And it isn't only a matter of financial profit. There's the honor and prestige. As to my views on that, if honor and prestige have to be bought by giving up dollar profits, that is too high a price to pay. But, when it is possible to have that *also*—then I—who probably am called Butter-and-egg-man Jensen because I deal in butter and eggs and do a big business in butter and eggs—I am not so silly or stupid that I wouldn't take the prestige along with the rest. If I could manage to run my butter and egg business in the name of our Lord Jesus Christ in such a way—please note, in such a way—that I had the same financial profit I now have, perhaps a bit more—I would certainly relish the pleasure of no longer scraping and bowing, as I do now, before the dealers who buy my butter—but having them come with their money and bowing deeply to me, embarrassed at having to mention money in my honored presence—naturally we have to be sure that I get the money!—scraping and bowing before a most eminent man of God. —The same applies to sitting at the head table at the social events. I completely agree with Holberg's Henrich[1396] that when being the most distinguished guest sitting at the head table merely means getting the first and worst cut of the roast, the trial cup of coffee—well, then I far prefer being the well-to-do guest who sits toward the end of the table but gets the best cut of roast and the best cup of coffee. But when they can be united, when one can be the well-to-do gentleman who gets the best cut of roast and the best cup of coffee and is *also* Number One, then I am not so silly or stupid that I do not know how to evaluate honor—if one, please note, also has the profit."

"See, this is why I have respect for that man and for Christianity and instill respect for them in my children; there is no man for whom I take off my hat and bow so low as for that man and for what he teaches me to respect: Christianity."

XI² A 298   *n.d.*, 1853–54

« **3781**

If someone entered in a race were to come to the track wearing heavy overshoes, three jackets, and not only that but his friends waited for him there with a huge cap, a regular wind-catcher, which he put on

—would it not be laughable? And why? Because his clothing would have no relationship or, more correctly, would have a misrelationship to his undertaking.

So, too, it is laughable if one, in proclaiming Christianity, that is, proclaiming self-denial, renunciation, and also how the truth must suffer in this world, arrays himself in velvet and medals and bands, steps forth accompanied by gold-braid arrayed attendants, etc.—for his appearance has no relationship, or more correctly, has a parodying misrelationship to his speaking. And yet no one laughs. His speaking is perhaps a masterpiece of eloquence; it produces a prodigious effect—but, strangely enough, not in the form of laughter—that is the most laughable of all.

XI² A 348   n.d., 1854

REPENTANCE

« **3782**

It will not do to plunge ahead as the moralists, even rejecting repentance—in the physical world do we not see the mist rise from the earth like a silent prayer and like a prayer granted return as refreshing dew—?

I A 81   *n.d.*, 1835

« **3783**

> *Je tiefer wir in uns versinken,*
> *Je näher dringen wir zur Hölle,*
> *Bald fühlen wir des Glutstroms Welle,*
> *Und mussen bald darin vertrinken;*
> *Er zehrt das Fleisch von unserm Leibe,*
> *Und öde wirds im Zeitvertreibe,*
> *In uns ist Tod!*
> *Die Welt ist Gott!*
> *O Mensch lass nicht vom Menschen los,*
> *Ist deine Sünde noch so gross*
> *Meid nur die* Sehnsucht nach den Sünden*
> *So kannst Du noch viel Gnade finden;*
> *Wer hat die Gnade noch ermessen?*
> *Es kann der Mensch so viel vergessen.* [1397]

Die Gräfinn Dolores [1398]
II, p. 260.

*for even in repentance there can hide a longing for sin, if repentance is more contemplatively deadening than awakening.

III A 85   *n.d.*, 1841

« **3784**

As far as Greek esthetics is concerned, Aristotle says a remarkable thing in book III of his *Ethics*, [1399] chapter 2: "An act done in ignorance cannot be regarded as intrinsically voluntary; only when an entirely involuntary act is done with dissatisfaction and later arouses repentance can it be regarded as voluntary." When it arouses repentance, it is construed to be voluntary,[1400] and yet it is really only at that moment that Aristotle believes it can be regarded as involuntary.

IV C 19 *n.d.*, 1842-43

« 3785

The fire of repentance and the accusing conscience is like that Grecian fire[1401] which could not be put out with water—so, too, this one can be extinguished only with tears.[1402]

VI B 173 *n.d.*, 1844-45

« 3786

Ecclesiastes 3:9 (What gain
has the worker from his toil?)

Everything has its time, says Solomon—

There is even that which has its time of preparation, but does this hold true of the confession of sin; is not contemplation all too slow in relation to the speed of repentance, in relation to what is to occur in that very moment.

VII¹ B 147 *n.d.*, 1846

« 3787

Gregory VIII[1403] says: Penance means to lament the sins that have been committed and not to commit any more the sins that have been lamented.

VIII¹ A 203 *n.d.*, 1847

« 3788

Sorrow, according to the world, is itself sin, and yet one often is or becomes conceited and self-important in his sadness. Sorrow, according to God, is essentially repentance[1404]—and when the sadness has lasted too long, it takes penitence to put sadness a little aside. It is quite certain that when penitence simultaneously maintains the relationship of guilt to God, one does not notice at all what he may have suffered in bearing sadness. Thus when a man becomes far too impatient in his sadness, God often punishes him by allowing him to sink into one sin or another. Now it takes penitence to lift him up; now he has something to weep over.

IX A 345 *n.d.*, 1848

« 3789

• How dead, externalized, and formalized everything in Christianity has become is seen even incidentally if one opens a book like Rothe's[1405] about the Church year, although I do not hereby mean to criticize him. Here it says that the Gospels for Advent are taken from the story of John the Baptist, for only by true penance can one prepare himself worthily for the great festival. And so it goes throughout. We read this kind of thing as if we were reading a dancing teacher's instructions on how a dance should be performed: one couple out and form a chain etc. etc. We are through with penitence on the fourth Sunday in Advent, Christmas-happy the first Christmas day, and how is one, then, on "pork-Sunday" or "fat-Tuesday," as these days were called in the old times?

x^1 A 515   *n.d.*, 1849

« 3790

The gospel says: Seek the kingdom of God first.
Experience teaches that when men have sought
    their peace and joy every other place they *finally* in the end
    turn to God.
If a man is to reach the point of beginning to seek the kingdom of God first, he must begin with repentance.[1406]

x^2 A 360   *n.d.*, 1850

REPETITION

« 3791

Even in insanity massive monotony is so predominant that (according to medical reports) one very seldom encounters a phenomenon which has not already been described many times before.

II A 445   May 24, 1839

« 3792

3. *Repetition*
   here doubt could be broken off—one assumes that there is no repetition. But it cannot be done without assuming a repetition.[1407]
4. *The Actuality of Repetition*
   Illusion

8. The first expression for the relationship between immediacy and mediacy is *REpetition.*
   In immediacy there is no repetition; it may be thought to depend on the dissimilarity of things; not at all, if everything in the world were absolutely identical there still would be no repetition.

9. But when the possibility of repetition is posited, and then the question of its actuality arises: is it actually a repetition.

Illusion
IV B 10:3, 4, 8, 9   n.d., 1842–43

« 3793

Repetition comes again everywhere. (1) When I am going to act, my action has existed in my consciousness in conception and thought —otherwise I act thoughtlessly—that is, I do not act. (2) Inasmuch as I am going to act, I presuppose that I am in an original integral state. Now comes the problem of sin, the problem of a second repetition,[1408] for now I must return to myself again. (3) The real paradox by which

I become the single individual, for if I remain in sin, understood as the universal, there is only repetition no. 2.

One may at this point compare the Aristotelian categories: *Das—Was—War—Sein.* See Marbach, *Geschichte der Philosophie des Mittelalters,* para. 128, pp. 4–5, and para. 102 in his *Geschichte der griechischen Philosophie.*[1409]

IV A 156   *n.d.,* 1843

« **3794**

"Repetition" is and remains a religious category.[1410] Constantin Constantius therefore cannot proceed further. He is clever, an ironist, battles the interesting[1411]—but is not aware that he himself is caught in it. The first form of the interesting is to love change; the second[1412] is to want repetition, but still in *selbstgenugsamkeit,* with no suffering— therefore Constantine is wrecked on what he himself has discovered, and the young man goes no further.

IV A 169   *n.d.,* 1844

« **3795**

Earnestness is acquired originality.
    Different from habit—which is the disappearance of self-awareness. (See Rosenkrantz, Psych.[1413])
Therefore genuine repetition is—earnestness.[1414]

V B 69   *n.d.,* 1844

ROMANTICISM, CLASSICISM

« **3796**

First of all I must protest against the view that the romantic can be captured in a definition, for the romantic lies essentially in flowing over all boundaries.

I A 130   n.d., 1836

« **3797**

I wonder if the romantic does not consist essentially in the lack of a relative standard which advances its claim right at this point; if only the manifold is considered, then something which is indeed romantic could not be subsumed under this concept. I think of a wide, wide desert,* such as the North African desert, for example, which according to Ehrenberg's writings (see note) is very romantic, also the Jutland heath (Blicher), the beginning of the novel *Telse.*[1415]

* See an interesting piece[1416] in the *Dansk. Ugeskrift* (IV, p. 153 etc., p. 154 n.): "It has been observed previously by many travelers that the lack of a standard for the relative size of bodies in the great, empty African desert gives occasion to curious confusion. I myself have often been disappointed this way. Thinking that I saw a vulture or some other large bird sitting on a rise nearby, I have approached with cocked gun until at last I discovered that it was not a bird close by but a camel on a faraway elevation. Similarly I have often hesitated and failed to shoot at a bird because I thought it to be a large animal in the distance . . . . . It is similar with hearing. To the ear of a European the dead silence which prevails at night in these deserts is something like the singularity which the flat, monotonous plain presents to the eye. At an unbelievable distance one can hear footsteps, conversation, yes, even a soft whisper." —And therefore one cannot determine whether the sound comes from far away or close by.

I A 131   n.d., 1836

« **3798**

Addition to 3797 (I A 131):

The dissimilarity in games may also be pointed out; the ancients used gymnastics, hurled the discus—the romantic period hunted and fished (both particularly romantic. All the dreaming about what one might possibly catch).

I A 132   March, 1836

« **3799**

Why is it that most, at least the most prominent, of the romantic school went over to Catholicism? Was it not simply because the Reformation, as that which returned to something original, for that very reason intimated that it had the coming into existence of the idea in the form, a present tense which it sought once again to make into a present tense, while Catholicism essentially aspired forward (but surely not because the Catholic Church service was more sensuous, etc.)

I A 134   March, 1836

« **3800**

An authentic romantic situation is that of Ingeborg[1417] sitting on the seashore following with her eyes Frithiof's departing sail, although the romantic element here would disappear if one imagined her dwelling more on the thought of her loss than on Frithiof's journey and his undertaking.

I A 136   March, 1836

« **3801**

The romantic actually arises from the two halves of one idea being kept apart by some intervening foreign element. When Adam was created, Adam's idea craved its supplement in Eve (the animals came to him and he gave them names—multiplicity is here—the chorus, if I may call it that, is here—irony is here—); Eve comes, and the romantic is over, there is repose. —Man is created, the sinner; this circumstance craves its supplement, namely, Christianity. Among the nations this halfness in existence now became conscious, the romantic developed —the rest formed the chorus, irony, etc.—Christ comes, there is repose —Christ's second coming could be treated this way again.

These statements are easily documented in the Middle Ages generally, as well as in the achievements which belong to the romantic.

Is echo romantic. Yes, but when it answers, the romantic is over. The romantic period always has something *in mente.*

I A 140   n.d. 1836

« **3802**

Furthermore, the romantic depends upon whether it is primarily a longing gazing into an eternity (the more sentimental) or a diversity conditioned by vigorous action.

I A 142   March, 1836

« **3803**

The romantic is demonstrated in the key phrase in Baggesen's *Thora fra Havsgaard*,[1418] the returning one, I shall return.

Is Joan of Arc romantic, and to what extent?

Does the romantic lie in variety, multiplicity? No, for the classical does indeed have nymphs, nereids, etc., but the romantic in variety consists in this, that an unsatisfied need has evoked it, yet without finding any satisfaction in it.

I A 155   April, 1836

« **3804**

When I speak of the contrast between the classical and the romantic, I of course do not have in mind any particular esthetic category but rather a basic contrast which must lend different coloration to every particular segment in esthetics.

I A 171   June 12, 1836

« **3805**

Now I understand something I frequently have wondered about—namely, that Thorvaldsen[1419] emerged in our age. He really belongs to Hegel's generation. The romantic has vanished, and the present tense of necessity (the classical) has commenced (sculpture belongs to the classical), and thus we have experienced a new classical stage. The romantic is reconciled with the world. The same thing happened in monasticism, which for a long time has been finished historically but whose last stage was essentially classical, the form in which it must also come again, if it ever does. In the beginning the monks lived completely outside the world, embattled with the world and wearing a special habit so that everyone could recognize them; finally they lived in the world, reconciled with it (Jesuits, etc.).

I A 200   July 2, 1836

« **3806**

Even the most classical restlessness (for example, Laocoön crushed by serpents) is still serene—the most romantic serenity is restless—for example:

Waldeinsamkeit
Wie liegst Du weit!
O dich gereut
Einst mit der Zeit.—
Ach einzige Freud
Waldeinsamkeit.

(Tieck, *Phantasus,* I, *Schriften,* IV, p. 161: *"der blonde Eckbert."*)[1420]

I A 203   July 10, 1836

« 3807

Does not I Corinthians 13:12 ($\beta\lambda\acute{\epsilon}\pi o\mu\epsilon\nu$ $\gamma\grave{\alpha}\rho$ $\H{\alpha}\rho\tau.$ $\delta\iota'\acute{\epsilon}\sigma\acute{o}\pi\tau\rho o\upsilon$ $\acute{\epsilon}\nu$ $\alpha\grave{\iota}\nu\acute{\iota}\gamma\mu\alpha\tau\iota$[1421]) imply a recognition of the necessity of *allegory* for our present condition?

The relation of allegory to the romantic?

Aug. 3, '36

since the whole idea cannot rest and be contained in the actual expression. —metaphor—

I A 214   *n.d.*

« 3808

Corresponding phenomena: scholasticism in the Middle Ages' fantasy-period; the romantic school in our day's period of reason.

I A 216   August 4, 1836

« 3809

The romantic has miracles; this the classical cannot have (Hegelians—Schleiermacher).

I A 217   August 4, 1836

« 3810

In a way the romantic can also be seen in the drapery which modern art gives its statues and paintings (a kind of allegory).

See Görres, p. 276, 11.7 ff., p. 302, 11.5 ff.[1422]

I A 218   August 4, 1836

« 3811

With respect to the distinction between the classical and the romantic, it may also be pointed out that the actor (in the romantic period) continually strives to create an illusion for the spectator, something he does not do at any particular moment or continuously but suggests with an appropriate facial expression, a line, etc.; whereas the actor in Greece or Rome, in his *cothurnus* or *soccus,* through the use of masks etc. entered the stage thus and so at the very outset and remained the same all evening, which was somewhat automatic and did not leave much opportunity for using facial expressions.

See Schlegel, *Werke,* V, middle of p. 61.[1423]

I A 219   August 9, 1836

« 3812

Why is hand organ music so often appealing? It is no doubt because of the romantic involved in the mode of its appearance. It is, so to speak, a kind of poetry on the street corner. One does not expect music at all, and suddenly he begins to play.

I A 228   August 25, 1836

« 3813

Since Goethe formed a link to the classical [*Antique*], why did the age not follow him, why does it not follow him, since Hegel did it, why is it not effective—because these two had narrowed the esthetic and speculative process to this; but the political process also must go through its romantic development, and for that reason the whole modern romantic school are—politicians.[1424]

I A 230   August 25, 1836

« 3814

The romantic was also expressed in a distinctive way in the Middle Ages by all the wandering about that went on: wandering knights, traveling scholars, itinerant singers, musicians, monks, etc.—
"fliegendes Blatt."[1425]

I A 262   *n.d.,* 1836

« 3815

When I consider the matter entirely *in abstracto,* I must in all consistency come to the conclusion that the romantic resolves itself in a classicism,* although every attempt to demonstrate the classical period in time is naturally of a mythological nature and arises only because of the human weakness which can never grasp a concept in all its infinite evanescence but always must stake it off by using boundaries —thus the expectations of the Jews were bound up with Christ's coming, Christ's coming was bound up with his return, etc., which again in all consistency must be regarded as pointing to a coming again, etc., because every attempt to say "Now it is finished" is an attempt to transform it into mythology.

Nov. 30, '36

*For line 3 on previous page: romantic striving is a self-consuming, and I cannot render it eternal, since then I would get an eternity consisting of an infinite aggregate of moments—yet all this *in abstracto.*

I A 294   n.d.

« 3816

It is no doubt true that Baggesen[1426] lacks that certain "inexpressible something" (according to a critique of Baggesen from the German in *Kiøbhsposten*[1427] for today), but this is the romantic itself, a continual grasping after something which eludes one, and therefore it can never be produced but only the image of the shadow etc., that is, *the allegory.* See my papers on the romantic. The classical really has no allegory.

I A 306   n.d., 1836

« 3817

The prolixity and diversity found in Indian poetry—which has led some to characterize it as romantic—is not romantic; it is *vegetative-prolification;* on the whole, life in the East is vegetative; indeed, their gods are borne by a calyx, grow out of flowers.

See *speculative Darstellung des Christenthums, v. M.,*[1428] Leipzig 1819, p. 168: "*Daher rühren die vielen Reitze des Pflanzenreichs, das unendliche Spiel von Formen und Farben, welches die Pflanzen in unschuldiger bewusstloser Offenheit vor den Augen des Zuschauers entfalten.*"[1429]—

Dec. 25, 1836

(I have this book.)

I A 315   Dec. 25, 1836

« 3818

Christian romanticism no doubt has an oriental aspect, but it is only the three kings from the East who have seen its star and now bring their *gifts,* gold and precious incense (the drapery).

II A 109   July 7, 1837

« 3819

There is so much talk about variety as a necessary factor in the romantic, but I could almost say the opposite, for absolute solitude, where not a breeze stirs* and no barking of dogs is heard in the distance—and yet the trees bow to each other and recount the memories of their childhood when the nymphs lived in them, and yet right in this moment the imagination revels in complete enjoyment—and what else is this if it is not romantic, and I would merely ask those concerned a Socratic question, whether the Pompeian taste is not very bound and very varied.

*And yet one feels the talkativeness of the air, just as on other occasions one feels its visibility.

II A 638   n.d., 1837

« 3820 *A Union of the Classic and the Romantic*

A nude Apollo with nothing on but a modern dress coat with long tails, and with one of them he modestly hides his nakedness.

II A 699   February 6, 1838

« 3821

In *A Thousand and One Nights*[1430] the oriental character is delineated also through the ingenious confusion with which the different tales entwine like the foliage of plants which luxuriantly intertwine upward, and over all this rests heaven—oppressing, alarming—it is Scheherezade, who preserves life by telling tales.

III A 113   n.d., 1841

« 3822

I find an absolutely perfect example of the romantic in the Old Testament, in the Book of Judith, chapter 10, verse 11:

"And Judith went out, she and her maidservant with her; but the men of the city watched her until she came down from the mountain, until she came through the valley and they could see her no more. And they proceeded onward in the valley."[1431]

III A 197   May, 1842

« 3823

Consequently it is a mistake if one believes that genuine romanticism is confined to Catholicism, if one believes, as does the author of *Either/Or,* that in our day it should be abolished—first in the esthetical, then in the ethical.[1432]

IV B 50:4   n.d., 1843

ROUSSEAU

« **3824**

That passage in Rousseau's *Emile*, [1433] book IV, is splendid, where the vicar says: "I have now, my young friend, given you my confession of faith . . . . . You are the first one to whom I have confessed this, perhaps you are the only one to whom I will ever confess it." Now comes the good part: "As long as any sound faith is to be found among men, one must not disturb the peaceful souls or trouble the simple souls in their faith by heaping up problems which they are unable to solve and which merely disquiet them without enlightening them. But if their faith happens to be shaken, then one must preserve the trunk by sacrificing the branches. The troubled, wavering, and almost dying consciences which find themselves in the situation in which I have seen you need to be strengthened and restored, and in order to establish them again on the foundations of eternal truth, it is necessary to complete the work by tearing down the shaky pillars on which they still believe themselves to be supported."

X^3 A 6   *n.d.*, 1850

« **3825**

There is psychological depth in a remark in *Emile* [1434] (in the story called "Emile and Sophie, or the Solitaries"): "I speak continually about forgiving (Sophie had been unfaithful to him) without taking into account that the offended party forgives often, but the offending party never." Why is it so difficult for the offending party to forgive? Because it is so difficult to humble oneself under one's own guilt. This accounts for the hate whereby the world never forgives its having wronged the good. For the most part Rousseau has not understood this, for the explanation Emile appends makes the sentence trivial: "Undoubtedly it was her intention to inflict on me all the evil she has inflicted on me. Ha, how she must hate me!" But this is not the dilemma at all. The trouble is that the guilty party still loves himself too much really to be able penitently to hate himself. In order to be able to forgive completely the guilty party must feel his guilt infinitely

772

—otherwise he prefers to be angry at the one he has wronged, or at least to avoid him, to shun his forgiveness. To accept the forgiveness of one wronged is the humiliation he cannot bear—which is why the offending party never forgives.

x^3 A 10   *n.d.*, 1850

« **3826**

Rousseau has an excellent observation on white lies (*Reveries d'un promeneur solitaire*, in Walk 4—quoted from Richard Rothe, *Ethik*,[1435] III, p. 569 n.):

cette question est très decidée, je le sais bien; negativement dans les livres, ou la plus austere morale ne coute rien a l'auteur; affirmativement dans la societe, ou la morale des livres passe pour un bavardage impossible a pratiquer.[1436]

But the same thing holds true also of all the preaching of Christianity. We have one language in the churches—it disturbs neither the speakers nor the listeners—in life we act entirely differently.

x^3 A 559   *n.d.*, 1850

« **3827** *Rousseau*

His *Confessions*,[1437] volume IV (*Walking Tours*), is excellent; the fifth walking tour, for example, is esthetically unparalleled.

Incidentally, this is an example of what it means not to be taught and brought up in Christianity.

Rousseau's life contains analogies to the genuinely Christian collisions (to do the good and suffer for it, to do the good and thereby manage to make oneself and others unhappy[1438]). This is what he cannot bear; he complains that it cripples him so indescribably. How it would have strengthened him to have had a clear understanding that this is the genuine Christian collision.

But since he is totally ignorant of Christianity, he is on the one hand crippled and on the other he falls into the conceit that he is the only human being who has suffered this way.

x^4 A 223   *n.d.*, 1851

« **3828**

In margin of 3827 (x^4 A 223):

He lacks the ideal, the Christian ideal, which could humble him and teach him how little he suffers in comparison with the saint, the ideal which could keep him striving and prevent him from sinking into poetic dreaming and inactivity. He is an example of how hard it is for a man to die to the world.

x^4 A 224   *n.d.*

Bibliography
Collation of Entries
Notes

Bibliography

KIERKEGAARD'S WORKS IN ENGLISH

Editions referred to in the notes.

Listed according to the original order of publication or the time of writing.

The Concept of Irony, tr. Lee Capel. New York: Harper and Row, 1966; Bloomington: Indiana University Press, 1968. (*Om Begrebet Ironi,* by S. A. Kierkegaard, 1841.)

Either/Or, I, tr. David F. Swenson and Lillian Marvin Swenson; II, tr. Walter Lowrie; 2 ed. rev. Howard A. Johnson. Princeton: Princeton University Press, 1971. (*Enten-Eller,* I–II, ed. Victor Eremita, 1843.)

Johannes Climacus or De omnibus dubitandum est and *A Sermon,* tr. T. H. Croxall. London: Adam and Charles Black, 1958. ("Johannes Climacus eller *De omnibus dubitandum est,"* written 1842–43, unpubl., *Papirer* IV B 1; *Demis-Prædiken,* 1844, unpubl., IV C 1.)

Upbuilding [*Edifying*] *Discourses,* I–IV, tr. David F. Swenson and Lillian Marvin Swenson. Minneapolis: Augsburg Publishing House, 1943–46. (*Opbyggelige Taler,* by S. Kierkegaard, 1843, 1844.)

Fear and Trembling (with *The Sickness unto Death*), tr. Walter Lowrie. Princeton: Princeton University Press, 1968. (*Frygt og Bæven,* by Johannes de Silentio, 1843.)

Repetition, tr. Walter Lowrie. Princeton: Princeton University Press, 1941. (*Gjentagelsen,* by Constantin Constantius, 1843.)

Philosophical Fragments, tr. David F. Swenson, 2 ed. rev. Howard Hong. Princeton: Princeton University Press, 1962. (*Philosophiske Smuler,* by Johannes Climacus, ed. S. Kierkegaard, 1844.)

The Concept of Anxiety [*Dread*], tr. Walter Lowrie, 2 ed. Princeton: Princeton University Press, 1957. (*Begrebet Angest,* by Vigilius Haufniensis, ed. S. Kierkegaard, 1844.)

Three Discourses on Imagined Occasions [*Thoughts on Crucial Situations in Human Life*], tr. David F. Swenson, ed. Lillian Marvin Swenson. Minneapolis: Augsburg Publishing House, 1941. (*Tre Taler ved tænkte Leiligheder,* by S. Kierkegaard, 1845.)

Stages on Life's Way, tr. Walter Lowrie. Princeton: Princeton University Press, 1940. (*Stadier paa Livets Vej,* ed. Hilarius Bogbinder, 1845.)

Concluding Unscientific Postscript, tr. David F. Swenson and Walter Lowrie. Princeton: Princeton University Press for American-Scandinavian Foundation, 1941. (*Afsluttende uvidenskabelig Efterskrift*, by Johannes Climacus, ed. S. Kierkegaard, 1846.)

The Present Age [part of *Two Ages: the Age of Revolution and the Present Age. A Literary Review*] and *Two Minor Ethical-Religious Essays* [*Treatises*], tr. Alexander Dru, Walter Lowrie. London and New York: Oxford University Press, 1940. (*En literair Anmeldelse. To Tidsaldre*, by S. Kierkegaard, 1846; *Tvende ethisk-religieuse Smaa-Afhandlinger*, by H. H., 1849.)

On Authority and Revelation, The Book on Adler, tr. Walter Lowrie. Princeton: Princeton University Press, 1955. (*Bogen om Adler*, written 1846–47, unpubl., Papirer VII² B 235.)

Upbuilding Discourses in Various Spirits. (*Opbyggelige Taler i forskjellig Aand*, by S. Kierkegaard, 1847.) Part One, *Purity of Heart* [*"En Leiligheds-Tale"*], tr. Douglas Steere. New York: Harper, 2 ed., 1948. Part Three and Part Two, *The Gospel of Suffering* and *The Lilies of the Field* [*"Lidelsernes Evangelium"* and *"Hvad man lærer af Lilierne paa Marken og Himlens Fugle"*], tr. David F. Swenson and Lillian Marvin Swenson. Minneapolis: Augsburg Publishing House, 1948.

Works of Love, tr. Howard and Edna Hong. New York: Harper and Row, 1962. (*Kjerlighedens Gjerninger*, by S. Kierkegaard, 1847.)

Crisis [*and a Crisis*] *in the Life of an Actress*, tr. Stephen Crites. New York: Harper and Row, 1967. (*Krisen og en Krise i en Skuespillerindes Liv*, by Inter et Inter, *Fædrelandet*, 188–91, July 24–27, 1848.)

Christian Discourses, including *The Lily of the Field and the Bird of the Air* and *Three Discourses at the Communion on Fridays*, tr. Walter Lowrie. London and New York: Oxford University Press, 1940. (*Christelige Taler*, by S. Kierkegaard, 1848; *Lilien paa Marken og Fuglen under Himlen*, by S. Kierkegaard, 1849; *"Ypperstepræsten"—"Tolderen"—"Synderinden,"* Tre Taler ved Altergangen om Fredagen, by S. Kierkegaard, 1849.)

The Sickness unto Death (with *Fear and Trembling*), tr. Walter Lowrie. Princeton: Princeton University Press, 1968. (*Sygdommen til Døden*, by Anti-Climacus, ed. S. Kierkegaard, 1849.)

Practice [*Training*] *in Christianity*, including "The Woman Who Was a Sinner," tr. Walter Lowrie. London and New York: Oxford University Press, 1941; repr. Princeton: Princeton University Press, 1944. (*Indøvelse i Christendom*, by Anti-Climacus, ed. S. Kierkegaard, 1850; *En opbyggelig Tale*, by S. Kierkegaard, 1850.)

Armed Neutrality and *An Open Letter*, tr. Howard V. Hong and Edna H. Hong. Bloomington and London: Indiana University Press, 1968. (*Den bevæbnede Neutralitet*, written 1848–49, publ. 1965; *Foranledigt ved en Yttring af Dr. Rudelbach mig betræffende*, *Fædrelandet*, no. 26, January 31, 1851.)

The Point of View for My Work as an Author, including the Appendix " 'The Single Individual' Two 'Notes' Concerning My Work as an Author" and *On My Work as an Author,* tr. Walter Lowrie. London and New York: Oxford University Press, 1939. (*Synspunktet for min Forfatter-Virksomhed,* by S. Kierkegaard, written 1848, publ. 1859; *Om min Forfatter-Virksomhed,* by S. Kierkegaard, 1851.)

For Self-Examination, tr. Edna and Howard Hong. Minneapolis: Augsburg Publishing House, 1940. (*Til Selvprøvelse,* by S. Kierkegaard, 1851.)

Judge for Yourselves!, including *For Self-Examination, Two Discourses at the Communion on Fridays,* and *The Unchangeableness of God* (tr. David F. Swenson), tr. Walter Lowrie. Princeton: Princeton University Press, 1944. (*Dommer Selv!* by S. Kierkegaard, 1852; *To Taler ved Altergangen om Fredagen,* by S. Kierkegaard, 1851; *Guds Uforanderlighed,* by S. Kierkegaard, 1855.)

Kierkegaard's Attack upon "Christendom," tr. Walter Lowrie. Princeton: Princeton University Press, 1944. (*Bladartikler* I–XXI, by S. Kierkegaard, *Fædrelandet,* 1854–55; *Dette skal siges; saa være det da sagt,* by S. Kierkegaard, 1855; *Øieblikket,* by S. Kierkegaard, 1–9, 1855; 10, 1905; *Hvad Christus dømmer om officiel Christendom,* by S. Kierkegaard, 1855.)

The Journals of Søren Kierkegaard, tr. Alexander Dru. London and New York: Oxford University Press, 1938. (From *Søren Kierkegaards Papirer,* I–XI[1] in 18 volumes, 1909–1936.)

The Last Years, tr. Ronald C. Smith. New York: Harper and Row, 1965. (From *Papirer* XI[1]–XI[3], 1936–48.)

Søren Kierkegaard's Journals and Papers, tr. Howard V. Hong and Edna H. Hong, assisted by Gregor Malantschuk. Bloomington and London: Indiana University Press, I, 1967; II, 1970; III–IV, 1975, V–VII in preparation. (From *Papirer* I–XI[3], suppl. vols. XII, XIII, 1969–70, and *Breve og Aktstykker vedrørende Søren Kierkegaard,* ed. Niels Thulstrup, I–II, 1953–54.)

At various times in recent years over twenty-five paperback editions of twenty Kierkegaard titles have appeared in English translation. For paperback editions currently available, see the latest issue of *Paperback Books in Print,* published by R. R. Bowker Co., 1180 Avenue of the Americas, New York, N.Y.

General works on Kierkegaard are listed in the Bibliography, *Søren Kierkegaard's Journals and Papers,* I, pp. 482–88. Studies of a more limited and specific nature are listed in the appropriate section of topical notes in each volume of *Søren Kierkegaard's Journals and Papers.*

Collation of Entries in this Volume
With Kierkegaard's *Papirer*

Numbers in the left-hand columns are the standard international references to the *Papirer*. Numbers in parentheses are the serially ordered references in the present edition.

Volume I A		Volume I A		Volume I A		Volume II A	
10	(3542)	195	(3046)	298	(2855)	155	(2309)
19	(3543)	200	(3805)	300	(2799)	156	(2310)
20	(3544)	203	(3806)	306	(3816)	157	(2311)
22	(3545)	213	(2698)	315	(3817)	158	(2312)
26	(2854)	214	(3807)	**Volume I C**		159	(2313)
31	(2806)	216	(3808)			160	(2314)
35	(3243)	217	(3809)	113	(2703)	161	(2315)
43	(3546)	218	(3810)	**Volume II A**		176	(3255)
45	(3045)	219	(3811)			177	(3256)
81	(3782)	226	(2699)	11	(3251)	198	(3257)
87	(3244)	228	(3812)	24	(2380)	201	(3364)
94	(3245)	230	(3813)	25	(2381)	230	(3699)
98	(3246)	240	(2785)	32	(3551)	239	(3259)
99	(3247)	241	(2798)	33	(3552)	244	(2578)
107	(3721)	243	(3656)	57	(3698)	262	(2738)
117	(3125)	250	(2304)	59	(3252)	266	(3365)
127	(3248)	251	(2305)	62	(2307)	268	(2705)
128	(3697)	253	(3250)	69	(3363)	273	(2382)
130	(3796)	261	(2306)	76	(3722)	285	(3366)
131	(3797)	262	(3814)	77	(3253)	289	(2458)
132	(3798)	267	(2745)	86	(2734)	292	(2746)
134	(3799)	269	(2700)	87	(2735)	299	(3264)
136	(3800)	270	(2786)	88	(2736)	308	(3367)
140	(3801)	278	(2787)	89	(2737)	309	(3368)
142	(3802)	281	(2701)	96	(3605)	313	(3369)
153	(3249)	283	(2456)	99	(2801)	314	(3370)
155	(3803)	284	(2702)	109	(3818)	318	(3371)
165	(2922)	291	(2788)	111	(2308)	320	(3372)
168	(2794)	294	(3815)	145	(2457)	325	(3134)
171	(3804)	295	(3547)	149	(2856)	327	(3373)

Volume II A	Volume II A	Volume III A	Volume III C
334 (3374)	554 (3381)	70 (2796)	32 (3285)
336 (3375)	558 (3553)	76 (2829)	Volume IV A
342 (3376)	559 (3554)	78 (2830)	3 (2739)
353 (3270)	586 (3254)	82 (2585)	11 (2360)
356 (3271)	587 (2800)	85 (3783)	12 (2361)
368 (2857)	588 (3555)	86 (3385)	19 (3289)
370 (2383)	589 (3556)	89 (2388)	20 (3290)
374 (2579)	631 (2704)	107 (3284)	26 (2362)
375 (2580)	633 (2825)	108 (3072)	29 (2363)
377 (3377)	638 (3819)	113 (3821)	35 (3340)
379 (2858)	665 (2316)	117 (2586)	47 (3075)
380 (2706)	676 (3058)	120 (2389)	51 (3701)
396 (3190)	681 (3627)	126 (3386)	54 (3294)
399 (3548)	699 (3820)	137 (2390)	55 (3295)
423 (3378)	701 (3258)	138 (2391)	62 (3076)
426 (3272)	704 (2385)	144 (2587)	78 (2591)
429 (2581)	706 (3265)	152 (2831)	95 (3239)
434 (2459)	722 (2317)	153 (2832)	103 (3077)
439 (3071)	724 (3700)	156 (2318)	116 (3078)
440 (3273)	755 (3070)	157 (2392)	145 (3390)
445 (3791)	763 (3598)	158 (3387)	156 (3793)
462 (2384)	786 (3266)	162 (3388)	159 (3325)
468 (2707)	787 (3267)	197 (3822)	163 (3296)
469 (2582)	788 (3268)	200 (2369)	169 (3794)
470 (2583)	789 (3059)	204 (3389)	171 (3396)
471 (2584)	790 (3269)	222 (2319)	183 (2402)
475 (2826)	814 (3280)	237 (2395)	195 (2396)
483 (2748)	Volume II C	244 (3286)	224 (2791)
491 (2789)	5 (2713)	Volume III B	230 (3326)
493 (3274)	8 (3189)	12 (3283)	237 (2592)
494 (2827)	54 (3260)	26 (3323)	Volume IV B
498 (2386)	55 (3261)	39 (2588)	6 (3291)
505 (2828)	56 (3262)	41:25 (2589)	10:3,4,8,9 (3792)
511 (3275)	57 (3263)	106 (2393)	14:6 (2320)
517 (3276)	61 (2747)	114 (2394)	50:4 (3823)
518 (3277)	Volume III A	179:34 (2790)	75 (3079)
519 (3278)	2 (3723)	183 (3287)	144 (2397)
529 (3279)	8 (2795)	192 (3288)	146 (2398)
537 (3379)	11 (3281)	Volume III C	147 (2399)
538 (3380)	24 (3282)	9 (3383)	148 (2400)
545 (3060)	32 (3382)	19 (3384)	149 (3391)
551 (3651)	61 (2387)	23 (3191)	150 (2401)

Volume IV B

164 (3392)
165 (3393)
171 (3394)
175 (3395)

Volume IV C

11 (2338)
12 (2339)
13 (2340)
19 (3784)
25 (3292)
28 (2590)
29 (3073)
30 (2364)
31 (2365)
36 (2366)
37 (2367)
38 (2368)
40 (3549)
57 (3126)
61 (3293)
70 (3324)
71 (3652)
78 (3657)
84 (3074)
89 (3658)

Volume V A

9 (3297)
12 (3465)
17 (3466)
31 (3298)
44 (3127)
46 (3299)
64 (2593)
74 (2341)
79 (3080)
98 (3300)

Volume V B

1:2 (2370)
1:3 (2342)
1:6 (3047)
5:10 (3081)
11:4 (3082)

Volume V B

14 (3301)
40:11 (3606)
49:1 (3653)
49:14 (2343)
53:9 (3557)
53:12 (2321)
53:35 (2802)
55:3 (3302)
55:6 (2740)
69 (3795)
115:2 (2322)
116:3 (3240)
150:21 (2344)
221 (3397)

Volume V C

1 (2345)
2 (2346)
3 (2347)
6 (2348)
7 (2349)
8 (2350)
9 (2351)
12 (2352)

Volume VI A

15 (3303)
33 (2353)
36 (2594)
37 (2708)
62 (3633)
66 (3304)
69 (2714)
89 (2833)
90 (2834)
91 (2835)
108 (2460)
110 (2632)
111 (2859)
126 (2836)
133 (3305)
138 (2837)
145 (3306)

Volume VI A

150 (3467)
151 (3468)
152 (3469)
153 (3192)
155 (3470)
156 (3471)

Volume VI B

25 (3607)
35:7 (2371)
35:30 (2354)
35:36 (3083)
40:31 (3562)
43 (3084)
45 (3085)
54:13, 14, 16 (3654)
54:19 (3702)
54:33 (3307)
58:8 (2749)
59:2 (3739)
98:26 (2355)
98:82 (3086)
136 (2372)
150 (3398)
154 (3399)
160 (3400)
161 (3401)
164 (3402)
173 (3785)

Volume VII[1] A

10 (3214)
38 (2741)
46 (2838)
56 (3403)
67 (2766)
70 (3327)
77 (2767)
82 (3308)
83 (2860)
88 (2839)
100 (2923)

Volume VII[1] A

102 (3128)
130 (3628)
131 (3404)
132 (3405)
133 (3406)
136 (3407)
137 (3408)
142 (3409)
151 (3103)
152 (3309)
170 (2742)
175 (2633)
182 (2807)
183 (2808)
186 (2809)
188 (2810)
189 (2811)
190 (2812)
191 (2813)
192 (2461)
194 (2814)
195 (2815)
196 (2816)
197 (2817)
198 (2818)
199 (2819)
200 (2820)
209 (2462)
225 (2403)
226 (2404)

Volume VII[1] B

147 (3786)
153:5 (3629)
177:4 (3472)
181:2 (3740)
205 (2840)
206 (2841)
207 (2842)
208 (2843)
209 (2844)
210 (2845)

Volume VII² B		Volume VIII¹ A		Volume VIII¹ A		Volume VIII² B	
235, pp.		196	(2410)	403	(2750)	36:11	(3231)
48–49fn.	(3724)	198	(2597)	411	(2848)	40	(3027)
235, p. 63		199	(2925)	418	(2636)	59:20	(3743)
fn.	(2669)	201	(3666)	427	(2849)	107	(3420)
235, pp.		203	(3787)	428	(2719)	133:5	(2792)
66–67	(3087)	206	(3193)	429	(3727)	143	(3423)
235, p. 88	(3473)	209	(2768)	434	(3477)	**Volume IX A**	
235, p.191	(3474)	211	(3741)	437	(2413)	11	(2467)
235, pp.		216	(3742)	441	(3563)	15	(3424)
113–14	(3202)	231	(2598)	456	(2928)	19	(2851)
249:4	(3725)	239	(2688)	461	(2929)	22	(2468)
256:9–10	(3088)	240	(2634)	465	(2463)	24	(3425)
256:20	(2846)	247	(3412)	471	(2930)	30	(2417)
257:9	(3104)	248	(2861)	474	(2850)	35	(2743)
257:12	(3203)	255	(3413)	477	(2931)	36	(3341)
261:22	(2356)	263	(2847)	510	(3352)	46	(2637)
Volume VIII¹ A		273	(3090)	521	(2414)	63	(2938)
11	(3089)	278	(3634)	527	(3635)	88	(2418)
26	(2715)	289	(2775)	529	(3050)	96	(2469)
29	(3011)	295	(2411)	532	(3421)	98	(2638)
39	(2716)	296	(2926)	538	(2933)	102	(2639)
51	(2405)	297	(2927)	539	(2934)	115	(3426)
52	(2595)	304	(3414)	541	(2464)	121	(3667)
55	(3410)	310	(3476)	546	(3422)	126	(2640)
65	(2717)	311	(2862)	566	(3051)	133	(3353)
69	(3012)	315	(2776)	571	(2935)	136	(3052)
70	(3310)	318	(2777)	572	(3744)	140	(3354)
86	(2406)	329	(3630)	585	(3028)	141	(2641)
89	(2407)	331	(3049)	592	(2709)	143	(2939)
91	(3665)	338	(2670)	610	(2415)	145	(2470)
92	(3129)	340	(2718)	611	(2936)	146	(2940)
98	(3475)	341	(2689)	620	(2937)	148	(3314)
103	(3726)	342	(3415)	627	(3313)	149	(2675)
110	(2323)	364	(3416)	642	(2465)	163	(3668)
118	(3048)	367	(3417)	656	(2932)	165	(2642)
132	(2924)	369	(2599)	664	(2466)	192	(3427)
149	(2408)	370	(3230)	668	(3478)	193	(3428)
152	(3311)	372	(3418)	680	(2416)	201	(3135)
159	(3411)	380	(3419)	681	(2357)	224	(3745)
166	(3312)	381	(3025)	**Volume VIII² B**		237	(2600)
173	(2409)	393	(2412)	15	(3026)	239	(3342)
188	(3351)	396	(2635)	16:8	(3703)	244	(3029)
190	(2596)						

Volume IX A	Volume IX A	Volume X¹ A	Volume X¹ A
245 (2601)	490 (2944)	291 (3435)	482 (2868)
246 (2602)	495 (2646)	297 (2485)	485 (2607)
248 (3704)	**Volume IX B**	303 (2486)	487 (2422)
253 (3030)	5:2 y (3204)	304 (2487)	489 (2423)
273 (3013)	63:11 (2647)	310 (2604)	514 (2424)
274 (2471)	63:12 (2648)	314 (2488)	515 (3789)
277 (2941)	63:13 (2649)	324 (2489)	526 (2498)
294 (2942)	**Volume X¹ A**	326 (2490)	540 (3485)
306 (2419)	2 (3215)	330 (3708)	545 (2499)
322 (3031)	6 (3479)	333 (2653)	561 (3564)
325 (2643)	10 (2475)	361 (2358)	565 (3033)
327 (2420)	16 (2650)	363 (2373)	573 (3565)
328 (3429)	18 (3216)	370 (2491)	595 (2500)
344 (3669)	19 (3480)	371 (2374)	600 (3061)
345 (3788)	21 (2476)	373 (2720)	609 (3566)
352 (3343)	25 (2477)	376 (2492)	623 (2655)
355 (2863)	32 (2478)	379 (2375)	628 (3217)
362 (2751)	34 (2852)	382 (2654)	630 (2501)
365 (3705)	47 (2479)	388 (3436)	633 (3440)
366 (2690)	55 (2769)	389 (3437)	635 (2425)
377 (2472)	66 (3707)	390 (3438)	638 (2426)
383 (3706)	85 (2480)	392 (3194)	642 (2692)
384 (2864)	119 (2651)	396 (3014)	651 (2502)
385 (2644)	125 (3481)	400 (2691)	655 (2869)
389 (2473)	144 (3482)	401 (3195)	666 (3558)
403 (2752)	154 (2481)	403 (2493)	675 (2427)
404 (2753)	172 (2482)	419 (2494)	679 (3567)
406 (3136)	173 (3232)	420 (2495)	680 (3091)
409 (3355)	182 (3483)	439 (2496)	**Volume X² A**
412 (3344)	197 (2483)	440 (2605)	5 (2770)
415 (3670)	205 (3332)	444 (2421)	21 (3486)
417 (3430)	207 (3484)	445 (2606)	30 (2503)
426 (3431)	210 (3433)	449 (2376)	41 (3197)
427 (3032)	211 (3434)	451 (3196)	63 (2428)
433 (2474)	213 (2484)	458 (2947)	77 (3441)
434 (2603)	220 (2652)	461 (3636)	95 (3487)
435 (2645)	221 (2865)	462 (3637)	107 (2429)
452 (2943)	231 (2945)	465 (2377)	114 (3345)
456 (3671)	237 (3233)	466 (2378)	115 (3638)
462 (3432)	268 (2946)	470 (3439)	116 (3660)
474 (3672)	287 (2866)	474 (2497)	117 (3034)
486 (3746)	288 (2867)	481 (3608)	121 (2948)

Volume X² A		Volume X² A		Volume X² A		Volume X³ A	
123	(2504)	383	(2951)	633	(3568)	153	(2518)
133	(3053)	389	(3035)	636	(3711)	154	(3504)
149	(3488)	390	(2952)	637	(3569)	165	(2873)
151	(3489)	412	(3241)	640	(3712)	166	(3749)
154	(3356)	418	(3141)	**Volume X³ A**		169	(2874)
156	(3639)	430	(3609)	6	(3824)	170	(2519)
162	(2505)	432	(3315)	10	(3825)	175	(2711)
173	(2506)	441	(3198)	11	(3449)	176	(3148)
181	(2608)	446	(3610)	16	(3347)	193	(3613)
190	(2656)	447	(3611)	19	(2432)	208	(3451)
197	(3655)	448	(2512)	20	(2954)	211	(2520)
202	(3346)	461	(3612)	21	(2955)	214	(2875)
218	(3490)	464	(2710)	23	(3646)	216	(2755)
227	(3491)	484	(3092)	28	(3661)	217	(2521)
230	(3492)	485	(2953)	32	(2870)	218	(2522)
235	(2324)	496	(3446)	33	(2871)	220	(3678)
238	(3137)	501	(3093)	34	(2872)	221	(2523)
244	(2507)	502	(3094)	40	(3143)	222	(3452)
245	(2508)	505	(3599)	48	(3498)	223	(3453)
247	(2430)	509	(3747)	49	(3450)	225	(3679)
262	(2431)	529	(2803)	52	(3559)	227	(3454)
263	(2509)	541	(3673)	56	(2754)	232	(3680)
288	(3493)	545	(3674)	57	(2671)	233	(2876)
289	(2657)	550	(3142)	58	(2515)	234	(2524)
294	(2949)	552	(3640)	59	(3499)	237	(3505)
296	(3645)	553	(3054)	62	(3144)	242	(3149)
310	(3494)	554	(3055)	93	(3145)	243	(3150)
312	(3218)	558	(2513)	102	(3500)	244	(3151)
323	(2658)	559	(2514)	113	(2610)	246	(3506)
334	(2510)	566	(2609)	120	(3146)	260	(3152)
340	(2797)	573	(3675)	121	(3570)	262	(2956)
341	(2793)	581	(3497)	122	(3571)	266	(3750)
342	(3443)	582	(3015)	124	(3676)	267	(3153)
343	(3444)	594	(3130)	125	(3677)	271	(3507)
344	(3445)	595	(3447)	127	(2516)	278	(3681)
357	(3140)	604	(3748)	129	(3501)	288	(3508)
360	(3790)	608	(3328)	130	(3502)	290	(3348)
362	(2821)	609	(3329)	132	(3147)	299	(3682)
363	(3495)	610	(3330)	138	(2517)	302	(2525)
364	(2511)	614	(3709)	141	(3503)	303	(2659)
369	(2950)	624	(3710)	143	(3357)	306	(3751)
382	(3496)	632	(3448)	149	(3234)	307	(3509)

Volume X³ A	Volume X³ A	Volume X³ A	Volume X⁴ A
316 (2611)	496 (3018)	605 (2531)	30 (3731)
317 (3455)	497 (3019)	606 (3158)	38 (3732)
325 (3154)	498 (2660)	608 (3729)	54 (2535)
326 (3728)	502 (3156)	609 (3109)	74 (3641)
328 (2877)	503 (2782)	610 (3159)	75 (3687)
329 (2878)	508 (2783)	622 (3037)	84 (3321)
330 (2879)	510 (2528)	626 (3110)	93 (2960)
333 (3036)	511 (2661)	630 (3111)	94 (3322)
335 (2526)	513 (2784)	631 (3112)	100 (2961)
336 (2527)	514 (3157)	632 (3113)	103 (2728)
337 (2756)	515 (3514)	633 (3114)	105 (2962)
351 (3752)	516 (2529)	634 (3115)	107 (2963)
352 (3753)	517 (2694)	639 (3116)	108 (2662)
361 (3754)	518 (2695)	640 (3117)	109 (2663)
364 (3510)	520 (2696)	641 (3118)	117 (3733)
371 (2778)	523 (2697)	642 (3119)	121 (3162)
377 (3683)	531 (3456)	644 (3120)	122 (2886)
383 (3016)	532 (2721)	645 (3121)	124 (3518)
384 (3017)	533 (2530)	646 (3122)	128 (3688)
392 (3572)	534 (3515)	656 (2958)	157 (2887)
398 (3573)	537 (2880)	657 (2959)	162 (3614)
407 (3511)	541 (2881)	674 (3038)	163 (3235)
412 (2779)	542 (3105)	676 (2727)	174 (3642)
419 (2612)	543 (3106)	682 (3320)	180 (3550)
424 (3095)	544 (3107)	683 (3242)	190 (3689)
428 (3333)	545 (3685)	692 (3517)	197 (2325)
431 (3684)	546 (3108)	696 (3686)	198 (2326)
436 (3155)	547 (3516)	698 (3160)	199 (2327)
437 (3318)	549 (2882)	700 (3458)	210 (3615)
451 (2957)	553 (2614)	722 (2885)	214 (3690)
456 (3755)	556 (3319)	739 (2434)	215 (3691)
457 (3756)	559 (3826)	740 (3662)	216 (3692)
459 (2780)	560 (3757)	741 (2435)	223 (3827)
460 (3358)	574 (3334)	751 (3161)	224 (3828)
461 (3359)	580 (3335)	752 (2757)	225 (2964)
467 (3199)	582 (2883)	Volume X⁴ A	227 (3519)
468 (2613)	583 (3131)	4 (2758)	229 (3459)
479 (3512)	584 (3132)	7 (2532)	232 (2822)
480 (2781)	588 (2712)	12 (2533)	236 (3574)
482 (3349)	590 (2884)	17 (3200)	237 (2536)
484 (3513)	594 (2722)	25 (2534)	255 (3713)
489 (2433)	595 (3457)	27 (3730)	258 (3647)

Volume X⁴ A	Volume X⁴ A	Volume X⁵ A	Volume X⁶ C
260 (2888)	450 (3316)	4 (3767)	6:1 (3331)
261 (3758)	451 (2542)	10 (3170)	**Volume XI¹ A**
263 (2771)	454 (2672)	12 (3022)	2 (3648)
266 (3759)	482 (2437)	14 (3659)	11 (3463)
281 (3460)	483 (2853)	15 (2894)	16 (2968)
287 (3520)	495 (3525)	19 (3768)	19 (3532)
289 (3693)	496 (3526)	25 (3769)	26 (2901)
295 (3694)	502 (3166)	29 (3770)	31 (3236)
298 (3790)	503 (3577)	34 (2441)	33 (3663)
309 (2436)	504 (3762)	47 (2561)	37 (2563)
313 (2328)	510 (3167)	48 (2895)	40 (2674)
315 (2889)	517 (3763)	50 (2442)	51 (3219)
316 (3760)	519 (2804)	53 (3771)	52 (2615)
317 (3521)	520 (2673)	57 (3529)	53 (3171)
324 (2537)	522 (3205)	58 (3772)	55 (3582)
325 (2538)	525 (3715)	62 (3530)	61 (2546)
326 (3761)	526 (2891)	66 (2896)	62 (3560)
330 (3522)	527 (2892)	68 (3773)	64 (2969)
332 (3163)	528 (3716)	73 (2823)	65 (2564)
336 (3695)	529 (3717)	75 (3123)	67 (3649)
338 (3020)	531 (2760)	78 (2897)	68 (3172)
345 (3734)	532 (3578)	79 (3774)	73 (2902)
355 (3523)	535 (2966)	86 (2562)	77 (2547)
357 (3714)	536 (3764)	96 (2898)	79 (3775)
360 (3524)	541 (3201)	100 (3206)	80 (2329)
368 (3164)	562 (3461)	102 (2729)	85 (2761)
371 (2539)	565 (3462)	111 (3207)	86 (3173)
372 (2540)	589 (2438)	113 (3317)	87 (3618)
374 (2759)	597 (3527)	117 (3531)	88 (3174)
393 (3165)	602 (3631)	122 (2730)	89 (3533)
394 (2541)	607 (2893)	123 (2967)	94 (2824)
398 (3575)	612 (2560)	130 (2723)	97 (3220)
403 (3021)	614 (3579)	135 (2899)	100 (3583)
405 (2965)	615 (3735)	140 (2900)	101 (3584)
413 (3056)	622 (3168)	142 (3097)	106 (3619)
414 (3600)	627 (3169)	143 (3350)	107 (2903)
416 (3360)	641 (3096)	159 (3064)	108 (2548)
428 (2890)	642 (2439)	163 (3138)	110 (2904)
442 (3062)	645 (3765)	164 (3139)	113 (3601)
443 (2557)	649 (3766)	**Volume X⁶ B**	114 (2664)
444 (2558)	655 (2440)	17 (3576)	116 (3776)
446 (2559)	662 (3057)	227 (3580)	126 (3133)
448 (3063)	671 (3528)	239 (3442)	127 (2549)

Volume XI¹ A		Volume XI¹ A		Volume XI¹ A		Volume XI² A	
129	(2616)	289	(3643)	466	(3603)	39	(2379)
134	(2762)	295	(2620)	467	(3588)	43	(2569)
138	(2905)	297	(2551)	473	(3589)	46	(3561)
143	(3777)	298	(2552)	477	(3535)	51	(3099)
150	(2617)	299	(3098)	480	(3604)	52	(3100)
154	(2906)	313	(2621)	482	(3042)	54	(2570)
155	(2907)	316	(2909)	486	(2566)	55	(2571)
156	(3336)	325	(2974)	489	(2732)	56	(2572)
157	(2908)	339	(3023)	495	(3650)	65	(3664)
161	(3337)	341	(3221)	504	(3536)	68	(2667)
162	(3338)	344	(3178)	511	(2666)	71	(3538)
169	(2618)	345	(2731)	512	(2980)	81	(3101)
172	(3534)	346	(2975)	513	(2981)	88	(2986)
186	(2724)	354	(3222)	514	(2982)	89	(2987)
187	(2725)	356	(2444)	520	(2332)	90	(2988)
193	(2550)	360	(3039)	523	(3024)	91	(2679)
195	(3065)	361	(2331)	525	(3736)	92	(2989)
196	(3066)	364	(3602)	532	(3182)	93	(2990)
198	(2763)	367	(3361)	548	(3183)	96	(3644)
199	(3620)	372	(2976)	549	(2677)	103	(2359)
202	(3585)	373	(2977)	552	(3209)	105	(2452)
203	(3586)	375	(3238)	569	(2693)	107	(3224)
204	(3041)	376	(3779)	571	(2913)	109	(2991)
205	(2330)	387	(2978)	572	(2554)	116	(2992)
213	(3621)	389	(3179)	578	(3464)	118	(2573)
217	(2805)	390	(3180)	581	(3590)	127	(2993)
224	(3622)	392	(2910)	582	(2983)	128	(2334)
227	(2970)	393	(3223)	584	(3184)	129	(2335)
228	(3175)	395	(2911)	585	(3043)	138	(2680)
229	(3176)	405	(2445)	589	(2567)	144	(2574)
230	(3177)	406	(2446)	590	(2568)	146	(2994)
234	(2971)	411	(2447)	Volume XI² A		147	(2336)
235	(2972)	414	(2448)	1	(2678)	148	(3185)
246	(3208)	417	(3181)	7	(3362)	150	(2622)
247	(3623)	435	(2565)	8	(2450)	151	(2995)
250	(2676)	437	(3624)	9	(2451)	152	(2575)
253	(2619)	442	(2553)	16	(3040)	153	(2623)
263	(2764)	443	(2765)	17	(2984)	154	(2624)
267	(3632)	450	(3587)	22	(2772)	155	(2996)
274	(3237)	452	(2912)	26	(2985)	156	(2997)
279	(2443)	454	(2979)	27	(3537)	159	(2998)
283	(3778)	459	(2449)	37	(2333)	160	(2625)
287	(2973)	462	(2665)	38	(3210)	162	(3625)

Volume XI² A		Volume XI² A		Volume XI² A		Volume XI² A	
163	(3044)	218	(3593)	305	(3617)	390	(2453)
166	(2576)	220	(3007)	316	(2916)	395	(2920)
167	(2999)	222	(2337)	323	(2681)	397	(2733)
168	(3000)	230	(3008)	324	(3010)	398	(3626)
169	(3001)	231	(2628)	325	(3212)	400	(3186)
172	(2626)	233	(3594)	326	(2682)	401	(3187)
174	(2914)	238	(2629)	327	(3124)	402	(3228)
176	(2627)	241	(2630)	332	(3696)	403	(2921)
177	(3225)	243	(3009)	338	(3616)	405	(2744)
178	(3226)	249	(3539)	339	(2726)	421	(2454)
181	(2915)	262	(2668)	340	(3720)	426	(2455)
184	(3002)	266	(2556)	346	(3737)	427	(2685)
185	(3003)	270	(3595)	347	(3339)	431	(3229)
187	(3211)	273	(3718)	348	(3781)	435	(2687)
194	(2555)	274	(3719)	355	(3738)		
209	(3591)	278	(2684)	363	(2773)	Volume XI³ B	
210	(3067)	281	(3540)	364	(2917)		
211	(3004)	289	(3541)	368	(3596)	43	(3068)
212	(3102)	295	(3581)	372	(2631)	109	(3069)
214	(3005)	298	(3780)	376	(3597)	115	(2774)
215	(3006)	301	(2543)	385	(2683)	175	(3213)
216	(3592)	303	(2544)	386	(2918)	177	(2686)
217	(3227)	304	(2545)	387	(2919)	197	(3188)
						260:8	(2577)

Notes, Commentary, and Topical Bibliography

The summary presentation of basic concepts is by Gregor Malantschuk and the notes and bibliography are by the editors.

The following abbreviations have been used throughout the notes:

S.V.   *Samlede Værker* by Søren Kierkegaard, I–XIV (Copenhagen: Gyldendal, 1901–1906).

Pap.   *Papirer* by Søren Kierkegaard, edited by P. A. Heiberg, V. Kuhr, and E. Torsting, I–XI³ (20 vols.) (Copenhagen: Gyldendal, 1909–1948); 2 ed. ed. Niels Thulstrup, I–XI³ and suppl. vols. XII–XIII (Copenhagen: Gyldendal, 1968–70). References to the *Papirer* and the appropriate serial number in *J* and *P* will usually be in the form of I A 1, etc.

ASKB   *Auktionsprotokol over Søren Kierkegaards Bogsamling* (Auction Catalog of Søren Kierkegaard's Book Collection), edited by H. P. Rohde (Copenhagen: Det Kongelige Bibliotek, 1967). This enlarged edition of the auction catalog contains the basic serially numbered list of books indicated by number (*ASKB* 200), two appendices designated by I and II (*ASKB* II 200), and a section on books otherwise unlisted but in various ways known to have belonged to Kierkegaard, designated by U (*ASKB* U 100).

Titles of studies pertinent to a particular theme are given under the appropriate heading. The editions of Kierkegaard's works referred to in the notes are listed in the bibliography.

LANGUAGE

Kierkegaard thoroughly analyzed the problem of language and the use of language in social intercourse (communication), because the very development and usefulness of his dialectic of communication required him to.

Language, he maintained, was no accidental discovery; man as a mental-spiritual being is predisposed to language. Language makes it possible for man to apprehend things in the medium of thought (i.e., to have an abbreviation of actuality). Kierkegaard worked hard to find an adequate linguistic expression for the actuality he describes; frequently he searched long for the right word to express a particular thought.

Kierkegaard also points out that in presenting Christian truths one must remember that Christianity's use of language is qualitatively different from ordinary usage, "for Christianity makes manifest one sphere more or a higher sphere than the one in which we men naturally live, and in this sphere ordinary human language is reflected inversely. For example, Christianity says that to lose the earthly is a gain, that to possess it is a loss. We also use the words "loss" and "gain." But we do not in any way include the sphere of the spirit and therfore by loss and gain we understand the opposite of what Christianity understands" (XI² A 37).

Charlesworth, J. H. "Kierkegaard and Optical Linguistics." *Kierkegaardiana*, vol. VII, 1968.

Heinecken, Martin. *The Moment before God*. Philadelphia: Muhlenberg, 1956.

Holmer, Paul L. "Kierkegaard and Kinds of Discourse." *Meddelelser fra S. K. Selskabet*, no. 4, 1953.

————. "Kierkegaard and Religious Propositions." *Journal of Religion*, vol. 35, 1955.

Zuurdeeg, Willem F. "Some Aspects of Kierkegaard's Language Philosophy." *Atti del XII Congresso Internazionale di Filosofia XII: Storia della filosofia moderna e contemporanea*. Firenze: Sansoni, 1961.

In Kierkegaard's works there are numerous references to language. See, for example, *Either/Or*, I, pp. 53 ff., 66 ff., 267 f.; *Fear and Trembling*, pp. 91 ff.; *The Concept of Anxiety* [*Dread*], pp. 38 ff.; *Upbuilding* [*Edifying*] *Discourses*, IV, pp. 11 f.; *Stages*, pp. 175, 206, 219 f., 248, 290, 440 f.; *Postscript*, pp. 26, 270; *Works of Love*, pp. 23, 92, 95, 199 f., 239, 245; *The Sickness unto Death*, pp. 184 f.

1. Emphasis by the length of a syllable.

2. Emphasis by the accent on a syllable.

3. Henrich Steffens, *Caricaturen des Heiligsten*, I–II (Leipzig: 1819–21). *ASKB* 793–94.

4. European languages are only sound: the letters, the syllables, the words have meaning only for the ear. The sound fastens itself on the innermost, liveliest, most agile existence, and that language, especially, which puts emphasis on expression, where the sounds, rising and falling, emphasized or repressed, cling closely and lightly to the inner meaning of the movement of the soul, can rightly be called a *Christian** language, and hints at the victory of love over law.

5. See, for example, *Works of Love*, pp. 199 ff.

6. See note 3.

7. L. Achim von Arnim and Clemens Brentano, *Des Knaben Wunderhorn*, I–III (Heidelberg: 1806). *ASKB* 1494–96.

8. Gottfried A. Bürger, "Lenore," in *Bürgers Gedichte* (Gotha, New York: 1828), I, pp. 48 ff.

9. G. H. Schubert, *Die Symbolik des Traumes* (Bamberg: 2 ed., 1821). *ASKB* 776.

10. Earnestness, gravity. See II A 92, Kierkegaard's notes on reading Karl Rosenkranz, "*Eine Parallele zur Religionsphilosophie*" (*Bauers Zeitschrift*, II, pp. 1–32), in which this expression occurs, p. 9. *ASKB* 354–57.

11. Severin Bindesbøll, review in *Maanedsskrift for Litteratur*, XVIII (1837), pp. 127 ff., of two articles by E. F. Bojesen, "*Om græsk Musik.*"

12. Tage Algreen-Ussing (1797–1872), provincial high-court judge, member of the Roskilde assembly, and a controversial figure in constitutional politics. See *Repetition*, p. 35.

13. See *Stages*, pp. 440 f., for Kierkegaard's eulogy of his native tongue.

14. See *Either/Or*, I, pp. 53, 267 f.; *Postscript*, p. 270; *Upbuilding* [*Edifying*] *Discourses*, IV, pp. 11 f.

15. The entry is from a draft of *Johannes Climacus or, De omnibus dubitandum est;* see first full paragraph on p. 147 of English translation.

16. J. N. Madvig (1804–1886), Danish philologist and politician. See *Indbydelsskrift til Kjøbenhavns Universitets Fest* . . ., September 18, 1842, p. 8; *Stages*, pp. 206, 440; *The Concept of Anxiety* [*Dread*], p. 43 fn., from the draft of which the present entry is taken.

17. *Love of Fame*, II, 1. 208: "And men talk only to conceal the mind." Talleyrand (1754–1838) is supposed to have used this expression to a Spanish diplomat. A "later writer" refers to one of Kierkegaard's own pseudonyms, Vigilius Haufniensis, author of *Begrebet Angest* (*The Concept of Anxiety* [*Dread*]), p. 96. See *Stages*, p. 312.

18. See note 14.

19. Psalms 10:14.

20. Christian Scriver, *Seelen-Schatz*, I–V (Leipzig: 1715), I, p. 35. *ASKB* 261–63.

21. I Corinthians 1:28; James 2:5.

22. See note 20.

23. So that it is easy to perceive something divine in sacred Scriptures.

24. Paul Henry, *Das Leben Johan Calvins des grossen Reformators* (Hamburg: 1835). Kierkegaard had six volumes of Calvin's works in Latin [*ASKB* 92–95, 455–56], but the *Auktionsprotokol* (*ASKB*) does not list the volume by Henry. This is one of numerous instances which indicate that Kierkegaard's library was larger than implied by the catalog and/or that he made use of other collections, such as those of his father and brother, the Student Union, the University Library, and the Royal Library. He was also a member of Athenæum, which had a good collection.

25. H. L. Martensen was named Mynster's successor in 1854. See *JP*, V, passim.

26. See, for example, *The Sickness unto Death*, pp. 84 f.

27. See *Works of Love*, pp. 199 ff.

28. Philippians 3:7.

29. See Diogenes Laertius, VIII, 10 (*ASKB* 1109–11); *From the Papers of One Still Living*, *S.V.*, XIII, p. 63; also *For Self-Examination*, pp. 54 ff.

LEAP

In his thorough investigation of existential issues Kierkegaard discovered that it is impossible to carry through a continuous movement either in thought or in existence. Thought and existence encounter very definite limits, and the next level or next sphere cannot be reached without a leap. Since thought and existence are the two media within which human life develops, there are first of all two kinds of leap: the dialectical and the pathos-filled (IV C 11), but there are also the leaps from each of these to the other, of which the leap from thought to existence is the more important. Kierkegaard found the definition of the leap in Aristotle's theory of κίνησις (motion, movement, change), understood as "the transition from possibility," or from the sphere of thought "to actuality" (IV C 47) or existence. This leap is the most important part of Kierkegaard's elaborated "theory of the leap" (V C 12) and is used particularly in his development of the theory of the stages. He lamented that even though it was necessary to use the leap, no philosopher before him had been aware of the decisive significance of the leap in life and in thought.

Replogle, J. "Auden's Religious Leap." *Wisconsin Studies in Contemporary Literature*, vol. 7, Winter, 1966.

30. R. Descartes, *Meditationes de prima philosophia, Opera philosophica* (Amsterdam: 1678), no. IV, pp. 26 ff. *ASKB* 473.

31. See, for example, *Fear and Trembling*, p. 53 fn.; *Postscript*, pp. 347 ff.

32. W. G. Tennemann, *Geschichte der Philosophie*, I–XI (Leipzig: 1798–1819). *ASKB* 815–26.

33. Descartes' theory of God's cooperation in effecting interaction between body and soul.

34. Pre-established harmony.

35. B. Spinoza, *Opera philosophica omnia* (Stuttgart: 1830). *ASKB* 788.

36. Such as the principles of identity and contradiction.

37. F. A. Trendelenburg, *Logische Untersuchungen*, I–II (Berlin: 1840), II, pp. 113 ff., 30 f. *ASKB* 843.

38. See, for example, *The Concept of Irony*, p. 66; *Fear and Trembling*, pp. 47, 51 ff.; *Fragments*, p. 53; *The Concept of Anxiety* [*Dread*], pp. 16 fn., 28 f., 34 ff., 42, 54, 71, 76, 99 ff.; *Postscript*, pp. 15, 38 fn., 86–97, 105, 134 fn., 231, 234, 262, 302, 306, 340, 343; *Two Ages* [*The Present Age*, pp. 8, 36, 65 ff.]; *Practice* [*Training*] *in Christianity*, pp. 50, 158.

39. See *Fragments*, pp. 53 ff.

40. F. A. Trendelenburg, *Elementa logices Aristolicae, Editio altera recognita et aucta* (Berlin: 1842). *ASKB* 844.

41. F. A. Trendelenburg, *Erläuterungen zu den Elementen der Aristotelischen Logik* (Berlin: 1842). *ASKB* 845.

42. Ibid., pp. 72, 78, 81 f.

43. See V C 12.

44. G. E. Lessing, *Sämmtliche Schriften*, I–XXXII (Berlin: 1825–28). *ASKB* 1747–62. Entry is from draft of *Postscript*. See pp. 90–97; also *The Concept of Anxiety* [*Dread*], pp. 27 f. and fn.

45. See *Fear and Trembling*, pp. 47, 51 f., 53 fn.

46. Entry is from draft of ibid., p. 20, end of first full paragraph.

47. H. T. Rötscher, *Die Kunst der dramatischen Darstellung*, I–II (Berlin: 1841–44), II, pp. 99 ff. *ASKB* 1391.

48. *Goethes Werke*, I–LV (Stuttgart, Tübingen: 1828–33), XIX, pp. 70 ff., 73 ff. 255 ff.

49. See *The Concept of Anxiety* [*Dread*], pp. 74 ff. and fn.

50. See ibid., pp. 28 f., 34 f., 54, 69, 82; *Fragments*, p. 53; *Postscript*, pp. 262, 302.

51. See note 38.

52. See V B 515.

53. G. W. F. Hegel, *Phänomenologie des Geistes*, I–II (Berlin: 1832), II, p. 71. *ASKB* 550. In entry IV A 59, Hegel is cited as saying that "something goes on behind the back of consciousness."

54. G. E. Lessing, *Sämmtliche Schriften*, II, p. 516.

55. The consequence in Hegel's philosophy of the absence of the concept "the leap."

56. See *The Concept of Anxiety* [*Dread*], p. 10; also p. 12 fn. and p. 28 fn.

57. See I Corinthians 2:9; *Fragments*, p. 45.

58. J. H. Fichte, *Grundzüge zum Systeme der Philosophie*, I–II (Heidelberg: 1833), I, pp. iv ff. (*Das Erkennen als Selbsterkennen*). *ASKB* 502–3.

59. Knowledge as self-knowledge.

60. See Kierkegaard's account of Schelling's lecture no. 10 (III C 27); *The Concept of Anxiety* [*Dread*], p. 11; *Postscript*, p. 96.

61. See *Postscript*, pp. 163 f.

62. See *Dansk poetisk Anthologie*, ed. Chr. Molbech (Copenhagen: 1840), IV, 1, p. 275.

63. See *Postscript*, p. 327.

64. See *Fragments*, pp. 100 ff.

65. See note 32.

66. See *Fragments*, pp. 88 ff.; "Interlude."

67. Ibid., p. 53.

68. See *Postscript*, pp. 134 fn., 302.

69. See *The Concept of Anxiety* [*Dread*], pp. 42, 49, 99 f., 109.

70. See note 44.

71. See *Postscript*, pp. 91 ff.

72. See F. H. Jacobi, *Werke*, I–VI (Leipzig: 1812–25). *ASKB* 1722–28.

73. Henrich Steffens, *Erindringer*, I–X (Breslau: 1843). *ASKB* 1834–43.

74. On Hegel and ethics, directly or by implication, see, for example, *Postscript*, pp. 110, 119–30, 132 f., 135–43, 292 ff., 309, 376 f.

75. Aristotle's *Rhetorik*, I–II, *Werke* (Stuttgart: 1833–41; *ASKB* 1092), I, 1, 1355 a, 3 ff.; 2, 1356 b, 1 ff.; 1358 a, 2 ff.; II, 22, 1395 b, 20 ff.

76. This entry is from a draft of *Concluding Unscientific Postscript*, end of paragraph, pp. 90–91.

77. See ibid., p. 91.

78. Entry is a note omitted from final text of *Postscript*, l. 10, p. 86, part of which became ll. 23–30 and ll. 33–35, p. 90, and ll. 1–3, p. 91.

79. See *Fragments*, p. 5 and note.

80. Entry is from draft of *Bogen om Adler* (*On Authority and Revelation*), pp. 125–26, end of paragraph.

81. M. Luther, *En christelig Postille*, tr. J. Thisted, I–II (Copenhagen: 1828), I, p. 273. *ASKB* 283.

82. See *Postscript*, p. 337.

83. See ibid., pp. 25 ff.

84. Change into another category or kind; see *Philosophical Fragments*, p. 90.

LEIBNIZ

Kierkegaard found Leibniz (1646–1716) helpful for his own detailed, penetrating analysis of freedom. He had thoroughly studied Leibniz's *Theodicy*, in which Leibniz not only presents his own views on human freedom and its relation to God and God's foreknowledge but also adduces many instances of other philosophers' attempts to solve these questions. Kierkegaard notes particularly Leibniz's controversy with Bayle (1647–1706): "The whole conflict between Leibniz and Bayle is very much to one point, and it is astonishing to compare it with controversy in our time, for we have actually gone backward, and I believe Hegel has not really understood what it was all about" (IV C 29; see also IV C 33 and 39).

Kierkegaard also notes Leibniz's view of Christian truth as being "above reason and against reason" (IV C 29). Leibniz defends the use of these two expressions. Kierkegaard, in using the concept of the absurd for Christianity, might characterize its truth as being "against understanding" [*Forstand*] (*Postscript*, p. 503; X² A 354).

Grimsley, R. "Kierkegaard and Leibniz." *Journal of the History of Ideas*, vol. 26, July, 1965.

85. See *Fear and Trembling*, p. 48; *Repetition*, p. 105; *Philosophical Fragments*, p. 103 n.; *Stages on Life's Way*, pp. 401, 425.

86. G. W. Leibniz, *Theodicee,* ed. J. C. Gottscheden (Hannover, Leipzig: 5 ed. 1763), p. 72. *ASKB* 619. The auction catalog also lists Leibniz's *Opera philosophica quae extant latina gallica germanica omnia,* ed. J. E. Erdmann, I–II (Berlin: 1840). *ASKB* 620. For references to Leibniz in the works, see, for example, *Either/Or,* I, p. 355; II, pp. 20, 128; *Fear and Trembling,* p. 56; *Repetition,* p. 3; *Fragments,* pp. 52 fn., 99; *The Concept of Anxiety* [*Dread*], p. 100.

87. See note 86.

88. W. G. Tennemann, *Geschichte der Philosophie,* I–XI (Leipzig: 1798–1819). *ASKB* 815–26.

89. See *The Concept of Anxiety* [*Dread*]. p. 100. Para. 55 refers to *Theodicee,* p. 518 in the Erdmann edition. Lazy Sophism.

90. See note 86.

91. See *Stages on Life's Way,* p. 300; the more lost, the less repentant.

92. See *Prefaces, S. V.,* V, p. 51, where this quotation is used as a chapter heading; Horace, *Satires,* II, 5, 59.

93. See Gottscheden, ed. (note 86), para. 169, p. 335, a quotation from article on Epicurus in Bayle's *Dictionary.*

94. Ibid.; pp. 137 ff., "On the Justice of God."

95. Ibid.; natural inertia of bodies.

96. Ibid., pp. 126 ff., 140; the ideal reasons which restrict it.

97. See *Fragments,* pp. 52 fn., 99.

98. *Theodicee* (Gottscheden, ed.), pp. 105 f.

99. Ibid., para. 37 ff., pp. 146 ff., esp. 42 (p. 151); the knowledge of mere intelligence, the knowledge of intuition, mediate knowledge (para. 40).

100. Ibid., para. 44 ff., pp. 153 ff., esp. 46 (p. 156); see also para. 35 (p. 144); indifference of equipoise.

101. Ibid., para. 311 ff., 319; the reason of the good.

102. Ibid., pp. 396 ff.

103. See *The Concept of Anxiety* [*Dread*], p. 28 n.

104. Leibniz defines "equals" as entities whose quantities are the same and "similars" as those not differing according to qualities.

105. If you add like to like, then the whole is like.

106. If you add similar things to similar things in like manner, the whole is similar.

107. But the part of the best whole is not of necessity the best that could have been made of this part.

108. *Theodicee.*

109. See ibid., para. 271.

LESSING

Both in the journals and papers and in the published works Kierkegaard frequently expresses great appreciation for Lessing's (1729–81) clear and unprejudiced views on various important questions relating to esthetics as well as to Christianity. In *Either/Or* Lessing is commended, for example, for "determining the boundaries between poetry and visual art in his well-known treatise Laokoön" by showing "that art lies in the qualification of space, poetry in that of time, that art expresses repose, poetry movement" (I, p. 167). In *Fear and Trembling* (pp. 99–100 fn.) Johannes de Silentio thanks Lessing for the hint he gives in his *Hamburgische Dramaturgie* about the problems in using Christianity as material for poetic productions. But what Kierkegaard appreciates most in Lessing is his disclosure of the difficulties in the transition from the human to the religious, and the fact that he, as Climacus says, "attacks the direct transition from historical trustworthiness to the determination of an eternal salvation" (*Postscript*, p. 88). Kierkegaard says: "This is and remains the main problem with respect to the relationship between Christianity and philosophy. Lessing is the only one who has dealt with this" (V B 1:2). In *Concluding Unscientific Postscript* Kierkegaard has Climacus detail how a person becomes a Christian. In this connection there are three specific points he is pleased to find treated by Lessing. The first is that the Christian truth "does not allow itself to be taught directly" (the dialectic of communication); next, "that accidental historical truths can never serve as proofs for eternal truths of reason; and that the transition by which it is proposed to build an eternal truth on historical testimony is a leap" (*Postscript*, p. 86); and third, that for man the truth is the infinite striving for it, which Climacus uses as an argument against Hegel's claim that "the system" provides the whole truth.

In his later years Kierkegaard takes a more critical attitude toward Lessing, particularly to his pronouncements in *Von dem Zwecke Jesu und seiner Jünger. Noch ein Fragment des Wolfenbüttelschen Ungenannten* (Braunschweig: 1778). Of course Søren Kierkegaard finds Lessing's untraditional treatment of the subject both bold and ingenious (X¹ A 449), and his reflection is detectible not only in the journal entries where Lessing is mentioned; but Kierkegaard nevertheless believes that Lessing here ridicules Christianity without being "sufficiently developed dialectically to know what he was doing" (X¹ A 465; see also X⁴ A 335 and XI¹ A 482). Kierkegaard also criticizes Lessing's words about the infinite striving which Climacus embraces (*Postscript*, p. 97), since in his opinion Lessing emphasizes this striving so strongly that it becomes more important than the object—namely, the truth (X¹ A 478).

Campbell, Richard. "Lessing's Problem and Kierkegaard's Answer." *Scottish Journal of Theology*, vol. XIX, 1966.

110. *"Lied aus dem Spanischen,"* G. E. *Lessings sämmtliche Schriften*, I–XXXII (Berlin: 1825–28). *ASKB* 1747–62. Kierkegaard also had Lessing's *Emilia Galotti* (Leipzig: 1844). *ASKB* 1763. For other references to Lessing in the works see, for example, *Either/Or*, I, pp. 164, 167; *Fear and Trembling*, p. 136 fn.; *Repetition*, p. 20; *The Concept of Anxiety* [*Dread*], p. 83 fn.; *Upbuilding* [*Edifying*] *Discourses*, III, p. 119; *Stages*, pp. 352, 396; *Postscript*, p. 36, pt. I, ch. I, pp. 59–66, ch. II, pp.

67–113; *The Concept of Irony*, pp. 72, 295; " 'The Single Individual' Two 'Notes' " together with *The Point of View*, p. 133; *Attack*, p. 68.

111. Yesterday I loved,
Today I suffer,
Tomorrow I die,
Yet, today and tomorrow
I like to think
Of yesterday.

112. See II Samuel 15:18, 8:18; the Cherethites and the Pelethites.

113. Entry is from a sketch for *Philosophical Fragments;* see title page, also *Postscript*, pp. 86 ff.

114. Entry is from draft of *Concluding Unscientific Postscript*, p. 67, heading of para. 3.

115. Entry is from draft of an unused preface (VI B 133) to *Three Discourses on Imagined Occasions* [*Thoughts on Crucial Situations in Human Life*].

116. For edition, see note 110.

117. Ibid.

118. *Von dem Zwecke Jesu und seiner Jünger. Noch ein Fragment des Wolfenbüttelschen Ungenannten*, ed. G. E. Lessing (Braunschweig: 1778), p. 18.

119. Ibid., p. 235.

120. Ibid.

121. Carl Schwarz, *Gotthold Ephraim Lessing als Theologe dargestellt* (Halle: 1854), pp. 211 ff. *ASKB* 622.

LOVE

The engagement with Regine and its unhappy outcome gave Kierkegaard a profound experience of love between man and woman and of its many problems: "In a year and a half I myself experienced more poetry than [is found] in all the novels put together" (IV A 107). This rich but painful experience obliged him to think through the possibilities involved in love between man and woman, and he used the new knowledge in the first period of his authorship. His pseudonyms describe both the ideal marriage (Judge William) and also the collisions of erotic love with the demands of the ethical and the religious (*Repetition, Fear and Trembling*, and part three of *Stages on Life's Way*). However, the five speeches making up "In Vino Veritas," part one of *Stages*, present a caricature of the relationship between man and woman.

But for Kierkegaard the highest form of love is not human love but the love of God, which ought to have "priority" (X^2 A 63) over all other love. In the first part of *Works of Love* Kierkegaard distinguishes all human love from the love commanded in "You shall love your neighbor as yourself" and which has God as the "middle term." The object of this love is, therefore, not a specially chosen person, as in the case of erotic love and friendship, but every human being. In erotic love and friendship, too, love for another as one's neighbor must be primary. Otherwise all love, erotic love, friendship, even mother-love (X^1 A 635), is by itself only an expression of self-love.

Only the command "you shall love your neighbor as yourself" raises love to a new level and establishes the point of departure for Christian love, which is portrayed in part two of *Works of Love*.

The view that love can develop in the right way only if it is person-centered and concrete is characteristic of Kierkegaard's conception of love. It should be oriented to individual persons or to God, rather than to abstractions such as humanity, race, society, nation.

De Rosa, Peter. "Some Reflections on Kierkegaard and Christian Love." *Clergy Review*, vol. 44, 1959.

Lindström, Valter. "A Contribution to the Interpretation of Kierkegaard's Book: *The Works of Love*." *Studia Theologica* (Lund), 1952–53.

Niebuhr, Reinhold. "Kierkegaard and Love." *New York Times Book Review*, vol. 51, no. 33, 1946.

Rougemont, Denis de. "Two Danish Princes: Kierkegaard and Hamlet." *In Love Declared: Essays on the Myths of Love*. New York: Pantheon Books, 1963.

Shideler, Mary McDermott. *The Theology of Romantic Love*. New York, Harper, 1962.

122. See *Works of Love*, Introduction, pp. 13 ff. Love—its different varieties and their roots and manifestations—is a constant theme in Kierkegaard's various works. *Works of Love* is the one volume which concentrates particularly on this theme.

123. See *Either/Or*, I, p. 24.

124. See *Works of Love*, pp. 34 ff.

125. H. Kornmann, *Mons Veneris* . . . (Frankfurt/M: 1614).

126. An undated letter to Regine, presumably written late in 1840, begins with Plato's praise of love. *Letters*, no. 21.

127. See *Either/Or*, II, pp. 206 ff.

128. See ibid., p. 236.

129. See *Upbuilding* [*Edifying*] *Discourses*, I, pp. 87, 90.

130. See ibid., p. 86.

131. See *Either/Or*, I, pp. 411 f.

132. Ibid.

133. See Pliny, *Natural History*, XXXVI, 17.

134. Numbers I and II of *Tre Opbyggelige Taler* (Copenhagen: 1843) have a similar title. See *Upbuilding* [*Edifying*] *Discourses*, I, pp. 61, 79. Number III has an entirely different title (ibid., p. 93). The substance of this entry is found in Number I (ibid., pp. 76, f.) and in Number II (ibid., pp. 89 f.). See also *Works of Love*, pp. 261 ff.

135. See *Upbuilding* [*Edifying*] *Discourses*, I, pp. 76 f., 89 f.

136. See ibid., I, p. 89.

137. See *Works of Love*, pp. 49–53.

138. See ibid., pp. 46 f.

139. See ibid., pp. 34 ff.

140. *Augustini Aurelii Opera*, I–XVII (Venice: 1797–1807), which Kierkegaard bought in May, 1843. *ASKB* 117–34.

141. Entry is from draft of *Tre Opbyggelige Taler* (1834), Upbuilding [*Edifying*] *Discourses*, I, pp. 61 ff.

142. Ibid.

143. See *Philosophical Fragments*, pp. 30 ff.

144. See *Works of Love*, pp. 99 ff.

145. See Matthew 9:32; Mark 7:32.

146. See *Works of Love*, pp. 148 f.

147. See ibid., p. 149.

148. Plato, *Symposium*.

149. Luke 7:36 ff.

150. This entry was not used in the preface to *Works of Love*, but the central idea (without the emperor and corps of writers) was used. See *Works of Love*, p. 19. The emperor, somewhat altered, found his place in chapter II (p. 51).

151. A presupposition for the whole *Works of Love*.

152. Emilie Carlèn, *En Nat ved Bullar-Søen*, serialized in *Berlingske Tidende*, 43–206, February 20, 1847–September 4, 1847.

153. See *Works of Love*, pp. 341 ff.

154. See, for example, ibid., pp. 65 ff.

155. *Ludovicii Blosii Opera Omnia* (Louvain: 1568). *ASKB* 429. The love of Jesus affects me; his fragrance mortifies me. My mortal mind fails me; love alone suffices the loving one.

156. See Ephesians 5:28.

157. See *Practice* [*Training*] *in Christianity*, pp. 174 ff., esp. 176.

158. On various aspects of the theme of love and happiness, see, for example, *Either/Or*, II, pp. 23, 43; *Stages on Life's way*, pp. 46, 210, 272 f., 320; *Fragments*, pp. 30 ff.; *Postscript*, pp. 399 ff., 521 ff; *The Point of View*, p. 77; *Attack upon Christendom*, pp. 189 f.

159. See *Works of Love*, pp. 58 ff., 164, 237 ff., 248 ff., 280 ff.

160. See note 158.

161. See *Works of Love*, p. 79.

162. John 14:21.

163. See *Works of Love*, pp. 171 ff.

164. M. Luther, *En christelig Postille* (see note 81), I, pp. 519 ff.

165. Ibid., p. 520.

166. Deuteronomy 6:5.

167. See, for example, *Stages on Life's Way*, pp. 136 ff.; *Works of Love*, pp. 203 f.

168. See ibid, pp. 123 f., 133.

169. Ibid., pp. 35 f., 117 ff., 131 ff.

170. Ibid., p. 48.

171. See Matthew 25:45.

172. See Matthew 10:42.

173. M. Luther, *En christelig Postille* (see note 81), I, pp. 149 ff.

174. See *Philosophical Fragments*, pp. 39 ff.

175. See *Works of Love*, pp. 34 ff.

176. Sextus Propertius, *Carmina, Elegies*, II, 8, 1.3. No enmity but love's can be so bitter.

177. I John 3:17.

178. See *Works of Love*, pp. 58 ff.

179. I John 3:16.

180. See, for example, *Attack upon Christendom*, pp. 7, 17, 35.

181. Matthew 8:22.

182. See *Attack upon Christendom*, pp. 30 ff., 105, 212 ff., 221 ff.

183. See *Works of Love*, for example, pp. 122 ff., 247 ff.

184. II Corinthians 5:14. See *Works of Love*, Introduction, pp. 15 ff., pp. 347 ff.

185. See *Attack upon Christendom*, pp. 286 f.

186. Mark 10:21.

187. Plato, *Symposium*, 222 b.

188. See *Stages on Life's Way*, p. 161; *Two Ages* [*The Present Age*, pp. 32 f.]; esp. *Practice* [*Training*] *In Christianity*, pp. 181 ff., 190.

189. See ibid., pp. 214 ff.; *Postscript*, pp. 520 ff.

190. See *Philosophical Fragments*, pp. 30 ff.

191. See *Works of Love*, pp. 117 ff., 119.

192. See *For Self-Examination*, pp. 88 ff.

193. See *Attack upon Christendom*, p. 142.

194. See *Works of Love*, pp. 341 ff.

LUTHER

In a journal entry of 1847 Kierkegaard writes, "I have never really read anything by Luther" (VIII¹ A 465). He meant that until then he was merely acquainted with Luther (1483–1546) because of his theological studies in a Protestant university and that he had not intensively studied any of Luther's writings.

However, as early as 1846 Kierkegaard had begun more thorough work with Luther, as revealed in an entry on Luther's expression "the anguished conscience" (VII¹ A 192). Typically, when Kierkegaard wanted to become better acquainted with Luther, he chose Luther's devotional writings, available in a Danish edition entitled *En christelig Postille, sammendragen af Dr. Morten Luthers Kirke- og Huuspostiller ... i Oversættelse af Jørgen Thisted.* Kbh. 1828 (*A Collection of Christian Sermons selected from Dr. Martin Luther's Church- and Home-Sermons ...* translated by Jørgen Thisted [I-II]. Copenhagen: 1828). Just as Kierkegaard regarded his own devotional (*opbyggelige:* upbuilding, edifying) writings as the central portion of his works, he turned to Luther's devotional writings as the most important part of his works.

Kierkegaard was for years afterward a diligent reader of Luther's *Postille*, as numerous journal entries indicate. Yet Kierkegaard was not uncritical of Luther. When he began reading Luther, he already had his own clear conception of "the upbuilding," and there was a confrontation of his views and Luther's.

In most of his observations on Luther's sermons Kierkegaard completely agrees with Luther. For example: "Today I have read Luther's sermon according to plan; it was the Gospel about the ten lepers. O, Luther is still the master of us all" (VIII^1 A 642). He writes that Luther's sermons should be used much more (see, for example, X^1 A 370, 376); furthermore, if Luther's sermons were read, we would discover how far removed we are from Luther (X^1 A 403).

But Kierkegaard was also critical of Luther on various points, increasingly over the years. The main objections are:

(1) "Luther was no dialectician; he always saw only one side of the matter" (X^4 A 394); Luther lacked a comprehensive view, but "to reform Christianity requires first and foremost a comprehensive view of the whole of Christianity" (XI^1 A 193).

(2) Luther "did not go back far enough, did not make a person contemporary enough with Christ" (IX A 95). The encounter with Christ in the situation of contemporaneity is one of the central points in Kierkegaard's understanding of Christianity.

(3) Luther "onesidedly draws Paul forward and uses the gospels less" (X^2 A 244, XI^1 A 572).

(4) "Luther has actually done incalculable harm by not becoming a martyr" (XI^1 A 61), a conclusion Kierkegaard arrived at along with his later emphasis upon imitation [*Efterfølgelsen*]. Luther's attitude has promoted secular mentality, related to the political cast the Reformation took on (X^1 A 154, XI^1 A 442). This critique of the role of the political during the Reformation has particular clarity in a journal entry comparing Reformation times with the present: "The future will correspond inversely to the Reformation: then everything appeared as a religious movement and became political; now everything appears as politics but will become a religious movement" (IX B 63:7).

Despite his later strong criticisms of Luther, Kierkegaard still emphasizes Luther's special merit in making a stand against the naïve conception that a person could "come up to the prototype," and in this connection he says, "Next to the N.T. [New Testament] Luther is the truest figure" (X^5 A 96).

Hess, M. W. "Browning and Kierkegaard as Heirs of Luther." *Christian Century,* LXXX, 1963.

———. "What Luther Meant by Faith Alone." *Catholic World,* vol. 199, May, 1964.

Koenker, Ernest B. "Søren Kierkegaard on Luther." In *Interpreters of Luther,* ed. Juroslav Pelikan. Philadelphia: Fortress Press, 1968.

Lønning, Per. *The Dilemma of Contemporary Theology Prefigured in Luther, Pascal, Kierkegaard, Nietzsche.* Oslo: Universitetsforlaget, 1962.

Pelikan, Jaroslav. *From Luther to Kierkegaard.* St. Louis: Concordia, 1950.

Refsell, Lloyd, "Kierkegaard and Luther." S.T.D. dissertation, Chicago Lutheran Seminary, 1949.

Sløk, Johannes. "Kierkegaard and Luther." In *A Kierkegaard Critique.* New York: Harper, 1962.

Luther—his life, writings, and significance—appears frequently in the *Papirer* from volume I through volume XI^3 in the works, all out of proportion to the frequency of references in the works. There, too, however, Luther is referred to from the earliest newspaper letters through the last (published posthumously) issue of *The Moment* (*Øieblikket,* X). See, for example, *Kjøbenhavnsposten,* 43, February 12, 1836 (*S. V.,* XIII, p. 14); *Fragments,* p. 67; *The Concept of Anxiety [Dread],* p. 139; *Postscript,* pp. 28, 50, 145, 304 327; *Upbuilding Discourses in Various Spirits,* Part Three [*The Gospel of Suffering,* p. 73]; *Works of Love,* pp. 30, 88, 193; *Christian Discourses,* p. 199; *Practice [Training] in Christianity,* pp. 72, 190; *For Self-Examination,* pp. 12 ff.; *Two Upbuilding [Edifying] Discourses,* together with *Judge for Yourselves!,* p. 19; *On My Work as an Author,* together with *The Point of View,* p. 161; *Attack,* pp. 11, 32, 204, 282–83 fn.

195. Finally the devil *deceived* him *honestly.*

196. See K. G. Bretschneider, *Handbuch der Dogmatik der evangelisch-lutherischen Kirche,* I–II (Leipzig: 4 ed., 1838), I, p. 34; *Hutterus redivivus* (Leipzig: 4 ed., 1839), p. 119. *ASKB* 437–38 and 581.

197. Matthew 7:29.

198. See *Postscript,* p. 327.

199. M. Luther, *En christelig Postille* (see note 81), I, p. 28; II, p. 46.

200. See *Works of Love,* p. 193.

201. Ibid., II, p. 11.

202. See M. Luther, *Werke* (Erlangen ed.), XV, p. 43; *The Gospel of Suffering,* p. 31.

203. G. Büchner, *Biblische Real- und Verbal-Hand-Concordanz* (Halle: 6 ed., 1837–40). *ASKB* 79.

204. *Either/Or,* II, p. 356.

205. *En christelig Postille* (see note 81), I, pp. 17 and 16.

206. See VIII^1 A 465 (1847), where Kierkegaard notes that Luther had emphasized "the category: 'for you,' " that he had "never really read anything by Luther," and that he had begun reading Luther's *En christelig Postille* (see

note 81). This work he read regularly for many years. It is significant that with intensive, continued, although still limited, reading of Luther, Kierkegaard usually found a reinforcing, kindred spirit in Luther and also became critical, especially of the use others had made of Luther.

207. Fourteenth Sunday after Trinity (Luke 17:11–19), *En christelig Postille* (see note 81), I, pp. 501 ff.

208. Ibid., I, p. 559.

209. Ibid., I, pp. 164 ff., 605 ff.

210. Matthew 8:10, 9:22. See M. Luther, *En christelig Postille* (see note 81), I, pp. 165, 608.

211. Matthew 26:39.

212. M. Luther, *En christelig Postille* (see note 81), II, p. 91.

213. Ibid., II, pp. 240 ff.

214. John 10:16.

215. M. Luther, *En christelig Postille* (see note 81), I, p. 302.

216. Ibid., I, p. 380.

217. Ibid., I, p. 402 [error in the pagination, printed as 420].

218. Luke 15:1–10.

219. M. Luther, *En christelig Postille* (see note 81), I. pp. 483 ff.

220. Ibid., I, p. 609.

221. M. Luther, *En christelig Postille* (see note 81), I, pp. 632 ff.

222. Matthew 25:1 ff.

223. M. Luther, *En christelig Postille* (see note 81), II, p. 20.

224. Ibid., II, p. 28.

225. Ibid., II, p. 53.

226. Ibid., II, p. 161.

227. See *Judge for Yourselves!*, pp. 201 ff.

228. M. Luther, *En christelig Postille* (see note 81), II, pp. 329 ff.

229. Ibid., II, p. 378.

230. Ibid., I, pp. 132 ff.

231. Ibid., I, p. 156.

232. Ibid., I, p. 161.

233. Matthew 8:4.

234. M. Luther, *En christelig Postille* (see note 81), I, pp. 168 ff.

235. Ibid., I, pp. 199 ff.

236. See *Christian Discourses*, p. 199; also *Practice* [*Training*] *in Christianity*, p. 72.

237. M. Luther, *En christelig Postille* (see note 81) I, p. 207.

238. Ibid., I, pp. 299 ff.

239. Ibid., pp. 297 ff.

240. Ibid., pp. 301 f.

241. Ibid., I, p. 358. In 1849 this sermon for Whit Monday came on May

28. Inasmuch as Kierkegaard read the *Postille* regularly, this entry most likely was written around that date.

242. Ibid., I, p. 349.

243. Kierkegaard left for Berlin on October 11, 1841, and returned March 6, 1842. During this time he (as well as Engels and J. Burkhardt) heard many of Schelling's lectures on Philosophy of Revelation. Among the unpublished *Papirer* (recently published in Danish as a supplement to the current photo-offset reissue of the *Papirer*) are his accounts of forty-one of the lectures.

244. Luke 14:15 ff.

245. M. Luther, *En christelig Postille* (see note 81), I, p. 391.

246. Ibid., pp. 396 ff.

247. Ibid., p. 475.

248. Ibid., II, p. 59.

249. Ibid., II, p. 113.

250. Ibid., II, p. 163.

251. See *Fragments*, pp. 103 f. and ch. V-VI, pp. 111–38; *Postscript*, pp. 89 f.

252. M. Luther, *En christelig Postille* (see note 81), II, p. 279.

253. Ibid., II, pp. 320 ff.

254. Ibid., II, pp. 329 ff.

255. Ibid., II, pp. 331 ff.

256. *Works of Love*, pp. 185 ff.

257. M. Luther, *En christelig Postille* (see note 81), I, pp. xii f.

258. Ibid., p. xiii.

259. Ibid., pp. xiii f.

260. Ibid., p. 273.

261. Ibid., I, pp. 420 f.

262. Ibid., I, p. 433.

263. See *Attack*, pp. 282–83 fn.

264. See *Postscript*, p. 28.

265. M. Luther, *En christelig Postille* (see note 81), I, p. 625.

266. Ibid., II, pp. 99 ff.

267. Luther uses the expression "he wants joyous and willing servants," ibid.

268. One is reminded here of Nietzsche's "Blessed are the drowsy, for they shall soon sleep" (*Thus Spake Zarathustra*, I, 2, end). Kierkegaard and Nietzsche were not chronological contemporaries but they faced common issues, frequently in the same way and frequently very differently. Georg Brandes (letter, February 19, 1888) urged Nietzsche to read Kierkegaard, but apparently nothing came of it. It would have been a fruitful meeting of somewhat kindred yet different spirits. Someday a philosopher-poet will write "Nietzsche and Kierkegaard: Imaginary Conversations" or "Imaginary Correspondence."

269. M. Luther, *En christelig Postille* (see note 81), II, p. 66.

270. Ibid., II, pp. 241 ff.

271. Ibid., II, p. 290.

272. See *Judge for Yourselves!*, pp. 179 f., 201 ff., 213.

273. M. Luther, *En christelig Postille* (see note 81), I, pp. 236 f.

274. Ibid., p. 348.

275. Ibid., pp. 168 f.

276. Ibid., pp. 471 ff.

277. Ibid., p. 613.

278. See *For Self-Examination*, pp. 10 f.

279. See *Postscript*, p. 218. The Danish is *Fuglekonger*.

280. M. Luther, *En christelig Postille* (see note 81), I, pp. 625 ff.

281. "On a Prince Who Lent Out Money at Usury in His Last Hours."

282. Thus it has gone so far now, unfortunately, that one says, O good work, my piety does not save me; so I will be covetous, usurious, and do what pleases and benefits me. . . .

283. Ibid., I, p. 624.

284. See *For Self-Examination*, p. 10.

285. M. Luther, *En christelig Postille* (see note 81), II, pp. 122 ff.

286. Matthew 13:21.

287. M. Luther, *Geist- und Sinnreiche auserlesene Tisch-Reden*, ed. B. Lindner, I-II (Salfeld: 1745), pt. I, pp. 754 f). *ASKB* 225-26.

288. M. Luther, *En christelig Postille* (see note 81), II, p. 182.

289. See *Judge for Yourselves!*, pp. 201 ff.

290. M. Luther, *En christelig Postille* (see note 81), I, p. 15.

291. See, for example, *Armed Neutrality*, p. 37.

292. Ibid., II, pp. 406 ff.

293. Exodus 34:30.

294. Matthew 17:2 ff.

295. M. Luther, *En christelig Postille* (see note 81), II, pp. 420 f.

296. See, for example, *An Open Letter*, together with *Armed Neutrality*, p. 54.

297. M. Luther, *En christelig Postille* (see note 81), II, p. 486.

298. August Petersen, *Die Idee der Kirche*, I-III (Leipzig: 1839-46). *ASKB* 717-19.

299. See note 296.

300. Paul Henry, *Das Leben Johann Calvins des grossen Reformators*, I-III (Hamburg: 1835-44).

301. L. Holberg, *Erasmus Montanus*, I, sc. 3.

302. Morten Fredriksen, while imprisoned in Roskilde, fashioned a leg out of cloth and straw and got the guards to put the chain around it, whereupon he escaped (November 23, 1812). See *S.V.*, V, p. 22.

303. J. L. Heiberg, *De Uadskillelige*, sc. 11.

304. M. Luther, *En christelig Postille* (see note 81), I, pp. 625 ff., 629.

305. Arthur Schopenhauer, *Die Welt Als Wille und Vorstellung*, I-II (Leipzig: 2 ed., 1844). *ASKB* 773–73a.

306. M. Luther, *En christelig Postille* (see note 81), I, pp. 41 ff.

307. See *Attack*, pp. 282–83 fn.

308. See *Postscript*, p. 304; *Works of Love*, p. 88; *Practice* [*Training*] *in Christianity*, p. 190.

MAJESTY

According to Kierkegaard, the relation between God's majesty and man may take the following forms: (1) God's majesty may be so elevated that one is freed from coming into a closer relationship with God. Occasionally Kierkegaard mentions situations in which "God has been made so majestic and has been so fantastically infinitized that he really has been smuggled out of everything to some point infinitely distant from actuality" (X^5 A 47; XI^1 A 37; XI^2 A 116). (2) But a person can also be related to God in such a way that he loses respect for the majesty of God and thereby rebels and sins against God. To sin in this way means to draw punishment upon oneself or, as Kierkegaard says, one punishes himself, for even though one apparently avoids punishment in this life, it cannot be escaped because "God has eternity," in which a full accounting must be made. "Consequently, to sin against God is to punish oneself, and in this way God's majesty is assured" (XI^1 A 589). Yet in this life God can punish a man with the greatest punishment: "Even if a person heaps crime upon crime and it goes unpunished, yes, his life is sheer good luck and conquest, he should not be deceived, for God sees it, God is very near but he overlooks him; he is punished with the most frightful punishment of all—he is ignored by God" (XI^2 A 166).

Kierkegaard also points out that in God's eyes the race and the mass have no significance: "the greater the number the less one enters into relationship with God" (XI^1 A 589).

The condition for the individual's true approach to God is obedience, and the more inward the relationship to God becomes, the more one discovers his distance from God (XI^1 A 590). In this way God's majesty is maintained also in true worship.

Gerry, Joseph. "Kierkegaard: the Problem of Transcendence; an Interpretation of the Stages." Ph.D. dissertation, Fordham University, 1959.

For various uses of "majesty" in the works, see, for example, *Stages*, p. 111, 244; *Postscript*, pp. 19, 161, 325, 375, 475 fn. and note; *Works of Love*, pp. 74, 353 f. (high treason); *Christian Discourses*, p. 175, 302; *Practice* [*Training*] *in Christianity*, p. 222 (high treason); "Two Notes" together with *The Point of View*, p. 135; *Attack*, pp. 14 (high treason), 36, 82.

309. Ch. xxxii ff.

310. Ibid., ch. xxxiv.

311. See *S.V.*, XIV, pp. 80 f.

312. See Matthew 24:44; I Thessalonians 5:2.

313. Just L. Jacobi, *Die Lehre der Irvingiten verglichen mit der heiligen Schrift* (Berlin: 1853).

314. See *Attack*, pp. 35 f.

315. See *Postscript*, p. 178; SUBJECTIVITY, OBJECTIVITY.

316. See XI^2 A 54; " 'The Single Individual,' " together with *The Point of View*, p. 135.

317. Matthew 5:11.

318. Matthew 5:12.

319. Matthew 5:40.

320. Matthew 6:26 ff.

321. "Du" is the familiar nominative of address in Danish, used for family members and close friends. Strangely, however, the familiar forms in English, "thou" and "thee," have become words of distance, elevation, rather than of closeness, so that the "relationship turns about" in reverse.

322. Marginal note to draft of *The Moment*, No. 2. See *Attack*, p. 110, last paragraph.

MARRIAGE

Quite early in Kierkegaard's writings (1838) there is a moderate criticism of the view that marriage is superior to the single state: "paganism levied a tax upon bachelorhood; Christianity recommended celibacy" (II A 244). And indirectly: "Marriage is a physical unity, not a unity in spirit and truth . . ." (II A 469; VIII^1 A 231). Kierkegaard, however, does give through his pseudonym Judge William an attractive and extensive presentation of what a marriage should be, according to his conception (*Either/Or*, II, pp. 5–157; *Stages on Life's Way*, pp. 95–178). Judge William, it should be noted, strongly emphasizes the element of the eternal in marriage, as well as the sensuous aspect, and thereby maintains that marriage has a spiritual aspect too. Later Kierkegaard wrote that in this work he had written "one of the most substantial and inspired defenses of marriage" (X^6 B 115).

Gradually discovering that a marriage seldom turns out according to one's idea of it and that frequently in Christendom marriage is advanced as the highest earnestness in life, as a substitute for the idea of imitation and the eternal (which to Kierkegaard are ultimately the only earnestness), Kierkegaard launched, from a Christian viewpoint, a violent criticism of the overvaluing of marriage. At the same time he avowed that Christianity is particularly interested in "virginity—that is, religion of the spirit" (XI^1 A 150).

In a few instances Kierkegaard links propagation with original sin, pointing out that through it original sin is continued. He also thinks that when marriage and propagation of the species play a dominant role, as in paganism and Judaism, they are a "substitute for the immortality of the individual" (XI¹ A 150, XI² A 176). Only in Christianity, which regards the individual person's spiritual development as most important and marriage as subordinate, does immortality emerge as reality.

Croxall, T. H. *Kierkegaard Commentary.* New York: Harper, 1956.

323. See *Stages,* pp. 70, 111 ff., 144 f. On marriage especially especially Judge William's discussions, *Either/Or,* II, pp. 5–157; *Stages,* pp. 97–178.

324. See *Either/Or,* II, pp. 28, 63, 277; *Stages,* pp. 106 f., 111.

325. See *Either/Or,* II, pp. 37, 62, 70, 99; also *Stages,* pp. 226 f., 340.

326. J. G. G. Büsching, *Ritterzeit und Ritterwesen,* I–II (Leipzig: 1823), II, p. 286. *ASKB* 1408.

327. Quoted from W. M. L. de Wette, *Lærebog i den christelige sædelære og sammes Historie,* tr. C. E. Scharling (Copenhagen: 1835), p. 236. *ASKB* 871. A second marriage is adultery in an honorable form.

328. Something different.

329. See W. M. L. de Wette, p. 129.

330. The City of God would be completed much more rapidly and the end of the age would be hastened.

331. See Diogenes Laertius, II, 53 (*Diogen Laërtses filosofiske Historie,* tr. B. Riisbrigh, I–II; Copenhagen: 1811–12; *ASKB* 1110–11); *Either/Or,* I, p. 37; *The Concept of Irony,* p. 98.

332. *Velbekomme,* a polite expression used by the host after a meal; there is no equivalent in English. The form *volbekom's* is equivalent to the German *wohl bekomm's* (*Ordbog over det danske Sprog,* XXVI, Col. 975).

333. See *Either/Or,* p. 430.

334. See ibid., pp. 430 f.; Euripides, *Medea,* ll. 250 ff.

335. A note for *Either/Or,* see II, p. 106. "Confidence" as in "confide" or "in someone's confidence."

336. See *Either/Or,* I, pp. 282, 425.

337. *Die Politik des Aristoteles,* tr. C. Garve (Breslau: 1799). *ASKB* 1088. *Politics* [ch. 8], I, 3, 1253 b, ll. 3 ff.

338. *Addresseavisen,* no. 85, April 10, 1843.

339. See *Repetition,* p. 107.

340. Marginal note in copy of *Either/Or,* II, p. 3.

341. See *Either/Or,* I, pp. 64 f., 430.

342. See *Works of Love,* pp. 249 ff.

343. See *Fear and Trembling,* p. 112, where a reference is made to *Longi Pastoralia,* i.e., *Longi Pastoralia Græce & Latine,* ed. E. Seiler (Leipzig: 1843), which Kierkegaard had in his library. *ASKB* 1128.

344 Peter C. Kierkegaard (1805–1888), a brother, the oldest son of M. P. Kierkegaard.

345. *Nyt theologisk Bibliothek,* ed. Jens Møller (Copenhagen: 1821–32). *ASKB* 336–45.

346. Ibid., VI, pp. 158 ff.

347. Entries on the relationship between Kierkegaard and Regine Olsen will appear primarily in volumes V–VI of *Søren Kierkegaard's Journals and Papers*.

348. "Yes, not for ten years." See X⁵ A 149:12.

349. See A. Neander, *Denkwürdigkeiten aus der Geschichte des christlichen Lebens*, I-II (Berlin: 1823), I, pp. 136 ff.; II, p. 226. *ASKB* 179–80.

350. John 2:1 ff.

351. *Libri symbolici ecclesiæ evangelicæ sive Concordia*, ed. C. A. Hase (Leipzig: 2 ed., 1837), pp. 456 f. *ASKB* 624.

352. See note 351.

353. Plato, *Symposium*, 206 e ff.

354. Aristotle, *Nicomachean Ethics*, VIII, 12; IX, 7.

355. Friedrich Böhringer, *Die Kirche Christi und ihre Zeugen oder Kirchengeschichte in Biographien*, I, 1–4; II, 1–5 (Zürich: 1842–49), I, p. 387. *ASKB* 173–77 (bound in five volumes).

356. I Corinthians 7:9.

357. Matthew 10:16.

358. I Corinthians 7:9.

359. Matthew 10:16.

360. See notes 353 and 354.

361. *Don Juan, Opera i tvende Akter*, adapted by L. Kruse (Copenhagen: 1807), p. 19.

362. See *Visebog inholdende udvalgte Danske Selskabssange; med tillæg af nogle svenske og tyske*, ed. Andreas Seidlin (Copenhagen: 1814), pp. 86 f.; *ASKB* 1483; Kierkegaard's piece in *Fædrelandet*, 83, April 11, 1855; *S.V.*, XIV, p. 59.

363. I. H. Fichte, *System der Ethik*, I–II (Leipzig: 1850—53), II, 2, pp. 101 f. *ASKB* 504 (II, *Die Gesellschaft Wissenschaft*).

MARTYR

The highest ideal for the Christian life, according to Kierkegaard, is the martyr. "Just as all the nerves converge in the fingertips, so the entire nervous system of Christianity converges in the reality [*Realitet*] of martyrdom" (XI¹ A 61). By this Kierkegaard does not mean that all Christians should become martyrs but that a criterion is needed according to which one should determine his own distance from the ideal.

The highest model of the martyr is Christ himself (i.e., Christ "as prototype"); therefore Kierkegaard calls martyrs and witnesses of the truth "the derivative prototypes" (*Attack*, p. 242, ed. tr.). But since Christ's life has a significance still higher than being the prototype—that of being Redeemer—and since Christ is God, Kierkegaard does not consider it justifiable to call Christ a martyr. "Why cannot Christ be called a martyr. Because he was not a witness to truth but was 'the truth,' and his death was not a martyrdom but the Atonement" (X¹ A 119).

According to Kierkegaard, there are various forms of martyrdom (see, for example, X³ A 303, X⁴ A 108), just as there are various levels of the Christian life (*Judge for Yourselves!*, pp. 209 ff.) in their approach toward or departure from the highest form of the Christian ideal. Here each individual must honestly seek clarity about his own position.

Kierkegaard's view is that only the martyr can advance the cause of Christianity in a decisive way: "And martyrs are the only ones who are needed" (X¹ A 16), but at the same time he adds that in a very reflective period "the most eminent reflection" will be required in order to penetrate the errors of the time and to find out how to go about the task. From this point of view, one sees that when Kierkegaard speaks of the "martyr of the future" (IX B 63: 12–13), he attributes to him "an eminent reflection."

Kierkegaard himself was faced with the question of becoming a martyr. But his pecuniary concerns and his conception that he was a "penitent" kept him from going so far.

364. See *Two Minor Ethical-Religious Essays* [*Treatises*], together with *The Present Age*, pp. 120 ff. On the theme of martyr and martyrdom in the works, see for example, *The Concept of Irony*, p. 298; *Either/Or*, I, p. 226; *Fear and Trembling*, p. 90; *Stages*, pp. 374, 380; *Postscript*, pp. 31 f., 208, 238, 259, 405 f., 453, 496, 529; *Upbuilding Discourses in Various Spirits*, Part Three; [*The Gospel of Suffering*, pp. 75, 140, 155 f.]; *Works of Love*, p. 28; *Christian Discourses*, p. 188; *Two Minor Ethical-Religious Essays* [*Treatises*], together with *The Present Age*, p. 81; *Practice*, pp. 215 f., 219, 224; *Judge for Yourselves!*, pp. 118, 137, 203 f.; *Armed Neutrality* and *An Open Letter*, pp. 39 ff., 51; *On My Work as an Author*, together with *The Point of View*, p. 160; ibid., p. 35, 90, 100 f.; " 'The Single Individual' Two 'Notes' Concerning My Work as an Author," Appendix to ibid., p. 116.

365. See Moriz Carriere, *Die philosophische Weltanschauung der Reformationszeit in ihren Beziehungen zur Gegenwart* (Stuttgart, Tübingen: 1847), p. 410. *ASKB* 458.

366. II Corinthians 12:7. See *Upbuilding* [*Edifying*] *Discourses*, IV, pp. 49 ff.

367. See *The Point of View*, pp. 100 ff.

368. See Hebrews 11:38; J. P. Mynster, *Prædikener*, I-II (Copenhagen: 1826–32), I, pp. 26 f., 50 f. *ASKB* 228.

369. See *Upbuilding Discourses in Various Spirits*, Part Three [*The Gospel of Suffering*, pp. 155 f.].

370. H. Steffens, *Anthropologie*, I–II (Breslau: 1822); *ASKB* 795–96; see also Steffens, *Religionsphilosophie*, I–II (Breslau: 1839).

371. See *Postscript*, p. 496.

372. As early as *Repetition* (p. 9) Kierkegaard uses the expression *Spion*, "secret agent" or "spy," "in a higher service," and it appears frequently in the

Papirer, for example, X⁵ A 511. In the posthumously published *The Point of View for My Work as an Author* (p. 87) he writes, "I am like a secret agent in a higher service," and in " 'The Single Individual' Two 'Notes' Concerning My Work as an Author" (p. 136, Appendix to *The Point of View*) he writes, "Not even the most trusted spy [secret agent] of the shrewdest detective agency can more confidently vouch for the content of his report than I, a mere practitioner, a spy [secret agent] *si placet,* will vouch for the correctness of this."

373. See *Works of Love,* pp. 183 f., 236 f., 346; *Three Discourses at the Communion on Fridays,* together with *Christian Discourses,* pp. 345 f.; *Practice [Training] in Christianity,* pp. 223 f.; *For Self-Examination,* pp. 101 ff.; *The Point of View,* p. 87; *The Moment,* no. 7, in *Attack upon Christendom,* pp. 223 ff.

374. See *Armed Neutrality* and *An Open Letter,* p. 41.

375. Entry from draft of "Three 'Notes' Concerning My Work as an Author"; see *The Point of View,* p. 90; see also *On Authority and Revelation,* pp. 23, 46.

376. See *The Point of View,* p. 138.

377. See note 375.

378. See *Armed Neutrality,* pp. 44 f.

379. See ibid.; *The Point of View,* p. 100.

380. See *The Point of View,* pp. 38–41, 73–75, 90.

381. See note 375.

382. A German politician and writer (1807–1848), executed following an uprising in Vienna. See *Fædrelandet,* 291, Nov. 1848; M. Goldschmidt, *Nord og Syd,* IV, 4 (1848), pp. 19 ff.

383. See *Postscript,* p. 529.

384. Perfect in every respect. See *Stages on Life's Way,* p. 380; *Has a Man the Right to Let Himself Be Put to Death for the Truth?,* together with *The Present Age,* pp. 144, 122.

385. See *Two Minor Ethical-Religious Essays [Treatises],* together with *The Present Age,* pp. 71 ff.

386. See *Upbuilding Discourses in Various Spirits,* Part Three [*The Gospel of Suffering,* p. 75].

387. See *Practice [Training] in Christianity,* pp. 215 f., 219; *Judge for Yourselves!,* pp. 203 f.

388. See note 372.

389. See Friedrich Böhringer, *Die Kirche Christi* (see note 355), I, 1, p. 387.

390. See *Fear and Trembling,* p. 90.

391. See Plutarch, *Marcellus,* XIV; *Stages on Life's Way,* p. 245.

392. Hebrews 12:5.

393. C. T. E. Engeltoft, Bishop of Fyn, father of triplets, April 29, 1854.

394. Basil in Friedrich Böhringer, I, 2, p. 190.
395. See note 364.
396. See note 387.

MARY

In references to Mary, the mother of God, in his works and journal entries, Kierkegaard does not dwell so much on her elevation by being chosen but on the suffering and misunderstanding to which such selection must have exposed her among her contemporaries. The pseudonym Johannes de Silentio says: "To be sure, the angel was a ministering spirit, but it was not a cooperative spirit which went around to the other young maidens of Israel and said, 'Despise not Mary. What befalls her is the extraordinary.' But the angel came only to Mary, and no one could understand her. After all, what woman was so mortified as Mary? And is it not true in this instance also that one whom God blesses He curses in the same breath? This is the spirit's interpretation of Mary, and she is not (as it shocks one to say, but shocks one still more to think, that they have thoughtlessly and superficially interpreted her thus)—she is not a fine lady who sits in state and plays with an infant God. Nevertheless, when she says, 'Behold the handmaid of the Lord'—then she is great, and I think it will not be found difficult to explain why she became the mother of God" (*Fear and Trembling*, pp. 75 f.).

Mary's difficult position is expressed by calling her "the despised maiden" (*Christian Discourses*, p. 45). "Mary thought of herself as sacrificed; happy she was not; and the prophecy also said that a sword would pierce her heart" (X^3 A 57. Of her willingness to become an instrument in God's plan, Kierkegaard says: "but it is precisely this which goes beyond a human being's power, beyond even the utmost exertion of a person's ultimate strength" (X^4 A 54). The suffering side of being chosen is emphasized in these words: "You will live your life scorned by other maidens, treated as a frivolous, conceited wench or a poor, half-crazy wretch or a loose woman ... exposed to all possible suffering, and finally, because God, too, seems to have deceived you, a sword will pierce your heart—this is the glad tidings" (XI^1 A 40). In the last quotation it seems that Kierkegaard wants to draw attention to Mary's suffering in the world as a human analogy to Christ's passion suffering. With the words "as if God, too, has deceived you" a parallel is drawn to Christ's cry, "My God, my God! Why have you forsaken me" (Matthew 27:46).

There are no extended discussions of Mary in the works. For references see, for example, *Either/Or*, I, pp. 196, 312, 328; *Fear and Trembling*, p. 75; *Upbuilding* [*Edifying*] *Discourses*, III, pp. 40, 124; *Fragments*, p. 42; *Postscript*, p. 232; *Upbuilding Discourses in Various Spirits*, Part One [*Purity of Heart*, p. 139]; Part Three [*The Gospel of Suffering*, p. 52]; *Christian Discourses*, p. 45; *Practice* [*Training*] *in Christianity*, p. 167; *An Upbuilding* [*Edifying*] *Discourse*, together with ibid., p. 261; *Judge for Yourselves!*, p. 171; *Attack*, p. 25.

397. Entry from ms. of *Bogen om Adler*. See *On Authority and Revelation*, p. 50 fn.

398. Luke 1:48.

399. Luke 2:35.

400. Luke 1:38.

401. See Genesis 18:12.

402. See note 399.

403. See note 398.

MEDIOCRITY

With his high ideals for human existence, Kierkegaard could not be other than critical of mediocrity as the attitude of preferring to live superficially and not wanting to have a deeper encounter with spiritual values. He frequently points out that mediocrity knows how to interpret Scriptures in such a way that it manages to get around the strenuousness and the demands of which the Scriptures speak (for example, XI² A 91; *For Self-Examination*, p. 85; *Attack*, p. 196).

Kierkegaard never criticizes mediocrity in the sense of deficiency of capacities, but he does rigorously judge mediocrity as a lack of passion in decisively willing the good. "What makes it so enormously difficult to get Christianity hauled through the mire in our time is that it is stalled in mediocrity, passionlessness, and absence of spirit, something far more dangerous than heresies and schisms, where there nevertheless is passion" (XI² A 323).

On the theme of mediocrity, see, for example, *The Concept of Irony*, p. 157; *Three Discourses on Imagined Occasions* [*Thoughts on Crucial Situations*, pp. 11, 15, 66]; *Postscript*, p. 487; *Upbuilding Discourses in Various Spirits*, Part One [*Purity of Heart*, pp. 63, 98]; Part Three [*The Gospel of Suffering*, p. 148]; *Christian Discourses*, p. 215; *Two Minor Ethical-Religious Essays* [*Treatises*], together with *The Present Age*, pp. 126 f.; *Judge for Yourselves!*, pp. 169, 182; *Attack*, pp. 34, 108, 228, 248, 281.

404. See *Stages*, p. 282.

405. See " 'The Single Individual' Two 'Notes' Concerning My Work as an Author," Appendix to *The Point of View*, p. 140; *Attack*, pp. 34, 102, 117, 175, 177, 197, 262, 277.

406. Matthew 16:23.

407. Romans 12:16.

408. Luke 14:8.

409. Character in L. Tieck, *Der gestiefelte Kater, ein Kindermärchen*. See *S. V.*, XIII, p. 26; *The Concept of Irony*, p. 97.

410. James 1:5.

411. See *Attack*, p. 108.

412. Ibid., p. 277.

413. Luke 22:32.

MELANCHOLY

Throughout his life Kierkegaard struggled with a melancholy related to the depression of his father as well as to home environment. He writes: "Already in my earliest childhood I broke down under the grave impression which the melancholy old man who laid it upon me himself sank under. A child—what a crazy thing!—travestied as an old man!" (*The Point of View,* p. 76).

But Kierkegaard took on this melancholy as a task for his thought and for his existence. Through his existential penetration of the nature of melancholy and depression he uncovered its deeper connections with human existence. In a later work, *The Sickness unto Death,* the profound and exhaustive description of the forms of despair is derived from his thorough experience of and reflection upon melancholy and depression. Melancholy and despair are parallel existence-concepts, with the difference that "despair" stresses the cognitional aspect and "melancholy" or "depression" emphasizes the emotional character of the same basic condition.

In journal entry VIII¹ A 239 Kierkegaard says that either a melancholic seeks to forget his melancholy by escape into external diversions (*The Sickness unto Death,* p. 189) or he closes himself up with it in order to battle it out. Kierkegaard chose the second way, the prerequisite for a solution of the riddle of melancholy, which he regarded as solved.

Grimsley, R. "Romantic Melancholy in Chateaubriand and Kierkegaard." *Comparative Literature,* vol. 8, no. 3, 1956.

Direct references in the works to melancholy are infrequent and are confined to the earliest esthetic works. See *Either/Or,* I, pp. 20, 74 f., 77, 392, 430; II, pp. 26, 237, 312; *Repetition,* pp. 7, 11 f., 82, 89 f., 93, 137; *The Concept of Anxiety* [*Dread*], p. 53 fn. ("Schelling speaks of a melancholy brooding over nature . . .").

414. Thomas à Kempis, *Om Christi Efterfølgelse,* tr. J. A. L. Holm (Copenhagen: 3 ed., 1848), p. 10. *ASKB* 273.

METHODISTS

While reading a biography of John Wesley (1703–1791) (Robert Southey, *John Wesleys Leben* . . . , Hamburg: 1841), Kierkegaard made a few notes in his journal which presumably are all he wrote on Methodism. However, these entries are of particular interest because they are an early indication that whatever in his reading touched his personal problems made an impression upon him.

Methodism, which has much in common with the Moravian Brethren (*Hernhutters*), whose meetings in Copenhagen Kierkegaard's father often attended, must have appealed to Kierkegaard because it attached the greatest importance to personal engagement (X³ A 518) and the practical consequences of faith. Its emphasis on being led to conversion and sanctification through Methodist guidance must have evoked a response in Kierkegaard, who also thought that man should go through a definite spiritual development in order to reach a personal appropriation of Christianity.

The great importance Methodists placed upon the personal manifested itself in their prerequisites for performing the duties of a pastor, a question Kierkegaard himself struggled with during the years he pondered becoming a pastor. In one entry (X^3 A 517) he compares the Methodists' requirements with the requirements placed upon the pastors of the Danish Church, for whom, in Kierkegaard's opinion, the ministry was more and more a means of making a living (see also X^3 A 530). Therefore, the Danish pastors' preaching was practically "pure falsehood with respect to the existential" (X^3 A 519), whereas Kierkegaard must have thought that the Methodist pastors had the proper existential background for their preaching, since it was well known that they sought out the common people, preached on the street, and often risked assault by the rabble. In another entry from the period, in comparing his own proclamation with that of the state-appointed clergy, he declares that he "did it *gratis*," exposed himself "to mob-persecution, lived in the street" (X^3 A 530).

But the first sentence of journal entry X^2 A 519 surely must be interpreted as a dissociation from the pietistic severity (see PIETISM) which Kierkegaard found among the Methodists, since the note probably was made at the time he was reading about John Wesley.

Finally, in Wesley's counseling with his friends, who urged upon him the marriage he was tempted to enter (X^3 A 523), Kierkegaard finds confirmation of his own conviction that when a man wants to take the ultimate consequences of the imitation of Christ, his friends will try to prevent it *Practice* [*Training*] *in Christianity*, p. 120: "the precaution to have no friend").

415. See Robert Southey, *John Wesleys Leben*, tr. F. S. Krummacher, I–II (Hamburg: 1841). *ASKB* 785–86.

416. See VOCATION.

417. See Robert Southey (note 415), II, p. 220.

418. Ibid., pp. 270 ff., 281.

419. See note 415.

MIDDLE AGES

In many journal entries Kierkegaard points out that the chief characteristic of the Middle Ages was its doubleness, a cleft (II A 468) which divided society into two camps representing the higher and the lower. On one side were the monks, knights, and clergy, and on the other the laity. Or, "the scholastics and the fools" were in opposite camps. Speaking of this "cleft," Kierkegaard declares that it almost seems "as if it takes two individuals to form one whole man . . ." (I A 145). The overcoming of this onesidedness was "reserved for a later age." Kierkegaard's idea is to unite the higher and the lower through "the individual's synthesis of these elements." This is analogous to Kierkegaard's conception of man as a synthesis of the eternal and the temporal. (See also MONASTICISM.)

For traces of various interests in the Middle Ages in the works, see, for example, *From the Papers of One Still Living, S.V.*, XIII, p. 91; *The Concept of Irony*, pp. 270, 295, 319; *Either/Or*, I, pp. 86 f., 222; II, pp. 8, 26, 141, 250, 332; *Fear and Trembling*, pp. 101 fn., 107; *The Concept of Anxiety* [*Dread*], pp. 10, 95, 134 fn.; *Stages*, pp. 111, 166, 168, 190, 271, 410; *Postscript*, pp. 108, 262, 360, 362, 365, 370, 372 f., 375, 410, 422, 430, 440, 467, 482 f., 486, 501; *The Sickness unto Death*, p. 198; *For Self-Examination*, pp. 8 f., 79; *Judge for Yourselves!*, pp. 201, 213.

420. See MYTHOLOGY.

421. See "To Mr. Orla Lehman," *S.V.*, XIII, p. 35.

422. C. L. Stieglitz, "Die Sage vom Doctor Faust," in von Raumer's *Taschenbuch*, V.

423. "On the Possible Age and Interpretation of the Poem on the Wartburg War."

424. August Koberstein, *Ueber das wahrscheinliche Alter und die Bedeutung des Gedichtes vom Wartburger Kriege* (Naumburg: 1823). *ASKB* 1742.

425. "The riddle game between Wolfram von Eschenback and Klinsor."

426. So, as was said, it was from the tendency to exalt Wolfram and from this predilection for the allegorical and the enigmatic that our riddle game sprang, in which the teasing, mischievous magic in Klinsor, which, derived from natural religion and harking back to its fatherland the pagan Orient, attempts to prove the inadequacy of Christianity and make the Christian doubt himself, encounters Wolfram, solid in his faith and convinced of Christianity's infallibility and universal validity. And since it is not able to do so, it calls the devil himself for help, as the element of eternal negation, abandonment, and destruction.

427. See "*Kjøre Ved og Kjøre Vatn,*" Norwegian folksong, in J. Davidsen, *Ny Sangbog* (Copenhagen: 1814), pp. 286 f.

428. J. M. Thiele, *Danske Folkesagn*, I–II (Copenhagen: 1818–23). *ASKB* 1591–92.

429. Refers to *catena patrum*, a chain or a collection of Bible interpretations drawn from the writings of the Church Fathers.

430. An orphan Amen.

431. If I am not mistaken.

432. See *The Concept of Anxiety* [*Dread*], p. 95; *Stages*, pp. 271, 410; *Postscript*, p. 362, 372 f.; *For Self-Examination*, pp. 8 f., 179.

433. Ibid.

434. Ibid.

MIRACLES

The possibility of miracles must always be presupposed in Christianity because of faith in God, who is omnipotent. When faith is lacking, there is no belief in miracles: "when there are no longer any miracles, Christianity no longer exists at all" (XI^1 A 187). Even though miracles are always possible according to Christianity, one must not rashly play with ideas of miracles but "should be edified or built up by the thought of the power of the Almighty, be built up and quieted by the release which miracle provides" (VIII^1 A 26).

In addition one should consider that miracles are not merely temporal aids but may also involve difficulties. In this connection Kierkegaard refers not only to the healing of the congenitally blind man who was excluded from the synagogue after being healed (VIII^1 A 428) but also to the fact that miracles can force the individual to confront important decisions.

It is significant that Kierkegaard considers certain spiritual changes in the human personality to be greater miracles than those in the external world of nature, for example, a person led by God's help who becomes "infinitely nothing in humility." We may think that this miracle, in comparison with feeding the five thousand (John 6:1 ff.) "is much easier, but it is not so. Every qualitative change, every infinite change in quality, is genuinely a miracle" (X^3 A 532).

Along the same line but on a higher level is Kierkegaard's statement that it was a "miracle" that he who could command the weather and the wind became, in the passion story, impotent (X^5 A 130), one who was incapable of anything.

435. Professor H. N. Clausen (1793–1877), whose lectures on exegesis in the winter semesters of 1832–33 and 1838–39 and on dogmatics in the winter and summer semesters of 1833–34 and 1839–40 Kierkegaard presumably heard or followed in some way. See I C 7; I C 19 (in Supplement, *Papirer*, XII, 2 ed., 1968–); II C 1; I C 34–36 (also in Supplement, *Papirer*, XII, 2 ed.).

436. On this theme in the works, see, for example, *Either/Or*, I, p. 34; *Fear and Trembling*, p. 63; *Fragments*, pp. 41 f., 136; *Prefaces, S.V.*, V, p. 67; *Stages*, p. 98; *Postscript*, pp. 510, 535; *Upbuilding Discourses in Various Spirits*, Part Three [*The Gospel of Suffering*, p. 158]; *Works of Love*, pp. 274, 304; *Christian Discourses*, p. 302; *Two Minor Ethical-Religious Essays* [*Treatises*], together with *The Present Age*, p. 146; *The Sickness unto Death*, p. 172; *Practice* [*Training*] *in Christianity*, pp. 44 f., 94, 98 f., 125 f., 135, 170; *Judge for Yourselves!*, p. 173.

437. Matthew 21:1 ff.

438. Matthew 14:13 ff.; Mark 6:34 ff.; Luke 9:12 ff.; John 6:5 ff.

439. Ibid.

440. Mark 5:22 ff.; Luke 8:41 ff.

441. See *Christian Discourses*, p. 302.

442. Ibid.; see note 438.

443. See *Postscript*, pp. 88 f.

444. *Fragmente des Wolfenbüttelschen Ungenannten . . . Bekanntgemacht von G. E. Lessing* (Berlin: 1788), pp. 69 ff.

445. See note 438.

446. A. Neander, *Der heilige Bernhard und sein Zeitalter* (Hamburg, Gotha: 2 ed., 1848).

447. Matthew 8:26; Mark 4:39; Luke 8:24.

448. See *Postscript*, pp. 510, 535; *Works of Love*, p. 138; *The Sickness unto Death*, p. 172.

MISSION

For Kierkegaard there was no doubt that true Christianity must always have a universal and missionary character. "According to the New Testament, Christianity is a continuing mission, every Christian a missionary: Go out and proclaim my teaching" (X^5 A 122). If one forgets this task and settles down in repose, Christianity loses its significance for him and the falling away begins. Kierkegaard thinks that the individual needs to be reminded again of this task. "Christianity in repose is *eo ipso* not Christianity. As soon as anything of that sort appears, it means: 'Become a missionary' " (XI^1 A 345).

Among the few direct references to this theme in the works, see *Stages*, p. 315; *Postscript*, pp. 535 f., *The Point of View*, pp. 23, 30, 43; " 'The Single Individual' Two 'Notes' Concerning My Work as an Author," Appendix to ibid., p. 138.

449. Without more ado.

450. An abbreviated and indigenized form of *anno domini* used on title pages.

451. See *The Point of View*, p. 30.

452. See *Practice [Training] in Christianity*, pp. 124 ff.; QUALITATIVE DIFFERENCE.

MOHAMMEDANISM

Kierkegaard clarified his conception of Mohammedanism particularly through his reading of Karl Rosenkranz's treatise, "Eine Parallel zur Religionsphilosophie" in Bruno Baur's *Zeitschrift für spekulative Theologie* (1837), in which Rosenkranz makes a comparison of world religions. Mohammedanism is characterized (II A 86) as "abstract monotheism" as distinguished from Judaism's "concretized monotheism" and Christianity's doctrine of God's incarnation. In "God is one" Mohammedanism stresses the number "one" in contrast to Judaism's personal, concrete "I am who I am" (Exodus 3:14).

Kierkegaard says that in Mohammedanism everything "stops" at the halfway point since it does not go beyond its abstract point of departure. The relationship of Mohammedanism to Christianity can best be rendered in the symbol used by Mohammedans themselves: "the moon, which borrows its light from the sun" (II A 88), that is, from Christianity.

References to Mohammedanism in the works are few and brief. See *From the Papers of One Still Living*, S. V., XIII, p. 77; *The Concept of Irony*, pp. 85, 180, 297; *Either/Or*, I, p. 424; *Postscript*, pp. 45, 49, 369 fn., 512.

453. See Colossians 1:2; Philippians 1:14.
454. Galatians 3:20.

MOMENT, THE MOMENTARY

A portion (pp. 78 ff.) of *The Concept of Anxiety* (pseudonymous author, Vigilius Haufniensis) gives a coherent and detailed exposition of the important and difficult category "the moment" (*øjeblikket*). The moment comes into existence when "time and eternity touch one another." Without eternity the moment does not exist in the proper sense, because the nature of time is "only that it goes by," and the stream of time consists of fugitive discrete moments. Only when the eternal strikes the stream of time and forms a synthesis of time and eternity does the particular moment gain significance: "for the moment is really time's atom, but not until eternity is posited, and this is why one may properly say that eternity is always ἐν ἀτόμῳ (V B 55:6).

When the pseudonym Climacus wants to give expression to Christ's coming into the world, he calls Christ "the moment." This, he says, is the entrance of the eternal into the world expressed "in its most abbreviated form" (*Philosophical Fragments*, p. 64).

As a lower-level analogy, Kiekegaard used the name *The Moment* for his pamphlets during his attack on the Church. The title was intended to mean a judging of Christendom by the earnestness of the eternal. This judgment could first be expressed when the right man was on hand: " 'The moment' occurs when the person is there, the right person" (XI² A 405).

Croxall, T. H. "The Christian Doctrine of Hope and the Kierkegaardian Doctrine of the Moment." *Expository Times*, vol. 56, 1944-45.

Daane, James. "Kierkegaard's Concept of the Moment." Th.D. dissertation, Princeton Theological Seminary, 1947.

Jones, O. T. "The Meaning of the 'Moment' in Existential Encounter according to Kierkegaard." S.T.D. dissertation, Temple University, 1962.

Direct or extended considerations of this important concept are not numerous in either the works or the *Papirer*. See, for example, *The Concept of Irony*, p. 228; *Either/Or*, II, pp. 22, 167; *Fear and Trembling*, p. 51; *Fragments*, title page, pp. 13 ff., 22, 37, 64 f., 71 ff., 77; *The Concept of Anxiety* [*Dread*], pp. 47, 74 and fn., 78 ff. and fn.; *Three Discourses on Imagined Occasions* [*Thoughts on Crucial Situations*, p. 36]; *Stages*, p. 108; *Postscript*, p. 346; *Works of Love*, pp. 101, 231 ff., 280, 289 f.; *Christian Discourses*, pp. 103 f.; *The Lily of the Field and the Bird of the Air*, together with ibid., pp. 325 f., 340; *Attack*, pp. 41 and note, 91.

455. See *Upbuilding* [*Edifying*] *Discourses*, I, p. 62.

456. A portion in draft of *The Concept of Anxiety* [*Dread*]. It closes the first sentence in the footnote, p. 79.

457. For this ordinary view of "moment" or "the momentary" in the works, see, for example, *The Concept of Irony*, p. 228; *Either/Or*, I, pp. 427, 431; II, p. 22; *Fear and Trembling*, p. 51; *Upbuilding Discourses in Various Spirits*, Part One [*Purity of Heart*, p. 147]; Part Two [*What We Learn from the Lilies of the Field*

and the Birds of the Air,] together with Part Three [*The Gospel of Suffering,* pp. 214]; *Works of Love,* pp. 337 ff.; *Christian Discourses,* pp. 232 f., 236 f.

458. See *The Point of View,* pp. 101 f. and previous note.

459. Genesis 27:38 ff.

460. See *The Moment* [*Instant*], no. X, in *Attack,* pp. 280 ff.

MONASTICISM

In the monastic movement Kierkegaard saw the willingness of men to renounce the world for the sake of an absolute purpose. His pseudonym Climacus therefore calls the monastic movement "a passionate decision, as is becoming in relation to the absolute *telos*" (*Postscript,* p. 360). It is really the movement of renunciation which Kierkegaard-Climacus sees actualized in the monastic movement. It is also this renunciation Kierkegaard has in mind when he says in a journal entry: " 'The monastery' is an essential dialectical element in Christianity; therefore we need to have it out there like a buoy at sea in order to see where we are, even though I myself would not enter it" (VIII¹ A 403).

Kierkegaard's objections to monastic life center around two points: (1) it is wrong to emphasize an inner change by an external withdrawal from the world and then in addition to stress such a withdrawal by, for example, a mode of dress. According to his conception, it is greater and more difficult to remain in the world and to practice continually the movement of renunciation; such a life in the world could be called "hidden inwardness" (*Postscript,* p. 424, ed. tr.; *Practice* [*Training*] *in Christianity,* p. 211); (2) the monks were regarded as extraordinary Christians, and even though there are various levels of appropriation of Christianity, all Christians are to be judged according to the same high criterion.

Most likely this "hidden inwardness" would be practiced particularly in Protestantism, but Kierkegaard gradually came to the conclusion that in Protestantism, through the omission of renunciation as the presupposition for "hidden awareness," one would end up in sheer secular-mindedness. Therefore in his later years Kierkegaard tended to stress the monastic life as an element in the appropriation of the essentially Christian: "Back to the monastery—the question must be brought back to the monastery from which Luther broke out (this is probably the truth)." But at the same time he emphasizes that it was a mistake to regard the monks as extraordinary Christians: "the error in the Middle Ages was not the monastery and asceticism but that basically the secular mentality had conquered in the monk's parading as the extraordinary Christian" (XI¹ A 134). The monk, by stopping with renunciation and withdrawal, gained a kind of secular recognition. Kierkegaard ironizes over Protestantism's misuse of "hidden inwardness": "The monastery dropped out. In place of monasticism's unreasonable worship there appeared the true Christian worship, for we, we Protestants, we do not flee like cowards from life, and neither did Christ—no, we remain, as did Christ, in the world—lost in unmitigated profane secularism, worse than paganism" (XI¹ A 263). See RENUNCIATION, RESIGNATION.

Roos, H. (S.J.). *Søren Kierkegaard and Catholicism.* Westminster, Md.: Newman Press, 1954.
For a variety of references to monasticism etc. in the works, see, for example, *From the Papers of One Still Living, S.V.,* XIII, p. 91; *The Concept of Irony,* p. 301; *Either/Or,* I, pp. 181, 189, 197; II, pp. 250, 332 f.; *Fear and Trembling,* pp. 107 ff.; *The Concept of Anxiety* [*Dread*], pp. 63 f.; *Preface, S.V.,* V, p. 33; *Stages,* pp. 75 f., 174 f., 190; *Postscript,* pp. 283, 359 f., 362 f., 366 f., 370 f., 372 ff., 412, 423 ff., 439 f., 446, 451, 458, 482 f., 502; *Works of Love,* pp. 144 f.; *Practice* [*Training*] *in Christianity,* p. 223; *For Self-Examination,* pp. 8 f.; *Judge for Yourselves!,* pp. 179, 201 ff.; *The Point of View,* p. 18.

461. Ludwig Tieck, *Sehr wunderbare Historie von der Melusina,* in *Sämmtliche Werke,* I–II (Paris: 1837), II, pp. 417 ff. *ASKB* 1848–49.

462. K. Rosenkranz. *ASKB* 35.

463. *Einsiedelei,* hermitage.

464. See *Stages,* pp. 75 f.; *Postscript,* pp. 362 f., 366 f., 372 f., 412, 422 f., 439 f., 446, 451, 458, 502; *Works of Love,* p. 144 f.

465. Entry is from draft of *Concluding Unscientific Postscript,* p. 363 end; see also pp. 359 f., 372 f., 422 f., 434–40, 482 f.

466. See *Christian Discourses,* pp. 180 f.

467. See *For Self-Examination,* pp. 8 ff.

468. See *Works of Love,* p. 138; *For Self-Examination,* pp. 55 ff.

469. See *Works of Love,* pp. 188 ff. and note, p. 196; *Practice* [*Training*] *in Christianity,* p. 217.

470. See *Postscript,* pp. 370 ff.

471. See INWARDNESS; note 629.

472. See Hosea 1:2.

473. See *Postscript,* pp. 373 f.

474. May 19, 1850.

475. See *Either/Or,* II, p. 171; *Stages,* p. 351 (present English translation omits "When Cato had taken his own life").

476. A. Neander, *Der Heilige Johannes Chrysostomus und die Kirche,* I–II (Berlin: 1821).

477. Ibid.

478. Monk of monks.

479. C. Ullmann, *Reformatoren vor der Reformation,* I–II (Hamburg: 1842).

480. See notes 464 and 465.

481. Ibid.

482. See *Postscript,* pp. 359 f., 422 f.; *Judge for Yourselves!,* pp. 179, 201 ff.

MONEY

In the works there are scores of metaphors and illustrations involving money. For more direct references, see, for example, *The Concept of Irony*, pp. 211 f., 310 f.; *Either/Or*, II, pp. 101 f.; *Fragments*, pp. 4, 28; *Stages*, pp. 281, 354, 426; *Postscript*, pp. 353, 382, 467; *Upbuilding Discourses in Various Spirits*, Part One [*Purity of Heart*, pp. 59 f., 70 f., 129, 143]; Part Three [*The Gospel of Suffering*, p. 153]; *Works of Love*, p. 350; *Christian Discourses*, pp. 21, 37 f., 120, 233; *Judge for Yourselves!*, pp. 144, 173 f.; *Attack*, pp. 72, 83, 210.

483. See A. Oehlenschläger, *Digte* (Copenhagen: 1803), pp. 238 f.

484. See *Works of Love*, pp. 292 ff.

485. J. L. A. Kolderup-Rosenvinge (1792–1850), professor of law, University of Copenhagen.

486. *Cyropædia*, II, 2, 26.

487. See *Either/Or*, II, pp. 101 f.

488. See letter to *Fædrelandet*, 97, April 27, 1855, in *Attack*, pp. 45 f.

489. See ibid., p. 72.

490. See ibid., pp. 41, 50, 83, 123, 134, 209.

MONTAIGNE

Kierkegaard owned a German translation of Montaigne's (1533–1592) essays entitled *Gedanken und Meinungen über allerley Gegenstände*, I–VII (Berlin: 1793–99). In all probability Kierkegaard began reading Montaigne in 1847. Not satisfied with superficial knowledge about man's motives, Kierkegaard was attracted by Montaigne's skeptical outlook on man's preconceived ideas and his lack of a critical sense.

In addition to a few entries in the journals, Kierkegaard mentions Montaigne in a published work, where he calls him a "wise man" because he points out that even if one is not overtly punished for his transgressions, he nevertheless suffers under them secretly, which also is a punishment (*Christian Discourses*, p. 140; VIII^1 A 278).

Especially interesting is Kierkegaard's revision (X^3 A 501) of Montaigne's remark that "remarkably enough, what we all owe our existence to is something to be despised." Kierkegaard maintains over against this that in procreation "there is also present a creative factor" whereby God makes the individual man a being with the possibility of eternity within him.

491. Michael Montaigne, *Gedanken und Meinungen über allerley Gegenstände*, I–VII (Berlin: 1793–99). *ASKB* 681–87. The only direct reference to Montaigne in the works apparently is in *Christian Discourses*, p. 140.

492. Ibid.

493. We (Christians) should be ashamed that no adherent of a human sect has yet been found who did not to an extent base his conduct and life on

its tenets, no matter how peculiar and difficult they were. And such a divine and heavenly doctrine (Christianity) characterizes Christians merely in their language.

494. Spinoza, *Tractatus theologica politicus,* ed. H. E. G. Paulus (Jena: 1802). Matters have long since reached the point where one can only pronounce a man Christian, Turk, Jew, or heathen by his general appearance and attire, by his choice of a place of worship, or by his use of the phraseology of a particular sect—as for way of life, it is in all cases the same.

495. He who spins too fine gets himself snarled up.

496. Montaigne, III, p. 481.

497. Ibid.

498. Ibid., V, p. 376.

499. Ibid., V. 150.

500. Ibid., II, p. 172 (ch. 38).

501. Ibid., p. 22.

502. Ibid., pp. 267 f.

MOZART

Presumably Kierkegaard became acquainted with Mozart's (1756–1791) operas as early as autumn 1835. Mozart's music impressed him deeply, and he arrived at the idea that Mozart's three well-known operas, *Figaro, The Magic Flute,* and *Don Juan,* constitute an expression of the three levels of the erotic in the stage of immediacy: *Figaro* as representing the Oriental erotic, *The Magic Flute* the Greek, and *Don Juan* the protest of the immediate erotic against Christianity.

In a journal entry from January 1837 we find: "Tonight for the first time I shall see *The Magic Flute.* It has occurred to me that it might have significance with respect to Don Juan and fill out the stage between him and the Page in *Figaro.* I am of the opinion that in these three stages Mozart has consummately and perfectly presented development of love on the level of immediacy" (I C 125).

In the same entry Kierkegaard gives a precise description of what is disclosed by a closer look at the "three stages" and of their relationship to one another. Kierkegaard's pseudonym, adopting these observations essentially unchanged, develops them as "The Immediate Stages of the Erotic or the Musical Erotic" (*Either/Or,* I, pp. 43 ff.).

Maintaining that music has "its absolute object" in "the genius of sensuousness" (ibid., p. 70) as represented by Don Juan, he must regard the music of *Don Juan* as the ultimate achievable in music. In fact, the demonic in Don Juan's eroticism is the essential sphere of music.

This music had a great effect on Kierkegaard himself, because he encountered it just at the time he was trying to free himself from the effects of his father's rigorous training involving the erotic. Referring to the seductive effect of Mozart's music in *Don Juan,* he says: "it is this piece which affected me so diabolically that I can never forget it; it was this piece which drove me, like Elvira, out of the cloister's quiet night" (II A 491).

To the same effect, although in another way, are the words underlined by Kierkegaard in his copy of *Either/Or:* "Immortal Mozart! You to whom I owe everything, because of whom I lost my reason . . . (IV A 224; see *Either/Or,* I, p. 47). With the words "lost my reason," Kierkegaard undoubtedly refers to the years 1836–37, when he tried to live as an esthete.

Clive, G. "Demonic in Mozart (Kierkegaard's criticism of Mozart)." *Music and Letters,* vol. 37, 1956.

Cochrane, Arthur C. "On the Anniversaries of Mozart, Kierkegaard, and Barth." *Scottish Journal of Theology,* vol. 9, 1956.

Croxall, T. H. "Kierkegaard and Mozart." *Music Letters,* 1945.

Croxall, T. H. "Kierkegaard on Music." *Proceedings of Royal Music Association,* 1946–47.

Grimsley, Ronald. "The Don Juan Theme in Molière and Kierkegaard." *Comparative Literature,* no. 4, 1954.

Poole, Roger. "Irony Ironized." *New Blackfriars,* vol. 49, 1967.

Turner, W. J. *Mozart.* New York: Doubleday, 1954.

For a consideration of Mozart in the works, see *The Concept of Irony,* p. 308; *Either/Or,* I, pp. 29, 43–133 (which some critics regard as one of the finest essays, if not the best, on Mozart), 298; II, pp. 25, 43; *Stages,* p. 43; *Postscript,* p. 253 fn.; "A Fleeting Observation Concerning a Detail in *Don Juan,*" in *Fædrelandet,* 1890–91, May 19–20, 1845, *S.V.,* XIII, pp. 445–52.

503. See "On *Fædrelandet's* Polemic," in *Kjøbenhavns flyvende Post,* 82, March 12, 1836, *S.V.,* XIII, p. 16; *Either/Or,* I, pp. 188 ff.

504. *Don Juan,* adapted by L. Kruse (Copenhagen: 1807), p. 18.

505. See *Either/Or,* I, pp. 29 f.

506. Ibid., p. 47.

MYSTERY

Kierkegaard always maintains that in Christianity the truth is "hidden mystery" (II A 78) even when it is revealed to men, because Christianity can never be fathomed by thought. Because of his concern to draw human existence within the mystery through touch with higher reality, Kierkegaard seeks to "emphasize another side of the concept mystery: the ethical-religious" (X^2 A 341). This kind of mystery means "initiation" into the truth of Christianity, which grips the individual profoundly and cannot be rationally explained. Judge William's words are an instance of initiation within the purely ethical realm: "So when all has become still around one, as solemn as a starlit night, when the soul is alone in the whole world, then there appears before one, not a distinguished man, but the eternal Power itself. The heavens part, as it were, and the I chooses itself—or rather, receives itself. Then has the soul beheld the loftiest sight that mortal eye can see and which never can be forgotten, then the personality receives the accolade of knighthood which ennobles it for an eternity" (*Either/Or*, II, p. 181). This initiation grows in significance along with the growth of inwardness.

For uses of "mystery" in the works, see, for example, *Either/Or*, I, p. 330; *Fear and Trembling*, p. 113; *Repetition*, p. 84; *The Concept of Anxiety* [*Dread*], p. 91; *Stages*, p. 126; *Postscript*, p. 191; *The Sickness unto Death*, pp. 233, 246; *Practice* [*Training*] *in Christianity*, pp. 134–35.

507. Entry is from "Has a Man the Right to Let Himself Be Put to Death for the Truth?", one of *Two Minor Ethical-Religious Essays* [*Treatises*], together with *The Present Age*, p. 87.

508. See I Corinthians 2:7. The Danish translation of I Corinthians 2:7 is quite different from the English rendering in the RSV.

509. See *Practice* [*Training*] *in Christianity*, pp. 134 f.; II A 78.

510. James 2:6.

MYSTIC, MYSTICISM

In Kierkegaard's library there was a fair number of works on mysticism, and various utterances in the *Papirer* as well as in the works indicate his acquaintance with Christian mysticism. Judge William attempted to characterize mysticism: "The mystic chooses himself abstractly and so must repent abstractly. . . . One can therefore say that he constantly chooses himself out of the world. But the consequence is that he is unable to choose himself back again into the world" (*Either/Or*, II, p. 253). Because of this isolation, Kierkegaard says, "a mystic generally does not have as much significance for his noisy contemporaries as for the listening kindred spirit in the stillness of history after the passage of time" (III A 70).

In evaluating the various forms of mysticism, Kierkegaard uses his criteria for the relation between the abstract and the concrete in his concept of existence. Accordingly, philosophy itself approaches mysticism if it overstresses the abstract element. "The system *begins* with 'nothing'; the mystic always ends with 'nothing'" (X^2 A 340). (The word "system" always refers to Hegel's philosophy.)

Catteau, Georges. "Bergson, Kierkegaard, and Mysticism." *Dublin Review*, January, 1933.

Michalson, C. "Existentialism is a Mysticism." *Theology Today*, vol. 12, 1955.

For consideration of mystics and mysticism in the works, see, for example, *The Concept of Irony*, pp. 114, 275; *Either/Or*, II, pp. 245–55, 327 f. See also the use of "mystical" in *The Concept of Irony*, p. 54; *Fear and Trembling*, p. 60; *Postscript*, p. 278.

511. See *The Concept of Irony*, p. 275.

512. Ibid.

MYTH, MYTHOLOGY

In journal entry I A 300 Kierkegaard gives his concise view of mythology, a view which he continued to hold. Mythology is defined as "the beachhead (suppressed being) of the idea of eternity (the eternal idea) in the categories of time and space. . . . " What is meant is that eternal being is drawn into time and space and is thereby suppressed with respect to its eternal essence. In its earliest form this outlook belongs to the childhood of mankind, and every individual experiences it in foreshortened perspective during his own childhood. The mythological elements (mythology of the gods, myths, fairy stories, etc.) which men create in childhood are taken as direct representations of reality.

Kierkegaard's point is that whenever the attempt is made to incorporate the perfect or the eternal directly into the categories, the result is always mythology. All promises of perfect conditions here on earth by social-political reformers (Chiliasm) fall within mythology. This is also the case when a "finite personality" arrogates to himself the attributes of a god.

Christianity, too, can become a mythology if within Christendom there are tendencies to accommodate Christianity wholly to earthly conditions, a process that Kierkegaard thought was underway in his generation: "Christianity has disappeared; 'the race' has been put in the place of the individual; in official preaching Christianity has become mythology, poesy" (X⁴ A 642). The way to halt this transmogrification of Christianity is to point constantly to the absurd in Christianity and its incommensurability with the world. The absurd stresses that Christianity lies beyond the narrow limits of human thought.

In opposition to assertions that Christianity contains mythological elements, it must be affirmed constantly that Christianity exists in "the reduplication of its content. There is nothing mythical here" (X² A 529). One who seeks to practice in existence the content of Christianity (Kierkegaard uses the term "reduplication" for this practice) will also discover the reality of the Resurrection and the Ascension (*For Self-Examination*, pp. 78 ff., 89 f.), and consequently discover the reality of the two Christian truths most exposed to criticism as being mythological.

For references to these themes in the works, see, for example, *The Concept of Irony*, pp. 69, 78 f., 98, 128 ff., 140, 151, 153, 294; *Either/Or*, I, p. 407; *Fragments*, 137; *Postscript*, pp. 195, 513, 523, 531; *The Sickness unto Death*, p. 262; *Judge For Yourselves!*, p. 197.

513. See *The Concept of Irony*, pp. 133–34 fn.

514. See note 513.

515. Genesis 3:15.

516. Entry is from the draft of *The Concept of Anxiety* [*Dread*]; see pp. 27 f., ll. 11 ff.

517. See *Postscript*, pp. 195, 513; *The Sickness unto Death*, p. 262.

518. See *Postscript*, pp. 523, 531; *Judge For Yourselves!*, p. 197.

519. See, for example, *Fragments*, p. 79; *Postscript*, 530; *Practice* [*Training*] *in Christianity*, pp. 27 f., 127–32; *The Point of View*, p. 16.

520. See *Postscript*, pp. 523, 531.

521. *Judge For Yourselves!*, p. 197.

NATURAL SCIENCES

In a letter to the natural scientist P. W. Lund, in which Kierkegaard tells of his study plans, he writes sympathetically of research in the natural sciences, with the important reservation that the natural scientist ought to strive to find "that Archimedean point" outside the world from which he is able to see particulars in their proper context. At the outset Kierkegaard had a positive attitude toward the natural sciences, understood as having limits. What he later opposed strongly was the increasing belief that the natural sciences could be used to explain spiritual phenomena.

According to Kierkegaard, since nature belongs to finitude, the natural scientist is able to find laws only for this finitude and can never by this path reach the world of spirit, which belongs to the infinite and which Kierkegaard regarded as a reality. However great the advances of empirical research may be, it will never be enough to speak in an essential way of spiritual conditions. "If there were anything by way of the natural sciences which would help define spirit," Kierkegaard declares, "I should be the first to get hold of a microscope, and I think my perseverance would equal anyone's. But when by qualitative dialectic I easily perceive that, qualitatively understood, in 100,000 years the world will not have advanced one single step, I shall do the very opposite, preserve my soul and not waste one single second of my life on curiosity" (VII[1] A 191).

Consequently Kierkegaard thinks that the transition from the natural sciences, representing finitude, to the world of the spirit can occur only by a leap. Kierkegaard's most important argument against overestimation of the natural sciences is that, although their sphere of research is finitude, they also try to encompass ethics. With an ironic undertone Kierkegaard observes that ethics will be made into "natural-scientific statistical information about the human moral condition as a natural product explained by geography, air currents, wind, annual rainfall, water level, etc." (*Judge For Yourselves!*, p. 169, ed. tr.).

In a journal entry Kierkegaard points to some additional consequences of a one-sided natural scientific view: "The conflict between God and man will therefore culminate in the withdrawal of man behind natural science. And it is perhaps the trend of the future that Christianity now wants to shake off illusions, with the result that there will be hosts of people whose religion will become natural science" (X[5] A 73).

Nakamura, Kohei. "On the Relation of Human Being and Science by Kierkegaard." *Kierkegaard-Studiet*, I, 1964.

For references to the natural sciences and natural scientists in the works, see, for example, *Either/Or*, I, p. 310; *Fragments*, pp. 46 f.; *The Concept of Anxiety* [*Dread*], pp. 52 fn., 54; *Stages*, p. 129, 181 ff.; *Postscript*, pp. 134, 221; *Works of Love*, pp. 263, 280; *Judge For Yourselves!*, p. 169 (should read, ll. 6 ff.: natural-scientific statistical information about the human moral condition as a natural product explained by etc.).

522. Genesis 2:19 f.

523. See *Postscript*, pp. 23 f.

524. See *Judge For Yourselves!*, p. 169; see paragraph above on references to natural sciences.

525. See *Postscript*, pp. 484 f.; *Upbuilding* [*Edifying*] *Discourses*, II, p. 63.

526. One fool always finds another fool who admires him (Boileau). See *Fear and Trembling*, p. 66.

527. See Carl G. Carus, *Psyche: zur Entwicklungsgeschichte der Seele* (Pforzheim: 1846), "*Von dem Ersten Hervorbilden des Bewusstseins aus dem Unbewusstsein,*" [Concerning the initial shaping of the consciousness out of the unconscious], pp. 98 ff., "*Von der Art und Weise, wie das bewusste Seelenleben auf das unbewusste einwirkt,*" [Concerning the way the conscious soul-life influences the unconscious soul-life], pp. 195 ff. Kierkegaard bought this book November 20, 1846. *ASKB* 459.

528. See ibid., pp. 350 f.

529. II Corinthians 4:16.

530. See Carl G. Carus, *Psyche* . . . , pp. 96 f.

531. See ibid.

532. See ibid., p. 98.

533. See ibid., pp. 98, 174. The law of the secret.

534. See ibid., pp. 112 ff., 120.

535. See ibid., pp. 32 f.

536. See note 527.

537. See *Stages on Life's Way*, p. 129; *Philosophical Fragments*, p. 108.

538. Infinite regression within the finite, therefore bad or negative infinity (Hegel).

539. The stethoscope was introduced into Denmark by O. Bang in 1824, and its use was advanced by S. Trier's *Anviisning til at kjende Lunge- og Hjerte-Sygdomme ved Percussion og middelbar Ausculation* (Copenhagen: 1830).

540. See *Postscript*, p. 313.

541. Kierkegaard's house-servant, Anders Westergaard Christensen.

542. See note 527.

543. See Ludvig Holberg, *Gert Westphaler*, sc. 7.

544. Here is Rhodes; now leap (or dance). In one of Aesop's fables a braggart says that on Rhodes he had made an extraordinary leap. A listener

replies: Here is Rhodes; now leap. See *Either/Or*, II, pp. 64, 257; *Stages on Life's Way*, p. 101.

545. See *Works of Love*, pp. 331 f.

546. Christian consciousness.

547. August Petersen, *Die Idee der christlichen Kirche*, I–III (Leipzig: 1839–46), pp. 346 f. *ASKB* 717–719.

NATURE

Nature, which in Kierkegaard's view is an expression of God's visible (esthetic) creative activity, was for him an impetus to thought in many ways. For example, he frequently affirms that nature obeys God completely: "In nature all is obedience, unconditional obedience" (*The Lily of the Field and the Bird of the Air*, together with *Christian Discourses*, pp. 336 f.). Man, however, as qualified under spirit, has the possibility of choice and can decide in opposition to his creator.

Of man's relation to nature, Climacus writes: "Nature, the totality of created things, is the work of God. And yet God is not there; but within the individual man there is a potentiality (man is potentially spirit) which is awakened in inwardness to become a God-relationship, and then it becomes possible to see God everywhere" (*Postscript*, pp. 220 f.). Thus nature stands on a level lower than man, who, even though a part of God's creation, contains the possibility that spirit can break through.

Nature's beauty and power can, however, play a part in awakening a man's sense of a higher reality. In Kierkegaard's "Gilleleie letter" of 1835 we read: "as I stood there solitary and abandoned, and the force of the sea and the conflict of the elements reminded me of my own nothingness, and on the other hand the sure flight of the birds reminded me of Christ's words: 'Not a sparrow shall fall to the ground without your Father's will'—then all at once I felt how great and how small I was; then did those two mighty powers, pride and humility, happily join together in friendship" (I A 68).

Later, in one of his discourses he compares the kind of adoration evoked by nature with Christian faith: "God's greatness in nature awakens at once *amazement*, and then *adoration*; God's greatness in showing mercy is first a *stumbling block* [*Forargelse*, offense] and then is *for faith*" (*Christian Discourses*, p. 299).

Also in small-scale, very concrete situations, nature can offer analogies to something higher. Kierkegaard sensitively elaborates and utilizes Christ's examples of the lily and the bird to illuminate man's relation to God. A typical example of his use of nature to illustrate spirit is found in *For Self-Examination* (pp. 101 ff.) and *Judge for Yourselves!*, (pp. 105 f.), where a royal coachman's handling of horses is a metaphor of the way the spiritual element is supposed to guide man's natural being.

Löwith, Karl. *Nature, History, and Existentialism*. Evanston: Northwestern University Press, 1966.

References in the works to nature are numerous and varied. See, for example, *Either/Or*, I, p. 66; II, p. 277; *Fragments*, pp. 94, 97, 120 f.; *The Concept of Anxiety* [*Dread*], pp. 53 f., 79; *Postscript*, pp. 46, 127, 188, 220, 484; *Upbuilding Discourses in Various Spirits*, Part Two [*What We Learn from the Lilies of the Field and the Birds of the Air*, together with *The Gospel of Suffering*, pp. 224, 227]; *Works of Love*, pp. 207, 252, 263; *The Lily of the Field and the Bird of the Air*, together with *Christian Discourses*, pp. 336 ff., 349.

548. During the period July 19 to August 6, 1840, Kierkegaard made a visit to Sæding in Jutland, his father's birthplace and boyhood home.

549. Psalm 139:7.

550. See *S.V.*, XIII, pp. 473 ff.

551. See *Upbuilding Discourses in Various Spirits*, Part One [*Purity of Heart*, p. 48].

552. The giant Ymer, slain by Bor's sons (Odin, Vili, and Ve), who then made the universe out of Ymer's body. His flesh became the earth, his bones mountains and stones, his hair trees and grass, his skull the heavens, his blood the seas and rivers, his brains the clouds, and his marrow the dwarfs who live under the earth and under stones. From his eyebrows the gods later made a fortress, Midgaard, a defense against the giants.

Kierkegaard's library included a number of works on mythology and folklore, such as: N. F. S. Grundtvig, *Nordens Mythologie eller Udsigt over Eddal-æren* (Copenhagen: 1808), *ASKB* 1948; *Nordens Mythologie eller Sindsbilledsprog* (Copenhagen: 1832), *ASKB* 1949; *Irische Elfenmärchen*, tr. Brothers Grimm (Leipzig: 1826), *ASKB* 1423; K. P. Moritz, *Guderlære* (Copenhagen: 1847), *ASKB* 1946; P. F. Nitsch, *Neues mythologisches Wörterbuch*, I–II (Leipzig, Sorau: 1821), *ASKB* 1944–45; W. Vollmer, *Vollständiges Wörterbuch der Mythologie alles Nationen* (Stuttgart: 1836), *ASKB* 1942–43.

553. A. P. Adler, about whom Kierkegaard wrote *Bogen om Adler (The Book about Adler)*, which remained unpublished in the *Papirer* (VII² B 235, pp. 5–230). The English version by Walter Lowrie is under the title *On Authority and Revelation* (Princeton: Princeton University Press, 1955).

554. Michael Montaigne, *Gedanken und Meinungen* (see note 491), III, pp. 323 ff.

555. Henrich Steffens, *Christliche Religionsphilosophie*, I–II (Breslau: 1839), I, p. 29. *ASKB* 797–98.

556. Gustav Theodor Fechner, *Nanna oder über das Seelenleben der Pflanzen* (Leipzig: 1848).

557. Ibid., pp. 64 f.

558. See Matthew 10:29.

NEW TESTAMENT

Kierkegaard was a keen and diligent reader of the Bible and continually sought to penetrate more deeply the essential core of its message to men. In the Old Testament the figures of Job and Abraham particularly absorbed him, and he tried, in *Repetition* and *Fear and Trembling*, respectively, to actualize their religious significance for our time.

But it was the New Testament's testimony about Christ that engaged him most of all. He regarded the Old Testament with its optimistic view of man's temporal life as the proper *background* for Christianity, whose ultimate goal is eternity. Numerous journal entries stress this difference between the Old and the New Testaments. He writes, for example, "Judaic religion relates to this life, has promise for this life—the Christian religion is essentially promise for the next life, since essential Christianity is the suffering truth" (X^3 A 138). Or he writes: "Christianity means renunciation—therefore it is brought to bear upon Judaism, for Judaism is characterized particularly by promises of all kinds for this life, with everything concentrated in this life" (XI^1 A 151). Through the unconditional affirmation of the reality of the eternal in the New Testament, an entirely new light is cast upon human life, and all mundane, common, human phenomena thereby become less significant. Kierkegaard thinks that anyone who reads the New Testament impartially will agree with his conception, but one is hindered by the numerous interpretations and commentaries which usually shade off the clear message of the New Testament. We have, he says, "locked up the New Testament with the help of scientific scholarship" (X^3 A 34).

Later on, with the intensification of the requirement of Christianity, culminating in stress upon contemporaneity with Christ (see *Attack*, pp. 239 ff.), Kierkegaard distinguished between the Gospels and the Epistles on the grounds that already in the Epistles a modification of the requirements takes place (see PAUL).

Despite this pressing of Christianity's demand up "to a peak of ideality" and thereby making it difficult for a person to come into relationship with it, one is not released from seeking to fulfill the New Testament requirement. On the contrary, according to Kierkegaard, after recognizing his distance from the ideal, a person must humble himself under it (see GRACE) and move from where he is toward Christianity. Here Kierkegaard's idea of "admission" is very important. He expected this admission from his contemporaries, and when it was not given, Kierkegaard's attack on the Church followed.

It is typical of Kierkegaard's relation to the New Testament that he is not bothered by its being "written in a poor language" (X^4 A 313) or by inconsistencies between various portions. He thinks, instead, that because of this uncertainty "the choice of faith takes place or that faith becomes a choice and the possibility of offense gives tension to faith" (X^3 A 702).

In contrast to numerous conceptions of the use of the New Testament, Kierkegaard gives his own excellent and detailed instructions in his comparison of "God's Word" with "a letter from the beloved" (*For Self-Examination*, pp. 23 ff.).

Dewey, B. R. "Kierkegaard and the Blue Testament." *Harvard Theological Review*, vol. 60, October 1967.

Dunstan, J. Leslie. "The Bible in *Either/Or.*" *Interpretation,* vol. VI, 1952.

Lewis, Edwin. *A Philosophy of the Christian Revelation.* New York: Harper, 1940; London: Epworth, 1948.

Minear, P. S., and Morimoto, Paul S., eds. *Kierkegaard and the Bible, an Index.* Princeton: Princeton Pamphlets, 9, 1953.

Perry, Edmund. "Was Kierkegaard a Biblical Existentialist?" *Journal of Religion,* vol. 36, 1956.

Thomas, John Heyward. "The Relevance of Kierkegaard to the Demythologizing Controversy." *Scottish Journal of Theology,* vol. 10, 1957.

Wolf, Herbert C. *Kierkegaard and Bultmann.* Minneapolis: Augsburg, 1964.

For Kierkegaard's use of the New Testament and Old Testament in the works, see thirteen columns of entries under "Bibelen" in the author-index (*Forfatter Register*), A. Ibsen, *Register til Søren Kierkegaards Samlede Værker* (Copenhagen: 1936), *S.V.,* XV. For extended discussions, see *Postscript,* pp. 25–35; *Works of Love,* pp. 199 ff., 231; *For Self-Examination,* pp. 23–61.

559. Luke 16:31.

560. Not only "in this age," but also "in the world to come."

561. Prophecy; speaking in tongues.

562. See *Two Ages* [*The Present Age,* pp. 60 f.].

563. Thomas Hansen Kingo (1634–1703), one of the great Danish hymn writers.

564. Luke 18:9 ff., the Gospel for the Eleventh Sunday after Trinity, which in 1847 was on August 15.

565. See *Works of Love,* p. 294.

566. Hebrews 10:39.

567. Johan Arndt, *Sämtliche Geistreiche Bücher vom wahren Christentum.* (Tübingen: 2 ed., 1777). *ASKB* 276. *Fire Bøger om den sande Christendom* (Christiania: 1829). *ASKB* 277.

568. Zacharias Werner, *Poetische Werke,* I–XIII (Grimma: 1835–41). *ASKB* 1851–54.

569. See *For Self-Examination,* pp. 23 ff.

570. See ibid., pp. 32 ff.

571. See ibid., pp. 33 ff.

572. Luke 15:4 ff.

573. Luke 10:23.

574. See *Repetition,* p. 149; *The Concept of Anxiety* [*Dread*], p. 16 n.

575. Mark 2:1 ff.

576. Matthew 18:23 ff.

577. John 2:32 ff.

578. Matthew 3:14.

579. M. Luther, *En christelig Postille* (see note 81), II, pp. 395–96.

580. John 10:11 ff.

581. I Peter 2:21 ff., in 1852 the Epistle for April 25.

582. See Luke 14:26.

583. Luke 14:15 ff.

584. Luke 10:26.

585. Luke 10:30 ff.

586. Acts 2:1 ff.

587. *Confessio Augustina invariator* (Havniæ: 1817), p. 40. *ASKB* 469. *Den rette uforandredede Augsburske Troesbjekendelse,* tr. A. G. Rudelbach (Copenhagen: 1825), p. 76. *ASKB* 386.

588. Matthew 20:1 ff.

589. Matthew 7:13.

590. M. Luther, *En christelig Postille* (see note 81), I, p. 559.

591. See Matthew 7:14, 10:22; John 16:2.

592. Matthew 11:28.

593. John 12:47.

594. See J. L. Heiberg, *Kong Solomon og Jørgen Hattemager,* sc. 26; *Stages on Life's Way,* pp. 317, 337.

595. Hatred of the human race. See Tacitus, *Annals,* 15, 44; *Practice [Training] in Christianity,* p. 119 and note. Kierkegaard had two editions of Tacitus: *Opera ex recensione Ernestiana,* ed. I. Bekker, I–III (Hamburg: 1765–66); *ASKB* 1283–85; and C. C. Tacitus, tr. J. Baden, I–III (Copenhagen: 1850). *ASKB* 1286–88.

596. I Corinthians 7:9.

597. Matthew 7:14. See *For Self-Examination,* pp. 63 ff.

598. A work on trolls, magic, etc., corresponding to the Faust books in Germany and *Svarteboken* (black catechism) in Norway. *Cyprianus, den over ald Verden vidtberømte Sorte Konstner, Paany gjennemseet og forbedret af høilaerde Doctoribus.* Manuscript. *ASKB* 1462.

NUMBERS, CROWD, MASS, PUBLIC

The highest ideal for human life, maintains Kierkegaard, is to be a "single individual" (see INDIVIDUAL). This implies that in all his activities a person relates himself to the eternal, which must always be understood as a relationship to God. If one has not reached this firm standpoint or has abandoned it, he is determined by merely external and finite ends, and the highest authority for man becomes the nation, the race, the party, or some other transitory power (seen from the viewpoint of eternity). To Kierkegaard the lowest in rank of these external determining factors are numbers, the public, the crowd, the mass, whereas the nation and the race are expressions of an organic whole. Numbers, the public, the crowd, the mass lack any relation to something higher, and without this support in his life the individual is abandoned to all accidental influences and thereby loses his spiritual independence. Then, together with the others, one forms a compliant mass which wants to act as a power but has no room for personal responsibility. Because of this irresponsibility Kierkegaard says that the crowd is "untruth" (" 'The Single Individual' Two 'Notes' Concerning My Work as an Author," Appendix to *The Point of View*, p. 112). Since "the public," "the crowd," etc. are marks of man's deep demoralization, Kierkegaard regards the crowd in action as a form of "the evil" (for example, VIII[1] A 611) which particularly marks our age, in which a sense and respect for eternal values has diminished. His many observations on numbers, the public, the crowd, and the press (which he regards as the prime promoter of spiritless human agglomerations) are very sharp and sarcastic.

Kierkegaard thought it was possible to oppose this tendency by constant reference to the single individual who, by being first of all responsible before God and by gaining and maintaining his own independence, can avoid being a plaything in the game of irresponsible powers.

Kierkegaard's deepest contempt for the crowd is expressed in his assertion that "the man never was born and never will be born with courage and insolence enough" (" 'The Single Individual' ...," p. 115; see also VIII[1] A 296) to spit upon Christ (Matthew 27:30), but the crowd, whose predominant trait is "cowardice," could do that.

On these themes, always related, sometimes synonymous, in the works, see, for example: *Either/Or*, II, pp. 291, 301; *The Concept of Anxiety* [*Dread*], p. 61; *Three Discourses on Imagined Occasions* [*Thoughts on Crucial Situations in Human Life*, pp. 33, 94]; *Stages*, pp. 432–33; *Postscript*, pp. 120, 131, 486; *Two Ages* [*The Present Age*, pp. 37 ff.]; *Upbuilding Discourses in Various Spirits*, Part One [*Purity of Heart*, pp. 143, 184 ff., 196]; Part Three [*The Gospel of Suffering*, pp. 53, 145 f.]; *Works of Love*, pp. 109, 120, 153, 165 f.; *Christian Discourses*, pp. 238, 278 ff., 285; *The Sickness unto Death*, pp. 160, 166f., 249, 251, 253 f.; *For Self-Examination*, pp. 9, 15, 56; *Judge For Yourselves!*, pp. 138, 166, 177, 181; *The Point of View*, pp. 23, 47, 56, 59; " 'The Single Individual' Two 'Notes' Concerning My Work as an Author," Appendix to ibid., pp. 112–22, 124.

Hamilton, Kenneth. *The Promise of Kierkegaard*. New York: Lippincott, 1969.

599. See I A 166.

600. Goethe, *Faust* (Stuttgart, Tübingen: 1834), *ASKB* 1669; *Werke*, I–LV (Stuttgart, Tübingen: 1828–63), *ASKB* 1641–68.

601. See *Postscript*, pp. 546 f.

602. See " 'The Single Individual' Two 'Notes' Concerning My Work as an Author," Appendix to *The Point of View*, p. 137.

603. See *Works of Love*, pp. 165 f.; *Christian Discourses*, pp. 266 f.

604. See *Works of Love*, p. 166.

605. *Stages on Life's Way*, p. 433; *The Sickness unto Death*, pp. 253 f.; *Works of Love*, pp. 120 f.

606. See *For Self-Examination*, p. 15.

607. See Matthew 27:21.

608. Ibid.

609. See " 'The Single Individual' . . . ," Appendix to *The Point of View*, pp. 112–22, 140; *Attack upon Christendom*, p. 283.

610. See "Has a Man the Right to Let Himself Be Put to Death for the Truth?" together with *Two Ages* [*The Present Age*, pp. 115 f., 133].

611. This entry is one of the drafts of a portion of " 'The Single Individual' Two 'Notes' Concerning My Work as an Author." See pp. 112 ff. in *The Point of View*.

612. See *Attack*, p. 186.

613. See " 'The Single Individual' Two 'Notes' Concerning My Work as an Author," Appendix to *The Point of View*, p. 124; *Works of Love*, p. 19.

614. See *On My Work as an Author*, together with *The Point of View*, p. 162; *An Open Letter* and *Armed Neutrality*, p. 52.

615. A Copenhagen newspaper, new at the time (1834–82) with the purpose of extending enlightenment and an interest in public affairs. Among the editors and writers were Professor C. N. David, J. Hage, O. Lehmann, B. Christensen, C. Ploug, and J. Giødwad. With the latter Kierkegaard was closely associated. *Fædrelandet* carried ten pieces by Kierkegaard between 1842 and 1851 (See *S.V.*, XIII, pp. 396 ff.), as well as twenty-one Mynster-Martensen pieces between December 18, 1854, and May 26, 1855 (See *S.V.*, XIV, pp. 5 ff.).

616. See, for example, *Either/Or*, II, p. 291; *Upbuilding Discourses in Various Spirits*, Part One [*Purity of Heart*, pp. 133 f.].

617. See "Has a Man the Right to Let Himself Be Put to Death for the Truth?" together with *Two Ages* [*The Present Age*, pp. 115, 133].

618. See " 'The Single Individual' Two 'Notes' Concerning My Work as an Author," Appendix to *The Point of View*, p. 137.

619. See "Of the Difference between a Genius and an Apostle," together with *The Present Age*, pp. 161 f.

620. J. P. M. Grüne (1805–78), editor of *Kjøbenhavnsposten*, 1839–59; P. C. Ploug (1813–94), editor of *Fædrelandet*, 1841–81. See *Attack*, p. 285.

621. The phallic symbol of Siva in popular Hindu mythology.

622. See *Works of Love*, p. 153; *On My Work as an Author*, "The Accounting," together with *The Point of View*, p. 153 fn.

623. See *Prefaces*, *S.V.*, V, p. 31.

624. See Aristotle, *Politics*, I, 2, III, 11; the crowd as a many-headed animal, Horace, *Epistles*, I, 76; *The Sickness unto Death*, p. 249.

625. See *Attack*, p. 285.

626. See *Postscript*, pp. 437 f.; *The Present Age*, pp. 49 ff.

627. See *Attack*, p. 229.

628. See, for Example, *Postscript*, pp. 97 ff., 223 f., 291 f.

629. See "the knight of faith" in *Fear and Trembling*, pp. 49 ff. The expression "knight of faith" does appear again (contra W. Lowrie, ibid., p. 19) in

Two Ages [*The Present Age*, p. 12] and *Postscript*, p. 447 fn. Yet "hidden inwardness," which the knight does personify (see *Postscript*, pp. 452, 489 ff.) lacks the tension of the existential becoming of the person and collision with the less than ideal actual world. Hence *Works of Love* and the numerous criticisms (*Practice* [*Training*] *in Christianity*, p. 209, for example) of sedentary piety, relaxed piety, etc., not because of inwardness (see *Armed Neutrality* and *An Open Letter*, pp. 41, 47 ff.) but because of an absence of inwardness (*Works of Love*, p. 140) and/or an absence of an expressive ethic (ibid., Introduction, pp. 13 ff.).

630. See *Practice* [*Training*] *in Christianity*, p. 39; *Attack upon Christendom*, pp. 32–33.

631. Anti-Climacus. See note 630.

632. A. G. Rudelbach, *Fædrelandet*, 38, February 14, 1851. A reply to Kierkegaard's "Open Letter" to Rudelbach, *Fædrelandet*, 26, January 31, 1851. See *Armed Neutrality* and *An Open Letter*, pp. 47 ff.

633. See *Prefaces*, *S.V.*, V, pp. 16 f.

634. See note 611.

635. See note 624.

636. See *Attack*, pp. 33 ff.

637. See ibid., p. 283.

638. See *The Point of View*, p. 23.

639. See V A 19 and notes.

640. See Poul Martin Møller, *Efterladte Skrifter*, I–III (Copenhagen: 1839–43), III, p. 26; ibid. (Copenhagen: 2 ed., 1850), F. C. Olsen, *Poul Møllers Levnet*, VI, pp. 96, 157.

641. See *Works of Love*, pp. 177 ff.

642. See *Two Ages* [*The Present Age*, pp. 21 ff.].

643. Supposedly Edward Meyer, editor of *Flyveposten*. See *Corsaren*, 407, July 7, 1848, col. 11; *Løse Blade af en dansk Journalists Album* (Copenhagen: 1855), I, pp. 41 f.

644. See, for example, *Postscript*, p. 178.

645. See, for example, ibid., pp. 218 ff.

646. See *Attack*, p. 186.

647. See note 624.

648. See *Attack*, p. 33 ff.

649. See *Works of Love*, p. 337; *For Self-Examination*, opening paragraphs on II Corinthians 5:11.

650. See *Attack*, p. 284.

651. See *Christian Discourses*, p. 238; *Works of Love*, p. 120.

652. See note 630.

653. See note 624.

654. See *Attack*, pp. 208 ff.

655. See *Stages on Life's Way*, p. 433; *The Sickness unto Death*, pp. 179, 253

f.; *Practice* [*Training*] *in Christianity*, p. 89; *Judge for Yourselves!*, pp. 168 f., 208; " 'The Single Individual' Two 'Notes' Concerning My Work as an Author," Appendix to *The Point of View*, pp. 135 f.; *Attack*, pp. 35, 39, 149, 168 f.

    656. See note 655.

    657. Matthew 10:17.

    658. See Gert Bundtmager's lines in L. Holberg, *Den politiske Kandestøber*, II, 3.

OBEDIENCE

    Kierkegaard considered it most important to learn obedience in relation to God. He clearly gives the reasons for this point of view in the following words: "Every human being who has ever once understood himself penetratingly understands further that he could never possibly be satisfied with being master of his fate, that for a human being there is satisfaction and joy and blessedness only in obeying" (VIII^1 A 525). Kierkegaard was thus armed against the temptation to use his uncommon capacities arbitrarily; instead he placed them obediently in the cause of Christianity. He mentions (VIII^1 A 549) that each day he would repeat to himself the "magic formula" (VIII^1 A 540) from I Samuel 15:22: "Obedience is dearer to God than the fat of rams." (See also II A 422.)

    The first condition for obedience is quietness and silence. These two adjustments must be regarded as analogous on a lower plane to the two higher forms of the movement of infinity: irony and renunciation and then repentance (see these sections). By seeking quiet, one is freed from disturbing external influences and is prepared for silence, which disciplines a person's own cravings. An inner receptivity is created that is responsive before God. Of this quiet, which creates silence and which must be accompanied by the earnestness of eternity, Kierkegaard writes: "But he who in truth has become at one with himself, he is in *silence*" (*Upbuilding Discourses in Various Spirits*, Part One [*Purity of Heart*, p. 47]). In the discourse *The Lily of the Field and the Bird of the Air* (together with *Christian Discourses*, pp. 322 ff.) Kierkegaard depicts in detail how "silence" is the condition for becoming "obedient" and how only this obedience can give "joy."

    For various references to obedience in the works, see, for example, *Either/ Or*, I, p. 148; II, p. 248; *Upbuilding* [*Edifying*] *Discourses*, I, pp. 55, 96, 100; IV, p. 102; *Stages*, pp. 167, 244; *Postscript*, p. 122; *Upbuilding Discourses in Various Spirits*, Part One [*Purity of Heart*, pp. 47 ff., 100]; Part Three [*The Gospel of Suffering*, pp. 10, 47 ff., 63 f., 79, 82, 102, 113]; *Works of Love*, pp. 36, 93, 103, 122, 124, 338; *Christian Discourses*, pp. 54, 83 f., 86 ff., 135, 247, 322 ff.; *The Lily of the Field and the Bird of the Air*, together with ibid., pp. 315, 350, 352, 354; *The Sickness unto Death*, pp. 169, 212; *Practice* [*Training*] *in Christianity*, pp. 92, 180, 182, 222; *Judge For Yourselves!*, p. 176; *The Unchangeableness of God*, together with ibid., pp. 227, 238.

659. See Matthew 21:28 ff.; *Works of Love*, pp. 100 ff.

660. *Theologia Germanica*, ch. L: "And in this Paradise all things are lawful, save one tree and the fruits thereof, that is to say: of all things that are, nothing is forbidden and nothing is contrary to God but one thing only: that is Self-will, or to will otherwise than as the Eternal Will would have it."

661. See, for example, *Postscript*, pp. 515 f.

662. Luke 18:8.

663. See *For Self-Examination*, pp. 31 ff.

664. See *Works of Love*, pp. 93, 122, 231; *Christian Discourses*, pp. 83 f., 247, 350 ff.; "Of the Difference between a Genius and an Apostle," together with *The Present Age*, pp. 151 ff.; *The Sickness unto Death*, p. 212; *Practice* [*Training*] *in Christianity*, p. 222; *Judge For Yourselves!*, p. 437; *The Unchangeableness of God*, together with *Judge For Yourselves!*, pp. 227, 230, 238.

665. See " 'The Single Individual' Two 'Notes' Concerning My Work as an Author," Appendix to *The Point of View*, pp. 135 f.

666. See *Fear and Trembling*, pp. 27 ff.

667. I understand in order that I may believe; I believe in order that I may understand. See Anselm, *Proslogium*, ch. I; *credo ut intelligam*, used by Schleiermacher as the title-page motto of *Der christliche Glaube* (Berlin: 3 ed., 1835; *ASKB* 2580); H. L. Martensen, *De autonomia conscientiæ sui humanæ* (Copenhagen: 1837; *ASKB* 648), pp. 6, 17, 97 ff.

OFFENSE

Christianity protects itself against a purely human interpretation of life by the paradox in the sphere of knowledge and by offense in the existential sphere. Offense is, therefore, a deeper expression of opposition to Christianity than the mere recognition of Christianity's paradoxicality. Kierkegaard regarded the concept of offense as one of the most central Christian concepts.

According to Kierkegaard, no one can become a Christian without encountering the possibility of offense, whether one then becomes a Christian or not. In the first case, offense acquires a positive significance for a person: he ceases his natural opposition to Christianity and humbles himself under it. This form of offense is presented in *Practice in Christianity*, where it is shown that even Christ's disciples had to go through offense, which reached its climax when they were confronted by Christ's suffering and death.

The second case, being offended and remaining in offense, is described in *The Sickness unto Death*. The culmination of this offense, active hostility toward Christianity, is, according to Kierkegaard, the sin against the Holy Spirit.

Anonymous. "The 'Offence' of the God-Man: Kierkegaard's Way of Faith." *Times Literary Supplement*, vol. 36, May 5, 1937.

For references to offense (sometimes in the English spelling, "offence," and sometimes translated "stumbling block," "scandal") in the works, see: *From the Papers of One Still Living*, S.V., XII, p. 65; *Either/Or*, I, p. 232; II, pp.

54, 95, 170, 346; *Fear and Trembling*, p. 122; *Repetition*, p. 40; *Upbuilding* [*Edifying*] *Discourses*, I, pp. 67, 97; III, p. 32; *Fragments*, pp. 40, 61–67, 117, 120; *The Concept of Anxiety* [*Dread*], pp. 27, 29, 129; *Stages*, p. 162; *Postscript*, pp. 139, 191, 200, 333, 400, 479, 518–19, 512 (Christ as "sign of offense" omitted in present English translation, ll. 13–14), 530, 535; *Two Ages* [*The Present Age*, p. 34]; *Upbuilding Discourses in Various Spirits*, Part Three [*The Gospel of Suffering*, p. 42, 71, 88]; *Works of Love*, pp. 41, 65, 70–71, 74, 145, 191–94, 214, 278; *Christian Discourses*, pp. 188, 299; *The Sickness unto Death*, pp. 214–35, 244–62; *Practice* [*Training*] *in Christianity*, pp. 9, 26, 28, 38, 43, 61, 64–65, 69, 75–144, 153–54; *For Self-Examination*, p. 4; *Judge for Yourselves!*, pp. 154, 163, 167, 172–73, 176, 209, 212; in *Fædrelandet*, in *Attack*, p. 22; *The Moment*, IV, in *Attack*, pp. 142, 150; V, in *Attack*, pp. 162, 189.

668. See, for example, Matthew 18:7.

669. See *Practice* [*Training*] *in Christianity*, pp. 86 ff.

670. See ibid., p. 96.

671. This entry is one of Kierkegaard's possible additions and changes (VIII² B 2–27) for *The Book on Adler* (VII² B 235), English version under title *Authority and Revelation*, end of paragraph on pp. 46–47.

672. Entry is from draft of *Works of Love*. See pp. 190 ff.: "What wonder then that Christianity and its salvation and tasks can no longer satisfy 'the Christians'—they cannot even be offended by it." Then follows VIII² B 240.

673. See references above to theme of offense in the works.

674. Matthew 26:31; Mark 14:27. RSV has "fall away" instead of "be offended."

675. See note 673.

676. See J. P. Mynster, *Prædikener*, I–II (3 printing, 1826–32), I, pp. 284 f., 302 ff.; *ASKB* 228; also OBEDIENCE, commentary.

677. M. Luther. *En christelig Postille* (see note 81), I, 467 ff.

678. See *Practice* [*Training*] *in Christianity*, pp. 124, ff.; PARADOX.

679. N. F. S. Grundtvig (1783–1872), religious leader, poet, historian, politician, and education theorist. See, for example, *Postscript*, pp. 36 ff.

680. See *Philosophical Fragments*, pp. 60 ff.

681. Hermann Reuchlin, *Geschichte von Port Royal*, I–II (Hamburg, Gotha: 1839–44), I, p. 521 et passim.

682. Matthew 11:2 ff.

683. Matthew 11:6; Luke 7:23.

684. See note 673.

685. See, for example, *Works of Love*, p. 191.

OPTIMISM–PESSIMISM

Kierkegaard's whole spiritual outlook involves a pessimistic view of the world, balanced by his optimistic view of eternity as man's ultimate goal.

According to Kierkegaard, a person begins as an optimist, and philosophy, which reproduces the natural man's view of life, is therefore always optimistic: "The philosopher must either embrace optimism—or despair" (I A 94, p. 66). With its hope for eternal life Christianity must gradually demolish a person's initial optimistic view of the world. The more this Christian hope comes to the fore, the more its pessimistic view of man and the world appears. When Kierkegaard affirms martyrdom to be the highest act the Christian can practice here on earth, his intense pessimism about the world is evident. Kierkegaard goes so far as to picture Christ as the unconditioned pessimist with respect to life here on earth (XI^1 A 482).

Kierkegaard, for whom the world is still God's creation, appreciates the positive aspects of this world, despite his pessimism. Contrary to Schopenhauer, Kierkegaard affirms that life in itself is not sheer suffering and that life is first brought essentially within the sphere of suffering by Christianity's teaching of a voluntary renunciation of the world's goods.

Kierkegaard thinks it necessary to maintain the optimistic, human life attitude as the point of departure for understanding the new view Christianity brings. It is possible to make the mistake of intensifying pessimism so sharply that one forgets that the optimistic life-view is the presupposition. Pertaining to this, Kierkegaard says: "In so many areas, wherever there is a dialectic, there is a zealousness which is so zealous in emphasizing the second that in its zeal it takes away the first and thereby basically makes the second impossible" (XI^1 A 181). With this perspective one understands Kierkegaard's pointing out that Christianity has as its "foreground the most intense zest for life," namely "Jewish optimism" (ibid).

For the infrequent direct references to these themes in the works, see, for example, *The Concept of Irony*, pp. 318 f., *Either/Or*, I, pp. 45, 316; II, p. 325; *Prefaces, S. V.*, V, pp. 43, 48; *Postscript*, p. 534.

686. *Von dem Zwecke Jesu und seiner Jünger. Noch ein Fragment des Wolfenbüttelschen Ungenannten*, ed. G. E. Lessing (Braunschweig: 1778), pp. 120 ff., 126 f.

687. Christoff in L. Holberg, *Jacob von Thyboe*, IV, 6, sings: "Round and round and round, so merrily, so merrily. ..." See *Kierkegaard's Attack upon Christendom*, p. 35.

688. Sirach 2:1.

689. See *The Concept of Irony*, pp. 318 f.

ORTHODOX, ORTHODOXY

According to Kierkegaard's view, ethical and religious truths must be reduplicated in the medium of actuality. Therefore he was a sharp critic of the orthodoxy which simply holds fast to the truth without asking how this truth is to be realized in actual life. As a counterweight to this one-sided stress on truth alone, Kierkegaard shows in his works how truth and actuality must correspond to each other in human existence. Thus he lays the basis of a new orthodoxy. For example, his pseudonym Climacus says of Kierkegaard's central dogmatic work *Philosophical Fragments* that it comes out with "old-fashioned orthodoxy in a suitable degree of severity" (*Postscript*, p. 245 fn.). With the aid of his insight into man's experiences in relation to Christianity, and with rigorous logical consistency, Kierkegaard tried to shape a new and correct (orthodox) view of Christianity. His numerous attacks on orthodoxy apply to the kind of orthodoxy that ends in rigid forms and in which the truth does not have a decisive and continually renewed meaning for existence. The pseudonym Vigilius Haufniensis criticizes the rigid orthodoxy that clings to the letter without the spirit by saying: "A partisan of the most rigid orthodoxy may be demoniacal" (*The Concept of Anxiety* [*Dread*], p. 124). Climacus speaks of "childlike Christianity" and "childish orthodoxy" (*Postscript*, p. 527, ed. tr.).

On this theme in the works, see, for example, *The Concept of Anxiety* [*Dread*], pp. 51, 84, 124, 127; *Postscript*, pp. 88 fn., 222, 340, 472, 499, 525 ff., 533 ff., 539, 542; *The Sickness unto Death*, p. 227; *Works of Love*, p. 70; *Practice* [*Training*] *in Christianity*, pp. 133, 181; *The Point of View*, p. 30; *Attack*, p. 108.

690. See *Postscript*, p. 35. Entry is from draft of *Fragments*.

691. See Moriz Carriere, *Die Philosophische Weltanschauung der Reformationszeit* . . . (Stuttgart, Tübingen: 1847), p. 368. *ASKB* 458.

692. Henrich Steffens, *Christliche Religionsphilosophie*, I–II (Breslau: 1839). *ASKB* 797.

693. See *Postscript*, p. 88 fn.

694. See *Works of Love*, p. 71.

695. See *The Point of View*, p. 30.

696. See, for example, *The Concept of Anxiety* [*Dread*], pp. 124, 127; *Postscript*, pp. 222, 499, 525 ff., 533 ff., 542.

697. It is not necessary to dispute whether contrition springs from love of righteousness or from fear of punishment, since it is mixed. . . . I remember that exactly the same people who carried on the dispute sang and drank here a whole night long: "They drank there the good, long night, until daylight dawned. They sang, leapt, and were drunk."

698. Friedrich Galle, *Versuch einer charakteristik der Melanchthon als theologen und einer Entwicklung seines Lehrbegriffs*.

PAGANISM

In Kierkegaard's view, paganism comprises the sensate sphere of life and the given developmental possibilities of the natural man (II A 79). Paganism culminates in Socrates, in whom the spiritual element breaks through. Only when a person comes into relation with the transcendent is he beyond the domain of paganism. From a philosophical point of view, paganism lies within immanence. According to Kierkegaard, even when Socrates in his faith ventured toward the transcendent, he remained essentially within paganism, since the transcendent itself did not meet him. Only in Judaism and in Christianity is man beyond paganism, because here the transcendent power confronts man with its claim.

Kierkegaard distinguishes between two kinds of paganism, one which (as in Greek paganism) moves in the direction of spirit, and the other, which, after coming to know the qualification of spirit, moves away from spirit. The latter form, occuring only within Christianity, is the particular object of his polemic.

On the theme of paganism in the works, see, for example, *The Concept of Irony*, p. 112; *Either/Or*, I, pp. 60 ff.; II, pp. 41, 175, 245; *Fear and Trembling*, p. 66; *Fragments*, p. 41; *The Concept of Anxiety* [*Dread*], pp. 19, 84 ff., 93; *Three Discourses on Imagined Occasions* [*Thoughts on Crucial Situations*, p. 109]; *Stages*, pp. 106 f., 111 ff., 125, 159, 383, 426; *Postscript*, pp. 34 fn., 116, 183, 218 ff., 248 f., 308, 323 f., 329, 335, 362, 387 fn., 438, 495 f., 514 f., 530 f.; *Upbuilding Discourses in Various Spirits*, Part Three [*The Gospel of Suffering*, pp. 70, 76, 78, 83 f., 139 ff., 157]; *Works of Love*, pp. 40 f., 58 f., 65 ff., 80 f., 137, 143, 163, 189, 190, 242; *Christian Discourses*, Pt. I, "The Cares of the Pagans," pp. 5–93; "Has a Man the Right to Let Himself Be Put to Death for the Truth?" together with *The Present Age*, p. 132; *The Sickness unto Death*, pp. 178, 211 f., 215, 220, 224, 230 ff., 247, 256; *Practice* [*Training*] *in Christianity*, pp. 38, 40, 84, 97, 109 f., 143, 246 f.; *The Point of View*, pp. 30, 37, 43, 74, 138; *Attack*, pp. 110, 133, 136, 149, 164, 166, 182, 223 f., 226 f., 279, 290.

699. John 18:38.

700. Cicero, *De natura deorum*, Bk. III, ch. 36. Kierkegaard had Cicero's works in Latin and German and in various editions. *ASKB* 1224–46, A I 149–52, A II 48–49.

701. Horace, *Odes*, II, 3, 1 ff., I, 16, 25 ff. Kierkegaard had two editions of Horace's *Opera* and a German translation of his letters. *ASKB* 1248, A I 162–65.

702. Personally I shall prefer a calm (or fair) attitude.

703. M. Luther, *En christelig Postille* (see note 81), I, pp. 473 ff.

PARABLES (S.K.)

Kierkegaard often uses the familiar parables of the New Testament when describing and elucidating ethical and religious correlations. Best known is his repeated and detailed use of the parable of "The Lilies of the Field and the Birds of the Air" (*Upbuilding Discourses in Various Spirits*, Part Two [*What We Learn from the Lilies of the Field and the Birds of the Air*], together with Part Three [*The Gospel of Suffering*, pp. 169 ff.]; *Christian Discourses*, pp. 11 ff.; and *The Lily of the Field and the Bird of the Air*, together with *Christian Discourses*, pp. 311 ff.). As examples of his superb use of other New Testament parables, we mention only "The Foolish Virgins" (*Upbuilding* [*Edifying*] *Discourses*, III, p. 47; *Upbuilding Discourses in Various Spirits*, Part Three [*The Gospel of Suffering*, p. 31]; and *Christian Discourses*, p. 219), "The Compassionate Samaritan" (*Upbuilding Discourses in Various Spirits*, Part Three [*The Gospel of Suffering*, pp. 98 f.]; *Works of Love*, p. 38; *For Self-Examination*, pp. 45 ff.), "The Unfaithful Steward" (*Christian Discourses*, p. 33), and "The Lord's Vineyard" (*Christian Discourses*, p. 165).

But Kierkegaard also illustrates ethical and religious actuality with his own parables. These include, for example, his depiction of the heavy lot of those who suffer in the strictest sense. He uses the metaphor of a horse that lives in a herd with the other horses and shares their occasional hardships but never hears anything about his own suffering (*Upbuilding Discourses in Various Spirits*, Part One [*Purity of Heart*, pp. 155 ff.]). In his portrayal of a badly driven team of horses he tries to show how man can waste imprudently his given powers and capacities (ibid., Part Three [*The Gospel of Suffering*, pp. 105 ff.]). He also uses the relationship between the coachman and the horses to illustrate the relationship between God and man—not until man is "driven" by God can he accomplish anything (*For Self-Examination*, pp. 101 ff.; *Judge For Yourselves!*, pp. 123 ff.). The "quiet lake" that gets its water from "hidden springs" is used as a picture of how a man's love must have its deep basis in God's love (*Works of Love*, p. 27). There is a similar figure in *The Unchangeableness of God* (together with *Judge For Yourselves!*, pp. 239 f.).

Mobilizing for the Church conflict, Kierkegaard the ironist stocked his journals with parables which either would strike at what to him were the empty forms of Christendom or would present his own position.

Thus the tame geese depict men who are Christians in name; whereas the true Christian is the wild goose (XI^1 A 195). The same metaphor reappears in a parable "The Tame Goose," which parodies the routine worship of God in Christendom (XI^2 A 210).

Kierkegaard compares his own position to that of an imprisoned artist in the service of "a mighty prince"; he could use and develop his talents and have a good life, but he is a prisoner and must adapt himself to the prince's will. Elsewhere he likens himself to an obedient hunting dog who, despite being teased, does not use his power before the master demands it. "For him everything depends on what the master's look commands" (XI^2 A 423). He uses the illustration of the fire chief who breaks up the crowd obstructing the fire-fighting to show that wherever "an idea is to be introduced" the crowd must be dispersed in order that he who "in a higher sense has and should have command" can have a chance (*The Moment*, no. 6, in *Attack*, p. 194).

704. This entry presumably was considered for inclusion in *The Moment* [*Øieblikket*], no. VIII. See XI^2 B 310: "Looking at the Stars."

705. J. P. Mynster, bishop of Sjælland, friend of Kierkegaard and of his father, a central figure in Kierkegaard's attack upon Christendom, December 18, 1854–55. See, for example, *Attack*, pp. 5–15.

706. "First picture" is crossed out in ms. The entire second picture is crossed out in the ms. Therefore "Third Picture" following is changed to "Second Picture."

PARADOX

According to Kierkegaard's conception, the sphere of knowledge and the sphere of faith are qualitatively different. From the standpoint of knowledge the sphere of faith is paradoxical or "absurd" (see this section). In the sphere of knowledge man reaches the culmination in metaphysics, which seeks to give direct and logically justifiable knowledge of the world and of man. But metaphysics cannot cope with existential relations, in which a person, either by self-deepening (Socrates) or by the prompting of a transcendent power, is confronted with the task of uniting two qualitative opposites, the temporal and the eternal. Here Kierkegaard employs the concept "paradox" or "the absurd." There are qualitative opposites when, for example, a person as an empirical (finite) being ("the first self") is supposed to be placed under the eternal requirement ("the deeper self"), the requirement with a *telos* (end) which does not lie within immanence (*Upbuilding* [*Edifying*] *Discourses*, IV, pp. 34 ff.). Using the examples of Socrates, Job, Abraham, and a Christian, Kierkegaard presents an ascending scale of paradoxical existential contrasts. Christ stands on a qualitative, new level and, seen from a logical and philosophical viewpoint, is "the absolute paradox . . . a stumbling block to the Jews, foolishness to the Greeks, and an absurdity to the understanding" (*Postscript*, p. 196; see also IV C 84).

Kierkegaard uses the expressions "paradox" and "absurd" interchangeably for the qualitative existential contrasts which are either to be united in a person or are already united in Christ. The expression "the absurd" stresses the existential more than the intellectual in a person's relation to a transcendent power or to Christ.

Allison, H. E. "Christianity and Nonsense." *Review of Metaphysics,* 1967.

Croxall, T. H. *Kierkegaard Studies.* London: Lutterworth Press, 1948.

Duncan, Elmer H. "Kierkegaard's Uses of Paradox—Yet Once More." *Journal of Existentialism,* 1967.

Earle, W. A. "The Paradox and Death of God: Kierkegaard and Nietzsche," in Christian, C. W. and Wittig, G. R., eds., *Radical Theology.* New York: Lippincott, 1967.

Eller, V. "Fact, Faith, and Foolishness: Kierkegaard and the New Quest." *Journal of Religion,* vol. 48, 1968.

Glicksberg, C. I. "The Kierkegaardian Paradox of the Absurd," in *The Tragic Vision in Twentieth Century Literature.* Carbondale, Ill.: Southern Illinois University Press, 1963.

Heinecken, Martin John. "The Absolute Paradox in Søren Kierkegaard," Ph. D. dissertation, University of Nebraska, 1941. *Abstracts of Doctoral Dissertations,* Lincoln, Neb.: 1942.

Herbert, Robert. "Two of Kierkegaard's Uses of 'Paradox,' " *Philosophical Review,* 1961.

Heywood, Thomas J. *Subjectivity and Paradox.* Oxford: Basil Blackwell, 1958.

Klemke, E. D. "Logicality versus Alogicality in Christian Faith." *Journal of Religion,* 1958.

Larsen, Robert E. "Kierkegaard's Absolute Paradox." *Journal of Religion,* 1962.

Lønning, Per. "Kierkegaard's 'Paradox.'" *Orbis Litterarum,* 1955. *The Dilemma of Contemporary Theology.* New York: Humanities Press, 1962.

McKinnon, Alastair. "Kierkegaard: 'Paradox' and Irrationalism." *Journal of Existentialism,* 1967.

Mackintosh, Hugh Ross. "Kierkegaard: The Theology of Paradox," in *Types of Modern Theology.* New York: Scribner, 1958.

Schmitt, Richard. "The Paradox in Kierkegaard's Religiousness A." *Inquiry* (Oslo), 1965.

Søe, N. H. "Kierkegaard's Doctrine of the Paradox," in *A Kierkegaard Critique,* ed. Niels Thulstrup and Howard Johnson. New York: Harper, 1962.

Sokel, W. H. "Kleist's Marquise of O., Kierkegaard's Abraham, and Musil's Tonka: Three Stages of the Absurd as the Touchstone of Faith." *Wisconsin Studies in Contemporary Literature,* vol. 8, 1967.

Thomas, F. M. Lloyd. "The Modernness of Kierkegaard." *Hibbert Journal,* 1947.

Thomas, John Heywood. *Subjectivity and Paradox (A Study of Kierkegaard).* New York: Oxford, 1957.

The terms "paradox," "paradoxical," and "the paradox" appear frequently in the pseudonymous works, the "edited" works, and the *Papirer* and much less frequently in the signed works. See, for example, *From the Papers of One Still Living, S. V.,* XIII, p. 55; *The Concept of Irony,* pp. 60, 107; *Either/Or,* I, pp. 37, 51, 64, 76, 177, 232, 236, 294; II, pp. 113, 265; *Fear and Trembling,* pp. 44, 48, 58 ff., 62 ff., 65, 72 f., 80 f., 84; *Fragments,* pp. 46–68, 72 f., 80 f., 87, 119, 123, 135; *The Concept of Anxiety* [*Dread*], pp. 92, 119, 123; *Postscript,* pp. 45, 89 fn., 95, 162, 177 f., 180, 183 ff., 186–98, 201 ff., 226, 229 (on distinction between immanental [*opbyggelige Taler*] and the paradoxically religious), 241 f., 244, 259, 265, 338, 348, 483 fn., 502, 505 fn., 518, 524, 528, 536, 540; "Of the Difference between A Genius and an Apostle," together with *The Present Age,* pp. 139, 141 ff., 147, 159 f., 163; *The Sickness unto Death,* pp. 155, 214, 224, 227, 231, 237, 248, 260; *Practice* [*Training*] *in Christianity,* pp. 28, 33, 67, 85, 102, 106, 123; *Attack,* p. 162; *On Authority and Revelation* (*Pap.* VII² B 235), pp. 58, 63, 79, 104, 106, 111 f., 117 f., 121 f., 164, 192.

707. See *Fragments,* p. 46; *Postscript,* p. 95.

708. See *Either/Or,* I, pp. 76, 180, 194; II, p. 113; *Fragments,* p. 46; *Postscript,* pp. 177 f., 206, 226.

709. See *Fear and Trembling,* p. 77; *Postscript,* p. 338.

710. Fifth edition.

711. See note 709.

712. Pp. 31 f., 66, 70 f., in the edition cited. *ASKB* 619.

713. God. Guil. Leibnitii, *Opera philosophica* . . . , ed. J. E. Erdmann, I–II (Berlin: 1839–40), I, pp. 486, 496. *ASKB* 620.

714. Peter Bayle, *Historisches und Kritisches Wörterbuch,* tr. J. C. Gottscheden, I–IV (Leipzig: 1741–44). *ASKB* 1961–64.

715. See, for example, *Philosophical Fragments,* pp. 46–68, 119; *Postscript,* p. 498.

716. See note 709.

717. See *Philosophical Fragments,* pp. 46–68; *Postscript,* pp. 248, 260; *Practice* [*Training*] *in Christianity,* pp. 28, 33, 67, 85.

718. See, for example, *Philosophical Fragments,* pp. 68 ff., 111 ff.

719. See *Fear and Trembling,* p. 76; *Philosophical Fragments,* pp. 68 ff.

720. See, for example, *Postscript,* p. 518; *The Sickness unto Death,* pp. 248, 260; *Practice* [*Training*] *in Christianity,* pp. 79–144.

721. See note 715.

722. See *Philosophical Fragments,* pp. 56, 69–70.

723. See ibid., pp. 56, 69–88.

724. See *Fear and Trembling,* p. 108, especially fn.

725. See *Fear and Trembling,* pp. 63 f., 76 f., 91, 129.

726. In a draft of *Philosophical Fragments,* following first partial paragraph on p. 57.

727. Compare entire entry with *Philosophical Fragments,* pp. 68 ff.

728. See *Philosophical Fragments,* p. 64, the draft of which has this entry following the initial partial paragraph.

729. See ibid., pp. 45, 206, 466 fn., 470, 498, 505 f., 508, 520, 524, 540; *The Sickness unto Death,* pp. 231, 248, 260; *Practice* [*Training*] *in Christianity,* pp. 28, 33, 85, 102, 123.

730. See *Postscript,* p. 96, the draft of which has this entry following "determination" in line 15.

731. See *Postscript,* pp. 197 f., 285, 502.

732. See ibid., pp. 184–85 fn.

733. See ibid., pp. 180, 191 f., 505 f., 536, 540.

734. See ibid., pp. 201 ff., 241 f., 316, 466 fn., 479 fn., 524.

735. See *Fear and Trembling,* p. 58; *Postscript,* pp. 186–198, 288, 506, 536.

736. See *Philosophical Fragments,* pp. 108 f.; *Postscript,* pp. 184–85 fn.

737. See *Postscript,* pp. 511 f.; *Comment,* also pp. 325–29, 532 f., 539.

738. See *Either/Or,* I, p. 232. See *Authority and Revelation* (English version of *The Book on Adler*), where this portion from the *Papirer* is omitted from p. 52.

739. From a draft of *The Book on Adler.* See *On Authority and Revelation,* pp. 103–120; "Of the Difference between a Genius and an Apostle," together with *Two Ages* [*The Present Age,* pp. 139, 141 ff., 147, 159 f., 163]. See also *Postscript,* pp. 348, 405, 452 fn., 535 fn.

740. See *The Concept of Irony,* p. 139 and note.

741. See *Fear and Trembling,* p. 84; *Postscript,* pp. 502, 514 f.

742. *Postscript*, p. 529.

743. See, for example, *Fear and Trembling*, p. 84; *Philosophical Fragments*, pp. 80 f.; *Postscript*, pp. 288, 496 fn., 505 f.

744. Julius Müller, *Die christliche Lehre von der Sünde*, I–II (Breslau: 1849, 3 printing), II, pp. 529 ff., 553 ff. *ASKB* 689–90.

745. See *Philosophical Fragments*, title page, p. 137; *Postscript*, pp. 18, 323.

746. See note 740.

747. See *Postscript*, pp. 180, 186–98.

748. See, for example, *For Self-Examination*, pp. 88 ff.; *Practice* [*Training*] *in Christianity*, p. 245.

749. Hermann Reuchlin, *Geschichte von Port Royal*, I–II (Hamburg, Gotha: 1839), pp. 680 f.

750. Daniel 1:8 ff.

751. See *Philosophical Fragments*, ch. III, pp. 46 ff.

752. John 19:5. "What a man!" is a more accurate translation of the Danish than "Here is the man," as in the RSV.

753. Matthew 6:33.

754. See "Of the Difference between a Genius and an Apostle," together with *The Present Age*, p. 139; *Attack*, p. 162.

PASCAL

Both as a person and as a thinker, Kierkegaard felt a kinship with Pascal. Like Kierkegaard, Pascal had to go through a school of suffering, and both men looked upon suffering as essential to Christianity. The only reference in the works to Pascal is in connection with a discussion of Christianity as suffering. Kierkegaard's pseudonymous author Frater Taciturnus cites Feuerbach's declaration that he agrees with Pascal in his claim that "suffering is the natural state of the Christian. . . ." The fact that two men of totally opposite views assert the same thing Frater Taciturnus-Kierkegaard takes as a confirmation of the soundness of his own view of Christianity as suffering. Incidentally, it is said of Pascal that he "spoke out of his own Christian experience" (*Stages*, p. 416), which was also the case with Kierkegaard.

In his reading of Pascal, Kierkegaard discovered other essential points of similarity between Pascal's view of Christianity and his own. For instance, Kierkegaard agrees with Pascal that "knowledge of the divine is essentially a transformation of the person" (X^3 A 609) and that God had "hidden himself even more by enveloping himself in humanness" (X^3 A 626). This last thought is found also in II A 78 and in the *Postscript*, pp. 219 f.

In addition, Kierkegaard, like Pascal, believes that grace should not be misused as an exemption from works (X^3 A 633). Kierkegaard subscribes to Pascal's view that "later Christianity with the help of some sacraments excuses itself from loving God" (X^5 A 144; see also XI^1 A 556, XI^2 A 327). Kierkegaard also finds in Pascal (X^3 A 640) the idea that if one knows God theoretically, that is, "in the imaginative medium of abstraction," then "God does not exist or is not present" for a person (VII¹ A 139).

Kierkegaard complains that Pascal's thoughts are utilized but no one tries to imitate his life (X⁴ A 537).

Allen, E. L. "Pascal and Kierkegaard." *London Quarterly Review,* 1937.

Patrick, Denzil G. M. *Pascal and Kierkegaard.* London: Lutterworth, 1947.

Thomas, J. M. "Pascal and Kierkegaard." *Hibbert Journal,* 1948.

Apparently the only reference to Pascal in the works is in *Stages,* p. 216, a quotation from Pascal by Ludwig Feuerbach in *Das Wesen des Christenthums* (Leipzig: 2 ed., 1843), p. 91. *ASKB* 488.

755. See B. Pascal, *Gedanken über die Religion und einige andere Gegenstände,* tr. K. A. Blech, I–II (Berlin: 1840), I (*Leben des Blaise Pascal, beschrieben von seiner Schwester Gilberta Verehl. Perier*), p. 33. *ASKB* 712–13.

756. See ibid., I, p. 306.

757. See ibid., I, pp. 336 f.

758. See ibid., I, p. 177.

759. H. L. Martensen, whose lectures on "speculative dogmatics" Kierkegaard heard at the University of Copenhagen during the winter semester, 1837–38. See II C 12 ff. See also "The Battle between the Old and the New Soap-Cellars" (1838), II B 1.

760. See Pascal, I, p. 145.

761. Athenæum Society's library, which Kierkegaard used considerably in addition to the other libraries in Copenhagen and his own.

762. A lecture given by A. Neander to the Berlin Academy, October 16, 1846. Second printing, 1847.

763. It is more suitable to ward off quibbling by making a few small changes which merely temper an expression than to be obliged to make a defense.

764. Hermann Reuchlin, *Geschichte von Port Royal,* I–II (Hamburg, Gotha: 1839).

765. Johannes Climacus, the pseudonymous author of *Philosophical Fragments* and *Concluding Unscientific Postscript.* See *Postscript,* pp. 35 fn., 191 f., 217 ff.

766. Hermann Reuchlin, *Pascals Leben und der Geist seiner Schriften zum Theil nach neu aufgefundenen Handschriften mit Untersuchungen über die Moral der Jesuiten* (Stuttgart, Tübingen, 1840).

767. A false opinion that makes me happy is worth a truth that presses me to the floor.

768. H. Reuchlin, *Pascals Leben*; see note 766.

769. Ibid.

770. Ibid.

771. In the scattered thoughts of Pascal it reads: Love is no metaphorical command. To say that Christ, who has come to take away the symbols and to

place the truth in their place, has come merely in order to take away the picture of love and real love, its responsibility, which was previously valued—to say that is detestable. (See *Pénsees*, 532, Brunschvieg, 665.)

The Messiah, according to the carnal Jews, was to be a great temporal prince. Jesus Christ, according to carnal Christians, has come to dispense us from the love of God and to give us sacraments which shall do everything without our help. Such is not the Christian religion, nor the Jewish. (See *Pénsees*, 546, Brunschvieg, 607.)

772. H. Reuchlin, *Pascals Leben*; see note 766.

773. Ibid.

774. Ibid.

775. Ibid.

776. Ibid.

777. See Hermann Reuchlin, *Geschichte von Port Royal*, I–II (Hamburg, Gotha: 1839), I, pp. 58 ff.

778. P. 269. Reuchlin has "saint" [*Heiligen*] rather than "pious man" [*en from Mand*].

779. See note 761.

780. See Pascal, *Gedanken über die Religion* (see note 755) I, p. 434. See X³ A 633; X⁵ A 144.

PASSION, PATHOS

Etymologically, "passion" [*Lidenskab*] is the Danish word for the Greek "pathos" [in Danish, *Patos*], and therefore these two words in the Danish language are in part synonymous. Passion, as well as pathos, contains two elements—namely, that one suffers from something but at the same time clings to what occasions the suffering. But for Kierkegaard the word "passion" is more comprehensive than the word "pathos" because it is equivocal (see *Three Discourses on Imagined Occasions* [*Thoughts on Crucial Situations*], p. 20) and thus may mean both something negative and something positive. Kierkegaard speaks this way, for example, of "the ungodly imposition of dark passions" (ibid., p. 35) and "the passion of impatience" (ibid., p. 95); but at the same time he uses the word "passion" to designate a positive emotion, uses it even for the highest religious relationship—as, for example, when he speaks of the passion of faith. The word "pathos," however, is used exclusively to indicate a positive passionate emotion.

As a contrast to the subjective relationship of passion and pathos to something, Kierkegaard cites reflection, which relates to its object objectively. Kierkegaard believed that there was at the time a universal tendency in philosophical and theological thinking to emphasize reflection unilaterally (see VIII¹ A 192), resulting in a withdrawal of the existential far into the background. Therefore he regarded it as his task to draw to the foreground in a decisive way the passionate and pathos-filled side of man as represented in feeling and will.

In connection with his concept of the stages, Kierkegaard and the pseudo-nymous authors distinguish between three kinds of pathos—the esthetic, the ethical, and the religious, each of which can take various forms within its own sphere. Thus esthetic pathos can be wholly spontaneous—for example, Judge William mentions "the pathos of spontaneity" (*Stages*, p. 150) in connection with erotic love; but it may also apply to a sublime relationship, to an idea—thus Climacus speaks of an individual's losing himself "in the idea" (*Postscript*, p. 347). But since esthetic pathos is either oriented toward the finite and is perishable or is related only in an abstract way to an idea, it does not manage to transform the individual's existence. Therefore Kierkegaard's primary interest is not in esthetic pathos, even if he has given us many examples of its various forms, but rather in ethical and religious pathos.

Ethical and religious pathos first brings a person into an existential relationship to the eternal, where for the first time there can be question of a transformation of existence and of inward deepening or inwardization (ibid., pp. 386 f.). But there are various levels in the intensification of this pathos. The highest pathos, which Climacus calls "the pathos of the absurd" (ibid., p. 494), is possible only in relation to Christianity, which as the absurd brings about a qualitative sharpening of ethical-religious pathos.

On passion, passions, and pathos in the works, see, for example, *The Concept of Irony*, pp. 111, 114, 212, 321; *Either/Or*, I, title page, pp. 27, 224 ff., 241, 251, 406; II, 161, 171, 289; *Upbuilding* [*Edifying*] *Discourses*, I, p. 26; *Fear and Trembling*, pp. 43, 88, 106, 130; *Repetition*, p. 125; *Fragments*, pp. 11, 26, 46, 48, 55, 59, 63, 67, 73, 76, 99, 105, 107 fn.; *The Concept of Anxiety* [*Dread*], pp. 16 fn., 25 fn., 97, 103, 110, 130 fn.; *Three Discourses on Imagined Occasions* [*Thoughts on Crucial Situations*, p. 34]; *Stages*, pp. 150, 160, 210, 211, 223, 238, 243, 321, 335 f., 368–77, 382, 394, 398, 407, 416 ff.; *Postscript*, pp. 32, 33, 83 f., 117 f., 176, 178 ff., 206 f., 217, 276, 313 f., 345–498, 510, 516 f., 538 f.; *Two Ages, S.V.,* VIII, pp. 32, 35 f., 40, 49, 53, 58–64; ibid. [*The Present Age*, pp. 3 f., 11 ff., 20 f., 48]; *Upbuilding Discourses in Various Spirits*, Part One [*Purity of Heart*, pp. 42, 202]; *Works of Love*, pp. 56, 59, 63, 347; *The Sickness unto Death*, pp. 172, 192; *Practice* [*Training*] *in Christianity*, pp. 114, 183; "The Sinner," ibid., p. 262; *For Self-Examination*, pp. 52, 77; *Judge For Yourselves!*, pp. 116 f., 131; *S.V.,* XIII, p. 413; *The Point of View*, pp. 28, 56, 90; " 'The Single Individual' Two 'Notes' Concerning My Work as an Author," Appendix to *The Point of View*, p. 136; *Attack*, pp. 97, 150 f., 185 f. Note that *"pathetiske"* (passionate, pathos-filled) is frequently rendered as "pathetic."

781. See W. G. Tennemann, *Geschichte der Philosophie*, I–XI (Leipzig: 1798–1819), IV, pp. 126 ff. *ASKB* 815–26.

782. See *Practice* [*Training*] *in Christianity*, pp. 127 ff.

783. See *Either/Or*, I, pp. 299 ff.

784. See *Fear and Trembling*, pp. 53 fn., 88 f.

785. C. H. Visby, Vor Frelserens Kirke, October 27, 1850.

PASTORS, CLERGY

When Søren Kierkegaard had taken his final theological examination at the university, he was qualified for a pastoral appointment. For many years there was the possibility of his becoming a pastor in the Danish Church. There were, however, various hindrances. The first was something entirely personal —for example, he speaks of a guilt he cannot reveal (see VI A 55–59); second, there was his desire to write; and third, it was not long before he developed a critical attitude toward the clergy.

Kierkegaard's criticism of the pastors of his day intensified concurrently with his increasing emphasis upon Christianity's requirement for the individual, because he believed that those who proclaim Christianity have a special responsibility and a special obligation to try to live in accord with its requirements or at least to confess their distance from them. In particular Kierkegaard charged the pastors with being pastors for the sake of their bread-and-butter and not for the sake of the call. His mounting criticism of the clergy culminated in the battle with the Church.

Since Kierkegaard himself had suffered through and fought through the whole problem of how truth is to be proclaimed, he was able to set forth the positive prototype for a pastor. He rated the significance of the authentic pastors very high, for he believed that the reversal of the downward, disintegrating tendencies of our time to something new must come about through pastors. He declares: "What is needed is *pastors.* There is the battleground; if there is a victory, it must needs come about through the pastors who, scholarly and scientifically well-educated, are trained in what could be called—as distinguished from scientific exercise in counting—engagements of composure for battle not so much with scientific and scholarly attacks and problems as with human passions, pastors capable of splitting the 'crowd' into individuals, pastors who would not make too great claims for studying and would desire anything but to dominate, pastors who, powerfully eloquent, if possible, would be no less powerful in keeping silent and enduring, pastors who, penetrators of the heart, if possible, would be no less learned in abstinence from judging and prejudging, pastors who would know how to use authority with the aid of the art of making sacrifices, pastors who would be prepared, brought up, and educated to obey and to suffer so that they would be able to mitigate, admonish, build up, move, but also compel—not by force, anything but—no, compel by their own obedience, and above all to suffer patiently . . ." (X^6 B 40).

Diamond, Malcolm L. "Kierkegaard and Apologetics." *Journal of Religion,* XLIV, 1964.

Forgey, Wallace. "A Pastor Looks at Kierkegaard." *Andover Bulletin,* vol. 47, no. 3, 1955.

Riviere, William T. *A Pastor Looks at Kierkegaard.* Grand Rapids, Michigan: Zondervan, 1941.

For references to the clergy in the works see, for example, *Either/ Or,* II, pp. 341 f.; *The Concept of Anxiety* [*Dread*], pp. 132 f.; *Three Discourses on Imagined Occasions* [*Thoughts on Crucial Situations*, pp. 8 f.]; *Postscript*, pp. 158 f., 221 f., 321 ff., 389–96, 399, 410 f., 416 f., 425 ff., 435 f., 478 f.; *Works of Love*, pp. 60 f., 139; *Christian Discourses*, pp. 172 f., 207; "Of The Difference between a Genius and an Apostle," together with *The Present Age*, p. 149; *The Sickness unto Death*, pp. 191, 209 f., 233 ff.; *Practice* [*Training*] *in Christianity*, pp. 134 f.; *For Self-Examination*, pp. 45 f., *Judge For Yourselves!*, pp. 126 ff., 139 ff., 169; *The Point of View*, pp. 36, 86; *Attack*, pp. 18 f., 26 f., 47 ff., 102 f., 112 f., 174 ff., 181 f., 208 ff., 226 ff., 268 ff., 288 ff.

786. Included in the watchman's call at nine o'clock.

787. L. Holberg, *Erasmus Montanus*, I, 4.

788. See *Attack*, p. 289.

789. Ibid.

790. On leave without pay.

791. See *Practice* [*Training*] *in Christianity*, pp. 39, 221 f., *Attack*, pp. 29 ff., 166 f., 182, 191 f., 277, especially pp. 32 f.

792. "In former times, when the subject of the lectures was not theology but mathaiology ($\mu\alpha\theta\alpha\iota\circ\lambda\circ\gamma\acute{\iota}\alpha$) . . . what crowds of priests there were, roaming about the world . . . but now we shun the subject, so that among the multitudes of students one can hardly [find one] who cares to concern himself with the subject . . . ."

793. Kierkegaard's work with this title was published September 27, 1850.

794. A Neander, *Der heilige Johannes Chrysostomus und die Kirche* . . ., I–II (Berlin: 1821–22).

795. Friedrich Böhringer, *Die Kirche Christi* (see note 355).

796. Adolf Müller, *Leben des Erasmus von Rotterdam. Mit einleitenden Betrachtungen über die analoge Entwicklung der Menschheit und des einzelnen Menschen.*

797. See, for example, *For Self-Examination*, pp. 80 ff.; *Practice* [*Training*] *in Christianity*, pp. 222–23.

798. Acts 5:1 ff.

799. See *Postscript*, p. 171; *On Authority and Revelation*, pp. 55 f.

800. Plato, *Apology*, 27 b.

801. A. Vinet, *Pastoraltheologie eller Theori af det evangeliske Præsteembede*, tr. C. A. Ravn (Copenhagen: 1854). *ASKB* 875.

802. See *Attack*, pp. 174 ff.

803. See ibid., pp. 103, 170 f.

804. Ibid.

805. See ibid., pp. 208 ff.

806. Ibid.

807. L. Holberg, *Erasmus Montanus*, I, 3. In discussing the price of a grave, Peer Degn says, "Do you want fine sand or just plain dirt?" See *Fear and Trembling*, p. 119.

808. The world wants to be deceived.

809. See note 791.

PAUL

Kierkegaard read Paul with great intensity and interest. An early journal entry (II A 392) gives an evaluation of Paul's thoughts (Romans 11) on God's plan of salvation: "one of the most profound expositions the world has ever heard." Kierkegaard's later pondering on Paul's words "O depth of richness" clearly shows that Paul's attempt to grasp God's salvation of the Jews and the pagans profoundly affected his own reflections on God's plan for the world and for the individual.

In his upbuilding or edifying works Kierkegaard very often uses Paul's words as the starting point for his own original elucidation of Christianity.

At two points Kierkegaard found analogies between his own God-relationship and Paul's. One of these was the suffering Paul calls "the thorn in the flesh," which was his lot because of the revelations he received. Through this, Kierkegaard says, Paul experienced "sufferings such as no man before him had experienced" (*Upbuilding* [*Edifying*] *Discourses*, IV, p. 54). The other was Paul's saying that he was "set apart" for the gospel of God (Romans 1:1). Because of his sufferings Kierkegaard also felt set apart for special service in the cause of Christianity. "Paul speaks of being ἀφωρισμένος [one set apart]—this I have been from my earliest youth" (VIII¹ A 185). Both men were humbled by sufferings in order to serve God.

In spite of his very great respect for Paul as Christ's "apostle," Kierkegaard allows his pseudonym Vigilius Haufniensis to correct Paul's teaching (*The Concept of Anxiety* [*Dread*], p. 30 fn.; see Romans 5:12–21, I Corinthians 15:21–22). Kierkegaard's later criticism of Paul is of a more general nature. Kierkegaard presents as the highest criterion for Christians a confrontation with Christ in "the situation of contemporaneity." Described in the gospels, this confrontation is the most rigorous form of Christianity. Kierkegaard charges Paul with mitigating the gospels: ". . . he has already relaxed in relation to the gospels" (XI¹ A 572); "as early as 'the apostle' the scaling down process begins, and it seems as if the natural man gets off a little easier in becoming a Christian" (XI² A 403). Kierkegaard, however, guards against the possible misunderstanding that he would place himself above the apostle. Viewed existentially, he always regards the apostle as standing far higher than he himself, but "intellectually" (i.e., with reference to clear characterization of Christian truth) he thinks he is vis-à-vis Paul in certain respects (see *Attack*, pp. 282 f., fn.).

For references to Paul in the works, see, for example, *Upbuilding* [*Edifying*] *Discourses*, I, pp. 73 f., 93 ff., III; pp. 103 ff.; IV, pp. 49 ff.; *The Concept of Anxiety* [*Dread*], p. 36; *Three Discourses on Imagined Occasions* [*Thoughts on Crucial Situations*, pp. 40 f.]; *Postscript*, pp. 164, 249, 406; *Upbuilding Discourses in Various Spirits*, Part One [*Purity of Heart*, p. 176]; Part Two [*What We Learn from the Lilies of the Field and the Birds of the Air*, together with *The Gospel of Suffering*, p. 220]; Part Three [ibid., pp. 19, 125, 129 f., 152 ff., 155 f.]; *Works of Love*, pp. 136

ff., 231 ff.; "Of the Difference between a Genius and an Apostle," together with *The Present Age*, pp. 140 ff., 145 ff., 160 ff.; *Attack*, pp. 182, 283 f.

810. See *Fear and Trembling* throughout.

811. Set apart for the gospel.

812. Romans 8:38 ff.

813. Ephesians 6:11.

814. See *Attack*, p. 182.

815. Romans 14:23.

816. See *The Sickness unto Death*, pp. 218 ff.

817. *Von dem Zwecke Jesu und seiner Jünger. Noch ein Fragment des Wolfenbüttelschen Ungenannten*, ed. G. E. Lessing (Braunschweig: 1778), p. 96.

818. But now (in baptism) one professes belief in a trinity in God, in a human becoming of the second person in God, and in a good many catechism articles as well, about which the first Christians and perhaps some of the apostles themselves would not know how to give an answer.

819. Galatians 1:16.

820. See *Attack*, p. 208.

821. Christian Scriver, *Seelen-Schatz* (Leipzig: 1715), pt. V, p. 980.

822. See note 791.

823. I Corinthians 7:21.

824. See *Upbuilding* [*Edifying*] *Discourses*, I, pp. 93 ff.; II, pp. 103 ff.; *Three Discourses on Imagined Occasions* [*Thoughts on Crucial Situations in Human Life*, pp. 40 f.]; *Upbuilding Discourses in Various Spirits*, Part Three [*The Gospel of Suffering*, pp. 19 ff., 125, 129 f., 152 ff.]; *Postscript*, p. 406.

PERFECTIBILITY

Søren Kierkegaard has explicitly distinguished Christianity from all other religions and all purely human conceptions of life. The essential mark of Christianity is that the eternal has revealed itself in the temporal at a specific historical point in time, something which will always be regarded by human understanding as a paradox and will be an occasion for offense. These are the elements in Christianity that Kierkegaard continually emphasizes.

This is why he opposed all attempts at adapting Christian truth to human knowledge, especially when one simultaneously maintains that this adaptation improves or perfects Christianity. He found attempts along this line in Lessing, among others (XI^2 A 39), but it was Hegel's philosophy in particular which promoted the view that Christianity is "perfectible," since philosophy, according to Hegel, could reproduce the content of Christianity in a more perfect form. This was supposed to be a step forward, but to Kierkegaard it was a step backward, since it obliterated the specific character and the paradoxicalness of Christian truth. It was Hegel's "theory of perfectibility" and his followers' elaboration of it that Kierkegaard particularly opposed (IX B 5:24).

During the battle with the Church, when Kierkegaard pointed to the striking difference between true Christianity and that which has accommodated itself to the world and human arrangements, he attacked most vigorously those who believe that "Christianity is perfectible" (*Attack*, pp. 28, 159 ff., 181, 210).

The first (1835) reference in the *Papirer* to "perfectibility" is in connection with the theory that Christianity is improvable with the years (I A 46, 47). During the following decade the pseudonymous writers occasionally use "perfectibility" in a more general way, including personal perfectibility (*The Concept of Anxiety* [*Dread*], p. 9; *Stages on Life's Way*, pp. 342, 344, 360, 419; *Postscript*, p. 421; and later, *Crisis in the Life of an Actress*, p. 90). With *The Book on Adler* (*On Authority and Revelation*) in 1846–47, Kierkegaard returns to a critique of the more specific theory of the perfectibility of Christianity. See, for example, *Attack*, pp. 28, 36, 105 f., 176, 181, 210, 279.

825. This portion from *The Book on Adler* is among those omitted from the present English version (*On Authority and Revelation*, pp. 84 ff.).

826. Entry is from a draft for "*A Cycle of Ethical-Religious Essays* [*Treatises*]," which included what became *Bogen om Adler* (*On Authority and Revelation*).

827. Ibid.

828. Galatians 4:4. See *Either/Or*, I, p. 140; *Upbuilding* [*Edifying*] *Discourses*, III, p. 40; *Fear and Trembling*, p. 55; *Upbuilding Discourses in Various Spirits*, Part Three [*The Gospel of Suffering*, p. 51]; *Fragments*, p. 22; *Postscript*, p. 523; *The Concept of Anxiety* [*Dread*], p. 81.

829. See *Attack*, pp. 158 f.

830. Ibid.

831. Ibid., pp. 36, 105, 176, 210, 279.

832. Ibid., p. 181.

833. Ibid., p. 279.

834. Friedrich Böhringer, *Die Kirche Christi* (see note 355), I, pt. 3, p. 342 ff.

835. *Den politiske Kandestøber*, II, 3.

836. I Corinthians 7:9.

837. Matthew 16:22.

PERSON, PERSONALITY

In Søren Kierkegaard's ranking of names for "man" (see INDIVIDUAL), "person" and "personality" rank alongside individuality. On the lowest rung is "copy" or "specimen" (*Eksemplar*), one who has only a dependent existence as man; then comes "individual" (*Individ*), one who primarily asserts his independence against the race; whereas "a person" has a distinctive characteristic that differentiates him from other persons. This distinctive characteristic is intensified in "individuality" and "personality." A personality must know his own special presuppositions and his peculiar task and must have the courage to manifest his purpose. Kierkegaard briefly characterizes these two aspects of personality in the following observation: " 'Personality' is derived from sound (*personare*); in another sense personality could be called transparency" (XI^2 A 107).

In the journals and papers as well as in the published works, Kierkegaard frequently stresses that personality should have external expression through one's conduct. He vigorously maintains that the person, or, more correctly, the personality, should have the courage to defend his convictions and must not shield himself behind the impersonal, the official, or the anonymous. Of the tendency to shield oneself, stemming from men's anxiety about each other, Kierkegaard says: "Every man shrinks from becoming personality, from standing face to face with others as a personality; he shrinks from it because he knows that this makes it possible for others to take aim at him" (XI^1 A 393; see also XI^1 A 51). A personal expression not only exposes a person to the possibility that others "take aim at him," but it also may prompt the interpretation that his conduct is an attack or an insult because it invites others to take personal positions. Kierkegaard observes that we express this in language when we say that speaking personally to a person is "being personal—that is, an insult" (X^1 A 18).

This external expression, which manifests a personal, that is, subjective, interest in the existence of one's fellow men, is still only one side of personality, since its subjective interest in its own existence is its unalterable presupposition. This is what Kierkegaard means by transparency [*Gennemsigtighed*], which in the lines just quoted he calls the other side of personality. For Kierkegaard it is essential that personality have this "transparency," and in many places in his writings he elaborates on how it is achieved and how the maturing to personality takes place. For example, in *Either/Or*, II, Judge William describes in detail how personality comes to be and shows how one arrives at an understanding of his concrete task for the first time through his relationship to the eternal power or "the absolute." The high value of the personality in this relationship to the absolute is evident in a passage where Judge William calls the personality "the Archimedean point," an expression Kierkegaard normally uses only about God. Judge William states: "If personality is the absolute, then it is itself the Archimedean point from which one can lift the world" (ibid., p. 270).

Allen, K. R. "Identity and the Individual: Personhood in the Thought of Erik Erikson and of Søren Kierkegaard." Ph.D. dissertation, Boston University, 1967.

Allport, Gordon. *Becoming*. New Haven: Yale University Press, 1955.

Barrett, William. *Irrational Man: A Study in Existential Philosophy*. London: Heinemann, 1961.

De George, Richard T. "Solitude and Communion: A Study of their Meaning and Relation in Human Existence." Ph.D. dissertation, Yale, 1959.

Elhard, Leland. "Faith and Identity." Ph.D. dissertation, University of Chicago, 1965.

Harper, Ralph. *Seventh Solitude.* Baltimore: Johns Hopkins University Press, 1965.

Markus, R. I. "Facts, Things, and Persons." *Hibbert Journal,* vol. 48, 1950.

Neumann, Harry. "Kierkegaard and Socrates on the Dignity of Man." *Personalist,* vol. 48, 1967.

Olafson, Frederick. "Principles and Persons: An Interpretation of Existentialism." Ph.D. dissertation, Johns Hopkins, 1967.

Skinhøj, Erik and Kirsten. "Kierkegaard in American Psychology." *Acta Psychiatrica et Neurologica,* vol. 30, no. 1–2, 1955.

Smith, Constance J. "Single One and the Other." *Hibbert Journal,* no. 4, 1947–48.

Smith, Elwyn Allen. "Psychological Aspects of Kierkegaard." *Character and Personality,* vol. 12, 1944.

Ziegler, L. "Personal Existence: A Study of Buber and Kierkegaard." *Journal of Religion,* vol. 40, April, 1960.

See titles in topical bibliography under INDIVIDUAL, SELF, and STAGES.

On the theme of person, personality, see, for example, *Either/Or,* II, pp. 159 ff., 164, 171, 181, 185, 187, 198, 216–17, 234, 236, 248, 255–56, 267, 275; *Repetition,* p. 43; *The Concept of Anxiety* [*Dread*], p. 132; *Stages on Life's Way,* p. 286; *Postscript,* pp. 277 f., 450; *Works of Love,* p. 218; *Christian Discourses,* p. 199; *The Sickness unto Death,* pp. 142, 162; *For Self-Examination,* p. 51; *The Concept of Irony,* p. 66.

838. See *The Sickness unto Death,* pp. 146 f., 210; *Works of Love,* pp. 136–52.

839. See *Postscript,* pp. 113, 449 f., and fn., 484 f.; *Christian Discourses,* p. 199 (*Personlighed,* personality, is there rendered as "personal concern," which is part of personality or being a person); *For Self-Examination,* pp. 39–45.

840. C. H. Visby.

841. See *Christian Discourses,* p. 199; *For Self-Examination,* pp. 39 f.; *Practice* [*Training*] *in Christianity,* pp. 229 f.; *Attack,* p. 172.

842. H. L. Martensen, *Den christelige Dogmatik* (Copenhagen: 1849), pp. 488 ff. *ASKB* 653.

843. See PARADOX and references to Kierkegaard's works.

844. Ibid.

845. M. Luther, *En christelig Postille* (see note 81), II, p. 290.

846. See *Philosophical Fragments,* pp. 17 ff.

847. Galatians 1:1.

848. I Corinthians 1:12.

849. See NUMBERS, CROWD, MASS, PUBLIC; *The Sickness unto Death,* pp. 166 f.; *Works of Love,* pp. 119 ff.

850. See *Postscript*, pp. 19, 108 f., 155, 172 f., 179, 271, 281, 312 f., 449 f., 484 f.; *For Self-Examination*, pp. 39 ff., 45 ff.; *S.V.*, XIII, p. 429.

851. *Politics*, V, 10, 1312 b 4 ff.

852. See *Attack*, pp. 153, 170 f.

853. Current discussions of the National Pension Fund appeared in *Fædrelandet*, no. 201, August 30, no. 205, September 4, no. 208, September 7, 1854; *Dagbladet*, no. 203, September 1, no. 204, September 2, no. 209, September 8, 1854.

854. See *Xenophons Mindesværk, om Cyri Ledingsfærd i Overasien og de ti Tusinde Grækeres Tilbagetog*, tr. O. Wolff (Copenhagen: 1800); Karl Becker's *Verdenhistorie*, tr. J. R. Riise, I–XII (Copenhagen: 1822–29), XI, pp. 671 ff. *ASKB* 1972–83.

855. See *Works of Love*, p. 98.

856. See *The Concept of Irony*, pp. 234 f.; *The Sickness unto Death*, pp. 147, 213, 262; *Works of Love*, p. 332.

857. See note 852.

858. See note 839.

PETER

Now and then in his writings Kierkegaard uses Bible passages from Peter's letters, but Peter's particular significance lies in his intense and impulsive personality, which frequently manifests itself in the gospels in crucial situations where the human and the divine clash. Thus Kierkegaard comments several times on Christ's joy over Peter's confession of Jesus as the Son of God. This no man can perceive by himself, and Kierkegaard declares that if God "was unrecognizable" when he became man, then it was "not flesh and blood, but the exact opposite of flesh and blood, which prompted Peter to know him" (*Practice* [*Training*] *in Christianity*, p. 128; see also pp. 82 and 102). But doubt sometimes got the best of Peter, as it did when he took Christ at his word and walked upon the waves but began to sink when he doubted (*Practice* [*Training*] *in Christianity*, p. 79). The divine and the human collide especially in the account of Peter's indignation when Christ begins to talk about his suffering and death. Kierkegaard says: "Peter is the most lovable edition of human sympathy—but it is human compassion and therefore an offense to Christ. Christ is the divine, the absolute, and therefore an offense to Peter" (ibid., pp. 120 f.; see also *Works of Love*, p. 115).

In many passages Kierkegaard examines the account of Peter's denial—see, for example, *Christian Discourses*, p. 286 f. Kierkegaard believes that Peter would not have denied Christ if he had regarded Christ as only a man; but that the Son of God "should be treated this way" "overwhelms Peter" to the point where he cannot bear it and therefore he deserts (VIII[1] A 370; see also *Practice* [*Training*] *in Christianity*, p. 106). It is interesting that in another discussion of Peter's denial Kierkegaard shows how Christ restores the relationship and, despite the treachery, saves Peter by showing him his faithful love by merely looking at him (*Works of Love*, pp. 166 ff.; see also p. 107).

Kierkegaard also closely examines Christ's thrice-repeated question: Peter, do you love me? To Kierkegaard this situation is yet another example of the collision or contradiction between the divine and the human, namely, "that he who is God loves humanly . . ." (*Works of Love*, pp. 154 f.; see also *Practice* [*Training*] *in Christianity*, p. 82). In his book *Christian Discourses* (p. 184) Kierkegaard uses the tension between the human and the divine polemically when he uses Peter's words to Christ, "Lo, we have left everything and followed you," to ironize over the Christendom which has not left anything for the sake of Christ.

For references to Peter in the works, see, for example, *Postscript*, p. 526; *Upbuilding Discourses in Various Spirits*, Part Three [*The Gospel of Suffering*, pp. 16, 39, 52 f.]; *Works of Love*, pp. 107, 115, 154 f., 166 ff., 304; *Christian Discourses*, pp. 184 ff., 190 ff., 288; *Practice* [*Training*] *in Christianity*, pp. 79, 82, 102, 106 f., 120, 128; *Judge For Yourselves!*, pp. 113 f.

859. See M. Luther, *En christelig Postille* (see note 81), II, pp. 337–38.

860. See "Has a Man the Right to Let Himself Be Killed for the Truth?" together with *The Present Age*, pp. 77 ff.

861. Matthew 26:40 ff.

862. Matthew 27:75.

863. Matthew 16:23.

PETRARCH

In *Stages on Life's Way*, where Kierkegaard's pseudonym Quidam gives examples of "unhappy love" (p. 370), mention is also made of the poet Petrarch's (1304–1374) love for Laura, who "belonged to another" (V B 116:3). Quidam emphasizes that all the examples cited are on a lower plane than his own situation inasmuch as his hindrance is of a religious nature. Something similar is expressed elsewhere in the journals, where Kierkegaard speaks of Petrarch's love and compares it with his own, which became an unhappy love because "a higher power forbade him" the relationship (V B 116:3).

Earlier in the same volume (p. 308), Quidam quotes a verse from Petrarch which to him properly describes an element in unhappy love—namely, the silence in which one is invaded by so many unhappy thoughts. But, generally speaking, one may say that Kierkegaard is critical of the way Petrarch depicts erotic love in his poetry (IV A 95). The erotic is most authentically expressed for Kierkegaard when—as Constantin Constantius says: "the idea . . . is in motion" (*Repetition*, p. 141)—that is, when the erotic is brought into relationship with the eternal.

864. "Amors Triumph" in F. Petrarca, *Sämmtliche italienische Gedichte*, tr. F. W. Brüchbau, I–V (Munich: 1827). *ASKB* 1932–33.

865. From draft of *Stages on Life's Way*, at end of partial paragraph at top of p. 322.

866. Innocent desire and chaste allurement.
Passing into Elysium and never dying.

867. C. L. Ferrow, *Francisco Petrarca* (Altenburg, Leipzig: 1818), p. 52.

PHILOSOPHY

According to Kierkegaard, Hegel had extended the domain of philosophy beyond its legitimate boundary. For example, the modern tendency to place knowledge higher than faith, whereby faith merely becomes a step on the way to a higher cognition, culminates in Hegel. It is amazing how early Kierkegaard realized the direction to take to make clear what belongs to the domain of philosophy and thus to demarcate it from theology. Already in 1835 in a journal entry Kierkegaard says of the difference between philosophy and Christianity: "Philosophy and Christianity can never be united." He substantiates this remark with the idea that redemption, which is "the most essential part of Christianity," is alien to philosophy. Philosophy's limitations are stressed even more strongly in a sentence (added to the entry) which gives the problem an existential turn by switching focus from philosophy to the philosopher: "The philosopher must either embrace optimism or—despair" (I A 94). This means that the philosopher will never be able to accept man's categorical bankruptcy, that he must always keep open the possibility for a change to the better; if he cannot, he must despair, and in that case philosophy will be unable to help him. This position is later given special prominence in Kierkegaard's works by Constantin Constantius, who says: "Repetition is the *interest* of metaphysics, and at the same time the interest upon which metaphysics founders" (*Repetition*, p. 34; see also *The Concept of Anxiety* [*Dread*], p. 16). He means that repetition (which here means redemption) cannot be found in philosophy.

From this position, then, Kierkegaard defines philosophy as "the purely human view of the world—the *human* viewpoint" (II A 77). Judge William defines the "spheres" of philosophy more closely as "logic, nature, history . . ." (*Either/Or*, II, p. 178), but it is only history in the general sense that falls within philosophy; it is unequal, however, to the man's inner history which comes into existence when his actions are motivated by the ethical as something eternal.

It is true that man can be led to the absolute good by means of philosophical self-deepening (which was the case with Socrates), but when a man wishes to act upon this, he abandons philosophy's envisioned objective and abstract certainty and ventures out into "objective uncertainty" (*Postscript*, p. 182). In the beginning the venture can be accompanied by a philosophical optimism, as with Socrates, but the more earnestly a person exerts himself, the more it will be apparent how little he achieves on his own. He is thereby brought to the point where he heeds dogmatics' offer of a new beginning. Thus ethics is a middle term between philosophy and dogmatics.

As long as one remains within the human, he can live on the basis of a philosophical view of life. But as soon as he is taken beyond the human, either by the disintegration of his life or through his ethical exertions, he existentially discovers the limits of man's abilities. Here he must either despair or take refuge in a transcendent power.

In other words, the domain of philosophy lies within immanence—that is, the sphere of human cognition and ability; whereas theology, which presupposes a personal God who is outside of the world and is the object of faith, is anchored in transcendence. Thus, according to Kierkegaard, faith is higher than philosophy.

Arendt, Hannah. "Tradition in the Modern Age." *Partisan Review*, vol. 21, no. 1, 1954.

Collins, James. "Kierkegaard and Christian Philosophy." *The Thomist*, vol. 14, 1952.

Dooyeweerd, H. *Philosophy and Christianity*. Leiden: E. J. Brill, 1965.

Hong, Howard V. "Søren Kierkegaard as a Christian Philosopher." *Scottish Journal of Theology*, 1941.

Jaspers, Karl. *Philosophical Faith and Revelation*. New York: Harper, 1967.

Kuhn, Helmut. "Existentialism and Metaphysics." *The Review of Metaphysics*, vol. 1, no. 2, 1947.

Mackey, L. "Kierkegaard and the Problem of Existential Philosophy." *Review of Metaphysics*, vol. 9, 1956.

Molina, Fernando. *Existentialism as Philosophy*. Englewood Cliffs, N. J.: Prentice-Hall, 1962.

Smith, John E. "The Revolt of Existence." *Yale Review*, vol. 43, no. 3, 1953–54.

Swenson, David. *Something about Kierkegaard*. Minneapolis: Augsburg, 1951.

Wild, John. *The Challenge of Existentialism*. Bloomington, Ind.: Indiana University Press, 1955.

Wild, John. *Existence and the World of Freedom*. Englewood Cliffs, N. J.: Prentice-Hall, 1963.

Wild, John. *Human Freedom and Social Order: an Essay in Christian Philosophy*. Durham, N.C.: Duke University Press, 1959.

Wild, John. "Kierkegaard and Contemporary Existentialist Philosophy," *A Kierkegaard Critique*. New York: Harper, 1962.

Wild, John. "Kierkegaard and Classic Philosophy." *Philosophical Review*, 1940.

For specific references to philosophy and philosophies in the works, see, for example, *S.V.*, XIV, p. 54; *The Concept of Irony,* passim; *Either/Or,* I, 37 f.; II, pp. 174 ff., 180; *Repetition,* pp. 3 ff.; *Fear and Trembling,* pp. 22 ff., 132; *The Concept of Anxiety* [*Dread*], pp. 73 ff., 130; *S.V.*, V, pp. 53 ff., 59 ff., 70; *Fragments,* passim; *Postscript,* pp. 34, 75 ff., 90 ff., 99 ff., 105, 110 ff., 153 ff., 163 f., 206 f., 263 f., 270 ff., 275, 279, 281, 289, 292, 293 ff., 322, 344 ff., 337 ff., 377, 459 ff., 548 ff.; *The Sickness unto Death,* pp. 218 ff., 227 f.; *Practice* [*Training*] *in Christianity,* pp. 82, 178, 201.

868. Reminiscent of Hamann's *Stein der Weisen.*

869. See *Postscript,* pp. 334 ff.

870. See *Postscript,* p. 337.

871. See note 869.

872. Ibid.

873. See *Baron von Münchhausens vidunderlige Reiser, Feldttog og Hændelser, fortalte af ham selv* (Roeskilde: 1834), p. 27; *Postscript,* pp. 50, 85, 250.

874. See note 869.

875. See Matthew 7:15.

876. Reference is made here to Hegel and later Hegelians. Kierkegaard was reading Hegel during the summer of 1838.

877. See I Corinthians 13:12.

878. See John 19:24.

879. He is an accursed man who raises a hog and teaches his own son Greek culture.

880. See Genesis 14:23.

881. See *Prefaces, S.V.,* V. p. 49.

882. Anton Günther, *Die Juste-Milieus in der deutschen Philosophie gegenwärtiger Zeit* (Vienna: 1838). *ASKB* 522.

883. As a six-year-old child, Kierkegaard had seen an antisemitic outburst (September, 1819).

884. Presumably a reference to Hegel's interpretation of Christianity.

885. In Hebrew a mark (:) under a consonant to express the absence of a following vowel sound (quiescent sheva), a neutral vowel sound (movable sheva), or a shaded vowel sound (compound sheva). See *Either/Or,* I, p. 22.

886. I. H. Fichte, the younger. See FICHTE.

887. See *Philosophical Fragments,* in which Kierkegaard, in contemporary philosophical terminology, considers the continuity or discontinuity of idealistic philosophy and Christianity.

888. *Zeitschrift für Philosophie und spekulative theologie* (Bonn: 1839). 1835–38. *ASKB* 354–57.

889. Ibid., pp. 239 ff.

890. Ibid.

891. Christianity is not only the conclusion and fulfillment of Jewish religion but is also the key to and interpreter of pagan polytheism.

892. See note 888.

893. Frederik Christian Sibbern (See VII¹ A 152), Kierkegaard's favorite philosophy professor (See VII¹ A 152) next to Poul Martin Møller. The concept of the collateral as organismic, parallel-lined thinking was hinted at by Sibbern and developed by Kierkegaard. For Kierkegaard this was a very important conception of thinking, and he employed his own form of it without forgetting the initial impetus given by Sibbern, even though it is mentioned only twice in the *Papirer* (II A 519 and IV C 78).

894. See *The Concept of Irony*, p. 243. According to Livy, Publius (Pulcher) Claudius, son of Appius Claudius, lost the battle of Drepanum in 249 B.C. because he treated the augurs' warning in this way.

895. Distinctions, even in a metaphysical sense.

896. See A. P. Adler, *Den isolerede Subjectivitet i dens vigtigste Skikkelser* (Copenhagen: 1840), pp. 4 ff.; J. L. Heiberg, *Perseus*, no. 2 (August 1838), p. 11. *ASKB* 569. See also *The Concept of Irony*, p. 75; *Postscript*, pp. 101 f., 104; *The Sickness unto Death*, p. 224.

897. Genesis 11:1 ff.

898. If contemporary philosophers would have disputed in a just manner, I would at any rate not have denied that they could be at liberty with impunity to devote themselves vigorously even to their disputations and to the deep-seated questions of importance in the field of philosophy, ignorant of the involvements; I say I would not have denied that they had persuaded me that it would have been better to look to the truth in such matters; if upon following those of earlier days we try not to systematize life and to interpret it from that point of view but nevertheless to obviate the systematic make an experimental approach, we thereby betray life. Both of these approaches ought to be avoided.

899. See *The Concept of Irony*, pp. 47 ff.

900. See *Musæus' Folkeæventyr*, tr. F. Schaldemose (Copenhagen: 1840), pp. 116 ff. *Volksmärchen der Deutschen*, I–V (Vienna: 1815). *ASKB* 1434–38.

901. Entry is from draft of *The Concept of Irony*.

902. See Kierkegaard's development of this and related themes in *Johannes Climacus or De omnibus dubitandum est.*

903. See ibid., pp. 116 ff.; *The Concept of Anxiety* [*Dread*], p. 130 fn.; *Postscript*, pp. 34 fn., 75 f.

904. For it is owing to their wonder that men both now and at first began to philosophize; . . . . Aristotle, *Metaphysics*, bk. A 2, 982 b 12 f.

905. For this feeling of wonder shows that you are a philosopher, since wonder is the only beginning of philosophy. Plato, *Theaetetus*, 155 d.

906. Karl F. Hermann, *Geschichte und System der Platonischen Philosophie* (Heidelberg: 1839). *ASKB* 576.

907. Ph. Marheineke, *Die Grundlehren der christlichen Dogmatik als Wissenschaft* (Berlin: 1827), pp. 123 ff. *ASKB* 644.

908. During the winter of 1841–42 Kierkegaard heard K. Werder's lectures in Berlin on *Logic and Metaphysics, with Special Reference to the Leading Systems in Ancient and Modern Philosophy*. See also Marheineke, pp. 189 ff.

909. Ibid., pp. 107 ff.

910. See end of *Either/Or*, II, pp. 341 f.

911. See *Prefaces, S.V.*, V, pp. 53 ff.

912. See *From the Papers of One Still Living, S.V.*, VIII, p. 54.

913. See *Philosophical Fragments*, p. 121.

914. Flavius Philostratus, the Elder, *Werke*, pts. 1–5 (Stuttgart: 1821–32), p. 106. *ASKB* 1143.

915. Ibid.

916. See *Fear and Trembling*, p. 132; *Repetition*, p. 33; *Postscript*, p. 277 fn.

917. See Matthew 23:4.

918. See *Postscript*, pp. 228 f.

919. From draft of *Johannes Climacus*. See ibid., p. 103; *Postscript*, pp. 275 f.

920. Technical skills, scientific knowledge, temperance (related to practical wisdom), intuitive reason, philosophic wisdom. *Nicomachean Ethics*, VI, 4, 1140 ff.

921. Mean.

922. Entry is an excerpt from G. O. Marbach, *Geschichte der Philosophie des Mittelalters* (Leipzig: 1841), pp. 220 ff. *ASKB* 643.

923. See W. G. Tennemann, *Geschichte der Philosophie*, I–XI (Leipzig: 1798–1819), I, pp. 37, 39 ff. *ASKB* 815–26. See also *Either/Or*, I, pp. 37 ff.; *The Concept of Anxiety* [*Dread*], pp. 73 ff.; *Postscript*, p. 75 fn., 99 f., 272 fn., 377.

924. See *Either/Or*, II, pp. 174–80; *Fragments*, pp. 14 and note, 47; *Postscript*, pp. 177 f., 330 ff., 354 ff., 373 f.

925. Tennemann, pp. 37, 39 ff.

926. See *Postscript*, pp. 206 f.

927. Time is like a river, which has brought down to us things light and puffed up, while those which are weighty and solid have sunk. Francis Bacon, *The New Organon*, preface to *The Great Instauration*, (Indianapolis: Bobbs-Merrill, 1960), p. 10.

928. F. H. Jacobi, *Sämmtliche Werke*, I–VI in 7 vols. (Leipzig: 1812–25). *ASKB* 1722–28.

929. See *Prefaces, S.V.*, V, pp. 53 ff.

930. See note 896.

931. See note 924.

932. See Shakespeare, *Hamlet*, I, 5; *Shakespeare's dramatische Werke*, tr. A. W. Schegel and L. Tieck, I–XII (Berlin: 1839), pp. 103 f. *ASKB* 1883–88.

933. *Aristotelis de anima Libri tres. Ad interpretum Graec. auctoritatem et codicum fidem recogn. comm. illustravit,* ed. F. A. Trendelenburg (Jena: 1833). *ASKB* 1079.

934. Ibid., pp. 83 ff.

935. Kierkegaard said (VIII¹ A 18, 1847) he was indebted to no other modern philosopher so much as to Trendelenburg and that he regretted not hearing him in Berlin in the winter of 1841–42. In his library he had the work cited above as well as *Platonis de ideis et numeris doctrina ex Aristotele illustrata* (Leipzig: 1826), *ASKB* 842; *Logische Untersuchungen* (Berlin: 1844), *ASKB* 843; *Elementa logices Aristotelicæ* (Berlin: 1842), *ASKB* 844; *Erläuterungen zu den Elementen der aristotelischen logik* (Berlin: 1842), *ASKB* 845; *Die logische Frage in Hegels System* (Leipzig: 1843), *ASKB* 846; *Niobe* (Berlin: 1846), *ASKB* 847; *Geschichte der Kategorienlehre* (Berlin: 1846), *ASKB* 848. See *Postscript,* pp. 100, 267 fn.

936. See *Nicomachean Ethics,* 1139 b, 18 ff. See IV C 23.

937. Entry from draft of *Philosophical Fragments,* following the first full paragraph on pp. 89 f.

938. Always unchanged and the same. See *Sophist,* 248 a; also *Timaeus* 35 a, 38 a, and *Phaedo* 78 d; *Johannes Climacus,* p. 147; *The Concept of Anxiety* [*Dread*], p. 74 fn.

939. Entry from draft of *The Concept of Anxiety* [*Dread*], following first word ("speculating") on p. 76. See also *Johannes Climacus,* pp. 144 f.

940. See *The Concept of Irony,* p. 241 fn.; *Postscript,* pp. 131–32 fn., 144, 180 f., 184 f., 502.

941. See *Postscript,* p. 59.

942. See ibid., pp. 99 ff.

943. See ibid., p. 34 fn.

944. See note 935.

945. See note 896.

946. According to the auction catalog (*ASKB*), Kierkegaard had twenty volumes of individual works by Hegel. *ASKB* 549–65, 1384–86.

947. *Memorabilia,* III, 6. Entry is from draft of *Postscript.*

948. See *The Sickness unto Death,* p. 177.

949. C. Siddons, "*Enkelte Træk til Skildring en af Nord-Americas videnskabelige, religiøse og kirkelige Tilstand.*"

950. 1828, edited by N. F. S. Grundtvig and A. G. Rudelbach. See *Armed Neutrality* and *An Open Letter,* pp. 30 ff.

951. F. C. Sibbern, professor of philosophy, University of Copenhagen. See note 893.

952. Siddons, p. 9.

953. Moriz Carriere, *Die philosophische Weltanschauung der Reformationszeit in ihren Beziehungen zur Gegenwart* (Stuttgart, Tübingen: 1847). *ASKB* 458.

954. When a philosopher was asked when he had begun to be a philosopher, he answered: When I began to be a friend to myself. If one were to ask

a Christian when he became a Christian, he would answer: When I began to be an enemy to myself.

955. See *Stages on Life's Way*, pp. 298 f.

956. Non-being consists of the three principles of impotence, ignorance, and hate.

957. Carriere.

958. P. 338.

959. See *Armed Neutrality*, p. 42.

960. *Philosophical Fragments*, p. 80 fn.

961. See *The Concept of Irony*, pp. 241–42 fn.

PIETISM

From earliest childhood Søren Kierkegaard was familiar with the pietistic view of Christianity. At home and in church he learned the hymns of the pietist H. A. Brorson, and his father owned and read books by German pietistic authors. In his own library Kierkegaard had books by Johann Arndt, Spener, and Tersteegen, to which he repeatedly returned.

Kierkegaard appreciated pietism for its existential view of Christianity and its earnest attempt to imitate Christ—in contrast to orthodoxy, which attached the greatest importance to pure doctrine. He calls pietism, "properly understood," "the one and only consequence of Christianity" (X³ A 437) and maintains that pietism will always "collide with the established" because it demands "inwardness in contrast to empty externalism" (*Practice* [*Training*] *in Christianity*, p. 87). When in his later years Kierkegaard occasionally seems to criticize pietism, without exception it is in connection with its strict insistence on a specific external form of conduct instead of first and foremost "speaking of the improvement of the heart" (X⁴ A 94). With this attitude toward pietism, Kierkegaard had to reject totally the attacks of his contemporaries to the effect that he wanted "to develop a pietistic severity which is a thing alien to my soul and nature" (*On My Work as an Author*, together with *The Point of View*, p. 160; see also X³ A 519).

962. Here Kierkegaard uses "pietism" according to its root, "piety." The expression "pietism" is used only twice in the published works (*Practice* [*Training*] *in Christianity*, p. 87, and "My Position as a Religious Writer in 'Christendom' and My Tactics," published in 1851 together with *On My Work as an Author*, in English version together with *The Point of View*, p. 160). "Piety" in the sense of religious commitment and integrity and also in a personal sense (filial piety toward his father and Bishop Mynster, for example) is used much more frequently.

963. Pp. 15 ff.

964. Wilhelm Hossbach, *Philipp Jakob Spener und seine Zeit* (Berlin: 1828), pt. II, pp. 389 ff.

965. H. E. F. Guericke, *August Hermann Francke* (Halle: 1827). I demand no new religion but new hearts.

966. Ibid.

PLATO

Kierkegaard's great interest in Socrates led him into a thorough study of the works of Plato (427–347 B.C.). In his doctoral dissertation, *The Concept of Irony* (p. 65), he describes his "somewhat youthful, perhaps, infatuation with Plato." Like many other scholars before him, Kierkegaard tries in this book to determine more precisely the relationship "between the *Platonic* Socrates and the *actual* Socrates" (ibid., p. 67). His conclusion in *The Concept of Irony,* as well as in later books, is that Socrates realizes various forms of existence in his life, for example, the ironic or the ethical, whereas Plato tries his hand at speculation and when he falls short avails himself of "the mythical" (ibid., p. 135). In *Concluding Unscientific Postscript* (pp. 184 f.) Climacus also stresses this difference, maintaining that "the principle that all knowledge is recollection . . . does indeed belong to both"; but while "Socrates is always departing from it in order to exist," Plato remains speculative "by pursuing the lure of recollection and immanence." In the few portions of the journals and papers where Plato is mentioned as a philosopher, it is to the speculative that Kierkegaard alludes, as, for example, in III A 5, which concerns Plato's remark that "all knowledge is recollection."

Of particular interest is Kierkegaard's commentary on Plato's assertion that "poets should be expelled from the state" (X^2 A 608). Kierkegaard believes that this thought actually must be attributed to Socrates, since only an ethicist and not a poet like Plato would make this demand. But Kierkegaard is also aware that the same sort of critical attitude toward the poet could be directed at him; however, he believes that there is a difference between himself and Plato—namely, that Plato, who had witnessed Socrates as ethicist expressing the ideal in his life, merely treats these ideals poetically and therefore represents a regression, whereas Kierkegaard himself must first of all poetically "clear the terrain," after which he moves toward the actualization of the ethical. (See also X^2 A 229.) In conclusion, it must be mentioned that Kierkegaard finds in Plato an analogy to Christianity's view that the just must suffer in this world (X^2 A 610).

Arendt, Hannah. "Tradition and the Modern Age." *Partisan Review,* 21, no. 1, 1954.

Munz, Peter. "Sum qui sum." *Hibbert Journal,* 1951–52.

On Plato and the Platonic in the works, see, for example, *The Concept of Irony,* pp. 52 f., 56, 59, 65–158, 174, 181 ff., 185 ff., 205, 230, 237, 243, 326, 349; *Either/Or,* I, p. 127, 412; II, p. 167; *The Concept of Anxiety [Dread],* pp. 74 f., 95 fn., 130 fn.; *Fragments,* pp. 14, 29, 74, 99, 103; *Stages,* pp. 58, 67, 73 f.;

Postscript, pp. 77, 184, 295; "Of the Difference between a Genius and an Apostle," together with *The Present Age*, p. 140. For the citing of Plato's works, see *S.V.*, XV, Plato as author.

967. Reference is to paragraph 244–57, ed. Steph., to I, pp. 164–94 in Kierkegaard's Greek edition of Plato, *Platonis quae exstant Opera*, ed. Fr. Astius, I–XI (Leipzig: 1819–32). *ASKB* 1144–54. For a discussion of Kierkegaard's reading of Plato see *Philosophical Fragments*, Commentary, pp. 164 ff. See also *The Concept of Irony*, pp. 65–158.

968. *Vorlesungen über die Geschichte der Philosophie*, I–III (Berlin: 1836). *ASKB* 557–59.

969. *Platons Werke*, tr. F. Schleiermacher, I–VI (Berlin: 1817–28), I, pp. 79 ff.

970. See Plato, *Parmenides* 151 e. Entry is an addition to IV C 63.

971. In Kierkegaard's account (III C 27, no. 13, December 10, 1841) of Schelling's lectures in Berlin, there is a discussion of Hegel's trilogy: art, religion, and philosophy.

972. See G. O. Marbach, *Geschichte der Philosophie des Mittelalters* (Leipzig: 1841), pp. 58, 63 f. *ASKB* 643.

973. See Plato, *Gorgias*, 483 a ff. This entry is a marginal note in a copy of *Either/Or*, I, p. 284, end of full paragraph.

974. *Unum cognoris, omnes noris* (Terence): If you know one, you know all.

975. Presumably a reference to Plato's *Republic*, 605 a ff. See X² A 229.

976. Change into another kind.

977. C. M. Wieland, *Sämmtliche Werke* (Leipzig: 1801).

978. This view of the Sophists coincides with that in Plato's *Republic*, bk. I.

979. Translation from the Danish version based upon German version in C. M. Wieland, XXXVI, pp. 66 f. See Plato, *Republic*, bk. II, 360 e ff.

980. E. Zeller, *Die Philosophie der Griechen*, I–II, pts. 1–4 (Tübingen: 1844). *ASKB* 913–14.

981. Disputatious art; to make contentious.

POLEMICAL, POLEMICS

In one of the journal entries on Hamann, Kierkegaard writes that "every man who in the proper sense is to fill out a period in history must always begin polemically, precisely because the subsequent stage is not purely and simply the result of the previous one" (I A 340). Since Kierkegaard himself advanced new, original points of view, his authorship ought to be of a polemical character, and scrutiny reveals that his entire authorship, from the very first work, *From the Papers of One Still Living*, to his attack on the Church, has a strong polemical cast.

For Kierkegaard the first prerequisite for any polemic and criticism is the provision of something positive as a replacement. Furthermore, the object of the polemic is very important. His clear perception of what should result and his complete mastery of the dialectic of communication meant that his own polemic was very well considered. For Kierkegaard a crucial point is that one who undertakes a showdown with the old and the introduction of something new must feel an ethical responsibility. He discusses this particularly in the beginning of *The Book on Adler* (VII² B 235; English title, *Authority and Revelation*, pp. 3 ff.).

For references in the works to polemics and the polemical, see, for example, *The Concept of Irony*, pp. 188, 192, 212, 233, 237, 239 f., 262, 293 f., 317, 321; *Either/Or*, II, p. 105; *Stages*, p. 426 (*polemisk* omitted in translation, l. 3); *Postscript*, pp. 28, 64, 226, 236, 243, 297, 546; *Two Ages*, S.V., VIII, p. 62; "Has a Man the Right to Let Himself Be Put to Death for the Truth?" together with *The Present Age*, pp. 114, 133; *For Self-Examination*, p. 18 (tr. "taking issue"); *Armed Neutrality* and *An Open Letter*, pp. 34, 38, 42, 52; *On My Work as an Author*, together with *The Point of View*, pp. 6, 50, 59; " 'The Single Individual' Two 'Notes' Concerning My Work as an Author," Appendix to *The Point of View*, p. 125 fn.; *Attack*, p. 127.

982. See *Attack*, p. 127: "The concept 'Christian' is a polemical concept," and *The Point of View*, p. 59: "The essentially religious author is always polemical."

POSSIBILITY

In order to fathom human existence, Kierkegaard tried to identify himself with other men's possibilities and to experiment with his own. This explains why possibility became central to Kierkegaard's existential thought. The prominence he gave to possibility and its significance in existence are apparent in the following statement by Vigilius Haufniensis: "only the man who is educated by possibility is educated in accordance with his infinity. Possibility is therefore the weightiest of all categories" (*The Concept of Anxiety* [*Dread*], p. 140). "In possibility everything is equally possible," but the possibilities which threaten existence lead men farther along.

Within the esthetic there is the possibility of misfortune that a person cannot cope with and that he feels is a threat to his existence. Only in "faith's anticipation" can this possibility be overcome (ibid., p. 141, ed. tr.; see also *Upbuilding* [*Edifying*] *Discourses*, I, p. 17).

In the ethical sphere "the possibility of despair" arises when one cannot fulfill the requirement of the eternal. But this possibility can mature one to the point of accepting Christianity's invitation (*Postscript*, pp. 492 f.).

In the confrontation with Christianity through the "possibility of offense," steadily increasing in intensity, one is placed over against salvation or damnation (*The Sickness unto Death*, pp. 253 ff.; *Practice* [*Training*] *in Christianity*, p. 83).

For Kierkegaard the category of possibility is closely connected to the category of freedom in such a way that possibility may be called the possibility for freedom. But freedom presupposes a choice; therefore Kierkegaard always operates by posing two opposite possibilities, an either/or, of which one is the possibility of the good. The choice between opposite possibilities becomes decisive for the first time within the ethical stage, and particularly in the Christian-religious stage.

In itself possibility is only "a thought actuality" (*Postscript*, p. 285, ed. tr.) and as such still a nothing, because in order for possibility to become actuality there must also be a resolution, a movement. As an existential thinker, Kierkegaard particularly stresses the importance of moving possibility out into actuality. There are many reminders in Kierkegaard's writing that one must not merely experiment with possibilities but must actualize them. Possibility can even be "a hint from God" (IX A 352).

Kierkegaard warns vigorously against the temptation to become enthusiastic about Christianity's possibilities while flinching from actualizing the possibility, a temptation to which even the apostles were exposed (X^2 A 202), for where "the essentially Christian" is concerned, "what looks so extraordinarily inviting in possibility becomes just the opposite when made into actuality" (X^3 A 482). (See REALITY, ACTUALITY.)

Barnes, Hazel E. *Humanistic Existentialism: The Literature of Possibility.* Lincoln, Neb.: University of Nebraska Press, 1959.

Eller, V. "Fact, Faith, and Foolishness: Kierkegaard and the New Quest." *Journal of Religion*, 1968.

On the theme of possibility in the works, see, for example, *The Concept of Irony*, pp. 216 ff., 221, 279, 302; *Either/Or*, II, p. 262; *Fragments*, pp. 91–107; *The Concept of Anxiety* [*Dread*], pp. 38 ff., 55, 81 f., 97 ff., 140 ff.; *Stages*, pp. 253, 351; *Postscript*, pp. 267 ff., 278 ff., 292 ff., 302 ff., 320, 514–15 fn., 532; *Works of Love*, pp. 47 f., 218, 233 ff.; *The Sickness unto Death*, pp. 162, 164, 166–75, 205; *Practice* [*Training*] *in Christianity*, p. 131.

On the theme of impossibility in the works see, for example, *The Concept of Anxiety* [*Dread*], p. 101; *Fear and Trembling*, pp. 53, 57 f.; *Postscript*, pp. 238, 477; *Works of Love*, pp. 233–46; *The Sickness unto Death*, pp. 166 ff., 170 ff., 205.

983. See *Stages* (tr. "reality"), p. 303.

984. *Plutarchs Moralische Abhandlungen*, tr. J. F. S. Kaltwasser, I–V, pts. 1–9 (Frankfurt/M: 1783), II, pp. 126 f. *ASKB* 1192–96.

985. See Matthew 15:32 ff.

986. Matthew 6:33.

987. See *Postscript*, pp. 282 f., 292, 295, 298, 302–4, 320.

988. See ibid., pp. 347 f.

989. See note 987.

990. See LEAP.

991. See, for example, *For Self-Examination*, pp. 12 ff.

PRACTICALITY, SENSIBLENESS

Søren Kierkegaard is often ironical about men's prudence, sensibleness, and sense for "the practical." He uses these terms when he wants to characterize the attitude which first and foremost aims at results in the secular, temporal world. At the esthetic level this attitude can result in deliberating so interminably that one "never allows the matter to go to judgment and decision in action" *Two Ages* [*The Present Age*, p. 3, ed. tr.]). Within the relationship to God, a man's prudence and practical common sense can result in his trusting his own opinion as to what is beneficial instead of relying on God (see, for example, *Upbuilding Discourses in Various Spirits*, Part one [*Purity of Heart*, pp. 164 ff.] and Part Two [*What We Learn from the Lilies of the Field and the Birds of the Air*], together with Part Three [*The Gospel of Suffering*, p. 186]). "Just when prudence is able to perceive advantage, faith cannot see God" (ibid., p. 32, ed. tr.). Ultimately "practical common sense" becomes "rebellion against the unconditioned," so that there is less and less concern "about God's requirement, about ideals" (*Judge for Yourselves!*, pp. 168 f., ed. tr.). When it becomes a matter of practicing Christianity, the requirement to give up human prudence and practical common sense is greatly intensified, inasmuch as for all relative τέλη (ends) Christianity actually reverses the relationship (X^2 A 154) in such a way that "the practicing of Christianity" in this world will appear to be "most impractical" (VIII^1 A 510). "Practical common sense" has perceived this for a long time, and this is why attempts are made to accommodate Christianity "to practical life and actuality." Thus Kierkegaard takes Mynster to task for believing "that it does not help any to require so much" (VIII^1 A 510). But thereby one is not only led into a "dreadful demoralization" but he is also prevented from pressing through toward "making decisions toward a dénouement" (X^4 A 416), which exposes his impotence.

On the themes of practicality, sensibleness, calculation of security, small-mindedness, etc. in the works, see, for example, *Either/Or*, II, pp. 43, 105; *Upbuilding* [*Edifying*] *Discourses*, III, p. 31; IV, pp. 85 f.; *The Concept of Anxiety* [*Dread*], pp. 26, 27, 63, 74 fn., 141 f.; *Stages*, pp. 71 f., 152, 155, 376, 444; *Postscript* (*S.V.*, VII, p. 259, on job-view of education; "philistinely" omitted in present English edition, p. 268), 346, 394, 482 f., 486 f; *Two Ages* [*The Present Age*, pp. 3 ff. (see note 1005), 15, 61]; *Works of Love*, pp. 25, 32; *Judge for Yourselves!*, pp. 131, 168, 208 ff.; *The Sickness unto Death*, pp. 159 f., 174 f., 189 ff., 232, 238; *Attack*, p. 203; " 'The Single Individual' Two 'Notes' Concerning My Work as an Author," Appendix to *The Point of View*, p. 109.

992. Matthew 11:6, see *Practice* [*Training*] *in Christianity*, pp. 86 ff. See OFFENSE.

993. See *Judge for Yourselves!*, pp. 208 ff.

994. See *Attack on Christendom*, p. 203.

995. See " 'The Single Individual' Two 'Notes' Concerning My Work as an Author," appendix to *The Point of View*, p. 109.

996. *Practice [Training] in Christianity*, pt. I, pp. 5 ff.

997. See *Postscript*, pp. 486 f.

998. See *Practice [Training] in Christianity*, p. 46.

999. See *Upbuilding Discourses in Various Spirits*, Part One [*Purity of Heart*, passim].

1000. See *Judge for Yourselves!*, p. 168.

1001. See *Postscript*, pp. 486 f.

1002. . . . that is not a middle course, it is no course at all, to play the part of men who have been merely awaiting the event with the intention of adapting our counsels to the decisions of fortune.

1003. See *Works of Love*, p. 32.

1004. Ibid.

1005. See *Two Ages* [*The Present Age*, p. 3 et passim], noting, however, that *den forstandige* and *Forstandighed* have been translated as "understanding" there, rather than as "practicality," "sensibleness."

1006. Plato, *Republic* 407 a.

1007. "As soon as a man has a livelihood, he should practice virtue."

1008. *Platons Stat*, tr. C. J. Heise (Copenhagen: 1851), p. 292. *ASKB* 1167.

1009. A. Schopenhauer, *Preisschrift über die Grundlage der Moral* (Frankfurt/M: 1841), para. 13. *ASKB* 772.

1010. M. P. Kierkegaard, a fine conversationalist and splendid storyteller.

1011. Johan H. Wessel, *Kierligheden uden Strømper*, V, 3.

PRAYER, PRAYERS

Kierkegaard began writing short prayers into his journals after his experience of "an indescribable joy" on May 19, 1838. After having lived for a few years as an esthete, this experience meant for him a return to the religious outlook inculcated by his father. From now on Kierkegaard sought to look at his life in the light of the God-relationship. He struggled for clarity about how a person comes closer to God. That this can only happen through existential experiences he makes clear in the following significant journal entry: "But it takes a long time before one really finds his way into the divine economy, comes to be at home there (knows where each thing has its place); he fumbles about amid a multiplicity of moods, does not even know how one ought to pray; Christ does not come to have any definite configuration in us—one does not know what the aid of the spirit means etc." (II A 756). Through the prayer entries in the journals over the next few years we can follow Kierkegaard's existential experience of man's impotence, solicitude, and mercy. Through these experiences he learned first and foremost that without God man achieves nothing at all (II A 327). In a gripping prayer, Kierkegaard speaks of feeling like someone who has lost his way and now wants to come back, and he asks God's help to walk his way, bound even more firmly to the Savior as his bondservant, now and for all eternity (II A 538).

During these years Kierkegaard's experience of man's absolute dependence upon God shapes the religious background for all his upbuilding or edifying works. For example, the thought that without God man "achieves nothing at all" (II A 327) is expanded to the edifying discourse "Man's Need of God is Man's Highest Perfection" (*Upbuilding* [*Edifying*] *Discourses*, IV, pp. 7 ff.), just as his own personal struggle with various woes (III A 32) suggests the overcoming of these cares in the discourse about the lilies of the field and the birds of the air (see *Upbuilding Discourses in Various Spirits*, Part Two [*What We Learn from the Lilies of the Field and the Birds of the Air*], together with *The Gospel of Suffering*, pp. 168 ff.; *Christian Discourses*, pp. 7 ff.; *The Lily of the Field and the Bird of the Air*, together with ibid., pp. 311 ff.). We find a reminder of III A 86 —that "Everything comes from God" and that God "satisfies everything that lives with his blessing"—in the motif of the prayer introducing his first discourse on the unchangeableness of God (*Upbuilding* [*Edifying*] *Discourses*, I, pp. 34 ff.), which is based on the Epistle of James 5:17. Kierkegaard uses this text repeatedly (*Upbuilding* [*Edifying*] *Discourses*, II, pp. 27 ff., 44 ff.), and he returns to it again in his last edifying discourse (*The Unchangeableness of God*, together with *Judge for Yourselves!*, pp. 223 ff.), published at the conclusion of the battle with the Church.

In the journal entry referred to above (II A 756), Kierkegaard declares that to begin with we do not even know "how we should pray." In 1844 he has come so far as to write in an edifying discourse that "the man praying aright strives in prayer and conquers—in that God conquers" (*Upbuilding* [*Edifying*] *Discourses*, IV, pp. 113 f.). In a later discourse he points out that "the mightiest is he who rightly folds his hands" (*Three Discourses on Imagined Occasions* [*Thoughts on Crucial Situations*, p. 13]). The might and power possessed by this "pray-er who prays aright" is still more strongly depicted in the following entry: "The Archimedean point outside the world is a prayer chamber where a true man of prayer prays in all honesty—and he will move the world" (IX A 115).

Kierkegaard as a pray-er learns to know ever new aspects of the God-relationship—for example, what it means to pray in Jesus' name (X^2 A 77). In later years, when Kierkegaard steadily intensifies the requirements for being a Christian, he also struggles to clarify how he himself should venture out, and through this learns that in order to become an obedient instrument in God's hand he must pray the prayer of "silent, trusting understanding with God" (X^2 A 595). In this confident frame of mind Kierkegaard begins his last difficult task —the attack upon Christendom. Now he has to ask himself if he has the courage to pray as a "witness-to-the-truth" that God will "give him strength to endure the suffering" (X^4 A 565).

For Kierkegaard, the truth for every situation in his life was that "to pray is to breathe" (IX A 462 and *The Sickness unto Death*, p. 173).

For references or examples of prayer in the works, see, for example, *Either/Or*, II, pp. 48, 51, 247, 319 f., 343; *Upbuilding [Edifying] Discourses*, I, pp. 6, 34, 48 f., 92; *Repetition*, pp. 8 f., 100; *Upbuilding [Edifying] Discourses*, II, p. 44; III, p. 8, 59 f.; IV, pp. 27, 31 ff., 53 f., 113 ff., 127 ff., 131 ff., 141 f.; *Three Discourses on Imagined Occasions [Thoughts on Crucial Situations*, pp. 1 f.]; *Stages*, pp. 219, 225, 237, 320, 368; *Postscript*, pp. 83, 145, 179 f., 389 fn., 435; *Upbuilding Discourses in Various Spirits*, Part One [*Purity of Heart*, pp. 31, 51, 182]; Part Three [*The Gospel of Suffering*, pp. 4, 53 f., 78 f.]; *Works of Love*, pp. 19, 64; *Christian Discourses*, pp. 18 f., 54, 67, 78, 176 f., 182; *Discourses at the Communion on Fridays*, together with *Christian Discourses*, pp. 259, 269, 275, 283, 289, 297, 305; *The Lily of the Field and the Bird of the Air*, together with *Christian Discourses*, pp. 315, 322, 344, 354 f.; *The Sickness unto Death*, pp. 174 f., 234, 260 fn.; *Three Discourses at the Communion on Fridays*, together with *Christian Discourses*, pp. 361, 371, 374 f., 379; *Practice [Training] in Christianity*, pp. 151, 156, 252 ff.; *Two Discourses at the Communion on Fridays*, together with *Judge for Yourselves!*, pp. 7, 18; *For Self-Examination*, pp. 7, 37, 63, 85, 104; *Judge for Yourselves!*, pp. 113, 161; *The Point of View*, pp. 52, 68, 116; *Attack*, p. 152; *The Unchangeableness of God*, together with *Judge for Yourselves!*, p. 227.

Barber, Samuel. *Prayers of Kierkegaard*. New York: G. Schirmer, 1954.

Le Fevre, Perry, ed. *The Prayers of Kierkegaard*. Chicago: University of Chicago Press, 1956.

Morier, J. P. "Subject Lesson. The Prayers of Kierkegaard." *Time and Tide* (London), 1957.

1012. See *Upbuilding [Edifying] Discourses*, IV, pp. 31 ff., *Postscript*, p. 435.

1013. See Eusebius, *Kirkens Historie gennem de tre første Aarhundrede*, tr. C. A. Muus (Copenhagen: 1832), p. 97. *ASKB* U 37.

1014. Philippians 2:12.

1015. Romans 8:15.

1016. Ibid.

1017. See *Upbuilding [Edifying] Discourses*, IV, pp. 27, 126 f.

1018. See *The Unchangeableness of God*, together with *Judge for Yourselves!*, pp. 226 ff.; *Upbuilding Discourses in Various Spirits*, Part One [*Purity of Heart*, p. 51]; *Christian Discourses*, p. 54; *Discourses at the Communion on Fridays*, together with *Christian Discourses*, p. 275.

1019. See *Upbuilding Discourses in Various Spirits*, Part One [*Purity of Heart*, p. 182].

1020. Luke 17:11 ff.

1021. See *Upbuilding [Edifying] Discourses*, I, p. 34.

1022. Seventh Sunday after Trinity, July 25 in 1841.

1023. In 1840 (July 19–August 6) Kierkegaard made a journey, almost a pilgrimage, to Sæding in Jutland, where his father, Michael Pedersen Kierkegaard, was born and grew up. The reference here is to a journal kept during that time: *Papirer* III A 14–84 (to appear in *Søren Kierkegaard's Journals and Papers*, V).

1024. *Upbuilding [Edifying] Discourses*, I, p. 34.

1025. See *Repetition*, p. 145.

1026. See *Upbuilding [Edifying] Discourses*, IV, pp. 131 ff.

1027. No. 2, the second of *Three Upbuilding Discourses*, published in 1843, is entitled "Love Shall Cover a Multitude of Sins."

1028. See *Postscript*, p. 145.

1029. See *Works of Love*, p. 20; *Christian Discourses*, pp. 202 f.; *Discourse at the Communion on Fridays*, together with *Christian Discourses*, p. 289.

1030. See *Upbuilding [Edifying] Discourses*, I, pp. 34 ff., 92; II, pp. 27 ff., 45 ff.; *Upbuilding Discourses in Various Spirits*, Part Two [*What We Learn from the Lilies of the Field and the Birds of the Air*, together with *The Gospel of Suffering*, p. 168].

1031. See *Upbuilding [Edifying] Discourses*, III, p. 59.

1032. Ibid., IV, pp. 113, 117 ff., 120 ff., 131 ff.

1033. See *Three Discourses on Imagined Occasions* [*Thoughts on Crucial Situations*, pp. 1 f.]. Entry is from draft.

1034. Matthew 5:8.

1035. See VI B 160; *Upbuilding Discourses in Various Spirits*, Part One [*Purity of Heart*, pp. 31 f.].

1036. Ibid. See VI B 154.

1037. See *Upbuilding Discourses in Various Spirits*, Part One [*Purity of Heart*, pp. 131 f., 142].

1038. This entry is from a draft of "Purity of Heart," Part One of *Upbuilding Discourses in Various Spirits*. A version of VI B 154 was used instead of this.

1039. See *Either/Or*, II, pp. 48, 247; *Upbuilding Discourses in Various Spirits*, Part One [*Purity of Heart*, p. 182].

1040. See ibid., Part Three [*The Gospel of Suffering*, pp. 53 ff.]. Kierkegaard frequently employs the elemental meanings and roots of words to clarify and sharpen an idea or relationship. Here, after stressing the poles of praying and hearing, he enriches both by joining hearing (the one who hears, *den Hørende*) to being obedient (*hørig*).

1041. Entries VII¹ A 129–46 (written during a visit to Berlin, May 2–May 16, 1846) include some which are serially numbered, with occasional unnumbered intervening entries, from 1 to 12. Number 5 is missing or the number has been omitted, and there are two entries (VII¹ A 142, 143) with the number 10. Most, but not all, of the numbered entries are prayers, and they are similar to those in the various upbuilding or edifying discourses. Number 4 (VII¹ A 134), number 8 (VII¹ A 138), number 11 (VII¹ A 144), and number 12 (VII¹ A 146) are in *Søren Kierkegaard's Journals and Papers*, I. Number 9 (VII¹ A 141) and number 10 (VII¹ A 143) are in ibid., II.

1042. See *The Lily of the Field and the Bird of the Air,* together with *Christian Discourses,* p. 322; also *For Self-Examination,* pp. 55 ff.

1043. See note 1030.

1044. See *Christian Discourses,* p. 289.

1045. Luke 15:11 ff.

1046. See note 1030.

1047. See *Christian Discourses,* pp. 111 f., 174 f.

1048. See *Works of Love,* pp. 353 f.

1049. See *Stages on Life's Way,* p. 320.

1050. See ibid.; *The Lily of the Field and the Bird of the Air,* together with *Christian Discourses,* p. 234.

1051. Hebrews 2:11.

1052. Luke 12:20.

1053. See *Practice [Training] in Christianity,* p. 151.

1054. Ibid.

1055. Ibid.

1056. John 16:24.

1057. See *Works of Love,* p. 64.

1058. Acts 7:60.

1059. This entry was not used in *The Sickness unto Death,* presumably for the reason given here (see ibid., pp. 142 f.). The title originally read *The Sickness unto Death. A Christian Upbuilding (opbyggelige) Exposition in the Form of a Discourse.* "Upbuilding" was changed to "Psychological." For a brief discussion of Kierkegaard's distinction among various forms of presentation, see *Works of Love,* Introduction, pp. 11 ff.

1060. *Either/Or,* I, p. 291; II, p. 270; *Repetition,* p. 94; *Postscript,* pp. 61, 93, 375; *Works of Love,* p. 138; *On Authority and Revelation,* p. 43.

1061. Luke 18:22.

1062. See *Christian Discourses,* pp. 78, 275.

1063. See *The Point of View,* p. 52.

1064. *Johann Arndt's Vier Bücher vom wahren Christentum* (Schiffbeck b. Hamburg: 1721).

1065. See note 1050.

1066. *Evangelisk-christelig Psalmebog* (Copenhagen: 1845), pp. 18 f. *ASKB* 197.

1067. See *Works of Love,* pp. 353 f.

1068. *Fenelons Sämmtliche Werke,* pts. 1–5, I–II (Leipzig: 1872), *ASKB* 1912–13; *Fenelons Werke religiösen Inhalts,* tr. M. Claudius, I–III (Hamburg: 1822), *ASKB* 1914.

1069. See *Repetition,* p. 109; *Stages,* p. 225; *Postscript,* p. 83.

1070. L. Holberg, *Erasmus Montanus,* I, 4.

1071. See *Upbuilding [Edifying] Discourses,* I, pp. 48 f.; III, p. 8.

1072. See ibid., IV, p. 27.

1073. See *The Gospel of Suffering,* pp. 47 ff.

1074. See *For Self-Examination,* pp. 7 f.

1075. See ibid., p. 63.

1076. *Johann Arndt,* pp. 296 f., 304.

1077. See *Either/Or,* II, p. 40.

1078. See *The Sickness unto Death,* p. 260 fn.

1079. See *Judge for Yourselves!,* p. 161.

1080. Christian Scriver, *Seelen-Schatz* (Leipzig: 1715).

1081. See note 1042.

1082. A. G. Rudelbach, *Hieronymus Savonarola und seine Zeit* (Hamburg: 1835).

1083. Johann Arndt, *Sechs Bücher vom Wahren Christenthume und dessen Paradiesgärtlein* (Leipzig: 1842), pp. 24 f.

PREACHING, PROCLAMATION

Kierkegaard's pseudonym Climacus declares that the sermon corresponds "to the essentially Christian, and to the sermon there corresponds a pastor, and a pastor is essentially what he is through ordination" (*Postscript,* p. 244). Later Kierkegaard stressed more strongly that where authority to preach is concerned, agreement between the pastor's life and his preaching is more important than ordination. Kierkegaard came very early to the awareness that a proclaimer's actions should stand in relationship to his proclamation (V A 12), but there is a long way to go for a proclaimer, too, before one experiences what the Christian life means. Kierkegaard describes this road in his upbuilding works, and it proceeds from the "ethical categories of immanence" in the direction of confrontation with the paradox (*Postscript,* p. 229). A person must then experience that Christianity is an "existential contradiction" and an "existential communication" (ibid., p. 339), and therefore for the single individual it means the transformation of existence, which in itself is the best sermon for others. Kierkegaard voices this in many places; for example, he says that the pastor's task in the most profound sense is "preaching with his life" (X^2 A 149; see also X^3 A 237, 307, etc.). He details the proclaimer's task thus: "(1) witnessing, (2) using authority, (3) then offering a life which is willing to take the consequences of this" (X^3 A 288).

In connection with his criticism of the pastors of the day, found in various later writings, Kierkegaard gives copious advice and instructions on the preparation of a sermon. For example, when gentleness is proclaimed, severity should not be omitted (*Practice* [*Training*] *in Christianity,* pp. 221 ff.), nor should the difficulties the Christian will encounter when he attempts to actualize Christianity's requirement. Kierkegaard also declares that if the rigorousness of Christianity is not stressed, it will not be possible to comfort those who feel like social misfits because of their heavy sufferings (X^3 A 129). Moreover, the sermon should be personal and directed to the single individual (X^2 A 230). Kierkegaard touches on this particularly in *Practice* [*Training*] *in Christianity* (pp.

227 ff.) in his criticism of Mynster's preaching, which to him consisted predominantly of objective "meditations" that did not encourage imitation. Kierkegaard points out in one place that "a penitent can best proclaim the truth" (X^3 A 271). This applies not only to Peter and Paul, whom he mentions, but also to Søren Kierkegaard himself.

Kierkegaard worked until the end with the question of authentic preaching, but did not believe that he had the authority to preach to others; this is why he does not call his religious discourses "sermons" (see note 1059). Even his last published discourse (*The Unchangeableness of God*, together with *Judge for Yourselves!*, pp. 223 ff.), which was preached as a sermon in Citadel Church and was an attempt on his part to clarify whether it was his future task to preach (X^4 A 323), Kierkegaard does not call a sermon.

Dargan, Edwin Charles. *A History of Preaching*. New York: Hodder & Stoughton, 1912.

Holmer, Paul. "Kierkegaard and the Sermon." *Journal of Religion*, 1957.

For references in the works to preaching, see, for example, *Either/ Or*, II, pp. 71 f., 109, 341 ff.; *Upbuilding [Edifying] Discourses*, I, pp. 5, 59; *Fear and Trembling*, pp. 40, 63; *Upbuilding [Edifying] Discourses*, II, p. 5; III, pp. 5, 69; IV, p. 5; *The Concept of Anxiety [Dread]*, p. 14; *Prefaces, S. V.*, pp. 35 ff.; *Three Discourses on Imagined Occasions [Thoughts on Crucial Situations*, pp. 8 f.]; *Stages*, pp. 139 f., 150, 168, 207, 211, 222, 281 f., 314, 419, *Postscript*, pp. 148, 191, 193, 201, 210, 217, 229, 239, 242, 243 fn., 254, 307, 334, 361, 374 fn., 425 f., 429, 436 f., 442, 461 fn., 478, 482, 526; *Upbuilding Discourses in Various Spirits*, Part Three [*The Gospel of Suffering*, pp. 3, 73 ff., 150 f.]; Part One [*Purity of Heart*, pp. 27 f., 179 ff.]; *Works of Love*, pp. 185 ff., 190, 192 f., 292 f.; *Christian Discourses*, pp. 171 f., 193 f., 195 f., 201 f., 224, 257, 267, 277; "Has a Man the Right to Let Himself Be Put to Death for the Truth?" together with *The Present Age*, p. 100; "Of the Difference between a Genius and an Apostle," ibid., p. 149 fn.; *The Sickness unto Death*, pp. 235, 248, 260 fn.; *Practice [Training] in Christianity*, pp. 97, 109, 111, 115 f., 134 f., 143, 173, 222 f., 227 f., 229 f., 240, 250; *Two Discourses at the Communion on Fridays*, together with *Judge for Yourselves!*, p. 19; *For Self-Examination*, pp. 3 ff., 14, 17, 18 f., 43, 63; *Judge for Yourselves!*, pp. 116, 125, 126 ff., 141, 170, 174, 179, 197 f.; *S.V.*, XIII, pp. 416 f.; " 'The Single Individual' Two 'Notes' Concerning My Work as an Author," Appendix to *The Point of View*, p. 112 fn.; *Attack*, pp. 5 f., 11, 13, 14 f., 16, 18 f., 172 f., 201 f., 210, 243, 276.

1084. Peter J. Spang (1796–1846); reference is presumably to sermon on John 16:23–28 in Helliggeistes Kirke, Copenhagen, on May 12, 1844. See *Postscript*, p. 436 fn.

1085. See *Postscript*, pp. 371 f., 410; *Works of Love*, Introduction, pp. 11 ff.

1086. See ibid., p. 371.

1087. See *Postscript*, pp. 427 ff. and notes.

1088. See ibid., pp. 373 ff.

1089. See VI A 146.

1090. L. Holberg, *Erasmus Montanus*, I, 4.

1091. This entry is from a draft of *What We Learn from the Lilies of the Field and the Birds of the Air* (together with *The Gospel of Suffering* in English edition), p. 198, just before the final sentence of the first discourse.

1092. See PARADOX; *Postscript*, p. 201; *Practice* [*Training*] *in Christianity*, p. 109; *Judge for Yourselves!*, p. 125.

1093. See *Either/Or*, II, p. 109; *Practice* [*Training*] *in Christianity*, pp. 229 f.; *For Self-Examination*, pp. 3 ff.; *Kierkegaard's Attack upon Christendom*, pp. 5 f., 11, 14 f., 172 f.

1094. This entry is a marginal note to the ms. of *The Book on Adler*, omitted on p. 66 of English version under title *Authority and Revelation*.

1095. Aristoteles *Dichtkunst*, tr. C. Curtius (Hannover: 1753), p. 2. *ASKB* 1094.

1096. See *Fear and Trembling*, p. 40; *Works of Love*, pp. 185 ff., 192 f.; *Christian Discourses*, pp. 172 ff.

1097. See *Bogen om Adler* (VII^2 B 235), pp. 225 f., fn., omitted on p. 185 of *Authority and Revelation; Judge for Yourselves!*, pp. 141, 197 f.

1098. See *Works of Love*, p. 71.

1099. See *Practice* [*Training*] *in Christianity*, pp. 222 ff.

1100. Luke 10:23 ff.

1101. Matthew 25:31 ff.

1102. See *Either/Or*, I, p. 19.

1103. See *Postscript*, p. 374 fn.; "Has a Man the Right to Let Himself Be Put to Death for the Truth?" together with *The Present Age*, p. 100; *Attack*, p. 243.

1104. See ibid., pp. 268 ff.

1105. See *Evangelisk-christelig Psalmebog* (Copenhagen: 1845), p. 4. *ASKB* 197.

1106. See *For Self-Examination*, p. 43; *Attack*, pp. 201 f.

1107. See ibid., pp. 227 ff.; *Judge for Yourselves!*, pp. 197 f.

1108. See *Practice* [*Training*] *in Christianity*, pp. 227 ff.

1109. See *Judge for Yourselves!*, p. 179.

1110. See *Postscript*, pp. 229, 374 fn.; *Works of Love*, p. 190, 192 f.; *Practice* [*Training*] *in Christianity*, p. 250; *For Self-Examination*, pp. 3–5.

1111. Peter J. Spang (1796–1846). See *Prædikener og Leilighedstaler*, Foreword by H. D. Kopp, (Copenhagen: 1847), pp. vi ff.

1112. See *Attack*, pp. 5 f., 172 f.

1113. See *For Self-Examination*, p. 14.

1114. See *Stages on Life's Way*, p. 419.

1115. H. L. Martensen became court preacher in 1845. See *Attack*, p. 276.

1116. See *For Self-Examination*, pp. 42 ff.

1117. Luke 7:12 ff.

1118. M. Luther, *En christelig Postille,* (see note 81), I, p. 534.

1119. Carl H. Visby, pastor of Vor Frelsers Kirke (now with outside tower-stairway) in Christianshavn, the port area of Amager, a small island a few hundred yards off the main port area of Copenhagen. For years Visby (prison chaplain, 1826–44) had had special concern for prison inmates and prison conditions. Thus Visby's parish and his concerns were quite the opposite of those in a court setting.

1120. Parliamentary (*Folketing*) election, December 4, 1849.

1121. Matthew 7:7, text for the First Sunday after Trinity, January 13 in 1850.

1122. Reference to a phrase by N. F. S. Grundtvig emphasizing the continuity of oral tradition and the vitality of the spoken word.

1123. See Seneca, *De ira*, III, 17, 3 f., on the treatment of Telesphorus by Lysimachus.

1124. See note 1106.

1125. On the preaching of J. P. Mynster, Bishop of Sjælland (Copenhagen) see, for example, *Prefaces, S.V.,* V, pp. 35 ff.; *Judge for Yourselves!,* p. 17; *Attack,* pp. 5 f., 13 ff.

1126. See *Works of Love,* pp. 185 ff., 190, 192 f.; *Christian Discourses,* pp. 201 f.; *Practice* [*Training*] *in Christianity,* pp. 109, 227 f., 250; "Has a Man the Right to Let Himself Be Put to Death for the Truth?" together with *The Present Age,* p. 100; *Judge for Yourselves!,* pp. 197 f.; *For Self-Examination,* p. 14; *Attack,* pp. 5 f., 172 f.

1127. See *Practice* [*Training*] *in Christianity,* pp. 115 f.

1128. See note 1126.

1129. See *For Self-Examination,* pp. 15 f.

1130. See note 1126.

1131. Ibid.

1132. Kierkegaard regarded authority as belonging to the apostle and to the Church in its mission of proclamation, therefore to ordination. See the repeated and also somewhat varied expression similar to this entry (an addition to the ms. of *Three Upbuilding Discourses,* 1843, in *Upbuilding* [*Edifying*] *Discourses,* I, p. 5); ibid., p. 49; II, p. 5; III, pp. 5, 69; IV, p. 5; *Three Discourses on Imagined Occasions* [*Thoughts on Crucial Situations in Human Life,* pp. 8 f.]; *Upbuilding Discourses in Various Spirits,* Part Two [*What We Learn from the Lilies of the Field and the Birds of the Air,* together with *The Gospel of Suffering,* p. 167]; "Of the Difference between a Genius and an Apostle," together with *The Present Age,* p. 149 fn.; *For Self-Examination,* pp. 18 f.

1133. See *Judge for Yourselves!,* p. 125.

1134. See note 1126.

1135. Jørgen O. Thisted (1795–1855), pastor, writer, translator, editor.

1136. See *For Self-Examination,* p. 63.

1137. Quintilian, *Institutio Oratoria,* VI, 2, 35; see *For Self-Examination,* p. 13.

1138. Ibid., VI, 2, 36.

1139. See *Attack*, pp. 201 f.

1140. See *For Self-Examination*, pp. 22 f.

1141. See ibid., pp. 16 ff.

1142. See note 1106; *Attack*, pp. 201 f.

1143. H. L. Martensen, professor of theology, Bishop Mynster's successor and the particular present object whom Kierkegaard was later to "write against."

1144. Kierkegaard's one request or demand: an admission, specifically from Bishop Mynster, that Christianity had been modified, domesticated, accommodated to human goals and desires. This he regarded as an act of simple human honesty. See, for example, *Armed Neutrality* and *An Open Letter*, index, "Admission"; *Attack*, pp. 6 f. fn.

1145. See *Armed Neutrality* and *An Open Letter*, passim.

1146. See *Upbuilding Discourses in Various Spirits*, Part One [*Purity of Heart*, pp. 180 f.].

1147. See note 1113.

1148. H. V. Paulli (1809–1865), pastor of Christiansborg Castle Church.

1149. See, for example, *Practice [Training] in Christianity*, pp. 222 f., 227 f.

1150. See note 1144.

1151. See *Fear and Trembling*, p. 40.

1152. See *For Self-Examination*, pp. 1 ff.

1153. See notes 1125 and 1144.

1154. *Apology*, 34 c ff.; see *For Self-Examination*, pp. 1 ff.

1155. See *Armed Neutrality* and *An Open Letter*, passim.

1156. See *Fear and Trembling*, p. 40.

1157. See note 1126.

1158. See *Works of Love*, pp. 199 ff.

1159. J. L. Heiberg, *Recensenten og Dyret* (Copenhagen: 1827), sc. 15.

1160. By Alcibiades in *Symposium*, 221 e-f.

1161. See *Upbuilding Discourses in Various Spirits*, Part One [*Purity of Heart*, pp. 27 f., 180 f.]; *Works of Love*, p. 190; *Christian Discourses*, pp. 201 f.; *Practice [Training] in Christianity*, p. 250; *Attack*, pp. 201 f.

1162. See note 1126.

1163. See note 1106.

1164. *Evangelisk-christelig Psalmebog* (Copenhagen: 1845), pp. 337 f., 350 f. *ASKB* 197.

1165. See *The Sickness unto Death*, p. 224.

1166. See *Prefaces*, *S.V.*, V, p. 47; *Historie om Tiile Ugelspegel* (Copenhagen: n.d.). *ASKB* 1469.

1167. See *The Concept of Anxiety [Dread]*, p. 61; *Attack upon Christendom*, p. 30.

1168. See note 1113.

1169. See notes 1137 and 1138.

PREDESTINATION

In the early summer of 1843 Søren Kierkegaard was tutored (lectures and discussions) by divinity graduate H. L. Martensen (later professor and bishop) in Schleiermacher's *Dogmatics.* * Martensen observes[†] that when they were going through the doctrine of election, Kierkegaard's "bent for sophistry" became especially apparent. However, it was Kierkegaard's keenness and thoroughness that did not allow him to relinquish the subject until he had grasped it. Kierkegaard worked very persistently on the problem of predestination in the days following, as revealed by his preoccupation with this theme in many of the earliest journal entries dating from the summer of 1834.

It gradually became clear to Kierkegaard that Schleiermacher's stress on the strict Calvinistic doctrine of predestination, according to which God predetermines everything, brings his teaching in close relationship to Hegel's philosophy: for both of them "a necessary development" takes place—according to Schleiermacher, because God alone determines everything, and according to Hegel, because the idea develops according to the principle of necessity (I A 170). But since Kierkegaard, in opposition to this view, maintained from the beginning the idea of man's freedom and the significance of decision, he could not accept a strict predestination because it denies the importance of human freedom. Since the doctrine of predestination does not solve the central problem of the relationship between "freedom and God's omnipotence," Kierkegaard calls it an "abortion" (I A 5). Moreover, he points out that accepting predestination leads to new difficulties—for example, he says that "a strict doctrine of predestination traces the origin of evil back to God" (I A 2).

Kierkegaard also points out that a distinction must be made between God's predetermining and God's foreknowledge (I A 20) in that the latter does not exclude human freedom in advance. This position, for which Kierkegaard finds support in Boëthius, is utilized by Climacus in the "Interlude" (*Philosophical Fragments*, pp. 98 f.; see also IV C 40).

In 1836 Kierkegaard arrived at a "solution of the problem of predestination" in the idea that predestination means that "the whole of Christianity, its manifestation in its wholeness, was determined from eternity," and that those who are called by meeting Christianity are thereby chosen for salvation or perdition (I C 40, I A 295; see also II A 399). According to Kierkegaard, this view, which is based on Romans 8:28, is similar to Schleiermacher's position that there can be no mention of predestination until man confronts Christianity.

This primary concept of predestination expressed in I A 295 is found again in the works, including *The Concept of Anxiety* [*Dread*], pp. 55 f., where Vigilius Haufniensis declares: "sin presupposes itself, not of course before it

*F. Schleiermacher, *Der christliche Glaube* (Berlin: 1830).
[†]See H. L. Martensen, *Af mit Levnet* (Copenhagen: 1882–83), p. 78.

is posited (that would be predestination). . . ." This means that a person first appears as sinner in his meeting Christ, but at the same time he manifests whether he is destined for salvation or for perdition, depending on whether he accepts God's offer of grace or rejects it.

Kierkegaard indicates many times that the very idea of predestination may have unfortunate results in the lives of individual men. For example, a man can be prevented from arriving at an ethical view of life from an esthetic position by being "ensnared by one expression or other of the theory of predestination" (*Either/Or*, II, p. 237), and the unhappy man who feels "predestined to pity" can be led to the demonic (*Fear and Trembling*, p. 151). Nevertheless, a person's acceptance of predestination may also be the humble explanation that he can be saved despite his sin (*Stages*, p. 431); whereas one who looks upon Christianity as a special "favor" particularly for his benefit makes himself guilty in "the desperate presumption of predestination" (*Postscript*, p. 516).

It is characteristic of Kierkegaard not to accept the strict doctrine of predestination that eliminates human freedom and decision. Contrary to Schleiermacher, who from an "esthetic-metaphysical" standpoint regards Christianity "only as a condition," Kierkegaard from an ethical and religious standpoint regards Christianity "as striving" and decision (X^2 A 417).

For various observations and allusions to predestination, see, for example, *Either/Or*, II, pp. 135, 237; *The Concept of Anxiety* [*Dread*], pp. 55 f.; *Fragments*, pp. 98 f.; *Stages on Life's Way*, p. 431; *Postscript*, p. 516.

1170. See *The Concept of Anxiety* [*Dread*], p. 102.

1171. See *The Concept of Irony*, p. 290.

1172. Origen, *Epist. ad Roman. Comm.*, VII, 7 ff.; Romans 8:28 ff.

1173. G. W. Leibniz, *Theodicee* (Hannover, Leipzig: 1763), p. 594. *ASKB* 619.

1174. Ibid., p. 619.

1175. Ibid., pp. 624 ff.

1176. See *Fragments*, p. 99.

1177. G. W. Leibniz.

PRESENTIMENT

In his journals Kierkegaard mentions that while growing up he often had misgivings (*bange Anelser*) about what awaited him in the future (IV A 144). He tried quite early to fathom the nature of presentiment, and in the first attempt (1837) he says that there must always be elements in consciousness that allow for presentiment in such a way that it does not appear "as the conclusion of given premises but always manifests itself in an undefined something" and in this way engenders uneasiness. Nevertheless, simply because of these "elements in consciousness," presentiment must be regarded as an aspect of a normal constitution (II A 22).

A journal entry (II A 558) from a few years later (1839) illuminates the way presentiment arises. With the aid of a diagram he explains how a person in the present, by becoming absorbed in the future, will be able to have presentiments of possibilities in the future. Therefore presentiment has a close relation to the category of possibility, which also points to the future. But the future possibilities that generally occupy men are always somewhat rationally grounded, whereas the possibilities of presentiment have a more ambiguous cast. Yet presentiment can approach sure knowledge, and therefore he can speak of "the infinite approximation of presentiment" (*The Concept of Irony*, p. 332).

According to Kierkegaard, presentiment may be regarded from various perspectives. There are presentiments designated as "historical presentiments," those which arise when one becomes absorbed in the driving forces of history. The "prophetic statement" about the future is also a form of presentiment, but with a religious background (II A 589). A special form of prophetic presentiment is found in Kierkegaard's characterization of himself as "a presentiment-filled individual who has indeed rightly oriented himself to the history of the future, to the turning which is to be made and which will be the history of the future" (IX B 64, p. 379).

Presentiment can also refer to purely personal matters; there are many examples in the journals, such as in X^5 A 146, p. 151: "There are two thoughts which were present in my soul so early that I really cannot say when they arose." One was that he was supposed to be "sacrificed for others in order to advance the idea," and the other was that he "would never be tested in trying to work for results." Possibly Kierkegaard considered that these thoughts arose in connection with his special qualifications and task.

As a psychologist, too, Kierkegaard had an interest in presentiment. He gives an example of how an experienced observer, on the basis of a person's single utterance, by a "concentration of presentiment" can get a survey of all the consequences in his life (*Repetition*, p. 29).

For uses of the term "presentiment" variously translated in the works, see, for example, *Either/Or*, I, pp. 33, 59, 64, 74, 75, 146; II, p. 117; *Repetition*, p. 29; *The Concept of Anxiety* [*Dread*], p. 55: *Upbuilding* [*Edifying*] *Discourses*, I, p. 39; II, p. 28; *Stages*, p. 388; *Postscript*, pp. 95, 484, f.; *The Concept of Irony*, pp. 130, 131, 134, 319, 335; *Johannes Climacus, or De omnibus dubitandum est*, pp. 122 ff.

1178. Clemens Brentano (1778–1842), German romantic poet and writer, "*Historien om den brave Kasper og skjøn Ane,*" *Harpen*, ed. A. P. Liunge, no. 53–60, 1820, included in *Phantasiestykker*, ed. A. P. Liunge (Copenhagen: 1821), pp. 80 ff.

1179. L. Achim von Arnim, Clemens Brentano, *Des Knaben Wunderhorn, Alte deutsche Lieder*, I-III (Heidelberg: 1806). *ASKB* 1494–96.

1180. Henrich Steffens, *De fire Normænd*, tr. J. R. Reiersen, I-III (Copenhagen: 1835). *ASKB* 1586–88.

1181. See *Postscript,* pp. 484 f.

1182. L. Achim von Armin, *Novellen,* ed. Wilhelm Grimm, I-VI (Berlin: 1839–42), I. *ASKB* 1612–17.

1183. Ibid.

1184. See note 1180.

1185. See *The Concept of Anxiety* [*Dread*], pp. 101 ff.

1186. See, for example, *Stages,* p. 263.

1187. See, for example, *The Concept of Irony,* p. 277; *Either/Or,* I, p. 83.

1188. See K. Rosenkranz, *Psychologie oder die Wissenschaft von subjectiven Geist* (Königsberg: 1837), p. 331. *ASKB* 744.

1189. See *The Concept of Anxiety* [*Dread*], p. 38. This entry is from a draft of p. 38.

PRIMITIVITY

For Kierkegaard the term "primitivity," or "the primitive," does not have the slightly disparaging ring of the undeveloped that it has in modern Danish. On the contrary, "primitivity" to Kierkegaard designates man's original and uncorrupted capacity to receive an impression without being influenced by "the others" (XI[1] A 62) or by current views.

Virgilius Haufniensis points out that this capacity manifests itself markedly in the genius, who is mainly differentiated from other men by the fact that within his historical presuppositions he consciously begins just as primitively as Adam did (*The Concept of Anxiety* [*Dread*], pp. 93 f., ed. tr.). He says further: "The genius is not as most people are . . . because he deals primitively with himself alone, and all other men and their explanations are of no help whatsover" (ibid., p. 96, ed. tr.). The genius's primitivity also reveals itself when the question arises of the relationship of freedom to fate or to guilt— "Here genius again shows itself by not leaping away from the primitive decision" (ibid., p. 97).

Climacus believes that in a reflected age the majority of men move "farther and farther away from the primitive existential impressions. . . . One does not love, does not believe, does not act, but knows what love is, what faith is . . ." (*Postscript,* p. 307, ed. tr.). When a person has "divested himself of his primitivity," he enters into "despairing narrowness," says Anti-Climacus in *The Sickness unto Death* (p. 166). In order for a man to become a single individual, become a self, he must go back to this primitivity so that he does not permit "his self to be defrauded by 'the others,' " "for every man is primitively planned as a self" (ibid.). But it is difficult for men who live "packed together all too closely" "to receive primitive impressions" (*Stages,* p. 346). A man's melancholy, which isolates him from others, may be of help by evoking the possibilities of human existence. Here, too, is the poet's task, since he must have the ability to experience primitively and to reproduce poetically the possibilities by which he may prompt in others "a primitive impression." On this point Climacus expresses his admiration for Lessing, "who had poetic

imagination enough to ... become contemporary with that event which occurred 1,812 years ago so primitively as to exclude every objectively-inverted
falsification" (*Postscript*, p. 61, ed. tr.).

Kierkegaard perceived that by means of his writings his task was to assist
men "whose misfortune it is to know too much" into a primitive relationship
to existence and especially to Christianity, the truth of which, "because everybody knows it, has gradually become such a triviality that it is difficult to get
a primitive impression of it" (ibid., p. 245).

Bugental, J. F. T. *Search for Authenticity.* Holt, 1965.

Henry, J. "The Term 'Primitive' in Kierkegaard and Heidegger" in A.
Montagu, ed., *The Concept of the Primitive.* New York: Free Press (Macmillan),
1968.

For references in the works to primitivity, see, for example, *The Concept
of Irony*, p. 66; *Fear and Trembling*, p. 130; *Fragments*, p. 124; *The Concept of Anxiety*
[*Dread*], pp. 23 (tr. "primordial"), 56 (tr. "pristine"), 93 f., 96 f.; *Stages* pp.
128, 346, 390; *Postscript*, pp. 61, 106, 245 fn., 250, 307; *Two Ages* [*The Present Age*,
p. 50 ("*der primitivt oplever noget*" translated as "who has a real experience")];
The Sickness unto Death, p. 50, *Practice* [*Training*] *in Christianity*, p. 88.

1190. See notes 839 and 849.

1191. See *Philosophical Fragments*, pp. 46 ff.

1192. See *The Concept of Irony*, p. 173.

1193. See *The Concept of Irony*, p. 66; *The Sickness unto Death*, p. 166.

1194. See *The Concept of Anxiety* [*Dread*], p. 94; *Stages*, p. 128; *Practice*
[*Training*] *in Christianity*, p. 88.

1195. See *Stages*, p. 390.

PROFESSOR

Søren Kierkegaard usually speaks more or less ironically of professors
and assistant professors; often his remarks are sharply critical and condemna-
tory. However, he objects neither to professors and scholarship in general nor
to theological scholarship in particular. His criticism is directed exclusively to
the professors and assistant professors in philosophy or theology who make
Christianity an object of scientific scholarship as "objective teaching, as mere
doctrine" (*Judge for Yourselves!*, p. 204) and completely forget the personal
relationship to it. He regards the steadily increasing influence of professors as
a sign that Christianity is disintegrating; they understand how to make everything vague and ambiguous, so that "the decision to become a Christian ...
is put off," so that "one can make life as comfortable as possible for oneself" (ibid., p. 204 ff.) and "evade doing God's will" (XI^2 A 376).

As the professor and assistant professor relate objectively to Christianity
instead of subjectively and passionately, they also seek to make it homogeneous with the world by explaining away the paradox in Christianity (see
Postscript, pp. 196 f.), but the professor is the very one who should "*comprehend*

that faith cannot be comprehended" (X¹ A 561). Instead of seeing his responsibility, the professor makes Christianity an occupation, makes "the sufferings of others into a paid career" (X⁴ A 398). By arranging to live off Christianity and at the same time calling himself its true friend and follower (XI¹ A 100), he acts in bad faith. In this way the professor and assistant professor intervene between the people and those who could be their true leaders, "the few who are truly in the service of God" (XI¹ A 473).

Kierkegaard believes that when it is the "professor" who misleads, the emphasis must be laid on "imitation" (*Judge for Yourselves!*, p. 205). Otherwise Christianity could well be smuggled out of the world with the help and countenance of "speculative theological professors" *Practice* [*Training*] *in Christianity*, p. 104).

For references in the works to professors see, for example, *Either/Or*, I, pp. 89, 205; *Fear and Trembling*, p. 73; *Fragments*, pp. 80, 120; *The Concept of Anxiety* [*Dread*], pp. 18, 120; *Postscript*, pp. 19, 112, 130, 134 fn., 154, 170 f., 172, 175, 181, 189, 194, 197, 202 fn., 203, 207, 224, 236, 249 ff., 266 fn., 282, 296, 308, 449 fn., 539, 541; *The Sickness unto Death*, p. 143; *Practice* [*Training*] *in Christianity*, pp. 98, 104, 123; *Judge for Yourselves!*, pp. 131, 134, 138, 145, 170, 189, 204 f.; *Attack*, pp. 5 f., 202, 219, 242, 275 f., 283.

1196. This entry is from a draft of *Concluding Unscientific Postscript;* see p. 203, also pp. 130, 170 f., 172, 282, 296, 308.

1197. L. Holberg, *Den Stundesløse*, I, 11.

1198. See *Fragments*, p. 120; *Postscript*, p. 197.

1199. See *Postscript*, pp. 99 ff.

1200. Jens Møller (1779–1833), professor of theology, University of Copenhagen 1808–.

1201. See *Postscript*, p. 346.

1202. See *The Sickness unto Death*, pp. 159 f., 174 f., 189 ff., 232, 238.

1203. See *Postscript*, pp. 170 f., 194, 250, 541; *Practice* [*Training*], *in Christianity*, p. 98; *Judge for Yourselves!*, pp. 131, 134, 138, 145, 170; *Attack*, pp. 5 f., 202, 219, 242.

1204. See Romans 12:6 ff.

1205. See *Postscript*, p. 198; *Practice* [*Training*] *in Christianity*, p. 104; *Judge for Yourselves!*, pp. 204 f.

1206. See *Postscript*, pp. 176 f., 276.

1207. See note 1205.

1208. Paul Henry, *Das Leben Johann Calvins* . . . , I–III (Hamburg: 1835–44), III, 1, pp. 209 ff.

1209. See *Fear and Trembling*, p. 73.

1210. This entry is from a draft of *Judge for Yourselves!;* see pp. 204 f.; also *Practice* [*Training*] *in Christianity*, p. 104.

1211. See *The Sickness unto Death*, pp. 208 ff.; *Works of Love*, pp. 59 ff.; *Practice* [*Training*] *in Christianity*, pp. 247 ff.; *Attack*, pp. 117, 201.

1212. Matthew 10:22, 24:9.

1213. Genesis 2:19 ff.

1214. Matthew 21:31.

1215. Matthew 27:46.

1216. See *Postscript*, pp. 202 fn., 541; *Attack*, p. 242.

1217. See J. V. Neergaard, *Hesteavlens Sørgerlige Forfald i Danmark* (Copenhagen: 1851), p. ix.; an advertisement of another publication on this theme appeared in *Addresseavisen*, no. 195, August 23, 1854.

1218. See, for example, *Attack*, p. 287.

1219. See note 791.

1220. See PERFECTIBILITY.

1221. See *Kinder- und Haus-Märchen, Gesammelt durch die Brüder Grimm*, I–III (Berlin: 1819), I, pp. 14 ff. *ASKB* 1425–27.

1222. Cyprian. See F. Böhringer, *Die Kirke Christi* (see note 355), I, 1, p. 424.

1223. See *For Self-Examination*, pp. 63 ff.

PROGRESS

Kierkegaard was mainly interested in man's ethical and religious development. He looked skeptically upon the glorification of external progress, whether technical, scientific, or social, because men are most often interested only in the quantitative—that is, in increasing their knowledge and control of the external world—but in this way a person faces the danger of being diverted from his real task of "relating himself to God only through the ethical" (VII[1] A 191). As far as the ethical is concerned, no external progress can lead man forward, for, as Kierkegaard says, "Qualitatively understood, in 100,000 years the world will not have advanced one single step" (VII[1] A 191). On the contrary, external progress most often leads to the leveling of ethical values; this is especially true of the natural sciences (see NATURAL SCIENCE).

Generally speaking, Kierkegaard believes that "the world goes neither forward nor backward, it remains essentially the same . . . ; it is and should be the element which can furnish the test for whether one is a Christian in it . . ." (*Practice* [*Training*] *In Christianity*, p. 226, ed. tr.).

In the works, see, for example, *Postscript*, pp. 164 ff., Johannes Climacus's whimsical musing upon the nineteenth century and its perfection through inventions; also *Fear and Trembling*, pp. 170 ff., on essential equality; and *The Sickness unto Death*, p. 223, on going beyond Socrates.

1224. See *Postscript*, p. 165.

1225. See *Postscript*, pp. 218, 246, 359, 360.

PROOF

According to Kierkegaard, all proof lies within the sphere of thought, where one proceeds from specific presuppositions and draws conclusions from them. We find the best example of this form of demonstration in logic, including mathematics, where a proof can be said to have absolute validity. In the sphere of being, however, there is a limit to rigorous demonstration, both because there are opposite possibilities (VII^1 A 215) and because, everything considered, it is impossible to reach being by a proof. To reach being there must be a transition from the sphere of demonstration (thought) to the sphere of actuality, a transition which can take place only by means of a leap. Climacus says of this: "Thus I always reason from existence, not toward existence, whether I move in the sphere of palpable sensible fact or in the world of thought" (*Fragments*, p. 50). The sensuous, immediate being neither can nor must be demonstrated, for it exists, and we always presuppose it when we draw conclusions about actuality. These conclusions are always leaps and may have more or less probability. But there is also a being which cannot be perceived or observed immediately, as, for example, the existence of God and the truth of Christianity, and it has always been within the interest of philosophy and of theology to reach this being by way of proofs. Like Kant, Kierkegaard totally rejects proofs of the existence of God. The most one can do is to use thought in "clarifying the concept of God" (ibid., p. 54), but the whole thing remains idea. Man can find the actuality of God only by means of the leap of faith. Kierkegaard goes so far as to say: "The idea of proving the existence [*Tilvær-else*] of God is of all things the most ridiculous. Either he exists [*er til*], and then one cannot prove it (no more than I can prove that a certain human being exists [*er til*]; the most I can do is to let something testify to it, but then I presuppose existence—or he does not exist, and then it cannot be proved at all" (V A 7; see also *Postscript*, pp. 485 f.).

Kierkegaard sharply protests proofs for the truth of Christianity as well as for Christ's being the God-man. In *Concluding Unscientific Postscript* Climacus rejects attempts to prove the truth of Christianity, whether by the "historical-critical" method (pp. 29 f.) or by "the proof of centuries" (p. 45; see also VI B 25), just as he vigorously attacks Hegel, who would prove the truth of Christianity by speculation. In *Practice* [*Training*] *in Christianity* Kierkegaard calls it outright "blasphemy" to want to prove that Christ was God by considering "the consequences of his life" (p. 32). It is also worth noting that Kierkegaard rejects the "proofs" which Scripture presents for Christ's divinity: "His miracles, His Resurrection from the dead, His Ascension" (p. 29)—they are "only for faith."

Kierkegaard's vigorous opposition to all attempts to prove the existence of God and the divinity of Christ is also based on his wanting to emphasize as strongly as possible the infinite distance between God and man and between man and the God-man, a distance which only faith can bridge and which in all eternity will never disappear ("Of the Difference between a Genius and an Apostle," together with *The Present Age*, pp. 151 ff.).

Diamond, Malcolm L. "Kierkegaard and Apologetics." *Journal of Religion*, XLIV, 1964.

Dupré, Louis. *Kierkegaard as Theologian*. New York: Sheed and Ward, 1963.

See titles in topical bibliography under CHRISTIANITY, GOD.

For references to proof in the works, see, for example, *The Concept of Irony*, pp. 98, 101, 108, 128 f.; *Either/Or*, I, pp. 34, 35 f.; II, 284; *Upbuilding* [*Edifying*] *Discourses*, III, p. 82; *Fragments*, pp. 49 ff., 117 ff.; *The Concept of Anxiety* [*Dread*], pp. 124 f., 131; *Prefaces*, *S.V.*, V, p. 44; *Three Discourses on Imagined Occasions* [*Thoughts on Crucial Situations*, p. 21]; *Stages*, pp. 71, 83, 114, 129, 413; *Postscript*, pp. 20, 26, 29, 31 f., 38 f., 45 ff., 64, 86, 88 f., 137, 152, 155 ff., 174, 180, 190, 232, 281, 282 f., 378, 407, 485, 491, 496, 532 f.; *Upbuilding Discourses in Various Spirits*, Part One [*Purity of Heart*, p. 84]; Part Three [*The Gospel of Suffering*, p. 84]; *Works of Love*, pp. 56, 193; *Christian Discourses*, pp. 88, 198, 210 ff.; *The Lily of the Field and the Bird of the Air*, together with *Christian Discourses*, pp. 345 f.; "Of the Difference between a Genius and an Apostle," together with *The Present Age*, pp. 144 f.; *The Sickness unto Death*, pp. 234 f.; *Practice* [*Training*] *in Christianity*, pp. 28 f., 31 f., 97, 107, 144, 243; *For Self-Examination*, p. 80; *Judge for Yourselves!*, pp. 114, 199, 211; *Attack*, pp. 145, 231, 271 f.

1226. "In spite of this demand there is freedom in history. The established, true fact ought to be one necessarily conditioned by miracle, so that miracle remains a matter of faith; necessity in nature ought to be ignored. For miracle, a free deed, should be thought of as a fact of nature—it should be experienced. Those present at the ascension of the Savior of the world saw only that he withdrew from the earth, but not the (unconditioned) freedom, the power of his remoteness. The truth, which this miracle is, realized itself; its reality lay not in the brief, past sight of the movement, but in its power. As long as they go on demanding the proof which would establish the truth of miracles on the basis of history or nature, the doubter and the unbeliever themselves prove that the conditioned freedom within them has been subordinated either to the law of causality, as in a pragmatizing historical science, or to the perceptions they have in common with animals, as in a merely empirical natural science. . . ."

1227. L. Holberg, *Erasmus Montanus*, II, 3; IV, 1.

1228. This entry was omitted from the final draft of the note on p. 54 of *Fragments*.

1229. This entry is from a draft of *Concluding Unscientific Postscript*. See ibid., pp. 45 ff., also pp. 180, 190; also *Practice* [*Training*] *In Christianity*, pp. 28–34, 144, 243.

1230. See note 1229.

1231. See *Postscript*, pp. 20, 26, 29, 31 f., 378; *Upbuilding Discourses in Various Spirits*, Part Three [*The Gospel of Suffering*, p. 84]; *Works of Love*, p. 193; *Practice* [*Training*] *in Christianity*, pp. 31 f., 97; *The Sickness unto Death*, pp. 234 f.; *For Self-Examination*, p. 80; *Judge for Yourselves!*, pp. 199, 211; *Attack*, pp. 271 f.

1232. *Postscript*, pp. 31 f., *Upbuilding Discourses in Various Spirits*, Part One [*Purity of Heart*, p. 84]; *Attack*, pp. 271 f.

1233. *Either/Or*, I, p. 32.

1234. See IV C 87–96.

1235. See *Postscript*, pp. 345 ff.

1236. See ibid., p. 180; *The Sickness unto Death*, pp. 234 f.

1237. See *Postscript*, pp. 155 ff.; *Christian Discourses*, p. 88; *Lily and the Bird*, together with *Christian Discourses*, pp. 345 f.; *For Self-Examination*, p. 80; *Judge for Yourselves!*, p. 199.

1238. See *The Concept of Anxiety* [*Dread*], pp. 129 f.; *Postscript*, pp. 26, 407; *Upbuilding Discourses in Various Spirits*, Part Three [*The Gospel of Suffering*, p. 84].

1239. Peter Engel Lind, prison pastor in Christianshavn and Copenhagen. Notice of lecture appeared in *Berlingske Tidende*, no. 29, February 5, 1850.

1240. See *Postscript*, pp. 31 f.; *Christian Discourses*, pp. 210 ff.; *The Sickness unto Death*, pp. 234 f.; *Judge for Yourselves!*, p. 211.

1241. See note 1229.

1242. See *Postscript*, pp. 495 f.

1243. See CONTEMPORANEITY.

1244. See *Judge for Yourselves!*, p. 211.

1245. See note 1229.

1246. Matthew 8:22.

1247. See *The Sickness unto Death*, pp. 146 f.

1248. See Friedrich Böhringer, *Die Kirche Christi* . . . (see note 355), I, 3, pp. 234 f.

1249. See *Postscript*, p. 298.

1250. See Böhringer.

1251. See ibid., II, 1, pp. 253 f.

PROTESTANTISM

Kierkegaard grew up in a Protestant milieu and was rigorously and earnestly "brought up in Christianity" (*The Point of View*, p. 76) by his father. Through his theological studies at the University of Copenhagen he became intimately acquainted with Protestant-Lutheran theology, and after taking his examination was qualified to become a pastor in the State Church of Denmark, which, however, he never did.

His strict religious upbringing provided him with personal experiences of Christianity's great requirement and of how it becomes an offense to the natural man. These existential experiences provided him with a criterion to assess the Christianity found within the Danish Church of his day, and later for assessment of the religious situation in all Christendom.

The following expression in *From the Papers of One Still Living* (*S.V.*, XIII, p. 64) reveals Kierkegaard's respect for Protestantism's original inwardness as well as his denunciation of the vulgarization to which Protestantism was subjected in his day: "Protestantism's deep and inward life-view reduced (in our day) *in absurdum zum Gebrauch für Jedermann.*"

Kierkegaard's criticism first applies to the Protestant theologians in Denmark who wanted to use Hegel's philosophy to substantiate Christian truths. But his criticism also applies to the Protestantism represented by Judge William in *Either/Or* and *Stages on Life's Way,* even if Protestantism is here depicted in its more ideal form. Although Judge William is familiar with Lutheran-Protestant Christianity and seeks to live his life according to it, his whole orientation to Christianity is still abstract. For example, he regards the movement of repentance as the most important; but this movement is made abstract, and thus he has no concrete use for grace. Moreover, his one-sided concentration on the Lutheran idea of serving God in one's occupation and position binds him too strongly to this world and to middle-class morality. But since Kierkegaard believes that the Christian's presupposition for participating in the life of the community must be a steady movement toward "the absolute *telos*" (*Postscript,* p. 359), he cannot accept Judge William's form of Christianity. This continuous "double movement" (ibid., p. 366) is given particular prominence by the pseudonym Climacus in his repudiation of the Protestant clergy's cheaply acquired criticism of "monasticism" (ibid., p. 360).

As his journals indicate, Kierkegaard's criticism of Protestantism intensifies with the years and culminates in the Church battle. While Kierkegaard throughout his life and in his entire authorship holds to grace as man's only refuge, he becomes more and more aware of the misuse of this most important Christian truth by "Protestantism, especially in Denmark" (*Attack,* p. 34). Men want merely to provide themselves with "tranquillity in order to enjoy life here" and therefore desire to be reassured that "man is saved by grace alone, yes, it is even arrogant to want to help oneself the least bit, and in this frame of mind we shove Christianity out entirely—and now the fun starts with getting a living, begetting children, endless activity, enjoyment of life etc. etc." (XI[1] A 76). Luther's assertions that "faith is a restless thing" and that "faith . . . should be discernible" in a man's life (*For Self-Examination,* p. 14) are completely forgotten. Kierkegaard even goes so far as to say that Protestantism is "man's mutiny against Christianity" (XI[1] A 76), and it becomes a question for him whether or not Protestantism is quite simply, from the essentially Christian point of view, "an untruth . . . just as soon as it is regarded as a principle for Christianity, not as a necessary remedy (corrective) at a given time and place" (*Attack,* p. 34; see also XI[2] A 305).

Angell, J. William. *Can the Church Be Saved?* Nashville: Broadman, 1967.

Barckett, Richard M. "Søren Kierkegaard: 'Back to Christianity!' " *Downside Review,* vol. 73, 1955.

Bonifazi, Conrad. *Christendom Attacked.* London: Rockliff, 1953.

Celestin, G. "Kierkegaard and Christian Renewal." *Dominican,* vol. L, 1964.

Demson, D. "Kierkegaard's Sociology with Notes on the Relevance to the Church." *Religion in Life,* vol. 27, no. 2, 1958.

Eller, Vernard. *Kierkegaard and Radical Discipleship.* Princeton: Princeton University Press, 1968.

Eller, V. M. "A Protestant's Protestant: Kierkegaard from a New Perspective." Th. D. dissertation, Pacific School of Religion, 1964.

Eller, Vernard. "Protestant Radicalism." *Christian Century,* Nov. 1, 1967.

Fitzpatrick, Mallary, Jr. "Kierkegaard and the Church." *Journal of Religion,* vol. 27, no. 4, 1947.

Gates, John Alexander. *Christendom Revisited; a Kierkegaardian View of the Church Today.* Philadelphia: Westminster Press, 1963.

Hartt, J. N. "The Philosopher, the Prophet, and the Church: Some Reflections on their Roles as Critics of Culture." *Journal of Religion,* vol. 35, 1955.

Lønning, Per. *The Dilemma of Contemporary Theology.* New York: Humanities Press, 1962.

Stewart, R. W. "Is Church Like a Theatre?" *Expository Times,* vol. 62, 1950–51.

For references to Protestantism in the works, see, for example, *From the Papers of One Still Living, S.V.,* XIII, pp. 64, 85; *The Concept of Anxiety* [*Dread*], pp. 24, 37; *Postscript,* p. 35, 360; *Attack,* pp. 12, 34, 145, 181, 223, 282–83 fn.

1252. See H. C. Andersen's observation on religious conditions in France, quoted in Kierkegaard's early work, *Fra en endnu Levendes Papirer, S.V.,* XIII, p. 85 fn.

1253. See CORRECTIVE; *Attack,* p. 34.

1254. See note 629.

1255. See note 1253.

1256. See Judge William's advice to the young esthete, *Either/Or,* II, p. 212.

1257. See note 629.

1258. See *Attack,* pp. 145, 181.

1259. Against its own nature.

1260. See note 1259.

1261. Opening line of Danish version of Usteri's drinking song *"Freut euch des Lebens," Visebog indeholdende udvalgte danske Selskabssange; med tillæg af nogle svenske og tydske,* ed., Andreas Seidelin (Copenhagen: 1814), pp. 86 f. *ASKB* 1483. See *Attack,* p. 42.

1262. Possibly an inverted recollection of H. C. Andersen's report on Paris. See Kierkegaard's *From the Papers of One Still Living, S.V.,* XIII, p. 85 fn.

1263. See G. H. Schubert, *Die Symbolik des Traumes* (Bamberg: 2 ed., 1821), p. 38. *ASKB* 776. See *Fragments*, p. 135 and note; *Postscript*, p. 297.

1264. See Plato, *Laws*, VIII, 829 a.

1265. Romans 2:24; I Timothy 6:1; Titus 2:5.

1266. See, for example, I Peter 2:1.

PROVIDENCE, GOVERNANCE

In one of his earliest journal entries (II A 681) Kierkegaard speaks of governance (*Styrelsen*), saying that while the world goes its way, God does not forget his great plans but intervenes in the world according to his own idea and often against man's. The idea of providence (*Forsynet*) and God's governance has special significance in Kierkegaard's view of existence. But just as there can be no demonstrative proof of the existence of God or the divinity of Christ, neither can it be proved that there is a providence and a just governance. Kierkegaard declares: "A providence is no easier to understand (to grasp) than redemption—both can only be believed" (VII[1] A 130). A person can arrive at faith in a providence only by coming in his existence to the limit of his ability. Kierkegaard points this out many times. For example, his pseudonym Vigilius Haufniensis describes how a person can overcome the anxiety of existence only by faith in providence. "By means of faith anxiety educates the individual to rest in providence" (*The Concept of Anxiety* [*Dread*], p. 144, ed. tr.). A person comes into relationship with providence also through guilt (ibid., p. 88); this is stressed with particular clarity in the following statement: "Providence and redemption are categories of despair" (VII[1] A 130), meaning that man's ethical exertions always end in despair, but through faith in providence and faith in the forgiveness of sins, one is freed from this despair.

Faith in providence and governance had a personally crucial significance for Kierkegaard, as many of his journal entries indicate. In his works there are two passages in particular that touch upon the role of governance. No doubt Kierkegaard is thinking of himself in a long account of governance's intervention in the life of the man who is grasped by Christ: "Thus Governance deals with him many times, and each time it helps him farther out into suffering, because he will not let go that picture which he desires to resemble" (*Practice* [*Training*] *in Christianity* p. 189). The other passage is in *The Point of View* (p. 69), where Kierkegaard tells of the influence of providential guidance in his life and authorship: "Thus it is that in the course of my whole activity as an author I have constantly needed God's aid."

Kierkegaard uses two words (*Forsyn* and *Styrelse*) which translators of the works usually have rendered as "providence." Frequently, however, *Styrelse* has been translated as "guidance" (preferred by David Swenson) or as "governance" (preferred by Walter Lowrie). At times Kierkegaard uses the two together (*Forsynets Styrelse*, guidance or act of providence, *Either/Or*, II, p. 290), which indicates the more active, specific character of *Styrelse*—hence "guidance," "governance," "management." Both terms are used in the works and the journals and papers from the earliest to the last. See, for example, *The Concept of Anxiety* [*Dread*], pp. 86 f., 90, 93, 140; *Postscript*, pp. 30, 363; *Upbuilding Discourses in Various Spirits*, Part One [*Purity of Heart*, pp. 110 f., 160, 172]; *Judge for Yourselves!*, p. 214; *Armed Neutrality*, pp. 19, 79, 98.

Gilkey, L. B. "Concept of Providence in Contemporary Theology." *Journal of Religion*, vol. 43, 1963.

1267. Into another (qualitatively different) kind.

1268. Kierkegaard's active use of Latin and Greek in his reading also finds an outlet in his writing through the easy adoption of Latin or Greek words or constructed words into his Danish. For this reason "autopsy" does not appear in the 28-volume *Ordbog over det danske Sprog*. In the works the word is found in *Fear and Trembling*, p. 98 fn.; *Fragments*, pp. 87, 128; *Postscript*, pp. 3 ("acquaintance"), 42 ("firsthand acquaintance"), 48 ("autopsy"). The term means the same in the restricted English usage: seeing with one's own eyes.

1269. This entry is from a draft of *Upbuilding Discourses in Various Spirits*, Part One [*Purity of Heart*, p. 87, ll. 32 ff.].

1270. See *Fear and Trembling*, p. 95.

1271. Matthew 10:29 f.

PUNISHMENT

A man's task is to actualize the good. Not to do so involves punishment. Thus Kierkegaard declares "that punishment exists only for the sake of transgressors" (*Upbuilding Discourses in Various Spirits*, Part One [*Purity of Heart*, p. 87]) and that God in his wisdom has connected "a punishment with every transgression" (ibid., p. 93). In a wider sense punishment must be understood as the restoration of the relationship to the good, whether it is society which carries it out or God. But society's punishment lies on a lower level and cannot be just; only God's punishment can, for, as Kierkegaard says, "the good and the punishment of the world are not identical" (ibid., p. 93). Therefore Kierkegaard was not greatly interested in a man's guilt and punishment in relation to society; he was interested mainly in the individual's guilt and punishment in relation to God.

However, it is not always apparent in this world that God's punishment is just. The man who encounters much opposition and suffering may doubt "what was punishment and what was incident" (*Upbuilding* [*Edifying*] *Discourses*, I, p. 54; see also *The Concept of Anxiety* [*Dread*], p. 107: "to what extent it is fate and to what extent guilt"), and if his guilt remains hidden from the world he may question whether he ought to bring the world's punishment upon himself by revealing his guilt (X² A 156; see also VI A 55–59).

According to Kierkegaard, it is wrong to believe "that atonement should exempt one from punishment"; on the contrary, the sinner gets "the bold confidence to dare believe that God is merciful to him; even though he still suffers his punishment" (X^1 A 462; see especially II A 63). Generally speaking, it is up to the person to learn to understand that punishment, "like all other things which fall to the lot of one who loves God, . . . is a helping hand" (*Upbuilding Discourses in Various Spirits*, Part One [*Purity of Heart*, p. 87]) and "a good . . . when it is gratefully received" (ibid., p. 93), yes, it is also a "medicine" (ibid., p. 82).

Thus it is far worse for a man not to be punished than to be punished (X^2 A 115). Even paganism regarded a deferment of punishment as a manifestation of God's cruelty (X^1 A 461), and even if the Christian, by contrast, may consider the absence of punishment as a sign of God's patience, he must also be aware of how serious it can be if the punishment does not occur and one is irresponsible, for it can mean that one goes astray again and thereby becomes hard of heart (*Judge for Yourselves!*, p. 234). The most dreadful thing that can happen to a man, however, is for God "to punish by ignoring" him to the extent that "the one punished does not even notice it" (XI^2 A 96). This punishment is bad enough in time, but the worst part of it for a person is that God "has eternity"; there are, then, crimes on such a scale that they "cannot be punished in this world" but can only "be punished in eternity" (*Attack*, p. 254).

That there is an eternal punishment which man can incur while living in time is, in Kierkegaard's view, a corollary of the question whether or not an eternal salvation is also decided in time (VI A 62; see also *Postscript*, p. 86). Kierkegaard maintains that this side of the issue must not be repressed in the proclamation, inasmuch as it must be a reminder to men to forsake the paths of sin, just as it was in "the militant church" which brought men up "in the fear and trembling" of the "punishment of eternity" *Practice* [*Training*] *in Christianity*, p. 224. On the other hand Kierkegaard does not believe that fear of punishment should motivate a man to do the good; for then he actually does what "he continually really would rather not do"; then he does not wholeheartedly will the good (*Upbuilding Discourses in Various Spirits*, Part One [*Purity of Heart*, p. 86]).

In his later years Kierkegaard vigorously emphasized that by suffering for the good and "by being punished in time" man is "saved for eternity" (*Attack*, p. 254), and he increasingly regarded this existence as the "suffering of punishment" (XI^1 A 292); therefore death is not a punishment for a Christian but a deliverance, "God's compassion" (XI^1 A 289).

For a variety of references to punishment in the works, see, for example, *Either/Or*, II, p. 336; *Upbuilding* [*Edifying*] *Discourses*, I, pp. 53 f.; *The Concept of Anxiety* [*Dread*], pp. 99–100 fn., 109, 111, 122; *Stages*, p. 444; *Postscript*, pp. 86 ff., 88 fn., 264 fn., 472, 481 ff., 489; *Upbuilding Discourses in Various Spirits*, Part One [*Purity of Heart*, pp. 79 ff., 93, 115 f., 122]; *Works of Love*, pp. 225, 356; *Christian Discourses*, pp. 82, 140; *The Sickness unto Death*, p. 211; *Practice* [*Training*] *in Christianity*, pp. 224 ff.; *The Point of View*, p. 55; *God's Unchangeableness*, together with *Judge for Yourselves!*, p. 234; *Attack*, p. 255.

1272. See *Postscript*, pp. 86 ff., 472; *The Sickness unto Death*, p. 211; *Practice* [*Training*] *in Christianity*, pp. 244 ff.

1273. Michael Montaigne, *Gedanken und Meinungen* (see note 491). See *Christian Discourses*, p. 140.

1274. *"Ueber den Verzug der göttlichen Strafen,"* *Plutarchs moralische Abhandlungen*, tr. J. F. S. Kaltwasser, I–V, 1–9 (Frankfurt/M: 1783), V, pp. 1 ff., esp. 45 ff. *ASKB* 1192–96. Kierkegaard also had twenty-four other volumes of Plutarch in Greek, German and Danish.

1275. See *Either/Or*, II, p. 336. Not quite the same formulation but the same meaning.

1276. On May 14, 1847, Kierkegaard began to number his journals with NB and a number (NB²). The previous journal, or more accurately "journals," was designated JJ (see VIII¹ A 107). The new series was given serial numbers, and the last journal was numbered NB³⁶ (see XI² 240).

1277. Of the hidden things the congregation is not to judge. See VI A 55.

1278. I. H. Fichte, *System der Ethik*, I–II (Leipzig: 1850–53), I, p. 108. *ASKB* 510–11.

1279. F. Böhringer, *Die Kirche Christi* (see note 355).

1280. See *Postscript*, p. 178.

1281. See *Attack*, p. 256.

1282. For example, XI¹ A 381, 554. See *The Concept of Anxiety* [*Dread*], pp. 99 f., fn.; *God's Unchangeableness*, together with *Judge for Yourselves!*, p. 234; *Attack*, pp. 253, 255; see also *Postscript*, pp. 264 fn., 482 ff., 489.

QUALITATIVE DIFFERENCE

Søren Kierkegaard was a man of distinctions; therefore his pseudonym Vigilius Haufniensis laments, "The age of distinctions is over; the system has overcome it" (*The Concept of Anxiety* [*Dread*], p. 2, ed. tr.). By placing thought higher than faith, Hegel, in Kierkegaard's opinion, placed philosophy and theology into a wrong relationship to each other and at the same time wiped out the qualitative difference between the two spheres. Kierkegaard, on the other hand, champions the principle that philosophy and theology lie on two qualitatively different levels, since philosophy's object is the temporal, visible world, while theology's interest is the eternal, to which thought is unequal. Hegel, too, uses the terms temporal-eternal, but the "supremacy of thought" (*Postscript*, p. 310) relativizes the absolute differences and creates confusion. In the medium of thought it is fairly easy to establish—as in Hegel—a transition from the idea as the eternal to finitude (the temporal) and from finitude again to the idea, because the movement is abstract and not actual. In contrast to this, Kierkegaard points out that as soon as the terms "temporal" and "eternal" are understood as realities, there is an absolute qualitative difference between them and nothing but a leap can span the two qualities.

This point of view becomes decisively important to Kierkegaard in his outlook on the relationship between man and God, between whom Kierkegaard posits an absolute qualitative difference that only the leap of faith can cope with. This difference manifests itself further by Christ's presenting himself to man as the absolute paradox and "the possibility of offense" (*Practice* [*Training*] *in Christianity*, p. 83), even though God did become man. This qualitative difference is clearest of all when man stands as a sinner before God. Anti-Climacus says: "As a sinner man is separated from God by a yawning qualitative abyss. And obviously God is separated from man by the same qualitative yawning abyss when he forgives sins" (*The Sickness unto Death*, p. 253).

Based on this principle of the absolute difference between man and God, between immanence and transcendence, Kierkegaard clearly distinguishes between the various spheres of existence man can traverse in his spiritual development. In making these distinctions, Kierkegaard accordingly stresses that the transition from the one sphere to the other can take place by means of a leap.

Gerry, Joseph. Kierkegaard: "The Problem of Transcendence: an Interpretation of the Stages." Ph. D. dissertation, Fordham, 1958. *Dissertation Abstracts*, 1958–59, pp. 153 ff.

Heinecken, Martin J. *The Moment before God.* Philadelphia: Muhlenberg, 1956.

Although the concept "qualitative difference" is of great importance in Kierkegaard's thought, the expression itself is used infrequently in the journals and in the works. See, for example, *Postscript*, pp. 195, 369, 439, 514 fn.; *On Authority and Revelation*, p. 112; "Of the Difference between a Genius and an Apostle," together with *Two Ages* [*The Present Age*, p. 151]; *The Sickness unto Death*, pp. 230, 253, 257 f. See OFFENSE, PARADOX.

1283. M. Luther, *En christelig Postille* (see note 81), II, p. 195.

1284. See note 1240.

1285. See note 1282.

REALITY, ACTUALITY

In philosophical usage the two concepts reality (*Realitet*) and actuality (*Virkelighed*) are often merged. For Kierkegaard each of these terms also has a special meaning. "Reality" indicates the presence of something or of a concrete situation without specific reference to their origin, but coming-into-existence plays a central role in "actuality." Here the emphasis is on the fact that something *comes into existence* or that something has come to exist.

When Kierkegaard speaks of reality, the crucial aspect is that something or the situation genuinely is. Kierkegaard sometimes uses the word "reality" for concrete, palpable actuality; therefore it is significant that this word appears quite frequently in *The Concept of Irony*, where, for example, Socrates is said to reject the external world, customarily called reality, and to seek a new form of actuality.

Kierkegaard's pseudonym Vigilius Haufniensis raises the question whether thinking as a medium of apprehension of things also has reality, which was "the assumption of all ancient philosophy as well as of the philosophy of the Middle Ages" (*The Concept of Anxiety* [*Dread*], p. 10). But Kant's philosophy raises doubts about this presupposition. Kierkegaard's pseudonym Climacus answers the question by saying that there is a "thought-reality" (*Postscript*, p. 292, ed. tr.), that is, a possibility for which there is backing in actuality itself, but which nevertheless must not be confused with actuality. "Yet to conclude from this that thought does not have reality is a misunderstanding" (ibid., p. 294 ed. tr.). But there is also thinking, "pure thought," to which "actuality, existence" does not correspond (see *Postscript*, pp. 278 f.), just as there also can be things and situations which do not correspond to the concept. Kierkegaard cites many examples of such a discrepancy between the concept of reality and reality itself. For example, he mentions that Socrates understood that "the reality of the concrete ethic had become vacillating (*The Concept of Irony*, p. 251), and he has Judge William say that life for esthete A had "lost its reality" (*Either/Or*, II, p. 200). Several times Kierkegaard uses the expression "the reality of actuality" (ibid., p. 36; *Fear and Trembling*, p. 52 fn.) in the sense that reality consists of a concentration upon a particular area or in a particular object within actuality.

Kierkegaard also expands the use of the term "reality" to the ethical and religious spheres. Only here is there true reality, meaning that actuality-position (an existential position expressed by a person) is expressed through a subject. For example, Anti-Climacus says: "And what an infinite reality the self acquires by being conscious of existing before God" (*The Sickness unto Death*, p. 210, ed. tr.), which is comparable to his expression "the reality of repentance" (ibid., p. 241; see also *Either/Or*, II, p. 179, there translated "the validity of repentance").

As early as *The Concept of Irony* (pp. 259 f.) Kierkegaard gives a formula for actuality, which he retains generally throughout his writings. Actuality is here regarded as indissolubly composed of two contrasting qualities: for example, the phenomenon and the concept of being and essence. Later Kierkegaard defines actuality simply as "the unity of possibility and necessity" (*The Sickness unto Death*, p. 169). In *The Concept of Irony* (p. 276) Kierkegaard says that "the word 'actuality' must primarily be taken to mean historical actuality, that is to say, the actuality given at a certain time and under certain conditions. This word may be taken not only in a metaphysical sense, as when one treats the metaphysical problem of the relation of the Idea to actuality, where there can be no question of this or that actuality but only of the Idea's concretion, i.e., its actuality; but the word 'actuality' may also be used with respect to the historically actualized Idea. This last-named actuality is different at various times." Kierkegaard's concern for historical actuality is also found in the "Interlude" (*Fragments*, pp. 88–110), where he gives a detailed and explicit account of the centrality of the category of coming-into-existence (*Tilblivelse*), which is a transition from possibility to actuality (ibid., p. 91). Consequently "coming-into-existence" signifies for Kierkegaard that something which is possible is actualized by action. Climacus stresses that change takes place only in the category of being (possibility, actuality), not in the category of essence (necessity). All movement or change presupposes something unmoved (see *Postscript*, p. 277). The movement, that is, the transition from possibility to actuality, was of special interest to Kierkegaard. In the "Interlude" Kierkegaard-Climacus affirms the contradiction and tension involved in this transition, and in all his writings he gives numerous examples of it.

In *Concluding Unscientific Postscript* (pp. 267 ff., 202 ff.) Climacus details how the actuality existing through the process of coming into existence in particular situations can be more specifically defined—that is, the nature of its quality. Climacus's interpretation of actuality is closely related to the theory of the stages. The sensuous, external actuality is transitory, and Climacus is unwilling to grant it the name of actuality in the proper sense. On the other hand, he affirms the eternal as actuality, and in the first phase this eternal can be actualized temporally only through man's ethical action. Climacus maintains that "the ethical actuality of the individual is the only actuality" (ibid., p. 291, ed. tr.). But the eternal has its ultimate ground in God, who is the one and only genuine actuality, and from whom all actuality has its origin; it is God who as an "absolute freely-effecting cause" sets the historical coming-into-existence in motion (*Fragments*, p. 94).

But for Kierkegaard the highest actuality is the absolute paradoxical (the universal historical actuality is only relatively paradoxical) actuality which is God's concrete revelation in history (*Postscript*, pp. 514 f.).

Barrett, W. "What Existentialism Offers Modern Man: a Philosophy of Fundamental Human Realities." *Commentary*, vol. 12, 1951.

Edie, J. M. "Transcendental Ontology and Existentialism." *Journal of Philosophy*, vol. 59, 1962.

Gerry, Joseph. "Kierkegaard: the Problem of Transcendence: an Interpretation of the Stages." Ph. D. dissertation, Fordham University, 1959.

Holmer, Paul. "Metaphysics and Existentialism." *Hanover Forum*, vol. V, 1958.

Mann, Jesse A. and Kreyche, G. F., eds. *Perspectives on Reality.* New York: Harcourt, 1966.

Wyschogrod, Michael. *Kierkegaard and Heidegger, The Ontology of Existence.* New York: Columbia University Press, 1954.

The term *Virkelighed*, here translated as "actuality," has given great trouble to translators of Kierkegaard's writings. (See Robert Widenman's discussion, "Kierkegaard's Terminology—and English," *Kierkegaardiana*, 1968). If *Virkelighed* is translated as "reality" in the broad vernacular sense, there may be a loss of precision, but no great and obvious difficulty is created. But when Kierkegaard uses *Realitet* (which is found much less frequently than *Virkelighed*), there is a genuine difficulty, most striking, for example, in the case of *"Vir-kelighedens Realitet"* (*Either/Or*, II, 36). Throughout the works *Realitet* appears about sixty times, particularly in such expressions as "ethical reality," "the reality of love," "reality for you," "reality of the religious movement," "true reality of marriage," "reality of the self," "virtue has its reality," "thought has its reality," "the reality of childhood," etc. The dominant meaning of *Realitet* is, therefore, genuineness, validity. *Virkeligheden,* used hundreds of times with stress on temporality and spatiality, is better translated as "actuality," which also corresponds more adequately to the German cognate *Wirklichkeit.* The "actual" is "real" but the "real" both encompasses and lies beyond "actuality." For example, possibility is real but not actual; actuality is embodied possibility. Concepts are real, but they may or may not be actual or phenomenal (see *The Concept of Irony,* pp. 259 f.). Ideals are real, and the ethical task is to actualize them. The use of *Realitet* in the *Papirer* is not typical and is very infrequent. See, for example, IV B 1–17, p. 146 f. (*Johannes Climacus, or De omnibus dubitandum est,* pp. 148 ff.; observe footnotes); IV C 2, IX A 179.

For the very extensive use of "actuality" (*Virkelighed*) in the works, see *S.V.,* XV (1936), pp. 466 f. For the uses of "reality" (*Realitet*) in the works (note that the translations vary), see for example, *The Concept of Irony,* pp. 133 fn., 135, 137 fn., 218, 236, 246, 250 fn., 251, 255, 259 f., 270, 274, 276, 287, 297, 301, 331; *Either/Or,* I, p. 146, 206, 221, 293, 295, 341, 363; II, 13, 36, 57, 106, 125, 136, 141, 143, 179, 197, 200, 203; *Fear and Trembling,* pp. 52 and fn., 84, 100, 108 fn.; *Repetition,* p. 95; *Johannes Climacus, or De omnibus dubitandum est,* pp. 148 ff. and fn., 153 and fn.; *The Concept of Anxiety* [*Dread*], pp. 10, 19; *Stages,* pp. 118, 134, 145 f., 169 f.; *Postscript,* p. 85 (tr. "validity"), 153, 291 (*"Virkelighed"* tr. as "reality"), 292 (*"Tanke-Realitet"* tr. as "valid thought"), 294 f., 299 (tr. "becomes valid"), 496 f., 511–15 fn. (Partial confusion of *Virkelighed* and *Realitet* in tr.), 550; *The Sickness unto Death,* p. 169 (*Virkelighed,* tr. as "reality"), 210, 214, 241, 245, 262.

1286. *Theodicee,* para. 44 ff.

1287. G. W. F. Hegel, *Wissenschaft der Logik,* I–III (Berlin: 1833), II, pt. 3. *ASKB* 552–54. See English translation of *Wirklichkeit* as "actuality" in *Hegel's Science of Logic,* tr. W. H. Johnston and L. G. Struthers (London: Allen Unwin; New York: Macmillan, 1929), II, pp. 9, 160 ff.

1288. The bracketed context for this fragment from the draft of *The Concept of Anxiety* [*Dread*] is on p. 9 of the present English version (ed. tr.).

1289. This entry is from a draft of *Concluding Unscientific Postscript,* at the end of paragraph on pp. 283 f.

1290. Precedes all my thinking.

1291. Entry is from draft of *Postscript* at end of first paragraph, p. 285.

REASON, UNDERSTANDING

To designate the human capacity and exercise of thought Kierkegaard uses common terms such as "understanding" (*Forstand*), "reason" (*Fornuft*), and "reflection" (*Refleksion*), each of which, however, acquires from him a particular perspective. His idea of the relationship between understanding and reason is close to Kant's (see II C 20–21, Kierkegaard's notes on Martensen's Kant lectures); understanding embraces the qualifications of finitude or the empirical, whereas reason designates the synoptic ideas that lie beyond experience. Kierkegaard therefore uses the term "understanding" when he wants to note the range and limits of human knowledge. For Kierkegaard it is extremely important to define precisely this sphere of human cognition because of its bearing upon his attempt to draw the exact boundary between knowledge and faith.

But since Kierkegaard believes that man is created by God and for God and therefore aspires beyond his temporal boundary, he believes that in the understanding, too, there is a longing for something beyond its sphere and that the understanding aspires beyond its boundaries. Climacus says that it is the supreme passion of the understanding "to seek a collision, although this collision must in one way or another prove its undoing. The supreme paradox of all thought is the attempt to discover something that thought itself cannot think" (*Fragments*, p. 46), or, "The last thing that human thinking can will to do is to transcend itself in the paradoxical" (*Postscript*, p. 95).

At the same time that Kierkegaard points to the limitations of the understanding, he can also say: "the understanding, reflection, is also a gift of God" (IX A 222) which is to be used. And Climacus says that one "must not think meanly of the understanding" (*Postscript*, p. 502) because not until the understanding has perceived its limitations is there room for faith. Faith means that one must "relinquish his understanding and his thinking" as the highest authority (ibid., p. 495). Climacus also speaks of "the crucifixion of understanding" when it subordinates itself to faith (ibid., p. 500).

Kierkegaard does not make simply an epistemological distinction between understanding and faith but above all an existential distinction, because a person commonly uses his understanding, whose domain is finitude, as the measure for his actions. Climacus says that such a person "undertakes nothing unless the understanding, with the aid of probability, can somehow make clear to him the profit and loss and can answer the questions why and wherefore" (*Practice* [*Training*] *in Christianity*, p. 118). When one allows himself to be guided by the understanding, his actions remain within the realm of probability, whereas faith, on the other hand, bases its actions upon the improbable and the absurd.

As mentioned previously, the term "reason" encompasses more than understanding, since man uses his reason to try to create a coherent view of existence. Thus reason has a speculative strain, and therefore Kierkegaard uses this term only when he wants to note the outside cognitive boundary within immanence. This happens most often in polemics against Hegel, since in Hegel the term "reason" plays the central role. When, for example, Kierkegaard says that Christianity "has married human reason" (*Works of Love,* p. 192) or when he has Anti-Climacus speak of demonstrating "that to be a rational reality which is at variance with reason" (*Practice [Training] in Christianity,* p. 29), he no doubt has Hegel in mind. Inasmuch as the understanding and reason, despite their differences, lie essentially within the same sphere, i.e., immanence, Kierkegaard at times uses both terms as a contrast to faith, which points to the transcendent. For example, he says: "for reason (*Fornuft*), understanding (*Forstand*), is, humanly speaking, the faculty of seeing, but faith is against the understanding" (*Three Discourses at the Communion on Fridays,* together with *Christian Discourses,* p. 375).

Throughout his sharp demarcation of the domains of the understanding and reason from that of faith, Kierkegaard does not want to disallow their significance for the believer, who must indeed use the understanding to "believe against the understanding" (*Postscript,* p. 503). For Kierkegaard it was important only to emphasize that faith lies on a qualitatively higher level than understanding and reason.

Angell, R. B. "Logic and Existentialist Ethics." *Journal of Philosophy,* vol. 58, 1961.

Beck, Maximillian. "Existentialism, Rationalism, and Christian Faith." *Journal of Religion,* vol. 26, 1946.

———. "Reason and Existence." *Journal of Philosophy,* vol. 44, 1947.

Blanshard, Brand. "Kierkegaard on Faith." *Personalist,* vol. 49, 1968.

Collins, James. "Faith and Reflection in Kierkegaard." *Journal of Religion,* vol. 37, 1957. In *Kierkegaard Critique,* ed. Howard Johnson and Niels Thulstrup. New York: Harper and Row, 1962.

Fabro, Cornelio. "Faith and Reason in Kierkegaard's Dialectic." In *A Kierkegaard Critique,* ed. Howard Johnson and Niels Thulstrup. New York: Harper and Row, 1962.

Garelick, Herbert. "The Irrationality and Supra-Rationality of Kierkegaard's Paradox." *The Southern Journal of Philosophy,* II, 1964.

Gerber, Rudolph. "Kierkegaard, Reason and Faith." *Thought,* vol. 25, 1969.

Held, Matthew. "The Historical Kierkegaard: Faith or Gnosis." *Journal of Religion,* no. 37, 1957.

Hick, John, ed. *Faith and the Philosophers.* New York: St. Mark's Press, 1964.

Holmer, Paul. "Kierkegaard and Logical Theory." *Kierkegaardiana,* 1957.

———. "Kierkegaard and Theology," *Union Seminary Quarterly Review,* vol. XII, 1957.

Klemke, E. D. "Logicality versus Alogicality in the Christian Faith." *Journal of Religion,* vol. 38, no. 2, 1958.

McInery, R. M. "Reason and Speculative Thought." *The New Scholasticism,* vol. XL, 1966.

McKinnon, Alastair. "Kierkegaard's Irrationalism Revisited." *International Philosophical Quarterly,* vol. 9, 1969.

Magel, Charles R. "An Analysis of Kierkegaard's Philosophic Categories." Ph. D. dissertation, University of Minnesota, 1960.

Murphy, J. L. "Faith and Reason in the Teaching of Kierkegaard." *American Ecclesiastical Review,* CXLV, 1961.

Niebuhr, Reinhold. "Coherence, Incoherence, and Christian Faith." *Journal of Religion,* no. 3, 1951.

Paul, William W. "Faith and Reason in Kierkegaard and Modern Existentialism." *Review of Religion,* vol. 20, 1956.

Popkin, R. H. "Kierkegaard and Scepticism." *Alg. Nederl. Tidschrift,* vol. 51, 1958–59.

Stack, George J. "Concern in Kierkegaard and Heidegger." *Philosophy Today,* vol. 13, 1969.

See also titles in topical bibliography under HEGEL and PARADOX.

See entries under REFLECTION.

The task of translating *Fornuft* and *Forstand* has vexed all who have shared the work of bringing Kierkegaard's works to English readers. Robert Widenman's article "Kierkegaard's Terminology—and English" (*Kierkegaardiana,* 1968; see also the discussion of *Virkelighed* under ACTUALITY, REALITY) presents the spectrum of translations and also the variations within the work of individual translators.

The main problem has been the translation of *Forstand.* The translation into German has been accomplished quite simply. Hayo Gerdes in the first volumes of *Kierkegaard's Tagebücher* renders *Fornuft* as *Vernunft* consistently and *Forstand* as *Verstand.* In English the problem has not been so easy to solve, and the question has persisted whether to translate *Forstand* as "reason" or as "understanding."

Walter Lowrie quite consistently uses "understanding," as does Lee Capel in *The Concept of Irony.* David Swenson uses "reason" in *Fragments.* In *Concluding Unscientific Postscript* (five-sixths by Swenson, one-sixth by Lowrie, who was "scrupulous not to use the terms I prefer but the locutions he had chosen [ibid., Preface, p. ix]"), *Forstand* is usually translated as "understanding" and very infrequently (p. 189) as "reason" (a few other times quite appropriately as "mind" or "wits" or "common sense"), Lowrie writes of this change of mind on Swenson's part (ibid., p. x). Therefore David Swenson's weighty observation in the first edition of *Fragments* (pp. 222 f. in second edition), in which he argues for "reason," would seem to be repudiated by the usage in *Postscript.*

Upon close reading, however, the note on "reason" in the *Fragments* proves to be not so much a defense of the selection of "reason" as an elaboration of the meaning of *Forstand*: the term "is not to be taken in any abstract-intellectual sense, but quite concretely, as the reflectively organized common sense of mankind, including as the essential core a sense of life's values. Over against the 'paradox,' it is therefore the self-assurance and self-assertiveness of man's nature in its totality. To identify it with any abstract intellectual function, like the function of scientific cognition, or of general ideas, or of the a priori, or of self-consistency in thinking, etc., is wholly to misunderstand the exposition of the *Fragments*." It is this very interpretation of *Forstand* which leads the present translators to follow the later Swenson and generally use "understanding," although out of respect for Swenson's pioneer translating and the special Hegelian idiom in *Fragments*, "reason" was left untouched in the revision of *Fragments* for the second edition. "Reason" is then used for *Fornuft* to denote man's capacity for and practice of thinking comprehensively and penetratingly in the attempt to achieve an encompassing, coherent view of life and the world.

For the use of "reason" (*Fornuft*) in the works, see, for example, *The Concept of Irony*, pp. 229, 300; *Either/Or*, I, p. 1; *The Concept of Anxiety* [*Dread*], pp. 100, 126; *Stages*, p. 433 fn.; *Postscript*, pp. 144 fn., 337, 461–62 fn.; *Works of Love*, p. 192 (should be translated "reason"); *Three Discourses at the Communion on Fridays*, together with *Christian Discourses*, p. 375 (*Fornuft* and *Forstand* used together); *Practice* [*Training*] *in Christianity*, pp. 28 f.; *S.V.*, XIII, pp. 6, 413.

For the use of "understanding" (*Forstand*) in the works, sometimes translated as "reason," "mind," etc., see, for example, *Either/Or*, I, p. 22, 47, 277, 294, 349, 383; II, pp. 16, 27, 195, 272; *Upbuilding* [*Edifying*] *Discourses*, I, pp. 46, 74, 83 f., 89, 116; III, pp. 7, 18, 28, 31, 89, 120; IV, pp. 64, 133, 136; *Fear and Trembling*, pp. 31, 47, 57, 95; *Repetition*, pp. 56, 99, 102, 115, 127; *Fragments* (see discussion above), pp. 32, 47, 48, 55, 61, 72 f., 76, 113, 128, 226; *The Concept of Anxiety* [*Dread*], pp. 29, 48, 102, 103, 145; *Three Discourses on Imagined Occasions* [*Thoughts on Crucial Situations*, pp. 22, 50]; *Stages*, pp. 82, 98, 117, 122, 163, 176, 190, 202, 204, 213, 216, 225, 252, 255, 266, 270, 318, 324, 334, 339, 355, 359, 385, 386, 388, 436, 450; *Postscript*, pp. 36, 78, 159, 174, 189, 191, 196, 201, 205, 208, 234, 258, 261, 310, 311, 337, 384, 399, 408, 441, 495, 501, 513 fn., 518, 522, 529, 531, 536; *S.V.*, VIII, pp. 63 ff.; *Two Ages* [*The Present Age* (*Forstandighed* does not mean "understanding," as on p. 1, but "practicality," "sensibleness"), p. 68]; *Upbuilding Discourses in Various Spirits*, Part One [*Purity of Heart*, pp. 31, 43, 218]; Part Three [*The Gospel of Suffering*, p. 48]; *Works of Love*, pp. 111, 144, 215, 228, 243, 331, 334; *Christian Discourses*, pp. 30, 87, 92, 243, 264; *The Lily of the Field and the Bird of the Air*, together with *Christian Discourses*, pp. 320, 328; "Of the Difference between a Genius and an Apostle," together with *The Present Age*, p. 161; *The Sickness unto Death*, pp. 171, 216, 231, 247, 256; *Three Discourses at the Communion on Fridays*, together with *Christian Discourses*, p. 375 (*Fornuft* and *Forstand* used together); *Practice* [*Training*] *in Christianity*, pp. 49, 85, 107, 117 f., 121; *For Self-Examination*, p. 96; *Judge for Yourselves!*, pp. 173, 185; *S.V.*, XIII, p. 471; *Attack*, pp. 65, 162, 277.

1292. The last (1577) of the classical Lutheran formulations of faith.

1293. See *Postscript*, p. 75.

1294. Ibid., pp. 107 ff.

1295. See *Prefaces*, *S.V.*, V, p. 37.

1296. See F. C. Sibbern, "Recension over Prof. Heibergs Perseus No. 1," *Maanedsskrift for Litteratur*, XIX (1838), pp. 294 ff., reprinted as *Bemærkninger og Undersøgelser . . .* (1838).

REDOUBLING

The concept of redoubling (*Fordoblelse*) is used by Kierkegaard as an ontological category for the kind of being (*Væren*) that belongs to the realm of faith. It is distinguished from the kind of being that constitutes the point of departure for ontology in philosophy, which is an empirical and limited being. By exploring this being, philosophical thought can arrive at certain abstract concepts that are an abbreviation of this being. The pseudonymous writer Climacus says that these concepts are an "abstract reflection of, or the abstract prototype for, what being is as concrete empirical being" (*Postscript*, p. 170). Philosophical concepts of being contain no actual redoubling, since they are an abstract version of empirical being. Only when both parts in the redoubling are actual does actual redoubling take place, according to Kierkegaard's view. This actual redoubling is possible only within the sphere of faith, because here there is a higher ethical or religious reality over against empirical being. Both of these elements, empirical being and the higher reality, give a redoubling of man's original being, which consists of two parts (body-mind) viewed empirically, but of only one part (the temporal) viewed from the possibility of genuine redoubling. A person's task, then, is to form a synthesis of these two parts in a redoubling. When the synthesis is actualized, each element in man's existence contains a doubleness in that it simultaneously has a temporal and an eternal expression. One reaches redoubling as an ontological category in the sphere of faith. Kierkegaard gives a description of this redoubling within temporality in *Works of Love* (p. 261): "But redoubling in itself never has a temporal object; as the temporal disappears in time, so also it exists only in its characteristics. If, on the other hand, the eternal is in a man, the eternal redoubles itself in him in such a way that it is in him in a double mode: in an outward direction and in an inward direction back into itself, but in such a way that it is one and the same, for otherwise it is not redoubling."

Redoubling as an ontological category thus serves to indicate that a person has an eternal self or is intended to become spirit. Kierkegaard also uses the expression "self-redoubling" to emphasize that in redoubling the lower self stands in relation to the spiritual element (the "deeper self") in man. Self-redoubling, however, can be either negative or positive, according to a person's trying to achieve it by his own efforts or his assigning it to God (see X² A 116). The negative form of self-redoubling is treated especially in *The Sickness unto Death* (pp. 201 ff.) and in his criticism of Kant's view that the higher self can master redoubling without the help of a transcendent power (see X² A 396).

Since redoubling is characteristic of the reality of spirit, Kierkegaard, in the journals, even speaks of redoubling in God in terms of two apparently opposite qualities, mildness and rigor, but one cannot comprehend this redoubling (XI² A 130). He also uses the expression "infinite redoubling" in characterizing God, by which he means that God as spirit redoubles by having an unlimited view and power over his own subjectivity (XI² A 97). This is never possible for man, either intellectually or existentially.

Finally, mention must be made of Kierkegaard's use of the expression "dialectical redoubling," which is related to his dialectic of communication. This means that a person's life is seen in the light of two qualitative contrasts, of which he can choose one or seek to synthesize them. He briefly describes dialectical redoubling as "composing qualitative opposites into unity" (*Practice* [*Training*] *in Christianity*, p. 132).

Most translators of Kierkegaard's works (including *Works of Love*) have ignored any distinction between redoubling (*Fordoblelse*) and reduplication (*Reduplikation*). Therefore if the reader uses the translated works referred to in this section he will usually find "reduplication," also "duplication," "doubly," "duplexity," "by pairs," "doubleness," etc. instead of "redoubling" as translations of Kierkegaard's distinctive term *Fordoblelse*. See *Either/Or*, II, p. 179 (here Kierkegaard does not use "redoubling," but the content is pertinent to the present entry); *Johannes Climacus, or De omnibus dubitandum est*, p. 154 (*Fordobling*); *Fragments*, p. 94 (*Fordobling*); *Christian Discourses*, p. 43; *The Sickness unto Death*, p. 202; *Practice* [*Training*] *in Christianity*, p. 159. See also *Postscript*, p. 307 f. (a helpful exploration of redoubling, although the term is not used). For other instances of redoubling, see *Stages*, pp. 170, 172, 449 fn.; *Works of Love*, pp. 37, 176, 261, 262; "Of the Difference between a Genius and an Apostle," together with *The Present Age*, p. 149; *Practice* [*Training*] *in Christianity*, pp. 132, 142, 189; *The Point of View*, pp. 10, 17.

In the initial printing of *Journals and Papers*, I, the "re" was omitted in line 1 of X² A 396; 188.

1297. See *On My Work as an Author*, together with *The Point of View*, p. 151 fn.

1298. See note 1297.

1299. There is no third.

1300. See note 1297. See also *Christian Discourses*, p. 208.

1301. See *Judge for Yourselves!*, p. 115; *Attack*, p. 162.

1302. See note 1301.

REDUPLICATION

Kierkegaard defines reduplication as follows: "To reduplicate is to be what one says" (IX A 208), or, as Anti-Climacus says: "to reduplicate is to exist in what one understands" (*Practice* [*Training*] *in Christianity*, p. 133). Reduplication always presupposes reflection, that is, a knowledge of the good to be actualized. Therefore reduplication is not possible in the sphere of spontaneity, where everything happens without the middle link of reflection. There can, however, be a kind of reduplication on the esthetic level where conscious and considered practice is required for example, where it is a matter of learning "physical competence (military exercises, dancing, etc.), physical-intellectual competence: to calculate, for example, the higher arts, for example, acting" (VIII² B 85:7).

Essential reduplication, however, belongs to the ethical and ethical-religious sphere, and it is this Kierkegaard deals with in detail. The ethical is to be actualized within both spheres, even though "a knowledge" of Christianity's offer of grace (VIII² B 82:13) must first be communicated within the ethical-religious sphere. To actualize the good is positive reduplication, but as a contrast there is a negative reduplication that takes place when one secretly carries out (reduplicates) his evil purposes and at the same time knows how to put on a good front in the outer world. Kierkegaard calls this kind of reduplication demonic (X⁴ A 214).

Reduplication always takes place in the medium of actuality, but Kierkegaard nevertheless speaks of a reduplication of his ethical-religious experiences in thinking itself, which he calls "dialectic raised to the second power" (VIII A 91) or "double reflection" (*Practice* [*Training*] *in Christianity*, p. 132). This special reduplication or double reflection provides the basis for his indirect method, since to Kierkegaard the ethical can never be communicated directly but only in such a way that the poles of the choice are set opposite each other (ibid., pp. 132 f.). Such a reduplication or double reflection should motivate other men to reduplicate in the medium of existence. Kierkegaard's mode of operation in this instance is as follows: Kierkegaard carries through the reduplication in his life, and he communicates this in reduplicated or doubly reflected form—that is, by indirect communication—in his authorship. In doing this he simultaneously reduplicates the idea he believes God has for his life—that he is to be an author.

The concept of reduplication plays an extraordinary role in Kierkegaard's life and writings, because his total interest is in putting stress on existence and action. Reduplication is closely related to redoubling (see this section) in that redoubling signifies a reduplication already completed. Here the weight is on the ontological, that is, on being, which already exists, whereas in his use of the word "reduplication" Kierkegaard points to the ethical task that must first be actualized.

For references in the works to reduplication, see, for example, *Stages,* pp. 75, 387; *Postscript,* p. 69 (a distinction is maintained here between "reduplication" and "double reflection"), 152, 170 f., 217, 222, 269, 297, 542 fn., 552; *On Authority and Revelation,* p. 43 fn.; "Of the Difference between a Genius and an Apostle," together with *The Present Age,* p. 148; *Practice [Training] in Christianity,* pp. 123, 133; *On My Work as an Author,* together with *The Point of View,* 151 fn.; " 'The Single Individual' . . .," Appendix to *The Point of View,* p. 133.

1303. See " 'The Single Individual' Two 'Notes' Concerning My Work as an Author," Appendix to *The Point of View,* p. 133; *On My Work as an Author,* ibid., p. 151 fn. In these two portions there is an indication of the relationship without synonymity between "reduplication" and "redoubling."

1304. See *Postscript,* pp. 69, 170 f., 217, 222, 269; *Practice [Training] in Christianity,* p. 133.

1305. See *Works of Love,* pp. 350 f.

1306. See *Fragments,* pp. 17 ff., 37 ff.

1307. See *Postscript,* p. 226; *Practice [Training] in Christianity,* pp. 123, 173.

1308. See J. P. Mynster, *Prædikener Holdte i Aaret 1848* (Copenhagen: 1849), pp. 47 ff. *ASKB* 232. Also *Prædikener paa alle Søn- og Hellig-Dage i Aaret,* I-II (Copenhagen: 3 pr. 1837), I, pp. 288 ff. *ASKB* 229–30.

1309. See, for example, *Postscript,* pp. 267 ff., 296;

PROFESSOR

1310. Matthew 27:4.

1311. See *En christelig Postille* (see note 81), I, p. 513.

1312. Ibid., p. 174.

1313. See "Of the Difference between a Genius and an Apostle," together with *The Point of View,* p. 148.

1314. Carl H. Visby, chaplain at the Copenhagen prison and Christianshavn prison and from 1844 pastor of Vor Frelsers Kirke in Christianshavn, where he preached, July 21, 1850, on Matthew 7:15–21.

1315. See *Practice [Training] in Christianity,* pp. 3, 5, and passim.

1316. See note 791.

1317. See *Practice [Training] in Christianity,* Pt. III, ch. 6, pp. 226 f. See also *Works of Love,* Introduction, pp. 11 ff. for further discussion of types of address and terms employed.

1318. See *Upbuilding Discourses in Various Spirits,* Part One [*Purity of Heart,* p. 203].

1319. See note 1144.

1320. Alexandre R. Vinet (1797–1847), French-Swiss literary critic and theologian, some of whose books Kierkegaard owned and read: *Ueber die Darlegung der religiösen Ueberzeugers und über die Trennung der Kirche und des Staates,* tr.

F. H. Spengler (Heidelberg: 1845); *Der Socialismus in seinem Princip betrachtet*, tr. D. Hofmeister (Berlin: 1849); *Pastoral theologie* . . . , tr. C. A. Ravn (Copenhagen: 1854). *ASKB* 873–75.

1321. X⁴ A 185, 186.

1322. See note 1165.

1323. "Reduplication" in the sense used here is suggested much earlier in *Stages*, p. 387.

1324. L. Holberg, *Hexerie eller Blind Allarm*, III, 3.

1325. L. Holberg, *Erasmus Montanus*, I, 3, 5.

1326. See *Postscript*, pp. 548 f.

1327. Change into another kind.

1328. See note 1320.

1329. Matthew 10:18 f.

REFLECTION, THOUGHT

See commentary and titles in topical bibliography under REASON, UNDERSTANDING.

For references in the works to reflection, see, for example, *S.V.*, XIII, pp. 65 ff., 71 f.; *The Concept of Irony*, pp. 133, 190, 191, 225, 227 f., 234 f.; *Either/Or*, I, pp. 146 ff., 168 f., 177 f., 186, 190, 209 f.; II, pp. 27 ff., 40 f., 47 f., 56 ff., 91 f., 95 f., 195; *Stages*, pp. 30 f., 79, 81, 123, 154, 157 f., 230, 252, 253, 375, 410; *Postscript*, pp. 37, 62, 67 ff., 68 fn., 68–73, 102 f., 171 ff., 376, 536; *Two Ages, S.V.*, VIII, (omitted in *The Present Age*), pp. 48 f., 62 f.; [*The Present Age*, pp. 3, 29 f., 36, 38, 42, 47, 61, 67 f.]; *On Authority and Revelation*, pp. 173 f., "Herr Phister as Captain Scipio," together with *Crisis in the Life of an Actress*, p. 110; *The Sickness unto Death*, pp. 162, 168, 182, 187 f.; *On My Work as an Author*, together with *The Point of View*, pp. 146 fn., 147; ibid., pp. 37, 38, 41 ff., 72, 73, 81, 90, 94, 103; "'*The Single Individual' Two 'Notes' Concerning My Work as an Author*," Appendix to ibid., p. 136.

1330. II Samuel 12:7. See *Either/Or*, II, p. 5; *Works of Love*, p. 31; *For Self-Examination*, pp. 41 ff.

1331. See *Stages*, p. 30.

1332. This entry is from a draft of *Concluding Unscientific Postscript*, pp. 301 f., end of paragraph.

1333. See *Poul Martin Møllers Levnet* by F. C. Olsen, together with Poul M. Møller, *Efterladte Skrifter*, I–III (Copenhagen: 1839–43), III, p. 109 fn. (separate pagination). *ASKB* 1574–76.

1334. See *On My Work as an Author*, together with *The Point of View*, p. 147; ibid., pp. 37 ff., 41 ff., 103.

1335. See ibid., p. 103.

1336. See *Postscript*, pp. 102 f.

1337. See Acts 9:16.

1338. See *Stages*, p. 375; *The Point of View*, p. 73.

1339. See note 1334.

1340. See, for example, "Of the Difference between a Genius and an Apostle," together with *The Present Age; On Authority and Revelation*, pp. 104 ff., 112 f., 118 ff.

1341. See *Either/Or*, I, p. 31; *Fear and Trembling*, p. 97.

1342. See *Postscript*, pp. 102 f.

1343. Wise men, lovers of wisdom. See *Armed Neutrality* and *An Open Letter*, p. 42.

1344. See *Stages*, pp. 230, 410.

1345. *Republic*, 406 a ff.

1346. *Platons Stat*, tr. C. J. Heise (Copenhagen: 1851). *ASKB* 1167.

1347. For other variations on this theme, see *Fear and Trembling*, pp. 27 ff.

1348. See *Two Ages* [*The Present Age*, passim].

REFORM, REFORMATION, REFORMER

Søren Kierkegaard regarded his age as an "age of disintegration" (IX B 64, 65), and he saw that there is always the danger in such a period that many intruders will step forward and play the reformer. Therefore Kierkegaard's critical remarks about reformation and reformers deal first and foremost with the contemporary self-appointing zeal for reformation. For example, he ironizes over "the nonsense about a whole age being reformation-minded" (VIII¹ A 429; see also X³ A 608 and *Judge for Yourselves!*, p. 219), and he rejects and ridicules the attempt of the age to reform by means of "general assemblies and voting" (IX B 10, p. 309; see also VIII¹ A 429). Moreover, he takes exception to anonymous criticism that pretends to want "to stick to the issue" and thus avoids the danger that accompanies any intervention under one's own name (X³ A 326).

Søren Kierkegaard categorically opposes the idea that reform can be accomplished by external measures, for example, by new "institutions." He clearly expresses this in his answer to Dr. Rudelbach: "Christianity will not be helped from the outside by institutions and constitutions, and least of all if these are not won by martyrs in the old-fashioned Christian way but are won in a social and amiable political way, by elections and by a lottery of numbers. On the contrary, to be aided in this way is the downfall of Christianity. Christianity is victorious inwardness. This is what should be worked for, that this victorious inwardness may be in every man, if possible, that the 'single individual' may become more and more truly a Christian" (*An Open Letter* and *Armed Neutrality*, p. 51).

In Kierkegaard's journal entries also we see that this "idea for a reformation" lies on the plane of inward deepening (X⁵ B 107, p. 293). In order to make room for such a reformation Kierkegaard himself must play the role of "a policeman who clears out all these false reformers" (X³ A 608). The true qualification for a reformer is "that the reformer stands alone in the whole world" (VIII¹ A 429) and that he is responsible only to God. "The concept 'reformer' corresponds qualitatively to: one" (X⁴ A 38). Kierkegaard himself actually came very close to this ideal reformer in that he was trained by God through heavy suffering to take an enormous responsibility. As the single individual he speaks to single individuals in order to awaken them to an inward deepening and thereby, according to his later understanding, "to introduce Christianity into Christendom" (*Practice* [*Training*] *in Christianity*, p. 39). Kierkegaard's works provide this reformation with "an entirely new military science" (*The Point of View*, p. 38) as an aid in the coming spiritual struggle. Looking to the future, Kierkegaard speaks of a forthcoming "dreadful reformation" (XI² A 346) compared to which the Protestant Reformation will seem like a jest, since it will involve millions of men who have fallen away from Christianity.

Thus Søren Kierkegaard did not regard himself as a reformer in the ordinary sense of the word, but he saw it as his task to call attention to the errors of Christendom and to speak to the single individual about inward deepening in order to provide the building stone for the coming renewal of Christianity. (See also LUTHER and PROTESTANTISM.)

For references to reform, reformers, Reformation in the works see, for example, *S.V.*, XIII, pp. 9, 14, 24, 34, 54; *The Concept of Irony*, pp. 276, 278, 306; *Postscript*, pp. 123, 547 f.; *Two Ages* [*The Present Age*, p. 34]; *For Self-Examination*, pp. 15, 18; *Judge for Yourselves!*, pp. 218 f., 220; *The Point of View*, p. 23; *Attack*, pp. 6 fn., 33.

1349. Entry is from draft of *The Book on Adler*, omitted from English translation, *On Authority and Revelation*, p. 41. Note is to the line (*On Authority and Revelation*, p. 41) "The same men who constitute the established order he (the movement-man, the spurious extraordinary) not only will need again but *he has need of them*, if only they will don a new uniform in accordance with his plan."

1350. Entry is an omission from later draft of *The Book on Adler* (included in *On Authority and Revelation*, p. 29).

1351. See *Two Ages* [*The Present Age*, pp. 67 f.].

1352. See early (1836) newspaper letters, *S.V.*, XIII, pp. 9, 14, 24, 34 f.

1353. See *Judge for Yourselves!*, p. 220.

1354. See *On Authority and Revelation*, p. 33.

1355. See *For Self-Examination*, p. 15.

1356. See VII² B 235, p. 42 (omitted in English translation of *The Book on Adler*, *On Authority and Revelation*, p. 36): "If a whole generation wants to be king and a whole generation dabbles at being extraordinary, it will be no good. And the result will only be delay."

1357. Ibid.: "first a forerunner must be sent, a servant who will have the task of clearing the air, of clearing out all the false prophets, of bringing a little sense and substance again into the enervated, thoughtless situation. If the whole generation has become a reformer, the true reformer cannot appear in truth at all—that is, to recall a former expression, if everyone is to give commands at a fire, the fire chief cannot command." The three treatises or essays referred to include *The Book on Adler* (*On Authority and Revelation*), which was not published until the *Papirer* appeared over fifty years later (VII^2 in 1927). The other two had been published in 1849 as *Tvende ethisk-religeuse Smaa-Afhandlinger* (*Two Minor Ethical-Religious Essays*), by H. H.

1358. See note 1144.

1359. Ibid.

1360. See notes 1356 and 1357.

1361. See *Armed Neutrality*, pp. 33–44.

1362. Ibid., p. 45.

1363. See note 1258.

1364. See Diogenes Laertius, *Lives and Opinions of Eminent Philosophers*, 2, 5, 31; *Works of Love*, p. 219; *The Sickness unto Death*, pp. 175 f.; *Attack*, p. 188.

RENUNCIATION, SELF-DENIAL

A person's spiritual or religious life begins, according to Kierkegaard, with "the movement of infinity" (*Fear and Trembling*, p. 46); that is, one turns away from the temporal in order to seek the eternal. The three principal forms of the movement of infinity are irony, renunciation, and repentance. Irony and renunciation can be sustained without a God-relationship but will not lead a person beyond immanence. Repentance, however, always stands in relationship to the transcendent (God). Irony negates finitude by seeing through its nothingness, and it is therefore primarily an intellectual movement, while renunciation is existentially concerned and is a real movement from finitude toward the eternal.

Every movement of infinity is the negative that one must carry out in order that God can give the positive. In Kierkegaard's opinion, without renunciation or infinite resignation it is impossible for a man to enter a true relationship with God. Renunciation, however, can adopt a progressively deeper existential expression the more earnestly men become involved with God or Christianity.

Kierkegaard customarily uses the expression "resignation" for the mildest form of renunciation, and infinite resignation, as in Abraham's case, may well be only temporary and come to be regarded as a test (*Christian Discourses*, p. 186). Christian renunciation has an enduring character, and the more deeply Kierkegaard enters into Christian existence, the stronger are the expressions he uses for it. Thus Climacus uses in addition to the term "resignation" the expression "dying away to the life of immediacy" (*Postscript,* p. 386, ed. tr.). In *Works of Love* we meet the still stronger expression "self-denial," or "self-renunciation," which as the negative is the prerequisite for the positive which always has God as the "middle term" (p. 66). Here Kierkegaard distinguishes between the self-renunciation which "does not approach God" but is merely "human self-denial" and a "Christian self-denial" (ibid., pp. 186 ff.) which forms the basis for the whole Christian ethic with all its high demands.

But Christian self-denial, too, can become "a new form of loving oneself, which must be dislodged by hating oneself" (X^5 A 53). In the last years Kierkegaard regarded this intensification and sharpening of self-denial as the authentic Christian requirement. For example, he says: "No, the purpose of the requirement to hate oneself is to teach one rightly to repent and to rely upon grace" (X^5 A 58).

Especially during the Church struggle Kierkegaard drew the ultimate consequences of renunciation and self-denial by comparing official Christianity with Christianity as it should be: "crucifying the flesh, hating oneself, suffering for the doctrine, being salt, being sacrificed . . ." (*Attack,* p. 34).

Eller, Vernard. *Kierkegaard and Radical Discipleship.* Princeton: Princeton University Press, 1968.

Smit, Harvey Albert. *Kierkegaard's Pilgrimage of Man: The Road of Self-Positing and Self-Abdication.* Delft: W. D. Meinema, 1965.

On the translation of the Danish term "*Resignation,*" see the perceptive but partial note by Karl Potter in his *Presuppositions of India's Philosophies* (New York: Prentice-Hall, 1962), p. 15: "One remarkable paradox about complete freedom, noted in various religious traditions,[f] is that in external appearances the man who is completely free, the *mukta,* resembles if anything the man who is least free, the man of minimal concern. The difference lies in their attitudes. Where the man of minimal concern is resigned, the free man has renounced." "[f]See, for example, Søren Kierkegaard's description of 'the man of faith' in *Fear and Trembling,* Anchor Books A 30, New York, 1954, p. 49. Kierkegaard's use of the word "resigned"—or at any rate his translator's use—is clearly different from mine, however."

The problem here lies neither in the translator's use (for the expression in *Fear and Trembling* and at times in the *Postscript* is "resignation [*Resignation*]) nor in Kierkegaard's use, but rather in a partial and static reading of Kierkegaard's writings, against which a reader should be warned by the polynymity of the pseudonymous works. In *Fear and Trembling* resignation is not only the mildest form of renunciation, but it may be only the beginning of "infinite resignation" and thereby only part of the "double movement of infinity," and in no case should it be regarded simply as apathy or "minimal concern," a state of "being resigned to be at the mercy of a large part of the environment" (*Presuppositions* . . . , p. 14), for it is a personal act.

For references to these themes in the works, see, for example, *Fear and Trembling*, pp. 46–64; *Fragments*, pp. 15, 40; *Upbuilding [Edifying] Discourses*, IV, p. 34; *Stages*, p. 430; *Postscript*, pp. 363, 377, 386, 411, 417, 501; *Two Ages [The Present Age*, p. 7]; *Upbuilding Discourses in Various Spirits*, Part One [*Purity of Heart*, p. 103 (tr. as self-forgetfulness)]; *Works of Love*, pp. 20, 41, 65 f., 93, 118, 133; *Christian Discourses*, pp. 151, 160, 180, 183, 233, 299; *Practice [Training] in Christianity*, pp. 129 ff., 138, 208, 242, 245; *For Self-Examination*, pp. 13, 88; *Judge for Yourselves!*, pp. 136, 139, 143, 213; *Attack*, p. 30.

1365. This entry is from the draft of *Concluding Unscientific Postscript*, at the end of the heading 2, p. 386. The Danish expression *Afdøen* used here, *Selvfornegtelse*, and *Forsagelse*, are the three primary terms in this section.

1366. See IMITATION.

1367. This entry is from a draft of *Upbuilding Discourses in Various Spirits*, Part Three [*The Gospel of Suffering*, at end of paragraph, pp. 13 f.].

Because of the biblical background (see ibid., p. 10) and because Kierkegaard's view of the self points to the proper fulfillment of selfhood rather than annihilation or extinction of selfhood, "self-denial" is judged a more suitable translation of *Selvfornegtelse* than "self-abnegation" or "self-renunciation," which have been used at times, along with "self-denial," by translators of the works. See *Upbuilding [Edifying] Discourses*, IV, pp. 29 ff.

1368. See Abraham à St. Clara, *Sämmtliche Werke*, I–XXI (Passau, Lindau: 1835–47), XV–XVI, p. 276; *ASKB* 294–311; *Christian Discourses*, p. 21.

1369. See Matthew 19:27; *Christian Discourses*, pp. 184 ff.

1370. This entry is from a draft of *Works of Love*. Compare entry with beginning of paragraph, p. 334.

1371. See *Judge for Yourselves!*, p. 136; *Attack*, p. 202.

1372. See *Works of Love*, pp. 188 ff.

1373. See note 1371.

1374. See *For Self-Examination*, p. 88.

1375. See ibid., pp. 89 ff.

1376. See *Upbuilding Discourses in Various Spirits*, Part Three [*The Gospel of Suffering*, pp. 3 ff.].

1377. See Matthew 10:22; *Works of Love*, p. 185.

1378. See *Works of Love*, p. 185; *Christian Discourses*, p. 180; *Attack*, p. 221.

1379. See *Works of Love*, p. 334.

1380. Paul Henry, *Das Leben Johann Calvins des grossen Reformators* (Hamburg: 1835).

1381. John 16:20.

1382. See *Postscript*, pp. 124, 350 f., 359, 366, 466; *Works of Love*, p. 59; *The Lily of the Field and the Bird of the Air*, together with *Christian Discourses*, p. 338; *Judge for Yourselves!*, pp. 148, 166; *Attack*, pp. 11, 17, 18, 250 f.

1383. See *Practice* [*Training*] *in Christianity*, pp. 208, 245; *Attack*, p. 279.
1384. Ibid.
1385. *Johann Arnd's sechs Bücher vom wahren Christenthume* ... (Leipzig: 1842), pp. 24 f.
1386. See note 1383.
1387. See note 1379.
1388. II Corinthians 12:9.
1389. See *Works of Love*, pp. 348 ff.
1390. See *Armed Neutrality* and *An Open Letter*, passim.
1391. Matthew 10:37; Luke 14:26.
1392. See *For Self-Examination*, pp. 85 ff.
1393. See *Attack*, p. 279.
1394. See note 1379.
1395. *Stages*, p. 87.
1396. L. Holberg, *Henrich og Pernille*, II, 9.

REPENTANCE

The movement of infinity has its deepest expression in repentance; it is the beginning of a personal God-relationship, because no one can come to God except as guilty and repentant. Kierkegaard and his pseudonyms express this in various ways. For example, Judge William says: "love for God has its absolute characteristic; its expression is repentance. And what is all other love in comparison with this? It is only childish prattle in this contrast" (*Either/Or*, II, p. 222). And in the first section of *Three Discourses on Imagined Occasions* [*Thoughts on Crucial Situations*] Kierkegaard says that no one can "take cognizance of God without becoming a sinner" (p. 25), just as in a journal entry he says, "Sorrow, according to God, is essentially repentance" (IX A 345).

But even if "a man's highest inward action is to repent," repentance as a movement of infinity is still "a negative movement" (*Stages*, p. 430) but as such it is the presupposition for the positive movement, namely, that "the paradox of the religious breaks through, that is, atonement, to which faith corresponds" (IV A 112). Thus it is God in Christ who gives the positive movement and the possibility for a new beginning.

Repentance provides the transition from the esthetic to the ethical and religious spheres, where it essentially belongs (see *Postscript*, p. 463), and Kierkegaard describes this transition in various passages. For example, Judge William shows that by repenting oneself out of the whole of existence (*Either/Or*, II, p. 229), one goes from the esthetic to the religious through this repentance, which is the presupposition for the ethical outlook. Johannes de Silentio in *Fear and Trembling* speaks of repentance as the boundary between the esthetic and the religious. He also mentions the form of repentance that stops before the religious and becomes demonic repentance (pp. 106 ff.).

Superb characterization of the refusal to enter into repentance is found in *The Concept of Anxiety* [*Dread*] (pp. 102 ff.). In *Stages on Life's Way* Quidam struggles with the question whether the unhappiness preventing him from realizing the universal is fate or guilt. The problem, which was also Søren Kierkegaard's, is formulated here as " 'Guilty?'/'Not guilty?' " (p. 179). Before this problem is cleared up, repentance is "dialectically prevented from coming to a head" (ibid., p. 404).

Kierkegaard also weaves the problem of repentance into the upbuilding or edifying works, especially in *Upbuilding Discourses in Various Spirits,* Part One [*Purity of Heart*], where he shows that a person's confession must always begin with repentance, and that because one continually fails to "will only one thing," he must constantly resort to repentance (pp. 37 ff., 216 ff.).

It is important to note that Kierkegaard warns against repentance in an abstract way, but also against a person's becoming despondently stuck on one particular sin. He says: "To repent of a trivial generality is a contradiction like offering the most profound passion a feast of superficialities, but to stick fast in remorse for some particular transgression is to repent on one's own responsibility, not before God, and to weaken one's resolve in self-love in melancholy of spirit (*Three Discourses on Imagined Occasions* [*Thoughts on Crucial Situations*], p. 34).

Yet Kierkegaard believes that one must always begin by repenting particular sins; this is the only way one can discover that sin is "an understanding before God of the continuity of sin in itself" (ibid., p. 30). Kierkegaard also calls it "an unfathomable continuity" (ibid., p. 33).

For references to repentance in the works, see, for example, *Either/Or,* I, pp. 146 (tr. as "remorse"), 304; II, pp. 179 f., 220 f., 229, 236, 242, 246; *Fear and Trembling,* p. 108 (crucial footnote); *Fragments,* pp. 23, 95; *The Concept of Anxiety* [*Dread*], pp. 11, 16, 92, 97 f., 102 ff.; *Three Discourses on Imagined Occasions* [*Thoughts on Crucial Situations,* pp. 24 f., 33 f.]; *Stages,* pp. 31, 114, 279, 293, 312, 386, 404 f., 407 f., 410, 423, 428 f., 432, 434, 438; *Postscript,* pp. 300, 304 fn., 463, 467, 485; *Two Ages, S.V.,* VIII, p. 71; *Upbuilding Discourses in Various Spirits,* Part One [*Purity of Heart,* pp. 31, 37, 39 ff., 112, 216 ff.]; *Works of Love,* pp. 101, 166; *Christian Discourses,* pp. 24, 92, 112, 271; *The Sickness unto Death,* pp. 193, 228, 240 f.

1397. The deeper we sink into ourselves,
  The closer we come to hell,
  Soon we feel the wave of the fire-river
  And we must soon drown in it.
  It shrinks the flesh from our body,
  And in time's passage it becomes waste.
  Within us is death!
  The world is God!
  O man, do not abandon man,
  However great your sins,

Shun only longing after sins
And you can yet find much grace;
Who has yet measured grace?
Man can forget so much.

1398. *Armuth, Schuld und Büsse der Grafinn Dolores,* L. A. von Arnim, *Eine Wahre Geschichte zur lehrreichen Unterhaltung armer Fräulein aufgeschrieben,* in *Novellen,* ed. Wilhelm Grimm, I–VI (Berlin: 1839–42). *ASKB* 1612–17.

1399. *Nicomachean Ethics,* 1110 b, 18 f.

1400. See *Either/Or,* II, pp. 220 f., 236; *The Concept of Anxiety* [*Dread*], pp. 97, 103.

1401. Greek fire was a combustible material capable of burning under water and was used by the Greek navy. Old books on fireworks have formulæ for Greek fire.

1402. Entry from draft of *Three Discourses on Imagined Occasions* [*Thoughts on Crucial Situations in Human Life*].

1403. See Abraham à St. Clara, *Sämmtliche Werke* (see note 1368), XV, p. 53.

1404. See *Either/Or,* I, pp. 146, 304; *Stages,* pp. 279, 423, 434; *The Sickness unto Death,* pp. 193, 240 f.

1405. Wilhelm Rothe, *Det danske Kirkeaar og dets Pericoper* (Copenhagen: 2 ed. 1843), pp. 90 ff. *ASKB* 747.

1406. See *Fear and Trembling,* p. 108 fn.; *Fragments,* pp. 23, 95; *The Concept of Anxiety* [*Dread*], p. 16; *Stages,* pp. 434, 438; *Postscript,* p. 463; *Christian Discourses,* p. 92.

REPETITION

In his book *Repetition* Constantin Constantius experiments with the various meanings the word "repetition" may have, from its everyday meanings to the more profound, essential meanings. He is especially interested in repetition as it relates to the esthetic and religious spheres. He points out that a repetition is impossible on the esthetic level, because everything here depends upon the play of chance, and he then indicates the areas where the concept of repetition finds its proper substance: "repetition is the *conditio sine qua non* of every issue in dogmatics" (p. 34, ed. tr.). As an example of a religious movement in the direction of repetition, he refers to the young man who after his unhappy love affair seeks a new point of departure through relationship to the transcendent.

In discussing the complex of problems in *Repetition* (IV B 117, pp. 281 ff.), Kierkegaard gives a condensed review of the role of repetition in the various stages, from the esthetic, through the ethical, to the religious. "Repetition's most profound expression" (p. 293) is in the religious sphere, in the Atonement, and this highest form of repetition is the goal toward which Kierkegaard's whole authorship is directed. But at the same time he gives many examples of repetition in the ethical sphere, where repetition means that one continually carries out his actions with the thought of the eternal. This outlook is given prominence particularly by Judge William, and it appears also in the upbuilding works, especially in *Works of Love*. As the negative counterpart to the ethical philosophy of life, there is the despondency that transforms "all life to a homogenized, meaningless repetition" (p. 279; see also p. 235: "dull repetition").

Two other particular forms of repetition must be mentioned: "each generation's repetition" (*Three Discourses on Imagined Occasions* [*Thoughts on Crucial Situations*, p. 14, ed. tr.]). which takes place because each generation is obliged to live through "the content of paganism," and the genius's repetition of "the past" in history in his own original way (*The Concept of Anxiety* [*Dread*], p. 94).

Chaning-Pearce, M. "Repetition: A Kierkegaard Study." *Hibbert Journal*, vol. 41, 1943.

Clive, Geoffrey. "The Teleological Suspension of the Ethical." *Journal of Religion*, vol. 34, 1954.

Grieve, Alexander. "Søren Kierkegaard," in *Encyclopaedia of Religion and Ethics*, XIII. London: 1926.

Heinemann, F. H. "Origin and Repetition." *The Review of Metaphysics*, vol. 4, 1950–51.

McLane, Henry E. "Kierkegaard's Use of the Category of Repetition." Yale University Ph.D. dissertation, 1961.

Martin, H. V. *Kierkegaard*. London: Epworth, 1950.

Stack, George J. "Kierkegaard and the Phenomenology of Repetition." *Journal of Existentialism*, vol. 7, 1966–67.

Repetition is another instance of a concept which is important in the works but is sparsely represented directly in the *Papirer*. See *Johannes Climacus, or De omnibus dubitandum est*, pp. 153 f.; *Repetition*, passim, particularly p. 34 fn.; *Either/Or*, I, pp. 52 f.; II, pp. 144, 246; *Upbuilding* [*Edifying*] *Discourses*, II, pp. 56, 81; *The Concept of Anxiety* [*Dread*], pp. 16 fn. (reference to p. 34 of *Repetition*), 83 fn., 95, 100, 132, 135; *Postscript*, pp. 110, 146, 235, 277; *En literair Anmeldelse, S.V.*, VIII, pp. 15, 22 (omitted in *The Present Age*). In the *Papirer* there is extensive interpretation of "repetition" and *Repetition* in a draft of a contemplated open letter by Constantin Constantius to Professor J. L. Heiberg, in response to Heiberg's review of *Repetition* in his *Urania, Aarbog for 1844* (Copenhagen: 1843). *ASKB* U57.

1407. This and the following entries are from a draft of *Johannes Climacus, or De omnibus dubitandum est*; see pp. 152 f.

1408. See *Fear and Trembling*, p. 108 fn.; *Repetition*, pp. 34, 144; *The Concept of Anxiety* [*Dread*], pp. 16–17 fn.

1409. G. O. Marbach, *Geschichte der Philosophie des Mittelalters* (Leipzig: 1841). *ASKB* 642.

1410. See *Repetition*, pp. 155 ff.

1411. Ibid., pp. 30 ff.

1412. Ibid., pp. 36 ff., 81 f.

1413. K. Rosenkranz, *Psychologie oder die Wissenschaft vom subjectiven Geist* (Königsberg: 1837), pp. 157 f. *ASKB* 744.

1414. See *The Concept of Anxiety* [*Dread*], p. 132.

ROMANTICISM, CLASSICISM

In an entry (I C 88) from March, 1836, Kierkegaard summarizes with comments several passages on romanticism as found in Christian Molbech's *Forlæsninger over den nyere danske Poesi*, II (Copenhagen: 1832), and this was the beginning of his intense preoccupation with Germans such as Jean Paul, August W. von Schlegel, Friedrich von Schlegel, Ludwig Tieck, and K. W. F. Solger, originators of the romantic movement. Many journal entries during this period disclose that Kierkegaard was attempting to place romanticism into a broader spiritual context; he was especially interested in the relation of romanticism to the classical period and to Christianity. The romantic movement appealed to Socrates' irony as its point of departure, and this led Kierkegaard to a closer study of Socratic irony. Thereafter he undertook a thorough examination of the relationship between irony and romanticism. Common to both of them is the negative outlook on the given actuality, which is rejected in order to make room for something higher. Just as Socrates before him, Kierkegaard conceived of this something higher as the ethical, which provides man with a goal beyond finitude. The German romanticism, however, did not arrive at this positive position after rejecting bourgeois morality; it degenerated into arbitrary experimentation with the values of life, even though J. G. Fichte, who with his philosophy laid the basis of romanticism, was ethically oriented (see *The Concept of Irony*, pp. 290 ff.).

During the period from 1836 to the spring of 1838, Kierkegaard tried to live in the romantic style, which only augmented his despair. But in the attempt he acquired both theoretical and practical insight into the content of irony and of romanticism. His doctoral dissertation, *The Concept of Irony*, utilizes his knowledge of irony and romanticism. Here he shows how Socratic irony, despite its negativity, makes room for something higher, namely, the ethical, while German romanticism by Christian standards is a retrogression—in the first place because it ends up in moral arbitrariness and, in the second place, because it does not respect the ethical, already expressed in Christianity in a qualitatively new and higher manner.

In *The Concept of Irony* Kierkegaard presents irony and romanticism each in its world-historical manifestations. His personal experience with irony and romanticism, however, he describes pseudonymously in the first part of *Either/*

Or. In harmony with Kierkegaard's existential outlook, the ethicist (Judge William) in the second volume of *Either/Or* calls to the attention of his romantic young friend from Volume I that the way forward for him involves choosing the ethical. Judge William does not deny that the romantic can contain something positive—for example, in the love-relationship between man and woman (*Either/Or*, II, pp. 20 ff.)—but it must not only not halt with romantic love and go no further but must become a presupposition for something higher.

In Constantin Constantius we have an example of the way irony and also romanticism lose their positive quality and become demonic. In *Repetition* his irony has something of a positive character, while in *Stages on Life's Way* (in the section "*In Vino Veritas*") it falls within the demonic, because he remains on the romantic level. At the same time it is important to note that although Constantin from the beginning shows an acquaintance with Christianity, his irony has a strain of romanticism. Despite its original yearning for the eternal, romanticism contains the possibility of the demonic, since it is actually a flight from the ethical requirement of Christianity (see *The Concept of Anxiety* [*Dread*], pp. 105 ff.).

Grimsley, R. "Romantic Melancholy in Chateaubriand and Kierkegaard." *Comparative Literature*, 1956.

In the works, "romantic" is usually used simply as an adjective. For the infrequent, more extended allusions to the romantic, see especially *The Concept of Irony*, pp. 282 fn., 304 f., 318 ff., 331 f., 341.

1415. S. S. Blicher, *Samlede Noveller*, I–V, suppl. (Copenhagen: 1833–39), II, pp. 1 ff. *ASKB* 1521–23.

1416. C. G. Ehrenberg, *De nordafricanske Ørkner*, in *Danske Ugeskrift*, 1834.

1417. See Esaias Tegner, *Frithiofs Saga* (Stockholm: 1825), p. 71; *The Concept of Anxiety* [*Dread*], p. 78.

1418. See Jens Baggesen, *Danske Værker*, I–XII (Copenhagen: 1827–32), VII, pp. 307 ff. *ASKB* 1509–20.

1419. Bertel A. Thorvaldsen (1768–1844), Denmark's most famous sculptor. His best-known works are Christ and the disciples in Vor Frue Kirke, Copenhagen.

1420. Ludwig Tieck, *Schriften*, I–IV (Berlin: 1828).

> Alone in wood so gay,
> Ah, far away!
> But thou wilt say
> Some other day,
> 'Twere best to stay
> Alone in wood so gay.

"The Fair-haired Eckbert," *German Romances*, tr. Thomas Carlyle, I–II (New York: Scribner, n.d.), I, p. 288.

1421. For now we see in a mirror dimly. . . .

1422. J. Gorres, *Die Teutschen Volksbücher* (Heidelberg: 1807). *ASKB* 1440.

1423. *Fr. Schelgels sämmtliche Werke*, I–X (Vienna: 1822–25). *ASKB* 1816–25.

1424. For Kierkegaard "these two" represented the reduction of esthetics and of philosophy, respectively, to the sphere of immanence. Only when esthetics and philosophy point beyond immanence is there the possibility of the romantic. Politics, the overriding interest of the period, must also go through its romantic phase, and therefore Goethe and Hegel were not being followed in their nonromantic reduction. Kierkegaard may have had in mind the politician Orla Lehman (see *S.V.*, XIII, pp. 55 f.).

1425. Flyer, circular, handbill. An expression used concerning Faust in L. Achim von Arnim and Clemens Brentano, *Das Knaben Wunderhorn. Alte deutsche Lieder*, I–III (Heidelberg: 1819), I, pp. 214 ff. *ASKB* 1494–96.

1426. Jens Baggesen (1764–1826), Danish writer, who wrote in both Danish and German.

1427. *Kiøbenhavnsposten*, 347, December 10, 1836.

1428. Nicolai Møller. *ASKB* 787.

1429. That is why the many charms of the plant kingdom, the endless play of forms and colors, which the plants unfold in innocent, unconscious openness before the eyes of the beholder, are so moving.

1430. *Tausend und eine Nacht*, tr. G. Weil, I–IV (Stuttgart, Pforsheim: 1838–41). *ASKB* 1414–17.

1431. See *Fear and Trembling*, p. 27.

1432. Lines of article "Lyrisk Poesie" underlined in red crayon by Kierkegaard in a copy of *Intelligensblade*, ed. J. L. Heiberg, 26–27 (April 15, 1843), p. 50.

ROUSSEAU

In his library Kierkegaard had J. J. Rousseau's (1712–78) *Confessions* in Danish translation (*ASKB* 1922–25) and *Émile* in both French (*ASKB* 939–40) and Danish (*ASKB* 941–43), and it is apparent in his journals that he had done at least some reading in them. In Kierkegaard's opinion Rousseau was a long way from Christianity since he did not perceive that the sufferings he was undergoing when he willed to do the good and which "cripple him so indescribably" (X[4] A 223) are analogous to the collisions a Christian experiences in this world. Rousseau's confused views on suffering led Kierkegaard to count him among the "confused heads" whose views on suffering are one thing in theory and another in practice (X[4] A 488). Thus Rousseau was for Kierkegaard another example of "how difficult it is for a man to die to the world" (X[4] A 224). Kierkegaard's quotation from *Émile* in X[3] A 6 is of particular interest because it harmonizes with his own views on how a counselor should conduct himself in the presence of faith and doubt in the Christian man. In an age which sought support for its tottering faith in the historical-critical (*Postscript,* pp. 26 ff.), in scientific research, or in a speculative philosophy (ibid., pp. 49 ff.), Kierkegaard saw it as his task to point to the paradox in Christianity and to the many difficulties that must be overcome before one comes to a new personal foundation for faith. But at the same time he believed, as does the Vicar in *Émile* (see X³ A 6), that rigorous discourse is only for those who doubt and not for the simple person "whose mind piously remains ignorant" of such doubt (*Upbuilding Discourses in Various Spirits,* Part One [*Purity of Heart,* p. 55]).

In the works Rousseau is directly referred to only once, in *Fear and Trembling,* p. 78.

1433. J. J. Rousseau, *Emil eller om Opdragelsen,* I–VI (Copenhagen: 1796–99), IV, pp. 256 f. *ASKB* 941–43. *Émile ou de l' Education,* I–IV (Aux Deux-Ponts: 1792). *ASKB* 939–40.

1434. J. J. Rousseau, *Emil eller om Opdragelsen,* VI, p. 271.

1435. Richard Rothe, *Theologische Ethik,* I–III (Wittenberg: 1848).

1436. This question is quite settled, I know, negatively in the books, where the strictest morals do not cost the author anything; affirmatively in society, where the morals of books are considered twaddle which cannot be practiced.

1437. *J. J. Rousseaus Bekjendelser eller hans Levnet,* tr. M. Hagerup, I, IV (Copenhagen: 1798), IV, pp. 102 ff. *ASKB* 1922–25.

1438. Ibid., IV, pp. 125 ff., especially pp. 134 ff.